# Consumer Behavior

## Building Marketing Strategy ELEVENTH EDITION

**Del I. Hawkins**
*University of Oregon*

**David L. Mothersbaugh**
*University of Alabama*

Boston   Burr Ridge, IL   Dubuque, IA   New York   San Francisco   St. Louis
Bangkok   Bogotá   Caracas   Kuala Lumpur   Lisbon   London   Madrid   Mexico City
Milan   Montreal   New Delhi   Santiago   Seoul   Singapore   Sydney   Taipei   Toronto

**McGraw-Hill Irwin**

CONSUMER BEHAVIOR: BUILDING MARKETING STRATEGY

Published by McGraw-Hill/Irwin, a business unit of The McGraw-Hill Companies, Inc., 1221 Avenue of the Americas, New York, NY, 10020.

Some ancillaries, including electronic and print components, may not be available to customers outside the United States.

This book is printed on acid-free paper.

1 2 3 4 5 6 7 8 9 0 DOW/DOW 0 9

ISBN      978-0-07-338110-7
MHID      0-07-338110-1

Vice president and editor-in-chief: *Brent Gordon*
Publisher: *Paul Ducham*
Executive editor: *Doug Hughes*
Editorial coordinator: *Kelly Pekelder*
Marketing manager: *Katie Mergen*
Lead project manager: *Christine A. Vaughan*
Senior manager, EDP: *Heather D. Burbridge*
Interior designer: *Laurie J. Entringer*
Senior photo research coordinator: *Lori Kramer*
Photo researcher: *Mike Hruby*
Senior media project manager: *Greg Bates*
Cover and interior design: *Laurie J. Entringer*
Cover image: *© Sylvain Sonnett, Getty Images*
Typeface: *10/12 Times Roman*
Compositor: *Macmillan Publishing Solutions*
Printer: *R. R. Donnelley*

**Library of Congress Cataloging-in-Publication Data**

Hawkins, Del I.
    Consumer behavior: building marketing strategy / Del I. Hawkins, David L. Mothersbaugh.—11th ed.
    p.   cm.
    Includes index.
    ISBN-13: 978-0-07-338110-7 (alk. paper)
    ISBN-10: 0-07-338110-1 (alk. paper)
    1. Consumer behavior—United States. 2. Market surveys—United States.
3. Consumer behavior—United States—Case studies. I. Mothersbaugh,
David L. II. Title.
HF5415.33.U6H38 2010
658.8'3420973—dc22

                                                        2008044958

# Preface

Marketing attempts to influence the way consumers behave. These attempts have implications for the organizations making them, the consumers they are trying to influence, and the society in which these attempts occur. We are all consumers and we are all members of society, so consumer behavior and attempts to influence it are critical to all of us. This text is designed to provide an understanding of consumer behavior. This understanding can make us better consumers, better marketers, and better citizens.

## MARKETING CAREERS AND CONSUMER BEHAVIOR

A primary purpose of this text is to provide the student with a usable, managerial understanding of consumer behavior. Most students in consumer behavior courses aspire to careers in marketing management, sales, or advertising. They hope to acquire knowledge and skills that will be useful to them in these careers. Unfortunately, some may be seeking the type of knowledge gained in introductory accounting classes; that is, a set of relatively invariant rules that can be applied across a variety of situations to achieve a fixed solution that is known to be correct. For these students, the uncertainty and lack of closure involved in dealing with living, breathing, changing, stubborn consumers can be very frustrating. However, if they can accept dealing with endless uncertainty, utilizing an understanding of consumer behavior in developing marketing strategy will become tremendously exciting.

It is our view that the use of knowledge of consumer behavior in the development of marketing strategy is an art. This is not to suggest that scientific principles and procedures are not applicable; rather, it means that the successful application of these principles to particular situations requires human judgment that we are not able to reduce to a fixed set of rules.

Let us consider the analogy with art in some detail. Suppose you want to become an expert artist. You would study known principles of the visual effects of blending various colors, of perspective, and so forth. Then you would practice applying these principles until you developed the ability to produce acceptable paintings. If you had certain natural talents, the right teacher, and the right topic, you might even produce a masterpiece. The same approach should be taken by one wishing to become a marketing manager, a salesperson, or an advertising director. The various factors or principles that influence consumer behavior should be thoroughly studied. Then, one should practice applying these principles until acceptable marketing strategies result. However, while knowledge and practice can in general produce acceptable strategies, great marketing strategies, like masterpieces, require special talents, effort, timing, and some degree of luck (what if Mona Lisa had not wanted her portrait painted?).

The art analogy is useful for another reason. All of us, professors and students alike, tend to ask, "How can I use the concept of, say, social class to develop a successful marketing strategy?" This makes as much sense as an artist asking, "How can I use blue to create a great picture?" Obviously, blue alone will seldom be sufficient for a great work of art. Instead, to be successful, the artist must understand when and how to use blue in conjunction with other elements in the picture. Likewise, the marketing manager must understand when and how to use a knowledge of social class in conjunction with a knowledge of other factors in designing a successful marketing strategy.

This book is based on the belief that knowledge of the factors that influence consumer behavior can, with practice, be used to develop sound marketing strategy. With this in mind, we have attempted to do three things. First, we present a reasonably comprehensive description of the various behavioral concepts and theories that have been found useful for understanding consumer behavior. This is generally done at the beginning of each chapter or at the beginning of major subsections in each chapter. We believe that a person must have a thorough understanding of a concept in order to successfully apply that concept across different situations.

Second, we present examples of how these concepts have been used in the development of marketing strategy. We have tried to make clear that these examples are not "how you use this concept." Rather, they are presented as "how one organization facing a particular marketing situation used this concept."

Third, at the end of each chapter and each major section, we present a number of questions, activities, or cases that require the student to apply the concepts.

# CONSUMING AND CONSUMER BEHAVIOR

The authors of this book are consumers, as is everyone reading this text. Most of us spend more time buying and consuming than we do working or sleeping. We consume products such as cars and fuel, services such as haircuts and home repairs, and entertainment such as television and concerts. Given the time and energy we devote to consuming, we should strive to be good at it. A knowledge of consumer behavior can be used to enhance our ability to consume wisely.

Marketers spend billions of dollars attempting to influence what, when, and how you and I consume. Marketers not only spend billions attempting to influence our behavior but also spend hundreds of millions of dollars studying our behavior. With a knowledge of consumer behavior and an understanding of how marketers use this knowledge, we can study marketers. A television commercial can be an annoying interruption of a favorite program. However, it can also be a fascinating opportunity to speculate on the commercial's objective, target audience, and underlying behavior assumptions. Indeed, given the ubiquitous nature of commercials, an understanding of how they are attempting to influence us or others is essential to understand our environment.

Throughout the text, we present examples that illustrate the objectives of specific marketing activities. By studying these examples and the principles on which they are based, we can develop the ability to discern the underlying logic of the marketing activities encountered daily.

# SOCIAL RESPONSIBILITY AND CONSUMER BEHAVIOR

What are the costs and benefits of direct-to-consumer (DTC) advertising of pharmaceutical products? How much more needs to be done to protect the online privacy of children? These issues are currently being debated by industry leaders and consumer advocacy groups. As educated citizens, we have a responsibility to take part in these sorts of debates and work toward positive solutions. However, developing sound positions on these issues requires an understanding of such factors as information processing as it relates to advertising—an important part of our understanding of consumer behavior.

The debates described above are just a few of the many that require an understanding of consumer behavior. We present a number of these topics throughout the text. The objective is to develop the ability to apply consumer behavior knowledge to social and regulatory issues as well as to business and personal issues.

# FEATURES OF THE ELEVENTH EDITION

Marketing and consumer behavior, like the rest of the world, are changing at a rapid pace. Both the way consumers behave and the practices of studying that behavior continue to evolve. To keep up with this dynamic environment, the eleventh edition includes a number of important features.

## Internet and Technology

The Internet and technology are rapidly changing many aspects of consumer behavior. We have integrated the latest research, practices, and examples concerning the Internet and technology throughout the text and the cases. Examples include:

- Online social media and Web 2.0
- Sears Goes Zwicky for Tweens and Teens
- Mobile marketing strategies
- Techniques for converting Web site visitors to buyers

## Global Marketing

Previous editions have included a wealth of global material, and this edition is no exception. Most chapters contain multiple global examples woven into the text. In addition, Chapter 2 and several of the cases are devoted to global issues. New global examples include:

- Wal-Mart adapts its strategy to developing countries
- Emerging segments of global citizens
- Seki Saba—repositioning Japanese Mackerel
- The changing nature of globalization

## Ethnic Subcultures

This edition continues our emphasis on the exciting issues surrounding marketing to ethnic subcultures. Ethnic diversity is increasing, and we draw on the latest research and emerging trends to shed light on this important topic. Examples include:

- P&G's My Black Is Beautiful Campaign
- Camry Goes Interactive to Attract Black Women
- Hispanic Teens—The New Bicultural Youth

## Strategic Application

This edition continues our emphasis on the application of consumer behavior concepts and theory to exciting marketing problems and important emerging trends. We do this through our opening examples, featured Consumer Insights, and cases. Examples include:

- Jack Link's Beef Jerky Going Hip and Healthy
- Positioning the Yaris
- Living in a DVR world
- Organic Hits Its Stride

# CHAPTER FEATURES

Each chapter contains a variety of features designed to enhance students' understanding of the material as well as to make the material more fun.

## Opening Vignettes

Each chapter begins with a practical example that introduces the material in the chapter. These involve situations in which businesses, government units, or nonprofit organizations have used or misused consumer behavior principles.

## Consumer Insights

These boxed discussions provide an in-depth look at a particularly interesting consumer study or marketing practice. Each has several questions with it that are designed to encourage critical thinking by the students.

## Integrated Coverage of Ethical and Social Issues

Marketers face numerous ethical issues as they apply their understanding of consumer behavior in the marketplace. We describe and discuss many of these issues. These discussions are highlighted in the text via an "ethics" icon in the margin. In addition, Chapter 20 is devoted to social and regulation issues relating to marketing practice. Several of the cases are also focused on ethical or regulatory issues, including all of the cases following Part Six.

## Internet Exercises

The Internet is a major source of data on consumer behavior and a medium in which marketers use their knowledge of consumer behavior to influence consumers. A section at the end of each chapter has Internet assignments to enhance students' understanding of how marketers are approaching consumers using this medium.

## DDB Life Style Study™ Data Analyses

Each relevant chapter poses a series of questions that require students to analyze data from the annual DDB Life Style Study™ survey. These data are available in spreadsheet format on the disk that accompanies this text. These exercises increase students' data analysis skills as well as their understanding of consumer behavior. The DDB data were completely updated for the tenth edition to include results of the 2004 survey. A major advantage of this new data is that it includes information on behaviors related to Internet use and shopping.

## Four-Color Illustrations

Print ads, Web pages, storyboards, and photos of point-of-purchase displays and packages appear throughout the text. Each is directly linked to the text material both by text references to each illustration and by the descriptive comments that accompany each illustration.

These illustrations, which we've continued to update with the eleventh edition, provide vivid examples and applications of the concepts and theories presented in the text.

## Review Questions

The review questions at the end of each chapter allow students or the instructor to test the acquisition of the facts contained in the chapter. The questions require memorization, which we believe is an important, though insufficient, part of learning.

## Discussion Questions

These questions can be used to help develop or test the students' understanding of the material in the chapter. Answering these questions requires the student to utilize the material in the chapter to reach a recommendation or solution. However, they can generally be answered without external activities such as customer interviews; therefore, they can be assigned as in-class activities.

## Application Activities

The final learning aid at the end of each chapter is a set of application exercises. These require the students to use the material in the chapter in conjunction with external activities such as visiting stores to observe point-of-purchase displays, interviewing customers or managers, or evaluating television ads. They range in complexity from short evening assignments to term projects.

# OTHER LEARNING AIDS IN THE TEXT

Three useful sets of learning material are presented outside the chapter format—cases, an overview of consumer research methods, and a format for a consumer behavior audit.

## Cases

There are cases at the end of each major section of the text except the first. Many of the cases can be read in class and used to generate discussion of a particular topic. Students like this approach, and many instructors find it a useful way to motivate class discussion.

Other cases are more complex and data intense. They require several hours of effort to analyze. Still others can serve as the basis for a term project. We have used several cases in this manner with success (the assignment is to develop a marketing plan clearly identifying the consumer behavior constructs that underlie the plan).

Each case can be approached from a variety of angles. A number of discussion questions are provided with each case. However, many other questions can be used. In fact, while the cases are placed at the end of the major sections, most lend themselves to discussion at other points in the text as well.

## Consumer Research Methods Overview

Appendix A provides a brief overview of the more commonly used research methods in consumer behavior. While not a substitute for a course or text in marketing research, it is a useful review for students who have completed a research course. It can also serve to provide students who have not had such a course with relevant terminology and a very basic understanding of the process and major techniques involved in consumer research.

## Consumer Behavior Audit

Appendix B provides a format for doing a consumer behavior audit for a proposed marketing strategy. This audit is basically a list of key consumer behavior questions that should be answered for every proposed marketing strategy. Many students have found it particularly useful if a term project relating consumer behavior to a firm's actual or proposed strategy is required.

# SUPPLEMENTAL LEARNING MATERIALS

We have developed a variety of learning materials to enhance the student's learning experience and to facilitate the instructor's teaching activities. Please contact your local Irwin/McGraw-Hill sales representative for assistance in obtaining ancillaries. Or visit the McGraw-Hill Higher Education Web site at www.mhhe.com.

## Instructor's Presentation CD ROM

The *Instructor's CD ROM to Accompany Consumer Behavior* includes all of the instructor's resources available for *Consumer Behavior* in electronic form and an easy interface that makes it even easier to access the specific items the instructor wants to use:

- **Instructor's Manual (New Supplemental Examples for Eleventh Edition)**
  The Instructor's Manual contains suggestions for teaching the course, learning objectives for each chapter, lecture tips and aids, answers to the end-of-chapter questions, suggested case teaching approaches, and discussion guides for each case. It also includes supplemental examples called *CB Press Highlights*. These examples are not found in the text and can help enhance classroom presentation and discussion.
- **Test Bank and Computerized Test Bank**
  A new and improved test bank was created for the tenth edition. The eleventh edition maintains our high standards of accuracy and completeness, with over 2,000 questions ranging from multiple-choice, to true-false, to short-answer. These questions are coded according to degree of difficulty and are designed with the flexibility to suit your students' needs and your teaching style. These questions cover all the chapters, including material in the opening

vignettes and in the Consumer Insights. Questions are marked with a page number so that instructors can make quick reference back to the book.

- **Digital Four-Color Ad Set**

  A set of digital four-color images of ads, picture boards, point-of-purchase displays, and so forth is included. These items are keyed to specific chapters in the text. The Instructor's Manual relates these items to the relevant concepts in the text.

- **PowerPoint Program (New Video Clips for the Eleventh Edition!)**

  The PowerPoint slides have again been substantially enhanced for each chapter. They include the key material from each chapter as well as additional illustrations and examples to enhance the overall classroom experience. A new feature of the Power-Points for the eleventh edition is that each chapter is accompanied by a one- to three-minute video clip that elaborates on one of the chapter concepts. The PowerPoints can be used "off the shelf," in combination with the instructor's own materials, and/or can be combined with the digital four-color ad set to create powerful presentations that include both text and nontext materials.

## Video Cases (Now on DVD!)

A set of 15 video cases is available to adopters. One third of the videos are new to the eleventh edition and since the tenth edition, all the videos have been replaced. These videos describe firm strategies or activities that relate to material in the text. A guide for teaching from the videos is contained in the Instructor's manual. Examples of videos in the set include:

- Geek Squad: Services and Satisfaction
- Oreo: Crafting a Truly Global Brand
- Targeting the Premium Dog Market
- MINI Cooper: Creating an Iconic Lifestyle Brand

## Text Web site

The book-specific Online Learning Center, located at www.mhhe.com/hawkins11e, offers comprehensive classroom support by providing resources for both instructors and students. For instructors, it gives access to downloadable teaching supplements (Instructor's Manual and PowerPoint slides), resource links, and PageOut. For students, it offers resource links and quizzes for self-testing.

# ACKNOWLEDGMENTS

We enjoy studying, teaching, consulting, and writing about consumer behavior. Most of the faculty we know feel the same. As with every edition of this book, our goal for the eleventh edition has been to make a book that students enjoy reading and that excites them about a fascinating topic.

Numerous individuals and organizations helped us in the task of writing this edition. We are grateful for their assistance. At the risk of not thanking all who deserve credit, we would like to thank Martin Horn at DDB, Tom Spencer at Claritas, Jessica Damico at Forrester Research, Dr. Sijun Wang at California State University at Pomona, Dr. Junwu Dong at Guangdong University, Rick Bruner at DoubleClick, Matt Bailey at Site Logic, and Carrie Hollenberg at SRI Consulting Business Intelligence. Maren Kirlin and Casey Findley (The University of Alabama) deserve special thanks for their countless hours of research and analysis.

We would also like to thank the many members of the McGraw-Hill Higher Education team, including Dough Hughes, Kelly Pekelder, Katie Mergen, Christine Vaughan, Heather Burbridge, Laurie Entringer, Lori Kramer, Mike Hruby, and Greg Bates. We believe that the eleventh edition is improved because of your efforts: Scott Anderson, Buena Vista University; Linda Anglin, Minnesota State University, Mankato; Yeqing Bao, University of Alabama-Huntsville; Mary E. Briseno, University of the Incarnate Word; Kathy Crockett, Lubbock Christian University; Brent Cunningham, Jacksonville State University; Michael T. Elliott, University of Missouri–St. Louis; Dr. Nitika Garg, University of Mississippi; David Hagenbuch, Messiah College; Karl A. Hickerson, St. Ambrose University; Samira B. Hussein, Johnson County Community College; Joseph Izzo, SUNY Fredonia; John C. Kozup, Villanova University; William Lundstrom, Cleveland State University; Kimberly McNeil, North Carolina A&T State University; Nancy J. Nentl, Metropolitan State University; Dr. Brooke Quigg, Pierce College; Dr. Donna Tillman, California State University–Pomona; and Ramaprasad Unni, Tennessee State University.

Finally, to our colleagues at Oregon and Alabama— Thanks for your ongoing support, encouragement and friendship.

Del I. Hawkins
David L. Mothersbaugh

# Walkthrough

## KNOWING CONSUMER BEHAVIOR

Marketing attempts to influence the way consumers behave. These attempts have implications for the organizations making the attempt, the consumers they are trying to influence, and the society in which these attempts occur. We are all consumers: the authors of this book are consumers, as is everyone reading this text, and we are all members of society, so consumer behavior, and attempts to influence it, are critical to all of us. This text is designed to provide an understanding of consumer behavior. This understanding can make us better consumers, better marketers, and better citizens.

Throughout the text, we present examples that illustrate the objectives of specific marketing activities. By studying these examples and the principles on which they are based, one can develop the ability to discern the underlying logic of the marketing activities encountered daily. Given the time and energy we devote to consuming, we should strive to be good at it, and a knowledge of consumer behavior can be used to enhance our ability to consume wisely.

## Opening Vignette

The chapter openers feature vignettes that focus on practical examples that introduce the consumer behavior concepts covered in the chapter.

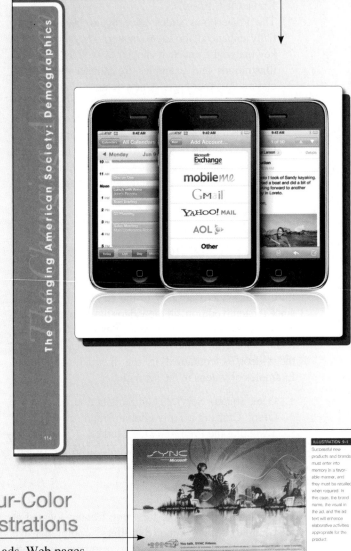

## Four-Color Illustrations

Print ads, Web pages, storyboards, and photos of point-of-purchase displays and packages appear throughout the text.

## Part-Ending Cases

There are cases at the end of each major section of the text that can be approached from a variety of angles. They can be utilized for class discussion, more intense efforts of analysis, or as the basis for a term project.

**Part Four | Cases**

CASE 4-1 SEARS GOES ZWINKY FOR TWEENS AND TEENS

Sears has struggled over the years. While some categories, such as Craftsman tools, have been a perennial hit, other categories, particularly apparel, have struggled. Sears has made numerous efforts, including the addition of Lands' End and the Covington collection, as well as the refurbishing of out-of-date stores. While Sears may not be the coolest brand around, the data in Table A for tween and teen girls suggest that in terms of store visits, Sears beats out retailers such as Gap, Macy's, and Wet Seal.

tool? Social networking! Their message? "Don't Just Go Back. Arrive." According to one source:

Thirteen sites have partnered with Sears to create custom animation, virtual worlds and social networking applications aimed at driving the target market to the Sears online "Arrive Lounge." [Arrive Lounge] features exclusive, interactive content from the entire Sears 2008 back to school offering.

## Ethical/Social Issues

The discussions regarding the numerous ethical issues facing marketers are highlighted in the margin throughout the text.

What Are the Ethical Implications of Marketing This Product in This Country?

All marketing programs should be evaluated on ethical as well as financial dimensions. As discussed at the beginning of the chapter, international marketing activities raise many ethical issues. The ethical dimension is particularly important and complex in marketing to Third World and developing countries. Consider Kellogg's attempt to introduce cold cereal as a breakfast food in a developing country. An ethical analysis would consider various factors including:

If we succeed, will the average nutrition level be increased or decreased?

If we succeed, will the funds spent on cereal be diverted from other uses with more beneficial long-term impacts for the individuals or society?

If we succeed, what impact will this have on the local producers of currently consumed breakfast products?

Such an ethical analysis not only is the right thing to do; it may head off conflicts with local governments or economic interests. Understanding and acting on ethical considerations in international marketing is a difficult task. However, it is also a necessary one.

**4**

# The Changing American Society: Demographics and Social Stratification

■ Technology is hot. And marketers want to know who the heavy users are and what traits characterize them so they can better understand this market and meet their needs. Scarborough Research recently conducted a national survey of adults 18 and older to find what they call the **Digital Savvy** consumer.[1] Digital Savvy consumers *are leading-edge digital users who are early adopters and diffusers of information related to technology in terms of (1) technology ownership, (2) Internet usage, and (3) cell phone feature usage.* Scarborough identified 18 different behaviors relating to these three dimensions that [...] generally [...] those [...] nolog [...] Havin [...] abou [...]

iors, demographics, lifestyle, and media usage. Some of the key results include:

- *Technology Behaviors:* The Digital Savvy outstrip the general population in every category of technology, including MP3 and DVR ownership, online banking, online streaming video, text messaging, and e-mail use via cell phone.

- *Demographics:* The Digital Savvy have a very distinct demographic profile. They trended younger, white collar, male, higher education, higher income. And while it is commonly believed that technology is mostly a

## DDB Life Style Study™ Data Analyses

Each relevant chapter poses a series of questions geared toward helping students increase their data analysis skills as well as their understanding of consumer behavior.

DDB LIFE STYLE STUDY™ DATA ANALYSES

1. Examine the DDB data in Tables 1B through 7B. What characterizes someone who *wants to look a little different from others*? Which factors contribute most? Which of McGuire's motives does this most relate to, and what are the marketing implications of your findings?

2. What characterizes someone who *views shopping as a form of entertainment* (Tables 1B through 7B)? Which factors contribute most? How do your

findings relate to the information presented in Consumer Insight 10–1?

3. Some people feel (and act) more self-confident than others. Based on the DDB data (Tables 1B through 7B), what factors are most characteristic of highly confident individuals? Which of the Big Five personality dimensions does self-confidence relate most to, and what are the marketing implications of your findings?

**Consumer Insight 7–1**

**Online Social Media, Consumer-Generated Content, and WOM**

Social media is part of an ongoing *revolution* online, sometimes referred to as Web 2.0, which involves technologies that allow users to leverage the unique interactive and collaborative capabilities of the Internet. These technologies and formats include online communities, social network sites of all types, consumer review sites, and blogs or online journals kept by individuals and companies and distributed across the Web. Online social media allow users not only to form, join, and communicate with groups and individuals online, but also to create and distribute original content in ways not possible in the past. Such *consumer-generated content* is changing the marketing landscape. Marketers no longer completely control the communications process but now are both observers and participants in an ongoing dialogue that often is driven by consumers themselves.[27]

An example of consumer-generated content in online social network sites is a video titled "Fully Submerged Jeep." It shows an amateur video posted on [...]

fans to create commercials using the same material Chevy provided. Or better yet—GM could have allowed them to use their own videos, images, and music to create truly personalized commercials.

In this new world of social media, there are numerous categories of participants. These include:[29]

- Creators—these folks create content of their own—Web pages, blogs, video and video uploads to places like YouTube. Creators tend to be in the teens and early twenties.

- Critics—these folks are bloggers and post ratings and reviews. Critics tend to be a bit older than creators—more in the late teens and mid-twenties.

- Joiners—these folks utilize social networking sites. Joiners range mostly from teens to late twenties. Joiners are a much larger proportion of the population than creators and critics.

- Spectators—these folks consume other people's content by reading blogs, watching videos, and [...]

APPLICATION ACTIVITIES

42. Interview two students from two different cultures. Determine the extent to which the following are used in those cultures and the variations in the values of those cultures that relate to the use of these products:
   a. Gift cards
   b. Energy drinks (like Red Bull)
   c. Fast-food restaurants
   d. Exercise equipment
   e. Music
   f. Internet

45. Interview a student from India. Report on the advice that the student would give an American firm marketing consumer products in India.

46. Interview two students from EU (European Union) countries. Report on the extent to which they feel the EU will be a homogeneous culture by 2025.

47. Imagine you are a consultant working with your state or province's tourism agency. You have been asked to advise the agency on the best promotional themes to use to attract foreign tourists. What would you recommend if Germany and Australia

## Consumer Insight

These boxed discussions provide an in-depth look at a particularly interesting consumer study or marketing practice.

## End-of-Chapter Materials

At the end of each chapter are a series of learning tools including Internet Exercises, Review Questions, Discussion Questions, and Application Activities.

# DDB Life Style Study™ Data Analyses

DDB Worldwide is one of the leading advertising agencies in the world. One of the many services it provides for its clients, as well as to support its own creative and strategy efforts, is a major annual lifestyle survey. This survey is conducted using a panel maintained by Synovate. In a panel such as this, consumers are recruited such that the panel has demographic characteristics similar to the U.S. population. Members of the panel agree to complete questions on a periodic basis.

## THE DATA

The 2004 DDB Life Style Study™ involved more than 3,300 completed questionnaires. These lengthy questionnaires included hundreds of attitude, activity, interest, opinion, and behavior items relating to consumers, their consumption, and their lifestyles. The questionnaires also contained numerous questions collecting demographic and media preference data.

DDB has allowed us to provide a portion of these data in spreadsheet format in the disk that accompanies this text. The data are presented in the form of cross-tabulations at an aggregate level with the cell values being percents. For example,

| | Household Size | | | |
|---|---|---|---|---|
| | **1** | **2** | **3–5** | **6+** |
| **Number in Sample** | 523 | 1294 | 1351 | 133 |
| Own a DVD Player | 49.0% | 68.2% | 84.3% | 88.5% |
| Purchased clothes online | 11.0 | 12.4 | 15.3 | 13.1 |
| Visited a fast-food restaurant | 46.6 | 54.1 | 69.1 | 74.7 |

The example indicates that 49.0 percent of the 523 respondents from one-person households own a DVD player, compared with 68.2 percent of the 1,294 from two-person households, 84.3 percent of those from households with three, four, or five members, and 88.5 percent of those from households with six or more members.

It is possible to combine columns within variables. That is, we can determine the percent of one- and two-person households combined that purchased clothes online. Because the number of respondents on which the percentages are based differs across columns, we can't simply average the cell percentage figures. Instead, we need to convert the cell percentages to numbers by multiplying each cell percentage times the number in the sample for that column. Add the numbers for the cells to be combined together and divide the result by the sum of the number in the sample for the combined cells' columns. The result is the percentage of the combined column categories that engaged in the behavior of interest.

The data available on the disk are described below.

## COLUMN VARIABLES FOR THE DATA TABLES

### Tables

1A & 1B  Household size, marital status, number of children at home, age of youngest child at home, age of oldest child at home.

2A & 2B  For married female respondents, their spouse's level of employment. For married male respondents, their spouse's level of employment.

3A & 3B  Household income, education level of respondent, perceived tech savvy.

4A & 4B  Occupation of respondent.

5A & 5B  Ethnic subculture, age, cognitive age (feel a lot younger than my age).

6A & 6B  Gender, geographic region.

7A & 7B    Ideal self-concept traits (adventurous, affectionate, ambitious, assertive, careful, competitive, easy-going, independent, masculine, sensitive, tolerant, traditional, youthful).

# ROW VARIABLES FOR TABLES 1A THROUGH 7A

## Heavier User Behaviors and Product Ownership

### General Behaviors
Read books/articles about health

Visited gourmet coffee bar or café

Visited fast-food restaurant

Went on weight reducing diet

Went dancing at a club

Played bingo

Worked in the garden

Jogged

Went camping

Rented a DVD

Traveled to another country

Attended church/place of worship

### Consumption Behaviors
Dessert

Diet sodas

Sports drinks

Cordials, liqueurs or other after-dinner drinks

Chocolate bars

Premium ice cream

### Shopping Activities
Purchased from mail order catalog

Shopped at a convenience store

Purchased items for home at discount retailer

Bought a store's own brand

Used a price coupon

### Product Ownership
DVD

PVR

MP3 player

Personal computer

Cellular phone

Individual retirement account

Car

Home

ATV or off-road motorcycle

Dog

Cat

### Types of TV Shows Watched Regularly
Children's shows

Comedy

Drama

Home improvement

News/political

Religious programming

Sports

Weather

# ROW VARIABLES FOR TABLES 1B THROUGH 7B

## Attitude/Activity/Interest/ Behavior Relating to . . .

### Culture
Enjoy shopping for items influenced by other cultures

Interested in the cultures of other countries

### Values
I work hard most of the time

Religion is a big part of my life

Men concerned with latest styles and fashions aren't masculine

Make a special effort to buy from environmentally friendly businesses

Work at trying to maintain a youthful appearance

A commercial that features people of my race speaks more directly to me

There is not enough ethnic diversity in commercials today

I make a strong effort to recycle

### Gender and Family

Individuality is an important value to pass down to kids

A woman's place is in the home

When making family decisions, consideration of the kids comes first

### Brands, Innovators, and Opinion Leadership

Friends and neighbors come to me for advice about brands and products

I am usually among the first to try a new product

I try to stick to well-known brand names

### Motivation, Personality, and Extended Self

View shopping as a form of entertainment

Want to look a little different from others

Have more self-confidence than friends

Brands I buy are a reflection of who I am

The car I drive is a reflection of who I am

Clothes I wear reflect who I am as a person

### Information Search and Decision Making

Consult consumer reports before making a major purchase

Nutritional information on label influences what I buy

Information in advertising helps me to make better decisions

The Internet is the best place to get information about products and services

Consider myself tech savvy

In making big decisions, I go with my heart rather than my head

Making purchases with a credit card over the Internet is too risky

Worry about others getting private information about me

### Shopping and Loyalty

Am an impulse buyer

Stick with favorite brand even if something else is on sale

Pay more for better service

Our family is in too much debt

### Marketing Regulation

Avoid buying products advertised on shows with sex or violence

TV commercials place too much emphasis on sex

Most big companies are just out for themselves

Advertising directed at children should be taken off TV

### Internet Use and Purchase

Used the Internet in the past 12 months

Purchased auto insurance online

Purchased clothes online

Purchased concert/play/sports tickets online

# Brief Contents

# Contents

# Consumer Behavior

Building Marketing Strategy

# Introduction

External
Influences

Culture
Subculture
Demographics
Social Status
Reference Groups
Family
Marketing Activities

Internal
Influences

Perception
Learning
Memory
Motives
Personality
Emotions
Attitudes

Self-Concept
and
Lifestyle

Experiences and Acquisitions

Experiences and Acquisitions

■ What is consumer behavior? Why should we study it? Do marketing managers, regulators, and consumer advocates actually use knowledge about consumer behavior to develop strategies and policy? How? Will a sound knowledge of consumer behavior help you in your career? Will it enable you to be a better citizen? How does consumer behavior impact the quality of all of our lives and of the environment? How can we organize our knowledge of consumer behavior to understand and use it more effectively?

■ Chapter 1 addresses these and a number of other interesting questions, describes the importance and usefulness of the material to be covered in this text, and provides an overview of the text. Chapter 1 also explains the logic of the model of consumer behavior shown below, which is presented again in Figure 1–3 and discussed toward the end of the chapter.

# Consumer Behavior and Marketing Strategy

Marketers face exciting and daunting challenges as the forces that drive and shape consumer behavior rapidly evolve. Domestic firms confront the challenges of international competition but also the opportunities of vast emerging markets such as China and India. In the United States, companies are responding to increased diversity and retailers face the challenges and opportunities of technology such as online shopping. Marketers and regulators struggle with tough ethical and social aspects of marketing including marketing to children. And this only scratches the surface! Let's take a closer look at a few of these areas.

*Online marketing*—Marketers are using the Internet to make their offerings more personalized and convenient. Historically, we don't think about buying fast food online. That has all changed. Papa John's recently announced that it hit the $1 billion mark through online and text message options, which represents 20 percent of its overall sales. Several factors are driving this trend. One is increased Internet access, recently estimated at about 75 percent of U.S. adults. Another is consumer desire for convenience. Consider the following quote of one busy mother:

> I'm so into the Internet and the ease of doing things that way. Being able to log in and [order] versus trying to talk over a baby crying or a 2½-year-old that's running around the house is probably one of the main reasons I like to order that way.

To further build in convenience, Papa John's offers consumers the opportunity to order ahead of time. Competitors are in the mix as well, with Domino's offering online pizza tracking.[1]

*Global marketing*—China's massive population, rising income, and emerging youth market make that country very attractive to marketers around the world. Consider the following:

> Urban Chinese teens download hip-hop tunes to trendy Nokia cell phones, guzzle icy Cokes after shooting hoops in Nike shoes and munch fries at McDonald's after school.

If this sounds like an American marketer's dream, you are partly right. However, there are challenges to marketing to this segment. Chinese history, values, and culture are factors that cannot be ignored. They create a unique teen market that U.S. marketers must understand and adapt to. As one marketing expert puts it:

> Successful advertising for youth brands carefully navigates the respect young consumers feel for their family, peer groups and country with their cautious desire to express individuality.

Still, key "passion points" exist—music, fashion, sports, and technology. Although these passion points are similar for teens around the globe, U.S. companies must adapt to the Chinese culture by identifying specific trends among urban Chinese teens. For example:

> Coke…has combined its partnerships with a popular girl band in China called S.H.E.; athletes like Liu Xiang; and the current video game hit in China, "World of Warcraft," to hit two or three passion points at the same time.[2]

*Social marketing*—OLPC, or One Laptop Per Child, is a nonprofit created by Nicholas Negroponte of MIT. The mission of OLPC is to "empower the children of developing countries to learn by providing one connected laptop to every school-age child."

OLPC is in a tough battle with for-profit firms for this market. As a consequence, OLPC has had to employ numerous marketing concepts. Starting with the product, OLPC has designed a computer specifically for developing countries. It is inexpensive (target price is $100) and durable, uses little power, and runs on free Linux software. Although these features are important, "compatibility" is still a driving factor, which has OLPC considering a dual operating system including Windows. According to Negroponte:

> When I went to Egypt for the first time, I met separately with the minister of communications, the minister of education, and the minister of science and technology, and the prime minister, and each one of them, within the first three sentences, said, "Can you run Windows?"

Promotional activities include efforts aimed at gaining donations so that OLPC can provide the computers for free. OLPC's Web site is one tool, which uses facts and emotions to persuade. It even provides a direct benefit by giving each donor one year's free access to T-Mobile HotSpot. Finally, social influence is used, including testimonials and viral marketing.[3]

---

The field of **consumer behavior** is *the study of individuals, groups, or organizations and the processes they use to select, secure, use, and dispose of products, services, experiences, or ideas to satisfy needs and the impacts that these processes have on the consumer and society.* This view of consumer behavior is broader than the traditional one, which focused more narrowly on the buyer and the immediate antecedents and consequences of the purchasing process. Our broader view will lead us to examine more indirect influences on consumption decisions as well as far-reaching consequences that involve more than just the purchaser and the seller.

The opening examples above summarize some attempts to apply an understanding of consumer behavior to develop an effective marketing strategy or to influence socially desirable behavior. Throughout this text, we will explore the factors and trends shaping consumer behavior and the ways marketers and regulators can use this information. The examples cited above reveal four key aspects regarding consumer behavior. First, and most basic, is that successful marketing decisions by commercial firms, nonprofit organizations, and regulatory agencies require extensive information about consumer behavior. It should be obvious from the examples that *organizations are applying theories and information about consumer behavior on a daily basis.* Knowledge of consumer behavior is critical for influencing decisions not only about which product to purchase but also about which college to attend, which charities to support, how much recycling to do, whether to seek help for an addiction, and so on.

Second, the examples indicate the need to collect information about the *specific* consumers involved in the marketing decision at hand. At its current state of development, consumer behavior theory provides the manager with the proper questions to ask. Given the importance of the specific situation or product category, it will often be necessary to *conduct research* to find the relevant answers to these questions. One executive explains the importance of consumer behavior research this way:

> Understanding and properly interpreting consumer wants is a whole lot easier said than done. Every week our marketing researchers talk to more than 4,000 consumers to find out
>
> * What they think of our products and those of our competitors.
> * What they think of possible improvements in our products.
> * How they use our products.
> * What attitudes they have about our products and our advertising.
> * What they feel about their roles in the family and society.
> * What their hopes and dreams are for themselves and their families.
>
> Today, as never before, we cannot take our business for granted. That's why understanding—and therefore learning to anticipate—consumer behavior is our key to planning and managing in this ever-changing environment.[4]

Marketers approach consumer research in a variety of ways (as discussed in Appendix A at the end of the text). An emerging approach involves online research. One estimate is that 60 percent of all product and service concept testing is done online. The most prominent reason is its efficiency in terms of time and money. Kellogg hired BuzzBack Market Research to conduct online research on kids and moms about its new Pop-Tarts Yogurt Blasts. They focused on picking a brand name and selecting key product benefits to feature in their promotions. They found that by having colorful and interesting packaging (kids) and emphasizing key health benefits (moms), they could satisfy both groups.[5]

Third, the examples in the chapter opener reveal that *consumer behavior is a complex, multidimensional process.* Coke, OLPC, and Papa John's have invested substantial time, money, and effort researching consumer behavior and much more trying to influence it; yet none of them are completely successful. Careful research is no guarantee—it simply increases the odds of success. Think of the complexity involved in Kellogg's Yogurt Blasts: Both kids and parents must be satisfied, and the benefits they want differ dramatically. Or consider the complex set of trade-offs consumers must often make to purchase and use products that are environmentally friendly.

Finally, the examples cited above suggest that *marketing practices designed to influence consumer behavior involve ethical issues that affect the firm, the individual, and society.* The issues are not always obvious and many times involve trade-offs at different levels. Coke, while providing benefits to individual consumers and profits for the company, raises resource use, disposition, and other issues that affect all of society. Coke may provide individual consumers with an enjoyable experience; however, dietary consequences of consuming sugar-laden beverages exist at both individual and societal levels, as highlighted,

**ILLUSTRATION 1–1**

These advertisements are targeting the same consumers with very similar products, yet they use two very different approaches. Why? They are based on different assumptions about consumer behavior and how to influence it.

for example, by increases in juvenile diabetes. More obvious concerns arise with marketing products such as cigarettes and alcohol, or when using marketing practices that target children. We will explore such ethical issues throughout the text.

Sufficient knowledge of consumer behavior currently exists to provide a usable guide to marketing practice for commercial firms, nonprofit organizations, and regulators, but the state of the art is not sufficient for us to write a cookbook with surefire recipes for success. We will illustrate how some organizations were able to combine certain ingredients for success under specific conditions. However, as conditions change, the quantities and even the ingredients required for success may change. It is up to you as a student and future marketing manager to develop the ability to apply this knowledge to specific situations. To assist you, we provide a variety of questions and exercises at the end of each chapter and a series of short cases at the end of each main part of the text that can be used to develop your application skills. Appendix B at the end of the text provides a list of key questions for a consumer behavior audit for developing marketing strategy.

Remember that *all marketing decisions and regulations are based on assumptions and knowledge about consumer behavior*. It is impossible to think of a marketing decision for which this is not the case. For example, OLPC's decision to use certain types of appeals on its Web site to target potential donors must be based on various assumptions about the characteristics of the donor base, the motives that drive people to make donations to worthy causes, and so forth. Likewise, a decision to match a competitor's price reduction must be based on some assumption about how consumers evaluate prices and how they would respond to a price differential between the two brands. Examine Illustration 1–1. Both these ads are targeted at the same consumers. *What assumptions about consumer behavior underlie each ad? Which approach is best? Why?*

# APPLICATIONS OF CONSUMER BEHAVIOR

## Marketing Strategy

All marketing strategies and tactics are based on explicit or implicit beliefs about consumer behavior. Decisions based on explicit assumptions and on sound theory and research are more likely to be successful than are decisions based solely on hunches or intuition. Thus, knowledge of consumer behavior can be an important competitive advantage. It can greatly reduce the odds of making bad decisions and creating market failures such as the following:

> S.C. Johnson recently pulled the plug on its Ziploc TableTops, a line of semi-disposable plates. TableTops was one of the company's most expensive launches with $65 million spent on marketing. A number of factors appear to have contributed to the failure including relatively high prices (which made consumers less likely to throw them away) and the fact that the products really weren't all that disposable. As one retailer explained, "There are no repeat purchases. The things last forever."[6]

A primary goal of this book is to help you obtain a usable managerial understanding of consumer behavior. The key here is *usable understanding*—we want to increase your understanding of consumer behavior to help you become a more effective marketing manager. Before we take a look at marketing strategy and consumer behavior, let's examine regulatory policy, social marketing, and the importance of being an informed individual.

## Regulatory Policy

Various regulatory bodies exist to develop, interpret, and/or implement policies designed to protect and aid consumers. For example, the Food and Drug Administration (FDA) administers the Nutrition Labeling and Education Act (NLEA). Among other things, NLEA requires that packaged foods prominently display nutrition information in the form of the Nutrition Facts panel.

A major goal of NLEA was to improve consumer dietary decisions by providing more nutrition information. Has NLEA succeeded? A recent study suggests that it depends. For example, the Nutrition Facts panel appears to be the most beneficial to highly motivated consumers who are low in nutritional knowledge. Regulations have both costs and benefits. For example, the benefits of NLEA can be viewed in light of the estimated $2 billion in compliance costs. The comparisons get increasingly difficult as one tries to place a dollar value on individual and societal benefits.[7]

Clearly, effective regulation of many marketing practices requires an extensive knowledge of consumer behavior. We will discuss this issue throughout the text and provide a detailed treatment in Chapter 20.

## Social Marketing

Some states invest cigarette tax revenues in high-quality, prime-time antismoking television commercials. Researchers at the University of Vermont spent $2 million on a four-year

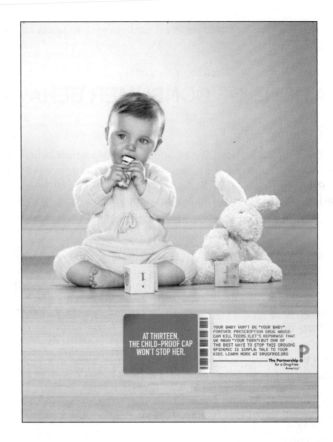

television campaign that showed popular kids disdaining cigarettes or smokers being unable to get dates. Smoking rates among teenagers were 35 percent lower in communities where the campaign was shown than in similar communities without the campaign. The effect was still strong two years after the campaign quit airing.[8]

How did these researchers decide to stress negative social consequences of smoking rather than negative health consequences? The decision was based on their knowledge and assumptions about the consumer behavior of teenagers.

**Social marketing** is *the application of marketing strategies and tactics to alter or create behaviors that have a positive effect on the targeted individuals or society as a whole.*[9] Social marketing has been used in attempts to reduce smoking, as noted above; to increase the percentage of children receiving their vaccinations in a timely manner; to encourage environmentally sound behaviors such as recycling; to reduce behaviors potentially leading to AIDS; to enhance support of charities; to reduce drug use; and to support many other important causes.

Just as for commercial marketing strategy, successful social marketing strategy requires a sound understanding of consumer behavior. For example, the Partnership for a Drug-Free America uses a fear-based campaign in its efforts to educate parents about the alarming increase in teen abuse of prescription drugs. Illustration 1–2 shows one such ad. In Chapter 11, we will analyze the conditions under which such campaigns are likely to succeed.

## Informed Individuals

Most economically developed societies are legitimately referred to as consumption societies. Most individuals in these societies spend more time engaged in consumption than in any other activity, including work or sleep (both of which also involve consumption). Therefore, knowledge of consumer behavior can enhance our understanding of our environment and ourselves. Such an understanding is essential for sound citizenship, effective purchasing behavior, and reasoned business ethics.

Literally thousands of firms are spending millions of dollars to influence you, your family, and your friends. These attempts to influence you occur in ads, in Web sites, on packages, as product features, in sales pitches, and in store environments. They also occur in the content of many television shows, in the products that are used in movies, and in the materials presented to children in schools.[10] Given the magnitude of these direct and indirect influence attempts, it is important that consumers accurately understand the strategies and tactics being used. It is equally important that all of us, as citizens, understand the consumer behavior basis of these strategies so that we can set appropriate limits on them when required.

# MARKETING STRATEGY AND CONSUMER BEHAVIOR

The applications of consumer behavior described above focus on the development, regulation, or effects of marketing strategy. We will now examine marketing strategy in more depth.

To survive in a competitive environment, an organization must provide its target customers more value than is provided to them by its competitors. **Customer value** is *the difference between all the benefits derived from a total product and all the costs of acquiring those benefits.* For example, owning a car can provide a number of benefits, depending on the person and the type of car, including flexible transportation, image, status, pleasure, comfort, and even companionship. However, securing these benefits requires paying not only for the car but also for gasoline, insurance, registration, maintenance, and parking fees, as well as risking injury from an accident, adding to environmental pollution, and dealing with traffic jams and other frustrations. It is the difference between the total benefits and the total costs that constitutes customer value.

It is critical that a firm consider value *from the customer's perspective.* Ziploc's TableTop failure, referred to earlier, demonstrates this. The product was overpriced relative to products of competitors in the category and much higher priced than truly disposable tableware. The high price made consumers hesitant to buy in the first place; if they did buy, the high price made them uncomfortable with throwing the tableware away. TableTop was too expensive and durable to be maximally useful to consumers and profitable for Ziploc.

*Providing superior customer value requires the organization to do a better job of anticipating and reacting to customer needs than the competition does.* This is the essence of a good marketing strategy. As Figure 1–1 indicates, an understanding of consumer behavior is the basis for marketing strategy formulation. Consumers' reactions to the marketing strategy determine the organization's success or failure. However, these reactions also determine the success of the consumers in meeting their needs, and they have significant impacts on the larger society in which they occur.

Marketing strategy, as described in Figure 1–1, is conceptually very simple. It begins with an analysis of the market the organization is considering. This requires a detailed analysis of the organization's capabilities, the strengths and weaknesses of competitors, the economic and technological forces affecting the market, and the current and potential customers in the market. On the basis of the consumer analysis undertaken in this step, the organization identifies groups of individuals, households, or firms with similar needs.

FIGURE 1–1        Marketing Strategy and Consumer Behavior

These market segments are described in terms of demographics, media preferences, geographic location, and so forth. Management then selects one or more of these segments as target markets on the basis of the firm's capabilities relative to those of its competition (given current and forecast economic and technological conditions).

Next, marketing strategy is formulated. Marketing strategy seeks to provide the customer with more value than the competition while still producing a profit for the firm. Marketing strategy is formulated in terms of the marketing mix; that is, it involves determining the product features, price, communications, distribution, and services that will provide customers with superior value. This entire set of characteristics is often referred to as the **total product.** The total product is presented to the target market, which is consistently engaged in processing information and making decisions designed to maintain or enhance its lifestyle (individuals and households) or performance (businesses and other organizations).

Look at Illustration 1–3. What is the Starbucks total product? Clearly, it is much more than coffee. Places such as Starbucks and the Hard Rock Cafe are selling experiences as much as or perhaps more than food and beverages—and they are doing so around the world.

An "experience" occurs when a company intentionally creates a memorable event for customers. While products and services are to a large extent external to the customer, an experience is largely internal to each customer. The experience exists in the mind of an individual who has been engaged on an emotional, physical, intellectual, or even spiritual level. Today, many firms are wrapping experiences around their traditional products and services in order to sell them better. Niketown, Cabela's, and REI all draw customers to their outlets in part because of the experiences that are available at those outlets.[11] Consumer Insight 1–1 shows how traditional retailers are drawing on this notion to develop lifestyle centers.

For the firm, the reaction of the target market to the total product produces an image of the product or brand or organization; sales (or lack thereof); and some level of customer satisfaction among those who did purchase. Sophisticated marketers seek to produce satisfied customers rather than mere sales—because satisfied customers are more profitable in the long run. For the individual, the process results in some level of need satisfaction, financial expenditure, attitude development or change, and/or behavioral changes. For society, the cumulative effect of the marketing process affects economic growth, pollution, social problems (e.g., illnesses caused by smoking and alcohol), and social benefits (e.g., improved nutrition, increased education). Since individual and societal impacts may or may not be in the best interests of the individual or society, the development and application of consumer behavior knowledge has many ethical implications.

Note again that an *analysis of consumers* is a key part of the foundation of marketing strategy, and *consumer reaction* to the total product determines the success or failure of the strategy. Before providing an overview of consumer behavior, we will examine marketing strategy formulation in more detail.

**Beyond Transactions: Retailers Build Lifestyle Centers**

Traditional "bricks-and-mortar" retailers are under increasing pressures to deliver customer value. Online shopping hasn't helped. It has created a situation in which consumers can easily and conveniently gather information and make purchases. So traditional retailers continue to struggle with what their value proposition should be. And increasingly, from the consumer's point of view, it is not in facilitating a transaction, since convenient transactions are much more likely online for many products.

To add additional value and remain competitive, retail developers have been moving to what are called lifestyle centers.[12] **Lifestyle centers** are "small, convenient, open-air retailing complexes laid out to evoke the small-town shopping districts of previous generations." In contrast to traditional enclosed malls with anchor stores, these lifestyle centers are anchored by more experiential offerings, such as restaurants and movie theaters, and also allow a relaxing stroll along the way. Lifestyle centers are on the increase while traditional malls are declining. The following excerpt about a typical lifestyle shopper (Kristen Kratus, a 29-year-old working professional and mother) helps explain why:

[Kristen] avoids the hassles of mall parking by making half her purchases online. Most of the rest is done at Broadway Plaza, a lifestyle center about 10 miles away in Walnut Creek with easy access to parking. "It's more convenient," says Kratus, who has a 10-month-old son, Charlie. "I can buy things, take them back to the car, and then shop again." She says the center has a better selection of restaurants and attractive pedestrian walkways, making shopping more enjoyable: "I can walk around with Charlie, drink a coffee outside, window shop, and see what's out there. It's like being at a park."

Clearly, shopping goes beyond transactions, and traditional retailers have responded in various ingenious ways, including lifestyle centers, that add an experiential component hard to match online.

**Critical Thinking Questions**

1. How do lifestyle centers add value hard to match by online retailers?

2. Can you see any negative aspects of lifestyle centers compared to traditional malls?

3. Do you think *virtual* lifestyle centers might be possible online? What would they look like?

# MARKET ANALYSIS COMPONENTS

Market analysis requires a thorough understanding of the organization's own capabilities, the capabilities of current and future competitors, the consumption process of potential customers, and the economic, physical, and technological environment in which these elements will interact.

## The Consumers

It is not possible to anticipate and react to customers' needs and desires without a complete understanding of consumer behavior. Discovering customers' needs is a complex process, but it can often be accomplished by marketing research. For example, Target wanted to tap into the $210 billion college market. In particular, Target was looking at the furnishings and accessories market and was interested in the specific needs and motivations of students making the transition from home to college dorm life. Jump Associates conducted the research for Target and took a unique approach:

[Jump Associates] sponsored a series of "game nights" at high school grads' homes, inviting incoming college freshmen as well as students with a year of dorm living under their belts. To get teens talking about dorm life, Jump devised a board game that involved issues associated with going to college. The game naturally led to informal conversations—and questions—about college life. Jump researchers were on the sidelines to observe, while a video camera recorded the proceedings.

On the basis of this research (which is a variation of focus groups—see Appendix A), Target successfully launched the Todd Oldham Dorm Room line, which included such products as Kitchen in a Box and Bath in a Box—all-in-one assortments of the types of products needed by college freshmen.[13] Target continues to appeal to the college market with logo merchandise and other dorm products.

Knowing the consumer requires understanding the behavioral principles that guide consumption behaviors. These principles are covered in depth in the remainder of this text.

## The Company

A firm must fully understand its own ability to meet customer needs. This involves evaluating all aspects of the firm, including its financial condition, general managerial skills, production capabilities, research and development capabilities, technological sophistication, reputation, and marketing skills. Marketing skills would include new-product development capabilities, channel strength, advertising abilities, service capabilities, marketing research abilities, market and consumer knowledge, and so forth.

Failure to adequately understand one's own strengths can cause serious problems. IBM's first attempt to enter the home computer market, with the PC Jr., was a failure in part for that reason. Although IBM had an excellent reputation with large business customers and a very strong direct sales force for serving them, these strengths were not relevant to the household consumer market. Its more recent move into high-end business consulting, through IBM Global Business Services, has been a major success and, interestingly, moves IBM back to a focus on its earlier core strengths.

## The Competitors

It is not possible to consistently do a better job than the competition of meeting customer needs without a thorough understanding of the competition's capabilities and strategies. This understanding requires the same level of knowledge of a firm's key competitors that is required of one's own firm. In addition, for any significant marketing action, the following questions must be answered:

1. If we are successful, which firms will be hurt (lose sales or sales opportunities)?
2. Of those firms that are injured, which have the capability (financial resources, marketing strengths) to respond?
3. How are they likely to respond (reduce prices, increase advertising, introduce a new product)?
4. Is our strategy (planned action) robust enough to withstand the likely actions of our competitors, or do we need additional contingency plans?

## The Conditions

The state of the economy, the physical environment, government regulations, and technological developments affect consumer needs and expectations as well as company and competitor capabilities. The deterioration of the physical environment has produced not only consumer demand for environmentally sound products but also government regulations affecting product design and manufacturing.

International agreements such as NAFTA (North American Free Trade Agreement) have greatly reduced international trade barriers and raised the level of both competition and consumer expectations for many products. And technology is changing the way people live, work, deal with disease, and so on. Blogging, podcasting, instant messaging, MP3s, and Apple's success with the iPod and iPhone are just some of the ways technology is changing the way consumers communicate and access media.

Clearly, a firm cannot develop a sound marketing strategy without anticipating the conditions under which that strategy will be implemented.

# MARKET SEGMENTATION

Perhaps the most important marketing decision a firm makes is the selection of one or more market segments on which to focus. A **market segment** is *a portion of a larger market whose needs differ somewhat from the larger market*. Since a market segment has unique needs, a firm that develops a total product focused solely on the needs of that segment will be able to meet the segment's desires better than a firm whose product or service attempts to meet the needs of multiple segments.

To be viable, a segment must be large enough to be served profitably. To some extent, each individual or household has unique needs for most products (a preferred color combination, for example). The smaller the segment, the closer the total product can be to that segment's desires. Historically, the smaller the segment, the more it costs to serve the segment. Thus, a tailor-made suit costs more than a mass-produced suit. However, flexible manufacturing and customized media (including online) are making it increasingly cost effective to develop products and communications for small segments or even individual consumers. *Behavioral targeting*, in which consumers' online activity is tracked and specific banner ads are delivered based on that activity, is another example of how technology is making individualized communication increasingly cost effective.

Market segmentation involves four steps:

1.   Identifying product-related need sets.
2.   Grouping customers with similar need sets.
3.   Describing each group.
4.   Selecting an attractive segment(s) to serve.

## Product-Related Need Sets

Organizations approach market segmentation with a set of current and potential capabilities. These capabilities may be a reputation, an existing product, a technology, or some other skill set. The first task of the firm is to identify need sets that the organization is capable, or could become capable, of meeting. The term **need set** is used to reflect the fact that most products in developed economies satisfy more than one need. Thus, a watch can meet more needs than just telling time. Some customers purchase watches to meet status needs, while others purchase them to meet style needs, and so on. Illustration 1–4 shows two ads for the same product. *What needs are these different ads appealing to?*

Customer needs are not restricted to product features. They also include types and sources of information about the product, outlets where the product is available, the price of the product, services associated with the product, the image of the product or firm, and even where and how the product is produced. For example, in the 1990s Nike lost sales as a result of publicity about child labor and abusive working conditions at some of the factories in developing countries where many of its products are made. In response, Nike changed practices and engaged in a variety of public relations activities. As a result, it seems to have turned its image around in the area of corporate social responsibility (CSR).[14]

Identifying the various need sets that the firm's current or potential product might satisfy typically involves consumer research, particularly focus groups and depth interviews, as well as logic and intuition. These need sets are often associated with other variables such as age, stage in the household life cycle, gender, social class, ethnic group, or lifestyle, and many firms start the segmentation process focusing first on one or more of the groups defined by one of these variables. Thus, a firm might start by identifying various ethnic groups and then attempt to discover similarities and differences in consumption-related needs across these groups. While better-defined segments will generally be discovered by focusing first on needs and then on consumer characteristics associated with those needs, both approaches are used in practice and both provide a useful basis for segmentation.

**ILLUSTRATION 1–4**

Both ads are for the same basic product. Yet, as these ads show, the products are designed to meet different sets of needs beyond their basic function.

## Customers with Similar Need Sets

The next step is to group consumers with similar need sets. For example, the need for moderately priced, fun, sporty automobiles appears to exist in many young single individuals, young couples with no children, and middle-aged couples whose children have left home. These consumers can be grouped into one segment as far as product features and perhaps even product image are concerned despite sharply different demographics.

This step generally involves consumer research, including focus group interviews, surveys, and product concept tests (see Appendix A). It could also involve an analysis of current consumption patterns.

## Description of Each Group

Once consumers with similar need sets are identified, they should be described in terms of their demographics, lifestyles, and media usage. Designing an effective marketing program requires having a complete understanding of the potential customers. It is only with such a complete understanding that we can be sure we have correctly identified the need set. In addition, we cannot communicate effectively with our customers if we do not understand the context in which our product is purchased and consumed, how it is thought about by our customers, and the language they use to describe it. Thus, while many young single individuals, young couples with no children, and middle-aged couples whose children have left home may want the same features in an automobile, the media required to reach each group and the appropriate language and themes to use with each group would likely differ.

## Attractive Segment(s) to Serve

Once we are sure we have a thorough understanding of each segment, we must select our **target market**—*that segment(s) of the larger market on which we will focus our marketing effort*. This decision is based on our ability to provide the selected segment(s) with superior customer value at a profit. Thus, the size and growth of the segment, the intensity of the current and anticipated competition, the cost of providing the superior value, and so forth are important considerations. Table 1–1 provides a simple worksheet for use in evaluating and comparing the attractiveness of various market segments.

As Table 1–1 indicates, segments that are sizable and growing are likely to appear attractive. However, profitability cannot be ignored. After all, a large unprofitable segment is still unprofitable. Finding profitable segments means identifying a maximal fit between customer needs and the firm's offerings. This means that some customers and segments will be unprofitable to serve and may need to be "fired." While firing customers may be difficult, it can lead to greater profits, as ING Direct has found. ING Direct is a bare-bones bank. It has limited offerings (no checking) and does most of its transactions online. ING Direct wants "low-maintenance" customers who are attracted by its higher interest rates. As their CEO notes:

> The difference between ING Direct and the rest of the financial industry is like the difference between take-out food and a sit-down restaurant. The business isn't based on relationships; it's based on a commodity product that's high-volume and low-margin. We need to keep expenses down, which doesn't work when customers want a lot of empathetic contact.[15]

ING Direct keeps costs lower and profits higher by identifying high-cost customers and (nicely) letting them go by suggesting they might be better served by a "high-touch" community bank. *Can you think of any potential risks of "firing" customers?*

**TABLE 1–1**

Market Segment
Attractiveness
Worksheet

| Criterion | Score* |
|---|---|
| Segment size | _____ |
| Segment growth rate | _____ |
| Competitor strength | _____ |
| Customer satisfaction with existing products | _____ |
| Fit with company image | _____ |
| Fit with company objectives | _____ |
| Fit with company resources | _____ |
| Distribution available | _____ |
| Investment required | _____ |
| Stability/predictability | _____ |
| Cost to serve | _____ |
| Sustainable advantage available | _____ |
| Communications channels available | _____ |
| Risk | _____ |
| Segment profitability | _____ |
| Other ( _____ ) | _____ |

*Score on a scale of 1 to 10, with 10 being most favorable.

It is important to remember that each market segment requires its own marketing strategy. Each element of the marketing mix should be examined to determine if changes are required from one segment to another. Sometimes each segment will require a completely different marketing mix, including the product. At other times, only the advertising message or retail outlets may need to differ.

# MARKETING STRATEGY

It is not possible to select target markets without simultaneously formulating a general marketing strategy for each segment. A decisive criterion in selecting target markets is the ability to provide superior value to those market segments. Since customer value is delivered by the marketing strategy, the firm must develop its general marketing strategy as it evaluates potential target markets.

**Marketing strategy** is basically the answer to the question, *How will we provide superior customer value to our target market?* The answer to this question requires the formulation of a consistent marketing mix. The **marketing mix** is *the product, price, communications, distribution, and services provided to the target market.* It is the combination of these elements that meets customer needs and provides customer value. For example, in Illustration 1–1, Crownline boats promise superior value, as compared with competitors' boats, in terms of quality and service. The J.D. Power and Associates award backs up those claims.

## The Product

A **product** is *anything a consumer acquires or might acquire to meet a perceived need.* Consumers are generally buying need satisfaction, not physical product attributes.[16] As the former head of Revlon said, "in the factory we make cosmetics, in the store we sell hope." Thus, consumers don't purchase quarter-inch drill bits but the ability to create quarter-inch holes. Federal Express lost much of its overnight letter delivery business not to UPS or Airborne but to fax machines and the Internet because these technologies could meet the same consumer needs faster, cheaper, or more conveniently.

We use the term *product* to refer to physical products and primary or core services. Thus, an automobile is a product, as is a transmission overhaul or a ride in a taxi. Packaged goods alone (food, beverages, pet products, household products) account for over 30,000 new product introductions each year.[17] Obviously, many of these will not succeed. To be successful, a product must meet the needs of the target market better than the competition's product does.

Consider the Chinese computer market. A few years ago, a state-owned company—Legend—appeared headed for oblivion as China opened its market to Western firms. Today, Legend is a major player. How? According to its general manager, "We have much more insight into the needs of Chinese customers." U.S. companies are learning that while attractive, the Chinese market is also a challenge. A joint venture between Legend and AOL to provide broadband access and service never became viable. As a consequence, Legend broke with AOL and formed an alliance to bundle its computers with China Telecom's China Vnet broadband service.[18]

## Communications

**Marketing communications** include *advertising, the sales force, public relations, packaging, and any other signal that the firm provides about itself and its products.* An effective communications strategy requires answers to the following questions:

1. *With whom, exactly, do we want to communicate?* While most messages are aimed at the target-market members, others are focused on channel members, or those who influence the target-market members. For example, pediatric nurses are often asked for advice concerning diapers and other nonmedical infant care items. A firm marketing such items would be wise to communicate directly with the nurses.

   Often it is necessary to determine who within the target market should receive the marketing message. For a children's breakfast cereal, should the communications be aimed at the children or the parents or both? The answer depends on the target market and varies by country.

2. *What effect do we want our communications to have on the target audience?* Often a manager will state that the purpose of advertising and other marketing communications is to increase sales. While this may be the ultimate objective, the behavioral objective for most marketing communications is often much more immediate. That is, it may seek to have the audience learn something about the product, seek more information about the product, like the product, recommend the product to others, feel good about having bought the product, or a host of other communications effects.

3. *What message will achieve the desired effect on our audience?* What words, pictures, and symbols should we use to capture attention and produce the desired effect? Marketing messages can range from purely factual statements to pure symbolism. The best approach depends on the situation at hand. Developing an effective message requires a thorough understanding of the meanings the target audience attaches to words and symbols, as well as knowledge of the perception process. Consider Illustration 1–5. Many older consumers may not relate to the approach of this ad. However, it communicates clearly to its intended youth market.

4. *What means and media should we use to reach the target audience?* Should we use personal sales to provide information? Can we rely on the package to provide needed information? Should we advertise in mass media, use direct mail, or rely on consumers to find us on the Internet? If we advertise in mass media, which media (television, radio, magazines, newspapers, Internet) and which specific vehicles (television

**ILLUSTRATION 1–5**

All aspects of the marketing mix should be designed around the needs and characteristics of the target audience. Many segments would not appreciate this ad, but it works with the targeted segment.

programs, specific magazines, Web sites, banner ads, and so forth) should we use? Answering these questions requires an understanding of both the media that the target audiences use and the effect that advertising in those media would have on the product's image.

Starburst recently launched a sweepstakes promotion targeting teens. The sweepstakes was promoted on 60 million packages and offered two ways to enter—via cell phone (using the code word "juicy") or online. Notice how the media fits the target audience.[19]

5. *When should we communicate with the target audience?* Should we concentrate our communications near the time that purchases tend to be made or evenly throughout the week, month, or year? Do consumers seek information shortly before purchasing our product? If so, where? Answering these questions requires knowledge of the decision process used by the target market for this product.

## Price

**Price** is *the amount of money one must pay to obtain the right to use the product.* One can buy ownership of a product or, for many products, limited usage rights (i.e., one can rent or lease the product, as with a video). Economists often assume that lower prices for the same product will result in more sales than higher prices. However, price sometimes serves as a signal of quality. A product priced "too low" might be perceived as having low quality. Owning expensive items also provides information about the owner. If nothing else, it indicates that the owner can afford the expensive item. This is a desirable feature to some consumers. Starbucks charges relatively high prices for its coffee. Yet it understands that the Starbucks brand allows consumers to "trade up" to a desired image and lifestyle without breaking the bank. Therefore, setting a price requires a thorough understanding of the symbolic role that price plays for the product and target market in question.

It is important to note that the price of a product is not the same as the cost of the product to the customer. **Consumer cost** is *everything the consumer must surrender in order to receive the benefits of owning/using the product.* As described earlier, the cost of owning/using an automobile includes insurance, gasoline, maintenance, finance charges, license fees, parking fees, time and discomfort while shopping for the car, and perhaps even discomfort about increasing pollution, in addition to the purchase price. One of the ways firms seek to provide customer value is to reduce the nonprice costs of owning or operating a product. If successful, the total cost to the customer decreases while the revenue to the marketer stays the same or even increases.

## Distribution

**Distribution,** *having the product available where target customers can buy it,* is essential to success. Only in rare cases will customers go to much trouble to secure a particular brand. Obviously, good channel decisions require a sound knowledge of where target customers shop for the product in question, as the following example shows:

> Huffy bikes created a *Cross Sport* bike which was a hybrid between a traditional lightweight 10-speed and a mountain bike. Research suggested strong consumer acceptance. However, Huffy distributed the bike through mass merchandisers like Kmart when the target buyer was more likely to go to a specialty bike shop—a mistake that cost them millions.[20]

Today's distribution decisions also require an understanding of cross-channel options. Savvy retailers are figuring out ways to let each distribution channel (e.g., online versus offline) do what it does best. For example, Coldwater Creek keeps retail inventories low by having in-store Internet kiosks where consumers can shop and get free shipping. Barnes and Noble bookstores use a similar approach. Obviously, retailers who adopt this approach have to choose an appropriate merchandising strategy where fast-moving, high-profit, seasonal items are in-store to attract customers while other merchandise is available online.[21]

## Service

Earlier, we defined *product* to include primary or core services such as haircuts, car repairs, and medical treatments. Here, **service** refers to *auxiliary or peripheral activities that are performed to enhance the primary product or primary service.* Thus, we would consider car repair to be a product (primary service), while free pickup and delivery of the car would be an auxiliary service. Although many texts do not treat service as a separate component of the marketing mix, we do because of the critical role it plays in determining market share and relative price in competitive markets. A firm that does not explicitly manage its auxiliary services is at a competitive disadvantage.

Auxiliary services cost money to provide. Therefore, it is essential that the firm furnish only those services that provide value to the target customers. Providing services that customers do not value can result in high costs and high prices without a corresponding increase in customer value.

# CONSUMER DECISIONS

As Figure 1–1 illustrated, the consumer decision process intervenes between the marketing strategy (as implemented in the marketing mix) and the outcomes. That is, the outcomes of the firm's marketing strategy are determined by its interaction with the consumer decision process. The firm can succeed only if consumers see a need that its product can solve, become aware of the product and its capabilities, decide that it is the best available solution, proceed to buy it, and become satisfied with the results of the purchase. A significant part of this entire text (Chapters 14 to 18) is devoted to developing an understanding of the consumer decision process.

# OUTCOMES

## Firm Outcomes

**Product Position**   The most basic outcome of a firm's marketing strategy is its **product position**—*an image of the product or brand in the consumer's mind relative to competing products and brands*. This image consists of a set of beliefs, pictorial representations, and feelings about the product or brand. It does not require purchase or use for it to develop. It is determined by communications about the brand from the firm and other sources, as well as by direct experience with it. Most marketing firms specify the product position they want their brands to have and measure these positions on an ongoing basis. This is because a brand whose position matches the desired position of a target market is likely to be purchased when a need for that product arises.

The ad in Illustration 1–6 is positioning the brand as a fun brand. This image and personality is facilitated and enhanced by the color and imagery used.

**Sales and Profits**   Sales and profits are critical outcomes, as they are necessary for the firm to continue in business. Therefore, virtually all firms evaluate the success of their marketing programs in terms of sales revenues and profits. As we have seen, sales and profits are likely to occur only if the initial consumer analysis was correct and if the marketing mix matches the consumer decision process.

**Customer Satisfaction**   Marketers have discovered that it is generally more profitable to maintain existing customers than to replace them with new customers. Retaining current customers requires that they be satisfied with their purchase and use of the product. Thus, **customer satisfaction** is a major concern of marketers.

As Figure 1–2 indicates, convincing consumers that your brand offers superior value is necessary in order to make the initial sale. Obviously, one must have a thorough understanding of the potential consumers' needs and of their information acquisition processes to succeed at this task. However, *creating satisfied customers,* and thus future sales, requires that customers continue to believe that your brand meets their needs and offers superior value *after they have used it.* You must deliver as much or more value than your customers initially expected, and it must be enough to satisfy their needs. Doing so requires an even greater understanding of consumer behavior.

## Individual Outcomes

**Need Satisfaction**   The most obvious outcome of the consumption process for an individual, whether or not a purchase is made, is some level of satisfaction of the need that initiated

ILLUSTRATION 1–6

This ad positions the brand as fun.

FIGURE 1–2        Creating Satisfied Customers

the consumption process. This can range from no satisfaction (or even a negative level if a purchase increases the need rather than reduces it) to complete satisfaction. Two key processes are involved—the actual need fulfillment and the perceived need fulfillment. These two processes are closely related and are often identical. However, at times they differ. For example, people might take food supplements because they believe the supplements are enhancing their health while in reality they could have no direct health effects or even negative effects. One objective of government regulation and a frequent goal of consumer groups is to ensure that consumers can adequately judge the extent to which products are meeting their needs.

Injurious Consumption    Although we tend to focus on the benefits of consumption, we must remain aware that consumer behavior has a dark side. **Injurious consumption** occurs *when individuals or groups make consumption decisions that have negative consequences for their long-run well-being.*

For most consumers, fulfilling one need affects their ability to fulfill other needs, because of either financial or time constraints. For example, some estimates indicate that most Americans are not saving at a level that will allow them to maintain a lifestyle near their current one when they retire.[22] The cumulative impact of many small decisions to spend financial resources to meet needs now will limit their ability to meet what may be critically important needs after retirement. For other consumers, readily available credit, unrelenting advertising, and widespread, aggressive merchandising result in a level of expenditure that cannot be sustained by their income.[23] The result is often financial distress, delayed or bypassed medical or dental care, family stress, inadequate resources for proper child care, bankruptcy, or even homelessness.

Cigarette consumption is encouraged by hundreds of millions of dollars in marketing expenditures, as is the consumption of alcoholic beverages, snacks with high sugar or fat content, and other potentially harmful products. These marketing expenditures cause some people to consume these products or to consume more of them. Some of these people, and their families, in turn are then harmed by this consumption.[24] Companies are not the only entities that promote potentially harmful products. Most states in the United States now promote state-sponsored gambling, which has caused devastating financial consequences for some individuals.

Although these are issues we should be concerned with, and we will address them throughout this text, we should also note that alcohol consumption seems to have arisen simultaneously with civilization and evidence of gambling is nearly as old. Consumers smoked and chewed tobacco long before mass media or advertising as we know it existed, and illegal drug consumption continues to grow worldwide despite the absence of large-scale marketing, or at least advertising. Thus, though marketing activities based on knowledge of consumer behavior undoubtedly exacerbate some forms of injurious consumption, they are not the sole cause and, as we will see shortly, such activities may be part of the cure.

## Society Outcomes

**Economic Outcomes**    The cumulative impact of consumers' purchase decisions, including the decision to forgo consumption, is a major determinant of the state of a given country's economy. Consumers' decisions on whether to buy or to save affect economic growth, the availability and cost of capital, employment levels, and so forth. The types of products and brands purchased influence the balance of payments, industry growth rates, and wage levels. Decisions made in one society, particularly large, wealthy societies such as those of the United States, Western Europe, and Japan, have a major impact on the economic health of many other countries.

**Physical Environment Outcomes**    Consumers make decisions that have a major impact on the physical environments of both their own and other societies. The cumulative effect of U.S. consumers' decisions to rely on relatively large private cars rather than mass transit results in significant air pollution in American cities as well as the consumption of nonrenewable resources from other countries. The decisions of people in most developed and in many developing economies to consume meat as a primary source of protein result in the clearing of rain forests for grazing land, the pollution of many watersheds due to large-scale feedlots, and an inefficient use of grain, water, and energy to produce protein. It also appears to produce health problems for many consumers. Similar effects are being seen as ethanol (made from corn, sugar cane, or rice) becomes a more popular alternative to oil as a source of fuel for automobiles. The high cost of fuel, along with the diversion of grain from food to fuel, is driving up food costs and threatens to increase poverty levels around the world.[25] Such outcomes attract substantial negative publicity. However, these resources are being used because of consumer demand, and consumer demand consists of the decisions you and I and our families and our friends make!

As we will see in Chapter 3, many consumers now recognize the indirect effects of consumption on the environment and are altering their behavior to minimize environmental harm.

**Social Welfare**   Consumer decisions affect the general social welfare of a society. Decisions concerning how much to spend for private goods (personal purchases) rather than public goods (support for public education, parks, health care, and the like) are generally made indirectly by consumers' elected representatives. These decisions have a major impact on the overall quality of life in a society.

Injurious consumption, as described above, affects society as well as the individuals involved. The social costs of smoking-induced illnesses, alcoholism, and drug abuse are staggering. To the extent that marketing activities increase or decrease injurious consumption, they have a major impact on the social welfare of a society. Consider the following:

> According to the U.S. Public Health Service, of the 10 leading causes of death in the United States, at least 7 could be reduced substantially if people at risk would change just 5 behaviors: compliance (e.g., use of antihypertensive medication), diet, smoking, lack of exercise, and alcohol and drug abuse. Each of these behaviors is inextricably linked with marketing efforts and the reactions of consumers to marketing campaigns. The link between consumer choices and social problems is clear.[26]

However, the same authors conclude: "Although these problems appear daunting, they are all problems that are solvable through altruistic [social] marketing." Thus, marketing and consumer behavior can both aggravate and reduce serious social problems.

# THE NATURE OF CONSUMER BEHAVIOR

Figure 1–3 is the model that we use to capture the general structure and process of consumer behavior and to organize this text. It is a **conceptual model**. It does not contain sufficient detail to predict particular behaviors; however, it does reflect our beliefs about the general nature of consumer behavior. Individuals develop self-concepts and subsequent lifestyles based on a variety of internal (mainly psychological and physical) and external (mainly sociological and demographic) influences. These self-concepts and lifestyles produce needs and desires, many of which require consumption decisions to satisfy. As individuals encounter relevant situations, the consumer decision process is activated. This process and the experiences and acquisitions it produces in turn influence the consumers' self-concept and lifestyle by affecting their internal and external characteristics.

The model in Figure 1–3, although simple, is both conceptually sound and intuitively appealing. We all have a view of ourselves (self-concept), and we try to live in a particular manner given our resources (lifestyle). Our view of ourselves and the way we try to live are determined by internal factors (such as our personality, values, emotions, and memory) and external factors (such as our culture, age, friends, family, and subculture). Our view of ourselves and the way we try to live result in desires and needs that we bring to the multitude of situations we encounter daily. Many of these situations will cause us to consider a purchase. Our decision, and even the process of making it, will cause learning and may affect many other internal and external factors that will change or reinforce our current self-concept and lifestyle.

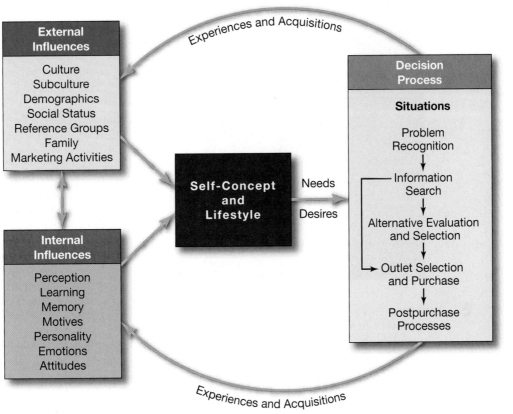

Of course life is rarely so structured as Figure 1–3 and our discussion of it so far may seem to suggest. Consumer behavior is hardly ever so simple, structured, conscious, mechanical, or linear. A quick analysis of your own behavior and that of your friends will reveal that on the contrary, consumer behavior is frequently complex, disorganized, nonconscious, organic, and circular. Remember—Figure 1–3 is only a model, a starting point for our analysis. It is meant to aid you in thinking about consumer behavior. As you look at the model and read the following chapters based on this model, continually relate the descriptions in the text to the rich world of consumer behavior that is all around you.

The factors shown in Figure 1–3 are given detailed treatment in the subsequent chapters of this book. Here we provide a brief overview so that you can initially see how they work and fit together. Our discussion here and in the following chapters moves through the model from left to right.

## External Influences (Part Two)

Dividing the factors that influence consumers into categories is somewhat arbitrary. For example, we treat learning as an internal influence despite the fact that much human learning involves interaction with, or imitation of, other individuals. Thus, learning could also be considered a group process. In Figure 1–3, the two-directional arrow connecting internal and external influences indicates that each set interacts with the other.

America is increas-ingly diverse. Ads such as this one reflect and embrace such diversity.

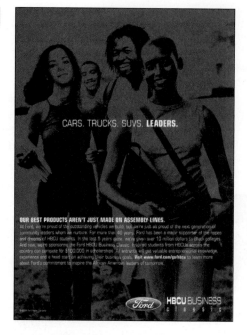

We organize our discussion of external influences from large-scale macrogroups to smaller, more microgroup influences. *Culture* is perhaps the most pervasive influence on consumer behavior. We begin our consider-ation of culture in Chapter 2 by examining differences in consumption patterns across cultures. In Chapters 3 through 6, we focus on American culture in detail. In Chapter 3, we examine cultural values. As we will see, while Americans share many values and consumption behaviors, there is also rich diversity and ongoing change in this society that create both marketing opportunities and unique social energy. Illustration 1–7 shows how marketers are embracing this diversity in their advertisements.

Chapter 4 continues our examination of American society by analyzing its demo-graphics (the number, education, age, income, occupation, and location of individuals in a society) and social stratification. Chapter 5 considers ethnic, religious, and regional sub-cultures. Chapter 6 analyzes families and households, including discussions of how they evolve over time, the role of families in teaching children how to consume, and household decision making. Finally, in Chapter 7, we look at the processes by which groups influence consumer behavior and group communication, including the role of groups in the accep-tance of new products and technologies. Taken together, Chapters 2 through 7 provide a means of comparing and contrasting the various external factors that influence consumer behavior in America—and around the world. Cross-cultural variations are highlighted when possible throughout the text.

## Internal Influences (Part Three)

Internal influences begin with perception, the process by which individuals receive and assign meaning to stimuli (Chapter 8). This is followed by learning—changes in the con-tent or structure of long-term memory (Chapter 9). Chapter 10 covers three closely related topics: motivation—the reason for a behavior; personality—an individual's characteristic response tendencies across similar situations; and emotion—strong, relatively uncontrolled feelings that affect our behavior. We conclude our coverage of internal influences by exam-ining attitudes in Chapter 11. An attitude is an enduring organization of motivational, emo-tional, perceptual, and cognitive processes with respect to some aspect of our environment. In essence an attitude is the way a person thinks, feels, and acts toward some aspect of his or her environment, such as a retail store, television program, or product. As such, our atti-tudes are heavily influenced by the external and internal factors that we will have discussed in the preceding chapters.

## Self-Concept and Lifestyle

Chapter 12 concludes Part Three with a detailed discussion of the key concepts of self-concept and lifestyle around which our model revolves. As a result of the interaction of the internal and external variables described earlier, individuals develop a self-concept that is reflected in a lifestyle. **Self-concept** is *the totality of an individual's thoughts and feelings about him- or herself.* **Lifestyle** is, quite simply, *how one lives,* including the products one buys, how one uses them, what one thinks about them, and how one feels about them. Lifestyle is the manifestation of the individual's self-concept, the total image the person has of him- or herself as a result of the culture he or she lives in and the individual situations and experiences that comprise his or her daily existence. It is the sum of the person's past decisions and future plans.

Both individuals and families exhibit distinct lifestyles. We often hear of "career-oriented individuals," "outdoor families," or "devoted parents." One's lifestyle is determined by both conscious and unconscious decisions. Often we make choices with full awareness of their impact on our lifestyle, but generally we are unaware of the extent to which our decisions are influenced by our current or desired lifestyle. Our model shows that consumers' self-concepts and lifestyles produce needs and desires that interact with the situations in which consumers find themselves to trigger the consumer decision process.

We do not mean to imply that consumers think in terms of lifestyle. None of us consciously thinks, "I'll have an Evian bottled water in order to enhance my lifestyle." Rather, we make decisions consistent with our lifestyles without deliberately considering lifestyle. Most consumer decisions involve very little effort or thought on the part of the consumer. They are what we call *low-involvement decisions.* Feelings and emotions are as important in many consumer decisions as logical analysis or physical product attributes. Nonetheless, most consumer purchases involve at least a modest amount of decision making, and most are influenced by the purchaser's current and desired lifestyle.

## Consumer Decision Process (Part Four)

Consumer decisions result from perceived problems ("I'm thirsty") and opportunities ("That looks like it would be fun to try"). We will use the term *problem* to refer both to problems and to opportunities. Consumer problems arise in specific situations and the nature of the situation influences the resulting consumer behavior. Therefore, we provide a detailed discussion of situational influences on the consumer decision process in Chapter 13.

As Figure 1–3 indicates, a consumer's needs/desires may trigger one or more levels of the consumer decision process. It is important to note that for most purchases, consumers devote very little effort to this process, and emotions and feelings often have as much or more influence on the outcome as do facts and product features. Despite the limited effort that consumers often devote to the decision process, the results have important effects on the individual consumer, the firm, and the larger society. Therefore, we provide detailed coverage of each stage of the process: problem recognition (Chapter 14), information search (Chapter 15), alternative evaluation and selection (Chapter 16), outlet selection and purchase (Chapter 17), and use, disposition, and purchase evaluation (Chapter 18). The increasing role of technology, particularly the Internet, in consumer decision making is highlighted throughout these chapters.

## Organizations (Part Five) and Regulation (Part Six)

In Chapter 19, we show how our model of individual and household consumer behavior can be modified to help understand the consumer behavior of organizations.

Chapter 20 focuses our attention on the regulation of marketing activities, especially those targeting children. We pay particular attention to the role that knowledge of consumer behavior plays or could play in regulation.

## The Meaning of Consumption

"I (Andre Hank) worked eight-hour shifts at one restaurant, then drove to the other one for another eight-hour shift. One day I came home and my girlfriend and our six-year-olds were gone. When she left, I fell apart. I stopped going to work, stopped sleeping. I wasn't doing anything, just going crazy . . . they took me to the hospital where I got a shot to help me sleep. I woke up in a psych ward. After three or four months, they released me.

"When I came out of the hospital I didn't have anything. I wanted to get my old job back, but they wouldn't give me a second chance. I tried to get another job but it's hard when you don't have a phone, or an answering machine, or a pager. And I was sleeping in abandoned buildings, then on the El for a long time.

"One day more than three years ago I was hungry and didn't have any money and I saw a guy selling newspapers. I asked him what he was selling and he told me about *StreetWise* (a nonprofit, independent newspaper sold by the homeless, formerly homeless, and economically disadvantaged men and women of Chicago). So I [began to sell *StreetWise*]. . . . I don't make a lot of money but I'm good at saving it. Right now I'm saving for a coat for next winter.

"I'm no longer homeless. I've got a nice little room in a hotel . . . I can buy food . . . I even saved for [and bought] Nikes."

Andre is not unique among low-income consumers in wanting and buying items such as Nike shoes. As one expert says: "These people (low-income consumers) want the same products and services other consumers want." He suggests that marketing efforts reflect those desires. Another expert states: "There's this stereotype that they don't have enough money for toothpaste, and that's just not true. There has to be some significance to them being called lower-income, but they do buy things."

The working poor are forced to spend a disproportionate percent of their income on housing, utilities, and medical care (because of a lack of insurance). They generally rely on public transportation. They spend a smaller portion of their relatively small incomes on meals away from home and on all forms of entertainment such as admissions, pets, and toys. They spend very little on their own financial security. However, as Andre illustrated, they spend the same percent of their income (though a smaller dollar amount) on apparel and accessories.[27]

### Critical Thinking Questions

1. What does the consumption of a product like Nikes mean to Andre?

2. What does this story say about our society and the impact and role of marketing?

# THE MEANING OF CONSUMPTION

As we proceed through this text, we will describe the results of studies of consumer behavior, discuss theories about consumer behavior, and present examples of marketing programs designed to influence consumer behavior. While reading this material, however, do not lose sight of the fact that consumer behavior is not just a topic of study or a basis for developing marketing or regulatory strategy. Consumption frequently has deep meaning for the consumer.[28]

Consider Consumer Insight 1–2. Andre, just escaping homelessness, is clearly proud that he was able to save for and buy a pair of Nikes. He could undoubtedly have purchased a different brand that would have met his physical needs just as well as the Nikes for much less money. Although he does not say why he bought the more expensive Nikes, a reasonable interpretation is that they serve as a visible symbol that Andre is back as a successful member of society. In fact, Nike is sometimes criticized for creating, through its marketing activities, symbols of success or status that are unduly expensive. *What do you think? Does Nike manipulate people like Andre into spending more than necessary for a product because of its symbolism? If ads were banned or restricted to showing only product features, would products and brands still acquire symbolic meaning?*

Perhaps some insight into these questions can be found in the following description of the attitudes of several goatherders in a narrow mountain valley in northeastern Mexico in 1964. Modern advertising was not part of their environment.

> I asked Juan what were his major economic concerns. He answered very quickly, "food and clothes," he said. "How about housing?" I asked. "That is never a problem," he said, "for I can always make a house." For Juan and the others, a house is not a prestige symbol but simply a place to sleep, a place to keep dry in, a place for family privacy, and a place in which to store things. It is not a place to live, as the word is so meaningfully used in the United States. It seems difficult to overestimate the importance of clothing. A clean set of clothes is for a pass into town or a fiesta. Clothes are the mark of a man's self-respect, and the ability of a man to clothe his family is in many ways the measure of a man."[29]

Thus, as you read the chapters that follow, keep in mind that we are dealing with real people with real lives, not mere abstractions.

## SUMMARY

This should be a fascinating course for you. The fact that you are enrolled in this class suggests that you are considering marketing or advertising as a possible career. If that is the case, you should be immensely curious about why people behave as they do. Such curiosity is essential for success in a marketing-related career. That is what marketing is all about—understanding and anticipating consumer needs and developing solutions for those needs.

Even if you do not pursue a career in marketing, analyzing the purpose behind advertisements, package designs, prices, and other marketing activities is an enjoyable activity. In addition, it will make you a better consumer and a more informed citizen.

Finally, much of the material is simply interesting. For example, it is fun to read about China's attempt to market Pansy brand men's underwear in America, or that Kellogg struggled in Sweden where Bran Buds translated to "burned farmer." So have fun, study hard, and expand your managerial skills as well as your understanding of the environment in which you live.

## KEY TERMS

Conceptual model  26
Consumer behavior  6
Consumer cost  22
Customer satisfaction  23
Customer value  11
Distribution  22
Injurious consumption  24
Lifestyle  29

Lifestyle centers  14
Marketing communications  20
Marketing mix  19
Marketing strategy  19
Market segment  16
Need set  16
Price  21

Product  19
Product position  23
Self-concept  29
Service  22
Social marketing  10
Target market  18
Total product  12

## INTERNET EXERCISES

1. Market segmentation is one of the most important parts of developing a marketing strategy. Many commercial firms provide information and services to help define and/or describe market segments. One is Yankelovich. Visit their Web site (www.yankelovich.com). Prepare a report on the various tools they have available to segment consumers. How valuable do you think this service would be to a marketer?

2. Visit the Global Media Monitor at (lass.calumet.purdue.edu/cca/gmm). What information can you find that is relevant to understanding consumer behavior?

3. Marketers are increasingly looking at the opportunities offered by older consumers. How will the number of adults 65 and over change between 2005 and 2010? What about 2005 and 2020? (Hint: visit www.census.gov and look under statistical abstract.)

4. Examine magazine ads for a product category that interests you. Visit two Web sites identified in the ads. Which is most effective? Why? What beliefs about consumer behavior are reflected in the ads?

5. What ethical and legal issues involving the interaction of consumers and marketing are currently the concern of the following?
   a. Federal Trade Commission (www.ftc.gov)
   b. Better Business Bureau (www.bbb.org)

6. Visit the FDA's Center for Food Safety and Applied Nutrition (www.cfsan.fda.gov). What food related issues are currently of concern? While there visit the food labeling and nutrition section and take the quiz on food labeling (go to www.cfsan.fda.gov/label.html and click on "Quiz Yourself"). How important do you feel the NLEA's Nutritional Facts Panel is in helping consumers make better food choices? Can this information still be misleading?

7. Evaluate several of PETA's Web sites (www.peta-online.org, www.circuses.com, www.nofishing.net, www.taxmeat.com, and www.furisdead.com).

8. Evaluate Apple's Web site (www.apple.com). What assumptions about consumer behavior are reflected in this Web site?

## DDB LIFE STYLE STUDY™ DATA ANALYSES

1. Examine the DDB data in Tables 1A through 7A for differences among heavier consumers of the following. Why do you think these differences exist? How would you use these insights to develop marketing strategy?
   a. Gourmet coffee bar
   b. DVD rental
   c. Sports drinks
   d. Mail order catalog

2. Some people are more prone to be influenced by nutritional labels than others. Use the DDB data (Tables 1B through 7B) to examine possible characteristics of these consumers. How might this information be used by the FDA in developing marketing campaigns related to nutrition?

## REVIEW QUESTIONS

1. How is the field of consumer behavior defined?

2. What conclusions can be drawn from the examples at the beginning of this chapter?

3. What are the four major uses or applications of an understanding of consumer behavior?

4. What is *social marketing*?

5. What is *customer value*, and why is it important to marketers?

6. What is required to provide superior customer value?

7. What is a *total product*?

8. What is involved in the *consumer* analysis phase of market analysis in Figure 1–1?

9. What is involved in the *company* analysis phase of market analysis in Figure 1–1?

10. What is involved in the *competitor* analysis phase of market analysis in Figure 1–1?

11. What is involved in the *conditions* analysis phase of market analysis in Figure 1–1?

12. Describe the process of *market segmentation*.

13. What is *marketing strategy*?

14. What is a *marketing mix*?

15. What is a *product*?

16. What does an effective communications strategy require?

17. What is a *price*? How does the price of a product differ from the *cost of the product to the consumer*?

18. How is *service* defined in the text?

19. What is involved in creating satisfied customers?

20. What are the major outcomes for the firm of the marketing process and consumers' responses to it?

21. What are the major outcomes for the individual of the marketing process and consumers' responses to it?

22. What are the major outcomes for society of the marketing process and consumers' responses to it?

23. What is *product position*?

24. What is meant by *injurious consumption*?

25. What is meant by *consumer lifestyle*?

26. Describe the consumer decision process.

## DISCUSSION QUESTIONS

27. Why would someone shop on the Internet? Buy an iPod? Eat at TGI Friday's frequently?
    a. Why would someone else not make those purchases?
    b. How would you choose one outlet, brand, or model over the others? Would others make the same choice in the same way?

28. Respond to the questions in Consumer Insight 1–1.

29. Of what use, if any, are models such as the one in Figure 1–3 to managers?

30. What changes would you suggest in the model in Figure 1–3? Why?

31. Describe your lifestyle. How does it differ from your parents' lifestyle?

32. Do you anticipate any changes in your lifestyle in the next five years? What will cause these changes? What new products or brands will you consume because of these changes?

33. Describe a recent purchase you made. To what extent did you follow the consumer decision-making process described in this chapter? How would you explain any differences?

34. Describe several *total products* that are more than their direct physical features.

35. Describe the needs that the following items might satisfy and the total cost to the consumer of obtaining the benefits of the total product.
    a. Digital video recorder (e.g., TiVo)
    b. Lasik eye surgery
    c. Motorcycle
    d. SUV

36. How would you define the product that the Hard Rock Cafe provides? What needs does it meet?

37. To what extent, if any, are marketers responsible for injurious consumption involving their products?

38. How could social marketing help alleviate some of society's problems?

39. Respond to the questions in Consumer Insight 1–2.

40. Is the criticism of Nike for creating a shoe that is symbolic of success to some groups (see Consumer Insight 1–2) valid? Why or why not?

41. Robert's American gourmet snack foods produces herbal-based snacks such as Spirulina Spirals and St. Johns Wort Tortilla Chips. According to the company president, "We're selling like crazy. We don't do research. We react as sort of a karma thing."[30] How would you explain the firm's success? What are the advantages and risks of this approach?

## APPLICATION ACTIVITIES

42. Interview the manager or marketing manager of a retail firm. Determine how this individual develops the marketing strategy. Compare this person's process with the approach described in the text.

43. Interview the managers of a local charity. Determine what their assumptions about the consumer behavior of their supporters are. To what extent do they use marketing strategy to increase support for the organization or compliance with its objectives?

44. Interview five students. Have them describe the last three restaurant meals they consumed and the situations in which they were consumed. What can you conclude about the impact of the situation on consumer behavior? What can you conclude about the impact of the individual on consumer behavior?

45. Visit one or more stores that sell the following items. Report on the sales techniques used (point-of-purchase displays, store design, salesperson comments, and so forth). What beliefs concerning consumer behavior appear to underlie these techniques? It is often worthwhile for a male and a female student to visit the same store and talk to the same salesperson at different times. The variation in salesperson behavior is sometimes quite revealing.
   a. Books and magazines
   b. Cellular phones
   c. Pet supplies
   d. Expensive art
   e. Expensive jewelry
   f. Personal computers

46. Interview individuals who sell the items listed below. Try to discover their personal models of consumer behavior for their products.
   a. Pleasure boats
   b. Pets
   c. Golfing equipment
   d. Plants and garden supplies
   e. Flowers
   f. Car insurance

47. Interview three individuals who recently made a major purchase and three others who made a minor purchase. In what ways were their decision processes similar? How were they different?

## REFERENCES

1. Sources for "Online marketing" section: "Who's Online" and "Online Activities," both from *Pew Internet & American Life Project,* 2008, www.pewinternet.org; and "Mamma Mia!," *CNN.com,* May 8, 2008, www.cnn.com.

2. Source for "Global marketing" section: N. Madden, "Report from China," *AdAge.com,* May 31, 2005, www.adage.com.

3. Sources for "Social marketing" section: Excerpts from OLPC's Web site (www.laptopgiving.org), accessed May 20, 2008, as well as J. Markoff, "For $150, Third-World Laptop Stirs Big Debate," *The New York Times,* November 30, 2006, www.nytimes.com, accessed May 20, 2008; B. Einhorn, "Intel Inside the Third World," *BusinessWeek,* July 9 and 16, 2007, pp. 38–40; and D. Talbot, "$100 Laptop Program's New President," *Technology Review,* May 2, 2008, www.technologyreview.com, accessed May 20, 2008.

4. "Marketing-Oriented Lever Uses Research," *Marketing News,* February 10, 1978, p. 9; see also B. O'Connor, "How Deep-Dive Consumer Research Defined an Emerging Market and Helped to Create a Brand," *Design Management Review,* Summer 2004, p. 64.

5. B. Light, "Kellogg's Goes Online for Consumer Research," *Packaging Digest,* July 2004, p. 40.

6. J. Neff, "S. C. Johnson Likely to Bag Ziploc TableTops," *Advertising Age,* November 25, 2002, p. 3; and J. Neff, "S. C. Johnson Faces a Clean-up Job," *Advertising Age,* November 29, 2004, p. 8.

7. See W. I. Ghani and N. M. Childs, "Wealth Effects of the Passage of the Nutrition Labeling and Education Act of 1990 for Large U.S. Multinational Food Corporations," *Journal of Public Policy and Marketing,* Fall 1999, pp. 147–58; and S. K. Balasubramanian and C. Cole, "Consumers' Search and Use of Nutrition Information," *Journal of Marketing,* July 2002, pp. 112–27.

8. "Slick TV Ads Divert Child Smoking," *Marketing News,* August 29, 1994, p. 30. See also C. Pechmann and S. Ratneshwar, "The Effects of Antismoking and Cigarette Advertising on Young Adolescents' Perceptions of Peers Who Smoke," *Journal of Consumer Research,* September 1994, pp. 236–51.

9. See A. R. Andreasen, "Social Marketing," *Journal of Public Policy & Marketing,* Spring 1994, pp. 108–14; and P. Kotler, N. Roberto, and N. Lee, *Social Marketing* (Thousand Oaks, CA: Sage, 2002).

10. See, e.g., C. A. Russell, "Investigating the Effectiveness of Product Placements in Television Shows," *Journal of Consumer Research,* December 2002, pp. 306–18.

11. B. J. Pine, Jr., and J. H. Gilmore, "Welcome to the Experience Economy," *Harvard Business Review,* July–August 1998, pp. 97–105.

12. This insight is based on J. Weber and A. T. Palmer, "How the Net Is Remaking the Mall," *BusinessWeek Online,* May 9, 2005. See also A. Serwer, "Hot Starbucks to Go," *Fortune,* January 26, 2004, pp. 61–74; and P. Bhatnagar, "Supermarkets Strike Back," *CNNMoney,* May 2, 2005, www.cnnmoney.com.

13. A. S. Wellner, "The New Science of Focus Groups," *American Demographics,* March 2003, pp. 29–33.

14. See W. McCall, "Nike Battles Backlash from Overseas Sweatshops," *Marketing News,* November 9, 1998, p. 14; and A. Hill, "Nike's Reputation in Spotlight Again," *PR Week,* April 1, 2005, p. 13.

15. E. Esfahani, "How to . . . Get Tough with Bad Customers," *Business 2.0,* October 2004, p. 52.

16. T. F. McMahon, "What Buyers Buy and Sellers Sell," *Journal of Professional Services Marketing* 2 (1996), pp. 3–16.

17. "'Build a Better Mousetrap' 2004 New Product Innovations of the Year," *Productscan Online* (press release), December 27, 2004 (www.productscan.com).

18. D. Roberts, "How Legend Lives Up to Its Name," *BusinessWeek,* February 15, 1999, pp. 75–76; and "China Industry," *EIU ViewsWire,* January 22, 2004 www.viewswire.com.

19. P. Odell, "Starburst Puts Texting Promo on 60 Million Wrappers," *Promo,* June 6, 2005, www.promomagazine.com.

20. C. Power, "Flops," *BusinessWeek,* August 16, 1993, pp. 79–80.

21. See, e.g., Weber and Palmer, "How the Net Is Remaking the Mall."

22. B. Morris, "The Future of Retirement," *Fortune,* August 19, 1996, pp. 86–94.

23. See D. N. Hassey and M. C. Smith, "Compulsive Buying," *Psychology & Marketing,* December 1996, pp. 741–52; and N. A. Mendoza and J. W. Pracejus, "Buy Now, Pay Later," *Advances in Consumer Research XXIV,* ed. M. Bruck and D. J. MacInnis (Provo, UT: Association for Consumer Research, 1997), pp. 499–503.

24. See P. Mergenhagen, "People Behaving Badly," *American Demographics,* August 1997, pp. 37–43.

25. "Price Rises Threaten Progress on Poverty," *Financial Times,* April 10, 2008, p. 8.

26. R. E. Petty and J. T. Cacioppo, "Addressing Disturbing and Disturbed Consumer Behavior," *Journal of Marketing Research,* February 1996, pp. 1–8.

27. C. Miller, "The Have-Nots," *Marketing News,* August 1, 1994, pp. 1–2; P. Mergenhagen, "What Can Minimum Wage Buy?" *American Demographics,* January 1996, pp. 32–36; and A. Hank, "Hank Finds Two Families," *StreetWise,* May 16–31, 1996, p. 7. See also R. P. Hill, "Disadvantaged Consumers," *Journal of Business Ethics* 80 (2008), pp. 77–83.

28. See M. L. Richins, "Special Possessions and the Expression of Material Values," *Journal of Consumer Research,* December 1994, pp. 522–33.

29. J. F. Epstein, "A Shirt for Juan Navarro," in *Foundations for a Theory of Consumer Behavior,* ed. W. T. Tucker (New York: Holt, Rinehart & Winston, 1967), p. 75.

30. M. W. Fellman, "New Age Dawns for Product Niche," *Marketing News,* April 27, 1998, p. 1.

# External Influences

External Influences

Culture
Subculture
Demographics
Social Status
Reference Groups
Family
Marketing Activities

Internal Influences

Perception
Learning
Memory
Motives
Personality
Emotions
Attitudes

Self-Concept and Lifestyle

Experiences and Acquisitions

Experiences and Acquisitions

■ The external influence area of our model shown at the left is the focal point of this part of the text. Any division of the factors that influence consumer behavior into separate and distinct categories is somewhat arbitrary. For example, we will consider learning in Part Three of the text, which focuses on internal influences. However, a substantial amount of learning involves interaction with, or imitation of, other individuals. Thus, learning clearly involves external influences such as family and peers. Our focus in this part is on the functioning of the various external groups, not the processes by which individuals react to these groups.

■ In this part, we begin with large-scale, macrogroup influences and move to smaller, more microgroup influences. As we progress, the nature of the influence exerted changes from general guidelines to explicit expectations for specific behaviors. In Chapter 2, we examine how cultures cause differing behaviors across countries and other cultural units. Chapters 3 through 6 focus primarily on the American society, examining its values, demographics, social stratification, subcultures, and family structure. Chapter 7 examines the mechanisms by which groups influence consumer behaviors. In combination, these chapters allow for a comparison and contrast of how external influences operate in America and around the world.

Needs

Desires

Decision
Process

Situations

Problem
Recognition

Information
Search

Alternative Evaluation
and Selection

Outlet Selection
and Purchase

Postpurchase
Processes

# Cross-Cultural Variations in Consumer Behavior

■ The three largest players in the global retailing scene are Wal-Mart (United States), Carrefour (France), and Tesco (United Kingdom). Each of these companies is engaged in ongoing global expansion focused heavily on Asia and Latin America. The size of these markets makes them attractive. The complex nature of these markets and their differences from Europe and America create major challenges.[1]

The superstores and hypermarkets, with their large size, one-stop shop, and enormous selection have worked well in Western markets, such as the United States or the United Kingdom. However, these same formats haven't always worked well in Latin America and Asia where large segments of consumers are lower income, prefer local markets close to home, and often shop daily to ensure the freshness of food products. The large, multinational retailers have had to adjust. Although supermarkets and hypermarkets are catching on, they represent only a small fraction of the retail activity. There are 500 small, independent stores for every 1 hyper- or supermarket in Mexico, for example. Wal-Mart has responded with Todo Día, a deep-discount supermarket in low-income areas, which carries only one-tenth of the selection of its Supercenters. Tesco has responded similarly in China with Tesco Express.

Clearly, however, having a larger number of smaller stores is not enough. Adaptations in service level and products to match regional needs and preferences are critical as well. For example, in China, where many customers arrive on foot or bicycle, Wal-Mart offers shuttle buses or free local delivery of heavy items such as refrigerators. In Mexico, Wal-Mart stumbled at first with product offerings such as riding lawn mowers, which didn't sell well because the country lacks the suburban-style lawns found in the United States. In China, where "wet markets" carry such delicacies as live turtles, snakes, and octopus, freshness is critical. As one Chinese shopper noted:

I will not buy a dead fish. How will I know how he died? Maybe he had an illness. I want to see him alive first and kill him myself.

As a consequence, Wal-Mart offers live turtles and snakes in its China stores. Tesco stores feature vats of boiled eggs stewing in black Chinese tea.

Marketing across cultural boundaries is a difficult and challenging task. As Figure 2–1 indicates, cultures may differ in demographics, language, nonverbal communications, and values. The success of global marketers depends on how well they understand and adapt to these differences.

In this chapter, we focus on cultural variations in *values* and *nonverbal communications*. In addition, we briefly describe how *demographic variations* across countries and cultures influence consumption patterns.

Before dealing with specifics, we must consider the broader issues of cross-cultural marketing, including globalization, attitudes toward multinational brands, and ethical considerations. Globalization means more than product exports and imports. Globalization can involve exporting and importing values, lifestyles, and attitudes. Historically, such influence has been thought of as primarily going one way—that is, large American and other Western multinational companies and brands influencing the values and lifestyles of the countries they enter. And, no doubt, such effects occur. For example, television advertising in countries such as China and India is extensive and reflects many Western values, such as individualism and an emphasis on youth. Over time, such advertising would be expected to influence not only how many Chinese and Indians choose to live (lifestyle) but also what they value and how they think and feel.[2]

**FIGURE 2–1        Cultural Factors Affect Consumer Behavior and Marketing Strategy**

**ILLUSTRATION 2–1**

Brazilian fashion is desired all over the world because of its unique blend of style, color, fabric, and fit.

Increasingly, however, globalization means mutual influence as products, brands, cultures, and values move back and forth across the world. So, while Western brands such as Mercedes still have cachet as luxury symbols in Eastern countries such as Japan, Eastern brands such as Japan's Lexus now have developed similar luxury status in Western countries such as the United States. Additional examples include:[3]

- Soccer is being imported into the United States particularly as symbolized by U.K. star David Beckham, while American-style football (termed *olive ball*) is being exported to China.
- Japanese baseball star Kosuke Fukudome has become an almost instant legend for the Chicago Cubs, and fans in right field now "bow" when he comes to the plate to bat.
- Brazilian products and fashion became all the rage in London as "Brazilian chic" was marketed through department stores, cultural events, and positive media coverage. Similar trends are occurring not only in the United States but also all over the world, as shown in Illustration 2–1.

Although globalization can influence cultural values, it would be a mistake to think that all cultures are becoming homogenized. While younger generations of consumers appear to be more similar, modern, and in some cases Western, older consumers in those same markets cling to traditional values that must be respected. For example, China appeared to eagerly (and profitably) copy TV contest shows like *American Idol* (*Supergirl* is a Chinese version). However, lawmakers there have clamped down with regulations to make the contestants act more conservatively and to keep the judges from embarrassing the contestants. According to one expert:

> The authorities are reacting against the sensationalistic, slightly rebellious nature of the contest programs, which promote individualism and personal achievement. The winners become idols with extreme influence on Chinese citizens. "Supergirl" also introduced Chinese to the concept of voting.[4]

Beyond elders and authorities attempting to maintain traditional cultural values, consumers across the globe often hold strong pride in their local heritage and sometimes mistrust or resent international brands, seeing them as irresponsible and hurtful to local culture and business. This can vary within and across countries. For example, whereas China and Japan have a strong preference for foreign products, Korea does not, which may help explain why many modern retailers have entered and then failed in Korea.[5] Indeed, a recent study indicates that regardless of country, there are four basic types of world citizens:[6]

- Global citizens (55 percent)—Positive toward international brands, view them as a signal of higher quality, most concerned about corporate responsibility to the local country. Prominent in Brazil, China, and Indonesia. Rare in the United States and the United Kingdom.
- Global dreamers (23 percent)—Positive toward international brands, and buy into their positive symbolic aspects, less concerned about corporate responsibility to the local country. Equally distributed across countries.
- Antiglobals (13 percent)—Negative toward international brands, don't like brands that preach American values, don't trust multinationals. Higher in the United Kingdom and China. Lower in Egypt and South Africa.
- Global agnostics (9 percent)—Don't base decisions on global brand name, evaluate as they would local brands, don't see global brands as special. Higher in the United States and South Africa. Lower in Japan, Indonesia, China, and Turkey.

Corporate responsibility and ethical issues can span from labor policies to influences on consumption of products linked to negative consequences. One example is American tobacco companies, which are aggressively marketing their products in the developing countries of Asia, Latin America, Africa, and Eastern Europe, where government restrictions and public attitudes are more favorable than in the United States. Their advertising and promotions, frequently using Western models and alluring settings, have been quite successful. Cigarette consumption in much of the world is increasing. Smoking-related deaths are now a leading killer in Asia, where increases in female smoking are a major concern.[7] As one World Health Organization (WHO) official notes:

> Here in Japan we see Western cigarette brands marketed as a kind of liberation tool. We see cigarette companies calling on young Japanese women to assert themselves, shed their inhibitions and smoke.[8]

Clearly, there are both subtle and direct ethical issues involved in international marketing.

# THE CONCEPT OF CULTURE

**Culture** is *the complex whole that includes knowledge, belief, art, law, morals, customs, and any other capabilities and habits acquired by humans as members of society.*

Several aspects of culture require elaboration. First, culture is a comprehensive concept. It includes almost everything that influences an individual's thought processes and behaviors. Although culture does not determine the nature or frequency of biological drives such as hunger or sex, it does influence if, when, and how these drives will be gratified. It influences not only our preferences but how we make decisions[9] and even how we perceive the world around us. Second, culture is acquired. It does not include inherited responses and predispositions. However, since much of human behavior is learned rather than innate, culture does affect a wide array of behaviors.

Third, the complexity of modern societies is such that culture seldom provides detailed prescriptions for appropriate behavior. Instead, in most industrial societies, culture supplies boundaries within which most individuals think and act. Finally, the nature of cultural influences is such that we are seldom aware of them. One behaves, thinks, and feels in a manner consistent with that of other members of the same culture because it seems "natural" or "right" to do so.

Imagine sweet corn. Most Americans think of it as a hot side dish. However, uses vary by country. Consider the following:

> Instead of being eaten as a hot side dish, the French add it to salad and eat it cold. In Britain, corn is used as a sandwich and pizza topping. In Japan, school children gobble down canned corn as an after-school treat. And in Korea, the sweet corn is sprinkled over ice cream.[10]

Some of these uses probably seem strange or disgusting to you but are perfectly natural to members of other cultures. This is the nature of culture. We don't think about the fact that many of our preferences are strongly influenced by our culture.

Culture operates primarily by setting rather loose boundaries for individual behavior and by influencing the functioning of such institutions as the family and mass media. Thus, culture provides the framework within which individual and household lifestyles evolve.

The boundaries that culture sets on behavior are called **norms,** which are simply rules that specify or prohibit certain behaviors in specific situations. Norms are derived from **cultural values,** or widely held beliefs that affirm what is desirable. Violation of cultural norms results in **sanctions,** or penalties ranging from mild social disapproval to banishment from the group. Thus, as Figure 2–2 indicates, cultural values give rise to norms and associated sanctions, which in turn influence consumption patterns.

The preceding discussion may leave the impression that people are aware of cultural values and norms and that violating any given norm carries a precise and known sanction. This is seldom the case. We tend to "obey" cultural norms without thinking because to do otherwise would seem unnatural. For example, we are seldom aware of how close we stand to other individuals while conducting business. Yet this distance is well defined and adhered to, even though it varies from culture to culture.

Cultures are not static. They typically evolve and change slowly over time. Marketing managers must understand both the existing cultural values and the emerging cultural values of the societies they serve. A failure to understand cultural differences can produce negative consequences, such as the following:

- Recently, an Indian entrepreneur flew in the Washington Redskin's cheerleaders for a cricket game. In a sexually conservative culture such as India's, this did not translate in a positive fashion. Lawmakers put pressure on the team and it switched to a band

**Values, Norms, Sanctions, and Consumption Patterns**    FIGURE 2–2

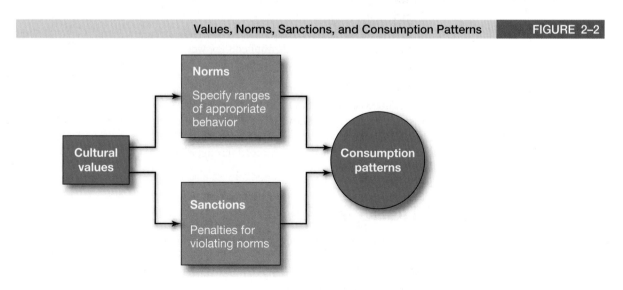

Many companies offer a mix of standard and customized products in their locations around the world. In many fast-food restaurants, rice and seafood dishes supplement traditional burgers and fries.

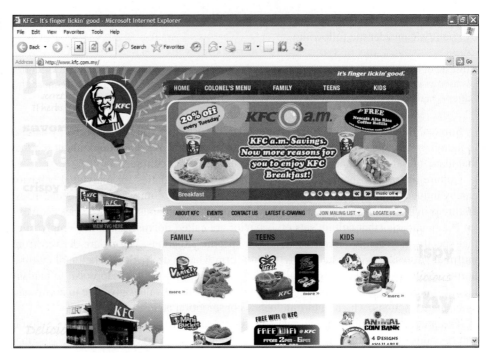

of local drummers. Their view of the cheerleaders was that they were "lewd and not appropriate for India's traditional culture."[11]

- A U.S. electronics firm landed a major contract with a Japanese buyer. The U.S. firm's president flew to Tokyo to sign the contract. The head of the Japanese firm read the contract intently for an extraordinary length of time. At last, the U.S. executive offered a price discount. The Japanese executive was surprised but didn't object. The U.S. executive's mistake was assuming that the long scrutiny was an attempt to reopen negotiations. Instead, the Japanese executive was demonstrating his concern and authority by closely and slowly examining the document.

- Lipton created a line of instant meals named *Side Dishes*. The meals sold well in the United States but not in Latin America, a large market that Lipton had hoped would fuel growth for the line. Latin American housewives, with more traditional views of their family role, felt that "instant" meals implied they were lazy or poor caretakers for their families.[12]

Starbucks' CEO offers this cautionary note for American businesses going global: "The biggest lesson is not to assume that the market or the consumers are just like Americans, even if they speak English or otherwise behave as if they were."[13] However, with appropriate strategies and an eye toward the needs and wants of local consumers, sophisticated retailers and manufacturers can and do succeed throughout the world, as shown in Illustration 2–2 for KFC Malaysia.

# VARIATIONS IN CULTURAL VALUES

Cultural values are widely held beliefs that affirm what is desirable. These values affect behavior through norms, which specify an acceptable range of responses to specific situations. A useful approach to understanding cultural variations in behavior is to understand the values embraced by different cultures.

Numerous values vary across cultures and affect consumption. We will present a classification scheme consisting of three broad forms of cultural values—*other-oriented, environment-oriented,* and *self-oriented.* The cultural values that have the most impact on consumer behavior can be classified in one of these three general categories.

**Other-oriented values** reflect a society's view of the appropriate relationships *between individuals and groups* within that society. These relationships have a major influence on marketing practice. For example, if the society values collective activity, consumers will look toward others for guidance in purchase decisions and will not respond favorably to promotional appeals to "be an individual."

**Environment-oriented values** prescribe a society's relationship *to its economic and technical as well as its physical environment.* As a manager, you would develop a very different marketing program for a society that stressed a problem-solving, risk-taking, performance-oriented approach to its environment than you would for a fatalistic, security- and status-oriented society.

**Self-oriented values** reflect the objectives and approaches to life *that the individual members of society find desirable.* Again, these values have strong implications for marketing management. For instance, the acceptance and use of credit is very much determined by a society's position on the value of postponed versus immediate gratification.

Table 2–1 provides a list of 18 values that are important in most cultures. Most of the values are shown as dichotomies (e.g., materialistic versus nonmaterialistic). However, this is not meant to represent an either/or situation but a continuum. For example, two societies can each value

Cultural Values of Relevance to Consumer Behavior     **TABLE 2–1**

### Other-Oriented Values

- *Individual/Collective.* Are individual activity and initiative valued more highly than collective activity and conformity?
- *Youth/Age.* Is family life organized to meet the needs of the children or the adults? Are younger or older people viewed as leaders and role models?
- *Extended/Limited family.* To what extent does one have a lifelong obligation to numerous family members?
- *Masculine/Feminine.* To what extent does social power automatically go to males?
- *Competitive/Cooperative.* Does one obtain success by excelling over others or by cooperating with them?
- *Diversity/Uniformity.* Does the culture embrace variation in religious belief, ethnic background, political views, and other important behaviors and attitudes?

### Environment-Oriented Values

- *Cleanliness.* To what extent is cleanliness pursued beyond the minimum needed for health?
- *Performance/Status.* Is the culture's reward system based on performance or on inherited factors such as family or class?
- *Tradition/Change.* Are existing patterns of behavior considered inherently superior to new patterns of behavior?
- *Risk taking/Security.* Are those who risk their established positions to overcome obstacles or achieve high goals admired more than those who do not?
- *Problem solving/Fatalistic.* Are people encouraged to overcome all problems, or do they take a "what will be, will be" attitude?
- *Nature.* Is nature regarded as something to be admired or overcome?

### Self-Oriented Values

- *Active/Passive.* Is a physically active approach to life valued more highly than a less active orientation?
- *Sensual gratification/Abstinence.* To what extent is it acceptable to enjoy sensual pleasures such as food, drink, and sex?
- *Material/Nonmaterial.* How much importance is attached to the acquisition of material wealth?
- *Hard work/Leisure.* Is a person who works harder than economically necessary admired more than one who does not?
- *Postponed gratification/Immediate gratification.* Are people encouraged to "save for a rainy day" or to "live for today"?
- *Religious/Secular.* To what extent are behaviors and attitudes based on the rules specified by a religious doctrine?

tradition, but one may value it more than the other. For several of the values, a natural dichotomy does not seem to exist. For a society to place a low value on cleanliness does not imply that it places a high value on dirtiness. These 18 values are described in the following paragraphs.

## Other-Oriented Values

**Individual/Collective**    Does the culture emphasize and reward individual initiative, or are cooperation with and conformity to a group more highly valued? Are individual differences appreciated or condemned? Are rewards and status given to individuals or to groups? Answers to these questions reveal the individual or collective orientation of a culture. Individualism is a defining characteristic of American culture. Australia, the United Kingdom, Canada, New Zealand, and Sweden are also relatively individualistic. Taiwan, Korea, Hong Kong, Mexico, Japan, India, and Russia are more collective in their orientation.[14]

This value is a key factor differentiating cultures, and it heavily influences the self-concept of individuals. Not surprisingly, consumers from cultures that differ on this value differ in their reactions to foreign products,[15] advertising,[16] and preferred sources of information.[17] Examples include:

- Eating alone is more prevalent in individualistic cultures such as the United States and Hungary than in collectivist cultures such as Russia and Romania.[18]
- In services such as health care and hair styling, consumers in Thailand place greater importance on personal relationships with the service provider than do U.S. consumers. These relationships drive loyalty more for consumers in Thailand.[19]
- Consumers from more collectivist countries tend to be more imitative and less innovative in their purchases than those from individualistic cultures.[20] Thus, ad themes such as "be yourself" and "stand out" are often effective in the United States but generally are not in Japan, Korea, or China.
- Advertising in collectivist countries such as Korea contains more celebrity appeals than does advertising in individualistic countries such as the United States.[21]

Interestingly, you might expect luxury items to be less important in collectivist cultures. However, they are quite important, but for different reasons. In individualistic cultures, luxury items are purchased as a means of self-expression or to stand out.[22] This is often not the case in more collectivist Asian societies. As one expert describes:

> Brands take on roles as symbols that extend well beyond the intrinsic features of the category. One is not buying a watch, or even a status brand, one is buying club membership, or an "I am just like you" (symbol).[23]

Similarly, the notion of conspicuous consumption is often associated with individualistic societies. However, a recent study finds that brand reputation influences decisions more for conspicuously consumed products in collectivist countries.[24] Another study finds that concern for appearance is 40 percent higher for those in collectivist countries. One explanation is that a given behavior is used for different reasons in different cultures. As one expert notes:

> Dressing well…might convey a sense of individuality in individualist cultures. However, it might be interpreted by collectivist-culture consumers as a way to demonstrate their in-group identity, show their concerns with in-group norms, follow in-group trends and avoid loss of face in front of in-group members.[25]

As useful as such generalizations are, it is important to realize that cultural values can and do evolve. This is particularly true among young, urban consumers in the developed and developing countries of Asia, where individualism is on the rise.[26] For example, 26 percent of Chinese teens consider individuality an important trait, more than double the rate of older Chinese.[27] Although this number is substantially lower than that of Western cultures, it represents an important shift. Consider the following description of a young Japanese woman:

> Mizuho Arai knows what she likes. A 20-year-old uniformed office worker by day, at night she wears loafers, a sweater, Levi's 501s, and a black parka. Shopping with an L.L. Bean bag over her shoulder, she prefers bargain outlets to traditional department stores and designer boutiques. "I don't like to be told what's trendy. I can make up my own mind."[28]

Arai is typical of the younger generation of Asian consumers, where traditional appeals may not work as they once did. For example, in the late 1980s, Shiseido Co. launched its very successful Perky Jean makeup line with the theme, "Everyone is buying it." "That would never work now," says a company executive.

The different values held by younger and older Asian consumers illustrate that few cultures are completely homogeneous. Marketers must be aware of differences both *between* cultures and *within* cultures.[29]

**Youth/Age**    To what extent do the primary family activities focus on the needs of the children instead of those of the adults? What role, if any, do children play in family decisions? What role do they play in decisions that primarily affect the child? Are prestige, rank, and important social roles assigned to younger or older members of society? Are the behavior, dress, and mannerisms of the younger or older members of a society imitated by the rest of the society?

While American society is clearly youth oriented, many Asian cultures have traditionally valued the wisdom that comes with age. Thus, mature spokespersons would tend to be more successful in these cultures than would younger ones. However, some Asian cultures are becoming increasingly youth oriented with increases in youth-oriented ads designed to target them.[30] Consider the following description of Taiwan:

> Taiwan is very, very youth-oriented, and it is a very hip culture....You have a consumer-based economy that is quite potent, and pitching to the youth is a good way of ensuring that your products are going to be bought.[31]

Illustration 2–3 demonstrates 7-Up's use of a youth theme in China. These unique outdoor "light pole" signs are common in China's major cities.

This youth trend can also be seen in Arab countries. One study of Arab consumers from Saudi Arabia, Bahrain, Kuwait, and the United Arab Emirates shows the rapid emergence of several youth segments. The largest (35 percent) consists of younger, more liberal, individualistic married couples living in nuclear (versus communal) families in which women are more likely to work outside the home and thus demand a greater voice in family decisions.[32]

Children's influence on purchases and the tactics they use vary according to the youth versus age value and this has implications for marketers.[33] For example, one study compared the tactics used by children in the Fiji Islands with those used in the United States. The Fiji Islands (and other Pacific Island nations) can be characterized as less individualistic and higher in respect for authority and seniority. As a consequence, Fiji children were more likely to "request" than "demand" and Fiji parents responded more favorably (i.e., bought the item) to "requests." In contrast, American children were more likely to demand than to request, and American parents responded more positively to demands.[34]

China's policy of limiting families to one child has produced a strong focus on the child, a shift toward youth, and increasing Westernization of children's commercials. In fact,

This outdoor signage for 7-Up in China demonstrates the youth trend that is emerging in Asian cultures, which have historically been quite traditional with a high value placed on age and wisdom.

many Chinese children receive so much attention that they are known in Asia as "little emperors."[35] Consider the following description of the Zhou family and their 10-year-old daughter Bella, who live in Shanghai:

> Under traditional Confucian teachings, respecting and obeying one's elders were paramount. In today's urban China, it is increasingly children who guide their parents through a fast-changing world. When the Zhous bought a new television set last year, Bella chose the brand. When they go out to eat, Bella insists on Pizza Hut.[36]

Obviously, while changes to traditional cultures such as those in Asia and the Gulf are occurring, it is important to remember that traditional segments and values still remain and that marketers must adapt not only across but within cultures.

**Extended/Limited Family**    The family unit is the basis for virtually all societies. Nonetheless, the definition of the family and the rights and obligations of family members vary widely across cultures. As we will see in Chapter 6, our families have a lifelong impact on us, both genetically and through our early socialization, no matter what culture we come from. However, cultures differ widely in the obligations one owes to other family members at various stages of life as well as who is considered to be a member of the family.

In the United States, the family is defined fairly narrowly and is less important than in many other cultures. In general, strong obligations are felt only to immediate family members, and these diminish as family members establish new families. In many other countries and regions, including South America, Fiji, Israel, and Asia, the role of the family is much stronger. Families, and obligations, often extend to cousins, nieces, nephews, and beyond. The following description indicates the complexity and extent of the extended Chinese family:

The family is critically important in all aspects of Chinese life and there is a distrust of nonfamily members. In response to this, the Chinese have developed family-like links to a greater extent than almost any other culture. It stretches to the furthest horizons, from close family, to slightly distant, to more distant, embracing people who are not really family but are connected to someone in one's family and to all their families. As such, the family is really a system of contacts, rather than purely an emotional unit as in the west.[37]

Clearly, marketers need to understand the role of families in the cultures they serve and adapt accordingly. For example:

- In Mexico, compared with the United States, adolescents are much more likely to seek parental advice or to respond positively to ads with parental figures in the purchase of items ranging from candy to movies to fashion clothing.[38]
- Young adults living on their own in Thailand, compared with those in the United States, are more likely to continue to be influenced by their parents and family in terms of consumption values and purchases.[39]
- Because Indian consumers tend to shop in groups and with their families, Biyani (a large discounter similar to Wal-Mart) has U- and C-shaped aisles to provide private corners where families can discuss their purchase decisions.[40]

**Masculine/Feminine**   Are rank, prestige, and important social roles assigned primarily to men? Can a female's life pattern be predicted at birth with a high degree of accuracy? Does the husband, wife, or both, make important family decisions? Basically, we live in a masculine-oriented world, yet the degree of masculine orientation varies widely, even across the relatively homogeneous countries of Western Europe.

This value dimension influences both obvious and subtle aspects of marketing (see Chapter 3). Obviously, the roles and manner in which one would portray women in advertisements in Muslim countries would differ from those in the United States.[41] However, suppose you were going to promote furniture in Taiwan or Japan. Would you focus on the husband, the wife, or both? Would the focus vary by country? Research indicates that a moderate focus on the wife would be best in both countries.[42] How would you portray a teenage Japanese girl in an ad to this audience? A more "girlish" (childlike, approval-seeking) portrayal than is common in U.S. ads (a more sultry, explicitly sexual portrayal) would be appropriate.[43]

The roles of women are changing and expanding throughout much of the world.[44] This is creating new opportunities as well as challenges for marketers.[45] For example, the increasing percentage of Japanese women who continue to work after marriage has led to increased demand for time-saving products as well as other products targeted at the working woman. For instance, long-lasting, no-smear lipstick didn't exist in Japan over a decade ago, but now is a huge market. Targeted at working women, Shiseido's brand, Reciente Perfect Rouge, featured a popular model racing through her busy day wearing the no-smear lipstick.[46]

Participation in sports and exercise is another aspect strongly influenced by the masculinity dimension. There tends to be a wide disparity between men and women participation rates (men higher) in countries and cultures high in masculine orientation such as South Korea, Mexico, Brazil, and France. However, as always, modern trends must be considered. In Mexico, for example, a strong masculine orientation toward sports is slowly giving way among younger Mexican women. One recent example is runner Ana Guevara, whose TV viewer numbers have sometimes been higher than those of men's soccer—something unheard of in the history of Mexican sports. One expert points to the "changing status of women in Mexico."[47] Lorena Ochoa is another recent example in golf. Ochoa, a young

The changing role of women around the world creates new marketing opportunities. The popularity and participation of women in sports is increasing in many cultures.

LPGA tour professional, has catapulted to the top of her sport and represents the new face of Mexican women in sports. Illustration 2–4 shows the changing role of women as represented by their ever-increasing participation in professional sports.

Again, it is important to remember that traditional segments and values certainly do still remain and that marketers must adapt not only across but within cultures. For example, a recent study of women in mainland China found both traditionalist and modern segments.[48] In Hong Kong, however, the traditional values are not necessarily giving way when economic and social independence are gained. Instead, the conflict is internalized, as indicated by the following quote:

> Women in Hong Kong, who are faced with both traditional Chinese culture and western culture, are at a crossroads of modernism and traditionalism. On one hand, they are having increasing amount of financial and decision power within the family and in the society. On the other hand, they are still under the pressure of traditional expectations on females as being a good wife and mother.[49]

For marketers, this conflict creates challenges in some cases to segment consumers into modern and traditional markets. In other cases the challenge is to help consumers (through products, positioning, advertising and so on) deal with tensions between traditional and modern values.

**Competitive/Cooperative**    Is the path to success found by outdoing other individuals or groups, or is success achieved by forming alliances with other individuals or groups? Does everyone admire a winner? Cultures with more masculine and individualistic orientations, such as the United Kingdom, the United States, and Australia, tend to value competitiveness and demonstrate it openly. Collectivist cultures, even if high in masculinity (e.g., Japan), tend to find *openly* competitive gestures offensive as they cause others to "lose face." [50]

Variations on this value can be seen in the ways different cultures react to comparative advertisements. For example, the United States encourages them, while their use in other cultures can lead to consumer (and even legal) backlash. As one would expect, the more collectivist Japanese have historically found comparative ads to be distasteful, as do the

Chinese, although Pepsi found Japanese youth somewhat more receptive if comparisons are done in a frank and funny way.[51] As a rule, comparative ads should be used with care and only after considerable testing.

**Diversity/Uniformity**   Do members of the culture embrace variety in terms of religions, ethnic backgrounds, political beliefs, and other important behaviors and attitudes? A culture that values diversity not only will accept a wide array of personal behaviors and attitudes but is also likely to welcome variety in terms of food, dress, and other products and services. In contrast, a society valuing uniformity is unlikely to accept a wide array of tastes and product preferences, though such a society may be subject to fads, fashions, and other changes over time.

Collectivist cultures tend to place a strong value on uniformity and conformity,[52] whereas more individualistic cultures tend to value diversity. For example, "in-group" influence (e.g., wanting to see the same movies as everyone else) tends to be higher in China and Japan than in the United Kingdom and the United States.[53] Obviously, however, economic and social changes associated with the youth movement in many collectivist societies mean relatively more acceptance of diversity than has been traditionally found, even if absolute levels trend lower than in their individualistic counterparts.

## Environment-Oriented Values

**Cleanliness**   Is cleanliness next to godliness, or is it a rather minor matter? Are homes, offices, and public spaces expected to be clean beyond reasonable health requirements? In the United States, a high value is placed on cleanliness, where germ-fighting liquid soaps alone are a $16 billion market.[54] In fact, people from many other cultures consider Americans to be paranoid on the subject of personal hygiene.

Although there are differences in the value placed on cleanliness among the economically developed cultures, the largest differences are between these cultures and many of the underdeveloped nations. In many poorer countries, cleanliness is not valued at a level sufficient to produce a healthy environment. This is true even in large parts of rapidly developing countries such as China and India, where a lack of basic hygiene still causes significant health problems.[55] While often criticized for having a negative impact on local cultures, McDonald's has been credited with introducing more hygienic food preparation and toilets in several East Asian markets, including China.[56]

**Performance/Status**   Are opportunities, rewards, and prestige based on an individual's performance or on the status associated with the person's family, position, or class? Do all people have an equal opportunity economically, socially, and politically at the start of life, or are certain groups given special privileges? Are products and brands valued for their ability to accomplish a task or for the reputation or status of the brand?

A status-oriented society is more likely to prefer "quality" or established and prestigious brand names and high-priced items to functionally equivalent items with unknown brand names or lower prices (e.g., private label or store brands).[57] As a result, compared with that in the United States, advertising in Japan, China, and India tends to involve more appeals to status or wealth.[58]

Performance/status is closely related to the concept of **power distance,** which refers to *the degree to which people accept inequality in power, authority, status, and wealth as natural or inherent in society.*[59] India, China, Brazil, Mexico, France, Hong Kong, and Japan are relatively high in their acceptance of power. Austria, Denmark, New Zealand, Sweden, and the United States are relatively low. Expert sources in ads have a greater impact in a high-power distance country than in a low one.[60] In addition, consumers in high-power distance countries are more likely to seek the opinions of others in making decisions.[61]

How power is used may depend on other cultural factors, however. In the United States, power is seen in terms of coercion and in Japan as relational. As a consequence, in negotiations where the buyer has more power, buyers are more likely to use that power to extract higher prices and profits in the United States, whereas that is not true in Japan. Marketers need to understand such nuances when negotiating with partners in other countries.[62]

**Tradition/Change**    Is tradition valued simply for the sake of tradition? Is change or "progress" an acceptable reason for altering established patterns? Compared with Americans, Korean and Chinese consumers have traditionally been much less comfortable dealing with new situations or ways of thinking.[63] Britain, too, has a culture laden with tradition. This value is reflected in their advertising where, compared to ads in America, those in Britain and China are more likely to emphasize tradition and history.[64]

It is important to note once again that change can and does live alongside traditional values. For example, both the Korean and Chinese cultures are now enthusiastically embracing change. In China, "modernness" (often symbolized by a Western name) is an important product attribute, particularly among younger, urban Chinese. A recent study found that advertisers in China segment their advertising depending on audience. For the mainstream audiences targeted by television, traditional appeals are used more often. In magazines targeted at younger Chinese (e.g., *Elle, Cosmopolitan,* and *Sanlian*), modern appeals focusing on technology, fashion, and leisure are used more often.[65]

A focus on technology as an indicator of change illustrates some dramatic differences. Obviously, these differences are a function of economic development as well as culture. The following table depicts Internet and cell phone users as a percentage of the total population:[66]

|  | Internet Users (%) | Cell Phone Users (%) |
|---|---|---|
| Brazil | 22 | 52 |
| Mexico | 20 | 52 |
| China | 12 | 35 |
| Japan | 69 | 80 |
| South Korea | 69 | 82 |
| United Kingdom | 56 | 115* |
| United States | 68 | 77 |

*Indicates multiple phones per person.

Clearly, there are differences across developed and developing countries. However, greater availability, appropriate pricing, and rising incomes in developing countries continue to fuel double-digit growth in these markets. In addition, given China's large population, the absolute market potential is staggering (China has 461 million cell phones compared with just 40 million in South Korea). And Vodafone found out just how demanding tech-hungry Asian consumers can be. Their market share in Japan plummeted when they failed to innovate and stay on the cutting edge.[67]

**Risk Taking/Security**    Do the "heroes" of the culture meet and overcome obstacles? Is the person who risks established position or wealth on a new venture admired or considered foolhardy? This value relates to tolerance for ambiguity and uncertainty avoidance. It has a strong influence on entrepreneurship and economic development as well as new-product acceptance. A society that does not admire risk taking is unlikely to develop enough entrepreneurs to achieve economic change and growth. New-product introductions, new channels of distribution, advertising themes, and reliance on brand name are affected by this value.[68]

**Problem Solving/Fatalistic**   Do people react to obstacles and disasters as challenges to be overcome, or do they take a "what will be, will be" attitude? Is there an optimistic, "we can do it" orientation? In the Caribbean, difficult or unmanageable problems are often dismissed with the expression "no problem." This actually means: "There is a problem, but we don't know what to do about it—so don't worry!" Western Europe and the United States tend to fall toward the problem-solving end of the continuum, whereas Mexico and most Middle Eastern countries fall toward the fatalistic end. Fatalists tend to feel they don't have control over the outcome of events. This has been shown to reduce consumer expectations of quality and decrease the likelihood that consumers make formal complaints when faced with an unsatisfactory purchase.[69]

**Nature**   Is nature assigned a positive value, or is it viewed as something to be overcome, conquered, or tamed? Americans historically considered nature as something to be overcome or improved. Most northern European countries place a high value on the environment. Packaging and other environmental regulations are stronger in these countries than in America. In fact, a British company recently developed a zero-emissions motorcycle that runs on hydrogen. They worry, however, because it also makes no sound! *Would you want a motorcycle that didn't growl when you revved it up?*[70]

In turn, Americans and Canadians appear to place a higher value on the environment than the southern European countries and most developing countries, though this may reflect variations in the financial ability to act on this value rather than the value itself. These differences in attitudes are reflected in consumers' purchase decisions, consumption practices, and recycling efforts.[71]

As with all the values we are discussing, there are wide ranges within as well as between countries, which create market opportunities. For example, overall, China does not have a strong environmental orientation. However, there are segments of the country that do have such an orientation and the means to buy products and services that reflect this focus.[72]

## Self-Oriented Values

**Active/Passive**   Are people expected to take a physically active approach to work and play? Are physical skills and feats valued more highly than nonphysical performances? Is emphasis placed on doing? Americans are much more prone to engage in physical activities and to take an action-oriented approach to problems. "Don't just stand there, do something" is a common response to problems in America. Participation in active exercise varies widely across countries, especially for women, as discussed earlier. While this obviously limits the market for exercise equipment in certain countries, it also affects advertising themes and formats. For example, an exercise or sports theme for bottled water would not be appropriate in a country such as Japan, where two-thirds of the men and three-fourths of the women exercise less than twice a year.

**Sensual Gratification/Abstinence**   Is it acceptable to pamper oneself, to satisfy one's desires for food, drink, or sex beyond the minimum requirement? Is one who forgoes such gratification considered virtuous or strange? Muslim cultures are extremely conservative on this value as are many Asian cultures, including Hong Kong and India. A full 37 percent of Saudis indicated modesty is important, compared with 9 percent in the United States.[73] Perhaps not surprisingly, compared with U.S. and Australian ads, ads in Hong Kong and

India contain fewer sex appeals.[74] And China has put legal restrictions on the use of sex appeals in ads.[75] Consider the following:

> In U.S. cigarette advertisements, it is not uncommon to find sensual models, males and females holding hands, and couples in intimate situations. In the eastern culture of India, such open display of intimacy between opposite sexes is not socially acceptable.[76]

In Arab countries, advertisements, packaging, and products must carefully conform to Muslim standards. Polaroid's instant cameras gained rapid acceptance because they allowed Arab men to photograph their wives and daughters without fear that a stranger in a film laboratory would see the women unveiled.

In contrast, Brazilian and European advertisements contain nudity and blatant (by U.S. standards) appeals to sensual gratification. Consider the following billboard ad for Gossard women's underwear appearing throughout the United Kingdom:

> The picture shows the upper half of a nude woman lying on a bed with her arms above her head, her back arched. Her bra and panties are on the floor along with a man's shoe and shirt. The text says "Bring him to his knees." The tagline is "*Gossard*. Find your *G* spot." Another version has the copy line—"If he's late you can always start without him."[77]

Illustration 2–5 shows how marketers make use of sensuality. While quite appropriate for some cultures, it would not be successful in a culture that did not accept sensual gratification.

### Material/Nonmaterial

Is the accumulation of material wealth a positive good in its own right? Does material wealth bring more status than family ties, knowledge, or other activities? Consider the following conclusion from a study of Chinese television ownership:

> The television one owns is very much a representation of one's own self-worth. For most, the television had become almost as much a part of getting married as saying their vows. One engaged man (age 24), who was saving for his TV so he could get married, noted that he wanted a 25" or 29" Japanese model. He was willing to save for up to two years (a commonly quoted time frame) before revising his sights downward. Price was not nearly as important as projecting "a good image" to others.[78]

There are two types of materialism. **Instrumental materialism** is *the acquisition of things to enable one to do something.* Skis can be acquired to allow one to ski. **Terminal materialism** is *the acquisition of items for the sake of owning the item itself.* Art is generally acquired for the pleasure of owning it rather than as a means to another goal. Cultures differ markedly in their relative emphasis on these two types of materialism.[79]

### Hard Work/Leisure

Is work valued for itself, independent of external rewards, or is work merely a means to an end? Will individuals continue to work hard even when their minimum economic needs are satisfied, or will they opt for more leisure time? For example, in parts of Latin America, work has traditionally been viewed as a necessary evil. However, generational gaps exist. For example, in Mexico, 100 percent of the older generation agreed with the statement "Today's emphasis on work is a bad thing" compared with only 28 percent of the younger generation. The trend was just the opposite in the United Kingdom, Netherlands, France, Canada, and Australia, where agreement by the older generation was around 55 percent while agreement by the younger generation was around 80 percent. In the United States and Hong Kong, younger and older generations were roughly the same (about 50 percent agreeing) on this value.[80]

These attitudes do not necessarily reflect *actual* work patterns. For example, hours worked per week are highest in Hong Kong (48.6 hours) and Mexico (41.6) and lowest in France (34.1) and Canada (34.8).[81] Nonetheless, this value has important consequences for lifestyle and demand for leisure activities.

**Postponed Gratification/Immediate Gratification**    Is one encouraged to "save for a rainy day," or should one "live for today"? Is it better to secure immediate benefits and pleasures, or is it better to suffer in the short run for benefits in the future, or in the here-after, or for future generations? The United States, the United Kingdom, and Australia tend to have short-term orientations, while India, Hungary, Brazil, Hong Kong, and China have long-term orientations. This value has implications for business strategies, efforts to encourage savings, and the use of credit. For example, valued business goals in short-term cultures tend to include "this year's profits" while those in long-term cultures included "profits 10 years from now."[82] In addition, use of credit is lower in long-term–oriented cultures, where cash and debit card usage is more common.[83]

**Religious/Secular**    To what extent are daily activities determined by religious doctrine? The United States is relatively secular. Many Islamic cultures as well as some Catholic cultures are much more religiously oriented.[84] In contrast, religion plays a very small role in Chinese culture. However, even in a country such as China, where few are actively involved with a formal religion, many of the culture's values were formed in part by historical religious influences. The same is true for the secular nations of the West. Understanding the extent and type of religious influences operating in a culture is essential for effectively designing all elements of the marketing mix.[85]

Clearly, the preceding discussion has not covered all the values operating in the various cultures. However, it should suffice to provide a feel for the importance of cultural values and how cultures differ along value dimensions.

# CULTURAL VARIATIONS IN NONVERBAL COMMUNICATIONS

Differences in **verbal communication systems** (languages) are immediately obvious to anyone entering a foreign culture. An American traveling in Britain or Australia will be able to communicate, but differences in pronunciation, timing, and meaning will still occur. For example, Dogpile, a U.S.-based meta search engine (www.dogpile.com), changed its name in Europe to WebFetch after realizing that in the United Kingdom "pile" refers to hemorrhoids or the result of a dog relieving itself![86]

Attempts to translate marketing communications from one language to another can result in ineffective communications, as shown in Table 2–2.

The problems of literal translations and slang expressions are compounded by symbolic meanings associated with words, the absence of some words from various languages, and the difficulty of pronouncing certain words:[87]

- In Japan, a global soft-drink company wanted to introduce a product with the attribute "creaminess." However, research showed that there was not a corresponding word in Japan for this attribute, so the company had to find something comparable, which turned out to be "milk feel."[88]
- Mars addressed the problem of making the M&M's name pronounceable in France, where neither ampersands nor the apostrophe "s" plural form exists, by advertising extensively that M&M's should be pronounced "aimainaimze."
- To market its Ziploc food storage bags in Brazil, Dow Chemical had to use extensive advertising to actually create the word *zipar,* meaning "to zip," since there was no such term in Portuguese.

| TABLE 2–2 | Translation Problems in International Marketing |
|---|---|

- Colgate's Cue toothpaste had problems in France, as *cue* is a crude term for "butt" in French.
- Sunbeam attempted to enter the German market with a mist-producing curling iron named the Mist-Stick. Unfortunately, *mist* translates as "dung" or "manure" in German.
- Parker Pen mistook *embarazar* (to impregnate) to mean "to embarrass" and ran an ad in Mexico stating "it won't leak in your pocket and make you pregnant."
- Pet milk encountered difficulties in French-speaking countries where *pet* means, among other things, "to break wind."
- Kellogg's Bran Buds translates to "burned farmer" in Swedish.
- United Airlines' in-flight magazine cover for its Pacific Rim routes showed Australian actor Paul Hogan in the outback. The caption stated, "Paul Hogan Camps It Up." *"Camps it up"* is Australian slang for "flaunts his homosexuality."
- China attempted to export Pansy brand men's underwear to America.
- American Airlines introduced its new leather first-class seats in Mexico with the theme "Fly in Leather" which, when translated literally, read "Fly Naked."

Factors Influencing Nonverbal Communications          FIGURE 2–3

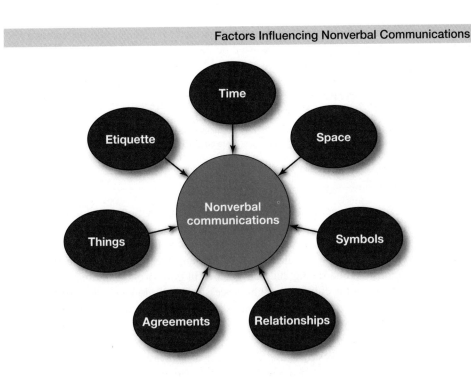

Additional communication factors that can cause problems include humor, style, and pace, for which preferences vary across cultures, even those speaking the same basic language.[89] Nonetheless, verbal language translations generally do not present major problems as long as we are careful. What many of us fail to recognize, however, is that each culture also has nonverbal communication systems or languages that, like verbal languages, are specific to each culture. **Nonverbal communication systems** are *the arbitrary meanings a culture assigns actions, events, and things other than words.*

The following discussion examines the seven variables shown in Figure 2–3, all of which influence nonverbal communications: time, space, symbols, relationships, agreements, things, and etiquette.

## Time

The meaning of time varies between cultures in two major ways. First is what we call time perspective, that is, a culture's overall orientation toward time.[90] The second is the interpretations assigned to specific uses of time.

**Time Perspective**   Most Americans, Canadians, Western Europeans, and Australians tend to view time as inescapable, linear, and fixed in nature. It is a road reaching into the future with distinct, separate sections (hours, days, weeks, and so on). Time is seen almost as a physical object; we can schedule it, waste it, lose it, and so forth. Believing that a person does one thing at a time, we have a strong orientation toward the present and the short-term future. This is known as a **monochronic time perspective.**

Most Latin Americans, Asians, and Indians tend to view time as being less discrete and less subject to scheduling. They view simultaneous involvement in many activities as natural. People and relationships take priority over schedules, and activities occur at their own pace rather than according to a predetermined timetable. Such cultures have an orientation toward the present and the past. This is known as a **polychronic time perspective.**

Some important differences between individuals with a monochronic perspective and those with a polychronic perspective are listed below.[91]

| Individuals in a Monochronic Culture | Individuals in a Polychronic Culture |
| --- | --- |
| Do one thing at a time | Do many things at once |
| Concentrate on the job | Are highly distractible and subject to interruptions |
| Take deadlines and schedules seriously | Consider deadlines and schedules secondary |
| Are committed to the job or task | Are committed to people and relationships |
| Emphasize promptness | Base promptness on the relationship |
| Are accustomed to short-term relationships | Prefer long-term relationships |

How would marketing activities vary between monochronic and polychronic cultures? Personal selling and negotiation styles and strategies would need to differ, as would many advertising themes. Contests and sales with deadlines would generally be more effective in monochronic than in polychronic cultures. Convenience foods frequently fail when positioned in terms of time saving and convenience in polychronic cultures, where "saving time" is not part of the cultural thought processes. The following quote illustrates the impact of time perspective on the positioning strategy of fast-food outlets in polychronic cultures:

In Argentina, McDonald's has an image of an expensive, modern restaurant where the majority of the customers are teenagers and young adults who patronize McDonald's to express their modern and liberated value systems. This is equally true in Turkey. In fact, a major reason for the popularity of fast-food restaurants in many developing countries is neither convenience nor reasonable prices. Time savings does not have the same priority in these countries as it does in the United States. What makes these restaurants popular in developing countries such as Argentina, Turkey, and many others is their "Americanness." Patronization of these restaurants enables consumers to express their "aspirational" links with developed nations.[92]

Interestingly, even within a culture, time perspectives can vary by age and by situation. For example, in Japan, work is approached in terms of monochronic time whereas leisure is approached, as their culture might suggest, in terms of polychronic time.[93] Also, while Americans have tended to be monochronic, younger consumers appear to demonstrate elements of polychronic time. This so-called MTV generation seems to have no attention span and may simultaneously be found doing homework, watching TV, and surfing the net! Not surprisingly, U.S. advertisers find it hard to capture and hold the attention of this audience.

Meanings in the Use of Time    Specific uses of time have varying meanings in different cultures. In much of the world, the time required for a decision is proportional to the importance of the decision. Americans, by being well prepared with ready answers, may adversely downplay the importance of the business being discussed. Likewise, both Japanese and Middle Eastern executives are put off by Americans' insistence on coming to the point directly and quickly in business transactions.

Promptness is considered very important in America and Japan. Furthermore, promptness is defined as being on time for appointments, whether you are the person making the call or the person receiving the caller. According to one expert:

Time is money and a symbol of status and responsibility. To be kept waiting is offensive in monochronic cultures, it is perceived as a message. It is not in polychronic cultures.[94]

What is meant by "being kept waiting" also varies substantially by culture. Thirty minutes might seem like an eternity in the United States, but seem like very little time in other countries, such as those in the Middle East. As you can see, understanding such differences *prior* to doing business in a given country is critical.

## Space

The use people make of space and the meanings they assign to their use of space constitute a second form of nonverbal communication.[95] In America, "bigger is better." Thus, office space in corporations generally is allocated according to rank or prestige rather than need. The president will have the largest office, followed by the executive vice president, and so on.

A second major use of space is **personal space.** It is the nearest that others can come to you in various situations without your feeling uncomfortable. In the United States, normal business conversations occur at distances of 3 to 5 feet and highly personal business from 18 inches to 3 feet. In parts of northern Europe, the distances are slightly longer; in most of Latin America, they are substantially shorter.

An American businessperson in Latin America will tend to back away from a Latin American counterpart in order to maintain his or her preferred personal distance. In turn, the host will tend to advance toward the American in order to maintain his or her personal space. The resulting "chase" would be comical if it were not for the results. Both parties generally are unaware of their actions or the reasons for them. Furthermore, each assigns a meaning to the other's actions according to what the action means in his or her own culture. Thus, the North American considers the Latin American to be pushy and aggressive. The Latin American, in turn, considers the North American to be cold, aloof, and snobbish.

## Symbols

An American seeing a baby wearing a pink outfit would most likely assume the child to be female. If the outfit were blue, the assumed gender would be male. These assumptions would be accurate most of the time in the United States but not in many other parts of the world, such as Holland. Colors, animals, shapes, numbers, and music have varying meanings across cultures. Failure to recognize the meaning assigned to a symbol can cause serious problems:

- AT&T had to change its "thumbs-up" ads in Russia and Poland, where showing the palm of the hand in this manner has an offensive meaning. The change was simple. The thumbs-up sign was given showing the back of the hand.
- Mont Blanc has a white marking on the end of its pens, meant to represent the snow-capped Alpine mountain peaks. However, Arab consumers reacted negatively because it looked like the "Star of David," which is Israel's national symbol. Mont Blanc worked to clear up the misunderstanding.[96]
- In the United States, blond hair color in women is often perceived as a symbol of beauty. In a study of seven European cities, the hair color most symbolic of beauty varied from dark brown (Madrid, Paris, and London), to black (Milan), to blond (Hamburg).[97]

Table 2–3 presents additional illustrations of varying meanings assigned to symbols across cultures.[98] Despite frequent cultural differences in symbols, many symbols work well across a wide range of cultures. Kellogg's Tony the Tiger works in the United States, China (see Illustration 2–6), and many other cultures.

| TABLE 2–3 | The Meaning of Numbers, Colors, and Other Symbols |
|---|---|

- White — Symbol for mourning or death in the Far East; purity in the United States.
- Purple — Associated with death in many Latin American countries.
- Blue — Connotation of femininity in Holland; masculinity in Sweden, United States.
- Red — Unlucky or negative in Chad, Nigeria, Germany; positive in Denmark, Rumania, Argentina.
- Yellow flowers — Sign of death in Mexico; infidelity in France.
- White lilies — Suggestion of death in England.
- The number 7 — Unlucky number in Ghana, Kenya, Singapore; lucky in Morocco, India, the Czech Republic, Nicaragua, United States.
- Triangle — Negative in Hong Kong, Korea, Taiwan; positive in Colombia.
- Owl — Wisdom in the United States; bad luck in India.
- Deer — Speed, grace in United States; homosexuality in Brazil.

**ILLUSTRATION 2–6**

Kellogg's tiger is an effective symbol in many cultures.

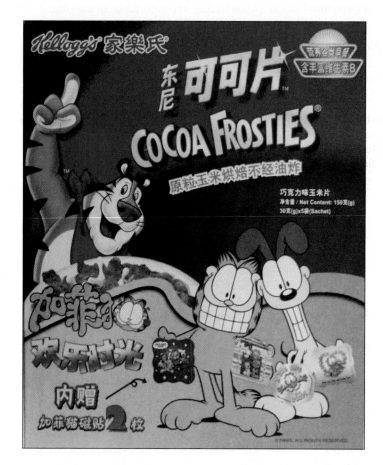

## Relationships

The rights and obligations imposed by relationships and friendship are another nonverbal cultural variable. Americans, more so than those in most other cultures, form relationships and make friends quickly and easily and drop them easily also. In large part, this may be because America has always had a great deal of both social and geographic mobility.

People who move every few years must be able to form friendships in a short time period and depart from them with a minimum of pain. In many other parts of the world, relationships and friendships are formed slowly and carefully because they imply deep and lasting obligations. As the following quote indicates, friendship and business are deeply intertwined in most of the world:

> To most Asians and Latin Americans, good personal relationships and feelings are all that really matter in a long-term agreement. After all, the written word is less important than personal ties. Once personal trust has been established, cooperation increases. The social contacts developed between the parties are often far more significant than the technical specifications and the price. In many countries the heart of the matter, the major point of the negotiations, is getting to know the people involved. Americans negotiate a contract; the Japanese negotiate a relationship. In many cultures, the written word is used simply to satisfy legalities. In their eyes, emotion and personal relations are more important than cold facts.[99]

In addition, long-run success in many cultures involves more than just "getting to know" someone in the Western sense of the expression. For example, Chinese relationships are complex and described under the concept of *guanxi:*

> *Guanxi* is literally translated as personal connections/relationships on which an individual can draw to secure resources or advantages when doing business as well as in the course of social life. Its main characteristics are (1) the notion of a continuing reciprocal relationship over an indefinite period of time, (2) favors are banked, (3) it extends beyond the relationship between two parties to include other parties within the social network (it can be transferred), (4) the relationship network is built among individuals not organizations, (5) status matters—relationships with a senior will extend to his subordinates but not vice versa, and (6) the social relationship is prior to and a prerequisite to the business relationship.[100]

## Agreements

Americans rely on an extensive and, generally, highly efficient legal system for ensuring that business obligations are honored and for resolving disagreements. Many other cultures have not developed such a system and rely instead on relationships, friendship, and kinship; local moral principles; or informal customs to guide business conduct. For example, the Chinese "tend to pay more attention to relationships than contracts."[101] Under the American system, we would examine a proposed contract closely. Under the Chinese system, we would examine the character of a potential trading partner closely. In the words of an American CEO based in China:

> Relationships are everything in China, more so than in the United States, which is more focused on business. The Chinese want to know and understand you before they buy from you.[102]

Americans generally assume that, in almost all instances, prices are uniform for all buyers, related to the service rendered, and reasonably close to the going rate. We order many products such as taxi rides without inquiring in advance about the cost. In many Latin American, Asian, and Middle East countries, the procedure is different. Virtually all prices are negotiated prior to the sale, including those for industrial products.[103]

## Things

The cultural meaning of things leads to purchase patterns that one would not otherwise predict. One observer noted a strong demand for expensive, status brands whose absolute cost was not too high among those Russians beginning to gain economically under capitalism. He concluded:

> They may stick to their locally produced toothpaste, but they want the Levi's, the Mont Blanc pens, the Moët & Chandon champagne to establish their self-esteem and their class position.[104]

The differing meanings that cultures attach to things, including products, make gift giving a particularly difficult task.[105] For example, giving a Chinese business customer or distributor a nice desk clock—a common gift in many countries—would be inappropriate. Why? In China, the word for *clock* is similar to the word for *funeral,* making clocks inappropriate gifts. When does receipt of a gift "require" a gift in return? In China this depends on the closeness of the relationship between the parties—the closer the relationship, the less a return gift is required.[106]

The business and social situations that call for a gift, and the items that are appropriate gifts, vary widely. For example, a gift of cutlery is generally inappropriate in Russia, Japan, Taiwan, and Germany. In Japan, small gifts are required in many business situations, yet in China they are less appropriate. In China, gifts should be presented privately, but in Arab countries, they should be given in front of others.

## Etiquette

*Etiquette* represents generally accepted ways of behaving in social situations. Assume that an American is preparing a commercial that shows people eating an evening meal, with one person about to take a bite of food from a fork. The person will have the fork in the right hand, and the left hand will be out of sight under the table. To an American audience this will seem natural. However, in many European cultures, a well-mannered individual would have the fork in the left hand and the right hand on the table.

Behaviors considered rude or obnoxious in one culture may be quite acceptable in another. The common and acceptable American habit, for males, of crossing one's legs while sitting, such that the sole of a shoe shows, is extremely insulting in many Eastern cultures. In these cultures, the sole of the foot or shoe should never be exposed to view. While most Americans are not hesitant to voice dissatisfaction with a service encounter, many Asians are. This also appears to be true of the British, who have traditionally been characterized by their reserved nature. Such factors can lead U.S. managers to misjudge customer response to their services abroad.[107]

Normal voice tone, pitch, and speed of speech differ among cultures and languages, as does the use of gestures. Westerners often mistake the seemingly loud, volatile speech of some Asian cultures as signifying anger or emotional distress (which it would if it were being used by a Westerner) when it is normal speech for the occasion.

As American trade with Japan increases, we continue to learn more of the subtle aspects of Japanese business etiquette. For example, a Japanese executive will seldom say "no" directly during negotiations; doing so would be considered impolite. Instead, he might say, "That will be very difficult," which would mean "no." A Japanese responding "yes" to a request often means, "Yes, I understand the request," not "Yes, I agree to the request." Many Japanese find the American tendency to look straight into another's eyes when talking to be aggressive and rude.

Another aspect of Japanese business etiquette is *meishi,* epitomized by "A man without a *meishi* has no identity in Japan." The exchange of meishi is the most basic of social rituals in a nation where social ritual matters very much. The act of exchanging meishi is weighted with meaning. Once the social minuet is completed, the two know where they stand in relation to each other and their respective statures within the hierarchy of corporate or government bureaucracy. What is "meishi"? It is the exchange of business cards when two people meet! A fairly common, simple activity in America, it is an essential, complex social exchange in Japan.

Other cultures also find it necessary to learn about the subtleties of doing business with Westerners. Business leaders in China are developing training programs to help sensitize Chinese businesspeople to other cultures. According to Jack Ma, who runs one such program:

> Chinese businessmen are shrewd, but they need to learn to be more polished. At a World Economic Forum held in Bejing, Mr. Ma was depressed at how many conducted themselves, noting— Many smoked constantly and held loud cellphone conversations, even during meetings.[108]

The importance of proper, culture-specific etiquette is obvious. Although people recognize that etiquette varies from culture to culture, there is still a strong emotional feeling that "our way is natural and right."

## Conclusions on Nonverbal Communications

Can you imagine yourself becoming upset or surprised because people in a different culture spoke to you in their native language, say Spanish or German, instead of English? Of course not. We all recognize that verbal languages vary around the world. Yet we generally feel that our nonverbal languages are natural or innate. Therefore, we misinterpret what is being "said" to us because we think we are hearing English when in reality it is Japanese, Italian, or Russian. It is this error that marketers can and must avoid.

# GLOBAL CULTURES

An important issue facing marketers is the extent to which one or more global consumer cultures or segments are emerging. Evidence suggests that there is indeed movement in this direction.[109] Such a culture would have a shared set of consumption-related symbols with common meaning and desirability among members. One such proposed global culture is that portion of local cultures that view themselves as cosmopolitan, knowledgeable, and modern. Such individuals share many values and consumption-related behaviors with similar individuals across a range of national cultures.

Such cultures are being created by the globalization of mass media, work, education, and travel. Some product categories (cell phones, Internet) and brands (Sony, Nike) have become symbolically related to this culture. This does not imply that these brands use the same advertising globally but rather that the underlying theme and symbolism may be the same. Thus, a combined shampoo and conditioner could be positioned as a time-saver for the time-pressured modern career woman. The advertisement might portray the shampoo being used in the context of a gym in the United States or Germany, where many females exercise, but in a home context in Japan, where few women visit gyms. Philips Electronic is one firm that has developed a global positioning strategy based on such a global culture.[110]

Perhaps the closest thing to a global culture today is urban youth, which we examine next.

## A Global Youth Culture?

Consider _____, a 19-year old hip-hop music producer scouting for a new pair of Air Force 1 sneakers at the Nike shop. . . . _____, who prefers to be addressed by his street name, "Jerzy King"—moved to _____ three years ago. . . . A music school dropout who has never set foot outside of _____, he totes a mini-disc player loaded with Eminem, Puff Daddy, and Fabolous. On this particular day he's looking phat in a blue-and-white fleece jacket bearing the logo of the Toronto Maple Leafs.[111]

Can you fill in the blanks with any degree of confidence? The young man is Wang Qi and he lives in Beijing. However, many of his behaviors and possessions echo those of millions of other teenagers in Europe, North and South America, and Asia. And as we discussed earlier, it is incorrect to think of the youth influence as a one-way street from America to the rest of the world with entities like Levi's, Coke, and Madonna leading the way:

Now it's a two-way street. Americans are learning Bollywood dance steps at their local health clubs. M.I.A., an up-and-coming pop singer who has Sri Lankan roots and was brought up in London, intermingles hip-hop, reggae, and South Asian influences. And Japanese *anime* has swept the globe.[112]

Similarities and convergence of lifestyles, values, and purchases make this global youth market compelling for companies, particularly given its large size. For example, a recent survey of global youth (age 14–29) across six countries found that 86 percent believe that products help to define and communicate their personality. It also found compelling similarities in the top three spending categories, as follows:[113]

|  | First Category | Second Category | Third Category |
|---|---|---|---|
| Amsterdam | Going out | Clothing | Food |
| Hong Kong | Clothing | Food | Transportation |
| Malaysia | Transportation | Food | Going out |
| Singapore | Food | Clothing | Entertainment |
| South Korea | Food | Clothing | Entertainment |
| United Kingdom | Going out | Clothing | Phone |
| United States | Clothing | Food | Music |

What is causing this convergence? The largest single influence is worldwide mass media, including, most recently, the Internet. Music, sports, and fashion appear to be major points of convergence, although the convergence often goes far beyond this to underlying values such as independence and risk taking. Marketers are using the similarities among youth across cultures to launch global brands or to reposition current brands to appeal to this large market. Levi's, reacting to the growing online trend among global teens, launched an online campaign in Asia targeted at "young, tech-savvy trendsetters." The Web site played heavily on Western music and style to promote its Levi's re-cut 501 Re-Born jeans. The theme emphasized that the jeans have been re-cut for today, with one page showing a teen being "reborn" or transformed by the new Levi's jeans.[114] Illustration 2–7 provides another example of an ad using a global youth appeal.

Several recent trends in the global youth market are critical for global marketers to understand. These include the following:[115]

- *Technology is mainstream.* Wired teens are a global phenomenon not restricted to developed countries. Fifty-six percent of teens globally are "superconnectors," meaning they use two or more electronic devices (e.g., cell phone and the Internet) daily.
- *U.S. teens no longer lead the way.* Now it's more about mind-set and the "creatives" are leading the way. Creatives are most prevalent in Europe (not the United States), are open to new ideas, and like expressing themselves in various ways, including personal Web pages and art.
- *U.S. brands are not currently the leaders.* U.S. brands used to be the leaders among global teens. Now the top three are Sony (Japan), Nokia (Finland), and Adidas (Germany).

As the global youth culture moves increasingly away from U.S. influence and brands, marketers in the United States must find ways to understand and connect with the trends and trendsetters across the globe. In addition, it is critical to understand that global youth also have a great many culturally unique behaviors, attitudes, and values. As one expert states, "European teens resent being thought of as Americans with an accent."[116] Also, the similarities described above are most noticeable among middle-class teens living in urban areas. Poorer, rural teens often conform more closely to their society's traditional culture. For example, Coke distinguishes between major urban centers and smaller cities and towns in China. Consider the following:

In the smaller cities and towns Coke uses a famous Chinese actor traveling the countryside in a hot bus and stresses taste and price. In China's largest markets its TV spot "features a hip Taiwanese VJ . . . who shows off his dance moves as he pretends his Coke can magnetically draw him to an attractive lady across the street." According to a Coke executive, "The (urban TV) ad is aimed at young adults who want to do things their own way, as opposed to following a famous actor as in the bus spot."[117]

## Bollywood Goes Global

Bollywood. India's Hollywood. India is the leading movie producer and consumer in the world (the United States is a distant second).[118] No wonder then that Indian culture is hot stuff, especially among global teens. Consider the following:

With riffs off India's cultural cachet showing up everywhere—from Madonna's use of mendhi, the traditional Indian henna art, to bhangra rhythms from northern India mixed into a Britney Spears single, advertisers are far from alone in embracing the colors and sounds of the subcontinent. The trend is even more entrenched overseas, where major campaigns with Bollywood themes are popping up from the Mediterranean to the South China Sea.

Marketers have not been shy about tapping this global hip status to market to teens in the United States, Asia, and Europe. A few examples include:

- In the United States, Absolut vodka has a 12-minute online "Bollywood ad" called Absolut Mulit.
- In Asia, Nokia has a TV spot in which "dozens of women clad in brightly colored saris … leap from a plane and sky-dive toward a bored-looking man standing on the side of the road. Alighting, they start gyrating to pulsating Indian music, while the man looks on in astonishment."
- In Spain, Italy, and Portugal, Coca-Cola runs an ad in which a Hindu waiter gets everyone at a stuffy European party to dance and liven up by singing a Bollywood-style song after drinking a Coke.[119]

Not everything coming out of Bollywood is good, however. A World Health Organization (WHO) study finds that over three-quarters of films coming out of Bollywood over the past 10 years contain smoking of some sort. In a country that accounts for one in three smoking-related deaths, WHO appears to have valid concerns.[120]

### Critical Thinking Questions

1. What cultural values are companies like Absolut, Nokia, and Coke tapping into in their advertising appeals?

2. How are these values different from or similar to traditional values in the countries where they are operating?

3. What ethical obligations does Bollywood have with respect to the smoking issue? Do you expect government regulations to follow?

It is fascinating to watch how teens across cultures continue to search for the new and interesting, and how different cultures influence each other. A recent example is India and its growing influence on teens worldwide, as discussed in Consumer Insight 2–1.

# GLOBAL DEMOGRAPHICS

Economies such as India and China have seen rapid growth, which has led to increased personal disposable income and strong and growing middle classes that are the envy of marketers worldwide.[121] Concerns about the extent to which economic growth in these and other countries will continue at current rates are beginning to appear due to rising fuel and food costs.[122] To the extent that growth continues at a relatively rapid pace, such expansion not only creates opportunities, but can also present challenges.

For example, the initial explosion in the use of motorbikes as replacements for bicycles in China triggered demand for gasoline in cities with no gasoline stations and few

**ILLUSTRATION 2–8**

The rapid growth in personal income in China has led to an explosion in motorbike owner- ship. The Chinese have responded with innovative distribution and service outlets.

available sites. Illustration 2–8 shows how one firm dealt with this challenge by devel- oping and deploying "mobile" service stations in the form of trucks with attached gaso- line pumps. More recently, an increase in automobile use (expected to increase 10 percent per year between 2005 and 2010) is creating environmental concerns related to emissions as well.[123]

Disposable income is one aspect of demographics. **Demographics** *describe a popula- tion in terms of its size, structure, and distribution. Size* refers to the number of individuals in the society. *Structure* describes the society in terms of age, income, education, and occu- pation. *Distribution* refers to the physical location of individuals in terms of geographic region and rural, suburban, and urban location.

Demographics are both a result and a cause of cultural values. Densely populated socie- ties are likely to have more of a collective orientation than an individualistic one because a collective orientation helps such societies function smoothly. Cultures that value hard work and the acquisition of material wealth are likely to advance economically, which alters their demographics both directly (income) and indirectly (families in economically advanced countries tend to be smaller).

A critical aspect of demographics for marketers is income, particularly the distribution of income. One country with a relatively low average income can have a sizable middle- income segment, while another country with the same average income may have most of the wealth in the hands of a few individuals. As shown below, Brazil's average per capita income is slightly higher than Romania's.[124] However, the distribution of that income dif- fers sharply. Forty-five percent of the income generated in Brazil goes to just 10 percent of the population. In contrast, the top 10 percent of households in Romania command only 21 percent of that country's income. *How will these and the other differences shown below affect consumption?*

| | Per Capita Income | Percent of Total Income to Top 10 Percent of Population | Per Capita PPP |
|---|---|---|---|
| Brazil | $ 4,791 | 45 | $ 8,596 |
| Canada | 35,133 | 25 | 35,078 |
| Chile | 7,305 | 45 | 12,262 |
| China | 1,721 | 35 | 4,091 |
| Egypt | 1,412 | 30 | 5,049 |
| France | 34,008 | 25 | 29,644 |
| India | 707 | 31 | 2,126 |
| Japan | 35,604 | 22 | 30,290 |
| Kenya | 531 | 37 | 1,395 |
| Mexico | 7,401 | 37 | 11,317 |
| Romania | 4,575 | 21 | 9,374 |
| United Kingdom | 37,266 | 29 | 31,580 |
| United States | 41,674 | 30 | 41,674 |

Source: Per Capita Income and Per Capita PPP: *2005 International Comparison Program* (International Bank for Reconstruction and Development/The World Bank, 2008): Percent of Total Income to Top 10 Percent of Population: *The World Factbook* (Washington, DC: Central Intelligence Agency, 2008).

Marketers increasingly use **purchasing power parity (PPP)** rather than average or median income to evaluate markets. PPP is based on the cost of a standard market basket of products bought in each country. An average household in one country may have a lower income in U.S. dollars. However, that household may be able to buy *more* than a household in other countries with higher income in U.S. dollars because of a lower local cost structure, government-provided health care, and so forth. The World Bank describes all countries in terms of PPP in its annual World Bank Atlas.[125] Notice how Brazil's purchasing power is substantially higher than its per capita income would suggest. *How might an understanding of PPP change marketer decisions about such things as market potential and entry?*

The estimated age distributions of the United States, the Philippines, Japan, and Canada are shown below.[126] Note that almost half the population of the Philippines is under 20 years of age, compared with around one-fourth for the United States and Canada, and about one-fifth for Japan. In the Middle East, a massive baby boom is under way, with two-thirds of the population under 25, fueling the youth movement in this region, which we discussed earlier.[127] *What product opportunities do this and the other age differences among these countries suggest?*

| Age | United States (%) | Philippines (%) | Japan (%) | Canada (%) |
|---|---|---|---|---|
| Under 10 | 13.4 | 26.6 | 9.2 | 11.3 |
| 10–19 | 14.0 | 22.6 | 10.3 | 13.3 |
| 20–29 | 14.0 | 17.5 | 13.3 | 13.8 |
| 30–39 | 13.7 | 13.4 | 14.2 | 14.5 |
| 40–49 | 15.1 | 8.9 | 12.4 | 16.6 |
| 50–59 | 12.9 | 5.5 | 15.0 | 13.0 |
| 60 and over | 16.9 | 5.4 | 25.5 | 17.7 |

# CROSS-CULTURAL MARKETING STRATEGY

There is continuing controversy over the extent to which cross-cultural marketing strategies should be standardized.[128] Standardized strategies can result in substantial cost savings. Maybelline's Manhattan line of cosmetics designed for the Asian market used one ad campaign in China, Taiwan, Hong Kong, Thailand, and Singapore. The ads featured an attractive Asian model in a low-cut, short dress against the Manhattan skyline at night. This combination of appeals to youth, beauty, and sophistication could be used in many other countries, though this ad would be inappropriate, and probably banned, in most Islamic countries.

Uniformity is sometimes possible, but companies must often adapt to cultural differences. We saw this earlier in the case of KFC in Malaysia. Consider McDonald's:

> McDonald's used to strive for uniformity around the Globe. Now it adapts its products as appropriate—adding fried eggs to burgers in Japan and offering Samurai Pork Burgers with a sweet barbecue sauce in Thailand. However, its most dramatic changes were made when it entered India for the first time. So, instead of the all-beef Big Macs, the menu featured the mutton [lamb] Maharaja Mac.[129]

McDonald's also adapts its store layout. As shown in Illustration 2–9, separate sections for families and singles are provided in Muslim countries.

In general, most companies will blend standardization and customization. A recent surge in people's pride in their local cultures (up 11 percent in Brazil and France and up 20 percent in Japan) means that at least some customization is necessary.[130] A critical success factor is achieving the right balance and determining where standardization is possible and where customization is critical.

## Considerations in Approaching a Foreign Market

There are seven key considerations for each geographic market that a firm is contemplating. An analysis of these seven variables provides the background necessary for deciding

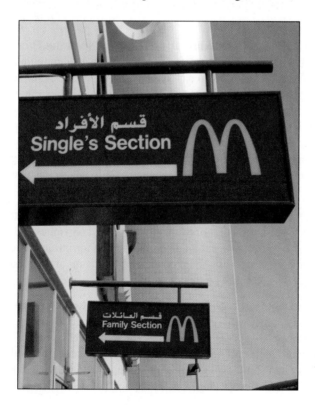

**ILLUSTRATION 2–9**

McDonald's offers both family and singles sections in Muslim countries to accommodate the cultural norms governing interactions between men and women. The singles section is for single men only.

whether or not to enter the market and to what extent, if any, an individualized marketing strategy is required. A small sample of experts, preferably native to the market under consideration, often will be able to furnish sufficient information on each variable.

### Is the Geographic Area Homogeneous or Heterogeneous with Respect to Culture?

Marketing efforts are generally directed at defined geographic areas, primarily political and economic entities. Legal requirements and existing distribution channels often encourage this approach. However, it is also supported by the implicit assumption that geographical or political boundaries coincide with cultural boundaries. As we have seen, country boundaries represent general tendencies, but differences *within* a given country are also critical to consider. For example, research suggests that strategies in Latin America need to consider not only cross-country (e.g., Brazil vs. Chile) but also within-country (e.g., regional; urban vs. rural) differences.[131]

Likewise, China has strong regional cultures (one authority has identified eight), urban and rural cultures, as well as sharp differences associated with income, age, and education.[132] Thus, marketing campaigns must be developed for cultural and demographic groups, not just countries.

### What Needs Can This Product or a Version of It Fill in This Culture?

Most firms examine a new market with an existing product or product technology in mind. The question they must answer is what needs their existing or modified product can fill in the culture involved. For example, bicycles and motorcycles serve primarily recreational needs in the United States, but they provide basic transportation in many other countries.

General Foods successfully positioned Tang as a substitute for orange juice at breakfast in the United States. However, in analyzing the French market, it found that the French drink little orange juice and almost none at breakfast. Therefore, a totally different positioning strategy was used; Tang was promoted as a new type of refreshing drink for any time of the day.

### Can Enough of the People Needing the Product Afford the Product?

An initial demographic analysis is required to determine the number of individuals or households that might need the product and who can actually afford it. For example, although China has over 1.3 billion consumers, the effective market for most Western goods is estimated to be less than 20 percent of this total.[133] Future economic expansion in countries like China and India is expected to enhance their market potential in coming years. In addition, the possibilities of establishing credit, obtaining a government subsidy, or making a less expensive version should be considered. This latter approach is being used by P&G in China, where a tiered pricing system was designed to help reach consumers with relatively low incomes.[134]

### What Values or Patterns of Values Are Relevant to the Purchase and Use of This Product?

The first section of this chapter focused on values and their role in consumer behavior. The value system should be investigated for influences on purchasing the product, owning the product, using the product, and disposing of the product. Much of the marketing strategy will be based on this analysis.

### What Are the Distribution, Political, and Legal Structures for the Product?

The legal structure of a country can have an impact on each aspect of a firm's marketing mix. China recently banned sex appeals, and TV ads for so-called "offensive" products such as feminine-hygiene products and hemorrhoid ointments have been banned during the three daily mealtimes (when families, including children, would be watching). China is also tightening regulations on the opening of new Internet cafes. The United Kingdom recently banned junk-food ads targeted at kids under the age of 16 and has put restrictions on product placements such that consumers must be reminded every 20 minutes which brands have been placed in a show (something unheard of in the United States). And Brazil has put laws in place that limit the amount of alcohol advertising.[135] Such legal restrictions limit the ability of companies to use standardized approaches to their marketing efforts. *What effect would China's ban on sex appeals have on Maybelline's advertising in Asia for its Manhattan line?*

**In What Ways Can We Communicate about the Product?**    This question requires an investigation into (1) available media and who attends to each type, (2) the needs the product fills, (3) values associated with the product and its use, and (4) the verbal and nonverbal communications systems in the culture(s). All aspects of the firm's promotional mix—including packaging, nonfunctional product design features, personal selling techniques, and advertising—should be based on these four factors.

The Internet seems like a natural media through which to communicate to consumers. However, as we saw earlier, Internet access varies widely across a country as does the percentage of consumers who will actually buy online.[136] Moreover, research suggests that tailoring Web sites to specific countries is critical to online marketing success because of cultural variations in Web site dimensions driving purchase and loyalty.[137]

**What Are the Ethical Implications of Marketing This Product in This Country?**
All marketing programs should be evaluated on ethical as well as financial dimensions. As discussed at the beginning of the chapter, international marketing activities raise many ethical issues. The ethical dimension is particularly important and complex in marketing to third world and developing countries. Consider Kellogg's attempt to introduce cold cereal as a breakfast food in a developing country. An ethical analysis would consider various factors, including:

If we succeed, will the average nutrition level be increased or decreased?

If we succeed, will the funds spent on cereal be diverted from other uses with more beneficial long-term impacts for the individuals or society?

If we succeed, what impact will this have on the local producers of currently consumed breakfast products?

Such an ethical analysis not only is the right thing to do but also may head off conflicts with local governments or economic interests. Understanding and acting on ethical considerations in international marketing is a difficult task. However, it is also a necessary one.

## SUMMARY

*Culture* is defined as the complex whole that includes knowledge, beliefs, art, law, morals, customs, and any other capabilities acquired by humans as members of society. It includes almost everything that influences an individual's thought processes and behaviors.

Culture operates primarily by setting boundaries for individual behavior and by influencing the functioning of such institutions as the family and mass media. The boundaries, or *norms,* are derived from *cultural val-* ues. Values are widely held beliefs that affirm what is desirable.

Cultural values are classified into three categories: other, environment, and self. *Other-oriented values* reflect a society's view of the appropriate relationships between individuals and groups within that society. Relevant values of this nature include *individual/collective, youth/age, extended/limited family, masculine/feminine, competitive/cooperative,* and *diversity/uniformity.*

*Environment-oriented values* prescribe a society's relationships with its economic, technical, and physical environments. Examples of environment values are *cleanliness, performance/status, tradition/change, risk taking/security, problem solving/fatalistic,* and *nature*. *Self-oriented values* reflect the objectives and approaches to life that individual members of society find desirable. These include *active/passive, sensual gratification/abstinence, material/nonmaterial, hard work/leisure, postponed gratification/immediate gratification,* and *religious/secular*.

Differences in *verbal communication systems* are immediately obvious across cultures and must be taken into account by marketers wishing to do business in those cultures. Probably more important, however, and certainly more difficult to recognize are *nonverbal communication systems*. Major examples of nonverbal communication variables that affect marketers are *time, space, symbols, relationships, agreements, things,* and *etiquette.*

There is evidence that urban youth around the world share at least some aspects of a common culture. This culture is driven by worldwide mass media and common music and sports stars. *Demographics* describe a population in terms of its size, structure, and distribution. Demographics differ widely across cultures and influence cultural values (and are influenced by them) as well as consumption patterns.

Seven questions are relevant for developing a cross-cultural marketing strategy: (1) Is the geographic area homogeneous or heterogeneous with respect to culture? (2) What needs can this product fill in this culture? (3) Can enough people afford the product? (4) What values are relevant to the purchase and use of the product? (5) What are the distribution, political, and legal structures for the product? (6) How can we communicate about the product? (7) What are the ethical implications of marketing this product in this country?

## KEY TERMS

Cultural values  43
Culture  42
Demographics  67
Environment-oriented values  45
*Guanxi*  61
Instrumental materialism  54
Monochronic time perspective  57

Nonverbal communication
  systems  57
Norms  43
Other-oriented values  45
Personal space  59
Polychronic time perspective  57
Power distance  51

Purchasing power parity
  (PPP)  68
Sanctions  43
Self-oriented values  45
Terminal materialism  54
Verbal communication
  systems  56

## INTERNET EXERCISES

1. Visit the Michigan State University international business resources Web site (www.globaledge.msu.edu/index.asp). Which of the resources listed is most useful for the following (hint: the global resources section is a good place to start)?
   *a.* Worldwide consumer data
   *b.* Data on consumer markets in China
   *c.* Data on consumer markets in Brazil
   *d.* Data on industrial markets in Canada

2. Using the Michigan State University site in Exercise 1 above, select and describe one of the sources listed. Evaluate its usefulness for understanding international markets and other cultures.

3. Using the Internet, prepare a brief report on the following as a market for automobiles. Provide addresses for all Web sites used.
   *a.* India
   *b.* United Kingdom
   *c.* Qatar
   *d.* China

4. Prepare a report that describes how useful, if at all, the information available at the World Bank Web site (www.worldbank.org) is in terms of helping you understand the following as a market for cell phones:
   *a.* United Kingdom        *c.* Australia
   *b.* South Korea           *d.* Argentina

5. Visit the CIA site (www.odci.gov). Evaluate the usefulness of this site for international marketers.

6. Visit the Kwintessential Web site (www .kwintessential.co.uk). Click on the "Cross Cultural Quizzes." Pick several topics/countries and take a quiz. Prepare a report on what you learned.

7. Visit Lands' End's various international sites (you can start at www.landsend.com). Beyond adapting to language differences, how much adapting have they done for each country? Based on your understanding of the cultural differences, would you have expected more or less adaptation?

## DDB LIFE STYLE STUDY™ DATA ANALYSES

1. What characterizes U.S. consumers who are interested in other cultures and interested in shopping for items influenced by other cultures? (Use the DDB data in Tables 1B through 7B.) How might travel agents use this in developing marketing strategies involving international travel?

## REVIEW QUESTIONS

1. What are some of the ethical issues involved in cross-cultural marketing?

2. What is meant by the term *culture*?

3. What does the statement "Culture sets boundaries on behaviors" mean?

4. What is a *norm*? From what are norms derived?

5. What is a *cultural value*?

6. What is a *sanction*?

7. Cultural values can be classified as affecting one of three types of relationships—other, environment, or self. Describe each of these, and differentiate each one from the others.

8. How does the first of the following paired orientations differ from the second?
   a. Individual/Collective
   b. Performance/Status
   c. Tradition/Change
   d. Limited/Extended family
   e. Active/Passive
   f. Material/Nonmaterial
   g. Hard work/Leisure
   h. Risk taking/Security
   i. Masculine/Feminine
   j. Competitive/Cooperative
   k. Youth/Age
   l. Problem solving/Fatalistic
   m. Diversity/Uniformity
   n. Postponed gratification/Immediate gratification
   o. Sensual gratification/Abstinence
   p. Religious/Secular

9. What is meant by *nonverbal communications*? Why is this a difficult area to adjust to?

10. What is meant by each of the following as a form of nonverbal communication?
    a. Time
    b. Space
    c. Symbols
    d. Relationships
    e. Agreements
    f. Things
    g. Etiquette

11. What is *guanxi*?

12. What is the difference between *instrumental* and *terminal* materialism?

13. What are the differences between a *monochronic* time perspective and a *polychronic* time perspective?

14. What forces seem to be creating a global youth culture?

15. What are *demographics*? Why are they important to international marketers?

16. What is *purchasing power parity*?

17. What are the seven key considerations in deciding whether or not to enter a given international market?

18. What does determining if a geographic area or political unit is homogeneous or heterogeneous with respect to culture mean? Why is this important?

## DISCUSSION QUESTIONS

19. Why should we study foreign cultures if we do not plan to engage in international or export marketing?

20. Is a country's culture more likely to be reflected in its art museums or its television commercials? Why?

21. Are the cultures of the world becoming more similar or more distinct?

22. Why do values differ across cultures?

23. The text lists 18 cultural values (in three categories) of relevance to marketing practice. Describe and place into one of the three categories two additional cultural values that have some relevance to marketing practice.

24. Select two cultural values from each of the three categories. Describe the boundaries (norms) relevant to that value in your society and the sanctions for violating those norms.

25. What are the most relevant cultural values affecting the consumption of each of the following? Describe how and why these values are particularly important.
    a. Internet
    b. MP3 player
    c. Milk
    d. Fast food
    e. Mountain bike
    f. Cell phones

26. What variations between the United States and other societies, *other than cultural variations,* may affect the relative level of usage of the following?
    a. Internet
    b. MP3 player
    c. Milk
    d. Fast food
    e. Mountain bike
    f. Cell phones

27. Is the European Union likely to become a relatively homogeneous culture by 2025?

28. What values underlie the differences between Fiji Island and U.S. children in terms of the strategies they use to influence their parents' decisions? What marketing implications emerge?

29. What are the marketing implications of the differences in the *masculine/feminine orientation* across countries?

30. Respond to the questions in Consumer Insight 2–1.

31. Why do nonverbal communication systems vary across cultures?

32. Which, if any, nonverbal communication factors might be relevant in the marketing of the following?
    a. Luxury automobiles
    b. Jewelry
    c. MP3 players
    d. Laundry detergent
    e. Lip balm
    f. Women's clothing

33. What are the implications of *guanxi* for a Western firm entering the Chinese market?

34. To what extent do you think youth are truly becoming a single, global culture?

35. Will today's youth still be a "global culture" when they are 40? Why or why not?

36. How do demographics affect a culture's values? How do a culture's values affect its demographics?

37. What causes the differences between purchasing power parity and income, as shown in the text?

38. The text provides a seven-step procedure for analyzing a foreign market. Using this procedure, analyze your country as a market for
    a. Laptop computers from Japan
    b. Automobiles from Germany
    c. Sunglasses from Italy
    d. Wine from Chile

39. What are the major ethical issues in introducing prepared foods such as fast foods to developing countries?

40. Should U.S. tobacco firms be allowed to market cigarettes in developing countries? Why or why not?

41. How can developing countries keep their cultures from being overly Westernized or Americanized?

## APPLICATION ACTIVITIES

42. Interview two students from two different cultures. Determine the extent to which the following are used in those cultures and the variations in the values of those cultures that relate to the use of these products:
    a. Gift cards
    b. Energy drinks (like Red Bull)
    c. Fast-food restaurants
    d. Exercise equipment
    e. Music
    f. Internet

43. Interview two students from two different foreign cultures. Report any differences in nonverbal communications they are aware of between their culture and your culture.

44. Interview two students from two different foreign cultures. Report their perceptions of the major differences in cultural values between their culture and your culture.

45. Interview a student from India. Report on the advice that the student would give an American firm marketing consumer products in India.

46. Interview two students from EU (European Union) countries. Report on the extent to which they feel the EU will be a homogeneous culture by 2025.

47. Imagine you are a consultant working with your state or province's tourism agency. You have been asked to advise the agency on the best promotional themes to use to attract foreign tourists. What would you recommend if Germany and Australia were the two target markets?

48. Analyze a foreign culture of your choice, and recommend a marketing program for a brand of one of the following made in your country:
    a. Automobile          d. Discount retailer
    b. Beer                e. Movies
    c. MP3 player          f. Cosmetics

## REFERENCES

1. Chapter opener based on C. Adese and M. Rueda, "Hello World," *Latin Trade,* July 2006, pp. 51–54; G. Samor, C. Rohwedder, and A. Zimmerman, "Wal-Mart Learns to Adapt to Asian Markets," *The Wall Street Journal Asia,* May 17, 2006, p. 26; E. Treewater, "Consumer Goods and Services in Latin American Distribution Channels," *NoticiasFinancieras,* August 24, 2007, p. 1; M. Calicchio, T. Francis, and A. Ramsay, "How Big Retailers Can Serve Brazil's Mass-Market Shoppers," *The McKinsey Quarterly,* 2007, www.mckinseyquarterly.com; and J. Arlidge, "Tesco Express Rolls into China," *Sunday Times,* April 13, 2008, p. 10.

2. See, e.g., M. Fielding, "Special Delivery," *Marketing News,* February 1, 2007, pp. 13–14; and T. Sangkhawasi and L. M. Johri, "Impact of Status Brand Strategy on Materialism in Thailand," *Journal of Consumer Marketing* 24, no. 5 (2007), pp. 275–82.

3. Examples from G. Burton, "Brazilian Lessons on Coolness and Imagination," *Brazzil,* April 2005, accessed April 27, 2008; N. Madden, "How the NFL Intends to Push 'Olive Ball' in China," *Advertising Age,* October 2, 2006, p. 45; I. Rowley, "Lexus," *Businessweek,* March 31, 2008, p. 72; and "Kosuke Fukudome Tastes Good," *SI.com,* April 29, 2008, www.si.com, accessed May 2, 2008.

4. N. Madden, "China Cracks Down on TV Talent Competitions," *Advertising Age,* April 3, 2006, p. 14.

5. M. Kotabe and C. Jiang, "Three Dimensional," *Marketing Management,* March–April 2006, pp. 39–43.

6. D. Holt, J. A. Quelch, and E. L. Taylor, "How Global Brands Compete," *Harvard Business Review,* September 2004, pp. 1–8.

7. See S. Mulley, "Young Women's Smoking Crisis Declared in Asia," *Medical Post,* January 11, 2000, p. 68; J. Mackay and M. Eriksen, *The Tobacco Atlas* (Brighton, U.K.: World Health Organization, 2002), p. 31; M. E. Goldberg and H. Baumgartner, "Cross-Country Attraction as a Motivation for Product Consumption," *Journal of Business Research* 55 (2002), pp. 901–6; and Mackay and Eriksen, *The Tobacco Atlas,* p. 89.

8. Mulley, "Young Women's Smoking Crisis Declared in Asia."

9. See, e.g., J. L. Aaker and J. Sengupta, "Additivity versus Attenuation," *Journal of Consumer Psychology* 2 (2000), pp. 67–82; and D. A. Briley, M. W. Morris, and I. Simonson, "Reasons as Carriers of Culture," *Journal of Consumer Research,* September 2000, pp. 157–77.

10. T. Parker-Pope, "Custom-Made," *The Wall Street Journal,* September 26, 1996, p. R22; see also M. Fielding, "Walk the Line," *Marketing News,* September 1, 2006, pp. 8–10.

11. "At Cricket Event, U.S. Cheerleaders Shake India's Conservative Values," *SI.com,* April 30, 2008, www.si.com, accessed April 30, 2008.

12. For this and other global missteps, see M. D. White, *A Short Course in International Marketing Blunders* (Petaluma: World Trade Press, 2002).

13. "It's a Grande-Latte World," *The Wall Street Journal,* December 15, 2003, p. B1.

14. G. Hofstede, *Culture's Consequences,* 2nd ed. (Thousand Oaks, CA: Sage, 2001).

15. Z. Gurhan-Canli and D. Maheswaran, "Cultural Variations in Country of Origin Effects," *Journal of Marketing Research,* August 2000, pp. 309–17.

16. C. Pornpitakpan and J. N. P. Francis, "The Effect of Cultural Differences, Source Expertise, and Argument Strength on Persuasion," *Journal of International Consumer Marketing* 1 (2001), pp. 77–101.

17. R. B. Money, M. C. Gilly, and J. L. Graham, "Explorations of National Culture and Word-of-Mouth Referral Behavior," *Journal of Marketing,* October 1998, pp. 76–87.

18. Based on data presented in *The Little Global Fact Book,* Ipsos World Monitor, 2004, www.ipsos-insight.com; and Hofstede, *Culture's Consequences.*

19. P. G. Patterson and T. Smith, "Relationship Benefits in Service Industries," *Journal of Services Marketing* 15, no. 6 (2001), pp. 425–43. See also A. S. Mattila and P. G. Patterson, "Service Recovery and Fairness Perceptions in Collectivist and Individual Contexts," *Journal of Service Research,* May 2004, pp. 336–46.

20. J. E. M. Steenkamp, F. Ter Hofstede, and M. Wedel, "A Cross-National Investigation into the Individual and National Cultural Antecedents of Consumer Innovativeness," *Journal of Marketing,* April 1999, pp. 55–69; and I. S. Yaveroglu and N. Donthu, "Cultural Differences on the Diffusion of New Products," *Journal of International Consumer Marketing* 14, no. 4 (2002), pp. 49–63.

21. S. M. Choi, W. Lee, and H. Kim, "Lessons from the Rich and Famous," *Journal of Advertising,* Summer 2005, pp. 85–98.

22. N. Y. Wong and A. C. Ahuvia, "Personal Taste and Family Face," *Psychology & Marketing,* August 1998, pp. 423–41.

23. C. Robinson, "Asian Culture," *Journal of the Market Research Society,* January 1996, pp. 55–62.

24. T. Erdem, J. Swait, and A. Valenzuala, "Brands as Signals," *Journal of Marketing,* January 2006, pp. 34–49.

25. T. Sun, M. Horn, and D. Merritt, "Values and Lifestyles of Individualists and Collectivists," *Journal of Consumer Marketing* 21, no. 5 (2004), pp. 318–31.

26. See, e.g., J. Zhang and S. Shavitt, "Cultural Values in Advertisements to the Chinese X-Generation," *Journal of Advertising* 32, no. 1 (2003), pp. 23–33.

27. "Global Teen Culture," *Brand Strategy,* January 2003, pp. 37–38.

28. K. L. Miller, "You Just Can't Talk to These Kids," *BusinessWeek,* April 19, 1993, pp. 104–6. See also W. Dou, G. Wang, and N. Zhou, "Generational and Regional Differences in Media Consumption Patterns of Chinese Generation X Consumers," *Journal of Advertising,* Summer 2006, pp. 101–10; and S. Okazaki and B. Mueller, "An Analysis of Advertising Appeals Employed in Japanese and American Print Advertising—Revisited," *Working Paper,* San Diego State University (San Diego, 2008).

29. See, e.g., K. C. C. Yang, "The Effects of Allocentrism and Idiocentrism on Consumers' Product Attribute Evaluation," *Journal of International Consumer Marketing* 16, no. 4 (2004), pp. 63–84.

30. B. Barak et al., "Perceptions of Age-Identity," *Psychology & Marketing,* October 2001, pp. 1003–29; C. A. Lin, "Cultural Values Reflected in Chinese and American Television Advertising," *Journal of Advertising,* Winter 2001, pp. 83–94; and D. H. Z. Khairullah and Z. Y. Khairullah, "Dominant Cultural Values," *Journal of Global Marketing* 16, no. 1/2 (2002), pp. 47–70.

31. P. L. Andruss, "Groups Make Fruits Apple of Taiwan's Eye," *Marketing News,* December 4, 2000, p. 5.

32. H. Fattah, "The New Arab Consumer," *American Demographics,* September 2002, p. 58.

33. J. Sherry, B. Greenberg, and H. Tokinoya, "Orientations to TV Advertising among Adolescents and Children in the U.S. and Japan," *International Journal of Advertising* 2 (1999), pp. 233–50; and A. Shoham and V. Dalakas, "Family Consumer Decision Making in Israel," *Journal of Consumer Marketing* 20, no. 3 (2003), pp. 238–51.

34. J. S. Wimalasiri, "A Comparison of Children's Purchase Influence and Parental Response in Fiji and the United States," *Journal of International Consumer Marketing* 4 (2000), pp. 55–73. See also J. S. Wimalasiri, "A Cross-National Study on Children's Purchasing Behavior and Parental Response," *Journal of Consumer Marketing* 21, no. 4 (2004), pp. 274–84.

35. M. F. Ji and J. U. McNeal, "How Chinese Children's Commercials Differ from Those of the United States," *Journal of Advertising,* Fall 2001, pp. 79–92; K. Chan and J. U. McNeal, "Parent–Child Communications about Consumption and Advertising in China," *Journal of Consumer Marketing* 20, no. 4 (2003), pp. 317–34; and "Little Emperors," *Fortune,* October 4, 2004, pp. 138–50.

36. L. Chang, "The New Stresses of Chinese Society Shape a Girl's Life," *The Wall Street Journal,* December 4, 2003, pp. A1, A13.

37. P. Kotler, S. W. Ang, and C. T. Tan, *Marketing Management: An Asian Perspective* (Singapore: Prentice Hall Pergamon, 1996), p. 524. But see M. Liu, "China's Empty Nest," *Newsweek,* March 10, 2008, p. 41, for evidence of how this is changing among younger generations of Chinese.

38. B. D. Keillor, R. S. Parker, and A. Schaffer, "Influences on Adolescent Brand Preferences in the United States and Mexico," *Journal of Advertising Research,* May–June 1996, pp. 47–56.

39. M. Viswanathan, T. L. Childers, and E. S. Moore, "The Measurement of Intergenerational Communication and Influence on Consumption," *Journal of the Academy of Marketing Science,* Summer 2000, pp. 406–24.

40. M. Kripalani, "Here Come the Wal-Mart Wannabes," *BusinessWeek,* April 4, 2005, p. 56.

41. See F. S. Al-Olayan and K. Karande, "A Content Analysis of Magazine Advertisements from the United States and the Arab World," *Journal of Advertising,* Fall 2000, pp. 69–82.

42. C.-N. Chen, M. Lai, and D. D. C. Tarn, "Feminism Orientation, Product Attributes, and Husband–Wife Decision Dominance," *Journal of Global Marketing* 3 (1999), pp. 23–39; and C. Webster, "Is Spousal Decision Making a Culturally Situated Phenomenon?" *Psychology & Marketing,* December 2000, pp. 1035–58.

43. M. L. Maynard and C. R. Taylor, "Girlish Images across Cultures," *Journal of Advertising,* Spring 1999, pp. 39–47.

44. S. M. Sidin et al., "The Effects of Sex Role Orientation on Family Purchase Decision Making in Malaysia," *Journal of Consumer Marketing* 21, no. 6 (2004), pp. 381–90; and "Rate of Chinese Businesswomen Higher than World Average," *China Daily,* March 20, 2005, www.chinadaily.com.

45. L. M. Milner and J. M. Collins, "Sex-Role Portrayals and the Gender of Nations," *Journal of Advertising,* Spring 2000, pp. 67–78; and G. Fowler, "China Cracks Down on Commercials," *The Wall Street Journal,* February 19, 2004, p. B7.

46. J. Russell, "Working Women Give Japan Culture Shock," *Advertising Age,* January 16, 1995, p. I24.

47. K. Simon, "A Rare Mexican Mania Over a Female Sporting Icon Ana Guevara May Like to Be Seen as an Inspiration to Girls Back Home," *Financial Times,* September 21, 2002, p. 24.

48. L. Y. Sin and O. H. Yau, "Female Role Orientation and Consumption Values," *Journal of International Consumer Marketing* 13, no. 2 (2001), pp. 49–75.

49. L. Y. M. Sin and O. H. M. Yau, "Female Role Orientation of Chinese Women," *Psychology & Marketing,* December 2004, pp. 1033–58.

50. For a related discussion, see M. de Mooij, *Global Marketing and Advertising* (Thousand Oaks, CA: Sage, 1998), pp. 252–53.

51. See Miller, "You Just Can't Talk to These Kids," p. 106; P. Sellers, "Pepsi Opens a Second Front," *Fortune,* August 8, 1994, pp. 70–76; and N. Donthu, "A Cross-Country Investigation of Recall of and Attitude toward Comparative Advertising," *Journal of Advertising,* Summer 1998, pp. 111–22.

52. See M. de Mooij, *Consumer Behavior and Culture* (Thousand Oaks, CA: Sage, 2004), pp. 162–64. For a discussion of how language can influence accessibility of cultural values, see D. A. Briley, M. W. Morris, and I. Simonson, "Cultural Chameleons," *Journal of Consumer Psychology* 15, no. 4 (2005), pp. 351–62.

53. T. Sun, M. Horn, and D. Merritt, "Values and Lifestyles of Individualists and Collectivists."

54. L. Shannahan, "Bugging Out over Germs," *Brandweek,* November 22, 2004, p. 17.

55. See, e.g., V. Kurian, "'Hand Wash' Campaign in Kerala Raises a Stink," *Businessline,* November 6, 2002, p. 1.

56. J. L. Watson, *Golden Arches East* (Stanford, CA: Stanford University Press, 1997).

57. For the related role of individualism/collectivism, see M. de Mooij and G. Hofstede, "Convergence and Divergence in Consumer Behavior," *Journal of Retailing* 78 (2002), pp. 61–69; see also S. H. C. Tai and R. Y. K. Chan, "Cross-Cultural Studies on the Information Content of Service Advertising," *Journal of Services Marketing* 15, no. 7 (2001), pp. 547–64.

58. H. Cheng and J. C. Schweitzer, "Cultural Values Reflected in Chinese and U.S. Television Commercials," *Journal of Advertising Research,* May–June 1996, pp. 27–45; Lin, "Cultural Values Reflected in Chinese and American Television Advertising"; and Khairullah and Khairullah, "Dominant Cultural Values"; and S. Okazaki and B. Mueller, "An Analysis of Advertising Appeals Employed in Japanese and American Print Advertising—Revisited."

59. For a related dimension, see S. Shavitt et al. "The Horizontal/Vertical Distinction in Cross-Cultural Consumer Research, *Journal of Consumer Psychology* 16, no. 4 (2006), pp. 325–56.

60. Pornpitakpan and Francis, "The Effect of Cultural Differences, Source Expertise, and Argument Strength on Persuasion"; see also B. R. Barnes et al., "Investigating the Impact of International Cosmetics Advertising in China," *International Journal of Advertising* 23 (2004), pp. 361–87.

61. C. Pornpitakpan, "Factors Associated with Opinion Seeking," *Journal of Global Marketing* 17, no. 2/3 (2004), pp. 91–113.

62. N. R. Buchan, R. T. A. Croson, and E. J. Johnson, "When Do Fair Beliefs Influence Bargaining Behavior?" *Journal of Consumer Research,* June 2004, pp. 181–90.

63. D. Kim, Y. Pan, and H. S. Park, "High- versus Low-Context Culture," *Psychology & Marketing,* September 1998, pp. 507–21.

64. Z. Caillat and B. Mueller, "The Influence of Culture on American and British Advertising," *Journal of Advertising Research,* May–June 1996, pp. 79–88; and Lin, "Cultural Values Reflected in Chinese and American Television Advertising."

65. Zhang and Shavitt, "Cultural Values in Advertisements to the Chinese X-Generation."

66. Table based on *The World Factbook* (Washington, DC: Central Intelligence Agency, 2008).

67. G. Parker, "Going Global Can Hit Snags," *The Wall Street Journal,* June 16, 2004, p. B1.

68. Steenkamp, Ter Hofstede, and Wedel, "A Cross-National Investigation into the Individual and National Cultural Antecedents of Consumer Innovativeness"; Pornpitakpan and Francis, "The Effect of Cultural Differences, Source Expertise, and Argument Strength on Persuasion"; J. M. Jung and J. J. Kellaris, "Cross-National Differences in Proneness to Scarcity Effects," *Psychology & Marketing,* September 2004, pp. 739–53; and T. Erdem, J. Swait, and A. Valenzuala, "Brands as Signals."

69. See, e.g., P. Raven and D. H. B. Welsh, "An Exploratory Study of Influences on Retail Service Quality," *Journal of Services Marketing* 18, no. 3 (2004), pp. 198–214.

70. "Quiet Motorcycle Seeks Added Vroom," *CNN.com,* March 17, 2005, www.cnn.com.

71. T. S. Chan, "Concerns for Environmental Issues," *Journal of International Consumer Marketing* 1 (1996), pp. 43–55.

72. See R. Y. K. Chan, "Environmental Attitudes and Behavior of Consumers in China," *Journal of International Consumer Marketing* 4 (1999), pp. 25–74; and R. Y. K. Chan, "Determinants of Chinese Consumers' Green Purchase Behavior," *Psychology & Marketing,* April 2001, pp. 389–413.

73. "Saudis and Americans," *NOP World* (New York: United Business Media), January 6, 2003, www.nopworld.com.

74. S. L. M. So, "A Comparative Content Analysis of Women's Magazine Advertisements from Hong Kong and Australia on Advertising Expressions," *Journal of Current Issues and Research in Advertising,* Spring 2004, pp. 47–58; and Khairullah and Khairullah, "Dominant Cultural Values."

75. K. Chen and L. Chang, "China Takes Aim at Racy, Violent TV Shows," *The Wall Street Journal,* May 24, 2004, p. B1.

76. Khairullah and Khairullah, "Dominant Cultural Values," p. 64.

77. "G, What Unusual Undie Ads," *Advertising Age,* October 23, 2000, p. 28.

78. K. B. Doran, "Symbolic Consumption in China," *Advances in Consumer Research,* vol. 24, ed. M. Bruck and D. J. MacInnis (Provo, UT: Association for Consumer Research, 1997), pp. 128–31.

79. C. Webster and R. C. Beatty, "Nationality, Materialism, and Possession Importance," *Advances in Consumer Research,* vol. 24, ed. Bruck and MacInnis, pp. 204–10.

80. P. Paul, "Global Generation Gap," *American Demographics,* March 2002, pp. 18–19.

81. "Work Hard? Play Hard? It's Not the Countries You Might Think," *NOP World* (New York: United Business Media), November 8, 2004, www.nopworld.com.

82. G. Hofstede et al., "What Goals Do Business Leaders Pursue?" *Journal of International Business Studies* 33, no. 4 (2002), pp. 785–803.

83. de Mooij and Hofstede, "Convergence and Divergence in Consumer Behavior."

84. See S. S. Al-Makaty, "Attitudes toward Advertising in Islam," *Journal of Advertising Research,* May–June 1996, pp. 16–25; and "Saudis and Americans."

85. See L. C. Huff and D. L. Alden, "An Investigation of Consumer Response to Sales Promotions in Developing Markets," *Journal of Advertising Research,* May–June 1998, pp. 47–56.

86. "Dogpile," *Kwintessential,* www.kwintessential.co.uk/translation/articles/cross-cultural-issues.htm, accessed March 20, 2005.

87. See S. Zhang and B. H. Schmitt, "Creating Local Brands in Multilingual International Markets," *Journal of Marketing Research,* August 2001, pp. 313–25.

88. D. L. Vence, "Proper Message, Design in Global Markets Require Tests," *Marketing News,* September 1, 2006, pp. 18, 24.

89. See M. F. Toncar, "The Use of Humor in Television Advertising," *International Journal of Advertising* 20 (2001), pp. 521–39.

90. See N. Spears, X. Lin, and J. C. Mowen, "Time Orientation in the United States, China, and Mexico," *Journal of International Consumer Marketing* 1 (2001), pp. 57–75.

91. L. A. Manrai and A. K. Manrai, "Effect of Cultural-Context, Gender, and Acculturation on Perceptions of Work versus Social/Leisure Time Usage," *Journal of Business Research,* February 1995, pp. 115–28; and J. D. Lindquist and C. F. Kaufman-Scarborough, "Polychronic Tendency Analysis," *Journal of Consumer Marketing* 21, no. 5 (2004), pp. 332–42.

92. Manrai and Manrai, "Effect of Cultural-Context, Gender, and Acculturation on Perceptions of Work versus Social/Leisure Time Usage." See also M. Lee and F. M. Ulgado, "Consumer Evaluations of Fast-Food Services," *Journal of Services Marketing* 1 (1997), pp. 39–52; and G. H. Brodowsky and B. B. Anderson, "A Cross-Cultural Study of Consumer Attitudes toward Time," *Journal of Global Marketing* 3 (2000), pp. 93–109.

93. de Mooij, *Global Marketing and Advertising.*

94. Ibid., p. 71.

95. See M. Chapman and A. Jamal, "Acculturation," *Advances in Consumer Research,* vol. 24, ed. Bruck and MacInnis, pp. 138–44.

96. From White, *A Short Course in International Marketing Blunders,* p. 39.

97. R. Bjerke and R. Polegato, "How Well Do Advertising Images of Health and Beauty Travel across Cultures?" *Psychology & Marketing,* October 2006, pp. 865–84.

98. See also de Mooij, *Global Marketing and Advertising;* and T. J. Madden, K. Hewett, and M. S. Roth, "Managing Images in Different Cultures," *Journal of International Marketing* 8, no. 4 (2000), pp. 90–107.

99. P. A. Herbig and H. E. Kramer, "Do's and Don'ts of Cross-Cultural Negotiations," *Industrial Marketing Management* 4 (1992), p. 293; see also P. Fan and Z. Zigang, "Cross-Cultural Challenges When Doing Business in China," *Singapore Management Review* 26, no. 1 (2004), pp. 81–90.

100. M. Ewing, A. Caruana, and H. Wong, "Some Consequences of *Guanxi,*" *Journal of International Consumer Marketing* 4 (2000), p. 77. See also F. Balfour, "You Say *Guanxi,* I Say Schmoozing," *BusinessWeek,* November 19, 2007, pp. 84–85.

101. Fan and Zigang, "Cross-Cultural Challenges When Doing Business in China," p. 85; and N. J. White and J. Lee, "Dispute Resolution in the Korean and U.S. Markets," *Mid-American Journal of Business* 19, no. 2 (2004), pp. 23–30.

102. G. Brewer, "An American in Shanghai," *Sales and Marketing Management,* November 1997, p. 42.

103. See H. McDonald, P. Darbyshire, and C. Jevons, "Shop Often, Buy Little," *Journal of Global Marketing* 4 (2000), pp. 53–72; and A. G. Abdul-Muhmin, "The Effect of Perceived Seller Reservation Prices on Buyers' Bargaining Behavior in a Flexible-Price Market," *Journal of International Consumer Marketing* 3 (2001), pp. 29–45.

104. C. Miller, "Not Quite Global," *Marketing News,* July 3, 1995, p. 9.

105. S. Y. Park, "A Comparison of Korean and American Gift-Giving Behaviors," *Psychology & Marketing,* September 1998, pp. 577–93.

106. A. Joy, "Gift Giving in Hong Kong and the Continuum of Social Ties," *Journal of Consumer Research,* September 2001, pp. 239–54. See also J. Wang, F. Piron, and M. V. Xuan, "Faring One Thousand Miles to Give Goose Feathers," *Advances in Consumer Research,* vol. 28, ed. M. C. Gilly and J. Meyers-Levy (Provo, UT: Association for Consumer Research, 2001), pp. 58–63.

107. M. K. Hui and K. Au, "Justice Perceptions of Complaint Handling," *Journal of Business Research* 52 (2001), pp. 161–73; and C. A. Voss et al., "A Tale of Two Countries' Conservatism, Service Quality, and Feedback on Customer Satisfaction," *Journal of Service Research,* February 2004, pp. 212–30.

108. M. Fong, "Chinese Charm School," *The Wall Street Journal,* January 13, 2004, pp. B1, B6.

109. B. D. Keillor, M. D'Amico, and V. Horton, "Global Consumer Tendencies," *Psychology & Marketing,* January 2000, pp. 1–19; and F. Ter Hofstede, M. Wedel, and J. E. M. Steenkamp, "Identifying Spacial Segments in International Markets," *Marketing Science,* Spring 2002, pp. 160–77.

110. C. Edy, "The Olympics of Marketing," *American Demographics,* June 1999, pp. 47–48.

111. "Little Emperors," p. 143.

112. S. Hamm, "Children of the Web," *BusinessWeek,* July 2, 2007, pp. 50–58.

113. "Global Youth Panel," *NGT,* www.nextgreatthing.com, accessed May 5, 2008.

114. N. Madden, "Levi's Enjoys 'Rebirth' on the Web in Asia," *Advertising Age,* April 19, 2004, p. N-10.

115. C. Walker, "Six Seismic Shifts in Global Teen Culture," *Chief Marketer,* www.chiefmarketer.com, accessed May 5, 2008.

116. L. Bertagnoli, "Continental Spendthrifts," *Marketing News,* October 22, 2001, p. 15.

117. N. Madden, "Coke Targets Second Cities," *Advertising Age,* August 16, 2004, p. 22.

118. S. Elder, "The Reel World," *National Geographic,* March 2005.

119. Examples and excerpt from C. Prystay, "It Is a Walk of Fame for Bollywood," *The Wall Street Journal Online,* December 24, 2004, www.wsj.com.

120. "Bollywood Told to Stub It Out," *BBC News,* February 18, 2003, http://news.bbc.co.uk, accessed March 21, 2005.

121. See, e.g., L. Tong, "Consumerism Sweeps the Mainland," *Marketing Management,* Winter 1998, pp. 32–35; and J. Slater, "In India, a Market Unleashed," *The Wall Street Journal,* March 12, 2004, p. A13.

122. "Picturing a World of Want," *Newsweek*, May 5, 2008, p. 7.

123. J. L. Lee, "China Senses Need for Cleaner Fuel," *The Wall Street Journal,* December 11, 2003, p. A16.

124. *The World Factbook* (Washington, DC: Central Intelligence Agency, 2008).

125. *2005 International Comparison Program,* International Bank for Reconstruction and Development/The World Bank, 2008, www.worldbank.org/data/quickreferences (per capita income in U.S. dollars; per capita PPP in international dollars).

126. *Statistical Abstract of the United States,* 2006, www.census.gov; *2000 Philippine Statistical Yearbook* (Makati City: National Statistical Information Center, 2000), p. 1.18; *Statistics Canada,* 2004, www.statcan.ca; *Japan Statistical Yearbook,* 2003, www.stat.go.jp.

127. H. Fattah, "The Middle East Baby Boom," *American Demographics,* September 2002, pp. 55–60.

128. See, e.g., de Mooij and Hofstede, "Convergence and Divergence in Consumer Behavior"; and A. Kanso and R. A. Nelson, "Advertising Localization Overshadows Standardization," *Journal of Advertising Research,* January–February 2002, pp. 79–89.

129. "When in Rome . . . ," *Businessline,* April 15, 2004, p. 1.

130. "Local Pride," *American Demographics,* September 2003, p. 16.

131. C. Rubel, "Survey," *Marketing News,* July 15, 1996, p. 5; and D. Barros, "Create Unique Strategy for Each Brazilian Culture," *Marketing News,* September 1, 2004, pp. 17–18.

132. G. Cui, "Segmenting China's Consumer Market," *Journal of International Consumer Marketing* 1 (1999), pp. 55–76; and T. Sun and G. Wu, "Consumption Patterns of Chinese Urban and Rural Consumers," *Journal of Consumer Marketing* 21, no. 4 (2004), pp. 245–53.

133. P. L. Andruss, "Slow Boat to China," *Marketing News,* September 10, 2001, p. 11.

134. N. Madden and J. Neff, "P&G Adapts Attitude toward Local Markets," *Advertising Age,* February 23, 2004, p. 28.

135. Examples come from Chen and Chang, "China Takes Aim at Racy, Violent TV Shows"; G. A. Fowler, "China Cracks Down on Commercials," *The Wall Street Journal,* February 19, 2004, p. B7; "Molson Airs Ad under New Rules," *Advertising Age,* February 23, 2004, p. 12; "China Bans Opening New Internet Cafes," *CNN.com,* March 2006, www.cnn.com; E. Hall, "Product Placement Faces Wary Welcome in Britain," *Advertising Age,* January 8, 2007, p. 27; and E. Hall, "In Europe, the Clash Over Junk-Food Ads Heats Up," *Advertising Age,* March 5, 2007, p. 32.

136. R. Gardyn, "Full Speed Ahead," *American Demographics,* October 2001, p. 12.

137. P. D. Lynch, R. J. Kent, and S. S. Srinivasan, "The Global Internet Shopper," *Journal of Advertising Research,* May–June 2001, pp. 15–23.

# The Changing American Society: Values

Gender roles and perceptions continue to evolve in the United States. At home, at work, and at play, women continue to redefine and reinvent themselves and their roles. This is the case at every level in the world of sports. Following are some examples in professional sports:[1]

- *Women's Motocross Association (WMA).* WMA was formed in 2004, and it owns and operates the women's professional motocross series. WMA continues the tradition of the Women's Motocross League (WML), a nonprofit that operated from the mid-1980s through 2004. Prior to the formation of the WML and WMA, few women raced professionally. Today, the WMA boasts over 40 pro riders and increased national media coverage. The WMA works to increase interest and participation in the sport through professional and amateur venues. In addition, the WMA has attracted major sponsors such as Kawasaki (bikes), thor (apparel), and The Original Pink Box (toolboxes). And ESPN recently added women's motocross to the X Games!

- *NASCAR.* NASCAR has long been dominated by men. Although there are still no women drivers in the premier NASCAR venue, the Nextel Cup Series, NASCAR is working to change this. In part this effort is being made because women are such a huge part of the fan base—at 40 percent. In addition, according to Fox Sports Network, NASCAR is the second most-watched sport on TV by women. And research shows that both men and women would like to see more women drivers. As a consequence, NASCAR has a program to develop women drivers. Several women are working their way up the NASCAR ladder, including Erin Crocker and Kelly Sutton, who currently drive in the NASCAR Craftsman Truck Series. Outside NASCAR, great strides are being made as well, with Danica Patrick leading the way for women in the Indy Racing League.

- *Women's National Basketball Association (WNBA).* The WNBA began in 1996 and represents a major force in professional sports. Its popularity can be seen in a number of ways, including its double-digit growth in TV viewer numbers on ESPN2. It is now the longest-running U.S. women's pro sports team league. The WNBA audience attests to its broad-based appeal, with 70 percent of stadium attendance and 50 percent of the TV audience being male. As a consequence of this broad appeal, major endorsement contracts flow to WNBA stars such as Sue Bird of the Seattle Storm, who has contracts with Nike, American Express, and Minute Maid.

Women are also active in amateur sports. Almost two-thirds engage in some general fitness activity, compared with only a third of males. Almost a third participate in a sport of some type. Half of women surveyed watch sports on television weekly, compared with 75 percent of males.[2] Moreover, women make up a large portion of the fan base of many "men's" sports, including baseball (47 percent), football (43 percent), hockey (41 percent), and NASCAR (40 percent).[3]

Spending on women's sports sponsorship exceeds $1 billion annually and is growing as more marketers attempt to capitalize on the increased popularity of women's sports.[4]

---

In Chapter 2, we discussed how variations in values influence consumption patterns *across* cultures. In this chapter, we will describe how changes in values over time influence consumption patterns *within* cultures, specifically the U.S. culture. The changing role of women in American society reflects changes in the "masculine/feminine" value described in Chapter 2. Obviously, cultural values are not constant. Rather, they evolve over time. In the first section of this chapter, we will examine the evolution of American values in general. Next, we examine four marketing trends that have evolved in response to changing values: green marketing, cause-related marketing, marketing to gay consumers, and gender-based marketing.

## CHANGES IN AMERICAN CULTURAL VALUES

Observable shifts in behavior, including consumption behavior, often reflect underlying shifts in **cultural values,** *widely held beliefs that affirm what is desirable.* Therefore, it is necessary to understand the underlying *value shifts* in order to understand current and future consumer behavior.[5] Thus, a shift away from a masculine-dominated to a more nearly balanced masculine/feminine value has produced a wide array of changes in the consumption behaviors of both men and women. Consumer Insight 3–1 describes an evolving trend in the United States: organic food consumption. Knowing which cultural values underlie it and how they are evolving enhances understanding of such a trend and its likely future course.

Although we discuss American values as though every American has the same values, in fact there is substantial variance in values across individuals and groups. In addition, changes in values tend to occur slowly and unevenly across individuals and groups. While traumatic events such as the September 11, 2001, attacks on the World Trade Center and the Pentagon, and the resultant military actions, can produce value shifts, a slow evolution is more common. Caution should be used in assuming that short-term behavioral or attitudinal changes in response to such events represent long-lasting value shifts.

Organic food is moving beyond the fringe and toward the mainstream of American eating.[6] The USDA developed and implemented nationwide standards in 2002 for the use of the term *organic* on food labels. Foods labeled "organic" must conform to specific guidelines, such as no use of pesticides, herbicides, and antibiotics. Food brands that meet USDA standards are certified, which enhances consumer trust. Certification and the resulting increase in consumer confidence have helped fuel double-digit growth in the category. Packaged Facts estimates that organic sales are now $26.3 million and expected to grow to $33 million by 2010. The mainstream nature of organic can be seen in several ways. First, roughly two-thirds of Americans have tried organic foods, with over half having purchased organic in the past year. Second, regular supermarkets account for the largest sales of organics, making organics very accessible. National food chains such as Whole Foods and Trader Joe's are another major outlet providing ease of access.

A number of underlying values and concerns account for the increased popularity of organic food. These include values relating to health, safety, family, and the environment. A Hartman Group study puts the top four motivators for organic purchases as health, taste, food safety, and the environment. A Whole Foods study indicates that 54 percent of Americans believe that organic is better for their heath and 58 percent believe that organic is better for the environment. The health and environment factors sometimes go hand in hand. Food grown without the use of chemicals keeps chemicals out of our bodies both directly (we don't consume them in our food) and indirectly (they don't end up in our drinking water through runoff).

Organic consumers tend to be younger and better educated, and organic purchases help create a lifestyle that is seen as healthy, family-friendly, and environmentally sound. The biggest barrier is price. However, as organic becomes more mainstream and continues to grow, companies like Wal-Mart are putting their muscle behind this trend, which will likely lead to lower prices. With lower price and greater access, it is likely that organic food purchases will increase. Certainly, the potential is there, since nearly two-thirds of U.S. consumers are still not regular purchasers of organic foods.

Not surprisingly, marketers are taking notice. Some recent examples of companies offering organic versions of their products include Bigelow (green tea), Del Monte (canned tomatoes), and Prego (pasta sauce). While many companies are just testing the waters with a few products, SUPERVALU (a leading grocery retailer) has launched its own organic store brand nationally. Its Wild Harvest brand is one of the first organic store brands to go national with a large selection, which will eventually include some 250 food items from eggs to cereals to snacks. According to a SUPERVALU executive:

> Significant research and consumer insights went into the development of the brand, which has enabled us to create a highly desirable offering that speaks directly to consumers' desire for fresh, wholesome and affordable foods that help them live a healthier lifestyle.

Lower prices, greater access, and consumers' continued concerns over food safety, family health, and the environment should help ensure that other companies follow SUPERVALU's lead in offering a broad array of products at a nationally branded level.

### Critical Thinking Questions

1. To what extent are organic food purchases influenced by values?
2. What factors do you think are contributing to the growth in the organic market?
3. How might marketers address U.S. consumers who are not regular organic purchasers?

**FIGURE 3–1**        **Traditional, Current, and Emerging American Values**

| | **Self-Oriented** | |
|---|---|---|
| Active | ECT* | Passive |
| Material | T      C      E | Nonmaterial |
| Hard work | T      C      E | Leisure |
| Postponed gratification | T                          EC | Immediate gratification |
| Sensual gratification | C      E              T | Abstinence |
| Religious | T              EC | Secular |

| | **Environment-Oriented** | |
|---|---|---|
| Maximum cleanliness | TC      E | Minimum cleanliness |
| Performance | T      E      C | Status |
| Tradition | EC      T | Change |
| Risk taking | T      E      C | Security |
| Problem solving | T      CE | Fatalistic |
| Admire nature | E      C              T | Overcome nature |

| | **Other-Oriented** | |
|---|---|---|
| Individual | T      CE | Collective |
| Limited family | TEC | Extended family |
| Diversity | EC              T | Uniformity |
| Competition | T      C      E | Cooperation |
| Youth | T      C      E | Age |
| Masculine | T      C      E | Feminine |

*T = Traditional, E = Emerging, and C = Current.

Figure 3–1 presents our estimate of how American values are changing. These are the same values used to describe different cultures in Chapter 2 (see page 45 for definitions). It must be emphasized that Figure 3–1 is based on the authors' *subjective* interpretation of the American society. You should feel free, indeed compelled, to challenge these judgments.

## Self-Oriented Values

Traditionally, Americans have been active, materialistic, hardworking, religious people inclined toward abstinence and postponed gratification. Beginning after the end of World War II and accelerating rapidly during the 1970s and early 1980s, Americans placed increased emphasis on leisure, immediate gratification, and sensual gratification. An examination of American advertising, product features, and personal debt levels indicates that these changes have significantly affected consumer behaviors and marketing practice. It appears that several of these trends have reversed direction and are moving back toward their traditional positions, however.

**Religious/Secular**    America is basically a secular society. A religious group does not control the educational system, government, or political process, and most people's daily behaviors are not guided by strict religious guidelines. Nonetheless, roughly 83 percent of American adults claim a religious affiliation,[7] 36 percent claim to attend a religious service at least once a month,[8] and more than 50 percent state that religion is very important in their lives.

While Americans often profess to be more religious than their behaviors would suggest, religious-based beliefs do influence decisions.[9] Many Americans for whom religion is especially important are conservative in their beliefs. They are quite active politically and as consumers. Their political activism involves attempts to regulate various marketing activities, including products (particularly "sin" products such as liquor, gambling, and pornography) and advertising. Their consumption patterns include both positive consumption (purchasing religious objects and books) and negative consumption (avoiding or boycotting products and companies). And when it comes to key policy issues such as abortion, gay rights, the death penalty, and welfare, devoutly religious consumers are becoming less tolerant of compromise by elected officials.[10]

Although conservative religious groups generate substantial publicity and have considerable political power, the culture remains relatively secular. Indeed, one expert estimates the devoutly religious at only 25 percent of the U.S. population, with the remainder made up of those mildly interested in religion (50 percent), and the secular (25 percent).[11] Increasing secularism is cited as one reason for the increase in interfaith marriages.[12] We treat religion and its impact on our society in considerable depth in Chapter 5 when we discuss subcultures.

**Sensual Gratification/Abstinence**   Closely tied to America's traditional religious orientation was a belief in the virtue of abstinence. As American society became more secular, sensual gratification became more acceptable. By the 1960s, sensual gratification was an important objective for many consumers. Now, sensual gratification is somewhat less acceptable than in the recent past. While it is still perfectly acceptable to consume products for the sensual pleasures they provide, the range of products and occasions for which this is acceptable has narrowed. In the advertising and fashion industries, there are signs that blatant appeals to sexuality *may* be losing their luster. According to one New York advertising executive:

> Everyone's gotten a little tired of in-your-face sexuality. Now there is an appreciation of things that are more prim and proper, with just a hint of depths lurking underneath.[13]

Although sensual and suggestive advertising is often used in an effective manner, some ads can go too far. For example, *Monday Night Football* and *Desperate Housewives* teamed up to do a joint promotion during prime time in which a scantily clad Nicollete Sheridan tries to seduce Terrell Owens, then with the Philadelphia Eagles. There was considerable backlash from the viewing public, who felt the ad was too racy for family viewing. In response to growing concerns over sex and violence on TV, the FCC has begun stepping up its efforts to curb indecency.[14]

In the food industry, tension between gratification and abstinence can be seen in consumers' seemingly contradictory behaviors toward food and diet. Even in the face of ongoing diet concerns and popular dietary programs, consumption of desserts and snacks remains strong. A recent study shows that roughly 90 percent of Americans eat dessert at least once a week, with the average being three times a week.[15] And while the overall cookie category has taken recent hits, sales of premium cookies such as Pepperidge Farm's Distinctive Cookies have gone up. According to one executive, their premium cookies offer a "small indulgence anytime, anywhere."[16]

Illustration 3–1 shows an ad that appeals to sensual gratification.

**Postponed/Immediate Gratification**   In line with the value they generally place on sensual gratification, Americans seem unwilling to delay pleasures, even in the face of discomfort over spending levels and debt. Although concern about personal debt is high[17]

and more consumers are shopping for value and waiting for sales, personal debt, personal
bankruptcies, and credit sales (often at very high rates) continue to climb. This trend is
particularly prominent in the younger generations, as evidenced by this quote by a 36-year-
old professional:

> Like many young professionals . . . I embraced the lessons of my seniors about hard work. Yet
> my generation racks up debt the way our grandparents used to squirrel away pennies. A [recent]
> study . . . finds that people ages 18 to 40 are most likely to say they're spending beyond their
> comfort range.[18]

**Hard Work/Leisure**   Americans continue their strong tradition of hard work, leading much of the industrialized world in hours worked. Average weekly hours worked is
around 39, with 28 percent of workers clocking more than 40 hours per week. The percentage of married women who work outside the home for wages has increased almost
50 percent since 1970, from 41 to 60 percent of all married women.[19] Americans work
long hours for many reasons. One is clearly their material orientation. Americans work to
have such things as a large home, two cars, and a nice vacation. Others work long hours
because they lack the skills or job opportunities to provide even a moderate lifestyle without doing so. However, Americans also work long and hard because work is meaningful
and valuable to them, in part because of the self-esteem and respect they gain from the
work they do.

Partly in response to the increase in work hours, the value placed on work relative
to leisure has dropped over the past two decades. For example, one study found that 81
percent of employed consumers felt the need to simplify their lives and create more time
for home and family.[20] This opens up opportunities for marketers who can deliver convenience. Still, we can't seem to get away from work. Forty-three percent of people in a

recent survey check in with the office while on vacation![21] Thus, we have a situation in which hard work and leisure are both valued (often by the same people) and commingled in people's lives.

**Material/Nonmaterial**    Americans have maintained a strong material orientation. An outcome of America's focus on materialism is a consumption-driven society. As we have seen, Americans are working longer hours, in part, to afford material possessions. That is, Americans are trading time and energy for things and services such as cars and travel. One factor found to influence materialism is television. As one group of researchers note:

> Television is a powerful medium . . . consumers often use information from television to construct perceptions of social reality including the prevalence of affluence. Heavier viewers tend to believe luxury products and services to be more commonplace than they actually are.[22]

There is, however, some evidence that materialism in the United States is moderating at least among some consumers. Role overload, burnout, and emotional exhaustion are causing some to rethink their priorities and consciously simplify their lives. Consider the following comment:

> I had all the stuff that was supposed to make me successful—my car and my clothes, the house in the right neighborhood and belonging to the right health club. All the external framework was excellent and inside I kind of had this pit eating away at me.[23]

Consumers' efforts to reduce their reliance on consumption and material possessions have been termed **voluntary simplicity.** Voluntary simplicity can span a continuum from minor life adjustments and reduced spending to drastic lifestyle adjustments, including downsized jobs, incomes, houses, and spending. A major influence in the decision to simplify appears to be reduced stress and increased life satisfaction, although other motivations, including environmentalism, can be involved. While the voluntary simplicity movement appears to represent a relatively small proportion of the U.S. population, its growth certainly holds economic and marketing consequences, including the market for secondhand products and green products.[24]

**Active/Passive**    Americans continue to value an active approach to life. Although less than half of all American adults exercise regularly, most Americans take an active approach to both leisure and problem solving activities. Television viewing as a primary form of entertainment has dropped sharply from its peak in the mid-1980s (young men [18 to 24 years of age] seem to be moving away from TV faster than any other group).[25] Alternative activities, including surfing the net, sports, cooking, and gardening are popular. And the amount of time children spend in scheduled activities continues to increase.[26] The following quote illustrates that Americans differ on this value, but most would agree more with the second speaker than the first.

> My idea of a vacation is a nice oceanfront resort, a beach chair, and a piña colada.
>
> Mine too. For a day or two. Then I'd go bug spit. I'd feel like I was in prison. I'd *do* something.[27]

Illustration 3–2 describes a resort designed for active leisure.

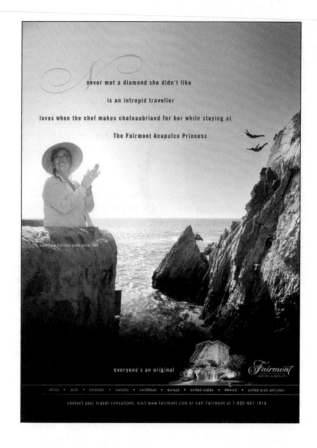

## Environment-Oriented Values

Environment-oriented values prescribe a society's relationship with its economic, technical, and physical environments. Americans have traditionally admired cleanliness, change, performance, risk taking, problem solving, and the conquest of nature. While this cluster of values remains basically intact, there are some significant shifts occurring.

**Cleanliness**   Americans have long valued cleanliness. This strong focus seems to be declining somewhat, particularly in terms of our homes. Likely due to increased time demands caused by work, messier homes are more acceptable.[28] However, such shifts don't appear to suggest major changes. The popularity of TV shows like *Mission: Organization* on HGTV suggest that while Americans may accept messier homes, they are not happy about them. This obviously presents marketing opportunities.[29] For example, the recent development of robotic vacuum cleaners such as Sharper Image's Roomba taps the desire for cleanliness while offering much needed convenience and time savings.

Personal hygiene, another aspect of cleanliness, remains very important to most Americans. A recent study shows that antibacterial hand sanitizers such as Purell are a new addition to the arsenal of products carried around by mothers.[30] Illustration 3–3 demonstrates the emphasis Americans place on cleanliness.

**Tradition/Change**   Americans have always been very receptive to change. *New* has traditionally been taken to mean *improved*. While still very appreciative of change, Americans are now less receptive to change for its own sake. New-product recalls, the expense and the failure of various government programs, and the energy required to keep pace with rapid

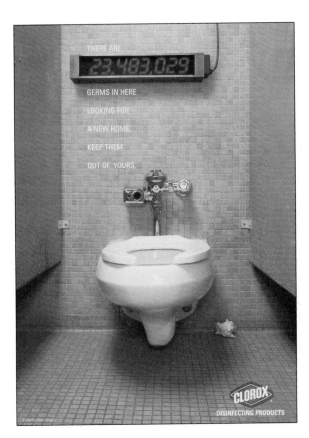

Americans continue to place a high value on cleanliness, as this ad demonstrates.

technological changes are some of the reasons for this shift. Another reason is the aging of the American population. As we will see in the next chapter, the average age of the population is increasing, and people generally become somewhat less accepting of change as they age. Still, much of America continues to embrace change, as evidenced by a growing segment of workers that one expert calls the *creative class*. The creative class includes those who work in such professions as architecture, science, engineering, and health care, and business who generate new ideas and technologies for a living or engage in complex problem solving. This group now constitutes about 33 percent of the workforce, compared with just 10 percent in 1900.[31]

**Risk Taking/Security**   Americans' risk-taking orientation seems to have changed somewhat over time. There was an increased emphasis on security during the period from 1930 through the mid-1980s. This attitude was a response to the tremendous upheavals and uncertainties caused by the Depression, World War II, and the cold war. However, risk taking remains highly valued and is gaining appreciation as Americans look to entrepreneurs for economic growth and to smaller firms and self-employment to obtain desired lifestyles. Increasing interest and investment in space tourism, culminating most recently in Virgin Galactic's SpaceShipTwo, is just one more example of America's spirit of change, innovation, and risk taking.

**Problem Solving/Fatalistic**   Americans take great pride in being problem solvers, and as we saw earlier, as a percentage of the workforce, problem solvers and creative types are on the increase. By and large, Americans believe that virtually anything can be fixed given sufficient time and effort. For example, over two-thirds of Americans believe that they can continue to grow the economy *and* improve environmental quality.[32] Marketers introduce thousands of new products each year with the theme that they will solve a problem better than existing products will. We will examine the results of this value later in this chapter in the sections on green marketing and cause marketing.

**Admire/Overcome Nature**    Traditionally, nature was viewed as an obstacle. Americans attempted to bend nature to fit their desires without realizing the negative consequences this could have for both nature and humanity. However, this attitude has shifted dramatically over the past 30 years.

Experts have been concerned that environmentalism is dead. Some cite the fact that the percentage of Americans who call themselves environmentalists dropped from 73 to 47 percent between 1990 and 2000. Part of the decline may be real. Part of the decline may simply be in how people define environmentalism. For example, a recent Gallop Poll shows that 80 percent of Americans are active or sympathetic to environmentalism (21 percent "active"; 49 percent "sympathetic" but not active). This puts active participation up by 5 percentage points since 2000. Other indications that concern for the environment among Americans remains strong and may be on the rise:

- Eighty-three percent report changing their lifestyle to protect the environment.
- Recycling (89 percent), energy reduction (85 percent), and environmentally friendly purchases (70 percent) remain strong.
- Environmental political activism (e.g., voting, contributing money) has increased since 2000.
- Roughly 70 percent are worried about global warming.[33]

One firm classifies consumers into the following segments in terms of their environmental activism:[34]

- *True Naturals* (11 percent): Express deeply felt environmental concerns and tailor their actions and purchases to these beliefs.
- *New Green Mainstream* (17 percent): Concerned about the environment but alter their actions and purchases only when it is convenient.
- *Affluent Healers* (11 percent): Most concerned about environmental issues that relate to their personal health; are less inclined to consider the environment when shopping.
- *Young Recyclers* (14 percent): Most concerned about environmental issues that relate to solid waste; are less inclined to consider the environment when shopping.
- *Overwhelmed* (22 percent): Feel too caught up in life's demands to worry about the environment; are unlikely to favor a product for environmental reasons.
- *Unconcerned* (25 percent): Do not pay attention to environmental issues, or do not feel that the environment is seriously threatened.

Firms that convince environmentally concerned consumers that their products are environmentally sound can reap huge rewards. Such an approach has been termed **enviropreneurial marketing.** Enviropreneurial marketing is *environmentally friendly marketing practices, strategies, and tactics initiated by a firm to achieve a competitive differentiation.* Research shows that such a marketing approach leads to increased new-product success and increased market share.[35]

We describe the marketing response to this value in the section of this chapter on green marketing.

**Performance/Status**    Americans are shifting back to a focus on performance rather than status. Although consumers are still willing to purchase "status" brands, these brands must provide style and functionality in addition to the prestige of the name. This has led to substantial increases in sales at stores that combine price, service, and quality, such as Wal-Mart and Target stores, and for quality retailer private-label brands such as those offered by Albertson's and Wal-Mart. In contrast, outlets with inappropriate cost structures or images, such as The Gap, Kmart, and Montgomery Ward, have struggled or failed.[36]

## Other-Oriented Values

Other-oriented values reflect a society's view of the appropriate relationships between individuals and groups within that society. Historically, American society has been oriented toward individualism, competitiveness, masculinity, youth, limited families, and uniformity. However, several aspects of this orientation are undergoing change.

**Individual/Collective**   A strong emphasis on individualism is one of the defining characteristics of American society. Watch any American hit movie. The leading character will virtually always behave as an individual, often despite pressures to conform to the group. Americans believe in "doing your own thing." Even the "uniforms" that each generation of teenagers invents for itself allow ample room for individual expression. This value affects incentive systems for salespeople, advertising themes, product design, and customer complaining behavior.[37] For example, consumers higher in individualism are more likely to complain, switch, or engage in negative word of mouth when faced with poor service performance.[38] Individualism is also evident in the customization craze for cars, trucks, and motorcycles, currently a market worth over $2 billion a year. Discovery Channel and CMT have tapped into this trend with shows such as *Orange County Chopper* and *Trick My Truck*, which attract the highly elusive younger male audience.[39]

**Diversity/Uniformity**   While American culture has always valued individualism, it has also valued a degree of uniformity, particularly with respect to groups. America was founded in part by people seeking religious freedom or fleeing from various forms of persecution. The Constitution and many laws seek to protect diverse religions, political beliefs, and so forth. Nonetheless, Americans historically insisted that immigrants quickly adopt the language, dress, values, and many other aspects of the majority. Those who did not were often subject to various forms of discrimination. This was particularly true for racial and some religious minorities.

Since World War II, Americans have increasingly valued diversity. Consider the following:[40]

> Hallmark markets a collection of greeting cards called "Common Threads," whose messages reflect a variety of world cultures, emphasizing global community and diverse cultural expression.

Researchers speculate that the market for products such as "Common Threads" is *"cultural creatives,"* the "26% of adult Americans who are concerned with self-actualization, spirituality, and self-expression and who like things that are foreign and exotic." Cultural creatives, regardless of ethnicity, are more likely to cross traditional ethnic boundaries in seeking out products.

Although far from being free of racial, religious, ethnic, or class prejudice, American culture is evolving toward valuing diversity more than uniformity. A recent study finds that 56 percent of Americans feel that over the past year they have become more likely to respect cultures with different values.[41] Illustration 3–4 reflects the positive view of diversity held by most Americans. We examine one aspect of America's

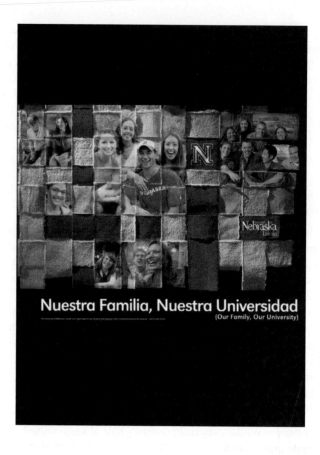

**Nuestra Familia, Nuestra Universidad**
(Our Family, Our University)

increasing acceptance of diversity–marketing to gay and lesbian consumers—later in this chapter.

**Limited/Extended Family**    America was settled by immigrants, people who left their extended families behind. As the nation grew, the western movement produced a similar phenomenon. Even today, frequent geographic moves as well as differential rates of social mobility mean that few children grow up in close interaction with aunts, uncles, cousins, nieces, or nephews.[42] It is also common for children to leave their hometowns and parents once they begin their own careers. The physical separation of traditional family members often reduces the sense of family among those members. This, in turn, reduces the impact that the family has on the individual.

This is not to say that Americans do not love their family members or that how an American is raised does not influence the person for life. Rather, it means that a 35-year-old American is unlikely to have a cousin who would feel obligated to respond positively to a loan request (this is not the case in many other cultures). Likewise, this 35-year-old would be unlikely to have one or more cousins, aunts, or nephews live with him or her for an extended time period. The role of families in the American culture is covered in depth in Chapter 6.

**Youth/Age**    Traditionally, older people were considered wiser than young people and were, therefore, looked to as models and leaders in almost all cultures. This has never been as true in American culture, probably because transforming a wilderness into a new type of producing nation required characteristics such as physical strength, stamina, youthful vigor, and imagination. The value on youth continued as America became an industrial nation. Since World War II, it has increased to such an extent that products such as cars, clothing, cosmetics, and hairstyles seem designed for and sold only to the young. For example, youth appeals in American advertising still appear to outstrip appeals to age and tradition.[43]

But a slow reversal of this value on youth seems to be occurring. Because of their increasing numbers and disposable income, older citizens have developed political and economic clout and are beginning to use it. As one expert says:

> It used to be that 25-year-old women drove the fashion industry; now it's 45-year-old women. Because when you are 45, you already know what you look good in. If a designer says, "Crepe is in," this group may confidently answer that "crepe is crap."[44]

Cosmetics, medicines, and hair care products are being marketed specifically to older consumers, and ads for these products increasingly feature older models, such as Julianne Moore, who are closer in age to the target audience. However, most of these products still have either a direct or indirect appeal of creating a younger appearance.

Age portrayal in advertising is a difficult issue. Since people often feel younger than their actual age, ads using younger models might generate a more positive reaction. In addition, for youth-oriented or conspicuously consumed products, using older models in ads may alienate younger consumers.[45] These two factors help explain the overrepresentation of younger models in ads.[46] There is the worry, however, that at some point older consumers may feel ignored by ads that portray overly young users. Clearly, marketers have a lot to learn in this area.[47]

**Competition/Cooperation**    America has long been a competitive society, and this value remains firmly entrenched. It is reflected in our social, political, and economic systems. We reward particularly successful competitors in business, entertainment, and sports with staggering levels of financial compensation. Although the focus on cooperation and teamwork in schools and businesses has increased, teamwork is generally instituted so that the team or group can outperform some other team or group.

It is no wonder that America was one of the first countries to allow comparative advertising.

**Masculine/Feminine**    American society, like most others, has reflected a masculine orientation for a long time. But as indicated by this chapter's opening vignette, this orientation is changing, as are gender roles. Although American society is becoming less masculine oriented, it still leans clearly in that direction. For example, 37 percent of parents indicate that they would prefer a boy if they could have only one child, compared with 28 percent who would opt for a girl.[48] And textbooks aimed at children still depict physical activity more often for boys (65 percent) than for girls (35 percent).[49] Still, there is a shift taking place in this value. For example, preference for male bosses continues to decline while preference for female bosses continues to increase.[50] The marketing implications resulting from evolving gender roles are discussed later in this chapter.

# MARKETING STRATEGY AND VALUES

We have examined a number of marketing implications of American values and changes in these values. It is critical that all aspects of the firm's marketing mix be consistent with the value system of its target market. We will now examine marketing responses to four evolving American values: green marketing, cause-related marketing, marketing to gay and lesbian consumers, and gender-based marketing.

## Green Marketing

Marketers have responded to Americans' increasing concern for the environment with an approach called **green marketing.**[51] Green marketing generally involves (1) developing products whose production, use, or disposal is less harmful to the environment than the traditional versions of the product; (2) developing products that have a positive impact on the environment; or (3) tying the purchase of a product to an environmental organization or event. For example:[52]

* Levi's recently launched its Levi's Eco line of 100 percent organic cotton jeans.
* Wal-Mart is making a huge "Green" push with many initiatives, including reducing energy waste, opening green supercenters, stocking more organic products, and working with suppliers to get them on board as well. As just one example, it is asking its detergent suppliers to cut the size of their packages (less waste) by concentrating their formulas.
* Office Depot offers Recycled EnviroCopy printer and copier paper, which contains 35 percent postconsumer, recycled fibers, with green-colored packaging and the name "Office Depot Green" to emphasize the environment.

As green claims have increased in number and scope, concern generated over the potential for marketers to mislead consumers. The Federal Trade Commission (FTC) has a set of voluntary guidelines called the "Green Guides," which provide dozens of examples of acceptable and unacceptable practices dealing with advertising and package claims relating to areas such as the environment in general (e.g., Eco-Safe) as well as the use of *biodegradable, recyclable, recycled content,* and *ozone friendly*. These guidelines have been estimated as 95 percent effective (to learn more, visit www.ftc.gov).

Green marketing is complex. Confusing terminology is a contributing factor. For example, *sustainable* products are a hot trend in food marketing. However, inconsistent use of the term makes it hard for consumers to make informed judgments. An emerging consensus is that **sustainability** involves methods that are (*a*) profitable for the farmer, (*b*) environmentally sound, and (*c*) socially responsible. The sustainability movement has become important in industries such as coffee.[53] In addition, environmental concerns are only one factor in consumer decisions.[54] Even among those who are environmentally concerned, factors such as lack of convenience, higher prices, skepticism about green claims, quality concerns, lack of availability, and a sense that individuals can't make a difference can inhibit green behaviors and purchases.[55] Overcoming these obstacles is critical to the success of green marketing. For example, Philips struggled in the compact fluorescent light (CFL) market until it effectively communicated the consumer benefits in terms of a $26 savings in energy costs (which is also environmentally friendly) over the lifetime of the bulb. This aspect was critical given the high price of the bulb. The Environmental Protection Agency's (EPA) Energy Star label also added credibility.[56] As discussed in Consumer Insight 3–2, the automotive industry is working hard to put these lessons to work on hybrid automobiles (also see Illustration 3–5).

## Cause-Related Marketing

The term *cause marketing* is sometimes used interchangeably with *social marketing* to refer to the application of marketing principles and tactics to advance a cause, such as a charity (United Way), an ideology (environmental protection), or an activity (breast cancer

## Hybrid Revolution?

Toyota's Prius was the first model to make a major move in the hybrid market.[57] The Prius still owns over half of the hybrid market, but hybrids still account for only around 2 percent of U.S. car sales. Americans, it seems, want it all. On the one hand, 60 percent favor energy conservation and 62 percent think that the environment should be a legislative priority. On the other hand, 98 percent of automobiles sold in the United States are not hybrids. A number of factors are behind this. First is a historical belief that gas prices will eventually come back down. Second is that simply being hybrid won't equate to greater sales. Consumers demand a return on the typically higher prices they are required to pay for hybrids. Take Honda, which in 2007 discontinued its Accord hybrid. This move doesn't make sense until you realize that the 2007 hybrid got 28 miles per gallon city and 35 miles per gallon highway and cost around $33,000. The gas-only Accord got 26 city and 34 highway miles per gallon with an entry price of $18,500!

Mind-sets are changing slowly, however. The notion that gas prices will go down is starting to be questioned as we understand that increased global demand from developing countries like China is here to stay. That, along with new legislative crackdowns on emissions, and new fuel-efficiency standards, has many auto manufacturers moving fast toward alternatives that include hybrids and electric cars. This is nowhere more true than at GM, which is racing to produce a plug-in hybrid that gets 100 miles per gallon and will cost between $30,000

and $45,000. The car, still in development, is called the Volt, a nod to the fact that it is mostly an electric car with a small gas engine to recharge the battery during trips. This is a huge reversal for GM, which walked away from a $1 billion investment in electric cars back in 2003. And it is still met with resistance by both company insiders and customers. As one customer notes, "I drove the Prius and the Civic, and although they were great on gas mileage, I just couldn't downgrade from a V-6."

Beyond the usual competitors, there is also a contingent of new brands to contend with, including the Obvio! from Brazil, which gets 29 city and 40 highway miles per gallon and is priced at $14,000. Indeed, even established players understand that they need to increase performance and reduce price. A Toyota executive stresses: "My quest is to produce a third-generation Prius quickly and cheaply."

### Critical Thinking Questions

1. Why is there so much demand for conventional SUVs, which are not environmentally friendly, when American values strongly support environmental protection?

2. What lessons does the Philips struggle in the compact fluorescent light (CFL) market referred to in the text provide for automobile manufacturers?

3. How important will continued high gasoline prices be to the growth of the hybrid market?

---

exams). Social marketing differs from traditional marketing in the intangible and abstract nature of the "product" and in the absence of a profit motive. At one extreme, such as a health-related campaign, there are potential direct benefits to the individual. In general, however, the benefits to the individual are indirect (a better society in which to live). Often the benefit is purely or primarily emotional. Individuals are requested to change beliefs or behaviors or provide funds because it is "the right thing to do" and they will "feel good" or "be a better person" because of it.

Examine the two ads in Illustration 3–6. *What are the benefits being promised to those who respond? Why might an individual "buy" one of these "products"?* As noted in Chapter 1, social marketing is marketing done to enhance the welfare of individuals or society

ILLUSTRATION 3–5

Hybrid automobiles
must emphasize
consumer benefits as
well as social benefits
to be successful.

without direct benefit to a firm. In contrast, cause marketing, or **cause-related marketing (CRM),** is *marketing that ties a company and its products to an issue or cause with the goal of improving sales or corporate image while providing benefits to the cause.*[58] Companies associate with causes to create long-term relationships with their customers, building corporate and brand equity that should eventually lead to increased sales. The ad on the left in Illustration 3–6 is an example of social marketing; it promotes a benefit to the world community without advancing the profits or image of a commercial firm. The ad on the right in Illustration 3–6 is an example of cause-related marketing; it attempts to benefit a cause *and* to enhance the image and sales of a commercial firm.

The foundation of CRM is marketing to consumers' values, and it can be very effective. Consumer acceptance of and response to CRM has increased dramatically over the past decade. Consider the following statistics (to learn more, visit the Cause Marketing Forum at www.causemarketingforum.com):

- Eighty percent say that corporate support of a cause increases their trust in the company.
- Seventy-four percent claim that a company's commitment to a social issue is important when deciding which products and services to recommend to other people.
- Eighty-six percent are likely to switch brands based on CRM when price and quality are equal (up from 66 percent in 1993).[59]

Cause-related marketing is often effective because it is consistent with strongly held American values.[60] For example, a common theme in most CRM programs taps

Help give breast cancer the brush off

America's problem-solving orientation by presenting a problem, such as breast cancer, AIDS, or pollution, and an action that individuals can take to help solve the problem. Given consumer receptivity to CRM, it is not surprising that corporate spending on it is on the rise. One area of spending, cause-related sponsorship, has grown from $120 million in 1990 to $1.5 billion in 2008, which represents the third-largest area of corporate sponsorship![61] Consumer skepticism and apathy remain a challenge, however, as illustrated by the following descriptions and quotes of four consumer types based on their responses to CRM:[62]

> *Skeptic* (doubts sincerity or effectiveness of CRM): I think those are fake, most of them. Because what they give is so little it doesn't amount to anything.

> *Balancer* (believes in CRM but generally doesn't act accordingly): I hate to say this, but, as far as grocery stores, I go to the one that is closest to me. It makes me feel better . . . about Food Lion that they were willing to do this (participate in CRM) . . . but, sometimes I don't put out that extra effort, but I guess I really should.

> *Attribution-oriented* (concerned about motives behind CRM): I always approach them with a skeptical eye, but I try and use good judgment and common sense based on who they are, what they're doing and try to see the end result.

> *Socially concerned* (driven by desire to help): I mean, as long as they're doing it, the motives can be questionable as far as I'm concerned. . . . Even if there's questionable motives, it's that much more important to support companies who do those things. Just to reinforce that good behavior.

**ILLUSTRATION 3–6**

The ad on the left promotes a benefit to the world community without advancing the profits or image of a commercial firm. That ad is an example of social marketing. The ad on the right represents cause-related marketing. It not only benefits a cause but also enhances the image and sales of a commercial firm.

An emerging consensus is that a "fit" between the company and the cause can improve results.[63] For example, ConAgra (a food marketing company) launched *Feeding Children Better* to combat child hunger while Crest and the Boys and Girls Club of America partnered to form *Healthy Smiles 2010* to teach kids about oral hygiene. In both cases there is a business–cause fit.[64]

## Marketing to Gay and Lesbian Consumers

As Americans in general are shifting to valuing diversity, they are increasingly embracing ethnic, religious, and racial diversity. Another group gaining increased public acceptance is the gay and lesbian community (we follow business press convention and refer to gay and lesbian consumers as the gay market). Recent data show that 54 percent of Americans feel that homosexuality should be considered an acceptable lifestyle, compared with only 34 percent in 1982.[65] Interestingly, the value that Americans place on individual rights and protection appears to transcend personal opinions about lifestyle. For example, over 70 percent support hate-crime protection laws and same-sex couple rights such as hospital visitation. These numbers are even stronger among younger consumers.[66] The emergence and popularity of TV shows with openly gay or lesbian characters, such as *Will and Grace* and *The L Word*, is additional evidence of increased public acceptance.

Before we begin, it is important to emphasize that gay consumers, like heterosexuals, vary in terms of ethnicity, geographic region, occupation, and age. These and other factors influence their behavior and, in most instances, play a much larger role in their consumption process than does their sexual orientation.

The gay market is substantial in both size and purchase power. The size of the gay market is estimated to be about 7 percent of the adult U.S. population, or 15.3 million people over the age of 18. Purchasing power is estimated at $723 billion and expected to grow to $835 billion by 2011.[67] Not surprisingly, many companies have concluded that the gay market is a highly attractive segment to pursue. Examples include the following:[68]

- Ikea generated considerable public outcry in 1994 for its gay-themed ad. It re-entered the gay market in 2006 with a spot that "shows a black and Asian male couple with their daughter and Golden Retriever and ends with the voiceover: 'Why shouldn't sofas come in flavors, just like families?'" Unlike the reaction in 1994, no public debate was created by this ad.
- American Airlines created a page on its Web site specifically for gay, lesbian, bisexual, and transgender (GLBT) consumers. Wyndham Hotels partnered with the airline by giving a 20 percent discount on all reservations made through the page.
- Wal-Mart has a GLBT employee group called Wal-Mart Pride and supports numerous gay causes.

Any firm that desires to capture the loyalty of the gay community must have internal policies that do not discriminate against gay employees. A recent survey found that 82 percent of gay consumers are more likely to buy from companies they know are gay friendly.[69] The Human Rights Campaign Foundation (www.hrc.org) helps provide such information through its corporate equality index (CEI), which measures how equitably a company treats its GLBT employees, customers, and investors.

**Product Issues**  In many cases the lifestyles of gay consumers do not differ sufficiently from those of other consumers to require product modifications. For example, three of the top four reasons for choosing a hotel were the same for GLBT customers as for heterosexuals. In order of importance, they were convenience, customer service, and recommendations from friends or family.[70] Companies such as IBM, Levi's, Coors, and Procter & Gamble have programs that target the gay market using their standard products. However, product modification opportunities are sometimes possible and beneficial. For example, in the realm of television, content that targets news, concerns, programs, and movies of specific interest to GLBT audiences is increasingly popular. Logo and here! networks have been launched recently in response to this growing demand. In addition, with the increased focus on same-sex marriage, companies such as Pottery Barn and Tiffany's are modifying their bridal registries to be gender neutral, and Web sites such as Gayweddings (www.gayweddings .com) are emerging to serve this market.

Another area in which product modifications are often necessary is financial services. As the director of segment marketing for American Express explains:

> Often, gay couples are very concerned about issues like Social Security benefits and estate planning, since same-sex marriages often are not recognized under the law.[71]

American Express Financial Advisors (now Ameriprise) has a GLBT Web page devoted to this market. In addition, the firm offers a product called Domestic Partner Planning services. An ad for this service stated in part:

> At American Express Financial Advisors we offer Domestic Partner Planning services that can help you address issues like protecting assets from unnecessary taxation and getting around restrictions placed on unmarried couples. We offer you the expertise and insight you need to make smart decisions.

**Communication Issues**   There are a large number of gay-oriented print media in the United States and Canada. Rivendell Marketing Company is a national advertising representative for over 200 such publications with a combined circulation of over 3.5 million. The National Gay Newspaper Guild has 12 publications with a readership of nearly 1 million. There are a number of gay-oriented magazines, with *Out* and *The Advocate* being two of the largest. Given the size and spending power of the gay market, it is not surprising that spending in gay-oriented print media has doubled since 1997 to its current level of over $200 million. Over 175 Fortune 500 companies now advertise in gay media, up from 19 in 1994.[72]

Compared with the general population, gay consumers tend to be more tech savvy, are more likely to be online, are more likely to have broadband access, and spend more hours online. Marketers are taking this into account in developing their Web sites.[73] For example, IBM has a GLBT Business Community page on its Web site, Orbitz has a gay and lesbian page on its travel site, and American Express often features financial issues specific to the gay market in its online advice columns. In addition, numerous gay Web sites have emerged. PlanetOut.com is a highly successful example. With over 3 million active members and over 5 million unique visits each month, the site has amazing access to the gay market and has attracted advertisers such as EarthLink, Visa, MG Rover, Ford, American Express, and ING.[74]

Since most products don't require alteration for the gay market, firms may decide to approach the market by placing one of their standard ads in gay-oriented media. Anheuser-Busch, Miller Brewing, Baileys Original Irish Cream, and American Express are among the firms that first approached this market with standard ads. However, these and other

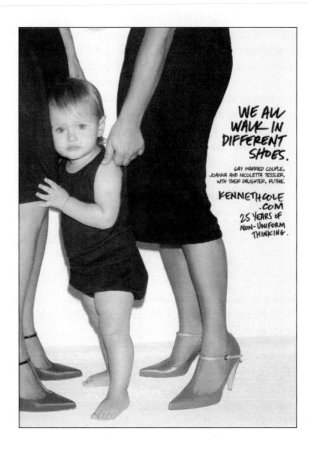

firms are increasingly creating ads specifically for the gay market, with 2004 being the first time a majority of the ads (59 percent) in gay print media were created specifically for gay consumers.[75] The ads may portray a gay couple instead of a heterosexual couple in a standard ad. Or the entire ad may contain a gay theme, as shown in Illustration 3–7.

It has been estimated that roughly half of the gay community rarely or never read gay-oriented publications and spend considerable time using standard media.[76] As one gay man stated, "We are not only reading *Out* and *The Advocate* all the time. If you go into any gay man's apartment you're very likely to see *Vanity Fair* and *People* as well."[77] This is also true online, where 8 of the 10 top Web sites visited by gay consumers are general sites, such as Yahoo!, Google, Amazon, CNN, and eBay, which are not specifically devoted to gay issues.[78]

Using ads with gay themes in standard mass media can generate concerns regarding backlash from the portion of the market that does not accept the gay community, as well as the desire to have ads that directly appeal to the largest number of viewers.[79] A recent study compared mainstream ads (heterosexual couples in the ad) with explicitly gay and lesbian ads (male or female couples) or implicit gay and lesbian ads (ads that had gay symbolic icons, such as the rainbow flag, pink triangle, and freedom rings). The study found that gays and heterosexuals equally liked the mainstream ads. In addition, although heterosexuals disliked explicit gay and lesbian ads, their attitudes were not negatively influenced by the implicit gay and lesbian ads. Finally, both explicit and implicit gay and lesbian ads were liked more than mainstream ads by those who identified themselves as gay or lesbian.[80] For marketers wanting to move into the mainstream market with appeals that are as broad as possible and still target gay consumers, this research suggests that using symbolic gay icons (which the mainstream market tends to be relatively unknowledgeable of) appears to be an effective tactic. This is important since research shows that gay consumers reward companies that advertise in gay media outlets and/or use gay themes in their advertising.

Finally, in addition to advertising in gay media, support of gay community events such as Gay Pride week is another important avenue firms use in approaching this market.

## Gender-Based Marketing

As we saw in the chapter's opening vignette, gender roles in the United States are shifting. It's hard to imagine that just one or two generations ago, the prevailing stereotype of an automobile purchase involved a male making the purchase alone. Today, women influence 80 percent of all vehicles sold, make over half of all new-vehicle purchases (up from 20 percent in 1984), and purchase 40 percent of all SUVs.[81]

Changes in gender roles for women have been dramatic, with increased participation in the workforce, increased wealth and purchase power, and increased participation in active lifestyles, to name just a few. Marketers of products and services ranging from automobiles, to sportswear, to financial services clearly understand the importance of women as a market segment. Consider the following examples:

- Women represent 40 percent of the market for casual lifestyle athletic shoes. Skechers, K-Swiss, and Reebok maintain strong positions in this market by offering products specifically tailored to the needs of active women.[82]
- Merrill Lynch recently launched its Women's Business Development Unit to target wealthy women investors who are entrepreneurs and executives.[83]
- *Good Housekeeping* now offers a "Women's Automobile Satisfaction Award" to brands that score 5 percent or more above the average satisfaction rating among female owners.

The terms *sex* and **gender** are used interchangeably to refer to *whether a person is biologically a male or a female.* **Gender identity** refers to *the traits of femininity* (expressive traits such as tenderness and compassion) *and masculinity* (instrumental traits such as aggressiveness and dominance). These traits represent the ends of a continuum, and individuals have varying levels of each trait, with biological males tending to be toward the masculine end of the continuum and biological females toward the feminine end.[84]

**Gender roles** are *the behaviors considered appropriate for males and females in a given society.* As the previous discussion of automobile purchasing indicates, gender roles in America have undergone massive changes over the past 30 years. The general nature of this shift has been for behaviors previously considered appropriate primarily for men to be acceptable for women too.[85]

Gender roles are ascribed roles. An **ascribed role** is based on *an attribute over which the individual has little or no control.* This can be contrasted with an **achievement role,** which is based on *performance criteria over which the individual has some degree of control.* Individuals can, within limits, select their occupational role (achievement role), but they cannot generally determine their gender (ascribed role).

Researchers find it useful to categorize women into **traditional** or **modern gender orientations** on the basis of their preference for one or the other of two contrasting lifestyles:

- *Traditional.* A marriage in which the husband assumes the responsibility for providing for the family and the wife runs the house and takes care of the children.
- *Modern.* A marriage in which husband and wife share responsibilities. Both work, and they share homemaking and child care responsibilities.

Americans have certainly moved toward a *preference* for a modern lifestyle, from only 35 percent in 1977 to 58 percent in the most recent polls.[86] In addition, only 25 percent agree that women should return to their traditional roles and 87 percent agree that fathers are just as capable as mothers of caring for their children.[87] However, while males and females both express strong preferences for the modern lifestyle as a general concept, most recognize that it comes with a cost, and attitudes and behaviors toward specific aspects of that lifestyle remain very conservative in some cases. For example, almost 70 percent of both women and men believe it would be best if mothers would "stay at home and just take care of the house and children."[88] And 80 percent of mothers with children age 5 or under would prefer to stay home with their children if it were totally up to them.[89]

Disparity still exists between men and women in terms of participation in household duties, although men's participation is on the rise. For example, recent research suggests that married men spend 50 percent more time on housework than they did 25 years ago. However, a recent Gallup Poll shows the following breakout of household chores in terms of who is most likely to do them. The figures for each activity represent the percent response to the question, "Who is most likely to do each of the following in your household?"

| Activity | Husband (%) | Wife (%) |
|---|---|---|
| Keep the car in good condition | 69 | 13 |
| Do yard work | 57 | 12 |
| Handle investments | 35 | 18 |
| Do grocery shopping | 16 | 53 |
| Do laundry | 10 | 68 |
| Clean house | 9 | 54 |

Source: F. Newport, "Wives Still Do Laundry, Men Do Yard Work," *Gallup*, 2008 www.gallup.com, accessed May 26, 2008.

These numbers have not changed much since the mid-1990s. One way to look at this is that there is a division of labor along relatively traditional lines. However, only 2 of the 11 activities were ones for which the male took majority responsibility, leaving wives to do most of the work at home even though they also work outside the home. This can lead to strong resentments, as the following quote demonstrates:

"It's a blowout fight every month," Hope (32 and a book editor) confesses. "It's the only thing we fight about." Hope says getting Cohen (34 and a medical resident) to do his agreed-upon tasks requires constant reminders. "He'll tell me he'll wash the dishes before we go to bed, and maybe he will," she says. "But by around 9:30, with dirty dishes still in the sink, I'm broiling."[90]

Conflict exists not only across gender groups but also within individuals who are torn between the two orientations. Many mothers who work outside the home experience considerable guilt, role conflict, and emotional burnout related to the heavy demands of their numerous roles.[91]

In fact, many Americans are realizing that they can't have it all, and where there is a choice, some are opting for change. Sometimes the change is toward the nontraditional, as in the increasing numbers of "stay-at-home" dads, which by one estimate has increased by

70 percent since 1990.[92] Sometimes the change is toward the traditional, as in the recent increase in "stay-at-home" moms, which reverses a three-decade trend of increasing numbers of young mothers in the workforce.[93]

As we have seen, women have a variety of role options and a range of attitudes concerning their gender roles. The ads in Illustration 3–8 reflect two sharply contrasting views of the female role. Next, we examine some of the marketing implications of the changing roles of women in American society.

**Market Segmentation**    Neither the women's nor the men's market is as homogeneous as it once was. At least four significant female market segments exist:[94]

1. *Traditional housewife.* Generally married. Prefers to stay at home. Very home and family centered. Desires to please husband and children. Seeks satisfaction and meaning from household and family maintenance as well as volunteer activities. Experiences strong pressure to work outside the home and is well aware of forgone income opportunity. Feels supported by family and is generally content with role.
2. *Trapped housewife.* Generally married. Would prefer to work, but stays at home because of young children, lack of outside opportunities, or family pressure. Seeks satisfaction and meaning outside the home. Does not enjoy most household chores. Has mixed feelings about current status and is concerned about lost opportunities.
3. *Trapped working woman.* Married or single. Would prefer to stay at home, but works because of economic necessity or social or family pressure. Does not derive satisfaction or meaning from employment. Enjoys most household activities, but is frustrated by lack of time. Feels conflict about her role, particularly if younger children are home.

**ILLUSTRATION 3–8**

Women fulfill a multitude of roles today and have a wide range of attitudes about their roles in society. These two ads take radically different approaches to the portrayal of women and women's attitudes.

Resents missed opportunities for family, volunteer, and social activities. Is proud of financial contribution to family.

4. *Career working woman.* Married or single. Prefers to work. Derives satisfaction and meaning from employment rather than, or in addition to, home and family. Experiences some conflict over her role if younger children are at home, but is generally content. Views home maintenance as a necessary evil. Feels pressed for time.

Although the above descriptions are oversimplified, they indicate the diverse nature of the adult female population. Notice that women may move in and out of these categories over their lifetimes. For example, an otherwise career working woman may feel more like a trapped working woman if she finds it necessary to work while her children are young. And while the career working woman category has grown significantly over the past three decades, the other segments are still sizable, unique, and important.

The male market is likewise diverse in both its attitudes and behaviors toward gender roles, work, and household chores.

**Product Strategy**   Many products are losing their traditional gender typing. Guns, cars, motorcycles, computer games and equipment, golf equipment, financial services, and many other once masculine products are now designed specifically with women in mind. The expanding wealth, independence, and purchase power of women, and the time pressure on them, make them an important target market. Consider the following:

- Women-headed households are expected to represent 28 percent of all households in 2010. The Barbara K tool line targeted at women was launched in 2003 and had sales of $5 million in 2004. According to CEO Barbara Kavovit, "Women have made so many strides but can't fix things in their homes." The tools are designed to be stylish and functional, have special features targeting women, such as cushioned handles, but don't come in "girly" colors.[95]
- Assaults against women are a major social problem. Smith & Wesson launched Lady-Smith, a line of guns designed specifically for women. They found that "if a woman is going to pull out a gun for personal protection, she doesn't want a cute gun." So rather than "feminize" men's guns with colored handles, Smith & Wesson targeted a key success criterion by redesigning its guns to fit women's hands.
- More women work more hours outside the home today than at any other time in our history.[96] This has created great time pressures on most households. As one working mother says, "The poor kids have to make do with you know, canned ravioli, or fish sticks or whatever I can round up."[97] A wealth of time-saving products and services has emerged to meet this need. One example is Betty Crocker's Web site, which focuses on meal planning and preparation. Illustration 3–9 demonstrates how companies are designing products to meet the need of reducing meal preparation time.

As women's roles have expanded, the consumption of potentially harmful products has become socially acceptable for women. This of course raises the ethical issue of targeting groups that have not historically been heavy users of products such as alcohol or tobacco.

**Marketing Communications**   A considerable amount of research suggests that males and females process and respond differently to various communications elements, including sexual appeals, music, verbal style, and so forth.[98] As just one example, females respond more favorably to a "help-others" type of appeal for a charity, whereas males respond best to a "self-help" appeal.[99] This is caused by differing worldviews that affect a range of communications responses as well as consumption behaviors.

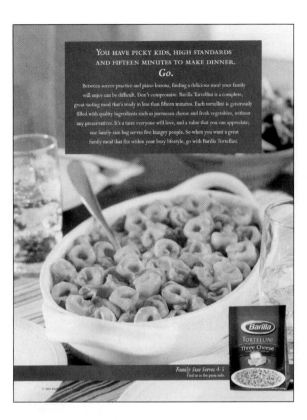

Men and women also consume different media. For example, while men and women are similar in their readership of newsmagazines, their top magazine category preferences vary dramatically:[100]

| Women | Men |
|---|---|
| General women's | Automotive |
| Parenting/child rearing | General men's |
| Health | Fishing/hunting |
| Home/home service | Sports |
| Epicurean | Motorcycles |

Reprinted with permission from the February 2002 issue of *American Demographics.* Copyright Crain Communications Inc. 2004.

Since women are quite diverse as a group, marketers must also consider such factors as ethnicity, age, life stage, and employment status differences when designing marketing communications. For example, State Farm Insurance targets working mothers who have children or who are expecting a child as prospects for their life insurance products. Its ads in magazines such as *Working Mother, Working Woman,* and *American Baby* have featured a picture of a woman life insurance agent with her own child. The copy from one ad reads in part:

A mother's love knows no bounds. And there's no better way to show how much you love them than with State Farm life insurance. Nobody knows better than Gail Coleman—a State Farm agent and mom. When she sits down with you to talk about life insurance, she knows you need a plan designed for working moms.

Advertisements portraying women must be careful about offending any of the various segments.[101] For example, an ad that implied that housework was unimportant or that

This ad is still somewhat unusual in that it portrays a male involved in a traditional female task. Although gender roles are changing, it is much more common to portray women performing traditional male tasks than the reverse.

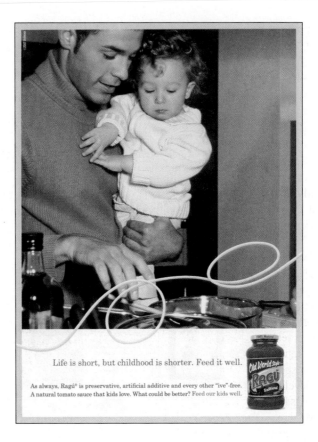

Life is short, but childhood is shorter. Feed it well.

As always, Ragú® is preservative, artificial additive and every other "ive"-free. A natural tomato sauce that kids love. What could be better? Feed our kids well.

women who work outside the home are somehow superior to those who do not could insult traditional housewives. Ads that show women primarily as decoration or as clearly inferior to males tend to produce negative responses across all female segments.[102] Despite such negative reactions, many ads still use these tactics. However, some companies are hitting this issue straight on. Dove launched its "Real Beauty" campaign, which features realistic depictions of women, in response to idealized and unrealistic portrayals of women in advertising that have been shown to reduce self-esteem.

Finally, in terms of gender role portrayal, there are still relatively few ads showing men using products traditionally designed for women or performing tasks traditionally performed by women. Illustration 3–10 shows an exception. Increases in such portrayals are likely over time, but the household chore data presented earlier suggest why such portrayals won't likely increase dramatically anytime soon.

Retail Strategy   Men are increasingly (though still the minority) shopping for household and other products traditionally purchased by females,[103] and females are shopping for traditionally masculine products such as lawn mowers and power tools. In response to these changes, retailers such as Kmart have begun showing very masculine men shopping for household products at their stores, while stores such as Bloomingdales and Target carry power tools targeted at women, such as the Barbara K line discussed earlier.

In addition, men and women react differently to various aspects of retail and service environments. For example, when there is a service failure, men appear to focus mostly on problem resolution, whereas women also focus on the process by which the problem is resolved. Being able to have a voice in the resolution process is much more important for women than men. Such differences need to be built into employee training programs.[104]

## SUMMARY

American values have evolved and will continue to evolve. In terms of those values that influence an individual's relationship with *others,* Americans remain individualistic. We have substantially less of a masculine orientation now than in the past. We also place a greater value on older persons and diversity.

Values that affect our relationship to our *environment* have become somewhat more performance oriented and slightly less oriented toward change. There is a strong and growing value placed on protecting the natural environment, and we increasingly value risk taking.

*Self-oriented* values have also undergone change. We place somewhat less emphasis on hard work as an end in itself and on sensual gratification, although we tend to desire immediate gratification considerably more than has been traditionally true. While religion is important, America remains a relatively secular culture.

Americans assign a high value to the environment. Marketers have responded to this concern with *green marketing:* (1) developing products whose production, use, or disposition is less harmful to the environment than the traditional versions of the product; (2) developing products that have a positive impact on the environment;

or (3) tying the purchase of a product to an environmental organization or event.

*Cause-related marketing* is marketing that ties a company and its products to an issue or cause with the goal of improving sales and corporate image while providing benefits to the cause. Companies associate with causes to create long-term relationships with their customers, building corporate and brand equity that should eventually lead to increased sales.

The *gay market* is estimated at 15.3 million people over the age of 18, with a purchase power of $723 billion. Many companies view the gay market as highly attractive and have committed considerable resources to targeting this market with specific products and promotional efforts. Supportive internal policies toward gay employees as well as support for important gay causes are among the critical factors in approaching this market.

*Gender roles* have undergone radical changes in the past 30 years. A fundamental shift has been for the female role to become more like the traditional male role. Male roles are also evolving, with men beginning to take on what have traditionally been considered female tasks. Virtually all aspects of our society, including marketing activities, have been affected by these shifts.

## KEY TERMS

Achievement role  101
Ascribed role  101
Cause-related marketing
    (CRM)  96
Cultural values  82

Enviropreneurial marketing  90
Gender  101
Gender identity  101
Gender role  101
Green marketing  94

Modern gender orientation  101
Sustainability  94
Traditional gender orientation  101
Voluntary simplicity  87

## INTERNET EXERCISES

1. Visit a site such as the Internet Newspaper (www .trib.com/NEWS). What value does it have in helping track American values? What other sites are useful for this?

2. Search for a newsgroup that is relevant for understanding the following. Report on the insights that it can provide.
    *a.* American values in general
    *b.* Cause-related marketing
    *c.* Green marketing
    *d.* Gender roles

3. Visit www.publicagenda.org. Pick an issue that is relevant to one or more of the values discussed in this chapter and report on the data available relevant to that value.

4. Use the Internet to discover what, if any, cause-related marketing activities the following firms are involved with:
    *a.* IBM
    *b.* Subway
    *c.* Estée Lauder Cosmetics
    *d.* A firm for which you would like to work

5. Visit www.ftc.gov/bcp/grnrule/guides980427 .htm (FTC's most recent "Green Guide.") and write a report about several acceptable and unacceptable advertising practices relating to Green Marketing.

6. Use the Internet to explore key issues facing GLBT (gay, lesbian, bisexual, transgender) consumers (one useful site is the Human Rights Campaign at www.hrc.org).

7. Use the Internet to determine the role of women in purchasing the following:
   a. Houses
   b. Motorcycles
   c. Greeting cards

## DDB LIFE STYLE STUDY™ DATA ANALYSES

1. What characterizes individuals with a traditional view of the female role? How do these individuals differ from those with a more modern view? (Use the DDB data in Tables 1B through 7B.)

2. Based on the data in the DDB Tables 1B through 7B, what characterizes individuals who believe that individuality is an important value to pass on to kids?

3. What characterizes consumers who are particularly responsive to green marketing? What are the marketing strategy implications of this? (See DDB data in Tables 1B through 7B.)

4. Examine the DDB data in Tables 1B through 7B. What characterizes individuals who are active recyclers? What are the marketing strategy implications of this?

## REVIEW QUESTIONS

1. What is a *cultural value*? Do all members of a culture share cultural values?

2. Describe the current American culture in terms of each of the 18 values discussed in this chapter.

3. How is *voluntary simplicity* related to the materialism value? What are the marketing implications of voluntary simplicity? Do these implications vary by product class?

4. What is *green marketing*?

5. What values underlie green marketing?

6. How is *enviropreneurial marketing* related to new product success and market share? Link this to the value of green marketing in creating a competitive advantage.

7. Describe the basic conflict between the environmental movement and many businesses.

8. What is *cause-related marketing*? Why is it often successful?

9. What are the major decisions a firm faces with respect to the gay market?

10. What is meant by *gender*?

11. What is *gender identity*?

12. What is a *gender role*?

13. How does an *ascribed role* differ from an *achievement role*?

14. What is happening to male and female gender roles in America?

15. What are the differences between a traditional and a modern gender role orientation?

16. Describe a segmentation system for the female market based on employment status and gender role orientation.

17. What are some of the major marketing implications of the changing role of women?

## DISCUSSION QUESTIONS

18. Describe additional values you feel could, or should, be added to Figure 3–1. Describe the marketing implications of each.

19. Pick the three values you feel the authors of this book were most *in*accurate about in the chapter in describing the *current* American values. Justify your answers.

20. Pick the three values you feel the authors were most *in*accurate about in describing the *emerging* American values. Justify your answers.

21. Respond to the questions in Consumer Insight 3–1.

22. Which values are most relevant to the purchase or use of the following? Are they currently favorable or unfavorable for ownership/use? Are they shifting at all? If so, is the shift in a favorable or unfavorable direction?
    a. Dietary supplements
    b. The SPCA
    c. Financial investments (stocks, mutual funds, etc.)
    d. Home theater systems
    e. Tanning salon
    f. Visa card

23. Do you believe Americans' concern for the environment is a stronger value than their materialism?

24. What ethical issues do you see relating to green marketing?

25. Respond to the questions in Consumer Insight 3–2.

26. Cause-related marketing is done to enhance a firm's sales or image. Some critics consider such marketing to be unethical. What is your position?

27. In which of the four categories of responders to cause-related marketing (page 97) are you? Why?

28. Suppose AT&T showed a gay couple using its long-distance service or P&G showed a gay couple using one of its laundry products in ads on network television. Is a backlash by those who do not accept the gay community a likely response? How are such consumers likely to respond? Why?

29. Do you think housewives may be defensive or sensitive about not having employment outside of the home? If so, what implications will this have for marketing practice?

30. Develop an advertisement for the following for each of the four female market segments described in the chapter (see pages 103 and 104).
    a. Bicycles
    b. Online banking
    c. Exercise equipment
    d. Breakfast cereal
    e. Vacations
    f. Cosmetics

## APPLICATION ACTIVITIES

31. Find and copy or describe an advertisement for an item that reflects Americans' position on the following values.
    a. Active/Passive
    b. Material/Nonmaterial
    c. Hard work/Leisure
    d. Postponed/Immediate gratification
    e. Sensual gratification/Abstinence
    f. Religious/Secular
    g. Cleanliness
    h. Performance/Status
    i. Tradition/Change
    j. Risk taking/Security
    k. Problem solving/Fatalistic
    l. Admire/Overcome nature
    m. Individual/Collective
    n. Limited/Extended family
    o. Diversity/Uniformity
    p. Competition/Cooperation
    q. Youth/Age
    r. Masculine/Feminine

32. Interview a vegetarian and a person with a strong vegetarian orientation. What values influence their decision to adopt this eating pattern?

33. Interview a salesperson who has been selling the following for at least 10 years. See if this individual has noticed a change in the purchasing roles of women over time.
    a. Motorcycles
    b. Cell phones
    c. Computers
    d. Homes
    e. Financial services

34. Interview a career-oriented working wife and a traditional housewife of a similar age. Report on differences in attitudes toward shopping, products, and so forth.

35. Form a team of five. Have each team member interview five married adult males. Based on these interviews, develop a typology that classifies them by their attitude toward and participation in household or child-rearing activities.

36. Pick two different environmental activism segments (e.g., True Naturals versus Overwhelmed). Find one advertisement you think is particularly appropriate or effective for each. Copy or describe each ad and justify its selection.

37. Interview a salesperson for each of the following. Ascertain the interest shown in the item by males and females. Determine if males and females are concerned with different characteristics of the item and if they have different purchase motivations.
    a. Art
    b. Automobiles
    c. Golf clubs
    d. Pets
    e. Clothing
    f. Flowers

38. Interview 10 male and 10 female students. Ask each to describe the typical owner or consumer of the following. If they do not specify, ask for the gender of the typical owner. Then probe to find out why they think the typical owner is of the gender they indicated. Also determine the perceived marital and occupational status of the typical owner and the reasons for these beliefs.
    a. Pet snake
    b. MP3 player
    c. Large life insurance policy
    d. Power tools
    e. Habitat for Humanity contributor
    f. Electric guitar

## REFERENCES

1. Sources include J. Batsell, "Seattle Basketball Guard to Appear on Local Nike Billboard," *Knight Ridder Tribune Business News,* September 30, 2003, p. 1; "New 2008 WNBA Collective Bargaining Agreement," *InsideHoops.com NewsWire,* January 28, 2008 www.insidehoops.com, accessed May 21, 2008; T. Warren, "Women Drive NASCAR's Fast Lane," *Edmunds.com,* www.edmunds.com accessed May 21, 2008; and information about the various associations garnered from their Web sites at www.womensmotocrossassociation.com, www.NASCAR.com, and www.wnba.com.

2. From Ipsos's global consumer and civic trends reporting service, *World Monitor,* 2nd quarter, 2001. Profiled data were collected on Ipsos's *Global Express* omnibus survey in 34 countries in November–December 2000.

3. "Women's Sports and Physical Activity Facts and Statistics," *Women's Sports Foundation*, May 17, 2008, accessed www .womenssportsfoundation.org.

4. S. G. Edry, "No Longer Just Fun and Games," *American Demographics,* May 2001, p. 38.

5. See, e.g., M. W. Allen and S. H. Ng, "The Direct and Indirect Influences of Human Values on Product Ownership," *Journal of Economic Psychology,* February 1999, pp. 5–39.

6. Consumer Insight 3–1 is based on "Consumers Choose Where They Shop," *The Hartman Group,* August 30, 2002, www .hartman-group.com, accessed May 23, 2008; R. Gardyn, "The Big O," *American Demographics,* October 2002, p. 20; "Nearly Two-Thirds of Americans Have Tried Organic Foods and Beverages," *Whole Foods Market,* press release, November 8, 2005, http://media.wholefoodsmarket.com, accessed May 23, 2008; "Natural and Organic Food and Beverage Industry Trends," *Packaged Facts,* June 2006; "Large Majorities See Organic Food as Safer, Better for the Environment and Healthier," *HealthNewsDigest .com,* October 18, 2007, www.healthnewsdigest.com, accessed May 23, 2008; and "SUPERVALU Launches New Wild Harvest™ Brand of Organic, Natural Foods Nationwide," *Business Wire,* April 9, 2008.

7. "U.S. Religious Landscape Survey," *The Pew Forum on Religion and Public Life*, 2008.

8. H. Taylor, "While Most Americans Believe in God, Only 36% Attend a Religious Service Once a Month or More Often," *The Harris Poll*®, no. 59, October 15, 2003, at www.harrisinteractive .com.

9. See P. S. La Barbera and Z. Gurhan, "The Role of Materialism, Religiosity, and Demographics in Subjective Well-Being," *Psychology & Marketing,* January 1997, pp. 71–97.

10. "New Survey Shows Religious Americans Less Likely to Support Compromise," *Public Agenda,* press release, January 23, 2005, www.publicagenda.org.

11. B. A. Robinson, "How Many People Go Regularly to Weekly Religious Services?" Ontario Consultants on Religious Tolerance, November 26, 2001, www.religioustolerance.org.

12. R. Gardyn, "Breaking the Rules of Engagement," *American Demographics,* July–August 2002, p. 35.

13. R. La Ferla, "Sex Doesn't Sell," *The Tuscaloosa News,* February 16, 2004, p. B1.

14. J. Flint, "Angry NFL Slams ABC's 'Desperate Housewives' Promo," *The Wall Street Journal Online,* November 17, 2004, www.wsj.com.

15. "What (and Who) Is Really Cooking at Your House?" *Parade Magazine,* November 16, 2003, pp. 4–5.

16. S. Thompson, "Minor Indulgence Keeps Cookies from Tanking," *Advertising Age,* June 28, 2004, p. S-18.

17. See, e.g., "Paper or Plastic," *American Demographics,* May 2003, p. 14.

18. E. Conant, "A Penny Saved Is a Penny Spent," *Newsweek,* March 24, 2008, p. 58.

19. These statistics drawn from *Statistical Abstract of the United States* (Washington, DC: U.S. Census Bureau, 2008), Section 12, Labor Force, Employment, and Earnings, tables 583, 584, and 580, respectively.

20. A. Miller, "The Millennial Mind-Set," *American Demographics,* January 1999, pp. 62–63.

21. R. Gardyn, "Nowhere to Hide," *American Demographics,* July–August 2002, pp. 12–13.

22. L. J. Shrum, J. E. Burroughs, and A. Rindfleisch, "Television's Cultivation of Material Values," *Journal of Consumer Research*, December 2005, pp. 473–79.

23. S. Zavestoski, "The Social-Psychological Bases of Anticonsumption Attitudes," *Psychology & Marketing,* February 2002, p. 155.

24. A. Etzioni, "Voluntary Simplicity," *Journal of Economic Psychology* 19 (1998), pp. 619–43; Zavestoski, "The Social-Psychological Bases of Anticonsumption Attitudes"; M. Craig-Lees and C. Hill, "Understanding Voluntary Simplifiers," *Psychology & Marketing,* February 2002, pp. 197–210; and S. McDonald et al., "Toward Sustainable Consumption," *Psychology & Marketing*, June 2006, pp. 515–34.

25. See P. Paul, "Targeting Boomers," *American Demographics,* March 2003, pp. 24–26; and J. Consoli, "Where Have All the Young Men Gone?" *Mediaweek,* October 20, 2003, pp. 4–5.

26. M. Slatalla, "Overscheduled?" *Time,* July 24, 2000, p. 79.

27. T. Cahill, "Exotic Places Made Me Do It," *Outside,* March 2002, p. 60.

28. See J. P. Robinson and M. Milke, "Dances with Dust Bunnies," *American Demographics,* January 1997, pp. 37–40; and Miller, "The Millennial Mind-Set."

29. P. Tyre, "Clean Freaks," *Newsweek,* June 7, 2004, p. 42.

30. "Cash and Carry," *American Demographics,* May 2000, p. 45.

31. "Creativity at Work," *American Demographics,* December 2002–January 2003, pp. 22–23.

32. "Earth in the Balance," *American Demographics,* January 2001, p. 24.

33. R. E. Dunlap, "The State of Environmentalism in the U.S.," *Gallup,* 2007, www.gallup.com, accessed May 25, 2008; J. M. Jones, "In the U.S., 28% Report Major Changes to Live 'Green,'" *Gallup,* 2008, www.gallup.com, accessed May 25, 2008 and *Public Agenda Online,* www.publicagenda.org, accessed May 25, 2008.

34. D. J. Lipke, "Good for Whom?" *American Demographics,* January 2001, p. 37.

35. P. R. Varadarajan, "Marketing's Contribution to the Strategy Dialogue," *Journal of the Academy of Marketing Science* 20 no. 4 (1992), pp. 335–44; and W. E. Baker and J. M. Sinkula, "Environmental Marketing Strategy and Firm Performance," *Journal of the Academy of Marketing Science* 33, no. 4 (2005), pp. 461–75.

36. A. C. Cuneo, "What's in Store," *Advertising Age,* February 25, 2002, p. 1.

37. M. J. Dutta-Bergman and W. D. Wells, "The Values and Lifestyles of Idiocentrics and Allocentrics in an Individualistic Culture," *Journal of Consumer Psychology* 12, no. 3 (2002), pp. 231–42.

38. B. S. C. Liu, O. Furrer, and D. Sudharshan, "The Relationship between Culture and Behavioral Intentions toward Services," *Journal of Service Research,* November 2001, pp. 118–29.

39. J. Halliday, "Tuners Fit In with Customizer Fare," *Advertising Age,* May 31, 2004, p. S-8.

40. S. A. Grier, A. M. Brumbaugh, and C. G. Thornton, "Crossover Dreams," *Journal of Marketing*, April 2006, pp. 35–51.

41. "Americans See Themselves as More Respectful than They Were a Year Ago toward Cultures with Different Values," *Ipsos News Center,* press release, November 7, 2002, www.ipsosna.com/news/pressrelease.

42. R. Suro, "Movement at Warp Speed," *American Demographics,* August 2000, pp. 61–64.

43. See, e.g., C. A. Lin, "Cultural Values Reflected in Chinese and American Television Advertising," *Journal of Advertising,* Winter 2001, pp. 83–94.

44. Miller, "The Millennial Mind-Set," p. 65.

45. E. Day and M. R. Stafford, "Age-related Cues in Retail Services Advertising," *Journal of Retailing,* Summer 1997, pp. 211–33.

46. C. R. Wiles, J. A. Wiles, and A. Tjernlund, "The Ideology of Advertising," *Journal of Advertising Research,* May–June 1996, pp. 57–66. See also P. Simcock and L. Sudbury, "The Invisible Majority?" *International Journal of Advertising* 25, no. 1 (2006), pp. 87–106.

47. For a discussion, see M. Carrigan and I. Szmigin, "The Usage and Portrayal of Older Consumers in Contemporary Consumer Advertising," *Journal of Marketing Practice* 4, no. 8 (1998), pp. 231–48.

48. F. Newport, "Americans Continue to Express Slight Preference for Boys," *Gallup,* July 5, 2007, www.gallup.com, accessed May 26, 2008.

49. *Women's Sports and Physical Activity Facts and Statistics* (East Meadow: *Women's Sports Foundation*, May 17, 2008).

50. D. W. Moore, "Americans More Accepting of Female Bosses Than Ever," *Gallup,* May 10, 2002, www.gallup.com, accessed May 26, 2008.

51. J. Ottman, "Innovative Marketers Give New Products the Green Light," *Marketing News,* March 1998, p. 10; and "Investors, Big Businesses See Green in Being Green," *CNN.com,* August 20, 2007, www.cnn.com, accessed December 1, 2008.

52. J. Neff, "Wal-Mart Persuades P&G, Others to Try Smaller Packaging," *Advertising Age*, June 12, 2006, p. 9; M. Gunther, "The Green Machine," *Fortune,* August 7, 2006, pp. 42–57; and information available through corporate Web sites.

53. "Environmental Groups Unveil Eco-Friendly Coffee Guidelines," *Gourmet News,* July 2001, p. 5; and K. McLaughlin, "Is Your Grocery List Politically Correct?" *The Wall Street Journal,* February 17, 2004, p. D1.

54. See J. A. Lee and S. J. S. Holden, "Understanding the Determinants of Environmentally Conscious Behavior," *Psychology & Marketing,* August 1999, pp. 373–92; and A. Biswas et al., "The Recycling Cycle," *Journal of Public Policy & Marketing,* Spring 2000, pp. 93–105.

55. J. Cohen and J. Darian, "Disposable Products and the Environment," *Research in Consumer Behavior* 9 (2000), pp. 227–57; H.-K. Bang et al., "Consumer Concern, Knowledge, Belief, and

Attitude toward Renewable Energy," *Psychology & Marketing,* June 2000, pp. 449–68; R. Gardyn, "Being Green," *American Demographics,* September 2002, pp. 10–11; and R. Gardyn, "Eco-Friend or Foe?" *American Demographics,* October 2003, pp. 12–13.

56. J. A. Ottman, "Green Marketing, Eco-Innovation and Your Consumer," www.greenmarketing.com/articles/Green-Graveyard.html.

57. Consumer Insight 3–2 is based on "The Environment," *Public Agenda,* www.publicagenda.org/issues, accessed April 18, 2005; L. Armstrong, "Are You Ready for a Hybrid?" *Business-Week,* April 25, 2005, pp. 118–26; A. Taylor III, "The Birth of the Prius," *Fortune,* March 6, 2006, pp. 111–24; M. Margolis, "Coming to America," *Newsweek,* October 2, 2006, p. E18; M. Glover, "Why Honda Accord Hybrid Ran Out of Gas," *Knight Ridder Tribune Business News,* June 13, 2007, p. 1; D. Welch, "GM: Live Green or Die," *BusinessWeek,* May 26, 2008, pp. 36–41; and R. Beene, "Prius Widens Hybrid Sales Lead," *Automotive News,* November 19, 2007, p. 22F.

58. See, e.g., P. S. Bronn and A. B. Vrioni, "Corporate Social Responsibility and Cause-Related Marketing," *International Journal of Advertising* 2 (2001), pp. 207–21.

59. "Multi-Year Study Finds 21% Increase in Americans Who Say Corporate Support for Social Issues is Important in Building Trust," Cone Incorporated press release, December 8, 2004, www.coneinc.com.

60. See also M. Strahilevitz, "The Effects of Product Type and Donation Magnitude on Willingness to Pay More for a Charity-Linked Brand," *Journal of Consumer Psychology* 3 (1999), pp. 215–41; M. J. Barone, A. D. Miyazaki, and K. A. Taylor, "The Influence of Cause-Related Marketing on Consumer Choice," *Journal of the Academy of Marketing Science,* Spring 2000, pp. 248–62; and S. Sen and C. B. Bhattacharya, "Does Doing Good Always Lead to Doing Better?" *Journal Marketing Research,* May 2001, pp. 225–43.

61. "The Growth of Cause Marketing," *Cause Marketing Forum,* www.causemarketingforum.com, accessed May 26, 2008.

62. D. J. Webb and L. A. Mohr, "A Typology of Consumer Responses to Cause-Related Marketing," *Journal of Public Policy & Marketing,* Fall 1998, pp. 226–38.

63. J. W. Pracejus and G. D. Olsen, "The Role of Brand/Cause Fit in the Effectiveness of Cause-Related Marketing Campaigns," *Journal of Business Research* 57 (2004), pp. 635–40; and N. J. Rifon et al., "Congruence Effects in Sponsorship," *Journal of Advertising,* Spring 2004, pp. 29–42.

64. Additional information about these programs can be found on each company's Web site. See also the Cause Marketing Forum at www.causemarketingforum.com.

65. "Gay Rights: Acceptance of Homosexuality Has Grown Significantly," *Public Agenda Online,* www.publicagenda.org, accessed May 27, 2008.

66. "Gay Rights: Seven in 10 Americans Say They Would Favor Hate Crime Laws to Protect Gays and Lesbians," *Public Agenda Online,* www.publicagenda.org, accessed April 18, 2005; and "Everything but the Ring," *American Demographics,* December 2002–January 2003, p. 20.

67. "The Gay and Lesbian Market in the U.S." *Packaged Facts,* February 2007.

68. Ibid., pp. 181–82; and M. Gunther, "Wal-Mart Becomes Gay-Friendly," *CNNMoney.com,* November 30, 2006, www.cnnmoney.com, accessed May 27, 2008.

69. D. L. Vence, "Pride Power," *Marketing News,* September 1, 2004, pp. 1, 13.

70. "The Gay and Lesbian Market in the U.S."

71. L. Koss-Feder, "Out and About," *Marketing News,* May 25, 1998, pp. 1, 20.

72. *2004 Gay Press Report* (Mountainside, NJ: 11th Annual Report by Prime Access Inc. and Rivendell Media Company Inc., 2004), available at www.gaymarket.com/agency_reports.html; and M. Gunther, "Courting the Gay Consumer," *CNNMoney.com,* December 7, 2006. See also S. Yin, "Coming Out in Print," *American Demographics,* February 2003, pp. 18–21.

73. R. Greenspan, "Advertisers May Find Gay Dollars Online," July 30, 2003, at www.clickz.com.

74. Information from corporate Web site at www.planetoutinc.com.

75. *2004 Gay Press Report;* see also S. M. Kates, "Making the Ad Perfectly Queer," *Journal of Advertising,* Spring 1999, pp. 25–35.

76. "The Gay and Lesbian Market in the U.S."

77. R. Gardyn, "A Market Kept in the Closet," *American Demographics,* November 2001, pp. 37–42; see also J. J. Burnett, "Gays," *Journal of Advertising Research,* January 2000, pp. 75–83.

78. R. Greenspan, "Gays Access News, Influenced by Ads," May 17, 2004, www.clickz.com.

79. S. Bhat, T. W. Leigh, and D. L. Wardlow, "The Effect of Consumer Prejudices on Ad Processing," *Journal of Advertising,* Winter 1998, pp. 9–28; S. A. Grier and A. M. Brumbaugh, "Noticing Cultural Differences," *Journal of Advertising,* Spring 1999, pp. 79–91; J. L. Aaker, A. M. Brumbaugh, and S. A. Grier, "Nontarget Market and Viewer Distinctiveness," *Journal of Consumer Psychology* 3 (2000), pp. 127–40; and G. Oakenfull and T. Greenlee, "The Three Rules of Crossing Over from Gay Media to Mainstream Media Advertising," *Journal of Business Research* 57 (2004), pp. 1276–85.

80. G. K. Oakenfull and T. B. Greenlee, "Queer Eye for a Gay Guy," *Psychology & Marketing*, May 2005, pp. 421–39.

81. For these and other statistics, go to the *About 4-Wheel Drive/ Offroading* Web site, at http://4wheeldrive.about.com.

82. M. Powell, "Eye on Footwear," *Sporting Goods Business,* December 2002, p. 38.

83. J. B. Bernstal, "The Power of the Purse," *ABA Bank Marketing,* November 2004, pp. 18–23.

84. E. Fischer and S. J. Arnold, "Sex, Gender Identity, Gender Role Attitudes, and Consumer Behavior," *Psychology & Marketing,* March 1994, pp. 163–82; see also K. M. Palan, C. S. Areni, and P. Kiecker, "Gender Role Incongruity and Memorable Gift Exchange Experiences," in *Advances in Consumer Research,* ed. M. Gilly and J. Meyers-Levy (Provo, UT: Association for Consumer Research, 2001), pp. 51–57.

85. See P. Ireland, *What Women Want* (New York: Dutton, 1996); D. J. Swiss, *Women Breaking Through* (Princeton, NJ: Peterson's/ Pacesetter Books, 1996); and P. McCorduck and N. Ramsey, *The Futures of Women* (Reading, MA: Addison-Wesley 1996).

86. J. S. Grigsby, "Women Change Places," *American Demographics,* November 1992, p. 48; and N. Speulda and M. McIntosh, "Global Gender Gaps," *Pew Research Center for the People & the Press,* Commentary, May 13, 2004, http://people-press.org/commentary/display.php3?AnalysisID=90.

87. "Child Care: Most People Say Fathers Can Be Just as Caring as Mothers and that Women Should Not Return to Their Traditional Roles," *Public Agenda Online,* www.publicagenda.org, accessed April 24, 2005.

88. "The Family," *Public Agenda Online,* www.publicagenda.org, accessed February 28, 2002.

89. "Child Care: Most Women Say that Mothers Who Work Outside the Home Are under More Stress than Mothers Who Stay Home and Most Mothers Say They Would Prefer to Stay at Home," *Public Agenda Online,* www.publicagenda.org, accessed April 24, 2005.

90. P. Paul, "Whose Job Is This Anyway?" *Time,* October 4, 2004, p. 83.

91. See, e.g., M. Posig and J. Kickul, "Work-Role Expectations and Work Family Conflict," *Women in Management Review* 19, no. 7/8 (2004), pp. 373–86; J. Warner, "Mommy Madness," *Newsweek,* February 21, 2005, p. 42; and "The Female Midlife Crisis," *The Wall Street Journal,* April 7, 2005, p. D1.

92. A. Taylor, "Many Fathers Begin to Stay at Home with Children," *Knight Ridder Tribune Business News,* June 20, 2004, p. 1.

93. A. Rock, "From Two Incomes to One," *Money,* January 2005, p. 34.

94. These segments are similar to the four categories popularized by Bartos. See C. M. Schaninger, M. C. Nelson, and W. D. Danko, "An Empirical Evaluation of the Bartos Model," *Journal of Advertising Research,* May 1993, pp. 49–63; and R. Bartos, "Bartos Responds to 'The Bartos Model,'" *Journal of Advertising Research,* January 1994, pp. 54–56.

95. A. Tsao, "Retooling Home Improvement," *BusinessWeek Online,* February 15, 2005, www.businessweek.com.

96. See J. Larson, "The New Homemakers," *American Demographics,* September 1997, pp. 45–50.

97. C. J. Thompson, "Caring Consumers," *Journal of Consumer Research,* March 1996, pp. 388, 395–96.

98. See, e.g., L. D. Wolin, "Gender Issues in Advertising," *Journal of Advertising Research,* March 2003, pp. 111–29; and S. Putrevu, "Communicating with the Sexes," *Journal of Advertising,* Fall 2004, pp. 51–62.

99. F. F. Brunel and M. R. Nelson, "Explaining Gender Responses to 'Help-Self' and 'Help-Others' Charity Ad Appeals," *Journal of Advertising,* Fall 2000, pp. 15–28.

100. From Simmons Market Research Bureau, in A. S. Wellner, "The Female Persuasion," *American Demographics,* February 2002, p. 25.

101. See L. J. Jaffe, "The Unique Predictive Ability of Sex-Role Identity in Explaining Women's Response to Advertising," *Psychology & Marketing,* September 1994, pp. 467–82; J. B. Ford and M. S. LaTour, "Contemporary Female Perspectives of Female Role Portrayals in Advertising," *Journal of Current Issues and Research in Advertising,* Spring 1996, pp. 81–95; and R. Widgery, M. G. Angur, and R. Nataraajan, "The Impact of Employment Status on Married Women's Perceptions of Advertising Message Appeals," *Journal of Advertising Research,* January 1997, pp. 54–62.

102. M. S. LaTour, T. L. Henthorne, and A. J. Williams, "Is Industrial Advertising Still Sexist?" *Industrial Marketing Management,* 1998, pp. 247–55; and M. Y. Jones, A. J. S. Stanaland, and B. D. Gelb, "Beefcake and Cheesecake," *Journal of Advertising,* Summer 1998, pp. 33–51.

103. For a description and theory of male shopping behavior, see C. Otnes and M. A. McGrath, "Perceptions and Realities of Male Shopping Behavior," *Journal of Retailing,* Spring 2001, pp. 111–37.

104. J. R. McColl-Kennedy, C. S. Daus, and B. A. Sparks, "The Role of Gender in Reactions to Service Failure and Recovery," *Journal of Service Research,* August 2003, pp. 66–82; see also A. S. Mattila, A. A. Grandey, and G. M. Fisk, "The Interplay of Gender and Affective Tone in Service Encounter Satisfaction," *Journal of Service Research,* November 2003, pp. 136–43.

# The Changing American Society: Demographics and Social Stratification

Technology is hot. And marketers want to know who the heavy users are and what traits characterize them so they can better understand this market and meet their needs. Scarborough Research recently conducted a national survey of adults 18 and older to find what they call the **Digital Savvy** consumer.[1] Digital Savvy consumers *are leading-edge digital users who are early adopters and diffusers of information related to technology in terms of (1) technology ownership, (2) Internet usage, and (3) cell phone feature usage.* Scarborough identified 18 different behaviors relating to these three dimensions that differentiated the Digital Savvy from the general population. Digital Savvy consumers are those who meet 8 or more of the 18 total technology behaviors. They represent 6 percent of the U.S. population, or roughly 14 million adults! Having identified this group, Scarborough went about characterizing it in terms of tech behav-

iors, demographics, lifestyle, and media usage. Some of the key results include:

- *Technology Behaviors:* The Digital Savvy outstrip the general population in every category of technology, including MP3 and DVR ownership, online banking, online streaming video, text messaging, and e-mail use via cell phone.

- *Demographics:* The Digital Savvy have a very distinct demographic profile. They trended younger, white collar, male, higher education, higher income. And while it is commonly believed that technology is mostly a youth market, Digital Savvy consumers are found across all age categories, and the youngest age category is not even the most Digital Savvy. The table below shows the age distribution of Digital Savvy consumers compared with the general population.

| Age | General Population (%) | Digital Savvy (%) |
|-----|------------------------|-------------------|
| 18–24 | 13 | 22 |
| 25–34 | 18 | 31 |
| 35–44 | 19 | 24 |
| 45–54 | 19 | 16 |
| 55–64 | 14 | 7 |
| 65+ | 17 | 1 |

Source: Adapted from "Understanding the Digital Savvy Consumer," *Scarborough Research,* 2008

- *Lifestyle:* The Digital Savvy's lifestyles are characterized by luxury purchases (upscale restaurants and luxury cars) and travel to exotic destinations, such as East Asia, the Middle East, and Hawaii. They are heavy online spenders who are also active and athletic (yoga, golf, bowling, adult education) and are sports fans.

- *Media:* The Digital Savvy are heavy users of digital media. In terms of traditional media, they tend to be slightly higher in radio, about average in newspapers, and somewhat lower in TV except for high-end TV such as pay-per-view and premium channels. They watch news, sports, and family programs (many are married with kids). They also tend to watch ethnically oriented programming since this group trends higher Asian and Hispanic.

Marketers must segment and understand their markets. Demographics are an important aspect in this process, as the opening example suggests. In this chapter, we will discuss the closely related concepts of demographics and social status. As we will see, several demographic variables—income, education, and occupation— serve as dimensions of social status, and they combine with others to determine social class. We will first take a broad look at the demographics of the American society, with particular attention to age and its related concept, generations. Then we will consider social status and the role that demographics play in social status.

# DEMOGRAPHICS

**Demographics** *describe a population in terms of its size, distribution, and structure* (see also Chapter 2). Demographics influence consumption behaviors both directly and by affecting other attributes of individuals, such as their personal values and decision styles.[2] Consider the demographics of the devoted high-end coffee shop crowd:

Today's most devoted coffee shop patrons are 18- to 34-year-olds and those with annual incomes over $75,000. Forty-two percent of the 18- to 34-year-olds and 46 percent of those who earn more than $75,000 say that when they drink coffee away from home, they head straight for Starbucks-like shops, compared with just 32 percent of all away-from-home coffee drinkers. The younger folks are attracted to the coffee-bar atmosphere, music selections and what tends to be a younger customer base, while the wealthy simply want the best.[3]

Not surprisingly, marketers frequently segment and describe their markets on the basis of demographics and use that information to select appropriate media and develop effective promotional themes. As the opening example suggests, demographics are often related to values, lifestyles, and media patterns in important ways.

## Population Size and Distribution

The population of the United States is approximately 309 million and is expected to surpass 320 million by 2015. The population grew steadily from 1960 through 2003, despite a declining birthrate, because of longer life expectancies, the large baby boom generation moving through the child-bearing years, and significant immigration. Population growth has continued to be steady, and starting in 2003, the overall birthrate began to increase again. In 2006 for example, there were roughly 4.37 million births, the single largest birth year since 1961! Growth in birthrates is occurring for those in their twenties, but the growth among those in their thirties has been the largest over time.[4]

Population growth has not been even throughout the United States, nor is it expected to be so in the future. For example, from 2005 to 2015, states like Arizona, Nevada, Texas, and Florida are predicted to grow by at least 15 percent. Growth in these states is being fueled in part by the retirement and migration of older consumers. In contrast, states like New York, Ohio, Iowa, and North Dakota are expected to grow by less than 2 percent.[5] As we discuss in the next chapter, regions of the country serve as important subcultures whose members have unique tastes and preferences. Several examples of these differences are shown in Figure 4–1.

## Occupation

Occupation is probably the most widely applied single cue we use to initially evaluate and define individuals we meet. This should be obvious when you stop to think of the most common bit of information we seek from a new acquaintance: "What do you do?" Almost invariably we want to know someone's occupation to make inferences about his or her probable lifestyle. Occupation is strongly associated with education (which to some extent determines occupation) and income (which to some extent is determined by occupation).

One's occupation provides status and income. In addition, the type of work one does and the types of individuals one works with over time also directly influence one's values, lifestyle, and all aspects of the consumption process. Differences in consumption between occupational classes have been found for products such as beer, detergents, dog food, shampoo, and paper towels. Media preferences, hobbies, and shopping patterns are also influenced by occupational class (see Table 4–1).

## Education

Approximately 86 percent of Americans have a high school degree, and 28 percent have completed college. Education is increasingly critical for a "family wage" job. Traditional high-paying manufacturing jobs that required relatively little education are rapidly disappearing. High-paying jobs in the manufacturing and service sectors today require technical skills, abstract reasoning, and the ability to read and learn new skills rapidly. Individuals without these skills are generally forced into minimum wage and often part-time jobs, which will rarely keep a family above the poverty level.[6] As the following data show, education clearly drives income in today's economy.

Since individuals tend to have spouses with similar education levels, these differences are magnified when spousal income is considered.

## FIGURE 4–1    A Tale of Three Cities

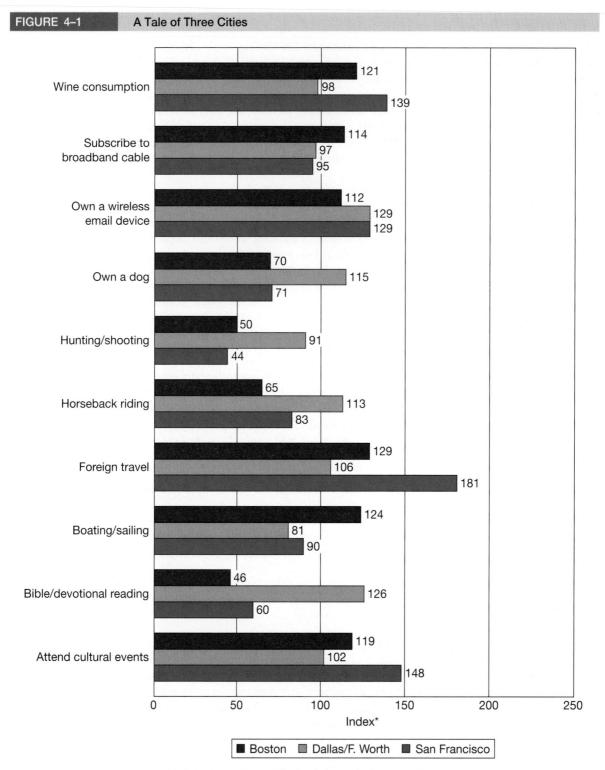

*An Index of 100 represents the average for the entire United States

Source: Data from "The Lifestyle Analyst, 2008 Edition," published by SRDS with data supplied by Equifax Marketing Services. Used by permission.

| | Wholesale and Retail Trade | Professional, Scientific, and Technical | Mining and Construction |
|---|---|---|---|
| **Products** | | | |
| Domestic Beer | 122 | 132 | 150 |
| Cigarettes | 121 | 67 | 129 |
| Diet Colas | 84 | 120 | 70 |
| Satellite Radio System | 93 | 339 | 144 |
| **Activities** | | | |
| Sailing | 129 | 230 | 243 |
| Surfing/Windsurfing | 122 | 140 | 251 |
| Archery | 87 | 49 | 327 |
| Movies (last 6 months) | 108 | 125 | 100 |
| **Shopping** | | | |
| Wal-Mart | 84 | 65 | 109 |
| American Eagle | 134 | 16 | 18 |
| Toys R Us | 62 | 37 | 114 |
| Lowe's | 87 | 137 | 139 |
| **Media** | | | |
| Comedy Central (5–7 hours/week) | 100 | 141 | 201 |
| Food Network (5–7 hours/week) | 61 | 138 | 45 |
| Classic rock radio | 96 | 107 | 154 |
| Religious radio | 124 | 70 | 84 |

**TABLE 4–1**

Occupational Influences on Consumption

Note: 100 = Average level of use, purchase, or consumption.

Source: *SMRB* 2006

| Income: Workers 18 and Older[7] | | |
|---|---|---|
| **Education Level** | **Males** | **Females** |
| No high school degree | $ 23,222 | $14,294 |
| High school degree | 35,248 | 22,208 |
| Associate's degree | 46,201 | 30,912 |
| Bachelor's degree | 67,980 | 40,684 |
| Master's degree | 86,667 | 49,573 |
| Professional degree | 139,773 | 82,268 |

Education influences what one can purchase by partially determining one's income and occupation. It also influences how one thinks, makes decisions, and relates to others.[8] Those with a limited education are generally at a disadvantage.[9] This is discussed in more detail in Consumer Insight 4–1.

Not surprisingly, education has a strong influence on one's tastes and preferences, as shown in Table 4–2. However, education seldom provides a complete explanation for consumption patterns. For example, a lawyer earning $30,000 per year as a public defender will have a different lifestyle from a lawyer earning $250,000 per year in private practice, despite similar educational backgrounds.

## Income

A household's income level combined with its accumulated wealth determines its purchasing power. While many purchases are made on credit, one's ability to buy on credit is ultimately determined by one's current and past income (wealth).

### Marketing and the Low Literate Consumer

Consumer literacy is a major issue in American society. Statistics reveal that 20 percent of American adults are functionally illiterate while an additional 34 percent are marginally literate. Both groups struggle with reading, comprehension, and inference making in ways that are atypical of literate consumers. **Consumer literacy** is defined as *"the ability to find and manipulate text and numbers to accomplish consumption-related tasks within a specific market context in which other skills and knowledge are also employed."*[10]

Low consumer literacy has many negative consequences for consumers in terms of making bad choices, paying too much, and being taken advantage of by unscrupulous marketers. The following quote from a daughter trying to help her mother makes this point:

> And, well, like she can't count. And, one day I was into the store with her, and she bought two boxes of cereal for $5.00. And, she gave the guy a $10.00 bill. And the guy didn't give her the change back. Well, which two boxes of cereal was only $5.00? So I went back and I got onto his back about it . . . And he felt kind of bad, you know, for trying to cheat her, but he did give her $5.00 change back.

Certain low literate consumers feel isolated and allow the negative social stigma to keep them from seeking help and allowing it to limit their purchasing. They use coping strategies such as memorizing brand logos from advertising to help them identify the correct brands or visual package cues to help them select the right product. They also choose a limited number or types of retailers with whom they are familiar and/or trust, so they feel safe. Finally, they will rely on trusted friends and family members to help them operate effectively and avoid major pitfalls. One consumer indicated that she would "drag her feet" when salespeople try to get her to buy something and she doesn't understand a critical aspect by telling the salesperson "I've got to go talk to my husband."

Others actively work to reject the stigma and to increase their skills through literacy programs. A key finding is that those who reject or fight against the negative social stigma tend to have higher levels of esteem, are more likely to work to change their literacy status, and thus are less likely in the long run to experience negative market outcomes as often or to the extent of those who simply accept their situation.

Many programs designed to protect consumers presume adequate consumer literacy. Clearly, low literacy itself becomes a threat to consumer well-being. For example, FDA food labeling laws are likely to be of little consequence to low literacy consumers. Clearly, more needs to be done to provide programs that encourage consumer literacy, enhance coping strategies, and help consumers overcome the fear and stigma associated with low literacy.

### Critical Thinking Questions

1. What is consumer literacy? How is it related to the quality of consumer choices?

2. What ethical issues are associated with marketing to low literate consumers?

3. Search the Internet for programs in your state that deal with the literacy issue. Are the resources abundant?

Most of American history has been characterized by consistently increasing real per capita income. For most middle- and lower-income Americans, this increasing trend stopped in the 1980s, and household incomes were stagnant or declining until they increased again in the mid-1990s.[11] Several notable economic expansions have taken place from the mid-1990s through 2006. The first was from 1993 through 2000 and the second from 2002 through 2006. Economic expansion results in higher incomes and spending

| | Graduated College | Attended College | Graduated High School | Did Not Graduate High School |
|---|---|---|---|---|
| **Products** | | | | |
| Champagne/Sparkling wine | 153 | 109 | 80 | 49 |
| Energy drinks | 89 | 109 | 101 | 116 |
| Motorcycles | 74 | 103 | 124 | 80 |
| Camcorder/Videocamera | 110 | 108 | 101 | 70 |
| **Activities** | | | | |
| Skiing | 203 | 96 | 61 | 34 |
| Playing Bingo | 51 | 109 | 120 | 116 |
| Cruise ship vacation | 145 | 117 | 82 | 46 |
| Recycle metal beverage cans | 132 | 103 | 95 | 57 |
| **Shopping** | | | | |
| Kmart | 69 | 94 | 124 | 100 |
| Neiman Marcus | 246 | 79 | 51 | 13 |
| Kentucky Fried Chicken | 74 | 99 | 112 | 113 |
| Outback Steakhouse | 124 | 120 | 87 | 64 |
| **Media** | | | | |
| *The National Enquirer* | 58 | 90 | 124 | 124 |
| *Forbes* | 173 | 101 | 68 | 58 |
| Nick at Nite (5–7 hours/week) | 18 | 127 | 151 | 69 |
| CNN (5–7 hours/week) | 108 | 73 | 112 | 98 |

**TABLE 4–2**

Education Level Influences on Consumption

Note: 100 = Average level of use, purchase, or consumption.

Source: *SMRB*, 2006

power. A major concern, however, is the growing income divide. One study shows that during the 1993–2000 expansion, real incomes of the top 1 percent grew by 10.1 percent while the remaining 99 percent grew by only 2.4 percent. Even more striking, during the 2002–2006 expansion, the top 1 percent of incomes grew by 11 percent compared with just 0.9 percent for the remaining 99 percent. Such increases in wealth concentration mean that not all Americans are benefiting equally from economic expansion in the United States.[12]

The economic repercussions surrounding rapidly increasing fuel prices and the bursting of the real estate bubble have yet to fully play themselves out, but are likely to affect the entire economy as they increase uncertainty and inflation and decrease purchase power.[13] Consumers are buying smaller cars and smaller houses, building fewer new homes, remodeling less, and drinking more coffee at McDonalds while Starbucks has suffered.[14]

How long these trends hold remains to be seen. Consumers with modest incomes often want to "trade up" to luxury brands. Companies, in a strategy termed **class to mass,** have responded by expanding opportunities for less affluent consumers to afford luxury. However, today more than ever, this may require trade-offs. As one retail expert notes:

Consumers are still willing to trade up. But if someone wants the designer jeans, they'll cut back on something else.[15]

A recent development could actually get a boost from a faltering economy—the luxury rental market for such products as purses and cars. One company, called Bag Borrow or Steal, allows customers to rent high-end bags, such as Coach, Louis Vuitton, and Prada, for a membership fee of $9.95 a month and a rental fee that varies by bag. As one expert notes:

> For those who have only been dabbling in luxury or admiring luxury from afar, this gives them the opportunity to actually taste it.[16]

Income *enables* purchases but *does not generally cause or explain them*. For example, a college professor or lawyer may have the same income as a truck driver or plumber. None-theless, it is likely that their consumption processes for a variety of products will differ. Occupation and education directly influence preferences for products, media, and activities; income provides the means to acquire them.[17] Thus, income is generally more effective as a segmentation variable when used in conjunction with other demographic variables.

How wealthy one feels may be as important as actual income for some purchases.[18] **Subjective discretionary income (SDI)** is *an estimate by the consumer of how much money he or she has available to spend on nonessentials.* Several studies show that SDI adds considerable predictive power to actual total family income (TFI) measures.[19]

## Age

Proper age positioning is critical for many products. Age carries with it culturally defined behavioral and attitudinal norms.[20] It affects our self-concept and lifestyles.[21] Not surpris-ingly, age influences the consumption of products ranging from beer to toilet paper to vacations. Our age shapes which media we use, where we shop, how we use products, and how we think and feel about marketing activities.[22] Table 4–3 illustrates some consumption behaviors that vary with age. Illustration 4–1 shows an ad with the type of humor appreci-ated by many young adults.

| TABLE 4–3 | | 18–24 | 25–34 | 35–44 | 45–54 | 55–64 | 65+ |
|---|---|---|---|---|---|---|---|
| Age Influences on Consumption | **Products** | | | | | | |
| | Tequilla | 104 | 140 | 130 | 114 | 90 | 33 |
| | Scotch Whiskey | 69 | 65 | 98 | 98 | 120 | 129 |
| | Botox | 3 | 60 | 85 | 220 | 60 | 104 |
| | Laser Printer | 117 | 115 | 126 | 125 | 92 | 39 |
| | **Activities** | | | | | | |
| | Skateboarding | 436 | 104 | 111 | 89 | 26 | 17 |
| | Yoga | 135 | 163 | 126 | 114 | 64 | 25 |
| | Volunteer for Cause | 86 | 86 | 91 | 92 | 108 | 127 |
| | Visiting Museums | 108 | 102 | 126 | 100 | 92 | 77 |
| | **Shopping** | | | | | | |
| | J.C. Penney | 75 | 90 | 105 | 115 | 108 | 93 |
| | Banana Republic | 162 | 206 | 109 | 77 | 71 | 24 |
| | Chuck E. Cheese | 164 | 243 | 131 | 52 | 46 | 16 |
| | Marie Callender's | 38 | 50 | 72 | 105 | 157 | 144 |
| | **Media** | | | | | | |
| | *Reader's Digest* | 25 | 34 | 64 | 105 | 123 | 194 |
| | *Maxim* | 273 | 223 | 113 | 62 | 25 | 10 |
| | *Glamour* | 200 | 184 | 116 | 85 | 51 | 28 |
| | *AARP, The Magazine* | 5 | 5 | 13 | 80 | 178 | 256 |

Note: 100 = Average level of use, purchase, or consumption.
Source: *SMRB,* 2006

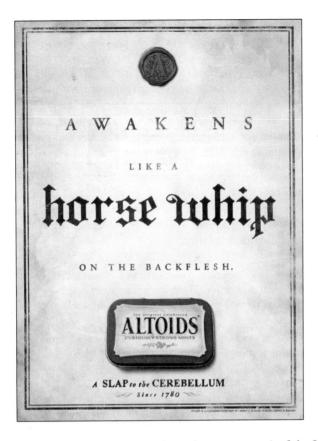

The estimated age distributions (millions in each age category) of the U.S. population for 2010 and 2020 are[23]

| Age Category | 2010 | 2020 | Percentage Change |
|---|---|---|---|
| Under 10 | 42,132 | 45,496 | +8.0% |
| 10–19 | 41,103 | 43,392 | +5.6 |
| 20–29 | 43,051 | 43,112 | +0.1 |
| 30–39 | 40,408 | 44,847 | +11.0 |
| 40–49 | 43,638 | 40,892 | −6.3 |
| 50–59 | 41,680 | 42,578 | +2.2 |
| 60–69 | 28,851 | 38,474 | +33.4 |
| Over 69 | 28,071 | 37,013 | +31.9 |

Even a quick look at these age distributions indicates important changes. Some of the marketing implications include:

- Demand for children's products, such as toys, diapers, and clothes, will grow moderately, as the population under 10 years of age will grow 8 percent over this period.
- The teen market is growing again at a modest rate after a decade in which growth had been minimal or negative. This signals a growth in demand for fashion, music, and technology targeting the teen market.
- Given that marriage and childbirth often occur in the twenties but are increasingly delayed until the thirties, growth in the 30–39 market should provide growth in homes, child care products and services, family cars, and insurance to offset the lack of growth in the 20–29 age group.

- Products consumed by those aged 40 to 49 will decline as this population group grows smaller. This will have significant implications for such industries as financial services for which this is a key age group.
- The largest growth area is in the 60 and over groups, which will grow at greater than 30 percent. The 60–69 group will be primarily one- or two-person households, with many retired or near retirement. Vacations, restaurants, second homes, and financial services aimed at this market should flourish. Growth in the 69 and over group will create many opportunities for marketers ranging from beauty aids and travel and leisure to retirement homes and health care.

Age groups, as defined by the census and as presented above, can be useful as a means of understanding and segmenting a market. For example, P&G launched the Oil of Olay ProVital line, targeting women over 50 years old. One of the first spokeswomen for the product was 51-year-old actress Anne Roberts. However, the product line has not been positioned as just an antiwrinkle solution:

> Age is just a number. Many women 50 and over have told us that as they age, they feel more confident, wiser, and freer than ever before. These women are redefining beauty. Our research shows that when it comes to skin, dryness and vitality are their key concerns, not just a few wrinkles.[24]

These comments suggest an important distinction between chronological age (how old you are) and cognitive age (how old you feel). **Cognitive age** is defined as *one's perceived age, a part of one's self-concept.*[25] It is measured by asking people what age they would associate with how they look, feel, and behave. For older consumers, cognitive age is often 10 to 15 years less than chronological age. Similar results have been found for cognitive age in Japan.[26] Better health and higher education, income, and social support lead to reductions in cognitive age. And for many behaviors, cognitive age is more important than chronological age, making age perception a critical marketing consideration.

Generational influences, which provide additional richness and insight beyond standard age categories, are discussed next.

## UNDERSTANDING AMERICAN GENERATIONS

A **generation,** or **age cohort,** is *a group of persons who have experienced a common social, political, historical, and economic environment.* Age cohorts, because their shared histories produce unique shared values and behaviors, often function as unique market segments.[27]

**Cohort analysis** is the process of describing and explaining the attitudes, values, and behaviors of an age group as well as predicting its future attitudes, values, and behaviors.[28] A critical fact uncovered by cohort analysis is that each generation behaves differently from other generations as it passes through various age categories. For example, in 2011 the leading edge of the baby boom generation will be eligible to retire at the traditional age of 65. Many, of course, have opted for earlier retirement while some will continue to work. However, it would be a mistake to assume that retiring baby boomers will behave like the pre-Depression generation does today. The forces that shaped the lives of these generations were different, and their behaviors will differ throughout their life cycles. As just one example, the computer and Internet skills that baby boomers have acquired will make them much heavier Internet users in their retirement years than is currently true of their parents, who in many cases were bypassed by the most recent technology revolution.

In the following sections, we will examine the six generations that compose the primary American market.[29] It is important to emphasize that generation is only one factor influencing behavior and the differences within generations are often larger than the differences across generations. In addition, generations do not have sharp boundaries. Those near the age breaks between generations often do not belong clearly to either generation.

## Pre-Depression Generation

The pre-Depression generation is composed of those individuals born before 1930. Some 12 million Americans are in this generation. These individuals grew up in traumatic times. Most were children during the Depression and entered young adulthood during World War II. They have witnessed radical social, economic, and technological change. As a group, they are conservative and concerned with financial and personal security.

As with all generations, the pre-Depression generation is composed of many distinct segments, and marketing to it requires a strategy that incorporates such factors as gender, ethnicity, and social class.[30] In fact, this generation is part of a broader category of consumers called the **mature market.** The mature market (often categorized as 55 years of age and over) now spans three generations (pre-Depression, Depression, and baby boom) and is a large and growing market with numerous subsegments. **Gerontographics** is *one segmentation approach to the mature market that incorporates aging processes and life events related to the physical health and mental outlook of older consumers* (see Consumer Insight 4–2).

The pre-Depression generation faces numerous consumption-related decisions. One is the disposition of valued belongings that they no longer use or that are not appropriate in nursing or retirement homes. These can be emotional decisions for both the elderly person and their family members.

> The pin means a great deal to me. I would love for my granddaughter to have it. It will be strange not seeing it in my jewelry box anymore.[31]

Communications strategies need to consider media selection, message content, and message structure. For example, some aspects of information processing, memory, and cognitive performance decline with age. The rapid, brief presentation of information that younger consumers respond to is generally not appropriate for older consumers.[32]

Products related to the unique needs of this segment range from health services to single-serving sizes of prepared foods. As this generation continues to age, assisted-living services are growing rapidly. As more members of this generation experience reduced mobility, shopping will become an increasing problem. Although Internet shopping would seem a good solution, relatively few members of this generation use the Internet.

## Depression Generation

This is the cohort born between 1930 and 1945. These people were small children during the Depression or World War II. They matured during the prosperous years of the 1950s and early 60s. They discovered both Sinatra and Presley. They "invented" rock and roll and grew up with music and television as important parts of their lives.

There are about 28 million individuals in this group. Most have retired or will soon do so. Many have accumulated substantial wealth in the form of home equity and savings. Those who still work often dominate the top positions in both business and government. Members of this generation are also grandparents with sufficient incomes to indulge their grandchildren, making them a major market for upscale children's furniture, toys, strollers, car seats, and clothing.

Many in this generation are still in excellent health and are quite active. Active lifestyles translate into demand for recreational vehicles, second homes, new cars, travel services, and recreational adult education.[33] So-called "active adult communities" such as Sun City in Phoenix, Arizona, are also a major growth arena and will continue to be so as the baby boomers

## Targeting the Mature Market

One approach to segmenting older consumers is gerontographics, based on the theory that people change their outlook on life when they experience major life events such as becoming a grandparent, retiring, losing a spouse, or developing chronic health conditions. Individuals who have confronted similar events are likely to have a similar outlook on life and, given similar economic resources, similar lifestyles. Gerontographics has identified four segments of the mature market. Interestingly, age is not the major distinguishing factor across segments (for example, frail recluses can be in any age range from 55 and above), which attests to the power of life events, health, and financial status.[34]

**Healthy Indulgers** This segment is physically and mentally healthy, has the most in common with the baby boomers than any other segment, and will increasingly be composed of baby boomers as they age. Both spouses are generally still alive. They have prepared for retirement both financially and psychologically. They are basically content and set to enjoy life. They often sell their fairly large homes and move into apartments, townhouses, or condos. They like activities, convenience, personal service, and high-tech home appliances. They are a strong part of the market for cruises and group travel.

**Ailing Outgoers** These people have experienced health problems that limit their physical abilities and frequently, their financial capability. Ailing outgoers are a key market for retirement communities and assisted-living housing. People in this group acknowledge their limits, maintain positive self-esteem, and seek to get the most out of life. Independence and socializing are important as is remaining stylish in their dress. However, limited funds are an issue as are physical limitations. Thus, value pricing and discounts are viewed positively as are ease and convenience, such as Velcro fasteners on clothes.

**Healthy Hermits** People in this group retain their physical health, but life events, often the death of a spouse, have reduced their self-concept. They have reacted by becoming withdrawn. Many then resent the isolation and the feeling that they are expected to act like old people. This group does not want to stand out. They prefer clothing styles that are popular with other seniors. They will pay a premium for well-known brands. They tend to stay in the homes in which they raised their families, and they are an important part of the do-it-yourself market.

**Frail Recluses** Those in this segment have accepted their old-age status and have adjusted their lifestyles to

enter their retirement years. These age-restricted communities offer an amazing array of activities and attract relatively wealthy households, many of whom can pay cash for their homes.[35]

Marketers targeting this segment are increasingly using themes that stress an active lifestyle and breaking with stereotypical portrayals of older consumers. Illustration 4–2 would appeal to the "healthy indulger" segment described in Consumer Insight 4–2.

Nonetheless, this generation is dealing with the physical effects of aging, with nursing home stays and in-home care an increasing likelihood as people move beyond their sixties (those in the pre-Depression and Depression generations).[36] In terms of clothing, comfort as well as style is important. Levi's Action Slacks have been a major success with this generation. These slacks, which have an elastic waistband, are cut for the less lean, more mature body. Easy Spirit shoes also targets this segment with comfort in mind. Health care is a major concern and a major expenditure.

Asset management is important to this group, and firms such as Merrill Lynch have developed products and services to meet these needs.[37] Lawyers, accountants, and financial planners have also been attracted to the "wealth transfer" that is expected to occur as the baby boomers inherit the wealth accumulated by their parents. Numbers vary dramatically reflect reduced physical capabilities and social roles. They focus on becoming spiritually stronger. Frail recluses may have been in any one of the other categories at an earlier age. They tend to stay at home, and many require home and lawn care services. They are a major market for health care products, home exercise and health testing equipment, and emergency response systems. Locational convenience is often a critical factor for this group.

One recent study found striking differences across these market segments in terms of how they choose physicians and surgeons. The following table examines the importance of several key criteria (numbers represent percentage in each group who indicate that the criterion is important):[38]

|  | Healthy Hermits (%) | Healthy Indulgers (%) | Ailing Outgoers (%) | Frail Recluses (%) |
| --- | --- | --- | --- | --- |
| Reasonable fees | 25 | 24 | 43 | 29 |
| Convenient location | 54 | 57 | 53 | 62 |
| Related services at same location | 39 | 36 | 35 | 34 |
| Staff explanation of services | 34 | 45 | 39 | 35 |

Not surprisingly, what drives patronage for one group is not necessarily a key factor for others, a finding that is true across a variety of products and services, including restaurants and financial services.

**Critical Thinking Questions**

1. The percentage of the American population that is mature is going to increase dramatically over the next decade. How is this going to change the nature of American society?

2. What explains the key differences in the importance of criteria used to select physicians and surgeons across the segments?

3. What ethical and social responsibilities do marketers have when marketing to older consumers?

due to stock market fluctuations and rising health care costs. However, even the most conservative estimate puts the value at $1 trillion over the next decade.[39]

In addition, this group of consumers is downsizing homes and possessions just like the pre-Depression generation. And increasing numbers are becoming more tech savvy, even to the point of using eBay to help them downsize! As one 60-something eBay user jokes:

The end of the bidding cycle is quite exciting, especially for older people whose lives like mine are not that exciting anymore.

SeniorNet is a nonprofit group that helps older consumers learn about computers by offering classes in nursing homes and recreation centers. eBay has donated over $5 million to SeniorNet to help the group expand its classes and computer centers.[40]

## Baby Boom Generation

The baby boom generation refers to those individuals born during the dramatic increase of births between the end of World War II and 1964. There are almost 80 million baby

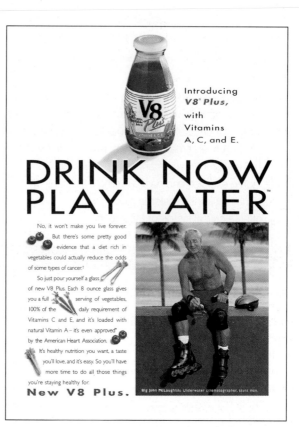

boomers, which is substantially more than the two preceding generations combined. Most of this group grew up during the prosperous 1950s and 1960s. They were heavily influenced by the Kennedy assassination, the Vietnam War, recreational drugs, the sexual revolution, the energy crisis, the rapid growth of divorce, and the cold war, as well as rock and roll and the Beatles. Although there are significant differences between the boomers born early in this generation and those born later, boomers are considered to be more self-centered, individualistic, economically optimistic, skeptical, suspicious of authority, and focused on the present than other generations.[41]

Baby boomers are characterized by high education levels, high incomes, and dual-career households. They are also often characterized by time poverty (particularly young boomers) as they try to manage two careers and family responsibilities. In 2010 their age range is 46 to 64, a range characterized by children leaving home, marrying, and producing grandchildren. The "empty nest" is rapidly becoming the norm for this generation, a circumstance that is providing them with both increased discretionary income and time. In fact, baby boomers are 48 percent more likely than the average adult to earn $100,000 or more.[42] As a result, sales of adventure vacations, expensive restaurant meals, second homes, recreational vehicles, maintenance-free homes, personal chefs, personal trainers, and even motorcycles should continue to grow rapidly.[43] Importantly, not all activities and spending is self-focused. One study finds that over a third of boomers consider themselves to be environmentally conscious, a number that is expected to increase as they continue to age. Obvious implications for the green movement and brands and products such as Toyota's Prius emerge when considering the considerable size and resources of this group.[44]

TV is still a major route through which to target this generation. However, baby boomers are more tech savvy than previous generations, a trend that will increasingly make the mature market an important target for online marketers, particularly given their high level of discretionary income.[45] The Internet offers the convenience and customization that this generation will increasingly demand. In addition, the Internet allows access to health information of importance to this aging segment. Baby boomers are at least twice as likely as the previous two generations to use the Internet and to use it to get access to health-related information. In fact, Internet usage among boomers is over 70 percent.[46]

Retirement is no longer something in the distant future, and many have already made that step. However, surveys indicate that boomers plan to continue and expand the concept of "active retirement" begun by the Depression generation. For example, households in this age segment spend 21 percent more on travel than the average household.[47] However, baby boomers don't just want to travel; they want to learn new skills, work actively both for pay and in charities, and otherwise continue to grow. Two-thirds of a recent survey of 50- to 75-year-olds selected as a definition of retirement: To begin a new, active, and involved chapter in life, starting new activities and setting new goals.[48] Or as one boomer who recently took early retirement stated: "I'm not retiring; I'm re-engineering my life."

In fact, it is expected that the baby boom generation will continue to work longer than previous generations. The reasons vary from necessity, among those with lower incomes or poor pension plans; to changes in Social Security, which are increasing the age at which full benefits can be drawn; to an increased desire to stay active in interesting and rewarding careers.[49]

Boomers are also facing the aging and often failing health of their parents. Becoming the caregiver rather than the care-receiver is a major challenge for this group. One result of this is the rapid growth of assisted-living centers. This type of living arrangement is a major innovation, and it arose because many baby boomers did not want their parents living with them and the healthy and active pre-Depression and Depression generations did not want to be dependent on or impose on their children.[50]

As boomers age, their physical needs are changing. Weight gain has become an increasing concern, and demand for plastic surgery, baldness treatments, health clubs, cosmetics for both men and women, hair coloring, health foods, and related products is exploding.

> When lotions failed to smooth the crow's feet around Cheryl Hoover's eyes and restore the firmness to her skin, the 41-year-old turned to Botox, collagen, and laser treatments. "I try to be proactive in heading off things. You want, as you get older, to appear youthful or at least look your age and not older. Our generation is looking for the fountain of youth, where it would have been more acceptable to age in previous generations."[51]

Illustration 4–3 shows an ad focused on the needs of this group. Other examples of firms focusing on the maturing needs of this generation include:

- Kellogg dropped its Special K ads featuring young, slim, attractive women putting on tight-fitting jeans or short skirts. Research revealed that boomers were alienated by those ads: "They told us they couldn't relate to advertising techniques that used unrealistic body images."[52]
- Sony spent $25 million to target what it calls the "zoomers," a name that reflects the active lifestyle of this generation. One of their ads featured a "grey-haired astronaut filming Earth with his own camcorder." The tagline: "When your kids ask where the money went, show them the tape." Sony credits a surge in camcorder sales to its renewed focus on this increasingly important segment.[53]

## Generation X

Generation X, often referred to as the baby bust generation, was born between 1965 and 1976. It is a smaller generation than its predecessor (about 45 million). This generation

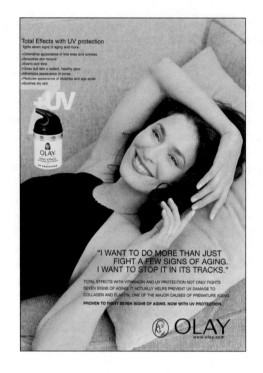

reached adulthood during difficult economic times. It is the first generation to be raised mainly in dual-career households, and 40 percent spent at least some time in a single-parent household before the age of 16. The divorce of their parents is often a cause of stress and other problems for the children involved.[54] However, these changes have also caused many members of Generation X to have a very broad view of a family, which may include parents, siblings, stepparents, half-siblings, close friends, live-in lovers, and others.

This is the first American generation to seriously confront the issue of reduced expectations. These reduced expectations are based on reality for many "busters" as wages and job opportunities for young workers were limited until the economic boom that started in the mid-1990s.[55] This relative lack of opportunity was in part responsible for this generation's tendency to leave home later and also to return home to live with their parents as younger adults. Not only has the path to success been less certain for this generation, but many Generation Xers do not believe in sacrificing time, energy, and relations to the extent the boomers did for the sake of career or economic advancement.

This generation faces a world racked by regional conflicts and terrorism, an environment that continues to deteriorate, and an AIDS epidemic that threatens their lives. Members of this group tend to blame the "me generation" and the materialism associated with the baby boom generation for the difficult future they see for themselves.

However, Generation X is highly educated, with more college attendance and graduates than previous generations. And Xer women are more highly educated than men, giving them increased leverage in the workforce. Given their early economic challenges, it is perhaps not surprising that this generation appears to be more entrepreneurial in its approach to jobs and less prone to devote their lives to large public corporations. For example, a recent survey found that Xers are 25 percent more likely than previous generations to be self-employed professionals.[56] The empowerment of Xer women extends beyond their careers. One study shows that across all generations, Xer women are the highest viewers of home improvement media and the most likely to engage in home improvement projects, including adding a room onto the house.[57]

This generation is moving into the middle and latter stages of the vaunted 18–49 demographic that advertisers and marketers covet. Considerable attention has recently focused on the inability of traditional network TV to attract this demographic, particularly men in the 18–34 range. One explanation is the explosion of media options, including cable and the Internet, which are increasingly luring these consumers away. Both Xers and their younger counterparts in Generation Y are more avid users of the Internet and related technologies than previous generations. Advertisers are responding by increasingly using alternative media to reach these consumers.[58]

In 2010, this generation is 34 to 45 years old. Although they tended to delay marriage, 63 percent of Xer households are now families with children under 18.[59] This helped keep the housing market strong during the economic downturn in the early 2000s. It is also the reason that this generation increasingly feels the time crunch typical of child-rearing years. This generation will be a major force in the market for cars, appliances, and children's products. The ad in Illustration 4–4 targets Xer parents.

While an important market, Generation X is not always easy to reach. It is both cynical and sophisticated about products, ads, and shopping. It is materialistic and impatient. In many aspects, its tastes are "not baby boom." Thus, it created the grunge look and snowboarding. Magazines such as *Spin, Details,* and *Maxim* were created for this generation as was the X Games. It responds to irreverence in advertising but not always as well to traditional approaches. Generation Xers want products and messages designed uniquely for their tastes and lifestyles. Marketers are increasingly targeting this group.

- Volvo redesigned its marketing mix for the S40 sedan to go after the Generation X market and some older Generation Yers. The automaker did tie-ins with Microsoft's

**ILLUSTRATION 4–4**

Generation X consumers are now becoming parents and companies are targeting their needs in this area.

Xbox and Virgin Group and created commercials with a hip-hop feel using the band Dilated Peoples. Signs and banners of the S40 were posted in such places as Virgin's Megastores.[60]

- State Farm began targeting Generation Xers with media buys on MTV, ESPN, and Comedy Central. They also placed banner ads on Web sites such as Rollingstone.com.[61]

As these examples suggest, companies are beginning to understand that Generation Xers are moving into a new life stage accompanied by increased buying power and families to care for. Additionally, these companies are adapting their media strategies beyond traditional approaches to speak to this segment on its own terms.

## Generation Y

Traditional mass-marketing approaches that were so successful with older generations often don't work well with younger consumers, including those in Generation Y. Companies must continually push the creative envelope with respect to media and promotional themes to capture this audience. Event sponsorships and electronic media are just a few of the ways marketers are finding to connect with this generation. Music and fashion are often key touch points, as shown in Illustration 4–5. Pepsi hit it big with this generation with the "P-Diddy Driving Pepsi" commercial spot in which the rapper catches a ride to an awards ceremony in a Diet Pepsi truck and unwittingly starts a pop icon frenzy that is mimicked by other stars. The ad helped Pepsi win the 2005 Super Bowl ad wars, with 63 percent awareness among 14- to 24-year-olds.[62]

Today's thirtysomethings are the leading edge of this generation of 71 million members, a number that rivals that of the baby boom. These children of the original baby boomers were born between 1977 and 1994 and are sometimes referred to as the "echo boom." Overall, it is the first generation to grow up with virtually full-employment opportunities for women, with dual-income households the standard, with a wide array of family types

**ILLUSTRATION 4–5**

Attracting Generation Y often requires unique and creative marketing approaches often involving music, fashion, and technology.

seen as normal, with significant respect for ethnic and cultural diversity, with computers in the home and schools, and with the Internet. It has also grown up with divorce as the norm,[63] AIDS, visible homelessness (including many teenagers), drug abuse, gang violence, and economic uncertainty. The Columbine shootings, the Oklahoma City bombing, the Clinton–Lewinsky scandal, the collapse of the Soviet Union, and Kosovo were key events for this generation.[64]

Generation Y is characterized by a strong sense of independence and autonomy. They are assertive, self-reliant, emotionally and intellectually expressive, innovative, and curious. They understand that advertisements exist to sell products and are unlikely to respond to marketing hype. They prefer ads that use humor or irony and have an element of truth about them. They like the ability to customize products to their unique needs. Brand names are important to them.[65]

Generation Y's age range in 2010 is 16 to 33. This market is thus characterized as older teens and young adults. This generation, as a whole, is expected to be the highest-educated generation to date, with incomes that should follow. Many in this generation are in college or have entered the workforce. These consumers are Internet savvy and use e-mail, cell phones, and text messaging to communicate. Over 90 percent of the 18–29 group is online, which is higher than any preceding generation,[66] and the 18–24 group leads all other age groups in every cell phone data service from text messaging to Web browsing.[67] This group is accustomed to media and TV programs designed for them, such as MTV, *Maxim, American Idol, Big Brother 4,* and *CSI.*

Ads targeting this generation must be placed in appropriate magazines and on appropriate Internet sites, television and radio programs, and video games—a strategy called "advergaming."[68] The portrayal of multiple racial and ethnic groups in ads aimed at this generation is common. This is a multiethnic generation, and single-race ads would seem unnatural to them. In addition, urban African American teenagers and Hispanic teenagers are frequently the style leaders of this generation.[69] As important as effective advertising are public relations (e.g., creating buzz) and event sponsorship.

The teenage segment of this generation receives a lot of attention. Many reside in dual-income or single-parent households and have grown up assisting in household management, including shopping. Coupled with the ubiquitous presence of advertising throughout their lives, this has made them savvy shoppers. They are also tech savvy, and cell phones are an important communication tool.

The teenage market is attractive to marketers for two reasons. First, preferences and tastes formed during the teenage years can influence purchases throughout life. As the Ford Focus brand manager states, "Although very few of [teenagers] are car buyers now, it is vital to create a relationship with them so they'll think of Ford when it is time to buy a car."[70] Second, teenagers currently spend over $150 billion annually for personal consumption,[71] spend billions more while doing the household shopping, and influence the purchase of many additional items, such as cars and vacations.

Marketers targeting teens need to use appropriate language, music, and images. Retailers are realizing that they need to constantly adjust and update their offerings to drive traffic among this active shopper segment that is also easily bored. Consider the following statement by a retail consultant:

This is the challenge for any store catering to mall rats—the kids come back so often that you're forced to constantly change the displays. Otherwise they get bored and stop coming at all. It's one reason stores need to know how often the regulars return—to see whether the windows and front tables should be changed every week or every seventeen days.[72]

ILLUSTRATION 4–6

This site promises a
place where teens
can focus on their
concerns and issues.

Honesty, humor, uniqueness, and information appear to be important to teens, as are social networking sites that allow them to connect with their peers regarding important issues, as shown in Illustration 4–6.[73]

Successful approaches to targeting this market include the following:

- Heinz's Bagel Bites were originally marketed only to mothers (to buy for their teens and others). Heinz revamped its strategy to focus directly on teens. It signed on as a sponsor of ESPN's Winter X Games and sales jumped 25 percent.[74]
- Hollister, a retailer, sells apparel, accessories, and body care products. According to a retail expert, "The brand encompasses a surfer lifestyle through merchandise selection and décor, which includes surfboards, a lounge area stocked with alternative magazines and listening stations." Hollister has also seamlessly integrated its in-store themes and personality into its Web site.[75]

The young adults segment of this generation is also critical to marketers as this generation begins to move out of its teens and into its twenties and thirties. This segment has created both challenges and opportunities. For example, while relatively few teens own cars, young adults are entering the car market, often for the first time, making Generation Y a major market for automobiles. It is expected Generation Y as a whole will represent 40 percent of the auto market in 10 years, a number that has automakers like Toyota and Ford clamoring to attract this group early and earn its loyalty. Toyota's Scion has been successful in attracting a younger crowd by offering lower pricing and edgy styling. Scion's marketing is also eclectic and edgy with an "urban youth" touch, including hosting dance parties with emerging DJs and artists.[76]

Another growth market for Generation Yers is apparel, for which 18- to 34-year-olds spend more than all other age categories.[77] Successful teen marketers needed to adapt and understand; as one expert puts it, "Where are all these folks going to go when they get tired of shopping in teenage land?" Abercrombie & Fitch is one retailer making the transition to the young adult market, while still keeping its traditional stores, as the following excerpt suggests:

In 2004 [Abercrombie & Fitch] started a new store, Ruehl No. 925, that is aimed at the 20- to-35-year-olds. It now has 10 stores in cities like Tampa, Fla.; Columbus, Ohio; and San Diego. At the Manhattan store on Bleeker Street – close to bars, cafes and smaller retail shops – pricey leather handbags and paper-thin T-shirts are sold in a space with dark wood and assorted mirrors that feels like a cross between a New York brownstone and a swanky boutique hotel.[78]

Finally, as this group gets married and has children, they should help fuel growth in housing and child-related products as well.

## Tweens

Marketers have yet to fully define the age cohort following Generation Y. This newest generation was born after 1994. However, it seems natural to look at the oldest of this group, now in the so-called tween years (8 to 14). Tweens have many of the same characteristics as the teens discussed earlier and will likely continue trends in increased education, diversity, and technology usage. In terms of diversity, for example, 40 percent of tweens belong to ethnic subcultures, with Hispanics and African Americans the two largest groups.[79] On the international front, they face global terrorism and the aftermath of 9/11. On the domestic front, they face school violence such as the Virginia Tech shootings, as well as economic uncertainty relating to the mortgage crisis. And while divorce is still a reality, today's tweens are benefiting from the fact that divorce rates have been on the decline since around 1990 and the fact that parents who marry later (more typical now) are less likely to get divorced. As a consequence, two-thirds of tweens live in households containing both parents.[80]

Tweens are late adolescents and early teens. This segment represents 29 million people and $43 billion in spending power.[81] Not surprisingly, marketers are increasingly targeting this segment, going after early loyalty and hefty allowances. Opportunities exist in music, fashion, cosmetics, video games, and so on. Consider the following excerpt:

Cosmetic and personal care companies are targeting kids and tweens this fall with products that include tasty lip balm branded Dairy Queen and Snapple, Bratz cosmetics and toothpaste featuring characters from Blues Clues, Looney Tunes and Dragon Tales.[82]

We discuss marketing to children in more detail in Chapter 6 in our discussion of families.

# SOCIAL STRATIFICATION

We are all familiar with the concept of social class, but most of us would have difficulty explaining our class system to a foreigner. The following quote illustrates the vague nature of social class:

Like it or not, all of us are largely defined, at least in the eyes of others, according to a complex set of criteria—how much we earn, what we do for a living, who our parents are, where and how long we attended school, how we speak, what we wear, where we live, and how we react to the issues of the day. It all adds up to our socioeconomic status, our ranking in U.S. society.[83]

The words *social class* and *social standing* are used interchangeably to mean **societal rank**—*one's position relative to others on one or more dimensions valued by society.* How do we obtain a social standing? Your social standing is a result of characteristics you possess that others in society desire and hold in high esteem. Your education, occupation,

| FIGURE 4–2 | Social Standing Is Derived and Influences Behavior |

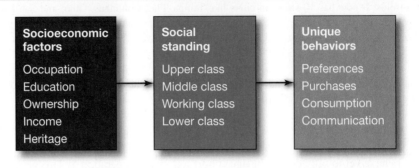

ownership of property, income level, and heritage (racial or ethnic background, parents' status) influence your social standing, as shown in Figure 4–2. Social standing ranges from the lower class, those with few or none of the socioeconomic factors desired by society, to the upper class, who possess many of the socioeconomic characteristics considered by society as desirable. Individuals with different social standings tend to have different needs and consumption patterns. Thus, a **social class system** can be defined as *a hierarchical division of a society into relatively distinct and homogeneous groups with respect to attitudes, values, and lifestyles.*

"Pure" social classes do not exist in the United States or most other industrialized societies. However, it is apparent that these same societies do have hierarchical groups of individuals and that individuals in those groups do exhibit unique behavior patterns that are different from behaviors in other groups.

What exists is *not a set of social classes* but a *series of status continua.*[84] These status continua reflect various dimensions or factors that the overall society values. In an achievement-oriented society such as the United States, *achievement-related factors* constitute the primary status dimensions. Thus, education, occupation, income, and to a lesser extent, quality of residence and place of residence are important status dimensions in the United States. Race and gender are *ascribed* dimensions of social status that are not related to achievement but still influence status in the United States. Likewise, the status of a person's parents is an ascribed status dimension that also exists in the United States. However, heritage is a more important factor in a more traditional society such as England.[85]

The various status dimensions are clearly related to each other. In a functional sense, the status of one's parents influences one's education, which in turn influences occupation that generates income, which sets limits on one's lifestyle, including one's residence. Does this mean that an individual with high status based on one dimension will have high status based on the other dimensions? This is a question of **status crystallization.** The more consistent an individual is on all status dimensions, the greater the degree of status crystallization for the individual. Status crystallization is moderate in the United States. For example, many blue-collar workers (such as plumbers and electricians) earn higher incomes than many professionals (such as public school teachers).

# SOCIAL STRUCTURE IN THE UNITED STATES

The moderate level of status crystallization in the United States supports the contention that a social class system is not a perfect categorization of social position. However, this does not mean that the population cannot be subdivided into status groups whose members share similar lifestyles, at least with respect to particular product categories or activities.

**Upper Americans**
- *Upper-Upper (0.3%).* The "capital S society" world of inherited wealth, aristocratic names.
- *Lower-Upper (1.2%).* The newer social elite, drawn from current professional, corporate leadership.
- *Upper-Middle (12.5%).* The rest of college graduate managers and professionals; lifestyle centers on careers, private clubs, causes, and the arts.

**Middle Americans**
- *Middle Class (32%).* Average-pay white-collar workers and their blue-collar friends; live on "the better side of town," try to "do the proper things."
- *Working Class (38%).* Average-pay blue-collar workers; lead "working-class lifestyle" whatever the income, school background, and job.

**Lower Americans**
- *Upper-Lower (9%).* "A lower group of people but not the lowest"; working, not on welfare; living standard is just above poverty.
- *Lower-Lower (7%).* On welfare, visibly poverty-stricken, usually out of work (or have "the dirtiest jobs").

**TABLE 4–4**

The Coleman–Rainwater Social Class Hierarchy

| Social Class | Percent | Typical Profile | | |
| --- | --- | --- | --- | --- |
| | | Income | Education | Occupation |
| **Upper Americans** | | | | |
| Upper-upper | 0.3% | $600,000 | Master's degree | Board chairman |
| Lower-upper | 1.2 | 450,000 | Master's degree | Corporate president |
| Upper-middle | 12.5 | 150,000 | Medical degree | Physician |
| **Middle Americans** | | | | |
| Middle class | 32.0 | 28,000 | College degree | High school teacher |
| Working class | 38.0 | 15,000 | High school | Assembly worker |
| **Lower Americans** | | | | |
| Upper-lower | 9.0 | 9,000 | Some high school | Janitor |
| Lower-lower | 7.0 | 5,000 | Grade school | Unemployed |

Source: R. P. Coleman, "The Continuing Significance of Social Class in Marketing," *Journal of Consumer Research*, December 1983, p. 267. Copyright 1983 by The University of Chicago. Used by permission.

Furthermore, there are many people with high levels of status crystallization who exhibit many of the behaviors associated with a class system. It is useful for the marketing manager to know the characteristics of these relatively pure class types, even though the descriptions represent a simplified abstraction from reality.

A number of different sets of social classes have been proposed to describe the United States. We will use the one developed by Coleman and Rainwater.[86] In their system, shown in Table 4–4, the *upper class* (14 percent) is divided into three groups primarily by differences in occupation and social affiliations. The *middle class* (70 percent) is divided into a middle class (32 percent) of average-income white- and blue-collar workers living in better neighborhoods and a working class (38 percent) of average-income blue-collar workers who lead a "working-class lifestyle." The *lower class* (16 percent) is divided into two groups, one living just above the poverty level and the other visibly poverty-stricken. Note that the average income associated with each class will have increased, in some cases dramatically, since Table 4–4 was developed. For example, the top 1 percent income group in the United States averages in excess of $1 million, while middle Americans likely fall in the $35,000 to $100,000 range.[87]

The percentage of the American population assigned to each class in the Coleman–Rainwater system closely parallels the way Americans classify themselves.[88] The Coleman–Rainwater groups are described in more detail in the following sections.

## Upper Americans

**The Upper-Upper Class**   Members of the upper-upper social class are aristocratic families who make up the social elite. Members with this level of social status generally are the nucleus of the best country clubs and sponsors of major charitable events. They provide leadership and funds for community and civic activities and often serve as trustees for hospitals, colleges, and civic organizations.

The Kennedy family is a national example of the upper-upper class. Most communities in America have one or more families with significant "old money." These individuals live in excellent homes, drive luxury automobiles, own original art, and travel extensively. They generally stay out of the public spotlight unless it is to enter politics or support a charity or community event.

**The Lower-Upper Class**   The lower-upper class is often referred to as "new rich—the current generation's new successful elite." These families are relatively new in terms of upper-class social status and have not yet been accepted by the upper crust of the community. In some cases, their incomes are greater than those of families in the upper-upper social strata. Bill Gates, founder of Microsoft, and Ted Turner, founder of CNN, are national examples of the lower-upper class. Most communities have one or more families who have acquired great wealth during one generation, many from the high-tech and dot-com boom of the 1990s.

Many members of this group continue to live lifestyles similar to those of the upper-middle class. Other members of the lower-upper class strive to emulate the established upper-upper class. Entrepreneurs, sports stars, and entertainers who suddenly acquire substantial wealth often engage in this type of behavior. However, they are frequently unable to join the same exclusive clubs or command the social respect accorded the true "blue bloods." Many respond by aggressively engaging in **conspicuous consumption;** that is, they purchase and use automobiles, homes, yachts, clothes, and so forth primarily to demonstrate their great wealth.[89] Thus, it is not unusual to read about a star professional athlete who owns 5 or 10 luxury cars, multiple homes, and so forth. These individuals are referred as the **nouveaux riches.** Doing the "in thing" on a grand scale is important to this group. High-status brands and activities are actively sought out by the nouveaux riches.

Although small, these groups serve as important market segments for some products and as a symbol of "the good life" to the upper-middle class. Illustration 4–7 shows a service that would appeal to the upper classes.

**The Upper-Middle Class**   The upper-middle class consists of families who possess neither family status derived from heritage nor unusual wealth. Occupation and education are key aspects of this social stratum, as it consists of successful professionals, independent businesspeople, and corporate managers. As shown in Table 4–4, members of this social class are typically college graduates, many with professional or graduate degrees.

Upper-middle-class individuals tend to be confident and forward-looking. They worry about the ability of their children to have the same lifestyle they enjoy. They realize that their success depends

It's not just a card. It's a choice.℠

A choice to speed up your life.

A choice to slow it down.

*Marquis Jet Card℠ Owners enjoy the quality, consistency & safety of NetJets®, 25 hours at a time. Accomplish more with the best fleet, pilots and service.*
1.866.538.1400 MarquisJet.com

All program flights operated by NetJets® companies under their respective FAR Part 135 Air Carrier Certificates.

**Upward-Pull Strategy Targeted at Middle Class**     **FIGURE 4–3**

| Middle class | | Aspirations | | Prefer | | Positioning |
|---|---|---|---|---|---|---|
| | → | To belong to upper-middle class | → | Products consumed by upper-middle class | → | Upper-class symbolism for middle-class products |

on their careers, which in turn depend on education. As a result, having their children get a sound education from the right schools is very important to them.

This group is highly involved in the arts and charities of their local communities. They belong to private clubs where they tend to be quite active. They are a prime market for financial services that focus on retirement planning, estate planning, and college funding issues. They consume fine homes, expensive automobiles, quality furniture, good wines, and nice resorts. Illustration 4–8 contains an advertisement aimed at this group.

This segment of the U.S. population is highly visible, and many Americans would like to belong to it. Because it is aspired to by many, it is an important positioning variable for some products. Figure 4–3 describes the upward-pull strategy often associated with the *class to mass* approach discussed earlier in the chapter. Illustration 4–9 is an example of the upward-pull strategy as it provides "affordable luxury."

This is an example of an upward-pull strategy—positioning a moderately priced product as one that will allow its users to experience some elements of the upper-middle-class lifestyle.

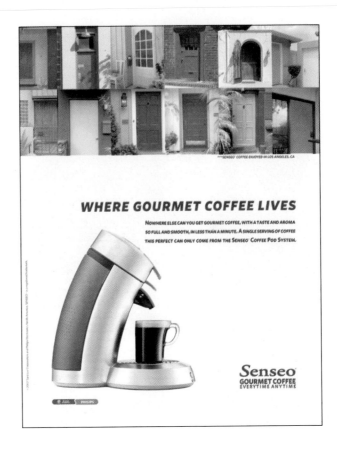

## Middle Americans

**The Middle Class**   The middle class is composed of white-collar workers (office workers, school teachers, lower-level managers) and high-paid blue-collar workers (plumbers, factory supervisors). Thus, the middle class represents the majority of the white-collar group and the top of the blue-collar group. The middle-class core typically has some college education though not a degree, a white-collar or a factory supervisor position, and an average income. Many members of this class feel very insecure because of downsizing, outsourcing, and fluctuations in the economy.[90]

The middle class is concerned about respectability. They care what the neighbors think. They generally live in modest suburban homes. They are deeply concerned about the quality of public schools, crime, drugs, the weakening of "traditional family values," and their family's financial security. Retirement is an increasing concern as firms reduce pension plans and health care costs escalate.

Members of the middle class are likely to get involved in do-it-yourself projects. They represent the primary target market for the goods and services of home improvement centers, garden shops, automotive parts houses, as well as mouthwashes and deodorants. With limited incomes, they must balance their desire for current consumption with aspirations for future security. Illustration 4–10 shows a company meeting the needs of this segment.

**The Working Class**   The working class consists of skilled and semiskilled factory, service, and sales workers. Though some households in this social stratum seek advancement, members are more likely to seek security for and protection of what they already have. This segment suffered seriously during the first half of the 1990s as their average real earnings

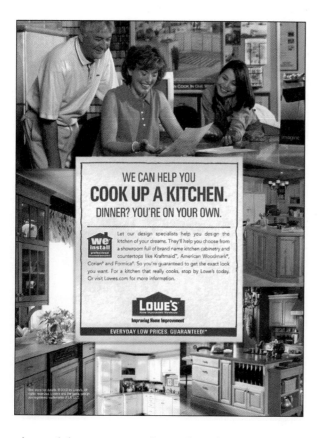

declined. Automation and the movement of manufacturing activities to developing countries also led to economic insecurity. Few of these individuals benefited from the stock market boom of the late 1990s, and many are likely to suffer as a consequence of the most recent economic downturn.

Working-class families live in modest homes or apartments that are often located in marginal urban neighborhoods, decaying suburbs, or rural areas. They are greatly concerned about crime, gangs, drugs, and neighborhood deterioration. They generally cannot afford to move to a different area should their current neighborhood or school become unsafe or otherwise undesirable. With modest education and skill levels, the more marginal members of this class are in danger of falling into one of the lower classes.

Many **working-class aristocrats** dislike the upper-middle class and prefer products and stores positioned at their social-class level.[91] These individuals are proud of their ability to do "real work" and see themselves as the often-unappreciated backbone of America. They are heavy consumers of pickups and campers, hunting equipment, power boats, and beer. Miller Brewing Company gave up attempts to attract a broad audience for its Miller High Life beer. Instead, it is targeting working-class aristocrats with ads that feature bowling alleys, diners, and country music. The ad shown in Illustration 4–11 would appeal to this group.

## Lower Americans

**The Upper-Lower Class**    The upper-lower class consists of individuals who are poorly educated, have very low incomes, and work as unskilled laborers.[92] Most have minimum-wage jobs. The Fair Minimum Wage Act of 2007 took an important step in helping this group by moving the minimum wage to $7.25 per hour by 2009. This is a substantial

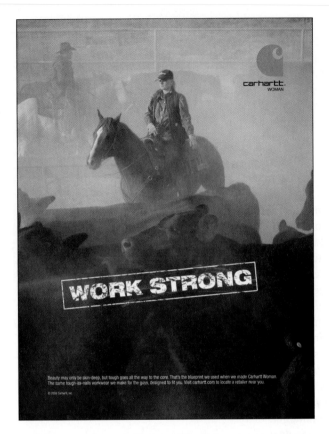

improvement but still means that a full-time, 50-week-a-year minimum-wage job is not enough to keep a family of three above the poverty line. This is a major change from the late 1960s, when the minimum wage would support a family of three. Compounding the problem is that many of these jobs are part-time and few provide benefits such as health insurance or a retirement plan. Consider John Gibson, a 50-year-old part-time janitor in Nashville who makes somewhat more than minimum wage:

"I'd like to work more," John says. However, he is not qualified for many jobs. "I have to make sacrifices but I get by. When I get my check, the first thing I do is pay my rent." John lives alone in a small efficiency apartment. One of the things John sacrifices in order to get by is eating at fast-food restaurants. Although he likes the food and the convenience, a co-worker convinced him that it was much cheaper to prepare food at home. He minimizes his expenses on clothing by shopping at thrift stores such as the one operated by the Salvation Army.

As a part-time employee, he has no company health insurance, but he is now eligible for some coverage from the state of Tennessee. A few years before he had this coverage he was hospitalized. Afterward, his wages were garnished to cover his bills, and he was forced to rely on social service agencies. Today he spends a great deal of his spare time volunteering at these same agencies. He would enjoy golf but is seldom able to play. He has no pension plan or personal insurance and wonders what his retirement years will be like.[93]

Lack of education tends to be a defining characteristic of this group.[94] Members of the upper-lower class live in marginal housing that is often located in depressed and decayed neighborhoods. Crime, drugs, and gangs are often close at hand and represent very real threats. They are concerned about the safety of their families and their children's future. The lack of education, role models, and opportunities often produces despair that can result in harmful consumption, such as cigarettes and alcohol. It may also produce inefficient purchasing and a short-term time focus.[95]

The marketing system has not served this group effectively. They have a particularly difficult time securing financial services, and many do not have bank accounts. This means that they generally must pay a fee for cashing paychecks and other checks. However, research indicates substantial marketing opportunities in this group. They tend to be value-oriented rather than just cost-focused. They tend to be very brand loyal. Firms such as Wal-Mart and Dollar General have done a good and profitable job serving these consumers.[96]

**The Lower-Lower Class**    Members of the lower-lower social stratum have very low incomes and minimal education. This segment of society is often unemployed for long periods of time and is the major recipient of government support and services provided by nonprofit organizations. Andre Hank, as described in Chapter 1 in Consumer Insight 1–2, is an example of an individual who was in the upper-lower class and then wound up in the lower-lower class when he lost his job.

Marketing to the lower classes is frequently controversial. The rent-to-own business flourishes by renting durable goods, such as televisions and refrigerators, to lower-class households who frequently cannot afford to acquire them for cash and lack the credit rating to charge the purchases at regular outlets. While this service appears to meet a real need, the industry is frequently criticized for charging exorbitant interest rates on the purchases.[97]

The marketing of "sin" products to this group is even more controversial. Malt liquors and fortified wines sell heavily in lower-class neighborhoods. However, firms that actively promote such products to this market risk significant negative publicity. When R. J. Reynolds tried to market its Uptown cigarettes to lower-class urban blacks, public protests became so strong that the product was withdrawn. Although some might applaud this outcome, the unstated assumption of the protest is that these individuals lack the ability to make sound consumption decisions and thus require protections that other social classes do not require—an assumption that is certainly controversial.

Other firms are criticized for not marketing to the lower classes. Major retail chains, particularly food chains, and financial firms seldom provide services in lower-class neighborhoods. Critics argue that such businesses have a social responsibility to locate in these areas. The businesses thus criticized respond that this is a problem for all of society and the solution should not be forced on a few firms. However, a few sophisticated chain retailers such as Dollar General Corporation have begun to meet the unique needs of this segment. As one specialist in this area said:

> People with lower household incomes are still consumers. They still have to buy food. They still wear clothing. They still have to take care of their kids.[98]

The challenge for business is to develop marketing strategies that will meet the needs of these consumers efficiently and at a reasonable profit to the firm.

# THE MEASUREMENT OF SOCIAL CLASS

There are two basic approaches to measuring social status: a single-item index and a multi-item index. **Single-item indexes** estimate social status on the basis of a single dimension such as education, income, or occupation. Since an individual's overall status is influenced by several dimensions, single-item indexes are generally less accurate. **Multi-item indexes** take into account numerous variables simultaneously and weight these according to a scheme that reflects societal views. We focus here on the classic multi-item approach of Hollingshead.[99]

**TABLE 4–5**

Hollingshead Index
of Social Position
(ISP)

| Occupation Scale (Weight of 7) | |
|---|---|
| Description | Score |
| Higher executives of large concerns, proprietors, and major professionals | 1 |
| Business managers, proprietors of medium-sized businesses, and lesser professionals | 2 |
| Administrative personnel, owners of small businesses, and minor professionals | 3 |
| Clerical and sales workers, technicians, and owners of little businesses | 4 |
| Skilled manual employees | 5 |
| Machine operators and semiskilled employees | 6 |
| Unskilled employees | 7 |

| Education Scale (Weight of 4) | |
|---|---|
| Description | Score |
| Professional (MA, MS, ME, MD, PhD, LLD, and the like) | 1 |
| Four-year college graduate (BA, BS, BM) | 2 |
| One to three years of college (also business schools) | 3 |
| High school graduate | 4 |
| Ten to eleven years of school (part high school) | 5 |
| Seven to nine years of school | 6 |
| Less than seven years of school | 7 |

ISP score = (Occupation score $\times$ 7) + (Education score $\times$ 4)

| Classification System | |
|---|---|
| Social Strata | Range of Scores |
| Upper | 11–17 |
| Upper-middle | 18–31 |
| Middle | 32–47 |
| Lower-middle | 48–63 |
| Lower | 64–77 |

Source: Adapted from A. B. Hollingshead and F. C. Redlich, *Social Class and Mental Illness* (New York: Wiley, 1958).

The Hollingshead **Index of Social Position (ISP)** is a two-item index that is well developed and widely used. The item scales, weights, formulas, and social-class scores are shown in Table 4–5. Notice how in the United States, occupation is given a higher weight than education. *Why is this?*

It is important to note that multi-item indexes were designed to measure or reflect *an individual's or family's overall social position within a community.* Because of this, it is possible for a high score on one variable to offset a low score on another. Thus, the following three individuals would all be classified as middle class on the ISP scale: (1) someone with an eighth-grade education who is a successful owner of a medium-sized firm; (2) a four-year college graduate working as a salesperson; and (3) a graduate of a junior college working in an administrative position in the civil service. All of these individuals may well have similar standing in the community. However, it seems likely that their consumption processes for at least some products will differ, pointing out the fact that overall status may mask potentially useful associations between individual status dimensions and the consumption process for particular products.

Another important aspect of these measures is that *they were developed before the rapid expansion of the role of women.* No scale has been developed that fully accounts for the new reality of dual sources of status (both men and women) for a household.

Finally, it is important to realize that in some cases, the individual demographic variables that make up social status (multi-item indexes) may be of more relevance in answering a specific marketing question. For example, media habits might relate most closely to education while leisure activities might relate most closely to occupation. In these instances, marketers are better off using these direct measures of demographics than the more global measures of status. Only when an overall indication of an individual or family's status is of particular relevance should measures such as the ISP be used. Recent research does suggest that social class is still an important determinant of various consumer behaviors in the United States.[100]

# SOCIAL STRATIFICATION AND MARKETING STRATEGY

While social stratification does not explain all consumption behaviors, it is certainly relevant for some product categories. For clear evidence of this, visit a furniture store in a working-class neighborhood and then an upper-class store such as Ethan Allen Galleries.

The consumption of imported wine, liqueurs, and original art varies with social class. Beer is consumed across all social classes, but Michelob is more popular at the upper end and Pabst is more popular at the lower end. A product or brand may have different meanings to members of different social strata. Blue jeans may serve as economical, functional clothing items to working-class members and as stylish, self-expressive items to upper-class individuals. Likewise, different purchase motivations for the same product may exist between social strata. Individuals in higher social classes use credit cards for convenience (they pay off the entire balance each month); individuals in lower social classes use them for installment purchases (they do not pay off the entire bill at the end of each month).

Figure 4–4 on the next page illustrates how Anheuser-Busch covers a large portion of the U.S. population by carefully positioning three different brands. While Anheuser-Busch's product portfolio has expanded since the research underlying Figure 4–4 was conducted, the major brands, themes, and social class connections still ring true. Table 4–6 indicates that consumers perceive these brands very clearly in terms of social class.

| | Social Class* | | | | | | TABLE 4–6 |
| Brand | Upper/Upper Middle | Middle | Lower Middle | Upper Lower/Lower | All Classes | | Perceived Social Class Appeal of Various Beer Brands |
|---|---|---|---|---|---|---|---|
| Coors | 22% | 54% | 16% | 2% | 3% | | |
| Budweiser | 4 | 46 | 37 | 7 | 4 | | |
| Miller | 14 | 50 | 22 | 6 | 6 | | |
| Michelob | 67 | 23 | 4 | 1 | 2 | | |
| Old Style† | 3 | 33 | 36 | 22 | 1 | | |
| Bud Light | 22 | 53 | 14 | 3 | 5 | | |
| Heineken | 88 | 9 | 1 | — | 1 | | |

*Percentage classifying the brand as most appropriate for a particular social class.
† Local beer on tap.

Source: K. Grønhaug and P. S. Trapp, "Perceived Social Class Appeals of Branded Goods," *Journal of Consumer Marketing,* Winter 1989, p. 27.

**FIGURE 4–4**    Marketing Classic: Anheuser-Busch Positioning to Social Class Segments

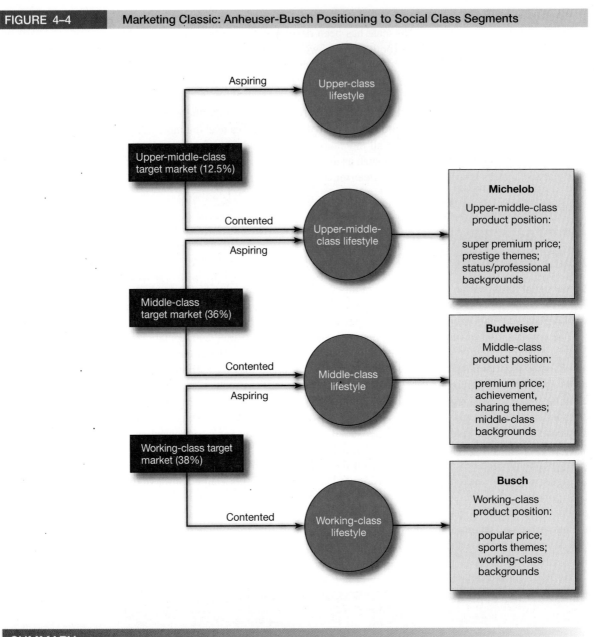

## SUMMARY

American society is described in part by its *demographics,* which include a population's size, distribution, and structure. The structure of a population refers to its age, income, education, and occupation makeup. Demographics are not static. At present, the rate of population growth is moderate, average age is increasing, southern and western regions are growing, and the workforce contains more women and white-collar workers than ever before. Marketers frequently segment markets based on a combination of two or more demographic descriptors.

In addition to actual measures of age and income, subjective measures can provide additional understanding of consumption. *Cognitive age* is how old a person feels. Many older consumers feel 10 to 15 years younger than their chronological age. *Subjective discretionary income,* which measures how much money consumers feel they have available for nonessentials, has been found to be a better predictor of some purchases than actual income.

An *age cohort* or *generation* is a group of persons who have experienced a common social, political, historical, and economic environment. *Cohort analysis* is the process of describing and explaining the attitudes, values, and behaviors of an age group as well as predicting its future attitudes, values, and behaviors. There are six major generations functioning in America today—pre-Depression, Depression, baby boom, Generation X, Generation Y, and Tweens.

A *social class system* is defined as the hierarchical division of a society into relatively permanent and homogeneous groups with respect to attitudes, values, and lifestyles. A tightly defined social class system does not exist in the United States. What does seem to exist is a series of status continua that reflect various dimensions or factors that the overall society values. Educa-

tion, occupation, income, and, to a lesser extent, type of residence are important status dimensions in this country. *Status crystallization* refers to the consistency of individuals and families on all relevant status dimensions (e.g., high income and high educational level).

Although pure social classes do not exist in the United States, it is useful for marketing managers to know and understand the general characteristics of major social classes. Using Coleman and Rainwater's system, we described American society in terms of seven major categories—*upper-upper, lower-upper, upper-middle, middle, working class, upper-lower,* and *lower-lower.*

There are two basic approaches to the measurement of social classes: (1) Use a combination of several dimensions, a *multi-item index;* or (2) use a single dimension, a *single-item index.* Multi-item indexes are designed to measure an individual's overall rank or social position within the community.

## KEY TERMS

Age cohort  124
Class to mass  121
Cognitive age  124
Cohort analysis  124
Conspicuous consumption  138
Consumer literacy  120
Demographics  116

Digital Savvy  115
Generation  124
Gerontographics  125
Index of Social Position (ISP)  144
Mature market  125
Multi-item indexes  143
Nouveaux riches  138

Single-item indexes  143
Social class system  136
Societal rank  135
Status crystallization  136
Subjective discretionary income
  (SDI)  122
Working-class aristocrats  141

## INTERNET EXERCISES

1. Use the Internet to describe the following characteristics of the U.S. population in 2020 (www.census .gov is a good place to start). How will this differ from the way it is today? What are the marketing strategy implications of these shifts?
   a. Total size and size by major census region
   b. Age distribution
   c. Education level
   d. Occupation structure
   e. Income level

2. Evaluate the services and data provided at www .easidemographics.com.

3. Visit www.freedemographics.com. Register for their free demographic information. Pick two

cities of interest and use the site to develop a demographic comparison using the most recent data available.

4. Compare and evaluate two teen Web sites such as about.com/teens, delias.com, alloy.com, teenpeople .com, gurl.com, bolt.com, and seventeen.com.

5. Visit the Tripod Web site (www.tripod.lycos.com). Evaluate this site in terms of its potential appeal to Generation X.

6. Visit AARP'S Web site (www.aarp.org). On the basis of what you read there, do you think AARP is doing a good job of appealing to baby boomers?

## DDB LIFE STYLE STUDY™ DATA ANALYSES

1. Which demographic variables are most closely associated with heavier consumption of the following? What would explain this association? Which contributes most to causing the consumption? (See Tables 1A through 6A.)
   a. Dessert
   b. DVD rental
   c. Fast-food restaurant
   d. Read books/articles about health

2. Which demographic variables are most closely associated with ownership of the following? What would explain this association? Which contributes most to causing the ownership? (See Tables 1A through 6A.)
   a. MP3 player
   b. Personal computer
   c. Individual retirement account
   d. Dog

3. Examine the DDB data in Tables 1A through 6A. Which demographic variables are most closely associated with watching the following types of shows on a regular basis? What would explain this association? Which contributes most to causing this enjoyment?
   a. News
   b. Children's shows
   c. Home improvement
   d. Sports

4. Which demographic variables are most closely associated with the following? What would explain this association? Which contributes most to causing each? (See Tables 1B through 6B.)
   a. Working hard
   b. View shopping as a form of entertainment
   c. View self as tech savvy
   d. Purchase clothes online

5. Using the DDB data in Table 5A, create age groups that approximate the generations described in the text. For which products and activities are there the greatest differences in heavier consumption across the generations? Why is this the case?

6. Using the DDB data in Table 5A, examine how actual age and cognitive age relate (positive, negative, no relationship) to the following behaviors. Compare and contrast the effects of actual age and cognitive age. Explain any similarities and differences you find.
   a. Read books/magazines about health
   b. Visit gourmet coffee bar
   c. Own cell phone
   d. Own personal computer
   e. Watch sports regularly

## REVIEW QUESTIONS

1. What are demographics?
2. Why is population growth an important concept for marketers?
3. What trend(s) characterizes the occupational structure of the United States?
4. What trend(s) characterizes the level of education in the United States?
5. What trend(s) characterizes the level of income in the United States?
6. What is meant by subjective discretionary income? How does it affect purchases?
7. What trend(s) characterizes the age distribution of the American population?
8. What is cognitive age? How is it measured?
9. What is an *age cohort*? A *cohort analysis*?
10. Describe each of the major generations in America.
11. What is a social class system?
12. What is meant by the statement, "What exists is not a set of social classes but a series of status continua"?
13. What underlying cultural value determines most of the status dimensions in the United States?
14. What is meant by *status crystallization*? Is the degree of status crystallization relatively high or low in the United States? Explain.
15. Briefly describe the primary characteristics of each of the classes described in the text (assume a high level of status crystallization).
16. What is meant by the phrase *class to mass* and how does it relate to *upward-pull*?

17. What ethical issues arise in marketing to the lower social classes?
18. What are the two basic approaches used by marketers to measure social class?

19. What are the advantages of multi-item indexes? The disadvantages?
20. Describe the Hollingshead Index of Social Position. Why is occupation weighted more heavily? Would this weighting hold in other cultures?

## DISCUSSION QUESTIONS

21. Which demographic shifts, if any, do you feel will have a noticeable impact on the market for the following in the next 10 years? Justify your answer.
    a. Upscale restaurants
    b. Botox treatments
    c. Prescription drugs
    d. Internet shopping
    e. Green products
    f. Newspapers
    g. Charity contributions
22. Given the projected changes in America's demographics, name five products that will face increasing demand and five that will face declining demand.
23. Why do the regional differences shown in Figure 4–1 exist? What are the implications of such differences for marketers of products such as soft drinks?
24. Will the increasing median age of our population affect the general tone of our society? In what ways?
25. Respond to the questions in Consumer Insight 4–1.
26. Which demographic variable, if any, is most related to the following?
    a. Watching extreme sports on TV
    b. Skiing
    c. International travel
    d. Motorcycle ownership
    e. Spa treatments
    f. Going to a NASCAR event
27. Describe how each of the following firm's product managers should approach the (i) pre-Depression generation, (ii) Depression generation, (iii) baby boom generation, (iv) Generation X, (v) Generation Y, and (vi) Tweens.
    a. Pepsi
    b. Panera Bread
    c. The Golf Channel
    d. About.com
    e. The Humane Society

f. iPod
g. Google.com
h. Crest Whitener System

28. Respond to the questions in Consumer Insight 4–2.
29. How will your lifestyle differ from your parents' when you are your parents' age?
30. How could a knowledge of social stratification be used in the development of a marketing strategy for the following?
    a. Boots
    b. Expensive jewelry
    c. Fishing
    d. Breakfast cereal
    e. Museum attendance
    f. Habitat for Humanity
31. Do you think the United States is becoming more or less stratified over time?
32. Do your parents have a high or low level of status crystallization? Explain.
33. Based on the Hollingshead two-item index, what social class would your father be in? Your mother? What class will you be in at their age?
34. Name two products for which each of the three following demographic variables would be most influential in determining consumption. If you could combine two of the three, which would be the second demographic you would add to each? Justify your answer.
    a. Income
    b. Education
    c. Occupation
35. Name three products for which subjective discretionary income might be a better predictor of consumption than actual income. Justify your answer.
36. How do you feel about each of the ethical issues or controversies the text describes with respect to marketing to the lower classes? What other ethical issues do you see in this area?

37. Is it ethical for marketers to use the mass media to promote products that most members of the lower classes and working class cannot afford?

38. Would your answer to question 37 change if the products were limited to children's toys?

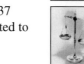

39. Name five products for which the upward-pull strategy shown in Figure 4–3 would be appropriate. Name five for which it would be inappropriate. Justify your answers.

40. What causes the results shown in Table 4–6?

## APPLICATION ACTIVITIES

41. On the basis of the demographics of devoted coffee shop patrons (p. 116), select two magazines in which the industry should advertise (use Standard Rate and Data [SRDS], Mediamark, or Simmons Research Bureau data). Justify your answer.

42. Interview a salesperson at the following locations and obtain a description of the average purchaser in demographic terms. Are the demographic shifts predicted in the text going to increase or decrease the size of this average-purchaser segment?
    a. Volvo dealership
    b. Electronics store
    c. Life insurance agent (vacation travel)
    d. Express
    e. Harley-Davidson dealership
    f. Pet store

43. Using Standard Rate and Data, Mediamark, or Simmons Research Bureau studies, pick three magazines that are oriented toward the different groups listed below. Analyze the differences in the products advertised and in the types of ads.
    a. Income groups
    b. Age groups
    c. Occupation groups
    d. Education levels

44. Interview three people over 50. Measure their cognitive age and the variables that presumably influence it. Do the variables appear to "cause" cognitive age? Try to ascertain if cognitive age or their chronological age is most influential on their consumption behavior.

45. Interview two members of the following generations. Determine the extent to which they feel the text description of their generation is accurate and how they think their generation differs from the larger society. Also determine what they think about how they are portrayed in the mass media and how well they are served by business today.
    a. Pre-Depression
    b. Depression
    c. Baby boom
    d. Generation X
    e. Generation Y
    f. Tween

46. Interview a salesperson from an expensive, moderate, and inexpensive outlet for the following. Ascertain their perceptions of the social classes or status of their customers. Determine if their sales approach differs with differing classes.
    a. Men's clothing
    b. Women's clothing
    c. Furniture
    d. Wine

47. Examine a variety of magazines/newspapers and clip or copy an advertisement that positions a product as appropriate for each of the seven social classes described in the text (one ad per class). Explain how each ad appeals to that class.

48. Interview an unskilled worker, schoolteacher, retail clerk, and successful businessperson all in their 30s or 40s. Measure their social status using one of the multi-item measurement devices. Evaluate their status crystallization.

49. Visit a bowling alley and a golf course parking lot. Analyze the differences in the types of cars, dress, and behaviors of those patronizing these two sports.

50. Volunteer to work two days or evenings at a homeless shelter, soup kitchen, or other program aimed at very low income families. Write a brief report on your experiences and reactions.

# REFERENCES

1. Consumer Insight 4–1 is based on "Understanding the Digital Savvy Consumer," *Scarborough Research,* 2008, www.scarborough.com.

2. See, e.g., M. R. Stafford, "Demographic Discriminators of Service Quality in the Banking Industry," *Journal of Services Marketing* 4 (1996), pp. 6–22; and I. M. Rosa-Diaz, "Price Knowledge," *Journal of Product and Brand Management* 13, no. 6 (2004), pp. 406–28.

3. K. Dawidowska, "Caffeine Overload," *American Demographics,* April 2002, p. 16.

4. B. E. Hamilton, J. A. Martin, and S. J. Ventura, "Births: Preliminary Data for 2006," *National Vital Statistics Reports,* December 5, 2007, www.cdc.gov. accessed August 22, 2008, and information from the Centers for Disease Control and Prevention, www.cdc.gov.

5. U.S. Census Bureau, Population Division, Interim State Population Projections, April 21, 2005.

6. P. Mergenhagen, "What Can Minimum Wage Buy?" *American Demographics,* January 1996, pp. 32–36; and W. O'Hare and J. Schwartz, "One Step Forward, Two Steps Back," *American Demographics,* September 1997, pp. 53–56.

7. "Mean Earnings by Highest Degree Earned: 2005," *Education* (Washington, DC: U.S. Bureau of the Census, 2008), Table 220.

8. See, e.g., M. Mittila, H. Karjaluoto, and T. Pento, "Internet Banking Adoption among Mature Consumers," *Journal of Services Marketing* 17, no. 5 (2003), pp. 514–28; and V. Mittal, W. A. Kamakura, and R. Govind, "Geographic Patterns in Customer Service and Satisfaction," *Journal of Marketing,* July 2004, pp. 48–62.

9. See A. D. Mathios, "Socioeconomic Factors, Nutrition, and Food Choice," *Journal of Public Policy & Marketing,* Spring 1996, pp. 45–54.

10. N. R. Adkins and J. L. Ozanne, "The Low Literate Consumer," *Journal of Consumer Research,* June 2005, pp. 93–105. See also J. L. Harrison-Walker, "The Import of Illiteracy to Marketing Communication," *Journal of Consumer Marketing* 12, no. 1 (1995), pp. 50–62; and H. Jae and D. DelVecchio, "Decision-Making by Low-Literacy Consumers in the Presence of Point-of-Purchase Information," *Journal of Consumer Affairs* 38, no. 2 (2004), pp. 342–354.

11. S. Fulwood III, "Americans Draw Fatter Paychecks," *(Eugene, OR) Register-Guard,* September 27, 1996, p. 1; and E. Kacapyr, "Are You Middle Class?" *American Demographics,* October 1996, pp. 31–35.

12. E. Saez, "Striking It Richer: The Evolution of Top Incomes in the United States," *Pathways Magazine,* Stanford Center for the Study of Poverty and Inequality, Winter 2008, pp. 6–7; updates and data tables available at http://elsa.berkeley.edu/~saez.

13. See, e.g., P. R. La Monica, "Welcome to the 'Recession,'" *CNNMoney.com,* May 27, 2008; and T. Luhby, "Making a Good Living, But Still Feeling Strapped," *CNNMoney.com,* May 28, 2008.

14. D. Gross, "The Latte Era Grinds Down," *Newsweek,* October 22, 2007, pp. 46–47.

15. Ibid.

16. E. Chuck, "Leasing Luxury," *MSNBC.com,* October 31, 2006, www.msnbc.msn.com, accessed June 1, 2008.

17. For an example, see F. J. Mulhern, J. D. Williams, and R. P. Leone, "Variability of Brand Price Elasticities across Retail Stores," *Journal of Retailing* 3 (1998), pp. 427–45.

18. Consumer confidence indexes also consider the subjective nature of spending and represent "leading indicators" of consumer spending. For a discussion, see M. J. Weiss, "Inside Consumer Confidence Surveys," *American Demographics,* February 2003, pp. 22–29.

19. T. C. O'Guinn and W. D. Wells, "Subjective Discretionary Income," *Marketing Research,* March 1989, pp. 32–41; see also P. L. Wachtel and S. J. Blatt, "Perceptions of Economic Needs and of Anticipated Future Income," *Journal of Economic Psychology,* September 1990, pp. 403–15; and J. R. Rossiter, "'Spending Power' and the Subjective Discretionary Income (SDI) Scale," *Advances in Consumer Research,* vol. 22, ed. F. R. Kardes and M. Sujan (Provo, UT: Association for Consumer Research, 1995), pp. 236–40.

20. P. L. Alreck, "Consumer Age Role Norms," *Psychology & Marketing,* October 2000, pp. 891–909.

21. P. Henry, "Modes of Thought That Vary Systematically with Both Social Class and Age," *Psychology & Marketing,* May 2000, pp. 421–40.

22. For example, see R. Gardyn, "Shopping Attitudes by Life Stage," *American Demographics,* November 2002, p. 33; and D. M. Phillips and J. L. Stanton, "Age-related Differences in Advertising," *Journal of Targeting, Measurement and Analysis for Marketing* 13, no. 1 (2004), pp. 7–20.

23. "Resident Population Projections by Sex and Age: 2010 to 2050," *Statistical Abstract of the United States 2008* (Washington, DC: U.S. Bureau of the Census, 2008), Table 10.

24. P. Sloan and J. Neff, "With Aging Boomers in Mind, P&G, Den-Mat Plan Launches," *Advertising Age,* April 13, 1998, p. 3.

25. See K. P. Gwinner and N. Stephens, "Testing the Implied Mediational Role of Cognitive Age," *Psychology & Marketing,* October 2001, pp. 1031–48; and A. Mathur and G. P. Moschis, "Antecedents of Cognitive Age," *Psychology & Marketing,* December 2005, pp. 969–94.

26. S. Van Auken, T. E. Barry, and R. P. Bagozzi, "A Cross-Country Construct Validation of Cognitive Age," *Journal of the Academy of Marketing Science,* Summer 2006, pp. 439–55.

27. See A. S. Wellner, "Generational Divide," *American Demographics,* October 2000, pp. 53–58.

28. A. Rindfleisch, "Cohort Generational Influences on Consumer Socialization," in *Advances in Consumer Research,* vol. 21, ed. C. T. Allen and D. R. John (Provo, UT: Association for Consumer Research, 1994), pp. 470–76; and R. T. Rust and K. W. Y. Yeung, "Tracking the Age Wave," *Advances in Consumer Research,* vol. 22, ed. Kardes and Sujan, pp. 680–85.

29. For a detailed treatment, see J. W. Smith and A. Clurman, *Rocking the Ages* (New York: Harper Business, 1997).

30. See N. Long, "Broken Down by Age and Sex," *Journal of the Market Research Society,* April 1998, pp. 73–91; and G. P. Moschis, "Life Stages of the Mature Market," *American Demographics,* September 1996, pp. 44–51.

31. L. L. Price, E. J. Arnould, and C. F. Curasi, "Older Consumers' Disposition of Special Possessions," *Journal of Consumer Research,* September 2000, p. 192.

32. See C. Yoon, "Age Differences in Consumers' Processing Strategies," *Journal of Consumer Research,* December 1997, pp. 329–40; S. Law, S. A. Hawkins, and F. I. M. Craik, "Repetition-Induced Belief in the Elderly," *Journal of Consumer Research,* September 1998, pp. 91–107; G. P. Moschis, "Consumer Behavior in Later Life," *Research in Consumer Behavior* 9 (2000), pp. 103–28; and G. P. Moschis, "Marketing to Older Adults," *Journal of Consumer Marketing* 20, no. 6 (2003), pp. 516–25.

33. P. Francese, "The Exotic Travel Boom," *American Demographics,* June 2002, pp. 48–49.

34. Moschis, "Life Stages of the Mature Market"; Moschis, "Marketing to Older Adults"; G. P. Moschis, C. F. Curasi, and D. Bellenger, "Restaurant-Selection Preferences of Mature Consumers," *Cornell Hotel and Restaurant Administration Quarterly,* August 2003, pp. 51–60; and G. P. Moschis, C. F. Curasi, and D. Bellenger, "Patronage Motives of Mature Consumers in the Selection of Food and Grocery Stores," *Journal of Consumer Marketing* 21, no. 2 (2004), pp. 123–33. For an alternative segmentation scheme, see C. M. Morgan and D. J. Levy, "The Boomer Attitude," *American Demographics,* October 2002, pp. 42–45.

35. J. Schleimer, "Active Adults Uncovered," *Builder,* February 2001, pp. 336–40.

36. M. J. Weiss, "Great Expectations," *American Demographics,* May 2003, pp. 26–35.

37. K. Parker, "Reaping What They've Sown," *American Demographics,* December 1999, pp. 34–38; and R. G. Javalgi, E. G. Thomas, and S. R. Rao, "Meeting the Needs of the Elderly in the Financial Services Market," *Journal of Professional Services Marketing* 2, no. 2 (2000), pp. 87–105.

38. Table adapted from G. P. Moschis, D. N. Bellenger, and C. F. Curasi, "What Influences the Mature Consumer?" *Marketing Health Services,* Winter 2003, p. 19.

39. Weiss, "Great Expectations."

40. J. Saranow, "Online Deaccessioning," *The Wall Street Journal,* June 28, 2004, pp. B1–B2.

41. C. Gibson, "The Four Baby Booms," *American Demographics,* November 1993, pp. 36–41; and P. Braus, "The Baby Boom at Mid-Decade," *American Demographics,* April 1995, pp. 40–45. For an alternative look at younger versus older baby boomers, see T. Reisenwitz and R. Iyer, "A Comparison of Younger and Older Baby Boomers," *Journal of Consumer Marketing* 24, no. 4 (2007), pp. 202–13.

42. *U.S. Baby Boomer Attitudes and Opportunities* (Rockville: Packaged Facts, June 2008).

43. J. Raymond, "The Joy of Empty Nesting," *American Demographics,* May 2000, pp. 49–54; P. Francese, "Big Spenders," *American Demographics,* September 2001, pp. 30–31; P. Francese, "The Coming Boom in Second-Home Ownership," *American Demographics,* October 2001, pp. 26–27; S. Yin, "More at Home on the Road," *American Demographics,* June 2003,

44. *U.S. Baby Boomer Attitudes and Opportunities,* Packaged Facts.

45. P. Paul, "Targeting Boomers," *American Demographics,* March 2003, pp. 24–26.

46. See, e.g., "Online Health Information Poised to Become Important for Seniors," press release, Kaiser Family Foundation, January 12, 2005, www.kff.org; and "Demographics of Internet Users," *Pew Internet & American Life Project,* 2007.

47. Francese, "The Exotic Travel Boom."

48. See R. Gardyn, "Retirement Redefined," *American Demographics,* November 2000, pp. 52–57.

49. P. Francese, "Working Women," *American Demographics,* March 2003, pp. 40–41.

50. J. Raymond, "Senior Living," *American Demographics,* November 2000, pp. 58–63.

51. L. Singhania, "Boomers Spend Big on Skin," *(Eugene, OR) Register-Guard,* February 27, 2002, p. E1; see also J. Taylor, "A Second Coming of Age," *American Demographics,* June 2004, pp. 36–38.

52. D. Goodman, "Special K Drops Thin Models for Health Theme," *Marketing News,* March 2, 1998, p. 8.

53. K. Greene, "Marketing Surprise," *The Wall Street Journal,* April 6, 2004, pp. A1, 12.

54. N. Zill and J. Robinson, "The Generation X Difference," *American Demographics,* April 1995, pp. 24–33.

55. Ibid.

56. C. Reynolds, "Gen X," *American Demographics,* May 2004, pp. 8–9.

57. "Farther ALONG the X Axis," *American Demographics,* May 2004, pp. 20–24.

58. J. Engebretson, "Odd Gen Out," *American Demographics,* May 2004, pp. 14–17; B. Barnes, "TV Ratings Show Stable Viewership by Young Males," *The Wall Street Journal,* May 27, 2004, p. B6; and C. Atkinson, "NBC's Grip on Prime Time Slips as Young Viewers Flee," *Advertising Age,* November 8, 2004, pp. 4, 65.

59. P. Francese, "In the Shadow of the Boom," *American Demographics,* May 2004, pp. 40–41.

60. J. Halliday, "Volvo Goes After Younger Buyers," *Advertising Age,* January 19, 2004, p. 12.

61. M. Grimm, "Insurance Gets Hip," *American Demographics,* January 2002, pp. 48–49.

62. "P. Diddy Helps Pepsi Win the Super Bowl Ad Wars among Young Adults," *STRATEGiY,* press release, February 14, 2005, www.strategiy.com.

63. For a discussion of the consequences of this, see A. Rindfleisch, J. E. Burroughs, and F. Denton, "Family Structure, Materialism, and Compulsive Consumption," *Journal of Consumer Research,* March 1997, pp. 312–25.

64. P. Paul, "Getting inside Gen Y," *American Demographics,* September 2001, pp. 43–49.

65. J. Napoli and M. T. Ewing, "The Net Generation," *Journal of International Consumer Marketing* 13, no. 1 (2001), pp. 21–34.

66. "Demographics of Internet Users," *Pew Internet & American Life Project,* 2007, http://pewinternet.org, accessed June 2, 2008.

67. N. R. Brier, "Coming of Age," *American Demographics,* November 2004, pp. 16–19.

68. C. La Ferle, S. M. Edwards, and W. Lee, "Teens' Use of Traditional Media and the Internet," *Journal of Advertising Research,* May 2000, pp. 55–65; and H. Fattah and P. Paul, "Gaming Gets Serious," *American Demographics,* May 2002, pp. 38–43.

69. M. Spiegler, "Marketing Street Culture," *American Demographics,* November 1996, pp. 29–34; and J. D. Zbar, "Hispanic Teens Set Urban Beat," *Advertising Age,* June 25, 2001, p. S6.

70. N. Shepherdson, "New Kids on the Lot," *American Demographics,* January 2000, p. 47.

71. M. Harvey, "Let's Hear it for the Boys," *American Demographics,* August 2000, p. 30; and "TRU Projects Teens Will Spend $169 Billion in 2004," TRU, press release, December 1, 2004.

72. P. Underhill, *Call of the Mall* (New York: Simon and Schuster, 2004), p. 160; see also D. L. Haytko and J. Baker, "It's All at the Mall," *Journal of Retailing* 80 (2004), pp. 67–83.

73. D. Chaplin, "The Truth Hurts," *American Demographics,* April 1999, pp. 68–69; for discussion of other issues related to Generation Y and advertising, see Y. Bao and A. T. Shao, "Nonconformity Advertising to Teens," *Journal of Advertising Research,* May–June 2002, pp. 56–65; and A. J. Bush, C. A. Martin, and V. D. Bush, "Sports Celebrity Influence on the Behavioral Intentions of Generation Y," *Journal of Advertising Research,* March 2004, pp. 108–18.

74. K. Cleland, "Action Sports Form Fabric of Generation," *Advertising Age,* April 16, 2001, p. S22.

75. Y. Moroz, "Image and Personality Key to Branding Gen Y Appeal," *Retailing Today,* January 7, 2008, pp. 5, 26.

76. N. Shirouzu, "Scion Plays Hip-Hop Impresario to Impress Younger Drivers," *The Wall Street Journal Online,* October 5, 2004, www.wsj.com.

77. P. Paul, "Echo Boomerang," *American Demographics,* June 2001, pp. 45–49; and A. Merrick, "Gap's Greatest Generation?" *The Wall Street Journal Online,* September 15, 2004, www.wsj.com.

78. S. Kang, "Chasing Generation Y," *The Wall Street Journal,* September 1, 2006, p. A11.

79. *The U.S. Tweens and Young Teens Market* (New York: Packaged Facts, May 2005).

80. "Marriages and Divorces," *Statistical Abstract of the United States 2008* (Washington, DC: U.S. Bureau of the Census, 2008), Table 121; and "The U.S. Tweens and Young Teens Market," Packaged Facts.

81. *The U.S. Tweens and Young Teens Market,* Packaged Facts. See also L. J. Seymour, "Tweens 'R' Shoppers," *The New York Times,* April 22, 2007, www.nytimes.com, accessed June 3, 2008.

82. S. Thompson, "Cosmetic Change," *Advertising Age,* June 28, 2004, p. 4.

83. K. Labich, "Class in America," *Fortune,* February 7, 1994, p. 114.

84. J. E. Fisher, "Social Class and Consumer Behavior," in *Advances in Consumer Research,* vol. 14, ed. M. Wallendorf and P. Anderson (Provo, UT: Association for Consumer Research, 1987), pp. 492–96.

85. See R. P. Heath, "The New Working Class," *American Demographics,* January 1998, pp. 51–55.

86. R. Coleman, "The Continuing Significance of Social Class in Marketing," *Journal of Consumer Research,* December 1983, p. 265. For a recent discussion of social class in America, see J. Scott and D. Leonhardt, "Shadowy Lines That Still Divide," *The New York Times,* May 15, 2005, www.nytimes.com, accessed May 28, 2008.

87. R. Greenstein and I. Shapiro, *The New Definitive CBO Data on Income and Tax Trends,* Report by the Center on Budget and Policy Priorities, September 23, 2003, www.cbpp.org; and G. Prante, "New Census Data on Income Gives a Welcome Dose of Fact Checking to 'Middle-Class' Rhetoric," *Tax Foundation,* September 11, 2007, www.taxfoundation.org, accessed June 3, 2008.

88. See Heath, "The New Working Class." See also E. Sivadas, G. Mathew, and D. J. Curry," A Preliminary Examination of the Continuing Significance of Social Class to Marketing," *Journal of Consumer Marketing* 14, no. 6 (1997), pp. 463–79.

89. See A. M. Kerwin, "Brands Pursue Old, New Money," *Advertising Age,* June 11, 2001, p. S1.

90. See, e.g., R. J. Samuelson, "The End of Entitlement," *Newsweek,* May 26, 2008, p. 39.

91. See J. P. Dickson and D. L. MacLachlan, "Social Distance and Shopping Behavior," *Journal of the Academy of Marketing Science,* Spring 1990, pp. 153–62.

92. See also D. Watson, "In Search of the Poor," *Journal of Economic Psychology* 21 (2000), pp. 495–515.

93. Mergenhagen, "What Can Minimum Wage Buy?"

94. H. Fattah, "The Rising Tide," *American Demographics,* April 2001, pp. 48–53.

95. For a theoretical examination, see P. Henry, "Hope, Hopelessness, and Coping," *Psychology & Marketing,* May 2004, pp. 375–403.

96. Fattah, "The Rising Tide."

97. R. H. Hill, D. L. Ramp, and L. Silver, "The Rent-to-Own Industry and Pricing Disclosure Tactics," *Journal of Public Policy & Marketing,* Spring 1998, pp. 1–10.

98. C. Miller, "The Have-Nots," *Marketing News,* August 1, 1994, p. 2.

99. See A. B. Hollingshead, *Elmstown's Youth* (New York: Wiley, 1949); and W. L. Warner, M. Meeker, and K. Eels, *Social Class in America: A Manual of Procedure for the Measurement of Social Status* (Chicago: Science Research Associates, 1949).

100. E. Sivadas, G. Mathew, and D. J. Curry," A Preliminary Examination of the Continuing Significance of Social Class to Marketing;" and T. G. Williams, "Social Class Influences on Purchase Evaluation Criteria," *Journal of Consumer Marketing* 19, no. 3 (2002), pp. 249–76.

# The Changing American Society: Subcultures

■ American ethnic subcultures continue to lead the way today in fashion, music, and culture.[1] While we are all Americans, those from specific ethnic subcultures bring with them values, heritage, and culture that influences their choices in ways that are different from so-called mainstream America. African Americans, for example, feel a strong need to embrace their specific ethnic subculture as it relates to activities and family traditions. They also are very likely to support retailers who affirm and respect their cultural heritage by carrying ethnic items and employing people who "look like me."

Proctor & Gamble has made a concerted effort to affirm its commitment to black women through a campaign called *My Black is Beautiful.* Research shows that the average African American woman spends three times more on beauty products than the average woman. It also shows that 77 percent are concerned with how African Americans are portrayed in the popular media.

Najoh Tita-Reid, Associate Director of Multicultural Marketing at P&G and brainchild of this effort, explains the motivation as follows:

[It] is an initiative we've created at Proctor & Gamble to celebrate the personal and collective beauty of Black women. *My Black is Beautiful* is a movement designed to ignite a national conversation by, for, and about Black women to effect positive change in the way Black women are reflected in the popular culture. *My Black is Beautiful* encourages African American women to define and promote a beauty standard that is an authentic reflection of their spirit.

The initiative was kicked off at the 2007 BET (Black Entertainment Television) Pre-Awards Dinner. Key aspects of the initiative, which are supported by such P&G brands as Pantene, Pro-V Relaxed & Natural, and Cover Girl Queen Collection, include:

- A 12-page advertorial in *Essence* magazine that includes a personal journal and discussion guide relating to the image, media, and life issues of black women.
- A Web site (www.myblackisbeautiful.com) that provides a forum for discussion as well as information on ongoing initiatives.
- A *My Black is Beautiful* Conversation Tour in various U.S. locations.
- Grants to community-based organizations related to health and education of black women.

Notice how this initiative goes well beyond simply offering products to serve black women or featuring black women in advertising. *My Black is Beautiful* is designed to create a grassroots movement that is facilitated and supported by P&G but whose driving force is ultimately black women all over America coming together in large and small groups around this important issue.

In the previous chapter, we described how changes in American demographics are creating challenges and opportunities for marketers. Another extremely important aspect of the American society is its numerous subcultures, such as the African American subculture described above. Although American society has always contained numerous subcultures, until recently, many marketers treated it as a homogeneous culture based primarily on Western European values. This view of America was never very accurate, and it is even less so today as non-European immigration, differential birthrates, and increased ethnic identification accentuate the heterogeneous nature of our society.

An array of racial, ethnic, nationality, religious, and regional groups or subcultures characterize American society today. These subcultures are growing at different rates and are themselves undergoing change. In this chapter, we describe the more important subcultures in America. We also highlight the marketing strategy implications of a heterogeneous rather than a homogeneous society.

## THE NATURE OF SUBCULTURES

A **subculture** is *a segment of a larger culture whose members share distinguishing values and patterns of behavior.* The unique values and patterns of behavior shared by subculture group members are based on the social history of the group as well as its current situation. Subculture members are also part of the larger culture in which they exist, and they generally share most behaviors and beliefs with the core culture. As Figure 5–1 indicates, the degree to which an individual behaves in a manner unique to a subculture depends on the extent to which the individual identifies with that subculture.

America has traditionally been viewed as a melting pot or a soup bowl. Immigrants from various countries came to America and quickly (at least by the second generation) surrendered their old languages, values, behaviors, and even religions. In their place, they acquired American characteristics that were largely a slight adaptation of Western European, particularly British, features. The base American culture was vast enough that new immigrants did not change the flavor of the mixture to any noticeable extent. Although this is a reasonable approximation of the experience of most Western European immigrants, it

**FIGURE 5–1**          Identification with a Subculture Produces Unique Market Behaviors isn't very accurate for African, Hispanic, Asian, or Arabic immigrants. Nor does it accurately describe the experience of Native Americans.

Today, America is perhaps better described as a salad rather than a melting pot or a soup bowl.[2] When a small amount of a new ingredient is added to a soup, it generally loses its identity completely and blends into the overall flavor of the soup. In a salad, each ingredient retains its own unique identity while adding to the color and flavor of the overall salad.[3] However, even in the salad bowl analogy, we should add a large serving of salad dressing, which represents the core American culture and blends the diverse groups into a cohesive society.[4]

Ethnic groups are the most commonly described subcultures, but religions and geographic regions are also the bases for strong subcultures in the United States. Generations, as described in the previous chapter, also function like subcultures. Thus, *we are all members of several subcultures.* Each subculture may influence different aspects of our lifestyle. Our attitudes toward new products or imported products may be strongly influenced by our regional subculture, our taste in music by our generation subculture, our food preferences by our ethnic subculture, and our alcohol consumption by our religious subculture. The communications manager at Miller Brewing described his firm's view of the influence of ethnicity and age on consumption:

> We used to have an ethnic marketing department up until several years ago. . . . [But now we believe] the things that young Hispanic or young African American or young white people have in common are much stronger and more important than any ethnic difference.[5]

This manager believes that age is more important than ethnicity in influencing the behaviors of the members of his target market for his product. Clearly, however, there are times when adapting specifically to key aspects of a subculture is critical. The ad shown in Illustration 5–1 takes a middle-ground approach. This ad, targeting young Hispanics, speaks to their cultural heritage and youth simultaneously, using Spanish copy.

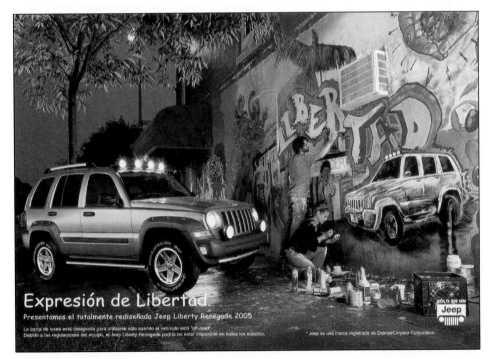

Expresión de Libertad

Presentamos el totalmente rediseñado Jeep Liberty Renegade 2005

**ILLUSTRATION 5–1**

The degree to which an ad needs to be customized for an ethnic audience varies by product and strategy. This ad blends Hispanic and youth themes.

Identifying which subculture, if any, is an important determinant of behavior for a specific product is a key task for marketing managers. In the sections that follow, we describe the major ethnic, religious, and regional subcultures in America. While we will describe the general nature of these subcultures, it must be emphasized that *large variations exist within each subculture.* Our focus in this chapter is on America, but all countries have a variety of subcultures that marketers must consider.

# ETHNIC SUBCULTURES

We define **ethnic subcultures** broadly as *those whose members' unique shared behaviors are based on a common racial, language, or national background.* In this chapter, we describe the major ethnic subcultures separately. However, there are many Americans who identify with more than one ethnic group. Romona Douglas, of white, black, and American Indian descent, described her feelings as follows:

> The assumption is that black people are a certain way, and white people are a particular way, and Asians are a certain way. Well, what about multi-racial families? I don't appreciate a McDonald's commercial with a street-wise black person. That is not me, that is not my upbringing. A lot of marketing campaigns are based on stereotypes of mono-racial communities.[6]

We describe the general characteristics of the major ethnic subcultures as a starting point, recognizing that further understanding can be gained by examining multi-ethnic groups as well. Figure 5–2 provides the current and projected sizes of the major ethnic groups in America. As this figure makes clear, non-European ethnic groups constitute a significant and growing part of our population, from 36 percent in 2010 to 44 percent by 2030. The percentages shown in the figure understate the importance of these ethnic groups to specific geographic regions.[7] Thus, Hispanics are the largest population group in parts of Arizona, California, Florida, New Mexico, and Texas; Asian Americans are the largest group in Honolulu; and African Americans are a majority in parts of the South and urban

| FIGURE 5–2 | Major Ethnic Subcultures in the United States: 2010–2030 |
| --- | --- |

*May be of any race.

‡Includes American Indian, Alaskan Native, Native Hawaiian, Pacific Islander, and two or more races.

Source: "Table 1a. Projected Population of the United States, by Race and Hispanic Origin: 2000 to 2050," *U.S. Interim Projections by Age, Sex, Race, and Hispanic Origin* (Washington, DC: U.S. Bureau of the Census, 2004).

areas in the Northeast and Midwest. In contrast, states such as Maine, Vermont, and West Virginia are more than 95 percent white.

The relatively faster growth rate of non-European groups is due to a higher birthrate among some of these groups and to greater immigration. Immigration has accounted for over a third of the U.S. population growth over the past several decades. Roughly 1 million legal immigrants arrive each year. In 2007, the sources of these immigrants were as follows (the percentages have been relatively stable over time).[8]

| | |
|---|---|
| Asia | 36.4% |
| Mexico | 14.1 |
| Europe | 11.5 |
| Caribbean | 11.3 |
| South America | 10.1 |
| Africa | 9.0 |
| Central America | 5.3 |

The influx of ethnic immigrants not only increases the size of ethnic subcultures, but also reinforces the unique behaviors and attitudes derived from the group's home culture. In the following sections, we describe the major ethnic subcultures. It is critical to remember that *all subcultures are very diverse, and general descriptions do not apply to all of the members.*[9]

Although one's ethnic heritage is a permanent characteristic, its influence is situational. That is, the degree to which a person's consumption is influenced by his or her ethnicity depends on such factors as who he or she is with, where he or she is, and other physical and social cues.[10] Thus, one's ethnicity might play no role in a decision to grab a quick bite for lunch during a business meeting and a large role in deciding what to prepare for family dinner.

In addition, ethnicity is only one factor that influences an individual's behavior. As we saw in the previous chapter, demographic factors also play a role. For example, a 45-year-old black doctor earning $90,000 per year and a 45-year-old white doctor with the same income would probably have more consumption behaviors in common than they would with members of their own race who were low-income service workers. As shown below, the various ethnic groups have distinct demographic profiles.[11] Thus, one must use caution in assuming that observed consumption differences between ethnic groups are caused by their ethnicity. These differences often disappear when demographic variables such as income are held constant.

| | **Whites** | **Blacks** | **Hispanics** | **Asians/Pacific Islanders** |
|---|---|---|---|---|
| Median age (in 2010) | 38 | 31 | 27 | 36 |
| High school or more (25 or older) | 86% | 81% | 59% | 87% |
| Bachelor's or more (25 or older) | 28% | 19% | 12% | 50% |
| Children under 18 | 46% | 56% | 63% | N/A |
| Growth rate (2000–2020) | 13% | 10% | 25% | 11% |
| Median household income | $52,423 | $31,969 | $37,781 | $63,402 |

Examine Table 5–1. Which of these differences are caused mainly by ethnicity or race, and which are caused by other factors?

Astute marketers are aggressively pursuing opportunities created by increased ethnic diversity. However, successful marketing campaigns targeted at different ethnic groups must be based on a thorough understanding of the attitudes and values of each group, which are discussed next.

| TABLE 5–1 | | White | Black | Hispanic |
|---|---|---|---|---|
| **Products** | | | | |
| | Ground coffee | 107 | 67 | 94 |
| | Diet colas | 108 | 62 | 83 |
| | Charcoal | 88 | 171 | 128 |
| | Electric steamer/rice cooker | 90 | 78 | 135 |
| **Activities** | | | | |
| | Bird watching | 114 | 41 | 58 |
| | Auto racing or rallying | 95 | 81 | 118 |
| | Soccer | 92 | 63 | 259 |
| | CD/tape club membership | 88 | 189 | 144 |
| **Shopping** | | | | |
| | Payless Shoes | 79 | 228 | 259 |
| | Talbots | 110 | 53 | 23 |
| | Starbucks | 100 | 56 | 127 |
| | Red Lobster | 94 | 145 | 82 |
| **Media** | | | | |
| | *Cosmopolitan* | 94 | 93 | 129 |
| | *GQ* | 64 | 283 | 111 |
| | *Field and Stream* | 111 | 60 | 50 |
| | MTV | 91 | 133 | 119 |

Ethnic Subcultures and Consumption

Note: 100 = Average level of use, purchase, or consumption.
Source: *SMRB*, 2006.

# AFRICAN AMERICANS

Debra Sandler, director of Flavor Brands (Slice, Mountain Dew, Mug Root Beer, and others) for PepsiCo, recently discussed the differences in marketing to the overall market and marketing to African Americans:

> The strategy does not differ, the tactics differ. For example, if we say we want to be the beverage of choice to all teens, one of the things we have to do if we want to get to where teens are, to where they live and breathe, is to be wherever they are. We want to be available; we also want to be seen as part of their lifestyle. The difference is we may go about that differently for an 18-year-old Anglo male who lives in the suburbs than for an 18-year-old African American male who happens to live in an urban environment.
>
> For example, we did a promotion where we gave away prizes—jet skis and convertibles. One thing we heard loud and clear from the urban teens was that they didn't participate in the promotion because they didn't think the prizes were relevant. So sometimes the tactics must change. . . . While we, African American consumers, are our own segment, we are also very much a part of the mainstream. In fact, in many cases we are driving the mainstream. . . . Again, in reaching teens, if I can produce television creative that appeals to an urban 18-year-old male, chances are that creative will appeal to all teens. It doesn't always work the other way around.[12]

African Americans, or blacks (surveys do not indicate a clear preference for either term among African Americans),[13] constitute 13 percent of the American population. Concentrated in the South and the major metropolitan areas outside the South, African Americans are, on average, younger than the white population and tend to have less education and lower household income levels, though the differences continue to decrease, particularly as a function of education. One-third of black households earn $50,000 or more and nearly 10 percent earn $100,000 or more.[14]

Education, income, and purchasing power have risen dramatically among African Americans over the past several decades, trends that are expected to continue. For example, African Americans represent $799 billion in buying power, which is expected to grow by some 34 percent through 2011.[15] Thus, it is not surprising that marketers are very interested in this group. Jaguar North America targeted the wealthier portion of this group with a direct-mail campaign to a list of 675,000 African Americans between the ages of 35 and 54 with annual incomes over $75,000 who do not own Jaguars. Spike Lee's agency created the mailing, which included a lifestyle-oriented brochure and an eight-minute video. The video showed a black female surgeon and her sculptor husband preparing for a jaunt to Martha's Vineyard from New York's Harlem in their Jaguar. The theme to the campaign was, "It's not luck that got you where you are."

## Consumer Groups

It would be a mistake to treat African Americans as a single segment. Numerous distinct segments exist as a function of demographics, life stage, and lifestyle. For example, Market Segment Research found four segments relating to aspirations, occupation, income, and life stage. The segments were *Contented* (mature and content with life, followers not leaders, not status conscious); *Upwardly Mobile* (active, status-conscious professionals, financially secure, optimistic about future); *Living for the Moment* (young, socially active, carefree, and image conscious); and *Living Day to Day* (low education and income, price conscious, pessimistic about future).[16]

Marketers are also finding important differences in terms of brand and style consciousness. While African Americans are more brand and style conscious than whites, research by Yankelovich finds wide differences *among* African Americans represented by two distinct segments labeled "market leaders" and "market followers":[17]

- *Market leaders* want to be on the cutting edge and to set trends. This group tends to have higher incomes that allow them to buy the "latest and greatest." This group has a relatively strong need to be seen as "hip and cool," and sees brands as communicating their unique style and identity. This group tends not to be price sensitive and tends to be brand loyal.
- *Market followers* tend to follow trends rather than lead the way. Compared with market leaders, this group has less of a need to be seen as "hip and cool," and they are considerably less likely to see brands as an indicator of their style and identity. This group often has financial constraints that make them more conservative, more price sensitive, and less brand loyal.

Generational differences also exist and have important marketing implications.[18] African American Baby Boomers and aging Generation Xers are driving growth in income and purchase power through education and professional achievement. Many of these consumers are migrating to the suburbs surrounding major metropolitan areas.[19] Such changes are creating challenges and opportunities for marketers. Consider the following quote by Pepper Miller, president of Hunter-Miller Group, an African American consulting firm:

> Black Generation Xers spawned one of the greatest marketing and lifestyle phenomena: the Hip Hop Culture. However, not all African American Generation Xers are Hip Hoppers. Yet marketing communications targeting the African American Generation X segment continue to reflect typical and often stereotypical images of Hip Hop's rap culture.[20]

Moreover, the aging Xers are increasingly focused on professional accomplishments and leveraging their higher educations toward higher incomes. The challenge for marketers is how to reflect these ongoing generational changes while still embracing core cultural values.[21]

Obviously, these are just some of the ways that the African American market can be segmented, reflecting the diversity that exists both within and across ethnic subcultures. Marketing strategies that target African Americans as a single market are likely to fail.

## Media Usage

African Americans make greater use of mass media than do whites, have different preferences, and report more influence by mass media ads than do whites.[22] While they consume general media, they often prefer media specifically targeted at African American culture, as shown below in terms of top magazines.

| Black Men's Top 10 Magazines | Black Women's Top 10 Magazines |
|---|---|
| 1. Smartsource | 1. Smartsource |
| 2. Parade | 2. Ebony |
| 3. Ebony | 3. Parade |
| 4. Jet | 4. Jet |
| 5. USA Weekend | 5. Essence |
| 6. Sports Illustrated | 6. USA Weekend |
| 7. Vibe | 7. Vibe |
| 8. Essence | 8. People Weekly |
| 9. Black Enterprise | 9. Woman's Day |
| 10. Source | 10. Better Homes & Gardens |

Source: Simmons Market Research Bureau, *Spring 2003 National Consumer Survey.*

The type of TV programming viewed by blacks and whites has evidenced some convergence in the past several decades. However, as with magazines, differences in TV viewing exist that relate to shows dealing with African American themes, concerns, and issues. Consider comments from an advertiser in the automobile industry who has worked with Black Entertainment Television (BET):

> We've been working with BET for 15 years. There are precious few TV outlets that specifically target the African American audience. BET is far and away the flagship operation for that. What we like about BET is that it has continued to evolve and diversify its programming. The African American market isn't really one big monolithic market, even though that's what people think. There's a lot of diversity in the market. BET's current programming speaks to the old, the young, and everyone in between.[23]

Although African Americans have historically lagged behind the population as a whole in terms of computer ownership and Internet usage, Internet usage is on the rise, and on some online dimensions, such as broadband access, African Americans outstrip the general population. One recent estimate is that 62 percent of African American adults are online, which is lower than the overall rate of around 75 percent. However, factors like education play a major role, with black college graduates having the highest Internet usage, at 93 percent.[24] In addition, African American Web users:[25]

- Spend more time per day surfing (5 hours) compared with the general population (2.9 hours).

- Are more likely to have broadband connections (66 percent) than the general population (53 percent).
- Are more likely than the general population to access the Web for news and information across a number of categories, including general news, health, finances, and sports.
- Prefer a black perspective on news and information.

Not surprisingly, black-focused sites such as NetNoir (www.netnoir.net) and AOL's BlackVoices (www.blackvoices.com) are attracting advertisers such as IBM, Hewlett-Packard, Wells Fargo, Walt Disney, and McDonald's. BlackPlanet.com is currently the largest online community for African Americans. It features news, entertainment, and career information from a black perspective and has over 16 million members.

Clearly, ongoing opportunities for marketing to African Americans can be found in a host of media outlets, some of which are specifically tailored to the needs of this market.

## Marketing to African Americans

Marketing to African Americans should be based on the same principles as marketing to any other group. That is, the market should be analyzed carefully, relevant needs should be identified among one or more segments of the market, and the entire marketing mix should be designed to meet the needs of the target segments. At times, the relevant segment of the African American market will require a unique product. At other times, it will require a unique package, advertising medium, or message. Or no change may be required from the marketing mix used to reach a broader market.

**Products**   African Americans have different skin tones and hair from white Americans. Cosmetics and similar products developed for white consumers are often inappropriate for black consumers. Recognition of this fact by major firms has created aggressive competition for the $6.2 billion that African Americans spend each year on personal care products and services, including cosmetics, hair care, and skin care.[26] L'Oréal created its SoftSheen-Carson division specifically to serve women in this market. Iman's line of cosmetics, which is sold through such retailers as Walgreens and Target, is similarly targeted to this market (www.i-iman.com). Illustration 5–2 shows a print advertisement for a product designed specifically for the unique needs of the African American market and another for a product designed to meet the needs of all ethnic groups but that is being promoted to African Americans.

Numerous companies have found it worthwhile to alter their products and target them specifically to African Americans. Some examples include:[27]

- Hallmark has a Mahogany line of greeting cards that features black characters and sayings.
- Barbie offers African American dolls.
- GM has designed the Escalade and other models specifically with African Americans in mind.
- Wal-Mart has introduced an urban fashion brand called Exsto.

**Communications**   A common mistake when communicating with any ethnic group is to assume that its members are the same as the larger culture except for superficial differences. Failure to recognize this often results in commercials targeted at African Americans that simply place the firm's standard ad in black media or that replace white actors with black actors, without changing the script, language, or setting. For example, Greyhound Bus targeted blacks by placing its standard commercials on black radio stations. Unfortunately,

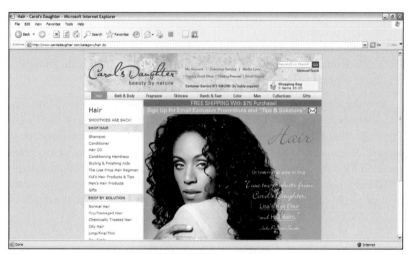

African American consumers have both unique and shared needs relative to other ethnic groups.

the sound track for the commercials was country-and-western music, which is not popular with most black audiences.

The extent to which messages targeted to African Americans need to differ from those targeting other groups varies by situation. For example, sometimes advertisers can simply change the race of the models in the ads and perhaps the consumption setting to help indicate that the product is appropriate for the needs of African Americans. This works when the product, the appeal, and the appropriate language are the same for the black target market and the other groups being targeted. The ad on the left side in Illustration 5–2 is a good example of this approach. This ad also recognizes the life-stage transition of many Generation Xers. In other cases, more specific changes need to be made to communicate how the product is designed to meet the specific needs of African Americans, as in the case of the ad on the right side in Illustration 5–2. The appeal of this ad is the desire for attractiveness, which is the same for whites and blacks, though the product is designed to meet the unique grooming needs of black women. In general, the use of black actors and spokespersons is important.[28] This is particularly the case for ethnically relevant products such as cosmetics and for those with strong ethnic identities.[29] Ads such as those in Illustration 5–2 can be run effectively in both black media and general media with a substantial black audience.

Another means of communicating with the African American and other ethnic communities is **event marketing,** which involves *creating or sponsoring an event that has a particular appeal to a market segment.* For example, church is a major force in the lives of many African Americans. In order to tap into black churchgoers, Chrysler was a sponsor of Patti LaBelle's "The Gospel According to Patti" concert tour in 2006. As part of the sponsorship, Chrysler offered test drives before each concert and donated $5 for each test drive to LaBelle's chosen charity, the University of Pennsylvania's Abramson Cancer Center.[30]

Retailing    Retailers often adjust the merchandising mix to meet the needs of African American shoppers. JCPenney had great success with its Authentic African boutiques in stores located near significant African American populations. These small shops, located inside JCPenney stores, featured clothing, handbags, hats, and other accessories imported from Africa. Albertson's, a national grocery retailer, adapts its merchandising mix in African American neighborhoods. One store in Oak Cliff, Texas, has a full grocery aisle devoted to

African American hair care products. And its food selections also cater to African American tastes, with products such as offal (organ meat) and brands such as Glory.[31]

Surveys reveal that three major store-selection factors for blacks are that the store carries ethnic products (51 percent say that is important), employs people who "look like me" (40 percent), and treats customers of all races and ethnicities with respect (84 percent).[32] This focus on respect is caused by the sad fact that many black shoppers still encounter obviously disrespectful acts such as being closely watched while shopping as well as more subtle discrimination such as slower service.[33] The need for cultural sensitivity training for retail and service employees is clear.[34]

African Americans also use shopping as a form of recreation more than whites.[35] This suggests that stores with black customers should pay particular attention to providing a pleasant and fun shopping environment. Blacks also respond to sales differently than do whites and have differing desires with respect to credit card, cash, and check payments.[36] Thus, all aspects of the shopping experience need to be carefully aligned to the needs of the target shoppers.

# HISPANICS

The Bureau of the Census defines **Hispanic** as *a person of Cuban, Mexican, Puerto Rican, South or Central American, or other Spanish culture or origin regardless of race.* It is measured by a person's response to the question: Are you Spanish/Hispanic/Latino? The Hispanic market is now the largest and fastest-growing ethnic subculture in the United States. By 2030 Hispanics are expected to represent 20 percent of the U.S. population. Marketers are definitely taking notice.

Like the other ethnic groups in America, Hispanics are diverse. Many marketers feel that the Hispanic subculture is not a single ethnic subculture but instead is three main and several minor nationality subcultures: Mexican Americans (64 percent), Puerto Ricans (10 percent), Cubans (4 percent), and other Latinos, mainly from Central and South America (13 percent).[37] Each group speaks a slightly different version of Spanish and has somewhat distinct values and lifestyles. Further, each group tends to live in distinct regions of the country: Mexican Americans in the Southwest and California, Puerto Ricans in New York and New Jersey, Cubans in Florida, and other Latinos in California, New York, and Florida. Income levels also vary across the groups, with those of Cuban descent having somewhat higher incomes than those of Mexican or Puerto Rican descent.

Others argue that while one must be sensitive to nationality-based differences, the common language, the common religion (Roman Catholic for most Hispanics), and the emergence of national Spanish-language media and entertainment figures create sufficient cultural homogeneity for most products and advertising campaigns. However, at a minimum, the decision to treat Hispanics as a single ethnic subculture needs to take into consideration factors relating to acculturation, language, and generational influences, which we discuss next.

## Acculturation, Language, and Generational Influences

Given that over 40 percent of growth in the Hispanic population is attributable to immigration, the level of acculturation plays a major role in the attitudes and behaviors of Hispanic consumers.[38] **Acculturation** is *the degree to which an immigrant has adapted to his or her new culture.*[39] Acculturation is highly related to language use and both are strongly

**Hispanic Teens: The New Bicultural Youth**

Hispanic teens constitute about 20 percent of all teen-agers but are far more important to marketers than that percentage suggests.[40] First, they currently represent $20 billion in spending power. This is likely to grow dramatically since this segment is projected to grow by 62 percent through 2020, which is six times faster than the overall teen market. More important, these teens are joining black teenagers as fashion and style leaders for the overall teenage market.

Hispanic teens often differ from their parents, who in many cases felt strong pressures to blend in and "be American" (i.e., act and speak like white Americans). These teens don't. Rather, the trend for Hispanic teens is to be bicultural, that is, *acculturating by adding a second culture, not replacing their first culture.* To do so requires a balancing act, particularly in how the divide between inside and outside the home is accomplished. This is particularly challenging given the importance of family, both nuclear and extended, in the Hispanic culture. How this balancing act is enacted is shown in the table on the next page.

And the balancing process leading to biculturalism seems to be working. As three experts describe:

I'm always amazed by the "Hispanicness" of Hispanic teens. They're speaking Spanish at home, both with friends, English for college and the Inter-net, but they're very much into the Hispanic cul-ture. Even when they're born here. It's downright breathtaking.

It's not about being bilingual. It's about being bicultural. They are engrossed in the American culture, but they take an incredible amount of pride in being Latino.

It's very cool to be Hispanic at this age. It almost makes them more attractive, exotic. Hispanic teens are brushing up on their Spanish and celebrating their culture.

These bicultural teens read the same English-language magazines and watch the same television programs as their non-Hispanic counterparts. In fact, they are much more likely to read such teen magazines as *Seventeen* and *YM*. One of the magazines targeting the female Hispanic teenager, *Latina,* is mostly English, though most of the ads are in Spanish. However, they also utilize Spanish-language magazines, television, and radio. They grew up listening not only to hip-hop and other popular music but to Hispanic-based rhythms as well—mariachi, banda, and norteño in California; tejano in Texas; salsa in Florida; and meringue in New York.

influenced by generational factors. A recent study by the Pew Hispanic Center identifies three generations of Hispanic adults:

*First-generation adults* (63 percent) are those born outside the United States. This generation has the lowest income and education, is most likely to identify themselves as Hispanic (including coun-try of origin), is most likely to have Spanish as their primary language (72 percent), and is most likely to possess traditional values including a masculine view of the family decision hierarchy.

*Second-generation adults* (19 percent) are those born in the United States to immigrant par-ents. Compared to the first generation, this generation has higher income and education, is more likely to identify themselves as Americans (though 62 percent still identify as Hispanic), is equally split between bilingual and English as primary language, and is somewhat less likely to ascribe to traditional values.

*Third-generation (and beyond) adults* (17 percent) are those born in the United States to U.S.-born parents. This group has the highest education and income, is most likely to identify as Americans (57 percent, versus 41 percent who identify themselves as Hispanic), is most likely to have English as the primary language (only 22 percent are bilingual; none are Spanish only), and is also somewhat less likely to ascribe to traditional values.[41]

| Identity (Their Base):<br>In-home and Family | Belong/Blend: Out-of-home and Friends | Differentiate: U.S. Mainstream |
| --- | --- | --- |
| Family | Hispanic friends, but also friends of other nationalities | Use their culture and heritage to show they are different |
| Experience Latino food and drinks | Latin food and drinks blended with mainstream products—Tacos and Lays Potato Chips | * |
| Speak Spanish | Speak English | Speak English, Spanish, and Spanglish |
| Presence of Latin American icons | Mainstream products/brands are more effective in helping them "belong" and be cool and accepted | Successful brands that compete against mainstream brands with Urban or Spanglish twist provides pride in that they are the drivers of those brands |
| Listen to and watch Spanish music and TV | * | Listen to and watch Spanish *and* English radio and TV |
| Family helps maintain cultural identity | Friends provide reassurance it's okay to be who you are and they hang out with other cultures | Are starting to set the trends as African American (Hip-Hop) culture becomes mainstream |

Source: Adapted from *Nuestro Futuro* (Redwood Shores, CA: Cheskin, 2006), p. 24.
*Data on specific behaviors and attitudes not available.

Now they are helping popularize these sounds and variations of them throughout the larger teen population.

## Critical Thinking Questions

1. To what extent are Hispanic teenagers leading the teenage market? Justify your response.

2. Many Hispanic teenagers are truly bicultural. What challenges does this present marketers?

3. Explain the role of family in Hispanic teenagers' tendency toward biculturalism.

As this discussion indicates, income, education, language, and identification with Hispanic culture change across generations. However, it is also important to note that most Hispanic adults identify more or less strongly with a Hispanic culture.[42] This strong cultural identity is also true of Hispanic teens, many of whom were born in the United States and would thus be classified as second- and third-generation teens.[43] As discussed in Consumer Insight 5–1, Hispanic teens are blending language and culture, setting cultural trends in the general U.S. population, and living truly bicultural and bilingual experiences.

The Hispanic culture is heavily influenced by the Roman Catholic religion. It is family oriented, with the extended family playing an important role across generations (unlike the general U.S. population in which extended family has lost its importance). It is also a masculine culture, and sports are very important to Hispanics, particularly boxing, baseball, and soccer. This masculine orientation manifests itself in many ways, including husband-dominant household decision making.[44] Examine Illustration 5–3. Note the family focus and the strong presence of the male.

The Hispanic culture generally has a fairly traditional view of the appropriate role of women. For example, the wife is expected to prepare the food for the family. This produces

The family is very important to the Hispanic subculture, and the male plays a major role. This ad has a strong family theme with a strong male presence.

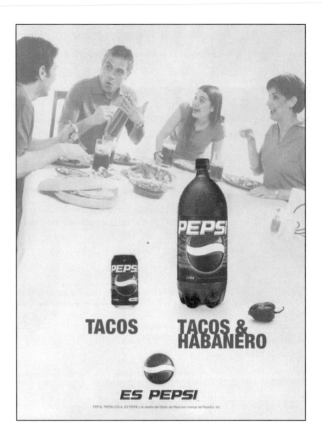

challenges and opportunities for marketers. Church's Chicken encountered resistance to its restaurant and takeout foods among Hispanic consumers. Church's vice president of marketing stated, "In the Latino community, there are a number of cultural barriers to not cooking." A result of these barriers is a social stigma against women who do not prepare meals for their families. To counter this, Church's launched an advertising campaign to make eating out more acceptable. The campaign positioned the chain as a place that provides a value-price dinner that frees up consumers to engage in more pressing activities.[45]

Language is clearly important to the Hispanic market and often strongly intertwined with cultural identity. Despite generational differences that are clearly emerging, a recent study finds that 69 percent of Hispanic households speak mostly Spanish at home and 83 percent speak at least some. Perhaps even more important is that Spanish-language ads are often more effective.[46] Consider the following:

> When asked about advertising effectiveness, 38% of Hispanics surveyed found English language ads less effective than Spanish ads in terms of recall and 70% less effective than Spanish ads in terms of persuasion. Many younger and acculturated Latinos mix languages in the form of "Spanglish," in which they speak English peppered with Spanish words. But, when it comes to selling, 56% of Latino adults respond best to advertising when it is presented in Spanish.[47]

Given these numbers, it should not be surprising that Univision, a Spanish-language network, is the fifth-largest network in the United States[48] and that there are over 30 cable stations targeted at the Hispanic market. In addition, recent research shows that the top 53 TV shows watched by Hispanics in the 18-to-49 demographic were in Spanish.[49]

# Marketing to Hispanics

Although average Hispanic household income is relatively low, the purchase power of the Hispanic market is estimated at $798 billion and is expected to grow by 50 percent through 2011.[50] In addition, Hispanic consumers tend to be highly brand loyal, particularly to marketers who they feel are working to adapt their products and services to meet their distinctive needs. Price is important, but so too is the availability of high-quality national brands. Hispanics tend to be less receptive than the general market to store brands.[51] Marketers are responding with adaptations to various aspects of their marketing mix.

**Communications**    As we saw earlier, Hispanics often speak Spanish and often prefer Spanish-language media. Therefore, although it is possible to reach part of this market using mass media, serious attempts to target Hispanics will often involve Spanish-language media as well. Univision, Telefutura, and Telemundo are the top three Spanish-language TV networks in the United States. Spanish-language radio is widespread, with both local and network stations. And there are numerous Spanish-language magazines, including Spanish versions of *Cosmopolitan, Sports Illustrated, Maxim, Men's Health, People,* and *Reader's Digest. Latina* targets younger, affluent Hispanic women, and *Latina Style* targets more mature but contemporary Hispanic women. There are also many Spanish-language newspapers.

With respect to communication and media, it is important to note that a youth trend is emerging, which will likely shape the future of Hispanic media strategy. Specifically, the 14-to-24-year-old demographic (which will grow rapidly over the next decade)[52] spends more time viewing English-language TV, radio, and print media than Spanish. This group tends to be U.S.-born and more English-dominant in terms of language. In addition, the 18-to-34 demographic views Spanish- and English-language media about equally. In response, Telemundo is offering both bilingual and Spanish-language programming and is developing shows more in touch with the Hispanic youth market, such as the reality show *Protagonistas de Novela*. SiTV is a relatively new cable network that creates and delivers English-language programming with a Latino theme targeted toward a younger demographic.[53]

Hispanics have historically lagged behind the general population in terms of Internet usage. However, this is changing, particularly for more acculturated, English-dominant Hispanics. For example, while overall Hispanic Internet usage is at 56 percent, English-speaking Hispanics are at around 78 percent, which is higher than the general population.[54] In response, sites focused on Hispanics are increasingly coming online (see Illustration 5–4). Gateway, Colgate-Palmolive, Coca-Cola, MasterCard, and GM are some of the firms that advertise on these sites. Online sports are available through such sites as ESPNdeportes.com, and Spanish-language versions of Yahoo! and AOL have been developed. Online Spanish-language communities such as CiudadFutura.com are also emerging. Hispanic Internet users tend to be relatively young, frequent both English- and Spanish-language sites, and in many cases prefer English-language media.[55] As with traditional media providers, online Hispanic providers will be challenged to deliver content that is relevant to acculturated Hispanics, regardless of language.

Successfully communicating to Hispanic consumers involves more than directly translating ad copy from English to Spanish. For example, when Mattel launched BarbieLatina .com, it was not merely a translation of the successful Barbie.com. While both Hispanic and non-Hispanic girls aged three to eight have a passion for fantasy and nurturing behavior, the Hispanic girls had less interest in games and more interest in activity-based play. The content of the two sites was designed to reflect these differences.[56]

Use of the Internet by Hispanics is exploding. Sites such as this one are being developed to appeal to the unique needs of this market.

Language translation is a challenge. For example, Tang introduced itself in its Spanish ads as *jugo de chino,* which worked well with Puerto Ricans, who knew it meant orange juice, but the phrase had no meaning to most other Hispanics. Other examples of translation difficulties include the following:

- Frank Perdue's chicken slogan, "It Takes a Tough Man to Make a Tender Chicken," was translated as "It Takes a Sexually Excited Man to Make a Chick Affectionate."
- Budweiser's slogan ended up being "The Queen of Beers," and Miller's was "Filling; Less Delicious."
- Coors' recent campaign uses the word "guey," which in modern slang terms can mean the equivalent of "dude." However, the word can also be used as slang for "idiot" or "stupid." According to one expert, whether or not consumers get the humor is generational.[57]

Successful marketing to Hispanics moves beyond accurate translations into unique appeals and symbols. It requires marketers to be "in-culture," that is, to understand the value system and the overall cultural context of the various Hispanic groups. In fact, value congruence has been found to overcome persuasion shortfalls for second-language ads (e.g., English-language ads to bilingual Hispanics).[58]

- Sears recognized the importance of the extended family in a successful ad for baby furniture. In the English ad, a husband and wife are shown selecting the furniture. In the Spanish ad, a teenage daughter and the grandparents join the expectant couple.
- Hispanic teens are particularly difficult to target with effective communications. Frito-Lay's successful campaign for Doritos was themed *Sabor a todo volumen* (roughly, "The loudest taste on earth"). TV ads featured loud Hispanic music and Hispanic teens, with an emphasis on Doritos' bold and spicy taste. Research revealed that the music was key to the success of the campaign. According to a spokesperson, "Music is one of the major attributes of Hispanic teens that bind them together. The styles differ from salsa to Latin pop, but all are based on Latin roots."[59]
- Best Buy created a TV spot designed to bridge the gap between younger tech-savvy Hispanic teens and their older less acculturated fathers who often are uncomfortable with technology but, given the patriarchal hierarchy, must "sign off" on the purchase. The slogan reads "If you're far away, get closer with Best Buy." Best Buy says they designed the spot to get kids and their fathers talking.[60]

**Products**   Historically, other than specialty food products, few marketers developed unique products or services for the Hispanic market. However, given the size and growth of this market, that is changing. For example:

- In Colorado, Wal-Mart created Denver Bronco T-shirts specifically targeting Hispanic consumers. One version had the phrase "de todo corazón," meaning "with all my heart" in Spanish. Wal-Mart's goal was to combine American sports tradition with symbols of Hispanic culture. The T-shirts became the most popular Denver Bronco's merchandise of the season.[61]
- Ford Motor Company is tapping into the increasingly lucrative Hispanic auto market by offering the F-150 Lobo truck. *Lobo* means "wolf" in Spanish and the Lobo truck, offered only in bright red, features a monochrome exterior and Lobo badging. Ford is leveraging the fact that the Lobo is made in Mexico and that many Hispanics are from Mexico. It has also signed Pablo Montero (a popular Mexican singer) as a celebrity spokesperson.[62]
- In addition, marketers are capturing the loyalty developed with their products in Central and South America by distributing them in areas of the United States with large Hispanic populations. For example, Colgate-Palmolive distributes its Mexican household cleaner Fabuloso in Los Angeles and Miami.

Some attempts at adapting products to the Hispanic market have failed because of a failure to truly understand the needs of this market. For example, many Hispanics find the current trend in houses of having the kitchen open onto the family room to be repugnant (Hispanics tend to be uncomfortable having strangers in their kitchens) and find the homes built for Hispanic buyers to be too stereotypical.[63]

Retailing   The primary retailing responses to this market have been an increase in the number of bilingual salespeople; the use of Spanish-language signs, directions, and point-of-purchase displays; and merchandise assortments that reflect the needs of the local Hispanic community. The following provide specific examples:

- Tiangus, a grocery chain aimed at the Mexican American market in southern California, was launched with a fiesta atmosphere. Stands served a wide variety of Mexican foods, the walls were splashed with bright colors, and shoppers were serenaded with maria-chi bands. The shelves were stocked with empanadas, handmade tortillas, and other items typically found only in specialty stores. The stores are not just standard stores with a Latin flair and a few specialty items. The chain is based on extensive research. For example, it was found that the Hispanic shopper "is fussier about freshness, so she shops more frequently and uses less refrigeration. She may have less disposable income but she'll spend a higher share of it on food." On the basis of these findings, Tiangus stores emphasize fresh food. Half the selling space is devoted to fresh food, with reduced space for packaged items and freezer foods.[64]
- Home Depot has launched a paint line called *Colores Origenes* in some 400 stores that have a heavily Hispanic customer base. Based on research, the names of the colors are designed to specifically communicate to Hispanic customers in terms that evoke Latin tastes, scents, and images.[65]
- Target has retooled its marketing, product, and retailing strategies to focus on the Hispanic market. Its retail stores now have many products targeted at Hispanic con-sumers. And Target also has a Spanish-language Web site called *Nuestra Gente*, which is a Hispanic Heritage sitelet.

# ASIAN AMERICANS

Asian Americans represent an important subculture. Although relatively small in size this group will continue to grow. Of particular importance to marketers is that Asian Americans are the highest-educated and highest-income group, with substantial purchasing power. Asian American purchase power is estimated at $427 billion and is expected to grow by 46 percent through 2011.[66] However, Asian Americans are also the most diverse group, with numerous nationalities, languages, and religions. The U.S. Census includes Asian-Indians in its summary figures for this group. However, we will discuss them separately in the next section.

Asian Americans are not a single subculture. Consider the Web site in Illustration 5–5. Ads on this site are probably quite effective with many of the Chinese members of this subculture. However, as Figure 5–3 shows, Chinese represent only a little over a fourth of all Asian Americans and they share neither a common language nor culture with most of the other groups.

As with Hispanics, language is a major factor. One estimate is that 80 percent of Asian Americans can be reached with "in-language" promotions. Two-thirds of Asian Ameri-cans are immigrants, and the percentage of each nationality group that uses primarily its native language is high, except for Filipinos.[67] In addition, the percentage who prefer "in-language" communication is also high, even for Filipinos.[68]

Ads on this site would appeal to many Chinese consumers but would not reach most other Asian Americans.

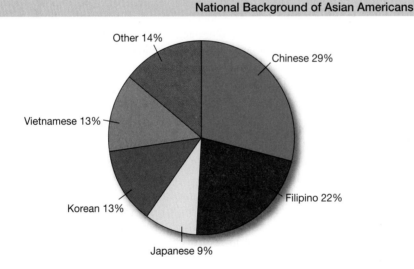

**National Background of Asian Americans**    FIGURE 5–3

- Other 14%
- Chinese 29%
- Filipino 22%
- Japanese 9%
- Korean 13%
- Vietnamese 13%

| Country | Primarily Use Native Language (%) | Prefer Communication in Native Language (%) |
|---|---|---|
| Vietnam | 85 | 93 |
| Hong Kong | 82 | N/A* |
| China | 64 | 83 |
| Korea | 64 | 81 |
| Taiwan | 64 | N/A* |
| Japan | 46 | 42 |
| Philippines | 27 | 66 |

*N/A is not available.

More than languages differ among the groups. In fact, the concept and term *Asian American* was developed and used by marketers and others who study these groups rather than the members themselves. Members of the various nationalities involved generally refer to themselves by their nationality without the term *American,* that is, Vietnamese, not Vietnamese American. An exception are Japanese Americans.[69]

While each nationality group is a distinct culture with its own language and traditions, there are some commonalities across most of these groups. All have experienced the need to adjust to the American culture while being physically distinct from the larger population. Most come from home cultures influenced by Confucianism. Confucianism emphasizes subordination of the son to the father, the younger to the elder, and the wife to the husband. It values conservatism and prescribes strict manners. Their base cultures have also typically placed a very strong value on traditional, extended families. Education, collective effort, and advancement are also highly valued.[70]

## Consumer Segments and Trends

Market Segment Research found three groups of Asian Americans on the basis of their demographics and attitudes that cut across nationality groups. Such commonalities can be useful starting points when designing marketing campaigns even if language and cultural symbols must be adapted. *Traditionalists* are older, often retired, have strong identification with original culture, native language tends to be primary language, and are not concerned about status. *Established* are older, conservative professionals; are well educated, with strong incomes; have relatively weak identification with native culture; have less need or desire for native-language programming; and will pay premium prices for high quality. *Living for the Moment* are younger, have moderate identification with native culture, tend to be bilingual, and are spontaneous, materialistic, and impulsive shoppers who are concerned with status and quality.[71]

Several emerging trends are worth watching, some of which will make the Asian American population somewhat easier to target over time. First is geographic concentration, which has historically been high and appears to be increasing. In 1990, for example, 54 percent of Asian Americans resided in just five cities (Los Angeles, San Francisco, New York, Honolulu, and Chicago). In 2000 that number had increased to 59 percent. The concentration is even higher if you look at the state level, with roughly 75 percent of all Asian Americans living in just six states (California, New York, New Jersey, Hawaii, Texas, and Illinois).[72]

Immigration is one of the factors fueling the growth of the Asian American population. One trend is toward an increase in skilled workers from Mandarin-speaking regions of mainland China. This trend appears to be causing a "gradual shift to Mandarin from Cantonese in Chinese communications."[73]

A final trend is one which is common to all subcultures, and that is the youth trend. Roughly a third of Asian Americans are under the age of 25, which is comparable to whites.[74] In addition, this second generation (sometimes referred to as Generation 2.0), which was born in the United States, is, like the African American and Hispanic youth, still tied to its roots, but blending languages and cultures, influencing general U.S. culture, and fueling trends in fashion and music. As in the Hispanic market, English-language media options with Asian American content targeted at this second generation are increasing. Pepsi is airing ads in English on one such venue called *Stir* TV.[75] Also consider the Honda initiative:

Honda Motor Co. chose to piggyback on Boba, a beverage developed in Taiwan that is all the rage in Asian youth circles. The beverage, also known as bubble tea, consists of "pearls" of black, gummy, tapioca balls that float in the mixture of sweetened iced tea. It has quickly caught on as the soft drink of Asian youth. Honda's idea was to develop drink sleeves that surround hot beverages in the U.S. to promote its youth-oriented cars, like the Civic and Acura RSX. Ponce (manager of emerging markets) got the idea from one of her young Asian co-workers who frequents Boba stores and noticed the number of young Asians who pulled up in Hondas.[76]

## Marketing to Asian Americans

As we've seen, there are several Asian American markets, based primarily on nationality and language. Each of these in turn can be further segmented on degree of acculturation,[77] social class, generation, lifestyle, and other variables. And while this creates challenges for marketers, the purchase power of this group and its various segments is increasingly attractive to marketers and causing them to address these niche markets with creative product, merchandising, and media approaches.

Geographic concentration is increasing, which helps marketing efficiency. Where there is a concentration of any of the nationality groups, there are native-language television and radio stations as well as newspapers.[78] Thus, targeted nationalities can be reached efficiently with native-language ads. For example, in San Francisco, KTSF offers in-language news and entertainment programming for Chinese and Japanese viewers. Many KTSF advertisers, such as McDonald's, dub their existing ads in Cantonese. Others, such as Colgate-Palmolive, run the ads they are using for the same products in Asia. McDonald's is bringing branded entertainment to the United States with its top-rated *McDonald's Minutes to Fame* from Hong Kong, coming to KTSF in Cantonese with Chinese subtitles.

Direct broadcast satellite (DBS) is also an important TV option. DBS provides a means of reaching virtually all the native-language speakers of any nationality nationwide. For example, EchoStar's Dish network offers a "Chinese Package" called the "Great Wall TV Package," which started with 3 channels several years ago and is now at over 25 channels. DirecTV offers the gamut of language options to the Asian American audience, including three services for South Asian languages, VietnameseDirect, and three Chinese-language services in both Cantonese and Mandarin, which are broadcast from China, Hong Kong, and Taiwan.[79]

Asian Americans are highly tech savvy and heavy users of the Internet. Internet penetration of Asian Americans is estimated at 90 percent.[80] Internet-based marketing to the Asian community is growing rapidly. Firms can reach Chinese consumers in their native language on sites such as that shown in Illustration 5–5. Similar sites are gaining popularity among other Asian nationality groups, and firms such as Charles Schwab are using them as communications channels.

Marketing to the various Asian nationality groups should follow the same basic guidelines discussed earlier for Hispanics. Thus, effective communication is more than simply translating ad copy. It also requires adopting and infusing ads with cultural symbols and meanings relevant to each nationality segment. Examine Illustration 5–6. It is bilingual and can communicate to Vietnamese with differing language preferences. More important, it is a special promotion based on the Lunar New Year that is meaningful to this group. It shows that Bank of America is doing more than just translating an ad used for the broader market but is focusing special attention on the Vietnamese market.

Marketing to Asian
Americans involves
more than translating
ads into the appro-
priate languages.
This promotion is
based on the Lunar
New Year, which
is special to many
Asian cultures.

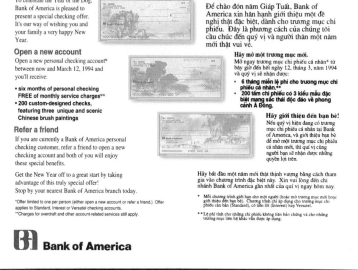

Other examples of successful marketing to Asian Americans include:

- A Los Angeles chain selected four outlets with large numbers of Chinese and Vietnamese customers. At the time of the Moon Festival (an important holiday in many
  Asian cultures), the store ran ads and distributed coupons for free moon cakes and
  lanterns. Sales increased by 30 percent in these stores during the promotion. Likewise,
  Sears advertises the Moon Festival in Mandarin, Cantonese, Vietnamese, or Korean,
  depending on the population near each outlet. It provides nationality-relevant gifts and
  entertainment such as traditional dances.
- Western Union sponsors numerous Asian cultural events, such as the Asian-American
  Expo for the Chinese New Year in Los Angeles. It also partnered with *World Journal*
  to publish the *Chinese Immigrant Handbook* to offer practical guidance to new immigrants. These represent grassroot, community-based efforts to target the very specific
  needs of various nationality groups. These efforts supplement their more traditional
  mass-media approaches using TV, radio, and magazines.[81]

# NATIVE AMERICANS

The number of Native Americans (American Indians and Alaska Natives, in U.S. Census
terms) depends on the measurement used. The Census Bureau reports three numbers for
Native Americans: (1) one tribe only, (2) one tribe only or in combination with another tribe,

and (3) number 2 plus in combination with any other race. The first definition produces an estimate of 2.8 million Native Americans; the total jumps to 4.1 million when the third definition is used. Nearly half live in the West, and 30 percent reside in the South. While many Native Americans live on or near reservations, others are dispersed throughout the country.

There are approximately 550 Native American tribes, each with its own language and traditions. Many of the tribes have reservations and quasi-independent political status. In general, Native Americans have limited incomes,[82] but this varies widely by tribe. The overall buying power of this group is estimated at $54 billion and is expected to grow by 35 percent through 2011.[83] The larger tribes are as follows:

| Tribes | One Tribe Only | Multiracial |
|---|---|---|
| Cherokee | 281,000 | 730,000 |
| Navajo | 269,000 | 298,000 |
| Sioux | 109,000 | 153,000 |
| Chippewa | 106,000 | 150,000 |
| Choctaw | 87,000 | 159,000 |
| Pueblo | 60,000 | 74,000 |
| Apache | 57,000 | 97,000 |
| Eskimo | 46,000 | 55,000 |

In recent years, Native Americans have taken increasing pride in their heritage and are less tolerant of inaccurate stereotypes of either their history or their current status. Thus, marketers using Native American names or portrayals must ensure accurate and appropriate use. Native American cuisine is making its way into the American mainstream with efforts from Native American chefs like Arnold Olson. Olson blends European and Native American styles to create interesting dishes such as bison carpaccio and caribou bruschetta. As American interest in and acceptance of diversity continues to grow, unique Native American offerings such as this will become increasingly relevant and popular.[84]

The larger tribes all have their own newspapers and radio stations. In addition, there are two national Native American–oriented newspapers and several national radio shows and magazines.[85] Although each tribe is small relative to the total population, the geographic concentration of each tribe provides easy access for marketers. Sponsorship of tribal events and support for tribal colleges, training centers, and community centers can produce good results for firms that do so over time. For example, Nike has teamed up with the Indian Health Service to set up educational programs to teach and promote health and fitness on reservations.[86]

# ASIAN-INDIAN AMERICANS

There are approximately 2.25 million Americans of Indian heritage (from India). This segment of the population is growing rapidly as a result of immigration. Asian-Indian Americans are concentrated in New York and California, with significant numbers in New Jersey, Illinois, and Texas as well. As a group, they are well educated, affluent, and fluent in English; yet most retain cultural ties to their Indian background.

Those unfamiliar with India often assume that it is a homogeneous country. However, in some ways it is more like Europe than America. It has 28 states, six union territories, 15 official languages, and dozens of other languages and dialects. Thus, while those who immigrate to America have much in common, they also have many differences based on their background in India.

Although diverse in many ways, most share a number of important cultural traits:

- They place great value on education, particularly their children's education.
- They are concerned with financial security and save at a rate much higher than the average American.
- They do not have a "throw-away" mentality. They shop for value and look for quality and durability.
- Husbands tend to have a dominant role in family decisions.

Asian-Indian Americans attend to the general mass media. They can also be targeted via specialty magazines such as *Matram* and *Indian Life & Style,* online sites such as IndiaAbroad.com, as well as cable TV, radio stations, and newspapers in regions with significant populations. For example, Western Union advertises to this segment on Eye on Asia, a cable channel focused on this group. National reach is now possible through EchoStar's Dish Network's South Asia Package with various channels from India. Long-term involvement in the Indian community is an effective way to gain support from this segment:

> Metropolitan Life was a major sponsor of a Navaratri, a religious festival that attracted 100,000 participants from around New York and New Jersey. As one participant said, "One of the chief executives of the company attended the festival, and the company took out a series of ads in the souvenir program. Now we feel we should reward the company for taking an interest in us."[87]

The Internet is also an effective way to market to these consumers. However, such an effort requires a sound knowledge of the community:

> It's December but Namaste.com's holiday rush has been over for two months. Christmas is not the big season for its customers. "To suggest gifting to Indians around Christmas time doesn't make sense. It's the wrong marketing message. Diwali [a festival of lights that happens in late October] is the Indian 'Christmas.'"[88]

# ARAB AMERICANS

The 2000 Census identified 1.25 million self-identified Arab Americans in the United States. However the Arab American Institute (the Census Bureau's official designee for analyzing data related to Arab Americans) estimates underreporting by a factor of 3 and based on additional research has estimated the Arab American population at about 3.5 million. Perhaps no group in America has a more inaccurate stereotype. For example: What is the most common religion of Arab Americans? Sixty-six percent identify themselves as Christians (up from about 50 percent in the early 1990s), and 24 percent are Muslim (down from about 50 percent in the early 1990s).

Arab Americans come from a variety of countries, including Morocco, Algeria, Egypt, Lebanon, Jordan, Saudi Arabia, and Kuwait. They share a common Arabic heritage and the Arabic language. Since World War II, many Arab immigrants have been business proprietors, landowners, or influential families fleeing political turmoil in their home countries. Many of these individuals attended Western or Westernized schools and were fluent in English before arriving.

More than 80 percent of Arab Americans are U.S. citizens, and a recent study finds that 75 percent were born in the United States. They are somewhat younger than the general population, are better educated, and have a higher-than-average income. They are also much more likely to be entrepreneurs. A third of all Arab Americans live in California, New York, and Michigan.

Most Arab Americans are tired of negative stereotyping and misrepresentations about their culture. Even the film *Aladdin* contained insults and mistakes. Aladdin sings about the "barbaric" country from which he came. A guard threatened to cut off a young girl's hand for stealing food for a hungry child. Such an action would be contrary to Islamic law. The storefront signs in the mythical Arabic land had symbols that made no sense in Arabic or any other language. The aftermath of the September 11, 2001, attacks on the World Trade Center and the Pentagon has aroused some prejudice against these citizens—as well as some enhanced knowledge of their backgrounds and beliefs.

The first rule in reaching this market is to treat its members with respect and accuracy. There are specialized newspapers, magazines, and radio and television stations focused on this market. EchoStar's Dish Network offers an Arabic-language package. And, Wal-Mart has begun to adjust its product selection in areas with strong Arab American populations, such as Dearborn, Michigan, with offerings such as falafel, olives, and Islamic greeting cards. Attention to the unique traditions of this community can pay large dividends.[89]

# RELIGIOUS SUBCULTURES

As discussed in Chapter 3, America is basically a **secular society.** That is, the educational system, government, and political process are not controlled by a religious group, and most people's daily behaviors are not guided by strict religious guidelines. Nonetheless, roughly 83 percent of American adults claim a religious affiliation,[90] 36 percent claim to attend a religious service at least once a month,[91] and more than 50 percent state that religion is very important in their lives.[92] Interestingly, while some are leaving religion altogether, which accounts for the ongoing decrease in those identifying with a religious affiliation over time, others are switching. A recent study indicates that 44 percent of adults have moved to another religion, moved within the Protestant denomination, or moved out of religion altogether.[93]

The fact that the American culture is largely secular is not viewed as optimal by all of society. Many conservative Christians would prefer a society and legal system more in line with their faith. The intense debates over abortion, prayer in schools, the teaching of evolution versus creationism, homosexual rights, and a host of other issues are evidence of this division in American society.

Religion is important to, and directly influences the behaviors of, many Americans. This includes consuming religiously themed products[94] and avoiding the consumption of other products such as alcohol. The different religions in America prescribe differing values and behaviors. Thus, a number of **religious subcultures** exist in America.

## Christian Subcultures

Much of the American value system and the resultant political and social institutions are derived from the Christian, and largely Protestant, beliefs of the early settlers. Although American culture is basically secular, many of its traditions and values are derived from the Judeo–Christian heritage of the majority of Americans. Most of the major American holidays, including Christmas, Easter, and Thanksgiving, have a religious base. However, except for Easter, the pure religious base of these holidays is no longer the central theme that it once was.

ILLUSTRATION 5-7

This Web site
would appeal to the
"young religious"
segment identified by
Yankelovich.

Although the United States is predominantly Christian, the percentage of American adults claiming Christianity as their religion was 78.4 percent in 2007, down from 86.2 percent in 1990.[95] However, Yankelovich has been tracking a psychographic segment it calls the "young religious," composed of Gen X and Y. Following up on the huge success of the movie *The Passion of the Christ*, clothing firms have begun marketing trendy fashions with an edge to this younger audience, including T-shirts with the slogan "Jesus is my homeboy." Some retailers have embraced this trend while others, concerned about offending customers, have declined.[96] The Web site shown in Illustration 5–7 appears to be targeting this group.

Christianity takes many forms in this country, each with some unique beliefs and behaviors, as discussed next.

**Roman Catholic Subculture**   Roughly 24 percent of American adults are Roman Catholic. The Catholic church is highly structured and hierarchical. The pope is the central religious authority, and individual interpretation of scripture and events is minimal. A basic tenet of the Catholic church is that a primary purpose of a marital union is procreation. Therefore, the use of birth control devices is prohibited, though many Catholics deviate from this. A result of this is a larger average family size for Catholics than for Protestants or Jews. The larger family size makes economic gains and upward social mobility more difficult. It also has a major influence on the types of products consumed by Catholics relative to many other religions.

The Catholic church is ethnically diverse, with some 35 percent of its adult membership coming from ethnic subcultures. Recall from our earlier discussion that the predominant religion among Hispanics is Catholicism. Hispanics have fueled much of the Catholic growth since 1960. Twenty-nine percent of adult Catholics are Hispanic, 3 percent are African American, and 3 percent are Asian.[97] Catholics tend to be concentrated in the Northeast and in areas with large Hispanic populations. *Encuentro* is one manifestation of this cultural diversity. It is a gathering of U.S. Hispanic Catholics held every few years. *Encuentro*

*2000: Many Faces in God's House* was a special event that embraced people of all ethnic and racial backgrounds. The conference included Latin music, an ethnic village, workshops reflecting the Asian experience, and speakers from various ethnic backgrounds.[98]

Like Protestants, Catholics vary in their commitment and conservatism. The more conservative members share many values and behaviors with Protestant religious conservatives. Catholics have few consumption restrictions or requirements associated with their religion. Marketers targeting this group can reach the more committed members through specialized magazines and radio programs.

**Protestant Subcultures**    Approximately 51 percent of American adults identify themselves as Protestant. While there are many types of Protestant faiths, with significant differences between them, most emphasize direct individual experience with God as a core tenet. In general, Protestant faiths emphasize individual responsibility and control. This focus has been credited with creating a strong work ethic, a desire for scientific knowledge, a willingness to sacrifice for the future, and relatively small families. These characteristics in turn have created upward social mobility and produced the majority of the ruling elite in America.

Protestant values and attitudes have tended to shape the core American culture. This is particularly true for white Protestants of Western European heritage—WASPs (white Anglo-Saxon Protestants). This group has historically dominated America in terms of numbers, wealth, and power, with power historically belonging to the male members of this group.

Although Protestants constitute the basic core culture of America, the diversity across and within denominations creates numerous subcultures within the larger group. Many of these religious groups have unique beliefs of direct relevance to marketers. These generally involve the consumption of products containing stimulants such as caffeine (prohibited by the Mormon Church) or alcohol (prohibited by the Southern Baptist church, among others). However, the basic distinction among Protestants, as among Catholics, is the degree of conservatism in their religious beliefs. The majority of Protestants are middle-of-the-road in terms of conservatism. This is consistent with America's dominant cultural values. However, a sizable minority are very conservative and, along with conservative Catholics, represent a significant subculture.

**The Born-Again Christian Subculture**    Born-again Christians have been referred to as the Christian Right, Religious Right, Conservative Christians, Evangelical Christians, and Fundamentalist Christians. **Born-again Christians** are *characterized by a strong belief in the literal truth of the Bible, a very strong commitment to their religious beliefs, having had a "born-again" experience, and encouraging others to believe in Jesus Christ.*

Born-again Christians tend to have somewhat lower education and income levels than the general population. They tend to have a more traditional gender role orientation. Born-again Christians are best known for their political stands on issues such as abortion, homosexual rights, and prayer in the schools.

Their beliefs also influence their consumption patterns. They generally oppose the use of alcohol and drugs. They do not consume movies or television programs that are overly focused on sex or other activities that they consider to be immoral. In fact, various groups of born-again Christians have organized boycotts against advertisers that sponsor shows they find inappropriate.

In contrast, they are very receptive to programs, books, and movies that depict traditional (i.e., Protestant) family (husband, wife, children) values. Firms with a reputation for supporting similar values are well received by this segment. In contrast, Disney products have faced boycotts because of Disney's personnel policies relating to same-sex couples.

## Non-Christian Subcultures

**Jewish Subculture**   Judaism represents 1.7 percent of American adults and is unique in that historically it has been an inseparable combination of ethnic and religious identity. Historically, Jews in America tended to marry other Jews, although that has changed somewhat over time.[99] In fact, a recent study of Match.com members found that 81 percent of Jewish single men and 72 percent of Jewish single women said they would date outside their race, ethnicity, or religion (these percentages were similar to those found for most other religions).[100]

Jews are heavily concentrated in the Northeast but are increasingly dispersing throughout the United States, particularly into the Sunbelt.[101] American Jews tend to have higher-than-average incomes and education levels. In most ways, Jewish consumption patterns are similar to those of other Americans with similar education and income levels.

Like other religious groups, the committed, conservative Jews represent a subculture distinct from mainstream Jews. Orthodox Jews have strict dietary rules that prohibit some foods such as pork and specify strict preparation requirements for other foods (see Illustration 5–8). They also strictly observe Jewish holidays, and many do not participate in even the secular aspects of the major Christian holiday, Christmas. Reformed Jews and Jews less committed to the strict interpretations of Judaism are less influenced by these practices.[102]

**Muslim Subculture**   It is important to recall from our earlier discussion that Arab Americans are often not Muslims, and by the same token Muslims in America are not necessarily Arabs. Muslims in America (representing roughly 0.6 percent of the American adult population)[103] are culturally diverse, including Arab Americans, African Americans, Asian Americans, and Hispanics. Like the Protestants, there are a variety of Muslim sects with varying belief patterns, though all are based on the Koran. As with Protestants, Catholics,

**ILLUSTRATION 5–8**

Many religions prescribe dietary practices for their members. This company uses its Web site to highlight its ongoing commitment to provide foods that follow the guidelines of the Jewish religion.

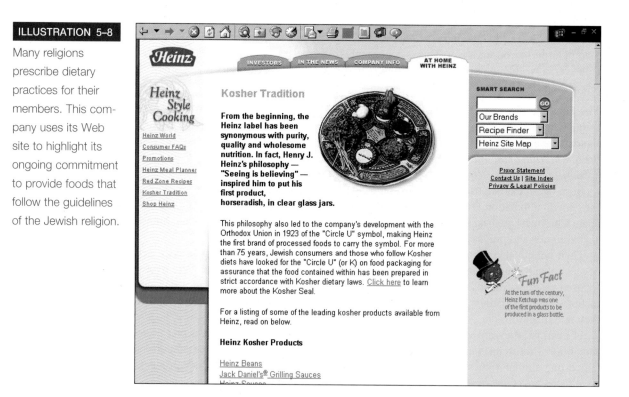

and Jews, the most obvious division among Muslims is the degree of conservatism and the importance attached to the literal teachings of the religion. As with the other religious groups in America, most Muslims' lives are centered on work, family, school, and the pursuit of success and happiness.

In general, Muslims tend to be conservative with respect to drug and alcohol use and sexual permissiveness. In fact, many oppose dating. They also place considerable emphasis on the family, with the eldest male as the head of the family, and on respect for elders. The more devout Muslims avoid not only pork products but also any foods that have not been prepared in accordance with the strict rules of Islam. The following quote from a devout Pakistani Muslim on why he does not eat in Western restaurants illustrates the stress this can cause:

> Well, how can I be sure that the cook who has cooked pork or bacon in a pan did not cook my vegetables in the same pan? How can I be sure that even if he used different pans he washed his hands in between cooking bacon and a vegetable? I do not think there is any way I can get a pure food out there.[104]

These beliefs conflict with the practices in the larger society and the images portrayed on television and in the movies and are also a source of conflict between older Muslims who immigrated to America and their children who were raised here.[105] Muslims in America have their own magazines, schools, social clubs, marriage services, and bookstores. There are more than 1,100 Muslim mosques and sanctuaries in America. In general, this subculture has not attracted the attention of marketers except as it overlaps with the Arab American subculture.

**Buddhist Subculture**   There are nearly as many Buddhists in America as there are Muslims. They are primarily Asian American or white, although Asian Americans are more likely to be Christian (roughly 43 percent) than Buddhist (roughly 6 percent). Buddhists tend to be slightly above average in income and education, and they are concentrated in the West.

There are a variety of Buddhist sects in America. All emphasize the basic idea that all beings are caught in *samsara,* a cycle of suffering and rebirth that is basically caused by desire and actions that produce unfavorable *karma.* Samsara can be escaped and a state of *nirvana* reached by following the noble *Eightfold Path.* This combines ethical and disciplinary practices, training in concentration and meditation, and the development of enlightened wisdom.

Thus far, marketers have largely ignored this market. Its small size and diverse ethnic composition make it difficult to target. However, as specialized media evolve to serve Buddhists, opportunities will exist for astute marketers.

# REGIONAL SUBCULTURES

Distinct **regional subcultures** arise as a result of climatic conditions, the natural environment and resources, the characteristics of the various immigrant groups that have settled in each region, and significant social and political events. These distinct subcultures present numerous opportunities and challenges for marketers. Examples include,

- TGI Friday's has a customizable menu which includes a set of 70 standard items plus 30 regional items, including chicken-fried steak, which is a hit in the Southeast but not in some other regions, and a baked brie cheese appetizer that is offered only in Michigan.

| TABLE 5-2 | | Northeast | Midwest | South | West |
|---|---|---|---|---|
| **Products** | | | | | |
| | Imported beer | 124 | 80 | 89 | 120 |
| | Tooth whiteners | 99 | 96 | 107 | 94 |
| | Breakfast pastries | 87 | 106 | 106 | 94 |
| | Bagels | 129 | 102 | 82 | 83 |
| **Activities** | | | | | |
| | Going to bars/nightclubs/dancing | 109 | 112 | 95 | 87 |
| | Fly fishing | 78 | 73 | 102 | 145 |
| | Snowboarding | 104 | 87 | 82 | 143 |
| | College football fan | 54 | 126 | 129 | 62 |
| **Shopping** | | | | | |
| | OfficeMax | 90 | 130 | 107 | 65 |
| | GAP | 145 | 59 | 103 | 99 |
| | Domino's Pizza | 91 | 68 | 117 | 112 |
| | Applebee's | 110 | 129 | 91 | 76 |
| **Media** | | | | | |
| | The New Yorker | 216 | 60 | 62 | 106 |
| | North American Hunter | 91 | 178 | 64 | 86 |
| | The Amazing Race (CBS) | 78 | 109 | 109 | 95 |
| | The Simpsons (FOX) | 93 | 95 | 95 | 120 |

Regional Consumption Differences

Note: 100 = Average level of use, purchase, or consumption.
Source: *SMRB*, 2006.

- Many national magazines run regional editions. *TV Guide,* for example, had 25 different regional covers for their NFL preview issue. And, *Sports Illustrated* often offers special issues devoted to sports in a specific city such as the *Sports Illustrated Boston Collection.*[106]
- Wahoo's, a restaurant in Southern California and Colorado (and also now online at www.wahoos.com), offers fish tacos, a menu item that may sound a bit odd to some, but which is popular among Hispanic consumers.

Although the most effective regional marketing strategies are often based on small geographic areas, we can observe significant consumption differences across much larger regions. Table 5–2 illustrates some of the consumption differences across the four U.S. census regions. Given such clear differences in consumption patterns, marketers realize that, for at least some product categories, the United States is no more a single market than the European Union. Since specialized (regional) marketing programs generally cost more than standardized (national) programs, marketers must balance potential sales increases against increased costs. This decision process is exactly the same as described in the section on multinational marketing decisions in Chapter 2.

## SUMMARY

The United States is becoming increasingly diverse. Much of this diversity is fueled by immigration and an increase in ethnic pride and by identification with non-European heritages among numerous Americans. Most members of a culture share most of the core values, beliefs, and behaviors of that culture. However, most individuals also belong to several subcultures. A *subculture* is a segment of a larger culture whose members share distinguishing patterns of behavior. An array of ethnic, nationality, religious, and regional subcultures characterizes American society. The existence of these subcultures provides marketers with the opportunity to develop unique marketing programs to match the unique needs of each.

*Ethnic subcultures* are defined broadly as those whose members' unique shared behaviors are based on a common racial, language, or nationality background. Non-European ethnic groups constitute a significant and growing part of the U.S. population, from 36 percent in 2010 to 44 percent by 2030.

*African Americans* represent a substantial non-European ethnic group at roughly 13 percent of the U.S. population. Although African Americans are younger and tend to have lower incomes than the general population, their rapidly growing education, income, purchasing power, and cultural influence continue to attract marketers to this large and diverse subculture.

*Hispanics* represent the largest and fastest-growing ethnic subculture in the United States. Even though Hispanics have a variety of national backgrounds (Mexico, Puerto Rico, Cuba, and so on), the Spanish language, a common religion (Roman Catholicism), and national Spanish-language media and entertainment figures have created a somewhat homogeneous Hispanic subculture.

*Asian Americans* are the most diverse of the major ethnic subcultures. They are characterized by a variety of nationalities, languages, and religions. From a marketing perspective, it is not appropriate to consider Asian Americans as a single group. Instead, Asian Americans are best approached as a number of nationality subcultures.

*Native Americans, Asian-Indian Americans,* and *Arab Americans* are smaller but important subcultures. Each is diverse yet shares enough common values and behaviors to be approached as a single segment for at least some products. Geographic concentration and specialized media allow targeted marketing campaigns.

Although the United States is a relatively secular society, roughly 78 percent of American adults claim a religious affiliation and a majority state that religion is important in their lives. A majority of American adults identify themselves as Christian although the percentage has declined over time. And a variety of *religious subcultures* exist within both the Christian faiths and the Jewish, Muslim, and Buddhist faiths. Within each faith, the largest contrast is the degree of conservatism of the members.

*Regional subcultures* arise as a result of climatic conditions, the natural environment and resources, the characteristics of the various immigrant groups that have settled in each region, and significant social and political events. Regional subcultures affect all aspects of consumption behavior, and sophisticated marketers recognize that the United States is composed of numerous regional markets.

## KEY TERMS

Acculturation  165
Born-again Christians  181
Ethnic subcultures  158

Event marketing  164
Hispanic  165
Regional subcultures  183

Religious subcultures  179
Secular society  179
Subculture  156

## INTERNET EXERCISES

1. Visit the U.S. Census Web site (www.census.gov). What data are available there on the following? Which of this is most useful to marketers? Why?
   a. Native Americans
   b. African Americans
   c. Hispanics
   d. Asian Americans

2. Use the Internet to determine the cities in the United States that have the largest population of the following. Why is this useful to marketers?
   a. Native Americans
   b. African Americans

   c. Hispanics
   d. Asian-Indian Americans
   e. Arab Americans

3. Visit www.adherents.com. Evaluate its usefulness as an information source on the following.
   a. Roman Catholic subculture
   b. Protestant subcultures
   c. Jewish subculture
   d. Muslim subculture
   e. Buddhist subculture

4. Visit Native Nations Network (www.nativenationsnet .net). Based on this site, what seem to be some

of the major issues facing Native Americans today?

5. Visit Accent Marketing (a Hispanic advertising agency) at www.accentmarketing.com. Click on "Portfolio" to view examples of the campaigns they have created. Prepare a brief report on one of these campaigns and how the agency has customized its ads to the unique needs of this segment.

6. Visit Kang & Lee Advertising (an Asian American advertising agency) at www.kanglee.com. Use the resources they provide to learn more about the Asian American market.

## DDB LIFE STYLE STUDY™ DATA ANALYSES

1. Based on the DDB data in Table 5A, which heavier-user categories have the greatest differences across the ethnic subcultures? Why is this the case?

2. For which products does ownership differ the most across ethnic groups (Table 5A)? Why is this the case?

3. For which types of television shows (Table 5A) do preferences differ the most across the ethnic subcultures? Why is this the case?

4. Use the DDB data in Table 5B to examine differences in the following characteristics across ethnic subcultures. What might explain these differences?
   a. Enjoy shopping for items influenced by other cultures.
   b. Religion is a big part of my life.
   c. Try to maintain a youthful appearance.
   d. When making family decisions, consideration of kids comes first.
   e. There is not enough ethnic diversity in commercials today.
   f. Want to look a little different from others.

## REVIEW QUESTIONS

1. What is a *subculture*?
2. What determines the degree to which a subculture will influence an individual's behavior?
3. Is the American culture more like a soup or a salad?
4. What is an *ethnic subculture*?
5. How large are the major ethnic subcultures in America? Which are growing most rapidly?
6. What countries/regions are the major sources of America's immigrants?
7. Are the various ethnic subcultures homogeneous or heterogeneous?
8. Describe the influence of education on the Internet use of African Americans. What are the marketing implications?
9. Describe the two African American consumer groups found by the Yankelovich group.
10. What are the basic principles that should be followed in marketing to an African American market segment?
11. To what extent is the Spanish language used by American Hispanics? How does language and acculturation affect Internet use among Hispanics?
12. Can Hispanics be treated as a single market?
13. Describe the three Hispanic generational groups identified by the Pew Hispanic Center.
14. How homogeneous are Asian Americans?
15. To what extent do Asian Americans use their native language?
16. Describe three emerging trends which may make the Asian American population somewhat easier to target.
17. Why is the United States considered to be a *secular society*?
18. Describe the *Roman Catholic subculture*.
19. Describe the *born-again Christian subculture*.
20. Describe the *Jewish subculture*.
21. Describe the *Muslim subculture*.
22. Describe the *Buddhist subculture*.
23. What is a regional subculture? Give some examples.

## DISCUSSION QUESTIONS

24. Examine Table 5–1. Which of these differences are mainly caused by ethnicity or race, and which are caused by other factors?

25. Do you agree that America is becoming more like a salad than a soup in terms of the integration of ethnic groups? Is this good or bad?

26. Do you agree with Miller Brewing that "the things that young Hispanic or young African American or young white people have in common are much stronger and more important than any ethnic difference"? For what types of products is this view most correct? Least correct?

27. Most new immigrants to America are non-European and have limited English-language skills. What opportunities does this present to marketers? Does this raise any ethical issues for marketers?

28. Does a firm's social responsibility play a role in marketing to consumers from various ethnic subcultures whose incomes fall below the poverty line? If so, what?

29. Respond to the questions in Consumer Insight 5–1.

30. Although many of the following have very limited incomes, others are quite prosperous. Does marketing to prosperous members of these groups require a marketing mix different from the one used to reach other prosperous consumers?
    a. African Americans
    b. Hispanics
    c. Asian Americans

31. Describe how each of the following firms' product managers should approach (*i*) the African American, (*ii*) the Hispanic, (*iii*) the Asian American,

(*iv*) the Asian-Indian American, (*v*) the Arab American, or (*vi*) the Native American markets.
    a. Red Bull
    b. McDonald's
    c. NBA
    d. *Sports Illustrated* magazine
    e. The United Way
    f. Dell laptops
    g. Google.com
    h. Coach handbags

32. What, if any, unique ethical responsibilities exist when marketing to ethnic subcultures?

33. Do you agree that the United States is a secular society? Why or why not?

34. Describe how each of the following firms' product managers should approach the (*i*) Catholic, (*ii*) Protestant, (*iii*) born-again Christian, (*iv*) Jewish, (*v*) Muslim, and (*vi*) Buddhist subcultures.
    a. Red Bull
    b. Wendy's
    c. NBA
    d. *Maxim* magazine
    e. The United Way
    f. Dell laptops
    g. eBay.com
    h. Coach handbags

35. Will regional subcultures become more or less distinct over the next 20 years? Why?

36. Select one product, service, or activity from each category in Table 5–2 and explain the differences in consumption for the item across the regions shown.

## APPLICATION ACTIVITIES

37. Watch two hours of prime-time major network (ABC, CBS, FOX, or NBC) television. What subculture groups are portrayed in the programs? Describe how they are portrayed. Do these portrayals match the descriptions in this text? How would you explain the differences? Repeat these tasks for the ads shown during the programs.

38. Pick a product of interest and examine the Simmons Market Research Bureau or MediaMark studies on the product in your library (these are often in the journalism library on CD-ROM). Determine the extent to which its consumption varies by ethnic group and region. Does consumption also vary by age, income, or other variables? Are the differences in ethnic and regional

consumption due primarily to ethnicity and region or to the fact that the ethnic group or region is older, richer, or otherwise different from the larger culture?

39. Examine several magazines or newspapers aimed at a non-European ethnic or nationality group. What types of products are advertised? Why?

40. Interview three members of the following sub-cultures and ascertain their opinions of how their ethnic or nationality group is portrayed on network television shows and in national ads.
    a. African Americans
    b. Asian Americans
    c. Hispanics
    d. Arab Americans
    e. Asian-Indian Americans
    f. Native Americans

41. Interview three members of the following subcultures and ascertain the extent to which they identify with the core American culture, their ethnic subculture within America, or their nationality subculture. Also determine the extent to which they feel others of their ethnic/race

group feel as they do and the reasons for any differences.
    a. African Americans
    b. Asian Americans
    c. Hispanics
    d. Arab Americans
    e. Asian-Indian Americans
    f. Native Americans

42. Interview three members of the following religious subcultures and determine the extent to which their consumption patterns are influenced by their religion.
    a. Catholics
    b. Protestants
    c. Born-again Christians
    d. Jews
    e. Muslims
    f. Buddhists

43. Interview two students from other regions of the United States and determine the behavior and attitudinal differences they have noticed between their home and your present location. Try to determine the causes of these differences.

## REFERENCES

1. Chapter opener is based on "L. M. Keefe, "P&G's Multicultural Marketing DNA," *Marketing News*, March 1, 2004, pp. 13–14; "Proctor & Gamble Launched 'My Black is Beautiful' Campaign at 2007 BET Awards," *My Black is Beautiful*, press release, July 3, 2007; J. Neff, "My Black is Beautiful," *Advertising Age*, August 27, 2007, www.adage.com, accessed June 4, 2008; "Proctor & Gamble Unveils "My Black is Beautiful," *My Black is Beautiful*, press release, August 8, 2007; M. Bush, "P&G Unveils 'My Black is Beautiful' Campaign," *PRweek*, December 3, 2007, p. 5; and excerpts from *My Black is Beautiful Personal Journal and Discussion Guide*, www.myblackisbeautiful.com, accessed June 5, 2008.

2. See R. Suro, "Recasting the Melting Pot," *American Demographics*, March 1999, pp. 30–32.

3. For conflicting data, see S. Reese, "When Whites Aren't a Mass Market," *American Demographics*, March 1997, pp. 51–54.

4. L. Wentz, "Reverse English," *Advertising Age*, November 19, 2001, p. S1.

5. M. G. Briones, "Coors Turns Up the Heat," *Marketing News*, June 22, 1998, p. 15.

6. C. Fisher, "It's All in the Details," *American Demographics*, April 1998, p. 45.

7. W. H. Frey, "Micro Melting Pots," *American Demographics*, June 2001, pp. 20–23.

8. K. Jefferys and R. Monger, *U.S. Legal Permanent Residents: 2007* (Washington, DC: U.S. Department of Homeland Security, 2007), p. 4.

9. See L. R. Oswald, "Culture Swapping," *Journal of Consumer Research*, March 1999, pp. 303–18.

10. M. R. Forehand and R. Deshpande, "What We See Makes Us Who We Are," *Journal of Marketing Research*, August 2001, pp. 336–48.

11. Median age, growth rate, and children under 18: *Statistical Abstract of the United States 2004–2005* (Washington, DC: U.S. Census Bureau, 2004–2005); except growth rate from *Hispanics: A People in Motion* (Washington, DC: Pew Research Center, 2005); education: *Statistical Abstract of the United States 2008* (Washington, DC: U.S. Census Bureau, data for 2006); income: *2007 Annual Social and Economic Supplement* (Washington, DC: U.S. Census Bureau, 2007).

12. M. L. Rossman, *Multicultural Marketing* (New York: American Management Association, 1994), pp. 153–57.

13. E. Morris, "The Difference in Black and White," *American Demographics*, January 1993, p. 46.

14. "Households by Total Money Income in 2006," *2007 Annual Social and Economic Supplement* (Washington, DC: U.S. Bureau of the Census, 2007).

15. J. M. Humphreys, "The Multicultural Economy 2006," *Georgia Business and Economic Conditions* 66, no. 3 (2006).

16. *The 1993 Minority Market Report* (Coral Gables, FL: Market Segment Research, 1993).

17. D. M. Ayers, "What Does Brand Have to Do With It?" *Market Snapshot* (Chicago: Hunter-Miller Group, July 2004), www.huntermillergroup.com.

18. See A. S. Wellner, "The Forgotten Baby Boom," *American Demographics,* February 2001, pp. 47–51.

19. D. M. Ayers, "Moving On Up," *Market Snapshot,* January 2004, www.huntermillergroup.com.

20. P. Miller, *African Americans Are a Heterogeneous, Not a Homogeneous, Market,* Cablevision Advertising Bureau, 2005, www.onetvworld.org.

21. "Black Baby Boomers," *Market Snapshot,* May 2002, www.huntermillergroup.com.

22. Y. K. Kim and J. Kang, "The Effects of Ethnicity and Product on Purchase Decision Making," *Journal of Advertising Research,* March 2001, pp. 39–48.

23. J. Adler, "Marketers, Agencies Praise BET's Savvy," *Advertising Age,* April 11, 2005, p. B16.

24. *Latinos Online* (Washington, D.C.: Pew Internet & American Life Project, March 14, 2007).

25. E. Burns, "African American Online Population Is Growing," *The ClickZ Network,* October 10, 2005, www.clickz.com, accessed June 7, 2008; and "AOL: Some 80 Percent of African-Americans Online," *MarketingVOX,* October 17, 2005, www.marketingvox.com, accessed June 7, 2008.

26. "African-American Buying Power 2002 vs. 2001," *Marketing News,* July 15, 2004, p. 11.

27. See, e.g., L. Sanders, "How to Target Blacks?" *Advertising Age,* July 3, 2006, p. 19.

28. E. M. Simpson et al., "Race, Homophily, and Purchase Intentions and the Black Consumer," *Psychology & Marketing,* October 2000, pp. 877–99. See also L. A. Perkins, K. M. Thomas, and G. A. Taylor, "Advertising and Recruitment," *Psychology & Marketing,* March 2000, pp. 235–55.

29. C. L. Green, "Ethnic Evaluations of Advertising," *Journal of Advertising,* Spring 1999, pp. 49–63; O. Appiah, "Ethnic Identification on Adolescents' Evaluations of Advertisements," *Journal of Advertising Research,* September 2001, pp. 7–21; and T. E. Whittler and J. S. Spira, "Model's Race," *Journal of Consumer Psychology* 12, no. 4 (2002), pp. 291–301.

30. *The African-American Market in the U.S.* (New York: *Packaged Facts,* 2008).

31. D. Howell, "Albertson's Caters to Different Ethnic Markets," *DSN Retailing Today,* October 1, 2001, p. 18.

32. Keefe, "P&G's Multicultural Marketing DNA."

33. T. L. Ainscough and C. M. Motley, "Will You Help Me Please?" *Marketing Letters,* May 2000, pp. 129–36.

34. See V. D. Bush et al., "Managing Culturally Diverse Buyer–Seller Relationships," *Journal of the Academy of Marketing Science,* Fall 2001, pp. 391–404.

35. M. F. Floyd and K. J. Shinew, "Convergence in Leisure Style and Whites and African Americans," *Journal of Leisure Research* 31, no. 4 (1999), pp. 359–84. See also, *The African-American Market in the U.S.* (New York: *Packaged Facts,* 2008).

36. N. Delener, "Consumer Payment System Attribute Perceptions and Preferences," *Journal of Professional Services Marketing* 1 (1995), pp. 53–71; and F. J. Mulhern, J. D. Williams, and R. P. Leone, "Variability of Brand Price Elasticities across Retail Stores," *Journal of Retailing* 3 (1998), pp. 427–45. See also, *The African-American Market in the U.S.* (New York: *Packaged Facts,* 2008).

37. *The American Community—Hispanics, 2004* (Washington, DC: U.S. Census Bureau, 2007), p. 2.

38. W. R. Ortiz, "Answering the Language Question," CableTelevision Advertising Bureau, press release, www.onetvworld.org, accessed May 9, 2005.

39. An excellent description of this process for Mexican immigrants appears in L. Penaloza, "*Atravesando Fronteras*/Border Crossings," *Journal of Consumer Research,* June 1994, pp. 32–54.

40. Based on R. X. Weissman, "Los Niños Go Shopping," *American Demographics,* May 1999, pp. 37–39; H. Stapinski, "Generación Latino," *American Demographics,* July 1999, pp. 63–68; R. Gardyn, "Habla English," *American Demographics,* April 2001, pp. 54–57; J. D. Zbar, "Hispanic Teens Set Urban Beat," *Advertising Age,* June 2001, p. S6; H. Chura, "Sweet Spot," *Advertising Age,* November 12, 2001, p. 1; *Nuestro Futuro* (Redwood Shores, Cheskin, 2006); and *Hispanic/Latino Market Profile* (New York: Mediamark Research, 2007).

41. *Generational Differences* (Washington, DC: Pew Hispanic Center/Kaiser Family Foundation, March 2004); (Source: © 2004, Pew Hispanic Center, www.pewhispanic.org).

42. G. Berman, *Portrait of the New America* (Coral Gables, FL: Market Segment Group, 2002), p. 21.

43. See *Hispanics: A People in Motion.*

44. C. Webster, "The Effects of Hispanic Identification on Marital Roles in the Purchase Decision Process," *Journal of Consumer Research,* September 1994, pp. 319–31.

45. L. Kramer, "Church's Chicken Chain Courts Latino Audience," *Advertising Age,* October 19, 1998, p. 12.

46. *The U.S. Hispanic Market* (New York: *Packaged Facts,* October 2003).

47. L. Sonderup, "Hispanic Marketing," *Advertising & Marketing Review,* April 2004, www.ad-mkt-review.com.

48. Ibid.

49. Ortiz, "Answering the Language Question."

50. Humphreys, "The Multicultural Economy 2006."

51. "The U.S. Hispanic Market."

52. L. Wentz, "Rapid Change Sweeps Hispanic Advertising Industry," *AdAge.com,* May 3, 2005, www.adage.com.

53. *The U.S. Hispanic Market.*

54. *Latinos Online.*

55. "YupiMSN and ESPNdeportes.com Team Up to Deliver the Best in Online Sports to Spanish-Speaking Fans throughout the Americas," Microsoft, press release, June 4, 2002; and "A Year in Review," ComScore Networks, press release, November 12, 2003.

56. C. P. Taylor, "BarbieLatina Says 'Hola' to Net," *Advertising Age,* October 1, 2001, p. 54.

57. For these and other examples, see "Marketing to Hispanics," *Advertising Age,* February 8, 1987, p. S23; M. Westerman, "Death of the Frito Bandito," March 1989, pp. 28–32; and L. Wentz, "Debate Swirls over Slang in Coors Spot," *Advertising Age,* May 17, 2004, p. 6.

58. See D. Luna, L. A. Peracchio, and M. D. de Juan, "The Impact of Language and Congruity on Persuasion in Multicultural E-Marketing," *Journal of Consumer Psychology* 13, no. 1/2 (2003), pp. 41–50; see also Gardyn, "Habla English."

59. L. Giegoldt, "Brand Loyalty Opportunities Abound," *Advertising Age,* August 24, 1998, p. S10. See also S. Shim and K. C. Gehrt, "Hispanic and Native American Adolescents," *Journal of Retailing* 3 (1996), pp. 307–24.

60. L. Wentz, "Best Buy Targets Hispanic Patriarchs," *Advertising Age,* August 2, 2004, p. 20.

61. J. Garcia and R. Gerdes, "To Win Latino Market, Know Pitfalls, Learn Rewards," *Marketing News,* March 1, 2004, pp. 14, 19.

62. J. Halliday, "Ford Unveils First Truck for U.S. Hispanic Market," *AdAge.com,* April 26, 2005, www.adage.com; and "Ford Celebrates Cinco de Mayo with 'Lobo' F-150," *Edmunds.com,* press release, April 26, 2005.

63. A. S. Wellner, "Gen X Homes In," *American Demographics,* August 1999, p. 61.

64. M. Johnson, "The Application of Geodemographics to Retailing," *Journal of the Market Research Society,* January 1997, p. 213.

65. L. Wentz, "Home Depot Paint Line Connects with Hispanics," *Advertising Age,* July 3, 2006, p. 19.

66. Humphreys, "The Multicultural Economy 2006."

67. See B. Edmundson, "Asian Americans in 2001," *American Demographics,* February 1997, pp. 16–17.

68. "Asia Rising," *American Demographics,* July–August 2002, pp. 38–43.

69. M. C. Tharp, *Marketing and Consumer Identity in Multicultural America* (Thousand Oaks, CA: Sage, 2001), p. 259.

70. Ibid., pp. 253–57.

71. *The 1993 Minority Market Report.*

72. D. L. Vence, "Growth in Asian-Am. Spending Fuels Targeted Marketing," *Marketing News,* June 1, 2004, pp. 11–13.

73. "Asia Rising."

74. *Annual Estimates of the Resident Population by Race, Age and Sex for the United States: April 1, 2000 to July 1, 2006* (Washington, DC: U.S. Census Bureau, 2007).

75. Vence, "Growth in Asian-Am. Spending Fuels Targeted Marketing."

76. "Reaching Generation 2.0," *Advertising Age,* July–August 2002, p. 42.

77. S. F. Ownby and P. E. Horridge, "Acculturation Level and Shopping Orientations of Asian American Consumers," *Psychology & Marketing,* January 1997, pp. 1–18; D. D'Rozario and S. P. Douglas, "Effects of Assimilation on Prepurchase External Information-Search Tendencies," *Journal of Consumer Psychology* 8, no. 2 (1999), pp. 187–209; and Y.-K. Kim and J. Kang, "Effects of Asian-Americans' Ethnicity and Accul-

turation on Personal Influences," *Journal of Current Issues and Research in Advertising,* Spring 2001, pp. 43–53.

78. See P. Paul, "Mediachannels," *American Demographics,* November 2001, pp. 26–31.

79. Information accessed from corporate Web sites.

80. "Annual Asian American Consumer Behavior Study Reveals Key Findings in Retail, Automobile, Insurance, and Telecom Industries," *DiversityBusiness.com,* March 7, 2007, www.diversitybusiness.com, accessed June 8, 2008.

81. Vence, "Growth in Asian-Am. Spending Fuels Targeted Marketing."

82. "Diversity in America," *American Demographics,* November 2002, p. S17.

83. Humphreys, "The Multicultural Economy 2006."

84. "Native American Food Goes Haute Cuisine," *CNN.com,* September 30, 2004, www.cnn.com.

85. See A. S. Wellner, "Discovering Native America," *American Demographics,* August 2001, p. 21.

86. A. M. Peterson, "Nike Boosts Indians' Health, Its Reputation," *Marketing News,* June 1, 2004, p. 10.

87. This section is based on M. Mogelonsky, "Asian Indian Americans," *American Demographics,* August 1995, pp. 32–39. See also M. M. Cardona, "Segment Marketing Grows as Tool for Financial Services Leaders," *Advertising Age,* November 20, 2000, p. S1.

88. A. S. Wellner, "Every Day's a Holiday," *American Demographics,* December 2000, p. 63.

89. "Arab Americans" section is based on S. El-Badry, "The Arab-American Market," *American Demographics,* January 1994, pp. 22–30; L. P. Morton, "Segmenting to Target Arab Americans," *Public Relations Quarterly,* Winter 2001, pp. 47–48; "Survey Reveals Arab American Experiences and Reactions Following 9/11," Arab American Institute, press release, August 19, 2002; "Arab American Demographics," Arab American Institute, www.aaiusa.org/demographics.htm, accessed May 14, 2005; and K. Naughton, "Arab-America's Store," *Newsweek,* March 10, 2008, p. 42.

90. "U.S. Religious Landscape Survey," *The Pew Forum on Religion and Public Life,* 2008.

91. H. Taylor, "While Most Americans Believe in God, Only 36% Attend a Religious Service Once a Month or More Often," *The Harris Poll®,* October 15, 2003, www.harrisinteractive.com.

92. B. A. Robinson, "How Many People Go Regularly to Weekly Religious Services?" Ontario Consultants on Religious Tolerance, November 26, 2001, www.religioustolerance.org.

93. "Survey: Americans Switching Faiths, Dropping Out," *CNN.com,* February 25, 2008, www.cnn.com, accessed February 25, 2008.

94. See R. Cimino and D. Lattin, "Choosing My Religion," *American Demographics,* April 1999, pp. 6–65.

95. "U.S. Religious Landscape Survey." Additional information on religion in the United States can be found at Adherents.com (www.adherents.com), which collects and disseminates statistics from various sources, including two of the most comprehensive surveys of religion in the United States, namely, the National

Survey of Religious Identification (NSRI: 1990) and the American Religious Identity Survey (ARIS: 2001) conducted by B. A. Kosmin, S. P. Lachman, and associates.

96. B. Ebenkamp, "The Young and Righteous," *Brandweek,* April 5, 2004, p. 18; and S. Kang, "Pop Culture Gets Religion," *The Wall Street Journal,* May 5, 2004, pp. B1, B2.

97. Information on ethnic diversity from ARIS research briefs, www.gc.cuny.edu.

98. Information on *Encuentro 2000* from press releases by the United States Conference of Catholic Bishops (Washington, DC), including "Growing Asian Impact on Church to Be Felt at *Encuentro 2000,*" May 22, 2000; "Latin Music, Movie on Cuba, Hispanic Cultural Expressions Part of *Encuento 2000* Celebration of Multi-ethnic Church," May 30, 2000; and "Bishops' Agenda Includes Pastoral Framework for Hispanic Ministry," October 11, 2002, www.usccb.org.

99. B. A. Kosmin and P. Lachman, *One Nation under God* (New York: Harmony Books, 1993), p. 245.

100. "Breaking the Rules of Engagement," *American Demographics,* July–August 2002, p. 35.

101. R. Thau, "The New Jewish Exodus," *American Demographics,* June 1994, p. 11.

102. Kosmin and Lachman, *One Nation under God,* p. 12.

103. Estimates here have been hotly debated. For an excellent discussion, see "The Largest Religious Groups in the United States of America," Adherents.com, www.adherents.com.

104. M. Chapman and A. Jamal, "The Floodgates Open," *Enhancing Knowledge Development in Marketing* (Chicago: American Marketing Association, 1996), p. 198.

105. See S. El-Badry, "Understanding Islam in America," *American Demographics,* January 1994, p. 10.

106. B. Horovitz, "Down-home Marketing," *USA Today,* October 3, 1997, p. 1B.

# The American Society:
# Families and Households

■ The kids' market is large and growing, and taking some amazing turns when it comes to high-end luxury.[1] *Packaged Facts* estimates that spending *on* kids 3 to 12 is around $178 billion per year and spending *by* kids the same age is around $26 billion, making total spending by and for this group over $200 billion annually! Spending crosses numerous categories, including food (at home and away), apparel, toys and video games.

New research by NPD Group uncovered several important aspects relating to this market:

- Top spending categories are apparel (23 percent of mom's discretionary income), and entertainment products such as toys, video games, books (48 percent). Spending on fast food was only 12 percent, which is clearly a move in the right direction from a health-related perspective.
- The main driver of spending on kids is not household income but rather age of child. Those with children over age five spend 35 percent more than those with children five and under.
- Children's influence on purchases is strong for 60 percent of mothers. The influence was strongest for video games and weakest for apparel.
- Gender does not influence amount spent except in two cases—apparel for girls and video games for boys.
- Brands are important in some categories, but style and look were important in all categories.

Although all these findings are important, the last point stands out—style and look are important even for young children. This is not lost at all on a number of companies, particularly those targeting young girls. Examples are numerous just in the area of spas, parties, and salon services. Companies are offering high-end lux treatment for young girls, including "snip, style, and sparkle" hair styling, and Tutti Frutti Manicures and Chocolate Pedicures. Demand appears to be strong, with double-digit growth in stores and revenues for companies such as Sweet & Sassy, Monkey Dooz, and Club Libby Lu. Obviously, this trend is not without concern. However, marketers counter that it's about fun and fantasy and that they wouldn't do anything to "keep a child from being a child." In addition, marketers see this as a triple win. First are the revenues earned now from this market. Second is building loyalty that can be leveraged in the future. This is particularly true for those like Club Libby Lu, which operates under the Saks nameplate. Finally is the added revenue from moms who come into the stores with their children and end up shopping for themselves as well.

The household is the basic consumption unit for most consumer goods. Major items such as housing, automobiles, and appliances are consumed more by household units than by individuals. Furthermore, the consumption patterns of individual household members seldom are independent from those of other household members. For example, deciding to grant a child's request for a bicycle may mean spending discretionary funds that could have been used to purchase a weekend away for the parents, new clothing for a sister or brother, or otherwise used by another member of the household. Therefore, it is essential that marketers understand the household as a consumption unit, as shown in Figure 6–1.

Households are important not only for their direct role in the consumption process but also for the critical role they perform in socializing children. The family household is the primary mechanism whereby cultural and subcultural values and behavior patterns are passed on to the next generation. Purchasing and consumption patterns are among those attitudes and skills strongly influenced by the family household unit.

This chapter examines (1) the nature and importance of families and households in contemporary American society, (2) the household life cycle, (3) the nature of the family decision process, and (4) consumer socialization.

| FIGURE 6–1 | The Household Influences Most Consumption Decisions |
| --- | --- |

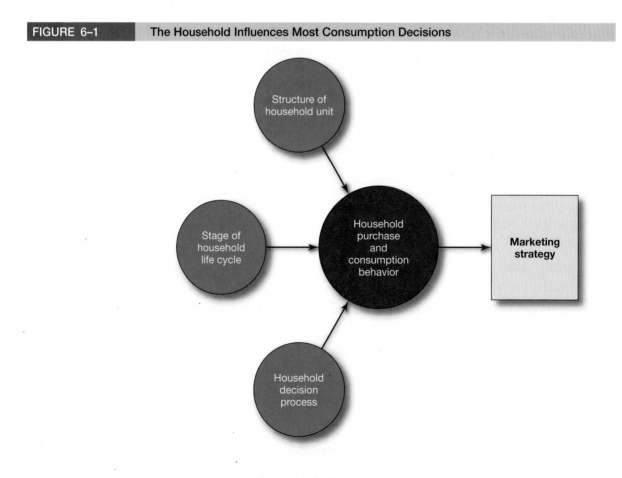

# THE NATURE OF AMERICAN HOUSEHOLDS

## Types of Households

There are a variety of types of households. The Census Bureau defines a **household** as *all the people who occupy a housing unit* (a house, apartment, group of rooms, or single room designed to be occupied as separate living quarters). It defines a **family household** as one having *at least two members related by birth, marriage, or adoption, one of whom is the householder* (householder owns or rents the residence). A **nonfamily household** is a *householder living alone or exclusively with others to whom he or she is not related.* Table 6–1 indicates the current distribution of household types in the United States.

These definitions are important because the Census Bureau, which provides most of the available data on households, uses them. Unfortunately, these terms do not capture the richness of the American family structure. The **blended family**—*a family consisting of a couple, one or both of whom were previously married, their children, and the children from the previous marriage of one or both parents*—is one missing form.[2] While more than 40 percent of first marriages end in divorce, most of these divorced individuals remarry.[3] Thus, a significant percentage of American children grow up with stepparents and stepsiblings. Many of these children spend significant time in two such families, one formed by their mother and the other by their father.

The term **traditional family** refers to *a married couple and their own or adopted children living at home.* Much publicity has been given to its demise, and this type of family has clearly declined over time. This is particularly true if one considers a traditional family to be one headed by a never-divorced couple. However, roughly half (51 percent) of all households are headed by married couples (down from 71 percent in 1970) and roughly 67 percent of households with children under 18 are headed by a married couple.[4] The decline in traditional families is due in part to an increase in single-parent households as a result of divorce. A larger cause is a significant increase in single individuals. This increase has been largely a result of the overall delay in the median age of marriage—from 23.2 and 20.8 years for males and females, respectively, in 1970 to 27.5 and 25.9 in 2006—and by an increase in sole survivors as the percentage of the population over 65 has grown significantly.

Other common household structures are also not adequately captured by Census reports or other major data sources such as Mediamark, Simmons, or Nielsen. Unmarried

**TABLE 6–1**

Family and Nonfamily Households, 2006

| Type of Household | Number (000s omitted) | Percentage |
|---|---|---|
| **All households** | **114,384** | **100.0%** |
| **Family households** | **77,402** | **67.7** |
| Married couples | 58,179 | 50.9 |
| *Children under 18 at home* | *25,919* | *22.6* |
| *No children under 18 at home* | *32,197* | *28.2* |
| Single fathers (children under 18 at home) | 2,095 | 1.8 |
| Single mothers (children under 18 at home) | 8,389 | 7.3 |
| Other families | 8,739 | 7.6 |
| **Nonfamily households** | **36,982** | **32.3** |
| Male householder | 16,753 | 14.7 |
| *Living alone* | *13,061* | *11.4* |
| Female householder | 20,230 | 17.7 |
| *Living alone* | *17,392* | *15.2* |

Source: *Households, Families, Subfamilies, and Married Couples: 1980–2006* (Washington, DC: U.S. Census Bureau, 2008), Table 58.

## Unmarried Families

There are over 5 million unmarried, opposite-sex households in the United States, a 30 percent increase in five years.[5] For some, cohabitation is a temporary arrangement before marriage; for others, it represents a long-term relationship:

> Our relationship has lasted longer than those of any of our friends near our own age—married or not. We are actually looked up to as a model couple. I don't want to mess with what works.

Unmarried couples increasingly resemble the general population in terms of age, presence of children, and so on. And, in many ways, the needs of unmarried couples are the same as those of married couples with similar demographics. However, there are exceptions, such as finding knowledgeable assistance with legal and financial issues concerning joint home ownership, estate planning, and so forth.

> When Dorain and Marshall—both twenty-something and cohabiting for eight years—applied for joint tenants insurance, they were told by a local agent that their only choice was to apply for individual policies at almost twice the cost. They eventually found an agency catering to the gay and lesbian community that signed them up for joint tenants and auto insurance with no problem. In fact, many heterosexual couples turn to gay professionals who are better equipped to navigate the complex legal and financial issues that unmarried couples often face.

One reason marketers rarely target unmarried couples is that they are not easy to identify or reach. There are no media dedicated to this audience, and they are not demographically unique. Another reason is that cohabitation is not fully accepted:

Companies that might benefit from targeting this group—banks, lawyers, and so forth—don't want to be viewed as doing anything that undermines marriage because they could be viewed as promoting an uncommitted lifestyle.

Most unmarried couples realize and deal with the difficulties and prejudices associated with their status. However, they would also like some recognition that they matter. Boutique card companies, for example, are increasingly looking for growth in the area of non-traditional families. A company called Cool Cards offers a line of Love Cards, described as "distinctly non-traditional Love Cards for distinctly non-traditional Friends and Lovers." Hallmark Cards initially responded with a line of cards called "Ties That Bind." Now they appear to simply intersperse such cards within their overall line. However, their move to include cards for nontraditional families still rings true:

> Our cards reflect the times. Relationships today are so nebulous that they are hard to pin down, but in creating products, we have to be aware that they are there. Companies need to respect and be sensitive to how people are truly living their lives now, and not how they might wish or hope for them to live.

### Critical Thinking Questions

1. Do you agree that unmarried couples will become increasingly more common?

2. What needs do unmarried couples have that demographically similar married couples do not have?

3. Should firms such as banks develop and advertise products to meet the unique needs of this group?

couples, both same-sex and opposite-sex, have consumption patterns similar to married couples but, in the absence of children, would not be classified as a family household by the Census. Consumer Insight 6–1 describes one subset of unmarried families, namely opposite-sex households, and some of the marketing issues and opportunities these consumers create.

Kraft recognizes the diversity and importance of families, with ads that portray various family types in scenarios revolving around food. A recent spot features a father and his daughter enjoying a quiet conversation.

Recognizing and adapting to the differing needs of various family members can be a critical success factor (see Illustration 6–1).

# THE HOUSEHOLD LIFE CYCLE

The traditional view of the American household life cycle was quite simple. People married by their early twenties; they had several children; these children grew up and started their own families; the original couple retired; and the male would eventually die, followed after a few years by the female. This was known as the *family life cycle,* and it was a useful tool for segmenting markets and developing marketing strategy. The basic assumption underlying the family life cycle approach is that most families pass through an orderly progression of stages, each with its own characteristics, financial situations, and purchasing patterns.

Members of the same family often have differing desires. Marketers that can appeal to all members of the family unit have an advantage.

However, as described earlier, American households follow much more complex and varied cycles today. Therefore, researchers have developed several models of the **household life cycle (HLC).**[6] All are based on the age and marital status of the adult members of the household and the presence and age of children. A useful version is shown in Figure 6–2.

The HLC assumes that households move into a variety of relatively distinct and well-defined categories over time. There are a variety of routes into most of the categories shown in Figure 6–2, and movement from one category into another frequently occurs. For example, it is common for singles to marry and then divorce within a few years without having children (moving from single to young married back to young single). Or one can become a single parent through divorce or through birth or adoption without a cohabiting partner.

Each category in the household life cycle poses a set of problems that household decision makers must solve. The solution to these problems is bound intimately to the selection and maintenance of a lifestyle and, thus, to consumption. For example, all young couples with no children face a need for relaxation or recreation. Solutions to this common problem differ, with some opting for an outdoors-oriented lifestyle and others choosing a sophisticated urban lifestyle. As these families move into another stage in the HLC, such as the "full nest I" stage, the problems they face change. The amount of time and resources available for recreation usually diminishes. New problems related to raising a child become more urgent.

Each stage presents unique needs and wants as well as financial conditions and experiences. Thus, the HLC provides marketers with relatively homogeneous household segments that share similar needs with respect to household-related problems and purchases.

While Figure 6–2 categorizes households into married and unmarried, it is "coupleness" rather than the legal status of the relationship that drives most of the behavior of the

| FIGURE 6-2 | Stages of the Household Life Cycle |
| --- | --- |

| Stage | Marital Status | | Children at Home | | |
| --- | --- | --- | --- | --- | --- |
|  | Single | Married | None | < 6 years | > 6 years |
| **Younger (< 35)** |  |  |  |  |  |
| Single I | × |  | × |  |  |
| Young married |  | × | × |  |  |
| Full nest I |  | × |  | × |  |
| Single parent I | × |  |  | × |  |
|  |  |  |  |  |  |
| **Middle-aged (35–64)** |  |  |  |  |  |
| Single II | × |  | × |  |  |
| Delayed full nest I |  | × |  | × |  |
| Full nest II |  | × |  |  | × |
| Single parent II | × |  |  |  | × |
| Empty nest I |  | × | × |  |  |
|  |  |  |  |  |  |
| **Older (> 64)** |  |  |  |  |  |
| Empty nest II |  | × | × |  |  |
| Single III | × |  | × |  |  |
|  |  |  |  |  |  |

household. Committed couples, of the same sex or of opposite sexes, tend to exhibit most of the category-specific behaviors described below whether or not they are married.

Single I    This group consists of young (ages 18 to 34), unmarried individuals. In 2006, there were roughly 67.4 million people in this age group, with 68 percent of men and 60 percent of women being single. Single I is basically the unmarried members of the Generation Yers, as described in Chapter 4. The aging of the larger Generation Y cohort along with continued delay of marriage has fueled growth in this market.[7] During this time, individuals generally leave home and establish their own distinct identities. It is a time of growth and change, both exciting and positive, and frightening and painful. As one thirty-something said:

> I wouldn't go through my 20s again for all the money in the world. You are out of undergraduate school and it's like, "What's expected of me?" You still haven't come to know yourself, and it's like that there is this gigantic world out there and you must somehow get all the experiences you can under your belt before you can get to know yourself. So you try on a lot of labels and I guess that somehow you think that assemblage is you, when it isn't.[8]

This group can be subdivided into those who live with one or both parents and those who live alone or with other individuals. The roughly 43 million single individuals in this age range live as follows:

|  | Males (%) | Females (%) | Total (%) |
| --- | --- | --- | --- |
| Live alone | 14 | 12 | 13 |
| Live with parent(s) | 46 | 40 | 43 |
| Live with others | 39 | 48 | 43 |

Those who live with parents tend to be younger; 75 percent are under 25. A significant number are in school or have recently graduated from high school or college and are beginning their working careers. Though people in this group have lower relative incomes, they also have few fixed expenses. They lead active, social lives. They go to bars, movies, and concerts, and purchase sports equipment, clothes, and personal care items.

Although some of those who live with others are involved with a partner, many share quarters with one or more housemates. These individuals have more fixed living expenses than do those who live with their parents, but they generally have ample disposable income as they share rent and other fixed housing costs.

These singles are a good market for the same types of products as those who live at home as well as for convenience-oriented household products. They are also a prime market for nice apartments, sports cars, Club Med vacations, and similar activities. They are beginning to develop financial portfolios such as life insurance, savings, and stocks or mutual funds. The ad shown in Illustration 6–2 would appeal to both groups.

Singles who live alone are older; 70 percent are over 25. In general, they have higher incomes than the others but also higher expenses because they have no one with whom to share the fixed cost of a house or apartment. They are a good market for most of the same products and services as the other singles.

**Young Couples: No Children**   The decision to marry, or to live together, brings about a new stage in the household life cycle. Marriage is much more likely for the 25- to 34-year-olds (50 percent) than it is for the under-25 crowd (8 percent). The lifestyles of two young singles are greatly altered as they develop a shared lifestyle. Joint decisions and

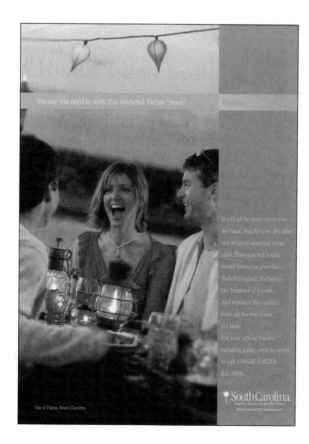

**ILLUSTRATION 6–2**

Young singles are active and often have significant discretionary income. They are an excellent market for a wide array of recreational and leisure items. This ad would appeal to their desire for action and romance.

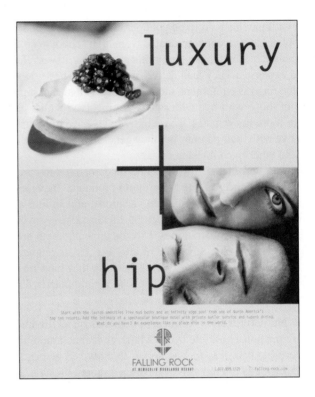

luxury

+

hip

FALLING ROCK

shared roles in household responsibilities are in many instances new experiences.[9] Savings, household furnishings, major appliances, and more comprehensive insurance coverage are among the new areas of problem recognition and decision making to which a young married couple must give serious consideration.

Like the young single stage, the time spent by a young couple in this stage of the HLC has grown as couples either delay their start in having children or choose to remain childless.

Most households in this group have dual incomes and thus are relatively affluent. Compared with full nest I families, this group spends heavily on theater tickets, expensive clothes, luxury vacations, restaurant meals, and alcoholic beverages. They can afford nice cars, stylish apartments, and high-quality home appliances.

Illustration 6–3 contains an ad that would appeal to this group as well as to some members of the single I and full nest I segments. Note that romance plays a major role in the ad. It also plays on the desire to escape worries and everyday responsibilities.

**Full Nest I: Young Married with Children**    Roughly 7 percent of households are young married couples with children. The addition of the first child to a family creates many changes in lifestyle and consumption. Naturally, new purchases in the areas of baby clothes, furniture, food, and health care products occur in this stage. Lifestyles are also greatly altered. The wife may withdraw fully or partly from the labor force (in roughly 60 percent of married couples with a child under six the wife works outside the home)[10] for several months to several years, with a resulting decline in household income. The couple may have to move to another place of residence since their current apartment may not be appropriate for children. Likewise, choices of vacations, restaurants, and automobiles must be changed to accommodate young children.

Some of the changes in income and annual expenditures that occur as a household moves from childless to the young child stage in their late twenties and early thirties include the following:[11]

| Expenditure | Percentage Change |
|---|---|
| Income | −9.4% |
| Food at home | 24.3 |
| Meals out | −9.6 |
| Alcoholic beverages | −25.0 |
| Adult apparel | −8.3 |
| Children's apparel | 215.7 |
| Health care | 16.1 |
| Education | −28.8 |
| Personal care products | −2.6 |

As shown above, discretionary and adult expenditures are reduced by the need to spend on child-related products such as food, health care, and children's apparel as well as to offset the decline in income.

Obtaining competent child care becomes an issue at this stage and remains a major concern of parents at all HLC stages. Households with a stay-at-home spouse confront this issue mainly for evenings out or weekends away. Single-parent and dual-earner households generally require daily child care, which is expensive and often requires parents to make trade-offs from their ideal situation.

ClubMom is an online loyalty program aimed at the $1.7 trillion in spending power of moms (across all HLC stages). Among other things, it provides advice, resources, and discounts to moms. Chrysler has been an automobile partner of ClubMom. In this arrangement, Chrysler promoted ClubMom in its ads and, in turn, ClubMom gave "points" that provided discounts on other products to members who purchased Dodge brands like the Durango.[12] McDonald's attempts to attract this segment by providing recreational equipment at its outlets that cater heavily to families with young children. Illustration 6–4 contains an ad aimed at this market segment. It shows how the choice of recreational activities may change with the addition of young children.

**Single Parent I: Young Single Parents**    Birth or adoption by singles is increasingly common. Roughly 37 percent of children are born to unmarried mothers, a number that has risen by 10 percentage points since 1990. However, as many as 40 percent of these children may actually be born to cohabiting unmarried parents.[13] Divorce, while on the decline since 1980, continues to be a significant part of American society, with 40 percent of first marriages ending in divorce.[14] Although most divorced individuals remarry and most women who bear children out of wedlock eventually get married, 9 percent of American households are single-parent families, and 79 percent of these are headed by women.

The younger members of this group, particularly those who have never been married, tend to have a limited education and a very low income. These individuals are often members of one of the lower social classes, as described in Chapter 4. The older members of this segment and the divorced members receiving support from their ex-spouses are somewhat better off financially, but most are still under significant stress as they raise their young children without the support of a partner who is physically present.

This type of family situation creates many unique needs in the areas of child care, easy-to-prepare foods, and recreation. The need to work and raise younger children creates enormous time pressures and places tremendous demands on the energy of these parents.

Parenthood brings both great pleasures and great responsibilities. This ad emphasizes the pleasures of family activities.

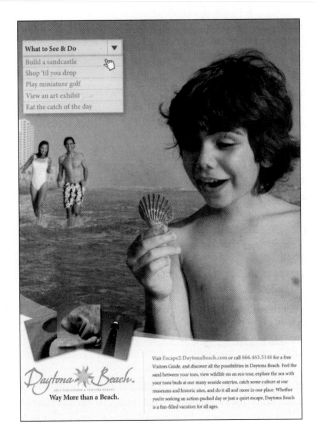

Most are renters and so are not a major market for home appliances and improvements. Their purchases focus on getting by and on time- and energy-saving products and services that are not overly expensive.

Few firms have developed marketing campaigns that explicitly focus on this group. An exception is John Hancock Financial Services, which targeted divorced mothers with this ad:

> In a dimly lit suburban kitchen, a divorced couple is quarreling bitterly. The thirty-something woman tells her ex-husband that he's not doing enough for their son. He retaliates that he's never missed a payment. She responds that he just doesn't get it. And then, almost as if he's trying to prove her point, the man says that his girlfriend wants him to move to California. "You tell Joey that, you tell him," she replies.[15]

**Middle-Aged Single**    The middle-aged single category is made up of people who have never married and those who are divorced and have no child-rearing responsibilities. These individuals are in the 35-to-64 age category, which includes the Generation X and baby boomers, as discussed in Chapter 4.

Middle-aged singles often live alone. In fact, living alone is increasingly viewed as a lifestyle choice that many are willing and able to make, given higher incomes. Middle-aged singles who live alone represented roughly 14.4 million households in 2006, which is about 47 percent of all single-person households. Middle-aged singles have higher incomes than young singles. However, all live-alone singles suffer from a lack of scale economies. That is, a couple or family needs only one dishwasher, clothes dryer, and so forth for everyone in the household; but the single-person household needs the same basic household infrastructure even though only one person uses it. Likewise, many foods and other items come in sizes inappropriate for singles, or the small sizes are disproportionately expensive. Thus, opportunities appear to exist to fill unmet needs among this important and growing market.[16]

The needs of middle-aged singles in many ways reflect those of young singles. But middle-aged singles are likely to have more money to spend on their lifestyles and they are willing to indulge themselves. Thus, they may live in nice condominiums, frequent expensive restaurants, own a luxury automobile, and travel often. They are a major market for gifts, and the males buy significant amounts of jewelry as gifts.

### Empty Nest I: Middle-Aged Married with No Children

The lifestyle changes in the 1980s and 1990s influenced many young couples to not have children.[17] In other cases, these households represent second marriages in which children from a first marriage are not living with the parent. This group also includes married couples whose children have left home. These three forces have produced a huge market consisting of middle-aged couples without children at home. Roughly 50 percent of married couples in this age group (35 to 64) don't have children under the age of 18. This segment will continue to be sizable and important as baby boomers move through the latter stages of middle age and into retirement.

Both adults typically will have jobs, so they are very busy. However, the absence of responsibilities for children creates more free time than they have enjoyed since their youth. They also have money to spend on dining out, expensive vacations, second homes, luxury cars, and time-saving services such as housecleaning, laundry, and shopping. They are a prime market for financial services. Less obvious, they are also heavy purchasers of upscale children's products, as gifts for nieces, nephews, grandchildren, and friends' children. One estimate puts baby boomer spending on grandchildren at $35 billion a year. They are purchasing products ranging from clothing and books to electronics products, and represent a growing market for upscale brands.[18]

The ad and product in Illustration 6–5 would appeal to this group.

### Delayed Full Nest I: Older Married with Young Children

Many members of the baby boom generation and Generation X delayed having their first child until they were in their mid-thirties. This produced the new phenomenon of a large number of middle-aged, established families entering into parenthood for the first time. Recall from Table 6–1 that married couples with children under 18 make up 22.6 percent of all households. And young married couples make up only 7 percent of all households. However, middle-aged (35 to 64) married couples with children (both delayed full nest I and full nest II) make up roughly 16 percent of all households and represent 69 percent of all married couples with children under 18.

A major difference between delayed full nest I and younger new parents is income. Older new parents' incomes are significantly larger than those of younger new parents. They have had this income flow longer and so have acquired more capital and possessions. They spend heavily on child care, mortgage payments, home maintenance, lawn care, and household furnishings. In addition, they want only the best for their children and are willing and able to spend on them. For example, the specialty diaper and toiletries market is expected to have double-digit growth. Brands such as Estée Lauder are getting into the game. And traditional mass marketers such as Kimberly-Clark are pushing high-end products like "pull-up" diapers with glow-in-the-dark animated characters such as Buzz Lightyear.[19] In addition to child-focused spending, delayed full nest I can also spend more on nonchild expenditures such as food, alcohol, and entertainment, and can make more savings and retirement contributions than can younger new parents.

### Full Nest II: Middle-Aged Married with Children at Home

A major difference between this group and delayed full nest I is age of the children. The children of full nest II are generally over age six and are becoming more independent. The presence of older children creates unique consumption needs, however. Families with children six and older are the primary consumers of lessons of all types (piano, dance, gymnastics, and so on), dental care, soft drinks, presweetened cereals, and a wide variety of snack foods.

Greater demands for space create a need for larger homes and cars. Transporting children to multiple events places time demands on the parents and increases transportation-related expenditures. These factors, coupled with heavy demand for clothing and an increased need to save for college, create a considerable financial burden on households in this stage of the HLC. This is offset somewhat by the tendency of the wife to return to work as the children enter school. This return to work usually entails greater time pressures. ConAgra Foods has found great success tapping parents' desire to simplify mealtime with their easy-to-prepare Banquet Crock-Pot Classics, which have all needed ingredients and can cook all day and be ready to eat in the evening with minimal hassle.[20]

As we saw in Chapter 4, the teenage members of this segment, as well as teens in the single parent II segment, are important consumers in their own right as well as important influencers on household consumption decisions.

**Single Parent II: Middle-Aged Single with Children at Home**    Single individuals in the 35-to-64 age group who have children are often faced with serious financial pressures. The same demands that are placed on the middle-aged married couple with children are present in the life of a middle-aged single with children. However, the single parent often lacks some or all of the financial, emotional, and time support that the presence of a spouse generally provides. Many individuals in this position are thus inclined to use time-saving alternatives such as ready-to-eat food, and they are likely to eat at fast-food restaurants. The children of this segment are given extensive household responsibilities.

It is important to note that becoming a single parent (through adoption or conception) is increasingly viewed as a lifestyle choice for older, more financially secure women who may or may not plan to marry in the future. Single Mothers by Choice (http://mattes.home .pipeline.com) is an organization that recognizes this and offers support and assistance. According to the organization, single women by choice are well-educated, career-oriented women in their thirties and forties. As a consequence, they often have higher income and financial security than many single parents.[21]

**Empty Nest II: Older Married Couples**    There are about 12.2 million households in this segment, and it is expected to grow rapidly over the next 10 years as baby boomers age. Many couples in the over-64 age group are either fully or partially retired. However, as we discussed in Chapter 4, improvements in health care and longevity, desire to stay active, and changes in Social Security will likely push retirement age upward over the decades to come. The younger members of this group are healthy, active, and often financially well-off. They have ample time. They are a big market for RVs, cruises, and second homes. They also spend considerable time and money on grandchildren. Increasingly, they take their grandchildren and occasionally their children on vacations. As described in Chapter 4, as they advance in age, health care and assisted living become more important. Illustration 6–6 shows an ad for a product designed to meet one of this segment's needs.

**Older Single**    There are more than 16 million older singles in the United States, and this group will continue to grow as baby boomers age. Approximately 70 percent of all older singles are female, and roughly two-thirds of all older singles live alone. The conditions of being older, single, and generally retired create many unique needs for housing, social-ization, travel, and recreation. Many financial firms have set up special programs to work

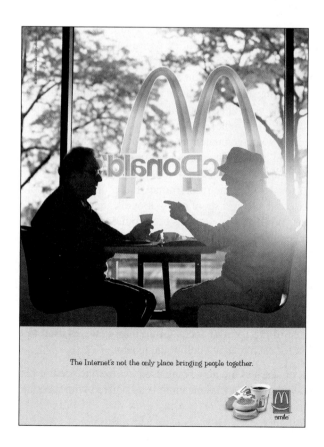

The Internet's not the only place bringing people together.

with these individuals. They often have experienced a spouse's death and now are taking on many of the financial responsibilities once handled by the other person. A recent study labeled consumers who were single as the result of the death of a spouse as "single by circumstance" rather than single by choice. Many older singles would fall into the single by circumstance category. Results of the research suggest that older singles who are single by circumstance will be less innovative, more risk averse, more price sensitive, and more likely to engage in coping behaviors, such as spending more time watching television, than their single by choice counterparts.[22] *What are the social and ethical issues involved in marketing to older consumers who are single by circumstance?*

# MARKETING STRATEGY BASED ON THE HOUSEHOLD LIFE CYCLE

The preceding sections have illustrated the power of the HLC as a segmentation variable. The purchase and consumption of many products are driven by the HLC because each stage poses unique problems or opportunities to the household members, and resolving these problems or taking advantage of these opportunities often requires the consumption of products or services. Our earlier discussion and illustrations indicated how marketers are responding to the unique needs of each stage in the HLC.

While a stage in the HLC causes many of the problems or opportunities individuals confront as they mature, it does not provide solutions. For example, whereas all full nest I families face similar needs and restrictions with respect to recreation, such factors as their income, occupation, and education heavily influence how they will meet those needs. Thus, it makes sense to combine a stage in the HLC with one of these variables to aid in market segmentation and strategy formulation.

For example, think of how the need for vacations differs as one moves across the stages of the household life cycle. Young singles often desire vacations focused on activities, adventure, and the chance for romance. Young married couples without children would have similar needs but without the desire to meet potential romantic partners. Full nest I and single parent I families need vacations that allow both parents and young children to enjoy themselves. The manner in which these needs will be met will vary sharply across occupational, income, and educational categories. For example, a young professional couple may vacation in Paris or at a resort in the tropics. A white-collar couple may visit a domestic ski resort or visit Hawaii on a package deal. A young blue-collar couple may visit family or go camping.

Table 6–2 presents the **HLC/occupational category matrix.** The vertical axis is the particular stage in the HLC, which determines the problems the household will likely encounter; the horizontal axis is a set of occupational categories, which provide a range of acceptable solutions. While this version has been found to be useful across a range of products, using income, education, or social class instead of occupation should be considered for some product categories.

This matrix can be used to segment the market for many products and to develop appropriate marketing strategies for the targeted segments. An effective use of the matrix is to isolate an activity or problem of interest to the firm, such as preparing the evening meal or providing nutritious snacks, scheduling weekend recreation or planning a summer vacation. Research, often in the form of focus group interviews, is used to determine the following information for each relevant cell in the matrix:

1. What products or services are now being used to meet the need or perform the activity?
2. What, if any, symbolic or social meaning is associated with meeting the need or using the current products?

TABLE 6-2    HLC/Occupational Category Matrix

| HLC Stage | Occupational Category | | | | |
|---|---|---|---|---|---|
|  | Executive/Elite Professional | Administrative/ Professional | Technical/Sales/ Clerical | Crafts | Unskilled/ Manual |
| Single I | | | | | |
| Young married | | | | | |
| Full nest I | | | | | |
| Single parent I | | | | | |
| Single II | | | | | |
| Delayed full nest I | | | | | |
| Full nest II | | | | | |
| Single parent II | | | | | |
| Empty nest I | | | | | |
| Empty nest II | | | | | |
| Single III | | | | | |

3.    Exactly how are the current products or services being used?

4.    How satisfied are the segment members with the current solutions, and what improvements are desired?

Attractive segments are those that are large enough to meet the firm's objectives and that have needs that current products are not fully satisfying. This approach has been used successfully for movies, regional bakeries, and financial services.[23] *What type of automobile would be best suited for each cell, and what type of ad should promote it?*

# FAMILY DECISION MAKING

**Family decision making** is *the process by which decisions that directly or indirectly involve two or more family members are made.* Decision making by a group such as a family differs in many ways from decisions made by an individual. Consider the purchase of a breakfast cereal that children, and perhaps the adults, will consume. Who recognizes the need for the product? How is a type and brand selected? Does everyone consider the same attributes? A parent typically makes the actual *purchase;* does that mean that the parent also makes the *choice?* Or is the choice made by the children, the other parent, or some combination? Which parents are involved, and how does this change across products and over time? How does it differ by stage in the household life cycle?

Family purchases are often compared with organizational buying decisions. Although this comparison can produce useful insights, it fails to capture the essence of family decision making. Organizations have relatively objective criteria, such as profit maximization, that guide purchases. Families generally lack such explicit, overarching goals. Most industrial purchases are made by strangers or have little impact on those not involved in the purchase. Most family purchases directly affect the other members of the family.

Most important, *many family purchases are inherently emotional and affect the relationships between the family members.*[24] The decision to buy a child a requested toy or new school clothes is more than simply an acquisition. It is a symbol of love and commitment to the child. The decision to take the family to a restaurant for a meal or to purchase a new

**FIGURE 6–3**   **The Household Decision-Making Process for Children's Products**

television has emotional meaning to the other family members. Disagreements about how to spend money are a major cause of marital discord. The processes families use to make purchase decisions and the outcomes of those processes have important effects on the well-being of the individual family members and the family itself. Thus, while family decision making has some things in common with organizational decision making, it is not the same.

## The Nature of Family Purchase Roles

Figure 6–3 illustrates the six roles that frequently occur in family decision making, using a cereal purchase as an example.[25] It is important to note that individuals will play various roles for different decisions.

- *Initiator(s).* The family member who first recognizes a need or starts the purchase process.
- *Information gatherer(s).* The individual who has expertise and interest in a particular purchase. Different individuals may seek information at different times or on different aspects of the purchase.
- *Influencer(s).* The person who influences the alternatives evaluated, the criteria considered, and the final choice.
- *Decision maker(s).* The individual who makes the final decision. Of course, joint decisions also are likely to occur.
- *Purchaser(s).* The family member who actually purchases the product. This is typically an adult or teenager.
- *User(s).* The user of the product. For many products there are multiple users.

Marketers must determine who in the family plays which role before they can affect the family decision process. After thorough study, Crayola shifted its advertising budget from children's television to women's magazines. Its research revealed that mothers rather than children were more likely to recognize the problem, evaluate alternatives, and make the purchase. Illustration 6–7 shows a product designed for use by children that is selected by both the children and the parents and purchased by the parents.

Family decision making has been categorized as *husband-dominant, wife-dominant, joint,* or *individualized.* Husband-dominant decisions have traditionally occurred with the purchase of such products as automobiles, liquor, and life insurance. Wife-dominant decisions were more common in the purchase of household maintenance items, food, and kitchen appliances. Joint decisions were most likely when buying a house, living room furniture, and vacations. These patterns are much less pronounced today. As women's occupational roles have expanded, so has the range of family decisions in which they participate or dominate.[26]

A moment's reflection will reveal that the above four categories omit critical participants in many family decisions. Until recently, most studies have ignored the influence of children.[27] Yet children, particularly teenagers, often exert a substantial influence on family purchase decisions.[28] Thus, we need to recognize that *child-dominant* and various combinations of *husband, wife,* and *child joint decisions* are also common.

Studies of family decisions have focused on direct influence and ignored indirect influence. For example, a wife might report that she purchased an automobile without discussing it with any member of her family. Yet she might purchase a van to meet her perceptions of the desires of the family rather than the sports car that she personally would prefer. Most research studies would classify the above decision as strictly wife-dominated. Clearly, however, other family members influenced the decision.

Different family members often become involved at different stages of the decision process. Figure 6–4 shows the influence of wives and husbands at each stage of the decision process for a variety of services. As can be seen, roles vary across services and across stages in the decision process.

## FIGURE 6–4    Husband–Wife Decision Roles for Services

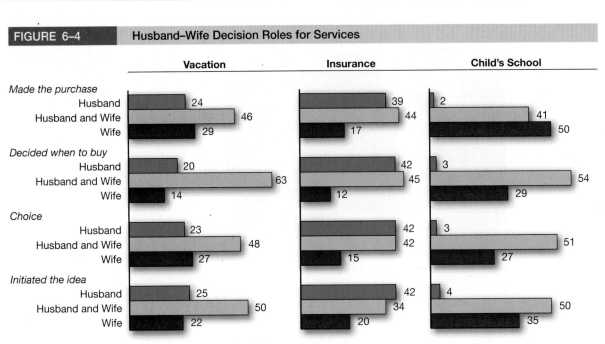

Note: Totals do not add to 100 because other individuals were involved in some decisions.

Source: M. R. Stafford, G. K. Ganesh, and B. C. Garland, "Marital Influence in the Decision-Making Process for Services," *Journal of Services Marketing* 10, no. 1 (1996), p. 15.

Family decisions also allow different members to make specific subdecisions of the overall decision. When an individual makes a decision, he or she evaluates all the relevant attributes of each alternative and combines these evaluations into a single decision. In a family decision, different members often focus on specific attributes. For example, a child may evaluate the color and style of a bicycle while one or both parents evaluate price, warranty, and safety features.

## Determinants of Family Purchase Roles

How family members interact in a purchase decision is largely dependent on the *culture and subculture* in which the family exists, the *role specialization* of different family members, the degree of *involvement* each has in the product area of concern, and the *personal characteristics* of the family members.[29]

Today, America has less of a masculine orientation than many other cultures. As one would expect, wives are more involved in a wider range of decisions in the United States than they are in cultures with a more masculine focus.[30] However, subcultures and other groups in the United States vary on this value. As we saw in Chapter 5, the Hispanic subculture has more of a masculine orientation than the broader culture. Research indicates that Hispanics who identify strongly with the Hispanic culture tend to make more husband-dominant decisions than do others.

Over time, each spouse develops more specialized roles as a part of the family lifestyle and family responsibilities. Husbands traditionally specialized in mechanical and technical areas, while wives specialized in home care and child rearing. Although particular roles are no longer automatically assigned to one gender in the marriage, they still tend to evolve over time. It is simply much more efficient for one person to specialize in some decisions than it is to have to reach a joint decision for every purchase.

Involvement or expertise in a product area is another major factor that affects how a family purchase decision will be made. Naturally, the more involved a spouse or other family

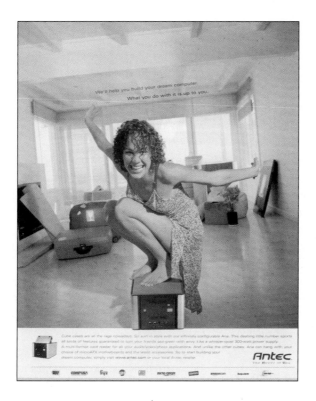

member is with a product area, the more influence this person will have. For example, when children are the primary users of a product (e.g., toys, snacks, breakfast cereal) they tend to have more influence. Teenagers who are involved with computers often strongly influence the decision for a family computer or the choice of an Internet access service.[31] The ad in Illustration 6–8 recognizes the strong role that teens can play in technology decisions.

As Consumer Insight 6–2 shows, teenagers are also garnering increased power over nontechnology purchases through their tech-savvy status within the family.

Several personal characteristics have an effect on the influence individuals will have on purchase decisions.[32] Education is one such personal characteristic. The higher a wife's education, the more she will participate in major decisions.[33] Personality is an important determinant of family decision roles. Traits such as aggressiveness, locus of control (belief in controlling one's own situation), detachment, and compliance influence family decision power.[34] For children, age matters, with older children and teens playing an increasingly stronger role. For example, one study found that 40 percent of kids age 12 to 14 told their parents to buy a certain kind of furniture, compared with only 25 percent of kids age 6 to 8. Marketers are responding. Ikea makes references to "living with parents" in its catalogs and Pottery Barn has children and teen lines and a teen catalog *PBteen* with products to fit the teen lifestyle.[35]

Finally, stage of the decision process influences decision roles. Purchase decisions evolve from the early stages of problem recognition and information search through choice and purchase. Children and teens tend to have more influence on earlier stages of the family decision process than on later stages.[36]

## Conflict Resolution

Given the number of decisions families make daily, disagreements are inevitable. How they are resolved is important to marketers as well as to the health of the family unit. One study

**Teen Internet Mavens as Family Influencers**

The influence and purchase power of teens are well documented. So too is their heavy online and technology usage. So it shouldn't be surprising that one area where teens have influence in family decisions is in technology-related categories like computers and the Internet.

However, research is now finding that technology is giving teens more power in family purchase decisions *not* directly related to technology, such as family vacations.[37] The idea is that the Internet provides a wealth of information access that can be used in making family decisions of all kinds. Tech-savvy teens who can provide their families with access to this world should have greater influence on the decision-making process. These teens are called Internet mavens and have the following characteristics:

- Greater enjoyment and interest in the Internet in general.
- Greater knowledge about the Web-based marketplace (e.g., new sites, where to get deals).
- More expertise in searching out and finding information and resources on the Web.
- Greater enjoyment and desire to help others by providing information found on the Web.

Not all teens are Internet mavens. Teen Internet mavens are more likely than nonmavens to be heavy users of the Internet and to use the Internet for fun.

Interestingly, teens who perceive themselves as Internet mavens are usually seen as mavens by their parents, who in turn seek them out as a gateway to the Internet marketplace.

Research looking specifically at family vacation decisions finds that teen Internet mavens had greater influence than nonmavens at both the earlier (initiation and search) and later (evaluation and choice) stages of the decision process. Teen influence was lower at the later stages even for the Internet mavens, suggesting that the maven's primary role is in information search and access. However, the Internet mavens also maintained a stronger influence at the later stages than did nonmavens, perhaps a carryover from their involvement in earlier stages.

Clearly, family decision making presents unique challenges to marketers, including how to simultaneously and effectively communicate with diverse members of a household unit.

**Critical Thinking Questions**

1. Were you or any of your siblings the Internet maven in your household?
2. What role does parent online expertise play in terms of the power of teen Internet mavens in the family decision process?
3. What unique challenges does the existence of teen Internet mavens present to marketers?

revealed six basic approaches that individuals use to resolve purchase conflicts after they have arisen (most couples generally seek to avoid open conflicts):[38]

- *Bargaining.* Trying to reach a compromise.
- *Impression management.* Misrepresenting the facts in order to win.
- *Use of authority.* Claiming superior expertise or role appropriateness (the husband/wife should make such decisions).
- *Reasoning.* Using logical argument to win.
- *Playing on emotion.* Using the silent treatment or withdrawing from the discussion.
- *Additional information.* Getting additional data or a third-party opinion.

Another study found that spouses adapt their strategies across decisions and that when they use coercive means (e.g., silent treatment) to get their way, they are satisfied with the decision *outcome* but dissatisfied with the decision *process*.[39] Although neither study included children, a study focused on how children and parents attempt to influence each other found a similar though more complex set of influence strategies.[40]

## Conclusions on Family Decision Making

Much remains to be learned about family decision making. But we can offer five general conclusions:

1. Different family members are often involved at different stages of the decision process.
2. Different family members often evaluate different attributes of a product or brand.
3. The direct involvement of family members in each stage of the decision process represents only a small part of the picture. Taking into account the desires of other family members is also important, though seldom studied.
4. Who participates at each stage of the decision process and the method by which conflicts are resolved are primarily a function of the product category and secondarily a function of the characteristics of the individual family members and the characteristics of the family. The product category is important because it is closely related to who uses the product.
5. Overt conflicts in decision making are less common than agreement.

# MARKETING STRATEGY AND FAMILY DECISION MAKING

Formulating an effective marketing strategy for most consumer products requires a thorough understanding of the family decision-making process in the selected target markets with respect to that product. Table 6–3 provides a framework for such an analysis.

The family decision-making process often varies across market segments such as stages in the family life cycle or subculture. Therefore, a marketer must analyze family decision making *within* each of the firm's defined target markets. Within each target market, the marketer needs to:

- Discover which family members are involved at each stage of the decision process.
- Determine what their motivations and interests are.
- Develop a marketing strategy that will meet the needs of each participant.

For example, younger children are often involved in the problem recognition stage related to breakfast. They may note a new cartoon character–based cereal or discover that

**TABLE 6–3**

Marketing Strategy Based on the Family Decision-Making Process

Segment: _____

| Stage in the Decision Process | Family Members Involved | Family Members' Motivation and Interests | Marketing Strategy and Tactics |
|---|---|---|---|
| Problem recognition | | | |
| Information search | | | |
| Alternative evaluation | | | |
| Purchase | | | |
| User/consumption | | | |
| Disposition | | | |
| Evaluation | | | |

their friends are eating a new cereal. They are interested in identifying with the cartoon character or being like their friends. When they request the new cereal, the parents, generally the mother, may become interested. However, she is more likely to focus on nutrition and price. Thus, a marketer needs to communicate fun, taste, and excitement to children—and nutrition, value, and taste to parents. The children can be reached on Saturday cartoons, appropriate Internet sites, and similar media, while the mother may be more effectively communicated with through magazine ads, on package information, and on the Internet.

# CONSUMER SOCIALIZATION

The family provides the basic framework in which consumer socialization occurs. **Consumer socialization** is *the process by which young people acquire skills, knowledge, and attitudes relevant to their functioning as consumers in the marketplace.*[41] We are concerned with understanding both the content of consumer socialization and the process of consumer socialization. The content of consumer socialization refers to what children learn with respect to consumption; the process refers to how they learn it. Before we address these two issues, we need to consider the ability of children of various ages to learn consumption-related skills.

## The Ability of Children to Learn

Younger children have limited abilities to process certain types of information. **Piaget's stages of cognitive development** are a widely accepted set of stages of cognitive development:

> *Stage 1: The period of sensorimotor intelligence (0 to 2 years).* During this period, behavior is primarily motor. The child does not yet "think" conceptually, though cognitive development is seen.

> *Stage 2: The period of preoperational thoughts (3 to 7 years).* This period is characterized by the development of language and rapid conceptual development.

> *Stage 3: The period of concrete operations (8 to 11 years).* During these years, the child develops the ability to apply logical thought to concrete problems.

> *Stage 4: The period of formal operations (12 to 15 years).* During this period, the child's cognitive structures reach their greatest level of development, and the child becomes able to apply logic to all classes of problems.

Other researchers have proposed other stages, with learning rather than aging as the underlying cause of observed differences. However, the general pattern of less ability to deal with abstract, generalized, unfamiliar, or large amounts of information by younger children is common to all approaches.[42]

The changing capabilities of children to process information as they age present challenges to parents who are attempting to teach their children appropriate consumption behaviors.[43] As we will discuss shortly, this also poses ethical and practical issues for marketers.[44] Children's limited learning capacity is the basis for substantial regulation of advertising to children. We describe existing and proposed regulations of marketing to children in depth in Chapter 20.

## The Content of Consumer Socialization

The content of consumer learning can be broken down into three categories: consumer skills, consumption-related preferences, and consumption-related attitudes.[45] **Consumer skills** are *those capabilities necessary for purchases to occur such as understanding money, budgeting, product evaluation, and so forth.* A child has to learn how to shop, how to compare similar brands, how to budget available income, and the like. The following example shows an attempt by a parent to teach her adolescent appropriate, from the parent's perspective, shopping rules:

> Son, look at this. This is just going to wash nicer, it will come through the laundry nicer, and you do a lot of the laundry yourself, and I just would rather that it's something that would wash easy, that doesn't have to be ironed, that isn't 100 percent cotton. (Mother with son, age 13)[46]

**Consumption-related preferences** are *the knowledge, attitudes, and values that cause people to attach differential evaluations to products, brands, and retail outlets.* For example, some parents through their comments and purchases may "teach" their children that Calvin Klein is a prestigious brand name and that prestigious brands are desirable. This information about Calvin Klein's prestige is not necessary to carry out the actual purchase (consumer skills), but it is extremely important in deciding to make a purchase and in deciding what to purchase (consumption-related preferences).[47]

**Consumption-related attitudes** are *cognitive and affective orientations toward marketplace stimuli such as advertisements, salespeople, warranties, and so forth.*[48] For example, children may learn from their parents or other family members that "you get what you pay for." This would lead them to assume a strong price–quality relationship. Or they may be taught that salespeople are not trustworthy. These attitudes will influence how they react to the various activities undertaken by marketers. What type of attitude is being formed in the following interaction?

> I'm always trying to get her to learn the relative value of things and particularly the impact of advertising and its effect on driving purchases and desires. So we try to talk about that. I point out manipulative or deceptive advertising, and give her a sense of being a critical consumer. (Father with daughter, age 13)[49]

## The Process of Consumer Socialization

Consumer socialization occurs through a number of avenues, including advertising and friends. However, family is a primary source of consumer socialization. For example, a recent study of eating patterns found that children cite parents as the most important influence regarding the kinds of foods they eat. This was even true of teenagers, where parental influence was highest, and friends and advertising played a much lesser role.[50] Parents teach their children consumer skills, consumption-related preferences, and consumption-related attitudes. They do so both deliberately and casually through instrumental training, modeling, and mediation.

**Instrumental training** *occurs when a parent or sibling specifically and directly attempts to bring about certain responses through reasoning or reinforcement.* In other words, a parent may try directly to teach a child which snack foods should be consumed by explicitly discussing nutrition. Or a parent may establish rules that limit the consumption of some snack foods and encourage the consumption of others. The following example shows an approach used with older children:

> One thing that we always talk about when we're looking at something is the price of it. "For what you're buying, is the price worth the quality of what you're buying?" (Mother with son, age 13)[51]

Parents often worry that marketing messages will simply drown out any instrumental training they try to provide. In Illustration 6–9 there is an attempt on the part of the firm to be a partner in the socialization process by offering nutritional options for kids that parents can live with.

ILLUSTRATION 6–9

ILLUSTRATION 6–9

This company clearly recognizes the concerns of parents in the socialization process.

**Modeling** *occurs when a child learns appropriate, or inappropriate, consumption behaviors by observing others.* Modeling generally, though not always, occurs without direct instruction from the role model and frequently without conscious thought or effort on the part of the child. Modeling is an extremely important way for children to learn relevant skills, knowledge, and attitudes. Children learn both positive and negative consumption patterns through modeling. For example, children whose parents smoke are more likely to start smoking than are children whose parents do not smoke.

**Mediation** *occurs when a parent alters a child's initial interpretation of, or response to, a marketing or other stimulus.* This can easily be seen in the following example:

CHILD: Can I have one of those? See, it can walk!

PARENT: No. That's just an advertisement. It won't really walk. They just make it look like it will so kids will buy them.

The advertisement illustrated a product attribute and triggered a desire, but the parent altered the belief in the attribute and in the believability of advertising in general. This is not to suggest that family members mediate all commercials. However, children often learn about the purchase and use of products during interactions with other family members. Thus, a firm wishing to influence children must do so in a manner consistent with the values of the rest of the family.

## The Supermarket as a Classroom

Professor James McNeal developed a five-stage model of how children learn to shop by visiting supermarkets and other retail outlets with a parent.[52]

**Stage I: Observing**   Parents begin taking children to the store with them at a median age of two months. During this stage, children make sensory contact with the marketplace and begin forming mental images of marketplace objects and symbols. In the early months, only sights and sounds are being processed. However, by 12 to 15 months, most children can begin to recall some of these items. This stage ends when children understand that a visit to the market may produce rewards beyond the stimulation caused by the environment.

**Stage II: Making Requests**   At this stage (median age is two years), children begin requesting items in the store from their parents. They use pointing and gesturing as well as statements to indicate that they want an item. Throughout most of this stage, children make requests only when the item is physically present, as they do not yet carry mental images of the products in their minds. In the latter months of stage II, they begin to make requests for items at home, particularly when they are seen on television.

**Stage III: Making Selections**   Actually getting an item off the shelf without assistance is the first act of an independent consumer (median age is three and a half years). At its simplest level, a child's desire is triggered by an item in his or her immediate presence and this item is selected. Soon, however, children begin to remember the store location of desirable items, and they are allowed to go to those areas independently or to lead the parent there.

**Stage IV: Making Assisted Purchases**   Most children learn by observing (modeling) that money needs to be given in order to get things from a store. They learn to value money given to them by their parents and others as a means to acquire things. Soon they are allowed to select and pay for items with their own money. They are now primary consumers (median age is five and a half years).

**Stage V: Making Independent Purchases**   Making a purchase without a parent to oversee it requires a fairly sophisticated understanding of value as well as the ability to visit a store, or a section of a store, safely without a parent. Most children remain in stage IV a long time before their parents allow them to move into stage V (median age is eight years).

McNeal's research indicates that children learn to shop, at least in part, by going shopping. Retailers are developing programs based on these learning patterns. Examples include child-sized shopping carts and kids' clubs.

# MARKETING TO CHILDREN

As seen in the opening example, children are a large and growing market. Brand loyalties developed at this age may produce returns for many years. Thus, it is no surprise that marketers are aggressively pursuing these young consumers.

However, marketing to children is fraught with ethical concerns. The major source of these concerns is the limited ability of younger children to process information and to make informed purchase decisions. There are also concerns that marketing activities, particularly advertising, produce undesirable values in children, result in inappropriate diets, and cause unhealthy levels of family conflict. We will examine questionable marketing practices focused on children and the regulations designed to control them in detail in Chapter 20.

Although marketers need to be very sensitive to the limited information-processing skills of younger consumers, ethical and effective marketing campaigns can be designed to meet the needs of children and their parents. All aspects of the marketing mix must consider the capabilities of the child. Consider the following ad and the responses to the ad from children of different ages:

> The ad reads "Inhale a lethal dose of carbon monoxide and it's called suicide. Inhale a smaller amount and it's called smoking. Believe it or not, cigarette smoke contains the same poisonous gas as automobile exhaust. So if you wouldn't consider sucking on a tailpipe, why would you want to smoke?" A picture of a smoking exhaust pipe was below the copy.
>
> **Seven- and eight-year-olds' responses:**
> "Never stand behind a bus because you could get poisonous in your face."
> "People sometimes get sick from exhaust."
>
> **Nine- and ten-year-olds' responses:**
> "The person who is driving is smoking."
> "No matter what kind of smoking it is, it can always make you sick."
>
> **Eleven-year-olds' responses:**
> "You could hurt yourself with that stuff. The same stuff in car exhaust is in cigarettes."
> "The tailpipe of a car is like the same as smoking and smoking could kill you . . . both of them could kill you."

Only the older children could fully engage in the analogical reasoning required to completely understand the ad. In contrast, a simpler ad that showed a dirty, grimy sock next to an ashtray full of cigarette butts with the word *gross* under the sock and *really gross* under the ashtray was understood by children of all ages (7 through 11).[53]

Reaching children used to mean advertising on Saturday morning cartoons. Now there are many more options, even for the very young. *National Geographic Kids, Martha Steward Kids,* and *Discovery Girls* are just a few of the many magazines with strong readership among children. CD-ROMs with interactive capabilities and titles such as "The Magic School Bus" are becoming big sellers. They provide the opportunity to offer entertainment, education, and commercial messages to children and their parents. Children as young as three are active Internet users. Sites such as Foxkids.com, Cartoonnetwork.com, Nick.com, Pokemon.com, and Barbie.com are visited by millions of children aged 2 to 11. And, Yahooligans! (www.yahooligans.yahoo.com) is an online Web guide designed specifically for kids, including games, news, and music videos. Radio is popular with older children who are very much into pop music and stars such as Miley Cyrus.

Direct mail can be an effective means to reach even very young children. Many firms target children or families with young children by forming "kids' clubs." Unfortunately, these clubs sometimes engage in sales techniques that are controversial if not clearly unethical. If done properly, however, they can be fun and educational for the children while delivering responsible commercial messages.

## SUMMARY

The household is the basic purchasing and consuming unit and is, therefore, of great importance to marketing managers of most products. Family households are also the primary mechanism whereby cultural and social-class values and behavior patterns are passed on to the next generation.

The *family household* consists of two or more related persons living together in a dwelling unit. *Nonfamily households* are dwelling units occupied by one or more unrelated individuals.

The *household life cycle* is the classification of the household into stages through which it passes over time based on the age and marital status of the adults and the presence and age of children. The household life cycle is a valuable marketing tool because members within each stage or category face similar consumption problems. Thus, they represent potential market segments.

The *household life cycle/occupational category matrix* is a useful way to use the HLC to develop marketing strategy. One axis is the stages in the HLC, which determine the problems the household will likely encounter; the other is a set of occupational categories, which provide a range of acceptable solutions. Each cell represents a market segment.

*Family decision making* involves consideration of questions such as who buys, who decides, and who uses. Family decision making is complex and involves emotion and interpersonal relations as well as product evaluation and acquisition.

Marketing managers must analyze the household decision process separately for each product category within each target market. Household member participation in the decision process varies by *involvement with the specific product, role specialization, personal characteristics,* and one's *culture and subculture.* Participation also varies by stage in the decision process. Most decisions are reached by consensus. If not, a variety of conflict resolution strategies may be employed.

*Consumer socialization* deals with the processes by which young people (from birth until 18 years of age)

learn how to become consumers. Children's learning abilities are limited at birth, then slowly evolve with experience over time. Consumer socialization deals with the learning of consumer skills, consumption-related preferences, and consumption-related attitudes. Families influence consumer socialization through direct *instrumental training, modeling,* and *mediation.* Young consumers appear to go through five stages of learning how to shop. This learning takes place primarily in retail outlets in interaction with the parents.

Marketing to children is fraught with ethical issues. The main source of ethical concern is the limited ability of children to process information and make sound purchase decisions or requests. There are also concerns about the role of advertising in forming children's values, influencing their diets, and causing family conflict. However, ethical and effective marketing programs can be developed for children.

## KEY TERMS

Blended family  195
Consumer skills  214
Consumer socialization  214
Consumption-related attitudes  215
Consumption-related preferences  215
Family decision making  207

Family household  195
HLC/occupational category
  matrix  206
Household  195
Household life cycle (HLC)  197
Instrumental training  215

Mediation  216
Modeling  216
Nonfamily household  195
Piaget's stages of cognitive
  development  214
Traditional family  195

## INTERNET EXERCISES

1. Prepare a report on the information available on the Internet concerning the percentage of the U.S. population that is in each stage of the household life cycle. Provide the addresses for all sites used.

2. Search Canadian government Web sites and compare the U.S. Census household definitions with those of the Canadian government. Which country seems to be best adapting to the evolution of household structures?

3. Visit the Federal Trade Commission (www.ftc.gov) and Better Business Bureau (www.bbb.org) sites. What ethical and legal issues involving marketing to children appear?

4. Visit one of the sites listed below. Evaluate the effectiveness of the site in terms of marketing to children and the degree to which it represents an ethically sound approach to marketing to children.
   a. www.kelloggs.com
   b. www.fritolay.com

    c. www.warnerbros.com
    d. www.crayola.com
    e. www.nabisco.com
    f. www.barbie.com

5. Visit one of the sites listed below. Evaluate the effectiveness of the site in terms of marketing to children and the degree to which it represents an ethically sound approach to marketing to children. What ages is it best suited for?
   a. www.kids.gov
   b. www.pbskids.org
   c. www.disney.com
   d. www.nick.com
   e. www.cartoonnetwork.com
   f. www.mtv.com

6. Find and describe two sites targeting children under six. What is your evaluation of these sites?

with respect to their purchase decisions. Also determine how conflicts are resolved.

*a.* Less than 1 year

*b.* 1–5 years

*c.* 6–10 years

*d.* More than 10 years

43. Pick a product and market segment of interest, and interview three households. Collect sufficient data to complete Table 6–3.

44. Pick a product of interest and, with several fellow students, complete enough interviews to fill the relevant cells in Table 6–2 using the four questions in the text (see pp. 206–207). Develop an appropriate marketing strategy based on this information.

45. Interview several parents of preschool children. Determine the extent to which they agree with Piaget's four stages and McNeal's five stages.

46. Watch several hours of Saturday morning cartoons. What ethical concerns, if any, do they cause?

## REFERENCES

1. The Chapter 6 opener is based on *The U.S. Kids Market* (New York: *Packaged Facts,* April 2004); L. Lee, "Pretty Babies," *Business-Week*, July 2, 2007, p. 18; *Apparel and Entertainment Make up Bulk of a Mom's Discretionary Spending on Her Kids* (Port Washington, NY: NPD Group, May 27, 2008), press release; "US: Apparel Makes up Bulk of Spending on Kids—Research," *just-style.com,* May 28, 2008, www.just-style.com, accessed June, 11, 2008.

2. See P. Kiecker and N. R. McClure, "Redefining the Extended Family in Recognition of Blended Family Structures," *Enhancing Knowledge Development in Marketing* (Chicago: American Marketing Association, 1996), pp. 242–43.

3. See F. F. Furstenberg, Jr., "The Future of Families," *American Demographics,* June 1996, pp. 34–40; R. Gardyn, "Unmarried Bliss," *American Demographics,* December 2000, pp. 56–61; S. Raymond, "The Ex-Files," *American Demographics,* February 2001, pp. 60–64; and P. Paul, "Millennial Myths," *American Demographics,* December 2001, p. 20.

4. Statistics in this section are drawn primarily from *America's Families and Living Arrangements: 2006* (Washington, DC: U.S. Census Bureau, 2007) and other relevant U.S. Census Bureau reports and updates.

5. Consumer Insight 6–1 is based on Gardyn, "Unmarried Bliss;" and *Unmarried-Partner Households by Sex of Partners: 2005* (Washington, DC: U.S. Census Bureau, 2008); and other information from the U.S. Census.

6. See C. M. Schaninger and W. D. Danko, "A Conceptual and Empirical Comparison of Alternative Household Life Cycle Models," *Journal of Consumer Research,* March 1993, pp. 580–94; R. E. Wilkes, "Household Life-Cycle Stages, Transitions, and Product Expenditures," *Journal of Consumer Research,* June 1995, pp. 27–42; and C. M. Schaninger and D. H. Lee, "A New Full-Nest Classification Approach," *Psychology & Marketing,* January 2002, pp. 25–58.

7. See, e.g., N. Donthu and D. I. Gilliland, "The Single Consumer," *Journal of Advertising Research,* November–December 2002, pp. 77–84.

8. G. J. Thompson, "Interpreting Consumers," *Journal of Marketing Research,* November 1997, p. 448.

9. See J. Raymond, "For Richer or Poorer," *American Demographics,* July 2000, pp. 59–64.

10. "Employment Status of Women by Marital Status and Presence and Age of Children: 1975 to 2005," *Statistical Abstract of the United States 2008* (Washington, DC: U.S. Bureau of the Census, 2008); see also R. Rosenwein, "The Baby Sabbatical," *American Demographics,* February 2002, pp. 36–38.

11. Estimates based on *Consumer Expenditure Survey* (Washington, DC: U.S. Bureau of Labor Statistics, 2005–2006).

12. S. Thompson, "ClubMom Prepares National Rollout," *Advertising Age,* May 3, 2004, p. 24.

13. Gardyn, "Unmarried Bliss," p. 61.

14. For a discussion, including differences across groups, see www .divorcereform.org; and D. Hurley, "Divorce Rate," *The New York Times,* April 19, 2005, p. F7.

15. Raymond, "The Ex-Files," p. 60.

16. See, e.g., J. Morrow, "A Place for One," *American Demographics,* November 2003, pp. 25–29; and P. Francese, "Well Enough Alone," *American Demographics,* November 2003, pp. 32–33.

17. P. Paul, "Childless by Choice," *American Demographics,* November 2001, pp. 45–50.

18. P. Paul, "Make Room for Granddaddy," *American Demographics,* April 2002, pp. 40–45.

19. J. Fetto, "The Baby Business," *American Demographics,* May 2003, p. 40; and J. Neff, "P&G Challenges Rival K-C in Trainers Battle," *Advertising Age,* May 17, 2004, p. 10.

20. "New Survey Finds Parents and Children Alike Crave More Time to Talk and Relax Together," ConAgra, press release, January 17, 2005.

21. Information from organization's Web site at http://mattes.home .pipeline.com.

22. Donthu and Gilliland, "The Single Consumer."

23. For a different approach, see L. G. Pol and S. Pak, "Consumer Unit Types and Expenditures on Food Away from Home," *Journal of Consumer Affairs,* Winter 1995, pp. 403–28.

24. See J. Park, P. Tansuhaj, and E. R. Spangenberg, "An Emotion-Based Perspective of Family Purchase Decisions," *Advances in Consumer Research,* vol. 22, ed. F. R. Kardes and M. Sujan (Provo, UT: Association for Consumer Research, 1995), pp. 723–28.

25. C. Lackman and J. M. Lanasa, "Family Decision-Making Theory," *Psychology & Marketing,* March–April 1993, pp. 81–113.

26. See, e.g., M. A. Belch and L. A. Willis, "Family Decision at the Turn of the Century," *Journal of Consumer Behaviour* 2, no. 2 (2002), pp. 111–24; and N. Razzouk, V. Seitz, and K. P. Capo, "A Comparison of Consumer Decision-Making Behavior of Married and Cohabiting Couples," *Journal of Consumer Marketing* 24; no. 5 (2007), pp. 264–74.

27. An exception is S. E. Beatty and S. Talpade, "Adolescent Influence in Family Decision Making," *Journal of Consumer Research,* September 1994, pp. 332–41.

28. See J. Cotte and S. L. Wood, "Families and Innovative Consumer Behavior," *Journal of Consumer Research*, June 2004, pp. 78–86; A. Shoham and V. Dalakas, "He Said, She Said . . . They Said," *Journal of Consumer Marketing* 22, no. 3 (2005), pp. 152–60; and E. Bridges and R. A. Briesch, "The 'Nag Factor' and Children's Product Categories," *International Journal of Advertising* 25, no. 2 (2006), pp. 157–87.

29. See C.-N. Chen, M. Lai, and D. D. C. Tarn, "Feminism Orientation, Product Attributes and Husband–Wife Decision Dominance," *Journal of Global Marketing* 12, no. 3 (1999), pp. 23–39; and C. Webster and M. C. Reiss, "Do Established Antecedents of Purchase Decision-Making Power Apply to Contemporary Couples?" *Psychology & Marketing,* September 2001, pp. 951–72.

30. J. B. Ford, L. E. Pelton, and J. R. Lumpkin, "Perception of Marital Roles in Purchase Decision Processes," *Journal of the Academy of Marketing Science,* Spring 1995, pp. 120–31.

31. See C. K. C. Lee and S. E. Beatty, "Family Structure and Influence in Family Decision Making," *Journal of Consumer Marketing* 19, no. 1 (2002), pp. 24–41; and G. Slattery and J. Butler, "Teens Are Primary Influencer on Holiday Technology Purchases," *Business Wire,* November 23, 2004, p. 1.

32. See M. C. Reiss and C. Webster, "Relative Influence in Purchase Decision Making," *Advances in Consumer Research,* vol. 24, eds. M. Bruck and D. J. MacInnis (Provo, UT: Association for Consumer Research, 1997), pp. 42–47; and C. Webster, "The Meaning and Measurement of Marital Power," *Advances in Consumer Research,* vol. 25, eds. J. W. Alba and J. W. Hutchinson (Provo, UT: Association for Consumer Research, 1998), pp. 395–99.

33. D. Crispell, "Dual-Earner Diversity," *American Demographics,* July 1995, pp. 32–37.

34. C. Webster, "Is Spousal Decision Making a Culturally Situated Phenomenon?" *Psychology & Marketing,* December 2000, pp. 1035–58.

35. T. Meyers, "Kids Gaining Voice in How Home Looks," *Advertising Age,* March 29, 2004, p. S-4.

36. See, e.g., Belch, Krentler, and Willis-Flurry, "Teen Internet Mavens."

37. Consumer Insight 6–2 is based on M. A. Belch, K. A. Krentler, and L. A. Willis-Flurry, "Teen Internet Mavens," *Journal of Business Research* 58 (2005), pp. 569–75.

38. C. Kim and H. Lee, "A Taxonomy of Couples Based on Influence Strategies," *Journal of Business Research,* June 1996, pp. 157–68.

39. C. Su, E. F. Fern, and K. Ye, "A Temporal Dynamic Model of Spousal Family Purchase-Decision Behavior," *Journal of Marketing Research,* August 2003, pp. 268–81.

40. K. M. Palan and R. E. Wilkes, "Adolescent–Parent Interaction in Family Decision Making," *Journal of Consumer Research,* September 1997, pp. 159–69; see also A. Aribarg, N. Arora, and H. O. Bodur, "Understanding the Role of Preference Revision and Concession in Group Decisions," *Journal of Marketing Research,* August 2002, pp. 336–49.

41. For a thorough review, see D. R. John, "Consumer Socialization of Children," *Journal of Consumer Research,* December 1999, pp. 183–209. See also M. J. Dotson and E. M. Hyatt, "Major Influence Factors in Children's Consumer Socialization," *Journal of Consumer Marketing* 22, no. 1 (2005), pp. 35–42.

42. See J. Gregan-Paxton and D. R. John, "The Emergence of Adaptive Decision Making in Children," *Journal of Consumer Research,* June 1997, pp. 43–56; T. Davis, "What Children Understand about Consumption Constellations," *Advances in Consumer Research,* vol. 27, eds. Hoch and Meyer, pp. 72–78; and E. S. Moore and R. J. Lutz, "Children, Advertising, and Product Experiences," *Journal of Consumer Research,* June 2000, pp. 31–47.

43. Parental responses differ across cultures; see G. M. Rose, "Consumer Socialization, Parental Style, and Developmental Timetables in the United States and Japan," *Journal of Marketing,* July 1999, pp. 105–19.

44. For example, see M. C. Macklin, "Preschoolers' Learning of Brand Names from Visual Cues," *Journal of Consumer Research,* December 1996, pp. 251–61; and D. R. Pawlowski, D. M. Badzinski, and N. Mitchell, "Effects of Metaphors on Children's Comprehension and Perception of Print Advertisements," *Journal of Advertising,* Summer 1998, pp. 83–98.

45. M. Viswanathan, T. L. Childers, and E. S. Moore, "The Measurement of Intergenerational Communication and Influence on Consumption," *Journal of the Academy of Marketing Science,* Summer 2000, pp. 406–24.

46. Palan and Wilkes, "Adolescent–Parent Interaction in Family Decision Making."

47. M. F. Ji, "Children's Relationships with Brands," *Psychology & Marketing,* April 2002, pp. 369–87; and E. S. Moore, W. L. Wilkie, and R. J. Lutz, "Passing the Torch," *Journal of Marketing,* April 2002, pp. 17–37.

48. See T. F. Mangleburg and T. Bristol, "Socialization and Adolescents' Skepticism toward Advertising," *Journal of Advertising,* Fall 1998, pp. 11–20; L. Carlson, R. N. Laczniak, and J. E. Keith, "Socializing Children about Television," *Journal of the Academy of Marketing Science,* Summer 2001, pp. 276–88; and P. Wright, M. Friestad, and D. M. Boush, "The Development of Marketplace Persuasion Knowledge in Children, Adolescents, and Young Adults," *Journal of Public Policy and Marketing,* Fall 2005, pp. 222–33.

49. Palan and Wilkes, "Adolescent–Parent Interaction in Family Decision Making."

50. P. Dando, "Healthier Fast-Food a Reality," *Advertising Age,* March 29, 2004, p. S-7.

51. Palan and Wilkes, "Adolescent–Parent Interaction in Family Decision Making."

52. J. U. McNeal, *Kids as Consumers* (New York: Lexington Books, 1992); and J. U. McNeal and C. Yeh, "Born to Shop," *American Demographics,* June 1993, pp. 34–39. See also J. B. Schor, *Born to Buy* (New York: Scribner, 2004).

53. L. A. Peracchio and D. Luna, "The Development of an Advertising Campaign to Discourage Smoking Initiation among Children and Youth," *Journal of Advertising,* Fall 1998, pp. 49–56.

# Group Influences on Consumer Behavior

For most products and brands, the basic purchase motivation relates to the ability of the product or service itself to meet a need of the consumer. Other purchases are fundamentally different in that consumers buy membership into a group as well. A prime example is the Jeep brand.[1] Many Jeep owners elect to become members of a "Jeep community." These owners attend "brandfests" such as Jeep Jamborees, Jeep 101, and Camp Jeep. At these events, they meet and form relationships with other geographically dispersed owners, deepen their involvement with their Jeep vehicles, and become acculturated into the rituals and traditions of the community. The following quote illustrates how Susan, a first-time Jeep owner, began to become a member of this community:

> I've been very happy. I get a lot of communications from Jeep, which I've been so impressed with. Usually you buy a car and you're a forgotten soul. It's kinda like they want you to be part of the family. As soon as I got the invitation for Jeep 101, I registered. I was very excited. But I was also nervous. I didn't think I would end up driving. I was very relieved to see someone in the car with you, 'cause it gave you the confidence to do what you're supposed to. Otherwise, I had visions of abandoning the truck on the hill and saying, "I can't do it!" I thought I might wimp out, but I didn't (smiles).

The Jeep brand has a long tradition of fostering a community spirit, with efforts that are ongoing and far-reaching. It strives for a balance between grassroots organizing and enthusiasm and corporate-guided efforts. The Jeep brand creates events for enthusiasts and venues where members contribute, thereby fostering a sense of community. In addition, Jeep owners organize their own events and clubs that have nothing to do with the company all centered on their jeeps, off-road experiences, and lifestyles. The Jeep community started offline. Events, organizations, and activities include the following:

- Camp Jeep—This event hosted each year by Jeep is a family event with activities including camping, crafts, concerts by such acts as Tim McGraw and, of course, off-road driving on a specially designed course where owners can test their skills and their Jeep vehicles.

- Jeep Jamboree—These are Jeep sponsored off-road treks that are fully focused on the off-road driving experience and are held all over the country in such 4×4 destinations as Moab, Utah.
- Local Jeep Clubs—These are member created clubs with their own rules, regulations, culture, and leadership. One such long-standing club is the Sacramento Jeepers club which was established in 1957. Membership into this group requires owning a 4 wheel drive Jeep vehicle, attending 3 meetings a year, and driving in 3 club trips a year.

While the community started offline, it has moved online as well in a number of ways including:

- Jeep Jamboree USA Interact—According to their website, this is a "…free on-line community for *anyone*—family, friends, drivers, riders, and visitors—interested or involved in our off-road adventure weekends that bring together the outdoors, down-to-earth people, and their Jeep 4×4s. [H]elp build a community around your stories, pictures, videos, and discussions." The site has features such as MyTrips!, MyVideos, MyRides, MyClassifieds, Forums, and Industry news.
- Jeep's YouTube Channel—The Jeep brand also has a YouTube Channel which is a sponsored YouTube area where Jeep and community members can post videos. Some of the videos are Jeep commercials posted by Jeep and some are videos from members taken at Jeep Jamborees and other off-road events.
- Local Club Web sites—Local clubs also have their own websites which provide information, news, classified ads, discussion forums, and so on. These sites range from simple to elaborate depending on the group's culture, values, and goals.

The Jeep brand has been fostering this community for decades—sometimes leading, sometimes following, and sometimes helping. Though some Jeep owners do not join this community, members tend to be intense, active, and devoted. They are connected to the Jeep brand, the Jeep community, and the lifestyle it represents in a very deep way that permeates their lives and helps define who they are.

---

As demonstrated in the opening example, even in an individualistic society like America, group memberships and identity are very important to all of us. And while we don't like to think of ourselves as conformists, most of us conform to group expectations most of the time.

When you decided what to wear to the last party you attended, you probably based your decision in part on the anticipated responses of the other individuals at the party. Likewise, your behavior at an anniversary celebration for your grandparents probably would differ from your behavior at a graduation party for a close friend. These behaviors are responses to group influences and expectations.

## TYPES OF GROUPS

The terms *group* and *reference group* need to be distinguished. A **group** is defined as *two or more individuals who share a set of norms, values, or beliefs and have certain implicitly or explicitly defined relationships to one another such that their behaviors are interdependent.*

## Reference Groups Change as the Situation Changes    FIGURE 7–1

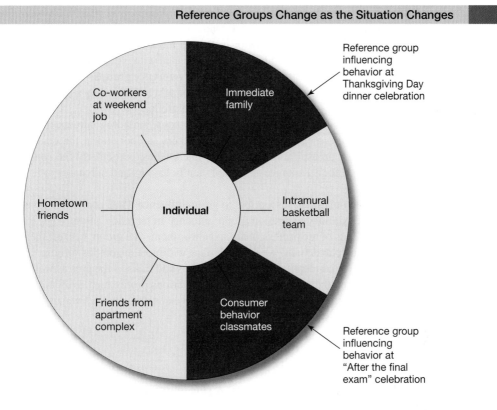

A **reference group** is *a group whose presumed perspectives or values are being used by an individual as the basis for his or her current behavior.* Thus, a reference group is simply a group that an individual uses as a guide for behavior in a specific situation.

Most of us belong to a number of different groups and perhaps would like to belong to several others. When we are actively involved with a particular group, it generally functions as a reference group. As the situation changes, we may base our behavior on an entirely different group, which then becomes our reference group. We may belong to many groups simultaneously, but we generally use only one group as our primary point of reference in any given situation. This tendency is illustrated in Figure 7–1.

Groups may be classified according to a number of variables. Four criteria are particularly useful: (1) membership, (2) strength of social tie, (3) type of contact, and (4) attraction.

The *membership* criterion is dichotomous: Either one is a member of a particular group or one is not a member of that group. Of course, some members are more secure in their membership than others are; that is, some members feel they really belong to a group, while others lack this confidence.

*Strength of social tie* refers to the closeness and intimacy of the group linkages. **Primary groups,** such as family and friends, involve strong ties and frequent interaction. Primary groups often wield considerable influence. **Secondary groups,** such as professional and neighborhood associations, involve weaker ties and less frequent interaction.

*Type of contact* refers to whether the interaction is direct or indirect. Direct contact involves face-to-face interaction, indirect contact does not. The Internet, in particular, has increased the importance of indirect reference groups in the form of *online communities,* which are discussed in more detail later in the chapter.

*Attraction* refers to the desirability that membership in a given group has for the individual. This can range from negative to positive. Groups with negative desirability—**dissociative reference groups**—can influence behavior just as do those with positive desirability.[2] For example, teenagers tend to avoid clothing styles associated with older consumers. Nonmembership groups with a positive attraction—**aspiration reference groups**—also exert a strong influence. Individuals frequently purchase products thought to be used by a desired group in order to achieve actual or symbolic membership in the group.

Recent research has identified various groups of teens, including influencers and conformers. *Influencers* are seen by themselves and others as cool and at the center of the action. Influencers are an aspirational group for many teens, particularly the *conformers,* who have a high need for acceptance and adapt their behaviors and purchases to fit in with the influencers.[3]

Teens are not the only ones susceptible to group influence. Golf equipment companies make heavy use of symbolic aspiration group influence in targeting adults. They get their equipment in the hands of the professionals and allow them, as a group, to exert their influence on the amateur players and weekend duffers with no illusions of turning pro. The influence revolves around identifying with core values and traits of the pros as well as their expertise.[4] Titleist used this in a clever ad in which various professional golfers talk about all their differences (right-handed versus left-, fade versus draw, boxers versus briefs) but one key similarity—their use of the Titleist golf ball.

## Consumption Subcultures

A consumption-based group, often termed a **consumption subculture,** is a distinctive subgroup of society that self-selects on the basis of a shared commitment to a particular product class, brand, or consumption activity. These groups have (1) an identifiable, hierarchical social structure; (2) a set of shared beliefs or values; and (3) unique jargon, rituals, and modes of symbolic expression.[5] Thus, they are reference groups for their members as well as those who aspire to join or avoid them.

A number of such subcultures, ranging from hip-hop to skydiving, have been examined. Activity-based subcultures are common. Snowboarding, golfing, rock climbing, and gardening all have consumption subcultures built around them. Each has a set of self-selecting members. They have hierarchies at the local and national levels. And they also have shared beliefs and unique jargon and rituals. Most hobbies and participation sports have consumption-based group subcultures built around them.

Consumption need not be shared physically to be a shared ritual that creates and sustains a group.[6] Serious fans of professional football or *Star Trek* form consumption subcultures. For example, following a team gives a fan something in common with other fans of the same team, and enthusiasm for the sport itself provides a common ground for all members of the group.[7]

Note that not all, or even most, product owners or participants in an activity become members of the consumption subculture associated with it. For example, one can enjoy the *Star Trek* TV shows without becoming a member of the associated subculture. Self-selecting into a consumption subculture involves more than merely participating in the activity or owning the product. Commitment is required, as are the acquisition of the group's beliefs and values, participation in its indirect activities, and use of its jargon and rituals.

It is a feeling of family. When I visit other dojos for a judo competition, I feel like I came back home. No other sports that I know do this and have the community judo has.[8]

As with other types of groups, members of consumption subcultures vary in their commitment to and interpretation of the group's values and norms. Members of the Star Trek consumption subculture tend to vary along a continuum from fandom to Trekkers to Trekkies (varying in part by when and how many Star Trek symbols, such as clothing, are worn). Members are quite cognizant of these gradients:

> To me, a "Trekkie" is someone who is pretty much lost in the fantasy world of "Star Trek," someone who has taken an escapist approach to the show and almost literally "escaped" into it. I like to think I am a fan with a more appropriate detachment to the show.[9]

**Marketing and Consumption Subcultures**   Consumption subcultures based on activities obviously are markets for the requirements of the activity itself, such as golf clubs for golfers. However, these groups develop rituals and modes of symbolic communication that often involve other products or services. Golf is renowned for the "uniform" that many of its adherents wear. Clothes, hats, and other items designed for golfers are based as much on providing symbolic meaning as they are for functional benefits.

While these subcultures adopt consumption patterns in large part to affirm their unique identity, the larger market often appropriates all or parts of their symbols, at least for a time. Thus, clothing initially worn by a consumption subculture, such as snowboarders or surfers, for functional or symbolic reasons may emerge as a style for a much larger group (see Illustration 7–1). Marketers such as Nike observe such groups closely for clues to new trends.

Participating in a shared consumption experience is a means of developing and maintaining social relationships among individuals. When two or more individuals share a

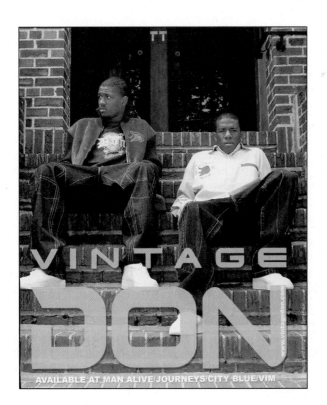

**ILLUSTRATION 7–1**

Clothing styles originating in consumption subcultures for functional or symbolic reasons are often adopted by other groups as well. Rappers and hip-hop artists continue to initiate so-called urban youth trends that gain widespread popularity.

consumption event, such as attending a performance, the consumption experience is not just the direct effect of seeing the performance. It includes the social interactions with the other individuals, the fact of sharing, and the meanings attached to these interactions. Thus, organizations marketing the arts, as well as sports marketers and others, should focus on providing and promoting the social, group aspects of the experience as well as the artistic and entertaining features.

## Brand Communities

Consumption subcultures focus on the interactions of individuals around an activity, product category, or occasionally a brand. A **brand community** is *a nongeographically bound community, based on a structured set of social relationships among owners of a brand and the psychological relationship they have with the brand itself, the product in use, and the firm.*[10] A **community** is *characterized by consciousness of kind, shared rituals and traditions, and a sense of moral responsibility.*[11]

Jeep, along with its owner-enthusiasts, has created a brand community, as described at the beginning of this chapter, as have Harley-Davidson, Saab, Ford Bronco, and MG (a British sports car). The following examples illustrate the nature of brand communities.[12]

**Consciousness of Kind**
Who else drives Broncos? Guys like myself and guys who like engines.

There are several new classes of riders fouling the wind with the misapprehension that merely owning a Harley [Davidson] will transform them into a biker. This is the same type of dangerous ignorance that suggests that giving a dog an artichoke turns him into a gourmet.

**Rituals and Traditions**
If you drove a Saab, whenever you passed someone else driving a Saab, you beeped or flashed your headlights.

For the past 7 years, we have sponsored a fall trip. [W]e always go the first weekend in October. [W]e . . . get on the Blue Ridge Parkway [which was] made for MGs, you know—high mountain roads, curves, and hills. We spend Friday and Saturday night in the mountains and then come back. The 1st year we had seven or eight people, last year we had 23 cars.

**Moral Responsibility**
Yeah, we see another Saab on the side of the road; we pull over to help, no matter what it is.

An MG owner and enthusiast indicates a sense of dedication to help other MG owners even to the point of letting a stranger (who eventually became a friend) stay at his home for free for several nights while waiting on repair parts. "I love it because anyone who has an MG is immediately accepted. . . . I'd help anyone who has an interest in British cars."

**Marketing and Brand Communities**    Brand communities can add value to the ownership of the product and build intense loyalty. A "mere" Jeep owner derives the functional and symbolic benefits associated with owning a Jeep. A member of the Jeep community derives these benefits plus increases in self-esteem from gaining skill in the off-road operation of a Jeep, the ability and confidence to use the Jeep in a wider range of situations, new friendships and social interactions, a feeling of belongingness, a positive association with Chrysler LLC, and a deeper relationship with his or her Jeep.

If a consumer anticipates these benefits in advance and values them, he or she is much more likely to buy the brand. Once a consumer becomes a member of a brand community, remaining in the community generally requires continuing to own and use the brand. This can create a very intense brand loyalty. Thus, a mere Jeep owner who needed to replace his Jeep might compare a new Jeep with other competing brands by comparing attributes across the brands. However, a Jeep community member would also consider the social and psychological costs of leaving the Jeep community.

A number of firms work diligently to foster brand communities. An initial question a manager must ask is, Does a brand community make sense for this product and brand? Brand communities seem most relevant for high-involvement, activity-based products.

A second condition for a strong brand community appears to be a degree of uniqueness to the brand itself. Harley-Davidson has its historical association with "outlaw bikers." Jeep conjures up images from endless World War II movies. Saab has its unique design and foreign origin. Much of the MG mystique is its unique British heritage and authenticity. It would certainly be more difficult to build a strong brand community around a mundane brand.

Given that a brand community is feasible, what is required to foster one? Fundamentally, it requires the firm to establish a relationship with the owner and help owners establish relationships with each other through Web sites and brand-related events. Brand-related events are often termed "brand fests," which are *gatherings of owners and others for the purposes of interacting with one another in the context of learning about and using the brand.* Jeep makes extensive use of its brand fests through Jeep Jamborees and Camp Jeep.

## Online Communities and Social Networks

An **online community** is *a community that interacts over time around a topic of interest on the Internet.*[13] These interactions can take place in various forms, including online message boards and discussion groups, blogs, as well as corporate and nonprofit Web sites. Research indicates that online communities exist for many participants and that there is often a sense of community online, which moves beyond mere interactions to include an affective or emotional attachment to the online group. Studies have found ongoing communications among subsets of these interest groups. In addition, the patterns of communication indicate a group structure, with the more experienced members serving as experts and leaders and the newer members seeking advice and information. These groups develop unique vocabularies, netiquette, and means for dealing with behaviors deemed inappropriate.

Extent of connection can vary dramatically across members. Many members observe the group discussions without participating. Others participate but only at a limited level. Others manage and create content for the group.[14]

The most recent and ongoing evolution relating to online communities are online social network sites. An **online social network site** is *a Web-based service that allows individuals to (1) construct a public or sempublic profile within a bounded system, (2) articulate a list of other users with whom they share a connection, and (3) view and traverse their list of connections and those made by others within the system.*[15] Online social network sites take many forms, including friendship (Facebook and MySpace), media sharing (Flickr and YouTube), events (NASCAR Hookup), and corporate (P&G's Capessa site for women).

Illustration 7–2 shows how a company is using a *branded* online social network site to foster an online community and further solidify brand loyalty.

**Marketing and Online Communities and Social Networks**    Marketing in online communities and social networks is possible and potentially beneficial. In fact, marketers are spending over $2 billion on advertising on social network sites alone, which is nearly 10 percent of all online advertising.[16] Options range from relative standard banner and

Online social network sites are increasingly popular for both consumers and brands as a way to foster and be connected to a community with similar lifestyles, values, and interests.

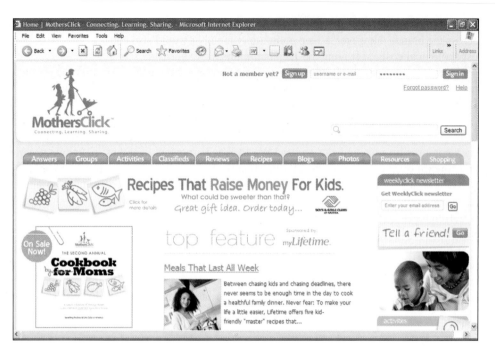

pop-up ads to more tailored approaches that maximize the specific characteristics of the venue. We discuss several guiding principles and specific examples that demonstrate these principles.[17]

The first guiding principle is to be *transparent.* In online communities it is critical that companies identify themselves and any posted content as such. Marketers who fail to do so risk being found out and subject to massive criticism from the community. Consider the case of Sony's PSP "Flog," or fake blog, as reported on *The Consumerist* blog:[18]

> [T]he forces of the internet outed a marketing company working for Sony for creating fake PSP blog. The ps3do site says it's written by "Charlie" who wants to get the parents of his friend, "Jeremy," to buy "Jeremy" a PSP for Christmas. The domain name is registered to the *Zipatoni* marketing company.

Since blogs can and often are a part of social network sites, this example is directly relevant. More generally it shows how important transparency is when companies interact with online groups.

The second principle is to *be a part of the community.* Online communities often expect that the company will be part of the community and not just market to it. A recent study examined an online newsgroup devoted to those interested in multisport events such as triathlons (MSN—or multisport network—with 17,000 daily readers). Some members of this community were sporting goods vendors who had to play a delicate balancing act:

> These sporting goods members . . . are expected to be "community members" first and vendors second. Other MSN members appreciate their views on equipment, but vendors lose their credibility if they appear to participate in MSN primarily to promote their own products. By adhering to this "good member" policy, one vendor reported that on days he posted a message to MSN, he could expect an additional 4000 hits on his Web site.[19]

A third principle is to *adapt marketing efforts to fit the nature of the site*. Some sites are more commercially oriented and thus more traditional forms of banner ads and commercial content are accepted and even welcomed. However, some sites, even those designed by companies, are positioned as being more for the user community and thus must be approached with care. Consider P&G. It has developed two very different social network sites—one is the more commercially oriented site called the People's Choice Community (related to the People's Choice Awards, which P&G produces). The other, Capessa, is much less commercial and designed toward women's issues such as health, work, and pregnancy. Consider the following comments from P&G relating to these sites:[20]

The two sites both target 18- to 49-year-olds, but differ in other ways. The entertainment site [Peoples Choice] will have a very jazzy, energized look and feel to it and feature some ads for P&G products and other products. [On the Capessa site] there won't be any P&G ads there.

As one expert notes, "With Capessa, they are providing women with a place where they can learn from and talk with each other, rather than listening to specific views by P&G or some expert. [As such] the site shouldn't be over-commercialized."

A fourth principle is to *take advantage of the unique capabilities of each venue*. Many of the social network sites have special areas for corporate advertising and activities that extend beyond traditional banner and pop-up ads. For example, companies can have their own channel on YouTube, which they manage, monitor, and facilitate, as Jeep does. An additional example is the "friends" component of MySpace:[21]

If an advertiser simply created a MySpace page and started sending thousands of requests for friends, recipients would likely be suspicious of something so commercial and mark it as spam. MySpace facilitates the process of helping the advertiser create a program in advertising areas. MySpace users then "opt in" as friends of the brand, and the marketer can start compiling a list of users to email and send MySpace bulletins.

  Wendy's . . . created a likable character, a square hamburger, humanizing the brand and having over 95,000 friends at its peak. The average page is visited 30 times, so the exposure for Wendy's on a daily basis was exponential.

# REFERENCE GROUP INFLUENCES ON THE CONSUMPTION PROCESS

We all conform in a variety of ways to numerous groups. Look around your classroom. The odds are that, except for gender differences, most of you will be dressed in a similar manner. In fact, a student who comes to class dressed in a suit will generally be asked about the job interview that others will assume is the cause of the more formal clothing. Note that we, as individuals, do not generally consider these behaviors to constitute conformity. Normally, we conform without even being aware of doing so; however, we also frequently face conscious decisions as to whether or not to go along with the group. Reference groups have been found to influence a wide range of consumption behaviors. Before examining the marketing implications of these findings, we need to examine the nature of reference group influence more closely.

# The Nature of Reference Group Influence

Reference group influence can take three forms: *informational, normative,* and *identification.* It is important to distinguish among these types since the marketing strategy required depends on the type of influence involved.

**Informational influence** *occurs when an individual uses the behaviors and opinions of reference group members as potentially useful bits of information.* This influence is based on either the similarity of the group's members to the individual or the expertise of the influencing group member.[22] Thus, a person may notice that runners on the track team use a specific brand of nutrition bar. He or she may then decide to try that brand because these healthy and active runners use it. Use by the track team members thus provides information about the brand. Illustration 7–3 shows another form of informational influence whereby a positive nonmember expert referent group endorses or recommends the brand.

**Normative influence,** sometimes referred to as *utilitarian* influence, *occurs when an individual fulfills group expectations to gain a direct reward or to avoid a sanction.*[23] You may purchase a particular brand of wine to win approval from a colleague. Or you may refrain from wearing the latest fashion for fear of being teased by friends or to fit in with or be accepted by them. As you might expect, normative influence is strongest when individuals have strong ties to the group and the product involved is socially conspicuous.[24] Ads that promise social acceptance or approval if a product is used are relying on normative influence. Likewise, ads that suggest group disapproval if a product is not used, such as a mouthwash or deodorant, are based on normative influence.

**ILLUSTRATION 7–3**

Consumers often use nonmember expert referent groups as a source of information for their purchase decisions.

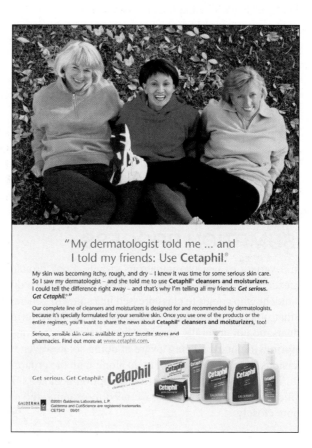

**Identification influence,** also called *value-expressive* influence, *occurs when individuals have internalized the group's values and norms.* These then guide the individuals' behaviors without any thought of reference group sanctions or rewards. The individual has accepted the group's values as his or her own. The individual behaves in a manner consistent with the group's values because his or her values and the group's values are the same.

Figure 7–2 illustrates a series of consumption situations and the type of reference group influence that is operating in each case.

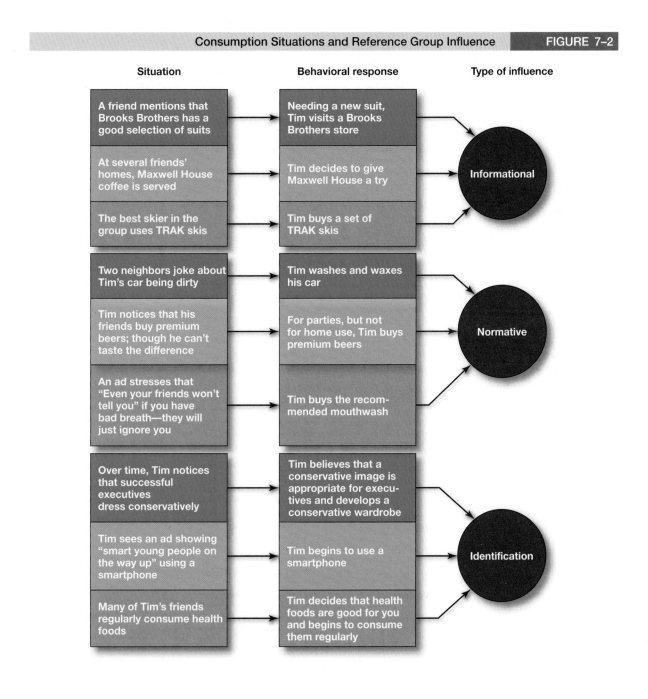

**Consumption Situations and Reference Group Influence    FIGURE 7–2**

TABLE 7-1

Two Consumption
Situation Charac-
teristics and
Product/Brand
Choice

| | Degree Needed | |
|---|---|---|
| **Consumption** | **Necessity**<br>Weak reference group influence on product | **Nonnecessity**<br>Strong reference group influence on product |
| **Visible**<br>Strong reference group influence on brand | *Public Necessities*<br>Influence: Weak product and strong brand<br>Examples:<br>    Shoes<br>    Automobiles | *Public Luxuries*<br>Influence: Strong product and brand<br>Examples:<br>    Snowboard<br>    Health club |
| **Private**<br>Weak reference group influence on brand | *Private Necessities*<br>Influence: Weak product and brand<br>Examples:<br>    Clothes washer<br>    Insurance | *Private Luxuries*<br>Influence: Strong product and weak brand<br>Examples:<br>    Hot tub<br>    Home theater system |

## Degree of Reference Group Influence

Reference groups may have no influence in a given situation, or they may influence usage of the product category, the type of product used, or the brand used. Brand influence is most likely to be a category influence rather than a specific brand; that is, a group is likely to approve, or disapprove, a range of brands such as imported beers or luxury automobiles.

Table 7–1 shows how two consumption situation characteristics—necessity/nonnecessity and visible/private consumption—combine to affect the degree of reference group influence likely to operate in a specific situation. In the following paragraphs, we will discuss these two characteristics and three additional determinants of reference group influences.

1. Group influence is strongest *when the use of product or brand is visible to the group.* Products such as running shoes are highly visible. Products such as vitamins are generally not. Reference group influence typically affects only those aspects (e.g., category or brand) that are visible to the group.[25]
2. Reference group influence is higher *the less of a necessity an item is.* Thus, reference groups have strong influence on the ownership of products such as snowboards and designer clothes, but much less influence on necessities such as refrigerators.
3. In general, *the more commitment an individual feels to a group, the more the individual will conform to the group norms.*
4. *The more relevant a particular activity is to the group's functioning, the stronger the pressure to conform to the group norms concerning that activity.* Thus, style of dress may be important to a social group that frequently eats dinner together at nice restaurants and unimportant to a group that meets for basketball on Thursday nights.
5. The final factor that affects the degree of reference group influence is *the individual's confidence in the purchase situation.* This can happen even if the product is not visible or important to group functioning as a result of the importance of the decision and a lack of personal decision confidence. Individual personality traits can influence confidence and thus susceptible to reference group influence.[26]

Figure 7–3 summarizes the major determinants of the degree to which a reference group is likely to influence product and brand usage. Marketing managers can use this structure to determine the likely degree of group influence on the consumption of their brand.

**Consumption Situation Determinants of Reference Group Influence**     FIGURE 7–3

# MARKETING STRATEGIES BASED ON REFERENCE GROUP INFLUENCES

The first task a manager faces in using reference group influence is to determine the degree and nature of the influence that exists, *or can be created,* for the product in question. Figure 7–3 provides the starting point for this analysis.

## Personal Sales Strategies

The power of groups was initially demonstrated in a classic series of studies. Eight subjects are shown four straight lines on a board—three unequal lines are grouped close together, and another appears some distance from them. The subjects are asked to determine which one of the three unequal lines is closest to the length of the fourth line shown some distance away. The subjects are to announce their judgments publicly. Seven of the subjects are working for the experimenter, and they announce incorrect matches. The order of announcement is arranged so that the naive subject responds last. The naive subject almost always agrees with the incorrect judgment of the others. This is known as the **Asch phenomenon.** Imagine how much stronger the pressures to conform are among friends or when the task is less well defined, such as preferring one brand or style to another.

Consider this direct application of the Asch phenomenon in personal selling. A group of potential customers is brought together for a sales presentation. As each design is presented, the salesperson scans the expressions of the people in the group, looking for the one who shows approval (e.g., head nodding) of the design. The salesperson then asks that person for an opinion, since the opinion is certain to be favorable. The person is asked to elaborate. Meanwhile, the salesperson scans the faces of the other people, looking for more support, and then asks for an opinion of the person now showing most approval. The salesperson continues until the person who initially showed the most disapproval is reached. In this way, by using the first person as a model, and by social group pressure on the last person, the salesperson gets all or most of the people in the group to make a positive public

French champagne is viewed by many as being appropriate only for very special occasions. This ad indicates that it is appropriate for fun, casual group activities.

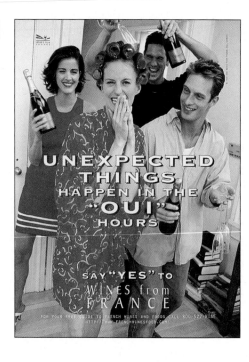

statement about the design. *Do you see any ethical issues in using group influences in this way?*

## Advertising Strategies

Marketers often position products as appropriate for group activities. French wines gained an image of being somewhat expensive and snobbish. Many consumers viewed them as appropriate only for very special occasions. A trade group, Food and Wines from France, launched a campaign to broaden their appeal. Illustration 7–4 shows an ad that positions French champagne as appropriate for casual group parties.

Marketers use all three types of reference group influence when developing advertisements. Informational influence in advertising was shown earlier in Illustration 7–3. This type of ad uses an expert reference group (e.g., dentists, doctors, and teachers) as the information agent. Another approach is showing members of a group using a product. The message, generally unstated, is that "these types of people find this brand to be the best; if you are like them, you will too."

Normative group influence is not portrayed in ads as much as it once was. It involves the explicit or implicit suggestion that using, or not using, the brand will result in having members of a group you belong to or wish to join rewarding or punishing you. One reason for the reduced use of this technique is the ethical questions raised by implying that a person's friends would base their reactions to the individual according to his or her purchases. Ads showing a person's friends saying negative things about them behind their back because their coffee was not great (yes, there was such an ad campaign) were criticized for playing on people's insecurities and fears.

Identification influence is based on the fact that the individual has internalized the group's values and attitudes. The advertising task is to demonstrate that the product is consistent with the group's and therefore the individual's beliefs. This often involves showing the brand being used by a particular type of group, such as socially active young singles or parents of young children.

# COMMUNICATIONS WITHIN GROUPS AND OPINION LEADERSHIP

We learn about new products, services, and brands, as well as retail and information outlets, from our friends and other reference groups in two basic ways. First is by observing or participating with them as they use products and services. Second is by seeking or receiving advice and information from them in the form of **word-of-mouth (WOM) communications.** WOM involves *individuals sharing information with other individuals in a verbal form, including face-to-face, phone, and the Internet.* As indicated in Consumer Insight 7–1, online social media and the Internet continue to transform interpersonal communications and WOM.

## Online Social Media, Consumer-Generated Content, and WOM

Social media is part of an ongoing *revolution* online, sometimes referred to as Web 2.0, which involves technologies that allow users to leverage the unique interactive and collaborative capabilities of the Internet. These technologies and formats include online communities, social network sites of all types, consumer review sites, and blogs or online journals kept by individuals and companies and distributed across the Web. Online social media allow users not only to form, join, and communicate with groups and individuals online, but also to create and distribute original content in ways not possible in the past. Such *consumer-generated content* is changing the marketing landscape. Marketers no longer completely control the communications process but now are both observers and participants in an ongoing dialogue that often is driven by consumers themselves.[27]

An example of consumer-generated content in online social network sites is a video titled "Fully Submerged Jeep." It shows an amateur video posted on Metacafe of a Jeep event in which someone takes their Jeep into a pit of water that covers the vehicle completely and comes out the other side unscathed. The video has had over 350,000 views! Jeep is not in control of this content. On the other hand, one Jeep enthusiast provided not only vicarious learning about Jeep but implicit positive WOM about the qualities of Jeep. Others then joined in and posted comments about the video and about Jeep, which kept the "conversation" going. This is the positive side, and for Jeep derives from the devoted members of its brand community.

On the negative side was the Chevy Apprentice Challenge, in which Chevy invited consumers to create their own Tahoe ads with online components and tools provided by the company. The problem was that one in five ads was negative, focusing on the gas guzzler aspect and coming from environmentalists. As one expert noted, the mistake was not in the use of new media, but in the mass approach that the company took:[28]

A much better approach would have been for GM to approach all owners of Tahoes—from soccer moms to hip-hop artists. They could have asked those loyal fans to create commercials using the same material Chevy provided. Or better yet—GM could have allowed them to use their own videos, images, and music to create truly personalized commercials.

In this new world of social media, there are numerous categories of participants. These include:[29]

- Creators—these folks create content of their own—Web pages, blogs, video and video uploads to places like YouTube. Creators tend to be in the teens and early twenties.
- Critics—these folks are bloggers and post ratings and reviews. Critics tend to be a bit older than creators—more in the late teens and mid-twenties.
- Joiners—these folks utilize social networking sites. Joiners range mostly from teens to late twenties. Joiners are a much larger proportion of the population than creators and critics.
- Spectators—these folks consume other people's content by reading blogs, watching videos, and so on. Spectators trend young as well, but also garner more members of the older generations.
- Inactives—these folks are online but don't participate in social media. Inactives trend older.

Creators and critics are the true leaders of conversation and opinion in Web 2.0. They are, in essence, the opinion leaders and e-fluentials, which we discuss shortly, whose influence cannot be underestimated. Marketers are finding that in this new world of social media, they must think more in terms of joining and participating in the conversation rather than driving and controlling it.

### Critical Thinking Questions

1. How do online social media change marketers from controlling communications to participating in and observing it?

2. Beyond age, what do you think are typical characteristics of creators and critics?

3. What strategies might marketers use to work in partnership with creators and critics? What pitfalls do you see?

Consumers generally trust the opinions of people (family, friends, acquaintances) more than marketing communications because, unlike marketing communications, these personal sources have no reason not to express their true opinions and feelings. As a consequence, WOM via personal sources such as family and friends can have a critical influence on consumer decisions and business success. In fact, it is estimated that two-thirds of all consumer product decisions are influenced by WOM.[30] Recent research shows just how much faith consumers put in personal WOM versus advertising across a number of products and services. The information below shows the percentage of adults who put people (WOM from friends, family, or other people), as compared with advertising, at the top of their list of best sources for information.

|  | People | Advertising |
| --- | --- | --- |
| Restaurants | 83% | 35% |
| Places | 71 | 33 |
| Prescription drugs | 71 | 21 |
| Hotels | 63 | 27 |
| Health tips | 61 | 19 |
| Movies | 61 | 67 |
| Best brands | 60 | 33 |
| Retirement planning | 58 | 9 |
| Automobiles | 58 | 36 |
| Clothes | 50 | 59 |
| Computer equipment | 40 | 18 |
| Web sites to visit | 37 | 12 |

Source: Adapted with the permission of The Free Press, a Division of Simon & Schuster, Inc., from *The Influentials: One American in Ten Tells the Other Nine How to Vote, Where to Eat, and What to Buy,* by Edward Keller and Jonathan Berry. Copyright © 2003 by Roper ASW, LLC. All rights reserved.

As this information suggests, the importance of WOM is generally high, and its importance relative to advertising varies somewhat across product types. In addition, traditional mass-media advertising still plays a role, particularly at the earlier stages of the decision process, including building brand awareness.

Negative experiences are powerful motivators of WOM, a factor that must be considered by marketers, since negative WOM can strongly influence recipients' attitudes and behaviors.[31] Negative experiences, which are highly emotional and memorable, motivate consumers to talk. While the number varies by situation and product, it is not at all uncommon to find that dissatisfied consumers tell twice as many people about their experience than do satisfied consumers.[32] While merely satisfying consumers (delivering what they expected) may not always motivate WOM, going beyond satisfaction to deliver more than was expected also appears to have the potential to generate substantial WOM. Thus, companies may consider strategies for "delighting" consumers or otherwise creating positive emotional experiences that consumers are motivated to pass along in the form of positive WOM (see Chapter 18).[33] Obviously, it is imperative for companies to provide both consistent product and service quality and quick, positive responses to consumer complaints.

Moreover, it is important to note that not all personal sources are equal in value. Some folks are known in their circles as the "go-to person" for specific types of information. These individuals actively filter, interpret, or provide product and brand-relevant information to their family, friends, and colleagues. An individual who does this is known as an **opinion leader.** The process of one person's receiving information from

**Mass Communication Information Flows**    **FIGURE 7–4**

the mass media or other sources and passing it on to others is known as the **two-step flow of communication.** The two-step flow explains some aspects of communication within groups, but it is too simplistic to account for most communication flows. What usually happens is a multistep flow of communication. Figure 7–4 contrasts the direct flow of information from a firm to customers with the more realistic multistep flow of mass communications.

The **multistep flow of communication** involves opinion leaders for a particular product area who actively seek relevant information from the mass media as well as other sources. These opinion leaders process this information and transmit their interpretations of it to some members of their groups. These group members also receive information from the mass media as well as from group members who are not opinion leaders. Figure 7–4 also indicates that these non–opinion leaders often initiate requests for information and supply feedback to the opinion leaders. Likewise, opinion leaders receive information from their followers as well as from other opinion leaders. Note how social media facilitates this multistep flow process online.

## Situations in Which WOM and Opinion Leadership Occur

The exchange of advice and information between group members can occur *directly* in the form of WOM when (1) one individual seeks information from another or (2) when one individual volunteers information. It can also occur *indirectly* through observation as a by-product of normal group interaction.[34]

Imagine that you are about to make a purchase in a product category with which you are not very familiar. Further imagine that the purchase is important to you—perhaps a new sound system, skis, or a bicycle. How would you go about deciding what type and brand to buy? Chances are you would, among other things, ask someone you know who you believe is knowledgeable about the product category. This person would be an opinion leader for you. Notice that we have described a *high-involvement* purchase situation in which the purchaser has limited product knowledge about an important decision. Figure 7–5 illustrates how these factors lead to varying levels of opinion leadership.[35]

**FIGURE 7–5**          Likelihood of Seeking an Opinion Leader

In addition to *explicitly* seeking or volunteering information, group members provide information to each other through observable behaviors. Consider Hard Candy nail polish:

> Dinah Mohajer, a student at the University of Southern California, made some funky-colored nail polish to match a pair of sandals. Other students saw her and wanted similar polishes. Soon she and her boyfriend were making nail polish in her bathtub. Next she obtained distribution for the polish, now named Hard Candy, in trendy local salons. News photos showing Quentin Tarantino and Drew Barrymore wearing it generated more interest. The actress Alicia Silverstone wore and praised the product on David Letterman. In three years sales grew to $30 million.[36]

Hard Candy succeeded mainly through observation. Stylish individuals were seen wearing it on campus (Dinah and her friends). Then other individual style leaders used it (by being distributed through trendy salons it was seen and purchased by style-conscious individuals). Finally, celebrities were seen in mass media wearing Hard Candy.

Obviously, observation and direct WOM often operate together. For example, you might be in the market for a digital camera and notice that a friend uses an Olympus. This might jump-start a conversation about digital cameras, the Olympus brand, and where to find the best deals. And while Hard Candy's success depended heavily on observation, WOM was also involved as friends told other friends.

## Characteristics of Opinion Leaders

What characterizes opinion leaders? The most salient characteristic is greater long-term involvement with the product category than the non–opinion leaders in the group. This is referred to as **enduring involvement,** and it leads to enhanced knowledge about and experience with the product category or activity.[37] This knowledge and experience makes opinion leadership possible.[38] Thus, an individual tends to be an opinion leader only for specific product or activity clusters.

Opinion leadership functions primarily through interpersonal communications and observation. These activities occur most frequently among individuals with similar demographic characteristics. Thus, it is not surprising that opinion leaders are found within all demo-graphic segments of the population and seldom differ significantly on demographic variables from the people they influence. Opinion leaders tend to be more gregarious than others are, which may explain their tendency to provide information to others. They also have higher levels of exposure to relevant media than do non–opinion leaders. And opinion leaders around the world appear to possess similar traits.[39]

Opinion leaders can be identified using self-designating questionnaires with questions such as "I often persuade other people to buy the _____ that I like," which allow researchers to adapt the area of opinion leadership to fit their needs. While such measures allow you to identify opinion leaders through direct research, what if you want to know who the opinion leaders are for a product on a national scale? Opinion leaders are hard to identify a priori because they tend to be demographically similar to those they influence.

The fact that opinion leaders are heavily involved with the mass media, particularly media that focus on their area of leadership, provides a partial solution to the identifica-tion problem. For example, Nike could assume that many subscribers to *Runner's World* serve as opinion leaders for jogging and running shoes.[40] Likewise, the fact that opinion leaders tend to be gregarious and tend to belong to clubs and associations suggests that Nike could also consider members, and particularly leaders, of local running clubs to be opinion leaders.

Some product categories have professional opinion leaders. For products related to live-stock, county extension agents are generally very influential. Barbers and hair stylists serve as opinion leaders for hair care products. Pharmacists are important opinion leaders for a wide range of health care products.

### Market Mavens, Influentials, and e-Fluentials

Opinion leaders tend to be special-ists. That is, their knowledge and involvement tend to be product or activity specific. Therefore, while a person might be an opinion leader for motorcycles, she or he is likely to be an opinion seeker for other products, such as cell phones or stereo equipment. However, some individuals have information about many different kinds of products, places to shop, and other aspects of markets. They both initiate discussions with others about products and shopping, and respond to requests for market information. These generalized market influencers are **market mavens.** In essence, then, market mavens are a special type of opinion leader.

Market mavens provide significant amounts of information to others across a wide array of products, including durables and nondurables, services, and store types. They provide information on product quality, sales, usual prices, product availability, store personnel characteristics, and other features of relevance to consumers. Market mavens are extensive users of media.[41] They are also more extroverted and conscientious, which drives their tendency to share information with others.[42] Demographically, market mavens tend to be similar to those they influence.

Roper Starch (a market research company) has been tracking a group of generalized market influencers, which are very similar in nature to market mavens, for over 30 years. These consumers, which Roper Starch calls the *Influentials,* represent about 10 percent of the population and have broad social networks that allow them to influence the attitudes and behaviors of the other 90 percent of the population. Influentials are heavy users of print media, such as newspapers and magazines, as well as the Internet and are more likely than the general population to engage in WOM recommendations about products, services, brands, and even what new Web sites to visit.[43]

Internet mavens also exist. As we saw in Chapter 6, teen Internet mavens are able to influence family decisions that their parents make by operating as important gatekeepers to information on the Web.[44] Roper Starch and Burston-Marsteller have identified a related group of consumers they call *e-fluentials*. E-fluentials represent about 10 percent of the adult online community, but their influence is extensive as they communicate news, information, and experiences to a vast array of people both online and offline. These e-fluentials actively use the Internet to gather and disseminate information through online bulletin boards, newsgroups, listservs, and corporate Web sites. Their number one factor in opening unsolicited e-mails is brand familiarity. Clearly a trusted brand and solid online presence are critical to targeting e-fluentials.[45]

## Marketing Strategy, WOM, and Opinion Leadership

Marketers are increasingly relying on WOM and influential consumers as part of their marketing strategies. Driving factors include fragmented markets that are more difficult to reach through traditional mass media, greater consumer skepticism toward advertising, and a realization that opinion leaders can provide invaluable insights in the research and development process. For example, *Teen People* has a group of 4,000 young "trend spotters" on call. The magazine encourages them to submit story ideas and respond to published articles. It invites them to monthly meetings at regional offices to discuss what's cool and what is not.

This is not to say that marketers have given up on traditional advertising and mass media approaches. Instead, they realize that in many cases they could make their traditional media spending go a lot further if they could tap into these influential consumers who will spread the word either indirectly through observation or directly through WOM. We examine some marketing strategies designed to generate WOM and encourage opinion leadership next.

**Advertising**   Advertising can stimulate and simulate WOM and opinion leadership. *Stimulation* can involve themes designed to encourage current owners to talk about the brand (tell a friend about) or prospective owners to ask current owners (ask someone who owns one) for their impressions. Ads can attempt to stimulate WOM by generating interest and excitement. Dove generated interest using a combination of advertising and so-called "pass-it-on" tools to stimulate WOM. They ran an ad offering two free bars of Dove to anyone who would recommend three friends who also got a free bar of soap that was gift-wrapped with the name of the initiating friend on the outside. So instead of a sample from a giant company, it felt like a gift from a friend.[46]

*Simulating* opinion leadership involves having an acknowledged opinion leader—such as LeBron James or Sheryl Swoopes for basketball equipment—endorse a brand. Illustration 7–5 is an example of this approach for cookware. Or it can involve having an apparent opinion leader recommend the product in a "slice of life" commercial. These commercials involve an "overheard" conversation between two individuals in which one person provides brand advice to the other. Finally, advertising can present the results of surveys showing that a high percentage of either knowledgeable individuals ("9 out of 10 dentists surveyed recommend . . .") or typical users recommend the brand.[47]

**Product Sampling**   *Sampling,* sometimes called "seeding," involves getting a sample of a product into the hands of a group of potential consumers. Sampling can be a particularly potent WOM tool when it involves individuals likely to be opinion leaders.

In an attempt to increase the preference for Dockers among the key 24- to 35-year-old urban market, Levi Strauss created the position of "urban networker" in key cities. The networkers identified emerging trendsetters in their cities and tied them to Dockers. This could involve noticing a new band that was beginning to catch on and providing Dockers

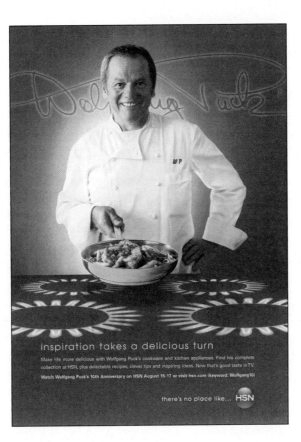

inspiration takes a delicious turn

Make life more delicious with Wolfgang Puck's cookware and kitchen appliances. Find his complete
collection at HSN, plus delectable recipes, clever tips and inspiring ideas. Now that's good taste in TV.
Watch Wolfgang Puck's 10th Anniversary on HSN August 15-17 or visit hsn.com (keyword: Wolfgang10)

there's no place like... HSN

to the members. The objective was to be associated with emerging urban "happenings" and young influentials as they evolved.[48]

BzzAgent (www.BzzAgent.com) recruits everyday people to actively spread WOM about products they like. BzzAgent is adamant that its "agents" acknowledge their association with BzzAgent and provide honest opinions. Most of the WOM occurs offline in normal con-versations. Agents receive a free product sample to use and are coached on various WOM approaches. Agents report back to BzzAgent about each WOM episode and redeemable points are rewarded. Importantly, the motive of most is not the points since many don't redeem them. BzzAgent's client list is long and growing and includes Kraft Foods, Goodyear, and Wharton School Publishing. Companies hire BzzAgent to create and field a WOM campaign. Costs vary, but a 12-week campaign involving 1,000 agents can cost $100,000.[49]

**Retailing/Personal Selling**   Numerous opportunities exist for retailers and sales per-sonnel to use opinion leadership. Clothing stores can create "fashion advisory boards" composed of likely style leaders from their target market. An example would be cheerlead-ers and class officers for a store like Abercrombie & Fitch, which caters to older teens and college students.

Retailers and sales personnel can encourage their current customers to pass along infor-mation to potential new customers. When those consumers are given rewards such as dis-counts, it is called a referral reward program. For example, an automobile salesperson, or the dealership, might provide a free car wash or oil change to current customers who send friends in to look at a new car. Such programs are growing in popularity and companies such as United Airlines, Cingular, and RE/MAX are using them. Research demonstrates

## Online Strategies to Leverage Buzz and WOM

As we've seen, the Internet continues to change the nature of interpersonal communications. New avenues are rapidly evolving, and the rewards can be huge for companies who can harness the speed and ease of interconnectivity that the Internet allows. Here are a few examples:

- **Viral marketing** is an online "pass-it-along" strategy. It "uses electronic communications to trigger brand messages throughout a widespread network of buyers." Viral marketing comes in many forms, but often involves e-mail. Honda U.K. developed a successful viral marketing campaign that started with "cutting-edge" creative in the form of a two-minute advertisement called "The Cog." The ad aired in the U.K. during the Brazilian Formula 1 Grand Prix to hit likely opinion leaders and was available on Honda's Web site. That's when the viral aspect kicked in as people "wowed" by the ad e-mailed it to friends and acquaintances around the world. Honda had record sales in the United Kingdom, and buzz spread to America, where Web traffic and sales jumped. Honda, Volvo, and Gillette are among a growing list of companies using viral techniques.[50]

- **Blogs** are personalized journals where people and organizations can keep a running dialogue. People can read, comment on, and connect to your blog, creating a powerful network that also includes other topical and news blogs. Blogs can be used in several ways by marketers. First, they can place banner ads in blogs and package ads with blog feeds. Second, they can use product sampling by getting their products in the hands of well-known bloggers in the category with the idea that they will create buzz about them on their blogs. This strategy was used successfully by a new wine company which bypassed the traditional launch approach of going through wine magazines. The result was a doubling of sales in one year. A third way marketers can use blogs is by observing important blog sites for marketing intelligence. As one expert indicates: "A manufacturer who is not paying attention to Web sites, chat rooms, and blogs is either clueless or

that the programs are effective, particularly for encouraging positive WOM to those with whom consumers have weak rather than strong ties.[51]

**Creating Buzz**    **Buzz** can be defined as *the exponential expansion of WOM*. It happens when "word spreads like wildfire" with no or limited mass media advertising supporting it. "Buzz" drove demand for Hard Candy nail polish, as described earlier. It also made massive successes of Pokémon, Beanie Babies, the original *Blair Witch Project,* and the Harry Potter books.[52] Marketers create buzz by providing opinion leaders advance information and product samples, having celebrities use the product, placing the product in movies, sponsoring "in" events tied to the product, restricting supply, courting publicity, and otherwise generating excitement and mystique about the brand.

Buzz is generally not supported by large advertising budgets, but it is often created by marketing activities. In fact, creating buzz is a key aspect of *guerrilla marketing*—marketing with a limited budget using nonconventional communications strategies. Guerrilla marketing is about making an "intense connection with individuals and speed[ing] up the natural word-of-mouth process."[53] Examples of guerrilla techniques include:

- Sony Ericsson hired attractive actors to pose as tourists in various metro areas. They would then hand their cell phone/digital camera to locals and ask them to take a picture in an attempt to get the camera in their hands and get them talking about it.

it doesn't care." A fourth way is for a company to create its own blog and put a company representative in charge of blogging, as Dell has done with Direct2Dell and its chief blogger Lionel Menchaca. A fifth way is to create blogs and recruit consumer evangelists to run them. This is what Vespa set out to do several years ago. However, the Vespa story provides a cautionary note in that the company apparently didn't put enough ongoing resources behind the initiative and the sites have been abandoned.[54]

- **Consumer review sites** provide consumer product and service reviews in a host of different formats. Formats can include consumer reviews within online retailers such as Amazon, reviews within Web sites devoted to specific topics such as those found on the automobile site Edmunds.com, as well as stand-alone recommendation sites such as Angie's List. Angie's List is interesting in that it is one of the many emerging "local" sites. It focuses on finding service providers in your specific area based on the recommendations of others in your area who have used the service. A key to the credibility of this site is that it allows no business on the site unless it has been recommended by a user and it fact-checks to make sure that a company is not posing as a recommender. Credibility is a key issue in any recommendation system, and credible consumer review sites have been shown to be important sources of influence in the choice process for various products.[55]

Clearly marketers are learning how to leverage the WOM potential of the Internet. It will be interesting to see what the future brings!

### Critical Thinking Questions

1. What other Internet alternatives exist for interpersonal communication?

2. Do you trust online sources to provide accurate information? What can marketers do to increase consumer trust in online sources?

3. What do you think are typical characteristics of those who are heavy bloggers?

- Blue Cross Blue Shield (BC/BS) hired people to be painted blue and then asked them to roam around Pittsburgh. Nobody knew what the "Blue Crew" campaign was about and it generated enormous buzz. When BC/BS revealed its linkage to the campaign, Web site traffic increased.[56]

Buzz is not just guerrilla marketing, and guerrilla tactics must be used with care. Consumer advocates are increasingly concerned about certain guerrilla tactics. *What ethical concerns surround "hired representatives" who do not identify their affiliation with the company? How is BzzAgent's approach different from Sony Ericsson's?*

Creating buzz is often part of a larger strategy that includes significant mass media advertising. Clairol attempted to create WOM for its True Intense Color line via an online sampling program. It also launched a sweepstakes, "Be the Attraction," with a grand prize of an all-expenses-paid trip for four to the premiere of *Legally Blonde* to fuel the buzz. However, these efforts were soon supplemented with a major mass media advertising campaign.[57]

Buzz and WOM are not confined to traditional offline strategies. As discussed in Consumer Insight 7–2, marketers are leveraging increasing numbers of online strategies as well.

Illustration 7–6 shows how Hershey's used viral marketing to encourage positive buzz about its Take 5 candy bar.

# DIFFUSION OF INNOVATIONS

An **innovation** is *an idea, practice, or product perceived to be new by the relevant individual or group.* Whether or not a given product *is* an innovation is determined by the perceptions of the potential market, not by an objective measure of technological change. The manner by which a new product is accepted or spreads through a market is basically a group phenomenon. In this section, we will examine this process in some detail.[58]

## Categories of Innovations

Try to recall new products that you have encountered in the past two or three years. As you reflect on these, it may occur to you that there are degrees of innovation. For example, MP3 players are more of an innovation than a new fat-free snack. The changes required in one's behavior, including attitudes and beliefs, or lifestyle if a person adopts the new product or service determine the degree of innovation, not the technical or functional changes in the product.

We can place any new product somewhere on a continuum ranging from no change to radical change, depending on the target market's perception of the item. This continuum is often divided into three categories or types of innovations.

**Continuous Innovation**    Adoption of this type of innovation requires relatively minor changes in behavior or changes in behaviors that are unimportant to the consumer. Examples include Crest Vivid White Night toothpaste, Wheaties Energy Crunch cereal, Pria (an afternoon snack bar), and DVD players. Note that several of these products are complex technological breakthroughs. However, their use requires little change in the owner's behavior or attitude. Illustration 7–7 is another example of a continuous innovation.

**Dynamically Continuous Innovation**    Adoption of this type of innovation requires a moderate change in an important behavior or a major change in a behavior of low or moderate importance to the individual. Examples include digital cameras, personal navigators,

**ILLUSTRATION 7–7**

This new product would be considered a continuous innovation by most despite the fact that it meets an important need for some.

and Bella and Birch textured paints that are applied like wallpaper but without glue, using a special applicator. Illustration 7–8 shows a product that is a dynamically continuous innovation for most consumer groups.

**Discontinuous Innovation**    Adoption of this type of innovation requires major changes in behavior of significant importance to the individual or group. Examples would include the Norplant contraceptive, becoming a vegetarian, the Honda FCX Clarity hydrogen car, and perhaps even more so, Honda's home energy system for generating hydrogen for their cars and electricity for your home using natural gas (see Illustration 7–9).

Most of the new products or alterations introduced each year tend toward the no-change end of the continuum. Much of the theoretical and empirical research, however, has been based on discontinuous innovations. For example, individual consumers presumably go through a series of distinct steps or stages known as the **adoption process** when purchasing an innovation. These stages are shown in Figure 7–6.

Figure 7–6 also shows the steps in extended decision making, described in Chapter 1. As can be seen, the *adoption process* is basically a term used to describe extended decision making when a new product is involved. As we will discuss in detail in Chapter 14, extended decision making occurs when the consumer is *highly involved* in the purchase. High purchase involvement is likely for discontinuous innovations such as the decision to purchase a hybrid car, and most studies of innovations of this nature have found that consumers use extended decision making.

However, it would be a mistake to assume that all innovations are evaluated using extended decision making (the adoption process). In fact, most continuous innovations

**ILLUSTRATION 7–8**

Using this product would require a major change in an area of moderate importance for most individuals. For these individuals, it would be a dynamically continuous innovation.

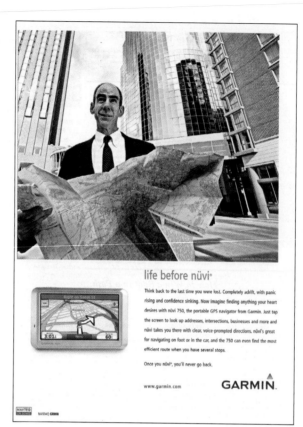

**ILLUSTRATION 7–9**

Most consumers will react to this as a discontinuous innovation.

**Adoption Process and Extended Decision Making** — **FIGURE 7–6**

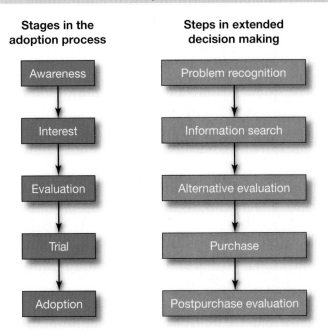

probably trigger limited decision making. As consumers, we generally don't put a great deal of effort into deciding to purchase innovations such as Jolt's new Wild Grape flavored drink or the new Glad microwave steaming bags.

## Diffusion Process

The **diffusion process** is *the manner in which innovations spread throughout a market.* The term *spread* refers to purchase behavior in which the product is purchased with some degree of regularity.[59] The market can range from virtually the entire society (for a new soft drink, perhaps) to the students at a particular high school (for an automated fast-food and snack outlet).

For most innovations, the diffusion process appears to follow a similar pattern over time: a period of relatively slow growth, followed by a period of rapid growth, followed by a final period of slower growth. This pattern is shown in Figure 7–7. However, there are exceptions to this pattern. In particular, it appears that for continuous innovations such as new ready-to-eat cereals, the initial slow-growth stage may be skipped.

An overview of innovation studies reveals that the time involved from introduction until a given market segment is saturated (i.e., sales growth has slowed or stopped) varies from a few days or weeks to years. This leads to two interesting questions: (1) What determines how rapidly a particular innovation will spread through a given market segment? and (2) In what ways do those who purchase innovations relatively early differ from those who purchase them later?

**Factors Affecting the Spread of Innovations**     The rate at which an innovation is diffused is a function of the following 10 factors.

1. *Type of group.* Some groups are more accepting of change than others. In general, young, affluent, and highly educated groups accept change, including new products,

**FIGURE 7-7**    **Diffusion Rate of an Innovation over Time**

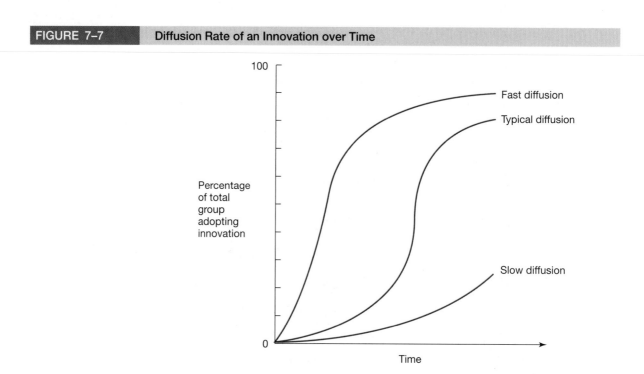

readily. Thus, the target market for the innovation is an important determinant of the rate of diffusion.[60]

2. *Type of decision.* The type of decision refers to an individual versus a group decision. The fewer the individuals involved in the purchase decision, the more rapidly an innovation will spread.

3. *Marketing effort.* The rate of diffusion is heavily influenced by the extent of marketing effort involved. Thus, the rate of diffusion is not completely beyond the control of the firm.[61]

4. *Fulfillment of felt need.* The more manifest or obvious the need that the innovation satisfies, the faster the diffusion. Rogaine, a cure for some types of hair loss, gained rapid trial among those uncomfortable with thin hair or baldness.

5. *Compatibility.* The more the purchase and use of the innovation are consistent with the individual's and group's values or beliefs, the more rapid the diffusion.[62]

6. *Relative advantage.* The better the innovation is perceived to meet the relevant need compared with existing methods, the more rapid the diffusion. Both the performance and the cost of the product are included in relative advantage. The digital audio tape (DAT) had neither advantage compared with CDs and DVDs and thus never took off.

7. *Complexity.* The more difficult the innovation is to understand and use, the slower the diffusion. The key to this dimension is ease of use, *not* complexity of product. Specialized blogging software is making an otherwise complex task easy and fun.[63]

8. *Observability.* The more easily consumers can observe the positive effects of adopting an innovation, the more rapid its diffusion will be. Cell phones are relatively visible. Laser eye surgery, while less visible, may be a frequent topic of conversation. On the other hand, new headache remedies are less obvious and generally less likely to be discussed.

**Diffusion Rates for Consumer Electronics**    FIGURE 7–8

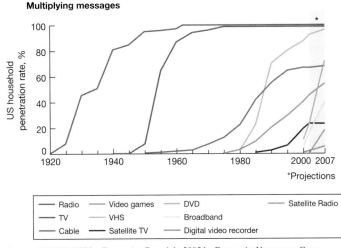

Source: *ECONOMIST* by *Economist*. Copyright 2005 by Economist Newspaper Group.
Reproduced with permission of Economist Newspaper Group in the format Textbook via
Copyright Clearance Center.

9.  *Trialability.* The easier it is to have a low-cost or low-risk trial of the innovation, the more rapid is its diffusion. The diffusion of products like laser eye surgery has been hampered by the difficulty of trying out the product in a realistic manner. This is much less of a problem with low-cost items such as headache remedies, or such items as camera phones, which can be borrowed or tried at a retail outlet.

10. *Perceived risk.* The more risk associated with trying an innovation, the slower the diffusion. Risk can be financial, physical, or social. Perceived risk is a function of three dimensions: (1) *the probability that the innovation will not perform as desired;* (2) *the consequences of its not performing as desired;* and (3) *the ability (and cost) to reverse any negative consequences.*[64] Thus, many consumers may feel a need for the benefits offered by laser eye surgery and view the probability of its working successfully as being quite high. However, they perceive the consequences of failure as being extreme and irreversible and therefore do not adopt this innovation.

Figure 7–8 shows the diffusion curves for various consumer electronic products. How would you explain the differences in diffusion rates across these products in U.S. households?

**Characteristics of Individuals Who Adopt an Innovation at Varying Points in Time**    The curves shown in Figures 7–7 and 7–8 are cumulative curves that illustrate the increase in the percentage of adopters over time. If we change those curves from a cumulative format to one that shows the percentage of a market that adopts the innovation at any given point in time, we will have the familiar bell-shaped curves shown in Figure 7–9.

Figure 7–9 reemphasizes the fact that a few individuals adopt an innovation very quickly, another limited group is reluctant to adopt the innovation, and the majority of the group adopts at some time in between the two extremes. Researchers have found it useful to divide the adopters of any given innovation into five groups based on the relative time at which they adopt. These groups, called **adopter categories,** are shown in Figure 7–9 and defined below:

Innovators: The first 2.5 percent to adopt an innovation.

Early adopters: The next 13.5 percent to adopt.

**FIGURE 7–9**     **Adoptions of an Innovation over Time**

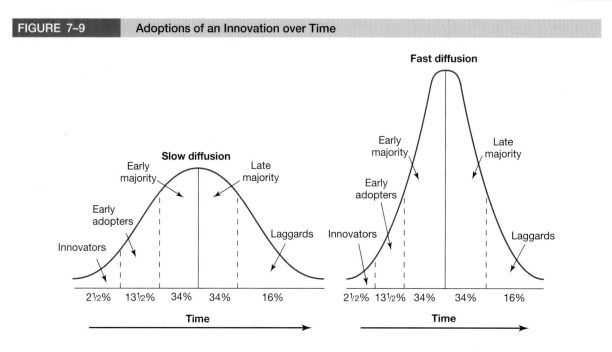

Early majority: The next 34 percent to adopt.

Late majority: The next 34 percent to adopt.

Laggards: The final 16 percent to adopt.

How do these groups differ? The following descriptions, though general, provide a good starting point. Clearly, however, research by product category would be necessary in fully understanding specific marketing situations.

**Innovators** are venturesome risk takers. They are capable of absorbing the financial and social costs of adopting an unsuccessful product. They are cosmopolitan in outlook and use other innovators rather than local peers as a reference group. They tend to be younger, better educated, and more socially mobile than their peers. Innovators make extensive use of commercial media, sales personnel, and professional sources in learning of new products.

**Early adopters** tend to be opinion leaders in local reference groups. They are successful, well educated, and somewhat younger than their peers. They are willing to take a calculated risk on an innovation but are concerned with failure. Early adopters also use commercial, professional, and interpersonal information sources, and they provide information to others.

**Early majority** consumers tend to be cautious about innovations. They adopt sooner than most of their social group but also after the innovation has proved successful with others. They are socially active but seldom leaders. They tend to be somewhat older, less well educated, and less socially mobile than the early adopters. The early majority relies heavily on interpersonal sources of information.

**Late majority** members are skeptical about innovations. They often adopt more in response to social pressures or a decreased availability of the previous product than because of a positive evaluation of the innovation. They tend to be older and have less social status and mobility than those who adopt earlier.

**Laggards** are locally oriented and engage in limited social interaction. They tend to be relatively dogmatic and oriented toward the past. Laggards adopt innovations only with reluctance.

## Marketing Strategies and the Diffusion Process

**Market Segmentation**    Since earlier purchasers of an innovation differ from later purchasers, firms should consider a "moving target market" approach. That is, after selecting a general target market, the firm should initially focus on those individuals within the target market most likely to be innovators and early adopters.[65] Messages to this group can often emphasize the newness and innovative characteristics of the product as well as its functional features. Since this group is frequently very involved with, and knowledgeable about, the product category, marketing communications may be able to focus on the new technical features of the product and rely on the audience to understand the benefits these features will provide.[66]

As the innovation gains acceptance, the focus of attention should shift to the early and late majority. This will frequently require different media. In addition, message themes should generally move away from a focus on radical newness. Instead, they should emphasize the acceptance the product has gained and its proven performance record.

**Diffusion Enhancement Strategies**    Table 7–2 provides a framework for developing strategies to enhance the market acceptance of an innovation. The critical aspect of this process is to analyze the innovation *from the target market's perspective*. This analysis will indicate potential obstacles—*diffusion inhibitors*—to rapid market acceptance. The manager's task is then to overcome these inhibitors with *diffusion enhancement strategies*. Table 7–2 lists a number of potential enhancement strategies, but many others are possible.

Consider the innovation shown in Illustration 7–10. Which factors will inhibit its diffusion, and what strategies can be used to overcome them?

| Diffusion Determinant | Diffusion Inhibitor | Diffusion Enhancement Strategies |
|---|---|---|
| 1.  Nature of group | Conservative | Search for other markets<br>Target innovators within group |
| 2.  Type of decision | Group | Choose media to reach all deciders<br>Provide conflict reduction themes |
| 3.  Marketing effort | Limited | Target innovators within group<br>Use regional rollout<br>Leverage buzz |
| 4.  Felt need | Weak | Extensive advertising showing importance of benefits |
| 5.  Compatibility | Conflict | Stress attributes consistent with normative values |
| 6.  Relative advantage | Low | Lower price<br>Redesign product |
| 7.  Complexity | High | Distribute through high-service outlets<br>Use skilled sales force<br>Use product demonstrations<br>Extensive marketing efforts |
| 8.  Observability | Low | Use extensive advertising<br>Target visible events when appropriate |
| 9.  Trialability | Difficult | Use free samples to early adopter types<br>Special prices to rental agencies<br>Use high-service outlets |
| 10.  Perceived risk | High | Success documentation<br>Endorsement by credible sources<br>Guarantees |

**TABLE 7–2**

Innovation Analysis and Diffusion Enhancement Strategies

**ILLUSTRATION 7–10**

Ten factors determine the success of innovations. How do you think this innovation will fare based on these 10 factors?

## SUMMARY

A *group* in its broadest sense includes two or more individuals who share a set of norms, values, or beliefs and have certain implicit or explicit relationships such that their behaviors are interdependent. Some groups require membership; others (e.g., aspiration groups) do not. *Primary groups* are those with strong social ties and frequent interaction, whereas *secondary groups* involve weaker ties and less frequent interaction. *Attraction* refers to the degree of positive or negative desirability the group has to the individual.

The degree of *conformity* to a group is a function of (1) the visibility of the usage situation, (2) the level of commitment the individual feels to the group, (3) the relevance of the behavior to the functioning of the group, (4) the individual's confidence in his or her own judgment in the area, and (5) the level of necessity reflected by the nature of the product.

A *consumption subculture* is a group that self-selects on the basis of a shared commitment to a particular product or consumption activity. These subcultures also have (1) an identifiable, hierarchical social structure; (2) a set of shared beliefs or values; and (3) unique jargon, rituals, and modes of symbolic expression.

A *brand community* is a nongeographically bound community, based on a structured set of social relationships among owners of a brand and the psychological relationship they have with the brand itself, the product in use, and the firm. Brand communities can add value to the ownership of the product and build intense loyalty. An *online community* is a community that interacts over time around a topic of interest on the Internet. Online communities have evolved over time to include *online social network sites,* which are Web-based services that allow individuals to (1) construct a public or semipublic profile within a bounded system, (2) articulate a list of other users with whom they share a connection, and (3) view and traverse their list of connections and those made by others within the system.

Group influence varies across situations. *Informational influence* occurs when individuals simply acquire information shared by group members. *Normative influence* happens when an individual conforms to group expectations to gain approval or avoid disapproval. *Identification influence* exists when an individual identifies with the group norms as a part of his or her self-concept and identity.

Communication within groups is a major source of information about certain products. It is a particularly important source when an individual has a high level of *purchase involvement* and a low level of *product knowledge*. In such cases, the consumer is likely to seek information from a more knowledgeable group member. This person is known as an *opinion leader*. Opinion leaders are product-category or activity-group specific. They tend to have greater product knowledge, more exposure to relevant media, and more gregarious personalities than their followers. They tend to have demographics similar to their followers.

The terms *market mavens* and *Influentials* describe individuals who are general market influencers. They have information about many different kinds of products, places to shop, and other aspects of markets. *Internet mavens* and *e-fluentials* describe their online counterparts. Social media such as blogs, online social networking sites, and consumer review sites are facilitating interpersonal communication in ways never before imagined. Information is communicated within groups either directly through *word-of-mouth (WOM)* communication or indirectly through observation. Negative experiences are a strong driver of negative WOM for all consumers.

Marketers attempt to identify opinion leaders primarily through their media habits and social activities.

Identified opinion leaders then can be used in marketing research, product sampling, retailing/personal selling, advertising, and creating buzz. Various offline and online strategies exist for stimulating WOM, opinion leadership, and buzz. Online strategies include viral marketing, blogs, and consumer review sites.

Groups greatly affect the diffusion of innovations. *Innovations* vary in degree of behavioral change required and the rate at which they are diffused. The first purchasers of an innovative product or service are termed *innovators;* those who follow over time are known as *early adopters, early majority, late majority,* and *laggards.* Each of these groups differs in personality, age, education, and reference group membership. These characteristics help marketers identify and appeal to different classes of adopters at different stages of an innovation's diffusion.

The time it takes for an innovation to spread from innovators to laggards is affected by several factors: (1) nature of the group involved, (2) type of innovation decision required, (3) extent of marketing effort, (4) strength of felt need, (5) compatibility of the innovation with existing values, (6) relative advantage, (7) complexity of the innovation, (8) ease in observing usage of the innovation, (9) ease in trying the innovation, and (10) perceived risk in trying the innovation.

## KEY TERMS

## INTERNET EXERCISES

1. Monitor a forum, bulletin board, or blog on a topic that interests you for a week. Are the participants in this activity a group? A reference group? An online community? Opinion leaders?

2. Find a consumption-based group or subculture that uses the Internet as one means of communication. What can you learn about this group by monitoring the Internet?

3. Join an online social networking site of your choosing (e.g., MySpace, Facebook, Linkedin). Observe and/or participate in various activities for a week. Write a report that examines the various strategies that marketers are using on this site.

4. Visit the Web sites for the following and describe the firms' efforts to foster brand communities.
   a. Jolt
   b. Harley-Davidson
   c. Jeep
   d. Saturn
   e. Proctor & Gamble
   f. Hobie lifejackets
   g. NASCAR

5. Find and describe evidence of market maven and/or opinion leadership on the Internet.

6. Pick a recent innovation of interest. Prepare a report on the information available about this innovation on the Internet.

## DDB LIFE STYLE STUDY™ DATA ANALYSES

1. Use the DDB data (Tables 1B through 7B) to determine the characteristics of new-product innovators. Why is this the case? What are the marketing implications?

2. Use the DDB data (Tables 1B through 7B) to determine the characteristics of opinion leaders.

Why is this the case? What are the marketing implications?

3. What are the characteristics of those who like to "play it safe" by *sticking with well-known brand names* (Tables 1B through 7B)? How do these consumers compare with the innovators you found in Question 1?

## REVIEW QUESTIONS

1. How does a *group* differ from a *reference group*?

2. What criteria are used by marketers to classify groups?

3. What is a *dissociative reference group*? In what way can dissociative reference groups influence consumer behavior?

4. What is an *aspiration reference group*? How can an aspiration reference group influence behavior?

5. What is a *consumption-based group* or a *consumption subculture*? How can marketers develop strategy based on consumption subcultures?

6. What is a *brand community*? What are the characteristics of such a group?

7. For what products are brand communities most appropriate? How can a marketer foster a brand community?

8. What is an *online social network site*? What are the guidelines for marketers operating in online communities and social networking sites?

9. What types of group influence exist? Why must a marketing manager be aware of these separate types of group influence?

10. What five factors determine the strength of reference group influence in a situation?

11. What is the *Asch phenomenon* and how do marketers utilize it?

12. How can a marketer use knowledge of reference group influences to develop advertising strategies?

13. What is an *opinion leader*? How does an opinion leader relate to the *multistep flow of communication*?

14. What characterizes an opinion leader?

15. What determines the likelihood that a consumer will seek information from an opinion leader?

16. How does a *market maven* differ from an *opinion leader*?

17. Explain the role of *enduring involvement* in driving opinion leadership.

18. How can marketing managers identify opinion leaders?

19. How can marketers utilize opinion leaders?

20. What is *buzz*? How can marketers create it?

21. What is a *blog*?

22. What is an *innovation*? Who determines whether a given product is an innovation?

23. What are the various categories of innovations? How do they differ?

24. What is the *diffusion process*? What pattern does the diffusion process appear to follow over time?

25. Describe the factors that affect the diffusion rate for an innovation. How can these factors be utilized in developing marketing strategy?

26. What are *adopter* categories? Describe each of the adopter categories.

27. How can a marketer use knowledge of adopter categories to develop marketing strategy?

## DISCUSSION QUESTIONS

28. Respond to the questions in Consumer Insight 7–1.

29. Using college students as the market segment, describe the most relevant reference group(s) and indicate the probable degree of influence on decisions for each of the following:
    a. Brand of toothpaste
    b. Purchase of a hybrid car
    c. Purchase of an iPod
    d. Becoming a vegetarian
    e. Choice of a music DVD

    *Answer Questions 30 to 33 using (a) shoes, (b) barbeque grill, (c) car, (d) toaster, (e) pet, and (f) volunteering with a nonprofit organization.*

30. How important are reference groups to the purchase of the above-mentioned products or activities? Would their influence also affect the brand or model? Would their influence be informational, normative, or identification? Justify your answers.

31. What reference groups would be relevant to the decision to purchase the product or activity (based on students on your campus)?

32. What are the norms of the social groups of which you are a member concerning the product or activity?

33. Could an Asch-type situation be used to sell the product or activity?

34. Describe two groups that serve as aspiration reference groups for you. In what ways, if any, have they influenced your consumption patterns?

35. Describe two groups to which you belong. For each, give two examples of instances when the group has exerted (*a*) informational, (*b*) normative, and (*c*) identification influence on you.

36. Develop two approaches using reference group theory to reduce drug, alcohol, or cigarette consumption among teenagers.

37. What ethical concerns arise in using reference group theory to sell products?

38. Describe a consumption subculture to which you belong. How does it affect your consumption behavior? How do marketers attempt to influence your behavior with respect to this subculture?

39. Do you belong to a brand community? If so, describe the benefits you derive from this group and how it affects your consumption.

40. Do you belong to an online community or social network site? If so, describe the benefits you derive from this group and how it affects your consumption.

41. Answer the following questions for (*i*) MP3 players, (*ii*) space flight, (*iii*) cell phone–based GPS.
    a. Is the product an innovation? Justify your answer.
    b. Using the student body on your campus as a market segment, evaluate the perceived attributes of the product.
    c. Who on your campus would serve as opinion leaders for the product?
    d. Will the early adopters of the product use the adoption process (extended decision making), or is a simpler decision process likely?

42. Describe two situations in which you have served as or sought information from an opinion leader. Are these situations consistent with the discussion in the text?

43. Are you aware of market mavens on your campus? Describe their characteristics, behaviors, and motivation.

44. Have you used a blog recently? Why? How did it work? What marketing implications does this suggest?

45. Identify a recent (*a*) continuous innovation, (*b*) dynamically continuous innovation, and (*c*) discontinuous innovation. Justify your selections.

46. Analyze the Roomba (robotic vacuum cleaner) in terms of the determinants in Table 7–2 and suggest appropriate marketing strategies.

47. Conduct a diffusion analysis and recommend appropriate strategies for the innovation shown in Illustration 7–10.

48. Assume that you are a consultant to firms with new products. You have members of the appropriate market segments rate innovations on the 10 characteristics described in Table 7–2. Based on these ratings, you develop marketing strategies. Assume that a rating of 9 is extremely favorable (e.g., strong relative advantage or a lack of complexity), and 1 is extremely unfavorable. Suggest appropriate strategies for each of the following consumer electronic products (see table).

| Attribute | Product | | | | | | | | |
|---|---|---|---|---|---|---|---|---|---|
| | A | B | C | D | E | F | G | H | I |
| Fulfillment of felt need | 9 | 7 | 3 | 8 | 8 | 5 | 7 | 8 | 9 |
| Compatibility | 8 | 8 | 8 | 8 | 9 | 2 | 8 | 9 | 8 |
| Relative advantage | 9 | 2 | 8 | 9 | 7 | 8 | 9 | 8 | 8 |
| Complexity | 9 | 9 | 9 | 9 | 9 | 3 | 8 | 8 | 7 |
| Observability | 8 | 8 | 9 | 1 | 9 | 4 | 8 | 8 | 8 |
| Trialability | 8 | 9 | 8 | 9 | 9 | 2 | 9 | 2 | 9 |
| Nature of group | 3 | 8 | 7 | 8 | 9 | 9 | 7 | 7 | 3 |
| Type of decision | 3 | 7 | 8 | 8 | 6 | 7 | 7 | 3 | 7 |
| Marketing effort | 6 | 7 | 8 | 7 | 8 | 6 | 3 | 8 | 7 |
| Perceived risk | 3 | 8 | 7 | 7 | 3 | 7 | 8 | 8 | 5 |

## APPLICATION ACTIVITIES

49. Find two advertisements that use reference groups in an attempt to gain patronage. Describe the advertisement, the type of reference group being used, and the type of influence being used.

50. Develop an advertisement for (*i*) breath strips, (*ii*) energy drink, (*iii*) upscale club, (*iv*) Habitat for Humanity, (*v*) scooters, or (*vi*) watches using the following.
    *a.* An informational reference group influence
    *b.* A normative reference group influence
    *c.* An identification reference group influence

51. Interview two individuals who are strongly involved in a consumption subculture. Determine how it affects their consumption patterns and what actions marketers take toward them.

52. Interview an individual who is involved in a brand community. Describe the role the firm plays in maintaining the community, the benefits the person gets from the community, and how it affects his or her consumption behavior.

53. Identify and interview several opinion leaders on your campus for the following. To what extent do they match the profile of an opinion leader as described in the text?
    *a.* Local restaurants
    *b.* Sports equipment
    *c.* Music
    *d.* Computer equipment

54. Interview two salespersons for the following products. Determine the role that opinion leaders play in the purchase of their product and how they adjust their sales process in light of these influences.
    *a.* Cell phones
    *b.* Golf equipment
    *c.* Computers
    *d.* Art
    *e.* Jewelry
    *f.* Sunglasses

## REFERENCES

1. Chapter 7 opener is based on J. H. McAlexander, J. W. Schouten, and H. F. Koenig, "Building Brand Community," *Journal of Marketing,* January 2002, pp. 38–54, as well as information from various Web sites, including www.jeep.com, www.youtube.com/user/thejeepchannel, and www.jeepjamboreeusa.com.

2. K. White and D. W. Dahl, "To Be or *Not* Be?" *Journal of Consumer Psychology* 16, no. 4, 2006, pp. 404–14.

3. "'Getting Wiser to Teens' Offers a Snapshot of Teen Social Hierarchy," Teenage Research Unlimited (TRU), press release, June 21, 2004. See also J. E. Escalas and J. R. Bettman, "Self-Construal, Reference Groups, and Brand Meaning," *Journal of Consumer Research,* December 2005, pp. 378–89; and D. B. Wooten, "From Labeling Possessions to Possessing Labels," *Journal of Consumer Research,* September 2006, pp. 188–98.

4. For the role that consumer self-enhancement needs play in the process, see J. E. Escalas and J. R. Bettman, "You Are What They Eat," *Journal of Consumer Psychology* 13, no. 3 (2003), pp. 339–48.

5. J. W. Schouten and J. H. McAlexander, "Subcultures of Consumption," *Journal of Consumer Research*, June 1995, p. 43.

6. B. Gainer, "Ritual and Relationships," *Journal of Business Research,* March 1995, pp. 253–60. See also E. J. Arnould and P. L. Price, "River Magic," *Journal of Consumer Research,* June 1993, pp. 24–45.

7. See R. J. Fisher, "Group-Derived Consumption," *Advances in Consumer Research,* vol. 25, eds. J. W. Alba and J. W. Hutchinson (Provo, UT: Association for Consumer Research, 1998), pp. 283–88; and R. J. Fisher and K. Wakefield, "Factors Leading to Group Identification," *Psychology & Marketing,* January 1998, pp. 23–40.

8. J. H. McAlexander, K. Fushimi, and J. W. Schouten, "A Cross-Cultural Examination of a Subculture of Consumption," *Research in Consumer Behavior* 9 (2000), p. 66.

9. R. V. Kozinets, "Utopian Enterprise," *Journal of Consumer Research,* June 2001, p. 72.

10. Based on McAlexander, Schouten, and Koenig, "Building Brand Community."

11. A. M. Muniz Jr. and T. C. O'Guinn, "Brand Community," *Journal of Consumer Research,* March 2001, p. 413. See also R. P. Bagozzi, "On the Concept of Intentional Social Action in Consumer Behavior," *Journal of Consumer Research,* December 2000, pp. 388–96; and A. M. Muniz Jr. and H. J. Schau, "Religiosity in the Abandoned Apple Newton Brand Community," *Journal of Consumer Research,* March 2005, pp. 737–47.

12. Bronco and Saab examples come from Muniz Jr. and O'Guinn, "Brand Community." Harley example comes from Schouten and McAlexander, "Subcultures of Consumption." Jeep example comes from McAlexander, Schouten, and Koenig, "Building Brand Community." MG examples come from T. W. Leigh, C. Peters, and J. Shelton, "The Consumer Quest for Authenticity," *Journal of the Academy of Marketing Science* 34, no. 4 (2006), pp. 481–93.

13. Q. Jones, "Virtual Communities, Virtual Settlements, and CyberArchaeology," *Journal of Computer-Mediated Communication* 3, no. 3 (1997), www.ascusc.org/jcmc/vol3/issue3/jones.html; C. Okleshen and S. Grossbart, "Usenet Groups, Virtual Community and Consumer Behaviors," and S. Dann and S. Dann, "Cybercommuning," both in *Advances in Consumer Research,* vol. 25, eds. Alba and Hutchinson, pp. 276–82 and 379–85, respectively; C. L. Beau, "Cracking the Niche," *American Demographics,* June 2000, pp. 38–40; and P. Maclaran and M. Catterall, "Researching the Social Web," *Marketing Intelligence and Planning* 20, no. 6 (2002), pp. 319–26.

14. A. L. Blanchard and M. L. Markus, "The Experienced 'Sense' of a Virtual Community," *Database for Advances in Information Systems,* Winter 2004, pp. 65–79.

15. D. M. Boyd and N. B. Ellison, "Social Network Sites," *Journal of Computer-Mediated Communication* 13, no. 1 (2007), http://jcmc.indiana.edu, accessed June 17, 2008.

16. "Digital Marketing and Media Fact Pack," *Advertising Age,* April 23, 2007.

17. For additional information and expertise, visit *Site Logic Marketing* at www.sitelogicmarketing.com and the online marketing blog, "Marketing Logic," written by Matt Bailey, Site Logic's President.

18. Excerpt from http://consumerist.com/consumer/blogs/sonys-psp-blog-flog-revealed-221384.php.

19. Blanchard and Markus, "The Experienced 'Sense' of a Virtual Community."

20. L. Cornwell, "P&G Launches Two Social Networking Sites," *Marketing News,* February 1, 2007, p. 21.

21. "Q&A with MySpace's Gold," *Advertising Age,* June 5, 2006, pp. S4–S5; and B. S. Bulik, "The Man Moves in on MySpace," *Advertising Age,* June 12, 2006, p. 9.

22. See T. F. Mangleburg and T. Bristol, "Socialization and Adolescents' Skepticism toward Advertising," *Journal of Advertising,* Fall 1998, pp. 11–20. See also T. F. Mangleburg, P. M. Doney, and T. Bristol, "Shopping with Friends and Teens' Susceptibility to Peer Influence," *Journal of Retailing* 80 (2004), pp. 101–16.

23. See R. J. Fisher and D. Ackerman, "The Effects of Recognition and Group Need on Volunteerism," *Journal of Consumer Research,* December 1998, pp. 262–77.

24. See K. R. Lord, M.-S. Lee, and P. Choong, "Differences in Normative and Informational Social Influence," *Advances in Consumer Research,* vol. 28, eds. M. C. Gilly and J. Meyers-Levy (Provo, UT: Association for Consumer Research, 2001), pp. 280–85.

25. See W. Amaldoss and S. Jain, "Pricing and Conspicuous Goods," *Journal of Marketing Research,* February 2005, pp. 30–42.

26. See, e.g., M. Mourali, M. Laroche, and F. Pons, "Individualistic Orientation and Consumer Susceptibility to Interpersonal Influence," *Journal of Services Marketing* 19, no. 3 (2005), pp. 164–73.

27. M. Creamer, "How to Win Web 2.0," *Advertising Age,* November 13, 2006, pp. 3, 57; and "How Businesses Are Using Web 2.0, *McKinsey Quarterly,* March 2007, www.mckinseyquarterly.com, accessed January 18, 2008.

28. "New Media Marketing Plays," *AdvancedBusinessBlogging.com,* May 15, 2006.

29. J. Hempel, "Web Strategies That Cater to Customers," *Inside Innovation* (a *BusinessWeek* publication), June 2007, p. 6.

30. M. Gladwell, "Alternative Marketing Vehicles," *Consumer Insight Magazine* (an ACNielsen Publication), Spring 2003, pp. 6–11, www2.acnielsen.com.

31. See e.g., R. N. Laczniak, T. E. DeCarlo, and S. N. Ramaswami, "Consumers' Responses to Negative Word-of-Mouth Communication," *Journal of Consumer Psychology* 11, no. 1 (2001), pp. 57–73.

32. E. Rosen, *The Anatomy of Buzz* (New York: Doubleday, 2000); see also D. S. Sundaram, K. Mitra, and C. Webster, "Word-of-Mouth Communications," *Advances in Consumer Research,* vol. 25, eds. Alba and Hutchinson, pp. 527–31; and A. A. Bailey, "The Interplay of Social Influence and Nature of Fulfillment," *Psychology & Marketing,* April 2004, pp. 263–78.

33. M. Johnson, G. M. Zinkhan, and G. S. Ayala, "The Impact of Outcome, Competency, and Affect on Service Referral," *Journal of Services Marketing* 5 (1998), pp. 397–415.

34. See W. G. Mangold, F. Miller, and G. R. Brockway, "Word-of-Mouth Communication in the Service Marketplace," *Journal of Services Marketing* 13, no. 1 (1999), pp. 73–89.

35. For a thorough discussion, see D. F. Duhan, S. D. Johnson, J. B. Wilcox, and G. D. Harrell, "Influences on Consumer Use of Word-of-Mouth Recommendation Sources," *Journal of the Academy of Marketing Science,* Fall 1997, pp. 283–95; and C. Pornpitakpan, "Factors Associated with Opinion Seeking," *Journal of Global Marketing* 17, no. 2/3 (2004), pp. 91–113.

36. R. Dye, "The Buzz on Buzz," *Harvard Business Review,* November 2000, p. 145.

37. G. M. Rose, L. R. Kahle, and A. Shoham, "The Influence of Employment-Status and Personal Values on Time-Related Food Consumption Behavior and Opinion Leadership," in *Advances in Consumer Research,* vol. 22, eds. F. R. Kardes and M. Sujan (Provo, UT: Association for Consumer Research, 1995), pp. 367–72; and U. M. Dholakia, "Involvement-Response Models of Joint Effects," *Advances in Consumer Research,* vol. 25, eds. Alba and Hutchinson, pp. 499–506.

38. See M. C. Gilly, J. L. Graham, M. F. Wolfinbarger, and L. J. Yale, "A Dyadic Study of Interpersonal Information Search," *Journal of the Academy of Marketing Science,* Spring 1998, pp. 83–100.

39. R. Marshall and I. Gitosudarmo, "Variation in the Characteristics of Opinion Leaders across Borders," *Journal of International Consumer Marketing* 8, no. 1 (1995), pp. 5–22.

40. See I. M. Chaney, "Opinion Leaders as a Segment for Marketing Communications," *Marketing Intelligence and Planning* 19, no. 5 (2001), pp. 302–8.

41. L. F. Feick and L. L. Price, "The Market Maven," *Journal of Marketing,* January 1987, pp. 83–97. See also R. A. Higie, L. F. Feick, and L. L. Price, "Types and Amount of Word-of-Mouth Communications about Retailers," *Journal of Retailing,* Fall 1987, pp. 260–78; K. C. Schneider and W. C. Rodgers, "Generalized Marketplace Influencers' Attitudes toward Direct Mail as a Source of Information," *Journal of Direct Marketing,* Autumn 1993, pp. 20–28; and J. E. Urbany, P. R. Dickson, and R. Kalapurakal, "Price Search in the Retail Grocery Market," *Journal of Marketing,* April 1996, pp. 91–104.

42. T. A. Mooradian, "The Five Factor Model and Market Mavenism," *Advances in Consumer Research,* vol. 23, eds. K. P. Corfman and J. G. Lynch (Provo, UT: Association for Consumer Research, 1996), pp. 260–63. For additional motivations driving mavens, see G. Walsh, K. P. Gwinner, and S. R. Swanson, "What Makes Mavens Tick?" *Journal of Consumer Marketing* 21, no. 2 (2004), pp. 109–22.

43. E. Keller and J. Berry, *The Influentials* (New York: Free Press, 2003). See also D. Godes and D. Mayzlin, "Firm-Created Word-of-Mouth Communication," *Harvard Business School Marketing Research Papers,* no. 04-03 (July 2004).

44. M. A. Belch, K. A. Krentler, and L. A. Willis-Flurry, "Teen Internet Mavens," *Journal of Business Research* 58 (2005), pp. 569–75.

45. I. Cakim, "E-Fluentials Expand Viral Marketing," *iMedia Connection,* October 28, 2002, www.imediaconnection.com; see also information on Burson-Marsteller's Web site at www.efluentials.com.

46. Rosen, *The Anatomy of Buzz.*

47. See C. S. Areni, M. E. Ferrell, and J. B. Wilcox, "The Persuasive Impact of Reported Group Opinions on Individuals Low vs. High in Need for Cognition," *Psychology & Marketing,* October 2000, pp. 855–75.

48. A. Z. Cuneo, "Dockers Strives for Urban Credibility," *Advertising Age,* May 25, 1998, p. 6.

49. See R. Walker, "The Hidden (In Plain Sight) Persuaders," *New York Times Magazine,* December 5, 2004; and materials on BzzAgent's Web site at www.BzzAgent.com.

50. A. Dobele, D. Toleman, M. Beverland, "Controlled Infection!" *Business Horizons* 48 (2005), pp. 143–49.

51. See E. Biyalogorsky, E. Gerstner, and B. Libai, "Customer Referral Management," *Marketing Science,* Winter 2001, pp. 82–95; and G. Ryu and L. Feick, "A Penny for Your Thoughts," *Journal of Marketing,* January 2007, pp. 84–94.

52. Dye, "The Buzz on Buzz," p. 140.

53. T. F. Lindeman, "More Firms Use Unique 'Guerrilla Marketing' Techniques to Garner Attention," *Knight Ridder Tribune Business News,* January 18, 2004, p. 1.

54. "Two Years After Launching Brand Blogs, Vespa Forgets Them," http://blog.clickz.com, January 2, 2007; R. Ford, "No Wrench Required," *Knight Ridder Tribune Business News,* January 8, 2007, p. 1; J. Jarvis, "Dell Learns to Listen," *BusinessWeek,* October 29, 2007, pp. 118, 120; and presentation by Matt Bailey, President of Site Logic Marketing, November 27, 2007.

55. S. Senecal and J. Nantel, "The Influence of Online Product Recommendations on Consumers' Online Choices," *Journal of Retailing* 80 (2004), pp. 159–69; D. Smith, S. Menon, and K. Sivakumar, "Online Peer and Editorial Recommendations, Trust, and Choice in Virtual Markets," *Journal of Interactive Marketing,* Summer 2005, pp. 15–37; T. K. Grose, "50 Ways to Improve Your Life in 2007," *US News and World Report,* December 17, 2006; and information from Angie's List at www.angieslist.com.

56. Ibid.

57. K. Fitzgerald, "Bristol-Meyers Builds Buzz," *Advertising Age,* April 23, 2001, p. 18.

58. See also V. Mahajan, E. Muller, and F. M. Bass, "New Product Diffusion Models in Marketing," *Journal of Marketing,* January 1990, pp. 1–26; E. M. Rogers, *Diffusion of Innovations,* 4th ed. (New York: Free Press, 1995). For an alternative to the traditional adoption diffusion model, see C.-F. Shih and A. Venkatesh, "Beyond Adoption," *Journal of Marketing,* January 2004, pp. 59–72.

59. See M. I. Nabith, S. G. Bloem, and T. B. C. Poiesz, "Conceptual Issues in the Study of Innovation Adoption Behavior," *Advances in Consumer Research,* vol. 24, eds. M. Bruck and D. J. MacInnis (Provo, UT: Association for Consumer Research, 1997), pp. 190–96.

60. See, e.g., S. L. Wood and J. Swait, "Psychological Indicators of Innovation Adoption," *Journal of Consumer Psychology* 12, no. 1 (2002), pp. 1–13.

61. See, e.g., E.-J. Lee, J. Lee, and D. W. Schumann, "The Influence of Communication Source and Mode on Consumer Adoption of Technological Innovations," *Journal of Consumer Affairs,* Summer 2002, pp. 1–27.

62. See N. Y.-M. Siu and M. M.-S. Cheng, "A Study of the Expected Adoption of Online Shopping," *Journal of International Consumer Marketing* 13, no. 3 (2001), pp. 87–106.

63. For a discussion of how type of innovation and consumer expertise interact, see C. P. Moreau, D. R. Lehmann, and A. B. Markman, "Entrenched Knowledge Structures and Consumer Response to New Products," *Journal of Marketing Research,* February 2001, pp. 14–29.

64. For a more complete analysis, see U. M. Dholakia, "An Investigation of the Relationship between Perceived Risk and Product Involvement," *Advances in Consumer Research,* vol. 24, eds. Bruck and MacInnis, pp. 159–67; and M. Herzenstein, S. S. Posavac, and J. J. Brakus, "Adoption of New and Really New Products," *Journal of Marketing Research,* May 2007, pp. 251–60.

65. For a discussion of when this is not appropriate, see V. Mahajan and E. Muller, "When Is It Worthwhile Targeting the Majority Instead of the Innovators in a New Product Launch?" *Journal of Marketing Research,* November 1998, pp. 488–95.

66. See, e.g., Chaney, "Opinion Leaders as a Segment for Marketing Communications."

# Part Two | Cases

Asia, particularly China, is well known for its love of tea. So it may be a bit surprising how enthusiastic Starbucks is about the Chinese market. Consider the following quote from a Starbucks executive:

> I am so excited about China right now I can hardly stand it. I was in Shanghai a few weeks ago. The stores there are full of customers. I thought China would always be a great market for us eventually. But it is clearly a tea-drinking society—unlike Japan, which we think of as a tea-drinking society but they also drink a lot of coffee. In China, that really isn't true. I thought it would be a much longer education process. But they're picking that up so fast.

And there certainly is reason for excitement. China is a major consumer market. With an overall population of around 1.3 billion, rising incomes, and increasingly global attitudes, particularly in the major cities, numerous companies around the world are clamoring to tap this gold mine.

However, the reality of China's coffee market is still far behind the hype. Consider the fact that despite a 90 percent growth in coffee sales in China in recent years, per capita consumption is still under one kilogram per person compared with four kilograms in the United States. Tea is still the number one beverage in China (by volume), is a part of China's national heritage, and is strongly embedded in their culture. Here is how one expert on food marketing put it:

> Despite the potential of a 1.3 billion population base, coffee marketers are wary of the difficulty in transforming a tea-drinking nation into a coffee-drinking nation. Tea is the Chinese national drink and deemed to have medicinal qualities that coffee does not have, which means that it will continue to be an integral part of Chinese daily life in the next two or three decades. Added to this the fact that coffee is still prohibitively expensive and not familiar to the majority of the population, the indications are that despite potential being massive, the growth of coffee will continue to be slow.

In a population so large, it might surprise you to know that recent statistics put the number of Starbucks outlets in China at nearly 200, a drop in the bucket compared with over 6,500 Starbucks-owned stores in the United States. Various factors will influence the Chinese coffee market and must be considered in Starbucks' marketing strategy.

## DEMOGRAPHICS AND GEOGRAPHY

Pure population statistics don't tell the whole story. The potential 1.3 billion population base is largely rural and lower income. The economy is growing and the middle class is increasing in size. The middle- and upper-class Chinese tend to be located in the major cities, such as Guangzhou, Beijing, and Shanghai, where incomes have risen substantially. One estimate puts the number of Chinese with "middle-class" incomes at 50 million and growing, with incomes expected to increase rapidly in coming years. The coastal market between Shanghai and Shenzhen represents roughly 200 million people and is therefore highly attractive.

## COMPETITION

Beyond tea, which is clearly a major "beverage" competitor, challengers in terms of the "fresh-ground" market include Pacific Coffee (Hong Kong), Blenz Coffee (Canada), Figaro (Philippines), and McCafe (a McDonald's coffee house). However, instant coffee is the major player. According to one report, this is because coffee is just taking off and the Chinese don't yet appreciate the taste of coffee or the taste difference among types of coffee. Currently, inexpensive mixes (coffee, milk, and sugar) are popular as a time-saving device among time-pressed professionals. In fact, Nescafé (a Nestlé brand) holds nearly half the market share and has become the Chinese generic term for coffee.

# CULTURE, HABITS, AND PERCEPTIONS

Obviously, a population of 1.3 billion is impossible to generalize. However, some interesting information is available as a guide. General insights come from a recent survey of consumers in the four Chinese cities of Beijing, Shanghai, Chengdu, and Shenyang by Kurt Salmon Associates. The survey found that the top five factors in choosing a brand were "high quality," "good for health," "cares about customer," "fits self-image," and "fair price." Given the highly collectivist nature of Chinese culture, the self-image component is significant.

Another general insight regarding foods and beverages is the notion of balance, as embodied by the concepts of yin versus yang. Frito-Lay learned its lesson when it found that certain flavors and colors are associated with yin and others with yang. In terms of seasonal marketing, the difference is critical since yin is associated with cool and yang is associated with hot. Frito-Lay developed a cool lemon chip with pastel packaging to highlight yin for summer months since its traditional fried potato chip was associated with yang.

More specific insights in terms of the coffee and food market, especially for younger, wealthier, professional Chinese, include:

- Enjoy eating out.
- Associate coffee with Western lifestyles.
- See coffee as a fashionable drink.
- Associate Starbucks with wealth and status.
- Prefer food products from local (versus foreign) merchants.
- Enjoy sweet-tasting foods and beverages, particularly desserts.

As if the Chinese market were not enough, Starbucks is finalizing a deal to enter India. Clearly, it is betting on the Asian market to fuel growth as the U.S. market matures. Whether Starbucks can fully capitalize on this bet remains to be seen.

## Discussion Questions

1. What are the barriers facing Starbucks as they try to "teach" people to change their consumption habits from tea and instant coffee?

2. To what extent can/should Starbucks customize their offerings to local tastes and preferences? What are the risks of extreme customization?

3. What values are involved in the Starbucks "experience"?

4. Examine the 10 factors that influence the spread of innovations using Table 7–2 (thinking now that Starbucks is still quite novel and an innovative concept as is coffee to many in China), and create a grid for the Chinese market relative to coffee and Starbucks.

5. Based on your analysis in Question 4, what can Starbucks do to successfully encourage greater coffee consumption? Develop an advertising campaign that not only would encourage greater coffee consumption in general, but also more demand for Starbucks. Specify key themes, copy points, and visuals.

6. Develop a marketing strategy for taking Starbucks into smaller Chinese cities and communities. What barriers would be faced? Could they be successful?

7. Discuss the demographic, cultural, and media factors that make India more attractive for Starbucks than it was 10 years ago. Compare and contrast India and China in terms of the key elements Starbucks must address.

Source: "It's a Grande-Latte World," *The Wall Street Journal*, December 15, 2003, pp. B1, B4; G. A. Fowler and R. Setoodeh, "Outsiders Get Smarter about China's Tastes," *The Wall Street Journal*, August 5, 2004, p. B1; L. Chang, "China's Consumers Put Product Quality over Price," *The Wall Street Journal*, August 6, 2004, p. A7; "China Wakes Up to Instant Coffee," *AP-Foodtechnology.com*, September 27, 2004; D. Farkas, "China Patterns," *Chain Leader*, March 2005, pp. 20, 22; M. S. Ouchi, "Starbucks Ventures that China Will Like Java, Too," *Knight Ridder Business News*, June 10, 2005, p. 1; "Starbucks Lifts Stake in South China Venture," *The Wall Street Journal*, June 10, 2005, p. 1; J. Harrison et al., "Exporting a North American Concept to Asia," *Cornell Hotel and Restaurant Administration Quarterly*, May 2005, pp. 275–83; and R. Delaney and C. Chan, "Starbucks Buys Outlets in China," *International Herald Tribune*, October 25, 2006.

## CASE 2–2 THE CREST WHITESTRIP CHALLENGE

The market for oral care products is strong at $7.5 billion. However, growth is relatively slow in this mature market and companies continue to innovate to stay competitive. A recent innovation has been the teeth whitener systems, including trays, gels, and strips. The whitener market was launched with Crest Whitestrips and has attracted considerable competition. Growth was initially very strong in this product niche, with sales reaching almost $500 million at their peak. However, growth has slowed considerably and whiteners are actually losing ground, with the most recent sales data putting the market at around $300 million. And while the market is sizable, at 32 million adults, that represents only 15 percent of all U.S. adults.

Despite the downward sales trend and relatively low overall market penetration, companies such as Crest are bullish on the whitener market if approached correctly. As the market leader in this category with over 65 percent market share, Crest is taking two steps to bolster this market. First is new products aimed at new market segments. For example, they launched Crest Whitestrips Renewal Age-Defying Strips to go after an older demographic, including Gen X and younger baby boomers. One description of the product and its target segment is as follows:

*Description:* In just 10 days, you'll eliminate up to 20 years of stain build-up. Crest Whitestrips Renewal uses the same, enamel-safe ingredients dentists use for tooth whitening so your stains are safely removed.

*Target Segment:* The product [Crest's first in the anti-aging arena] is geared toward women aged 35 to 54 who are interested in whiter teeth, but have not purchased over-the-counter whitening systems in the past.

A more detailed analysis of various whitening strips offered by Crest, as described on its Web site, is as follows:

| Type | Days to Whiten | Number of Strips | Effective for | Amount of Whitener |
|---|---|---|---|---|
| Classic | 14 days | 28 upper 28 lower | 12 months | Less than other Crest strips |
| Premium | 7 days | 14 upper 14 lower | 12 months | More than Crest Classic |
| Renewal | 10 days | 20 upper 20 lower | 18 months | Different formula but similar whitening benefits of Crest Premium |

According to a P&G spokesperson, this move relates to an overall push in the whitener category:

It is a good story on creating an innovative product that reaches a new consumer target in a new way. That is really the theme for where Crest thinks the whitener category needs to go, which is developing specific products for specific consumers.

A second aspect of the Crest strategy revolves around better communicating the whitener effectiveness message.

The idea of just whitening is not enough to keep the category growing at its historical rate. [W]e will have ads coming out that show how Crest Whitestrips can actually provide consumers with the same benefits as a professional whitening that can cost $500. I don't think we have as clearly communicated that in the past.

Table A provides demographic data on the users of whiteners overall and by type.

| TABLE A | Demographics and Whitener Use |
|---|---|

| | Type | | |
| | All Whiteners | Whitening Gels | Whitening Strips |
|---|---|---|---|
| Percent adults using | 15.2% | 5.5% | 8.3% |
| **Gender** | | | |
| Male | 69 | 67 | 66 |
| Female | 129 | 131 | 132 |
| **Age** | | | |
| 18–24 years | 140 | 140 | 162 |
| 25–34 | 104 | 105 | 108 |
| 35–44 | 115 | 105 | 129 |
| 45–54 | 114 | 125 | 113 |
| 55–64 | 85 | 93 | 69 |
| 65–74 | 54 | 51 | 37 |
| 75 and over | 42 | 28 | 23 |
| **Education** | | | |
| College graduate | 111 | 93 | 132 |
| Some college | 110 | 103 | 119 |
| High school graduate | 94 | 102 | 88 |
| No degree | 93 | 104 | 82 |
| **Occupation** | | | |
| Manager | 129 | 117 | 149 |
| Legal/education | 116 | 96 | 143 |
| Health care | 139 | 129 | 151 |
| Sales | 132 | 129 | 157 |
| Office support | 104 | 120 | 101 |
| Production | 83 | 91 | 65 |
| **Race/ethnic group** | | | |
| White | 96 | 92 | 104 |
| Black | 133 | 52 | 99 |
| Asian | 79 | 46 | 97 |
| Hispanic | 105 | 113 | 87 |
| **Region** | | | |
| Northeast | 93 | 99 | 98 |
| Southeast | 114 | 114 | 104 |
| Southwest | 99 | 109 | 88 |
| Pacific | 103 | 97 | 106 |
| **Household income** | | | |
| Under $10,000 | 82 | 81 | 78 |
| $10,000–19,999 | 89 | 118 | 60 |
| $20,000–29,999 | 97 | 113 | 77 |
| $30,000–39,999 | 83 | 78 | 74 |
| $40,000–49,999 | 110 | 90 | 117 |
| $50,000–59,999 | 89 | 102 | 85 |
| $60,000–74,999 | 99 | 87 | 105 |
| $75,000–99,000 | 105 | 90 | 129 |
| $100,000–149,999 | 111 | 117 | 115 |
| $150,000 and over | 121 | 117 | 136 |
| **Marital status** | | | |
| Single | 124 | 123 | 138 |
| Married | 92 | 89 | 92 |
| Divorced/separated | 114 | 130 | 99 |
| Widowed | 59 | 60 | 38 |

Note: 100 = Average use or consumption unless a percent is indicated. Base is all adults.

Source: Simmons Market Research Bureau, Spring 2006.

## Discussion Questions

1. Prepare a two-page summary, accompanied by no more than four graphs, that conveys the key information in Table A to a manager.
2. Describe the typical user of whiteners overall, gel whiteners, and whitener strips in one paragraph each.
3. Conduct an innovation analysis of Crest Renewal Strips using Table 7–2 as the basis. What insights does the innovation analysis provide into its probable sales growth?
4. Which of the demographic factors are most relevant for developing marketing strategy for Crest Renewal Strips? Why?
5. Using demographics, describe the best target market for the Crest Renewal Strips.
6. What areas of opportunity does Table A suggest for Crest to expand the total market for whiteners beyond 15 percent of the adult market? What barriers exist to adoption of whitener products by these groups?
7. Which ethnic groups are more inclined to use whitener products? For each ethnic group listed, develop an advertising campaign including key positioning statement (how you want your brand to be perceived), and key advertising elements, such as spokesperson, copy points, and other symbolic elements.
8. Do an HLC analysis relating to age and household structure. What aspects emerge that help explain why consumers of various age groups and marital status are more or less likely to use whiteners?
9. What do you feel are the major barriers to growing the whitening market overall? Discuss how these might be overcome.

Source: A. Alexander, "Boomers Make Whitener Sales Gleam," *Drug Store News*, August 28, 2006, p. 92; *Oral Care Products in the U.S.* (Rockville, MD: *Packaged Facts*, February 2007); information from reviews.pricegrabber.com/oral-care/m/13414114/, accessed June 21, 2008; and information from www.whitestrips.com, accessed June 21, 2008.

## CASE 2–3 CAMRY GOES INTERACTIVE TO ATTRACT BLACK WOMEN

The Camry is by most accounts a success story. It has been Toyota's best-selling car for 9 out of the last 10 years. It consistently ranks high in quality by such authorities as J.D. Power, and nearly 60 percent of consumers who reviewed the Camry on Cars.com said they would recommend it to a friend. So what's the problem? Camry does not appeal to professional African American women. One could point to income—except that college-educated black women earn more than college-educated white women. One could argue that African American women just don't like mid-sized sedans—except that they buy other mid-sized competitors, such as the Nissan Altima, Honda Accord, and Dodge Avenger.

The real problem, Toyota is finding, is image. According to Toyota's ad agency:

> Here's a nameplate that's ubiquitous. But for an African-American woman, it's not even in her consideration set. Our preliminary testing found they think of it as suburban, not urban; as solid but boring. And for this woman, she doesn't see herself as boring.

To challenge these perceptions, Toyota tried a cutting-edge interactive approach called an "episodic interactive campaign." The campaign was a $5 million endeavor that included print, radio, and online media, with a primarily black audience designed to get the target customer to go to its "If Looks Could Kill" Web site. There, they found themselves embroiled in an urban, upscale, drama mystery game with interactive Webisodes. The campaign lasted several months during the summer of 2008. At the center of attention were two key elements. First was Bianca, a young African American career woman in the fashion industry, who becomes embroiled in a "world of espionage." Second was the Toyota Camry, which she drives in her ongoing adventures. The Camry's Bluetooth navigation and push-button start system were seamlessly integrated into the ongoing drama. During the Webisodes, interactive features allowed viewers to participate in the drama and help Bianca. Viewers could also register to win prizes, view Bianca's journal, and of course, view what Bianca is driving!

According to Toyota's ad agency:

> The game . . . is designed to target exactly those professional black women between 25 and 40 who earn at least $70,000 a year—the same group that had previously written off the car as a suburban yawn. No one has ever targeted African-American women like this.

### Discussion Questions

1. There are three types of reference group influence—informational, normative, and identification. Assuming Bianca is a representative for the group consisting of successful, urban, professional African American

women, which type(s) of group influence do you see operating in this campaign?

2. What are the primary core American values that this campaign is attempting to tap into?

3. What values and aspirations does this campaign tap into relating to the subgroups of professional women and professional African American women?

4. Yankelovich described two African American segments, namely, Market Leaders and Market Followers (Chapter 5). Which group do you think the target market of professional African American women represents? Explain.

5. Does the target market of professional African American women fit the message and media that Camry used in this campaign? Be specific in your explanations for both message (what you thought the overall themes were) and media (what types of

media such as print and Internet) that were used and how they fit the target audience.

6. Beyond simply replacing a young white professional woman with one who is black, is this campaign at its core truly tapping into the unique cultural aspects of African American women? Explain.

7. Why do you think Camry chose to try to change perceptions of their car rather than changing the car itself?

8. Do you think this campaign succeeded in changing the perceptions of African American professional women? Explain. How might you have altered your approach to have a stronger impact?

Source: C. Brodesser-akner, "Toyota," *Advertising Age*, June 9, 2008, www .adage.com, accessed June 23, 2008; and general information from J.D. Power and Associates, www.jdpower.com, from *Cars.com*, and from www .iflookscouldkill.com, accessed June 23, 2008.

## CASE 2–4  RENAULT'S LOGAN TAPS EMERGING GLOBAL MARKETS

In 1999, Renault bought Romanian automaker Dacia. The idea was to retool the plant and manufacture an ultra-low-priced automobile that would be attractive to consumers in developing countries where 80 percent have never owned a car. Renault's chairman at the time, Louis Schweitzer, indicates that he had

. . . always been slightly nervous about the constant escalating costs of ordinary family cars. Adding more and more features just pushed up costs with no real benefit for buyer or carmaker.

The move was a bold one. Consider that in 1999, with gasoline prices still in check, consumer demand was still high for larger and more powerful automobiles. And cars often are an important status symbol for at least some consumers. Many luxury brands continue to tap this "aspirational" market with lower-priced versions of their luxury brands. These aspirational buyers pay a lower but still hefty price for the status of owning a luxury nameplate.

Renault's Logan is anything but luxury. However, it is a well-designed, reliable, and easy-to-repair car. It is a roomy sedan that can seat five people, but has simple design features, such as a flat windshield, minimal electronics, a single-piece dashboard, and so on to reduce manufacturing costs. Simple, low-cost manufacturing that can be executed in factories located in countries like Russia, Morocco, Colombia, and Iran has been the goal, since production close to their key markets also reduces costs.

The Logan has been an unqualified success, beating even Renault's most optimistic projections. Perhaps not so surprising is Logan's success in developing countries like Romania. The automobile is currently priced at about 6,000 euros, putting it at the ultra-low end of the price spectrum, but also into the price range of large masses of consumers in developing countries. Consider these two illustrative statistics:

- In Poland, entry-level autos account for 30 percent of the market.
- In Russia, 90 percent of the auto market falls in the 8,000 to 10,000 euro range.

Renault has a stated goal for the Logan of 1 million units in annual worldwide sales by 2010, an amazing number for a brand that began with only 23,000 units in 2004 and considering that the best-selling auto in the United States sells only between 300,000 and 400,000 units per year. Obviously, large developing countries with increasing incomes, such as India and China, are part of the plan.

However, what has really surprised Renault is that buyers in Western Europe are also flocking to the Logan. In response, Renault has added some additional features, but has still kept the price well below that of comparable competitors. These Western European buyers are far from aspirational in their view of cars. Consider the following comment by one happy owner in France (one of the top-selling countries for the Logan): "For me a car is only a means of transportation. The Logan is a genius idea."

Renault is well on its way to attaining its 2010 sales goal, with 2007 sales estimated at around 250,000 units worldwide. Not surprisingly, given Renault's success, competitors are on their way, including Volkswagen (going after China) and Tata (an Indian auto manufacturer).

### Discussion Questions

1. Beyond income, can you see other barriers to selling cars to consumers in developing countries where 80 percent have *never* owned a car? Be as specific as you can about the consumer behavior–related barriers, including culture, values, new-product adoption, etc.

2. Based on your answer to Question 1, develop an action plan for Renault that would help overcome these barriers.

3. Do you think the Logan would be successful in the United States? If Renault thought it could be successful, would it make sense for them to put resources here given their goal of 1 million units per year worldwide?

4. Develop an advertising campaign to market the Logan in the following countries. Be specific with respect to core theme, copy points, and visuals. Detail the role you think different media (e.g., TV, print, radio, mobile phone, Internet) might play in these different countries.
   *a.* Russia
   *b.* India
   *c.* China

5. Do you think a branding strategy that includes Renault's name (e.g., Logan by Renault) is wise? What are the potential risks and benefits?

6. What sorts of word-of-mouth strategies might be effective in marketing the Logan?

7. As incomes in the developing countries increase, do you expect these consumers to continue to have strong demand for ultra-low-priced cars such as the Logan?

Source: A. Lewis, "Renault's Romanian Route," *Automotive Industries*, Februrary 2005, pp. 6–7; "Renault's Logan 'World Car' Begins Production in Moscow," www.edmunds.com, April 4, 2005; "Got 5,000 Euros?" *Business-Week*, July 4, 2005, p. 49; "Renault's Low-Cost Logan Beats Sales Forecasts," www.forbes.com, July 10, 2005; "Renault's $6,000 Sedan," www.biz-architect .com, July 18, 2005; and T. Jensen, "2007 Toyota Camry Review," *Autotropolis .com*, accessed June 23, 2008; and information from Renault's Web site, www .daciagroup.com.

## CASE 2–5 OFFICE DEPOT LEADS IN GREEN

In 2004, Office Depot issued its first annual *Environmental Stewardship Report*. It was audited by an independent third party, namely, the sustainability experts at PricewaterhouseCoopers LLP. The report was the "office supply industry's first independently verified report of environmental performance." Office Depot has continued to be an industry leader on the environment. The cornerstone of its environmental policy is the "Office Depot Environmental Paper Procurement Policy and Vision Statement," which is posted on its Web site. This policy statement has formed the basis for the company's ongoing efforts and benchmarking on their achievements regarding the environment. An overview of the three core areas and 10 key guiding principles, which are articulated in considerably more detail in their Policy and Vision Statement, are as follows:

### Recycling and Pollution Reduction

- Give preference to paper products containing recycled materials including those made with post-consumer waste fiber.
- Increase the scope of products containing recycled materials.
- Increase the total volume of paper recovered from recycling and the amount of this material that is in the paper Office Depot distributes.

- Encourage suppliers to continue to reduce pollution, including the phasing out of elemental chlorine bleaching agents in the paper-making process.

### Responsible Forest Management and Conservation

- Give preference to products made of wood fiber sourced from operations that are certified as well managed by an independent third party and that use procurement systems that require landowners to meet or exceed government requirements on their forestlands.
- Give preference to products from suppliers that are genuinely and meaningfully engaged in initiatives with the conservation science community to develop and apply best practices to advance sustainable forest management and the conservation of biodiversity values.
- Not knowingly extend preferred status to products sourced from industrial forest operations that convert, or explicitly promote the conversion of, naturally diverse forests to monoculture plantations.
- Not knowingly extend preferred status to products sourced from forest operations that use genetically modified trees to reforest naturally diverse forest ecosystems.

## Issue Awareness and Market Development

- Pursue the promotion and development of markets for environmentally sound products by communicating the value of our environmental policies and the benefits of purchasing products that contribute to environmental stewardship.
- Fund independent research to develop a better understanding of issues such as conservation of biodiversity in production forests and responsible forest management.

## Discussion Questions

1. Review materials on Office Depot's Web site (www.officedepot.com) pertaining to their environmental stewardship efforts, including their ongoing reports. Prepare a report that details accomplishments that Office Depot has made relating to its 10 guiding principles. How would you judge Office Depot's environmental stewardship?

2. Based on your review in Question 1, do you think that consumers are generally aware of the positive things that Office Depot does? If not, should it more heavily promote these positive activities? If it decided to do so, how should it go about it?

3. What effect does PricewaterhouseCoopers' auditing have on your overall evaluation of Office Depot's efforts in the area of the environment?

4. Office Depot argues that being "green" makes both environmental and business sense. What consumer values does environmental stewardship tap into, and how do you think these can translate to the "bottom line" of businesses?

5. Develop promotional materials that would help Office Depot achieve its goal of "promotion and development of markets for environmentally sound products" to a consumer target market.

Source: *2004 Environmental Stewardship Report* (Delray Beach, FL: Office Depot, 2004); and "Office Depot Environmental Paper Procurement Policy and Vision Statement," www.community.officedepot.com/paperproc.asp, accessed June 26, 2008.

## CASE 2–6 REDE GOLF DISPOSABLE GOLF CLEATS

Golf is a sport with a uniform. One part of that uniform is shoes. Not just any shoes to be certain. Golf requires powerful moves and solid footing. Professional golfers wear shoes with metal cleats or spikes for the most effective traction. Amateurs tend to purchase shoes with rigid plastic cleats. Golf shoes are not cheap. They start at $60 a pair and can go on up to over $300. Golf shoes are bulky so they don't fit in a golf bag easily. They take up precious room when traveling, and are sometimes just plain easy to forget. On top of that, they aren't always as comfortable as your favorite pair of sneakers.

In response to all of this, Rede Golf has come out with adhesive-backed cleats that can be put on almost any shoe. Rede Golf cleats are red and are in the shape of an "e"; hence the name. Their Web site states the following:

Why buy golf shoes? Now turn any shoes into golf shoes for just $9.95. Enjoy 20 or more rounds of golf in your comfortable shoes before replacing cleats. Carry PRO LINE Round Savers in your golf bag for the Perfect Replacement Cleat for All Brands of Golf Shoes [for those who have golf shoes but lose a cleat].

Why pack golf shoes when you travel? Attach PRO LINE Round Savers to your shoes—play golf—remove cleats after round and save for another time. And Round Savers are "Approved Under The Rules of Golf By Both the USGA And the Royal & Ancient Golf Association."

## Discussion Questions

1. What type of innovation is the new Rede Golf adhesive-backed cleat? Evaluate it as an innovation using Table 7–2 as a structure.

2. How can the firm use opinion leaders to help their PRO LINE Round Savers succeed?

3. How can the firm use reference group influence to help their PRO LINE Round Savers succeed?

4. What values will help this product succeed?

5. Would you target professionals or amateurs? How would your approach differ between the two groups?

6. What demographic groups would you target?

7. Develop an advertisement for Rede Golf's PRO LINE Round Savers. Be sure to articulate the advantages of the product and also utilize reference group influence.

8. How would you market the Rede Golf's PRO LINE Round Savers in these countries?
   a. Japan
   b. European Union
   c. Mexico

Source: Rede Golf Web site, www.redegolf.com; D. Foust, "Golf 911," *BusinessWeek*, July 31, 2006, p. 77.

## CASE 2–7 THE MOSQUITO MAGNET

Female mosquitoes bite humans and other creatures to acquire blood for the protein they need to lay eggs. They are attracted to humans by the carbon dioxide and other compounds in their breath as well as body heat, moisture, and organic compounds on the skin. Mosquitoes typically do not fly more than a few hundred yards from where they are hatched (unless wind-blown) during their short (several weeks) lives. Thus, if most females are continuously killed in an area, the population should collapse in six to eight weeks.

The Mosquito Magnet was launched on the basis of these facts. It looks a bit like a small gas barbecue grill, complete with propane tank. It mimics a large mammal by emitting a plume of carbon dioxide, heat and moisture, and octenol (a chemical in human breath). This plume attracts female mosquitoes, no-see-ums, biting midges, black flies, and sand flies. It attracts only blood-sucking insects. As the insects approach the Magnet, they are vacuumed into a net where they dehydrate and die. Tests indicate that this system is the most effective available.

The system needs to operate 24 hours a day as it works by creating a mosquito-free (or low-density) area. It takes about two weeks for there to be a noticeable decrease in the mosquito population. The company claims that the population will typically collapse in four to six weeks, leaving only occasional, wind-blown mosquitoes in the area.

The propane tank needs to be refilled approximately every three weeks ($15 to $20). The octenol cartridge (which is not essential but improves the attraction power of the system) also needs to be replaced every three weeks (about $9 each). The net needs to be emptied when half full (frequency depends on the mosquito density in the area).

Mosquito Magnet currently has three models as described below (prices do not include the propane tank):

- *Defender:* covers one-half acre; requires a 110-volt plug to operate; $319.99.

- *Liberty:* covers one acre; requires a 110-volt plug to operate; $519.99.
- *Liberty Plus:* covers one acre; generates its own electricity; $719.99.

While the original Mosquito Magnet was launched earlier this decade, the market for this product appears to still be in the early phases of the adoption cycle.

### Discussion Questions

1. Is the Mosquito Magnet an innovation? If so, what type?

2. Conduct an innovation analysis on the Mosquito Magnet, and develop appropriate marketing strategies based on this analysis.

3. Based on your innovation analysis in Question 2, provide an explanation for why the Mosquito Magnet is still in the early phases of the adoption cycle despite its having been on the market for some time.

4. Examine the firm's Web site at www.mosquitomagnet.com. Are they using any cutting-edge technology online to encourage buzz or WOM? How can the firm encourage word-of-mouth communications about the Mosquito Magnet?

5. Who do you think the opinion leaders will be for this product, and how can the firm use them?

6. What, if any, values are relevant to marketing this product?

7. List the top five countries outside the United States in order of their attractiveness as an export market for this product. Justify your selection.

8. Which family members will be involved in the purchase decision? What roles will they play?

Source: Mosquito Magnet Web site, www.mosquitomagnet.com; J. E. Guyette, "Easing Summer's Sting," *LP/Gas,* August 2001, p. 1; F. Antowiewicz, "Mosquitoes Help Save Firm from Bankruptcy," *Plastics News,* June 24, 2002, p. 1; S. O'Neill, "Skeeter Snuffers," *Kiplinger's Personal Finance,* June 2002, p. 3; P. Grimaldi, "Mosquito Magnet Bought for $6 Million," *Knight Ridder Tribune Business News,* April 18, 2007, p. 1; and H. Svokos, "Skeeters be Gone!" *Knight Ridder Tribune Business News,* July 26, 2007, p. 1.

## CASE 2–8 TAPPING THE ETHNIC HOUSING MARKET

Fannie Mae was established in 1968 and provides financial products and services that help low-, moderate-, and middle-income households buy homes. Its goal is to increase home ownership, particularly among underserved populations. Fannie Mae recently commissioned a survey to

look at the perceptions and knowledge of the home-buying process across ethnic subcultures. Three major areas were assessed, namely (*a*) reasons to buy a home, (*b*) knowledge about the home-buying process, and (*c*) confidence in the home-buying process. Results were as follows.

| TABLE A | | Safe Investment with Potential | Renting Is Bad | Feeling of Ownership | Can Pick Neighborhood | Always My Dream |
|---|---|---|---|---|---|---|
| Key Reasons to Purchase a Home by Ethnicity | General population | 61% | 77% | 74% | 67% | 65% |
| | African American | 54 | 67 | 82 | 66 | 67 |
| | English Hispanic | 67 | 77 | 82 | 71 | 77 |
| | Spanish Hispanic | 60 | 75 | 79 | 65 | 63 |

"Key Reasons to Purchase a Home by Ethnicity" from *Understanding America's Homeownership Gaps: 2003 Fannie Mae National Housing Survey* (Washington, DC: Fannie Mae, 2003). Used by permission.

## HOME-BUYING REASONS

Key reasons for buying or wanting to buy a home are shown in Table A. (Note that English Hispanics are those for whom English is the dominant language, and Spanish Hispanics are those for whom Spanish is dominant.)

## HOME-BUYING KNOWLEDGE

Knowledge about the home-buying process was assessed by the percentage of respondents who identified each of the following statements (S) as false (which they are) as shown in Table B.

**S1:** Information on buying a home is only available in English.

**S2:** You need to hire an attorney to fill out your paperwork when you buy a house.

**S3:** If you want a mortgage, you have to accept a 30-year commitment.

**S4:** Housing lenders are required by law to give you the best possible rates on loans.

**S5:** The person buying the home pays the real estate professional.

**S6:** You need to have a perfect credit rating to qualify for a mortgage.

| TABLE B | | Home-Buying Knowledge by Ethnicity | | | | |
|---|---|---|---|---|---|---|
| | **S1** | **S2** | **S3** | **S4** | **S5** | **S6** |
| General population | 89% | 70% | 74% | 59% | 48% | 73% |
| African American | 92 | 53 | 60 | 36 | 34 | 57 |
| English Hispanic | 93 | 70 | 65 | 42 | 47 | 64 |
| Spanish Hispanic | 60 | 39 | 27 | 25 | 23 | 22 |

Note: Read each column as percentage who know the statement is false. For example, 89 percent of the general population knows that Statement 1 is false.

"Home-buying Knowledge by Ethnicity," from *Understanding America's Homeownership Gaps: 2003 Fannie Mae National Housing Survey* (Washington, DC: Fannie Mae, 2003). Used by permission.

## HOME-BUYING CONFIDENCE

Confidence in home-buying skill and in avoiding discrimination were examined, as shown in Table C.

| TABLE C | Perceptions of Home-Buying Confidence by Ethnicity | | |
|---|---|---|---|
| | **Understand Process Well*** | **Process too Complex** | **Avoiding Discrimination†** |
| General population | 33% | 13% | 4.0 |
| African American | 23 | 25 | 3.4 |
| English Hispanic | 29 | 18 | 3.9 |
| Spanish Hispanic | 18 | 23 | 3.6 |

*Think they have above-average knowledge of the home-buying process.

†Measured on a 1–5 scale, where 1 is lowest confidence and 5 is highest confidence that they will avoid discrimination in the home-buying process.

"Perceptions of Home Buying Confidence by Ethnicity," from *Understanding America's Homeownership Gaps: 2003 Fannie Mae National Housing Survey* (Washington, DC: Fannie Mae, 2003). Used by permission.

### Discussion Questions

1. What are the opportunities and challenges facing housing lenders and real estate agents across ethnic subcultures?

2. Based on the information in Tables A, B, and C, develop an overall marketing strategy for targeting each of the following groups:
   a. African Americans
   b. English Hispanics
   c. Spanish Hispanics

3. Based on the information in Tables A, B, and C, develop advertising campaigns including (*i*) overall positioning strategy and core theme, (*ii*) key advertising copy points, (*iii*) visual elements, and (*iv*) key media outlets for:
   a. African Americans
   b. English Hispanics
   c. Spanish Hispanics

4. Based on the information in Tables A, B, and C, develop training materials for lenders and real estate agents to enhance their interactions with consumers from various ethnic backgrounds. Analyze lenders and real estate agents separately, and develop materials relating to both verbal (written and oral) and nonverbal communications.

Source: Tables from *Understanding America's Homeownership Gaps: 2003 Fannie Mae National Housing Survey* (Washington, DC: Fannie Mae, 2003); general information about Fannie Mae from www.fanniemae.com.

## CASE 2–9 FIGHTING OBESITY IN KIDS

In the mid-60s, less than 5 percent of children aged 6 to 11 or 12 to 19 were significantly overweight. By the end of the century, the percentage for both groups was approaching 15 percent. A diet rich in high-fat, high-calorie foods coupled with limited physical activity is acknowledged as the cause.

Earlier in this decade, the Centers for Disease Control and Prevention (CDC) launched a $125 million campaign, including $50 million for media purchases and $43 million for various marketing and public relations activities; funding for subsequent years was to be substantial but less. The funding legislation from Congress directed the CDC to target childhood obesity but left it wide latitude as to how. It did require that the CDC "communicate messages that help foster good health over a lifetime, including diet, physical activity, and avoidance of illicit drugs, tobacco and alcohol."

The CDC opted to narrow the approach to increased physical activity, particularly among 9- to 13-year-olds. Mike Greenwell, communications director for the CDC, stated, "What we want is behavior change. That would be success for us."

The barriers to physical activity for kids are substantial. First, nonphysical entertainment options have exploded in recent years. Not only has cable television greatly expanded the number of television channels targeting kids, but magazines focusing on them have also expanded. Videos and video games are now a major recreational choice for children. Of course, the time spent online has grown dramatically as well.

Coupled with the vast growth in nonphysical exercise options, there has been a radical decline in required physical education in school. CDC estimates that the number of kids getting physical education in schools has dropped from 50 percent to 21 percent in the past decade.

An initial 15-second spot launched in July showed computer animation of action words turning into an image of a boy running. The theme was "Verb: It's what you do." This and similar teaser spots ran on kid-targeted network and cable TV shows. In September, the full campaign began. The ads all promoted the fun of a physically active lifestyle rather than warning about the dangers of not exercising or of excess weight.

The CDC campaign was the exclusive sponsor of a weekly live-action Nickelodeon show called "WACK" (Wild & Crazy Kids), a related nine-city tour, Nick.com's WACK Web site, and a "Nick News" special program.

There was controversy about the positive-lifestyle approach of the campaign. Antidrug ads targeting the same age were not successful. In explaining why, the Partnership for a Drug-Free America argued that the positive-lifestyle approach does not motivate nearly as well as ads warning about drug dangers.

### Discussion Questions

1. The campaign focused primarily on children, with limited attention to parents. Teachers and other potential influencers were not directly targeted. What do you think is the appropriate balance among these groups? Why?

2. Is the positive approach better than the negative approach in this situation? Why?

3. Describe a series of three positive-lifestyle ads you would use to encourage physical activity among 9- to 13-year-olds.

4. Describe a series of three warning ads you would use to encourage physical activity among 9- to 13-year-olds.

5. Describe a series of three positive-lifestyle ads targeting parents that you would use to encourage physical activity among their 9- to 13-year-old children.

6. Describe a series of three warning ads targeting parents that you would use to encourage physical activity among their 9- to 13-year-old children.

Source: I. Teinowitz and W. Friedman, "U.S. Launches $125 Mil Push to Combat Obesity," *Advertising Age*, July 17, 2002, p. 4; and Centers for Disease Control and Prevention, www.cdc.gov.

# Internal Influences

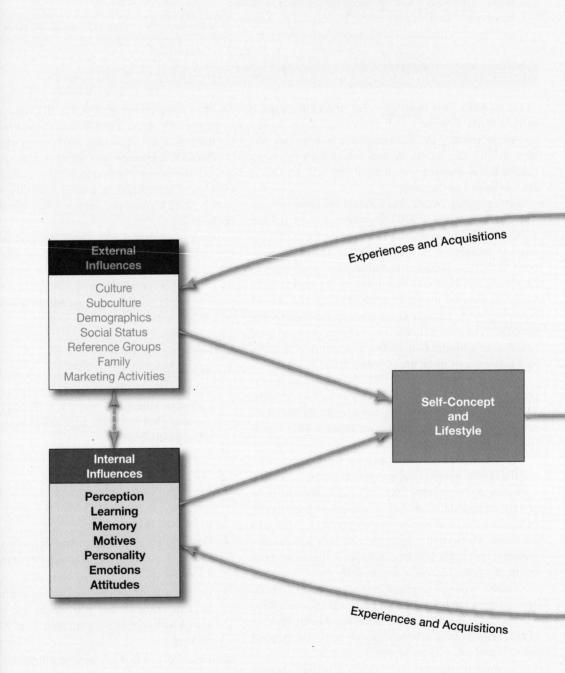

External
Influences

Culture
Subculture
Demographics
Social Status
Reference Groups
Family
Marketing Activities

Internal
Influences

Perception
Learning
Memory
Motives
Personality
Emotions
Attitudes

Self-Concept
and
Lifestyle

Experiences and Acquisitions

Experiences and Acquisitions

The highlighted areas of our model, internal influences and self-concept and lifestyle, are the focal points of this part of the text. Our attention shifts from forces that are basically outside the individual to processes that occur primarily within the individual.

Part Three begins with a discussion of perception, the process by which individuals access and assign meaning to environmental stimuli. In Chapter 9, we consider learning and memory. Chapter 10 covers motivation, personality, and emotion. Chapter 11 focuses on the critical concept of attitudes and the various ways attitudes are formed and changed.

As a result of the interaction of the external influences described in the previous part of the text and the internal processes examined in this part, individuals form self-concepts and desired lifestyles, as discussed in Chapter 12. These are the hub of our model of consumer behavior. Self-concept refers to the way individuals think and feel about themselves as well as how they would like to think and feel about themselves. Their actual and desired lifestyles are the way they translate their self-concepts into daily behaviors, including consumption behaviors.

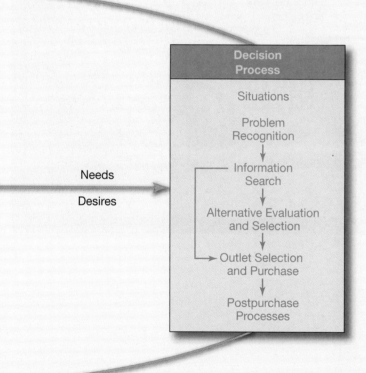

Needs

Desires

Decision Process

Situations

Problem Recognition

Information Search

Alternative Evaluation and Selection

Outlet Selection and Purchase

Postpurchase Processes

# Perception

■ Consumers on vegetarian and vegan diets are searching for foods that balance taste and dietary requirements. In response, Gardenburger introduced its first "meatless" patty in 1985 and has gone on to create other meatless alternatives, including Meatless Meatloaf and Buffalo Chik'n Wings. Their products substitute grain-based proteins and vegetables for meat. Many of their meatless patties include mushrooms as a key ingredient.

In early 2002, Gardenburger became concerned when a competitor introduced foods containing mycoprotein and wanted to claim they were "mushroom in origin." As Gardenburger's CEO Scott Wallace explained it, "After extensive consumer research and discussion with scientific experts, we feel that this labeling is misleading, and could potentially damage those who legitimately use mushrooms in their products."

To understand Gardenburger's concern, you might ask yourself the following question:

"What does it mean to me if a product claims it is 'mushroom in origin'?" Gardenburger launched an extensive survey to answer this very question. Sixty percent of the consumers they surveyed believed that a product labeled as "mushroom in origin" would contain actual mushrooms! Is that what you thought it meant as well? If so, look more carefully at the phrase. It never explicitly states that the product contains mushrooms.

Gardenburger's concerns were justified. Labeling mycoprotein as "mushroom in origin" rather than with the more accurate "edible protein derived from fungus" increases the odds that consumers will infer the presence of mushrooms when they aren't there. It also enhances consumer perceptions and willingess to try the product over that garnered by the more accurate label. As a consequence, Gardenburger petitioned the Food and Drug Administration to regulate the labeling of mycoprotein.[1]

Perception is a process that begins with consumer exposure and attention to marketing stimuli and ends with consumer interpretation. As we will see, exposure and attention are highly selective—meaning that consumers process only a small fraction of the available information. And as the opening example suggests, interpretation can be a highly subjective process. Thus reality and consumer perceptions of that reality are often quite different. Marketers wishing to communicate their brand message effectively to consumers must understand the nature of perception and the many factors influencing it.

# THE NATURE OF PERCEPTION

**Information processing** is a series of activities by which stimuli are perceived, transformed into information, and stored. Figure 8–1 illustrates a useful information-processing model having four major steps or stages: exposure, attention, interpretation, and memory. The first three of these constitute **perception.**

*Exposure* occurs when a stimulus such as a banner ad comes within range of a person's sensory receptor nerves—vision, in this example. *Attention* occurs when the stimulus

---

**FIGURE 8–1**        Information Processing for Consumer Decision Making

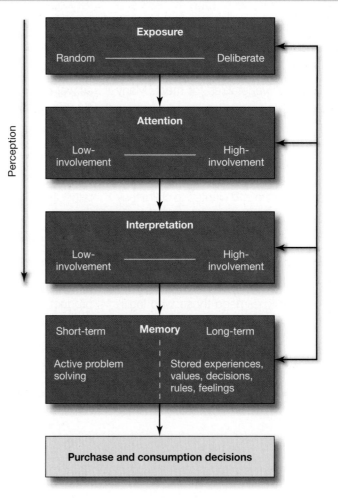

(banner ad) is "seen" (the receptor nerves pass the sensations on to the brain for process-ing). *Interpretation* is the assignment of meaning to the received sensations. *Memory* is the short-term use of the meaning for immediate decision making or the longer-term retention of the meaning.

Figure 8–1 and the above discussion suggest a linear flow from exposure to memory. However, *these processes occur virtually simultaneously and are clearly interactive.* For example, a person's memory influences the information he or she is exposed to and attends to and the interpretations the person assigns to that information. At the same time, memory itself is being shaped by the information it is receiving.

Both perception and memory are extremely selective. Of the massive amount of infor-mation available, individuals can be exposed and attend to only a limited amount. The meaning assigned to a stimulus is as much or more a function of the individual as it is the stimulus itself. Further, much of the interpreted information will not be available to active memory when the individual makes a purchase decision.

This selectivity, sometimes referred to as **perceptual defenses,** means that *individuals are not passive recipients of marketing messages.* Rather, consumers largely determine the mes-sages they will encounter and notice as well as the meaning they will assign them. Clearly, the marketing manager faces a challenging task when communicating with consumers.

# EXPOSURE

**Exposure** *occurs when a stimulus is placed within a person's relevant environment and comes within range of their sensory receptor nerves.* Exposure provides consumers with the *opportunity* to pay attention to available information but in no way guarantees it. For example, have you ever been watching television and realized that you were not paying attention to the commercials being aired? In this case, exposure occurred, but the commer-cials will probably have little influence due to your lack of attention.

An individual can be exposed to only a minuscule fraction of the available stimuli. There are now hundreds of television channels, thousands of radio stations, and innumerable maga-zines and Web sites. In-store environments are also cluttered with tens of thousands of indi-vidual items and in-store advertising. Even in today's multitasking society there are limits.[2]

So what determines exposure? Is it a random process, or is it purposeful? Most of the stimuli to which individuals are exposed are "self-selected." That is, people deliberately seek out exposure to certain stimuli and avoid others. Generally, people seek *information that they think will help them achieve their goals.* Immediate goals could involve seeking stimuli such as a television program for amusement or a Web site to make a purchase. Long-range goals might involve examining corporate Web sites to determine how environmentally friendly they are in hopes of making your community a safer place to live. An individual's goals and the types of information needed to achieve those goals are a function of that per-son's existing and desired lifestyle and such short-term motives as hunger or curiosity.

Of course, people are also exposed to a large number of stimuli on a more or less ran-dom basis during their daily activities. While driving, they may hear commercials, see billboards and display ads, and so on that they did not purposefully seek out.

## Selective Exposure

The highly selective nature of consumer exposure is a major concern for marketers since failure to gain exposure results in lost communication and sales opportunities. For exam-ple, consumers are highly selective in the way they shop once they enter a store. One study found that only 21 percent of U.S. shoppers visited each aisle in the store. The remainder avoided exposure to products in aisles they didn't shop. Consumers in France, Belgium and Holland are also highly selective shoppers, while consumers in Brazil and the United Kingdom are more likely to shop all the aisles.[3]

Media exposure is also of great concern to marketers. Media are where marketers put their commercial messages and include television, radio, magazines, direct mail, billboards, and the Internet. The impact of the active, self-selecting nature of media exposure can be seen in the zipping, zapping, and muting of television commercials. **Zipping** occurs when one fast-forwards through a commercial on a prerecorded program. **Zapping** involves switching channels when a commercial appears. **Muting** is turning the sound off during commercial breaks. Zipping, zapping, and muting are simply mechanical ways for consumers to selectively avoid exposure to advertising messages, often referred to as **ad avoidance.**

The nearly universal presence of remote controls makes zipping, zapping, and muting very simple. Indeed, existing and emerging technologies give consumers more and more control over exposure to television commercials. One such technology is the digital video recorder (DVR) offered by companies such as TiVo. Consumer Insight 8–1 explores how the DVR is reshaping the media landscape and how marketers are responding.

Avoidance of commercials is a global phenomenon that extends beyond TV to include radio, the Internet, magazines, and newspapers. Ad avoidance depends on numerous psychological and demographic factors. A study by Initiative examined ad avoidance globally and across various media. The study found that ad avoidance is increased by lifestyle (busy and hectic lifestyle), social class (higher social class), and demographics (men and younger consumers).[4]

In addition, ad avoidance appears to increase as advertising clutter increases and as consumer attitudes toward advertising become more negative. Consumers tend to dislike (and actively avoid) advertising when it is perceived to be boring, uninformative, and intrusive.[5] In China, for example, where the novelty of advertising and product variety is wearing off, ad avoidance is on the rise and feelings about advertising are becoming more negative.[6] In online settings, marketers have devised "pop-up" ads that are difficult or impossible for viewers to eliminate. At the extreme, movie theaters have begun airing ads *prior* to the movie since the theater provides a captive audience and enhances ad recall beyond that of TV.[7] Such techniques should be used with care, however, since consumers may react very negatively to such forced exposure.[8] In fact, one study found that between 20 and 37 percent of online users are so turned off by pop-up ads that they download "anti-pop-up" software to avoid them completely![9]

In response to consumers' tendency to avoid ads, marketers increasingly seek to gain exposure by placing their brands within entertainment media, such as in movies and television programs, in exchange for payment or promotional or other consideration. Such **product placement** provides exposure that consumers don't try to avoid, it shows how and when to use the product, and it enhances the product's image. Product placement agents read scripts and meet with set designers to identify optimal placement opportunities. The goal is realism and subtle, unobtrusive exposure to the brand. Placements work best when the principal actor is present and the placement is well integrated into the scene. For example, as hybrid cars began taking hold in the United States, Toyota's Prius was featured prominently in an episode of the political drama *The West Wing*. The Prius was integral to a principal character and positively woven into the core plot dealing with fuel economy standards.[10]

Movies and television are just some of the avenues being used. Marketers increasingly seek exposure by placing their messages in ever more unique media, such as on the side of trucks and taxis, in airplanes, at events, and in video games. Outdoor and video games are major growth areas for advertisers in this regard. Outdoor is branching out in many new

## Living in a DVR World

DVRs allow for digital recording of programs and "time-shifted" viewing. Currently 20 percent of U.S. households have a DVR and that number is expected to increase to 41 percent by 2009.[11] A major concern for marketers is increased ad avoidance. DVR viewers of pre-recorded content skip ads at more than twice the rate of those who view the same content live. And 50 to 90 percent of DVR users fast-forward through at least some commercials.[12]

Other research is more optimistic. Several studies point out that most viewers who zip through DVR commercials still "notice" the ads and, in fact, will stop and view commercials they are interested in.[13] And Innerscope Research recently found that DVR users who fast-forwarded through TV ads were more "engaged" with the ads than those who did not.[14]

Clearly, marketers need to think beyond traditional models as DVR technology transforms how consumers watch TV. One strategy being tested is compressing ads so consumers see a shortened version of the ad, which plays in real time during fast forwarding.[15] Other strategies now in use include the following:[16]

- *Still-frame ads.* This strategy keeps the visual relatively static for 30 seconds, giving marketers a chance to present their package, brand, and logo and have it visible even during fast forwarding. *Brotherhood,* a show set in Providence, Rhode Island, used the cityscape focal visual. When fast-forwarded, the clouds move and the audio is made to be quite dramatic.
- *Hybrid ads.* Hybrid ads mimic the show the audience is watching. These tie-ins to shows seem to be particularly effective at staving off ad skipping. Guinness used a hybrid to mimic *Mythbusters,* the

show in which the ad aired. This ad yielded 41 percent higher recall than a regular Guinness ad!
- *Interactive ads.* TiVo recently added an interactive "tag" icon that appears while the ad is playing, which takes consumers to more detailed brand information and additional ads. Sony has created ads with multiple endings that viewers select with their remote. Interactivity provides marketers with *more* freedom in a DVR context to deliver relevant brand information and content to consumers who want it.

Some companies are not ready to embrace this new world. ABC, for example, has expressed its desire that DVR manufacturers "disable the fast-forward [button]" rather than train a new generation to skip commercials just because they can.[17] Perhaps reacting to such comments, Time Warner Cable now offers a free DVR feature that won't allow fast-forwarding.[18] Other companies are embracing the change and looking for ways to adapt and be relevant.

### Critical Thinking Questions

1. Do you think that later adopters of DVRs will be less interested in "ad avoidance" capabilities? Will this change as they "learn" to use their DVR?

2. How much influence "should" large broadcasters, such as ABC, CBS, and NBC, have over what controls are and are not allowed on DVR and related technology? What ethical issues are involved?

3. Can you think of other strategies beyond those discussed that could be used to reduce consumers' tendency to skip ads even with a DVR?

ways beyond traditional billboards. Adidas created an outdoor display to launch a new store in Amsterdam that mimicked a shoe box except that it was 6 feet tall, 6 feet deep, and 24 feet wide! And for the World Cup in Germany, Adidas used a 215-foot-long cutout image of Oliver Kahn (a goalkeeper for one of the German teams) diving for a soccer ball that spanned across the autobahn (see Illustration 8–1).[19] Such outdoor efforts provide eye-catching visuals that are virtually impossible to ignore.

Video game advertising is perhaps the fastest-growing alternative media. It allows for exposure to younger males, who tend to be the gamers and avoid traditional media. As one expert notes:

> Advertisers have seen that young males, specifically 18- to-24-year-olds, are increasingly turning their backs on TV and multiplexes in favor of video games and the Internet. Making the area [ads in video games] even more attractive [is] a recent study from Nielson and game publisher Activision [which] shows that gamers not only accept brands embedded into games but can be persuaded to buy the products if the integration is relevant and authentic.[20]

As a result, the Yankee Group estimates that while ad spending in some media is growing in the 4 to 5 percent range (TV and magazines) and some is even shrinking (newspapers), ad spending in video games is growing by over 30 percent per year and is expected to reach around $800 million by 2009.[21]

## Voluntary Exposure

Although consumers often avoid commercials and other marketing stimuli, sometimes they actively seek them out for various reasons, including purchase goals, entertainment, and information. As we saw earlier, consumers actively seek out aisles containing items they want to buy.[22] And many viewers look forward to the commercials developed for the Super Bowl. Perhaps more impressive is the positive response consumers have to **infomercials**—program-length television commercials with a toll-free number and/or Web address through which to order or request additional information. These positively affect brand attitudes and purchase intentions.[23] And they are more likely to be viewed by early adopters and opinion leaders.[24] This latter effect implicates a critical indirect influence of infomercials through word-of-mouth communications. It also highlights the role that information and relevance play in driving voluntary exposure to marketing messages.

Exposure to online messages and advertising can also be voluntary or involuntary. As we saw earlier, exposure to banner ads and pop-ups is generally *involuntary,* as consumers encounter them while seeking other information or entertainment. However, a consumer who clicks on the banner or pop-up (*click through*) is now *voluntarily* being exposed to the target site and its marketing message.

Consumers also voluntarily expose themselves to marketing messages by deliberately visiting firms' homepages and other marketer sites. For example, if you are buying a new car, you might visit manufacturer sites such as www.toyota.com and independent sites such as www.edmunds.com. In fact, recent car buyers using the Web visited up to seven sites and spent almost five hours online![25] You might also register online to receive coupons or regular updates or newsletters about a company's products and services. When you register at www.eversave.com, the site provides you with coupons and newsletters from various consumer goods marketers such as Procter & Gamble. The voluntary and self-selected nature of such online offerings, where consumers "opt in" to receive e-mail-based promotions, is often referred to as **permission-based marketing.**[26] Permission-based marketing concepts are also being used to enhance the effectiveness of *mobile marketing* on cell phones.[27] Consumers control the messages they are exposed to and, consequently, are more receptive and responsive to those messages.

# ATTENTION

**Attention** *occurs when the stimulus activates one or more sensory receptor nerves, and the resulting sensations go to the brain for processing.* Attention requires consumers to allocate limited mental resources toward the processing of incoming stimuli, such as packages seen on store shelves or banner ads on the Web. As we discussed earlier, the marketing environment is highly cluttered and consumers are constantly bombarded by thousands of times more stimuli than they can process. Therefore, consumer attention is selective.

This selectivity has major implications for marketers. As the following example illustrates, after obtaining exposure, anyone wishing to communicate effectively with consumers must understand how to gain their attention.

> The Federal Crop Insurance Corporation (FCIC) spent $13.5 million over a four-year period on an advertising campaign to increase awareness and knowledge among farmers of the federal crop insurance program. The campaign included radio ads, direct mail brochures, and news releases. However, "farmers ended up knowing no more about this program after the ad campaign than they did before." A spokesperson described the problem: "It was very good and very effective advertising. The trouble is that we had a hard time getting people to read it."[28]

"Very good and very effective advertising" that no one reads is neither good nor effective. People must attend to the messages. As one advertising agency director stated,

> Every year it gets more and more important to stand out and be noticed, to be loud but simple, and to say something relevant and compelling because there is less and less opportunity to talk to consumers and you can't waste any chances.[29]

The ad in Illustration 8–2 is very likely to attract attention. What factors determine and influence attention? Perhaps you are in the market for a DVD player. Once in the DVD aisle, you focus your attention on the various brands to make a purchase. However, a loud announcement briefly pulls your attention away from the display. Later, you lose concentration and begin focusing on nearby products you hadn't noticed before. These products were available

© 2007 Adams Respiratory Therapeutics, Fort Worth, TX 76155, 638 100107

**ILLUSTRATION 8–2**

This ad uses stimulus factors including color and interestingness to capture attention.

all the time but were not processed until a deliberate effort was made to do so. As this example demonstrates, attention always occurs within the context of a situation. The *same individual* may devote different levels of attention to the *same stimulus* in *different situations*. Attention is determined by these three factors: the *stimulus,* the *individual,* and the *situation.*

## Stimulus Factors

*Stimulus factors* are physical characteristics of the stimulus itself. Stimulus characteristics such as ad size and color are under the marketer's control and can attract attention

**The Impact of Size on Advertising Readership**     FIGURE 8–2

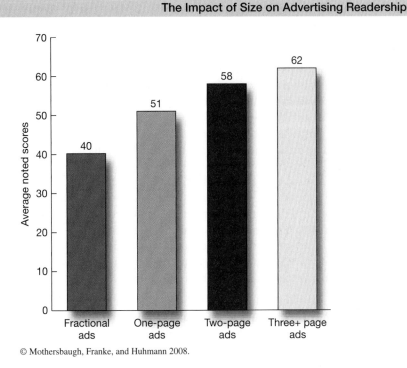

© Mothersbaugh, Franke, and Huhmann 2008.

independent of individual or situational characteristics. The attention garnered by stimulus factors tends to be relatively automatic. So even if you *think* you are not interested in a car (individual characteristic), a large and colorful car ad (stimulus characteristics) may be hard to ignore.

Size   Larger stimuli are more likely to be noticed than smaller ones. This is certainly the case on store shelves where shelf space is at a premium and more shelf space can translate into greater attention and sales.[30] As a consequence, consumer-products companies often pay what are called *slotting allowances* to retailers to secure shelf space. The Federal Trade Commission estimates that companies spend $9 billion annually on such slotting fees.[31]

Size also affects attention to advertising. Figure 8–2 indicates the relative attention-attracting ability of various sizes of magazine ads, with larger ads garnering more attention than smaller ads. Larger banner ads also attract more attention, which might help explain why banner and online ads continue to increase in size.[32] And larger Yellow Pages ads get more attention and have higher call rates. In one study, consumers seeking a business from the Yellow Pages attended to more than 90 percent of the quarter-page ads but only a quarter of the small listings.[33]

Intensity   The *intensity* (e.g., loudness, brightness, length) of a stimulus can increase attention. For instance, the longer a scene in an advertisement is held on-screen, the more likely it is to be noticed and recalled.[34] In online contexts, one aspect of intensity is *intrusiveness,* or the degree to which one is forced to see or interact with a banner ad or pop-up in order to see the desired content. A study in which the banner ad was the only thing on the screen for a brief period before the consumer was connected to the sought-after site produced over three times the level of noticing the ad compared with a standard banner format, and almost 25 times the clickthrough rate.[35] As we saw earlier, however, caution is advised in using intrusiveness because of negative attitudes and ad avoidance.

*Repetition* is related to intensity. It is the number of times an individual is exposed to a given stimulus, such as an ad or brand logo, over time. Attention generally decreases across repeated exposures, particularly when those exposures occur in a short period of time (intensity is high). For example, attention to multiple inserts of the same print ad within the same magazine issue has been found to drop by 50 percent from the first to the third exposure.[36]

However, the decrease in overall attention caused by repetition needs to be interpreted in view of two factors. First, consumers may shift the *focus* of their attention from one part of the ad to another across repetitions. Have you ever noticed something new about an ad after you've seen it a couple of times? This is a result of a shift in your attention as you become more familiar with the ad. One study suggests that consumers shift their attention away from the brand component of the ad (name, logo, etc.) and toward the text component.[37] This *attention reallocation* is important since many of a brand's features can be communicated through the ad's text, but convincing consumers to read is difficult. The second factor is that repetition often increases recall.[38] As we will discuss in Chapter 9, subsequent exposures, while generating less attention, appear to reinforce the learning that occurred on the first exposure.

### Attractive Visuals

Individuals tend to be attracted to pleasant stimuli and repelled by unpleasant stimuli. This explains the ability of *attractive visuals,* such as mountain scenes and attractive models, to draw consumer attention to an advertisement. In fact, an ad's visual or pictorial component can have a strong influence on attention independent of other characteristics. One study found that greater graphics content increased how much time consumers spent at an online retailer's Web site.[39] Another study of over 1,300 print ads found that the ad's picture garnered more attention than any other ad element (e.g., brand and text elements) regardless of its size. This *picture superiority* effect on attention demonstrates the importance of an ad's visual component and suggests why the heavy use of pictures in contemporary print advertising may be justified. However, since attention is limited, drawing attention to one element of an ad can detract from others. For example, increasing picture size in a print ad reduces the amount of attention consumers pay to the brand.[40]

Any factor that draws attention to itself and away from the brand and its selling points has to be used with caution. An ad's visual component represents one such factor. Attractive models represent another. One company found that putting a provocatively dressed model in its print ad drew attention away from their product and toward the model. As a consequence, consumer recall of their brand name 72 hours after exposure to the ad was reduced by 27 percent![41]

### Color and Movement

Both *color* and *movement* serve to attract attention, with brightly colored and moving items being more noticeable. Certain colors and color characteristics create feelings of excitement and arousal, which are related to attention. Brighter colors are more arousing than dull. And *warm* colors, such as reds and yellows, are more arousing than *cool* colors, such as blues and grays.[42]

In-store, a brightly colored package or display is more apt to receive attention. Retailers interested in encouraging impulse purchases may utilize red in their displays given its ability to attract attention and generate feelings of excitement.[43] Also, point-of-purchase displays with moving parts and signage are more likely to draw attention and increase sales. Thus, companies like Eddie Bauer are choosing dynamic digital signage over static displays.[44]

Color and movement are also important in advertising. Thus, banner ads with dynamic animation attract more attention than similar ads without dynamic animation.[45] In a study of Yellow Pages advertising, color ads were attended to sooner, more frequently, and longer than noncolor ads.[46] Figure 8–3 shows the relative attention-attracting ability of black-and-white and of four-color magazine ads of different sizes.

Illustration 8–3 shows two ads that are identical except for the use of color. The ad with the color was noticed by significantly more readers than was the black-and-white ad.

**Position**   *Position* refers to the placement of an object in physical space or time. In retail stores, items that are easy to find or that stand out are more likely to attract attention. End caps and kiosks are used for this reason. In addition, since items near the center of a

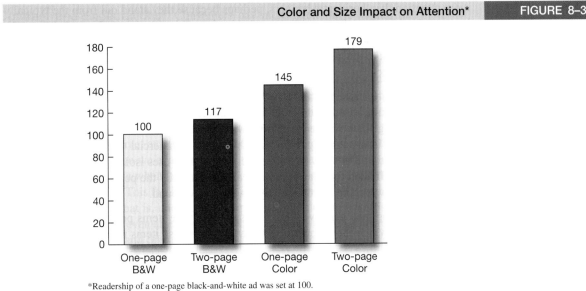

**Color and Size Impact on Attention***                                    **FIGURE  8–3**

*Readership of a one-page black-and-white ad was set at 100.

Source: "How Important Is Color to an Ad?" *Starch Tested Copy,* February 1989, p. 1, Roper Starch Worldwide, Inc.

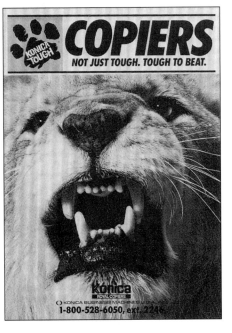

**ILLUSTRATION 8–3**

Color can attract attention to an ad. In this case, the color ad had a noted score of 62 percent, compared with 44 percent for the identical black-and-white ad.

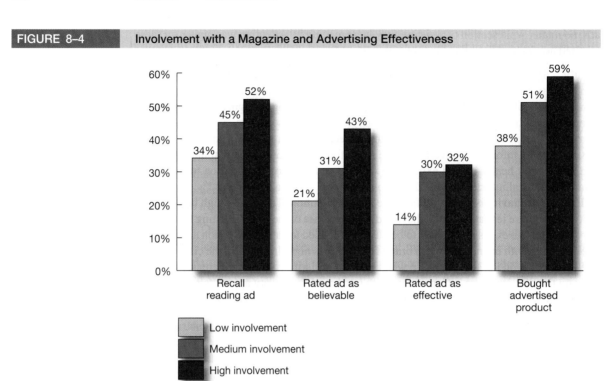

**FIGURE 8–4**    **Involvement with a Magazine and Advertising Effectiveness**

Source: *Cahners Advertising Research Report 120.1 and 120.12* (Boston: Cahners Publishing, undated).

or conscious focusing of attention. A classic example is the *cocktail party effect,* whereby an individual engaged in a conversation with a friend isn't consciously aware of other conversations at a crowded party until someone in another group says something relevant such as mentioning her name. This example suggests we are processing a host of stimuli at a subconscious level and mechanisms in our brain evaluate this information to decide what warrants deliberate and conscious attention.[71] In fact, the idea behind *hemispheric lateralization* is that different parts of our brain are better suited for focused versus nonfocused attention.

Hemispheric Lateralization    **Hemispheric lateralization** is a term applied to activities that take place on each side of the brain. The left side of the brain is primarily responsible for verbal information, symbolic representation, sequential analysis, and the ability to be conscious and report what is happening. It controls those activities we typically call *rational thought.* The right side of the brain deals with pictorial, geometric, timeless, and nonverbal information without the individual being able to verbally report it. It works with images and impressions.

The left brain needs fairly frequent rest. However, the right brain can easily scan large amounts of information over an extended time period. This led Krugman to suggest that "it is the right brain's picture-taking ability that permits the rapid screening of the environment—to select what it is the left brain should focus on."[72] One study of banner ads found evidence of preconscious screening. Web surfers seem able to spot a banner ad without actually looking directly at it. As a consequence, direct attention to banner ads occurred only 49 percent of the time. It seems that experience with the Web allows consumers to build up knowledge about banner characteristics (typical size and location) that is used to avoid direct attention.[73]

However, just because consumers don't pay direct attention to an advertisement doesn't mean it can't influence them. For example, brands contained in ads to which subjects are exposed but pay little or no attention (incidental exposure) nonetheless are more likely to be considered for purchase.[74]

Subliminal Stimuli   A message presented so fast or so softly or so masked by other messages that one is not aware of seeing or hearing it is called a **subliminal stimulus.** A subliminal ad is different from a "normal" ad in that it "hides" key persuasive information within the ad by making it so weak that it is difficult or impossible for an individual to physically detect. Normal ads present key persuasive information to consumers so that it is easily perceived.

Subliminal advertising has been the focus of intense study and public concern. It's one thing for consumers to decide not to pay attention to an ad. It's quite another for advertisers to try to bypass consumers' perceptual defenses by using subliminal stimuli.

Two books triggered public interest in masked subliminal advertising.[75] The author "documents" numerous advertisements that, once you are told where to look and what to look for, appear to contain the word *sex* in ice cubes, phalli in mixed drinks, and nude bodies in the shadows. Such masked symbols, deliberate or accidental, do not appear to affect standard measures of advertising effectiveness or influence consumption behavior. Likewise, research on messages presented too rapidly to elicit awareness indicates that such messages have little or no effect.[76] In addition, there is no evidence marketers are using subliminal messages.[77]

# INTERPRETATION

**Interpretation** is *the assignment of meaning to sensations.* Interpretation is related to how we comprehend and make sense of incoming information based on characteristics of the stimulus, the individual, and the situation.

Several aspects of interpretation are important to consider. First, it is generally a relative process rather than absolute, often referred to as **perceptual relativity.** It is often difficult for people to make interpretations in the absence of some reference point. Consider the following actual scenario:

> An episode of QVC Network's *Extreme Shopping* program offers Muhammad Ali's boxing robe (priced at over $12,000), followed by Jane Mansfield's former mansion (almost $3.5 million), and a Volkswagen Beetle painted by Peter Max ($100,000). Then, signed and personalized Peter Max prints were offered for about $200.

In line with the notion of relativity, consumers interpreted the print price as lower when it followed the higher-priced items.[78]

A second aspect of interpretation is that it tends to be subjective and open to a host of psychological biases. The subjective nature of interpretation can be seen in the distinction between *semantic meaning,* the conventional meaning assigned to a word such as found in the dictionary, and *psychological meaning,* the specific meaning assigned a word by a given individual or group of individuals based on their experiences, expectations, and the context in which the term is used.

Marketers must be concerned with psychological meaning as it is the subjective experience, not objective reality, that drives consumer behavior. A firm may introduce a high-quality new brand at a lower price than competitors because the firm is more efficient. However, if consumers interpret the lower price to mean lower quality (and they often do), the new brand will not be successful regardless of the objective reality.[79]

Consumers have emotional responses to or interpretations of ads as well as cognitive ones. This ad is likely to produce an emotional or feeling response in many members of its target audience.

A final aspect of interpretation is that it can be a cognitive "thinking" process or an affective "emotional" process. **Cognitive interpretation** is *a process whereby stimuli are placed into existing categories of meaning.*[80] As we saw earlier, ads are categorized as expected or unexpected, a process that can vary by culture and individual.[81] In countries like France where ads are more sexually explicit, nudity may be seen as more appropriate than in the United States. Products are also categorized. When DVD players were first introduced, most consumers probably grouped them in the same category as VCRs, but with further experience put them in separate categories. Radically "new" products (discontinuous innovation) are the most difficult to categorize, and marketers need to provide consumers with assistance to gain understanding and acceptance.[82]

**Affective interpretation** is *the emotional or feeling response triggered by a stimulus such as an ad.* Emotional responses can range from positive (upbeat, exciting, warm) to neutral (disinterested) to negative (anger, fear, frustration). Like cognitive interpretation, there are "normal" (within-culture) emotional responses to many stimuli (e.g., most Americans experience a feeling of warmth when seeing pictures of young children with kittens). Likewise, there are also individual variations to this response (a person allergic to cats might have a negative emotional response to such a picture). Consumers confronting new products or brands often assign them to emotional as well as cognitive categories.[83] The ad shown in Illustration 8–6 is likely to trigger an emotional interpretation as well as a cognitive one.

## Individual Characteristics

Marketing stimuli have meaning *only* as individuals interpret them.[84] Individuals are not passive interpreters of marketing and other messages but actively assign meaning based on their needs, desires, experiences, and expectations.

**Traits**    Inherent physiological and psychological traits, which drive our needs and desires, influence how a stimulus is interpreted. From a *physiological* standpoint, consumers differ in their sensitivity to stimuli. Some children are more sensitive to the bitter taste of certain chemicals found in green, leafy vegetables such as spinach.[85] Tab (a diet cola containing saccharine) maintains a small but fiercely loyal customer base, most likely among those who (unlike most of us) don't physiologically perceive saccharine as bitter.

From a *psychological* standpoint, consumers have natural cognitive, emotional, and behavioral predispositions. As just one example, some people experience emotions more strongly than others, a trait known as *affect intensity*. A number of studies have found that consumers who are higher in affect intensity experience stronger emotional reactions to any given advertisement.[86] We discuss other personality differences in Chapter 10.

**Learning and Knowledge**    The meanings attached to such "natural" things as time, space, relationships, and colors are learned and vary widely across cultures, as we saw in Chapter 2. Consumers also learn about marketer-created stimuli like brands and promotions through their experiences with them. This experience and knowledge affects

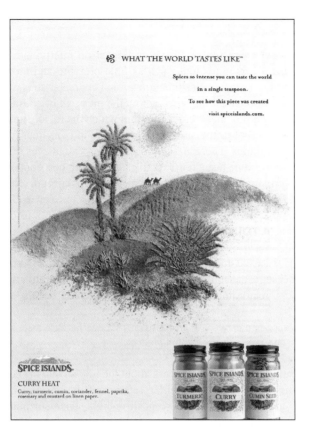

**ILLUSTRATION 8–7**

Colors often have learned associations that are used in ads to convey product characteristics and meanings.

interpretations. One general finding is that consumers tend to interpret information in ways that favor their preferred brands. In one study, those higher in loyalty to a firm tended to discredit negative publicity about the firm and thus were less affected by it.[87] Similarly, another study found that consumers infer more positive motives from a company's price increase if the company has a strong reputation.[88]

The ad in Illustration 8–7 uses color to reinforce an interpretation that consumers have learned. *What meanings are associated with the colors in Illustration 8–7?*

**Expectations**    Individuals' interpretations of stimuli tend to be consistent with their *expectations,* an effect referred to as the *expectation bias.* Most consumers expect dark brown pudding to taste like chocolate, not vanilla, because dark pudding is generally chocolate flavored and vanilla pudding is generally cream colored. In a taste test, 100 percent of a sample of college students accepted dark brown *vanilla* pudding as chocolate.[89] Thus, their expectations, cued by color, led to an interpretation that was inconsistent with objective reality.

Consumers' expectations are the result of learning and can be formed very quickly, as the old saying "first impressions matter" suggests. Once established, these expectations can wield enormous influence[90] and can be hard to change. Many consumers expect, for example, that well-known brands are higher quality. As a consequence, consumers frequently evaluate the performance of a well-known brand as higher than that of an *identical* product with an unknown brand name. Many consumers have also come to expect that brands with some sort of in-store signage are on sale. As a consequence, one study found that brands with promotional signs on them in retail stores are interpreted as having reduced prices even though the signs don't indicate a price reduction and the prices aren't actually reduced.[91]

## Situational Characteristics

A variety of situational characteristics have an impact on interpretation, including temporary characteristics of the individual, such as time pressure and mood,[92] and physical characteristics of the situation, such as the number and characteristics of other individuals present and the nature of the material surrounding the message in question.

Basically, the situation provides a context within which the focal stimulus is interpreted. The **contextual cues** present in the situation play a role in consumer interpretation *independent* of the actual stimulus. There are innumerable contextual cues in any given marketing context—here we examine just a few examples. *Color* can be a contextual cue. A recent study of online advertising examined various aspects of background color present during Web page loads. Certain color characteristics were found to elicit feelings of relaxation (blue more relaxing than red) and these feelings increased perceptions of faster Web page loading even when actual speed was identical.[93]

The *nature of the programming* surrounding a brand's advertisements can also be a contextual cue. Both Coca-Cola and General Foods have refused to advertise some products during news broadcasts because they believe that "bad" news might affect the interpretation of their products. According to a Coca-Cola spokesperson:

> It's a Coca-Cola corporate policy not to advertise on TV news because there's going to be some bad news in there, and Coke is an upbeat, fun product.[94]

The previous example expresses a concern about the impact that the content of the material surrounding an ad will have on the interpretation of the ad. As Coca-Cola suspects, it appears that ads are evaluated in a more positive light when surrounded with positive programming.[95]

## Stimulus Characteristics

The stimulus is the basic entity to which an individual responds and includes the product, package, advertisement, in-store display, and so on. Consumers react to and interpret basic traits of the stimulus (size, shape, color), the way the stimulus is organized, and changes in the stimulus. As we have seen, all these processes are likely to be heavily influenced by the individual and the situation.

**Traits**    Specific traits of the stimulus, such as size, shape, and color, affect interpretation. The meaning of many stimulus traits is learned. Color is one trait in which learning affects meaning. Canada Dry's sugar-free ginger ale sales increased dramatically when the can was changed to green and white from red. Red is interpreted as a "cola" color and thus conflicted with the taste of ginger ale.[96] White space in ads is another trait involving learned meaning. That is, over time consumers have come to believe that white space in an ad means prestige, high price, and quality. As a consequence, marketers can positively influence product perceptions by what they *don't* say in an ad![97]

Another general trait is the extent to which the stimulus is unexpected, a trait sometimes referred to as *incongruity*. Incongruity increases attention, as we saw earlier. However, it also increases liking, in part because of the pleasure consumers derive from "solving the puzzle" presented by the incongruity. As a consequence, products and ads that deviate somewhat from established norms (without going too far) are often better liked. Incongruity often requires that consumers go beyond what is directly stated or presented in order to make sense of the stimulus. These inferences, which we discuss later in the chapter, are an important part of interpretation. Consumer Insight 8–2 provides a closer look at how

### Rhetorical Figures and Perception

Examine the ad in Illustration 8–8. Is this ad unique in any way? How does it impact your thoughts and feelings? As media outlets become more cluttered, companies struggle to find advertising tactics that grab consumer attention and draw them into the ad. One tactic that seems to have potential is the use of rhetorical figures. **Rhetorical figures** *involve the use of an unexpected twist or artful deviation in how a message is communicated either visually in the ad's picture or verbally in the ad's text or headline.*[98] Common rhetorical figures include rhymes such as Bounty's "quicker picker-upper," or Uni-ball's "write the good write," and metaphors such as Kiwi's "Unpolished shoes are the open fly of footwear" or Srixon's (golf ball) "Fire in the hole."

The unexpected nature of rhetorical figures attracts and holds attention as consumers decipher the ad's meaning. In one study of over 800 print ads, rhetorical figures in the ad's headline increased readership (a measure of total attention) between 15 and 42 percent over literal headlines. Clearly, rhetorical figures have the power to attract and hold attention!

Rhetorical figures also influence how consumers interpret an ad. Unpolished shoes aren't *literally* an unzipped garment (open fly). However, the meanings associated with "open fly" (embarrassing, distasteful, bad for your image) are what Kiwi hopes consumers will relate to unpolished shoes. Such meaning would be harder to communicate and probably less convincing if directly stated in the ad. In addition, the artful twist or deviation of rhetorical figures tends to generate more positive attitudes toward the ad.

Marketers need to be careful when using rhetorical figures across ethnic subcultures since their interpretation often requires an understanding of embedded cultural meanings which don't always transfer across cultures. Thus, the "open fly" in Kiwi's ad might work well with native English speakers but not so well with first-generation Asian Americans.

### Critical Thinking Questions

1. How do rhetorical figures work?
2. What other types of rhetorical figures can you think of?
3. Besides ethnicity, what other factors might influence the effectiveness of rhetorical figures?
4. What ethical concerns, if any, can you see with the use of rhetorical figures?

*rhetorical figures* can be used to enhance incongruity and influence both attention and interpretation.

Organization    **Stimulus organization** refers to *the physical arrangement of the stimulus objects.* Organization affects consumer interpretation and categorization. For example, you likely perceive the letters that make up the words you are reading as words rather than as individual letters. This effect is enhanced by the fact that each word has letters that are close together and is separated by larger spaces, a principle called proximity. We discuss this and other principles next.

**Proximity** refers to the fact that *stimuli positioned close together are perceived as belonging to the same category.* Sometimes proximity comes from the stimulus itself. For example, when consumers read the headline "Have a safe winter. Drive Bridgestone Tires," they tend to infer from the proximity of the two statements that the ad means Bridgestone Tires will help them have a safe winter. However, the headline does not explicitly make that claim. *What ethical implications exist?*

Sometimes proximity results from the relationship of the stimulus to its context, as in ambush marketing. **Ambush marketing** involves *any communication or activity that*

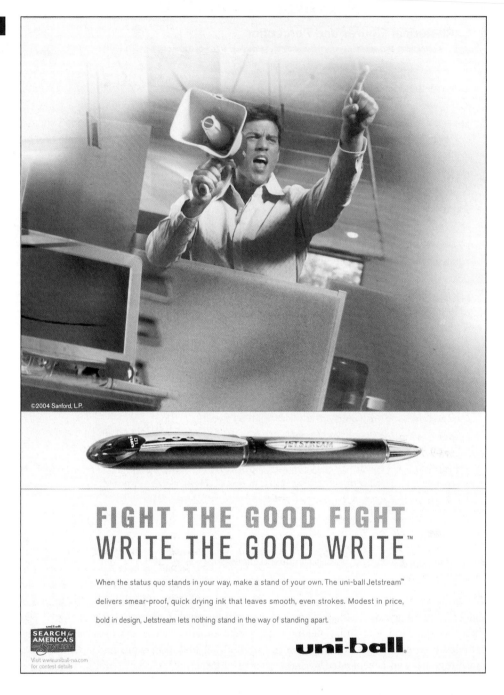

*implies, or from which one could reasonably infer, that an organization is associated with an event, when in fact it is not.* A common form of ambush marketing is to advertise heavily during the event. Proximity would lead many to believe that the company was a sponsor of the event even if it was not.[99]

**Closure** involves *presenting an incomplete stimulus with the goal of getting consumers to complete it and thus become more engaged and involved.* Advertisers will often use incomplete stimuli in this manner since closure is often an automatic response engaged

AN AMERICAN R=VOLUTION

MULTI-TALENTED, MULTI-DIMENSIONAL MULTI-TASKERS:
MEET YOUR MATCH.

malibu maxx | POWER-ADJUSTABLE PEDALS | SLIDING/RECLINING REAR SEATS | BEST-IN-CLASS REAR LEGROOM* | REAR SKYLIGHT | AVAILABLE DVD, ONSTAR® AND REMOTE START | NO WONDER WE CALL IT THE MAXX | CHEVYMALIBU.COM

in by consumers in order to interpret message meaning. Not surprisingly, increasing consumer ad involvement also increases recall, as we will discuss more in Chapter 9.[100] Illustration 8–9 demonstrates the closure concept. Interpretation is enhanced by perceiving the three parallel lines as the letter E. The red color of the lines draws attention to the incompleteness and also reinforces the core meaning of the ad.

**Figure–ground** involves *presenting the stimulus in such a way that it is perceived as the focal object to be attended to and all other stimuli are perceived as the background.* This strategy is often used in advertising, where the goal is to make the brand stand out as the prominent focal object to which consumers will attend. Absolut, a Swedish vodka, uses figure–ground very effectively. Each ad uses the natural elements in the ad to "form" the figure of a bottle, as with Absolut Mandarin where the bottle is formed by pieces of orange peel.

Changes    In order to interpret stimulus change, consumers must be able to categorize and interpret the new stimulus relative to the old. Interpreting change requires both the ability to detect change and then assign meaning to that change. Sometimes consumers won't be able to detect a change. Sometimes they can detect a change but interpret it as unimportant.

The physiological ability of an individual to distinguish between similar stimuli is called **sensory discrimination.** This involves such variables as the sound of stereo systems, the taste of food products, or the clarity of display screens. The minimum amount that one brand can differ from another (or from its previous version) with the difference still being noticed is referred to as the **just noticeable difference (j.n.d.).** The higher the initial level of an attribute, the greater that attribute must be changed before the change will be noticed. Thus, a small addition of salt to a pretzel would not likely be noticed unless that pretzel contained only a small amount of salt to begin with.

As a general rule, *individuals typically do not notice relatively small differences between brands or changes in brand attributes.* Makers of candy bars have used this principle for years. Since the price of cocoa fluctuates widely, they simply make small adjustments in the size of the candy bar rather than altering price. Since marketers want some product changes, such as reductions in the size, to go unnoticed, they may attempt to make changes that fall below the j.n.d. This strategy, sometimes referred to as *weighting out,* appears to be on the increase. However, if and when consumers do notice, the potential backlash may be quite severe.[101] *What is your evaluation of the ethics of this practice?*

After *noticing* a change or difference, consumers must *interpret* it. Some changes are meaningful and some are not. The relationship between change and consumers' valuation of that change tends to follow the pattern discussed for j.n.d. The higher the initial level of an attribute, the greater the attribute must change before it is seen as meaningful. For example, consumers underestimate the calories in a meal more as the portion size of the meal increases. This *mis*interpretation has important individual and societal consequences for obesity and portion control.[102]

Change is often interpreted with respect to some *referent state.* The referent state might be a brand's prior model or a competitor model. *Reference price* is also a referent state. Consumers can bring *internal* reference prices with them based on prior experience. Also, marketers can provide a reference in the form of *manufacturer suggested retail price (MSRP).* Consumers then are more likely to interpret the sale price with respect to the MSRP which, if favorable, should increase perceived value of the offer and likelihood of purchase.[103]

## Consumer Inferences

When it comes to marketing, "what you see is not what you get." That's because interpretation often requires consumers to make inferences. An **inference** *goes beyond what is directly stated or presented.* Consumers use available data *and* their own ideas to draw conclusions about information that is not provided.

**Quality Signals**     Inferences are as numerous and divergent as consumers themselves. However, some inferences related to product quality are relatively consistent across consumers. Here consumers use their own experiences and knowledge to draw inferences about product quality based on a nonquality cue.

*Price-perceived quality* is an inference based on the popular adage "you get what you pay for." Consumers often infer that higher-priced brands possess higher quality than do lower-priced brands.[104] Consumers sometimes take price discounts as a signal of lower quality, which is a major concern for companies such as General Motors who rely heavily on such tactics.[105]

*Advertising intensity* is also a quality signal. Consumers tend to infer that more heavily advertised brands are higher quality.[106] One reason is that effort is believed to predict success, and ad spending is seen as an indicator of effort. Any factor related to advertising expense such as medium, use of color, and repetition, can increase quality perceptions and choice.[107]

*Warranties* are another quality signal, with longer warranties generally signaling higher quality. Consumers infer that a firm wouldn't offer a longer warranty if it weren't confident in the quality of its products, since honoring the warranty would be expensive.[108]

Price, advertising, and warranties are just a few quality cues. Others include *country of origin (COO),* in which consumers interpret products more positively when they are manufactured in a country they perceive positively,[109] as well as *brand* effects, where well-known brands are perceived as higher quality than are unknown brands.

In general, quality signals operate more strongly when consumers lack the expertise to make informed judgments on their own, when consumer motivation or interest in the decision is low, and when other quality-related information is lacking.

**Interpreting Images**    Consumer inferences from visual images are becoming increasingly important as advertisers increase their use of visual imagery.[110] Note how visuals dominate many print ads. For example, Clinique ran an ad that pictured a tall, clear glass of mineral water and ice cubes. A large slice of lime was positioned on the lip of the glass. In the glass with the ice cubes and mineral water were a tube of Clinique lipstick and a container of cheek base. Nothing else appeared in the ad. *What does this mean?*

Obviously, in order to interpret the Clinique ad, consumers must infer meaning. Until recently, pictures in ads were thought to convey reality. If so, the Clinique ad is nonsensical. Is Clinique guilty of ineffective advertising? No. All of us intuitively recognize that pictures do more than represent reality; they supply meaning. Thus, one interpretation of the Clinique ad is "Clinique's new summer line of makeup is as refreshing as a tall glass of soda with a twist."

The verbal translation of the meaning conveyed by images is generally incomplete and inadequate. A picture is worth a thousand words not just because it may convey reality more efficiently than words but because it may convey meanings that words cannot adequately express.

Marketers must understand the meanings their audiences assign to various images and words, and use them in combination to construct messages that will convey the desired meaning. They must be sensitive to cultural differences since interpretation is highly contingent on shared cultural experience. For example, consumers in some cultures (termed high-context cultures) tend to "read between the lines." These consumers are very sensitive to cues in the communications setting such as tone of voice. On the other hand, consumers in low-context cultures tend to ignore such cues and focus more on the message's literal or explicit meaning. A recent study finds that consumers in high-context cultures such as the Philippines are more likely to infer implicit meanings from ad visuals than are those in low-context cultures such as the United States.[111] Illustration 8–10 is an example of an ad based heavily on imagery. *What does this ad mean to you? Would it mean the same to older consumers? Consumers from other cultures?*

**Missing Information and Ethical Concerns**    When data about an attribute are missing, consumers may assign it a value based on a presumed relationship between that attribute and one for which data are available; they may assign it the average of their assessments of the available attributes; they may assume it to be weaker than the attributes for which data are supplied; or any of a large number of other strategies may be used.[112]

Consider the following hypothetical ad copy:

- The Subaru Outback gets better gas mileage than the Pontiac Aztek.
- It has more cargo space than the Saturn VUE.
- It has more power than the Toyota RAV4.

Some consumers would infer from this that the Subaru gets better gas mileage than the VUE and the RAV4; has more cargo space than the Aztek and the RAV4; and has more power than the Aztek and the VUE.[113] These claims are not stated in the ad, making it clear that certain types of information portrayal may lead to incorrect inferences and suboptimal consumer decisions. Thus, a factually correct ad could still mislead some consumers. *Are such ads ethical?*

As we saw in the opening example, consumers can be misled in a number of different ways. One way is that companies can make *direct claims* that are false. Claiming that something is mushroom in origin when it is really a fungus or mold appears to fall into this category. This is the easiest form of deception to detect and prosecute under the law. However, other types of deception are more subtle. These fall under the broad category of *claim-belief discrepancies,* whereby a communication leads consumers to believe something about the product that is not true even though it doesn't present a direct false claim. For example, the Federal Trade Commission (FTC) felt that Kraft Foods' early ads for Kraft Cheese Singles might be misleading based on claim-belief discrepancy. That's because their ads focused on the importance of calcium and the fact that each slice was made from 5 ounces of milk. The FTC's concern was that reasonable consumers would infer that Kraft Cheese Singles contained the same amount of calcium as five ounces of milk even though this was not directly stated in their ads. This inference is wrong since processing milk into cheese reduces calcium content. Since parents might use Kraft Cheese Singles as a calcium source for their kids, this was of particular concern. Although more difficult from a legal standpoint, the FTC can and does hold companies responsible for claim-belief discrepancies as we see with Kraft.[114] Our understanding and regulation of deception continues to evolve as we gain a better understanding of consumer information processing. This is discussed in more detail in Chapter 20.

# PERCEPTION AND MARKETING STRATEGY

Perception holds critical implications for marketing strategy in a number of areas. We turn to these next.

## Retail Strategy

Retailers often use exposure very effectively. Store interiors are designed with frequently purchased items (canned goods, fresh fruits and vegetables, meats) separated so that the average consumer will travel through more of the store. This increases total exposure. High-margin items are often placed in high-traffic areas to capitalize on increased exposure.

Shelf position and amount of shelf space influence which items and brands are allocated attention. Point-of-purchase displays also attract attention and boost sales.[115] And **cross-promotions,** whereby signage in one area of the store promotes complementary products in another (milk signage in the cookie aisle), can also be effective. Recently, retailers have begun to reduce clutter by cutting out marginal, unimportant, and redundant SKUs (stock keeping units—individual items such as brands, sizes, and versions) within a category. Consumer perceptions and sales tend to go up when the reduction in clutter does not reduce variety and choice.[116]

Another important aspect of the retail environment is *ambient scent*. Pleasant smells in a retail store can increase product evaluations by boosting emotions. In some cases this occurs even when the scent is inconsistent with the product being evaluated (e.g., pine scent and orange juice).

## Brand Name and Logo Development

Shakespeare notwithstanding, marketers do not believe that "a rose by any other name would smell as sweet." Mountain Dew's marketing director ascribes part of the success of Code Red to its name: "Had it been called 'Mountain Dew Cherry' it would've done very differently."[117] Brand names can influence anything from color preference to food taste. One study found that people preferred avocado to light green even though the actual color was exactly the same. Another found that young kids liked the taste of foods such as carrots, milk, and apple juice more when they came in a McDonald's package![118] Effects such as this can be related back to expectation biases. That is, the name sets up an expectation which, in turn, biases people's perceptions of the actual experience. Given the tendency toward global brands, it is easy to imagine how complex creating an appropriate name can be.[119]

**Linguistic Considerations**    Sometimes brand names start out having no inherent meaning, but gain associations over time as consumers gain experience with them. Ford and Toyota are examples. However, marketers increasingly tap into linguistic characteristics of words to create brand names with inherent meaning right from the start. One aspect is inherent *semantic meaning* or *morpheme*. NutraSweet took advantage of morphemes to imply nutritious and sweet. And Dodge has brought back its "Hemi" engine, a name associated with high performance.[120] A second aspect is sound or *phonemes*. Sounds of letters and words can symbolize product attributes. For example, heavier sounding vowels (Frosh) might be better used to suggest richer creamier ice cream than lighter sounding vowels (Frish).[121]

Lexicon and other naming companies such as NameLab use these concepts to create names that convey appropriate meanings. Lexicon selected the Blackberry name for Research in Motion's handheld device because Berry suggests small, the "b" sound is associated strongly with relaxation, and the two "b" sounds at the beginning of black and berry are light and crisp, suggesting speed. Thus, a name that suggests a handheld that is small, easy to use, and fast—every consumer's dream![122]

**Branding Strategies**    Marketers engage in numerous strategies to leverage strong existing brand names. One is **brand extension** where an existing brand extends to a new

FIGURE 8–5    **Logos Influence the Image Consumers Have of Firms**

| Name Only | Rated Very High | Name and Logo | Rated Very High | Percent Change |
|---|---|---|---|---|
| UPS | 68% | UPS | 58% | −15% |
| FedEx | 67 | FedEx | 50 | −25 |
| Federal Express | 62 | FEDERAL EXPRESS | 68 | +10 |
| United States Postal Service | 53 | UNITED STATES POSTAL SERVICE | 54 | +2 |

Note: The percentage shown on the Name and Logo columns is average top-box ratings ("agree strongly") within a 5-point rating scale on the image contribution attributes, based only on respondents who are aware of the company or brand.

category with the same name such as Levi Strauss putting its Levi name on a line of upscale men's suits. Another is **co-branding,** an alliance in which two brands are put together on a single product. An example is "Intel Inside" Compaq computers. Brand extensions and co-branding can be positive or negative, as we'll discuss in Chapter 9. A key issue is *perceived fit* between the core brand and the extension or the two co-brands. Really poor fit (too much incongruity) is bad, as people find it hard to categorize and make sense of the new brand. For example, the Levi men's suit was a flop because the core Levi image of relaxed and casual did not fit a formal, upscale suit.[123]

Logo Design and Typographics    How a product or service name is presented—its *logo*—is also important.[124] Figure 8–5 shows the additional positive or negative impact the graphic part of a logo can have on the image associated with a name. Image was an overall measure based on such attributes as "trustworthy" and "high quality." One rating was obtained from consumers who saw only the company name; the second was in response to the full logo including the name.[125] *What advice would you offer these firms?*

Perhaps in trying to answer this last question, you realized that you don't have any criteria for making suggestions. Such criteria are hard to come by and we are just now beginning to understand why some logos work better than others. One study provides guidance, finding that logo symbols (such as Prudential's Rock) which are natural, moderately elaborate, and symmetrically balanced lead to higher levels of logo liking. *Natural* logos depict commonly experienced objects; *elaborate* logos entail complexity; *symmetrical* logos are visually balanced.

Beyond the logo symbol is also the shape and form of the letters in their name which relates to typeface and type font. Intuitively, for example, you might think that a fancy *scripted* font signals elegance and is better suited for a fountain pen than for a mountain bike. Turns out you would be right! Different fonts do evoke different meanings and an appropriate fit between the font and product can increase choice of the brand, independent of the name.[126] *Given these various criteria, can you now make suggestions to the firms?*[127]

# Media Strategy

The explosion of media alternatives makes it difficult and expensive to gain exposure to key target audiences.[128] However, the fact that the exposure process is often selective rather than random is the underlying basis for effective media strategies. Specifically, firms must determine to which media the consumers in the target market are most frequently exposed and place ad messages in those media. As one executive stated:

> We must look increasingly for matching media that will enable us best to reach carefully targeted, emerging markets. The rifle approach rather than the old shotgun.[129]

Consumer involvement can drive media exposure and strategy. For high-involvement products, ads should be placed in media outlets with content relevant to the product. Specialized media such as *Runner's World* or *Vogue* tend to attract readers who are interested in and receptive to ads for related products. In contrast, ads for low-involvement products should be placed in reputable media independent of content, as long as it is frequented by the target market.[130] In a situation such as this, the marketer must find media that the target market is interested in and place the advertising message in those media. Target markets as defined by age, ethnic group, social class, or stage in the family life cycle have differing media preferences which can then be used to select media outlets. Table 8–1 illustrates selective exposure to several magazines based on demographic characteristics.

As we saw earlier, video game player demographics skew toward young males (for console games, average age is 26 and 68 percent are male). Companies like Burger King, who are desperate to obtain media exposure among this demographic, are moving ad dollars to in-game video ads and product placements.[131]

| Demographic Characteristics | Better Homes & Gardens | Cosmopolitan | Maxim | National Geographic | Family Circle |
|---|---|---|---|---|---|
| **Gender** | | | | | |
| Male | 24 | 20 | 186 | 120 | 11 |
| Female | 152 | 154 | 42 | 86 | 161 |
| **Age** | | | | | |
| 18–24 | 36 | 296 | 274 | 52 | 32 |
| 25–34 | 60 | 149 | 223 | 58 | 55 |
| 35–44 | 76 | 113 | 113 | 77 | 76 |
| 45–54 | 104 | 83 | 62 | 112 | 93 |
| 55–64 | 145 | 45 | 25 | 120 | 131 |
| 65 and over | 142 | 26 | 10 | 149 | 129 |
| **Education** | | | | | |
| College graduate | 94 | 105 | 118 | 116 | 73 |
| High school graduate | 107 | 94 | 100 | 81 | 118 |
| **Household income** | | | | | |
| Less than $25,000 | 90 | 97 | 61 | 94 | 112 |
| $25,000–$49,999 | 105 | 99 | 96 | 100 | 109 |
| $50,000–$59,999 | 100 | 103 | 122 | 104 | 105 |
| $60,000–$74,999 | 101 | 96 | 146 | 104 | 90 |
| $75,000 or more | 105 | 104 | 121 | 103 | 80 |

**TABLE 8–1**

Selective Exposure to Magazines Based on Demographic Characteristics

Note: 100 represents an average level of usage, purchase, or consumption.

Source: Simmons Market Research Bureau, 2006.

Technology continues to radically alter media targeting choices. Consider the impact of GPS technology on outdoor mobile ads:

> While a cab travels from one end of a city to the other, an electronic billboard on top changes according to location and time of day. Thanks to a satellite feed and Global Positioning System, the bright, attention-getting ads on the taxi roof keep changing. As the cab passes by a college, an ad for a bookstore appears. While the cab moves through the business district at noon, an ad for a local deli fills the screen. As the cab travels through a Hispanic neighborhood, a Spanish-language ad for a snack food is shown.[132]

## Advertisements

Advertisements must perform two critical tasks—capture attention and convey meaning. Unfortunately, the techniques appropriate for accomplishing one task are often counterproductive for the other.

What if you had to design a campaign to increase users for your firm's toilet bowl freshener but research shows your target market has little inherent interest in the product. What do you do? Two strategies seem reasonable. One is to *utilize stimulus characteristics* such as bright colors or surrealism to attract attention. The second is to *tie the message to a topic in which the target market is interested.*

However, using factors unrelated to the product category to attract attention must be done with caution. First, it may detract attention away from the core brand message since stimuli compete for limited attention. That's why companies often try to use humor, sex appeal, and celebrities in ways that are relevant to the product or message. Second, it may negatively affect *interpretation.* For example, humor in an insurance ad may result in the brand's being interpreted as unreliable.

## Package Design and Labeling

Packages must attract attention and convey information, and various aspects from color to shape to typography can interact in complex ways in affecting consumer perceptions.[133] Packaging has functional and perceptual components. Consider the candy coating of M&M's. It is functional because it keeps the chocolate from melting in your hands. But it is also perceptual. The bright colors are interesting and unique even though they don't taste different. One study varied the color variety (7 versus 10 colors) in a bowl of M&M's and found that as variety went up, consumers ate more![134] M&M's has refocused on color by introducing bolder colors and emphasizing color in its ads. As one executive states, "We've always had color as a unique point of difference, but we wanted to reinforce that message in a fresh, contemporary way."[135]

Bright colors, tall packages, and unusual shapes can be used to attract attention, convey meaning, and influence consumption.[136] For example, consumers tend to believe that taller, more elongated packages contain more than shorter packages of the same volume (e.g., a can of soda). As a consequence, a recent study shows that consumers of beverages buy fewer bottles than cans, but perceive that the volume they buy is the same. Notice how package options such as an elongated bottle can influence perceived consumption in ways that reduce product sales and revenues.[137] Look at Illustration 8–11. Which appears to contain more? If you said Acqua Panna, you were influenced by the elongation bias (they all contain exactly the same amount of liquid: 1 liter).

Packages also contain product information and warnings. Ethical and legal considerations require marketers to place warning labels on a wide array of products such as cigarettes, alcoholic beverages, and many over-the-counter drugs. On the one hand, there is the desire to effectively alert users to potential risks. On the other hand, there is a desire to avoid detracting unduly from product image. The key from an ethical and legal standpoint is to not err on the side of image at the expense of the consumer. Well-designed warnings appear to be at least somewhat effective. Factors reducing their effectiveness include overly technical or complex language and a failure to indicate the positive consequences of compliance.[138]

## SUMMARY

Perception consists of those activities by which an individual acquires and assigns meaning to stimuli. Perception begins with *exposure*. This occurs when a stimulus comes within range of one of an individual's primary sensory receptors. People are exposed to only a small fraction of the available stimuli, and this is usually the result of self-selection, as evidenced by high levels of *ad avoidance*. Marketers try to overcome avoidance by using tactics such as *product placement* and *hybrid ads*.

*Attention* occurs when the stimulus activates one or more of the sensory receptors and the resulting sensations go into the brain for processing. People *selectively attend* to stimuli as a function of stimulus, individual, and situational factors. *Stimulus factors* are physical characteristics of the stimulus itself, such as contrast, size, intensity, attractiveness, color, movement, position, isolation, format, and information quantity. *Individual factors* are characteristics of the individual, such as motivation and ability. *Situational factors* include stimuli in the environment other than the focal stimulus and temporary characteristics of the individual that are induced by the environment. Clutter and program involvement are situational factors of particular interest to marketers.

*Nonfocused attention* occurs when a person takes in information without deliberate effort. *Hemispheric lateralization* is a term applied to activities that take place on each side of the brain. The left side of the brain is concerned primarily with those activities typically called rational thought and the ability to be conscious and report what is happening. The right side of the brain deals with pictorial, geometric, timeless, and nonverbal information without the individual's being able to verbally report it.

A message presented so fast or so softly or so masked by other messages that one is not aware of seeing or hearing it is called a *subliminal message.* Subliminal messages have generated a great deal of interest but are not generally thought to affect brand choice or other aspects of consumer behavior in a meaningful way.

*Interpretation* is the assignment of meaning to stimuli that have been attended to. Interpretation tends to be relative rather than absolute (perceptual relativity) and subjective rather than objective. Two general forms of interpretation are cognitive and affective. *Cognitive interpretation* appears to involve a process whereby new stimuli are placed into existing categories of meaning. *Affective interpretation* is the emotional or feeling response triggered by the stimulus.

Interpretation is largely a function of individual traits, learning, and expectations that are triggered by the stimulus and moderated by the situation. Stimulus characteristics are critical. *Stimulus organization* is the physical arrangement of the stimulus objects and relates to the perceptual principles of *proximity, closure,* and *figure–ground.* Marketers can use these principles to design effective communication strategies. *Stimulus change* and consumer reactions to it are also of concern and have consequences in relation to such strategies as "weighting out," whereby marketers attempt to reduce the quantity offered in increments that consumers won't detect.

Interpretation often involves consumer inferences. *Inferences* go beyond what is directly stated or presented and help explain consumer use of *quality signals* (e.g., higher price means higher quality), their *interpretation of images,* and how they deal with *missing information.* Inferences also help explain how consumers can be misled by marketing messages even when those messages are *literally* true.

Marketers use their knowledge of perception to enhance strategies in a number of areas including media, retailing, branding, advertising, and package design.

## KEY TERMS

Ad avoidance  280
Adaptation level theory  289
Affective interpretation  294
Ambush marketing  297
Attention  283
Brand extension  303
Brand familiarity  291
Closure  298
Co-branding  304
Cognitive interpretation  294
Contextual cues  296
Cross-promotions  303

Exposure  279
Figure–ground  299
Hemispheric lateralization  292
Inference  300
Infomercials  282
Information overload  290
Information processing  278
Interpretation  293
Just noticeable difference
 (j.n.d.)  299
Muting  280
Perception  278

Perceptual defenses  279
Perceptual relativity  293
Permission-based marketing  283
Product placement  280
Proximity  297
Rhetorical figures  297
Sensory discrimination  299
Smart banners  290
Stimulus organization  297
Subliminal stimulus  293
Zapping  280
Zipping  280

## INTERNET EXERCISES

1. Examine several magazines. Copy two ads that do a good job of encouraging the reader to visit a Web site. Justify your selection using the principles of perception described in this chapter.

2. Visit one of the following Web sites. Evaluate the site on the principles of perception covered in this chapter.
   a. www.vonage.com
   b. www.skyy.com

*c.* www.toyota.com

*d.* www.cyberpet.com

3. Visit several company Web sites until you find one that you feel makes effective use of the principles of perception that we have covered and one that violates these principles. Provide the URL of each and justify your selections.

4. Visit the following blog (or other sites if you can find them) which track and comment on recent product placements (http://movieproductplacement.blogspot .com/). What comments and evaluations are being made about the placements? What criteria do people seem to be using to evaluate the placement? Do these seem to match those presented in the chapter?

## DDB LIFE STYLE STUDY™ DATA ANALYSES

1. Examine the DDB data in Tables 1B through 7B. What characterizes a person who *avoids buying products advertised on shows with sex or violence*? Why is this the case? What does it suggest about the importance of *programming context*?

## REVIEW QUESTIONS

1. What is *information processing*? How does it differ from *perception*?
2. What is meant by *exposure*? What determines which stimuli an individual will be exposed to? How do marketers utilize this knowledge?
3. What are *zipping, zapping,* and *muting*? Why are they a concern to marketers?
4. What are *infomercials*? How effective are they?
5. What is *ad avoidance*? How is *DVR technology* affecting it? How are marketers dealing with this phenomenon?
6. What is meant by *attention*? What determines which stimuli an individual will attend to? How do marketers utilize this?
7. What stimulus factors can be used to attract attention? What problems can arise when stimulus factors are used to attract attention?
8. What is *adaptation level theory*?
9. What is *information overload*? How should marketers deal with information overload?
10. What impact does *program involvement* have on the attention paid to commercials embedded in the program?
11. What is a *contextual cue*? Why is it of interest to marketers?
12. What is meant by *nonfocused attention*?
13. What is meant by *hemispheric lateralization*?
14. What is meant by *subliminal perception*? Is it a real phenomenon? Is it effective?

15. What is meant by *interpretation*?
16. What determines how an individual will interpret a given stimulus?
17. What is the difference between *cognitive* and *affective* interpretation?
18. What is the difference between *semantic* and *psychological* meaning?
19. What is *sensory discrimination*? What is a *just noticeable difference (j.n.d.)*?
20. What is a *consumer inference*? Why is this of interest to marketers?
21. How does a knowledge of information processing assist the manager in the following?
    *a.* Formulating retail strategy
    *b.* Developing brand names and logos
    *c.* Formulating media strategy
    *d.* Designing advertisements
    *e.* Package design and labels
22. What is *co-branding*? Is it effective?
23. What is a *cross-promotion* retail strategy? Provide two examples.
24. How can *rhetorical figures* enhance attention?
25. What is a *smart banner*? How does this relate to selective attention?
26. What is *figure–ground*?
27. What ethical concerns arise in applying knowledge of the perceptual process?
28. What is *ambush marketing*?

## DISCUSSION QUESTIONS

29. Given that smoking scenes in movies increase the positive image and intention to smoke among youth, what regulations, if any, should apply to this?

30. How could a marketing manager for the following use the material in this chapter to guide the development of a national advertising campaign (choose one)? To assist local retailers or organizations in developing their promotional activities? Would the usefulness of this material be limited to advertising decisions?
    a. Boys and Girls Clubs of America
    b. Cell phones
    c. Qdoba Mexican Grill
    d. Lucky Jeans
    e. Belkin WiFi equipment

31. Respond to the questions in Consumer Insight 8–1.

32. Hershey recently created a line of upscale chocolates called "Cacao Reserve *by Hershey's*." The company created fancy packaging, priced the product at the high end, and did little mass marketing for its new product. Initial sales were disappointingly slow even though the premium chocolate market is growing nicely, with brands like Ghirardelli faring well. As a consequence, Hershey almost immediately (within six months) dropped its prices and started mass advertising. Using concepts in this chapter, why do you think Hershey failed in its move into the premium chocolate market? Do you think the adjustments were the most appropriate, or could Hershey have taken other steps?

33. Pick three brand names that utilize a *morphemic* approach and three that utilize a *phonetic* approach. Are the morphemes and phonetics consistent with the overall positioning of these brands?

34. Develop a brand name for (*a*) an MP3 player, (*b*) an R&B music store, (*c*) an Internet grocery shopping service, (*d*) a national magazine for adults over 50, or (*e*) a pet-walking service. Justify your name.

35. Develop a logo for (*a*) an MP3 player, (*b*) an R&B music store, (*c*) an Internet grocery shopping service, (*d*) a national magazine for adults over 50, or (*e*) a pet-walking service. Justify your design.

36. Evaluate the in-text ads in Illustrations 8–1 through 8–10. Analyze the attention-attracting characteristics and the meaning they convey. Are they good ads? What risks are associated with each?

37. Develop three co-branded products: one that would be beneficial to both individual brands, one that would benefit one brand but not the other, and one that would benefit neither brand. Explain your logic.

38. Respond to the questions in Consumer Insight 8–2.

39. Find an ad that you feel might mislead consumers through a *claim–belief discrepancy*. What inference processes are you assuming?

## APPLICATION ACTIVITIES

40. Find and copy or describe examples of advertisements that specifically use stimulus factors to attract attention. Look for examples of each of the various factors discussed earlier in the chapter, and try to find their use in a variety of promotions. For each example, evaluate the effectiveness of the stimulus factors used.

41. Repeat Question 40, but this time look for advertisements using individual factors.

42. Complete Question 34, and test your names on a sample of students. Justify your testing procedure, and report your results.

43. Complete Question 35 and test your logos on a sample of students. Justify your testing procedure and report your results.

44. Find two brand names that you feel are particularly appropriate and two that you feel are not very appropriate. Explain your reasoning for each name.

45. Find and describe a logo that you feel is particularly appropriate and one that you feel is not very appropriate. Explain your reasoning.

46. Interview three students with a DVR about their behavior during television breaks when watching prerecorded programming. Do they watch any ads? Why? What do you conclude?

47. Interview three students about how they respond to banner ads and the extent to which they attend to various commercial messages on the Internet.

48. Go to a health food or alternative medicines store or section of a store. Find three products that make

health claims. Evaluate the likely effectiveness of any disclaimers that they contain.

49. Find and copy or describe an ad or other marketing message that you think makes unethical use of the perceptual process. Justify your selection.

50. Develop an ad but omit information about some key product attributes. Show the ad to five students.

After they have looked at the ad, give them a questionnaire that asks about the attributes featured in the ad and about the missing attributes. If they provide answers concerning the missing attributes, ask them how they arrived at these answers. What do you conclude?

## REFERENCES

1. Chapter 8 opener is based on K. Weisberg, "Vegetarian Delight," *Foodservice Director,* October 15, 2004; "Gardenburger Takes a Stand against Deceptive Labeling," corporate press release, April 10, 2002; and additional information from Gardenburger's corporate Web site, www.gardenburger.com, including a "Roper ASW Study," March 15, 2002.

2. For an interesting discussion, see J. J. Pilotta and D. Schultz, "Simultaneous Media Experience and Synesthesia," *Journal of Advertising Research,* March 2005, pp. 19–26.

3. R. Liljenwall, "Global Trends in Point-of-Purchase Advertising," in *The Power of Point-of-Purchase Advertising,* ed. R. Liljenwall (Washington, DC: Point-of-Purchase Advertising International, 2004), chap. 10.

4. "Ad Avoidance Highest among Key Target Groups, Says Study," *Businessline,* October 21, 2004, p. 1.

5. S. M. Edwards, H. Li, and J.-H. Lee, "Forced Exposure and Psychological Reactance," *Journal of Advertising,* Fall 2002, pp. 83–95; H. Li, S. M. Edwards, and J.-H. Lee, "Measuring the Intrusiveness of Advertisements," *Journal of Advertising,* Summer 2002, pp. 37–47; S. Shavitt, P. Vargas, and P. Lowrey, "Exploring the Pole of Memory for Self-Selected Ad Experiences," *Psychology & Marketing,* December 2004, pp. 1011–32; and C. H. Cho and H. J. Cheon, "Why Do People Avoid Advertising on the Internet?" *Journal of Advertising,* Winter 2004, pp. 89–97.

6. A. C. B. Tse and R. P. W. Lee, "Zapping Behavior during Commercial Breaks," *Journal of Advertising Research,* May 2001, pp. 25–28; M. Savage, "China Turning On, but Tuning Out," *Media,* May 7, 2004, p. 19.

7. P. Paul, "Coming Soon: More Ads Tailored to Your Tastes," *American Demographics,* August 2001, pp. 28–31.

8. Edwards, Li, and Lee, "Forced Exposure and Psychological Reactance."

9. "Pop-Ups—End of an Era?" *NOP World United Business Media,* www.unitedbusinessmedia.com, September 29, 2003.

10. R. Ferraro and R. J. Avery, "Brand Appearances on Prime-Time Television," *Journal of Current Issues and Research in Advertising,* Fall 2000, pp. 1–25; C. A. Russell, "Investigating the Effectiveness of Product Placements in Television Shows," *Journal of Consumer Research,* December 2002, pp. 306–18; S. A. McKechnie and J. Zhou, "Product Placement in Movies," *International Journal of Advertising* 22, no. 3 (2003), pp. 349–74.

11. "Ad Spots in the DVD Era," *Broadcast Engineering,* August 2007, p. 106; and "DVR Viewers Play Catch-up Quickly Says Palisades MediaGroup," *Business Wire,* December 11, 2007.

12. R. Greenspan, "DVRs Not Necessarily Ad-Killers," *ClickZ.com,* May 24, 2004; "Jupiter: DVR Ad Skipping Threatens $8B in Advertising," *MarketingVOX.com,* May 4, 2006; "Ad Spots in the DVD Era; and R. Dana and S. Kang, "Answer to Vexing Question: Who's Not Watching Ads," *The Wall Street Journal,* October 17, 2007, p. B2.

13. J. Mandese, "Study: DVRs 'Recapture' 96% of TV Ad Zapping," *MediaPost's Media Daily News,* May 25, 2004, www.mediapost.com; "New Age for Ads," *Cablefax Daily,* December 6, 2007, www.cablefax.com H. Dawley, "As to Worries Over Ad-Skipping, Skip It," *Media Life Research* www.medialifemagazine.com, May 18, 2006.

14. A. Ambruster, "Don't Give Up on TV Ads Just Yet," *Television-Week,* July 23–30, 2007, p. 16.

15. B. A. S. Martin, V. T. L. Nguyen, and J.-Y. Wi, "Remote Control Marketing," *Marketing Intelligence and Planning* 20, no. 1 (2002), pp. 44–48.

16. See D. Kiley, "Learning to Love the Dreaded TiVo," *BusinessWeek,* April 17, 2006, p. 88; C. Limbardi, "TV Advertising's DVR Challenge," *News.com,* May 23, 2006; K Ritchi, "Fast-Forwarding Is So Passe Advertisers Want in on DVR and Providers Are Finally Listening," *Boards,* January 2007, p. 13; B. Steinberg, "In the End, It's the Last Ad in a Pod They Recall," *Television Week,* June 11, 2007, p. 13; and S. Vranica, "New Ads Take on TiVo," *The Wall Street Journal,* October 5, 2007, p. B4.

17. D. Goetzl and W. Friedman, "ABC Looks Beyond Upfront to DVR, Commercial Ratings Issues," *MediaPostPublications,* mediapost.com, July 6, 2006.

18. L. Story, "A Variation on the DVR, Without Ad Skipping," *The New York Times,* nytimes.com, August 13, 2007.

19. The Adidas outdoor efforts found in the following: "Adidas and Guerrilla Marketing," *Outdoor Advertising Blog,* 1outdooradvertising.blogspot.com, August 13, 2007; and "Giant Adidas Ad," *Advertising Age,* June 5, 2006, p. 15.

20. T. L. Stanley, "Advergames, Content Role Juice up Marketer's Game," *Advertising Age,* February 6, 2006, p. S-3; see also L. Schneider, "Cashing in on Crashes via Brand Placement in Computer Games," *International Journal of Advertising* 24 no. 3 (pp. 321–43).

21. P. Lehman, "Mad Ave Clicks with the Gamers," *IN,* November 2007, p. 28; and "Interactive Marketing and Media Fact Pack," *Advertising Age,* 2006, p. 46.

22. Liljenwall, "Global Trends in Point-of-Purchase Advertising."

23. M. Singh, S. K. Balasubramanian, and G. Chakraborty, "A Comparative Analysis of Three Communication Formats," *Journal of Advertising,* Winter 2000, pp. 59–75.

24. M. T. Elliot and P. S. Speck, "Antecedents and Consequences of Infomercials," *Journal of Direct Marketing,* Spring 1995, pp. 39–51.

25. R. Park, "Consumers Kick the Tires on the Web before They Drive New Cars off the Lot," *iMedia Connection.com,* September 23, 2004, imediaconnection.com.

26. "DoubleClick's 2004 Consumer Email Study," October 2004, www.doubleckick.com.

27. A. Z. Cuneo, "Wireless Giants Leap into Third-Screen Marketing," *Advertising Age,* September 11, 2006, p. 39.

28. "Farm Ads Win Golden Fleece," *Stars and Stripes,* July 10, 1984, p. 6.

29. S. Thompson, "Media Recipe," *Advertising Age,* October 23, 2000, p. 42.

30. K. Bouffard, "Analyst Says Grocers' Cut in Shelf Space for Orange Juice Hurts Citrus Sales," *Knight Ridder Tribune Business News,* July 22, 2004, p. 1.

31. M. Rappaport, "Food Product Makers Secure Supermarket Shelf Space by Paying Slotting Fees," *Knight Ridder Tribune Business News,* January 14, 2004, p. 1.

32. X. Drèze and F. Xavier Hussherr, "Internet Advertising," *Journal of Interactive Marketing,* Autumn 2003, pp. 8–23; "A Not-So-Banner Year," *Marketing News,* April 29, 2002, p. 3; and H. Robinson, A. Wysocka, and C. Hand, "Internet Advertising Effectiveness," *International Journal of Advertising* 26, no. 4 (2007), pp. 527–41.

33. G. L. Lohse, "Consumer Eye Movement Patterns on Yellow Pages Advertising," *Journal of Advertising,* Spring 1997, pp. 61–73; A. M. Abernethy and D. N. Laband, "The Customer Pulling Power of Different-sized Yellow Pages Advertisements," *Journal of Advertising Research,* May–June 2002, pp. 66–72; and A. M. Abernethy and D. N. Laband, "The Impact of Trademarks and Advertising Size on Yellow Page Call Rates," *Journal of Advertising Research,* March 2004, pp. 119–25.

34. J. R. Rossiter and R. B. Silberstein, "Brain-Imaging Detection of Visual Scene Encoding in Long-Term Memory for TV Commercials," *Journal of Advertising Research,* March 2001, pp. 13–21. See also S. L. Crites, Jr., and S. N. Aikman-Eckenrode, "Making Inferences Concerning Physiological Responses," *Journal of Advertising Research,* March 2001, p. 25; and J. R. Rossiter et al., "So What?" *Journal of Advertising Research,* May 2001, pp. 59–61.

35. C.-H. Cho, J.-G. Lee, and M. Tharp, "Different Forced-Exposure Levels to Banner Ads," *Journal of Advertising Research,* July 2001, pp. 45–54; and W. W. Moe, "A Field Experiment to Assess the Interruption Effect of Pop-Up Promotions," *Journal of Interactive Marketing,* Winter 2006, pp. 34–44.

36. R. Pieters, E. Rosbergen, and M. Wedel, "Visual Attention to Repeated Print Advertising," *Journal of Marketing Research,* November 1999, pp. 424–38.

37. R. Pieters and M. Wedel, "Attention Capture and Transfer in Advertising," *Journal of Marketing,* April 2004, pp. 36–50.

38. S. N. Singh et al., "Does Your Ad Have Too Many Pictures?" *Journal of Advertising Research,* January 2000, pp. 11–27.

39. P. J. Danaher, G. W. Mullarkey, and S. Essegaier, "Factors Affecting Web Site Visit Duration," *Journal of Marketing Research,* May 2006, pp. 182–94.

40. Pieters and Wedel, "Attention Capture and Transfer in Advertising."

41. *What the Eye Does Not See, the Mind Does Not Remember,* Telecom Research, Inc., undated.

42. G. J. Gorn, A. Chattopadhyay, T. Yi, and D. W. Dahl, "Effects of Color as an Executional Cue in Advertising," *Management Science,* October 1997, pp. 1387–99.

43. L. Haugen and C. Weems, "P-O-P Advertising Design and Creativity," in *The Power of Point-of-Purchase Advertising,* chap. 6.

44. L. Rostoks, "Sales from POP Advertising Are Measureable," *Canadian Grocer,* July–August 2001, p. 19; and J. McCarthy, "Point of Purchase Last Chance to Dance," *Marketing Magazine,* March 2004, p. 33.

45. C.-H. Cho, "How Advertising Works on the WWW," *Journal of Current Issues and Research in Advertising,* Spring 1999, pp. 33–49; see also S. S. Sunder and S. Kalyanaraman, "Arousal, Memory, and Impression-Formation Effects of Animation Speed in Web Advertising," *Journal of Advertising,* Spring 2004, pp. 7–17.

46. Lohse, "Consumer Eye Movement Patterns on Yellow Pages Advertising." See also K. V. Fernandez and D. L. Rosen, "The Effectiveness of Information and Color in Yellow Pages Advertising," *Journal of Advertising,* Summer 2000, pp. 62–73.

47. D. Alexander, "Food Industry Giants Spend Big Money for Prime Supermarket Shelf Space," *Knight Ridder Tribune Business News,* December 14, 2003, p. 1.

48. C. Garcia, V. Ponsoda, and H. Estebaranz, "Scanning Ads," *Advances in Consumer Research,* vol. 27, eds. S. J. Hoch and R. J. Meyer (Provo, UT: Association for Consumer Research, 2000), pp. 104–9.

49. Drèze and Hussherr, "Internet Advertising."

50. D. D. McAdams, "Is Anybody Paying Attention?" *Broadcasting and Cable,* August 7, 2000, p. 38.

51. See G. D. Olsen, "Creating the Contrast," *Journal of Advertising,* Winter 1995, pp. 29–44.

52. C. Janiszewski, "The Influence of Display Characteristics on Visual Exploratory Search Behavior," *Journal of Consumer Research,* December 1998, pp. 290–301.

53. A. Chattopadhyay, D. W. Dahl, R. J. B. Ritchie, and K. N. Shahin, "Hearing Voices," *Journal of Consumer Psychology* 13, no. 3 (2003), pp. 198–204.

54. J. Roumelis, "How to Get Noticed . . . Fast," *Marketing Magazine,* May 6, 2002, p. 26.

55. R. C. Goodstein, "Category-Based Applications and Extensions in Advertising," *Journal of Consumer Research,* June 1993, pp. 87–99; see also Y. H. Lee, "Manipulating Ad Message," *Journal of Advertising,* Summer 2000, pp. 29–43.

56. R. Pieters, L. Warlop, and M. Wedel, "Breaking through the Clutter," *Management Science,* June 2002, pp. 765–81.

57. "Signposts," *Advertising Age,* May 21, 2001, p. 3.

58. T. Elkin, "PVR Not Yet a Big Threat," *Advertising Age,* May 6, 2002, p. 55. See also L. F. Allwitt, "Effects of Interestingness

on Evaluations of TV Commercials," *Journal of Current Issues and Research in Advertising,* Spring 2000, pp. 41–53; and W. Friedman, "72.3% of PVR Viewers Skip Commercials," *AdAge.com,* July 2, 2002, www.adage.com.

59. J. W. Elpers, M. Wedel, and R. Pieters, "Why Do Consumers Stop Viewing Television Commercials?" *Journal of Marketing Research,* November 2003, pp. 437–53.

60. Pieters, Warlop, and Wedel, "Breaking through the Clutter"; and Elpers, Wedel, and Pieters, "Why Do Consumers Stop Viewing Television Commercials?"

61. B. Lee and W. Lee, "The Effect of Information Overload on Consumer Choice Quality in an On-Line Environment," *Psychology & Marketing,* March 2004, pp. 159–83.

62. Pieters and Wedel, "Attention Capture and Transfer in Advertising"; and R. Pieters and M. Wedel, "Goal Control of Attention to Advertising," *Journal of Consumer Research,* August 2007, pp. 224–33.

63. C.-H. Cho, "The Effectiveness of Banner Advertisements," *Journalism and Mass Communication Quarterly,* Autumn 2003, pp. 623–45.

64. See W. Dou, R. Linn, and S. Yang, "How Smart Are 'Smart Banners'?" *Journal of Advertising Research,* July 2001, pp. 31–43.

65. K. Oser, "Targeting Web Behavior Pays, American Airlines Study Says," *Advertising Age,* May 17, 2004, p. 8; see also L. Sherman and J. Deighton, "Banner Advertising," *Journal of Interactive Marketing,* Spring 2001, pp. 60–64.

66. A. M. Menon, A. D. Deshpande, M. Perri III, and G. M. Zinkhan, "Consumers' Attention to the Brief Summary in Print Direct-to-Consumer Advertisements," *Journal of Public Policy and Marketing,* Fall 2003, pp. 181–91.

67. M. Dahlen, "Banner Advertisements through a New Lens," *Journal of Advertising Research,* July 2001, pp. 23–30.

68. J. Spaeth, "Post-Promotion Evaluation," chap. 6, and Liljenwall, "Global Trends in Point-of-Purchase Advertising," chap. 10, both in *The Power of Point-of-Purchase Advertising.*

69. R. G. M. Pieters and T. H. A. Bijmolt, "Consumer Memory for Television Advertising," *Journal of Consumer Research,* March 1997, pp. 362–72; see also E. Riebe and J. Dawes, "Recall of Radio Advertising in Low and High Advertising Clutter Formats," *International Journal of Advertising* 25, no. 1 (2006), pp. 71–86.

70. "The Involvement Index," *Magazine Involvement Alliance,* 2004.

71. For more detail, see T. L. Chartrand, "The Role of Conscious Awareness in Consumer Behavior," *Journal of Consumer Psychology* 15, no. 3 (2005), pp. 203–10; A. Dijksterhuis and P. K. Smith, "What Do We Do Unconsciously?" *Journal of Consumer Psychology* 15, no. 3 (2005), pp. 225–29; and L. A. Peracchio and D. Luna, "The Role of Thin-Slice Judgments in Consumer Psychology," *Journal of Consumer Psychology* 16, no. 1 (2006), pp. 25–32.

72. H. E. Krugman, "Sustained Viewing of Television," *Journal of Advertising Research,* June 1980, p. 65; and H. E. Krugman, "Low Recall and High Recognition of Advertising," *Journal of Advertising Research,* February–March 1986, pp. 79–86.

73. Drèze and Hussherr, "Internet Advertising."

74. S. Shapiro, D. J. MacInnis, and S. E. Heckler, "The Effects of Incidental Ad Exposure on the Formation of Consideration Sets," *Journal of Consumer Research,* June 1997, pp. 94–104; and S. Shapiro, "When an Ad's Influence Is beyond Our Conscious Control," *Journal of Consumer Research,* June 1999, pp. 16–36.

75. W. B. Key, *Subliminal Seduction* (Englewood Cliffs, NJ: Prentice Hall, 1973); and W. B. Key, *Media Sexploitation* (Englewood Cliffs, NJ: Prentice Hall, 1976).

76. C. Trappey, "A Meta-Analysis of Consumer Choice and Subliminal Advertising," *Psychology & Marketing,* August 1996, pp. 517–30; S. J. Broyles, "Subliminal Advertising and the Perpetual Popularity of Playing to People's Paranoia, *Journal of Consumer Affairs* 40, no. 2 (2006), pp. 392–406. In contrast, see A. B. Aylesworth, R. C. Goodstein, and A. Kalra, "Effect of Archetypical Embeds on Feelings," *Journal of Advertising,* Fall 1999, pp. 73–81.

77. M. Rogers and C. A. Seiler, "The Answer Is No," *Journal of Advertising Research,* March 1994, pp. 36–45.

78. T. F. Stafford, "Alert or Oblivious?" *Psychology & Marketing,* September 2000, pp. 745–60.

79. See D. Grewal, K. B. Monroe, and R. Krishnan, "The Effects of Price-Comparison Advertising," *Journal of Marketing,* April 1998, pp. 46–59; and D. Grewal, R. Krishnan, J. Baker, and N. Borin, "The Effects of Store Name, Brand Name, and Price Discounts," *Journal of Retailing* 3 (1998), pp. 331–52.

80. M. Viswanathan and T. L. Childers, "Understanding How Product Attributes Influence Product Categorization," *Journal of Marketing Research,* February 1999, pp. 75–94; and J. Gregan-Paxton, S. Hoeffler, and M. Zhao, "When Categorization Is Ambiguous," *Journal of Consumer Psychology* 15, no. 2 (2005), pp. 127–40.

81. Goodstein, "Category-Based Applications and Extensions in Advertising."

82. G. P. Moreau, D. R. Lehmann, and A. B. Markman, "Entrenched Knowledge Structures and Consumer Responses to New Products," *Journal of Marketing Research,* February 2001, pp. 14–29; and G. Page Moreau, A. B. Markham, and D. R. Lehmann, "'What Is It?' Categorization Flexibility and Consumers' Responses to Really New Products," *Journal of Consumer Research,* March 2001, pp. 489–98.

83. J. Z. Sojka and J. L. Giese, "Thinking and/or Feeling," *Advances in Consumer Research,* vol. 24, eds. M. Bruck and D. J. MacInnis (Provo, UT: Association for Consumer Research, 1997), pp. 438–42; and J. A. Ruth, "Promoting a Brand's Emotional Benefits," *Journal of Consumer Psychology* 11, no. 2 (2001), pp. 99–113.

84. See S. Ratneshwar, "Goal-Derived Categories," *Journal of Consumer Psychology* 10, no. 3 (2001), pp. 147–57.

85. B. Turnbull and E. Matisoo-Smith, "Taste Sensitivity to 6-*n*-propylthiouracil Predicts Acceptance of Bitter-Tasting Spinach in 3–6-y-Old Children," *American Journal of Clinical Nutrition* 76 (2002), pp. 1101–5.

86. For a discussion, see J. E. Escalas, M. C. Moore, and J. E. Britton, "Fishing for Feelings?" *Journal of Consumer Psychology* 14, nos. 1 & 2 (2004), pp. 105–14.

87. R. Ahluwalia, R. E. Burnkrant, and H. R. Unnava, "Consumer Response to Negative Publicity," *Journal of Marketing Research,* May 2000, pp. 203–14.

88. M. C. Campbell, "Perceptions of Price Unfairness," *Journal of Marketing Research,* May 1999, pp. 187–99; see also L. Xia, K. B. Monroe, and J. L. Cox, "The Price Is Unfair!" *Journal of Marketing,* October 2004, pp. 1–15.

89. G. Tom et al., "Cueing the Consumer," *Journal of Consumer Marketing,* Spring 1987, pp. 23–27. See also D. S. Kempf and R. N. Laczniak, "Advertising's Influence on Subsequent Product Trial Processing," *Journal of Advertising,* Fall 2001, pp. 27–40.

90. See K. R. Evans et al., "How First Impressions of a Customer Impact Effectiveness in an Initial Sales Encounter," *Journal of the Academy of Marketing Science,* Fall 2000, pp. 512–26.

91. J. J. Inman, L. McAlister, and W. D. Hoyer, "Promotion Signal," *Journal of Consumer Research,* June 1990, pp. 74–81.

92. See M. G. Meloy, "Mood-Driven Distortion of Product Information," *Journal of Consumer Research,* December 2000, pp. 345–58.

93. G. J. Gorn, A. Chattopadhyay, J. Sengupta, and S. Tripathi, "Waiting for the Web," *Journal of Marketing Research,* May 2004, pp. 215–25.

94. "GF, Coke Tell Why They Shun TV News," *Advertising Age,* January 28, 1980, p. 39.

95. A. B. Aylesworth and S. B. MacKenzie, "Context Is Key," *Journal of Advertising,* Summer 1998, pp. 17–31; Q. Chen and W. D. Wells, "Attitude toward the Site," *Journal of Advertising Research,* September 1999, pp. 27–37; and B. M. Tennis and A. B. Bakker, "Stay Tuned," *Journal of Advertising,* Fall 2001, pp. 15–25. See also S. Shapiro, D. J. MacInnis, and C.W. Park, "Understanding Program-Induced Mood Effects," *Journal of Advertising,* Winter 2002, pp. 15–26.

96. R. Alsop, "Color Grows More Important in Catching Consumers' Eyes," *The Wall Street Journal,* November 29, 1989, p. B1.

97. J. W. Pracejus, G. D. Olsen, and T. C. O'Guinn, "How Nothing Became Something," *Journal of Consumer Research,* June 2006, pp. 82–90.

98. Consumer Insight 8–2 is based on D. L. Mothersbaugh, B. A. Huhmann, and G. R. Franke, "Combinatory and Separative Effects of Rhetorical Figures on Consumers' Effort and Focus in Ad Processing," *Journal of Consumer Research,* March 2002, pp. 589–602; E. F. McQuarrie and D. Glenn Mick, "Visual and Verbal Rhetorical Figures under Directed Processing versus Incidental Exposure to Advertising," *Journal of Consumer Research,* March 2003, pp. 579–87; and S. Bulmer and M. Buchanan-Oliver, "Advertising Across Cultures," *Journal of Current Issues and Research in Advertising,* Spring 2006, pp. 57–71.

99. T. Meenaghan, ed., "Ambush Marketing," special issue, *Psychology & Marketing,* July 1998.

100. J. Sengupta and G. J. Gorn, "Absence Makes the Mind Grow Sharper," *Journal of Marketing Research,* May 2002, pp. 186–201.

101. T. Howard, "Pay the Same, Get Less as Package Volume Falls," *USA Today,* March 17, 2003, p. 3b.

102. R. Bryant and L. Dundes, "Portion Distortion," *The Journal of Consumer Affairs,* Winter 2005, pp. 399–408; and P. Chandon and B. Wansink, "Is Obesity Caused by Calorie Underestimation?" *Journal of Marketing Research,* February 2007, pp. 84–99.

103. A. Krishna, R. Briesch, D. R. Lehmann, and H. Yuan, "A Meta-Analysis of the Impact of Price Presentation on Perceived Savings," *Journal of Retailing* 78 (2002), pp. 101–18; L. D. Compeau, J. Lindsey-Mullikin, D. Grewal, and R. D. Petty, "Consumers' Interpretations of the Semantic Phrases Found in Reference Price Advertisements," *Journal of Consumer Affairs,* Summer 2004, pp. 178–87; and T. Mazumdar, S. P. Raj, and I. Sinha, "Reference Price Research," *Journal of Marketing,* October 2005, pp. 84–102.

104. P. Raghubir, "Free Gift with Purchase," *Journal of Consumer Psychology* 14, nos. 1 & 2 (2004), pp. 181–86.

105. S. Chatterjee, T. B. Heath, and S. Basuroy, "Failing to Suspect Collusion in Price-Matching Guarantees," *Journal of Consumer Psychology* 13, no. 3 (2003), pp. 255–67; and J. Halliday, "GM Incentive Plans Could Damage Brand," *Advertising Age,* September 27, 2004, p. 1.

106. A. Kirmani, "Advertising Repetition as a Signal of Quality," *Journal of Advertising,* Fall 1997, pp. 77–86.

107. G. L. Lohse and D. L. Rosen, "Signaling Quality and Credibility in Yellow Pages Advertising," *Journal of Advertising,* Summer 2001, pp. 73–85.

108. A. Kirmani and A. R. Rao, "No Pain, No Gain," *Journal of Marketing,* April 2000, pp. 66–79; and D. Soberman, "Simultaneous Signaling and Screening with Warranties," *Journal of Marketing Research,* May 2003, pp. 176–92.

109. Z. Gurhan-Canli and D. Maheswaran, "Cultural Variations in Country of Origin Effects," *Journal of Marketing Research,* August 2000, pp. 309–17; Z. Gurhan-Canli and D. Maheswaran, "Determinants of Country-of-Origin Effects," *Journal of Consumer Research,* June 2000, pp. 96–108; and P. Chao, G. Wuhrer, and T. Werani, "Celebrity and Foreign Brand Name as Moderators of Country-of-Origin Effects," *International Journal of Advertising* 24, no. 2 (2005), pp. 173–92.

110. B. J. Phillips and E. F. McQuarrie, "The Development, Change, and Transformation of Rhetorical Style in Magazine Advertisements 1954–1999," *Journal of Advertising* 31, no. 4 (2003), pp. 1–13; L. A Peracchio and J. Meyers-Levy, "Using Stylistic Properties of Ad Pictures to Communicate with Consumers," *Journal of Consumer Research,* June 2005, pp. 29–40; J. Z. Sojka and J. L. Giese, "Communicating Through Pictures and Words," *Psychology & Marketing,* December 2006, pp. 995–1014.

111. B. J. Phillips, "The Impact of Verbal Anchoring on Consumer Response to Image Ads," *Journal of Advertising,* Spring 2000, pp. 15–24; E. F. McQuarrie and D. G. Mick, "Visual Rhetoric in Advertising," *Journal of Consumer Research,* June 1999, pp. 37–54; and M. Callow and L. Schiffman, "Implicit Meaning in Visual Print Advertisements," *International Journal of Advertising,* 21, 2002, pp. 259–77.

112. See R. Kivetz and I. Simonson, "The Effects of Incomplete Information on Consumer Choice," *Journal of Marketing Research,* November 2000, pp. 427–48.

113. M. J. Barone and P. J. Miniard, "How and When Factual Ad Claims Mislead Consumers," *Journal of Marketing Research,* February 1999, pp. 58–74; M. J. Barone, K. M. Palan, and P. W. Miniard, "Brand Usage and Gender as Moderators of the Potential Deception Associated with Partial Comparative Advertising," *Journal of Advertising,* Spring 2004, pp. 19–28; and M. J. Barone, K. C. Manning, and P. W. Miniard, "Consumer

Response to Retailers' Use of Partially Comparative Pricing," *Journal of Marketing,* July 2004, pp. 37–47.

114. For an excellent discussion, see I. L. Preston, *The Tangled Web They Weave* (Madison, WI: University of Madison Press, 1994).

115. L. Petrak, "Capturing Consumer Attention," *National Provisioner,* October 2003, pp. 52–53.

116. P. Boatwright and J. C. Nunes, "Reducing Assortment," *Journal of Marketing,* July 2001, pp. 50–63. See also E. van Herpen and R. Pieters, "The Variety of an Assortment," and S. J. Hoch, E. T. Bradlow, and B. Wansink, "Rejoinder to 'The Variety of an Assortment,'" both in *Marketing Science,* Summer 2002, pp. 331–41 and pp. 342–46, respectively; A. Chernev, "When More Is Less and Less Is More," *Journal of Consumer Research,* September 2003, pp. 170–83; and S. Thompson, "Kraft Vows to Kick Addiction to Extensions," *Advertising Age,* August 23, 2004, p. 1.

117. H. Chura, "Pepsi-Cola's Code Red Is White Hot," *Advertising Age,* August 27, 2001, p. 24.

118. "What's in a Name?" *Global Cosmetics Industry,* August 2002, p. 42. See also E. G. Miller and B. E. Kahn, "Shades of Meaning," *Journal of Consumer Research,* June 2005, pp. 86–92; J. L. Skorinko et al., "A Rose by Any Other Name . . . ," *Psychology and Marketing,* December 2006, pp. 975–93; and "Study: Food in McDonald's Wrapper Tastes Better to Kids," *CNN .com,* accessed August 7, 2007. See also R. Raghunathan, R. W. Naylor, and W. D. Hoyer, "The Unhealthy = Tasty Intuition," *Journal of Marketing,* October 2006, pp. 170–84.

119. S. Zhang and B. H. Schmitt, "Creating Local Brands in Multilingual International Markets," *Journal of Marketing Research,* August 2001, pp. 313–25.

120. S. Freeman, "Revived 'Hemi' Engine Helps Chrysler Juice Up Its Sales," *The Wall Street Journal,* April 30, 2004, p. B1.

121. R. R. Klink, "Creating Brand Names with Meaning," *Marketing Letters* 11, no. 1 (2000), pp. 5–20; and E. Yorkston and G. Menon, "A Sound Idea," *Journal of Consumer Research,* June 2004, pp. 43–51.

122. S. Begley, "New ABCs of Branding," *The Wall Street Journal,* August 26, 2002, p. B1.

123. I. P. Levin and A. M. Levin, "Modeling the Role of Brand Alliances in the Assimilation of Product Evaluations," *Journal of Consumer Psychology* 9, no. 1 (2000), pp. 43–52; and K. K. Desai and K. I. Keller, "The Effects of Ingredient Branding Strategies on Host Brand Extendibility," *Journal of Marketing,* January 2002, pp. 73–93.

124. See J. Tantillo, J. D. Lorenzo-Aiss, and R. E. Mathisen, "Quantifying Perceived Differences in Type Styles," *Psychology & Marketing,* August 1995, pp. 447–57; and C. Janiszewski and T. Meyvis, "Effects of Brand Logo Complexity, Repetition, and Spacing on Processing Fluency and Judgment," *Journal of Marketing Research,* June 2001, pp. 18–32.

125. A. H. Schechter, "Measuring the Value of Corporate and Brand Logos," *Design Management Journal,* Winter 1993, pp. 33–39.

126. T. L. Childers and J. Jass, "All Dressed Up with Something to Say," *Journal of Consumer Psychology* 12, no. 2 (2002), pp. 93–106; J. R. Doyle and P. A. Bottomley, "Font Appropriateness and Brand Choice," *Journal of Business Research* 57 (2004), pp. 873–80; and J. R. Doyle and P. A. Bottomley, "Dressed for the Occasion," *Journal of Consumer Psychology* 16, no. 2 (2006), pp. 112–23. See also P. W. Henderson, J. L. Giese, and J. A. Cote, "Impression Management Using Typeface Design," *Journal of Marketing,* October 2004, pp. 60–72.

127. P. W. Henderson and J. A. Cote, "Guidelines for Selecting or Modifying Logos," *Journal of Marketing,* April 1998, pp. 14–30; and J. T. Landry, "Making Logos Matter," *Harvard Business Review,* March–April 1998, pp. 16–17.

128. M. Peers, "Buddy, Can You Spare Some Time?" *The Wall Street Journal,* January 26, 2004, p. B1; and B. Frank, "'Missing' Men Prove Prescient," *Advertising Age,* August 23, 2004, p. 16.

129. "Ford Boss Outlines Shift to 'Rifle' Media," *Advertising Age,* October 26, 1981, p. 89. See also P. J. Danaher, "Wearout Effects in Target Marketing," *Marketing Letters* 3 (1996), pp. 275–87.

130. P. N. Shamdasani, A. J. S. Stanaland, and J. Tan, "Location, Location, Location," *Journal of Advertising Research,* July 2001, pp. 7–20.

131. P. Lehman, "Mad Ave Clicks with the Gamers."

132. J. Guterman, "Outdoor Interactive," *American Demographics,* August 2001, p. 32.

133. O. Ampuero and N. Vila, "Consumer Perceptions of Product Packaging," *Journal of Consumer Marketing* 23, no. 2 (2006), pp. 100–112.

134. B. E. Kahn and B. Wansink, "The Influence of Assortment Structure on Perceived Variety and Consumption Quantities," *Journal of Consumer Research,* March 2004, pp. 519–33.

135. S. Thompson, "M&M's Wraps Up Promo with Color," *Advertising Age,* March 8, 2004, p. 4.

136. B. Wansink and K. Van Ittersum, "Bottoms Up!" *Journal of Consumer Research,* December 2003, pp. 455–63; V. Folkes and S. Matta, "The Effect of Package Shape on Consumers' Judgments of Product Volume," *Journal of Consumer Research,* September 2004, pp. 390–401; and J. Hoegg and J. W. Alba, "Taste Perception," *Journal of Consumer Research,* March 2007, pp. 490–498.

137. S. Yang and P. Raghubir, "Can Bottles Speak Volumes?" *Journal of Retailing* 81, no. 4 (2005), pp. 269–81.

138. E. Lepkowska-White and A. L. Parsons, *Journal of Consumer Affairs,* Winter 2001, pp. 278–94; and V. A. Taylor and A. B. Bower, "Improving Product Instruction Compliance," *Psychology & Marketing,* March 2004, pp. 229–45; see also J. J. Argo and K. J. Main, "Meta-Analyses of the Effectiveness of Warning Labels," *Journal of Public Policy and Marketing,* Fall 2004, pp. 193–208.

# Learning, Memory, and Product Positioning

Sushi has a long and respected history in Japan since its introduction there over a thousand years ago. Sushi itself has undergone many transformations in the hands of highly skilled Japanese chefs whose expertise and creativity have long been revered. Imagine, then, trying to introduce a fish that consumers and sushi chefs feel very negatively about into this market and then turning it into a delicacy!

That's just what Kishichiro Okamoto, head of Japan's Oita Prefecture Fisherman's Cooperative did with a fish called the mackerel (*saba* in Japanese). Mackerel is a relatively common fish and considered the "poor man's fish" because of its low price, oily texture, and tendency to spoil rapidly. Negative perceptions of the fish are so entrenched in local lore that the Japanese say that it starts to stink while it is still swimming!

Okamoto started with the product itself. He noticed that mackerel from the Saganoseki region was more flavorful and less prone to spoilage because strong currents in that region decreased the fat content. He also noticed that certain cleaning techniques called *ikejime* helped increase quality. From here, Okamoto developed the brand name Seki to link it to the region and then developed a strict set of guidelines that were to become the hallmarks of this premium brand. Specifically, Seki saba (a) must be "rod-caught" since nets damage the flesh, (b) must be cleaned using the ikejime method, and (c) must not be weighed or measured since that increases handling and spoilage.

Having a good product is one thing. Teaching consumers about it is another. Okamoto's strategy was to showcase the Seki brand at major fish markets so that buyers could learn about his product through direct experience. Even this direct approach, however, took years. He also focused on specific buyers he knew would be opinion leaders, whose behavior would be mimicked by others. His strategy finally paid off.

When the prestigious Otani Hotel began serving Seki saba, other top restaurants and sushi bars followed close behind.

As Okamoto notes, "With Seki saba we proved that a brand is really about building credibility." That credibility was hard earned and required consumer learning. Today, however, Seki saba is considered a delicacy in Japan and around the world, with respected restaurant owners touting its fine texture and high quality. It sells for some $58 per fish compared with regular mackerel which sells for around $9. Pretty good for an ordinary fish that sophisticated buyers had virtually written off.[1]

---

As the Seki saba example illustrates, brands seek to reduce existing negative associations (e.g., common, smelly), and create new positive associations (e.g., firm texture, high quality, premium). When possible, brands also try to reinforce existing positive associations, although saba appears to historically have had none in the Japanese market. These associations are at the heart of learning. They are also the key to successful brand image development, positioning, and repositioning.

In this chapter, we discuss the nature of learning and memory, conditioning and cognitive theories of learning, and factors affecting retrieval. Implications for marketing managers are discussed throughout, culminating with an examination of product positioning and brand equity in the final sections.

## NATURE OF LEARNING AND MEMORY

Learning is essential to the consumption process. In fact, consumer behavior is largely *learned* behavior. People acquire most of their attitudes, values, tastes, behaviors, preferences, symbolic meanings, and feelings through learning. Culture, family, friends, mass media, and advertising provide learning experiences that affect the type of lifestyle people seek and the products they consume. Consider, for example, how often your movie choices are influenced by what you read online and discussions you have with friends.

**Learning** is *any change in the content or organization of long-term memory or behavior*[2] and is the result of information processing. In the previous chapter, we described information processing as *a series of activities by which stimuli are perceived, transformed into information, and stored.* The four activities in the series are exposure, attention, interpretation, and memory.

As Figure 9–1 indicates, different information processing systems handle different aspects of learning. The perceptual system deals with information intake through exposure and attention and, as we discussed in Chapter 8, may be conscious or unconscious. Short-term memory (STM) deals with holding information temporarily while it is interpreted and transferred into long-term memory. Long-term memory (LTM) deals with storing and retrieving information to be used in decisions.

These processes are highly interrelated. For example, a consumer may notice their favorite brand of soda on the store shelf because of a purchase goal stored in long-term memory. The soda's current price is brought into short-term memory through the perceptual system for processing. But a reference price may also be retrieved from long-term memory as a comparison point. Finally, price perceptions associated with their favorite brand may be updated and stored in long-term memory as a consequence of the comparison process.

**Information Processing, Learning, and Memory**    **FIGURE 9–1**

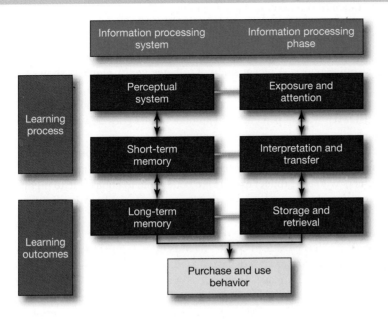

# MEMORY'S ROLE IN LEARNING

Memory is the total accumulation of prior learning experiences. As Figure 9–1 suggests, memory is critical to learning. It consists of two interrelated components: short-term and long-term memory.[3] These are *not* distinct physiological entities. Instead, **short-term memory (STM),** or *working memory,* is that portion of total memory that is currently activated or in use. **Long-term memory (LTM)** is that portion of total memory devoted to permanent information storage.

## Short-Term Memory

Short-term memory has a limited capacity to store information and sensations. In fact, it is not used for storage in the usual sense of that term. It is more like a computer file that is currently in use. Active files hold information while it is being processed. After processing is complete, the reconfigured information is printed or returned to more permanent storage such as the hard drive. A similar process occurs with short-term memory. Individuals use short-term memory to hold information while they analyze and interpret it. They may then transfer it to another system (write or type it), place it in long-term memory, or both. Thus, short-term memory is closely analogous to what we normally call thinking. *It is an active, dynamic process, not a static structure.*

**STM Is Short Lived**    Information in working memory decays quickly. The memory span for prices, for example, is about 3.7 seconds.[4] The short-lived nature of STM means that consumers must constantly refresh information through **maintenance rehearsal** or it will be lost. Maintenance rehearsal is the continual repetition of a piece of information in order to hold it in current memory for use in problem solving or transferal to long-term memory. Repeating the same formula or definition several times before taking an exam is an example. Marketers frequently simulate this by repeating the brand name or a key benefit in a prominent manner several times in an ad.

**STM Has Limited Capacity**   The limited capacity of STM means that consumers can hold only so much information in current memory. The capacity of STM is thought to be in the range of 5 to 9 bits of information. A bit can be an individual item or a related set of items. Organizing individual items into groups of related items that can be processed as a single unit is called *chunking*. Chunking can greatly aid in the transfer (and recall) of information from memory. A recent study of toll-free *vanity numbers* shows the power of chunking. Memory for completely numeric numbers was 8 percent, memory for combinations of numbers and words (800-555-HOME) was 44 percent, and memory for all words (800-NEW-HOME) was 58 percent! The number of bits goes down as the words become meaningful chunks replacing meaningless numbers.[5]

Marketers can help consumers chunk product information by organizing detailed attribute information in messages around the more general benefits that they create. Interestingly, consumers who are product experts are better able to chunk due to highly organized memory structures. As a consequence, experts are better able to learn information and avoid information overload.[6]

**Elaborative Activities Occur in STM**   STM is often termed working memory because that's where information is analyzed, categorized, and interpreted—that is, STM is where **elaborative activities** take place. Elaborative activities are *the use of previously stored experiences, values, attitudes, beliefs, and feelings to interpret and evaluate information in working memory as well as to add relevant previously stored information.* Elaborative activities serve to redefine or add new elements to memory.

Suppose your firm has developed a new product for consumers who want to use their electronic devices safely while driving. The product is a voice-activated program that allows you to give commands to your MP3 player and to your cell phone, hands free. How will this product be categorized? The answer depends in large part on *how* it is presented. How it is presented will influence the nature of the elaborative activities that will occur, which in turn will determine how the product is remembered.

Illustration 9–1 shows how Ford, with Microsoft, launched such a product. First, it used an image-rich name that conveys much of the product's function. SYNC is short for synchronize, which suggests how the product helps orchestrate and coordinate in-car technology activities. The visual in the ad clearly, if symbolically, suggests the easy flow and interplay of the various technologies as they relate to the workday commute. The text expands on this theme and helps relay key benefits. Thus, this ad should help trigger elaborative activities that will allow consumers to define this as a new and useful product for safely using a cell phone and MP3 player while driving. The high-imagery name should help retention and recall of the key benefits of the product.

Elaborative activities can involve both concepts and imagery. **Concepts** are abstractions of reality that capture the meaning of an item in terms of other concepts. They are similar to a dictionary definition of a word. Thus, a consumer might bring to mind concepts such as harmonize, coordinate, and bring together, when first processing the new concept SYNC.

**Imagery** involves concrete sensory representations of ideas, feelings, and objects. It permits a direct recovery of aspects of past experiences. Thus, imagery processing involves the recall and mental manipulation of sensory images, including sight, smell, taste, and tactile (touch) sensations.

Pictures can increase imagery, particularly when they are *vivid,* meaning they are relatively concrete representations of reality rather than an abstraction. In the SYNC ad, for example, the visual depicts a car moving toward the city. In between are images of actual musicians, office buildings, and electronic devices. These concrete images may induce some consumers to think about their morning commute to work, prior experiences trying to operate their radios and cell phones with difficulty, and then imagine how pleasurable it

Special Advertising Section

**ILLUSTRATION 9–1**

Successful new products and brands must enter into memory in a favorable manner, and they must be recalled when required. In this case, the brand name, the visual in the ad, and the ad text will enhance elaborative activities appropriate for the product.

would be to have hands-free capabilities. Pictures are not the only factor to increase imagery, however. Words and phrases in an ad can also encourage consumers to conjure up their own images (e.g., "picture it . . . ," "feel it . . . ," "imagine . . .").

Marketers need to make sure that the words and pictures work together. For example, if the ad text invites consumers to engage in imagery processing, but provides them with a boring picture, then consumers will be turned off to the message and less likely to buy the brand.[7]

Whether consumers are processing concepts or images, a key issue in learning and memory is the *extent of elaboration.* A major determinant of elaboration is consumer motivation or involvement. Elaboration is enhanced when consumers are more involved or interested in the brand, product, or message at hand (as we saw earlier, it also is facilitated by consumer expertise). Elaboration increases the chances that information will be transferred to LTM and be retrieved at a later time by increasing the processing attention directed at that information and by establishing meaningful linkages between the new information and existing information. These linkages or associations are an important part of LTM, as discussed next.

## Long-Term Memory

**Long-term memory** is viewed as *an unlimited, permanent storage.* It can store numerous types of information, such as concepts, decision rules, processes, and affective (emotional) states. Marketers are particularly interested in **semantic memory,** which is *the basic knowledge and feelings an individual has about a concept.* It represents the person's understanding of an object or event at its simplest level. At this level, a brand such as Acura might be categorized as "a luxury car."

Another type of memory of interest to marketers is **episodic memory.** This is *the memory of a sequence of events in which a person participated.* These personal memories of events such as a first date, graduation, or learning to drive can be quite strong. They often

## Burned into the Brain: Creating "Flashbulb" Memories for Brands

Given the cluttered marketing landscape, brands fight not only for attention but also to be remembered. This is a difficult task. However, researchers have recently uncovered the fact that some brand encounters create highly vivid and enduring episodic memories called flashbulb memories. **Flashbulb memory** is *acute memory for the circumstances surrounding a surprising and novel event.*[8] Key aspects of flashbulb memories include the following:

- They are vividly detailed and therefore highly enduring over time.
- They contain specific situational detail about location, people, activities, and felt emotions.
- They are held with a high degree of confidence.
- They are perceived as special and different from memories of ordinary or mundane experiences.

One 37-year-old consumer reported the following flashbulb memory for Krispy Kreme donuts:

I remember it just like it was yesterday. I was 11, and we were visiting my cousins, who lived in the South at the time. As a special treat, my aunt and my cousin and I went to the Krispy Kreme one morning. There were hot donuts that had just been made, and we had them right after they were done. I remember the smell, the taste of the donuts. I remember my cousin making fun of me, because I ate mine so fast, and I got glaze all over myself, on my face, my hands, everything.

Notice how much situational detail is recalled and how vivid and positive the recollection is over 25 years after the experience!

Clearly, brand managers would love to have such experiences seared into the minds of their consumers, as they would help enhance brand recall, attitudes, and purchases. The question is, *Can all brand encounters be expected to create such flashbulb memories?* The answer appears to be no. Brands that are undifferentiated, boring, and not unique are less likely to create the emotional response of surprise critical to flashbulb memories. One study, for example, found that Krispy Kreme donuts and Build-A-Bear created more flashbulb memories than Dunkin' Donuts and KB Toys. Also, first experiences with a brand are by their nature more novel and surprising and therefore more likely to involve flashbulb memories. So, even for Krispy Kreme and Build-A-Bear, subsequent visits failed to produce flashbulb memories.

Later in this chapter we will discuss brand equity and positioning. It is apparent that a unique, positive, position in the marketplace is critical to vivid and enduring flashbulb-like memories of first-time encounters with brands, which can last a lifetime.

### Critical Thinking Questions

1. How is episodic memory related to flashbulb memory?

2. Can you think of other brands you feel would engender flashbulb memories? Explain.

3. Do you have a flashbulb memory of a first brand encounter? Do you feel it influences your brand purchase behavior?

---

elicit imagery and feelings. Marketers frequently attempt to evoke episodic memories either because their brand was involved in them or to associate the positive feelings they generate with the brand. Consumer Insight 9–1 discusses flashbulb memories, a special type of episodic memory.

Marketers worry not only about *what* information is stored in LTM but also *how* this information is organized. Two important memory structures are schemas and scripts.

**Schemas** Both concepts and episodes acquire depth of meaning by becoming associated with other concepts and episodes. A pattern of such associations around a particular concept is termed a **schema** or *schematic memory*, sometimes called a *knowledge structure*.

| A Partial Schematic Memory for Mountain Dew | FIGURE 9–2 |

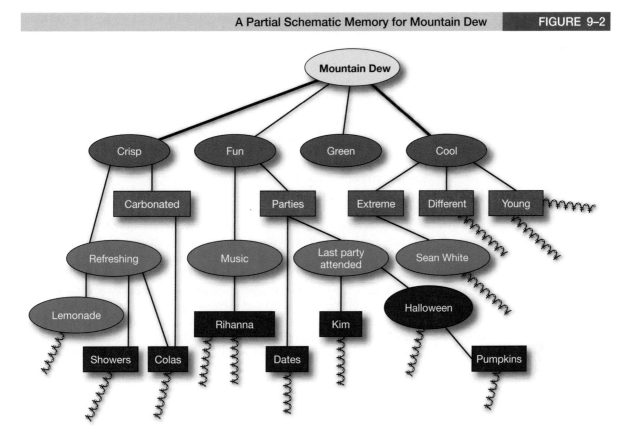

Schematic memory is a complex web of associations. Figure 9–2 provides a simplified example of a schema by showing how one might associate various concepts with Mountain Dew to form a network of meaning for that brand. Notice that our hypothetical schema contains *product characteristics, usage situations, episodes,* and *affective reactions.* The source of some of the schema is personal experience, but other aspects may be completely or partially based on marketing activities.[9] The schematic memory of a brand is the same as the brand image, which we discuss later in the chapter. It is what the consumer thinks of and feels when the brand name is mentioned.

In the partial schema shown in Figure 9–2, concepts, events, and feelings are stored in *nodes* within memory. Thus, the concept "cool" is stored in a node, as are "music," "fun," and "Halloween." Each of these is associated either directly or indirectly with Mountain Dew. *Associative links* connect various concepts to form the complete meaning assigned to an item.

Associative links vary in terms of how strongly and how directly they are associated with a node. In our example, crisp, fun, green, and cool are directly associated with Mountain Dew. However, one or two of these may be strongly associated with the brand, as crisp and cool are shown to be by the bold lines in our example. Other nodes, such as fun and green, may have weaker links. Without reinforcement, the weaker links may disappear or fade over time (e.g., the Halloween party linkage). Over the longer run, so will the stronger ones (e.g., the cool linkage). Marketers spend enormous effort attempting to develop strong, easily activated links between their brands and desirable product benefits.[10] The various ways in which these linkages are established and strengthened (reinforced) are discussed in the next section, on learning.

The memory activation shown in Figure 9–2 originated with the name of a particular brand. If the activation had begun with the concept "cool," would Mountain Dew arise as a node directly linked to cool? It would depend on the total context in which the memory was being activated. In general, multiple memory nodes are activated simultaneously. Thus, a question like "What is a cool soft drink?" might quickly activate a memory schema that links Mountain Dew directly to cool. However, a more abstract question like "What is cool?" might not, because of its relatively weak and indirect connection to beverages and sodas.[11] Marketers expend substantial effort to influence the schema consumers have for their brands. We will discuss this process in detail later in the chapter.

Marketers also strive to influence the schema consumers have for consumption situations. For example, consumers likely have very different beverage schemas for situations such as jogging, where thirst is a key component, than for a party, where socializing and relaxing are key components. The beverage schema for jogging might include products such as water and soda and brands such as Dasani and Pepsi. The beverage schema for a party might include products such as wine and beer and brands such as Yellow Tail and Budweiser. Brands in the schematic memory that come to mind (are recalled) for a specific problem or situation such as thirst are known as the *evoked set.*

The usage situation schema a brand attaches itself to can have major ramifications. For example, if Canada Dry Ginger Ale associated itself strongly with a "party" situation as a mixer for cocktails, then it is much less likely to be retrieved as part of the evoked set when consumers are thinking of other usage situations, such as those involving thirst.[12] We will discuss how the evoked set influences consumer decision making in Chapter 15.

Scripts    *Memory of how an action sequence should occur,* such as purchasing and drinking a soft drink to relieve thirst, is a special type of schema known as a **script.** Scripts are necessary for consumers to shop effectively. One of the difficulties new forms of retailing have is teaching consumers the appropriate script for acquiring items in a new manner. This is the problem facing firms wanting to sell products via the Internet. Before these firms can succeed, their target markets must learn appropriate scripts for Internet shopping.

Marketers and public policy officials want consumers to develop scripts for appropriate product acquisition, use, and disposal behavior. For example, using a product or service requires one to learn a process. This process often includes the disposition of the package or some part of the product.[13] Unfortunately, many consumers have learned consumption scripts that do not include appropriate disposition activities such as recycling. Thus, both government agencies and environmental groups spend substantial effort attempting to teach consumers consumption scripts that include recycling.

Retrieval from LTM    The likelihood and ease with which information can be recalled from LTM is termed **accessibility.** Every time an informational node or a link between nodes is activated (accessed) in memory, it is strengthened. Thus, accessibility can be enhanced by rehearsal, repetition, and elaboration. For example, Coca-Cola might be one of the brands that always comes to mind (is retrieved) when you think of sodas because you have seen so many ads for that brand. This accessibility effect for brands is called *top-of-mind awareness.* In addition, accessibility is related to the strength and number of incoming linkages. In essence, when a concept is linked to other concepts in memory, its accessibility increases as a result of the multiple retrieval pathways. Thus, elaboration enhances retrieval by creating a rich associative network. Finally, accessibility is related to the strength and directness of links to nodes, with stronger and more direct linkages being more accessible. Thus, cool and crisp are highly accessible associations related to Mountain Dew, while parties and refreshing are less accessible. Clearly, marketers want strong and direct linkages between their brand and critical product features.

Retrieving information from LTM is not a completely objective or mechanical task. If asked to recall the sponsor of the last summer Olympics, some consumers will not remember instantly and certainly. These individuals may *construct* a memory based on limited recall and a series of judgments or inferences. For example, many might "recall" Nike because it is a dominant firm in sports equipment and apparel. Thus, it would "make sense" for Nike to be the sponsor, which could lead some consumers to believe that Nike was indeed a sponsor of the event even if it was not.[14] Therefore, memory is sometimes shaped and changed as it is accessed. Likewise, memory of an actual event may be altered as new or additional information about that event is received.[15] In fact, one study found that an ad which prompted imagery responses about a childhood trip to Disney increased consumers' confidence that they had actually experienced an event at Disney (shaking hands with a non-Disney character such as Bugs Bunny) that could not have happened.[16] *What are the ethical concerns relating to this sort of memory construction and distortion?*

Finally, retrieval may involve *explicit* or *implicit* memories. Traditionally, we have thought of remembering, and thus memory, as the ability to recall specific items or events. If you read this chapter and then try to answer the review questions at the end without referring back to the chapter, you are engaging in traditional memory recall. This is referred to as **explicit memory,** which is characterized by *the conscious recollection of an exposure event.* In contrast, **implicit memory** involves *the nonconscious retrieval of previously encountered stimuli.* It is a sense of familiarity, a feeling, or a set of beliefs about an item without conscious awareness of when and how they were acquired. An example of implicit memory relates to brand placements. One study found that over time, a brand's image becomes increasingly similar to the TV show in which it appears, even when consumers don't remember seeing the brand placements![17]

# LEARNING UNDER HIGH AND LOW INVOLVEMENT

We have described learning as any change in the content or organization of long-term memory or behavior. In addition, we have described long-term memory in terms of schemas or associational networks. So how do people *learn* these associations? For example, how do consumers *learn* that Mountain Dew is cool or that Wal-Mart has low prices?

A moment's reflection will reveal that people learn things in different ways. For example, buying a car or stereo generally involves intense, focused attention and processing. The outcome of these efforts is rewarded by better choices. However, most learning is of a much different nature. Even if they don't care for baseball, most people know who is playing in the World Series each year because they hear about it frequently. And people can identify clothes that are stylish even though they never really think much about clothing styles.

As just described, learning may occur in either a high-involvement or a low-involvement situation. Recall from Chapter 8 that information processing (and therefore learning) may be conscious and deliberate in high-involvement situations. Or it may be nonfocused and even nonconscious in low-involvement situations. A **high-involvement learning** situation is one in which *the consumer is motivated to process or learn the material.* For example, an individual reading *PC Magazine* prior to purchasing a computer is probably highly motivated to learn relevant material dealing with the various computer brands. A **low-involvement learning** situation is one in which *the consumer has little or no motivation to process or learn the material.* A consumer whose television program is interrupted by a commercial for a product he or she doesn't currently use or feel a desire for generally has little motivation to learn the material presented in the commercial. Much, if not most, consumer learning occurs in relatively low-involvement contexts.[18]

As we will see in the following sections, the way a communication should be structured differs depending on the level of involvement the audience is expected to have. Illustration 9–2 shows one ad that assumes high-involvement learning and another based on low-involvement learning. *Why does one ad assume a highly involved audience and the other a low-involvement audience? What differences do you notice between these two ads? Do those differences make sense?*

Figure 9–3 shows the two general situations and the five specific learning theories that we are going to consider. *Level of involvement is the primary determinant of how material is learned.* The solid lines in the figure indicate that operant conditioning and analytical reasoning are common learning processes in high-involvement situations. Classical conditioning and iconic rote learning tend to occur in low-involvement situations. And vicarious learning/modeling is common in both low- and high-involvement situations. We will discuss each of these theories in the following pages.

## Conditioning

**Conditioning** is probably most appropriately described as a set of procedures that marketers can use to increase the chances that an association between two stimuli is formed or learned. The word *conditioning* has a negative connotation to many people and brings forth images of robot-like humans. However, the general procedure simply involves presenting two stimuli in close proximity so that eventually the two are perceived (consciously or

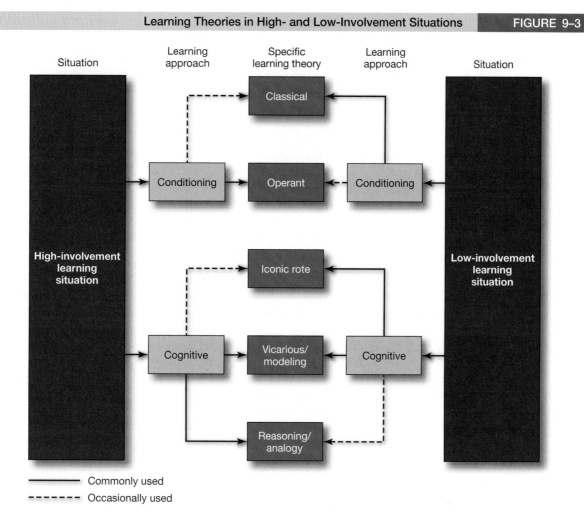

**Learning Theories in High- and Low-Involvement Situations**    FIGURE 9–3

unconsciously) to be related or associated. That is, consumers learn that the stimuli go (or do not go) together.

There are two basic forms of conditioned learning—classical and operant. *Classical conditioning* attempts to create an association between a stimulus (e.g., brand name) and some response (e.g., behavior or feeling). *Operant conditioning* attempts to create an association between a response (e.g., buying a brand) and some outcome (e.g., satisfaction) that serves to reinforce the response.

**Classical Conditioning**    Imagine that you are marketing a new brand of pen and want consumers to feel positively about that pen. How might classical conditioning help you to associate positive feelings with your unfamiliar brand? The classical conditioning procedure would have you pair the unknown brand repeatedly together with some other stimulus that you know already *automatically* elicits positive feelings or emotions, such as popular music in an ad. The goal would be that, eventually, after repeatedly pairing the brand name and the music, the brand name alone will elicit the same positive feelings produced by the music.

The process of using an established relationship between one stimulus (music) and response (pleasant feelings) to bring about the learning of the same response (pleasant

**FIGURE 9–4**        **Consumer Learning through Classical Conditioning**

UCS = Unconditioned stimulus        UCR = Unconditioned response
CS = Conditioned stimulus        CR = Conditioned response

feelings) to a different stimulus (the brand) is called **classical conditioning.** Figure 9–4 illustrates this type of learning. Hearing popular music (unconditioned stimulus) automatically elicits a positive emotion (unconditioned response) in many individuals. If this music is consistently paired with a particular brand of pen or other product (conditioned stimulus), the brand itself may come to elicit the same positive emotion (conditioned response).[19] In addition, some features, such as the masculine/feminine qualities of the unconditioned stimulus, may also become associated with the conditioned stimulus. That is, using a scene showing males or females in an activity that elicits positive emotions may not only cause a positive emotional response to a brand consistently paired with it, but also cause the brand to have a masculine or a feminine image.[20] Thus, classical conditioning can lead to positive attitudes by influencing brand feelings and beliefs. This is important because, as we will see in later chapters, attitudes influence information search, trial, and brand choice.

Other marketing applications of classical conditioning include:

* Consistently advertising a product on exciting sports programs may result in the product itself generating an excitement response.
* An unknown political candidate may elicit patriotic feelings by consistently playing patriotic background music in his or her commercials and appearances.
* Christmas music played in stores may elicit emotional responses associated with giving and sharing, which in turn may increase the propensity to purchase.

Learning via classical conditioning is most common in low-involvement situations, where relatively low levels of processing effort and awareness are involved.[21] However, after a sufficient number of low-involvement "scannings" or "glances at" the advertisement, the association may be formed or learned.

Operant Conditioning    **Operant conditioning** (or instrumental learning) involves rewarding desirable behaviors such as brand purchases with a positive outcome that serves to reinforce the behavior.[22] The more often a response is reinforced, the more likely it will be repeated in the future as consumers *learn* that the response is associated with a positive outcome.

Imagine that you are marketing a snack called Pacific Snax's Rice Popcorn. You believe your product has a light, crisp taste that consumers will like. But how can you influence them to learn to consume your brand? One option, based on the operant conditioning procedure, would be to distribute a large number of free samples through the mail, at shopping malls, or in stores. Many consumers would try the free sample (desired response). To the extent that the taste of Rice Popcorn is indeed pleasant (a positive outcome that serves as a reinforcement), the probability of continued consumption is increased. This is shown graphically in Figure 9–5.

**Consumer Learning by Operant Conditioning**    FIGURE 9–5

Unlike the relatively automatic associations created by classical conditioning, operant conditioning requires that consumers first engage in a deliberate behavior and come to understand its power in predicting positive outcomes that serve as reinforcement. As suggested in Figure 9–3, such learning is common under conditions of higher involvement.

Operant conditioning often involves influencing consumers to purchase a specific brand or product (desired response). Thus, a great deal of marketing strategy is aimed at securing an initial trial. Free samples (at home or in the store), special price discounts on new products, and contests all represent rewards offered to consumers to try a particular product or brand. If they try the brand under these conditions and like it (reinforcement), they are likely to take the next step and purchase it in the future. This process of encouraging partial responses leading to the final desired response (consume a free sample, buy at a discount, buy at full price) is known as **shaping** and is illustrated in Figure 9–6.

In one study, 84 percent of those given a free sample of a chocolate while in a candy store made a purchase, whereas only 59 percent of those not provided a sample made a purchase. Thus, shaping can be very effective. Illustration 9–3 shows an ad designed to induce trial, the first step in shaping.

While reinforcement increases the likelihood of behavior such as a purchase being repeated, a negative consequence (punishment) has exactly the opposite effect. Thus, the purchase of a brand that does not function properly greatly reduces the chances of future purchases of that brand. This underscores the critical importance of consistent product quality.

**The Process of Shaping in Purchase Behavior**    FIGURE 9–6

Operant conditioning is used widely by marketers. The most common application is to offer consistent-quality products so that the use of the product to meet a consumer need is reinforcing. Other applications include:

- Direct mail or personal contact after a sale that congratulates the purchaser for making a wise purchase.
- Giving extra reinforcement for purchasing a particular brand, such as rebates, toys in cereal boxes, or discount coupons.
- Giving free product samples or introductory coupons to encourage product trial (shaping).
- Making store interiors, shopping malls, or downtown areas pleasant places to shop (reinforcing) by providing entertainment, controlled temperature, exciting displays, and so forth.

The power of operant conditioning was demonstrated by an experiment conducted by an insurance company. More than 2,000 consumers who purchased life insurance over a one-month period were randomly divided into three groups. Two of the groups received reinforcement after each monthly payment in the form of a nice "thank-you" letter or telephone call. The third group received no such reinforcement. Six months later, 10 percent of the members of the two groups that received reinforcement had terminated their policies, while 23 percent of those who had not received reinforcement had done so! Reinforcement (being thanked) led to continued behavior (sending in the monthly premium).[23]

# Cognitive Learning

**Cognitive learning** encompasses all the mental activities of humans as they work to solve problems or cope with situations. It involves learning ideas, concepts, attitudes, and facts that contribute to our ability to reason, solve problems, and learn relationships without direct experience or reinforcement. Cognitive learning can range from very simple information acquisition (as in iconic rote learning) to complex, creative problem solving (as in analytical reasoning). Three types of cognitive learning are important to marketers.

## Iconic Rote Learning
Learning *a concept or the association between two or more concepts in the absence of conditioning* is known as **iconic rote learning.** For example, one may see an ad that states "Ketoprofin is a headache remedy" and associate the new concept "ketoprofin" with the existing concept "headache remedy." Notice the distinction from conditioning in that there is neither an unconditioned stimulus (classical) nor a direct reward or reinforcement (operant) involved.

Also, it is important to point out that unlike more complex forms of cognitive learning, iconic rote learning generally involves considerably less cognitive effort and elaboration.[24] A substantial amount of low-involvement learning involves iconic rote learning. Numerous repetitions of a simple message that occur as the consumer scans the environment may result in the essence of the message being learned. Through iconic rote learning, consumers may form beliefs about the characteristics or attributes of products without being aware of the source of the information. When the need arises, a purchase may be made based on those beliefs.[25]

## Vicarious Learning or Modeling
It is not necessary for consumers to directly experience a reward or punishment to learn. Instead, they can observe the outcomes of others' behaviors and adjust their own accordingly.[26] Similarly, they can use imagery to anticipate the outcome of various courses of action. This is known as **vicarious learning** or **modeling.**

This type of learning is common in both low- and high-involvement situations. In a high-involvement situation, such as purchasing a new suit shortly after taking a job, a consumer may deliberately observe the styles worn by others at work or by role models from other environments, including advertisements. Many ads encourage consumers to imagine the feelings and experience of using a product.[27] Such images not only enhance learning about the product, but may even influence how the product is evaluated after an actual trial.

A substantial amount of modeling also occurs in low-involvement situations. Throughout the course of their lives, people observe others using products and behaving in a great variety of situations. Most of the time they pay little attention to these behaviors. However, over time they learn that certain behaviors, and products, are appropriate in some situations and others are not.

## Analytical Reasoning
The most complex form of cognitive learning is **analytical reasoning.** In reasoning, individuals engage in creative thinking to restructure and recombine existing information as well as new information to form new associations and concepts. Information from a credible source that contradicts or challenges one's existing beliefs will often trigger reasoning.[28] The ad for Merck in Illustration 9–4 challenges consumer beliefs regarding the sources of bad cholesterol.

One form of analytical reasoning is the use of analogy. **Analogical reasoning** is an inference process that allows consumers to use an existing knowledge base to understand a new situation or object. That is, it allows consumers to use knowledge about something

Ads not only convey information and elicit feelings; they can challenge existing assumptions and cause readers to think and reexamine their beliefs.

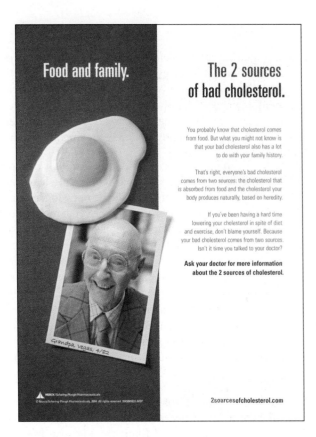

they are familiar with to help them understand something they are not familiar with. For example, if you have not tried or adopted a DVR, you may learn about it by

relating it to something you understand better such as VCRs. You may notice that DVRs and VCRs are designed to record and replay media content. Given this similarity of purpose, you may infer that they share other capabilities such as fast-forward, pause, mute, and so on. You may also conclude that since you feel VCR players are difficult to program, DVRs will also be difficult to use. At the end of this process, you may have a fairly complete set of beliefs about the DVR based on very minimal exposure to the product or product information.[29]

## Learning to Generalize and Differentiate

Regardless of which approach to learning is applicable in a given situation, consumers' ability to differentiate and generalize from one stimulus to another (for example, one brand to another) is critical to marketers.

**Stimulus discrimination** or differentiation refers to the *process of learning to respond differently to similar but distinct stimuli.* This process is critical for marketers who want consumers to perceive their brands as possessing unique and important features compared with other brands. For example, the management of Bayer aspirin feels that consumers should not see its aspirin as being the same as other brands. In order to obtain a premium price or a large market share, Bayer must teach consumers that its aspirin is distinct from other brands. Stimulus discrimination is an important consideration in brand image and product positioning, discussed later in the chapter.[30]

Stimulus discrimination is critical when brand scandals erupt. Scandals don't always hurt just the scandalized brand but can damage competitors in that industry, an effect termed *spillover.* One of the best ways for competitors to protect against spillover from scandals is to be highly differentiated from the scandalized brand.[31]

**Stimulus generalization,** often referred to as the *rub-off effect, occurs when a response to one stimulus is elicited by a similar but distinct stimulus.*[32] Thus, a consumer who learns that Nabisco's Oreo Cookies taste good and therefore assumes that the company's new Oreo Chocolate Cones will also taste good has engaged in stimulus generalization. Stimulus generalization is common and provides a major source of brand equity and opportunities for brand extensions, which are discussed later in the chapter.

## Summary of Learning Theories

Theories of learning help us understand how consumers learn across a variety of situations. We have examined five specific learning theories: classical conditioning, operant conditioning, iconic rote learning, vicarious learning/modeling, and analytical reasoning. Each of these learning theories can operate in a high- or a low-involvement situation, although some are more common in one type of situation than another. Table 9–1 summarizes these theories and provides examples from both high- and low-involvement contexts.

Summary of Learning Theories with Examples of Involvement Level    **TABLE 9–1**

| Theory | Description | High-Involvement Example | Low-Involvement Example |
|---|---|---|---|
| Classical Conditioning | A response elicited by one object is elicited by a second object if both objects frequently occur together. | The favorable emotional response elicited by the word *America* comes to be elicited by a car brand after repeated exposure to its *Made in America* campaign. This response is in addition to any cognitive learning that may have occurred. | The favorable emotional response elicited by a song in an ad for a new breath mint comes to be elicited by that brand after repeated pairing with the song even though the consumer pays little attention to the ad. |
| Operant Conditioning | A response that is reinforced is more likely to be repeated when the same (or similar) situation arises in the future. | A suit is purchased after extensive thought and the consumer finds that it is comfortable and doesn't wrinkle. A sport coat made by the same firm is later purchased because of the positive experience with the firm's suits. | A familiar brand of peas is purchased without much thought—because of the low importance of the decision. The peas taste "fresh" so the consumer continues to purchase this brand. |
| Iconic Rote Learning | A concept or the association between two concepts is learned without conditioning. | A consumer with little expertise about CD players tries hard to learn brand information by examining it carefully several times. Learning is limited, however, because his or her lack of expertise inhibits elaboration. | A consumer learns a company's most recent jingle because it is catchy and can't stop replaying it in his or her head. |
| Vicarious Learning or Modeling | Behaviors are learned by watching the outcomes of others' behaviors or by imagining the outcome of a potential behavior. | A consumer carefully watches the reactions that other co-workers have to her friend's new briefcase before deciding to buy one. | A child learns that people dress up for special occasions without really ever thinking about it. |
| Analytical Reasoning | Individuals use thinking to restructure and recombine existing and new information to form new associations and concepts. | A consumer buying a car carefully processes information about a new gas/electric hybrid car by using the analogy of homes powered by solar energy. | When a store is out of black pepper, a consumer buys white pepper instead based on the quick reasoning that "pepper is pepper." |

# LEARNING, MEMORY, AND RETRIEVAL

Gillette's growth slowed considerably in the early 2000s,[33] as did Saturn's in the early 1990s,[34] and L&M cigarettes' in the 1980s.[35] In each case, at least some of the decline in growth was attributed to sharply reduced advertising. As one executive stated,

> Some time after the company moved away from advertising and marketing, it became clear that people would quickly forget about our products if we didn't support them in the marketplace.[36]

These examples emphasize that marketers want consumers to learn *and* remember positive features, feelings, and behaviors associated with their brands. However, consumers forget. In conditioned learning, forgetting is often referred to as **extinction,** since the desired response (e.g., pleasant feelings or brand purchase) decays or dies out if learning is not repeated and reinforced. In cognitive learning, forgetting is often referred to as a **retrieval failure,** since information that is available in LTM cannot be accessed, that is, retrieved from LTM into STM.

Two aspects of forgetting that are of concern to marketers are the *likelihood of forgetting* in any given situation and the *rate of forgetting.* Figure 9–7 illustrates a commonly found rate of forgetting for advertising. In this study, aided and unaided recall of four advertisements

---

**FIGURE 9–7**     **Forgetting over Time: Magazine Advertisement**

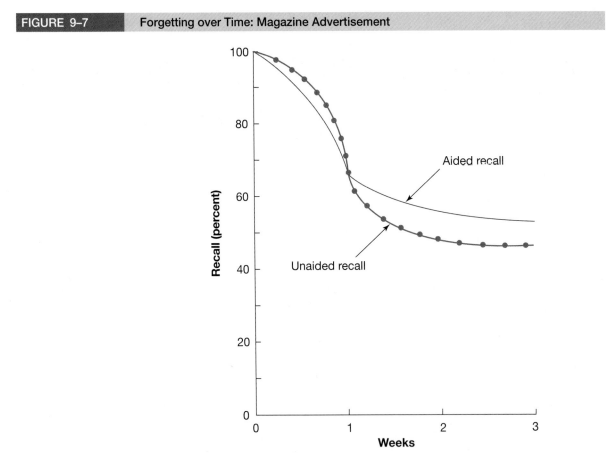

Source: LAP Report #5260.1 (New York: Weeks McGraw-Hill, undated). Reprinted with permission from McGraw-Hill Companies, Inc.

from *American Machinist* magazine was measured. As can be seen, the probability of ad recall (likelihood) dropped rapidly over the first five days and then stabilized (rate).

At times, marketers or regulatory groups desire to accelerate forgetting or extinction. For example, the American Cancer Society and other organizations offer programs designed to help individuals "unlearn" smoking behavior. Manufacturers want consumers to forget unfavorable publicity or outdated product images. *Corrective advertising,* a government requirement that firms remove inaccurate learning caused by past advertising, is described in Chapter 20.

Consumers forget brands, brand associations, and other information for a variety of reasons. First, learning may be weak to begin with. Second, information from competing brands and ads may cause memory interference. Third, the response environment (e.g., the retail store) may not be set up to encourage retrieval of previously learned information (e.g., from advertising). We turn to these issues next.

## Strength of Learning

How can the HIV Alliance teach you to minimize your AIDS risk so that you will not forget? Or how can Neutrogena teach you about its line of sunless tanning products so you remember key features when shopping at CVS? That is, what is required to bring about a long-lasting learned response?

One factor is strength of learning. The stronger the original learning (e.g., of nodes and links between nodes), the more likely relevant information will be retrieved when required. *Strength of learning* is enhanced by six factors: *importance, message involvement, mood, reinforcement, repetition,* and *dual coding.*

**Importance**     Importance refers to the value that consumers place on the information to be learned. Importance might be driven by inherent interest in the product or brand, or might be driven by the need to make a decision in the near future. The more important it is for the individual to learn a particular behavior or piece of information, the more effective and efficient he or she becomes in the learning process. This is largely due to the greater elaborative activities involved in fully processing and categorizing the material.

One emerging area of interest to marketers is how bilingual consumers process and recall second-language ads. For example, if Hispanic consumers process an ad in English, will it still be as effective as when they process the same ad in Spanish? Generally speaking, processing an ad in a second language is more difficult. This tends to reduce learning and recall for ads in a consumer's second language. Does this mean that second-language ads can never be effective? The answer appears to depend on importance. When importance is high, bilingual consumers expend more processing effort to understand the second-language ad, leading to greater learning and recall.[37]

Importance is one dimension that separates high-involvement learning situations from low-involvement situations. Therefore, high-involvement learning tends to be more complete than low-involvement learning.[38] Unfortunately, marketers are most often confronted with consumers in low-involvement learning situations.

**Message Involvement**     When a consumer is not motivated to learn the material, processing can be increased by causing the person to become involved *with the message itself.* For example, playing an instrumental version of a popular song with lyrics related to product attributes ("Like a rock" in Chevrolet pickup ads) may cause people to "sing along," either out loud or mentally. This deepened involvement with the message, relative to merely listening to the lyrics being sung, increases the extent of processing of the message and memory of the associated features or theme.[39]

In Chapter 8 we discussed various strategies for increasing consumer attention including incongruity, rhetoric, incomplete messages, and interesting ads with plots and surprise endings. These strategies also tend to enhance message involvement and thus lead to stronger learning and memory.[40]

Several issues regarding message involvement are important to consider. First, there is evidence that scent may be important to memory. One study found that positive scents present during exposure to an ad increased attention to the ad and resulted in higher brand recall. Not surprisingly, marketers are currently in the early stages of developing technologies that will allow for "scent-emitting" technologies for Internet applications and in-store kiosks![41]

A second issue is the role of suspense. Sometimes marketers wait until the very end of a message to reveal the brand name in an attempt to attract interest and attention. However, this strategy must be used with caution because waiting until the end of an ad to reveal the brand gives consumers little opportunity to integrate new information into their existing brand schemas. As a result, the associative linkages are weaker and memory is reduced. These results suggest that marketers should strongly consider mentioning the brand relatively early in any marketing message.[42]

A final issue regards message strategies that highlight a brand's personal relevance to the consumer. One such strategy is self-referencing. **Self-referencing** indicates that consumers are relating brand information to themselves. The "self" is a powerful memory schema and integrating brand information into this schema enhances learning and memory. Self-referencing can be encouraged in ads by using nostalgia appeals, which encourage consumers to remember past personal experiences.[43] It can also be encouraged by using language such as "you" and "your" (second-person pronoun). The SYNC ad in Illustration 9–1 effectively uses self-referencing. It encourages self–brand links with statements such as "lets *you* voice-activate *your* MP3 player," and "*You* talk. SYNC listens."

**Mood**    Get happy, learn more? Research indicates that this is indeed true. A positive mood during the presentation of information such as brand names enhances learning. A positive mood during the reception of information appears to enhance its relational elaboration—it is compared with and evaluated against more categories. This produces a more complete and stronger set of linkages among a variety of other brands and concepts, which in turn enhances retrieval (access to the information).[44]

Learning enhancement caused by a positive mood suggests the types of programs that marketers attempting to encourage consumer learning should advertise on. Likewise, it suggests that those commercials that enhance one's mood would also increase learning.[45]

**Reinforcement**    Anything that increases the likelihood that a given response will be repeated in the future is considered **reinforcement.** While learning frequently occurs in the absence of reinforcement, reinforcement has a significant impact on the speed at which learning occurs and the duration of its effect.

A *positive reinforcement* is a pleasant or desired consequence. A couple who likes Mexican food sees an ad for a new Chipotle Mexican Grill in their area and decides to try it. They enjoy the food, service, and atmosphere. They are now more likely to select the Chipotle Mexican Grill the next time they dine out.

A *negative reinforcement* involves the removal or the avoidance of an unpleasant consequence. In Illustration 9–5, Vicks promises to relieve sinus pain and pressure. If the ad convinces a consumer to try the sinus formula and it performs well, this consumer is likely to purchase and use it again in the future and, based on stimulus generalization, perhaps try other Vicks products as well.

**Punishment** is the opposite of reinforcement. It is any consequence that decreases the likelihood that a given response will be repeated in the future. If the couple who tried the

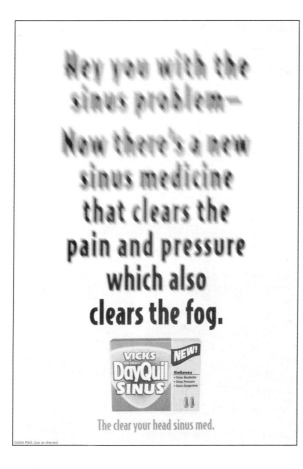

**ILLUSTRATION 9–5**
Reinforcement is anything that increases the probability that a response will be repeated in the future. It can involve a positive outcome such as providing pleasure, or the removal or avoidance of a negative outcome, such as sinus problems.

Chipotle Mexican Grill described earlier thought that the service was bad or that the food was poorly prepared, they would be unlikely to patronize it in the future.

Obviously, it is critical for marketers to determine precisely what reinforces consumer purchases so they can design promotional messages and products that encourage initial and repeat purchases.

**Repetition**    Repetition enhances learning and memory by increasing the accessibility of information in memory or by strengthening the associative linkages between concepts.[46] Quite simply, the more times people are exposed to information or engage in a behavior, the more likely they are to learn and remember it. For example, compared with one showing of a Miller Lite beer commercial, three showings during a championship baseball game produced two-and-one-third times the recall.[47]

The effects of repetition depend, of course, on importance and reinforcement. Less repetition of an advertising message is necessary for someone to learn the message if the subject matter is important or if there is a great deal of relevant reinforcement. Since many advertisements do not contain information of current importance to consumers or direct rewards for learning, repetition plays a critical role in the promotion process for many products.[48] As we saw earlier, classical conditioning and iconic rote learning (low-involvement learning) rely heavily on repetition.

Figure 9–8, based on a study of 16,500 respondents, shows the impact of various levels of advertising repetition over a 48-week period on brands that had either high or low levels of initial awareness. Several features stand out. First, the initial exposure has the largest

## FIGURE 9–8 | Impact of Repetition on Brand Awareness for High- and Low-Awareness Brands

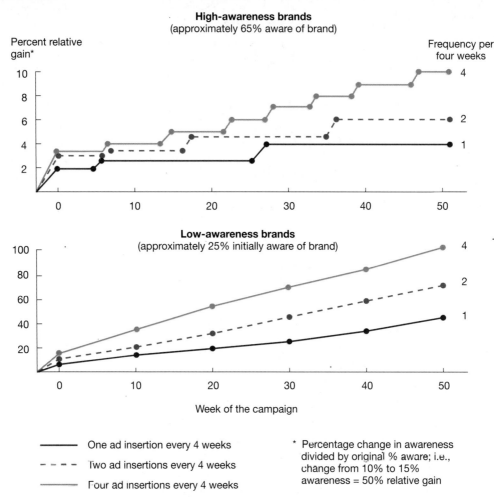

Source: *A Study of the Effectiveness of Advertising Frequency in Magazines.* © 1993 Time Inc. Reprinted by permission.

impact.[49] Second, frequent repetition (once a week) outperforms limited repetition (once every other week or every four weeks). This advantage grows the longer the campaign lasts. Finally, relative gains are much greater for unknown brands.

Both the number of times a message is repeated and the timing of those repetitions affect the extent and duration of learning and memory.[50] Figure 9–9 illustrates the relationship between repetition timing and product recall for a food product. One group of homemakers, represented by the curved line in the figure, was exposed to a food product advertisement once a week for 13 consecutive weeks. For this group, product recall increased rapidly and reached its highest level during the 13th week. Forgetting occurred rapidly when advertising stopped, and recall was virtually zero by the end of the year.

A second group of homemakers was exposed to the same 13 direct-mail advertisements. However, they received one ad every four weeks. The zigzag line in the figure shows the recall pattern for this group. In this case, learning increased throughout the year, but substantial forgetting occurred between message exposures.

Repetition Timing and Advertising Recall    FIGURE 9–9

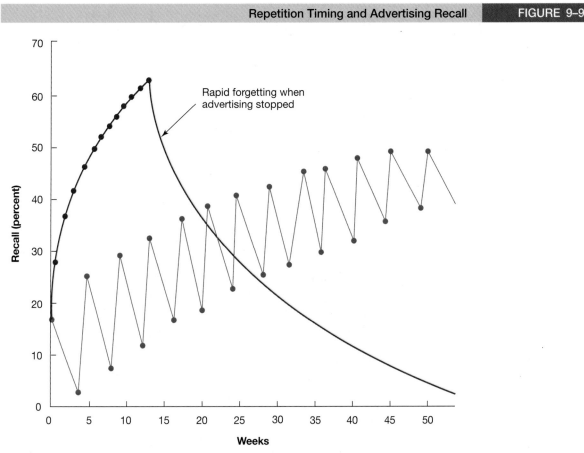

Source: Reprinted from H. J. Zielski, "The Remembering and Forgetting of Advertising," *Journal of Marketing,* January 1959, p. 240, with permission from The American Marketing Association. The actual data and a refined analysis were presented in J. L. Simon. "What Do Zielski's Data Really Show about Pulsing?" *Journal of Marketing Research,* August 1979, pp. 415–20.

Given a finite budget, how should a firm allocate its advertising across a budget cycle—should it concentrate it all at once or spread it out over time? The answer depends on the task. Any time it is important to produce widespread knowledge of the product rapidly, such as during a new-product introduction, frequent (close together) repetitions should be used. This is referred to as **pulsing.** Thus, political candidates frequently hold back a significant proportion of their media budgets until shortly before the election and then use a media blitz to ensure widespread knowledge of their desirable attributes. More long-range programs, such as store or brand image development, should use more widely spaced repetitions.[51]

Marketers must walk a fine line in terms of repetition. Too much repetition can cause consumers to actively shut out the message, evaluate it negatively, or disregard it, an effect called **advertising wearout.**[52] One strategy for avoiding wearout is to utilize variations on a common theme.[53] For example, ads for Target continually emphasize core brand themes and the "red dot" symbol. However, they do so in different and interesting ways including roaming animated spokes characters, a white dog with a red dot around one eye, and so on.

**Dual Coding**    Consumers can store (code) information in different ways. Storing the same information in different ways (dual coding) results in more internal pathways (associative links) for retrieving information. This in turn can increase learning and memory.

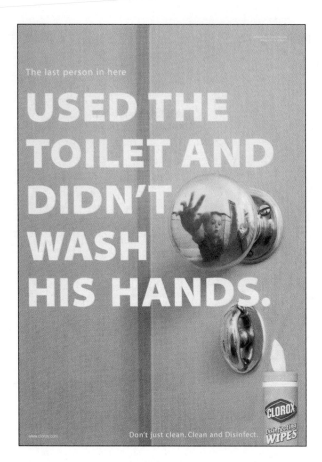

One example of dual coding is when consumers learn information in two different contexts—for example, a consumer sees two ads for the same brand of dandruff shampoo, one with an office theme and one with a social theme. The varied theme (context) provides multiple paths to the brand and therefore enhances recall later on. Illustration 9–6 shows one theme that Clorox uses for its disinfectant products. (Illustration 3–3 in Chapter 3 shows another.) By using multiple themes for its disinfectant products, Clorox can enhance consumer memory beyond its traditional bleach products.

Another example of dual coding relates to information being stored in different memory modes, such as verbal versus visual.[54] Dual coding helps explain why *imagery* enhances memory. High-imagery stimuli leave a dual code, because they are stored in memory on both verbal and pictorial dimensions, whereas low-imagery stimuli are coded only verbally. As a consequence, high-imagery brand names such as Jolt and Mustang are substantially easier to learn and remember than low-imagery names.

*Echoic memory*—memory of sounds, including words—is another memory mode that appears to have characteristics distinct from visual and verbal memory.[55] This provides the opportunity for dual coding when the sound component of a message (e.g., background music) conveys similar meanings to that being conveyed by the verbal message.[56]

Learning and memory appear to be enhanced when the key ideas communicated through one mode are consistent with those communicated through other modes.[57] For example, one study finds that having the picture (visual) and text (verbal) convey consistent ideas makes it easier for bilingual consumers to process an ad in their second language. The result is greater learning and memory of the second-language ad.[58]

# Memory Interference

Sometimes consumers have difficulty retrieving a specific piece of information because other related information in memory gets in the way. This effect is referred to as **memory interference.** A common form of interference in marketing is due to competitive advertising. For example, seeing an ad for Canada Dry Ginger Ale might interfere with your memory of Mountain Dew. Competitive advertising makes it harder for consumers to recall any given advertisement and its contents. And even if they can recall the contents of a specific ad, they will often have a hard time associating that ad with a specific brand. As a consequence, competitive advertising can either reduce memory for the brand claims made in a specific advertisement or lead to brand-claim confusions across advertisements for competing brands.[59]

Competitive advertising interference increases as the number of competing ads within the same product category increases and as the similarity of those ads to each other increases. Given the high levels of advertising clutter, it should not be surprising that this is an area of concern for marketers and advertisers. The major question is, *What can marketers do to decrease competitive interference?* A number of strategies exist, many related to the learning and memory concepts we discussed earlier.

**Avoid Competing Advertising**     One strategy is to avoid having your ad appear in the same set of ads (same pod in a TV format) as your competitors'. Some companies actually pay a premium to ensure this exclusivity. Another strategy, called *recency planning,* involves trying to plan advertising exposures so that they occur as close in time to a consumer purchase occasion as possible. The idea behind this concept is that reducing the time to purchase reduces the chances that an ad for a competing brand will be seen prior to purchase.[60]

**Strengthen Initial Learning**     Another strategy is to increase the strength of initial learning since stronger learning is less subject to memory interference. Evidence for the value of this strategy comes from the fact that memory interference is less pronounced in high-involvement contexts and for highly familiar brands. This is not surprising when you consider that high-involvement learning should result in stronger brand schemas and that brand schemas for familiar brands are stronger than those for unfamiliar brands.[61]

Additional evidence for the role of learning comes from advertising strategies that encourage dual coding. Specifically, brands can reduce competitive interference by showing different ad versions for the same brand (shampoo ad in office context and social context) or by varying the modality across exposures (radio ad followed by a print ad).[62]

Interestingly, while strong initial learning of a brand's key attributes can yield positive memory effects, it can also make it harder for the brand to add or change attributes. That is, the strong initial learning interferes with consumer learning and memory for new brand information.[63] This can make brand *repositioning* a challenging task. Repositioning is discussed later in the chapter.

**Reduce Similarity to Competing Ads**     Ads within the same product class (e.g., ads for different brands of cell phone) have been shown to increase interference, as have ads that are similar to competing ads. Similarity can be in terms of ad claims, emotional valence, and ad execution elements such as background music or pictures. Interestingly, similarity between ad execution elements can lead to memory interference even when the ads are for brands in different product categories (print ads for bleach and soda each picturing mountain scenes). Just as unique ads can break through advertising clutter to garner greater attention, unique ads are also more resistant to competitive memory interference.[64]

**Provide External Retrieval Cues**   Retrieval cues provide an external pathway to information that is stored in memory. The reason that brand names are so important is because they can serve as a retrieval cue. Seeing a brand name can trigger recall of brand information stored in memory, as well as retrieval of images and emotions associated with prior advertisements for the brand.

However, brand name is not always enough to trigger recall of prior advertising for the brand. For example, seeing the brand on a store shelf may not be sufficient to cue consumers' memory for prior advertising. This is of major consequence for marketers, since failure to recall prior advertising information and emotion during purchase reduces advertising effectiveness. In this case, marketers can use point-of-purchase displays or package cues that link directly back to the advertisements for that brand.[65] For example, during the "Got Milk?" campaign, in-store signage with the "Got Milk?" slogan was used to remind consumers about the TV ads which emphasized how awful it feels to run out of milk. Quaker Oats applied this concept as well by placing a photo of a scene from its Life cereal commercial on the cereal box. This enhanced the ability of consumers to recall both affect and information from the commercial and was very successful.

## Response Environment

Retrieval is also affected by the similarity of the retrieval (response) environment to the original learning environment and type of learning.[66] Thus, the more the retrieval situation offers cues similar to the cues present during learning, the more likely effective retrieval is to occur. One strategy is to configure the retrieval environment to resemble the original learning environment. The "Got Milk?" and Life cereal examples discussed earlier represent attempts by marketers to match the in-store retrieval environment to the learning environment by providing retrieval cues.

Another strategy is to configure the learning environment to resemble the most likely retrieval environment. Suppose a chewing gum brand knows that its retrieval environment will be in retail stores. In this case, conditioning a positive feeling to the *brand and package* by consistently pairing a visual image of the package with pleasant music would likely be most appropriate. This is because the response environment (the store shelf) visually presents consumers with brand packages. And, since learning was conditioned to a visual of the brand's package (learning environment configured to match the retrieval environment), seeing the package on the shelf will likely elicit the learned response.

# BRAND IMAGE AND PRODUCT POSITIONING

## Brand Image

**Brand image** refers to *the schematic memory of a brand.* It contains the target market's interpretation of the product's attributes, benefits, usage situations, users, and manufacturer/marketer characteristics. It is what people think of and feel when they hear or see a brand name. It is, in essence, the set of associations consumers have *learned* about the brand.[67] *Company image* and *store image* are similar except that they apply to companies and stores rather than brands.

The importance of branding and brand image can be seen in the fact that products that have traditionally been unbranded such as water, apples, and meat, are increasingly being branded. Consider the meat industry. It must deal with a number of issues, not the least of

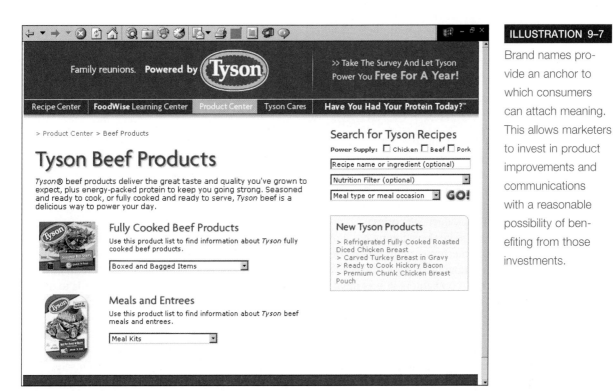

**ILLUSTRATION 9–7**

Brand names provide an anchor to which consumers can attach meaning. This allows marketers to invest in product improvements and communications with a reasonable possibility of benefiting from those investments.

which is that many consumers see meat as difficult and time-consuming to prepare. As one industry expert said:

> A lot of consumers don't have the time and expertise to take a raw roast and cook it for six to eight hours, so what we have to do in this industry is understand that and do something about it.[68]

Tyson has responded by offering a line of fully cooked chicken, pork, and beef meals that are fast, easy, and safe to prepare. This move builds nicely on Tyson's strong reputation for quality fresh meat products and its prepackaged lunch meats. Given today's consumers' dual concerns over convenience and food safety, Tyson is well positioned with a strong and consistent image that consumers trust and can relate to (see Illustration 9–7). The ability to benefit from a brand image is called *brand equity,* which we discuss in the next section.

Brand image is a major concern of both industrial and consumer goods marketers. Consider the following headlines from recent marketing publications:

Volvo Plans Ad Campaign to Clarify Automaker's Image
Making Coke *Iconic* Again
P&G Bets $100 mil on Crest Brand Plan

How powerful are brand images? Think of Nike, McDonald's, Kate Spade, Hershey's, Coke, Discovery Channel, Amazon.com, and Midas. For many consumers, each of these names conjures up a rich pattern of meanings and feelings. These meanings and imagery are powerful drivers of consumer decision making, which explains why strong brands also tend to be market leaders in terms of sales and profits.

Brand images can hinder as well as help products.[69] Hershey's recently tried to enter the upscale chocolate market with the name Cacao Reserve *by Hershey's.* The product has not performed well, most likely because consumers don't equate Hershey with premium. Hershey has a strong image. However, its image as an everyday chocolate hinders its move into the premium market. In this case, Hershey may have been better off using a *new brand strategy* with no ties to the Hershey name. We discuss this strategy later in the chapter.

## Product Positioning

**Product positioning** is a *decision by a marketer to try to achieve a defined brand image relative to competition within a market segment.* That is, marketers decide that they want the members of a market segment to think and feel in a certain way about a brand relative to competing brands. The term *product positioning* is most commonly applied to decisions concerning brands, but it is also used to describe the same decisions for stores, companies, and product categories.

Product positioning has a major impact on the long-term success of the brand, presuming the firm can create the desired position in the minds of consumers. A key issue in positioning relates to the need for brands to create product positions that differentiate them from competitors in ways that are meaningful to consumers.[70] A brand that fails to differentiate itself from competitors (stimulus discrimination) will generally find it difficult to generate consumer interest and sales.

Consider Saturn. Its original positioning emphasized customer service and the retail experience. This differentiated Saturn from the competition and resulted in strong sales. However, its ads stopped focusing on customer service in 2002 and since then sales have slumped. As a result, Saturn is moving its $190 million account to Deutsch advertising agency with the hopes of *repositioning* its brand in the minds of customers by focusing back on customer service.[71]

An important component of brand image is the appropriate usage situations for the product or brand. Often marketers have the opportunity to influence the usage situations for which a product or brand is seen as appropriate. What do you think of when you think of cranberry sauce? Odds are that Thanksgiving and perhaps Christmas are part of your image of cranberry sauce. In fact, these are probably the only usage situations that came to mind. However, in one study, sales for cranberry sauce increased almost 150 percent over a three-month period after consumers saw advertisements promoting nontraditional uses. Thus, expanding the usage situation component of cranberry sauce's product position could dramatically increase its sales.[72]

The terms *product position* and *brand image* are often used interchangeably. In general, however, product position involves an explicit reference to a brand's image relative to another brand or the overall industry. It is characterized by statements such as "HP printers are the most reliable printers available." Brand image generally considers the firm's image without a direct comparison to a competitor. It is characterized by statements such as "HP printers are extremely reliable."

Once a marketer decides on an appropriate product position, the marketing mix is manipulated in a manner designed to achieve that position in the target market.[73] For example, Sunkist Growers offers a fruit jelly candy called Sunkist Fruit Gems, which comes in various fruit flavors. It is positioned as a "healthful, natural" snack for adults and children. From a product standpoint, the candy is made from pectin (a natural ingredient from citrus peels) and contains no preservatives and less sugar than most fruit jelly candies. Thus, the product itself communicates the desired position.

However, other aspects of the marketing mix can also contribute. For example, Sunkist could distribute the candy through the produce departments of supermarkets. Notice how distribution then supports the desired product position or image. A consumer receiving a

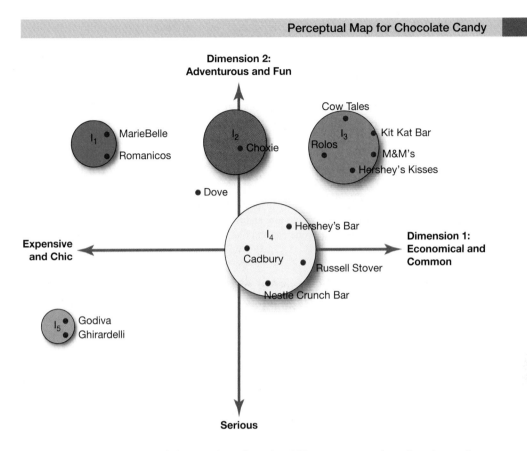

message that this is a healthful, natural product should be more receptive when the product is found near other healthful, natural products such as apples and oranges.

Marketing managers frequently fail to achieve the type of product image or position they desire because they fail to anticipate or test for consumer reactions. Toro's initial lightweight snowthrower was not successful. Why? It was named the Snowpup, and consumers interpreted this to mean that it was a toy or lacked sufficient power. Sales success came only after a more macho, power-based name was utilized—first Snowmaster and later Toro.

**Perceptual mapping** offers marketing managers a useful technique for measuring and developing a product's position. Perceptual mapping takes consumers' perceptions of how similar various brands or products are to each other and relates these perceptions to product attributes. Figure 9–10 is a perceptual map for various chocolate candy brands. This perceptual map also provides the ideal points for five market segments—$I_1$, $I_2$, $I_3$, $I_4$, $I_5$. The size of the circle around the ideal point represents the relative size of the segment, with segment 4 ($I_4$) being the largest and segment 5 ($I_5$) being the smallest. These ideal points represent the image or characteristics each segment desires in a chocolate candy. If the chocolate candies in this map were all that existed, it would indicate that segment 2 consumers are not being offered many of the products they want. Target has recently positioned a brand to target this segment with Choxie (the tagline is "Choxie is chocolate with moxie."). Still, opportunities remain to target segment 2. Is Dove well positioned? It appears not; that is, Dove would benefit from *repositioning* toward segment 2. We discuss repositioning in the next section. Notice that even though segment 3 is relatively large, there is also a considerable amount of competition, something of importance when deciding which segments to target with new brands. *What segment and competitor factors would make it more difficult to enter segment 5 than segment 2?*

## Product Repositioning

The images consumers have of brands change over time as a function of their own changing needs, as a function of changes in competitors, and as a function of changes initiated by the brand itself. For example, over the past few years, Volvo has introduced a number of new models targeting younger and less affluent consumers than it had in the past. As a Volvo representative stated:

> Consumers still think of the brand primarily in terms of safety but are unclear whether the cars are luxury vehicles, what their average prices are, and who the brand's target is. There is less clarity about Volvo now than when we had one car and one wagon. We are going to explain to people what we are.[74]

The lack of clarity of the Volvo image may signal that it is time for new strategies to help *reposition* the brand in the minds of consumers. **Product repositioning** refers to *a deliberate decision to significantly alter the way the market views a product.* This could involve its level of performance, the feelings it evokes, the situations in which it should be used, or even who uses it.[75]

Some years back, PepsiCo began repositioning its Mug Root Beer toward a younger audience. To accomplish this, it was advertised on television shows that appealed to young adults as well as on MTV. In one ad, a young man drinks Mug while flipping the city's master light switch on and off to the beat of a rock song. In addition to advertising, other changes have been made over the years to further enhance its position among a younger audience. First the package color was changed to one that better suited the youth market. Later, a funny and loveable bulldog *spokescharacter* named "Dog" was added to the package and promotions to emphasize youth and fun. Mug's Web site features Dog prominently, telling his background story, and inviting visitors to create their own Dog story and download it as computer wallpaper. Illustration 9–8 shows Mug's homepage. Notice how it reinforces Mug's ongoing repositioning efforts toward youth.

Other recent repositioning efforts include,

- H&R Block is moving from being a tax preparation specialist to "the accessible provider of financial services to Middle America."[76]
- Infiniti is attempting to move from a diffuse luxury car image to a "new brand image that is about performance."[77]
- Hyundai is attempting to move from a low-price image to one that is "refined and elegant."[78]

Repositioning can be very difficult and costly, requiring consumers to *unlearn* old associations and replace them with new ones.[79] This can take years to accomplish. In the auto industry, it is estimated that repositioning can take up to 10 years. According to one industry expert, "People's perceptions change very slowly."[80]

Repositioning may also require drastic action. For example, Hardee's was able to reverse plummeting sales only after completely walking away from the thin patties common in fast-food hamburgers and focusing exclusively on its now signature Thickburger made from Black Angus beef.[81] Sometimes companies will even change their brand name to allow a fresh start. For example, when Bell Atlantic and GTE Wireless merged, they changed their name to Verizon.

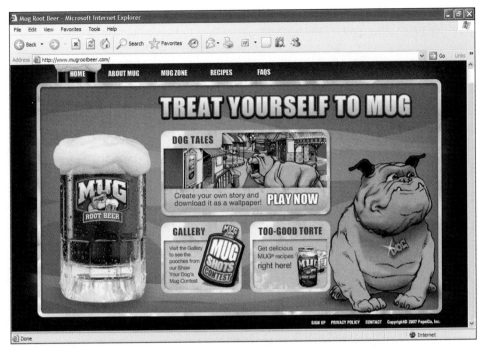

**ILLUSTRATION 9–8**

Repositioning a product involves making all aspects of the product consistent with the new position. This includes product features, price, communications, and distribution channels.

# BRAND EQUITY AND BRAND LEVERAGE

**Brand equity** is *the value consumers assign to a brand above and beyond the functional characteristics of the product.*[82] For example, many people pay a significant premium for Bayer aspirin relative to store brands of aspirin although they are chemically identical.

Brand equity is nearly synonymous with the reputation of the brand. However, the term *equity* implies economic value.[83] Thus, brands with "good" reputations have the potential for high levels of brand equity, whereas unknown brands or brands with weak or negative reputations do not. The outcomes of brand equity include increased market share, decreased consumer price sensitivity, and enhanced marketing efficiency.[84]

Brand equity is based on the product position of the brand. A consumer who believes that a brand delivers superior performance, is exciting to use, and is produced by a company with appropriate social values is likely to be willing to pay a premium for the brand, to go to extra trouble to locate and buy it, to recommend it to others, to forgive a mistake or product flaw, or to otherwise engage in behaviors that benefit the firm that markets the brand. Thus, one source of economic value from a positive brand image results from consumers' behaviors toward existing items with that brand name.[85]

Another source of value for a brand image is that consumers may assume that the favorable aspects of the image associated with an existing product will apply to a new product with the same brand name. This is based on the principle of stimulus generalization described earlier in this chapter. **Brand leverage,** often termed *family branding, brand extensions,* or *umbrella branding,* refers to *marketers capitalizing on brand equity by using an existing brand name for new products.*[86] If done correctly, consumers will assign some of the characteristics of the existing brand to the new product carrying that name. Relatively recent brand extensions include Starbucks ice cream, Listerine breath strips, and Campbell's tomato juice.

However, stimulus generalization does not occur just because two products have the same brand name. There must be a connection between the products. Pace is finally leveraging its brand equity beyond salsas by extending its name into related products such as refried beans, taco sauces, and bean dip. According to Pace's brand manager:

> We feel we have the ability to expand into Mexican meals, it's just now about choosing the right products and aligning with what consumers are making.[87]

In contrast, Campbell's was not able to introduce a spaghetti sauce under the Campbell's name (it used Prego instead). Consumer research found that

> Campbell's, to consumers, says it isn't authentic Italian. Consumers figured it would be orangy and runny like our tomato soup.[88]

Successful brand leverage generally requires that the original brand have a strong positive image and that the new product fit with the original product on at least one of four dimensions:[89]

1.  *Complement.* The two products are used together.
2.  *Substitute.* The new product can be used instead of the original.
3.  *Transfer.* Consumers see the new product as requiring the same manufacturing skills as the original.
4.  *Image.* The new product shares a key image component with the original.

It is important for marketers to understand what the key "fit" criteria are for consumers. For example, one study found that consumers would prefer Fruit Loops lollipops over Fruit Loops hot cereal. Apparently, the key fit criterion of concern was not the transfer of manufacturing capability, but rather the image component of taste.[90] Some brands are broad enough to be leveraged in multiple ways. For example, Porsche has a high-quality, sporty image among many consumers. It could logically extend its name to tires (complement), motorcycles (substitute), ski boats (transfer), or sunglasses (image). In fact, it has an entire line of golf accessories including a Porsche golf bag trolley with custom Porsche aluminum wheels designed to fit into the luggage compartment of its 911 Turbo and Boxster!

It is also important for marketers to understand that fit criteria may differ across consumer groups. For example, one study found that adults tend to look for deeper connections between the original product and the extension product, while children do not. So, despite the fact that crayons and guitars have virtually nothing in common, Crayola is able to successfully market both products to kids under the Crayola name![91]

Finally, it is important for marketers to realize that the more the new product category is a "stretch" for the brand, the more their advertising messages must help to explain how the products fit together. Such strategies help consumers transfer meaning from the existing brand to the new product by pointing out more subtle linkages than they might naturally think of on their own.[92] For example, Revlon tried to launch its own vitamins with the expression "Now, Revlon beauty begins from the inside-out." Notice how the slogan associates cosmetics and vitamins in terms of beauty.

Gucci has successfully extended its brand from leather goods and accessories to clothing and shoes. These extensions are very consistent with Gucci's luxury brand image. Illustration 9–9 shows ads for two different product offerings which demonstrate the concept of brand extension.

Other examples of successful and unsuccessful brand extensions include the following:

*   Harley-Davidson has applied its name successfully to a wide variety of products, but its Harley-Davidson wine coolers were not successful.

- Levi Strauss failed in its attempt to market Levi's tailored suits for men.
- Country Time could not expand from lemonade to apple cider.
- LifeSavers gum did not succeed.
- Coleman successfully expanded from camping stoves and lanterns into a complete line of camping equipment.
- Oil of Olay bar soap is successful in large part because of the equity of the Oil of Olay lotion.

Brand extensions are sometimes undertaken to bolster the image of the brand rather than to capitalize on its current equity. Mercedes launched a mountain bike with its name attached mostly because mountain bikes have a hip, active image. A marketer for Mercedes says the firm wants to "appeal to a larger, wider, younger audience."[93] Similarly, Courvoisier, a high-end cognac brand, is extending into luxury clothing to transform itself into a "lush lifestyle brand."[94] In these cases, the new product is designed to enhance the base brand image and increase its equity.

Sometimes brand extensions are not feasible. When marketers want to target distinct market segments with a distinct image from the original brand, they generally need to create a new brand rather than extend the existing one. AT&T did this by creating the Lucky Dog Phone Co. to offer low-cost dial-around phone service to cost-focused customers. Similarly, The Gap created Old Navy to target value-oriented students and young families. Miller Brewing uses the Plank Road Brewery to market specialty beers such as Red Dog, Southpaw, and Icehouse. These new brands have images that are distinct from the original brand. Using unique brand names for this purpose avoids diluting or confusing the original brand image.

**ILLUSTRATION 9–9**

Brand extensions are most likely to succeed when the new product is closer to existing products. However, the greatest rewards are sometimes associated with extensions into more distinct product categories.

Brand extensions can also involve risks, one being that a failure of any product with a brand name can hurt all the products with the same brand name (consumers generalize both good and bad outcomes).[95] Another risk is diluting the original brand image.[96] A strong image is generally focused on a fairly narrow set of characteristics. Each additional product added to that product name alters the image somewhat. If too many or too dissimilar products are added to the brand name, the brand image may become diffuse or confused.[97] For instance, were Porsche to offer a ski boat that competed on price rather than performance, it could damage its core image, particularly among existing owners.[98] Some observers feel that Nike is in danger of such a brand dilution as it attaches its name to an ever-wider array of products.

## SUMMARY

Consumers must learn almost everything related to being a consumer—product existence, performance, availability, values, preference, and so forth. Marketing managers, therefore, are very interested in the nature of consumer learning and memory.

Memory is the result of learning, which involves information processing. Most commonly, information goes directly into *short-term memory* for processing, where two basic activities occur—maintenance rehearsal and elaborative activities. *Maintenance rehearsal* is the continual repetition of a piece of information in order to hold it in current memory. *Elaborative activities* are the use of stored experiences, values, attitudes, and feelings to interpret and evaluate information in current memory.

*Long-term memory* is information from previous information processing that has been stored for future use. LTM undergoes continual restructuring as new information is acquired. Information is stored in long-term memory in associative networks, or schemas. Consumers often organize information in long-term memory around brands in the form of *brand schemas.* These schemas represent the brand's image in terms of key attributes, feelings, experiences, and so on.

*Learning* is defined as any change in the content or organization of long-term memory. Consumers learn in various ways, which can be broadly classified into high- versus low-involvement learning. *High-involvement learning* occurs when an individual is motivated to acquire the information. *Low-involvement learning* occurs when an individual is paying only limited or indirect attention to an advertisement or other message. Low-involvement learning tends to be limited as a result of a lack of elaborative activities.

Learning can also be classified as either conditioned or cognitive. There are two forms of conditioned learning—classical and operant. *Classical conditioning*

attempts to create an association between a stimulus (e.g., brand name) and some response (e.g., behavior or feeling) and is generally low involvement in nature. *Operant conditioning* attempts to create an association between a response (e.g., buying a brand) and some outcome (e.g., satisfaction) that serves to reinforce the response and is generally high involvement in nature.

The *cognitive* approach to learning encompasses the mental activities of humans as they work to solve problems, cope with complex situations, or function effectively in their environment. Cognitive learning includes *iconic rote learning* (generally low involvement), *vicarious learning/modeling* (low or high involvement), and *analytical reasoning* (generally high involvement).

*Stimulus generalization* is one way of transferring learning by generalizing from one stimulus situation to other, similar ones. *Stimulus discrimination* refers to the opposite process of learning—responding differently to somewhat similar stimuli. The ability of consumers to differentiate and generalize is critical for successful brand positioning and leverage.

Once learned, information is *retrieved* from long-term memory for use in evaluations and decisions. *Retrieval failures* or *extinction* of a learned response represents a reduction in marketing effectiveness. Retrieval depends on strength of initial learning, memory interference, and the response environment. *Strength of learning* depends on six basic factors: importance, message involvement, reinforcement, mood, repetition, and dual coding. *Importance* refers to the value that the consumer places on the information to be learned—greater importance increases learning and retrieval. *Message involvement* is the degree to which the consumer is interested in the message itself—the greater the message involvement, the greater the learning and retrieval. *Reinforcement* is anything that increases the likelihood that a response will be repeated in the future—the greater the reinforcement, the greater the learning and retrieval. *Mood* is the temporary mental state or feeling of the consumer. Learning and memory appear to be greater in positive mood conditions. *Repetition* refers to the number of times that we are exposed to the information or that we engage in a behavior. Repetition increases learning and memory, but can also lead to *wearout*. *Dual coding* involves creating multiple complementary pathways to a concept in long-term memory. Dual coding increases learning and retrieval.

*Memory interference* occurs when consumers have difficulty retrieving a specific piece of information because other related information in memory gets in the way. A common form of memory interference is due to competitive advertising. Competitive interference increases with increased advertising clutter. But it can be reduced by avoiding competitive clutter, strengthening learning, reducing similarity to competitor ads, and providing retrieval cues.

The *response environment* can also be critical to retrieval. Matching the response environment to the learning environment, or matching the learning environment to the response environment can enhance the ease and likelihood of retrieval.

*Brand image,* a market segment or individual consumer's schematic memory of a brand, is a major focus of marketing activity. *Product positioning* is a decision by a marketer to attempt to attain a defined and differentiated brand image, generally in relation to specific competitors. A brand image that matches a target market's needs and desires will be valued by that market segment. Such a brand is said to have *brand equity* because consumers respond favorably toward it in the market. In addition, these consumers may be willing to assume that other products with the same brand name will have some of the same features. Introducing new products under the same name as an existing product is referred to as *brand leverage* or *brand extension.*

## KEY TERMS

Accessibility  324
Advertising wearout  339
Analogical reasoning  331
Analytical reasoning  331
Brand equity  347
Brand image  342
Brand leverage  347
Classical conditioning  328
Cognitive learning  331
Concepts  320
Conditioning  326
Elaborative activities  320
Episodic memory  321
Explicit memory  325
Extinction  334

Flashbulb memory  322
High-involvement learning  325
Iconic rote learning  331
Imagery  320
Implicit memory  325
Learning  318
Long-term memory (LTM)  319
Low-involvement learning  325
Maintenance rehearsal  319
Memory interference  341
Modeling  331
Operant conditioning  328
Perceptual mapping  345
Product positioning  344
Product repositioning  346

Pulsing  339
Punishment  336
Reinforcement  336
Retrieval failure  334
Schema  322
Script  324
Self-referencing  336
Semantic memory  321
Shaping  329
Short-term memory (STM)  319
Stimulus discrimination  332
Stimulus generalization  333
Vicarious learning  331

## INTERNET EXERCISES

1. Visit one of the following Web sites. Evaluate the site in terms of its application of learning principles.
    *a.* www.chipotle.com
    *b.* www.motorola.com
    *c.* www.dior.com
    *d.* www.joltenergy.com

2. Visit several company Web sites until you find one that you feel makes particularly effective use of one or more of the learning theories we have

covered and one that makes very little use of these principles. Describe each and justify your selections.

3. Evaluate the following three Web sites in terms of their ability to create/support a good brand image and product position.
    *a.* www.minicooper.org
    *b.* www.toyota.com/yaris/
    *c.* www.bmw.com

## REVIEW QUESTIONS

1. What is *learning*?
2. What is *memory*?
3. Define *short-term memory* and *long-term memory*.
4. Discuss the nature of *short-term memory* in terms of its endurance and capacity.
5. What is *maintenance rehearsal*?
6. What is meant by *elaborative activities*?
7. What is meant by *imagery* in working memory?
8. What is *semantic memory*?
9. How does a *schema* differ from a *script*?
10. What is *episodic memory* and how does it relate to *flashbulb memory*?
11. Describe *low-involvement learning*. How does it differ from *high-involvement learning*?
12. What do we mean by *cognitive learning*, and how does it differ from the *conditioning theory* approach to learning?
13. Distinguish between learning via *classical conditioning* and learning that occurs via *operant conditioning*.
14. What is *iconic rote learning*? How does it differ from classical conditioning? Operant conditioning?
15. Define *modeling*.
16. What is meant by learning by *analytical reasoning*?
17. Describe *analogical reasoning*.
18. What is meant by *stimulus generalization*? When do marketers use it?
19. Define *stimulus discrimination*. Why is it important?
20. Explain *extinction* and *retrieval failure* and why marketing managers are interested in them.
21. What factors affect the *strength of learning*?
22. How does *self-referencing* relate to *strength of learning* and retrieval?
23. What is *memory interference,* and what strategies can marketers use to deal with it?
24. Why is it useful to match the retrieval and learning environments?
25. What is a *brand image*? Why is it important?
26. What is *product positioning*? *Repositioning*?
27. What is *perceptual mapping*?
28. What is *brand equity*?
29. What does *leveraging brand equity* mean?

## DISCUSSION QUESTIONS

30. How would you determine the best product position for the following?
    a. A candidate for student body president at your university
    b. A cell phone targeting children
    c. A local animal shelter
    d. A line of power tools targeting women
    e. A brand of toothpaste
31. Is low-involvement learning really widespread? Which products are most affected by low-involvement learning?
32. Almex and Company introduced a new coffee-flavored liqueur in direct competition with Hiram Walker's tremendously successful Kahlua brand. Almex named its new entry Kamora and packaged it in a bottle similar to that of Kahlua, using a pre-Columbian label design. The ad copy for Kamora reads, "If you like coffee—you'll love Kamora."

Explain Almex's marketing strategy in terms of learning theory.
33. Describe the brand images the following "brands" have among students on your campus.
    a. BlackBerry Smart Phone
    b. Your student government
    c. Coca Cola Zero
    d. Toyota Prius Hybrid
    e. The United Way
    f. Vegan
34. In what ways, if any, would the brand images you described in response to the previous question differ with different groups, such as (*a*) middle-aged professionals, (*b*) young blue-collar workers, (*c*) high school students, and (*d*) retired couples?
35. What role does *dual coding* play in the learning process?

36. Respond to the questions in Consumer Insight 9–1.

37. Evaluate Illustrations 9–1 through 9–5 in light of their apparent objectives and target market.

38. How would you teach teenagers an eating script that involved consistently washing one's hands first? A script for use of seat belts?

## APPLICATION ACTIVITIES

39. Fulfill the requirements of Question 33 by interviewing three male and three female students.

40. Answer Question 34 based on interviews with five individuals from each group.

41. Pick a consumer convenience product, perhaps a personal care product such as suntan lotion or toothpaste, and create advertising copy stressing (*a*) a positive reinforcement, (*b*) a negative reinforcement, and (*c*) a punishment.

42. Find and describe three advertisements, one based on cognitive learning, another based on operant conditioning, and the third based on classical conditioning. Discuss the nature of each advertisement and how it utilizes that type of learning.

43. Find and describe three advertisements that you believe are based on low-involvement learning and three that are based on high-involvement learning. Justify your selection.

44. Select a product and develop an advertisement based on low-involvement learning and one on high-involvement learning. When should each be used (be specific)?

45. Find two advertisements for competing brands that you feel do a good job of avoiding competitive advertising interference and two that you think do not. Justify your selection.

46. Visit a grocery store and examine product packages or point-of-purchase information that could serve as retrieval cues for a brand's ongoing advertising campaign. Write a brief report of your findings and describe the nature and effectiveness of the retrieval cues utilized. Could they have been better? Explain.

47. Select a product that you feel has a good product position and one that has a weak position. Justify your selection. Describe an ad or package for each product and indicate how it affects the product's position.

48. Select a product, store, or service of relevance to students on your campus. Using a sample of students, measure its brand image. Develop a marketing strategy to improve its image.

49. Develop a campaign to reduce the risk of AIDS for students on your campus by teaching them the value of
   *a.* Abstinence from sex outside of marriage
   *b.* Safe sex

50. Find a recent brand extension that you feel will be successful and one that you feel will fail. Explain each of your choices.

## REFERENCES

1. Chapter 9 opener is based on M. Mikami, "The Möet of Mackerel," *Business 2.0,* May 2006, p. 84; "The History of Sushi," *www.Sushi-master.com,* accessed January 24, 2008; and information found at the Oita City Tourist Association Web site, www.oishiimati-oita.jp/english/aji.html, accessed January 24, 2008.

2. A. A. Mitchell, "Cognitive Processes Initiated by Exposure to Advertising," in *Information Processing Research in Advertising,* ed. R. Harris (New York: Erlbaum, 1983), pp. 13–42.

3. For differing views, see A. J. Malter, "An Introduction to Embodied Cognition," *Advances in Consumer Research,* vol. 23, eds. K. P. Corfman and J. G. Lynch (Provo, UT: Association for Consumer Research, 1996), pp. 272–76; and M. E. Hill, R. Radtke, and M. King, "A Transfer Appropriate Processing View of Consumer Memory," *Journal of Current Issues and Research in Advertising,* Spring 1997, pp. 1–21.

4. M. Vanhuele, G. Laurent, and X. Drèze, "Consumers' Immediate Memory for Prices," *Journal of Consumer Research,* September 2006, pp. 163–72.

5. J. Fetto, "Call Me Vain," *American Demographics,* November 2002, p. 15.

6. See K. Mason, T. Jensen, S. Burton, and D. Roach, "The Accuracy of Brand and Attribute Judgments," *Journal of the Academy of Marketing Science,* Summer 2001, pp. 307–17; and S. Putrevu, J. Tan, and K. R. Lord, "Consumer Responses to Complex Advertisements," *Journal of Current Issues and Research in Advertising,* Spring 2004, pp. 9–24.

7. P. K. Petrova and R. B. Cialdini, "Fluency of Consumption Imagery and the Backfire Effects of Imagery Appeals," *Journal of Consumer Research,* December 2005, pp. 442–52.

8. Consumer Insight 8–1 is based on G. Wolters and J. J. Goodsmit, "Flashbulb and Event Memory of September 11, 2001, *Psychological Reports,* June 2005, pp. 605–19; H. A. Roehm, Jr. and M. L. Roehm, "Can Brand Encounters Inspire Flashbulb Memories?" *Psychology & Marketing,* January 2007, pp. 25–40; and A. Bohn and D. Bernsten, "Pleasantness Bias in Flashbulb Memories," *Memory and Cognition,* April 2007, pp. 565–77.

9. K. A. Braun, "Postexperience Advertising Effects on Consumer Memory," *Journal of Consumer Research,* March 1999, pp. 319–34; and M. Supphellen, O. Eismann, and L. E. Hem, "Can Advertisements for Brand Extensions Revitalize Flagship Products?" *International Journal of Advertising,* 23, 2004, pp. 173–96.

10. M. Morrin, J. Lee, and G. M. Allenby, "Determinants of Trademark Dilution," *Journal of Consumer Research,* September 2006, pp. 248–57.

11. See E. J. Cowley, "Recovering Forgotten Information," in *Advances in Consumer Research,* vol. 21, eds. C. T. Allen and D. R. John (Provo, UT: Association for Consumer Research, 1994), pp. 58–63.

12. K. K. Desai and W. Hoyer, "Descriptive Characteristics of Memory-Based Consideration Sets," *Journal of Consumer Research,* December 2000, pp. 309–23. See also P. Nedungadi, A. Chattopadyay, and A.V. Muthukrishnan, "Category Structure, Brand Recall, and Choice," *International Journal of Research in Marketing* 18 (2001), pp. 191–202; and E. Cowley and A. A. Mitchell, "The Moderating Effect of Product Knowledge on the Learning and Organization of Product Information," *Journal of Consumer Research,* December 2003, pp. 443–54.

13. See S. E. Heckler, "The Role of Memory in Understanding and Encouraging Recycling Behavior," *Psychology & Marketing,* July 1994, pp. 375–92.

14. G. Venkataramani and M. T. Pham, "Relatedness, Prominence, and Constructive Sponsor Identification," *Journal of Marketing Research,* August 1999, pp. 299–312.

15. E. Cowley and M. Caldwell, "Truth, Lies, and Videotape," *Advances in Consumer Research,* vol. 28, eds. M. C. Gilly and J. Meyers-Levy (Provo, UT: Association for Consumer Research, 2001), pp. 20–25.

16. K. A. Braun, R. Ellis, and E. F. Loftus, "Make My Memory," *Psychology & Marketing,* January 2002, pp. 1–23.

17. K. B. Monroe and A. Y. Lee, "Remembering versus Knowing," *Journal of the Academy of Marketing Science,* Spring 1999, pp. 207–25; and E. A. van Reijmersdal, P. C. Neijens, and E. G. Smit, "Effects of Television Brand Placement on Brand Image," *Psychology & Marketing,* May 2007, pp. 403–20.

18. S. A. Hawkins, S. J. Hoch, and J. Meyers-Levy, "Low-Involvement Learning," *Journal of Consumer Psychology* 11, no. 1 (2001), pp. 1–11.

19. See R. P. Grossman and B. D. Till, "The Persistence of Classically Conditioned Brand Attitudes," *Journal of Advertising,* Spring 1998, pp. 23–31; J. Kim, J.-S. Lim, and M. Bhargava, "The Role of Affect in Attitude Formation," *Journal of the Academy of Marketing Science,* Spring 1998, pp. 143–52; W. E. Baker, "When Can Affective Conditioning and Mere Exposure Directly Influence Brand Choice?" *Journal of Advertising,* Winter 1999, pp. 31–46; and B. D. Till and R. L. Priluck, "Stimulus Generalization in Classical Conditioning," *Psychology & Marketing,* January 2000, pp. 55–72.

20. B. D. Till and R. L. Priluck, "Conditioning of Meaning in Advertising," *Journal of Current Issues and Research in Advertising,* Fall 2001, pp. 1–8.

21. For discussions of the role of awareness in classical conditioning, see C. Janiszewski and L. Warlop, "The Influence of Classical Conditioning Procedures on Subsequent Attention to the Conditioned Brand," *Journal of Consumer Research,* September 1993, pp. 171–89; R. Priluck and B. D. Till, "The Role of Contingency Awareness, Involvement, and Need for Cognition in Attitude Formation," *Journal of the Academy of Marketing Science* 32, no. 3 (2004), pp. 329–44; and I. Kirsch et al., "The Role of Cognition in Classical and Operant Conditioning," *Journal of Clinical Psychology,* April 2004, pp. 369–92.

22. See, e.g., W. H. Motes and A. G. Woodside, "Purchase Experiments of Extra-ordinary and Regular Influence Strategies Using Artificial and Real Brands," *Journal of Business Research* 53 (2001), pp. 15–35; and Kirsch et al, "The Role of Cognition in Classical and Operant Conditioning."

23. B. J. Bergiel and C. Trosclair, "Instrumental Learning," *Journal of Consumer Marketing,* Fall 1985, pp. 23–28. See also W. Gaidis and J. Cross, "Behavior Modification as a Framework for Sales Promotion Management," *Journal of Consumer Marketing,* Spring 1987, pp. 65–74.

24. E. Heit, J. Briggs, and L. Bott, "Modeling the Effects of Prior Knowledge on Learning Incongruent Features of Category Members," *Journal of Experimental Psychology: Learning, Memory, and Cognition,* September 2004, pp. 1065–81.

25. See J. W. Pracejus, "Is More Always Better?" in *Advances in Consumer Research,* vol. 22, eds. F. R. Kardes and M. Sujan (Provo, UT: Association for Consumer Research, 1995), pp. 319–22; and K. P. Gwinner and J. Eaton, "Building Brand Image through Event Sponsorship," *Journal of Advertising,* Winter 1999, pp. 47–57.

26. T. P. Ballinger, M. G. Palumbo, and N. T. Wilcox, "Precautionary Saving and Social Learning across Generations," *The Economic Journal,* October 2003, pp. 920–47.

27. For a way to measure such images, see L. A. Babin and A. C. Burns, *Psychology & Marketing,* May 1998, pp. 261–78.

28. S. P. Jain and D. Maheswaran, "Motivated Reasoning," *Journal of Consumer Research,* March 2000, pp. 358–71.

29. J. Gregan-Paxton, J. D. Hibbard, F. F. Brunel, and P. Azar, "So That's What That Is," *Psychology & Marketing,* June 2002, pp. 533–50; and J. Gregan-Paxton and P. Moreau, "How Do Consumers Transfer Existing Knowledge?" *Journal of Consumer Psychology* 13, no. 4 (2003), pp. 422–30.

30. For an application to trademark infringement, see C. Pullig, C. J. Simmons, and R. G. Netemeyer, "Brand Dilution," *Journal of Marketing,* April 2006, pp. 52–66.

31. M. L. Roehm and A. M. Tybout, "When Will a Brand Scandal Spill Over, and How Should Competitors Respond?" *Journal of Marketing Research,* August 2006, pp. 366–373.

32. See Till and Priluck, "Stimulus Generalization in Classical Conditioning."

33. M. Maremont, "Gillette Chief Says Cost-Cutting Plan Will Take Time," *The Wall Street Journal,* June 7, 2001, p. B2.

34. "Behind Saturn's Stumble," *Advertising Age,* January 24, 1994, p. 22.

35. "L&M Lights Up Again," *Marketing & Media Decisions,* February 1984, p. 69.

36. Ibid.

37. D. Luna and L. A. Peracchio, "Where There Is a Will . . ." *Psychology & Marketing,* July–August 2002, pp. 573–93; see also R. S. Wyer, Jr., "Language and Advertising Effectiveness," *Psychology & Marketing,* July–August 2002, pp. 693–712.

38. See R. G. M. Pieters, E. Rosbergen, and M. Hartog, "Visual Attention to Advertising," *Advances in Consumer Research,* vol. 23, eds. Corfman and Lynch, pp. 242–48; and S. M. Leong, S. H. Ang, and L. L. Tham, "Increasing Brand Name Recall in Print Advertising among Asian Consumers," *Journal of Advertising,* Summer 1996, pp. 65–81.

39. M. L. Roehm, "Instrumental vs. Vocal Versions of Popular Music in Advertising," *Journal of Advertising Research,* May 2001, pp. 49–58. See also W. E. Baker and R. J. Lutz, "An Empirical Test of an Updated Relevance–Accessibility Model," *Journal of Advertising,* Spring 2000, pp. 1–13.

40. See, e.g., M. Wedel and R. Pieters, "Eye Fixations on Advertisements and Memory for Brands," *Marketing Science,* Fall 2000, pp. 297–312.

41. M. Morrin and S. Ratneshwar, "Does It Make Sense to Use Scents to Enhance Brand Memory?" *Journal of Marketing Research,* February 2003, pp. 10–25.

42. W. E. Baker, H. Honea, and C. A. Russell, "Do Not Wait to Reveal the Brand Name," *Journal of Advertising,* Fall 2004, pp. 77–85; see also W. E. Baker, "Does Brand Name Imprinting in Memory Increase Brand Information Retention?" *Psychology & Marketing,* December 2003, pp. 1119–35.

43. See R. E. Burnkrant and H. R. Unnava, "Effects of Self-Referencing on Persuasion," *Journal of Consumer Research,* June 1995, pp. 17–26; and P. Krishnamurthy and M. Sujan, "Retrospection versus Anticipation," *Journal of Consumer Research,* June 1999, pp. 55–69.

44. K. R. Lord, R. E. Burnkrant, and H. R. Unnava, "The Effects of Program-Induced Mood States on Memory for Commercial Information," *Journal of Current Issues and Research in Advertising,* Spring 2001, pp. 1–14; and S. J. Newell, K. V. Henderson, and B. T. Wu, "The Effects of Pleasure and Arousal on Recall of Advertisements during the Super Bowl," *Psychology & Marketing,* November 2001, pp. 1135–53.

45. T. Ambler and T. Burne, "The Impact of Affect on Memory of Advertising," *Journal of Advertising Research,* March 1999, pp. 25–39; and S. Youn et al., "Commercial Liking and Memory," *Journal of Advertising Research,* May 2001, pp. 7–13.

46. See P. Malaviya, J. Meyers-Levy, and B. Sternthal, "Ad Repetition in a Cluttered Environment," *Psychology & Marketing,* March 1999, pp. 99–118.

47. J. O. Eastlack, Jr., "How to Get More Bang from Your Television Bucks," *Journal of Consumer Marketing,* Third Quarter 1984, pp. 25–34. See also L. W. Turley and J. R. Shannon, "The Impact and Effectiveness of Advertisements in a Sports Arena," *Journal of Services Marketing* 14, no. 4 (2000), pp. 323–36.

48. See Hawkins, Hoch, and Meyers-Levy, "Low-Involvement Learning."

49. See also J. P. Jones, "Single-Source Research Begins to Fulfill Its Promise," *Journal of Advertising Research,* May 1995, pp. 9–16.

50. See S. N. Singh, S. Mishra, N. Bendapudi, and D. Linville, "Enhancing Memory of Television Commercials through Message Spacing," *Journal of Marketing Research,* August 1994, pp. 384–92; E. Ephron, "More Weeks, Less Weight," *Journal of Advertising Research,* May 1995, pp. 18–23; and H. Noel, "The Spacing Effect," *Journal of Consumer Psychology* 16, no. 3 (2006), pp. 306–20.

51. For more on spacing effects, see C. Janiszewski, H. Noel, and A. G. Sawyer, "A Meta-analysis of the Spacing Effect in Verbal Learning," *Journal of Consumer Research,* June 2003, pp. 138–49; and S. L. Appleton-Knapp, R. A. Bjork, and T. D. Wickens, "Examining the Spacing Effect in Advertising," *Journal of Consumer Research,* September 2005, pp. 266–76.

52. See M. H. Blair and M. J. Rabuck, "Advertising Wearin and Wearout," *Journal of Advertising Research,* September 1998, pp. 7–25; D. W. Stewart, "Advertising Wearout," *Journal of Advertising Research,* September 1999, pp. 39–42; M. C. Campbell and K. L. Keller, "Brand Familiarity and Advertising Repetition Effects," *Journal of Consumer Research,* September 2003, pp. 292–304.

53. D. Schumann, R. E. Petty, and D. S. Clemons, "Predicting the Effectiveness of Different Strategies of Advertising Variation," *Journal of Consumer Research,* September 1990, pp. 192–202.

54. W. J. Bryce and R. F. Yalch, "Hearing versus Seeing," *Journal of Current Issues and Research in Advertising,* Spring 1993, pp. 1–20; and A. C. Burns, A. Biswas, and L. A. Babin, "The Operation of Visual Imagery as a Mediator of Advertising Effects," *Journal of Advertising,* June 1993, pp. 71–85.

55. T. Clark, "Echoic Memory Explored and Applied," *Journal of Consumer Marketing,* Winter 1987, pp. 39–46. See also C. E. Young and M. Robinson, "Video Rhythms and Recall," *Journal of Advertising Research,* July 1989, pp. 22–25.

56. J. J. Kellaris, A. D. Cox, and D. Cox, "The Effect of Background Music on Ad Processing," *Journal of Marketing,* October 1993, pp. 114–25. See also M. Hahn and I. Hwang, "Effects of Tempo and Familiarity of Background Music on Message Processing in TV Advertising," *Psychology & Marketing,* December 1999, pp. 659–75.

57. K. R. Lord and S. Putrevu, "Communicating in Print," *Journal of Current Issues and Research in Advertising,* Fall 1998, pp. 1–18.

58. D. Luna and L. A. Peracchio, "Moderators of Language Effects in Advertising to Bilinguals," *Journal of Consumer Research,* September 2001, pp. 284–95.

59. See R. D. Jewell and H. R. Unnava, "When Competitive Interference Can Be Beneficial," *Journal of Consumer Research,* September 2003, pp. 283–91; and A. Kumar and S. Krishnan, "Memory Interference in Advertising," *Journal of Consumer Research,* March 2004, pp. 602–11.

60. See M. Dahlen and J. Nordfalt, "Interference Effects of a Purchase on Subsequent Advertising within the Category," *Journal of Current Issues and Research in Advertising,* Spring 2004, pp. 1–8.

61. R. J. Kent and C. T. Allen, "Competitive Interference Effects in Consumer Memory for Advertising," *Journal of Marketing,* July 1994, pp. 97–105; A. Kumar, "Interference Effects of Contextual Cues in Advertisements on Memory for Ad Content," *Journal of Consumer Psychology* 9, no. 3 (2000), 155–66; S. Law, "Can Repeating a Brand Claim Lead to Memory Confusion?" *Journal of Marketing Research,* August 2002, pp. 366–78; K. A. Braun-LaTour and M. S. LaTour, "Assessing the Long-Term Impact of a Consistent Advertising Campaign on Consumer Memory," *Journal of Advertising,* Summer 2004, pp. 49–61; and M. Laroche, M. Cleveland, and I. Maravelakis, "Competitive Advertising Interference and Ad Repetition Effects," *International Journal of Advertising* 25, no. 3 (2006), pp. 271–307.

62. H. R. Unnava and D. Sirdeshmukh, "Reducing Competitive Ad Interference," *Journal of Marketing Research,* August 1994, pp. 403–11.

63. Jewell and Unnava, "When Competitive Interference Can Be Beneficial"; and K. L. Keller, S. E. Heckler, and M. J. Houston, "The Effects of Brand Name Suggestiveness on Advertising Recall," *Journal of Marketing,* January 1998, pp. 48–57.

64. Kumar, "Interference Effects of Contextual Cues in Advertisements on Memory for Ad Content."

65. M. C. Macklin, "The Effects of an Advertising Retrieval Cue on Young Children's Memory and Brand Evaluations," *Psychology & Marketing,* May 1994, pp. 291–311; Keller, Heckler, and Houston, "The Effects of Brand Name Suggestiveness on Advertising Recall"; and N. T. Tavassoli and Y. H. Lee, "The Differential Interaction of Auditory and Visual Advertising Elements with Chinese and English," *Journal of Marketing Research,* November 2003, pp. 468–80.

66. See J. W. Park, "Memory-Based Product Judgments," and E. J. Cowley, "Altering Retrieval Sets," both in *Advances in Consumer Research,* vol. 22, eds. Kardes and Sujan, pp. 159–64 and 323–27, respectively; and M. E. Hill and M. King, "Comparative vs. Noncomparative Advertising," *Journal of Current Issues and Research in Advertising,* Fall 2001, pp. 33–52.

67. S. M. J. Van Osselaer and J. W. Alba, "Consumer Learning and Brand Equity," *Journal of Consumer Research,* June 2000, pp. 1–16; W. R. Dillon et al., "Understanding What's in a Brand Rating," *Journal of Marketing Research,* November 2001, pp. 415–29; and K. L. Keller, "Brand Synthesis," *Journal of Consumer Research,* March 2003, pp. 595–600.

68. S. Thompson, "Meat Gets Branded," *Advertising Age,* September 24, 2001, p. 6.

69. S. M. J. Van Osselaer and J. W. Alba, "Locus of Equity and Brand Extension," *Journal of Consumer Research,* March 2003, pp. 539–50.

70. For a discussion of perceived differences generated by trivial attributes, see S. M. Broniarczyk and A. D. Gershoff, "The Reciprocal Effects of Brand Equity and Trivial Attributes," *Journal of Marketing Research,* May 2003, pp. 161–75.

71. J. Halliday, "Losing Its Brand Soul," *Advertising Age,* February 5, 2007, pp. 4, 35.

72. B. Wansink, "Making Old Brands New," *American Demographics,* December 1998, pp. 53–58.

73. See, e.g., C. Young, "Brain Waves, Picture Sorts®, and Branding Moments," *Journal of Advertising Research,* August 2002, pp. 42–53.

74. J. Halliday, "Volvo Plans Ad Campaign to Clarify Automaker's Image," *Advertising Age,* October 9, 2000, p. 4.

75. See V. Gerson, "Showing Customers Your Best Face," *Bank Marketing,* January 1999, pp. 26–30; and D. James, "Image Makeovers Require Gentle Touch," *Marketing News,* July 2, 2001, p. 4.

76. M. Cardona, "Block's Less Taxing Future," *Advertising Age,* January 15, 2001, p. 6.

77. J. Halliday, "New Q45 Effort," *Advertising Age,* March 2001, p. 8.

78. J. Halliday, "Hyundai and Kia Head Upscale via Different Routes," *Advertising Age,* November 1, 2004, p. 12.

79. Jewell and Unnava, "When Competitive Interference Can Be Beneficial"; and K. K. Desai and S. Ratneshwar, "Consumer Perceptions of Product Variants Positioned on Atypical Attributes," *Journal of the Academy of Marketing Science,* Winter 2003, pp. 22–35.

80. J. Halliday, "Little Else Matters," *Advertising Age,* August 16, 2004, p. 6.

81. K. Macarthur, "Hardee's," *Advertising Age,* November 1, 2004, p. S-18.

82. M. Supphellen, "Understanding Core Brand Equity," *International Journal of Marketing Research* 42, no. 3 (2000), pp. 319–38; M. M. Mackay, "Application of Brand Equity Service Measures in Service Markets," *Journal of Services Marketing* 15, no. 3 (2001), pp. 21–29; D. A. Aaker and R. Jacobson, "The Value of Brand Attitude in High-Technology Markets," *Journal of Marketing Research,* November 2001, pp. 485–93; and S. Brown, R. V. Kozinets, and J. F. Sherry, Jr., "Teaching Old Brands New Tricks," *Journal of Marketing,* July 2003, pp. 19–33.

83. A. Chaudhuri, "How Brand Reputation Affects the Advertising–Brand Equity Link," *Journal of Advertising Research,* June 2002, pp. 33–43.

84. P. Chandon, B. Wansink, and G. Laurent, "A Benefit Congruency Framework of Sales Promotion Effectiveness," *Journal of Marketing,* October 2000, pp. 65–81.

85. N. Dawar and M. M. Pillutla, "Impact of Product-Harm Crises on Brand Equity," *Journal of Marketing Research,* May 2000, pp. 215–26; H. Kim, W. G. Kim, and J. A. An, "The Effect of Consumer-based Brand Equity on Firms' Financial Performance," *Journal of Consumer Marketing* 20, no. 4 (2003), pp. 335–51; and D. DelVecchio and D. C. Smith, "Brand-Extension Price Premiums," *Journal of the Academy of Marketing Science,* Spring 2005, pp. 184–96.

86. See T. Erdem and B. Sun, "An Empirical Investigation of the Spillover Effects of Advertising and Sales Promotions in Umbrella Branding," *Journal of Marketing Research,* November 2002, pp. 408–20; and J. H. Washburn, B. D. Till, and R. Priluck, "Brand Alliance and Customer-Based Brand-Equity Effects," *Psychology & Marketing,* July 2004, pp. 487–508.

87. S. Thompson, "Campbell Extends Pace beyond Salsa," *Advertising Age,* August 30, 2004, p. 10.

88. H. Schlossberg, "Slashing through Market Clutter," *Marketing News,* March 5, 1990, p. 6.

89. E. Maoz and A. M. Tybout, "The Moderating Role of Involvement and Differentiation in the Evaluation of Brand Extensions,"

*Journal of Consumer Psychology* 12, no. 2 (2002), pp. 119–31; F. Völckner and H. Sattler, "Drivers of Brand Extension Success," *Journal of Marketing,* April 2006, 18–34; and H. Mao and H. S. Krishnan, "Effects of Prototype and Exemplar Fit on Brand Extension Evaluations," *Journal of Consumer Research,* June 2006, pp. 41–49.

90. S. M. Broniarczyk and J. W. Alba, "The Importance of the Brand in Brand Extension," *Journal of Marketing Research,* May 1994, pp. 214–28; see also T. Meyvis and C. Janiszewski, "When Are Broader Brands Stronger Brands?" *Journal of Consumer Research,* pp. 346–57.

91. See S. Zhang and S. Sood, "'Deep' and 'Surface' Cues," *Journal of Consumer Research,* June 2002, pp. 129–41.

92. S. Bridges, K. L. Keller, and S. Sood, "Communication Strategies for Brand Extensions," *Journal of Advertising,* Winter 2000, pp. 1–12; and R. Klink and D. C. Smith, "Threats to the External Validity of Brand Extension Research," *Journal of Marketing Research,* August 2001, pp. 326–35; see also F. Völckner and H. Sattler, "Drivers of Brand Extension Success;" and C. Blankson and S. P. Kalafatis, "Congruence between Positioning and Brand Advertising," *Journal of Advertising Research,* March 2007, pp. 79–94.

93. B. Forrest, "Two-Wheel Drives," *Men's Journal,* November 1996, p. 34.

94. V. O'Connell, "Courvoisier to Launch Clothing Line," *The Wall Street Journal,* February 13, 2004, p. B2.

95. V. Swarminathan, R. J. Fox, and S. K. Reddy, "The Impact of Brand Extension Introduction on Choice," *Journal of Marketing,* October 2001, pp. 1–15.

96. Effects can be negative or positive. See, e.g., D. R. John, B. Loken, and C. Joiner, "The Negative Impact of Extensions," *Journal of Marketing,* January 1998, pp. 19–32; Z. Gurhan-Canli and D. Maheswaran, "The Effects of Extensions on Brand Name Dilution and Enhancement," *Journal of Marketing Research,* November 1998, pp. 464–73; S. Balachander and S. Ghose, "Reciprocal Spillover Effects," *Journal of Marketing,* January 2003, pp. 4–13.

97. For exceptions, see Meyvis and Janiszewski, "When Are Broader Brands Stronger Brands?"

98. A. Kirmani, S. Sood, and S. Bridges, "The Ownership Effect in Consumer Response to Brand Line Stretches," *Journal of Marketing,* January 1999, pp. 88–101.

# Motivation, Personality, and Emotion

How do people decide where to go on vacation? The answer to this question was of critical concern to New Zealand as it embarked on its first global branding initiative.[1] New Zealand, like many other countries, depends on tourism as a significant source of revenue. Tourism New Zealand (TNZ) was created to investigate the tourism market and to develop New Zealand into a destination spot with a high level of emotional pull.

TNZ's first step was extensive market research, with a particular focus on the United Kingdom (U.K.). An interesting early finding was that U.K. travelers had various underlying motivations for going on vacation. Their six motivations were:

- *Energizing*—take on the world
- *Sociability*—join in/have fun
- *Status*—feel superior to others
- *Connection*—getting together
- *Learning*—broaden the mind
- *Relaxation*—restore the spirit

A critical next step was to understand whether these needs and motives were different across types of traveler and travel situations. The answer was a resounding yes. Some vacationers were "fun and sun" types who wanted relaxation and socialization. Others were "serious" vacationers who wanted a vacation that was prestigious and energizing, and that provided opportunities for learning.

TNZ realized that it could not go after the "fun and sun" types. Their research clearly indicated that New Zealand was seen as potentially serious and boring because of its perceived lack of culture and night life. In addition, while warmer than the United Kingdom, New Zealand knew that it probably couldn't compete successfully against much closer resort destinations such as Venice in terms of sun and beaches.

All of this led TNZ to the conclusion that it had to position itself to go after the more serious vacationer. Its research showed that U.K. travelers saw New Zealand as friendly, down-to-earth, unpretentious, and adventurous. In addition, New Zealand is seen as "real and authentic." As one advertising executive on the account stated:

As the world becomes increasingly "manufactured," the world's nations have become

359

Appeals to self-actualization focus on individuals challenging themselves and reaching their full potential.

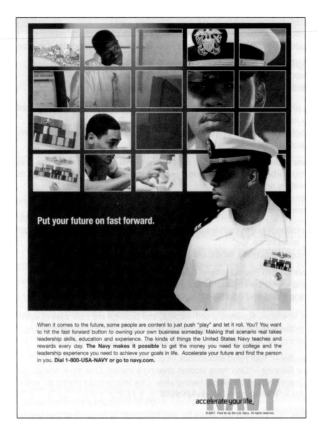

system that organizes these various theories into 16 categories.[5] This system helps marketers isolate motives likely to be involved in various consumption situations. McGuire first divides motivation into four main categories using two criteria:

1.  Is the mode of motivation cognitive or affective?
2.  Is the motive focused on preservation of the status quo or on growth?

*Cognitive* motives focus on the person's need for being adaptively oriented toward the environment and achieving a sense of meaning. *Affective* motives deal with the need to reach satisfying feeling states and to obtain personal goals. *Preservation-oriented* motives emphasize the individual as striving to maintain equilibrium, while *growth* motives emphasize development. These four main categories are then further subdivided on the bases of source and objective of the motive:

3.  Is this behavior actively initiated or in response to the environment?
4.  Does this behavior help the individual achieve a new internal or a new external relationship to the environment?

The third criterion distinguishes between motives that are actively or internally aroused versus those that are a more passive response to circumstances. The final criterion is used to categorize outcomes that are internal to the individual and those focused on a relationship with the environment.

McGuire's 16 motives and their implications for marketing are briefly described in the following sections.

Cognitive Preservation Motives     *Need for Consistency (active, internal)*     A basic desire is to have all facets of oneself consistent with each other.[6] These facets include attitudes, behaviors, opinions, self-images, views of others, and so forth. *Cognitive dissonance* is a common motive of this type. For example, making a major purchase is not consistent with the need to save money. This inconsistency motivates the individual to reduce it (see Chapter 18).

Understanding the need for consistency is also important for structuring advertising messages relating to attitude change. A need for internal consistency means consumers are reluctant to accept information that disagrees with existing beliefs. Thus, marketers wishing to change attitudes must use highly credible sources or other techniques to overcome this (see Chapter 11).

*Need for Attribution (active, external)*     This set of motives deals with our need to determine who or what causes the things that happen to us and relates to an area of research called **attribution theory.**[7] Do we attribute the cause of a favorable or unfavorable outcome to ourselves or to some outside force?

Need for attribution is extremely relevant to consumer reactions to promotional messages (in terms of credibility). Because consumers do not passively receive messages but rather attribute "selling" motives and tactics to ads and the advice of sales personnel, they do not believe or they discount many sales messages.[8] Marketers use a variety of means to overcome this. One approach is to use a credible spokesperson, as seen in Illustration 10–2. This technique is discussed in depth in Chapter 11.

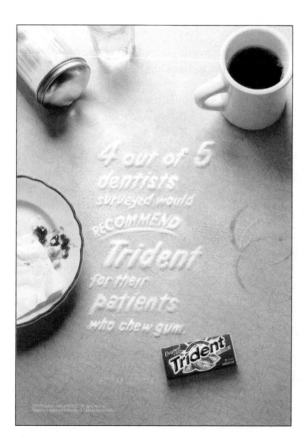

**ILLUSTRATION 10–2**

Consumers generally attribute selling motives to ads and disbelieve or discount the message. One approach to gain message acceptance is to use a credible source.

***Need to Categorize (passive, internal)***    People have a need to categorize and organize the vast array of information and experiences they encounter in a meaningful yet manageable way.[9] So they establish categories or mental partitions to help them do so. Prices are often categorized such that different prices connote different categories of goods. Automobiles over $20,000 and automobiles under $20,000 may elicit two different meanings because of information categorized on the basis of price level. Many firms price items at $9.95, $19.95, $49.95, and so forth. One reason is to avoid being categorized in the over $10, $20, or $50 group.

***Need for Objectification (passive, external)***    These motives reflect needs for observable cues or symbols that enable people to infer what they feel and know. Impressions, feelings, and attitudes are subtly established by viewing one's own behavior and that of others and drawing inferences as to what one feels and thinks. In many instances, clothing plays an important role in presenting the subtle meaning of a desired image and consumer lifestyle. Brands play a role in this as shown in Figure 10–1 (see page 368).

**Cognitive Growth Motives**    ***Need for Autonomy (active, internal)***    The need for independence and individuality is a characteristic of the American culture, as described in Chapter 2. All individuals in all cultures have this need at some level. Americans are taught that it is proper and even essential to express and fulfill this need (in contrast to Eastern countries such as Japan, which value affiliation).

Owning or using products and services that are unique is one way consumers express their autonomy.[10] Marketers have responded to this motive by developing limited editions of products and providing wide variety and customization options. In addition, many products are advertised and positioned with independence, uniqueness, or individuality themes, as shown in Illustration 10–3.

***Need for Stimulation (active, external)***    People often seek variety and difference out of a need for stimulation.[11] Such variety-seeking behavior may be a prime reason for brand switching and some so-called impulse purchasing.[12] The need for stimulation is curvilinear and changes over time.[13] That is, individuals experiencing rapid change generally become satiated and desire stability, whereas individuals in stable environments become bored and desire change.

**ILLUSTRATION 10–3**

Americans respond positively to ads and products that encourage uniqueness and individuality.

***Teleological Need (passive, internal)***    Consumers are pattern matchers who have images of desired outcomes or end states with which they compare their current situation. Behaviors are changed and the results are monitored in terms of movement toward the desired end state. This motive propels people to prefer mass media such as movies, television programs, and books with outcomes that match their view of how the world should work (e.g., the good guys win). This has obvious implications for advertising messages.

***Utilitarian Need (passive, external)***    These theories view the consumer as a problem solver who approaches situations as opportunities to acquire useful information or new skills. Thus, a consumer watching a situation comedy on

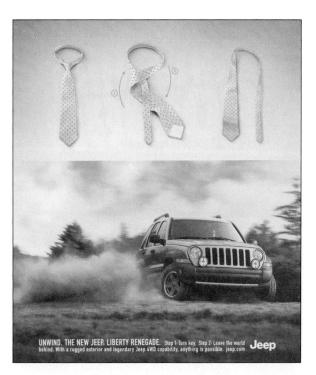

**ILLUSTRATION 10–4**

Today's hurried life-styles often produce uncomfortable levels of tension. Products that relieve this stress fulfill a fundamental need.

television not only is being entertained but is learning clothing styles, lifestyle options, and so forth. Likewise, consumers may approach ads and salespeople as a source of learning for future decisions as well as for the current one.

Affective Preservation Motives    *Need for Tension Reduction (active, internal)*    People encounter situations in their daily lives that create uncomfortable levels of stress. In order to effectively manage tension and stress, people are motivated to seek ways to reduce arousal. Recreational products and activities are often promoted in terms of tension relief. Illustration 10–4 contains a product and appeal focused on this need.

*Need for Expression (active, external)*    This motive deals with the need to express one's identity to others. People feel the need to let others know who and what they are by their actions, which include the purchase and use of goods. The purchase of many products, such as clothing and automobiles, allows consumers to express an identity to others, because the products have symbolic meanings. For example, fashion-oriented watches such as Swatch satisfy more than the functional need to tell time—they allow consumers to express who they are.

*Need for Ego Defense (passive, internal)*    The need to defend one's identity or ego is another important motive. When one's identity is threatened, the person is motivated to protect his or her self-concept and utilize defensive behaviors and attitudes. Many products can provide ego defense. A consumer who feels insecure may rely on well-known brands for socially visible products to avoid any chance of making a socially incorrect purchase.

*Need for Reinforcement (passive, external)*    People are often motivated to act in certain ways because they were rewarded for behaving that way in similar situations in the past. This is the basis for operant learning. Products designed to be used in public situations (clothing, furniture, and artwork) are frequently sold on the basis of the amount and type

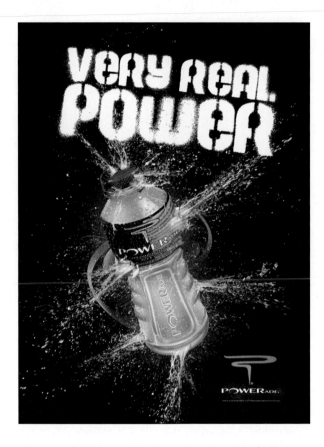

of reinforcement that will be received. Keepsake Diamonds exploits this motive with an ad that states, "Enter a room and you are immediately surrounded by friends sharing your excitement."

**Affective Growth Motives**   *Need for Assertion (active, internal)*   Many people are competitive achievers who seek success, admiration, and dominance. Important to them are power, accomplishment, and esteem. As Illustration 10–5 shows, the need for assertion underlies numerous ads.

*Need for Affiliation (active, external)*   Affiliation refers to the need to develop mutually helpful and satisfying relationships with others. It relates to altruism and seeking acceptance and affection in interpersonal relations. As we saw in Chapter 7, group membership is a critical part of most consumers' lives, and many consumer decisions are based on the need to maintain satisfying relationships with others. Marketers frequently use such affiliation-based themes as "Your kids will love you for it" in advertisements.[14]

*Need for Identification (passive, internal)*   The need for identification results in the consumer's playing various roles. A person may play the role of college student, sorority member, bookstore employee, fiancée, and many others. One gains pleasure from adding new, satisfying roles and by increasing the significance of roles already adopted. Marketers encourage consumers to assume new roles (become a skateboarder) and position products as critical for certain roles ("No working mother should be without one").

*Need for Modeling (passive, external)*   The need for modeling reflects a tendency to base behavior on that of others. Modeling is a major means by which children learn to become consumers. The tendency to model explains some of the conformity that occurs within reference groups. Marketers use this motive by showing desirable types of individuals using their brands. American Express, for example, uses Laird Hamilton and Tiger Woods in its "My life. My card" campaign.

# MOTIVATION THEORY AND MARKETING STRATEGY

Classico and Newman's Own spaghetti sauces are consumed by upscale, sophisticated adults. However, Classico buyers are motivated by indulgence and romance whereas Newman's Own buyers are showing ambition and individuality. Since the purchase of each of these brands is caused by a different motive, each requires a distinct marketing and advertising program.[15]

Consumers do not buy products; instead, they buy motive satisfaction or problem solutions. Thus, consumers do not buy perfume or cologne (or a chemical compound with certain odoriferous characteristics). Instead, they buy romance, sex appeal, sensual pleasure, sophistication, or a host of other emotional and psychological benefits. Managers must discover the motives that their products and brands can satisfy and develop marketing mixes around these motives.

An important question that often arises is, "Do marketers create needs?" The answer depends in part on what is meant by the term *need*. If it is used to refer to the basic motives described in this chapter, it is clear that marketers seldom if ever *create* a need. Human genetics and experience basically determine motives. Long before marketing or advertising appeared, individuals used perfumes, clothing, and other items to gain acceptance, display status, and so forth. However, marketers do create **demand.** Demand is *the willingness to buy a particular product or service.* It is caused by a need or motive, but it is not the motive. For example, a mouthwash ad might use a theme suggesting that without mouthwash people will not like you because you have bad breath. This message ties mouthwash to an existing need for affiliation in hopes of creating demand for the brand.

The preceding discussion makes clear the important role that motives play in consumer behavior and thus in marketing strategy. In the following sections, we examine how motives relate to various aspects of marketing strategy.

## Discovering Purchase Motives

Suppose a marketing researcher asked a consumer why he wears J. Crew clothes (or owns a mountain bike, or uses cologne, or whatever). Odds are the consumer would offer several reasons, such as "They're in style," "My friends wear them," "I like the way they fit," or "They look good on me." However, there may be other reasons that the consumer is reluctant to admit or perhaps is not even aware of: "They show that I have money," "They make me sexually desirable," or "They show I'm trendy and urbane." All or any combination of the above motives could influence the purchase of clothes or many other items.

The first group of motives mentioned above were known to the consumer and admitted to the researcher. Motives that are known and freely admitted are called **manifest motives.** Any of the motives we have discussed can be manifest; however, motives that conform to a society's prevailing value system are more likely to be manifest than are those in conflict with such values.

## FIGURE 10–1      Latent and Manifest Motives in a Purchase Situation

**Manifest Motives**

Their clothes are stylish and come in a variety of sizes and colors

Their clothes are high quality and comfortable

A number of my friends wear J. Crew clothes

**Consumption Behavior**

Purchase J. Crew clothes

**Latent Motives**

It will show that I'm sophisticated and trendy

It's an upscale and urbane brand that will help make me powerful and popular

The linkage between behavior and motives that are known and freely admitted

The linkage between behavior and motives that either are unknown or are such that the consumer is reluctant to admit or reveal them

The second group of motives described above either were unknown to the consumer or were such that she was reluctant to admit them. Such motives are **latent motives.** Figure 10–1 illustrates how the two types of motives might influence a purchase.

The first task of the marketing manager is to determine the combination of motives influencing the target market. Manifest motives are relatively easy to determine. Direct questions (Why do you purchase J. Crew clothing?) will generally produce reasonably accurate assessments of manifest motives.

Determining latent motives is substantially more complex. Motivation research or **projective techniques** are designed to provide information on latent motives. Examples include word associations whereby consumers respond to a list of brands or behaviors with the first word that comes to mind and third-person techniques whereby consumers provide reasons and motives as to why "other people" might buy a certain brand. The third-person technique assumes that consumers project their own motives onto other people and that talking about other people makes it easier and less threatening to reveal latent motives than talking about oneself. Oreo used projective techniques in a focus group setting to gain a fuller understanding of the brand. What surprised them was that "many regarded Oreo as almost 'magical.' " As a result, "Unlocking the Magic of Oreo" became a campaign theme.[16] For more details on projective techniques, see Appendix A and Appendix Table A–1.

Beyond projective techniques, a popular tool for identifying motives is **laddering,** or constructing a **means–end** or **benefit chain.**[17] A product or brand is shown to a consumer, who names all the benefits that product might provide. For each of these benefits, the respondent is then asked to identify further benefits. This is repeated until no additional benefits are identified.

For example, a respondent might mention "fewer colds" as a benefit of taking a daily vitamin. When asked the benefit of fewer colds, one respondent might identify "more efficient at work" and "more energy." Another might name "more skiing" and "looking better." Both use the vitamin to reduce colds but as a means to different ultimate benefits. *How should vitamin ads aimed at each of these two consumers differ?*

## Marketing Strategies Based on Multiple Motives

Once a manager has isolated the combination of motives influencing the target market, the next task is to design the marketing strategy around the appropriate set of motives. This involves everything from product design to marketing communications. The nature of these decisions is most apparent in the communications area. Suppose the motives shown in Figure 10–1 are an accurate reflection of a desired target market. *What communications strategy should the manager use?*

One consideration is the extent to which more than one motive is important. If multiple motives are important, the product and ads must provide and communicate them, respectively. A second consideration is whether the motive is manifest or latent. Communicating manifest benefits is relatively easy. For example, J. Crew's Web site provides hundreds of thumbnails of its many different products by category so that consumers can visually evaluate their products in terms of style, color, and quality. This is a *direct appeal* to manifest motives.

However, since latent motives often are less than completely socially desirable, *indirect appeals* frequently are used. While the bulk of J. Crew's Web site deals with showing very accurate but relatively bland pictures of their products, the most prominent aspects of the Web site provide *indirect appeals* to wealth and sophistication. For example, in the Women's Shop area, J. Crew clothes are modeled by attractive women in European settings, thus *suggesting* sophistication and worldliness. In the Men's Shop area, the Web site provides a visual list of the "12 Key Pieces" of fashion that every man must have. Included in this set (among various J. Crew products) is a vintage Rolex watch, which J. Crew doesn't actually sell. The Rolex watch *suggests indirectly* the notion that J. Crew is upscale, urbane, and powerful. The J. Crew Web site is thus taking a dual-appeal approach. The main body of the Web site provides direct visual evidence of the products, their styling, and so on. Other aspects of the Web site provide indirect evidence of the brand's cachet, class, and sophistication.

While any given advertisement for a product may focus on only one or a few purchasing motives, the campaign needs to cover all the important purchase motives of the target market. In essence, the overall campaign attempts to position the product in the schematic memory of the target market in a manner that corresponds with the target market's manifest and latent motives for purchasing the product. *To what motives does the ad shown in Illustration 10–6 appeal?*

Consumer Insight 10–1 looks at the various motives people have for shopping. Notice how some consumers have one basic motive for shopping while others have numerous motives.

## Motivation and Consumer Involvement

As we have seen in previous chapters, involvement is an important determinant of how consumers process information and learn. We will also see in future chapters that involvement is an important determinant of how consumers form attitudes and make purchase decisions. **Involvement** is a motivational state caused by consumer perceptions that a product, brand,

Most ads appeal to multiple motives and desires. Both the picture and the text should be based on the set of motives associated with acquiring and using the brand.

or advertisement is relevant or interesting.[18] Needs play a strong role in determining what is relevant or interesting to consumers. For example, watches may be involving because they tell time (utilitarian need), because they allow for self-expression (expressive need), or because they provide a way to fit in (affiliation need).[19] In addition, the situation itself may influence involvement. For example, some consumers may be involved with computers on an ongoing basis (enduring involvement), while others may only be involved in specific situations such as an upcoming purchase (situational involvement).

Involvement is important to marketers because it affects numerous consumer behaviors. For example, consumer involvement increases attention, analytical processing, information search, and word of mouth.[20] Involvement is also important to marketers because it affects marketing strategies. For example, high-involvement consumers tend to be product experts and are more persuaded by ads that include detailed product information. On the other hand, low-involvement consumers lack product expertise and are more persuaded by images, emotion, and message source. As a consequence, you will often find highly informational ads for automobiles in magazines, such as *Car and Driver,* that are targeted at high-involvement consumers. Alternatively, image and emotional approaches are often the norm in general interest magazines where involvement is likely moderate to low.

## Marketing Strategies Based on Motivation Conflict

With the many motives consumers have, there are frequent conflicts between motives. Resolution of a motivational conflict often affects consumption patterns. In many instances, the marketer can analyze situations that are likely to result in a motivational conflict, provide

**Consumers Have Fun at the Mall**

Consumers can shop for utilitarian reasons related to achieving specific purchase goals. Alternatively, they can shop for hedonic reasons related to having fun. As catalogs and the Web make it easier to satisfy utilitarian motives, traditional retailers are finding that they need to examine hedonic shopping motives and related marketing strategies. A recent study uncovered six hedonic shopping motives related to McGuire's typology.[21]

- *Adventure shopping* refers to shopping for fun and adventure and relates to the need for stimulation, e.g., "I enjoy shopping. It brings me great excitement and sometimes suspense as to what I'm going to find."
- *Social shopping* refers to the enjoyment that comes from socializing and bonding while shopping and relates to the need for affiliation, e.g., "Well, I shop because it gives me a chance to spend time with my friends and family."
- *Gratification shopping* relates to shopping to reduce stress or as a self-reward and relates to the tension reduction need, e.g., "I love to go shopping. It is my biggest stress reliever."
- *Idea shopping* involves shopping to keep up with trends and fashions and relates to categorization and objectification needs, e.g., "I like new gadgets, new technology and see the new toys that are out there. It is kind of a hobby."
- *Role shopping* relates to the enjoyment that consumers feel from shopping for others and relates

to the identification motivation, e.g., "I love to buy gifts for other people. It makes me feel good to buy something for someone that I know they are going to like."

- *Value shopping* involves shopping for deals and relates to assertion needs, e.g., "It's exciting, because you feel like you're winning. That's like the competitive part of shopping."

Interestingly, different segments of consumers emerged depending on their level of motivation on each hedonic dimension. These segments have interesting demographic characteristics that are important for marketers to consider. For example, there was a *minimalist* segment, motivated only by value. This segment consisted mostly of middle-aged males. There was also a *provider* segment, motivated primarily by role and value shopping. This segment consisted mostly of middle-aged females. There was also an *enthusiasts* segment, motivated by all the hedonic dimensions. This segment consisted primarily of young females.

**Critical Thinking Questions**

1. Can motivations vary by shopping situation (grocery versus clothes shopping)?
2. What implications do the demographic differences across shopping segments have for advertising and media selection?
3. What strategies can retailers use to target the various hedonic shopping motives?

a solution to the conflict, and thus encourage purchase of their brand. We address the three key types of motivation conflict next.

**Approach–Approach Motivational Conflict**   A consumer who must choose between two attractive alternatives faces **approach–approach conflict.** The more equal the attractions, the greater the conflict. A consumer who recently received a large cash gift for graduation (situational variable) might be torn between a trip to Hawaii (perhaps powered by a need for stimulation) and a new mountain bike (perhaps driven by the need for assertion). This conflict could be resolved by a timely ad designed to encourage one or the other action. Or a price modification, such as "buy now, pay later," could result in a resolution whereby both alternatives are selected.

**Approach–Avoidance Motivational Conflict**   A consumer facing a purchase choice with both positive and negative consequences confronts **approach–avoidance conflict.** Consumers who want a tan but don't want to risk the skin damage and health risks associated with extended sun exposure face this situation. Neutrogena's Instant Bronze sunless tanner resolves this problem by allowing consumers the aesthetic and social benefits of having a tan (approach) without the risk of skin cancer (avoidance).

**Avoidance–Avoidance Motivational Conflict**   A choice involving only undesirable outcomes produces **avoidance–avoidance conflict.** When a consumer's old washing machine fails, this conflict may occur. The person may not want to spend money on a new washing machine, or pay to have the old one repaired, or go without one. The availability of credit is one way of reducing this motivational conflict. Advertisements emphasizing the importance of regular maintenance for cars, such as oil filter changes, also use this type of motive conflict: "Pay me now, or pay me (more) later."

## Marketing Strategies Based on Regulatory Focus

Consumers are often strategic in terms of the behaviors they choose to attain a desired outcome. Some of this, we will see later, is a function of personality. Some of this relates to the particular set of motives that happen to be salient or important when consumers are reacting to stimuli and making decisions. The salience of particular sets of motives triggers consumers to regulate their behavior in different ways in order to achieve desired outcomes. Two prominent sets of motives are termed promotion and prevention. **Promotion-focused motives** revolve around a desire for growth and development and are related to consumers' hopes and aspirations. **Prevention-focused motives** revolve around a desire for safety and security and are related to consumers' sense of duties and obligations.[22]

**Regulatory focus theory** suggests that consumers will react differently depending on which broad set of motives is most salient. When promotion-focused motives are more salient, consumers seek to gain positive outcomes, think in more abstract terms, make decisions based more on affect and emotion, and prefer speed versus accuracy in their decision making. When prevention-focused motives are more salient, consumers seek to avoid negative outcomes, think in more concrete terms, make decisions based more on factual substantive information, and prefer accuracy over speed in their decision making. In essence, when promotion-focused motives are most salient, consumers are "eager," more risk-seeking decision makers looking for ways to maximize the possibility that they will attain the most positive possible outcomes. When prevention focused motives are most salient, consumers are "vigilant," more risk-averse decision makers looking for ways to minimize the chances that they will experience negative outcomes and attempt to avoid making mistakes.

Whether promotion or prevention motives are most salient depends both on the individual and on the situation. Both prevention and promotion motives reside in each person simultaneously. However, as a result of early childhood experiences, one or the other tends to dominate in each person. This aspect is called *chronic accessibility*. That is, these aspects have been a key focus for so long for these consumers that they tend to be brought to mind when stimuli and decisions are encountered. One aspect of this that has important implications for marketers and market segmentation is the fact that promotion-focused individuals tend to possess more independent self-concepts while prevention-focused individuals tend to possess more interdependent self-concepts. As we saw in Chapter 2, such differences relate to global differences across Western (individualistic) and Eastern (interdependent) cultures. Thus, marketers in Asia should expect that on average, consumers will be more

**TABLE 10–2**

Differences in
Regulatory Focus

| Dimension | Promotion-Focused | Prevention-Focused |
|---|---|---|
| *Motives* | Hopes, wishes, aspirations | Obligations, responsibilities |
| | Regulate nurturance needs | Regulate security needs |
| | Growth and development | Status quo |
| *Characteristics* | | |
| • Time | Long-term focus | Short-term focus |
| • Mental imagery | Abstract | Concrete |
| • Desired steady state | Change | Stability |
| • Desired feelings | Fun and enjoyment | Safety and security |
| • Failure emotions | Dejection | Agitation |
| • Desired self-trait | Creativity | Self-control |
| • Self-concept | Independent | Interdependent |
| *Decision Making* | | |
| • Style | Eager style to maximize gains | Vigilant style to minimize losses |
| • Meta-goals | Speed over accuracy | Accuracy over speed |
| • Ad cue Effects | Affect and emotion | Product facts |
| • Choice of compromise brand | Lower probability | Higher as compromise brand is less extreme and thus less risky |
| • Importance of "fit" in brand extensions | Less important | More important, as "fit" reduces risk |

naturally prevention focused than those in the United States and Western Europe and would benefit from adapting their strategies accordingly. For example, it appears that ads which "frame" the message in terms of acquiring positive outcomes work better in the United States than in China, whereas ads which frame the message in terms of avoiding losses work better in China than in the United States.

Situational factors, such as characteristics of the decision, the environment, and so on, can also *temporarily* make one orientation more prominent. Examples that marketers can use include:

* *Ad theme*—achievement (promotion) versus avoidance (prevention).
* *Message frame*—benefits to be gained (promotion) versus losses to be avoided (prevention).
* *Advertising context*—ad placement in shows, magazines, or Web sites that are likely to elicit a promotion focus (e.g., *O Magazine,* which focuses on ideals and aspirations) versus those likely to elicit a prevention focus (e.g., *The Evening News,* which tends to focus on negative events).

Considerable insight has been gained into the motives, characteristics, and decision-making styles that distinguish a promotion-focus from a prevention-focus. These differences have important marketing consequences, some of which we have already addressed, and some which will be addressed in later chapters. Table 10–2 describes differences and the marketing-related dimensions to which they relate.

# PERSONALITY

While motivations are the energizing and directing force that makes consumer behavior purposeful and goal directed, the personality of the consumer helps guide and further direct the behaviors chosen to accomplish goals in different situations. **Personality** is *an individual's characteristic response tendencies across similar situations.* Thus, two consumers might have equal needs for tension reduction, but differ in their level of extroversion, and as a consequence, engage in very different behaviors designed to satisfy that need.

While there are many theories of personality, those found to be most useful in a marketing context are called trait theories. Trait theories examine personality as an individual difference and thus allow marketers to segment consumers as a function of their personality differences. Trait theories assume that (1) all individuals have internal characteristics or traits related to action tendencies, and (2) there are consistent and measurable differences between individuals on those characteristics. To demonstrate, imagine how you might respond if you were asked to describe the personality of a friend. You might say that one of your friends is aggressive, competitive, and outgoing. What you have described are the behavioral tendencies or *traits* your friend has exhibited over time across a variety of situations. Most trait theories state that traits are inherited or formed at an early age and are relatively unchanging over the years. Differences between personality theories center on which traits or characteristics are the most important.

## Multitrait Approach

Some trait research attempts to examine a consumer's entire personality profile across a set of relatively exhaustive dimensions. Specifically, *multitrait personality theory* identifies several traits that in combination capture a substantial portion of the personality of the individual. The multitrait theory used most commonly by marketers is the **Five-Factor Model**.[23] This theory identifies five basic traits formed by genetics and early learning. These core traits interact and manifest themselves in behaviors triggered by situations. Table 10–3 lists the five traits and some of their manifestations.

The Five-Factor Model has proven useful in such areas as understanding bargaining and complaining behavior[24] and compulsive shopping.[25] There is evidence that it may have validity across cultures.[26] The advantage of a multitrait approach such as this is the broad picture it allows of the determinants of behavior. For example, suppose research focused on the single dimension of extroversion and found that those who complained about a dissatisfactory purchase tended to be extroverts. *What insights does this provide for training those who deal with consumer complaints? What training insights are added if we also*

| TABLE 10–3 | Core Trait | Manifestation |
|---|---|---|
| The Five-Factor Model of Personality | Extroversion | Prefer to be in a large group rather than alone <br> Talkative when with others <br> Bold |
| | Instability | Moody <br> Temperamental <br> Touchy |
| | Agreeableness | Sympathetic <br> Kind to others <br> Polite with others |
| | Openness to experience | Imaginative <br> Appreciative of art <br> Find novel solutions |
| | Conscientiousness | Careful <br> Precise <br> Efficient |

*learn such people are conscientious?* Clearly, the more we know, the better we can satisfy these customers.

## Single-Trait Approach

*Single-trait theories* emphasize one personality trait as being particularly relevant to understanding a particular set of behaviors. They do not suggest that other traits are nonexistent or unimportant. Rather, they study a single trait for its relevance to a set of behaviors, in our case, consumption-related behaviors. Examples of single-trait theories of relevance to marketing include those dealing with vanity,[27] trait anxiety,[28] sensation seeking,[29] compulsive buying,[30] materialism,[31] affect intensity,[32] and self-monitoring.[33]

Next, we examine three additional traits in more detail. We emphasize that given the strong interrelationship between motivation and personality, it is not uncommon for personality traits to evidence motivational aspects.[34] Traits labeled as "needs" often reflect these motivational bases.

**Consumer Ethnocentrism**    **Consumer ethnocentrism** reflects an individual difference in consumers' propensity to be biased against the purchase of foreign products.[35] Consumers low in ethnocentrism tend to be more open to other cultures, less conservative, and more open to purchasing foreign-made products. Consumers high in ethnocentrism tend to be less open to other cultures, more conservative, and more likely to reject foreign-made products in favor of domestics. As a consequence, Lexington furniture is tapping into pro-American sentiments by actively promoting the "Made in America" status of its Bob Timberlake line to retailers and consumers.[36] Consumer ethnocentrism is a global phenomenon, thus also affecting perceptions of American brands doing business in other countries.[37]

**Need for Cognition**    *Need for cognition (NFC)* reflects an individual difference in consumers' propensity to engage in and enjoy thinking.[38] Compared with low-NFC individuals, those high in NFC engage in more effortful processing of persuasive communications, prefer verbal to visual information, and are less swayed by the opinions of others. NFC has obvious implications for marketing communications. In addition, research linking NFC to demographic characteristics such as gender (e.g., women are generally higher in NFC) helps to make this personality factor more actionable in terms of media targeting.[39]

**Consumers' Need for Uniqueness**    *Consumers' need for uniqueness* reflects an individual difference in consumers' propensity to pursue differentness relative to others through the acquisition, utilization, and disposition of consumer goods.[40] It affects what consumers own and value, why they own it, and how they use it. The concept fits with the increasingly common marketing practice of deliberate scarcity—producing less of an item than the predicted demand. Such a strategy helps preserve the uniqueness of the product and enhances the distinctiveness and status of those who own it.

# THE USE OF PERSONALITY IN MARKETING PRACTICE

Sometimes consumers choose products that fit their personality. For example, a timid person might forgo a flashy car because "it's just not me." Other times, consumers use products to bolster an area of their personality where they feel weak. Thus, a timid person who

FIGURE 10-2        **Dimensions of Brand Personality**

Source: J. L. Aaker, "Dimensions of Brand Personality," *Journal of Marketing Research*, August 1997, p. 352. Used by permission of the American Marketing Association.

wants to feel more assertive might drive a powerful, flashy sports car. Clearly, products and brands help consumers express their personality.

Brand image is what people think of and feel when they hear or see a brand name (Chapter 9). A particular type of image that some brands acquire is a **brand personality.** Brand personality is *a set of human characteristics that become associated with a brand*. Consumers perceive brand personalities in terms of five basic dimensions, each with several facets as shown in Figure 10–2. A scale has been developed to measure brand personality in the United States and, with adaptations, in countries such as Russia and Chile.[41] Figure 10–2 applies most readily to "for-profit" firms. Non-profit personality dimensions have been shown to consist of integrity, nurturance, sophistication, and ruggedness.[42]

Marketers are paying increasing attention to brand personality given its power to influence purchases. Jaguar, Reebok, and Sprite are just a few of the many companies that are currently attempting to enhance their brand personalities to better target key customer groups. Jaguar is trying to be less "aloof," Reebok wants to be "hip and aggressive," and Sprite wants more "street cred."[43]

Researchers at Whirlpool found the following personality profiles for Whirlpool and KitchenAid appliances. Higher scores indicate the trait is more associated with the brand.[44] *What type of target market will each brand appeal to?*

| Whirlpool | KitchenAid |
|---|---|
| Gentle (146) | Sophisticated (206) |
| Sensitive (128) | Glamorous (186) |
| Quiet (117) | Wealthy (180) |
| Good-natured (114) | Elegant (178) |
| Sailing (125) | Theater (124) |
| Jazz (118) | Classical (126) |

Based on their investigation, researchers at Whirlpool also drew the following conclusions about brand personality:[45]

- Consumers readily assign human characteristics to brands even if the brands are not managed or the characteristics are not wanted by the marketers.

- Brand personalities create expectations about key characteristics, performance and benefits, and related services.
- Brand personalities are often the basis for a long-term relationship with the brand.

The ability of a brand's personality to affect customer relationships is critical, and one study provides key insights. Specifically, consumer relationships with "sincere" brands were found to deepen over time along the lines of a "friendship." Alternatively, consumer relationships with "exciting" brands were found to weaken over time along the lines of a "short-lived fling." This advantage for sincere brands required, however, that the brand consistently deliver high quality.[46]

## Communicating Brand Personality

Since brand personality can serve as a way to target specific market segments, marketers need to manage and communicate brand personality. Bourjois, a French cosmetics company, created unique makeup sets that communicate distinctive personalities. They used "various cocktails, holiday destinations, [and] fashion statements that have different personality attributes" on their packaging. One set, for example, used the martini and the name *Fabulous Flirtini*. According to their branding company Dragon Rouge, the strategy was to

> [offer] several different color stories with the same theme to capture as many consumers as possible and to promote a range of personalities to connect with a range of consumers. At the same time the sets reflected the core attributes of Bourjois: profusion of color, joi de vivre, whimsy, sassy and fun.[47]

As you can see, numerous elements can be used to communicate brand personality. Three important advertising tactics are celebrity endorsers, user imagery, and executional factors.[48]

**Celebrity Endorsers**     Celebrity endorsers are often a useful way to personify a brand since the characteristics and meanings of the celebrity can be transferred to the brand. Examples include:[49]

- Nike and Serena Williams—edgy, individualistic brand.
- Revlon and Halle Berry—sexy, confident brand.

**User Imagery**     User imagery involves showing a typical user along with images of the types of activities they engage in while using the brand. User imagery helps define who the typical user is in terms of their traits, activities, and emotions. The emotion and tone of the activities can also transfer to the brand. Examples include:[50]

- Mountain Dew—features young, active users engaged in fun and exciting activities.
- Hush Puppies—features "hip young people in a wooded setting."

**Executional Factors**     Executional factors go beyond the core message to include "how" it is communicated. The "tone" of the ad (serious vs. quirky), the appeal used (fear vs. humor), the logo and typeface characteristics (*scripted font* may signal sophistication), the pace of the ad, and even the media outlet chosen can all communicate a brand's personality. Examples include:[51]

- *Tone*. Listerine in Canada wanted a way to be both lighthearted and powerful, so it leveraged an action-hero theme from a popular movie. Listerine went from "old-fashioned and serious," to "powerful and larger than life."

ORIGINAL EQUIPMENT ON THE WORLD'S FINEST.
When you drive one of the best cars in the world, you don't want to compromise on performance, style and safety. That's why Pirelli is your official equipment, for ultimate control. Nothing less than the leader, always.

PIRELLI
POWER IS NOTHING WITHOUT CONTROL.

- *Media.* Hush Puppies placed ads in fashion magazines such as *W* and *InStyle* to establish a more hip, fashionable personality.
- *Pace.* Molson in Canada wanted a "spirited, adventurous and slightly naughty" personality. So it created TV ads in which "a festive Latin beat is punctuated with fast-moving, sexually charged party scenes."
- *Logo.* Reebok wanted to invigorate its brand toward a younger, hipper image. So it created the new "Rbk" logo. According to one executive, "Creating a short code gave permission to the youth culture to look at the brand again without the old baggage."

What type of brand personality is created by the ad in Illustration 10–7? What advertising elements are being used?

# EMOTION

Emotions are strong, relatively uncontrolled feelings that affect behavior.[52] Emotions are strongly linked to needs, motivation, and personality. Unmet needs create motivation which is related to the arousal component of emotion. Unmet needs generally yield negative emotions, while met needs generally yield positive emotions. As a result, products and brands that generate positive consumption emotions increase consumer satisfaction and loyalty.[53] Personality also plays a role. For example, some people are more emotional than others, a consumer trait termed *affect intensity*. Consumers higher in affect intensity experience stronger emotions and are more influenced by emotional appeals.[54]

All emotional experiences tend to have several common elements. First, emotions are often triggered by environmental events (e.g., viewing an ad, consuming a product that meets a need). However, they can also be initiated by internal processes such as imagery. As we have seen, advertisers frequently use imagery to evoke specific emotional responses.

Second, emotions are accompanied by *physiological changes* such as (1) eye pupil dilation, (2) increased perspiration, (3) more rapid breathing, (4) increased heart rate and blood pressure, and (5) enhanced blood sugar level. Third, emotions generally, though not necessarily, are accompanied by *cognitive thought*.[55] The types of thoughts and our ability to think rationally vary with the type and degree of emotion.[56]

A fourth characteristic is that emotions have associated *behaviors*. While the behaviors vary across individuals and within individuals across time and situations, there are unique behaviors characteristically associated with different emotions: fear triggers fleeing (avoidance) responses, anger triggers striking out (approach), grief triggers crying, and so forth.[57]

Finally, emotions involve *subjective feelings*. In fact, it is the feeling component we generally refer to when we think of emotions. Grief, joy, anger, and fear feel very different. These subjectively determined feelings are the essence of emotion. These feelings have a

**Nature of Emotions**    FIGURE 10–3

specific component we label as the emotion, such as sad or happy. In addition, emotions carry an evaluative, or a like–dislike, component.

We use **emotion** to refer to the identifiable, specific feeling, and *affect* to refer to the liking–disliking aspect of the specific feeling. Emotions are generally evaluated (liked and disliked) in a consistent manner across individuals and within individuals over time, but there are cultural, individual, and situational variations.[58] For example, few of us generally want to be sad or afraid, yet we occasionally enjoy a movie or book that scares or saddens us.

Figure 10–3 reflects current thinking on the nature of emotions.

## Types of Emotions

If asked, you could doubtless name numerous emotions. Thus, it is not surprising that researchers have attempted to categorize emotions into manageable clusters. Some researchers have suggested that three basic dimensions—pleasure, arousal, and dominance (PAD)—underlie all emotions. Specific emotions reflect various combinations and levels of these three dimensions. Table 10–4 lists the three primary PAD dimensions, a variety of emotions or emotional categories associated with each dimension, and indicators or items that can be used to measure each emotion.

# EMOTIONS AND MARKETING STRATEGY

Emotions play a role in a wide range of marketing situations relating to products, retailing, consumer coping, and advertising. We examine each of these in the following sections.

## Emotion Arousal as a Product and Retail Benefit

Emotions are characterized by positive or negative evaluations. Consumers actively seek products whose primary or secondary benefit is emotion arousal.[59] Movies, books, and music are obvious examples,[60] as are resort destinations such as Las Vegas and adventure travel programs. Recent advertisements designed to fuel consumer emotion and excitement

TABLE 10–4

Emotional
Dimensions,
Emotions, and
Emotional Indicators

| Dimension | Emotion | Indicator/Feeling |
|-----------|---------|-------------------|
| *Pleasure* | Duty | Moral, virtuous, dutiful |
| | Faith | Reverent, worshipful, spiritual |
| | Pride | Proud, superior, worthy |
| | Affection | Loving, affectionate, friendly |
| | Innocence | Innocent, pure, blameless |
| | Gratitude | Grateful, thankful, appreciative |
| | Serenity | Restful, serene, comfortable, soothed |
| | Desire | Desirous, wishful, craving, hopeful |
| | Joy | Joyful, happy, delighted, pleased |
| | Competence | Confident, in control, competent |
| *Arousal* | Interest | Attentive, curious |
| | Hypoactivation | Bored, drowsy, sluggish |
| | Activation | Aroused, active, excited |
| | Surprise | Surprised, annoyed, astonished |
| | Déjà vu | Unimpressed, uninformed, unexcited |
| | Involvement | Involved, informed, enlightened, benefited |
| | Distraction | Distracted, preoccupied, inattentive |
| | Surgency | Playful, entertained, lighthearted |
| | Contempt | Scornful, contemptuous, disdainful |
| *Dominance* | Conflict | Tense, frustrated, conflictful |
| | Guilt | Guilty, remorseful, regretful |
| | Helplessness | Poweless, helpless, dominated |
| | Sadness | Sad, distressed, sorrowful, dejected |
| | Fear | Fearful, afraid, anxious |
| | Shame | Ashamed, embarrassed, humiliated |
| | Anger | Angry, agitated, enraged, mad |
| | Hyperactivation | Panicked, confused, overstimulated |
| | Disgust | Disgusted, revolted, annoyed, full of loathing |
| | Skepticism | Skeptical, suspicious, distrustful |

Source: Adapted from M. B. Holbrook and R. Batra, "Assessing the Role of Emotions on Consumer Responses to Advertising," *Journal of Consumer Research*, December 1987, pp. 404–20. Copyright © 1987 by the University of the Chicago. Used by permission.

about brands include Bacardi rum's "Shake up your night," Pontiac G6's "Move like a shaker," and Chevrolet's "An American Revolution." Beyond products and brands, retailers also feature events and environments that arouse emotions such as excitement. For example, Web sites using avatars are perceived as more social, which enhances pleasure, arousal, perceived hedonic value, and purchase intentions.[61]

Although consumers seek positive emotions the majority of the time, this is not always the case, as when we enjoy a sad movie. Additionally, products can arouse negative emotions such as the frustration and anger we feel when high-tech gadgets are difficult to use.[62]

## Emotion Reduction as a Product and Retail Benefit

Few people like to feel sad, powerless, humiliated, or disgusted. Responding to this, marketers design or position many products to prevent or reduce the arousal of unpleasant emotions. The most obvious of these products are the various over-the-counter medications designed to deal with anxiety or depression. Food and alcohol are consumed, often harmfully, to reduce stress. Flowers are heavily promoted as an antidote to sadness. Weight-loss products and other self-improvement products are frequently positioned primarily in terms of guilt-, helplessness-, shame-, or disgust-reduction benefits. Personal grooming products often emphasize anxiety reduction as a major benefit. Charities frequently stress guilt reduction or avoidance as a reason for contributing.[63] Finally, as we saw in Consumer Insight 10–1, retail shopping is often used as a stress reducer.

## Consumer Coping in Product and Service Encounters

Consumers must cope with the negative emotions they experience in various marketing situations. **Coping** *involves consumer thoughts and behaviors in reaction to a stress-inducing situation designed to reduce stress and achieve more desired positive emotions.*[64] Avoidance is a common mechanism. For example, when a decision involves a trade-off that evokes strong negative emotions (e.g., price versus safety), consumers will often delay the purchase to avoid making a decision.[65] In retail settings, consumers in a bad mood attempt to cope by avoiding salespeople they perceive as happy. However, if they are forced to deal with a happy salesperson, it makes them feel worse, which reduces salesperson effectiveness.[66] *What marketing and training aspects relating to service personnel does this suggest?*

One typology of coping strategies categorizes three broad types in response to negative emotions emanating from stressful events such as bad customer service or product failure. The three types are:[67]

- *Active coping.* Thinking of ways to solve the problem, engaging in restraint to avoid rash behavior, and making the best of the situation.
- *Expressive support seeking.* Venting emotions and seeking emotional and problem-focused assistance from others.
- *Avoidance.* Avoiding the retailer mentally or physically or engaging in complete self-denial of the event.

Each strategy can have positive and negative marketing consequences. Active coping may involve working with the company to resolve the situation or switching from the firm altogether. Likewise, consumers may vent to the company (expressive support seeking), which is desirable, or they may vent to friends (negative WOM), which is damaging. Finally, denial (avoidance) may result in customer retention but physical avoidance of the retailer will result in lost sales. As you can see, proper training of service personnel to handle product and service failures as well as the careful design of retail and service facilities to reduce stressors are critical.

## Emotion in Advertising

Emotion arousal is often used in advertising regardless of whether it is specifically relevant to the brand's performance. Consider the following recent headlines:

- Under Armour taps raw emotion.
- Kleenex for Men to play on emotion in TV return.
- Emotional appeal of laundry to replace performance claims in ads.

Illustration 10–8 provides an example of the effective use of emotion to attract attention to an ad and to position a brand.

Emotions can play a variety of roles in advertising. Emotional content in ads *enhances their attention, attraction, and maintenance capabilities.* Advertising messages that trigger the emotional reactions of joy, warmth, and suspense[68] are more likely to be attended to than are more neutral ads. As we saw in Chapter 8, attention is a critical early step in the perception process.

Emotional appeals can play a powerful role in developing a brand image.

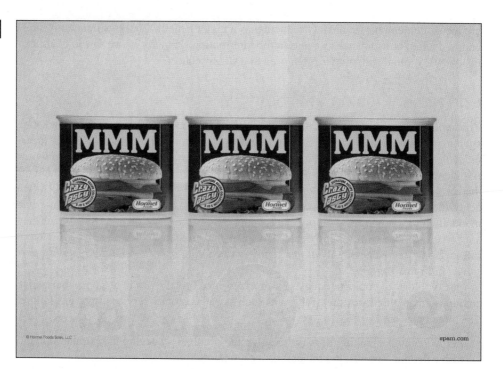

Emotions are characterized by a state of heightened physiological arousal. Individuals become more alert and active when aroused. Given this enhanced level of arousal, *emotional messages may be processed more thoroughly* than neutral messages. More effort and increased elaboration activities may occur in response to the emotional state.[69] As a consequence of this greater attention and processing, emotional ads *may be remembered better than neutral ads.*[70]

Emotional advertisements that *trigger a positively evaluated emotion will enhance liking of the ad itself.*[71] For example, warmth is a positively valued emotion that is triggered by experiencing directly or vicariously a love, family, or friendship relationship. Ads high in warmth are liked more than neutral ads. Liking an ad has a positive impact on liking the product and purchase intentions.[72] As you might suspect, ads that irritate or disgust consumers can create negative reactions to the advertised brand.[73]

Repeated exposure to positive-emotion-eliciting ads *may increase brand preference through classical conditioning.*[74] Repeated pairings of positive emotion (unconditioned response) with the brand name (conditioned stimulus) may result in the positive affect occurring when the brand name is presented. *Brand preference may also occur in a direct, high-involvement way.* A person having a single or few exposures to an emotional ad may simply decide they like the product. This is a much more conscious process than implied by classical conditioning. Such a process seems more likely for hedonic products involving high levels of emotional value rather than utilitarian products. For hedonic products, ad-evoked emotion is a relevant cue on which to base a product evaluation.[75]

Advertising using emotional appeals continues to be popular. For example, Zippo launched an emotion-based campaign for its lighters. It used eight print ads, each with a picture of an engraved lighter and a simple headline "True Love Is not Disposable." A spokesperson said of the campaign, "We wanted to make a human, emotional attachment."[76] Illustration 10–9 shows how Geico taps into emotions through the use of nostalgia.

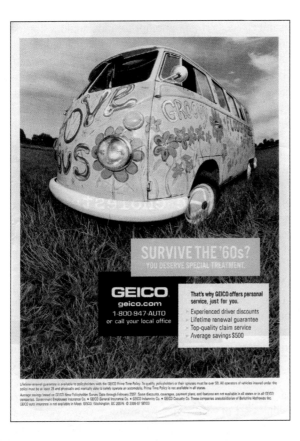

**ILLUSTRATION 10–9**

Emotional appeals can capture attention and enhance the retention of advertising messages. They can also help humanize the brand and associate feelings with it.

## SUMMARY

Consumer motivations are energizing forces that activate behavior and provide purpose and direction to that behavior. There are numerous motivation theories. Maslow's need hierarchy states that basic motives must be minimally satisfied before more advanced motives are activated. It proposes five levels of motivation: physiological, safety, belongingness, esteem, and self-actualization.

McGuire developed a more detailed set of motives— the needs for consistency, attribution, categorization, objectification, autonomy, stimulation, desired outcomes (teleological), utility, tension reduction, expression, ego defense, reinforcement, assertion, affiliation, identification, and modeling.

Consumers are often aware of and will admit to the motives causing their behavior. These are *manifest motives.* They can be discovered by standard marketing research techniques such as direct questioning. Direct advertising appeals can be made to these motives. At other times, consumers are unable or unwilling to admit to the motives that are influencing them. These are *latent motives.* They can be determined by motivation research

techniques such as word association, sentence completion, and picture response (see Appendix Table A–1). Although direct advertising appeals can be used, indirect appeals are often necessary. Both manifest and latent motives are operative in many purchase situations.

*Involvement* is a motivational state caused by consumer perceptions that a product, brand, or advertisement is relevant or interesting. Consumer needs play a strong role in shaping involvement and marketers must adapt their strategies depending on the level (high versus low) and type (enduring versus situational) of involvement exhibited by their target audience.

Because of the large number of motives and the many different situations that consumers face, motivational conflict can occur. In an *approach–approach conflict,* the consumer faces a choice between two attractive alternatives. In an *approach–avoidance conflict,* the consumer faces both positive and negative consequences in the purchase of a particular product. And finally, in an *avoidance–avoidance conflict,* the consumer faces two undesirable alternatives.

*Regulatory focus theory* suggests that consumers react differently depending on whether promotion-focused or prevention-focused motives are most salient. When promotion-focused motives are more salient, consumers seek to gain positive outcomes, think in more abstract terms, make decisions based more on affect and emotion, and prefer speed versus accuracy in their decision making. When prevention-focused motives are more salient, consumers seek to avoid negative outcomes, think in more concrete terms, make decisions based more on factual substantive information, and prefer accuracy over speed in their decision making. Which motive set is more salient can depend on individual and situational factors and has numerous marketing implications.

The *personality* of a consumer guides and directs the behavior chosen to accomplish goals in different situations. Trait theories of personality assume that (1) all individuals have internal characteristics or traits related to action tendencies, and (2) there are consistent and measurable differences between individuals on those characteristics. Most of these theories assume that traits are formed at an early age and are relatively unchanging over the years.

Multitrait theories attempt to capture a significant portion of a consumer's total personality using a set of personality attributes. The Five-Factor Model of personality is the most widely used multitrait approach. Single-trait theories focus on one aspect of personality in an attempt to understand a limited part of consumer behavior. Various traits related specifically to consumer behavior include consumer ethnocentricity, need for cognition, and consumers' need for uniqueness.

Brands, like individuals, have personalities, and consumers tend to prefer products with brand personalities that are pleasing to them. Consumers also prefer advertising messages that portray their own or a desired personality. Brand personality can be communicated in a number of ways, including celebrity endorsers, user imagery, and executional ad elements such as tone and pace.

*Emotions* are strong, relatively uncontrollable feelings that affect our behavior. Emotions occur when environmental events or our mental processes trigger physiological changes such as increased heart rate. These changes are interpreted as specific emotions resulting from the situation. They affect consumers' thoughts and behaviors. Marketers design and position products to both arouse and reduce emotions. In addition, consumers must cope with stressful marketing situations such as service and product failures. The various coping mechanisms can be beneficial or detrimental to the firm depending on various factors and requires that marketers consider not only their responses to failure but also service-setting design to reduce consumer stressors. Advertisements include emotion-arousing material to increase attention, degree of processing, remembering, and brand preference through classical conditioning or direct evaluation.

## KEY TERMS

Approach–approach conflict 371
Approach–avoidance conflict 372
Avoidance–avoidance conflict 372
Attribution theory 363
Benefit chain 368
Brand personality 376
Consumer ethnocentrism 375
Coping 381

Demand 367
Emotion 379
Five-Factor Model 374
Involvement 369
Laddering 368
Latent motives 368
Manifest motives 367
Maslow's hierarchy of needs 360

Means–end chain 368
Motivation 360
Motive 360
Personality 373
Prevention-focused motives 372
Projective techniques 368
Promotion-focused motives 372
Regulatory focus theory 372

## INTERNET EXERCISES

1. Visit several company Web sites. Find and describe one that makes effective use of an appeal or theme based on the following:
   *a.* One of Maslow's need hierarchy levels
   *b.* One of McGuire's motives
   *c.* An emotional appeal

2. Visit several general interest or entertainment sites on the Internet that contain ads. Find and describe an ad that uses the following:
   *a.* One of Maslow's need hierarchy levels
   *b.* One of McGuire's motives
   *c.* An emotional appeal

3. Monitor a hobby- or product-based interest group for a week. What types of motives and emotions are involved with the activity or product? What are the marketing implications of this?

4. Search for "emotional intelligence" on Google or another search engine. What do the results of this search indicate?

## DDB LIFE STYLE STUDY™ DATA ANALYSES

1. Examine the DDB data in Tables 1B through 7B. What characterizes someone who *wants to look a little different from others*? Which factors contribute most? Which of McGuire's motives does this most relate to, and what are the marketing implications of your findings?

2. What characterizes someone who *views shopping as a form of entertainment* (Tables 1B through 7B)? Which factors contribute most? How do your

findings relate to the information presented in Consumer Insight 10–1?

3. Some people feel (and act) more self-confident than others. Based on the DDB data (Tables 1B through 7B), what factors are most characteristic of highly confident individuals? Which of the Big Five personality dimensions does self-confidence relate most to, and what are the marketing implications of your findings?

## REVIEW QUESTIONS

1. What is a *motive*?
2. What is meant by a *motive hierarchy*? How does Maslow's hierarchy of needs function?
3. Describe each level of Maslow's hierarchy of needs.
4. Describe each of McGuire's motives.
5. Describe *attribution theory*.
6. What is meant by *motivational conflict,* and what relevance does it have for marketing managers?
7. What is a *manifest motive*? A *latent motive*? How is each measured?
8. How do you appeal to manifest motives? Latent motives?
9. Describe the following motivation research techniques (see Appendix A and Appendix Table A–1 for details):
   *a.* Association
   *b.* Completion
   *c.* Construction

10. What is the relationship between *involvement* and *motivation*?
11. Describe *regulatory focus theory.*
12. What is *personality*?
13. What is *consumer ethnocentrism* and why is it important to global marketers?
14. How can knowledge of personality be used to develop marketing strategy?
15. What is an *emotion*?
16. What physiological changes accompany emotional arousal?
17. What factors characterize emotions?
18. How can we type or categorize emotions?
19. How do marketers use emotions in product design and advertising?
20. What is *coping* and what are the general types of coping mechanisms used by consumers?

## DISCUSSION QUESTIONS

21. How could Maslow's motive hierarchy be used to develop marketing strategy for the following?
    *a.* American Bird Conservancy
    *b.* Redkin shampoo
    *c.* Dasani bottled water
    *d.* Chili's Bar and Grill
    *e.* BlackBerry
    *f.* Crest Whitestrips

22. Which of McGuire's motives would be useful in developing a promotional campaign for the following? Why?
    a. Cadillac CTS
    b. Precision Cuts (hair salon chain)
    c. Nokia cell phones
    d. Just for Men hair coloring
    e. Amazon.com
    f. Habitat for Humanity

23. Describe how motivational conflict might arise in purchasing, patronizing, or giving to, the following:
    a. Greenpeace
    b. Prius
    c. Wal-Mart
    d. Red Bull energy drink
    e. Taco Bell restaurant
    f. Home security system

24. Describe the manifest and latent motives that might arise in purchasing, shopping at, or giving to the following:
    a. Yukon hybrid
    b. Saks Fifth Avenue
    c. Bose sound system
    d. Kitten
    e. Mercedes Benz convertible
    f. iPhone

25. Do marketers create needs? Do they create demand? What ethical issues are relevant?

26. Respond to the questions in Consumer Insight 10–1.

27. How might knowledge of personality be used to develop an advertising campaign for the following?
    a. Rainforest Action Network (an environmental group)
    b. Smart phones
    c. American Express financial services
    d. Ready-to-drink iced tea
    e. J. Crew women's shoes
    f. Clinique cosmetics

28. Using Table 10–3, discuss how you would use one of the core personality source traits in developing a package design for an organic, shade-grown coffee.

29. How would the media preferences of those on each end of the consumer need for uniqueness continuum differ?

30. How would the shopping behaviors of those on each end of the ethnocentrism continuum differ?

31. How would you use emotion to develop a marketing strategy for each of the following?
    a. Visa card use
    b. Scuba diving
    c. Orthodontist
    d. Silk (soy milk)
    e. Honda Accord Hybrid
    f. Iceland

32. List all the emotions you can think of. Which ones are not explicitly mentioned in Table 10–4? Where would you place them in this table?

## APPLICATION ACTIVITIES

33. Develop an advertisement for one of the items in Question 21 based on relevant motives from McGuire's set.

34. Repeat Question 33 using Maslow's need hierarchy.

35. Repeat Question 33 using emotions.

36. Find and copy or describe two advertisements that appeal to each level of Maslow's hierarchy. Explain why the ads appeal to the particular levels, and speculate on why the firm decided to appeal to these levels.

37. Find and copy or describe an ad that contains direct appeals to manifest motives and indirect appeals to latent motives. Explain how and why the ad is using each approach.

38. Select a product of interest and use motivation research techniques to determine the latent purchase motives for five consumers (see Appendix A and Appendix Table A–1 for details).

39. Have five students describe the personality of the following. To what extent are their descriptions similar? Why are there differences?
    a. Timex watches
    b. Prada sunglasses
    c. Buick
    d. Macintosh computer
    e. Cheesecake Factory restaurant
    f. The university bookstore

40. Find and copy an ad that you feel communicates a strong brand personality. Describe that personality in terms of the dimensions in Figure 10–2. Describe the various techniques used in the ad (e.g., celebrity endorser, user imagery, and

executical factors) and how that links to the personality they are communicating.

41. Find and copy an ad with strong emotional appeals and another ad from the same product category with limited emotional appeals. Why do the companies use different appeals?

    a. Have 10 students rank or rate the ads in terms of their preferences and then explain their rankings or ratings.

    b. Have 10 different students talk about their reactions to each ad as they view it. What do you conclude?

42. Ask two students to describe the coping mechanisms they use when dealing with product or service failures. Identify factors that cause their coping to be beneficial (e.g., complaining to the company) rather than detrimental (e.g., negative WOM) to the firm.

## REFERENCES

1. The Chapter 10 opening vignette is based on N. Morgan, A. Pritchard, and R. Piggott, "New Zealand, 100% Pure," *Brand Management,* April 2002, pp. 335–54.

2. From R. Piggott, "Building a Brand for a Country," unpublished MBA dissertation, University of Hull, 2002, p. 79, as quoted in Morgan, Pritchard, and Piggott, "New Zealand, 100% Pure."

3. A. H. Maslow, *Motivation and Personality,* 2nd ed. (New York: Harper & Row, 1970).

4. See R. Yalch and F. Brunel, "Need Hierarchies in Consumer Judgments of Product Designs," *Advances in Consumer Research,* vol. 23, eds. K. P. Corfman and J. G. Lynch (Provo, UT: Association for Consumer Research, 1996), pp. 405–10.

5. W. J. McGuire, "Psychological Motives and Communication Gratification," in *The Uses of Mass Communications,* eds. J. G. Blumler and C. Katz (Newbury Park, CA: Sage, 1974), pp. 167–96; and W. J. McGuire, "Some Internal Psychological Factors Influencing Consumer Choice," *Journal of Consumer Research,* March 1976, pp. 302–19.

6. See A. G. Woodside and J.-C. Chebat, "Updating Heider's Balance Theory in Consumer Behavior," *Psychology & Marketing,* May 2001, pp. 475–95.

7. M. C. Campbell and A. Kirmani, "Consumers' Use of Persuasion Knowledge," *Journal of Consumer Research,* June 2000, pp. 69–83; and R. N. Laczniak, T. E. DeCarlo, and S. N. Ramaswami, "Consumers' Responses to Negative Word-of-Mouth Communication," *Journal of Consumer Psychology* 11, no. 31 (2001), pp. 57–73.

8. See M. Friestad and P. Wright, "Persuasion Knowledge," *Journal of Consumer Research,* June 1995, pp. 62–74.

9. See B. H. Schmit and S. Zhang, "Language Structure and Categorization," *Journal of Consumer Research,* September 1998, pp. 108–22; and J. A. Rosa and J. F. Porac, "Categorization Bases and Their Influence on Product Category Knowledge Structures," *Psychology & Marketing,* June 2002, pp. 503–32.

10. M. Lynn and J. Harris, "The Desire for Unique Consumer Products," *Psychology & Marketing,* September 1997, pp. 601–16.

11. R. K. Ratner, B. E. Kahn, and D. Kahneman, "Choosing Less-Preferred Experiences for the Sake of Variety," *Journal of Consumer Research,* June 1999, pp. 1–15; and R. K. Ratner and B. E. Kahn, "The Impact of Private versus Public Consumption on Variety-Seeking Behavior," *Journal of Consumer Research,* September 2002, pp. 246–57.

12. M. Trivedi, "Using Variety-Seeking-Based Segmentation to Study Promotional Response," *Journal of the Academy of Marketing Science,* Winter 1999, pp. 37–49; M. Trivedi and M. S. Morgan, "Promotional Evaluation and Response among Variety Seeking Segments," *Journal of Product and Brand Management* 12, no. 6 (2003), pp. 408–25; and J. Chen and S. Paliwoda, "The Influence of Company Name in Consumer Variety Seeking," *Brand Management,* February 2004, pp. 219–31.

13. See D. Goldman, "Pain? It's a Pleasure," *American Demographics,* January 2000, pp. 60–61; and J. J. Inman, "The Role of Sensory-Specific Satiety in Attribute-Level Variety Seeking," *Journal of Consumer Research,* June 2001, pp. 105–19.

14. See G. M. Zinkhan, J. W. Hong, and R. Lawson, "Achievement and Affiliation Motivation," *Journal of Business Research,* March 1990, pp. 135–43.

15. C. Miller, "Spaghetti Sauce Preference," *Marketing News,* August 31, 1992, p. 5.

16. C. Rubel, "Three Firms Show that Good Research Makes Good Ads," *Marketing News,* March 13, 1995, p. 18.

17. T. J. Reynolds and J. C. Olson, *Understanding Consumer Decision Making* (Mahwah, NJ: Erlbaum, 2001); G. S. Mort and T. Rose, "The Effect of Product Type on Value Linkages in the Means-End Chain," *Journal of Consumer Behaviour,* March 2004, pp. 221–34; and F. Huber, S. C. Beckmann, and A. Herrmann, "Means-End Analysis," *Psychology & Marketing,* September 2004, pp. 715–37.

18. See J. L. Zaichkowsky, "The Personal Involvement Inventory," *Journal of Advertising,* December 1994, pp. 59–70.

19. See P. Quester and A. L. Lim, "Product Involvement/Brand Loyalty," *Journal of Product and Brand Management* 12, no. 1 (2003), pp. 22–38.

20. See U. M. Dholakia, "A Motivational Process Model of Product Involvement and Consumer Risk Perception," *European Journal of Marketing* 35, no. 11/12 (2001), pp. 1340–60; and C.-W. Park and B.-J. Moon, "The Relationship between Product Involvement and Product Knowledge," *Psychology & Marketing,* November 2003, pp. 977–97.

21. Consumer Insight 10–1 is based on M. J. Arnold and K. E. Reynolds, "Hedonic Shopping Motivations," *Journal of Retailing* 79 (2003), pp. 77–95; see also T. L. Childers, C. L. Carr, J. Peck, and S. Carson, "Hedonic and Utilitarian Motivations for Online Retail Shopping Behavior," *Journal of Retailing* 77 (2001), pp. 511–35.

22. This section on regulatory focus, including Table 10–2 is based on the following: E. T. Higgins, "Beyond Pleasure and Pain," *American Psychologist*, December 1997, pp. 1280–1300; J. L. Aaker and A. Y. Lee, "'I' Seek Pleasures and 'We' Avoid Pains," *Journal of Consumer Research*, June 2001, pp. 33–49; A. Chernev, "Goal-Attribute Compatibility in Consumer Choice," *Journal of Consumer Psychology* 14, nos. 1 & 2 (2004), pp. 141–50; M. T. Pham and T. Avnet, "Ideals and Oughts and the Reliance on Affect versus Substance in Persuasion," *Journal of Consumer Research*, March 2004, pp. 503–18; A. Bosmans and H. Baumgartner, "Goal-Relevant Emotional Information," *Journal of Consumer Research*, December 2005, pp. 424–34; J. L. Aaker and A. Y. Lee, "Understanding Regulatory Fit," *Journal of Marketing Research*, February 2006, pp. 15–19; T. Avnet and E. T. Higgins, "How Regulatory Fit Affects Value in Consumer Choices and Opinions," *Journal of Marketing Research*, February 2006, pp. 1–10; Y-J. Kim, "The Role of Regulatory Focus in Message Framing in Antismoking Advertisements for Adolescents," *Journal of Advertising*, Spring 2006, pp. 143–51; J. Yeo and J. Park, "Effects of Parent-Extension Similarity and Self Regulatory Focus on Evaluations of Brand Extensions," *Journal of Consumer Psychology* 16, no. 3 (2006), pp. 272–82; and M. Mourali, U. Bockenholt, and M. Laroche, "Compromise and Attraction Effects under Prevention and Promotion Motivations," *Journal of Consumer Research*, August 2007, pp. 234–47.

23. See J. S. Wiggins, *The Five-Factor Model of Personality* (New York: Guilford Press, 1996).

24. E. G. Harris and J. C. Mowen, "The Influence of Cardinal-, Central-, and Surface-Level Personality Traits on Consumers' Bargaining and Complaint Behaviors," *Psychology & Marketing*, November 2001, pp. 1155–85.

25. J. C. Mowen and N. Spears, "Understanding Compulsive Buying among College Students," *Journal of Consumer Psychology* 8, no. 4 (1999), pp. 407–30.

26. W. Na and R. Marshall, "Validation of the 'Big Five' Personality Traits in Korea," *Journal of International Consumer Marketing* 12, no. 1 (1999), pp. 5–19.

27. R. G. Netemeyer, S. Burton, and D. R. Lichtenstein, "Trait Aspects of Vanity," *Journal of Consumer Research*, March 1995, pp. 612–26.

28. R. Suri and K. B. Monroe, "The Effects of Need for Cognition and Trait Anxiety on Price Acceptability," *Psychology & Marketing*, January 2001, pp. 21–42.

29. B. A. S. Martin, M. J. Sherrard, and D. Wentzel, "The Role of Sensation Seeking and Need for Cognition on Web-Site Evaluations," *Psychology & Marketing*, February 2005, pp 109–26.

30. D. J. Faber and T. C. O'Guinn, "A Clinical Screener for Compulsive Buying," *Journal of Consumer Research,* December 1992, pp. 459–69; and H. Kwak, G. M. Zinkhan, and D. E. Delorme, "Effects of Compulsive Buying Tendencies on Attitudes toward Advertising," *Journal of Current Issues and Research in Advertising,* Fall 2002, pp. 17–32.

31. See A. C. Ahuvia and N. Y. Wong, "Personality and Values Based Materialism," *Journal of Consumer Psychology* 12, no. 4 (2002), pp. 389–402.

32. M. Geuens and P. D. Pelsmacker, "Affect Intensity Revisited," *Psychology & Marketing,* May 1999, pp. 195–209; and D. J. Moore and P. M. Homer, "Dimensions of Temperament," *Journal of Consumer Psychology* 9, no. 4 (2000), pp. 231–42.

33. S. J. Hoch and R. J. Meyers (Provo, UT: Association for Consumer Research, 2000), pp. 119–24; and R. K. Ratner and B. E. Kahn, "The Impact of Private versus Public Consumption on Variety-Seeking Behavior," *Journal of Consumer Research,* September 2002, pp. 246–57.

34. See N. Brody and H. Ehrlichman, *Personality Psychology* (Englewood Cliffs, NJ: Prentice Hall, 1998); and A. Deponte, "Linking Motivation to Personality," *European Journal of Personality* 18 (2004), pp. 31–44.

35. See S. Sharma, T. A. Shimp, and J. Shin, "Consumer Ethnocentrism," *Journal of the Academy of Marketing Science,* Winter 1995, pp. 26–37; and G. Balabanis and A. Diamantopoulos, "Domestic Country Bias, Country-of-Origin Effects, and Consumer Ethnocentrism," *Journal of the Academy of Marketing Science,* Winter 2004, pp. 80–95.

36. J. Linville, "Lexington Touts Timberlake as "Made in America" Line," *Furniture Today,* October 13, 2003, p. 98.

37. M. Supphellen and K. Gronhaug, "Building Foreign Brand Personalities in Russia," *International Journal of Advertising* 22, no. 2 (2003), pp. 203–26; and H. Kwak, A. Jaju, T. Larsen, "Consumer Ethnocentrism Offline and Online," *Journal of the Academy of Marketing Science*, Summer 2006, pp. 367–85.

38. C. S. Areni, M. E. Ferrell, and J. B. Wilcox, "The Persuasive Impact of Reported Group Opinions on Individuals Low vs. High in Need for Cognition," *Psychology & Marketing,* October 2000, pp. 855–75; J. Z. Sojka and J. L. Giese, "The Influence of Personality Traits on the Processing of Visual and Verbal Information," *Marketing Letters,* February 2001, pp. 91–106.

39. See, e.g., L. K. Waters and T. D. Zakrajsek, "Correlates of Need for Cognition Total and Subscale Scores," *Educational and Psychological Measurement,* Spring 1990, pp. 213–17.

40. K. T. Tian, W. O. Bearden, and G. L. Hunter, "Consumers' Need for Uniqueness," *Journal of Consumer Research,* June 2001, pp. 50–66. See also K. T. Tian and K. McKenzie, "The Long-Term Predictive Validity of the Consumers' Need for Uniqueness Scale," *Journal of Consumer Psychology* 10, no. 3 (2001), pp. 171–93.

41. J. L. Aaker, "Dimensions of Brand Personality," *Journal of Marketing Research,* August 1997, pp. 347–56. For international adaptations, see Supphellen and Gronhaug, "Building Foreign Brand Personalities in Russia"; J. I. Rojas-Mendez, I. Erenchun-Podlech, and E. Silva-Olave, "The Ford Brand Personality in Chile," *Corporate Reputation Review,* Fall 2004, pp. 232–51; and Y. Sung and S. F. Tinkham, "Brand Personality Structures in the United States and Korea," *Journal of Consumer Psychology* 15, no. 4, (2005), pp. 334–50.

42. B. T. Venable et al., "The Role of Brand Personality in Charitable Giving," *Journal of the Academy of Marketing Science*, Summer 2005, pp. 295–312.

43. K. Greenberg, "Levinson: Jaguar Ads to Stress Quality, Youth, a Bit of Humor," *Brandweek,* April 26, 2004, p. 32; B. Russak, "Calling the Shots," *Footwear News,* October 25, 2004, p. 42; and K. MacArthur and J. Neff, "Sprite Shifts Gears in Quest for Street Cred," *Advertising Age,* January 26, 2004, p. 1.

44. B. F. Roberson, "Brand Personality and the Brand–Consumer Relationship," Whirlpool Corporation, April 5, 1994.

45. Ibid. Also see T. Triplett, "Brand Personality Must Be Managed or It Will Assume a Life of Its Own," *Marketing News,* May 9, 1994, p. 9.

46. J. Aaker, S. Fournier, and S. A. Brasel, "When Good Brands Do Bad," *Journal of Consumer Research,* June 2004, pp. 1–16.

47. From http://dragonrouge-usa.com/, accessed February 24, 2008.

48. For a detailed discussion, see D. A. Aaker, R. Batra, and J. G. Meyers, *Advertising Management,* 4th ed. (Englewood Cliffs, NJ: Prentice Hall, 1992), chap. 8. See also T. T. T. Wee, "Extending Human Personality to Brands," *Brand Management,* April 2004, pp. 317–30.

49. A. Nagel and M. Prior, "Revlon Gets Ready for 2005," *WWD,* August 13, 2004, p. 8; and S. Kang, "Nike, Serena Williams Partner Up," *The Wall Street Journal,* December 12, 2003, p. B2.

50. S. O'Loughlin, "Hush Puppies Steps into a New Image," *Brandweek,* June 23, 2003, p. 14.

51. Russak, "Calling the Shots"; O'Loughlin, "Hush Puppies Steps into a New Image"; "Listerine Mouthwash and PocketPaks," *Marketing Magazine,* November 18, 2002, p. C9; and M. Warren, "Molson Debuts a Saucy Brazilian," *Marketing Magazine,* March 24, 2003, p. 2.

52. For a thorough discussion, see R. P. Bagozzi, M. Gopinath, and P. U. Nyer, "The Role of Emotions in Marketing," *Journal of the Academy of Marketing Science,* Spring 1999, pp. 184–207. See also M. E. Hill et al., "The Conjoining Influences of Affect and Arousal on Attitude Formation," *Research in Consumer Behavior* 9 (2000), pp. 129–46.

53. See, e.g., D. M. Phillips and H. Baumgartner, "The Role of Consumption Emotions in the Satisfaction Response," *Journal of Consumer Psychology* 12, no. 3 (2002), pp. 243–52.

54. See, e.g., Moore and Homer, "Dimensions of Temperament."

55. J. A. Ruth, F. F. Brunel, and C. C. Otnes, "Linking Thoughts to Feelings," *Journal of the Academy of Marketing Science,* Winter 2002, pp. 44–58.

56. See B. J. Babin, J. S. Boles, and W. R. Darden, "Salesperson Stereotypes, Consumer Emotions, and Their Impact on Information Processing," *Journal of the Academy of Marketing Science,* Spring 1995, pp. 94–105.

57. For a discussion of coping strategies, see S. Yi and H. Baumgartner, "Coping with Negative Emotions in Purchase-Related Situations," *Journal of Consumer Psychology* 14, no. 3 (2004), pp. 303–17.

58. See L. Dube and M. S. Morgan, "Trend Effects and Gender Differences in Retrospective Judgments of Consumption Emotions," *Journal of Consumer Research,* September 1996, pp. 156–62; J. L. Aaker and P. Williams, "Empathy versus Pride," *Journal of Consumer Research,* December 1998, pp. 241–61; and M. Geuens and P. D. Pelsmacker, "Affect Intensity Revisited," *Psychology & Marketing,* May 1999, pp. 195–209.

59. J. A. Ruth, "Promoting a Brand's Emotion Benefits," *Journal of Consumer Psychology* 11, no. 2 (2001), pp. 99–113.

60. See K. T. Lacher and R. Mizerski, "An Exploratory Study of the Responses and Relationships Involved in the Evaluation of, and in the Intention to Purchase, New Rock Music," *Journal of Consumer Research,* September 1994, pp. 366–80.

61. L. C. Wang et al., "Can a Retail Web Site Be Social?" *Journal of Marketing,* July 2007, pp. 143–57.

62. S. L. Wood and C. Page Moreau, "From Fear to Loathing?" *Journal of Marketing*, July 2006, pp. 44–57.

63. B. A. Huhmann and T. P. Brotherton, "A Content Analysis of Guilt Appeals in Popular Magazine Advertisements," *Journal of Advertising,* Summer 1997, pp. 35–45.

64. Based on A. Duhachek, "Coping," *Journal of Consumer Research*, June 2005, pp. 41–53.

65. M. F. Luce, "Choosing to Avoid," *Journal of Consumer Research*, March 1998, pp. 409–33.

66. N. M. Puccinelli, "Putting Your Best Face Forward," *Journal of Consumer Psychology* 16, no. 2, (2006), pp. 156–62.

67. A. Duhachek, "Coping."

68. See L. F. Alwitt, "Suspense and Advertising Responses," *Journal of Consumer Psychology* 12, no. 1 (2002), pp. 35–49.

69. H. Mano, "Affect and Persuasion," *Psychology & Marketing,* July 1997, pp. 315–35; and A. M. Isen, "An Influence of Positive Affect on Decision Making in Complex Situations," *Journal of Consumer Psychology* 11, no. 2 (2001), pp. 75–85.

70. A. Y. Lee and B. Sternthal, "The Effects of Positive Mood on Memory," *Journal of Consumer Research,* September 1999, pp. 115–27; K. R. Lord, R. E. Burnkrant, and H. R. Unnava, "The Effects of Program-Induced Mood States on Memory for Commercial Information," *Journal of Current Issues and Research in Advertising,* Spring 2001, pp. 1–14; and S. J. Newell, K. V. Henderson, and B. T. Wu, "The Effects of Pleasure and Arousal on Recall of Advertisements during the Super Bowl," *Psychology & Marketing,* November 2001, pp. 1135–53.

71. M. Royo-Vela, "Emotional and Informational Content in Commercials," *Journal of Current Issues and Research in Advertising*, Fall 2005, pp. 13–38; and C. Chang, "Context-Induced and Ad-Induced Affect," *Psychology & Marketing*, September 2006, pp. 757–82.

72. W. Janssens and P. De Pelsmacker, "Emotional or Informative?" *International Journal of Advertising* 24, no. 3 (2005), pp. 373–94; and J. Kim and J. D. Morris, "The Power of Affective Response and Cognitive Structure in Product-Trial Attitude Formation," *Journal of Advertising*, Spring 2007, pp. 95–106.

73. B. M. Fennis and A. B. Bakker, "Stay Tuned—We Will Be Right Back after These Messages," *Journal of Advertising,* Fall 2001, pp. 15–25; J. D. Morris et al., "The Power of Affect," *Journal of Advertising Research,* May–June 2002, pp. 7–17; and T. A. Shimp and E. W. Stuart, "The Role of Disgust as an Emotional Mediator of Advertising Effects," *Journal of Advertising,* Spring 2004, pp. 43–53.

74. E. Walther and S. Grigoriadis, "Why Sad People Like Shoes Better," *Psychology & Marketing*, October 2004, pp. 755–73; and P. R. Darke, A. Chattapadhyay, and L. Ashworth, "The Importance and Functional Significance of Affective Cues in Consumer Choice," *Journal of Consumer Research*, December 2006, pp. 322–28.

75. See R. Adaval, "Sometimes It Just Feels Right," *Journal of Consumer Research*, June 2001, pp. 1–17.

76. C. Beardi, "Zippo's Eternal Flame," *Advertising Age*, August 13, 2001, p. 4.

# Attitudes and Influencing Attitudes

Pet overpopulation is a major concern in the United States.[1] Each day, roughly 70,000 puppies and kittens are born. Many of these animals end up in shelters or are abandoned as strays. According to the Humane Society of the United States (HSUS), an estimated 3 to 4 million cats and dogs are euthanized each year. That's one animal every eight seconds. Strays live short, harsh lives riddled with disease and hunger, while also contributing to the overpopulation problem.

Organizations such as the HSUS and the ASPCA (American Society for the Prevention of Cruelty to Animals) continue their crusade to persuade pet owners to spay or neuter. They see spaying and neutering as a key element in reducing the number of unwanted, abandoned, and abused animals. Consider these statistics: Just one cat and her offspring can create 420,000 cats in seven years; one dog and her offspring can create 67,000 dogs in six years.

Based on all its potential benefits, you might think spaying and neutering would be an easy sell. You would be wrong. Efforts to persuade pet owners to spay or neuter continue to come up against heavy resistance by those with strong negative attitudes toward the practice. These negative attitudes are often based on strongly held beliefs that simply have no scientific foundation.

For example, if you go to www.aspca.org you can find an informational brochure about spaying and neutering that discusses common misperceptions and tries to replace these with factual evidence, as the following excerpts demonstrate:

- *Myth*: My female cat or dog should have a litter before she is spayed.
  *Fact*: The sooner you spay your female, the better her health will be in the future. The longer a female goes unsprayed, the greater the likelihood of developing mammary tumors or uterine infections.

- *Myth*: Spaying or neutering will alter my pet's personality.

  *Fact*: Regardless of the age when spayed or neutered, your pet will remain a caring, loving, and protective companion. Any slight changes will be positive.

- *Myth*: Companion animals will become fat and lazy if they are neutered.

  *Fact*: Absolutely not! Lack of exercise and over-feeding make pets fat and lazy—not neutering.

Your pet will not gain weight if you provide exercise and monitor food intake.

As you can see, failure to spay or neuter does not indicate a lack of caring. On the contrary, it often appears to reflect important concerns of pet owners that are based on misperceptions. Changing these misperceptions (that is, replacing incorrect beliefs with correct beliefs) is at the heart of ongoing marketing efforts at the local, state, and federal level by organizations such as HSUS and ASPCA.

---

As the chapter's opening example indicates, organizations frequently attempt to alter consumer behavior by changing attitudes toward a product, service, or activity.

An **attitude** is an enduring organization of motivational, emotional, perceptual, and cognitive processes with respect to some aspect of our environment. It is a learned predisposition to respond in a consistently favorable or unfavorable manner with respect to a given object. Thus, an attitude is the way one thinks, feels, and acts toward some aspect of his or her environment, such as a retail store, television program, or product.[2] Attitudes are formed as the result of all the factors we have discussed in previous chapters, and they represent an important influence on an individual's lifestyle. In this chapter, we examine attitude components, general attitude change strategies, and the effect of marketing communications on attitudes.

# ATTITUDE COMPONENTS

As Figure 11–1 illustrates, it is useful to consider attitudes as having three components: cognitive (beliefs), affective (feelings), and behavioral (response tendencies). Each of these attitude components is discussed in more detail below.

## Cognitive Component

The **cognitive component** consists of *a consumer's beliefs about an object.* For most attitude objects, people have a number of beliefs. For example, an individual may believe that Mountain Dew

- Is popular with younger consumers.
- Contains a lot of caffeine.
- Is competitively priced.
- Is made by a large company.

The total configuration of beliefs about this brand of soda represents the cognitive component of an attitude toward Mountain Dew. Beliefs can be about the emotional benefits of owning or using a product (one can believe it would be exciting to own or drive a convertible) as well as about objective features.[3] Many beliefs about attributes are evaluative

| Attitude Components and Manifestations | **FIGURE 11–1** |

**Initiator**    **Component**    **Component manifestation**    **Attitude**

Stimuli:

Products, situations, retail outlets, sales personnel, advertisements, and other attitude objects

Affective — Emotions or feelings about specific attributes or overall object

Cognitive — Beliefs about specific attributes or overall object

Behavioral — Behavioral intentions with respect to specific attributes or overall object

Overall orientation toward object

in nature; for example, high gas mileage, attractive styling, and reliable performance are generally viewed as positive beliefs. This brings up the distinction between a *feature* and a *benefit*, both of which are beliefs. A product may have five milligrams of sodium per serving (a nonevaluative *feature* belief), which means that it is low in sodium and better for your health (both evaluative *benefit* beliefs). Marketers must promote benefits rather than features, especially for less knowledgeable consumers and for complex products. Otherwise consumers will not know how to evaluate and respond to the claims.[4] For example, Quaker Oats helps consumers interpret the nutritional information on their package with statements such as "the soluble fiber in oatmeal helps remove cholesterol!"

The more positive beliefs associated with a brand, the more positive each belief is, and the easier it is for the individual to recall the beliefs, the more favorable the overall cognitive component is presumed to be.[5] And because all the components of an attitude are generally consistent, the more favorable the overall attitude is. This logic underlies what is known as the **multiattribute attitude model.**

**Multiattribute Attitude Model**    There are several versions of this model. The simplest is

$$A_b = \sum_{i=1}^{n} X_{ib}$$

where

$A_b$ = Consumer's attitude toward a particular brand $b$
$X_{ib}$ = Consumer's belief about brand $b$'s performance on attribute $i$
$n$ = Number of attributes considered

This version assumes that all attributes are equally important in determining our overall evaluation. However, a moment's reflection suggests that frequently a few attributes, such as price, quality, or style, are more important than others. Thus, it is often necessary to add an importance weight for each attribute:

$$A_b = \sum_{i=1}^{n} W_i X_{ib}$$

where

$W_i$ = The importance the consumer attaches to attribute $i$

This version of the model is useful in a variety of situations. However, it assumes that more (or less) is always better. This is frequently the case. More miles to the gallon is always better than fewer miles to the gallon, all other things being equal. This version is completely adequate for such situations.

For some attributes, more (or less) is good up to a point, but then further increases (decreases) become bad. For example, adding salt to a saltless pretzel will generally improve the consumer's attitude toward the pretzel up to a point. After that point, additional amounts of salt will decrease the attitude. Thus, we need to introduce an *ideal point* into the multiattribute attitude model:

$$A_b = \sum_{i=1}^{n} W_i |I_i - X_{ib}|$$

where

$I_i$ = Consumer's ideal level of performance on attribute $i$

Because multiattribute attitude models are widely used by marketing researchers and managers, we will work through an example using the weighted, ideal point model. The simpler models would work in a similar manner.

Imagine that Coca-Cola gathers data on a set of beliefs about Diet Coke from a segment of consumers (more details on measuring the various attitude components can be found in Appendix A and Appendix Table A–3). These consumers perceive Diet Coke to have the following levels of performance (the $X$s) and desired performance (the $I$s) on four attributes:

|              | (1) | (2) | (3) | (4) | (5) | (6) | (7) |              |
|--------------|-----|-----|-----|-----|-----|-----|-----|--------------|
| Low price    |     |     | I   | X   |     |     |     | High price   |
| Sweet taste  |     | I   |     |     |     | X   |     | Bitter taste |
| High status  |     |     | I   |     | X   |     |     | Low status   |
| Low calories | IX  |     |     |     |     |     |     | High calories |

This segment of consumers believes (the $X$s) that Diet Coke is average priced, very bitter in taste, somewhat low in status, and extremely low in calories. Their ideal soda (the $I$s) would be slightly low priced, very sweet in taste, somewhat high in status, and extremely low in calories. Since these attributes are not equally important to consumers, they are assigned weights based on the relative importance a segment of consumers attaches to each.

A popular way of measuring importance weights is with a 100-point *constant-sum scale*. For example, the importance weights shown below express the relative importance of the four soft-drink attributes such that the total adds up to 100 points.

| Attribute | Importance |
|---|---|
| Price | 10 |
| Taste | 30 |
| Status | 20 |
| Calories | 40 |
| | 100 points |

In this case, calories are considered the most important attribute, with taste slightly less important. Price is given little importance.

From this information, we can index this segment's attitude toward Diet Coke as follows:

$$^{A}Diet\ Coke = (10)(|3 - 4|) + (30)(|2 - 6|) + (20)(|3 - 5|) + (40)(|1 - 1|)$$
$$= (10)(1) + (30)(4) + (20)(2) + (40)(0)$$
$$= 170$$

This involves taking the absolute difference between the consumer's ideal soft-drink attributes and beliefs about Diet Coke's attributes and multiplying these differences by the importance attached to each attribute. In this case, the attitude index is computed as 170. Is this good or bad? Since an attitude index is relative, to fully evaluate it, we must compare it with the segment's attitudes toward competing brands. However, if Diet Coke were perceived as the ideal soft drink, an attitude index of zero would result. Thus, the closer an attitude index calculated in this manner is to zero, the better.

We have been discussing the multiattribute view of the cognitive component as though consumers explicitly and consciously went through a series of deliberate evaluations and summed them to form an overall impression. However, this level of effort would occur only in very high-involvement purchase situations. In general, the multiattribute attitude model merely *represents* a process that is much less precise and structured than implied by the model.

## Affective Component

*Feelings* or *emotional reactions to an object* represent the **affective component** of an attitude. A consumer who states "I like Diet Coke" or "Diet Coke is a terrible soda" is expressing the results of an emotional or affective evaluation of the product. This overall evaluation may be simply a vague, general feeling developed without cognitive information or beliefs about the product. Or it may be the result of several evaluations of the product's performance on each of several attributes. Thus, the statements "Diet Coke tastes bad" and "Diet Coke is not good for your health" imply a negative affective reaction to specific aspects of the product that, in combination with feelings about other attributes, will determine the overall reaction to the brand.

Marketers are increasingly turning their attention to the affective or "feeling" component of attitudes to provide a richer understanding of attitudes than that based solely on the cognitive or "thinking" component. As a consequence, marketers now commonly distinguish *utilitarian* or functional benefits and attitudes from *hedonic* or emotional benefits and attitudes.[6] For example, one study found that consumer acceptance of handheld Internet devices was influenced by both utilitarian benefits such as usefulness and hedonic aspects such as fun to use.[7] Another study found that in some cases hedonic aspects of giving blood such as fear and joy were stronger determinants of overall attitude toward blood donation than utilitarian beliefs.[8]

In addition, marketers are beginning to consider both form *and* function in product designs and focus considerable attention on the aesthetic aspects of design (appearance, sensory experience). The iPod and iMac are examples of products with high **aesthetic appeal** that tap consumers' affective reactions by going beyond the cognitive associations of functionality.[9] Illustration 11–1 shows an ad for a product high in aesthetic appeal.

Affective reactions to a specific product or benefit can vary by situation and individual. For example, a consumer's belief that Diet Coke has caffeine may result in positive feelings if he or she needs to stay awake to work late but negative feelings if he or she wants to get to sleep quickly. And some individuals may have positive feelings toward the belief that "Diet Coke is made by a large multinational firm," whereas others could respond negatively. Would you enjoy an experience that induced the following? Illustration 11–2 is an example of an affective ad.

Marketers sometimes measure the affective component on verbal scales much like those used to measure the cognitive component (for more detail, see Appendix A and Appendix Table A–3). So, consumers might be asked to rate Diet Coke overall (or specific attributes such as taste) on the following dimensions by placing an *X* in the appropriate space:

|          | (1) | (2) | (3) | (4) | (5) | (6) | (7) |            |
|----------|-----|-----|-----|-----|-----|-----|-----|------------|
| Good     | ___ | ___ | ___ | ___ | ___ | ___ | ___ | Bad        |
| Like     | ___ | ___ | ___ | ___ | ___ | ___ | ___ | Dislike    |
| Happy    | ___ | ___ | ___ | ___ | ___ | ___ | ___ | Sad        |
| Pleasant | ___ | ___ | ___ | ___ | ___ | ___ | ___ | Unpleasant |

**SAM and AdSAM®** However, sometimes marketers want to tap feelings and emotions more directly and bypass the cognitive processing that often goes along with verbal scales. One such measure is based on the pleasure-arousal-dominance (PAD) approach to emotions discussed in Chapter 10. This measure, termed SAM (Self-Assessment Manikin), provides visual representations of 232 "emotional adjectives" underlying PAD. SAM (and AdSAM® [which applies SAM specifically to marketing, marketing communications, and strategic planning]) is a graphical character that is manipulated to portray emotions and more directly tap emotional responses. From a global standpoint, SAM is effective across different cultures and languages because the pictorial representations don't require translation or alteration.[10] Examples of AdSAM® for each dimension of PAD are shown below (top panel—pleasure; middle—arousal; bottom—dominance):

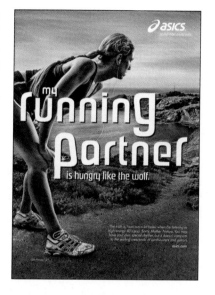

**ILLUSTRATION 11–2**

Individuals differ in their affective reactions to product characteristics. Likewise, the same individual will react differently to the same attribute in different situations.

Source: Copyright 2000 AdSAM Marketing LLC.

## Behavioral Component

The **behavioral component** of an attitude is *one's tendency to respond in a certain manner toward an object or activity*. A series of decisions to purchase or not purchase Diet Coke or to recommend it or other brands to friends would reflect the behavioral component.

Brand interest, as represented by tendencies to seek out the brand on store shelves or search for brand information, also reflects the behavioral component. The behavioral component provides response tendencies or behavioral intentions. *Actual behaviors reflect these intentions as they are modified by the situation in which the behavior will occur.*

**Direct versus Indirect Approach**    Actual behaviors and response tendencies are most often measured by fairly direct questioning (for more detail, see Appendix A and Appendix Table A–3). For example, consumers might be asked about their intentions to buy Diet Coke, as follows:

*How likely it is that you will buy Diet Coke the next time you purchase a soft drink (put an X in the appropriate space)?*

| Definitely Will | Probably Will | Might | Probably Will Not | Definitely Will Not |
|---|---|---|---|---|
| ___ | ___ | ___ | ___ | ___ |

Such direct questioning may work well for most consumption, but not so well for sensitive topics such as alcohol, pornography, and eating patterns where consumers may understate negative behaviors or intentions. In these cases, asking *indirect* questions such as estimating the behaviors of other people similar to themselves (neighbors, those with similar jobs, etc.) may help reduce the bias.

## Component Consistency

Figure 11–2 illustrates a critical aspect of attitudes: *All three attitude components tend to be consistent.*[11] This means that a change in one attitude component tends to produce related changes in the other components. This tendency is the basis for a substantial amount of marketing strategy.

Marketing managers are ultimately concerned with influencing behavior. But it is often difficult to influence behavior directly. Marketers generally are unable to directly cause consumers to buy, use, or recommend their products. However, consumers will often listen

| FIGURE 11–2 | Attitude Component Consistency |
|---|---|

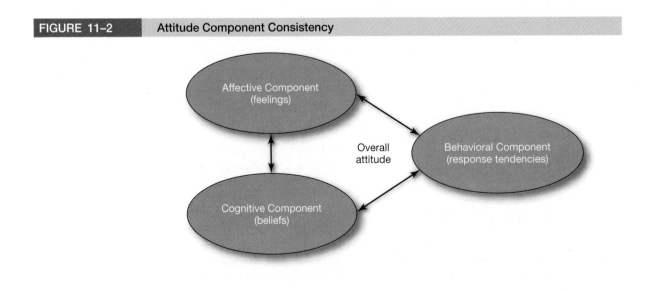

to sales personnel, attend to advertisements, or examine packages. Marketers can, therefore, indirectly influence behavior by providing information, music, or other stimuli that influence a belief or feeling about the product if the three components are indeed consistent with each other.

Some research has found only a limited relationship among the three components.[12] Let's examine the sources of this inconsistency by considering an example. Suppose an individual reports positive beliefs and affect toward the iPod but does not own an iPod or purchases another brand. At least eight factors may account for inconsistencies between *measures* of beliefs and feelings and *observations* of behavior.

1. *Lack of need.* A favorable attitude requires a need or motive before it can be translated into action. Thus, the consumer may not feel a need for a portable player or might already own an acceptable, though less preferred, brand.

2. *Lack of ability.* Translating favorable beliefs and feelings into ownership requires ability. The consumer might not have sufficient funds to purchase an iPod, thus she might purchase a less expensive brand.

3. *Relative attitudes.* In the prior example, only attitudes toward the iPod were considered. However, purchases often involve trade-offs across competing brands. Thus, a consumer may have a relatively high attitude toward iPod, but a slightly higher attitude toward a competing brand. In a choice situation, relative attitudes are a stronger predictor of behavior.

4. *Attitude ambivalence.* While consumers often strive to hold consistent beliefs, feelings, and intentions toward a specific attitude object, this is not always the case. Sometimes a consumer has an **ambivalent attitude,** which involves *holding mixed beliefs and/or feelings about an attitude object.* Think of seafood. A consumer with an ambivalent attitude toward seafood would agree that "Sometimes I feel seafood tastes good, but other times I feel it tastes bad." Ambivalent attitudes are less stable over time and less predictive of behavior. Firms should avoid ambivalent attitudes by creating consistent messages and experiences over time. Firms may also attempt to gain market share by creating ambivalence among customers of competing brands.[13]

5. *Weak beliefs and affect.* If the cognitive and affective components are weakly held, and if the consumer obtains additional information while shopping, then the initial attitudes may give way to new ones. Specifically, stronger attitudes or those attitudes held with more confidence tend to be stronger predictors of behavior. Attitudes can be weak because of ambivalence. However they can also be weak because of a general lack of experience with the brand. Thus, direct (and consistently positive) experience tends to yield attitudes that are more strongly and confidently held.[14] As a consequence, companies often spend enormous amounts of money on coupons and free samples to generate direct product experience.

   In addition to direct experience, factors related to strength of learning such as importance, message involvement, reinforcement, and repetition (see Chapter 9) are also related to attitude strength since attitudes are generally learned.

6. *Interpersonal influence.* An individual's attitudes were measured above. However, many purchase decisions involve others either directly or indirectly. Thus, for example, the shopper may purchase something other than an iPod to better meet the needs of the entire family.

7. *Situational factors.* Brand attitudes are often measured independent of the purchase situation. However, items are purchased for, or in, specific situations, which can modify behaviors as a function of various aspects of the situation, including social norms. The role of social norms was found in a recent study of Taiwanese consumers'

intentions to buy pirated DVDs. The positive influence of beliefs about cost savings was offset somewhat by the negative influence of social norms.[15]

8. *Measurement*. Measuring all relevant aspects of attitude is difficult. Consumers may be unwilling or unable to articulate all relevant feelings and beliefs. Therefore, attitude components are sometimes more consistent than the measures suggest. Also, some behavioral dimensions may be more easily influenced than others. For example, even weak positive beliefs about a brand may be enough to encourage information search but not sufficient to directly influence choice.

In summary, attitude components—cognitive, affective, and behavioral—tend to be consistent. However, as we see, the degree of apparent consistency can be reduced by a variety of factors. Marketers must incorporate these factors when developing persuasive messages and strategies.

# ATTITUDE CHANGE STRATEGIES

Marketers often attempt to influence consumer behavior by changing one or more of the underlying attitude components. Such influence can be positive, as we saw in the chapter's opening vignette. However, social, ethical, and regulatory concerns arise when companies attempt to promote potentially harmful consumption behaviors or when persuasion attempts are deemed deceptive.

## Change the Cognitive Component

A common and effective approach to changing attitudes is to focus on the cognitive component.[16] As we saw in the chapter's opening example, ASPCA is working to change existing negative beliefs. The theory is that by changing these beliefs, affect and behavior will then change.

Four basic marketing strategies are used for altering the cognitive structure of a consumer's attitude.

**Change Beliefs**  This strategy involves shifting beliefs about the performance of the brand on one or more attributes.[17] There is some evidence that beliefs tend to be consistent with each other.[18] Thus, changing one belief about a brand may result in other beliefs' changing to remain consistent with the changed belief. For example, causing consumers to believe that the Kia Sportage has a smooth ride rather than a rough ride may result in their having enhanced beliefs about its handling and safety.

Attempts to change beliefs generally involve providing facts or statements about performance. It is important to realize that some beliefs are strongly held and thus hard to change. As a consequence, marketers may have more success changing overall brand attitudes by targeting weaker brand beliefs that are more vulnerable to persuasion attempts.[19] Illustration 11–3 shows an ad for California Almonds. *What beliefs are they trying to change?*

**Shift Importance**  Most consumers consider some product attributes to be more important than others. Marketers often try to convince consumers that those attributes on which their brands are relatively strong are the most important. For example, General Motors uses detailed narratives of drivers in distress to emphasize the importance of instant communications and emergency assistance, which its proprietary OnStar system provides.

Sometimes evaluative factors that would otherwise not be prominent to consumers can be enhanced by cues in the ad. One study created ads with references to Asian culture (e.g.,

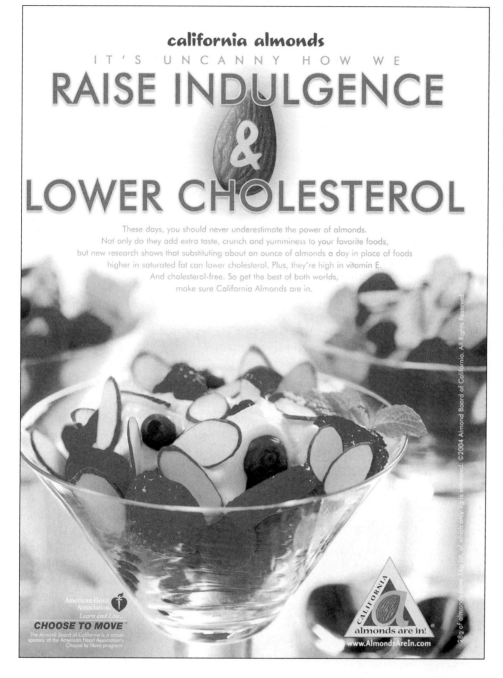

picture of the Great Wall of China) to enhance "ethnic self-awareness." When ethnic self-awareness was enhanced, Asian consumers reacted more positively to ads containing an Asian spokesperson.[20]

**Add Beliefs**   Another approach to changing the cognitive component of an attitude is to add new beliefs to the consumer's belief structure. For example, IBM introduced a "shock absorption" feature to protect its laptops from sudden jolts, as might occur if a computer is dropped. This technological breakthrough has created a benefit that consumers will increasingly incorporate in their laptop judgments.

**Change Ideal**    The final strategy for changing the cognitive component is to change the perceptions of the ideal brand or situation. Thus, many conservation organizations strive to influence our beliefs about the ideal product in terms of minimal packaging, nonpolluting manufacturing, extensive use of recycled materials, and nonpolluting disposition after its useful life.

## Change the Affective Component

Firms increasingly attempt to influence consumers' liking of their brands without directly influencing either beliefs or behavior. If the firm is successful, increased liking will tend to lead to increased positive beliefs,[21] which could lead to purchase behavior should a need for the product arise. Or, perhaps more common, increased liking will lead to a tendency to purchase the brand should a need arise,[22] with purchase and use leading to increased positive beliefs. Marketers use three basic approaches to directly increase affect: classical conditioning, affect toward the ad itself, and mere exposure.

**Classical Conditioning**    One way of directly influencing the affective component is through classical conditioning (see Chapter 9). In this approach, a stimulus the audience likes, such as music, is consistently paired with the brand name. Over time, some of the positive affect associated with the music will transfer to the brand.[23] Other liked stimuli, such as pictures, are frequently used for this reason.

**Affect toward the Ad or Web Site**    As we saw in Chapter 10, liking the advertisement (attitude toward the ad, or Aad) generally increases the tendency to like the brand (attitude toward the brand, or Abr).[24] Somewhat similar results are associated with liking the Web site on which an ad appears (Aweb).[25] Using humor, celebrities, or emotional appeals increases Aad and Aweb. For example, vivid Web sites with rich sensory content that appeal to multiple senses produce more positive Aweb than do less vivid sites.[26]

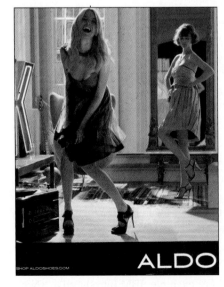

Illustration 11–4 contains an ad that relies on positive affect.

Ads that arouse negative affect or emotions such as fear, guilt, or sorrow can also enhance attitude change. For example, an ad for a charity assisting refugees could show pictures that would elicit a variety of unpleasant emotions such as disgust or anger and still be effective.[27]

**Mere Exposure**    While controversial, there is evidence that affect or brand preference may also be increased by **mere exposure.**[28] That is, simply presenting a brand to an individual on a large number of occasions might make the individual's attitude toward the brand more positive. A common explanation of the mere exposure effect is that "familiarity breeds liking." Thus, the repetition of advertisements for low-involvement products may well increase liking (through enhanced familiarity) and subsequent purchase of the advertised brands without altering the initial belief structure. Mere exposure effects underlie the use of simple reminder ads as well as product placements.[29]

Classical conditioning, Aad, and mere exposure can alter affect directly and, by altering affect, alter purchase behavior without first changing beliefs. This has a number of important implications:

- Ads designed to alter affect need not contain any cognitive (factual or attribute) information.
- Classical conditioning principles should guide such campaigns.
- Aad and ad-evoked affect are critical for this type of campaign unless mere exposure is being used.
- Repetition is critical for affect-based campaigns.
- Cognitively based measures may be inappropriate to assess advertising effectiveness.

As these guidelines suggest, classical conditioning, Aad, and mere exposure tend to occur in low-involvement situations (see Chapter 9). There is at least one major exception, however. When emotions and feelings are important product performance dimensions, then such feelings and emotions are relevant to the evaluation. In these situations, Aad can readily influence Abr under high involvement. As we discussed earlier in the chapter, hedonic (versus utilitarian) products are those for which affect and emotion are relevant performance criteria. Not surprisingly, hedonic products are those for which affect, emotions, and Aad can play a role in more conscious, high-involvement settings.[30]

## Change the Behavioral Component

Behavior, specifically purchase or use behavior, may precede the development of cognition and affect. Or it may occur in contrast to the cognitive and affective components. For example, a consumer may dislike the taste of diet soft drinks and believe that artificial sweeteners are unhealthy. However, rather than appear rude, the same consumer may accept a diet drink when offered one by a friend due to social norms. Drinking the beverage may alter her perceptions of its taste and lead to liking; this in turn may lead to increased learning, which changes the cognitive component.

Behavior can lead directly to affect, to cognitions, or to both simultaneously.[31] Consumers frequently try new brands or types of low-cost items in the absence of prior knowledge or affect. Such purchases are as much for information (Will I like this brand?) as for satisfaction of some underlying need such as hunger.

Internet marketers have been particularly concerned about their ability to simulate direct experiences for products in a virtual context. A recent study finds that for experiential products such as sunglasses, creating a *virtual direct experience* (in this case, a video which simulated viewing the content with and without the sunglasses) led to more positive beliefs, affect, and purchase intentions.[32] The ability to simulate experiences with products in an online context relates to the issue of "touch" which is a major online purchasing factor discussed in Chapter 17.

Changing behavior prior to changing affect or cognition is based primarily on operant conditioning (see Chapter 9). Thus, the key marketing task is to induce people to purchase or consume the product while ensuring that the purchase or consumption will indeed be rewarding.[33] Coupons, free samples, point-of-purchase displays, tie-in purchases, and price reductions are common techniques for inducing trial behavior. Since behavior often leads to strong positive attitudes toward the consumed brand, a sound distribution system (limited stockouts) is important to prevent current customers from trying competing brands.

# INDIVIDUAL AND SITUATIONAL CHARACTERISTICS THAT INFLUENCE ATTITUDE CHANGE

Attitude change is determined by individual and situational factors as well as marketing activities.[34] Individual factors include gender, need for cognition, consumer knowledge, ethnicity, and as we saw in Chapter 10, regulatory focus. Situational factors include program context, level of viewer distraction, and buying occasion.

Marketers continue to focus considerable attention on consumer involvement, which has both an individual (intrinsic interest) and situational (current need to make a purchase decision) component. Consumer involvement is an important motivational factor that influences elaborative processing, learning, and attitudes. The **elaboration likelihood model (ELM)** is a theory about how attitudes are formed and changed under varying conditions of involvement. Thus, the ELM integrates select individual, situational, and marketing factors to understand attitudes.[35]

The ELM suggests that involvement is a key determinant of how information is processed and attitudes are changed. High involvement results in a *central route* to attitude change by which consumers deliberately and consciously process those message elements that they believe are relevant to a meaningful and logical evaluation of the brand (see Figure 11–3). These elements are elaborated on and combined into an overall evaluation. The multiattribute attitude model represents a high-involvement view of attitude change.

In contrast, low involvement results in a *peripheral route* to attitude change in which consumers form impressions of the brand based on exposure to readily available cues in the message regardless of their relevance to the brand or decision. Attitudes formed through the peripheral route are based on little or no elaborative processing. Classical conditioning, Aad, and mere exposure represent low-involvement views of attitude change.

The ELM suggests that vastly different communications strategies are required to communicate effectively with high- versus low-involvement consumers. In general, detailed factual information (central cues) is effective in high-involvement, central route situations. Low-involvement, peripheral route situations generally require limited information and instead rely on simple affective and cognitive cues such as pictures, music, and characteristics of people in the ad (peripheral cues). *Which persuasion route is most likely being used in Illustration 11–4?*

## Cue Relevance and Competitive Situation

Generally speaking, compared with attitudes formed under the peripheral route, attitudes formed under the central route tend to be stronger, more resistant to counterpersuasion attempts, more accessible from memory, and more predictive of behavior.[36]

However, it is important to realize that central route processing involves extensive processing of *decision-relevant* information or cues. And what consumers find relevant can vary by product and situation. For example, an attractive picture can be peripheral or central. In an ad for orange soda, a picture of cute puppies would be a peripheral cue (and influence attitudes under low involvement) while a picture of fresh, juicy orange slices would be a central cue (and influence attitudes under high involvement).[37] Similarly, emotions likely represent a central cue for hedonic products and thus influence attitudes under high involvement.

In addition, the competitive situation can also work to enhance the role of peripheral cues even under high involvement. For example, if competing brands are comparable in terms of their product features (central cues), highly involved consumers prefer the brand with the strongest peripheral cues in its advertising.[38] The basic idea is that relative attitudes are critical in competitive settings and peripheral cues become the tiebreaker between

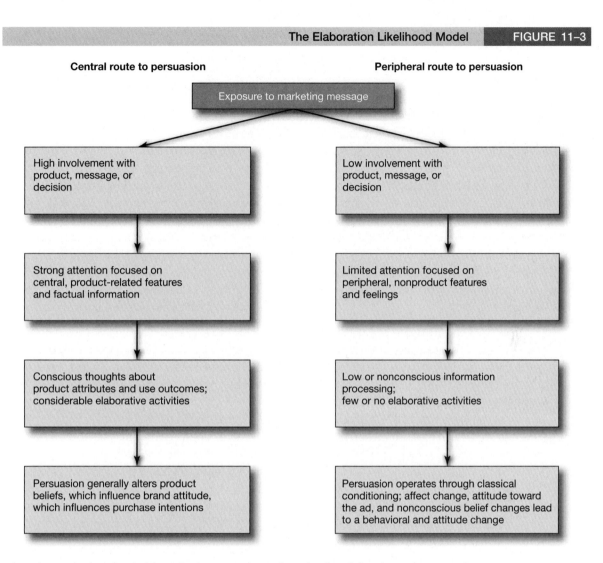

**FIGURE 11–3**

The Elaboration Likelihood Model

**Central route to persuasion**                    **Peripheral route to persuasion**

Exposure to marketing message

High involvement with product, message, or decision

Low involvement with product, message, or decision

Strong attention focused on central, product-related features and factual information

Limited attention focused on peripheral, nonproduct features and feelings

Conscious thoughts about product attributes and use outcomes; considerable elaborative activities

Low or nonconscious information processing; few or no elaborative activities

Persuasion generally alters product beliefs, which influence brand attitude, which influences purchase intentions

Persuasion operates through classical conditioning; affect change, attitude toward the ad, and nonconscious belief changes lead to a behavioral and attitude change

otherwise equivalent (parity) brands. As you can see, the role of peripheral cues can extend beyond low-involvement settings in certain competitive situations.

## Consumer Resistance to Persuasion

Consumers are not passive to persuasion attempts. Instead, consumers are often skeptical (an individual characteristic) and resist persuasion.[39] Also, consumers frequently infer an advertiser's intent and respond in light of that presumed selling intent.[40] For example, a consumer could respond to the California Almond ad in Illustration 11–3 as follows: "Of course they're going to tell me almonds are healthy for me. They're trying to sell more almonds. I'm still not convinced." To help reduce the likelihood of such responses, the ad makes use of the American Heart Association and scientific research to bolster its health claims.

Strongly held attitudes are harder to change than weakly held attitudes. Think of something you feel strongly about—perhaps your school or your favorite sports team. What would be required to change your attitude? Clearly, it would be difficult. Consumers tend to avoid messages that are counter to their attitudes (e.g., committed smokers tend to avoid antismoking ads). And if they do encounter such messages, they tend to discount them. Consumer Insight 11–1 examines various strategies that consumers use to resist persuasion attempts.

## Resisting Brand Attacks

Loyal and heavy users of a brand have highly developed associative networks regarding their favored brand. As a consequence, the attitude components are highly consistent and their brand attitudes are both positive and strongly held. Why is this important? One reason is that brands are often attacked by competitors or the media. Competitors can use comparative ads to suggest that a brand is weak in specific ways. The media might pick up a story regarding a potential scandal involving the brand. Either way, when a brand is under attack, customers loyal to that brand use a number of defense mechanisms to avoid changing their attitudes. These include:[41]

- *Discrediting.* When a consumer's favorite brand is attacked, the first strategy they use is to discredit the negative information. This is done through counterarguments, whereby consumers look for weaknesses in the attack. For example, if a competitor claimed that a customer's favorite running shoe was inferior in terms of shock absorption, but the evidence came from an unknown research firm with low credibility, it would be relatively easy for the customer to discredit this claim ("the competitor is biased," "the research was shoddy," and so on). Discrediting gets more difficult when the negative information is harder to refute, as when it comes from a highly credible source.

- *Discounting.* When discrediting won't work, loyal consumers will often resort to discounting. That is, they will, perhaps without even being aware of it, protect their brand by decreasing the importance they put on the attribute in question. For example, if it is hard to refute that their favorite brand is inferior in shock absorption, a loyal customer might simply reduce the importance placed on that attribute.

- *Containment.* If an attack can't be discredited, loyal consumers also engage in containment. It's as if they "seal off" the negative information as a way to quarantine it and avoid having it spill over and spoil their existing positive attitude. This is particularly important when the negative information is on an attribute that is highly correlated with other important product features. In the case of running shoes, other attributes you would expect to be related to shock absorption would be support and comfort. Loyal customers use containment by not changing their beliefs about other related and important attributes such as support and comfort.

As you can see, loyal customers are active defenders of their brands. If the attack is weak, they discredit it. If the attack is strong, they discount and contain it. On the other hand, consumers who are not loyal to the brand under attack do not engage in these behaviors. They fail to discredit even weak attacks, and they allow negative information from one attribute to "spill over" and influence their perceptions of other attributes. Thus, most marketers do not generally try to capture sales from consumers who are committed to competing brands. Rather, they focus on those who are less committed, as these consumers are more attentive and responsive to their messages.

### Critical Thinking Questions

1. How is discounting by consumers related to marketer's use of the cognitive attitude change strategy of "shifting importance"?

2. Can you think of any situations where loyal customers might be converted by competing brands?

3. Discuss how this insight relates to the difficulty marketers have when trying to get consumers to stop engaging in behaviors that are dangerous for them such as the use of illegal drugs?

# COMMUNICATION CHARACTERISTICS THAT INFLUENCE ATTITUDE FORMATION AND CHANGE

In this section, we describe communication techniques that can be used to form and change attitudes. Obviously, as with all aspects of consumer behavior, individual and situational characteristics interact with the communication features to determine effectiveness.

## Source Characteristics

The source of a communication represents "who" delivers the message. Sources include people (celebrities, typical consumers), animated spokescharacters (Jolly Green Giant, Mr. Peanut), and organizations (the company, a third-party endorser). The source of a message is important because consumers respond differently to the same message delivered by different sources.

**Source Credibility**    Persuasion is easier when the target market views the message source as highly credible. **Source credibility** consists of *trustworthiness* and *expertise*. A source that has no ulterior motive to provide anything other than complete and accurate information would generally be considered trustworthy. However, product knowledge is required for a source to have expertise. Thus a friend might be trustworthy but lack expertise. Alternatively, salespeople and advertisers may have ample knowledge but be viewed with skepticism by consumers.

Individuals who are recognized experts and who have no apparent motive to mislead can be powerful sources because of their ability to reduce risk.[42] An example is 1-800-PetMeds®, with its TV advertisements in which a veterinarian discusses pain management options for your pet. Relatively unknown individuals similar to those in the target market can be effective spokespersons as well, but for different reasons. In a **testimonial ad,** *a person, generally a typical member of the target market, recounts his or her successful use of the product, service, or idea.*[43] Testimonials are important on the Web as well. Amazon and other online marketers offer customer reviews, which appear to be important determinants of attitudes and purchase behavior.[44] Similarity of the source enhances the believability and relevance of these testimonials.

Independent *third-party endorsements* by organizations such as the American Dental Association (ADA) are widely viewed as both trustworthy and expert by consumers and are actively sought by marketers. Such endorsements appear to be used by consumers as brand quality cues.[45] The remarkable success of Crest toothpaste is largely attributable to the ADA endorsement. Other examples include:

- The American Heart Association—Kellogg's Smart Start and Subway.
- J.D. Power and Associates—Edward Jones.
- Good Housekeeping Seal of Approval—Charmin Toilet Tissue.

Of course, the company itself is the most obvious source of most marketing messages. This means developing a corporate reputation or image for trustworthiness can greatly enhance the impact of the firm's marketing messages.[46]

Source credibility can influence persuasion in various situations. First, a credible source can enhance attitudes when consumers lack the ability or motivation to form direct judgments of the product's performance.[47] This is more of a low-involvement process. Second, a credible source can enhance message processing and acceptance. In fact, expert sources can increase attitudes in some high-involvement settings as a result of their perceived decision relevance.[48]

Cultural differences can also play a role. For example, Thai consumers are more influenced by expert sources than are Canadian consumers. Thai consumers are more risk averse and more likely to defer to authority, thus making them more prone to external sources of influence.[49]

One factor that can diminish the credibility of any source is if consumers believe that the firm is paying the source for his or her endorsement.[50] This is especially relevant for celebrities and athletes who are paid large sums for their endorsements.

**Celebrity Sources**   Celebrities are widely used in advertising. Marketers are increasingly using culturally diverse celebrities to reach an ethnically diverse U.S. population. Eva Mendes, Shawn "Jay-Z" Carter, Queen Latifah, Tiger Woods, Mary J. Blige, Halle Berry, Penelope Cruz, and Michelle Wie are just a few such celebrities with endorsement contracts or product lines with companies such as General Motors, Elizabeth Arden, CoverGirl, L'Oréal, Nike, and Coke.

A visible use of celebrity endorsers in recent years has been the mustache campaign for milk. Illustration 11–5 clearly targets the growing ethnic market in the United States.

Celebrity sources are effective for a variety of reasons:[51]

- *Attention.* Celebrities may attract attention to the advertisement. Consumers tend to be curious about celebrities and are drawn to ads in which they appear.
- *Attitude toward the ad.* A celebrity's likeability and popularity often translate into higher Aad, which can enhance brand attitudes.
- *Trustworthiness.* Despite being paid for their endorsements, celebrities often develop strong and credible public personas that consumers trust. And this trust translates into purchases. A recent study finds that 26 percent of respondents are more likely to buy a product endorsed by Michael Jordan, one of the most trusted celebrity athletes. This same study finds that "62 percent of consumers say endorsers' private actions are just as important as professional achievements."[52]
- *Expertise.* Some celebrities are also experts. This occurs frequently in areas such as music and sports. Companies such as Nike, Reebok, and Prince build whole lines around celebrity athletes such as Serena Williams, Maria Sharapova, and Alan Iverson. Nike's partnership with Tiger Woods in golf equipment is a classic example of celebrity expertise.
- *Aspirational aspects.* Consumers may identify with or desire to emulate the celebrity. As a consequence, they may imitate the behavior and style of a celebrity through purchases of similar brands and styles. For example, popular actresses often lead the way in terms of clothing and hair styles for young women.
- *Meaning transfer.* Consumers may associate known characteristics of the celebrity with attributes of the product that coincide with their own needs or desires. For example, urban youth looking for "street cred" see celebrity athletes like Alan Iverson as powerful icons. As one executive states, "He's from the streets. They admire him."[53]

**Matching Endorser with Product and Target Audience**    FIGURE 11–4

As the last point suggests, effectiveness of a celebrity endorser can generally be improved by matching the image of the celebrity with the personality of the product and the actual or desired self-concept of the target market.

When the three components shown in Figure 11–4 are well matched, effective attitude formation or change can result.[54] For example, "Avril Lavigne, known for her pairing of frilly dresses and combat boots, will bring her style to the juniors department at Kohl's department stores. The edgy, pop-rock star's clothing line "Abbey Dawn" was named after her childhood nickname."[55] In this case, there should be a strong match between the celebrity, the clothing line, and the teen and Tween female consumers who want to emulate the singer's style and personality. Sometimes images don't mesh and should be avoided. For example, Burger King canceled talks with Paris Hilton when it decided her racy image might be too extreme for the franchise.[56]

Using a celebrity as a company spokesperson creates special risks. One risk is overexposure. If a celebrity endorses many products, consumers' reactions may become less positive. Thus, marketers might consider limiting the number of products "their" celebrities endorse.[57] An additional risk is that negative behavior involving the spokesperson will affect the individual's credibility and, in turn, damage the firm's image.[58] PepsiCo had problems with commercials featuring Madonna and Michael Jackson after these celebrities became embroiled in public controversy. Rawlings and Nike terminated their deals with Michael Vick after his indictment for dog fighting. And to protect its family image, NASCAR was quick to penalize Dale Earnhardt, Jr., for using profanity in an interview.

Rather than use celebrities, many firms are creating **spokescharacters.**[59] Tony the Tiger and the Green Giant are perhaps the most famous, although Geico's gecko and Aflac's duck have quickly become household names. Spokescharacters can be animated animals, people, products, or other objects. A major advantage of spokescharacters is complete image control. This eliminates many of the problems associated with real celebrities. Such characters come to symbolize the brand and give it an identity that competitors cannot easily duplicate. Illustration 11–6 shows how spokescharacters are used as product symbols.

Sponsorship    **Sponsorship,** *a company providing financial support for an event* such as the Olympics or a concert, is one of the most rapidly growing marketing activities and a multibillion-dollar industry.[60] Sponsorships in North America are expected to grow by 12.6 percent from 2007 to 2008, with spending estimated at $16.8 billion for 2008. Much of the spending and growth is in sports.[61] One high-profile example is Nextel's replacement

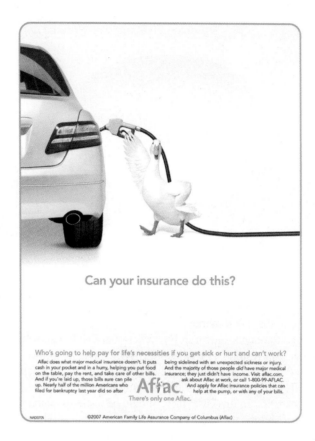

of Winston as NASCAR's title sponsor.[62] The potential to generate goodwill in sports sponsorships is particularly high among rabid fans.[63] These fans may react along these lines: "Reebok supports my team, so I'm going to support Reebok."

Sponsorships often work in much the same manner as using a celebrity endorser. That is, the characteristics of the sponsored event may become associated with the sponsoring organization. Such an association is most likely and most effective when the matchup described in Figure 11–4 occurs, with the event taking the place of the endorser.[64] Thus, fans seeing a new, upcoming band wearing Airwalk gear may come to see Airwalk as cool and "with it." Or consumers seeing a company sponsoring an event for a social cause they care about may see a boost in the company's image as a good corporate citizen.[65]

In addition to enhancing attitudes, an event serves to increase awareness just as traditional advertising does.[66] And, the evidence is clear that firms should promote their sponsorships through traditional media to further enhance their impact.[67]

Care must be taken, however, to avoid mismatches that generate consumer backlash. McDonald's had to discontinue its sponsorship of student report cards. Clearly, consumers find fast-food marketing to children (even in the guise of sponsorships) as inappropriate. Similar negative reactions are occurring over an Ohio hospital's plan to name its children's emergency and trauma center after Abercrombie & Fitch, a company that advocacy groups see as engaging in "not-exactly-child-friendly advertising."[68]

## Appeal Characteristics

As you would expect, the nature of the appeal, or "how" a message is communicated, affects attitude formation and change.

## Fear Appeals

The picture at the top of an ad is a snapshot of a young couple sitting together on their back deck. The headline reads: "I woke up in the hospital. Patti never woke up." The copy describes how carbon monoxide poisoning caused the tragedy. The ad, one of a series of similar ads, is for First Alert carbon monoxide detector.

**Fear appeals** use *the threat of negative (unpleasant) consequences if attitudes or behaviors are not altered.* Fear appeals have been studied primarily in terms of physical fear (physical harm from smoking, unsafe driving, and eating genetically modified foods), but social fears (disapproval of one's peers for incorrect clothing, bad breath, or smoking) are also used in advertising.[69]

There is some evidence that individuals avoid or distort extremely threatening messages. At the same time, fear appeals tend to be more effective as higher levels of fear are aroused. Thus, those using fear appeals want to maximize the level of fear aroused while not presenting a threat so intense as to cause the consumer to distort, reject, or avoid the message. This task is difficult because individuals respond differently to threats. Thus, the same "threatening" advertisement may arouse no fear in one individual or group and a high level of fear in another.[70] To further complicate matters, creating fear may not be enough. Recent research suggests that making people feel *accountable* to act by playing on guilt or regret emotions (e.g., ad for heart attack prevention medicine showing what the family goes through if you fail to act and die from a heart attack) may also be necessary to induce desired behaviors.[71]

Examine Illustration 11–7. *Is this an effective use of a fear appeal?*

Fear appeals are frequently criticized as unethical. Frequent targets of such criticisms are fear appeals based on social anxieties about bad breath, body odor, dandruff, or soiled clothes. The thrust of these complaints is that these appeals raise anxieties unnecessarily; that is, the injury or harm that they suggest will occur is unlikely to occur or is not really harmful. Fear appeals used to produce socially desirable behaviors such as avoiding drug use or avoiding acknowledged physical risks such as carbon monoxide poisoning are subject to much less criticism.[72]

**Humorous Appeals**   At almost the opposite end of the spectrum from fear appeals are **humorous appeals.**[73] Ads built around humor appear to increase attention to and liking of the ad, particularly for those individuals high in *need for humor*.[74] The overall effectiveness of humor is generally increased when the humor relates to the product or brand in a meaningful way and is viewed as appropriate for the product by the target audience.[75]

Illustration 11-8 shows an ad that makes effective use of humor.

Other humorous ads with relevance to the brand include:

- Mitsubishi's Montero Sport ad that showed the faces of several men applying mascara, eye shadow, and lipstick as another man drives on a country road. The point is made that the drive is smooth enough to allow the makeup to be applied accurately. At the end of the commercial, the men leave the vehicle as rodeo clowns.
- Clearblue's pregnancy test ad which spoofs Star Trek, with the device gliding through space while a baritone voice-over states: "It has arrived. The next generation of pregnancy tests. Its design is breathtakingly simple. Its circuitry incredibly precise. Without a doubt, it is the most sophisticated piece of technology . . . you will ever pee on." The humor relates to how this product is used and results from the irony of peeing on a high-tech device.

While it is generally recommended that humor be relevant, companies have been successful using humor that is only loosely tied to the product (e.g., Geico's Gecko ads in which the confusion between the two creates the humor even though the Gecko has nothing to do with auto insurance). In these cases, humor attracts attention, and the positive emotional response may transfer to the brand via classical conditioning or Aad.[76]

Humorous ads also involve risk. What is considered funny varies across individuals, cultures, and situations.[77] Humor viewed as demeaning or insulting can cost a company image and sales. One Subway campaign had a good idea—it's OK to cheat a bit on your diet if you eat at Subway. However, this idea was lost on viewers who saw people engaging in hurtful behaviors (cutting a child's kite string) and glibly justifying it with, "It's OK, I had a Subway." Subway benched this campaign. In another instance, Toyota issued a public apology to the African American community after it placed an ad in *Jet* with the headline, "Unlike your last boyfriend, it goes to work in the morning," which many viewed as insulting.

**Comparative Ads**   **Comparative ads** *directly compare the features or benefits of two or more brands* (see Illustration 11–9). Comparative ads are often more effective than noncomparative ads in generating attention, message and brand awareness, greater

**ILLUSTRATION 11–8**

Humor is widely used in advertising to attract attention and alter attitudes.

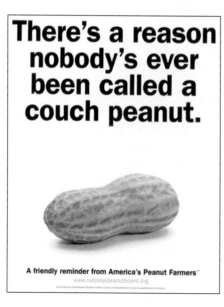

# There's a reason nobody's ever been called a couch peanut.

**A friendly reminder from America's Peanut Farmers**
www.nationalpeanutboard.org

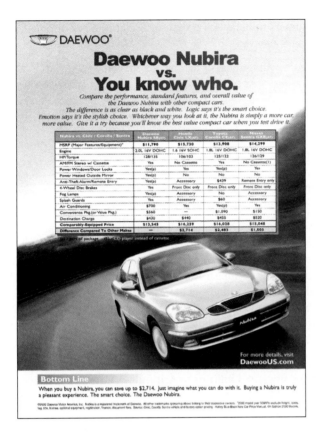

message processing, favorable sponsor brand attitudes, and increased purchase intentions and behaviors. However, comparative ads can also have negative consequences for the sponsor brand such as lower believability, lower attitude toward the ad and sponsor brand, and more positive attitude toward the competitor brand(s).[78] Available evidence suggests that comparative ads should follow these guidelines:[79]

- Comparative advertising may be particularly effective for promoting new or little-known brands with strong product attributes to create their position or to upgrade their image by association. When established brands use comparative ads, they may appear "defensive." This may be particularly true if comparisons are seen as overly derogatory.
- Comparative advertising is likely to be more effective if its claims are substantiated by credible sources. Also, research should be used to determine the optimal number of claims.
- Audience characteristics, especially brand loyalty associated with the sponsoring brand, are important. Users of the named competitor brands appear to resist comparative claims.
- Since comparative ads are more interesting than noncomparatives (and more offensive), they may be effective in stagnant categories where noncomparative ads have ceased to be effective.
- Print media appear to be better vehicles for comparative advertisements, because print lends itself to more thorough comparisons.
- Care must be used with *partially* comparative ads because of their misleading potential. A partially comparative ad contains comparative and noncomparative information and

may lead consumers to believe the sponsor brand is superior on all attributes not just the compared attributes.

**Emotional Appeals**   Emotional or feeling ads are being used with increasing frequency. **Emotional ads** are *designed primarily to elicit a positive affective response rather than to provide information or arguments.* Emotional ads such as those that arouse feelings of warmth trigger physiological reactions (see Chapter 10). Emotional advertisements may enhance persuasion by increasing[80]

- Attention and processing of the ad and, therefore, ad recall.
- Liking of the ad.
- Product liking through classical conditioning.
- Product liking through high-involvement processes.

As we discussed previously, whether emotional ads operate through classical conditioning and Aad (low involvement) or through more analytical high-involvement processes depends on the relevance of the emotion to evaluating key aspects of the product.

In addition, emotional ads appear to work better than rational or informational ads for heavy (versus light) users of a brand and more established (versus new) brands in a market. This effect may be due to the fact that heavy users and established brands already have an established knowledge base for attribute information, making emotions a more compelling differentiating feature.[81]

Illustration 11–10 is designed to elicit emotional responses.

**Value-Expressive versus Utilitarian Appeals**   **Value-expressive appeals** attempt to build a personality for the product or create an image of the product user. **Utilitarian appeals** involve informing the consumer of one or more functional benefits that are important to the target market. Which is best under what conditions?

Both theory and some empirical evidence indicate that *utilitarian* appeals are most effective for functional products and *value-expressive* appeals are most effective for products designed to enhance self-image or provide other intangible benefits.[82] Thus, marketers generally should not use image (value-expressive) advertising for lawn fertilizers or factual (utilitarian) advertising for perfumes. However, many products, such as automobiles, some cosmetics, and clothes, serve both utilitarian and value-expressive purposes.

For example, a recent survey finds that about 40 percent of car buyers see cars as an extension of their personality, while about 60 percent see them as functional.[83] Which approach is best for these products? There is no simple answer. Some marketers opt to present both types of appeals, others focus on one or the other, and still others vary their approach across market segments. Illustration 11–11 contains an example of each approach.

Research also indicates that banner ads on Web sites should differ for the two types of products. For utilitarian products, banner ads serve primarily to transport consumers to the more detailed target ads or sites. For value-expressive products, banner ads should influence attitudes on the basis of exposure to the banner ad itself, not on clickthrough to the target ad.[84]

## Message Structure Characteristics

**One-Sided versus Two-Sided Messages**    In advertisements and sales presentations, marketers generally present only the benefits of their product without mentioning any negative characteristics it might possess or any advantages a competitor might have. These are **one-sided messages,** since only one point of view is expressed. The idea of a **two-sided message,** presenting both good and bad points, is counterintuitive, and most marketers are reluctant to try such an approach. However, two-sided messages are generally more effective than one-sided messages in changing a strongly held attitude. One reason is because they are unexpected and increase consumer trust in the advertiser. They are particularly effective with highly educated consumers. One-sided messages are most effective at reinforcing existing attitudes. However, product type, situational variables, and advertisement format influence the relative effectiveness of the two approaches.[85]

**Positive versus Negative Framing**    **Message framing** refers to presenting one of two equivalent value outcomes either in positive or gain terms (positive framing) or in negative or loss terms (negative framing). There are various *types* of message frames and the type of frame influences whether positive or negative framing is best.[86] The simplest form appears to be **attribute framing** where only a single attribute is the focus of the frame. A classic example is describing ground beef as either 80 percent fat free (positive frame) or 20 percent fat (negative frame). In attribute framing situations, positive framing yields the most positive evaluations because it emphasizes the desirable aspects of the specific attribute.

   **Goal framing** is where "the message stresses either the positive consequences of performing an act or the negative consequences of not performing the act."[87] The act could be purchasing a specific brand, having a yearly mammogram, and so on. In both cases the act is beneficial. However, in the positive frame, the benefits of the act are emphasized (e.g., increased chance of finding tumor) while in the negative frame, the risks of not engaging in the act are emphasized (e.g., decreased chance of finding tumor). In goal framing situations the *negative* frame is generally more effective. This is likely due to the risk-averse nature of consumers coupled with the risk-enhancing nature of the negative goal frame.

Framing effects can vary across products, consumers, and situations. Thus, decisions to use positive or negative framing should ultimately be based on research for the specific product and market.[88]

**Nonverbal Components**    In Chapter 9, we discussed how pictures enhance imagery and facilitate learning. Pictures, music, surrealism, and other nonverbal cues are also effective in attitude change. Emotional ads, described earlier, often rely primarily or exclusively on nonverbal content to arouse an emotional response. Nonverbal ad content can also affect cognitions about a product. For example, an ad showing a person drinking a new beverage after exercise provides information about appropriate usage situations without stating "good to use after exercise." Thus, nonverbal components can influence attitudes through affect, cognition, or both.

# MARKET SEGMENTATION AND PRODUCT DEVELOPMENT STRATEGIES BASED ON ATTITUDES

## Market Segmentation

Identifying market segments is a key aspect of marketing. Properly designed marketing programs should be built around the unique needs of each market segment. The importance of various attributes is one way of defining customer needs for a given product. *Segmenting consumers on the basis of their most important attribute or attributes* is called **benefit segmentation.**[89]

To define benefit segments, a marketer needs to know the importance that consumers attached to various product or service features. This allows consumers who seek the same benefits to be grouped into segments. Additional information about consumers within each segment can then be obtained to develop a more complete picture of each segment. Based on this information, separate marketing programs can be developed for each of the selected target segments.

## Product Development

While the importance consumers attach to key attributes provides a meaningful way to understand needs and form benefit segments, the ideal levels of performance indicate the consumers' desired level of performance in satisfying those needs. These ideal levels of performance can provide valuable guidelines in developing a new product or reformulating an existing one.

Table 11–1 describes how Coca-Cola used this approach in developing a new soft drink.[90] The first step is constructing a profile of a consumer segment's ideal level of performance on key soft drink attributes. As shown in Table 11–1, four attributes were identified for a particular type of soft drink, and ideal performance was obtained from consumer ratings.

**TABLE 11–1**

Using the Multiattribute Attitude Model in the Product Development Process

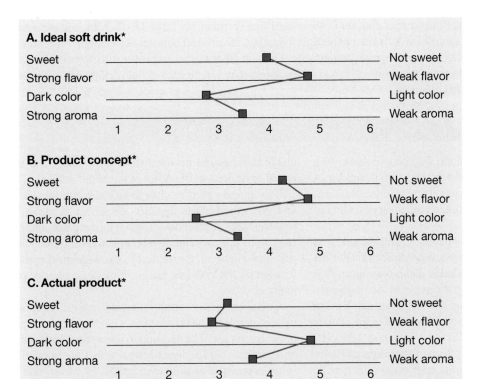

**A. Ideal soft drink***

Sweet / Not sweet
Strong flavor / Weak flavor
Dark color / Light color
Strong aroma / Weak aroma

1  2  3  4  5  6

**B. Product concept***

Sweet / Not sweet
Strong flavor / Weak flavor
Dark color / Light color
Strong aroma / Weak aroma

1  2  3  4  5  6

**C. Actual product***

Sweet / Not sweet
Strong flavor / Weak flavor
Dark color / Light color
Strong aroma / Weak aroma

1  2  3  4  5  6

**D. Attitude toward concept and product**

$$A_{concept} = 25\,|\,4.17 - 4.43\,| + 25\,|\,4.63 - 4.90\,| + 25\,|\,3.16 - 2.60\,| + 25\,|\,3.64 - 3.62\,|$$
$$= 25(.15) + 25(.27) + 25(.56) + 25(.02)$$
$$= 25$$

$$A_{product} = 25\,|\,4.17 - 3.25\,| + 25\,|\,4.63 - 3.17\,| + 25\,|\,3.16 - 4.64\,| + 25\,|\,3.64 - 3.68\,|$$
$$= 25(.92) + 25(1.46) + 25(1.48) + 25(.04)$$
$$= 97.5$$

0    200   300   400   500

Very favorable attitude

Actual product
Product concept

Very unfavorable attitude

*Measured on a six–point semantic differential scale.

A second step is creating a product concept that closely matches the ideal profile. The concept could be a written description, picture, or actual prototype. As section B in Table 11–1 shows, consumers evaluated the product concept developed by Coca-Cola as being fairly close to their ideal on each of the four attributes. Only color appears to be off target slightly by being a little too dark.

The next step is translating the concept into an actual product. When Coca-Cola did this and presented the product to the consumers, they did not perceive it to be similar to either the product concept or their ideal (see section C in Table 11–1). Although the actual product achieved a reasonable attitude rating, the product concept scored higher (section D, Table 11–1). Thus, the product could benefit from further improvements to better align it with the ideal profile. This same basic procedure can be used to help design ads, packages, or retail outlets.

## SUMMARY

*Attitudes* can be defined as the way people think, feel, and act toward some aspect of their environment. A result of all the factors discussed so far in the text, attitudes influence, as well as reflect, the lifestyle individuals pursue.

Attitudes have three components: cognitive, affective, and behavioral. The *cognitive component* consists of the individual's beliefs or knowledge about the object. It is generally assessed by using a version of the multiattribute attitude model. Feelings or emotional reactions to an object represent the *affective component* of the attitude and can be assessed in various ways including AdSAM®. The *behavioral component* reflects overt actions and statements of behavioral intentions with respect to specific attributes of the object or the overall object. In general, all three components tend to be consistent with each other.

Attitude change strategies can focus on affect, behavior, cognition, or some combination. Attempts to change affect generally rely on classical conditioning. Change strategies focusing on behavior rely more on operant conditioning. Changing cognitions usually involves information processing and cognitive learning. The influence of affect and emotion on attitudes under high involvement depends on their decision relevance. And, consumers with strongly held attitudes can resist brand attacks (attitude change attempts) by discrediting, discounting, or containing the attack.

*Source credibility* is composed of two dimensions: trustworthiness and expertise. Persuasion is much easier when the message source is viewed as highly credible. Celebrities are widely used as product or company spokespersons. They are most effective when their image matches the personality of the product and the actual or desired self-concept of the target market.

The appeals used to change attitudes are important and are varied. *Fear appeals* use threat of negative consequences if attitudes or behaviors are not altered. *Humorous appeals* can also be effective in influencing attitudes. However, the humorous message must remain focused on the brand or main selling point to be maximally effective.

*Comparative ads* produce mixed results. They are most effective for unknown brands having a strong functional advantage. The decision to use a *value-expressive* or *utilitarian appeal* depends on whether the brand fills value-expressive or utilitarian needs. However, this is complicated when the brand fills both types of needs. *Emotional appeals* have been found to have a strong effect on attitudes toward both the ad and the product.

Three aspects of the structure of the message affect its effectiveness. *Two-sided* (versus *one-sided*) *messages* can increase trust and message acceptance, but effects depend on characteristics of the individual and situation. *Message framing* effects—presenting equivalent value outcomes either in positive (positive framing) or negative (negative framing) terms—depend on type of frame. Positive *attribute framing* tends to work best whereas negative *goal framing* tends to work best. Nonverbal aspects of the ad, such as pictures, surrealism, and music, also affect attitudes.

Consumer evaluations, feelings, and beliefs about specific product features form the basis for market segmentation strategies, such as *benefit segmentation,* and for new-product development strategies.

## KEY TERMS

Aesthetic appeal  396
Affective component  395
Ambivalent attitude  399
Attitude  392
Attribute framing  415
Behavioral component  397

Benefit segmentation  416
Cognitive component  392
Comparative ads  412
Elaboration likelihood model (ELM)  404
Emotional ads  414

Fear appeals  411
Goal framing  415
Humorous appeals  412
Mere exposure  402
Message framing  415
Multiattribute attitude model  393

## INTERNET EXERCISES

1. Visit several general interest or entertainment sites on the Internet that contain ads. Find and describe an ad that attempts to change each of the following to help form or change attitudes:
   a. Affective component
   b. Cognitive component
   c. Behavioral component
2. Visit several company Web sites. Find and describe one that uses one of the following to help form or change attitudes:
   a. Credible source
   b. Celebrity source
   c. Humorous appeal

   d. Fear appeal
   e. Comparative appeal
   f. Emotional appeal
3. Visit www.adsam.com. Go to the "Take a Survey" section, read the instructions, and take a survey that involves ratings using the AdSAM approach. Evaluate AdSAM® compared with more cognitive approaches that utilize verbal scales.
4. Visit the Intergovernmental Panel on Climate Change (IPCC) Web site (www.ipcc.ch/). What attitude change techniques does it use? Are they effective?

## REVIEW QUESTIONS

1. What is an *attitude*?
2. What are the components of an attitude?
3. Are the components of an attitude consistent? What factors reduce the apparent consistency among attitude components?
4. What is the *multiattribute attitude model*?
5. What is *attitude ambivalence*?
6. What strategies can be used to change the following components of an attitude?
   a. Affective
   b. Behavioral
   c. Cognitive
7. What is meant by *mere exposure*?
8. What is the *elaboration likelihood model*?
9. What strategies can consumers use to resist persuasion? Which consumers are most likely to do so?
10. What are the two characteristics of the source of a message that influence its ability to change attitudes? Describe each.
11. What is *source credibility*? What causes it?
12. Why are celebrity sources sometimes effective? What risks are associated with using a celebrity source?
13. Name five possible characteristics of an appeal that would influence or change attitudes. Describe each.
14. Are *fear appeals* always effective in changing attitudes? Why?
15. What characteristics should *humorous ads* have?
16. Are *emotional appeals* effective? Why?
17. Are *comparative appeals* effective? Why?
18. What is a *value-expressive appeal*? A *utilitarian appeal*? When should each be used?
19. What are the three characteristics of the message structure that influence its ability to change attitudes? Describe each.
20. What is meant by *positive message framing* and *negative message framing*? How does the effectiveness of a positive versus negative frame vary depending on whether it's a *goal frame* or *attribute frame*?
21. What are the nonverbal components of an ad? What impact do they have on attitudes?
22. When is a *two-sided message* likely to be more effective than a *one-sided message*?
23. How can attitudes guide new-product development?
24. What is a *benefit segment*?

## DISCUSSION QUESTIONS

25. Which version of the multiattribute attitude model and which attributes would you use to assess student attitudes toward the following? Justify your answer.
    a. Student health system
    b. CVS pharmacy
    c. Hybrid automobiles
    d. Cats as pets
    e. Jolt

26. Respond to the questions in Consumer Insight 11–1.

27. Assume you wanted to improve or create favorable attitudes among college students toward the following. Would you focus primarily on the affective, cognitive, or behavioral component? Why?
    a. ASPCA
    b. Suzuki automobiles
    c. Organic eggs
    d. Sky diving
    e. Not driving after drinking
    f. Using the bus for most local trips
    g. Qdoba Mexican Grill
    h. Volunteering for Habitat for Humanity

28. Suppose you used the multiattribute attitude model and developed a fruit-based carbonated drink that was successful in the United States. Could you use the same model in the following countries? If not, how would it have to change?
    a. India
    b. Chile
    c. Qatar

29. Suppose you wanted to form highly negative attitudes toward smoking among college students.
    a. Which attitude component would you focus on? Why?

b. Which message characteristic would you use? Why?
    c. What type of appeal would you use? Why?

30. What communications characteristics would you use in an attempt to improve college students' attitudes toward the following?
    a. BlackBerry device
    b. Levis
    c. Volunteering at a local shelter
    d. Gmail
    e. MADD
    f. White-water rafting

31. Is it ethical to use fear appeals to increase demand for the following?
    a. Complexion medication among teenagers
    b. Dandruff-control shampoos among adults
    c. Emergency response devices among elderly consumers
    d. Weight loss supplements for young women

32. Name two appropriate and two inappropriate celebrity spokespersons for each of the products or causes in Question 27. Justify your selection.

33. What benefit segments do you think exist for the following?
    a. Live Aid concert
    b. NASCAR
    c. Major art museums
    d. Bluetooth earpiece

## APPLICATION ACTIVITIES

34. Find and copy two magazine or newspaper advertisements, one based on the affective component and the other on the cognitive component. Discuss the approach of each ad in terms of its copy and illustration and what effect it creates in terms of attitude. Also discuss why the marketer might have taken that approach in each advertisement.

35. Repeat Activity 34 for utilitarian and value-expressive appeals.

36. Identify a television commercial that uses a humorous appeal. Then interview five individuals not enrolled in your class and measure their
    a. Awareness of this commercial
    b. Recall of the brand advertised
    c. Recall of relevant information

*d.* Liking of the commercial

*e.* Preference for the brand advertised

Evaluate your results and assess the level of communication that has taken place in terms of these five consumers' exposure, attention, interpretation, and preferences for this product and commercial.

37. Describe a magazine, Internet, or television advertisement, or a package that uses the following. Evaluate the effectiveness of the ad or package.

   *a.* Aesthetic appeal

   *b.* Source credibility

   *c.* Celebrity source

   *d.* Testimonial

   *e.* Fear appeal

   *f.* Humorous appeal

   *g.* Emotional appeal

   *h.* Comparative approach

   *i.* Extensive nonverbal elements

   *j.* A two-sided appeal

   *k.* Positive message framing

   *l.* Negative message framing

38. Measure another student's ideal beliefs and belief importance for the following. Examine these ideal beliefs and importance weights and then develop a verbal description (i.e., concept) of a new brand for these items that would satisfy this student's needs. Next, measure that student's attitude toward the concept you have developed in your verbal description.

   *a.* Sunglasses

   *b.* Spa

   *c.* Automobile

   *d.* Credit card

   *e.* Laptop

   *f.* Charity

39. Use the multiattribute attitude model to assess 10 students' attitudes toward several brands in the following product categories. Measure the students' behavior with respect to these brands. Are they consistent? Explain any inconsistencies.

   *a.* Television news program

   *b.* Sports drinks

   *c.* Healthy dinners

   *d.* Fast-food restaurants

   *e.* Exercise

   *f.* Coffee shops

40. Develop two advertisements for the following with college students as the target. One ad should focus on the cognitive component and the other on the affective component.

   *a.* Crest Whitestrips

   *b.* Toyota Prius

   *c.* Red Bull energy drink

   *d.* Reducing smoking

   *e.* Increasing exercise

   *f.* Burger King

41. Repeat Activity 40 using utilitarian and value-expressive appeals.

42. Develop a positively framed and an equivalent negatively framed message about a product attribute. Have five students react to these messages. What do you conclude?

## REFERENCES

1. The Chapter 11 opening discussion is based on "Why Spay or Neuter?" ASPCA Brochure (2003), www.aspca.org; "HSUS Pet Overpopulation Estimates," HSUS Brochure (2004), www.hsus .org; and information from Northeast Arkansas for Animals, www.nafacares.org.

2. See R. E. Petty, D. T. Wegener, and L. R. Fabriger, "Attitudes and Attitude Change," *Annual Review of Psychology* 48 (1997), pp. 609–38.

3. J. A. Ruth, "Promoting a Brand's Emotional Benefits," *Journal of Consumer Psychology* 11, no. 2 (2001), pp. 99–113.

4. B. Wansink and M. M. Cheney, "Leveraging FDA Health Claims," *Journal of Consumer Affairs* 39, no. 2, (2005), pp, 386–98.

5. See M. Wanke, G. Bohner, and A. Jurkowitsch, "There Are Many Reasons to Drive a BMW," *Journal of Consumer Research,* September 1997, pp. 170–77.

6. K. E. Voss, E. R. Spangenberg, and B. Grohmann, "Measuring the Hedonic and Utilitarian Dimensions of Consumer Attitude,"

*Journal of Marketing Research,* August 2003, pp. 310–20; T. Lageat, S. Czellar, and G. Laurent, "Engineering Hedonic Attributes to Generate Perceptions of Luxury," *Marketing Letters,* July 2003, pp. 97–109; E. M. Okada, "Justification Effects on Consumer Choice of Hedonic and Utilitarian Goods," *Journal of Marketing Research*, February 2005, pp. 45–53.

7. G. C. Bruner II and A. Kumar, "Explaining Consumer Acceptance of Handheld Internet Devices," *Journal of Business Research* 58 (2005), pp. 553–58.

8. C. T. Allen et al., "A Place for Emotion in Attitude Models," *Journal of Business Research* 58 (2005), pp. 494–99.

9. C. Page and P. M. Herr, "An Investigation of the Processes by Which Product Design and Brand Strength Interact to Determine Initial Affect and Quality Judgments," *Journal of Consumer Psychology* 12, no. 2 (2002), pp. 133–47.

10. J. D. Morris et al., "The Power of Affect," *Journal of Advertising Research,* May–June 2002, pp. 7–17; and J. D. Morris,

"Observations: SAM," *Journal of Advertising Research,* November–December 1995, pp. 63–68.

11. For an excellent review, see P. A. Dabholkar, "Incorporating Choice into an Attitudinal Framework," *Journal of Consumer Research,* June 1994, pp. 100–18. See also Morris et al., "The Power of Affect"; and P. E. Grimm, "$A_b$ Components' Impact on Brand Preference," *Journal of Business Research* 58 (2005), pp. 508–17; and P. M. Homer, "Relationships among Ad-Induced Affect, Beliefs, and Attitudes," *Journal of Advertising*, Spring 2006, pp. 35–51.

12. R. E. Petty and J. A. Krosnick, *Attitude Strength* (Mahwah, NJ: Erlbaum, 1995); S. J. Kraus, "Attitudes and the Prediction of Behavior," *Personality and Social Psychology Bulletin* 21 (1995), pp. 58–75; R. Madrigal, "Social Identity Effects in a Belief-Attitude-Intentions Hierarchy," *Psychology & Marketing,* February 2001, pp. 145–65; and W. E. Baker, "The Diagnosticity of Advertising Generated Brand Attitudes in Brand Choice Contexts," *Journal of Consumer Psychology* 11, no. 2 (2001), pp. 129–39.

13. S. O. Olsen, J. Wilcox, and U. Olsson, "Consequences of Ambivalence on Satisfaction and Loyalty," *Psychology & Marketing*, March 2005, pp. 247–69; and C. Homburg, N. Koschate, and W. D. Hoyer, "The Role of Cognition and Affect in the Formation of Customer Satisfaction," *Journal of Marketing*, July 2006, pp. 21–31. See also Sparks, et al., "Ambivalence about Health-Related Behaviors," *British Journal of Health Psychology* 6, pp. 53–68.

14. See, e.g., J. R. Priester et al., "The $A^2SC^2$ Model," *Journal of Consumer Research,* March 2004, pp. 574–87; and B. Johnson, "Consumers Cite Past Experience as the No. 1 Influencer When Buying," *Advertising Age*, November 20, 2006, p. 21.

15. C.-C. Wang, "Factors That Influence the Piracy of DVD/VCD Motion Pictures," *Journal of American Academy of Business,* March 2005, pp. 231–37. See also R. P. Bagozzi et al., "Cultural and Situational Contingencies and the Theory of Reasoned Action," *Journal of Consumer Psychology* 9, no. 2 (2000), pp. 97–106.

16. See S. A. Hawkins, S. J. Hoch, and J. Meyers-Levy, "Low-Involvement Learning," *Journal of Consumer Psychology* 11, no. 31 (2001), pp. 1–11.

17. For guidelines on structuring message arguments to enhance beliefs, see C. S. Areni, "The Proposition–Probability Model of Argument Structure and Message Acceptance," *Journal of Consumer Research,* September 2002, pp. 168–87.

18. F. R. Kardes et al., "Down the Garden Path," *Journal of Consumer Psychology* 11, no. 3 (2001), pp. 159–68. See also J. Sengupta and G. V. Johar, "Effects of Inconsistent Attribute Information on the Predictive Value of Product Attitudes," *Journal of Consumer Research,* June 2002, pp. 39–56.

19. See A. Drolet and J. Aaker, "Off-Target?" *Journal of Consumer Psychology* 12, no. 1 (2002), pp. 59–68; and A. H. Tangari et al. "How Do Antitobacco Campaign Advertising and Smoking Status Affect Beliefs and Intentions?" *Journal of Public Policy and Marketing,* Spring 2007, pp. 60–74.

20. M. R. Forehand and R. Deshpande, "What We See Makes Us Who We Are," *Journal of Marketing Research,* August 2001, 336–48. See also J. K. Maher and M. Hu, "The Priming of Material Values on Consumer Information Processing of Print

Advertisements," *Journal of Current Issues and Research in Advertising,* Fall 2003, pp. 21–30.

21. For a discussion of program-induced affect and extremity of beliefs, see R. Adaval, "How Good Gets Better and Bad Gets Worse," *Journal of Consumer Research,* December 2003, pp. 352–67.

22. See M. J. J. M. Candel and J. M. E. Pennings, "Attitude-Based Models for Binary Choices," *Journal of Economic Psychology* 20 (1999), pp. 547–69; and H.-P. Erb, Antoine Bioy, and D. J. Hilton, "Choice Preferences without Inferences," *Journal of Behavioral Decision Making,* July 2002, pp. 251–62.

23. See, e.g., W. E. Baker, "When Can Affective Conditioning and Mere Exposure Directly Influence Brand Choice?" *Journal of Advertising,* Winter 1999, pp. 31–46; and B. D. Till and R. L. Priluck, "Stimulus Generalization in Classical Conditioning," *Psychology & Marketing,* January 2000, pp. 55–72.

24. See, e.g., R. E. Goldsmith, B. A. Lafferty, and S. J. Newell, "The Impact of Corporate Credibility and Celebrity Credibility on Consumer Reaction to Advertisements and Brands," *Journal of Advertising,* Fall 2000, pp. 43–54; and K. S. Coulter, "An Examination of Qualitative vs. Quantitative Elaboration Likelihood Effects," *Psychology & Marketing,* January 2005, pp. 31–49.

25. J. S. Stevenson, G. C. Bruner II, and A. Kumard, "Webpage Background and Viewer Attitudes," and G. C. Bruner II and A. Kumard, "Web Commercials and Advertising Hierarchy-of-Effects," both in *Journal of Advertising Research,* January 2000, pp. 29–34 and 35–43, respectively. See also L. Dailey, "Navigational Web Atmospherics," *Journal of Business Research* 57 (2004), 795–803.

26. J. R. Coyle and E. Thorson, "The Effects of Progressive Levels of Interactivity and Vividness in Web Marketing Sites," *Journal of Advertising,* Fall 2001, pp. 65–77.

27. See M.-H. Huang, "Is Negative Affect in Advertising General or Specific?" *Psychology Marketing,* May 1997, pp. 223–40. See also P. S. Ellen and P. F. Bone, "Does It Matter if It Smells?" *Journal of Advertising,* Winter 1998, pp. 29–39.

28. A. Rindfleisch and J. J. Inman, "Explaining the Familiarity-Liking Relationship," *Marketing Letters* 1 (1998), pp. 5–19; E. L. Olson and H. M. Thjomoe, "The Effects of Peripheral Exposure to Information on Brand Preference," *European Journal of Marketing* 37, no. 1/2 (2003), pp. 243–55; and G. Menon and P. Raghubir, "Ease-of-Retrieval as an Automatic Input in Judgments," *Journal of Consumer Research,* September 2003, pp. 230–43.

29. S. Auty and C. Lewis, "Exploring Children's Choice," *Psychology & Marketing,* September 2004, pp. 697–713.

30. See Ruth, "Promoting a Brand's Emotional Benefits"; R. Adaval, "Sometimes It Just Feels Right," *Journal of Consumer Research,* June 2001, pp. 1–17; M. T. Pham et al., "Affect Monitoring and the Primacy of Feelings in Judgment," *Journal of Consumer Research,* September 2001, pp. 167–88; and C. W. M. Yeung and R. S. Wyer, Jr., "Affect, Appraisal, and Consumer Judgment," *Journal of Consumer Research,* September 2004, pp. 412–24.

31. See D. S. Kempf, "Attitude Formation from Product Trial," *Psychology & Marketing,* January 1999, pp. 35–50.

32. D. A. Griffith and Q. Chen, "The Influence of Virtual Direct Experience (VDE) On On-line Ad Message Effectiveness," *Journal of Advertising,* Spring 2004, pp. 55–68.

33. See G. J. Gaeth et al., "Consumers' Attitude Change across Sequences of Successful and Unsuccessful Product Usage," *Marketing Letters* 1 (1997), pp. 41–53; and L. A. Brannon and T. C. Brock, "Limiting Time for Response Enhances Behavior Corresponding to the Merits of Compliance Appeals," *Journal of Consumer Psychology* 10, no. 3 (2001), pp. 135–46.

34. See, e.g., M. L. Roehm and B. Sternthal, "The Moderating Effect of Knowledge and Resources on the Persuasive Impact of Analogies," *Journal of Consumer Research,* September 2001, pp. 257–72; M. Moorman, P. C. Neijens, and E. G. Smit, "The Effects of Magazine-Induced Psychological Responses and Thematic Congruence on Memory and Attitude toward the Ad in a Real-Life Setting," *Journal of Advertising,* Winter 2002, pp. 27–40; and S. Putrevu, J. Tan, and K. R. Lord, "Consumer Responses to Complex Advertisements," *Journal of Current Issues and Research in Advertising,* Spring 2004, pp. 9–24.

35. See R. E. Petty, J. T. Cacioppo, and D. Schumann, "Central and Peripheral Routes to Advertising Effectiveness," *Journal of Consumer Research,* September 1993, pp. 135–46; J. Meyers-Levy and P. Malaviya, "Consumers' Processing of Persuasive Advertisements," *Journal of Marketing* 63 (1999), pp. 45–60; C. S. Areni, "The Effects of Structural and Grammatical Variables on Persuasion," *Psychology & Marketing,* April 2003, pp. 349–75; and D. D. Rucker and R. E. Petty, "Increasing the Effectiveness of Communications to Consumers," *Journal of Public Policy and Marketing*, Spring 2006, 39–52.

36. See, e.g., Petty and Krosnick, *Attitude Strength*. For a discussion of attitude persistence under low involvement, see J. Sengupta, R. C. Goodstein, and D. S. Boninger, "All Cues Are Not Created Equal," *Journal of Consumer Research,* March 1997, pp. 351–61.

37. P. W. Miniard et al., "Picture-based Persuasion Processes and the Moderating Role of Involvement," *Journal of Consumer Research,* June 1991, pp. 92–107.

38. P. W. Miniard, D. Sirdeshmukh, and D. E. Innis, "Peripheral Persuasion and Brand Choice," *Journal of Consumer Research*, September 1992, pp. 226–39; and T. B. Heath, M. S. McCarthy, and D. L. Mothersbaugh, "Spokesperson Fame and Vividness Effects in the Context of Issue-Relevant Thinking," *Journal of Consumer Research,* March 1994, pp. 520–34; See also B. Yoo and R. Mandhachitara, "Estimating Advertising Effects on Sales in a Competitive Setting," *Journal of Advertising Research,* September 2003, pp. 310–21; and S. S. Posavac et al., "The Brand Positivity Effect," *Journal of Consumer Research,* December 2004, pp. 643–51.

39. T. F. Mangleburg and T. Bristol, "Socialization and Adolescents' Skepticism toward Advertising," *Journal of Advertising,* Fall 1998, pp. 11–21; C. Obermiller and E. R. Spangenberg, "On the Origin and Distinctiveness of Skepticism toward Advertising," *Marketing Letters,* November 2000, pp. 311–22; and D. M. Hardesty, J. P. Carlson, and W. O. Bearden, "Brand Familiarity and Invoice Price Effects on Consumer Evaluations," *Journal of Advertising,* Summer 2002, pp. 1–15.

40. M. C. Campbell and A. Kirmani, "Consumers' Use of Persuasion Knowledge," *Journal of Consumer Research,* June 2000, pp. 69–83; R. Ahluwalia and R. E. Burnkrant, "Answering Questions about Questions," *Journal of Consumer Research,* June 2004, pp. 26–42; and D. M. Hardesty, W. O. Bearden, and J. P. Carlson, "Persuasion Knowledge and Consumer Reactions to Pricing Tactics," *Journal of Retailing* 83, no. 2 (2007), pp. 199–210.

41. Consumer 11-1 Insight is based on R. Ahlusalia, "Examination of Psychological Processes Underlying Resistance to Persuasion," *Journal of Consumer Research,* September 2000, pp. 217–32; R. D. Jewell and H. R. Unnava, "Exploring Differences in Attitudes between Light and Heavy Brand Users," *Journal of Consumer Psychology* 14, nos. 1 & 2, 2004, pp. 75–80; and Z. L. Tormala and R. E. Petty, "Source Credibility and Attitude Certainty," *Journal of Consumer Psychology* 14, no. 4 (2004), pp. 427–42.

42. A. Wang, "The Effects of Expert and Consumer Endorsements on Audience Response," *Journal of Advertising Research*, December 2005, pp. 402–12; R. Arora, C. Stoner, and A. Arora, "Using Framing and Credibility to Incorporate Exercise and Fitness in Individual's Lifestyle," *Journal of Consumer Marketing* 23, no. 4, (2006), pp. 199–207; and D. Biswas, A. Biswas, and N. Das, "The Differential Effects of Celebrity and Expert Endorsements on Consumer Risk Perceptions," *Journal of Advertising*, Summer 2006, pp. 17–31.

43. R. D. Reinartz, "Testimonial Ads," *Bank Marketing,* March 1996, pp. 25–30; and J. Nicholson, "Testimonial Ads Defend Client Turf," *Editor & Publisher,* October 23, 1999, p. 33.

44. A. Wang, "The Effects of Expert and Consumer Endorsements on Audience Response."

45. D. H. Dean, "Brand Endorsement, Popularity, and Event Sponsorship as Advertising Cues Affecting Pre-Purchase Attitudes," *Journal of Advertising,* Fall 1999, pp. 1–11; and D. H. Dean and A. Biswas, "Third-Party Organization Endorsement of Products," *Journal of Advertising,* Winter 2001, pp. 41–57.

46. Goldsmith, Lafferty, and Newell, "The Impact of Corporate Credibility and Celebrity Credibility on Consumer Reaction to Advertisements and Brands"; B. A. Lafferty, R. E. Goldsmith, and S. J. Newell, "The Dual Credibility Model," *Journal of Marketing Theory and Practice,* Summer 2002, pp. 1–12; and Z. Gurhan-Canli and R. Batra, "When Corporate Image Affects Product Evaluations," *Journal of Marketing Research,* May 2004, pp. 197–205.

47. S. P. Jain and S. S. Posavac, "Prepurchase Attribute Verifiability, Source Credibility, and Persuasion," *Journal of Consumer Psychology* 11, no. 3 (2001), pp. 169–80.

48. See P. M. Homer and L. R. Kahle, "Source Expertise, Time of Source Identification, and Involvement in Persuasion," *Journal of Advertising* 19, no. 1 (1990), pp. 30–39.

49. C. Pornpitakpan and J. N. P. Francis, "The Effect of Cultural Differences, Source Expertise, and Argument Strength on Persuasion," *Journal of International Consumer Marketing* 13, no. 1 (2001), pp. 77–101.

50. D. J. Moore, J. C. Mowen, and R. Reardon, "Multiple Sources in Advertising Appeals," *Journal of the Academy of Marketing Science,* Summer 1994, pp. 234–43. See also N. Artz and A. M. Tybout, "The Moderating Impact of Quantitative Information on the Relationship between Source Credibility and Persuasion," *Marketing Letters* 10, no. 1 (1999), pp. 51–62.

51. Sengupta, Goodstein, and Boninger, "All Cues Are Not Created Equal"; B. Z. Erdogan, M. J. Baker, and S. Tagg, "Selecting Celebrity Endorsers," *Journal of Advertising Research,* May–June 2001, pp. 39–48; M. R. Stafford, N. E. Spears, and

C.-K. Hsu, "Celebrity Images in Magazine Advertisements," *Journal of Current Issues and Research in Advertising,* Fall 2003, pp. 13–20; and A. J. Bush, C. A. Martin, and V. D. Bush, "Sports Celebrity Influence on the Behavioral Intentions of Generation Y," *Journal of Advertising Research*, March 2004, pp. 108–18.

52. "Michael Jordon Trumps Tiger, Lance in Influence on Purchase Consideration," press release, Knowledge Networks, October 27, 2003, www.knowledgenetworks.com.

53. M. Tenser, "Endorser Qualities Count More than Ever," *Advertising Age,* November 8, 2004, p. S2.

54. B. D. Till and M. Busler, "The Match-Up Hypothesis," *Journal of Advertising,* Fall 2000, pp. 1–13; Erdogan, Baker, and Tagg, "Selecting Celebrity Endorsers"; A. B. Bower and S. Landreth, "Is Beauty Best?" *Journal of Advertising,* Spring 2001, pp. 1–12; and R. Batra and P. M. Homer, "The Situational Impact of Brand Image Beliefs," *Journal of Consumer Psychology* 14, no. 3 (2004), pp. 318–30.

55. "Avril Lavigne's Style Comes to Kohl's," *StarNewsOnline.com*, March 12, 2008. See also J. Chebatoris, "Avril Lavigne Is Sew Cool," *Newsweek*, March 17, 2008, p. 69.

56. K. Macarthur, "BK and Paris," *Advertising Age,* August 30, 2004, p. 6.

57. C. Tripp, T. D. Jensen, and L. Carlson, "The Effects of Multiple Product Endorsements by Celebrities on Consumers' Attitudes and Intentions," *Journal of Consumer Research,* March 1994, pp. 535–47; and J. R. Priester and R. E. Petty, "The Influence of Spokesperson Trustworthiness on Message Elaboration, Attitude Strength, and Advertising Effectiveness," *Journal of Consumer Psychology* 13, no. 4 (2003), pp. 408–21.

58. B. D. Till and T. A. Shimp, "Endorsers in Advertising," *Journal of Advertising,* Spring 1998, pp. 67–82; and T. A. Louie, R. L. Kulik, and R. Jacobson, "When Bad Things Happen to the Endorsers of Good Products," *Marketing Letters,* February 2001, pp. 13–23.

59. J. A. Garretson and R. W. Niedrich, "Spokes-Characters," *Journal of Advertising,* Summer 2004, pp. 25–36; and J. A. Garretson and S. Burton, "The Role of Spokescharacters as Advertisement and Package Cues in Integrated Marketing Communications," *Journal of Marketing*, October 2005, pp. 118–32.

60. For an excellent overview, see T. Meenaghan, "Understanding Sponsorship Effects," *Psychology & Marketing,* February 2001, pp. 95–122; see also B. Walliser, "An International Review of Sponsorship Research," *International Journal of Advertising* 22 (2003), pp. 5–40.

61. "North American Sponsorship Spending Seen Up in '08," *Reuters.com*, January 22, 2008, www.reuters.com.

62. R. Thomaselli, "Nextel Sees Payoff as NASCAR Sponsor," *Advertising Age,* May 31, 2004, p. 3.

63. R. Madrigal, "The Influence of Social Alliances with Sports Teams on Intentions to Purchase Corporate Sponsors' Products," *Journal of Advertising,* Winter 2000, pp. 13–24.

64. S. R. McDaniel, "An Investigation of Match-Up Effects in Sport Sponsorship Advertising," *Psychology & Marketing,* March 1999, pp. 163–84; N. J. Rifon et al., "Congruence Effects in Sponsorships," *Journal of Advertising,* Spring 2004, pp. 29–42; and T. Bettina Cornwell, S. W. Pruitt, and J. M. Clark, "The Relationship between Major-League Sports' Official Sponsorship Announcements and the Stock Prices of Sponsoring Firms," *Journal of the Academy of Marketing Science* 33, no. 4 (2005), pp. 401–12.

65. B. Harvey, "Measuring the Effects of Sponsorship," *Journal of Advertising Research,* January 2001, pp. 59–65; S. Menon and B. E. Kahn, "Corporate Sponsorships of Philanthropic Activities," *Journal of Consumer Psychology* 13, no. 3 (2003), pp. 316–27. For a slightly different view, see L. R. Szykman, P. N. Bloom, and J. Blazing, "Does Corporate Sponsorship of a Socially Oriented Message Make a Difference?" *Journal of Consumer Psychology* 14, no. 1/2 (2004), pp. 13–20.

66. T. Lardinoit and C. Derbaix, "Sponsorship and Recall of Sponsors," *Psychology & Marketing,* February 2001, pp. 167–90.

67. P. G. Quester and B. Thompson, "Advertising and Promotion Leverage on Arts Sponsorship Effectiveness," *Journal of Advertising Research,* January 2001, pp. 33–47; and A. M. Levin, C. Joiner, and G. Cameron, "The Impact of Sports Sponsorship on Consumers' Brand Attitudes and Recall," *Journal of Current Issues and Research in Advertising,* Fall 2001, pp. 23–31. Conflicting evidence is in T. Lardinoit and P. G. Quester, "Attitudinal Effects of Combined Sponsorship and Sponsor's Prominence on Basketball in Europe," *Journal of Advertising Research,* January 2001, pp. 48–58.

68. N. Zmuda, "Children's Hospital in Hot Water Over Corporate Sponsorships," *AdAge.com,* March 12, 2008, http://adage.com.

69. C. Pechmann et al., "What to Convey in Antismoking Advertisements for Adolescents," *Journal of Marketing,* April 2003, pp. 1–18; M. S. LaTour and J. F. Tanner, Jr., "Randon," *Psychology & Marketing,* May 2003, 377–94; and J. P. Dillard and J. W. Anderson, "The Role of Fear in Persuasion," *Psychology & Marketing*, November 2004, pp. 909–26.

70. P. A. Keller and L. G. Block, "Increasing the Persuasiveness of Fear Appeals," *Journal of Consumer Research,* March 1996, pp. 448–60; M. S. LaTour and H. J. Rotfeld, "There Are Threats and (Maybe) Fear-Caused Arousal," *Journal of Advertising,* Fall 1997, pp. 45–59; and M. Laroche et al., "A Cross-Cultural Study of the Persuasive Effect of Fear Appeal Messages in Cigarette Advertising," *International Journal of Advertising* 3 (2001), pp. 297–317.

71. K. Passyn and M. Sujan, "Self-Accountability Emotions in Fear Appeals," *Journal of Consumer Research*, March 2006, pp. 583–89.

72. See M. S. LaTour, R. L. Snipes, and S. J. Bliss, "Don't Be Afraid to Use Fear Appeals," *Journal of Advertising Research,* March 1996, pp. 59–66.

73. D. L. Alden, A. Mukherjee, and W. D. Hoyer, "The Effects of Incongruity, Surprise and Positive Moderators and Perceived Humor in Television Advertising," *Journal of Advertising,* Summer 2000, pp. 1–14; K. Flaherty, M. G. Weinberger, and C. S. Gulas, "The Impact of Perceived Humor, Product Type, and Humor Style in Radio Advertising," *Journal of Current Issues and Research in Advertising,* Spring 2004, pp. 25–36; and J. Elpers, A. Mukherjee, and W. D. Hoyer, "Humor in Television Advertising," *Journal of Consumer Research,* December 2004, pp. 592–98.

74. T. W. Cline, M. B. Altsech, and J. J. Kellaris, "When Does Humor Enhance or Inhibit Ad Responses?" *Journal of Advertising,* Fall 2003, pp. 31–45.

75. See, e.g., H. S. Krishnan and D. Chakravarti, "A Process Analysis of the Effects of Humorous Advertising Executions on Brand Claims Memory," *Journal of Consumer Psychology* 13, no. 3 (2003), pp. 230–45.

76. H. Chung and X. Zhao, "Humour Effect on Memory and Attitude," *International Journal of Advertising* 22 (2003), pp. 117–44; and Y. Zhang and G. M. Zinkhan, "Responses to Humorous Ads," *Journal of Advertising*, Winter 2006, pp. 113–27.

77. D. L. Fugate, J. B. Gotlieb, and D. Bolton, "Humorous Services Advertising," *Journal of Professional Services Marketing* 21, no. 1 (2000), pp. 9–22; M. F. Toncar, "The Use of Humour in Television Advertising," *International Journal of Advertising* 20 (2001), pp. 521–39; K. Macarthur, "Subway Cans Schtick to Focus on Food in Its Creative," *Advertising Age,* March 1, 2004, p. 4.

78. D. Grewal et al., "Comparative versus Noncomparative Advertising," *Journal of Marketing,* October 1998, pp. 1–15; M. E. Hill and M. King, "Comparative vs. Noncomparative Advertising," *Journal of Current Issues and Research in Advertising,* Fall 2001, pp. 33–52; K. C. Manning et al., "Understanding the Mental Representations Created by Comparative Advertising," *Journal of Advertising,* Summer 2001, pp. 27–39; L. D. Compeau, D. Grewal, and R. Chandrashekaran, "Bits, Briefs, and Applications," *Journal of Consumer Affairs,* Winter 2002, pp. 284–94; and J. R. Priester et al., "Brand Congruity and Comparative Advertising," *Journal of Consumer Psychology* 14, no. 1/2 (2004), pp. 115–23.

79. A. Chattopadhyay, "When Does Comparative Advertising Influence Brand Attitude?" *Psychology & Marketing,* August 1998, pp. 461–75; M. J. Barone and P. W. Miniard, "How and When Factual Ad Claims Mislead Consumers," *Journal of Marketing Research,* February 1999, pp. 58–74; S. V. Auken and A. J. Adams, "Across- versus Within-Class Comparative Advertising," *Psychology & Marketing,* August 1999, pp. 429–50; A. B. Sorescu and B. D. Gelb, "Negative Comparative Advertising," *Journal of Advertising,* Winter 2000, pp. 25–40; S. P. Jain, B. Buchanan, and D. Maheswaran, "Comparative versus Noncomparative Advertising," *Journal of Consumer Psychology* 9, no. 4 (2000), pp. 201–11; A. V. Muthukrishnan, L. Warlop, and J. W. Alba, "The Piecemeal Approach to Comparative Advertising," *Marketing Letters* 12, no. 1 (2001), pp. 63–73; S. P. Jain and S. S. Posavac, "Valenced Comparisons," *Journal of Marketing Research,* February 2004, pp. 46–58; and M. J. Barone, K. M. Palan, and P. W. Miniard, "Brand Usage and Gender as Moderators of the Potential Deception Associated with Partial Comparative Advertising," *Journal of Advertising*, Spring 2004, pp. 19–28.

80. See, e.g., M. E. Hill et al., "The Conjoining Influences of Affect and Arousal on Attitude Formation," *Research in Consumer Behavior* 9 (2000), pp. 129–46; J. D. Morris et al., "The Power of Affect," *Journal of Advertising Research,* May–June 2002, pp. 7–17; M.-H. Huang, "Romantic Love and Sex," *Psychology & Marketing,* January 2004, pp. 53–73; and D. J. MacInnis and G. E. de Mello, "The Concept of Hope and Its Relevance to Product Evaluation and Choice," *Journal of Marketing,* January 2005, pp. 1–14.

81. R. K. Chandy et al., "What to Say When," *Journal of Marketing Research,* November 2001, pp. 399–414; and R. D. Jewell and H. R. Unnava, "Exploring Differences in Attitudes between Light and Heavy Brand Users," *Journal of Consumer Psychology* 14, no. 1/2 (2004), pp. 75–80.

82. J. S. Johar and M. J. Sirgy, "Value-Expressive versus Utilitarian Advertising Appeals," *Journal of Advertising,* September 1991, pp. 23–33; S. Shavitt, "Evidence for Predicting the Effectiveness of Value-Expressive versus Utilitarian Appeals," *Journal of Advertising,* June 1992, pp. 47–51; M. E. Slama and R. B. Singley, "Self-Monitoring and Value-Expressive vs. Utilitarian Ad Effectiveness," *Journal of Current Issues and Research in Advertising,* Fall 1996, pp. 39–49; L. Dube, A. Chattopadhyay, and A. Letarte, "Should Advertising Appeals Match the Basis of Consumers' Attitudes?" *Journal of Advertising Research,* November 1996, pp. 82–89; and J.-shen Chiou, "The Effectiveness of Different Advertising Message Appeals in the Eastern Emerging Society," *International Journal of Advertising* 21 (2002), pp. 217–36.

83. D. MacDonald, "Women & Wheels," *Design Engineering,* November–December 2004, p. 24.

84. M. Dahlen and J. Bergendahl, "Informing and Transforming on the Web," *International Journal of Advertising* 20, no. 2 (2001), pp. 189–205.

85. A. E. Crowley and W. D. Hoyer, "An Integrative Framework for Understanding Two-Sided Persuasion," *Journal of Consumer Research,* March 1994, pp. 561–74; G. Bohner et al., "When Small Means Comfortable," *Journal of Consumer Psychology* 13, no. 4 (2003), pp. 454–63; and M. Eisend, "Understanding Two-Sided Persuasion," *Psychology & Marketing*, July 2007, pp. 615–640.

86. I. P. Levin, S. L. Schneider, and G. J. Gaeth, "All Frames Are Not Created Equal," *Organizational Behavior and Human Decision Processes,* November 1998, pp. 149–88.

87. Ibid.

88. P. A. Keller, I. M. Lipkus, and B. K. Rimer, "Affect, Framing, and Persuasion," *Journal of Marketing Research,* February 2003, pp. 54–64; J. Meyers-Levy and D. Maheswaran, "Exploring Message Framing Outcomes When Systematic, Heuristic, or Both Types of Processing Occur," *Journal of Consumer Psychology* 14, no. 1/2 (2004), pp. 159–67; and B. Shiv, J. A. E. Britton, and J. W. Payne, "Does Elaboration Increase or Decrease the Effectiveness of Negatively versus Positively Framed Messages?" *Journal of Consumer Research,* June 2004, pp. 199–208.

89. See, e.g., J. W. Peltier and J. A. Schribrowsky, "The Use of Need-Based Segmentation for Developing Segment-Specific Direct Marketing Strategies," *Journal of Direct Marketing,* Fall 1997, pp. 53–62; and R. Ahmad, "Benefit Segmentation," *International Journal of Marketing Research* 45 (2003), pp. 373–88.

90. H. E. Bloom, "Match the Concept and the Product," *Journal of Advertising Research,* October 1977, pp. 25–27.

# Self-Concept and Lifestyle

■ Extreme is the name of the game![1] Snowboarding, wakeboarding, artificial wall climbing, and surfing have all seen double-digit growth in recent years. This comes at a time when many traditional sports are seeing their numbers decline. *Monday Night Football,* a perennial favorite with top-10 prime-time ratings, has seen its audience numbers slip in recent years. Participation in team sports, such as baseball, basketball, and softball, has seen double-digit declines. These changes are being fueled by dramatic shifts in the interests, values, and lifestyles of the youth market.

Harvey Lauer is president of American Sports Data, Inc. (ASD), a company that examines these trends. Lauer points out that the values underlying extreme sports are very different from those of traditional team sports. While team sports key in on working together and building character, extreme sports are rooted in "fierce individualism, alienation, and defiance."

The X Games and Gravity Games are two nationally televised events for extreme sports with a growing fan base, particularly among young men, a segment that marketers often find elusive and hard to reach. Extreme sports offer one way to connect, and marketers are scrambling to tap into the extreme, active, and adrenaline-pumped lifestyles that fuel this audience. Consider the following examples of marketing campaigns that blend extreme sports, culture, lifestyle, and music:

- Mountain Dew is a major sponsor of the X Games. It also has edgy ads with people engaged in extreme activities. Not surprisingly, teens increasingly see Mountain Dew as a "brand for them."

- Clear Channel is partnering with NBC and Mountain Dew to create an extreme sports tour, much like NASCAR's Nextel Cup Series.

- Aspen, Colorado, hosted the Winter X Games recently as a way to attract a younger audience and put a bit of edge into its stodgy image.

- Fender guitar, which sponsors athletes at the X Games, brings a truck loaded with guitars to the event and allows athletes and fans to jam right there in the snow! According to one executive at Fender, "What these guys are doing is art with their bodies and boards. They have a real desire to pursue creative outlets beyond just riding."

According to ASD's Lauer, "These sports are an authentic slice of the wider youth culture and not just a fad." Clearly, marketers should continue to look for ways to blend their brands into the lifestyles of this dynamic youth market.

---

In this chapter, we will discuss the meaning of lifestyle and the role it plays in developing marketing strategies. Lifestyle is, in many ways, an outward expression of one's self-concept. That is, the way an individual chooses to live, given the constraints of income and ability, is heavily influenced by that person's current and desired self-concept. Therefore, we begin the chapter with an analysis of the self-concept. We then describe lifestyles, the ways lifestyle is measured, and examples of how lifestyle is being used to develop marketing programs.

# SELF-CONCEPT

**Self-concept** is defined as *the totality of the individual's thoughts and feelings having reference to himself or herself as an object.* It is an individual's perception of and feelings toward him- or herself. In other words, your self-concept is composed of the attitudes you hold toward yourself.

The self-concept can be divided into four basic parts, as shown in Table 12–1: actual versus ideal, and private versus social. The actual–ideal distinction refers to the individual's perception of *who I am now* (**actual self-concept**) and *who I would like to be* (**ideal self-concept**). The private self refers to *how I am or would like to be to myself* (**private self-concept**), and the social self is *how I am seen by others or how I would like to be seen by others* (**social self-concept**).

## Interdependent/Independent Self-Concepts

The self-concept is important in all cultures. However, those aspects of the self that are most valued and most influence consumption and other behaviors vary across cultures. Researchers have found it useful to categorize self-concepts into two types—independent and interdependent, also referred to as one's separateness and connectedness.[2]

An independent construal of the self is based on the predominant Western cultural belief that individuals are inherently separate. The **independent self-concept** *emphasizes personal goals, characteristics, achievements, and desires.* Individuals with an independent self-concept tend to be individualistic, egocentric, autonomous, self-reliant, and self-contained. They define themselves in terms of what they have done, what they have, and their personal characteristics.[3]

An interdependent construal of the self is based more on the common Asian cultural belief in the fundamental connectedness of human beings. The **interdependent self-concept** *emphasizes family, cultural, professional, and social relationships.* Individuals with an interdependent self-concept tend to be obedient, sociocentric, holistic, connected, and

---

**TABLE 12–1**

Dimensions of a Consumer's Self-Concept

| Dimensions of Self-Concept | Actual Self-Concept | Ideal Self-Concept |
|---|---|---|
| *Private self* | How I actually see myself | How I would like to see myself |
| *Social self* | How others actually see me | How I would like others to see me |

relation oriented. They define themselves in terms of social roles, family relationships, and commonalities with other members of their groups.

Independent and interdependent self-concepts are not discrete categories; rather, they are constructs used to describe the opposite ends of a continuum along which most cultures lie. However, as we emphasized in Chapter 2, most cultures are heterogeneous. Therefore, within a given culture, subcultures and other groups will vary on this dimension, as will individuals.[4] For example, women across cultures tend to have more of an *interdependent* self-concept than do men.[5]

Variation in the degree to which an individual or culture is characterized by an independent versus an interdependent self-concept has been found to influence message preferences, consumption of luxury goods, and the types of products preferred. For example, ads emphasizing acting alone and autonomy tend to be effective with consumers with independent self-concepts, whereas ads emphasizing group membership work better with consumers with interdependent self-concepts.[6] The ad in Illustration 12–1 should be effective with individuals whose independent self-concept is dominant.

## Possessions and the Extended Self

Some products acquire substantial meaning to an individual or are used to signal particularly important aspects of that person's self to others. Belk developed a theory called the *extended self* to explain this.[7] The **extended self** consists of *the self plus possessions;* that is, people tend to define themselves in part by their possessions. Thus, some possessions are not just a manifestation of a person's self-concept; they are an integral part of that person's self-identity. People are, to some extent, what they possess. If one were to lose key possessions, he or she would be a somewhat different individual.[8]

While these key possessions might be major items, such as one's home or automobile, they are equally likely to be smaller items with unique meanings, such as a souvenir, a photograph, a pet, or a favorite cooking pan. Such objects have meaning to the individual beyond their market value. Consider these statements from consumers who lost their possessions in natural disasters and who had ample insurance to replace them:

Yea, we got better stuff, but it doesn't mean anything to us. It's just stuff.

You can't put back or replace what you had. It was too personal—it was customized.[9]

Products become part of one's extended self for a variety of reasons. Souvenirs often become part of the extended self as representations of memories and feelings:

You can't really tell what Paris is like . . . you know, a lot of it is just feelings; feelings you can't put into words, or [that] pictures cannot capture. . . . They [a hat and blouse] are just reminders.

I had a really wonderful trip and really sort of discovered myself; you know, I learned to be independent on my own. I really didn't have the money to buy this [necklace and boomerang charm], but I decided I wanted something really permanent. . . . The boomerang is a symbol of going back there sometime.[10]

Gifts often take on important meanings as representations of relationships:

That gift was my grandfather's ring. . . . Even now when I look at it, I think about its past with him and the journeys it took around the world in the Navy back in World War II.

The key chain is special because every so often, when I think about who gave it to me, it brings back old thoughts and feelings. It is a symbol of friendship between us, and it keeps us in touch.[11]

Some products become embedded with meaning, memories, and value as they are used over time, as with an old baseball glove. At other times, a single peak experience with a product such as a mountain bike can propel the product into the extended self. A **peak experience** is *an experience that surpasses the usual level of intensity, meaningfulness, and richness and produces feelings of joy and self-fulfillment.*[12] Finally, products that are acquired or used to help consumers with major life transitions (e.g., leaving home, first job, marriage) are also likely to be or become part of the extended self.[13]

As Consumer Insight 12–1 makes clear, extended self can also relate to nonproduct entities such as activities (golfing), other people (my best friend), TV shows (*Star Trek*), and sports teams (Green Bay Packers).

A scale has been developed to measure the extent to which an item has been incorporated into the extended self.[14] It is a Likert scale (see Appendix A) in which consumers express levels of agreement (from strongly agree to strongly disagree on a seven-point scale) to the following statements:

---

1. My _____ helps me achieve the identity I want to have.
2. My _____ helps me narrow the gap between what I am and what I try to be.
3. My _____ is central to my identity.
4. My _____ is part of who I am.
5. If my _____ is stolen from me I will feel as if my identity has been snatched from me.
6. I derive some of my identity from my _____.

---

Owning a product affects a person even if it does not become an important part of the person's extended self. The **mere ownership effect,** or the *endowment effect,* is *the tendency of an owner to evaluate an object more favorably than a nonowner.* This occurs almost immediately upon acquiring an object and increases with time of ownership. Thus, people tend to value an object more after acquiring it than before. People also tend to value objects they own more highly than they value similar objects owned by others.[15]

The concept of the extended self and the mere ownership effect have numerous implications for marketing strategy. One is that communications that cause potential consumers to *visualize product ownership* may result in enhanced product evaluations. Product sampling or other trial programs may have similar results.

## Measuring Self-Concept

Using the self-concept in marketing requires that it be measurable. The most common measurement approach is the semantic differential (see Appendix A). Malhotra has developed a set of 15 pairs of adjectives, shown in Table 12–2. These have proven effective in describing the ideal, actual, and social self-concepts of individuals as well as the images

You may know one. You may be one. A fan . . . of a music group, a sports team, a shoe line, a television show. . . . Fans are a devoted bunch. Their lives are often consumed by the object of their devotion.[16] Star Trek fans, or Trekkies, join clubs, attend conventions, and collect merchandise. Packers fans, or Cheeseheads, brave the cold at Lambeau Field and proudly wear headgear shaped like cheese. And NASCAR fans drive for days to attend races and get the chance to see their favorite drivers. Actually, fans come in all forms, from temporary to fanatical to dysfunctional. A key aspect driving fan devotion is the consumer's own assessment of how "being a fan is a necessary part of defining themselves and of presenting to others their self-identity." Within the realm of sports, a hierarchy of fandom has been discovered, where each successive level involves a stronger connection to the self, self-expression, and the extended self. The categories are as follows:

- *Temporary fans* are fans for a specific time-bound event and then go back to normal behaviors. An example might be the attention paid to baseball even by those who never follow baseball, when the Boston Red Sox were playing for a World Series which they had not won in over 80 years. Self-concept is not tied up at all with the team or identification with the team.
- *Local fans* are fans for geographic reasons such as the team is close by. You might be a fan of the Lansing Lugnuts (minor league baseball team) if you live in or near Lansing, Michigan. If you moved, you would cease being a fan. Again, self-concept is not tied up in the team.
- *Devoted and fanatical fans* are fans whose self-concepts are highly defined by identification and association with the team. They are active participants whose loyalty is not bound by time or geography.

- *Dysfunctional fans* are fans whose primary self-identification involves being a fan of a particular team. Obviously, such extreme identification can lead to antisocial behavior and other dysfunctional outcomes. Unruly fans who can't control their emotions and need to be managed fall into this category although more extreme consequences such as loss of job and family have been observed.

Just as consumers can be fans of sports teams, so too can they be devoted to brands such as Starbucks or McDonald's. As with sports fans, the devotion can range from low to high depending on the extent of identification with the self-concept. As one devoted Mercedes customer noted:

> I went up to Connecticut to buy my latest Mercedes because that dealer was able to deliver the newest model with the navigation system sooner than the [local] Miami dealer. So, I don't mind traveling for my Mercedes.

Indeed, devoted consumers are known to engage in numerous "self-reinforcing" or "sustaining" behaviors that keep the devotion alive, including sacrifice, rituals, sharing, and recruiting of others. Fans are committed and loyal. The sustaining behaviors involve not only purchases but also positive word of mouth and active recruiting. That is, devoted fans act as marketing representatives for their favorite brands, bands, teams, and so on. Building such loyalty represents an important marketing goal.

### Critical Thinking Questions

1. What strategies can marketers use to encourage fandom and devotion?

2. Is it possible that devoted consumers ever become disenchanted? What might cause this to happen?

3. Do you think there are instances when fans may feel a need to conceal that fact from others? What might motivate this?

| TABLE 12–2 | | | | | | | | | |
|---|---|---|---|---|---|---|---|---|---|
| 1. Rugged | ____ | ____ | ____ | ____ | ____ | ____ | ____ | | Delicate |
| 2. Excitable | ____ | ____ | ____ | ____ | ____ | ____ | ____ | | Calm |
| 3. Uncomfortable | ____ | ____ | ____ | ____ | ____ | ____ | ____ | | Comfortable |
| 4. Dominating | ____ | ____ | ____ | ____ | ____ | ____ | ____ | | Submissive |
| 5. Thrifty | ____ | ____ | ____ | ____ | ____ | ____ | ____ | | Indulgent |
| 6. Pleasant | ____ | ____ | ____ | ____ | ____ | ____ | ____ | | Unpleasant |
| 7. Contemporary | ____ | ____ | ____ | ____ | ____ | ____ | ____ | | Noncontemporary |
| 8. Organized | ____ | ____ | ____ | ____ | ____ | ____ | ____ | | Unorganized |
| 9. Rational | ____ | ____ | ____ | ____ | ____ | ____ | ____ | | Emotional |
| 10. Youthful | ____ | ____ | ____ | ____ | ____ | ____ | ____ | | Mature |
| 11. Formal | ____ | ____ | ____ | ____ | ____ | ____ | ____ | | Informal |
| 12. Orthodox | ____ | ____ | ____ | ____ | ____ | ____ | ____ | | Liberal |
| 13. Complex | ____ | ____ | ____ | ____ | ____ | ____ | ____ | | Simple |
| 14. Colorless | ____ | ____ | ____ | ____ | ____ | ____ | ____ | | Colorful |
| 15. Modest | ____ | ____ | ____ | ____ | ____ | ____ | ____ | | Vain |

Measurement Scales for Self-Concepts, Person Concepts, and Product Concepts

Source: N. K. Malhotra, "A Scale to Measure Self-Concepts, Person Concepts, and Product Concepts," *Journal of Marketing Research,* published by the American Marketing Association; reprinted with permission. November 1981, p. 462. Used by permission of the American Marketing Association.

of automobiles and celebrities. *Using this scale, determine your actual and desired private and social self-concepts.*

This instrument can be used to ensure a match between the self-concept (actual or ideal) of a target market, the image of a brand, and the characteristics of an advertising spokesperson. For example, in its decision to sign Serena Williams to a multiyear endorsement contract, Nike undoubtedly saw a match between the desired self-concept of young women, the desired image for Nike's women's athletic apparel line, and the image of Serena Williams.[17]

## Using Self-Concept to Position Products

People's attempts to obtain their ideal self-concept, or maintain their actual self-concept, often involve the purchase and consumption of products, services, and media.[18] This process is described in Figure 12–1. While this figure implies a rather conscious and deliberate process, many times that is not the case. For example, a person may drink diet colas because his desired self-concept includes a trim figure, but he is unlikely to think about the

## FIGURE 12–1 The Relationship between Self-Concept and Brand Image Influence

purchase in these terms. However, as the following statement illustrates, sometimes people do think in these terms:

And I feel if you present yourself in the right way, people will start to notice. But this leads back to image and self-worth, which can be achieved through having the right clothes and a good haircut . . . having a good portrait of yourself on the outside can eventually lead to an emotionally stable inside.[19]

All this suggests that marketers should strive to develop product images that are consistent with the self-concepts of their target markets.[20] While everyone's self-concept is unique, there is also significant overlap across individuals and groups, which is one basis for market segmentation. For example, many consumers see themselves as environmentalists. Companies and products that create an image of being concerned about or good for the environment are likely to be supported by these consumers.

Consumers maintain and enhance their self-concepts not only by what they consume, but by what they avoid.[21] Some consumers make a point of avoiding certain product categories, such as red meat, or certain brands, such as Nike, as part of maintaining "who they are."

In general, consumers prefer brands that match their self-concepts. However, it is important to realize that the degree to which such "self-image congruity" influences brand preference and choice depends on a number of product, situational, and individual factors. First, self-image congruity is likely to matter more for products such as perfume where value-expressive *symbolism* is critical than for more utilitarian products such as a garage door opener. Second, self-image congruity (especially ideal social self) is likely to matter more when the situation involves *public* or *conspicuous consumption* (e.g., having a beer with friends at a bar) than when consumption is private (e.g., having a beer at home).[22]

Finally, self-image congruity is likely to matter more for consumers who place heavy weight on the opinions and feelings of others (called *high self-monitors*) than for consumers who do not (called *low self-monitors*), particularly in public situations where consumption behaviors can be observed by others.[23]

Look at Illustration 12–2 and the various aspects of self-concept listed in Table 12–2. *Which aspect(s) of self-concept does this ad appeal to?*

## Marketing Ethics and the Self-Concept

The self-concept has many dimensions. Marketers have been criticized for focusing too much attention on the importance of being beautiful, with *beautiful* being defined as young and slim with a fairly narrow range of facial features. Virtually all societies appear to define and desire beauty, but the intense exposure to products and advertisements focused on beauty in America today is unique. Critics argue that this concern leads individuals to develop self-concepts that are heavily dependent on their physical appearance rather than other equally or more important attributes.

Consider the following statements from two young women:

I never felt that I looked right. Like I can see outfits that I'd love to wear, but I know that I could never wear them. I probably could wear them and get away with it, but I'd be so self-conscious walking around that I'd be like, "oh, my God." Like I always try to look thinner and I guess everybody does.

I am pretty content with my hair because I have good hair. I have good eyesight (laughs) so I don't have to wear glasses or anything that would make my face look different from what it is. In terms of bad points, well there is a lot. I got a lot of my father's features. I wish I had more of my mother's. My hands are pretty square. I have a kind of a big butt. Then, I don't have that great of a stomach.[24]

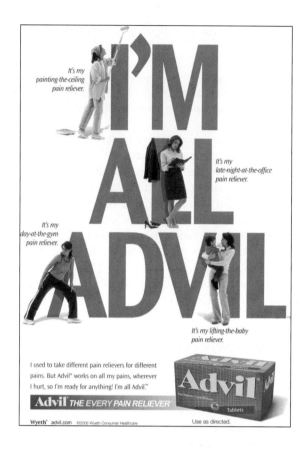

These young women have self-concepts that are partly negative as a result of their perceptions of their beauty relative to the standard portrayed in the media. Critics of advertising claim that most individuals, but particularly young women, acquire negative components to their self-concepts because very few can achieve the standards of beauty presented in advertising. Recent research indicates that similar negative self-evaluations occur in males as a result of idealized images of both physical attractiveness and financial success.[25]

The ethical question is complex. No one ad or company has this type of impact. It is the cumulative effect of many ads across many companies reinforced by the content of the mass media that presumably causes some to be overly focused on their physical beauty. And, as stated earlier, concern with beauty existed long before advertising.

## THE NATURE OF LIFESTYLE

As Figure 12–2 indicates, **lifestyle** is basically *how a person lives*. It is how a person enacts her or his self-concept, and is determined by past experiences, innate characteristics, and current situation. One's lifestyle influences all aspects of consumption behavior and is a function of inherent individual characteristics that have been shaped and formed through social interaction as the person has evolved through the life cycle.

The relationship between *lifestyle* and *self-concept* was demonstrated in a recent study comparing various lifestyle-related activities, interests, and behaviors across those with independent versus interdependent self-concepts. *Independents* were more likely to seek adventure and excitement through travel, sports, and entertainment; to be opinion leaders; and to prefer magazines over TV. *Interdependents* were more likely to engage in home and

**Lifestyle and the Consumption Process**    FIGURE 12–2

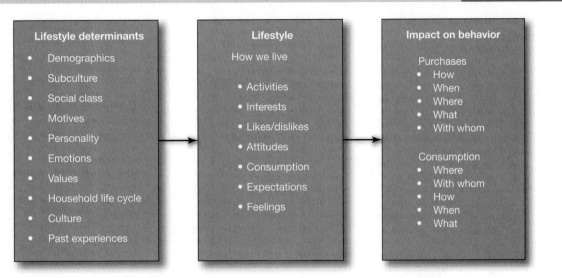

domestic-related activities and entertainment, including cooking at home and from scratch. Interdependents were also more likely to engage in social activities revolving around family and the community.[26]

Individuals and households both have lifestyles. Although household lifestyles are in part determined by the individual lifestyles of the household members, the reverse is also true.

Individuals' *desired* lifestyles influence their needs and desires and thus their purchase and use behavior. Desired lifestyle determines many of a person's consumption decisions, which in turn reinforce or alter that person's lifestyle.

Marketers can use lifestyle to segment and target specific markets. As the chapter's opening vignette illustrates, companies such as Mountain Dew and Fender guitars are targeting their promotions and brands toward the lifestyles of extreme sports fans and participants. Beer brands such as Heineken and Amstel would also see this group as a highly attractive segment, since its members are 107 percent more likely than the average consumer to drink imported beers.[27] Illustration 12–3 shows a Web site targeted at the extreme sports enthusiast.

Consumers are seldom explicitly aware of the role lifestyle plays in their purchase decisions. For example, few consumers would think, "I'll have a Starbucks coffee at a Starbucks outlet to maintain my lifestyle." However, individuals pursuing an active, social lifestyle might purchase Starbucks in part because of its convenience, its "in" status, and the presence of others at Starbucks outlets. Thus, lifestyle frequently provides the basic motivation and guidelines for purchases, although it generally does so in an indirect, subtle manner.

## Measurement of Lifestyle

Attempts to develop quantitative measures of lifestyle were initially referred to as **psychographics.**[28] In fact, the terms *psychographics* and *lifestyle* are frequently used interchangeably. Psychographics or lifestyle studies typically include the following:

- *Attitudes*—evaluative statements about other people, places, ideas, products, and so forth.
- *Values*—widely held beliefs about what is acceptable or desirable.

- *Activities and interests*—nonoccupational behaviors to which consumers devote time and effort, such as hobbies, sports, public service, and church.
- *Demographics*—age, education, income, occupation, family structure, ethnic background, gender, and geographic location.
- *Media patterns*—the specific media the consumers utilize.
- *Usage rates*—measurements of consumption within a specified product category; often consumers are categorized as heavy, medium, or light users or as nonusers.

A large number of individuals, often 500 or more, provide the above information. Statistical techniques are used to place them into groups whose members have similar response patterns. Most studies use the first two or three dimensions described above to group individuals. The other dimensions are used to provide fuller descriptions of each group. Other studies include demographics as part of the grouping process.[29]

## General versus Specific Lifestyle Schemes

Lifestyle measurements can be constructed with varying degrees of specificity. At one extreme, marketers can study the general lifestyle patterns of a population. These general lifestyle approaches are not specific to any one product or activity, so they have broad applicability in developing marketing strategies for a wide range of products and brands. General approaches include VALS and PRIZM, which are discussed in later sections of this chapter.

At the other extreme, firms can conduct very specific lifestyle studies focused on those aspects of individual or household lifestyles most relevant to their product or service. For these studies, lifestyle measurement is product or activity specific. Specific lifestyle schemes have been used to analyze complaint behavior by elderly patients dissatisfied with their health care,[30] to understand art gallery attendance in New Zealand,[31] to determine optimal marketing strategies for tourism in Spain,[32] and to develop dining menus at U.S. college campuses.[33] Let's take an in-depth look at three specific lifestyle schemes.

**Luxury Sports Cars**    Porsche examined the lifestyles of its buyers. What they found surprised them a bit, because although key demographics (e.g., high education and income) were similar across their buyers, their lifestyles and motivations were quite different. The segments and their descriptions are listed below:[34]

- *Top Guns* (27 percent). Ambitious and driven, this group values power and control and expects to be noticed.
- *Elitists* (24 percent). These old-family-money "blue-bloods" don't see a car as an extension of their personality. Cars are cars no matter what the price tag.
- *Proud Patrons* (23 percent). This group purchases a car to satisfy themselves, not to impress others. A car is a reward for their hard work.
- *Bon Vivants* (17 percent). These thrill seekers and "jet-setters" see cars as enhancing their already exciting lives.
- *Fantasists* (9 percent). This group uses their car as an escape, not as a means to impress others. In fact, they feel a bit of guilt for owning a Porsche.

*How would Porsche's marketing approach need to be changed across these different lifestyle segments?*

**Shopping**    In Chapter 10 (Consumer Insight 10–1) we discussed various hedonic motives underlying consumer shopping patterns. The motives were (1) adventure (fun), (2) gratification (reward/stress reduction), (3) role (shop for others), (4) value (good deal), (5) social (bonding), and (6) idea (trends). Five shopping lifestyle segments emerged based on these motives.[35]

- *Minimalists* (12 percent). Primarily motivated by value. Least motivated by fun and adventure. Minimalists are low in appreciation of retail aesthetics (look and feel of the mall/store), low in innovativeness, and don't tend to be browsers. This group is middle-aged, and 57 percent are men.
- *Gatherers* (15 percent). Primarily motivated by keeping up with trends and enjoyment of shopping for others. Least motivated by value. Gatherers are low in appreciation of retail aesthetics, low in innovativeness, but are moderate browsers. This group contains a mix of younger and older shoppers but is predominantly (70 percent) male.
- *Providers* (23 percent). Primarily motivated by enjoyment of shopping for others and by value. Not motivated by fun and adventure. Providers are moderate in their appreciation of retail aesthetics, low in innovativeness, and are moderate browsers. This is the oldest group and is predominantly (83 percent) female.
- *Enthusiasts* (27 percent). Highly motivated by all hedonic aspects, including fun and adventure, for which they are higher than any other group. Enthusiasts are highest in appreciation of retail aesthetics, the most innovative, and spend the most time browsing. This is the youngest group and is predominantly (90 percent) female.
- *Traditionalists* (23 percent). Moderately motivated by all hedonic aspects, with gratification high on the list. Traditionalists are moderate in appreciation of retail aesthetics, highly innovative, and moderate browsers. This group contains a mix of younger and older shoppers, and 58 percent are women.

*Which lifestyle segment(s) do you think shop at Banana Republic? What about at Target?*

**Technology**    How technology is used by consumers is of critical importance to marketers. Numerous technology and Internet lifestyle profiles exist, including Pew Internet User Types, Ebates.com Dot-shoppers, and TDS Shopper Clusters: Onliners Group.[36] Forrester

Research has created Technographics, a technology segmentation scheme that examines lifestyle segments across such technologies and activities as online access, PC ownership, instant messaging, and shopping online. Based on the responses of over 60,000 North American respondents, the following 10 segments emerged:[37]

- *Fast Forwards* (12 percent). Optimistic, high income, and motivated by career. Fast Forwards are time-pressed, driven, and heavy users of technology across the board. Most likely to own a PC and be online.
- *Techno-Strivers* (5 percent). Optimistic, low income, and motivated by career. Techno-Strivers are beginning to believe in the value of technology as a way to help advance their careers. More likely than average to be influenced by "what is hot." Average technology users.
- *Handshakers* (7 percent). Pessimistic, high income, and motivated by career. Handshakers are successful in their careers but have a low tolerance for technology. They are the lowest users of instant messaging and least likely to download music files. But they are still more likely than average to own a PC and be online.
- *New Age Nurturers* (8 percent). Optimistic, high income, and motivated by family. New Age Nurturers believe strongly in the value of technology for family and education. More likely than average to own a PC and be online.
- *Digital Hopefuls* (6 percent). Optimistic, low income, and motivated by family. Digital hopefuls are family-oriented technology lovers. Relatively high users of instant messaging. Perhaps due to lower income, they are less likely than average to own a PC and be online.
- *Traditionalists* (10 percent). Pessimistic, high income, and motivated by family. Traditionalists are suspicious of any technology beyond simple basics. Least likely to be influenced by "what's hot." One of the least likely groups to bank online and download music files.
- *Mouse Potatoes* (9 percent). Optimistic, high income, and motivated by entertainment. Mouse Potatoes are into interactive entertainment especially on the PC. Most likely of all groups to shop online, have a mobile phone, and bank online.
- *Gadget Grabbers* (7 percent). Optimistic, low income, and motivated by entertainment. Gadget Grabbers want affordable high-tech products. Most influenced by "what's hot," and most likely to use instant messaging and download music files. Lower income makes them slightly less likely than average to own a PC and be online.
- *Media Junkies* (6 percent). Pessimistic, high income, and motivated by entertainment. Media Junkies are especially interested in TV and such features as on-demand video.
- *Sidelined Citizens* (29 percent). Pessimistic and low income. Sidelined Citizens, by far the largest group, are frightened of technology and slow to adopt. This group is least receptive to technological innovations. Least likely to own a PC, be online, shop online, or bank online.

*To which of these groups will the ad in Illustration 12–4 appeal?*

**ILLUSTRATION 12–4**

Forrester Research has identified 10 lifestyle segments related to technology. To which segment(s) will this ad most appeal?

While specific lifestyle studies are useful, many firms have found general lifestyle studies to be of great value also. Two popular general systems are described next.[38]

# THE VALS™ SYSTEM

By far the most popular application of psychographic research by marketing managers is SRI Consulting Business Intelligence's (SRIC-BI) VALS™ program. Introduced in 1978 and significantly revised in 1989, **VALS** provides a systematic classification of American adults into eight distinct consumer segments.[39]

VALS is based on enduring psychological characteristics that correlate with purchase patterns. Respondents are classified according to their *primary motivation,* which serves as one of VALS's two dimensions. As we saw in Chapter 10, motives are critical determinants of behavior. Motives have strong linkages to personality and self-concept. Indeed, a core premise behind VALS is that "[a]n individual's primary motivation determines what in particular about the self or the world is the meaningful core that governs his or her activities." SRIC-BI has identified three primary motivations:

- *Ideals motivation.* These consumers are guided in their choices by their beliefs and principles rather than by feelings or desire for social approval. They purchase functionality and reliability.
- *Achievement motivation.* These consumers strive for a clear social position and are strongly influenced by the actions, approval, and opinions of others. They purchase status symbols.
- *Self-expression motivation.* These action-oriented consumers strive to express their individuality through their choices. They purchase experiences.

These three orientations determine the types of goals and behaviors that individuals will pursue. Table 12–3 provides more detailed descriptions of the goals, motivations, and behavioral tendencies of each motivational group.

The second dimension, termed *resources,* reflects the ability of individuals to pursue their dominant self-orientation. It refers to the full range of psychological, physical, demographic, and material means on which consumers can draw. Resources generally increase from adolescence through middle age and then remain relatively stable until they begin to decline with older age. Resources are an important part of VALS since they can aid or inhibit a consumer's ability to act on his or her primary motivation.

On the basis of these two concepts, SRIC-BI has identified eight general psychographic segments, as shown in Figure 12–3. Table 12–4 provides selected demographics for each

| Primary Motivation | | |
|---|---|---|
| **Ideals** | **Achievement** | **Self-Expression** |
| They are | | |
| Information seeking | Goal oriented | Spontaneous |
| They make | | |
| Choices based on principles | Choices to enhance position | Choices to have emotional impact |
| They buy | | |
| Functionality and reliability | Success symbols | Experiences |
| They seek | | |
| Understanding | Social approval | Adventure, excitement, novelty |
| They pursue | | |
| Self-development | Self-improvement | Self-reliance |
| They resist | | |
| Impulse | Risk | Authority |
| They ask | | |
| What "should" I do? | What are others like me doing? | What do I feel like doing? |

**TABLE 12–3**

Underlying Differences across VALS™ Motivational Types Selected Demographics of the VALS™

Source: SRI Consulting Business Intelligence, www.sric-bi.com/VALS/.

| FIGURE 12–3 | VALS™ Framework |

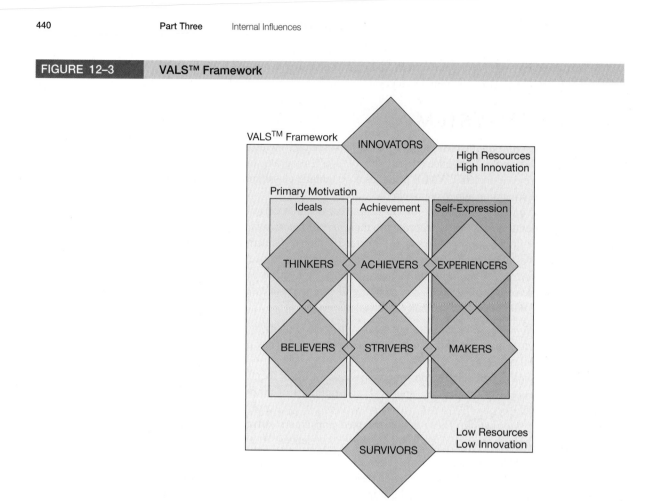

Source: SRI Consulting Business Intelligence, www.sric-bi.com/VALS/.

| TABLE 12–4 |
| Selected Demographics of the VALS™ System |

| Segment | Percent Female | Median Age | Median Income (000) |
|---|---|---|---|
| Innovators | 46% | 43 | $104 |
| Thinkers | 49 | 54 | 76 |
| Believers | 69 | 50 | 34 |
| Achievers | 56 | 40 | 67 |
| Strivers | 41 | 28 | 22 |
| Experiencers | 42 | 25 | 47 |
| Makers | 43 | 45 | 39 |
| Survivors | 63 | 70 | 15 |

Source: VALS/MediaMark Research Inc. (MRI) data from *The Survey of American Consumers;* SRI Consulting Business Intelligence, www.sric-bi.com/VAL/.

segment. Table 12–5 provides information on selected product ownership and activities for each segment. Each of these segments is described briefly next.

## The VALS™ Segments

**Innovators**  *Innovators* are successful, sophisticated, active, take-charge people with high self-esteem and abundant resources. Innovators are motivated by a blend of ideals, achievement, and self-expression. Image is important to Innovators, not as evidence of

| TABLE 12–5 | | VALS Segment: Selected Ownership and Activites* | | | | | | | |
| --- | --- | --- | --- | --- | --- | --- | --- | --- | --- |
| | **All** | **Innovators** | **Thinkers** | **Believers** | **Achievers** | **Strivers** | **Experiencers** | **Makers** | **Survivors** |
| Own a truck | 100 | 54 | 99 | 106 | 121 | 78 | 83 | 158 | 89 |
| Drink herb tea | 100 | 219 | 152 | 71 | 97 | 47 | 92 | 92 | 61 |
| Mountain bicycle $100+ | 100 | 145 | 36 | 14 | 141 | 146 | 221 | 122 | 0 |
| Attend country music performances | 100 | 59 | 95 | 107 | 116 | 87 | 92 | 159 | 74 |

*Note: Table based on index numbers (100 = average of U.S. adult population) and provide a basis of comparison across the VALS groups and the U.S. population overall. For example, Makers are 58 percent more likely to own a truck than the average U.S. adult consumer.

Source: VALS/MediaMark Research Inc. (MRI) data from *The Survey of American Consumers;* SRI Consulting Business Intelligence, www.sric-bi.com/VALS/.

status or power but as an expression of their taste, independence, and character. Their possessions and recreation reflect a cultivated taste for the finer things in life, and they often see brands and products as extensions of their personalities.

Innovators are among the established and emerging leaders in business and government, yet they continue to grow and seek new challenges. They have a wide range of interests, are concerned with social issues, and are the most receptive to new products, ideas, and technologies. The ad in Illustration 12–5 would appeal to Innovators.

**Thinkers and Believers: Ideals Motivated**    Ideals-motivated consumers base their decisions on abstract idealized criteria such as quality, integrity, and tradition. They seek to behave in ways that are consistent with their views of how the world is or should be.

*Thinkers* are mature, satisfied, comfortable, reflective people who value order, knowledge, and responsibility. Most are well educated, and in or recently retired from professional

London, tastefully delivered.

BRITISH AIRWAYS

**ILLUSTRATION 12–5**

This ad would appeal to Innovators' desire for growth and their taste for the finer things in life.

occupations. They are well informed about world and national events and are alert to opportunities to broaden their knowledge. Content with their careers, families, and station in life, they tend to center their leisure activities on the home.

Thinkers have a moderate respect for the status quo but are open-minded about new ideas and social change. They tend to base their decisions on strongly held principles and consequently appear calm and self-assured. Thinkers plan their purchases carefully and are particularly cautious concerning big-ticket items; they look for functionality, value, and durability in the products they buy.

*Believers* are conservative, conventional people with concrete beliefs based on traditional, established codes: family, church, community, and the nation. Many Believers express moral codes that are deeply rooted and literally interpreted. They follow established routines, organized in large part around their homes, families, and the social or religious organizations to which they belong. As consumers, they are conservative, predictable, and highly loyal. Believers favor American products and established brands, and are averse to change and new technology.

### Achievers and Strivers: Achievement Motivated

Achievement-oriented consumers make choices to enhance their position or to facilitate their move to a more desirable group. Strivers look to others to indicate what they should be and do, whereas Achievers look to their own peer group.

*Achievers* are successful career- and work-oriented people who like to, and generally do, feel in control of their lives. They value consensus, predictability, and stability over risk, intimacy, and self-discovery. They are deeply committed to work and family, with lives structured around family, church, and career. Achievers live conventional lives, tend to be politically conservative, and respect authority and the status quo. Image is important to them; they favor established, prestige products and services that demonstrate success to their peers. Convenience and time-saving products and services are also of interest to achievers given their hectic lifestyles.

The ad in Illustration 12–6 would appeal to Achievers.

*Strivers* are style conscious and trendy. They have limited education and tend to have narrow interests. Money defines success for Strivers, but they usually don't have enough of it. They favor stylish products that emulate the purchases of people with greater material wealth. Strivers have less self-confidence than Achievers. They often feel that life has given them a raw deal.

### Experiencers and Makers: Self-Expression Motivated

Self-expression–motivated consumers like to affect their environment in tangible ways. Makers do so by physically altering their environment at home—for example, building a new patio or adding a room. Alternatively, Experiencers seek to make an impact through their dress, speech, or adventurous experiences.

*Experiencers* are young, vital, enthusiastic, impulsive, and rebellious. They seek variety and excitement, savoring the new, the offbeat, and the risky. Still in the process of formulating life values and patterns of behavior, they quickly become enthusiastic about new possibilities but are equally quick to cool. At this stage of their lives, they are politically uncommitted, uninformed, and highly ambivalent about what they believe.

Experiencers combine an abstract disdain for conformity with an outsider's awe of others' wealth, prestige, and power. Their energy finds an outlet in exercise, sports, outdoor recreation, and social activities. Experiencers are avid consumers and spend much of their income on clothing, fast food, music, movies, and videos and technology. The ad in Illustration 12–7 would be particularly appealing to this segment.

*Makers* are practical people who have constructive skills and value self-sufficiency. They live within a traditional context of family, practical work, and physical recreation and have little interest in what lies outside that context. Makers express themselves and experience the world by working on it—building a house, raising children, fixing a car, or canning vegetables. Makers are politically conservative, suspicious of new ideas, respectful of government authority and organized labor, but resentful of government intrusion on individual rights. They are unimpressed by material possessions other than those with a practical or functional purpose (e.g., tools, pickup trucks, washing machines, or fishing equipment). The product shown in Illustration 12–8 would appeal to this group.

**ILLUSTRATION 12–7**

Experiencers are impulsive and social. They like new and offbeat things.

**ILLUSTRATION 12–8**

Makers focus on their families and homes. They are practical and value functional products. This product taps into their self-sufficiency motives.

**Survivors**    *Survivors'* lives are constricted. They live simply on limited incomes but are relatively satisfied. Frequently elderly and concerned about their health, they are not active in the marketplace. Survivors show no evidence of a strong primary motivation. They buy familiar, trusted products. Their chief concerns are for security and safety and for being with family. Survivors are cautious consumers who look for low prices. They represent a modest market for most products and services. As described in Chapter 4, meeting the needs of these consumers is a challenge for both marketers and public policy makers.

# GEO-LIFESTYLE ANALYSIS (PRIZM)

Claritas Inc., a leading firm in this industry, describes the logic of **geo-demographic analysis:**

> People with similar cultural backgrounds, means and perspectives naturally gravitate toward one another. They choose to live amongst their peers in neighborhoods offering affordable advantages and compatible lifestyles.
>
> Once settled in, people naturally emulate their neighbors. They adopt similar social values, tastes and expectations. They exhibit shared patterns of consumer behavior toward products, services, media and promotions.[40]

Geo-demographic analyses are based on the premise that lifestyle, and thus consumption, is largely driven by demographic factors, as described above.[41] The geographic regions analyzed can range from states and counties, to metropolitan statistical areas (urbanized areas of 50,000 people or more plus adjacent territory), to five-digit ZIP codes (1,500 to 15,000 or more households), to Census tracts (850–2,500 households), to Census blocks (8–25 households), to ZIP+4 (6–15 households), and even down to the individual household. Such data are used for target market selection, promotional emphasis, retail site selection, and so forth by numerous marketers.

Claritas has taken geo-demographic analysis one step further and incorporated extensive data on product consumption and media usage patterns. Claritas has updated their system on the basis of the most recent Census data and is now able to classify down to the level of individual households. The output is a set of 66 lifestyle segments called the **PRIZM®** system (the newest version being PRIZM NE, or New Evolution). Each household in the United States can be profiled in terms of these lifestyle groups.[42]

## PRIZM Social and Life Stage Groups

PRIZM organizes its 66 individual segments into broader social and lifestage groups. The broadest social groupings are based on "urbanicity." Urbanicity is determined by population density, relates to where people live and is strongly related to the lifestyles people lead. The four major social groups are:

- *Urban*—major cities with high population density.
- *Suburban*—moderately dense "suburban" areas surrounding metropolitan areas.
- *Second city*—smaller, less densely populated cities or satellites to major cities.
- *Town and country*—low-density towns and rural communities.

The broadest life stage groups are based on age and the presence of children. As we saw in Chapter 6, these factors strongly influence consumption patterns and lifestyle. The three major life stage groups are:

- *Younger years*—singles and couples under 45 years of age with no children.
- *Family life*—middle-aged (25–54) families with children.
- *Mature years*—singles and couples over 45 years of age.

PRIZM gets even finer-grained detail by further dividing each social and life stage group by level of affluence, (e.g., income and wealth) since affluence is a strong demographic determinant of activities, consumption patterns, and lifestyle. When possible, Claritas also merges its general PRIZM information with clients' customer databases as a way to further enhance precision.

## Sample PRIZM Segments

We briefly describe eight specific segments and use them in demonstrating how PRIZM can be used in developing successful marketing strategies (for information on all 66 segments, visit www.MyBestSegments.com).

- *Young Digerati* (Urban/Younger Years—PRIZM segment 04) are young, upscale, and technology savvy. They live in fashionable neighborhoods. They are highly educated professionals who are ethnically diverse, including a high concentration of Asians. They live near trendy boutiques, restaurants, and bars. They shop at stores like Banana Republic, travel and scuba dive, read newspapers, and listen to online radio.
- *Blue Blood Estates* (Suburban/Family—PRIZM segment 02) are middle-aged married couples with children. They live in exclusive neighborhoods with private clubs. They are highly educated, wealthy business executives and professionals. Ethnic diversity includes a high concentration of Asians. They shop at stores like Bloomingdale's. They travel extensively for business and read business magazines like *BusinessWeek*. They also eat at fast-food restaurants a lot with their kids.
- *Big Fish, Small Pond* (Town/Mature—PRIZM segment 09) are older "empty-nester" couples who are leaders in their small communities. They are affluent, typically Caucasian, college-educated professionals. They shop from catalog retailers like L.L.Bean, belong to country clubs, travel, and bird watch. They are also heavy listeners of radio and read magazines like *Travel and Leisure*.
- *Pools and Patios* (Suburban/Mature—PRIZM segment 15) are evolving into older "empty-nester" couples as their children grow up and leave home. They live in older, stable neighborhoods with pools and patios in their backyards. They are college-educated, typically Caucasian, middle-class managers and professionals who read the *Washington Post* and listen to classical radio. They order from QVC but will also shop Nordstrom. They travel, play the lottery, and bird watch.
- *Bohemian Mix* (Urban/Younger Years—PRIZM segment 16) are young, mobile, liberal singles. They are ethnically diverse, with high concentrations of Hispanics, Asians, and African-Americans. And they are professionally diverse, including students, artists, and professionals with reasonably high incomes. They are early adopters who shop at stores like J. Crew, travel, play tennis, and listen to online radio. They read magazines like *Maxim* and newspapers like *The New York Times*.
- *Urban Achievers* (Urban/Younger Years—PRIZM segment 31) are young singles often located in port cities. They are ethnically diverse, with high concentrations of African Americans, Asians, and Hispanics as well as recent immigrants. They are college-educated artists and professionals with modest incomes. They shop at stores like The Gap and eat out a lot at fast-food restaurants. They go to movies, order books online, watch MTV, and read magazines like *Spin* and *Vibe*.

- *Young & Rustic* (Town/Younger Years—PRIZM segment 48) are young, restless singles. They are less educated, typically Caucasian, work in low-paying blue-collar jobs, and live in tiny apartments. Despite their lower incomes, they try to live active lifestyles centered around sports, cars, and dating. They eat at fast-food restaurants, play volleyball, and go fishing and camping. They read magazines like S*pin, Bass Master,* and *Soap Opera Weekly.*
- *Golden Ponds* (Town/Mature—PRIZM segment 55) are retired (or soon to be) singles and couples. They are less educated, work (or worked) in blue-collar and farm jobs and are lower income. Many live in mobile homes or small apartments and lead sedentary lifestyles. They shop at stores like Wal-Mart, play bingo, and sew. They watch a lot of daytime TV and listen to oldies radio.

## Applications of PRIZM in Marketing Strategy

**Marketing a Las Vegas Casino**   One Las Vegas casino used PRIZM to identify its core consumers and markets and identify opportunities for future growth. They merged their own customer database with the PRIZM system in order to categorize each customer in their database into one of the 66 segments. With this data, they were able to find out which segments represented their core customers. These segments included *Young Digerati; Big Fish, Small Pond;* and *Pools and Patios.* While consumers in these segments differ in various ways, they are all highly educated, affluent professionals who like to travel.

The casino also looked at which segments were least attractive for their business. These included the *Young and Rustics* and *Golden Ponds.* Given the casino's core customer, these results make sense since both of these segments are less-educated, lower-income consumers who tend to engage in sedentary activities or activities close to home.

Finally, the casino searched for attractive segments that held opportunity but were currently being underleveraged. One such segment was the *Blue Blood Estates,* which holds key similarities to the casino's core customers in terms of education, income and travel.

Having identified high-opportunity segments, the casino re-aligned and refocused its marketing efforts to specifically target those groups while also staying true to its core. By understanding their core customers, and where households that looked like their core customers existed in target markets, they were successful in attracting new and profitable customers in a cost-effective manner.

**A Library Gets Hip to a Younger Crowd**   Lakewood Public Library (PL) in Lakewood, Ohio, realized that a major chunk of its residents hardly ever used their library.[43] One reason for this seemed to be that the population of the city was evolving and changing in ways that Lakewood PL had not fully understood or adapted to. As Lakewood PL's manager of electronic services noted:

> Many people had a perception of Lakewood as being a city of families and senior citizens. Our experiences at the library over the past several years suggested otherwise—that it was fast becoming a city dominated by young, professional (but non-mainstream) singles.

Unfortunately, Lakewood PL didn't have a library collection that was well-suited to attract this emerging customer base. And on top of that, the staff didn't know enough about these consumers to make the necessary changes.

In response, Lakewood PL engaged in marketing research including PRIZM.[44] They found that two of the largest segments in Lakewood included Urban Achievers and Bohemian Mix, two young, ethnically diverse segments who were intellectually, culturally, and socially engaged. Lakewood PL felt that they could attract these consumers to their library if the content were right.

So, based on the general lifestyle and media-usage information provided by Claritas and its own expertise in library design, Lakewood PL made adjustments in content and programming to better target these groups with "a rich array of programming and diverse book and CD collections just for them." Their efforts have been quite a success, enabling Lakewood PL to draw in the younger more diverse residents now so much a part of their community.

**The New Urban America: SoHo 10003**   "You are where you live" (YAWYL) is a core tenet of PRIZM. And PRIZM allows you to take a look at specific neighborhoods and get an up-close look at their distinctive composition, ethnic diversity, and lifestyle patterns. Let's take a quick tour of New York City's 10003 ZIP code, which includes or is in close proximity to chic and eclectic areas such as SoHo and the East Village and is home to the prestigious New York University. Key PRIZM segments include Bohemian Mix, Young Digerati, and Urban Achievers.

> The area indexes high as a young, tech-savvy, upwardly mobile, multicultural melting pot that most marketers of electronics, upscale clothing and imported autos often covet. Small wonder, then, that outdoor advertising here typically consists of beverage, fashion, movies and other "badge" brands looking to spark trends among nightcrawlers, show off their "coolness" factor and celebrate the diversity and independence echoing from these streets.[45]

# INTERNATIONAL LIFESTYLES

The VALS and PRIZM systems presented in this chapter are oriented to the United States. In addition, VALS has systems for Japan and the United Kingdom. As we saw in Chapter 2, marketing is increasingly a global activity. If there are discernible lifestyle segments that cut across cultures, marketers can develop cross-cultural strategies around these segments. Although language and other differences would exist, individuals pursuing similar lifestyles in different cultures should be responsive to similar product features and communication themes.

Not surprisingly, a number of attempts have been made to develop such systems.[46] Large international advertising agencies and marketing research firms are leading the way. Roper Starch Worldwide, a global marketing research and consulting company, surveyed roughly 35,000 consumers across 35 countries in Asia, North and South America, and Europe.[47] Their goal was a global segmentation scheme based on core underlying values. According to one executive,

> We're looking for the bedrock values, the fundamental stable things in people's lives that determine who they are, to understand the underlying motivations that drive their attitudes as well as their behavior.[48]

Their survey uncovered six global lifestyle segments as described in Table 12–6. While these segments exist in all the countries studied, the percentage of the population in each group varied by country. For example, Brazil had the highest proportion of Fun Seekers. Aside from language, the ad in Illustration 12–9 has a global appeal to the Fun Seekers segment. This type of ad is often used by marketers to target similar lifestyle groups across different cultures, allowing for a relatively standardized ad theme.

| TABLE 12–6 |
| --- |

Global Lifestyle Segments Identified by Roper Starch Worldwide

*Strivers* (23 percent)—value material and professional goals and are driven by wealth, status, and power. They like computers and cell phones but have little time for media beyond newspapers. Middle aged, and skewing male, Strivers are found disproportionately (33 percent) in Asia.

*Devouts* (22 percent)—value duty, tradition, faith, obedience, and respect for elders. They are the least media involved and least interested in Western brands. Skewing female, Devouts are most common in developing Asia (e.g., Philippines), Africa, and the Middle East and least common in developed Asia (e.g., Japan) and Western Europe.

*Altruists* (18 percent)—are interested in social issues and the welfare of society. They are well educated and older with a median age of 44. Skewing female, Altruists are most common in Latin America and Russia.

*Intimates* (15 percent)—value close personal relationships and family. They are heavy users of broadcast media, enjoy cooking and gardening, and are good targets for familiar consumer brands. Gender balanced, Intimates are more common in Europe and the United States (25 percent) and less common in developing Asia (7 percent).

*Fun Seekers* (12 percent)—value adventure, pleasure, and excitement. They are heavy users of electronic media, are fashion conscious, and like going to restaurants, bars, and clubs. Fun Seekers are the youngest, the most global in their lifestyles, roughly gender balanced, and more common in developed Asia.

*Creatives* (10 percent)—are interested in knowledge, education, and technology. They are the heaviest users of media, particularly books, magazines, and newspapers. They also lead the way in technology, including owning a computer and surfing the net. Gender balanced, Creatives are more common in Latin America and Western Europe.

Source: Global Lifestyle Segments, Roper Starch Worldwide.

| ILLUSTRATION 12–9 |
| --- |

This ad would have strong appeal to Fun Seekers.

## SUMMARY

The *self-concept* is one's beliefs and feelings about oneself. There are four types of self-concept: *actual self-concept, social self-concept, private self-concept,* and *ideal self-concept*. The self-concept is important to marketers because consumers purchase and use products to express, maintain, and enhance their self-concepts. Marketers, particularly those in international marketing, have found it useful to characterize individuals and cultures by whether they have a predominantly *independent self-concept* (the individual is the critical component) or an *interdependent self-concept* (relationships are of primary importance).

An individual's self-concept, the way one defines oneself, typically includes some of the person's possessions. The self-concept including the possessions one uses to define oneself is termed the *extended self.*

*Lifestyle* can be defined simply as how one lives. It is a function of a person's inherent individual characteristics that have been shaped through social interaction as the person moves through his or her life cycle. It is how an individual expresses one's self-concept through actions.

*Psychographics* is the primary way that lifestyle is made operationally useful to marketing managers. This is a way of describing the psychological makeup or lifestyle of consumers by assessing such lifestyle dimensions as activities, interests, opinions, values, and demographics. Lifestyle measures can be macro and reflect how individuals live in general, or micro and describe their attitudes and behaviors with respect to a specific product category or activity.

The *VALS* system, developed by SRIC-BI, divides the United States into eight groups—Innovators, Thinkers, Believers, Achievers, Strivers, Experiencers, Makers, and Survivors. These groups were derived on the basis of two dimensions. The first, *primary motivation,* has three categories: *ideals* (those guided by their basic beliefs and values); *achievement* (those striving for a clear social position and influenced by others); and *self-expression* (those who seek self-expression, physical activity, variety, and excitement). The second dimension is the physical, mental, and material *resources* to pursue one's dominant motivation.

*Geo-demographic* analysis is based on the premise that individuals with similar lifestyles tend to live near each other. PRIZM is one system that examines demographic and consumption data down to the individual household. Based on the most recent Census data, it has developed 66 lifestyle segments organized around social groupings and life stage.

In response to the rapid expansion of international marketing, a number of attempts have been made to develop lifestyle measures applicable across cultures. Roper Starch Worldwide conducted a large multinational survey and found six global lifestyle segments based on core values.

## KEY TERMS

Actual self-concept  428
Extended self  429
Geo-demographic analysis  444
Ideal self-concept  428
Independent self-concept  428

Interdependent self-concept  428
Lifestyle  434
Mere ownership effect  430
Peak experience  430
Private self-concept  428

PRIZM  444
Psychographics  435
Self-concept  428
Social self-concept  428
VALS  439

## INTERNET EXERCISES

1. Visit SRIC-BI's VALS Web site (www.sricbi.com/VALS). Complete the survey for yourself and your parents. Are you and your parents' classifications and the behaviors associated with them accurate?

2. Visit Claritas's Web site (www.claritas.com). Report on its PRIZM approach to lifestyle segmentation.

3. Visit the Lakewood Public Library Web site (www.lkwdpl.org). Has the library provided material and information on its Web site that will attract the city's Urban Achievers and Bohemian Mix segments? Explain.

## DDB LIFE STYLE STUDY™ DATA ANALYSES

1. DDB measures *ideal self-concept* on various dimensions. Based on the information in Table 7A answer the following:
   a. Do any of these ideal self-concept characteristics seem to be associated with any of the *heavier user behaviors* (general, consumption, shopping)? Why do you think this is?
   b. Do any of these ideal self-concept characteristics seem to be associated with *product ownership*? Why do you think this is?

*c.* Do any of these ideal self-concept characteristics seem to be associated with *television preferences*? Why do you think this is?

2. Based on the information in DDB Table 7B, identify which *ideal self-concept* characteristics are most versus least associated with the following Explain.

   *a.* Enjoy shopping for items influenced by other cultures.

   *b.* Religion is a big part of my life.

*c.* Work at trying to maintain a youthful appearance.

*d.* A woman's place is in the home.

*e.* I am usually among the first to try a new product.

*f.* I'm an impulse buyer.

*g.* In making big decisions I go with my heart rather than my head.

3. Examine the DDB data in Tables 1B through 7B. What characterizes someone who feels that (*a*) brands, (*b*) cars, or (*c*) clothing is part of his or her extended self?

## REVIEW QUESTIONS

1. What is a *self-concept*? What are the four types of self-concept?

2. How do marketers use insights about the self-concept?

3. How can one measure the self-concept?

4. How does an *interdependent self-concept* differ from an *independent self-concept*?

5. What is the *extended self*?

6. What is a *peak experience*?

7. What ethical issues arise in using the self-concept in marketing?

8. What do we mean by *lifestyle*? What factors determine and influence lifestyle?

9. What is *psychographics*?

10. When is a product- or activity-specific psychographic instrument superior to a general one?

11. What are the dimensions on which VALS is based? Describe each.

12. Describe the VALS system and each segment in it.

13. What is *geo-demographic analysis*?

14. Describe the PRIZM system.

15. Describe the global lifestyle segments identified by Roper Starch Worldwide.

## DISCUSSION QUESTIONS

16. Use Table 12–2 to measure your four self-concepts. To what extent are they similar? What causes the differences? To what extent do you think they influence your purchase behavior?

17. Use Table 12–2 to measure your self-concept (you choose which self-concept and justify your choice). Also measure the images of three celebrities you admire. What do you conclude?

18. Respond to the questions in Consumer Insight 12–1.

19. What possessions are part of your extended self? Why?

20. Is your self-concept predominantly independent or interdependent? Why?

21. What ethical concerns are associated with ads that portray a standardized ideal image of beauty?

22. For each of the following products, develop one ad that would appeal to a target market characterized by predominantly independent self-concepts and another ad for a target market characterized by predominantly interdependent self-concepts.

    *a.* Red Envelope Internet store

    *b.* Mini Cooper automobile

    *c.* Timex watch

    *d.* Nautica clothing

23. Use the self-concept theory to develop marketing strategies for the following products:

    *a.* The National Alzheimer Association contributions

    *b.* Barnesandnoble.com

    *c.* Army ROTC recruitment

    *d.* A&W root beer

    *e.* Purell

    *f.* Norwegian Cruiseline

24. Does VALS make sense to you? What do you like or dislike about it?

25. How would one use VALS to develop a marketing strategy?

26. Develop a marketing strategy based on VALS for
    a. Kohl's Department Store
    b. Grand Canyon Kayak vacation
    c. Sirius satellite radio
    d. Kawasaki Jet Ski
    e. Triumph motorcycles
    f. WPGA

27. Develop a marketing strategy for each of the eight VALS segments for
    a. Verizon wireless
    b. Vacation package
    c. DeVinci Gourmet coffee syrups
    d. CNN
    e. Facial cleansers
    f. Target

28. Does PRIZM make sense to you? What do you like or dislike about it? Is it really a measure of lifestyle?

29. How would one use PRIZM to develop a marketing strategy?

30. Develop a marketing strategy for each of the Roper Starch global lifestyle segments for the products in Question 26. What challenges do you face in trying to market these products to global market segments?

31. The following quote is from Paul Casi, president of Glenmore distilleries: "Selling cordials is a lot different from selling liquor. Cordials are like the perfume of our industry. You're really talking high fashion and you're talking generally to a different audience—I don't mean male versus female—I'm talking about lifestyle."
    a. In what ways do you think the lifestyle of cordial drinkers would differ from those who drink liquor but not cordials?
    b. How would you determine the nature of any such differences?
    c. Of what use would knowledge of such lifestyle differences be to a marketing manager introducing a new cordial?

32. How is one likely to change one's lifestyle at different stages of the household life cycle? Over one's life, is one likely to assume more than one of the VALS lifestyle profiles described?

33. To which VALS category do you belong? To which do your parents belong? Which will you belong to when you are your parents' age?

34. Based on the extreme activity lifestyles described in the chapter opening example, develop a marketing strategy for
    a. A mountain resort
    b. Wall-climbing equipment
    c. In-line skates
    d. Schwinn bicycles
    e. Snowboards
    f. Video games

## APPLICATION ACTIVITIES

35. Develop an instrument to measure the interdependent versus independent self-concept.

36. Use the instrument you developed in Activity 35 to measure the self-concepts of 10 male and 10 female students, all of the same nationality. What do you conclude?

37. Develop your own psychographic instrument (set of relevant questions) that measures the lifestyles of college students.

38. Using the psychographic instrument developed in Activity 37, interview 10 students (using the questionnaire instrument). On the basis of their responses, categorize them into lifestyle segments.

39. Find and copy or describe ads that would appeal to each of the eight VALS segments.

40. Find and copy or describe ads that would appeal to each of the PRIZM segments discussed in the text.

41. Repeat Activity 40 for the Roper Starch Worldwide global lifestyle segments.

42. Repeat Activity 40 for the Forrester Research Technographics segments.

## REFERENCES

1. The Chapter 12 opening is based on S. Yin, "Going to Extremes," *American Demographics,* June 2001, p. 26; J. Raymond, "Going to Extremes," *American Demographics,* June 2002, pp. 28–30; "Memorex Intros CD-Rs Depicting Extreme Lifestyles," *Twice,* March 24, 2003, p. 52; W. Friedman, "NBC, Clear Channel Will Form Extreme Sports Tour," *TelevisionWeek,* November 8, 2004, p. 12; J. Blevins, "Living the X-treme Life," *Denver Post,* January 30, 2005, p. A1; and T. R. Reid, "X Games Give Aspen an Extreme Makeover," *Seattle Times,* February 1, 2005, p. A2.

2. N. Y. Wong and A. C. Ahuvia, "Personal Taste and Family Face," *Psychology & Marketing,* August 1998, pp. 423–41; and T. Sun, M. Horn, and D. Merrit, "Values and Lifestyles of Individualists and Collectivists," *Journal of Consumer Marketing* 21, no. 5 (2004), pp. 318–31.

3. See, e.g., E. C. Hirschman, "Men, Dogs, Guns, and Cars: The Semiotics of Rugged Individualism," *Journal of Advertising,* Spring 2003, pp. 9–22.

4. C. L. Wang and J. C. Mowen, "The Separateness–Connectedness Self-Schema," *Psychology & Marketing,* March 1997, pp. 185–207.

5. C. L. Wang et al., "Alternative Modes of Self-Construal," *Journal of Consumer Psychology* 9, no. 2 (2000), pp. 107–15.

6. See A. Reed II, "Activating the Self-Importance of Consumer Selves," *Journal of Consumer Research,* September 2004, pp. 286–95; Sun, Horn, and Merrit, "Values and Lifestyles of Individualists and Collectivists;" N. Agrawal and D. Maheswaran, "The Effects of Self-Construal and Commitment on Persuasion," *Journal of Consumer Research,* March 2005, pp. 841–49; C. J. Torelli, "Individuality or Conformity?" *Journal of Consumer Psychology* 16, no. 3 (2006), 240–48; J. H. Leigh and Y. Choi, "The Impact of Attributions about Life Events on Perceptions of Foreign Products," *Psychology & Marketing,* January 2007, pp. 41–68; and A. B. Monga and L. Lau-Gesk, "Blending Cobrand Personalities," *Journal of Marketing Research,* August 2007, pp. 389–400.

7. R. W. Belk, "Possessions and the Extended Self," *Journal of Consumer Research,* September 1988, pp. 139–68; and R. Belk, "Extended Self and Extending Paradigmatic Perspective," *Journal of consumer Research,* June 1989, pp. 129–32. See also M. L. Richins, "Valuing Things" and "Special Possessions and the Expression of Material Values," both in *Journal of Consumer Research,* December 1994, pp. 504–21 and 522–31, respectively; and A. C. Ahuvia, "Beyond the Extended Self," *Journal of Consumer Research*, June 2005, pp. 171–84.

8. See S. S. Kleine, R. E. Kleine III, and C. T. Allen, "How Is a Possession 'Me' or 'Not Me'?" *Journal of Consumer Research,* December 1995, pp. 327–43.

9. S. Sayre and D. Horne, "I Shop, Therefore I Am," *Advances in Consumer Research,* vol. 23, eds. K. P. Corfman and J. G. Lynch (Provo, UT: Association for Consumer Research, 1996), pp. 323–28.

10. See L. L. Love and P. S. Sheldon, "Souvenirs," *Advances in Consumer Research,* vol. 25, eds. J. W. Alba and J. W. Hutchinson (Provo, UT: Association for Consumer Research, 1998), pp. 170–74.

11. C. S. Areni, P. Kiecker, and K. M. Palan, "Is It Better to Give Than to Receive?" *Psychology & Marketing,* January 1998, pp. 81–109. See also C. F. Curasi, L. L. Price, and E. J. Arnould, "How Individuals' Cherished Possessions Become Families' Inalienable Wealth," *Journal of Consumer Research,* December 2004, pp. 609–22.

12. K. J. Dodson, "Peak Experiences and Mountain Biking," *Advances in Consumer Research,* vol. 23, eds. Corfman and Lynch, pp. 317–22.

13. C. H. Noble and B. A. Walker, "Exploring the Relationships among Liminal Transitions, Symbolic Consumption, and the Extended Self," *Psychology & Marketing,* January 1997, pp. 29–47.

14. E. Sivadas and K. A. Machleit, "A Scale to Determine the Extent of Object Incorporation in the Extended Self," in *Marketing Theory and Applications,* vol. 5, eds. C. W. Park and D. C. Smith (Chicago: American Marketing Association, 1994).

15. S. Sen and E. J. Johnson, "Mere-Possession Effects without Possession in Consumer Choice," *Journal of Consumer Research,* June 1997, pp. 105–17; M. A. Strahilevitz and G. Loewenstein, "The Effect of Ownership History of the Valuation of Objects," *Journal of Consumer Research,* December 1998, pp. 276–89; and K. P. Nesselroade, Jr., J. K. Beggan, and S. T. Allison, "Possession Enhancement in an Interpersonal Context," *Psychology & Marketing,* January 1999, pp. 21–34.

16. Consumer Insight 12–1 based on K. A. Hunt, T. Bristol, and R. E. Bashaw, "A Conceptual Approach to Classifying Sports Fans," *Journal of Services Marketing* 13, no. 6 (1999), pp. 439–52; R. V. Kozinets, "Utopian Enterprise," *Journal of Consumer Research,* June 2001, pp. 67–88; R. W. Pimentel and K. E. Reynolds, "A Model for Consumer Devotion," *Academy of Marketing Science Review* www.amsreview.org 5 (2004), and A. Gregory, "NASCAR Fans Are Loyal to Their Drivers," *McClatchy-Tribune Business News* March 15, 2008, www.mcclatchy.com.

17. S. Kang, "Nike, Serena Williams Partner Up," *The Wall Street Journal,* December 12, 2003, p. B2.

18. J. G. Helgeson and M. Supphellen, "A Conceptual and Measurement Comparison of Self-Congruity and Brand Personality," *International Journal of Market Research* 46, no. 2 (2004), pp. 205–33; L. N. Chaplin and D. R. John, "The Development of Self-Brand Connections in Children and Adolescents," *Journal of Consumer Research,* June 2005, pp. 119–29; J. E. Escalas and J. R. Bettman, "Self-Construal, Reference Groups, and Brand Meaning," *Journal of Consumer Research,* December 2005, pp. 378–89; C. Yim, K. Chan, and K. Hung, "Multiple Reference Effects in Service Evaluations," *Journal of Retailing* 83, no.1 (2007), pp. 147–57; and V. Swaminathan, K. L. Page, and Z. Gurhan-Canli, " 'My' Brand or 'Our' Brand," *Journal of Consumer Research*, October 2007, pp. 248–59.

19. S. J. Gould, "An Interpretive Study of Purposeful, Mood Self-Regulating Consumption," *Psychology & Marketing,* July 1997, pp. 395–426.

20. See J. W. Hong and G. M. Zinkhan, "Self-Concept and Advertising Effectiveness," *Psychology & Marketing,* January 1995, pp. 53–77; A. Mehta, "Using Self-Concept to Assess Advertising

Effectiveness, *Journal of Advertising Research,* January 1999, pp. 81–89; and M. J. Barone, T. A. Shimp, and D. E. Sprott, "Product Ownership as a Moderator of Self-Congruity Effects," *Marketing Letters,* February 1999, pp. 75–85.

21. E. N. Banister and M. K. Hogg, "Mapping the Negative Self," and A. M. Muniz and L. O. Hamer, "Us versus Them," both in *Advances in Consumer Research,* vol. 28, eds. M. C. Gilly and J. Meyers-Levy (Provo, UT: Association for Consumer Research, 2001), pp. 242–48 and 355–61, respectively.

22. For a broader discussion of situational factors, see T. R. Graeff, "Consumption Situations and the Effects of Brand Image on Consumers' Brand Evaluations," *Psychology & Marketing,* January 1997, pp. 49–70.

23. M. K. Hogg, A. J. Cox, and K. Keeling, "The Impact of Self-Monitoring on Image Congruence and Product/Brand Evaluation," *European Journal of Marketing* 34, no. 5/6 (2000), pp. 641–66.

24. J. Meyers-Levy and L. A. Peracchio, "Understanding the Socialized Body," *Journal of Consumer Research,* September 1995, p. 147.

25. C. S. Gulas and K. McKeage, "Extending Social Comparison," *Journal of Advertising,* Summer 2000, pp. 17–28; and D. Smeesters and N. Mandel, "Positive and Negative Media Image Effects on the Self," *Journal of Consumer Research,* March 2006, pp. 576–82.

26. M. J. Dutta-Bergman and W. D. Wells, "The Values and Lifestyles of Idiocentrics and Allocentrics in an Individualistic Culture," *Journal of Consumer Psychology* 12, no. 3 (2002), pp. 231–42.

27. "Sports Fans Make Surprising Choices in Beers and Wines According to Scarborough Research," Abritron press release www.arbitron.com/newsroom/archive, April 24, 2002.

28. See E. H. Demby, "Psychographics Revisited," *Marketing Research,* Spring 1994, pp. 26–30.

29. See F. W. Gilbert and W. E. Warren, "Psychographic Constructs and Demographic Segments," *Psychology & Marketing,* May 1995, pp. 223–37.

30. A. L. Dolinsky et al., "The Role of Psychographic Characteristics as Determinants of Complaint Behavior by Elderly Consumers," *Journal of Hospital Marketing* 2 (1998), pp. 27–51.

31. S. Todd and R. Lawson, "Lifestyle Segmentation and Museum/Gallery Visiting Behavior," *International Journal of Nonprofit and Voluntary Sector Marketing* 6, no. 3 (2001), pp. 269–77.

32. A. M. Gonzalez and L. Bello, "The Construct 'Lifestyle' in Market Segmentation," *European Journal of Marketing* 36, no. 1/2 (2002), pp. 51–85.

33. D. J. Lipke, "You Are What You Eat," *American Demographics,* October 2000, pp. 42–46.

34. Based on A. Taylor III, "Porsche Slices Up Its Buyers," *Fortune,* January 16, 1995, p. 24.

35. Based on M. J. Arnold and K. E. Reynolds, "Hedonic Shopping Motivations," *Journal of Retailing* 79 (2003), pp. 77–95.

36. See M. J. Weiss, "Online America," *American Demographics,* March 2001, pp. 53–60.

37. Based on a Forrester Research report by J. Kolko, "Why Techno-Graphics *Still* Works," December 14, 2004. Used by permission of Forrester Research.

38. For a critical review and alternative approach, see D. B. Holt, "Poststructuralist Lifestyle Analysis," *Journal of Consumer Research,* March 1997, pp. 326–50. Alternative lifestyle systems are also described in C. Walker and E. Moses, "The Age of Self-Navigation," *American Demographics,* September 1996, pp. 36–42; and P. H. Ray, "The Emerging Culture," *American Demographics,* February 1997, pp. 29–56.

39. Based on material provided by SRI Consulting Business Intelligence.

40. *How to Use PRIZM* (Claritas Inc., 1986), p. 1.

41. See S. Mitchell, "Birds of a Feather," *American Demographics,* February 1995, pp. 40–48.

42. Based on materials provided by Claritas. Source: Claritas, Inc.

43. Based on E. St. Lifer, "Tapping into the Zen of Marketing," *Library Journal,* May 1, 2001, pp. 44–46.

44. This research was done prior to the most recent PRIZM NE system. However, the main thrust of this example is still germane.

45. B. Ebenkamp, "Urban America, Redefined," *Brandweek,* October 6, 2003, pp. 12–13.

46. For example, see M. T. Ewing, "Affluent Asia," *Journal of International Consumer Marketing* 12, no. 2 (1999), pp. 25–37.

47. This material, including information in Table 12–6, is based on S. Elliott, "Research Finds Consumers Worldwide Belong to Six Basic Groups That Cross National Lines," *The New York Times,* June 25, 1998, p. D8; and T. Miller, "Global Segments from 'Strivers' to 'Creatives,'" *Marketing News,* July 20, 1998, p. 11.

48. Elliott, "Research Finds Consumers Worldwide Belong to Six Basic Groups That Cross National Lines."

# Part Three | Cases

The market for pet products and services is large and growing, with a current estimated size of $47 billion. It's not just dry dog food anymore. Pet owners refer to themselves as "pet parents," put their animals in "pet motels," and pamper them with spa-like treatment. Pet owners, it seems, are a very interesting and committed group of folks. Increasingly, pet owners are "humanizing" their pets, with 92 percent considering their pets to be another member of the family. According to survey results from the American Animal Hospital Association, of pet owners surveyed, 63 percent tell their pets they love them at least once a day, 59 percent celebrate

their pet's birthday, and 66 percent prepare special foods for their pet!

These purchases, attitudes, and behaviors belong to the premium pet market, which consists of some 17 million people across a number of subsegments, including (1) affluents ($150,000+ annual income), (2) specialty shoppers (shop only in specialty stores and online), (3) married with children, (4) empty nesters, (5) dual-income households with no kids, and (6) singles with no children. No longer does the presence of children drive pet ownership and spending. Today, pet ownership and pampering is a lifestyle, with pets being part of the family. Table A contains

## TABLE A

Premium Pet Demographics versus Average Pet Owners

| | Premium Pet Owners | | Premium Pet Owners |
|---|---|---|---|
| **Percent of households** | 32.9% | **Gender** | |
| **Age** | | Male | 112 |
| 18–24 years | 91 | Female | 92 |
| 25–34 | 71 | **Region** | |
| 35–44 | 121 | Northeast | 125 |
| 45–54 | 128 | Southeast | 100 |
| 55–64 | 115 | Southwest | 85 |
| 65–74 | 47 | Pacific | 98 |
| 75+ | 41 | **Household Income** | |
| **Education** | | $50,000–$74,999 | 30 |
| Graduate degree | 201 | $75,000–$99,999 | 164 |
| College graduate | 154 | $100,000–$149,999 | 304 |
| High school graduate or less | 55 | $150,000+ | 304 |
| **Occupation** | | **Marital Status** | |
| Management | 181 | Single | 88 |
| Professional/technical | 149 | Married | 124 |
| Sales | 120 | Divorced | 64 |
| Administrative support | 110 | Widowed | 42 |
| Labor | 90 | **Number of Children** | |
| **Race/Ethnic Group** | | None | 104 |
| White | 103 | One | 92 |
| Hispanic | 76 | Two | 104 |
| Black | 74 | Three+ | 75 |
| Asian | 188 | | |

Note: 100 = Average household that owns a dog or cat.
Source: Simmons Market Research Bureau, *Study of Media and Markets,* Fall 2006.

demographic data pertaining to the premium pet market compared with the baseline of all households who own a dog or cat (for example, 18- to 24-year-olds index 91, which means they are 9 percent less likely to have premium pet owners in that age group than the average pet household).

While brands such as Purina and Hartz are major players in the mass market for pet supplies and products, numerous smaller brands exist which fill various niches in the market. One such company that is riding this premium pet wave is K9-Quencher, which sells flavored sports drinks for dogs through its online store and through specialty stores located around the country. K9-Quencher is a flavored powder that contains nutrients and electrolytes, much like human sports drinks. According to their Web site:

> K9-Quencher is a healthy sport drink mix, and treat for dogs. You'll find information about why you should give your dog K9-Quencher, testimonials from Veterinarians and other professionals, tips on numerous health issues related to your best friend, and links to stores that sell it. K9-Quencher is vital for many essential body functions. Just add it to the water bowl!

K9-Quencher comes in three flavors (Electryc Ice Cream, Smokin' Hot Dog, and Lickin' Chickin') and a 12-unit (1 unit per bowl of water) variety pack currently sells for $16.

## Discussion Questions

1. Visit K9-Quencher's Web site (www.k9-quencher .com). What types of attitude change strategies are they utilizing? Do you think they are effective?

2. What learning approach and principles would you use to teach consumers about K9-Quenchers? Is this reflected in the company's Web site?

3. Develop a psychographic profile relating to the type of person who would be most likely to purchase K9-Quenchers. That is, generate a list of attitudes, values, activities, and interests that are specifically related to having a dog that K9-Quencher buyers would likely possess.

4. Based on the demographic data in Table A, what would be the best target(s) market for K9-Quenchers assuming they are targeting the premium market?

5. Develop an ad or marketing approach to create a positive attitude toward K9-Quenchers, focusing on the following components:
   a. Cognitive
   b. Affective
   c. Behavioral

6. Develop an ad or marketing approach to create a positive attitude toward K9-Quenchers, using the following:
   a. Humor
   b. Emotion
   c. Utilitarian appeal
   d. Value-expressive appeal
   e. Celebrity endorser
   f. Self-concept
   g. Fear

7. What sorts of products, if any, could K9-Quencher develop for cats? What type of branding strategy would you suggest if they made such a move?

Source: J. Fetto, "'Woof, Woof' Means, 'I Love You,'" *American Demographics,* February 2002, p. 11; R. Gardyn, "Animal Magnetism," *American Demographics,* May 2002, pp. 30–37; *Market Trends: Premium Pet Demographics and Product Purchasing Preferences* (Rockville, MD: Packaged Facts, August 2007); and information from K9-Quencher's Web site, www.k9-quencher.com, accessed July 6, 2008.

## CASE 3–2 LEVI'S SIGNATURE STRETCH

Levi's US sales in 1996 were $7.1 billion. In 2001, sales had declined dramatically to $4.25 billion. Many teenagers and tweens view Levi's jeans as being for middle-aged consumers. And while the major slide appears to have halted, with annual sales in the $4 billion range, Levi's is still vulnerable. The most recent quarterly data show Levi's sales down by 6 percent. How did this happen? Super success in the 1980s led to complacency and a lack of focus on evolving customer needs. Levi's created women's jeans from men's patterns, resulting in a poor fit. It treated teenage girls and women as one segment, producing jeans too tight for many moms and too high-waisted for the teens.

It also ignored emerging style competitors such as Calvin Klein, Seven, and Blue Asphalt. Trendy and stylish competitors continue to emerge in increasing numbers at various price points, and this has not helped. As one 19-year-old consumer noted of Levi's, "They're too plain. There's just not enough style to them." Various efforts have been made by Levi's to stave off the decline and launch a comeback, including new advertising and new product designs to bolster its image and relevance, particularly among younger buyers. Their "Dangerously Low" campaign is one example.

Levi's has worked on distribution. For example, it tried to get into specialty chains, which are more popular with younger consumers, but met with resistance. Some chain buyers don't think the brand passes the "cool test." The VP of marketing for Wet Seal, Inc., said the chain will not carry Levi's because "it's not on the radar screen of young women now." One bright spot has been their push into upscale chains such as Bloomingdales and Barneys, with their premium lines. However, their success there has been spotty as well, with retailers like Neiman Marcus and SAKS Fifth Avenue no longer carrying the brand.

Levi's most recent attempt to revitalize its U.S. presence has been to restructure the product line into the following collections:

- *Levi's Capital E.* This is their premium offering, selling for $138 to $195 in their Levi's Stores and higher-end retailers, such as Barneys.
- *Levi's 501 Original.* This is their core brand offering and anchors their entire product line. It sells for $46 to $78 at retailers such as Macy's, Kohls, and JCPenney.
- *Levi's Eco.* The Eco is their newest offering, launched in 2006. It is made of all organic cotton and sells for $30 to $68.
- *Levi's Vintage Clothing.* LVC is custom-made, one-of-a-kind replicas of Levi's best-selling and most popular jean styles from the past. They can be ordered at www.levi.com and sell for $150 to $500.
- *LeviStrauss Signature.* This entry, launched in 2003, is their low-priced jean designed to tap the mass market. It has styles for the whole family and is sold through mass merchandisers such as Wal-Mart and Kmart in the $20 range.

The Signature line has been particularly important for Levi's over the past several years. It leverages the fact that 30 percent of all jeans are sold through discounter retailers. While overall, Levi's sales have been flat or slightly declining, the Signature line has seen double-digit growth and accounts for about 9 percent of Levi's sales. In what Levi's calls a "mass-tige" strategy of bringing its fashion and the unique authentic Levi's cachet to more people, this latest move takes its jeans "down market." Levi's Signature line has partnered with NASCAR, has its own Web site, and benefits from the distinct mass-merchandiser channel of distribution.

Critics argue that the Signature line will cannibalize sales of the core lines. They also argue that going discount means an even bigger hit on Levi's image. For example, the reaction of the Wet Seal marketing VP was, "The brand's not cool when you're at Target for detergent and you see a rack of Levi's."

Levi's remains positive. As one executive noted, "People are predisposed to the brand. So, if we get the product right, they'll buy." Consider another comment by a Levi's executive when asked if the Signature line hurts Levi's credibility in the premium market:

> That's [the premium market] such a different customer. Very few brands have the elasticity that we have, but we have it, so we should use it. It is the heritage of our company. That's what makes it so strong and why people of all socioeconomic levels want a pair of Levi's. We have the original patent on five-pocket jeans. The other brands are just copying us.

One looming problem for Levi's is that Wal-Mart recently launched its own private-label brand, which will compete directly with LeviStrauss Signature. One expert in the area suggests that while LeviStrauss Signature was a good idea, it has done little to differentiate itself. He states, "The real issue is that if the product [LeviStrauss Signature] is generic enough, the store [Wal-Mart] will do a better turn for itself by developing its own private label product."

## Discussion Questions

1. Do you think that Levi's was correct to keep the Levi Strauss name on its Signature line? Or would it have been better off creating a completely new brand name? Present both sides of the case. Take and justify a position.

2. What do you think Levi's image is among the following? What are the marketing implications of your response?
   *a.* Tween girls (aged 10 to 12)
   *b.* Tween boys (aged 10 to 12)
   *c.* Teenage girls
   *d.* Teenage boys
   *e.* Women aged 21 to 35
   *f.* Men aged 21 to 35
   *g.* Women aged 36 to 55
   *h.* Men aged 36 to 55

3. Do you believe that the Levi's brand is as "elastic" as Levi's executives believe it is? Or, have they "overstretched" the name with the Signature line?

4. Develop the "brand schema" that you think existed for the overall Levi's brand *before* and *after* the

introduction of the Signature line (i.e., an associative network map of links and nodes). What are the marketing implications of the differences?

5. Repeat Question 4 *before* and *after* the introduction of Levi's Eco. What are the marketing implications of the differences?

6. Which of the six environmental activism segments discussed in Chapter 3 (p. 90) does the Levi's Eco jean appeal to most? Explain.

7. Given what you know about organic buyers from Chapter 3, do you think Levi's Eco helps Levi's with younger consumers? Explain.

8. Do you think there is a core image of Levi's that can survive across the wide range of prices and outlets that it operates in? What is it?

9. Should Levi's consider a special brand for the specialty chains that cater to younger, hip consumers?

10. How can Levi's use each of the following to enhance its brand image?
    *a.* Emotion
    *b.* Humor

    *c.* Maslow's needs
    *d.* McGuire's needs
    *e.* Brand personality
    *f.* Self-concept

11. How should Levi's market to teen consumers in each of the following ethnic groups?
    *a.* African American
    *b.* Arab American
    *c.* Asian American
    *d.* Asian-Indian American
    *e.* Native American
    *f.* White

Source: A. Z. Cuneo, "Ailing Levi Strauss Refits U.S. Strategy," *Advertising Age,* July 15, 2002, p. 12; L. Lee, "Why Levi's Still Looks Faded," *BusinessWeek,* July 22, 2002, p. 54; G. Anderson, "Target Puts Signature on Levi's Deal," *retailwire,* www.retailwire.com, January 16, 2004; "Levi Strauss & Co. Announces Fiscal Year 2003 Financial Results" (Levi Strauss & Co., financial news release, March 1, 2004); "Levi's Dangerous Jean Therapy," *BusinessWeek,* August 8, 2005, p. 10; "Levi Strauss Seeing Green with Signature Blues," *BrandWeek,* July 25, 2005, p. 12; "Making Strides at Levi's," *BusinessWeek Online,* July 28, 2005; P. Sarkar, "Levi's Sales Slip Showing," *SFGate.com,* April 12, 2006; "Levi's Brand Launches 100% Organic Cotton Jeans," *Business Wire,* July 5, 2006, p. 1; and information from Levi Strauss & Co.'s Web site, www.levi.com.

## CASE 3–3 JACK LINK'S BEEF JERKY GOING HIP AND HEALTHY

Beef Jerky. Boring. Not cool. Eaten by men. Not good for you. If this is what you think of beef jerky then think again. Dried meat snacks, including beef jerky, have seen rising sales, which started with the low-carb craze. And while dried meat snacks are still a relatively small part of the overall snack market, at roughly 3 percent, Jack Link's is out to capture the category and change its image. Jack Link's leads the entire salted snack category in growth and is the market leader in beef jerky.

How are they doing this? One visit to their Web site and you see a brand working to create new products for a variety of users, an interesting and exciting brand personality, and awareness of the health benefits of the product. For example, their Web site has a "Who Are You?" page in which it tells consumers which of their products best fit a variety of personalities and lifestyles. These include:

- *The Enthusiast.* "Just because I'm outside doesn't mean I eat the bark."
- *The Health Nut.* "Life's a marathon. And I'm going to at least place."
- *The Adventure Seeker.* "I also enjoy extreme snacking, thank you.

- *The On-the-Go Mom.* "My kids move fast. I need a snack that can keep up."
- *The Armchair Quarterback.* "I'm looking to be inducted into the snacking hall of fame."
- *Wildly Original.* "Dare to be different. Bag the chips. Grab Jack Link's."

A focal point of their campaign and Web site is "Feed Your Wild Side" and their "Messin' with Sasquatch" commercials, which are quirky ads targeted at the youth market. One has a group of Gen Yers swimming at the lake when they see Sasquatch. One of the group "towel snaps" Sasquatch while he is trying to get a drink and gets thrown into the lake naked.

Not content with its existing demographic, Jack Link's is going after a new target—women. As one commentator notes:

Don't tell men, but beef jerky turns out to be an almost freakishly female food: low-fat, high-protein, more filling than chips.

In fact, two of the six profiles created (The Health Nut and The On-the-Go Mom) are women. And the

TABLE A   Snack Food Consumption by "Healthy" Snackers

| Snack Product | Index |
| --- | --- |
| Soy Chips | 147 |
| Energy and Diet Bars | 146 |
| Yogurt | 118 |
| Cereal and Granola Bars | 107 |
| Nuts as a snack | 107 |
| Popcorn | 96 |
| Pretzels | 93 |
| Potato Chips | 90 |
| Meat snack/Beef Jerky | 83 |

Note: 100 = Average household use or consumption in households where respondent agrees that they "usually snack on healthy foods."

Source: Simmons Market Research Bureau, *Study of Media and Markets,* Fall 2005.

Web site isn't just about quirky humor. Jack Link's is serious about communicating the health benefits of beef jerky—key they think, to attracting the female market both as consumers and as gatekeepers for their children's snack choices. The "Health Nut" persona speaks to health needs and Jack Link's desire to change perceptions in this area. They further push the health aspect by directly comparing their snacks with others, on such criteria as calories, fat, and carbohydrates, on which they compare quite favorably.

Good for you is not necessarily the first thing that comes to mind when thinking of beef jerky. One look at Table A tells you that. However, it is interesting to note that "healthy snacker" households are only 17 percent less likely than the average household to eat beef jerky.

Finally, Jack Link's is continually modifying its product offerings. Not content with the original tough dried strips of meat, it has created textures and flavors to satisfy a broader palate to attract younger consumers and women. Recent additions include the X Stick, Prime Rib Tender Cuts, and Original Beef Steak Nuggets. Flavors include sweet and spicy Thai and Buffalo chicken.

## Discussion Questions

1. What learning approaches and principles are being used by Jack Link's on their Web site to teach consumers about the health aspects of beef jerky? Do you think they are effective? Explain.

2. What role do you think children play in women's adoption of beef jerky as a household snack? How does Jack Link's play to the needs and wants of each group in its promotions (for insight, visit their Web site at www.jacklinks.com)?

3. What brand personality dimensions (see Chapter 10) do Jack Link's ad campaign and Web site create? Explain.

4. What tactics has Jack Link's used to establish its brand personality? Discuss.

5. Evaluate the attitude change strategy being used.

6. Evaluate the use of humor in their "Messin' with Sasquatch" ads. For which demographics do you think this approach would best work?

7. Evaluate their use of a nutritional fact sheet from a comparative advertising viewpoint. What other attitudinal change strategies might Jack Link's use to add more credibility to its health claims?

8. Compare Jack Link's Web site with that of one of its competitors, Slim Jim (a ConAgra Foods brand). What learning and attitude change strategies differentiate these competitors?

Source: "Snack Food Trends in the United States," *American-taste.com,* Summer 2006; *Snack Food Trends in the U.S.* (New York: Packaged Facts, July 2006); L. Skenazy, "Ladies Who Lunch Could Start Lunching on Dried Meat Snacks," *Advertising Age,* June 16, 2008; and information from Jack Link's Web site, www.jacklinks.com.

## CASE 3–4 CLOROX GREEN WORKS LINE

The $3 billion household cleaner market is a mature and stable market. Why did Clorox think it could introduce five new products into this market? The environment. Clorox's internal research showed that 25 percent of consumers worried about the harsh chemicals in cleaners and 40 percent wanted a natural product that worked. Clorox, under its Green Works line, now offers five such products, including a glass cleaner and a toilet bowl cleaner. Within six months of launch, Green Works had estimated sales of $20 million. There have been several key factors in the early success. First is the product, which Clorox advertises as a natural product that really works. Second is price, which is comparable with "regular" cleaners as opposed to the high prices of other "green" competitors, such as Method and Seventh Generation. Third is distribution through mass merchandisers rather than specialty stores. As one expert notes, "People want to make green choices, but they don't want to sacrifice."

Perhaps as significant as all of these factors is the alliance that Clorox has formed with the Sierra Club. As noted by Clorox CEO Don Knauss on its Web site:

> [I am proud to announce] an alliance with the Sierra Club, the oldest, largest, and most influential grassroots environmental organization in the United States. Our partnership with the Sierra Club is significant for Green Works and for our entire company. It is critical for the environment that industries such as ours move toward sustainability.
>
> As you can imagine, the dialogue with an organization so committed to the environment didn't happen overnight. Extensive conversations between the Sierra Club and Clorox took place over several months. They included tough questions and straight answers not only about Green Works, but about our complete product portfolio, sustainability initiatives and corporate practices.

The Sierra Club is allowing its logo to appear on the Green Works products, the first time it has ever done so. In return, the club will receive an undisclosed amount of the sales of these products as a way for Clorox to support its environmental work.

This partnership has not been without controversy. For instance, 4 of the 64 chapters opposed the partnership outright. Some have quit over the partnership and now blog about it, with entries expressing the opinion that the Sierra Club is "whoring the environment for financial gain, they've lost their mission and lost their way."

The negativity of individual members of this important alliance partner provides a cautionary note for companies and organizations looking for such endorsement deals. Particularly within social cause organizations with independent memberships, you have an activist mentality combined with today's Internet tools to execute effective attacks with relatively little support or funding. Says one expert in the area:

> You need to spend a lot of time upfront before you ink a deal and know that both brands are sharing reputations and halos.

Perhaps as a way to counter some of the negativity of disgruntled Sierra Club members, Clorox has also partnered with two other important entities: The U.S. EPA has given four of the five products its DfE (designed for the environment) designations, and *Better Homes and Gardens* is partnering with Clorox to conduct a "Living Green Tour."

## Discussion Questions

1. What attitude change strategies is Clorox using to persuade consumers to buy its Green Works products?

2. Which of the six environmental activism segments discussed in Chapter 3 (p. 90) does the Clorox Green Works line appeal to? Explain.

3. In what way is the "Green Works" name utilizing a rhetorical figure? Is it effective? Explain.

4. Should Clorox engage the negative bloggers directly by blogging as well, should it simply ignore them, or should it try other indirect methods of dealing with the negative fallout?

5. Why are the endorsements of Sierra Club, the EPA, and *Better Homes and Gardens* so important to Clorox and the success of Green Works?

6. Does it affect your attitude toward Green Works to know that the Sierra Club is receiving money from Clorox? Which aspect of the attitude process is at work here?

7. Clorox never in its history has put an ingredient list on its package. Now it does on Green Works. What attitude process is at work here?

8. Examine the packaging for Green Works. What perceptual processes are evident in the design and in how consumers will perceive and interpret the product?

Source: M. Frazier, "Clorox Eco-Friendly Line Finds Green Foes," *Advertising Age*, June 16, 2008, pp. 3, 25; and information found at www.cloroxgreenworks.com and www.greenworkscleaners.com.

## CASE 3–5 THE PSYCHOGRAPHICS OF LUXURY SHOPPERS

Marketers are always trying to fine-tune their segmentation strategies. For example, retailers may find that income is a necessary, but not sufficient, indicator of luxury spending or shopping patterns. To illustrate, Simmons Market Research recently conducted a psychographic analysis relating to luxury buying and shopping. The analysis, which examined middle-class and affluent single women who were heads of their households, also took into account demographics and life stage factors. The researchers identified five unique segments.

## Discussion Questions

1. For which segment(s) do you feel that products are most likely to become part of the extended self? What are the marketing implications of this?

2. Which segments appear to be more motivated by functional concerns versus those motivated by the need to keep up with the latest styles and trends? What are the marketing implications of this?

3. Can you explain why Savvy Career Women place great emphasis on clothing and fashion, while luxury automobiles really aren't that important?

4. Choose two segments which you feel would be viable but different markets for spas. Develop a marketing plan for each segment, to include core positioning statement, media venues, key product/service features, and promotional materials.

Source: Simmons Market Research Bureau 2002, as printed in R. Gardyn, "Oh, The Good Life," *American Demographics,* Nov 2002, p. 33; and J. D. Zbar, "Tony Travelers Seek out Quality," *Advertising Age,* September 13, 2004, pp. 5–6.

| Consumer Description | Savvy Career Women | Upscale Mature Women | Educated Working Women, No Kids | Single Working Moms | Active Grandmas |
|---|---|---|---|---|---|
| Median age | 41 | 60 | 33 | 39 | 61 |
| Median income | $166,425 | $69,605 | $49,789 | $48,916 | $35,431 |
| I am very happy with my life as it is | 94 | 103 | 87 | 92 | 95 |
| I enjoy entertaining people at home | 108 | 112 | 92 | 98 | 103 |
| It is worth paying extra for quality goods | 115 | 127 | 76 | 75 | 79 |
| Home décor is a particular interest | 131 | 139 | 103 | 123 | 123 |
| I can't resist expensive perfume/cologne | 172 | * | 151 | 218 | * |
| I like other people to think I'm rich | 116 | 98 | 91 | 97 | 83 |
| I tend to spend money without thinking | 143 | 81 | 121 | 132 | 102 |
| Most everything I wear is the highest quality | 150 | 121 | 86 | 124 | 101 |
| I spend more than I can afford for clothes | 201 | * | 164 | 136 | 127 |
| I plan far ahead to buy expensive items | 93 | 95 | 109 | 100 | 97 |
| Price isn't most important—what's important is getting what I want | 120 | 108 | 84 | 101 | 103 |
| Options on a car impress me | 111 | 75 | 84 | 121 | 71 |
| I prefer driving a luxury car | 106 | 95 | 59 | 83 | 70 |
| I try to keep up with changes in style/fashion | 152 | 101 | 114 | 125 | 111 |

Note: Except for age and income (where numbers are years and dollars, respectively), 100 is national average for adults. A 94 indicates group was 6 percent less likely than average adult to agree with statement.

*Sample size too small.

Source: Reprinted with permission from the November 2002 issue of *American Demographics.* Copyright Crain Communications, Inc. 2004.

## CASE 3–6 REVLON FOR MEN? UBERSEXUALS AND THE CHANGING MALE LANDSCAPE

Males have three reasons for trying to look good (which, in American society, also implies looking young). First, one's career may be enhanced by looking good, which includes being attractive, appearing fit, and being energetic (young), As one businesswoman stated:

Any guy who goes into consulting has to be attractive. It struck me one day: Every time I met a good-looking guy and asked him "So, little boy, what do you do?" he was a consultant. The ugly ones are all accountants.

A second reason for men's concern about looks is to be attractive to women. Many middle-aged men who go through divorce engage in a wide variety of "beauty" enhancement activities. Most women no longer need to rely on men for financial support, which allows them to focus more on the physical and personal characteristics of potential partners.

A final reason is a combination of ego and competitiveness. If looks matter, then competitive men will compete to look good. Knowing that one looks good or receiving compliments or "admiring glances" is also gratifying to a person's ego.

The men's grooming market is expected to be around $10 billion by the end of this decade, with a current market of $7.7 billion. The market can be broken out as shown in the following table. As you can see, the skin care market remains a relatively small part of the overall men's grooming market, although growth has been a steady 7 percent annually since the mid-1990s.

| | |
|---|---|
| Fragrances | $1,935 |
| Shaving | 3,560 |
| Deodorant | 1,470 |
| Hair care | 541 |
| Skin care | 154 |
| Bath and shower | 77 |

Source: Based on information from *The U.S. Market for Men's Grooming Products* (New York: Packaged Facts, January 2004), pp. 51, 62.

| | Hair Coloring Products | Facial Cleansers | Suncare Products | Moisturizers/ creams/lotions | |
|---|---|---|---|---|---|
| **Percent of males** | 5.5% | 19.1% | 34.4% | 33% | **TABLE A** |
| **Age** | | | | | Select Demographics Relating to Male Cosmetic Use |
| 18–24 years | 145 | 183 | 82 | 107 | |
| 25–34 | 60 | 141 | 108 | 113 | |
| 35–44 | 88 | 90 | 119 | 109 | |
| 45–54 | 120 | 63 | 106 | 95 | |
| 55–64 | 125 | 66 | 88 | 84 | |
| 65–74 | 95 | 49 | 84 | 73 | |
| 75+ | 61 | 55 | 74 | 91 | |
| **Race/Ethnic Group** | | | | | |
| White | 87 | 79 | 115 | 81 | |
| Black | 141 | 201 | SS | 180 | |
| Asian | 151 | 196 | 89 | 172 | |
| Hispanic | 141 | 127 | 75 | 146 | |
| **Household Income** | | | | | |
| $10,000–$19,999 | 106 | 138 | 73 | 115 | |
| $20,000–$29,999 | 113 | 112 | 85 | 109 | |
| $30,000–$39,999 | 112 | 85 | 105 | 97 | |
| $40,000–$49,999 | 96 | 94 | 119 | 98 | |
| $50,000–$59,999 | 66 | 86 | 118 | 104 | |
| $60,000–$74,999 | 86 | 75 | 133 | 94 | |
| $75,000–$99,999 | 76 | 71 | 154 | 89 | |
| $100,000–$149,999 | 62 | 71 | 160 | 92 | |

Note: 100 = Average use or consumption unless a percent is indicated. Base is U.S. Male Adults.
SS = sample size too small for a reliable index.
Source: Simmons Market Research Bureau, *Study of Media and Markets,* Spring 2003.

There is some uncertainty about the men's grooming market. A combination of demographics and psychographics may provide some clues. Table A presents select demographics for a number of men's cosmetic products.

Psychographics and gender-role attitudes can play a role as well and may present challenges among certain segments of the male population. According to one expert, the challenge is this:

How to entice more men to smell good, put gooey things in their hair, and oily lotions on their faces without feeling somehow unmanly.

Attitudes about what "manly" means and what male roles continue to change, further complicates the issue. One study identifies a number of male segments with distinct demographic and psychographic characteristics relating to women and changing gender roles. These are as follows:

- *Ubersexuals* (25 percent). With a mean age of 38 and a mean income of $60,600, this group sees no problems between the sexes and most agree that this is a good time to be a man.

- *Regular Joes* (27 percent). With a mean age of 43 and a mean income of $61,900, this group has no problems with how men are portrayed in the media and don't feel threatened by women.

- *Marked Grouchos* (30 percent). With a mean age of 47 and a mean income of $55,500, this group is confused about what women want and don't like the way women expect more of them.

- *Neutrals* (18 percent). With a mean age of 41 and a mean income of $53,500, this group is less resentful of women than Grouchos and are accepting of changing gender roles.

This study also suggests that ubersexuals may be taking the place of metrosexuals.

One of the telltale signs of metrosexuals is their willingness to indulge themselves, whether by springing for a Prada suit or spending a couple of hours at a spa to get a massage and facial. The ubersexual is less concerned with fashion and more inclined to develop his own sense of style. He dresses more for himself than for others. The ubersexual possesses a type of masculinity that combines the best of traditional manliness (strength, honor, character) with positive traits traditionally associated with females (nurturance, communicativeness, cooperation).

However, as one commentator, responding to these conclusions, noted:

Of course, men remain highly interested in style and grooming, and men's magazines are still littered with spreads for $3,000 suites and an array of fragrance and skin-care lines. And men's style magazines like Conde Nast's *Men's Vogue* continue to pop up.

Despite the uncertainty regarding current male perceptions and behaviors as well as the relative small size and modest growth of this market, numerous firms are entering with a variety of beauty-enhancing products that are generally positioned as skin care products. Companies such as Nivea, Clinique, Neutrogena, and *Mënaji* have full lines of men's grooming, skin care, and makeup products.

### Discussion Questions

1. Develop a marketing strategy for Revlon to enter the men's cosmetics market with a complete product line.

2. If Revlon were to enter the men's cosmetics market, what branding strategy should it use?

3. How, if at all, could Revlon use the following as the basis for its appeal for a men's cosmetic line?
   a. Personality
   b. Emotion
   c. Self-concept

4. Design an ad for a line of men's skin care products by Revlon. Explain how it will work at each stage of the perception process.

5. Evaluate Clinique's men's product line and branding strategy. Suggest changes where appropriate.

6. What motives should Clinique appeal to in promoting its men's line?

7. Persuading many men to use skin care products will require a significant attitude change. Which attitude change techniques would be most appropriate? Which would be least appropriate?

8. What learning theories would you use to teach your target market to take proper care of their skin?

9. Visit one of the Web sites listed below. Is it effective at promoting its products to men? What behavior principles and assumptions does it rely on?
   a. Clinique (www.clinique.com)
   b. Neutrogena (www.neutrogena.com)
   c. Mënaji (www.menaji.com)
   d. Nivea (www.nivea.com)

10. Using the demographic and psychographic information provided in the case, describe the traits that would make the most desirable target market for a line of cosmetics by Revlon. Explain.

11. Evaluate each of the following as a potential market for men's grooming products. Be specific as to the kinds of grooming products that might be best targeted to which segment.
    a. Ubersexual
    b. Regular Joe
    c. Marked Groucho

12. How might the emergence of the ubersexual influence how men's grooming care products are marketed?

Source: A. Wallenstein, "Boomers Put New Life in Hair Dye for Men," *Advertising Age,* September 1995, p. 1; A. Farnham, "You're So Vain," *Fortune,* September 9, 1996, pp. 66–82; G. Boulard, "Men's Personal Care Market," *I,* January 1999, pp. 50–54; K. Yamanouchi, "Men Wake Up to Makeup," *Hartford Courant,* May 24, 2002, p. 3; *The U.S. Market for Men's Grooming Products* (New York: Packaged Facts, January 2004); "Game for Anything," *Advertising Age,* May 22, 2006, p. S-1; T. Case, "Metrosexual Mortality," *Mediaweek,* September 4, 2006, pp. 17–18; and T. Valeo, "Ubersexual," *WebMD.com,* accessed July 8, 2008.

---

## CASE 3–7  POSITIONING THE YARIS

Toyota is trying to stake out a position among younger consumers with its Yaris brand. It hopes to attract 30 percent of its market share for the brand from the 18- to 34-year-old consumer. When it launched the brand several years ago, Toyota made it clear that it wanted to give the brand a personality. More specifically, it wanted the car to have a "cheeky, irreverent, mischievous" personality to match the car's styling. In doing so, Toyota humanized the Yaris:

We wrote a voice for this car, we gave it a personality and we created a world for it to live in. We knew that, rather than just speaking to our audience, the car had to behave as one of them.

In addition, Toyota envisioned an integrated campaign involving traditional TV melded with mobile marketing, Internet marketing, social networking, and so on. New media has been deemed critical to reaching this younger demographic.

Perceptual maps can be a critical tool in determining how well a company's efforts are working in attaining their desired position. The following perceptual map provides one view of the automobile market but does not include the Yaris. Brands are plotted as a function of consumer perceptions on the luxury-economy dimension on the vertical axis and dull-exciting on the horizontal axis. Market segment labels are labeled by ideal points on the map and the relative size of the circle represents the relative size of the segment.*

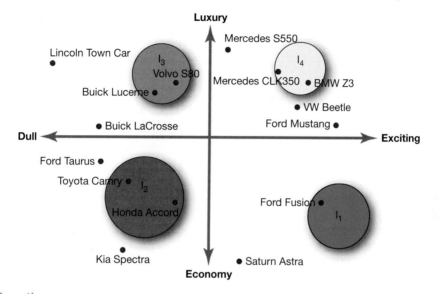

### Discussion Questions

1. Develop a questionnaire to assess the perceived position of the Yaris on the two dimensions of the perceptual map. Have 5 participants from Yaris' target age group complete the survey and plot their location on the map. Repeat this with 5 participants in the 45-65 year-old age group.

   Hint: You could use a −5 to +5 scale (See Appendix A for more detail on measuring attitudes and perceptions) with −5 being dull and +5 being exciting, and neutral being 0. You could then map the scale onto the axis with the extreme points anchoring the ends and the neutral or zero point being the intersection of the two dimensions. You would repeat this for luxury-economy dimension.

2. From the perceptual map, explain why Yaris wants to be an exciting economy car. According to your results in question 1, has Yaris achieved its objective of achieving that position? Does it depend on the age group? Discuss.

3. If your answer to Question 2 is no for the younger audience, develop a marketing strategy that would reposition the Yaris effectively. Detail all the elements of learning, attitude change, and so forth that you would use.

4. Examine all the Web activities that Yaris is engaged in, from their Web site to the social networking presence. Do you think that Yaris is doing a good job of leveraging these tools toward their younger audience and toward their desired position? Explain.

5. What does the perceptual map say about the Saturn Astra? What should Saturn do and what marketing strategies should it use to achieve its objective?

* The data in the perceptual map represents the subjective interpretation of the authors. This map is thus illustrative not definitive.
Source: M. Graser, "Toyota Hits Touch Points as It Hawks Yaris to Youth," *Advertising Age*, May 1, 2006, p. 28.

## CASE 3–8 HARDIPLANK'S PULL STRATEGY

In 1989, James Hardie Siding Products launched a line of fiber cement home siding products. The product was guaranteed against rotting or cracking for 50 years and had a warm, textured look that vinyl siding could not match. For most of the next decade, Hardie tried the traditional "push" approach of selling the product to builders, remodelers, and home improvement centers with ads and product demonstrations.

Unfortunately, builders did not like the siding. It was heavy, was hard on saw blades, and showed any flaws in a poor frame job. In addition, there were other fiber cement sidings available, so a builder or home improvement center that decided to use or carry the product would frequently buy on price.

In the late 1990s, Hardie's USA President Lewis Gries decided to build a brand image for the siding, which was named Hardiplank. The project began with a very small budget of $500,000. The head of the ad agency chosen for the project stated:

The first step was to do some research to find out what homeowners thought about the building materials used in their homes. Our assumption was that siding was a low-interest category but that turned out to be incorrect.

The research revealed that people are very emotional about their homes. When one focuses on what building materials provide, such as safety, security, beauty, and warmth, rather than what they actually are, home buyers and remodelers care a lot. This led the team to shift from a pure push (selling to builders and retailers who would then sell to home buyers) to more of a pull strategy (selling to home buyers who would then demand the product from builders and retailers).

Advertising was shifted from home building trade publications to lifestyle magazines, such as *Southern Living, Sunset,* and *Coastal Living.* The ads emphasized the emotional appeal of houses made with strong, weather-resistant materials. Trade ads were used to explain this positioning and emphasized the interest that would be generated on behalf of builders and remodelers.

Hardie's sales force also had to be trained. Historically, they had called on purchasing agents and talked price and delivery schedules. Now they needed to reach the marketing directors of major homebuilders and communicate the value this product and its emerging reputation could provide to their sales programs.

Another major effort was to put Hardiplank on model homes, in "dream homes" promoted by the lifestyle magazines, and in builder design centers.

While Hardiplank had to compete against wood siding and other fiber cement brands, vinyl was perhaps its strongest competitor. It lasted longer than wood, and builders liked it because it was easy to install. However, it did not look or feel like wood. So Hardie built displays that placed vinyl and Hardiplank side by side and encouraged consumers to do not only a visual comparison but also a "tap test." Unlike Hardiplank, vinyl is thin and rattles when tapped. According to Louis Sawyer, CEO of Hardie's advertising agency:

Vinyl siding met the functional requirements, but not the emotional ones. Our ads and displays spoke directly to the affluent baby boomer audience, and they appreciated the difference immediately.

## Discussion Questions

1. Will Hardie's pull strategy work? Why or why not?

2. What product position is Hardie trying to establish for Hardiplank?

3. What learning approach and principle would you use to teach consumers about Hardiplank?

4. How would you develop a favorable attitude toward Hardiplank?

5. Evaluate the name Hardiplank. Suggest and justify two others.

6. Conduct a diffusion analysis from the perspective of the home buyer, and develop appropriate strategies based on this analysis.

7. Conduct a diffusion analysis from the perspective of the builder, and develop appropriate strategies based on this analysis.

8. Develop two ads to create a positive attitude toward Hardiplank, one using a cognitive approach and one using an affective approach. Which is best? Why?

9. How can Hardie use emotion in marketing Hardiplank?

Source: B. Lamons, "Another Story about an Unlikely Brand," *Marketing News,* May 27, 2002, p. 8. Lamons is president of Robert Lamons & Associates in Houston, Texas.

## CASE 3–9 FRAMING PREVENTIVE CARE

Public health officials and other concerned groups have struggled for years trying to persuade women to have breast cancer examinations and men to be checked for prostate cancer. The technical ability to detect disease or disease-causing conditions has exploded in recent years. There are screening tests for high cholesterol (a heart attack risk factor), high blood pressure, osteoporosis, inherited breast cancer risk, HIV, and colon cancer, among others.

The advantages of early detection are great. Some diseases may be prevented entirely by early detection of potential causes (high cholesterol). Others are treated much more effectively and efficiently if detected and treated early. Thus, early detection can save lives, suffering, and money.

Despite such advantages, the use of early detection technology remains far below an optimal level. Some of this is due to the economics of the medical system. Lower-income individuals often lack adequate health insurance and are reluctant to spend scarce financial resources on tests for problems they may not have. However, even well-insured and prosperous individuals often forgo important tests. For example, it is estimated that 20 percent of American adults have dangerously high cholesterol, and many are unaware of this fact.

Why are consumers reluctant to take steps, often quite simple and inexpensive, that could literally save their lives? Some consumers believe that they are not susceptible to a particular health problem because of their age, genetics, or general condition. Given this belief, they do not see any value in taking a test that they are sure will merely confirm what they already "know." Marketers for Lipitor, a cholesterol-lowering drug, try to counter this by showing that apparently low-risk people, such as figure skater Peggy Fleming, have cholesterol levels that need treatment.

Other consumers are in the opposite camp. They are fearful that the tests might reveal a problem. Even if such a problem is correctable if caught early, it is still bad news to have any type of disease or likelihood of a disease. Further, such a diagnosis generally involves at least short-term unpleasantness—a change in diet, physical or drug treatments, and anxiety. People are ambivalent at best about seeking out potentially bad news.

In view of the above, how does a firm or a nonprofit or public agency persuade consumers to use appropriate early-detection technologies?

A number of opposing advertising approaches have been suggested. Should the ad use statistics or anecdotal evidence? Should the consequences be framed in terms of losses from not being tested or gains from being tested? Examples of each of these approaches are:

- *Statistical, gain.* "Many women have no family history of breast cancer and have never felt any lump in their breast. But they follow the advice of the American Cancer Society and start having annual screening mammograms when they turn fifty. Because of this, doctors are able to detect their tumors at an early, treatable stage, and they are 30 percent less likely to die of breast cancer."

- *Statistical, loss.* "Many women have no family history of breast cancer and have never felt any lump in their breast. So they don't follow the advice of the American Cancer Society to start having annual screening mammograms when they turn fifty. Because of this, doctors are not able to detect tumors at an early, treatable stage, and they are 43 percent more likely to die of breast cancer."

- *Anecdotal, gain.* "No one in Sara Johnson's family had ever gotten breast cancer, and she had never felt any lump in her breast. But she followed the advice of the American Cancer Society and started having annual screening mammograms when she turned fifty. Because of this, doctors were able to detect her breast tumor at an early, treatable stage, and now Sara can look forward to a long life, watching her grandson, Jeffrey, grow up."

- *Anecdotal, loss.* "No one in Sara Johnson's family had ever gotten breast cancer, and she had never felt any lump in her breast. So she didn't follow the advice of the American Cancer Society to start having annual screening mammograms when she turned fifty. Because of this, doctors were not able to detect her breast tumor at an early, treatable stage, and now Sara may miss out on a long life, watching her grandson, Jeffrey, grow up."

### Discussion Questions

1. Which of the four ads described above will work best? What consumer behavior theory helps you come to this conclusion?

2. Evaluate the four ads in terms of their use of fear appeal. What emotional responses linked to fear do these various messages promote? What consumer factors do you think will increase or decrease the level of fear that is experienced in response to any one of the ads (holding the ad itself constant)?

3. Create a survey to examine the effectiveness of each of the above ad formats in inducing changes in behavioral intentions (the focal behavior is your choice, and could include such things as intentions to take vitamins, engage in daily exercise, and so on). Which format works best? Why?

4. Develop a strategy to encourage people to test for a disease or health risk factor of your choice.

Source: D. Cox and A. D. Cox, "Communicating the Consequences of Early Detection," *Journal of Marketing,* July 2001, pp. 91–103; L. Sanders, "Aiming to Stay No. 1," *Advertising Age,* December 10, 2001, p. 4; and Centers for Disease Control and Prevention, www.cdc.gov.

# Consumer Decision Process

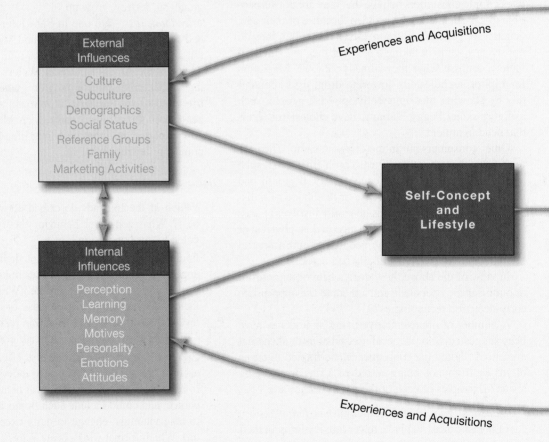

External Influences

Culture
Subculture
Demographics
Social Status
Reference Groups
Family
Marketing Activities

Internal Influences

Perception
Learning
Memory
Motives
Personality
Emotions
Attitudes

Self-Concept and Lifestyle

Experiences and Acquisitions

Experiences and Acquisitions

Up to now, we have focused on various sociological and psychological factors that contribute to different patterns of consumer behavior. Though these various influences play a significant role in behavior, all behavior takes place within the context of a situation. Chapter 13 provides a discussion of the impact situational variables have on consumer behavior.

Of particular importance to marketers is how situations and internal and external sources of influence affect the purchase decision process. The extended consumer decision process, shown on this page, is composed of a sequence of activities: problem recognition, information search, brand evaluation and selection, outlet choice and purchase, and postpurchase processes. However, extended decision making occurs only in those relatively rare situations when the consumer is highly involved in the purchase. Lower levels of purchase involvement produce limited or nominal decision making. Chapter 14 describes those various types of decisions and their relationship to involvement. It also analyzes the first stage of the process—problem recognition.

Information search, discussed in Chapter 15, constitutes the second stage of the consumer decision process. Chapter 16 examines the alternative evaluation and selection process. Chapter 17 deals with outlet selection and the in-store and online influences that often determine final brand choice. The final stage of the consumer decision process, presented in Chapter 18, involves behaviors after the purchase. These include postpurchase dissonance and regret, product use, satisfaction, disposition, and repurchase motivation. Both cognitive (thinking) and emotional (feeling) processes are important at each stage of the decision process.

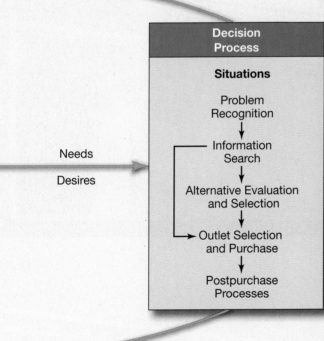

Needs

Desires

**Decision Process**

**Situations**

Problem Recognition

↓

Information Search

↓

Alternative Evaluation and Selection

↓

Outlet Selection and Purchase

↓

Postpurchase Processes

# Situational Influences

The transition from childhood to adulthood is an important life event. Different religious and ethnic subcultures have celebrations to mark the occasion.[1] For example, 13-year-old Jewish boys and girls celebrate bar mitzvahs and bat mitzvahs. Fifteen-year-old Hispanic girls celebrate quinceañera (keen-say-ah-NYAIR-ah). These occasions are often marked with religious ceremonies and after-ceremony parties. Traditionally, these events have tended to focus on religious aspects and responsibility to family and community:

The bar mitzvah is actually an ancient solemn event marking the coming of age of a Jewish male, undertaken after study of Jewish history, traditions and Hebrew. Bat mitzvahs, for girls, are a more recent phenomenon.[2]

In Latin America, the quinceañera, a celebration dating back to the Aztecs that commemorates the spiritual and physical coming of age of a 15-year-old girl, is typically observed with a ceremony in the Catholic church and a backyard party for family members.[3]

The "after-ceremony" celebrations range from simple and inexpensive to elaborate and costly. However, the trend is definitely toward more elaborate and costly parties with modern themes, expensive catering and entertainment, and interactive activities to entertain hundreds of guests. For example:

One Jewish family hired Big Wave International to convert their synagogue into a rainforest with its own waterfall for their son's bar mitzvah.

One Hispanic family spent $30,000 to celebrate their daughter's quinceañera with "a horsedrawn, pumpkin-shaped crystal carriage with liveried servants in powdered wigs, a silver tulle gown and a gala at which 260 guests danced until dawn in the shadow of Sleeping Beauty's castle at Disneyland."[4]

Marketers are definitely tapping into this more secularized luxury trend. For example, the Hartford Civic Center and others feature events such as the "Ultimate Bar and Bat Mitzvah Showcase" where vendors can market to prospective clients. Disneyland has event planners that custom-design quinceañeras for their clients. Royal Carribbean Cruises

469

offers quinceañera cruises for which demand has been strong. And Mattel issued a limited edition Quinceañera Barbie!

The modernization and secularization have gone so far that some non-Jewish teens are having what are called faux Mitzvahs—the lavish after-party without the religious ceremony. Clearly, the ongoing evolution of these ritual "coming of age" events will continue to present marketers with opportunities and challenges.

Bar and bat mitzvahs and quinceañeras are *ritual situations*. As the model we have used to organize this text indicates, the purchase decision and consumption process always occur in the context of a specific situation. Therefore, before examining the decision process, we must first develop an understanding of situations. In this chapter, we will examine the situations in which consumption occurs, the way situations influence consumption behaviors, key characteristics of situations, the nature of ritual situations, and situation-based marketing strategies.

# THE NATURE OF SITUATIONAL INFLUENCE

Consumers do not respond to stimuli such as advertisements and products presented by marketers in isolation; instead, they respond to marketing influences and the situation simultaneously. To understand a consumer's behavior, we must know about the *consumer;* about the primary *stimulus* object, such as a product or advertisement that the consumer is responding to; and about the *situation* in which the response is occurring.[5]

We define **situational influence** as *all those factors particular to a time and place that do not follow from a knowledge of the stable attributes of the consumer and the stimulus and that have an effect on current behavior.*[6] Thus, with one exception, the situation stands apart from the consumer and the stimulus. The exception is in the case of *temporary* (as opposed to stable) characteristics of a consumer or stimulus that are specific to the situation and sometimes even caused by it. For example, a consumer may generally be upbeat (stable trait), but just prior to viewing a firm's ad sees a disturbing news flash that puts her in a bad mood. This bad mood is a transient state (situational factor) caused by the surrounding media context in which the focal ad appears. Other such temporary conditions include illness and time pressure. Consumer involvement also includes a situation-specific component. That is, some consumers are involved only when they have to make a purchase.

A key marketing finding is that consumers often react and behave very differently depending on the situation. We discussed some of these effects in earlier chapters. For example, an ad or in-store display that might otherwise attract consumer attention may not do so in a cluttered environment (Chapter 8). Or an ad that might be persuasive in a non-purchase situation may be much less persuasive in a purchase situation where consumers are on the market to buy (Chapter 11). The interplay between situation, marketing, and the individual is shown in Figure 13–1.

Consumer behavior occurs within four broad categories or types of situations: the communications situation, the purchase situation, the usage situation, and the disposition situation.

## The Communications Situation

The situation in which consumers receive information has an impact on their behavior. Whether one is alone or in a group, in a good mood or bad, in a hurry or not influences the

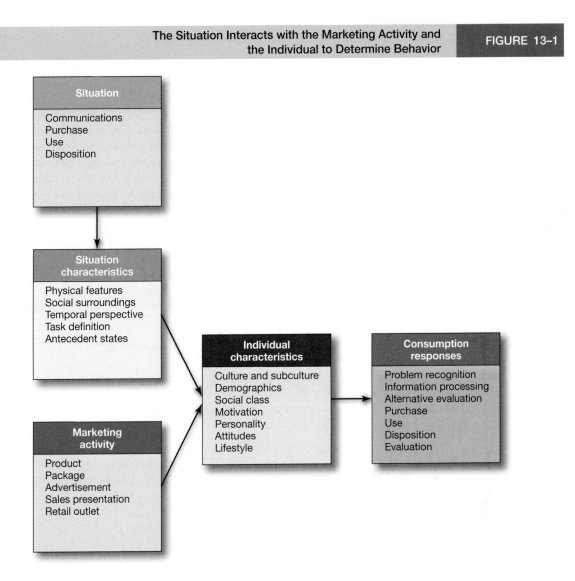

| The Situation Interacts with the Marketing Activity and the Individual to Determine Behavior | FIGURE 13–1 |

degree to which one sees and listens to marketing communications. Is it better to advertise on a happy or sad television program? A calm or exciting program? These are some of the questions managers must answer with respect to the **communications situation.**[7] Marketers often attempt to place their ads in appropriate media contexts to enhance their effectiveness. Some even go so far as to mandate that their ads be "pulled" when programming content negative to their company or industry will appear. Recent examples include Morgan Stanley and BP. *What are the ethical implications of such policies?*[8]

A marketer is able to deliver an effective message to consumers who are interested in the product and are in a receptive communications situation. However, finding high-interest potential buyers in receptive communications situations is a difficult challenge. For example, consider the difficulty a marketer would have in communicating to you in the following communications situations:

- Your favorite team just lost the most important game of the year.
- Final exams begin tomorrow.

- Your roommates watch only comedy programs.
- You have the flu.
- You are driving home on a cold night, and your car heater doesn't work.

## The Purchase Situation

The situation in which a purchase is made can influence consumer behavior. Mothers shopping with children are more apt to be influenced by the product preferences of their children than when shopping without them. A shortage of time, such as trying to make a purchase between classes, can affect the store-choice decision, the number of brands considered, and the price the shopper is willing to pay. At an even more basic level, whether or not a consumer is in a "purchase mode" influences a whole host of behaviors from advertising responses to shopping. Consider, for example, how differently you might behave at Best Buy if you were there only to browse versus being there to replace a broken DVD player.

Marketers must understand how **purchase situations** influence consumers in order to develop marketing strategies that enhance the purchase of their products. For example, how would you alter your decision to purchase a beverage in the following purchase situations?

- You are in a very bad mood.
- A good friend says, "That stuff is bad for you!"
- The store you visit does not carry your favorite brand.
- There is a long line at the checkout counter as you enter the store.
- You are with someone you want to impress.

## The Usage Situation

What beverage would you prefer to consume in each of the following usage situations?

- Friday afternoon after your last final exam.
- With your parents for lunch.
- After dinner on a cold, stormy evening.
- At a dinner with a friend you have not seen in several years.
- When you are feeling sad or homesick.

Marketers need to understand the **usage situations** for which their products are, or may become, appropriate. Using this knowledge, marketers can communicate how their products create consumer satisfaction in each relevant usage situation. For example, a recent study found that consuming two 1.5-cup servings of oat-based cereal a day could lower cholesterol. How could General Mills take advantage of this finding to increase sales of its oat-based cereal, Cheerios? A recent ad depicts a dad coming home late from work and having Cheerios for dinner. When asked why by his young daughter, he replies, "Because they taste just as good at night."

Research indicates that *expanded usage situation* strategies can produce major sales gains for established products.[9] Kraft has attempted to expand the appropriate usage situations for Grey Poupon mustard beyond sandwiches. Coach went away from the traditional two-occasion (everyday and dressy) approach to handbags and moved toward what it calls a "usage voids" approach. Now Coach offers a wide range of products, including weekend bags, coin purses, clutches, and wristlets in a variety of colors and fabrics (see Illustration 13–1). The goal is to get consumers more attuned to the various usage situations available in which to accessorize and then create bags to fit the situations.[10]

**ILLUSTRATION 13–1**

Many products become defined for particular usage situations. Firms that are able to expand the range of usage situations deemed appropriate for their brands can capture significant sales gains.

## The Disposition Situation

Consumers must frequently dispose of products or product packages after or before product use. As we will examine in detail in Chapter 18, decisions made by consumers regarding the **disposition situation** can create significant social problems as well as opportunities for marketers.

Some consumers consider ease of disposition an important product attribute. These people may purchase only items that can be easily recycled. Often disposition of an existing product must occur before or simultaneously with the acquisition of the new product. For example, most consumers must remove their existing bed before using a new one. Marketers need to understand how situational influences affect disposition decisions in order to develop more effective and ethical products and marketing programs. Government and environmental organizations need the same knowledge in order to encourage socially responsible disposition decisions.

How would your disposition decision differ in these situations?

- You have finished a soft drink in a can at a mall. There is a trashcan nearby, but there is no sign of a recycling container.
- You have finished reading the newspaper after class, and you note that you are running late for a basketball game.
- You and two friends have finished soft drinks. Both your friends toss the recyclable cans into a nearby garbage container.
- A local charity will accept old refrigerators if they are delivered to the charity. Your garbage service will haul one to the dump for $15. You just bought a new refrigerator. You don't know anyone (or you do know someone) with a pickup or van.

# SITUATIONAL CHARACTERISTICS AND CONSUMPTION BEHAVIOR

The situations discussed above can be described on a number of dimensions that determine their influence on consumer behavior. The five key dimensions or characteristics are physical surroundings, social surroundings, temporal perspectives, task definition, and antecedent states.[11] These characteristics have been studied primarily in the United States. While the same characteristics of the situation exist across cultures, a marketer should not assume that the response to these characteristics would be the same. For example, a crowded store might cause a different emotional reaction among American consumers than among Indian consumers.[12]

## Physical Surroundings

**Physical surroundings** include decor, sounds, aromas, lighting, weather, and configurations of merchandise or other materials surrounding the stimulus object. Physical surroundings are a widely used type of situational influence, particularly for retail applications.

The lifestyle centers we examined in Chapter 1 (Consumer Insight 1–1) show how important external factors such as the architecture, arrangement, and assortment of retailers can be in affecting consumers' shopping experiences. In addition, store interiors are often designed to create specific feelings in shoppers that can have an important cueing or reinforcing effect on purchase. All physical aspects of the store, including lighting, layout, presentation of merchandise, fixtures, floor coverings, colors, sounds, odors, and dress and behavior of sales personnel, combine to produce these feelings, which in turn influence purchase tendencies.[13] A retail clothing store specializing in extremely stylish, modern clothing would want its fixtures, furnishings, and colors to reflect an overall mood of style, flair, and newness (see Illustration 13–2). In addition, the store personnel should carry this theme in terms of their own appearance and apparel. Compare this interior with that of the men's clothing section of a so-called discount retailer that is also shown in the illustration. It is important to note that one is not superior to the other. Each attempts to create an appropriate atmosphere for its target audience.

**ILLUSTRATION 13–2**

Retail store interiors should provide a physical environment consistent with the nature of the target market, the product line, and the desired image of the outlet.

Typology of Service Environments   **FIGURE 13–2**

| Time Spent in Facility | Consumption Purpose | | |
|---|---|---|---|
| | Utilitarian ---------------------------------------------------------------- Hedonic | | |
| Short [minutes] | Dry cleaner Bank | Fast food Hair salon | Facial Coffee at Starbucks |
| Moderate [hour(s)] | Medical appointment Legal consultation | Business dinner Exercise class | **Theater Sporting event** |
| Extended [day(s)] | Hospital Trade show | **Conference hotel Training center** | **Cruise Resort** |

Note: The darker the shading, the more important the physical features of the servicescape are.

Source: Adapted from K. L.Wakefield and J. G. Blodgett, "Customer Response to Intangible and Tangible Service Factors," *Psychology & Marketing,* January 1999, p. 54. Copyright © 1999 John Wiley & Sons. Reprinted with permission of John Wiley & Sons, Inc.

*The sum of all the physical features of a retail environment* is referred to as the **store atmosphere** or environment (see Chapter 17). A store's atmosphere influences the consumers' judgments of the quality of the store and the store's image. It also has been shown to influence shoppers' moods and their willingness to visit and linger. **Atmospherics** is *the process managers use to manipulate the physical retail environment to create specific mood responses in shoppers.*[14] Atmospherics is also important online and is receiving increasing attention from marketers.[15]

Atmosphere is referred to as **servicescape** when describing a service business such as a hospital, bank, or restaurant.[16] Figure 13–2 classifies services according to the reason the customer is using the service and the length of time the service will be used. The consumption purpose is categorized along a continuum from strictly utilitarian, such as dry cleaning, to completely hedonic, such as a massage. The time can range from a few minutes to days or weeks. Physical characteristics and the feelings and image they create become increasingly important as hedonic motives and the time involved with the service increase. Thus, the physical characteristics of a vacation resort may be as important as or more important than the intangible services provided.

It is important that Figure 13–2 be interpreted correctly. It indicates that the physical environment at Starbucks is more important to the service experience than the physical features of dry cleaners are. *This does not mean that the physical aspects of dry cleaners are not important.* Indeed, an organized, professional-appearing dry cleaning establishment is likely to produce more satisfied customers than one with the opposite characteristics. What the figure does indicate is that the relative importance of tangible physical features increases as one moves to extended, hedonic consumption experiences.

Having established the importance of the physical environment, we will now examine some of its components.

Colors   As we saw in Chapter 8, certain colors and color characteristics create feelings of excitement and arousal that are related to attention. Bright colors are more arousing than dull colors. And *warm* colors, such as reds and yellows, are more arousing than *cool* colors, such as blues and greys.[17] Which color would be best for store interiors? The answer is, it depends. For the dominant interior color, cool colors (e.g., blue) should probably be used since they increase sales and customer satisfaction.[18] However, the attention-getting nature of warm colors should not be overlooked and can be used effectively as an accent color in areas where the retailer wants to attract attention and drive impulse purchases.[19] Cool colors also appear to be capable of reducing wait time perceptions by inducing feelings of relaxation.[20]

As we saw in Chapter 2, the meaning of colors varies across cultures. Therefore, this and all other aspects of the physical environment should be designed specifically for the cultures involved.

Aromas    There is increasing evidence that odors can affect consumer shopping.[21] One study found that a scented environment produced a greater intent to revisit the store, higher purchase intention for some items, and a reduced sense of time spent shopping.[22] Another study found that one aroma, but not another, increased slot machine usage in a Las Vegas casino.[23] A third study reported that a floral-scented environment increased sales of Nike shoes.[24] A fourth study found that a pleasantly scented environment enhanced brand recall and evaluations, particularly for unfamiliar brands. The pleasant scent increased the time spent evaluating the brands (attention), which, in turn, increased memory.[25]

Given these results, it is not surprising that a billion-dollar *environmental fragrancing* industry has developed around the use of ambient scents. However, marketers still have a lot to learn about if, when, and how scents can be used effectively in a retail environment.[26] In addition, scent preferences are highly individualized; a pleasant scent to one individual may be repulsive to another. Moreover, some shoppers object to anything being deliberately added to the air they breathe, and others worry about allergic reactions.[27]

Music    Music influences consumers' moods, which influence a variety of consumption behaviors.[28] Is slow-tempo or fast-tempo background music better for a restaurant? Table 13–1 indicates that slow music increased gross margin for one restaurant by almost 15 percent per customer group compared with fast music. However, before concluding that all restaurants should play slow music, examine the table carefully. Slow music appears to have relaxed and slowed down the customers, resulting in more time in the restaurant and substantially more purchases from the bar. Restaurants that rely on rapid customer turnover might be better off with fast-tempo music.

Other aspects of music besides tempo are also important. For example, research suggests that matching music to the musical preferences of the target audience is critical to positive retail outcomes such as satisfaction and enjoyment, browsing time, spending, perceived service quality, and positive word of mouth. In addition, research suggests that music which creates moderate levels of arousal (versus extremely low or high) yields the most positive retail outcomes.[29]

**TABLE 13–1**

The Impact of Background Music on Restaurant Patrons

| Variables | Slow Music | Fast Music |
|---|---|---|
| Service time | 29 min. | 27 min. |
| Customer time at table | 56 min. | 45 min. |
| Customer groups leaving before seated | 10.5% | 12.0% |
| Amount of food purchased | $55.81 | $55.12 |
| Amount of bar purchases | $30.47 | $21.62 |
| Estimated gross margin | $55.82 | $48.62 |

Source: R. E. Milliman, "The Influence of Background Music on the Behavior of Restaurant Patrons," in the *Journal of Consumer Research*, September 1986, p. 289. Copyright © 1986 by the University of Chicago. Used by permission.

Because of the impact that music can have on shopping behavior, firms exist to develop music programs to meet the unique needs of specific retailers. An emerging trend is having music more in the foreground so it becomes part of the shopping experience and drives store image. AEI, a major supplier of foreground music, does intense research on the demographics and psychographics of each client store's customers. The age mix, buying patterns, and traffic flows of each part of the day are analyzed. AEI characterizes its approach as:

> [Creating] environments where sounds, video, lighting and architecture blend together to give a brand a voice, creating emotional attachments that encourage consumers to shop longer, increase spending and return often.[30]

Firms such as Abercrombie & Fitch, Banana Republic, Bath & Body Works, and Eddie Bauer use companies like AEI to create appropriate and consistent shopping environments throughout their chains.

**Crowding**    Crowding generally produces negative outcomes for both the retail outlet and the consumer.[31] As more people enter a store or as more of the space of the store is filled with merchandise, an increasing percentage of the shoppers will experience a feeling of being crowded, confined, or claustrophobic. Most consumers find these feelings to be unpleasant and will take steps to change them. The primary means of doing so is to spend less time in the store by buying less, making faster decisions, and using less of the available information. This in turn tends to produce less satisfactory purchases, an unpleasant shopping trip, and a reduced likelihood of returning to the store.

Marketers should design their outlets in ways that will help reduce consumers' perceptions of crowding. This is difficult because retail shopping tends to occur at specific times, such as holiday weekends. Retailers must balance the expense of having a larger store than required most of the time against the cost of having dissatisfied customers during key shopping periods. Using extra personnel, opening additional checkout lines, and implementing similar measures can enhance the flow of consumers through a store during peak periods and reduce the crowding sensation. In addition, recent research shows that music tempo can be important. Specifically, music with a slow tempo offsets the negative emotions experienced as a result of crowding. Since music tempo adjustments are less expensive than store expansion or new personnel, this is an important finding for retail strategy.[32]

Marketers need to be sensitive to cross-cultural differences since personal space and resulting crowding perceptions can vary from culture to culture. For example, one study found that when the activity is for fun, such as an amusement park or concert, Middle East consumers perceive less crowding and appreciate crowding more than North American consumers.[33]

## Social Surroundings

**Social surroundings** are *the other individuals present in the particular situation*. People's actions are frequently influenced by those around them. What would you wear in each of the following situations?

- Studying alone for a final.
- Meeting at the library with a date to study for a final.
- Going to a nice restaurant with a date.
- Meeting a prospective employer for lunch.

Most people would change their apparel for at least some of these situations. Illustration 13–3 shows how Allen Edmonds designs shoes for different types of social situations.

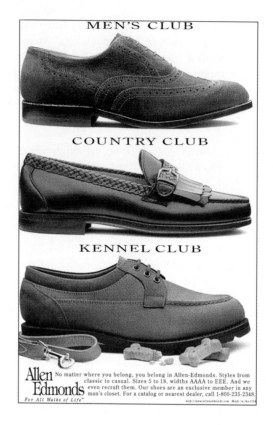

Social influence is a significant force acting on our behavior, since individuals tend to comply with group expectations, particularly when the behavior is visible (see Chapter 7). Thus, shopping, a highly visible activity, and the use of many publicly consumed brands are subject to social influences.[34] This is particularly true of those who are highly susceptible to interpersonal influence, a stable personality trait. As just one example, a recent study finds that consumers are more likely to engage in variety-seeking behavior in public (versus private) consumption situations even if it means consuming products they like less. The reason is that consumers feel that others view them more positively (more fun, interesting, exciting) if their purchases show more variety. This tendency is stronger for those more susceptible to interpersonal influence.[35]

Marketers have recently begun to examine the role of social influence on embarrassment. **Embarrassment** is a negative emotion influenced by both the product and the situation. Certain products are more embarrassing than others (condoms, hearing aids, etc.) and embarrassment is driven by the presence of others in the purchase or usage situation. Since embarrassment can deter purchases, this is an important area for marketers. One finding is that familiarity with purchasing the product reduces embarrassment, so marketers might try advertisements that show the purchase of a potentially embarrassing product in which no awkwardness or embarrassment occurs. For extremely sensitive products (e.g., adult diapers), strategies might include home delivery options with discreet labeling to completely avoid the social component.[36]

Shopping can provide a social experience outside the home for making new acquaintances, meeting existing friends, or just being near other people (Consumer Insight 10–1 discusses the social shopping motive). Some people seek status and authority in shopping since the salesperson's job is to wait on the customer. This allows these individuals a

### Does Shopping with Others Drive Impulse Buying?

Impulse buying can be defined as *a sudden and immediate unplanned purchase that occurs after experiencing a spontaneous urge to buy.* Some people are more prone to impulse purchases, and in extreme situations, impulse buying can create negative consequences such as large credit card debt. One question is whether the presence of other people during a shopping trip can influence impulse buying. To answer this question, a recent study examined several scenarios, two of which are highlighted below.[37]

**Scenario 1:** Mary is a 21-year-old college student with a part-time job. It is two days before Mary gets her next paycheck and she only has $25 left for necessities. In addition to food, Mary needs to buy a pair of warm socks for an outdoor party this weekend. *After work she goes with a group of her best friends to the mall to purchase the socks.* As she is walking through a final department store, Mary sees a great-looking sweater on sale for $75.

**Scenario 2:** Mary is a 21-year-old college student with a part-time job. It is two days before Mary gets her next paycheck and she only has $25 left for necessities. In addition to food, Mary needs to buy a pair of warm socks for an outdoor party this weekend. *After work, her family meets her at the mall to shop and purchase the socks. Mary and her family are very close-knit.* As she is walking through a final department store, Mary sees a great-looking sweater on sale for $75.

Now that you've read the two scenarios, when do you think impulse buying (that is, buying the socks *and* the sweater on credit) is higher? If you said Scenario 1, you were correct. In fact, compared with shopping alone, shopping with close friends increased impulse buying, while shopping with close family members decreased impulse buying.

The role of others in impulse buying can be explained by social norms that we examined in depth in Chapter 7. It was found that consumers generally believe that friends think impulse buying is more acceptable than does family. Thus, close friends and family influence impulse buying in a manner consistent with social norms. Notice that in the scenarios, strength of the social tie was high. When the social ties to friends and family were weak (for example, co-workers from her part-time job instead of best friends), the influence of others on impulse buying disappeared.

### Critical Thinking Questions

1. What insights can you find in this research for how retailers should advertise? What ethical implications are involved?

2. Relate this research to the different "self-concepts" discussed in Chapter 12.

3. What coping mechanisms could parents teach their children to help offset the influence of close friends on impulse buying?

measure of respect or prestige that may otherwise be lacking in their lives. Thus, consumers, on occasion, shop *for* social situations rather than, or in addition to, products. The presence of others *during* the shopping trip can also influence impulse buying, as discussed in Consumer Insight 13–1.

Frequently, marketing managers will not have any control over social characteristics of a situation. For example, when a television advertisement is sent into the home, the advertising manager cannot control whom the viewer is with at the time of reception. However, the manager can use the knowledge that some programs are generally viewed alone (weekday, daytime programs), some are viewed by the entire family (prime-time family comedies), and others are viewed by groups of friends (Super Bowl). The message presented can be structured to these viewing situations. Marketers can also use social consumption themes in their ads to enhance the likelihood that consumers will consider the social component in their decisions. For example, a recent study found that brand personality (fun and sophistication) conveyed by a celebrity endorser in an ad only enhanced purchase intentions when a social context was evoked.[38]

## Temporal Perspectives

**Temporal perspectives** are *situational characteristics that deal with the effect of time on consumer behavior*. Time as a situational factor can manifest itself in a number of ways.[39] The amount of time available for the purchase has a substantial impact on the consumer decision process. In general, the less time there is available (i.e., increased time pressure), the shorter will be the information search, the less available information will be used, and the more suboptimal purchases will be made.[40]

Limited purchase time can also result in a smaller number of product alternatives being considered. The increased time pressure experienced by many dual-career couples and single parents tends to increase the incidence of brand loyalty, particularly for nationally branded products. The obvious implication is that these consumers feel safer with nationally branded or "known" products, particularly when they do not have the time to engage in extensive comparison shopping.

Time as a situational influence affects consumers' choice of stores and behaviors in those stores.[41] A number of retail firms have taken advantage of the temporal perspective factor. Perhaps the most successful of these is the 7-Eleven chain, which caters almost exclusively to individuals who either are in a hurry or want to make a purchase after regular shopping hours.

Internet shopping is growing rapidly in part as a result of the time pressures felt by many dual-career and single-parent households. Shopping on the Internet has two important time-related dimensions. First, it has the potential to reduce the amount of time required to make a specific purchase. Second, it provides the consumer with almost total control over *when* the purchase is made (see Chapter 17). These features are among the major reasons for the rapid growth in Internet outlets and sales (see Illustration 13–4).

**ILLUSTRATION 13–4**

In the United States and other countries, dual-career and single-parent families have caused consumers to feel time starved. Internet shopping provides many such consumers both time savings and control over when they shop.

# Task Definition

**Task definition** is *the reason the consumption activity is occurring.* The major task dichotomy used by marketers is between purchases for self-use versus gift giving.

**Gift Giving**    Consumers use different shopping strategies and purchase criteria when shopping for gifts versus shopping for the same item for self-use.[42] Consumers give gifts for many reasons. Social expectations and ritualized consumption situations such as birthdays often require gift giving independent of the giver's actual desires.[43] Gifts are also given to elicit return favors in the form of either gifts or actions. And, of course, gifts are given as an expression of love and caring.[44]

The type of gift given and desired varies by occasion and gender.[45] One study found that wedding gifts tend to be *utilitarian,* while birthday gifts tend to be *fun.* Thus, both the general task definition (gift giving) and the specific task definition (gift-giving occasion) influence purchase behavior, as does the relationship between the giver and the recipient.

Gift giving produces anxieties on the part of both givers and receivers.[46] Gifts communicate symbolic meaning on several levels. The gift item itself generally has a known, or knowable, price that can be interpreted as a measure of the esteem the giver has for the receiver. The image and functionality of the gift implies the giver's impression of the image and personality of the receiver. It also reflects on the image and thoughtfulness of the giver.

The nature of a gift can signify the type of relationship the giver has or desires with the receiver.[47] A gift of stationery implies a very different desired relationship between two individuals than does a gift of cologne. Consider the following:

> The biggest moment of revelation, the moment I knew he was "serious" about me, was when he showed up with a gift for my daughter. Other men had shown the typical false affection for her in order to get on my good side, but he was only civil and polite to her, never gushy. One day, however, he showed up with a very nice skateboard for my daughter. . . . The gift marked a turning point in our relationship. I think for him it marked the time that he decided it would be OK to get serious about a woman with a child.[48]

As the example above indicates, the act of giving/receiving a gift can alter the relationship between the giver and receiver. In addition, items received as gifts often take on meaning associated with the relationship or the giver. For example a gift may be cherished and protected because it symbolizes an important friendship.[49]

Of course, gift giving is culture specific (see Chapter 2).[50] For example, in characterizing gift giving in Korea (collectivist) compared with the United States (individualistic), one expert summarized:

> Koreans reported more gift giving occasions, a wider exchange network, more frequent giving of practical gift items, especially cash gifts, strong face-saving and group conformity motivations, more social pressure to reciprocate, higher gift budget, and frequent workplace giving.[51]

# Antecedent States

*Features of the individual person that are not lasting characteristics,* such as momentary moods or conditions, are called **antecedent states.** For example, most people experience states of depression or excitement from time to time that are not normally part of their individual makeup.

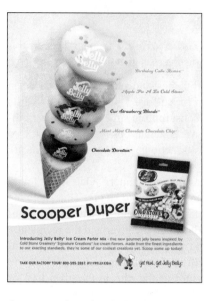

Scooper Duper

Introducing Jelly Belly® Ice Cream Parlor Mix – five new gourmet jelly beans inspired by Cold Stone Creamery® Signature Creations® ice cream flavors. made from the finest ingredients to our exacting standards, they're some of our coolest creations yet. Scoop some up today!

TAKE OUR FACTORY TOUR! 800-522-3267 JELLYBELLY.COM        get real. get Jelly Belly.

**Moods**  **Moods** are *transient feeling states that are generally not tied to a specific event or object.*[52] They tend to be less intense than emotions and may operate without the individual's awareness. Although moods may affect all aspects of a person's behavior, they generally do not completely interrupt ongoing behavior as an emotion might. Individuals use such terms as *happy, cheerful, peaceful, sad, blue,* and *depressed* to describe their moods.

Moods both affect and are affected by the consumption process.[53] Moods influence decision processes, the purchase and consumption of various products, and perceptions of service.[54] Positive moods appear to be associated with increased browsing and impulse purchasing. Negative moods also increase impulse and compulsive purchasing in some consumers. One explanation is that some shopping behaviors play both a mood maintenance (positive moods) and mood enhancement (negative moods) role.[55]

Mood can also play an important role in the communications situation. Such effects are often called *program context effects* and relate to the nature of the programming surrounding the focal ad (see Chapter 8). The television, radio, and magazine content viewed just prior to the focal ad can influence consumers' moods and arousal levels, which, in turn, influence their information-processing activities.[56] A basic finding is that ad and brand attitudes are often influenced in a mood-congruent manner. Thus, a TV show that puts a consumer in a positive mood (elicits positive affective reactions) should improve ad and brand attitudes compared with one that puts the consumer in a negative mood. However, in cases where so-called negative programming is also liked by the viewer (a sad movie that a viewer loves), then program liking can still provide a positive boost in ad and brand attitudes.[57] Given such complexities, marketers must pretest their ads in contexts as close to their expected programming environment as possible.

Consumers actively manage their mood states (see Illustration 13–5).[58] That is, consumers often seek situations, activities, or objects that will alleviate negative moods or enhance positive ones. Products and services are one means consumers use to manage their mood states. Thus, a person feeling bored, sad, or down might view a situation comedy on television, go to a cheerful movie, visit a fun store, eat at an upbeat restaurant, or purchase a new compact disc, shirt, or other fun product.[59] Consumers may engage in such mood-regulating behavior both at a nonconscious level and also at a deliberate, conscious level:

> [T]here are certain products that I purchase specifically to make me feel better. For instance, occasionally, I enjoy smoking a cigar. Certainly the cigar serves no other purpose than to make me feel good.
>
> While other cosmetics, perfumes and nice clothes can make me feel good, they seldom have the same power to transform my temperament like a manicure and pedicure can.[60]

Marketers attempt to influence moods and to time marketing activities with positive mood-inducing events.[61] Many companies prefer to advertise during light television programs because viewers tend to be in a good mood while watching these shows. Restaurants, bars, shopping malls, and many other retail outlets are designed to induce positive moods

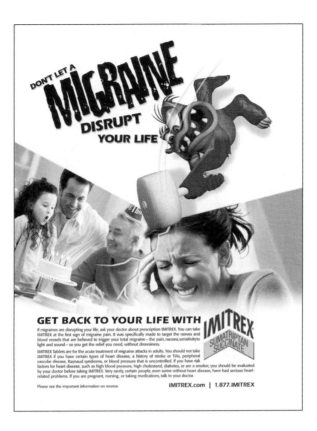

in patrons. As discussed earlier, music is often played for this reason. Finally, marketers can position their products and services in terms of mood enhancement.

**Momentary Conditions**   Whereas moods reflect states of mind, *momentary conditions reflect temporary states of being,* such as being tired, being ill, having extra money, being broke, and so forth. However, for conditions, as for moods, to fit under the definition of antecedent states, they must be momentary and not constantly with the individual. Hence, an individual who is short of cash only momentarily will act differently from someone who is always short of cash.[62]

As with moods, individuals attempt to manage their momentary conditions, often through the purchase or consumption of products and services. For example, individuals feeling tired or sleepy during the day may drink a cup of coffee or a soft drink or eat a candy bar. Massages are consumed to relieve sore muscles. A variety of medications are sold to relieve physical discomfort associated with overexertion, colds, allergies, and so forth. Pawnshops provide cash for individuals temporarily needing funds, as do banks and other financial institutions. Thus, a great deal of marketing activity is directed toward momentary conditions. Illustration 13–6 is an ad for a product designed to relieve a momentary condition.

# RITUAL SITUATIONS

Rituals are receiving increasing attention by marketing scholars and practitioners. A **ritual situation** can be described as a socially defined occasion that triggers a set of interrelated behaviors that occur in a structured format and that have symbolic meaning.[63] Ritual situations can range from completely private to completely public. A completely private ritual situation would be an individual's decision to drink a private toast or say a private prayer on the anniversary of an event with special meaning to the individual. A couple that celebrates their first date by returning to the same restaurant every year is involved in a more public ritual. Weddings tend to be even more public. Finally, national and global holidays present very public ritual situations.

Ritual situations are of major importance to marketers because they often involve prescribed consumption behaviors. Every major American holiday (ritual situation) has consumption rituals associated with it. For example, more than 60 percent of the toy industry's sales occur at Christmas.

While there is significant variation across individuals and households, there is enough shared behavior that marketers can develop products and promotions around the common ritual situations that arise each year. For example, candy marketers produce and promote a wide array of candies for Valentine's Day and Halloween. Illustration 13–7 shows how an online retailer is capitalizing on consumption rituals.

Marketers also attempt to change or create consumption patterns associated with ritual situations.[64] Mother's Day is a $10 billion occasion in which card giving is largely a ritual behavior created by marketers.[65] Halloween cards are now being promoted as part of the Halloween ritual.[66] And as we saw in the chapter's opening example, many firms seek to make their products and services part of the consumption pattern associated with "coming of age." The same is true for most other rites of passage in America, such as graduation.

Ritual situations can also result in injurious consumption. Binge or excessive drinking is a serious health and social problem on many college campuses, though its incidence appears to be on the decline. Recent research suggests that this can be understood as a ritual behavior in that it is triggered by social occasions (e.g., birthdays), involves a set of interrelated behaviors and routines (e.g., start drinking on game days at a specific time), and results in special meaning and rewards for participants (e.g., fun, acceptance by group). When approached from this perspective, more effective strategies for minimizing such behaviors may result.

# SITUATIONAL INFLUENCES AND MARKETING STRATEGY

In the previous sections, we described a variety of marketing strategies based on situational influences. Here we will focus more specifically on the process by which such strategies can be developed.

It is important to note that individuals do not encounter situations randomly. Instead, most people "create" many of the situations they face. Thus, individuals who choose to engage in physically demanding sports such as jogging, tennis, or racquetball are indirectly choosing to expose themselves to the situation of "being tired" or "being thirsty." This allows marketers to develop products, advertising, and segmentation strategies based on the situations that individuals selecting various lifestyles are likely to encounter.

After identifying the different situations that might involve the consumption of a product, marketers must determine which products or brands are most likely to be purchased or consumed across those situations. One method of approaching this is to jointly scale situations and products. An example is shown in Figure 13–3. Here, *use situations* that ranged from "private consumption at home" to "consumption away from home where there is a concern for other people's reaction to you" were scaled in terms of their similarity and relationship to products appropriate for that situation.

**Use Situations and Product Positioning**    **FIGURE 13–3**

I = Use situation: "To clean my mouth upon rising in the morning."
II = Use situation: "Before an important business meeting late in the afternoon."

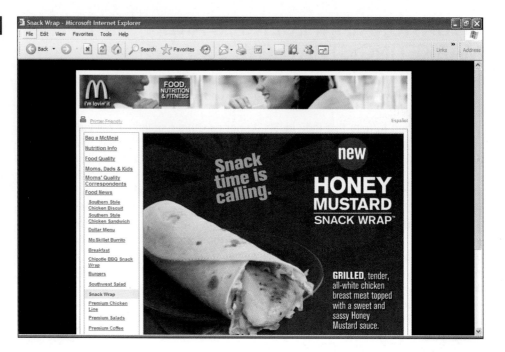

For use situation I, "to clean my mouth upon rising in the morning," toothpaste and mouthwash are viewed as most appropriate (see Figure 13–3). However, use situation II, "before an important business meeting late in the afternoon," involves both consumption away from home and a concern for the response from others. As a result, mint-flavored gums or candies are preferred. *Where do you think a product like Listerine Breath Strips would be located on this map?*

Determining how products are *currently used* across situations can help the marketer develop appropriate advertising and positioning strategies. In our example, Wrigley's might advertise its Spearmint Gum as having breath-freshening capabilities that make it appropriate for use in social situations away from home. Or a marketer may try to change the situations for which a product is used. In Figure 13–3, mouthwash is not seen as appropriate for consumption away from home. What if a version of Scope was developed that one swallowed after use? Could it successfully be promoted for use away from home? Would it be able to compete against breath strips? Illustration 13–8 shows a company that is adding products to expand the number of usage situations.

Another approach for developing situation-based marketing strategies is to follow these five steps:[67]

1. Use observational studies, focus group discussions, depth interviews, and secondary data to discover the various usage situations that influence the consumption of the product.
2. Survey a larger sample of consumers to better understand and quantify how the product is used and the benefits sought in the usage situation by the market segment.
3. Construct a person–situation segmentation matrix. The rows are the major usage situations and the columns are groups of users with unique needs or desires. Each cell contains the key benefits sought. (Table 13–2 illustrates such a matrix for suntan lotion.) Then:

TABLE 13–2

Person–Situation
Segments for
Suntan Lotions

| Potential Users of Suntan Lotion | | | | | |
|---|---|---|---|---|---|
| Suntan Lotion Use Situation | Young Children | Teenagers | Adult Women | Adult Men | General Situation Benefits |
| Beach/boat activities | Prevent sunburn/skin damage | Prevent sunburn while tanning | Prevent sunburn/skin change/dry skin | Prevent sunburn | Container floats |
| Home/pools sunbathing | Prevent sunburn/skin damage | Tanning without sunburn | Tanning without skin damage or dry skin | Tanning without sunburn/skin damage | Lotion won't stain clothes or furniture |
| Tanning booth | | Tanning | Tanning with moisturizer | Tanning | Designed for sunlamps |
| Snow skiing | | Prevent sunburn | Prevent sunburn/skin damage/dry skin | Prevent sunburn | Antifreeze formula |
| Person benefits | Protection | Tanning | Protection and tanning with soft skin | Protection and tanning | |

Source: "Potential Users of Suntan Lotion," adapted from P. Dickson, "Person–Situation: Segmentation's Missing Link," *Journal of Marketing,* Fall 1982, pp. 56–64. Used by permission of the American Marketing Association.

4.  Evaluate each cell in terms of potential (sales volume, price level, cost to serve, competitor strength, and so forth).
5.  Develop and implement a marketing strategy for those cells that offer sufficient profit potential given your capabilities.

## SUMMARY

Marketing managers should view the consumer and the marketing activities designed to affect and influence that consumer in light of the situations that the consumer faces. A *consumer situation* is a set of factors outside of and removed from stable characteristics of the individual consumer and focal stimulus. Four categories of situations are communications, purchase, usage, and disposition situations.

Situations have been classified into a scheme of five objectively measured variables. *Physical surroundings* include geographical and institutional location, decor, sound, aromas, lighting, weather, and displays of merchandise or other material surrounding the product. Retailers are particularly concerned with the effects of physical surroundings. The sum of all the physical features of a retail environment is referred to as the *store atmosphere* or environment. *Atmospherics* is the process managers use to manipulate the physical retail environment to create specific mood responses in shoppers. Atmosphere is referred to as *servicescape* when describing a service business such as a hospital, bank, or restaurant.

*Social surroundings* deal with other persons present who could have an impact on the individual consumer's behavior. The characteristics of the other persons present, their roles, and their interpersonal interactions are potentially important social situational influences.

*Temporal perspectives* relate to the effect of time on consumer behavior, such as effects of time of day, time since last purchase, time since or until meals or payday, and time constraints imposed by commitments. Convenience stores have evolved and been successful by taking advantage of the temporal perspective factor.

*Task definition* reflects the purpose or reason for engaging in the consumption behavior. The task may reflect different buyer and user roles anticipated by the individual. For example, a person shopping for dishes to be given as a wedding present is in a different situation from a person buying dishes for personal use.

*Antecedent states* are features of the individual person that are not lasting or relatively enduring characteristics. *Moods* are temporary states of depression or high excitement, and so on, which all people experience. *Momentary conditions* are such things as being tired, ill, having a great deal of money (or none at all), and so forth.

A *ritual situation* can be described as a set of interrelated behaviors that occur in a structured format, that have symbolic meaning, and that occur in response to socially defined occasions. Ritual situations can range from completely private to completely public. They are of major importance to marketers because they often involve prescribed consumption behaviors.

Situational influences may have direct influences, but they also interact with product and individual characteristics to influence behavior. In some cases, the situation will have no influence whatsoever, because the individual's characteristics or choices are so intense that they override everything else. But the situation is always potentially important and therefore of concern to marketing managers.

## KEY TERMS

Antecedent states  481
Atmospherics  475
Communications situation  471
Disposition situation  473
Embarrassment  478
Moods  482

Physical surroundings  474
Purchase situations  472
Ritual situation  483
Servicescape  475
Situational influence  470
Social surroundings  477

Store atmosphere  475
Task definition  481
Temporal perspectives  480
Usage situations  472

## INTERNET EXERCISES

1. Visit several online retailers. How would you characterize this shopping situation relative to shopping in a physical store?
2. What type of online environment does BarnesandNoble.com have?

3. Prepare a report listing and describing several useful sites for gathering current information about ritual situations such as marriages, high school graduation, Thanksgiving, or proms.
4. Evaluate WeddingWindow.com.

## REVIEW QUESTIONS

1. What is meant by the term *situation*? Why is it important for a marketing manager to understand situational influences on purchasing behavior?
2. What are *physical surroundings* (as a situational variable)? Give an example of how they can influence the consumption process.

3. How does crowding affect shopping behavior?
4. What is *store atmosphere*?
5. What is *atmospherics*?
6. What is a *servicescape*?

7. What are *social surroundings* (as a situational variable)? Give an example of how they can influence the consumption process.

8. What is *temporal perspective* (as a situational variable)? Give an example of how it can influence the consumption process.

9. What is *task definition* (as a situational variable)? Give an example of how it can influence the consumption process.

10. Why do people give gifts?

11. How might the receipt of a gift affect the relationship between the giver and the receiver?

12. What are *antecedent conditions* (as a situational variable)? Give an example of how they can influence the consumption process.

13. What is a *mood*? How does it differ from an *emotion*? How do moods influence consumption behavior?

14. How do people manage their moods?

15. How do moods differ from *momentary conditions*?

16. What is meant by the statement, "Situational variables may interact with product or personal characteristics"?

17. Are individuals randomly exposed to situational influences? Why or why not?

18. What are *ritual situations*? Why are they important?

19. Describe a process for developing a situation-based marketing strategy.

## DISCUSSION QUESTIONS

20. Discuss the potential importance of each type of situational influence in developing a marketing strategy to promote the purchase of (gifts to/shopping at):
    a. Audubon Society
    b. Applebee's
    c. iPhone
    d. Coca-Cola Zero
    e. Health insurance
    f. Eyewear

21. What product categories seem most susceptible to situational influences? Why?

22. Flowers are appropriate gifts for women for many situations but seem to be appropriate for men only when they are ill. Why is this so? How might 1-800-FLOWERS change this?

23. How could the store atmosphere at the following be improved?
    a. The main library on campus
    b. The bank lobby near campus
    c. A Mexican restaurant near campus
    d. A convenience store near campus
    e. The student advising office

24. Speculate on what a matrix like the one shown in Table 13–2 would look like for the following:
    a. Lemonade
    b. Eyewear
    c. Ice cream
    d. Shoes
    e. Bicycles
    f. Coffee

25. Does Table 13–1 have implications for outlets other than restaurants? If yes, which ones and why?

26. Do your shopping behavior and purchase criteria differ between purchases made for yourself and purchases made as gifts? How?

27. Describe a situation in which a mood (good or bad) caused you to make an unusual purchase.

28. Describe a relatively private ritual that you or someone you know has. What, if any, consumption pattern is associated with it?

29. Describe the consumption rituals your family has associated with the following ritual situations:
    a. Family birthdays
    b. Summer vacations
    c. Winter holiday
    d. Halloween
    e. Mother's Day
    f. Father's Day
    g. New Year's Eve

30. Respond to the questions in Consumer Insight 13–1.

## APPLICATION ACTIVITIES

31. Interview five people who have recently purchased the following. Determine the role, if any, played by situational factors.
    a. Cell phone
    b. Jewelry
    c. Motorcycle
    d. A fast-food restaurant meal
    e. A cup of coffee
    f. Health insurance

32. Interview a salesperson for the following. Determine the role, if any, this individual feels situational variables play in his or her sales.
    a. Renter's insurance
    b. BMX bikes
    c. Fine chocolates
    d. Flowers

33. Conduct a study using a small (five or so) sample of your friends in which you attempt to isolate the situational factors that influence the type, brand, or amount of the following purchased or used.
    a. Health club
    b. Energy bar
    c. Movie attendance
    d. Volunteer work
    e. TV dinners
    f. Audio books

34. Create a list of 10 to 20 use situations relevant to campus area restaurants. Then interview 10 students and have them indicate which of these situations they have encountered, and ask them to rank these situations in terms of how likely they are to occur. Discuss how a restaurant could use this information in trying to appeal to the student market.

35. Visit three stores selling the same product line. Describe how the atmosphere differs across the stores. Why do you think these differences exist?

36. Visit three local coffee shops. Describe how the servicescapes differ across the shops. Why do you think these differences exist?

37. What kind of online atmosphere does each of the following have? How would you improve it?
    a. Honda.com
    b. Harley-Davidson.com
    c. Reebok.com
    d. Charities.org
    e. Cabelas.com
    f. Cheerios.com

38. Copy or describe an advertisement that is clearly based on a situational appeal. Indicate
    a. Which situational variable is involved
    b. Why the company would use this variable
    c. Your evaluation of the effectiveness of this approach

39. Create a graduation gift, anniversary gift, and self-use ad for the following. Explain the differences across the ads:
    a. Savings bond
    b. Gourmet coffee maker
    c. Magazine subscription
    d. Set of dishes
    e. Blender
    f. Watch

40. Interview five students and determine instances where their mood affected their purchases. What do you conclude?

41. Interview five students and determine the consumption rituals they have with respect to the following. What do you conclude?
    a. New Year's Day
    b. Spring break
    c. Memorial Day
    d. Valentine's Day
    e. Mother's Day
    f. Father's Day

## REFERENCES

1. The Chapter 13 opening vignette is based on E. Bernstein, "You Don't Have to Be Jewish to Want a Bar Mitzvah," *The Wall Street Journal,* January 14, 2004, p. A1; T. Weiss, "Event Companies Cater Rising Demand for Elaborate Bar, Bat Mitzvahs," *Knight Ridder Tribune Business News,* March 10, 2004, p. 1; A. Chozick, "Fairy-Tale Fifteenths," *The Wall Street Journal,* October 15, 2004, p. B1; and D. M. Alba, "New Mexico Hispanics Emphasize 'Quinceanera' Celebrations," *Knight Ridder Tribune Business News,* February 7, 2005, p. 1.

2. Bernstein, "You Don't Have to Be Jewish to Want a Bar Mitzvah."

3. Chozick, "Fairy-Tale Fifteenths."

4. Ibid.

5. See K. S. Lim and M. A. Razzaque, "Brand Loyalty and Situational Effects," *Journal of International Consumer Marketing* 4 (1997), pp. 95–115.

6. R. W. Belk, "Situational Variables and Consumer Behavior," *Journal of Consumer Research,* December 1975, p. 158.

7. See K. R. Lord, R. E. Burnkrant, and H. R. Unnava, "The Effects of Program-Induced Mood States on Memory for Commercial Information," *Journal of Current Issues and Research in Advertising,* Spring 2001, pp. 1–14; S. Shapiro, D. J. MacInnis, and C. Whan Park, "Understanding Program-Induced Mood Effects," *Journal of Advertising,* Winter 2002, pp. 15–26; P. De Pelsmacker, M. Geuens, and P. Anckaert, "Media Context and Advertising Effectiveness," *Journal of Advertising,* Summer 2002, pp. 49–61; and S. Jun et al., "The Influence of Editorial Context on Consumer Response to Advertisements in a Specialty Magazine," *Journal of Current Issues and Research in Advertising,* Fall 2003, pp. 1–11.

8. L. Sanders and J. Halliday, "BP Institutes 'Ad-Pull' Policy for Print Publications," *AdAge.com,* May 24, 2005.

9. B. Wansink, "Making Old Brands New," *American Demographics,* December 1997, pp. 53–58.

10. E. Byron, "Case by Case," *The Wall Street Journal,* November 17, 2004, p. A1.

11. Ibid.; and I. Sinha, "A Conceptual Model of Situation Type on Consumer Choice Behavior and Consideration Sets," in *Advances in Consumer Research,* vol. 21, eds. C. T. Allen and D. R. John (Provo, UT: Association for Consumer Research, 1994), pp. 477–82.

12. See J. A. F. Nicholls et al., "Situational Influences on Shoppers," *Journal of International Consumer Marketing* 9, no. 2 (1996), pp. 21–39; and J. A. F. Nicholls, T. Li, and S. Roslow, "Oceans Apart," *Journal of International Consumer Marketing* 12, no. 1 (1999), pp. 57–72.

13. See E. Sherman, A. Mathur, and R. B. Smith, "Store Environment and Consumer Purchase Behavior," *Psychology & Marketing,* July 1997, pp. 361–78; and J. Baker et al., "The Influence of Multiple Design Cues on Perceived Merchandise Value and Patronage Intentions," *Journal of Marketing,* April 2002, pp. 120–41.

14. For an extensive review, see L. W. Turley and R. E. Milliman, "Atmospheric Effects on Shopping Behavior," *Journal of Business Research* 49 (2000), pp. 193–211. See also A. d'Astous, "Irritating Aspects of the Shopping Environment," and A. Sharma and T. F. Stafford, "The Effect of Retail Atmospherics on Customers' Perceptions of Salespeople and Customer Persuasion," both in *Journal of Business Research* 49 (2000), pp. 149–56 and 183–91, respectively.

15. P. Sautter, M. R. Hyman, and V. Lukosius, "E-Tail Atmospherics," *Journal of Electronic Commerce Research* 5, no. 1 (2004), pp. 14–24.

16. M. J. Bitner, "Servicescapes," *Journal of Marketing,* April 1992, pp. 57–71. See also K. D. Hoffman, S. W. Kelley, and B. C. Chung, "A CIT Investigation of Servicescape Failures and Associated Recovery Strategies," *Journal of Services Marketing* 17, no. 4/5 (2003), pp. 322–40.

17. G. J. Gorn, A. Chattopadhyay, T. Yi, and D. W. Dahl, "Effects of Color as an Executional Cue in Advertising," *Management Science,* October 1997, pp. 1387–99.

18. See J. A. Bellizzi and R. E. Hite, "Environmental Color, Consumer Feelings, and Purchase Likelihood," *Psychology & Marketing,* September 1992, pp. 347–63.

19. B. E. Kahn and L. McAlister, *Grocery Revolution* (Reading, MA: Addison-Wesley, 1997).

20. G. J. Gorn, A. Chattopadhyay, J. Sengupta, and S. Tripathi, "Waiting for the Web," *Journal of Marketing Research,* May 2004, pp. 215–25.

21. D. J. Mitchell, B. E. Kahn, and S. C. Knasko, "There's Something in the Air," *Journal of Consumer Research,* September 1995, pp. 229–38.

22. E. R. Spangenberg, A. E. Crowley, and P. W. Henderson, "Improving the Store Environment," *Journal of Marketing,* April 1996, pp. 67–80.

23. A. R. Hirsch, "Effects of Ambient Odors on Slot-Machine Usage in a Las Vegas Casino," *Psychology & Marketing,* October 1995, pp. 585–94.

24. M. Wilkie, "Scent of a Market," *American Demographics,* August 1995, pp. 40–49.

25. M. Morrin and S. Ratneshwar, "The Impact of Ambient Scent on Evaluation, Attention, and Memory for Familiar and Unfamiliar Brands," *Journal of Business Research* 49 (2000), pp. 157–65.

26. P. F. Bone and P. S. Ellen, "Scents in the Marketplace," *Journal of Retailing* 75, no. 2 (1999), pp. 243–62.

27. P. Sloan, "Smelling Trouble," *Advertising Age,* September 11, 1995, p. 1.

28. See S. Oakes, "The Influence of the Musicscape within Service Environments," *Journal of Services Marketing* 4, no. 7 (2000), pp. 539–56.

29. J. C. Sweeney and F. Wyber, "The Role of Cognitions and Emotions in the Music-Approach-Avoidance Behavior Relationship," *Journal of Services Marketing* 16, no. 1 (2002), pp. 51–69; and C. Caldwell and S. A. Hibbert, "The Influence of Music Tempo and Musical Preference on Restaurant Patrons' Behavior," *Psychology & Marketing,* November 2002, pp. 895–917.

30. B. Zimmers, "Business Deals Put AEI Music CEO in Good Mood," *Puget Sound Business Journal,* June 23, 2000, p. 44; see also C. A. Olson, "Shopping to the Music Made Easy," *Billboard,* July 31, 1999, pp. 73–74.

31. See K. A. Machleit, S. A. Eroglu, and S. P. Mantel, "Perceived Retail Crowding and Shopping Satisfaction," *Journal of Consumer Psychology* 9, no. 1 (2000), pp. 29–42. For an exception, see F. Pons, M. Laroche, and M. Mourali, "Consumer Reactions to Crowded Retail Settings," *Psychology & Marketing,* July 2006, pp. 555–72.

32. S. A. Eroglu, K. A. Machleit, and J. C. Chebat, "The Interaction of Retail Density and Music Tempo," *Psychology & Marketing,* July 2005, pp. 577–89.

33. F. Pons, M. Laroche, and M. Mourali, "Consumer Reactions to Crowded Retail Settings."

34. T. R. Graeth, "Consumption Situations and the Effects of Brand Image on Consumers' Brand Evaluations," *Psychology & Marketing,* January 1997, pp. 49–70.

35. R. K. Ratner and B. E. Kahn, "The Impact of Private versus Public Consumption on Variety-Seeking Behavior," *Journal of Consumer Research,* September 2002, pp. 246–57.

36. See, e.g., D. W. Dahl, R. V. Manchanda, and J. J. Argo, "Embarrassment in Consumer Purchase," *Journal of Consumer Research,* December 2001, pp. 473–81. See also D. Grace, "How Embarrassing!" *Journal of Service Research,* February 2007, pp. 271–84.

37. Consumer Insight 13–1 is based on S. E. Beatty and M. E. Ferrell, "Impulse Buying," *Journal of Retailing,* Summer 1998, pp. 161–91; and X. Luo, "How Does Shopping with Others Influence Impulsive Purchasing?" *Journal of Consumer Psychology* 15, no. 4 (2005), pp. 288–94.

38. R. Batra and P. M. Homer, "The Situational Impact of Brand Image Beliefs," *Journal of Consumer Psychology* 14, no. 3 (2004), pp. 318–30.

39. L. A. Brannon and T. C. Brock, "Limiting Time for Responding Enhances Behavior Corresponding to the Merits of Compliance Appeals," *Journal of Consumer Psychology* 10, no. 3 (2001), pp. 135–46; and R. Suri and K. B. Monroe, "The Effects of Time Constraints on Consumers' Judgments of Prices and Products," *Journal of Consumer Research,* June 2003, pp. 92–104.

40. S. M. Nowlis, "The Effect of Time Pressure on the Choice of Brands That Differ in Quality, Price, and Product Features," *Marketing Letters,* October 1995, pp. 287–96; R. Dhar and S. M. Nowlis, "The Effect of Time Pressure on Consumer Choice Deferral," *Journal of Consumer Research,* March 1999, pp. 369–84; and R. Pieters and L. Warlop, "Visual Attention during Brand Choice," *International Journal of Research in Marketing,* February 1999, pp. 1–16.

41. P. Van Kenhove, K. De Wulf, and W. Van Waterschoot, "The Impact of Task Definition on Store-Attribute Saliences and Store Choice," *Journal of Retailing* 75, no. 1 (1999), pp. 125–37; P. Van Kenhove and K. De Wulf, "Income and Time Pressure," *International Review of Retail, Distribution and Consumer Research,* April 2000, pp. 149–66.

42. See B. H. Schmitt and C. J. Shultz II, "Situational Effects on Brand Preferences for Image Products," *Psychology & Marketing,* August 1995, pp. 433–46.

43. T. M. Lowrey, C. C. Otnes, and J. A. Ruth, "Social Influences on Dyadic Giving over Time," *Journal of Consumer Research,* March 2004, pp. 547–58.

44. For a review and framework, see D. Larsen and J. J. Watson, "A Guide Map to the Terrain of Gift Value," *Psychology & Marketing,* August 2001, pp. 889–906; see also G. Saad and T. Gill, "An Evolutionary Psychology Perspective on Gift Giving among Young Adults," *Psychology & Marketing,* September 2003, pp. 765–84.

45. M. A. McGrath, "Gender Differences in Gift Exchanges," *Psychology & Marketing,* August 1995, pp. 371–93; K. M. Palan, C. S. Areni, and P. Kiecker, "Gender Role Incongruency and Memorable Gift Exchange Experiences," J. F. Durgee and T. Sego, "Gift-Giving as a Metaphor for Understanding New Products That Delight," both in *Advances in Consumer Research,* vol. 28, eds. M. C. Gilly and J. Meyers-Levy (Provo, UT: Association for Consumer Research, 2001), pp. 51–57 and 64–69, respectively.

46. D. B. Wooten, "Qualitative Steps toward an Expanded Model of Anxiety in Gift-Giving," *Journal of Consumer Research,* June 2000, pp. 84–95.

47. See, e.g., J. A. Ruth, C. C. Otnes, and F. F. Brunel, "Gift Receipt and the Reformulation of Interpersonal Relationships," *Journal of Consumer Research,* March 1999, pp. 385–402.

48. R. W. Belk and G. S. Coon, "Gift Giving as Agapic Love," *Journal of Consumer Research,* December 1993, pp. 404–5. See also J. A. Ruth, F. F. Brunel, and C. C. Otnes, "An Investigation of the Power of Emotions in Relationship Realignment," *Psychology & Marketing,* January 2004, pp. 29–52.

49. C. S. Areni, P. Kiecker, and K. M. Palan, "Is It Better to Give than to Receive?" *Psychology & Marketing,* January 1998, pp. 81–109.

50. A. Joy, "Gift Giving in Hong Kong and the Continuum of Social Ties," *Journal of Consumer Research,* September 2001, pp. 239–55; and S. L. Lotz, S. Shim, and K. C. Gehrt, "A Study of Japanese Consumers' Cognitive Hierarchies in Formal and Informal Gift-Giving Situations," *Psychology & Marketing,* January 2003, pp. 59–85.

51. S.-Y. Park, "A Comparison of Korean and American Gift-Giving Behaviors," *Psychology & Marketing,* September 1998, pp. 577–93.

52. See R. P. Bagozzi, M. Gopinath, and P. U. Nyer, "The Role of Emotion in Marketing," *Journal of the Academy of Marketing Science,* Spring 1999, pp. 184–206; and H. T. Luomala and M. Laaksonen, "Contributions from Mood Research," *Psychology & Marketing,* March 2000, pp. 195–233.

53. M. B. Holbrook and M. P. Gardner, "Illustrating a Dynamic Model of the Mood-Updating Process in Consumer Behavior," *Psychology & Marketing,* March 2000, pp. 165–94.

54. J. P. Forgas and J. Ciarrochi, "On Being Happy and Possessive," *Psychology & Marketing,* March 2001, pp. 239–60; and R. Adaval, "Sometimes It Just Feels Right," *Journal of Consumer Research,* June 2001, pp. 1–17.

55. D. W. Rook and M. P. Gardner, "In the Mood," *Research in Consumer Behavior* 6 (1993), pp. 1–28; W. R. Swinyard, "The Effects of Mood, Involvement, and Quality of Store Experience on Shopping Intentions," *Journal of Consumer Research,* September 1993, pp. 271–80; and R. J. Faber and G.A. Christenson, "In the Mood to Buy," *Psychology & Marketing,* December 1996, pp. 803–19.

56. See Reference 7.

57. See, e.g., K. S. Coulter, "The Effects of Affective Responses to Media Context on Advertising Evaluations," *Journal of Advertising,* Winter 1998, pp. 41–51.

58. H. T. Luomala and M. Laaksonen, "A Qualitative Exploration of Mood-Regulatory Self-Gift Behaviors," *Journal of Economic Psychology* 20 (1999), pp. 147–82.

59. H. Mano, "The Influence of Pre-Existing Negative Affect on Store Purchase Intentions," *Journal of Retailing* 75, no. 2 (1999), pp. 149–73.

60. S. J. Gould, "An Interpretive Study of Purposeful, Mood Self-Regulating Consumption," *Psychology & Marketing,* July 1997, pp. 395–426.

61. See M. G. Meloy, "Mood-Driven Distortion of Product Information," *Journal of Consumer Research,* December 2000, pp. 345–58.

62. See P. A. Walsh and S. Spiggle, "Consumer Spending Patterns," in *Advances in Consumer Research,* vol. 21, eds. Allen and John,

pp. 35–40; and N. Karlsson, T. Garling, and M. Selart, "Explanations of Prior Income Changes on Buying Decisions," *Journal of Economic Psychology* 20 (1999), pp. 449–63.

63. See B. Gainer, "Ritual and Relationships," *Journal of Business Research,* March 1995, pp. 253–60.

64. See C. C. Otnes and L. M. Scott, "Something Old, Something New," *Journal of Advertising,* Spring 1996, pp. 33–50.

65. "$10 Billion for Mom," *CNNmoney,* April 21, 2004, http://money.cnn.com/.

66. A. Z. Cuneo, "Using Halloween to Scare Up Sales," *Advertising Age,* October 8, 2001, p. 4.

67. For a similar approach, see R. Brodie, "Segmentation and Market Structure When Both Consumer and Situational Characteristics Are Explanatory," *Psychology & Marketing,* September 1992, pp. 395–408.

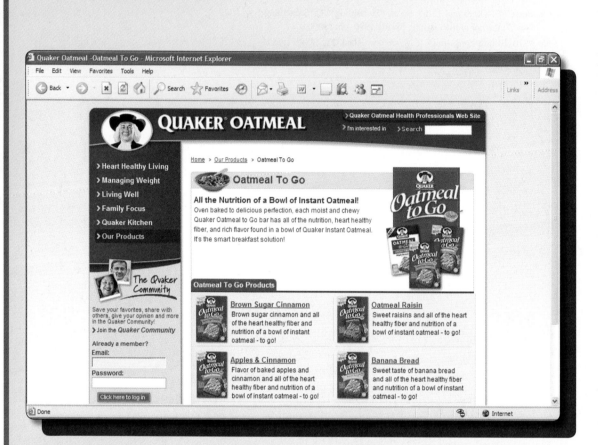

# Consumer Decision Process and Problem Recognition

■ Breakfast is big business—over $24 billion to be exact.[1] However, all is not well in the breakfast food category. Despite ongoing evidence from the scientific community about the health benefits of breakfast, it is not a top priority for many consumers. Some still don't buy into the importance of breakfast, with younger (ages 18 to 34), working, educated adults with higher incomes less likely than the average U.S. adult to believe that breakfast is more important than lunch or dinner. Others are simply too time pressed to eat breakfast or must settle for eating breakfast in the car or at their desks. Recent research puts the number of people eating breakfast at their desks at one in three.

Given the lack of importance placed on breakfast by many Americans and the time pressures that put limits on the nature of the morning meal, it is perhaps not surprising that the breakfast food industry is growing relatively slowly overall. The most recent statistics on cold cereal, for example, show it declining by 1.4 percent annually over a four-year period.

Two categories of breakfast food that are seeing high levels of growth are drinkable yogurt and breakfast bars. Yogurt drinks have seen annual growth of nearly 60 percent and breakfast bars of roughly 11 percent. The portability of yogurt drinks and breakfast bars clearly plays in their favor for those consumers who are time crunched and thus likely plays a large role in their growth. However, this growth obscures the fact that these categories are still relatively small, with each accounting for less than 4 percent of the overall breakfast food market.

Large cereal marketers such as Quaker Oats, General Mills, and Kellogg's clearly need a boost from convenient and healthy options such as breakfast bars. Not surprisingly, the number of new products in this category has grown exponentially in recent years. One such addition is Quaker Oat's "Quaker Oatmeal to Go" bar. This bar is meant to combine health and convenience. According to one health expert:

Too often, when people are on the go in the morning, they tend to reach for high-fat, nutrient-poor foods such as donuts, muffins, or pastries. [Launched] just in time for Heart Health Month, Quaker Oatmeal to Go is a great choice for busy people who want a nutritious, filling breakfast and the proven heart-health benefits of oatmeal.

By combining health and convenience, breakfast bars and drinkable yogurt seem poised to expand the breakfast category, particularly among younger working professionals. What is required is for these consumers to recognize a problem—that is, to recognize the importance of breakfast over other meals and make it a priority in their busy day.

---

This chapter examines the nature of the consumer decision process and analyzes the first step in that process—problem recognition. Within problem recognition, we focus on (1) the process of problem recognition, (2) the uncontrollable determinants of problem recognition, and (3) marketing strategies based on the problem recognition process.

# TYPES OF CONSUMER DECISIONS

The term *consumer decision* produces an image of an individual carefully evaluating the attributes of a set of products, brands, or services and rationally selecting the one that solves a clearly recognized need for the least cost. It has a rational, functional connotation. Consumers do make many decisions in this manner; however, many other decisions involve little conscious effort. Further, many consumer decisions focus not on brand attributes but rather on the feelings or emotions associated with acquiring or using the brand or with the situation in which the product is purchased or used. Thus, a brand may be selected not because of an attribute (price, style, functional characteristics) but because "it makes me feel good" or "my friends will like it."[2]

Although purchases and related consumption behavior driven by emotional or situational needs have characteristics distinct from the traditional attribute-based model, the decision process model provides useful insights into all types of consumer purchases. As we describe the process of consumer decision making in this and the next four chapters, we will indicate how it helps us understand emotion-, situation-, and attribute-based decisions.

Consumer decisions are frequently the result of a single problem, for example, running low on gasoline. At other times, they result from the convergence of several problems, such as an aging automobile and a growing feeling of inadequacy or low self-esteem. Furthermore, once the decision process begins, it may evolve and become more complex with multiple goals. A consumer noticing a simple need for gas may want to minimize the price paid, avoid one or more brands because of their environmental record, and decide to find a station with food service attached. This consumer may wind up choosing between a station with a lower price and its own food service, or another station with a higher price but with a preferred food outlet such as Taco Bell attached, or perhaps spending the extra time to buy gas at one and food at the other.[3]

As Figure 14–1 indicates, there are various types of consumer decision processes.[4] As the consumer moves from a very low level of involvement *with the purchase* to a high level of involvement, decision making becomes increasingly complex. While purchase involvement is a continuum, it is useful to consider nominal, limited, and extended decision making as general descriptions of the types of processes that occur along various points on the continuum. Keep in mind that the types of decision processes are not distinct but rather blend into each other.

## Involvement and Types of Decision Making    FIGURE 14–1

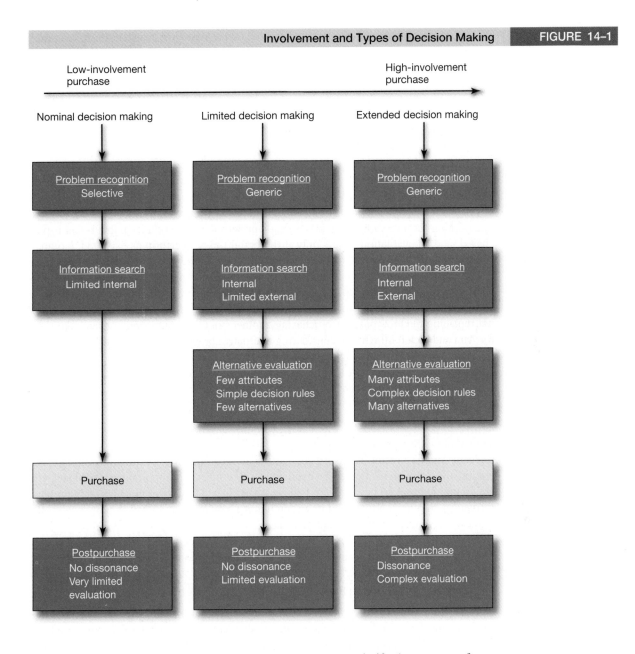

Before describing each type of decision process, we must clarify the concept of purchase involvement. We define **purchase involvement** as *the level of concern for, or interest in, the purchase process triggered by the need to consider a particular purchase.* Thus, purchase involvement is a *temporary state* of an individual or household. It is influenced by the interaction of individual, product, and situational characteristics.

Note that purchase involvement is *not* the same as **product involvement** or enduring involvement. A consumer may be very involved with a brand (Starbucks or Saturn) or a product category (coffee or cars) and yet have a very low level of involvement with a particular purchase of that product because of brand loyalty, time pressures, or other reasons. For example, think of your favorite brand of soft drink or other beverage. You may be quite loyal to that brand, think it is superior to other brands, and have strong, favorable feelings about it. However, when you want a soft drink, you probably just buy your preferred brand without much thought.

Or a consumer may have a rather low level of involvement with a product (school supplies or automobile tires) but have a high level of purchase involvement because he or she desires to set an example for a child, impress a friend who is on the shopping trip, or save money.

The following sections provide a brief description of how the purchasing process changes as purchase involvement increases.

## Nominal Decision Making

**Nominal decision making,** sometimes referred to as *habitual decision making,* in effect *involves no decision per se.* As Figure 14–1 indicates, a problem is recognized, internal search (long-term memory) provides a single preferred solution (brand), that brand is purchased, and an evaluation occurs only if the brand fails to perform as expected. Nominal decisions occur when there is very low involvement with the purchase.

A completely nominal decision does not even include consideration of the "do not purchase" alternative. For example, you might notice that you are nearly out of Aim toothpaste and resolve to purchase some the next time you are at the store. You don't even consider not replacing the toothpaste or purchasing another brand. At the store, you scan the shelf for Aim and pick it up without considering alternative brands, its price, or other potentially relevant factors.

Nominal decisions can be broken into two distinct categories: brand loyal decisions and repeat purchase decisions. These two categories are described briefly below and examined in detail in Chapter 18.

### Brand Loyal Purchases

At one time, you may have been highly involved in selecting a brand of toothpaste and, in response, used an extensive decision-making process. Having selected Aim as a result of this process, you may now purchase it without further consideration, even though using the best available toothpaste is still important to you. Thus, you are committed to Aim because you believe it best meets your overall needs and you have formed an emotional attachment to it (you like it). You are brand loyal. It will be very difficult for a competitor to gain your patronage.

In this example, you have a fairly high degree of product involvement but a low degree of purchase involvement because of your brand loyalty. Should you encounter a challenge to the superiority of Aim, perhaps through a news article, you would most likely engage in a high-involvement decision process before changing brands.

### Repeat Purchases

In contrast, you may believe that all ketchup is about the same and you may not attach much importance to the product category or purchase. Having tried Del Monte and found it satisfactory, you now purchase it whenever you need ketchup. Thus, you are a repeat purchaser of Del Monte ketchup, but you are not committed to it.

Should you encounter a challenge to the wisdom of buying Del Monte the next time you need ketchup, perhaps because of a point-of-sale price discount, you would probably engage in only a limited decision process before deciding on which brand to purchase.

## Limited Decision Making

**Limited decision making** involves internal and limited external search, few alternatives, simple decision rules on a few attributes, and little postpurchase evaluation. It covers the middle ground between nominal decision making and extended decision making. In its simplest form (lowest level of purchase involvement), limited decision making is similar to nominal decision making. For example, while in a store you may notice a point-of-purchase display for Jell-O and pick up two boxes without seeking information beyond your memory that "Jell-O tastes good," or "Gee, I haven't had Jell-O in a long time." In addition, you may have considered no other alternative except possibly a very limited examination of a "do not buy" option. Or you may have a decision rule that you buy the cheapest brand of instant coffee available. When you run low on coffee (problem recognition), you simply examine coffee prices the next time you are in the store and select the cheapest brand.

Limited decision making also occurs in response to some emotional or situational needs. For example, you may decide to purchase a new brand or product because you are bored with the current, otherwise satisfactory, brand. This decision might involve evaluating only the newness or novelty of the available alternatives.[5] Or you might evaluate a purchase in terms of the actual or anticipated behavior of others. For example, you might order or refrain from ordering wine with a meal depending on the observed or expected orders of your dinner companions.

In general, limited decision making involves recognizing a problem for which there are several possible solutions. There is internal and a limited amount of external search. A few alternatives are evaluated on a few dimensions using simple selection rules. The purchase and use of the product are given very little evaluation afterward, unless there is a service problem or product failure.

## Extended Decision Making

As Figure 14–1 indicates, **extended decision making** involves an extensive internal and external information search followed by a complex evaluation of multiple alternatives and significant postpurchase evaluation. It is the response to a high level of purchase involvement. After the purchase, doubt about its correctness is likely and a thorough evaluation of the purchase takes place. Relatively few consumer decisions reach this level of complexity. However, products such as homes, personal computers, and complex recreational items such as home theatre systems are frequently purchased via extended decision making.

Even decisions that are heavily emotional may involve substantial cognitive effort. For example, a consumer may agonize over a decision to take a ski trip or visit parents even though the needs being met and the criteria being evaluated are largely emotions or feelings rather than attributes per se, and are therefore typically fewer in number with less external information available.

As Figure 14–1 illustrates, problem recognition is the first stage of the decision process. We will describe this stage and discuss the marketing applications associated with it in the balance of this chapter. We devote the next four chapters to the remaining four stages of the consumer decision process and discuss the relevant marketing applications in those chapters.

Our discussion of the decision process is based primarily on studies conducted in America. Although the evidence is limited, it appears that consumers in other cultures use similar processes.[6]

# THE PROCESS OF PROBLEM RECOGNITION

A day rarely passes in which a person does not face multiple problems that are resolved by consuming products and services. Routine problems of depletion, such as the need to get gasoline as the gauge approaches empty or the need to replace a frequently used food item, are readily recognized, defined, and resolved. The unexpected breakdown of a major appliance such as a refrigerator creates an unplanned problem that is also easily recognized but is often more difficult to resolve. Recognition of other problems, such as the need for

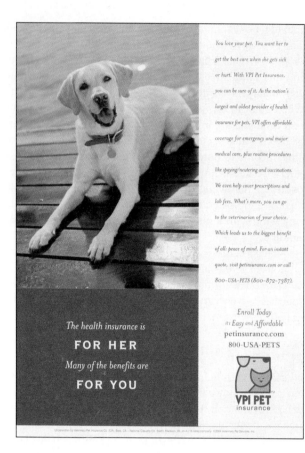

a camera phone or a GPS system in the car, may take longer, as they may be subtle and evolve slowly over time.

Feelings, such as boredom, anxiety, or the "blues," may arise quickly or slowly over time. Such feelings are often recognized as problems subject to solution by purchasing behavior (I'm sad, I think I'll go to the mall/to a movie/to a restaurant). At other times, such feelings may trigger consumption behaviors without deliberate decision making. A person feeling restless may eat snack food without really thinking about it. In this case, the problem remains unrecognized (at the conscious level) and the solutions tried are often inappropriate (eating may not reduce restlessness).

Marketers develop products to help consumers solve problems. They also attempt to help consumers recognize problems, sometimes well in advance of their occurrence (see Illustration 14–1).

## The Nature of Problem Recognition

Problem recognition is the first stage in the consumer decision process. **Problem recognition** is the result of a discrepancy between a desired state and an actual state that is sufficient to arouse and activate the decision process.[7] An **actual state** is the way an individual perceives his or her feelings and situation to be at the present time. A **desired state** is the way an individual *wants* to feel or be at the present time. For example, you probably don't want to be bored on Friday night. If you find yourself alone and becoming bored, you would treat this as a problem because your actual state (being bored) and your desired

**The Process of Problem Recognition** | FIGURE 14–2

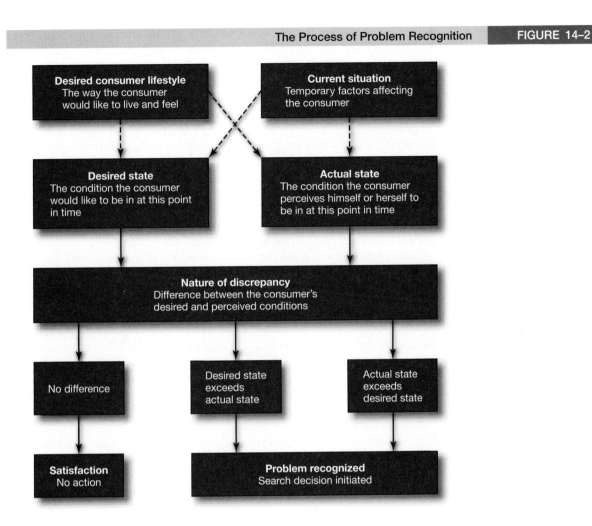

state (being pleasantly occupied) are different. You could then choose to watch a television program, rent a video, call a friend, go out, or take a wide array of other actions.

The kind of action taken by consumers in response to a recognized problem relates directly to the problem's importance to the consumer, the situation, and the dissatisfaction or inconvenience created by the problem.

Without recognition of a problem, there is no need for a decision. This condition is shown in Figure 14–2, when there is no discrepancy between the consumer's desired state (what the consumer would like) and the actual state (what the consumer perceives as already existing). Thus, if Friday night arrives and you find yourself engrossed in a novel, your desire to be pleasantly occupied (desired state) and your condition of enjoying a novel would be consistent, and you would have no reason to search for other activities.

On the other hand, when there is a discrepancy between a consumer desire and the perceived actual state, recognition of a problem occurs. Figure 14–2 indicates that any time the desired state is perceived as being greater than or less than the actual state, a problem exists. For example, being pleasantly occupied (desired state) would generally exceed being bored (actual state) and result in problem recognition. However, if your roommate suddenly showed up with a rowdy party, you might find yourself with more stimulation (actual state) than the medium level you actually desire. This too would result in problem recognition.

In Figure 14–2, consumer desires are shown to be the result of the desired lifestyle of the consumer (as described in Chapter 12) and the current situation (time pressures, physical surroundings, and so forth, as described in Chapter 13). Thus, a consumer whose self-concept and desired lifestyle focus on outdoor activities will desire frequent participation in such activities. A current situation of new snow in the mountains or warm weather at the beach would tend to increase that person's desire to be engaged in outdoor sports.

Perceptions of the actual state are also determined by a consumer's lifestyle and current situation. Consumers' lifestyles are a major determinant of their actual state because that is how they choose to live given the constraints imposed by their resources. Thus, a consumer who has chosen to raise a family, have significant material possessions, and pursue a demanding career is likely to have little free time for outdoor activities (actual state). The current situation—a day off work, a big project due, or a sick child—also has a major impact on how consumers perceive the actual situation.

It is important to note that it is the consumer's *perception* of the actual state that drives problem recognition, not some objective reality. Consumers who smoke cigars may believe that this activity is not harming their health because they do not inhale. These consumers do not recognize a problem with this behavior despite the reality that it is harmful.

**The Desire to Resolve Recognized Problems**    The level of one's desire to resolve a particular problem depends on two factors: (1) *the magnitude of the discrepancy between the desired and actual states,* and (2) *the relative importance of the problem.* An individual could desire to have a car that averages at least 25 miles per gallon while still meeting certain size and power desires. If his or her current car obtains an average of 22 miles per gallon, a discrepancy exists, but it may not be large enough to motivate the consumer to proceed to the next step in the decision process.

On the other hand, a large discrepancy may exist and the consumer may not proceed to information search because the *relative importance* of the problem is small. A consumer may desire a new Volkswagen and own a 15-year-old Toyota. The discrepancy is large. However, the relative importance of this particular discrepancy may be small compared with other consumption problems such as those related to housing, utilities, and food. Relative importance is a critical concept because all consumers have budget constraints, time constraints, or both. Only the relatively more important problems are likely to be solved. In general, importance is determined by how critical the problem is to the maintenance of the consumer's desired lifestyle.

## Types of Consumer Problems

Consumer problems may be either active or inactive. An **active problem** is *one the consumer is aware of or will become aware of in the normal course of events.* An **inactive problem** is *one of which the consumer is not aware.* (This concept is very similar to the concept of felt need discussed in the "Diffusion of Innovations" section of Chapter 7.) The following is a classic marketing example which should clarify the distinction between active and inactive problems.

Timberlane Lumber Co. acquired a source of supply of Honduran pitch pine. This natural product lights at the touch of a match even when damp and burns for 15 to 20 minutes. It will not flare up and is therefore relatively safe. It can be procured in sticks 15 to 18 inches long and 1 inch in diameter. These sticks can be used to ignite fireplace fires, or they can be shredded and used to ignite charcoal grills.

Prior to marketing the product, Timberlane commissioned a marketing study to estimate demand and guide in developing marketing strategy. Two large samples of potential consumers were interviewed. The first sample was asked how they lit their fireplace fires and what problems they had with this procedure. Almost all the respondents used newspaper, kindling, or both, and very few experienced any problems. The new product was then described, and the respondents were asked to express the likelihood that they would purchase such a product. Only a small percentage expressed any interest. However, a sample of consumers that were paid to use the new product for several weeks felt it was a substantial improvement over existing methods and expressed a strong desire to continue using the product. Thus, the problem was there (because the new product was strongly preferred over the old by those who tried it), but most consumers were not aware of it. This is an *inactive problem*. Before the product can be successfully sold, the firm must activate problem recognition.

In contrast, a substantial percentage of those interviewed about lighting charcoal fires expressed a strong concern about the safety of liquid charcoal lighter. These individuals expressed great interest in purchasing a safer product. This is an *active problem*. Timberlane need not worry about problem recognition in this case. Instead, it can concentrate on illustrating how its product solves the problem that the consumers already know exists.

As this example indicates, active and inactive problems require different marketing strategies. Active problems require the marketer only to convince consumers that its brand is the superior solution. Consumers are already aware of the problem. In contrast, inactive problems require the marketer to convince consumers that they *have* the problem *and* that the marketer's brand is a superior solution to the problem. This is a much more difficult task.

Illustration 14–2 shows two ads relating to active and inactive problems. The ad on the left first must make consumers aware of a problem (inactive) they likely didn't know of.

**ILLUSTRATION 14–2**

Often, marketers need to trigger problem recognition in market segments. However, at other times, the market is well aware of the problem and the communication can focus on the brand's ability to solve the problem.

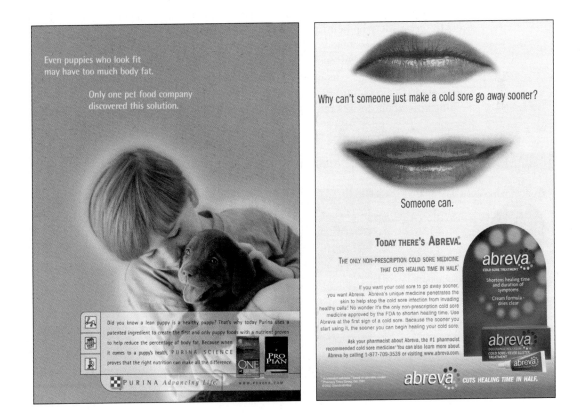

The ad on the right assumes consumers are aware of the problem (active) and simply focuses on its unique ability to solve it.

# UNCONTROLLABLE DETERMINANTS OF PROBLEM RECOGNITION

A discrepancy between what is desired by a consumer and what the consumer has is the necessary condition for problem recognition. A discrepancy can be the result of a variety of factors that influence consumer desires, perceptions of the existing state, or both. These factors are often beyond the direct influence of the marketing manager, such as a change in family composition. Figure 14–3 summarizes the major nonmarketing factors that influence problem recognition. The marketing factors influencing problem recognition are discussed in the next section of this chapter.

Most of the nonmarketing factors that affect problem recognition are fairly obvious and logical. Most were described in some detail in prior chapters. For example, as we discussed in Chapter 2, a person's culture affects almost all aspects of his or her desired state. Thus, the desire to be recognized as an independent, unique person with distinctive behaviors and possessions differs sharply between American and Japanese consumers because of cultural influences.

Previous decisions and individual development were not discussed in earlier chapters. A previous decision to buy a bike or skis could lead to a current desire to have a car rack to carry them. A decision to become a homeowner may trigger desires for numerous home and garden items. Past decisions may also deplete purchasing power with the result that fewer problems are recognized or are assigned sufficient importance to trigger action.[8] Consumer Insight 14-1 examines the role that prior consumption plays in driving consumers to seek variety in their future purchases.

Individual development causes many changes in the desired state. As people age, their needs and desires evolve noticeably. An ad for Scotch appearing in men's magazines recognized this—its headline, "When you were young, you didn't like girls either," appeared over a picture of an attractive woman and a bottle of Scotch. As individuals gain skills, their desires related to those skills change. Beginning skiers, musicians, and

## FIGURE 14–3      Nonmarketing Factors Affecting Problem Recognition

gardeners typically desire products and capabilities that will no longer be appropriate as their skills increase.

Government agencies and various consumer groups actively attempt to trigger problem recognition, often in relation to the consumption of various products. Warning labels on alcohol and cigarettes are two examples of these types of efforts as are antismoking campaigns, and campaigns that stress the dangers of drinking and driving (see Illustration 14–3).

# MARKETING STRATEGY AND PROBLEM RECOGNITION

Marketing managers have four concerns related to problem recognition. First, they need to know the problems consumers are facing. Second, they must know how to develop the marketing mix to solve consumer problems. Third, managers occasionally want

**ILLUSTRATION 14–3**

Government agencies and nonprofit groups often attempt to generate problem recognition in consumers. This is often done in an attempt to change behaviors that are harmful to the individual or society.

505

to cause consumers to recognize problems. Finally, there are times when they desire to suppress problem recognition among consumers. The remainder of this chapter discusses these issues.

## Discovering Consumer Problems

A wide variety of approaches are used to determine the problems consumers face. The most common approach undoubtedly is *intuition;* that is, a manager can analyze a given product category and logically determine where improvements could be made. Thus, soundless vacuum cleaners or lawnmowers are logical solutions to potential consumer problems. The difficulty with this approach is that the problem identified may actually be of low importance to most consumers. Therefore, several research techniques are also employed.

A common research technique is the *survey,* which asks relatively large numbers of individuals about the problems they are facing. This was the technique used by Timberlane, as described earlier. A second common technique is *focus groups*. Focus groups are composed of 8 to 12 similar individuals—such as male college students, lawyers, or teenage girls—brought together to discuss a particular topic. A moderator is present to keep the discussion moving and focused on the topic, but otherwise the sessions are free flowing (see Appendix A for more details).

Both surveys and focus groups tend to take one of three approaches to problem identification: *activity analysis, product analysis,* or *problem analysis*. A fourth approach, *human factors research,* does not rely on surveys or focus groups. *Emotion research,* a fifth effort, attempts to discover the role emotions play in problem recognition.

**Activity Analysis**    Activity analysis focuses on a particular activity, such as preparing dinner, maintaining the lawn, or swimming. The survey or focus group attempts to determine what problems consumers encounter during the performance of the activity. For example, Johnson Wax had a national panel of women report on how they cared for their hair and the problems they encountered. Their responses revealed a perceived problem with oiliness that existing brands could not resolve. As a result, Johnson Wax developed Agree Shampoo and Agree Crème Rinse, both of which were successful for some time. More recently, shampoos have been developed specifically for the hair-related problems associated with swimming in chlorinated pools.

**Product Analysis**    Product analysis is similar to activity analysis but examines the purchase or use of a particular product or brand. Thus, consumers may be asked about problems associated with using their mountain bikes or laptop computers. Curlee Clothing used focus groups to analyze the purchase and use of men's clothing. The results indicated a high level of insecurity in purchasing men's clothing. This insecurity was combined with a distrust of both the motivations and competence of retail sales personnel. As a result, Curlee initiated a major effort to train retail sales personnel through specially prepared films and training sessions.

**Problem Analysis**    Problem analysis takes the opposite approach from the previous techniques. It starts with a problem and asks respondents to indicate which activities, products, or brands are associated with (or perhaps could eliminate) those problems. For example, a study dealing with packaging problems could include questions such as these:

　　　　　　　———————— packages are hard to open.

　　Packages of ————— are hard to reseal.

_____ doesn't pour well.

Packages of _____ don't fit on the shelf.

Packages of _____ waste too many resources.

A recent survey examined a pervasive problem in America—namely, getting and staying organized. The study found that 89 percent of adults feel that they could use help organizing some aspect of their lives. In addition, 54 percent say they have or would purchase products or hire a service to get organized.[10] Marketers are responding with TV shows like "Mission: Organization" and stores like Organized Living, devoted solely to home-organization solutions. There is even a blog devoted to the topic (http://organized-living.com/tipblog.htm)!

**Human Factors Research**   Human factors research attempts to determine human capabilities in areas such as vision, strength, response time, flexibility, and fatigue and the effect on these capabilities of lighting, temperature, and sound. Many methods can be employed in human factors research. However, observational techniques such as slow-motion and time-lapse photography, video recording, and event recorders are particularly useful.

This type of research can sometimes identify functional problems that consumers are unaware of. For example, it can be used in the design of such products as vacuum cleaners, lawnmowers, kitchen utensils, and computers to minimize user fatigue. The growth in carpal tunnel syndrome (injury resulting from repeating the same movements such as inputting data into a computer over time) has resulted in substantial interest in this area.

**Emotion Research**   Marketers are increasingly conducting research on the role of emotions in problem recognition and resolution. Common approaches are focus group research and personal interviews that examine the emotions associated with certain problems. Surveys can also be used (see Table 10–4 for specific measures). For example, researchers are beginning to examine how consumers cope with the negative emotions associated with product or service failures. Findings suggest that certain emotions (e.g., anger) are associated with certain coping strategies (e.g., confrontation). This type of research is critical to marketers in helping them anticipate consumer reactions to problems and train their customer service personnel to respond appropriately.[11] For subtle or sensitive problems and emotions, projective techniques (see Appendix A, Table A–2) may be necessary.[12]

**ILLUSTRATION 14–4**

A key task of marketers is to identify consumer problems and to position their brands as solutions for them.

# Responding to Consumer Problems

Once a consumer problem is identified, the manager may structure the marketing mix to solve the problem. This can involve developing a new product or altering an existing one, modifying channels of distribution, changing pricing policy, or revising advertising strategy. For example, in Illustration 14–4 the product is being positioned as a unique solution to a problem.

As you approach graduation, you will be presented with opportunities to purchase insurance, acquire credit cards, and solve other problems associated with the onset of financial independence and a major change in lifestyle. These opportunities reflect various firms' knowledge that many individuals in your situation face problems that their products will help solve.

Weekend and night store hours and, in part, the rapid growth of Internet stores are a response of retailers to the consumer problem of limited weekday shopping opportunities. Solving this problem has become particularly important to families with both spouses employed.

The examples described above represent only a small sample of the ways marketers react to consumer problem recognition. Each firm must be aware of the consumer problems it can solve, which consumers have these problems, and the situations in which the problems arise.

## Helping Consumers Recognize Problems

There are occasions when the manager will want to cause problem recognition rather than react to it. In the earlier example, Timberlane faced having to activate problem recognition in order to sell its product as a fireplace starter. Toy marketers are attempting to reduce their dependence on the Christmas season by activating problem recognition at other times of the year. For example, Fisher-Price has had "rainy day" and "sunny day" promotions in the spring and summer months. Illustrations 14–1 and 14–2, presented earlier, show attempts to activate problem recognition.

**Generic versus Selective Problem Recognition**   Two basic approaches to causing problem recognition are *generic problem recognition* and *selective problem recognition*. These are analogous to the economic concepts of generic and selective demand.

**Generic problem recognition** involves a *discrepancy that a variety of brands within a product category can reduce*. Generally, a firm will attempt to influence generic problem recognition when the problem is latent or of low importance and one of the following conditions exists:

* It is early in the product life cycle.
* The firm has a high percentage of the market.
* External search after problem recognition is apt to be limited.
* It is an industrywide cooperative effort.

Telephone sales programs often attempt to arouse problem recognition, in part because the salesperson can then limit external search to one brand. Advertising for food-related cooperatives such as milk, beef, and pork frequently focuses on generic problem recognition. Illustration 14–5 is an example of one of the most notable ongoing campaigns of this type. Note that the ad does not promote a specific brand.

Firms with large market shares in a product category often focus on generic problem recognition because any sales increase will probably come to their brands. However, a smaller firm that generates generic problem recognition for its product category may be generating more sales for its competitors than for itself. But even firms with large market share can lose share if generic problem recognition campaigns are not done carefully. In the early 1990s, Borden increased marketing efforts for its popular Creamette pasta brand substantially and promoted recipes using pasta. Its sales increased only 1.6 percent, compared with the industry's growth of 5.5 percent.[13] Its efforts apparently helped the sales of its competitors more than its own sales.

**Selective problem recognition** involves *a discrepancy that only one brand can solve*. The ad shown in Illustration 14–6 is focused on creating selective problem recognition. Firms attempt to cause selective problem recognition to gain or maintain market share,

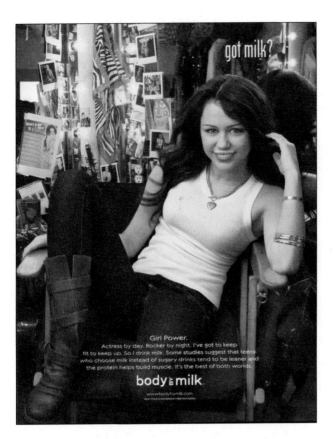

**ILLUSTRATION 14–5**

This ad will generate problem recognition that any brand could resolve. This is known as generic problem recognition.

whereas increasing generic problem recognition generally results in an expansion of the total market.

## Approaches to Activating Problem Recognition   How can a firm influence prob-

lem recognition? Recall that problem recognition is a function of the (1) *importance* and (2) *magnitude* of a discrepancy between the desired state and an existing state. Thus, a firm can attempt to influence the size of the discrepancy by altering the desired state or perceptions of the existing state. Or the firm can attempt to influence perceptions of the importance of an existing discrepancy.

Many marketing efforts attempt to *influence the desired state;* that is, marketers often advertise the benefits their products will provide, hoping that these benefits will become desired by consumers. The ad in Illustration 14–7 attempts to influence the desired state by showing just how good the product can make you look.

It is also possible to *influence perceptions of the existing state* through advertisements. Many personal care and social products take this approach.

**ILLUSTRATION 14–6**

This ad will generate problem recognition that is best solved by one brand. This is known as selective problem recognition.

This ad attempts to influence the desired state by showing the optimal outcomes that are possible.

"Even your best friend won't tell you . . ." or "Kim is a great worker but this coffee . . ." are examples of messages designed to generate concern about an existing state. The desired state is assumed to be fresh breath and good coffee. These messages are designed to cause individuals to question if their existing state coincides with this desired state.

Illustration 14–8 is designed to change consumer perceptions of the actual state which is described in the headline, and then change it.

Critics frequently question the ethics of activating problem recognition. This is particularly true for problems related to status or social acceptance. This debate is generally discussed in terms of marketers' "creating needs," which we discussed in Chapter 10.

**The Timing of Problem Recognition**   Consumers often recognize problems at times when purchasing a solution is difficult or impossible, as the following examples demonstrate:

- We decide we need snow chains when caught in a blizzard.
- We become aware of a need for insurance *after* an accident.
- We desire a flower bed full of tulips in the spring but forgot to plant bulbs in the fall.
- We want cold medicine when we are sick but don't feel like driving to the store.

In some instances, marketers attempt to help consumers solve such problems after they arise. For example, some pharmacies will make home deliveries. However, the more common strategy is to trigger problem recognition in advance of the actual problem (see Illustration 14–1). That is, it is often to the consumer's and marketer's advantage for the consumer to recognize and solve potential problems *before* they become actual problems.

Some companies, particularly insurance companies, attempt to initiate problem recognition through mass media advertising; others rely more on point-of-purchase displays and other in-store influences (see Chapter 17). Retailers, as well as manufacturers, are involved in this activity. For example, prior to snow season, the following sign was placed on a large rack of snow shovels in the main aisle of a large hardware store:

REMEMBER LAST WINTER
WHEN YOU *NEEDED*
A SNOW SHOVEL?
THIS YEAR BE PREPARED!

## Suppressing Problem Recognition

As we have seen, competition, consumer organizations, and governmental agencies occasionally introduce information in the marketplace that triggers problem recognition that particular marketers would prefer to avoid. The American tobacco industry has made strenuous attempts to minimize consumer recognition of the health problems associated with cigarette smoking. For example, a Newport cigarette advertisement showed a happy, laughing couple under the headline, "Alive with pleasure." This could easily be interpreted as an attempt to minimize any problem recognition caused by the mandatory warning at the bottom of the advertisement: "Warning: The Surgeon General has determined that cigarette smoking is dangerous to your health."

Obviously, marketers do not want their current customers to recognize problems with their brands. Effective quality control and distribution (limited out-of-stock situations) are important in this effort. Packages and package inserts that assure the consumer of the wisdom of their purchase are also common.

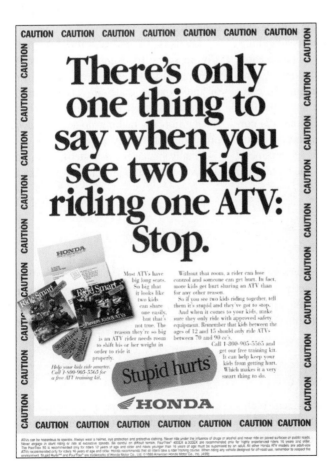

**ILLUSTRATION 14–8**

Changing perceptions about the actual state is a way to activate problem recognition and ultimately change behaviors.

## SUMMARY

Consumer decision making becomes more extensive and complex as *purchase involvement* increases. The lowest level of purchase involvement is represented by *nominal decisions:* A problem is recognized, long-term memory provides a single preferred brand, that brand is purchased, and only limited postpurchase evaluation occurs. As one moves from *limited decision making* toward *extended decision making,* information search increases, alternative evaluation becomes more extensive and complex, and postpurchase evaluation becomes more thorough.

*Problem recognition* involves the existence of a discrepancy between the consumer's desired state (what the consumer would like) and the actual state (what the consumer perceives as already existing). Both the desired state and the actual state are influenced by the consumer's lifestyle and current situation. If the discrepancy between these two states is sufficiently large and important, the consumer will begin to search for a solution to the problem.

A number of factors beyond the control of the marketing manager can affect problem recognition. The desired state is commonly influenced by (1) culture/subculture, (2) social status, (3) reference groups, (4) household characteristics, (5) financial status/expectations, (6) previous decisions, (7) individual development, (8) emotions, (9) motives, and (10) the current situation. The actual state is influenced by (1) past decisions, (2) normal depletion, (3) product/brand performance, (4) individual development, (5) emotions, (6) government/consumer groups, (7) availability of products, and the (8) current situation.

Before marketing managers can respond to problem recognition generated by outside factors, they must be able to *identify* consumer problems. Surveys and focus groups using *activity, product,* or *problem analysis* are commonly used. *Human factors research* approaches the same task from an observational perspective. *Emotion research* focuses on the role of emotions in problem recognition and resolution.

Once managers are aware of problem recognition patterns among their target market, they can react by designing the marketing mix to solve the recognized problem. This may involve product development or repositioning, a change in store hours, a different price, or a host of other marketing strategies.

Marketing managers often want to influence problem recognition rather than react to it. They may desire to generate *generic problem recognition,* a discrepancy that a variety of brands within a product category can reduce, or to induce *selective problem recognition,* a discrepancy that only one brand in the product category can solve.

Attempts to *activate problem recognition* generally do so by focusing on the desired state. However, attempts to make consumers aware of negative aspects of the existing state are also common. In addition, marketers attempt to influence the timing of problem recognition by making consumers aware of potential problems before they arise.

Finally, managers may attempt to minimize or suppress problem recognition by current users of their brands.

## KEY TERMS

Active problem  502
Actual state  500
Desired state  500
Extended decision making  499

Generic problem recognition  508
Inactive problem  502
Limited decision making  498
Nominal decision making  498

Problem recognition  500
Product involvement  497
Purchase involvement  497
Selective problem recognition  508

## INTERNET EXERCISES

1. Visit several general interest or entertainment Web sites that contain ads. Find and describe an ad that attempts to trigger problem recognition. How does it do this?

2. Visit several company Web sites. Find and describe one that attempts to trigger problem recognition. How does it do this?

3. Monitor several chat sites or interest groups for a week. Prepare a report on how a marketer could learn about the consumption problems of consumers by doing this.

## REVIEW QUESTIONS

1. What is meant by *purchase involvement*? How does it differ from product involvement?
2. How does consumer decision making change as purchase involvement increases?
3. What is the role of *emotion* in the consumer decision process?
4. How do *nominal, limited,* and *extended decision making* differ? How do the two types of nominal decision making differ?
5. What is *problem recognition*?
6. What influences the motivation to resolve a recognized problem?
7. What is the difference between an *active* and an *inactive problem*? Why is this distinction important?
8. How does lifestyle relate to problem recognition?
9. What are the main uncontrollable factors that influence the *desired* state?
10. What are the main uncontrollable factors that influence the *existing* state?
11. How can you measure problem recognition?
12. In what ways can marketers react to problem recognition? Give several examples.
13. How does *generic problem recognition* differ from *selective problem recognition*? Under what conditions would a firm attempt to influence generic problem recognition? Why?
14. How can a firm cause problem recognition? Give examples.
15. How can a firm suppress problem recognition?

## DISCUSSION QUESTIONS

16. What products do you think *generally* are associated with nominal, limited, and extended decision making? Under what conditions, if any, would these products be associated with a different form of decision making?
17. What products do you think *generally* are purchased or used for emotional reasons? How would the decision process differ for an emotion-driven purchase compared to a more functional purchase?
18. What products do you think *generally* are associated with brand loyal decision making and which with repeat purchase decision making? Justify your response.
19. Describe a purchase you made using nominal decision making, one using limited decision making, and one using extended decision making. What caused you to use each type of decision process?
20. Describe two recent purchases you have made. What uncontrollable factors, if any, triggered problem recognition? Did they affect the desired state, the actual state, or both?
21. How would you measure consumer problems among the following?
    a. College students
    b. Children aged 2 to 4
    c. Internet shoppers
    d. New residents in a town
    e. Vegans
    f. Newly married couples
22. How would you determine the existence of consumer problems of relevance to a marketer of the following?
    a. Women's spa
    b. Internet retail outlets
    c. Online health food store
    d. Public library
    e. Alaskan fishing lodge
    f. Mountain bikes
23. Discuss the types of products that resolve specific problems that occur for most consumers at different stages of their household life cycle.
24. How would you activate problem recognition among college students for the following?
    a. United Way blood drive
    b. Student recreation center
    c. A vegan diet
    d. Rooms To Go
    e. Using a designated driver if drinking
    f. Laundry service

25. How would you influence the time of problem recognition for the following?
    a. Fire alarm battery replacement
    b. Gift basket
    c. Car tune-up
    d. Air conditioner filters
    e. Health insurance
    f. Vitamins
26. Respond to the questions in Consumer Insight 14–1.

## APPLICATION ACTIVITIES

27. Interview five students and identify three consumer problems they have recognized recently. For each problem, determine
    a. The relative importance of the problem.
    b. How the problem occurred.
    c. What caused the problem (i.e., change in desired or actual states).
    d. What action they have taken.
    e. What action is planned to resolve each problem.
28. Find and describe an advertisement that is attempting to activate problem recognition. Analyze the advertisement in terms of the type of problem and the action the ad is suggesting. Also, discuss any changes you would recommend to improve the effectiveness of the ad in terms of activating problem recognition.
29. Interview three students and identify recent instances when they engaged in nominal, limited, and extended decision making (a total of nine decisions). What specific factors appear to be associated with each type of decision?
30. Interview three students and identify five products that each buys using a nominal decision process. Identify those that are based on brand loyalty and those that are merely repeat purchases. What characteristics, if any, distinguish the brand loyal products from the repeat products?
31. Find and describe an advertisement or point-of-purchase display that attempts to influence the timing of problem recognition. Evaluate its likely effectiveness.
32. Using two consumers from a relevant market segment, conduct an activity analysis for an activity that interests you. Prepare a report on the marketing opportunities suggested by your analysis.
33. Using two consumers from a relevant market segment, conduct a product analysis for a product that interests you. Prepare a report on the marketing opportunities suggested by your analysis.
34. Conduct a problem analysis, using a sample of five college freshmen. Prepare a report on the marketing opportunities suggested by your analysis.
35. Interview five smokers and ascertain what problems they see associated with smoking.
36. Interview someone from the local office of the American Cancer Society concerning their attempts to generate problem recognition among smokers.

## REFERENCES

1. *The U.S. Market for Breakfast Food and Beverages* (New York: Packaged Facts, March 2005); and "Quaker Gives People a Heart-Healthy Oatmeal to Go Just in Time for National Heart Health Month in February," *PR Newswire,* January 30, 2006, p. 1.
2. See B. Shiv and J. Huber, "The Impact of Anticipating Satisfaction on Consumer Choice," *Journal of Consumer Research,* September 2000, pp. 202–16; and M. T. Pham et al., "Affect Monitoring and the Primacy of Feelings in Judgment," *Journal of Consumer Research,* September 2001, pp. 167–88.
3. See J. R. Bettman, M. F. Luce, and J. W. Payne, "Constructive Consumer Choice," *Journal of Consumer Research,* December 1998, pp. 187–217.
4. For more complex but valuable approaches, see Bettman, Luce, and Payne, "Constructive Consumer Choice"; and R. Lawson, "Consumer Decision Making within a Goal-Driven Framework," *Psychology & Marketing,* August 1997, pp. 427–49.
5. M. Trivedi, F. M. Bass, and R. C. Rao, "A Model of Stochastic Variety-Seeking," *Marketing Science,* Summer 1994, pp. 274–97; S. Menon and B. E. Kahn, "The Impact of Context on Variety Seeking in Product Choice," *Journal of Consumer Research,* December 1995, pp. 285–95; and R. K. Ratner, B. E. Kahn, and D. Kahneman, "Choosing Less-Preferred Experiences for the Sake of Variety," *Journal of Consumer Research,* June 1999, pp. 1–15.
6. See W. J. McDonald, "Developing International Direct Marketing Strategies with a Consumer Decision-Making Content Analysis," *Journal of Direct Marketing,* Autumn 1994, pp. 18–27; and W. J. McDonald, "American versus Japanese Consumer Decision Making," *Journal of International Consumer Marketing* 7, no. 3 (1995), pp. 81–93.

7. See C. J. Hill, "The Nature of Problem Recognition and Search in the Extended Health Care Decision," *Journal of Services Marketing* 15, no. 6 (2001), pp. 454–79.

8. D. Soman, "Effects of Payment Mechanism on Spending Behavior," *Journal of Consumer Research,* March 2001, pp. 460–74.

9. Consumer Insight 14–1 is based on H. C. M. Van Trijp, W. D. Hoyer, and J. J. Inman, "Why Switch? Product Category-Level Explanations for True Variety-Seeking Behavior," *Journal of Marketing Research,* August 1996, pp. 281–92; and J. J. Inman, "The Role of Sensory-Specific Satiety in Attribute-Level Variety Seeking," *Journal of Consumer Research,* June 2001, pp. 105–20.

10. J. Fetto, "Get It Together," *American Demographics,* April 2003, pp. 10–11.

11. S. Yi and H. Baumgartner, "Coping with Negative Emotions in Purchase-Related Situations," *Journal of Consumer Psychology* 14, no. 3 (2004), pp. 303–17.

12. See, e.g., G. Zaltman, "Metaphorically Speaking," *Marketing Research,* Summer 1996, pp. 13–20; and C. B. Raffel, "Vague Notions," *Marketing Research,* Summer 1996, pp. 21–23.

13. E. Lesly, "Why Things Are So Sour at Borden," *BusinessWeek,* November 22, 1993, p. 84.

# Information Search

The ability of consumers to search for information has increased radically since the advent of the Internet. The Internet allows easy access to manufacturers' Web sites, to other consumers, and to third parties such as consumer groups and government agencies. It also greatly expands the ability of marketers to provide information to consumers. Marketers can provide information to consumers who are directly seeking information about the firm's products, typically through the company's or brand's home page or Web site. Marketers can also provide consumers information that they are not explicitly seeking by placing ads in other sites on the Web.

Internet strategies continue to evolve. However, most companies go well beyond simply providing company and product information in an electronic format. Consider the following:[1]

- Nike's Web site has various pages relating to its shoe and apparel lines. However, they go well beyond a simple place to find out information about shoes. For example, Nike+ is an online interactive tool that interfaces with special Nike equipment to allow runners to get real-time feedback while running through an armband or iPod, upload data and track goals, and connect and compete with others. It is so popular that 90 percent of Nike+ runners say they would recommend it to a friend. They have a runner's blog, a Q&A area with an expert trainer, and a member's newsletter. And this is only for running. They have similarly sophisticated sites for basketball, soccer, and so on.

- Kodak's site has various sections that provide product information to both amateur consumers and professional users. For cinematographers (and aspiring film students), Kodak offers film-comparison software, interviews with cinematographers, and information about its student film program. For the consumer market, it offers Kodak EasyShare Gallery, where digital pictures can be stored, printed, and shared online. Kodak also has a "Tips and Projects Center," which includes Web pages and podcasts full of information and advice regarding photography.

- Kraft Foods' site provides quick and easy help with food planning and preparation. It has searchable recipes and a recipe exchange, and delivers recipes by e-mail for those who sign up. It also has My Recipe Box, where members can enter, store, post, and rate recipes, as well as chat with "like minded foodies." My Recipe Box is integrated with Kraft's *food and family* magazine so that any recipes from an issue can be automatically uploaded. Kraft has also created a video-based "Cooking School" where consumers can watch video clips on how to prepare specific dishes.

Note that each of these Web sites provides basic product information similar to that which a consumer could get from a brochure or catalog. However, each site goes much further. It provides application and usage suggestions often personalized for each consumer. These suggestions add value for the consumer both in terms of providing easily accessible product information and by adding other information, activities, and applications of relevance to the consumer. These firms want consumers to use their sites not only when explicitly seeking product-specific information but also on a regular basis for a variety of purposes. This is one way a firm can build a relationship with the consumer.

---

Consumers continually recognize problems and opportunities, so internal and external searches for information to solve these problems are ongoing processes. Searching for information is not free. Information search involves mental as well as physical activities that consumers must perform. It takes time, energy, and money and can often require giving up more desirable activities.

The benefits of information search, however, often outweigh the costs of search. For example, a search may produce a lower price, a preferred style of merchandise, a higher-quality product, or greater confidence in the choice. In addition, the physical and mental processes involved in information search are, on occasion, rewarding in themselves.

Finally, marketers must keep in mind that consumers acquire a substantial amount of relevant information without deliberate search—through low-involvement learning (see Chapter 9).

# THE NATURE OF INFORMATION SEARCH

Suppose your television quit working, or you noticed that you were low on gas, or you felt particularly restless, or you decided you needed a bicycle. What would you do in response to each of these recognized problems? The odds are you would first remember how you usually solve this type of problem. This might produce a satisfactory solution (I'd better stop at the next BP station and fill up), which you would proceed to implement. Or you might decide that you needed to get additional information (I'll check the Yellow Pages to see who repairs my brand of television).

Once a problem is recognized, relevant information from long-term memory is used to determine if a satisfactory solution is known, what the characteristics of potential solutions are, what are appropriate ways to compare solutions, and so forth. This is **internal search.** If a resolution is not reached through internal search, then the search process is focused on external information relevant to solving the problem. This is **external search,** which can involve independent sources, personal sources, marketer-based information, and product experience. We discuss these sources in more detail later in the chapter. It is important to note that even in extended decision making with extensive external search, the initial internal search generally produces a set of guides or decision constraints that limit and guide external search. Such constraints might be a price range, a set of manufacturers, "must have" performance criteria, and so forth.[2]

Many problems are resolved by the consumer, using only previously stored information. If, in response to a problem, a consumer recalls a single, satisfactory solution (brand or store), no further information search or evaluation may occur. The consumer purchases the recalled brand and *nominal decision making* has occurred. For example, a consumer who catches a cold may recall that Dristan nasal spray provided relief in the past. He or she then purchases Dristan at the nearest store without further information search or evaluation.

Alternatively, a consumer might notice a new product in a store because of the attention-attracting power of a point-of-purchase display. He or she reads about the attributes of the product and recalls an unresolved problem that these attributes would resolve. The purchase is made without seeking additional information. This represents *limited decision making,* involving mainly internal information.

Had the consumer in the preceding example gone on and looked for other brands that would perform the same task or looked at another store for a lower price, we would have had an example of limited decision making using both internal and external information. As we move into *extended decision making,* the relative importance of external information search tends to increase.[3]

Deliberate external search also occurs in the absence of problem recognition. **Ongoing search** is done both *to acquire information for possible later use and because the process itself is pleasurable.* For example, individuals highly involved with an activity, such as tennis, are apt to seek information about tennis-related products on an ongoing basis without a recognized problem with their existing tennis equipment (recall that enduring involvement is characteristic of opinion leaders). This search could involve offline and online activities such as reading ads in tennis magazines, visiting tennis equipment shops, participating in tennis-related blogs, and so on. These activities would provide the individual both pleasure and information for future use.

# TYPES OF INFORMATION SOUGHT

A consumer decision requires information on the following:[4]

1. The appropriate evaluative criteria for the solution of a problem.
2. The existence of various alternative solutions.
3. The performance level or characteristic of each alternative solution on each evaluative criterion.

Information search, then, seeks each of these three types of information, as shown in Figure 15–1.

## Evaluative Criteria

Suppose you are provided with money to purchase a notebook computer, perhaps as a graduation present. Assuming you have not been in the market for a computer recently,

**Information Search in Consumer Decisions**    FIGURE 15–1

your first thought would probably be, "What features do I want in a computer?" You would then engage in internal search to determine the features or characteristics required to meet your needs. These desired characteristics are your *evaluative criteria*. If you have had limited experience with computers, you might also engage in external search to learn which characteristics a good computer should have. You could check with friends, read reviews in *PC Magazine* online, talk with sales personnel, visit computer Web sites, post questions on an online discussion board, or personally inspect several computers.

Thus, one potential objective of both internal and external search is *the determination of appropriate evaluative criteria*. Government agencies and consumer organizations want consumers to use sound evaluative criteria such as the nutrition content of foods. Marketers want consumers to use evaluative criteria that match their brand's strengths. Thus, both marketers and government agencies provide information designed to influence the evaluative criteria used by consumers. Illustration 15–1 shows an example of this in which the company is trying to focus consumers toward an attribute on which it excels but which consumers may not automatically have in mind when selecting a brand.

A detailed discussion of evaluative criteria appears in Chapter 16.

## Appropriate Alternatives

After and while searching for appropriate evaluative criteria, you would probably seek *appropriate alternatives*—in this case brands or, possibly, stores. Again, you would start with an internal search. You might say to yourself, "Lenova, Compaq, Toshiba, Apple, NEC, Sony, Fujitsu, Averatec, and HP all make notebook computers. After my brother's experience, I'd never buy Averatec. I've heard good things about Lenova, Apple, and

Compaq. I think I'll check them out." The nine brands you thought of as potential solutions are known as the **awareness set.** The awareness set is composed of three subcategories of considerable importance to marketers.

The three brands that you have decided to investigate are known as the **evoked set,** or the **consideration set.**[5] An evoked set is *those brands or products one will evaluate for the solution of a particular consumer problem.* It is important to note that the evoked set or consideration set will vary depending on the usage situation. For example, a person might choose from among cereal (perhaps several brands), a bagel, an Egg McMuffin, or just a cup of coffee for a weekday breakfast option but might consider eggs, waffles, or leftover pizza for a weekend breakfast.[6] Note that while evoked sets are frequently composed of brands from a single product category (brands of cereals or computers), this need not be the case.[7] For example, one landscaping company found that consumers often view landscaping as a "home improvement decision." As a consequence, their landscaping services often compete with other home improvement products such as interior decorating instead of, or in addition to, other landscaping services.

If you do not have an evoked set for notebook computers, or lack confidence that your evoked set is adequate, you will probably engage in external search to learn about additional alternatives. You may also learn about additional acceptable brands such as Acer and Sharp as an incidental aspect of moving through the decision process. Thus, an important outcome of information search is the development of a *complete* evoked set.

Whenever you are satisfied with your evoked set, your information search will focus on the performance of the brands in your evoked set on the evaluative criteria. Thus, the evoked set is of particular importance in structuring subsequent information search and purchase.

The brand you found completely unworthy of further consideration is a member of what is called the **inept set.** Brands in the inept set are *actively disliked or avoided by the consumer.* Positive information about these brands is not likely to be processed even if it is readily available.

In our example, Sony, Toshiba, NEC, Fujitsu, and HP were brands of which you were aware but were basically indifferent toward. They compose what is known as an **inert set.** Consumers will generally accept favorable information about brands in the inert set, although they do not seek out such information. Brands in this set are generally acceptable when preferred brands are not available. Thus, the nine brands in the initial awareness set can be subdivided as follows:

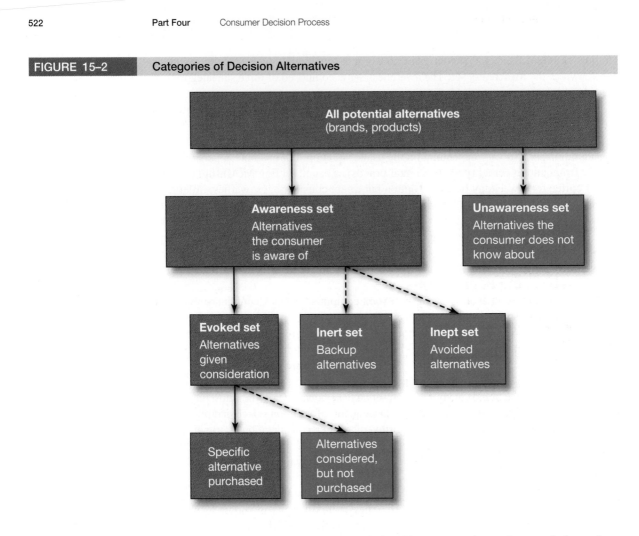

| FIGURE 15–2 | Categories of Decision Alternatives |

Figure 15–2 illustrates the general relationships among these classes of alternatives. Figure 15–3 illustrates the results of several studies comparing the size of the awareness and evoked sets for a variety of products. Notice that in all cases, the evoked set is substantially smaller than the awareness set. Because the evoked set generally is the one from which consumers make final evaluations and decisions, *marketing strategy that focuses only on creating awareness may be inadequate.* Thus, marketers must strive to have consumers recall their brand in response to a recognized problem *and* consider the brand a worthy potential solution.

A similar process operates with respect to retail outlet selection.[8]

## Alternative Characteristics

To choose among the brands in the evoked set, the consumer compares them on the relevant evaluative criteria. This process requires the consumer *to gather information about each brand on each pertinent evaluative criterion.* In our example of a computer purchase, you might collect information on the price, memory, processor, weight, screen clarity, and software package for each brand you are considering.

In summary, consumers engage in internal and external search for (1) appropriate evaluative criteria, (2) the existence of potential solutions, and (3) the characteristics of potential solutions. However, extensive search generally occurs for only a few consumption

**Awareness and Evoked Sets for Various Products**    FIGURE 15–3

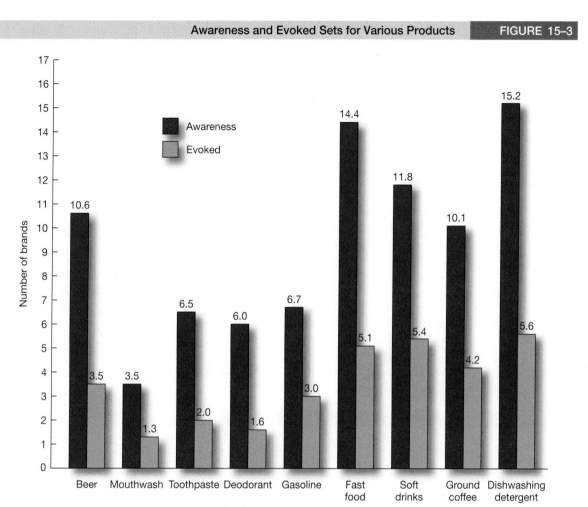

Source: J. Roberts, "A Grounded Model of Consideration Set Size and Composition," in *Advances in Consumer Research,* vol. 26, ed. T. K. Skrull (Provo, UT: Association for Consumer Research, 1989), p. 750.

decisions. Nominal and limited decisions that involve little or no active external search are the rule. In addition, consumers acquire substantial information without deliberate search through low-involvement learning. Finally, whereas our discussion has focused on searching for functional information, emotions and feelings are important in many purchases.

# SOURCES OF INFORMATION

Refer again to our notebook computer example. We suggested that you might recall what you know about computers, check with friends and an online discussion board, consult *Consumer Reports* and read reviews in *PC Magazine,* talk with sales personnel, or personally inspect several computers to collect relevant information. These represent the five primary sources of information available to consumers:

- *Memory* of past searches, personal experiences, and low-involvement learning.
- *Personal sources,* such as friends, family, and others.
- *Independent sources,* such as magazines, consumer groups, and government agencies.

- *Marketing sources,* such as sales personnel, Web sites, and advertising.
- *Experiential sources,* such as inspection or product trial.[9]

It is important to note that each of these sources has an online and an offline component. That is, memory could be from prior information search offline or on the Internet; offline personal sources correspond to online chatrooms, blogs, user groups, and social network sites; independent sources such as *Consumer Reports* magazine correspond to online independent sources; offline marketing sources such as TV advertising and brochures correspond to online banner ads and corporate Web sites.[10] And given the importance of product experiences in the attitude formation and purchase process, marketers are increasingly looking for ways to allow consumers to at least simulate an experience with their products via the Internet.[11] These sources are shown in Figure 15–4. Consumers decide how many and which sources of information to use at both the macro (personal sources) and micro (specific individuals) levels. Thus, a purchase decision requires a subset of decisions concerning information seeking.[12]

Internal information is the primary source used by most consumers most of the time (nominal and limited decision making). However, note that information in long-term memory was *initially* obtained from external sources. Thus, a consumer may resolve a consumption problem using only or mainly stored information. At some point, however, the individual acquired that information from an external source, such as direct product experience, friends, or low-involvement learning.

Marketing-originated messages are only one of five potential information sources, and they are frequently reported to be of limited *direct* value in consumer decisions.[13] However,

---

**FIGURE 15–4**    **Information Sources for a Purchase Decision**

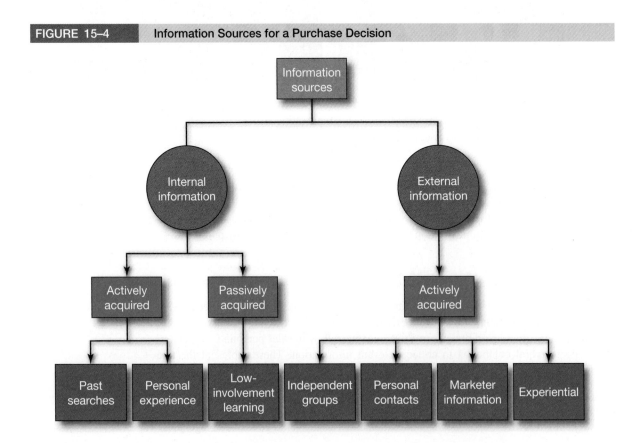

marketing activities influence all five sources. Thus, the characteristics of the product, the distribution of the product, and the promotional messages about the product provide the underlying or basic information available in the market. An independent source such as *Consumer Reports* bases its evaluation on the functional characteristics of the product. Personal sources such as friends also must base their information on experience with the product or its promotion, or on other sources that have had contact with the product or its promotion.

A substantial amount of marketing activity is designed to influence the information that consumers will receive from nonmarketing sources. For example, when Johnson & Johnson introduced a new-formula baby bath:

> Product information, demonstrations, monographs, journal ads, and direct-mail programs were targeted at pediatricians and nurses to capitalize on health care professionals' direct contact with new mothers. Print ads and coupons appeared in baby care publications, and a film exploring the parent–infant bonding process was distributed to teaching centers, hospitals, and medical schools.

In addition, although consumers may not use (or believe they use) advertising or other marketer-provided data as immediate input into many purchase decisions, there is no doubt that continual exposure to advertising frequently influences the perceived need for the product, the composition of the awareness and evoked sets, the evaluative criteria used, and beliefs about the performance levels of each brand.[14] As a consequence, the long-term influence of advertising and other marketer-provided information on consumer decision making and sales can be substantial.

## Information Search on the Internet

The Internet gives consumers unprecedented access to information. Global Internet usage continues to grow rapidly, and more than 1.4 billion people are online around the world. Asia (530 million), Europe (382 million), and North America (246 million) have the highest number of Internet users. Growth potential is strongest for regions such as Africa, Asia, and Latin America, where Internet usage as a percent of the total population is still relatively low. Asia overshadows other regions of the world in terms of current users and potential growth, in view of its population size (3.8 billion), growing middle class, and increased access to low-cost technology.[15] *What are the marketing implications of such global trends for American businesses?*

Just as there are global usage differences, as Figure 15–5 shows, the Internet is not used equally by all segments of the adult U.S. population. It is important to keep several points in mind while examining this figure. First, differences across groups have been rapidly decreasing and are expected to continue to do so, with growth in lower-use segments often outpacing that of higher-use segments.[16] Second, the estimate for Hispanics is specifically for English-speaking Hispanics. Research examining overall Hispanic usage generally finds lower use due to language barriers.[17] Third, as the baby boomers age, the large usage gap between those 65 and over and the rest of the population should decline sharply as these older consumers take their online skills into their latter years.[18] Finally, children and teenagers are also an important online market segment. One study shows that children as young as three years old are using the Internet and that Internet usage increases steadily from children to tweens to teens.[19]

The following list represents the top 10 activities of adult Internet users (number represents percent who have ever engaged in the activity):[20]

| E-mail | 92% |
| *Use search engine to find information* | *91* |
| Search for a map or driving directions | 86 |
| Look for information on a hobby or interest | 83 |
| *Research a product/service before buying it* | *81* |
| Look for health or medical information | 80 |
| Check the weather | 78 |
| Get travel information | 73 |
| Get news | 71 |
| *Buy a product* | *66* |

Source: Pew Internet & American Life Project, www.pewinternet.org.

**FIGURE 15–5**     Demographics of U.S. Adult Internet Users

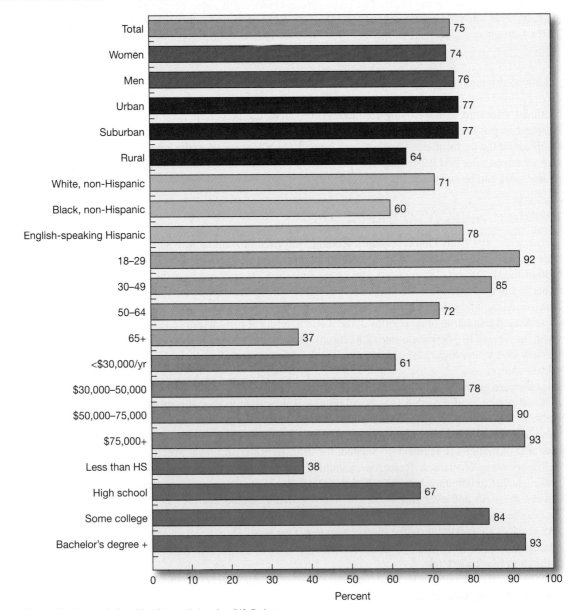

Source: Used by permission of Pew Internet & American Life Project.

This information shows just how important the Internet is in the search and decision process. Indeed, research suggests that the Internet is a preferred source of product-related information among Internet users.[21] Consider the following:[22]

- *Online information is expected.* A Pew survey finds that most Internet users *expect* to find information about a product or brand of interest to them on a company's Web site.
- *Online information boosts offline sales.* A Pew survey finds that nearly half of Internet users are more likely to purchase a company's product offline if its Web site provides product-related information.
- *Online sources are viewed as valuable.* A DoubleClick study finds that corporate and third-party Web sites matched or beat traditional TV and print advertising as an information source in 8 out of 10 product/service categories. A study of automobile buyers finds that 58 percent rate an Internet source (versus an offline source) as the most valuable.
- *Online sources reduce salesperson's role.* A DoubleClick study finds that 51 percent of Internet users across 11 product/service categories required considerably less assistance from a salesperson on their current purchase compared with their last. Three studies of automobile buyers found similar results.

Obviously, traditional media can be effective at guiding consumers' information search activities to company Web sites, as shown in Illustration 15–2.

Search engines such as Google, Yahoo, and MSN are an important search tool for consumers. A recent DoubleClick study examined search engine use in a 12-week period preceding an online purchase. Four product categories and seven to eight retailers within each of these categories were tracked using their panel of 1.5 million U.S. Internet users. They found that 50 percent of online purchases were preceded by information search using a search engine. Perhaps more interesting was the nature of search, where search terms were categorized as *brand only* (retailer's brand), *generic* (general product-related terms), and *brand-item* (brand plus generic). As shown in Figure 15–6, most of the search leading up to the purchase was generic—that is, general product-related terms that did not include any of the retailers being tracked in the study. As you might expect, generic search dominated early in the search process (3 to 12 weeks out), while branded search dominated just prior to purchase.[23] *What strategic implications do these results hold for online marketers?*

As we have seen, the Internet influences consumer information search. Obvious advantages of the Internet include the speed and efficiency with which vast amounts of information can be obtained. The result can be a more efficient search process and better decisions. For example, automobile buyers who used the Internet were able to make decisions faster and get a better buy—on average by $741.[24] Economic considerations appear to be a major motivator of online searching.[25]

Despite these and other benefits, one of the challenges facing consumers is sifting through the mountains of available information on the Internet. Thus, *information overload* (see Chapter 8) can be a major factor on the Internet. General search engines are useful. However, more specialized services and tools continue to evolve to aid consumers more specifically in their search and

**FIGURE 15–6**     The Nature of Search Using Online Search Engines

Source: "The Nature of Search Using Online Search Engines," *Search Before the Purchase* (New York: DoubleClick, February 2005), p. 2. Copyright: DoubleClick, Inc., 2005.

decision making.[26] For example, there are numerous shopping services on the Internet that can search out the lowest prices for specific items, search out online retailers of specific merchandise, suggest specific brands based on your prior purchases or prespecified criteria, and so on (see Illustration 15–3). These services use **bots,** which are software "robots" that do the shopping/searching for users, and are therefore often referred to as *shopping bots.* Examples include BizRate.com, mySimon.com, and NexTag.com.

In addition to marketer-based information, the Internet contains personal sources of information in bulletin boards and chat rooms as well as in the brand review features of many shopping services.[27] One study finds that consumers are increasingly using online WOM (word-of-mouth) as an information source prior to automobile purchases.[28] WOM and personal sources are highly influential because of consumer trust in these sources (Chapter 7).

**Marketing Strategy and Information Search on the Internet**    The online environment is continually evolving. For example, early on, the online consumer population was relatively homogeneous and characterized as young, white, educated, and male. As the online population increasingly mirrors the general population, segmentation and target marketing are becoming increasingly critical to online success. Consider the following:

> Where higher education marketing is different is the complexity of the audiences. A college . . . in particular has to please—if you are talking about the institutional Web site—alumni, donors, current students, prospective students, parents (and) the media. It's daunting sometimes.

Furman University decided that its general Web site was inadequate for admissions. So the university created a separate Web site to target high school students interested in the

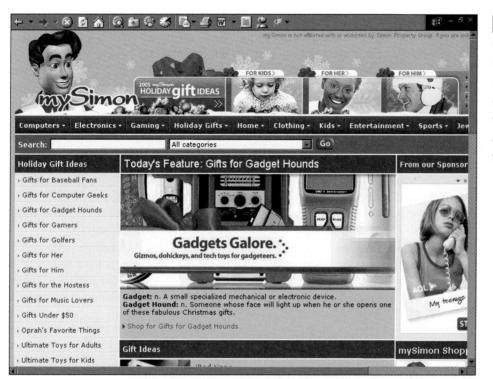

**ILLUSTRATION 15–3**

Online shopping ser-
vices are increasingly
popular as a way for
consumers to deal
with the enormous
amount of informa-
tion on the Internet.

institution. The site is designed to target this tech-savvy group specifically, with virtual tours, message boards, and online student journals (with no editing by administration!).[29]

Obviously, universities are not the only ones who must deal with diverse consumer needs and characteristics. For example, consumers of various ethnicities in the United States often prefer and primarily use ethnic (versus mainstream) Web sites.[30] Global marketers must adapt as well. A recent study finds that Japanese Web sites use less individualistic approaches than do U.S. Web sites.[31]

More specifically, with respect to the Internet's role in information search and decision making, marketers have at least three major strategic issues to deal with:

1. How can they drive their information to consumers?
2. How can they drive consumers to their information?
3. How (if at all) can online selling be utilized or integrated with existing channels?

The first two issues are addressed in this section. The third is covered in Chapter 17. The first two issues are highly interrelated in that many of the strategies companies use to drive information to consumers (e.g., banner ads) are also designed, ultimately, to drive consumers to additional sources of information about the company (e.g., the company's Web site).

*Driving a firm's information to consumers* is important since consumers are not always actively searching. One way is through Web advertising, including *banner ads.* Internet advertising spending is growing at around 25 percent per year and is projected to be $36.5 billion in 2011. This represents a marked increase from 2006 ($16.4 billion) but still is a relatively small proportion of total advertising expenditures in the United States (around $250 billion).[32] Broadband is changing the nature of online advertising, allowing for more use of streaming media. For example, in response to data showing that half of all new car buyers visit the Web prior to visiting a dealer, Honda placed its national TV ads for the Odyssey minivan on at least 14 Web sites. Viewers could click off the video or view it and ask for additional information. This goes beyond the traditional banner ad approach, and yet both drive the brand and information to the consumer.[33]

E-mail is also an important tool for pushing information to consumers. A study by DoubleClick shows that many consumers see e-mail as a replacement for direct mail. However, spam (unsolicited e-mails) continues to be a major concern and irritant. *Permission-based e-mail* (PBE), in which the consumer "opts in" to receive e-mail appears to be something consumers are highly receptive to. Even with PBE, marketers need to be careful—too many e-mails that lack relevance may still be viewed as spam.[34]

A new tool that is being used for online advertising is the widget. DoubleClick now offers companies the option to convert their interactive media into widgets so that viewers can "grab them" and post them on blogs or social networking sites such as Facebook. In this way, companies let consumers drive their information to other consumers who might be interested. This relates to online WOM and buzz, as discussed in Chapter 7.[35]

*Driving consumers to a firm's information* is a daunting and important task given the explosion in the amount and sources of information on the Web. Companies have Web sites to which they want consumers to go and return frequently.[36] Various strategies are possible. As we saw in Illustration 15–2, offline media are one avenue for calling attention to a Web site.

Banner ads are another way to drive traffic to Web sites. While click-through rates (percentage who click through to the corporate Web site) are generally low, marketers are looking beyond immediate click-through to measures that include brand awareness, brand attitudes, and purchase intentions. The idea is that boosting awareness and attitudes will drive *long-term* Web site visits and purchases.

DoubleClick terms Web site visits that occur as a result of exposure to an online ad but which do not occur at the time of exposure as *view-throughs*. They claim that they "typically see half or more of the ad-related visits in a campaign being attributed to the view-through effect as opposed to direct clicks." As online ads become more interactive, other metrics are also possible. Mini Cooper used an interactive banner that allowed viewers to see various owner profiles. Useful metrics here would be the interaction rate (percent that interacted in some way with the ad such as paging through the owner profiles) and time spent with the ad.[37]

As you might expect, appropriate or targeted ad placement is helpful in increasing online ad performance across various outcomes including click-through rates. For example, Dolby ran interactive banners relating to thunder and the outdoors. The campaign did well overall, but did markedly better (e.g., 60 percent higher click-through rate) when placed on the National Geographic site, because of the higher relevance of these themes to the site's viewers.[38] Social networking sites are also getting into the act. Sites like MySpace are offering targeted advertising based on the expressed interests and characteristics contained in the profiles of their members. MySpace indicates that ad performance increases by as much as 300 percent by using their targeted approach. However, member concerns over privacy led MySpace to allow users to opt out and brings attention to the fact that "commercializing" social networks has to be done carefully and appropriately given the culture of the site.[39]

Behavioral targeting is another form of targeting that is based not on what people say but what they actually do online. Specifically, **behavioral targeting** *involves tracking consumer click patterns on a Web site and using that information to decide on banner ad placement.*[40] For example, Snapple wanted to market its Snapple-a-Day product to health-conscious women. Snapple set its target as women who had visited iVillage's diet and fitness area three times in the previous 45 days. For those visitors, Snapple then delivered banner ads wherever they happened to be on the iVillage site. Behavioral targeting produced much better results for Snapple than standard Web-placement models because the ad and product were highly relevant to the targeted customer.[41]

As we saw earlier, online consumers are heavy users of search engines. Since search results are ordered and consumers often don't *drill down* beyond the first page of listings, keyword selection and other techniques relating to search engine optimization are critical for the firm in terms of getting their Web site the highest priority listing for the most appropriate search terms. **Search engine optimization (SEO)** *involves techniques designed to ensure that a company's Web pages "are accessible to search engines and focused in ways that help improve the chances they will be found."*[42] Programs such as Google's Adword program, in which companies pay for "sponsored" listings for specific search terms, are also available. The DoubleClick search-engine results suggest that consumers often begin their searches with general product-related terms. Therefore, finding and optimizing around the most likely generic search terms used by consumers would be a recommended strategy for getting the brand in front of the consumer during the decision process and increasing the odds that the consumer will visit the Web site as a consequence.

Web site design is also critical. While we will discuss this issue more in Chapter 17, it is clear that driving *ongoing and repeat* traffic to a Web site requires such factors as relevant and frequently updated content. That is, firms must provide consumers with ongoing incentives to return to their Web sites. Techniques can include product-related news features, user-related discussion forums, updates on new products and features, and so on. Increasingly, companies are relying on RSS (really simple syndication) feeds that pull information on an ongoing basis from various online sources to keep their sites relevant and current. The Web site can also offer consumers the option to receive regular e-mail updates, which can trigger site visits.[43]

Consumer Insight 15–1 examines the role of mobile marketing as it relates to information provision and gathering.

# AMOUNT OF EXTERNAL INFORMATION SEARCH

Marketing managers are particularly interested in external information search, as this provides them with direct access to the consumer. How much external information search do consumers actually undertake? Most purchases are a result of nominal or limited decision making and therefore involve limited external search immediately prior to purchase. This is particularly true for relatively low-priced convenience goods such as soft drinks, canned foods, and detergents. Therefore, the discussion in this section focuses on major purchases such as appliances, professional services, and automobiles. Intuitively, we would expect substantial amounts of direct external search prior to such purchases.

Various measures of external information search have been used: (1) number of stores visited, (2) number of alternatives considered, (3) number of personal sources used, and (4) overall or combination measures. Each of these measures of search effort assesses a different aspect of behavior, yet each measure supports one observation: *external information search is skewed toward limited search, with the greatest proportion of consumers performing little external search immediately prior to purchase.* For example, surveys of *shopping behavior* have shown a significant percentage of all durable purchases are made after the consumer has visited only one store.[44] The *number of alternatives* considered also shows a limited amount of prepurchase search. Although the number of alternative brands or models considered tends to increase as the price of the product increases, for some product

## Push and Pull Strategies in Mobile Marketing

Mobile phones are a critical tool for consumers. Not surprisingly, mobile marketing efforts are taking off as well. Efforts in this area can be viewed in much the same way as those on the Internet—that is, driving information to consumers (push strategies) and driving consumers to information (pull strategies).[45]

*Mobile Push.* Driving information to consumers on mobile devices can involve a variety of strategies. One strategy that will continue to grow as more consumers use mobile Internet is ads placed on mobile Web pages. As with computer-based approaches, mobile ads can be targeted to be most relevant to the specific mobile content being viewed. Another strategy is permission-based or opt-in text messaging promotions. Text messaging is growing in popularity across all age groups and is the second most popular activity on cell phones. According to SmartReply, a media consulting group, the best text message programs involve:

- Building an "opt-in" database—this can be done through traditional and e-mail marketing in which consumers are asked to text in or register at a specific Web site.
- Developing the text-message "ad"—should include (a) a hook relating to why they are being contacted; (b) a call to action, such as entering a code to get a discount; and (c) an "opt-out" option.
- Rolling out the campaign—involves delivering the text promotion to those on the opt-in list.

Adidas used a variation of this approach as sponsor of the 2007 NBA All-Star week. It had game information, store events, athlete appearances, and shoe releases as part of its promotions. Consumers opted in and then could access all the promotional materials at any time during the week by texting "originals."

*Mobile Pull.* Driving consumers to information on mobile devices can also involve a number of strategies. One is to use traditional media to build awareness about a mobile site or promotional event. AT&T held a mobile contest on U.S. college campuses for a free Dave Mathhews Band concert to the school that could generate the most "invitations" sent through text messaging for the band to play at their school. To generate awareness and drive students to its mobile space, AT&T blanketed college campuses with posters telling students to "Text DMB to 959" or "visit ATTBLUEROOM.COM to enter." Another emerging approach is mobile search. Mobile Internet users are increasing rapidly, with expected usage at over 64 million by 2011. At that time it is projected that some 56 million people will be using mobile search. Google, Yahoo, MSN, and AOL Mobile are currently the top mobile search providers and their search results drive traffic to traditional Web sites and mobile content.

### Critical Thinking Questions

1. With cell phones even less easily controlled and monitored than home computers, what ethical and regulatory issues are raised regarding mobile marketing to children?

2. Beyond the approaches discussed above, what other mobile marketing approaches are emerging? Are they effective? Explain.

3. What challenges do marketers face as they have to create campaigns that span mobile, Internet, and traditional media?

categories, such as watches, almost half of the purchasers considered only one brand *and* one model. Another study found that 27 percent of the purchasers of major appliances considered only one brand.[46] And while Internet use increased automobile search, those who used the Internet still examined only three models.[47]

Eight separate studies spanning almost 50 years, two product categories, four services, and two countries show remarkable consistency in terms of the total external information search undertaken. Consumers can be classified in terms of their total external information search as (1) nonsearchers—little or no search, (2) limited information searchers—low to moderate search, and (3) extended information searchers—high search.[48]

| Country/Product/Year | Nonsearchers | Limited Searchers | Extended Searchers |
|---|---|---|---|
| America/appliances/1955 | 65% | 25% | 10% |
| America/appliances/1972 | 49 | 38 | 13 |
| America/appliances/1974 | 65 | 27 | 08 |
| Australia/automobiles/1981 | 24 | 58 | 18 |
| America/appliances/1989 | 24 | 45 | 11 |
| America/professional services/1989 | 55 | 38 | 07 |
| Australia/professional services/1995 | 53 | 35 | 12 |
| America/automobiles/2003 | 20 | 40 | 20 |

As this information suggests, most consumers engage in minimal external information search immediately prior to the purchase of consumer durables and important professional services. The level of search for less important items is even lower. However, limited information search does not necessarily mean that the consumer is not following a sound purchasing strategy. Nor does it mean that substantial amounts of internal information are not being used.

# COSTS VERSUS BENEFITS OF EXTERNAL SEARCH

Why do buyers often engage in so little external search immediately prior to the purchase even for important durable goods and services? Part of the answer lies in the differences between the buyers' perceptions of the benefits and costs of search associated with a particular purchase situation. The benefits of external information search can be tangible, such as a lower price, a preferred style, or a higher-quality product. Or the benefits can be intangible—reduced risk or greater confidence in the purchase, or the search itself can even provide enjoyment.[49] Perceptions of these benefits are likely to vary with the consumer's experience in the market, his or her media habits, and the extent to which the consumer interacts with others or belongs to different reference groups. Therefore, one reason for limited external search in many cases is that consumers do not perceive significant benefits resulting from such an effort.

Furthermore, acquisition of external information is not free, and consumers may engage in limited search because the costs of search exceed the perceived benefits. The costs of search can be both monetary and nonmonetary. Monetary costs include the cost of transportation, parking, lost wages, charges for child care, and so forth. Nonmonetary costs of search are less obvious but may have an even greater impact than monetary costs. Almost every external search effort involves time and physical and psychological effort. Frustration and conflict between the search task and other more desirable activities, as well as fatigue, may shorten or otherwise alter the search effort. The Internet clearly has the potential to greatly lower search costs. When it does, it has been shown to increase search and result in better consumer decisions and a more enjoyable shopping experience.[50]

In this section, we examine four basic types of factors that influence the expected benefits and perceived costs of search: *market characteristics, product characteristics, consumer characteristics,* and *situation characteristics.*[51] These four factors and their components are shown in Table 15–1.

| Influencing Factor | Increasing the Influencing Factor Causes External Search To: |
|---|---|
| I.  Market characteristics | |
|   A. Number of alternatives | Increase |
|   B. Price range | Increase |
|   C. Store concentration | Increase |
|   D. Information availability | Increase |
|     1. Advertising | |
|     2. Point-of-purchase | |
|     3. Web sites | |
|     4. Sales personnel | |
|     5. Packaging | |
|     6. Experienced customers | |
|     7. Independent sources | |
| II.  Product characteristics | |
|   A. Price | Increase |
|   B. Differentiation | Increase |
|   C. Positive products | Increase |
| III.  Consumer characteristics | |
|   A. Learning and experience | Decrease |
|   B. Shopping orientation | Mixed |
|   C. Social status | Increase |
|   D. Age and household life cycle | Mixed |
|   E. Product involvement | Mixed |
|   F. Perceived risk | Increase |
| IV.  Situation characteristics | |
|   A. Time availability | Increase |
|   B. Purchase for self | Decrease |
|   C. Pleasant surroundings | Increase |
|   D. Social surroundings | Mixed |
|   E. Physical/mental energy | Increase |

## Market Characteristics

Market characteristics include the number of alternatives, price range, store distribution, and information availability. It is important to keep in mind that it is the consumer's perception of, or beliefs about, the market characteristics that influence shopping behavior, *not* the actual characteristics.[52] While beliefs and reality are usually related, often they are not identical.

Obviously, the greater the *number of alternatives* (products, stores, brands) available to resolve a particular problem, the more external search there is likely to be. At the extreme, there is no need to search for information in the face of a complete monopoly such as utilities or driver's licenses.

However, if too many models and brands are available, information overload may cause consumers to shop less. In particular, a wide range of models or brands may make the search process virtually impossible if the models vary across stores. That is, if one store has two brands with five models each and a second store has the same two brands but with five different models each, the consumer must compare 20 distinct brands/models. In response, many consumers will limit their shopping to a single retail outlet. This leads some marketers to develop a large number of models so that key accounts can have exclusive models and avoid direct price competition with other retailers on those exact models.[53]

The *perceived range of prices* among equivalent brands in a product class is a major factor in stimulating external search. For example, shopping 36 retail stores in Tucson for five popular-branded toys produced a total low cost of $51.27 and a total high cost of $105.95. Clearly, efficient shopping for those products in that market would provide a significant financial gain. Pricing strategies such as price matching can affect consumer price perceptions. A recent study suggests that consumers interpret such policies as signaling lower prices which, under high search costs, yields less search.[54]

It appears that the percentage savings available from shopping may be as important as the dollar amount. Consumers who perceive the chance to save $50 when purchasing a $200 item may be motivated to engage in search but not if the same savings were available for a $5,000 item.[55]

*Store distribution*—the number, location, and distances between retail stores in the market—affects the number of store visits a consumer will make before purchase. Because store visits take time, energy, and in many cases, money, a close proximity of stores will often increase this aspect of external search.[56]

In general, *information availability,* including format, is directly related to information use.[57] However, too much information can cause information overload and the use of less information. In addition, readily available information tends to produce learning over time, which may reduce the need for additional external information immediately prior to a purchase.[58] *Advertising, point-of-purchase displays, Web sites, sales personnel, packages, other consumers,* and *independent sources* such as *Consumer Reports* are major sources of consumer information.

## Product Characteristics

Product *differentiation*—feature and quality variation across brands—is associated with increased external search.

In addition, consumers appear to enjoy shopping for *positive products*—those whose acquisition results in positive reinforcement. Thus, shopping for flowers and plants, dress clothing, sports equipment, and cameras is viewed as a positive experience by most consumers. In contrast, shopping for *negative products*—those whose primary benefit is negative reinforcement (removal of an unpleasant condition)—is viewed as less pleasant. Shopping for groceries, extermination services, and auto repairs is not enjoyed by most individuals. Other things being equal, consumers are more likely to engage in external search for positive products.[59]

## Consumer Characteristics

A variety of consumer characteristics affect perceptions of expected benefits, search costs, and the need to carry out a particular level of external information search.[60] As described earlier, the first step a consumer normally takes in response to a problem or opportunity is a search of memory for an appropriate solution. If the consumer finds a solution that he or she is confident is satisfactory, external search is unlikely. Thus, confidence in one's knowledge of existing solutions is an important determinant of search.[61] However, a recent study concluded that "consumers are overconfident—they think they know more than they actually do."[62] Such overconfidence can lead to lower levels of search and lower-quality decisions. It can also make it harder for companies to reposition their brands when consumers feel they "know" about the brand if their knowledge and perceptions are inaccurate or outdated.

A satisfying *experience* with a particular brand is a positively reinforcing process. It increases the probability of a repeat purchase of that brand and decreases the likelihood of external search. As a result, external search is generally greater for consumers who have limited purchase experience with brands in a particular product category.[63]

However, there is evidence that at least some familiarity with a product class is necessary for external search to occur. For example, external search prior to purchasing a new automobile is high for consumers who have a high level of *general knowledge about cars* and low for those who have a substantial level of knowledge about existing brands.[64] Thus, consumers facing a completely unfamiliar product category may feel threatened by the amount of new information or may simply lack sufficient knowledge to conduct an external search.

External search tends to increase with various measures of *social status* (education, occupation, and income), though middle-income individuals search more than those at higher or lower levels. *Age* of the shopper is inversely related to information search. External search appears to decrease as the age of the shopper increases. This may be explained in part by increased learning and product familiarity gained with age. New households and individuals moving into new stages of the *household life cycle* have a greater need for external information than established households.

Consumers tend to form general approaches or patterns of external search. These general approaches are termed *shopping orientations*.[65] While individuals will exhibit substantial variation from the general pattern across situations and product categories, many do take a stable shopping approach to most products across a wide range of situations. Other individuals engage in extensive ongoing information search because they are market mavens, as described in Chapter 7.

Consumers who are *highly involved with a product category* generally seek information relevant to the product category on an ongoing basis.[66] This ongoing search and the knowledge base it produces may reduce their need for external search immediately before a purchase. However, this may vary with the nature of their involvement with the product category. One study found that wine enthusiasts who desired variety engaged in significantly more external search than those who were less interested in variety.[67]

**Perceived Risk**    The **perceived risk** associated with unsatisfactory product performance, either instrumental or symbolic, increases information search prior to purchase.[68] Higher perceived risk is associated with increased search and greater reliance on personal sources of information and personal experiences.

Perceived risk is a function of the individual, the product, and the situation. It varies from one consumer to another and for the same consumer from one product to another and from one situation to another. For example, the purchase of a bottle of wine may not involve much perceived risk when buying for one's own consumption. However, the choice of wine may involve considerable perceived risk when buying wine for a dinner party for one's boss. Likewise, it might be perceived as risky if the individual has little knowledge and is buying an expensive bottle for personal consumption.

While perceived risk varies across consumers and situations, some products and services are generally seen as riskier than others (see Table 17–2).[69] Likewise, perceived risk is high for products whose failure to perform as expected would result in a high

- *Social cost* (e.g., a new suit that is not appreciated by one's peers).
- *Financial cost* (e.g., an expensive vacation during which it rained all the time).
- *Time cost* (e.g., an automobile repair that required the car to be taken to the garage, left, and then picked up later).
- *Effort cost* (e.g., a computer that is loaded with important software before the hard drive crashes).
- *Physical cost* (e.g., a new medicine produces a harmful side effect).

## Situation Characteristics

As indicated in Chapter 13, situational variables can have a major impact on search behavior. For example, recall that one of the primary reactions of consumers to crowded store conditions is to minimize external information search. *Temporal perspective* is probably the most important situational variable with respect to search behavior. As the time available to solve a particular consumer problem decreases, so does the amount of external information search.[70]

Gift-giving situations (*task definition*) tend to increase perceived risk, which, as we have seen, increases external search. Likewise, multiple-item purchase tasks such as buying a bike and a bike rack or several items for a meal produce increased levels of information search.[71] Shoppers with limited physical or emotional energy (*antecedent state*) will search for less information than others. Pleasant *physical surroundings* increase the tendency to search for information, at least *within* that outlet. *Social surroundings* can increase or decrease search, depending on the nature of the social setting (see Chapter 13 for a more complete discussion of these issues).

# MARKETING STRATEGIES BASED ON INFORMATION SEARCH PATTERNS

Sound marketing strategies take into account the nature of information search engaged in by the target market prior to purchase. Two dimensions of search are particularly appropriate: The type of decision influences the level of search, and the nature of the evoked set influences the direction of the search. Table 15–2 illustrates a strategy matrix based on these two dimensions. This matrix suggests the six marketing strategies discussed in the following sections. As you will see, although there is considerable overlap between the strategies, each has a unique thrust.

## Maintenance Strategy

If the brand is purchased habitually by the target market, the marketer's strategy is to maintain that behavior. This requires consistent attention to product quality, distribution (avoiding out-of-stock situations), and a reinforcement advertising strategy. In addition, the marketer must defend against the disruptive tactics of competitors. Thus, it needs to maintain product development and improvements and to counter short-term competitive strategies, such as coupons, point-of-purchase displays, or rebates.

Morton salt and Del Monte canned vegetables have large repeat purchaser segments that they have successfully maintained. Budweiser, Marlboro, and Crest have large brand-loyal purchaser segments. They have successfully defended their market positions against assaults by major competitors in recent years. In contrast, Liggett & Myers lost 80 percent of its

| Position | Target Market Decision-Making Pattern | | |
|---|---|---|---|
| | Nominal Decision Making (no search) | Limited Decision Making (limited search) | Extended Decision Making (extensive search) |
| *Brand in evoked set* | Maintenance strategy | Capture strategy | Preference strategy |
| *Brand not in evoked set* | Disrupt strategy | Intercept strategy | Acceptance strategy |

**TABLE 15–2**

Marketing Strategies Based on Information Search Patterns

market share when it failed to engage in maintenance advertising.[72] Quality control problems caused Schlitz to lose substantial market share.

Illustration 15–4 shows the use of a maintenance strategy against the challenge of competitors. Note that the ad stresses the improvements to the product.

## Disrupt Strategy

If the brand is not part of the evoked set and the target market engages in nominal decision making, the marketer's first task is to *disrupt* the existing decision pattern. This is a difficult task since the consumer does not seek external information or even consider alternative brands before a purchase. Low-involvement learning over time could generate a positive product position for our brand, but this alone would be unlikely to shift behavior.

In the long run, a major product improvement accompanied by attention-attracting advertising could shift the target market into a more extensive form of decision making. In the short run, attention-attracting advertising aimed specifically at breaking habitual decision making can be successful. Free samples, coupons, rebates, and tie-in sales are common approaches to disrupting nominal decision making. Likewise, striking package designs and point-of-purchase displays may disrupt a habitual purchase sequence.[73] Comparative advertising is also often used for this purpose.

Illustration 15–5 is an example of a disrupt strategy. Silk has found that once consumers try its various soymilk products, many prefer them. However, most consumers drink either cow's milk or no milk at all. Therefore, Silk has tried a number of ways to disrupt these behaviors and induce trial. In this attention-attracting ad, Silk uses humor and a direct challenge.

## Capture Strategy

Limited decision making generally involves a few brands that are evaluated on only a few criteria, such as price or availability. Much of the information search occurs at the point-of-purchase or in readily available media prior to purchase. If the brand is one given this type of consideration by the target market, the marketer's objective is to capture as large a share of the purchases as practical.

Because these consumers engage in limited search, the marketer needs to know where they search and what information they are looking for. In general, the marketer will want to supply information, often on price and availability, in its Web site, in local media through cooperative advertising, and at the point of purchase through displays and adequate shelf space. The marketer will also be concerned with maintaining consistent product quality and adequate distribution.

## Intercept Strategy

If the target market engages in limited decision making and the brand is not part of the evoked set, the objective will be to intercept the consumer during the search for information on the brands in the evoked set or during general search for related information. Again, the emphasis will be on local media with cooperative advertising and at the point

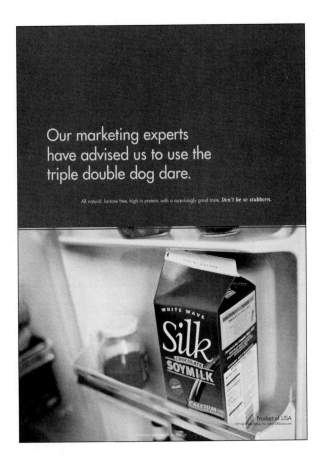

of purchase with displays, shelf space, package design, and so forth. Coupons can also be effective. The marketer will have to place considerable emphasis on attracting the consumers' attention, because they will not be seeking information on the brand. The behavioral targeting strategy used by Snapple on iVillage's Web site is a great example of an online intercept strategy. As one ad executive stated:

> The big trick with this product was changing [the audience's perception] of Snapple-a-Day from an on-the-go, quirky product to something that has real health benefits for women and that has to be more of a planned purchase.[74]

The promotion shown in Illustration 15–6 would be effective as part of a capture or intercept strategy.

In addition to the strategies mentioned above, low-involvement learning, product improvements, and free samples can be used to move the brand into the target market's evoked set.

## Preference Strategy

Extended decision making with the brand in the evoked set requires a preference strategy. Because extended decision making generally involves several brands, many attributes, and a number of information sources, a simple capture strategy may not be adequate. Instead, the marketer needs to structure an information campaign that will result in the brand being preferred by members of the target market.

The first step is a strong position on those attributes important to the target market.[75] This is discussed in considerable detail in Chapter 16. Next, information must be provided in all the appropriate sources. This may require extensive advertising to groups that do not purchase the item but recommend it to others (e.g., druggists for over-the-counter drugs, veterinarians, and county agents for agricultural products). Independent groups should be encouraged to test the brand, and sales personnel should be provided detailed information on the brand's attributes. In addition, it may be wise to provide the sales personnel with extra motivation (e.g., extra commissions paid by the manufacturer) to recommend the product. Point-of-purchase displays and pamphlets should also be available. A well-designed Web site is essential.

Illustration 15–7 shows part of an effective preference strategy. It assumes an involved search, provides detailed information relative to multiple product attributes, shopping venues, and so on.

## Acceptance Strategy

Acceptance strategy is similar to preference strategy. However, it is complicated by the fact that the target market is not seeking information about the brand. Therefore, in addition to the activities involved in the preference strategy described above, the marketer must attract the consumers' attention or otherwise motivate them to learn about the brand. Consider the following quote by Lee Iaccoca while he was head of Chrysler:

> Our biggest long-term job is to get people in [the showroom] to see how great these cars are—to get some traffic—and let them compare, so we're going head to head on price and value.[76]

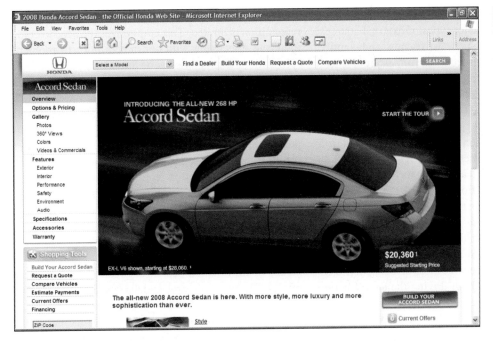

Because of this situation, Chrysler implemented an acceptance strategy. In addition to product improvements and heavy advertising, Chrysler literally paid consumers to seek information about their cars! They did this by offering cash to individuals who would test drive a Chrysler product prior to purchasing a new car.

Long-term advertising designed to enhance low-involvement learning is another useful technique for gaining acceptance. Extensive advertising with strong emphasis on attracting attention can also be effective. The primary objective of these two approaches is not to sell the brand; rather, the objective is to move the brand into the evoked set. Then, when a purchase situation arises, the consumer will seek additional information on this brand.

Finally, the Internet can play an important role in an acceptance strategy. As the search engine results of DoubleClick indicate, keyword searches prior to a purchase tend to be generic. This opens up important opportunities for companies that are not in the evoked set to engage in search engine optimization strategies (including paying for specific keywords) to give their brand exposure to the consumer during the decision process—hopefully, to the point of moving the brand into consumers' evoked sets. Obviously, a well-designed Web site is a critical part of this strategy.

## SUMMARY

Following problem recognition, consumers may engage in extensive internal and external search, limited internal and external search, or only internal search. Information may be sought on (1) the appropriate *evaluative criteria* for the solution of the problem, (2) the existence of various *alternative solutions,* and (3) the *performance* of each alternative solution on each evaluative criterion.

Most consumers, when faced with a problem, can recall a limited number of brands that they feel are probably acceptable solutions. These acceptable brands, the

*evoked set* (also known as the consideration set), are the initial ones that the consumer seeks additional information on during the remaining internal and external search process. Therefore, marketers are very concerned that their brands fall within the evoked set of most members of their target market.

Consumer internal information (information stored in memory) may have been actively acquired in previous searches and personal experiences, or it may have been passively acquired through low-involvement learning.

In addition to their own *memory,* consumers can seek information from four major types of external sources: (1) *personal sources,* such as friends and family; (2) *independent sources,* such as consumer groups, paid professionals, and government agencies; (3) *marketing sources,* such as sales personnel and advertising; and (4) *experiential sources,* such as direct product inspection or trial.

The Internet is commonly used as a source of information. While the Internet can decrease the costs of information search and lead to enhanced decisions, it can also lead to information overload. Online services that utilize *shopping bots* are increasingly popular with consumers as a means of establishing their consideration sets and for aiding in the decision itself. Marketing segmentation and targeted approaches are increasingly common as online users become more diverse. Marketers must be concerned with both driving their information to consumers and driving consumers to their information. Traditional offline media, Web advertising, search engine optimization, and behavioral targeting can help accomplish these goals.

Explicit external information search *after* problem recognition is limited. This emphasizes the need to communicate effectively with consumers prior to problem recognition. Characteristics of the market, the product, the consumer, and the situation interact to influence the level of search.

It is often suggested that consumers generally should engage in relatively extensive external search prior to purchasing an item. However, this view ignores the fact that information search is not free. It takes time, energy, and money, and can often require giving up more desirable activities. Therefore, consumers should engage in external search only to the extent that the expected benefits, such as a lower price or a more satisfactory purchase, outweigh the expected costs.

Sound marketing strategy takes into account the nature of information search engaged in by the target market. The level of search and the brand's position in or out of the evoked set are two key dimensions. Based on these two dimensions, six potential information strategies are suggested: (1) *maintenance,* (2) *disrupt,* (3) *capture,* (4) *intercept,* (5) *preference,* and (6) *acceptance.*

## KEY TERMS

Awareness set   521
Behavioral targeting   530
Bots   528
Consideration set   521
Evoked set   521

External search   518
Inept set   521
Inert set   521
Internal search   518
Ongoing search   519

Perceived risk   536
Search engine optimization
   (SEO)   531

## INTERNET EXERCISES

1. The demographic composition of Internet users in the United States is changing over time as are the activities that users engage in. Go to the Pew Internet and American Life Project Web site (www.pewinternet .org). Go to the section on trends and report on how demographics and activities have changed from those reported in the text (generally from 2007/08).

2. The Conference Board and TNS jointly sponsor the Consumer Internet Barometer at www .consumerinternetbarometer.us/. Report on the various dimensions they track and the major issues and perceptions of online users.

3. Go to www.searchenginewatch.com under their *search engine marketing 101* section. Examine the various resources in this section, including strategies

for search engine optimization (SEO). Prepare a brief report on the various techniques involved in SEO.

4. Find and describe a magazine ad that is particularly effective at causing readers to consult a Web site. Why is it effective?

5. Visit a firm's Web site in one of the product categories listed below. Report on the strategies this firm uses (if any) to generate repeat traffic. Which strategies are most effective?
   a. Boats
   b. Cosmetics
   c. Jewelry
   d. Food products company
   e. Health care organization
   f. Charities focused on poverty relief

6. Use an Internet shopping service such as mysimon.com to determine the "best buy" for a product that interests you. Evaluate this process. How could it be improved? If you were actually going to make the purchase, would you buy this one or would you purchase elsewhere? Why?

7. Visit Amazon.com, epionions.com, or a similar site. Examine the product reviews provided by other customers. How useful do you think these are? What could make them more useful?

8. Click on two banner ads for similar products. Describe where you encountered the banner ads, and evaluate each banner ad and the target site. Do you feel like behavioral targeting was being used? Explain.

## DDB LIFE STYLE STUDY™ DATA ANALYSES

1. Using the DDB data (Tables 1B through 7B), describe the major determinants of the following search-related behaviors and beliefs. What are the marketing implications?
   a. Consult consumer reports before making major purchases.
   b. Information in advertising helps me make better decisions.
   c. The Internet is the best place to get information about products and services.

2. Some consumers feel more *technology savvy* than others. Examine the DDB data in Tables 1B through 7B to determine what characterizes one who is likely to feel tech savvy.

3. Using Table 3B, specifically examine the relationship between consumer perceptions of being tech savvy and the three search-related variables in Question 1. What are the relationships and implications?

## REVIEW QUESTIONS

1. When does *information search* occur? What is the difference between internal and external information search?

2. What kind of information is sought in an external search for information?

3. What are *evaluative criteria* and how do they relate to information search?

4. How does a consumer's *awareness set* influence information search?

5. What roles do the *evoked set, inert set,* and *inept set* play in a consumer's information search?

6. What are the primary sources of information available to consumers?

7. What sources of information are available on the Internet?

8. What is *behavioral targeting*?

9. What is *search engine optimization*?

10. How do nonsearchers, limited information searchers, and extended information searchers differ in their search for information?

11. What factors might influence the search effort of consumers who are essentially one-stop shoppers? How do these factors differ in terms of how they influence limited information searchers and extended information searchers?

12. What factors have to be considered in the total cost of the information search? How might these factors be different for different consumers?

13. Explain how different *market characteristics* affect information search.

14. How do different *consumer characteristics* influence a consumer's information search effort?

15. How do *product characteristics* influence a consumer's information search effort?

16. How do *situational characteristics* influence a consumer's information search effort?

17. Describe the information search characteristics that should lead to each of the following strategies:
   a. Maintenance
   b. Disrupt
   c. Capture
   d. Intercept
   e. Preference
   f. Acceptance

18. Describe each of the strategies listed in Question 17.

## DISCUSSION QUESTIONS

19. Pick a product/brand that you believe would require each strategy in Table 15–2 (six products in total). Justify your selection. Develop a specific marketing strategy for each (six strategies in total).

20. Of the products shown in Figure 15–3, which product class is most likely to exhibit the most brand switching? Explain your answer in terms of the information provided in Figure 15–3.

21. Use a shopping service such as NexTag to help you choose a brand of digital camera. In what way does it help you form your evoked or consideration set? Is information overload a problem? Explain.

22. Have you used an Internet shopping service such as mysimon.com? If so, what is your evaluation of it? If no, why not?

23. What information sources do you think students on your campus use when acquiring the items listed below? Consider the various sources listed in Figure 15–4 in developing your answer. Do you think there will be individual differences? Why?
    a. Movies
    b. Restaurants
    c. Apartment
    d. Computer
    e. Fitness equipment
    f. A charity contribution
    g. Dress clothes
    h. Cell phones

24. What factors contribute to the size of the awareness set, evoked set, inert set, and inept set?

25. Discuss factors that may contribute to external information search and factors that act to reduce external search for information before purchase or adoption of the following:
    a. Car repairs
    b. International travel
    c. Exercise club
    d. Formal wear
    e. Organic foods
    f. Counseling services

26. Is it ever in the best interest of a marketer to encourage potential customers to carry out an extended prepurchase search? Why or why not?

27. What implications for marketing strategy does Figure 15–2 suggest?

28. What implications for online marketing strategy does Figure 15–6 suggest?

29. What role, if any, should the government play in ensuring that consumers have easy access to relevant product information? How should it accomplish this?

30. Respond to the questions in Consumer Insight 15–1.

31. Describe a recent purchase in which you engaged in extensive search and one in which you did little prepurchase search. What factors caused the difference?

32. What is your awareness set, evoked set, inert set, and inept set for the following? In what ways, if any, do you think your sets will differ from the average member of your class? Why?
    a. MP3 players
    b. Energy drinks
    c. Car insurance providers
    d. Jewelry stores
    e. Book stores
    f. Internet shopping services
    g. Restaurants

## APPLICATION ACTIVITIES

33. Develop an appropriate questionnaire and complete Question 23 using information from five students not in your class. Prepare a report discussing the marketing implications of your findings.

34. For the same products listed in Question 32, ask five students to list all the brands they are aware of in each product category. Then have them indicate which ones they might buy (evoked set), which ones they are indifferent toward (inert set), and which brands they strongly dislike and would not purchase (inept set). What are the marketing implications of your results?

35. Develop a short questionnaire designed to measure the information search consumers engage in

prior to purchasing an expensive recreational or entertainment item or service. Your questionnaire should include measures of types of information sought, as well as sources that provide this information. Also include measures of the relevant consumer characteristics that might influence information search, as well as some measure of past experience with the products. Then interview two recent purchasers of each product, using the questionnaire you have developed. Analyze each consumer's response and classify each consumer in terms of information search. What are the marketing implications of your results?

36. For each strategy in Table 15–2, find one brand that appears to be following that strategy. Describe in detail how it is implementing the strategy.

37. Develop a questionnaire to determine which products college students view as positive and which they view as negative. Measure the shopping effort associated with each type. Explain your overall results and any individual differences you find.

## REFERENCES

1. The Chapter 15 opener is based on information found on the various corporate Web sites.

2. G. Punji and R. Brookes, "Decision Constraints and Consideration-Set Formation in Consumer Durables," *Psychology & Marketing,* August 2001, pp. 843–63.

3. An outstanding discussion of the trade-off consumers make between memory-based decisions (internal search) and external search is in J. R. Bettman, M. F. Luce, and J. W. Payne, "Constructive Consumer Choice Processes," *Journal of Consumer Research,* December 1998, pp. 187–217.

4. For a more comprehensive view, see R. Lawson, "Consumer Decision Making within a Goal-Driven Framework," *Psychology & Marketing,* August 1997, pp. 427–49.

5. S. S. Posavac, D. M. Sanbonmatsu, and E. A. Ho, "The Effects of the Selective Consideration of Alternatives on Consumer Choice and Attitude-Decision Consistency," *Journal of Consumer Psychology* 12, no. 3 (2002), pp. 203–13; T. Erdem and J. Swait, "Brand Credibility, Brand Consideration, and Choice," *Journal of Consumer Research,* June 2004, pp. 191–98; and M. Paulssen and R. P. Bagozzi, "A Self-Regulatory Model of Consideration Set Formation," *Psychology & Marketing,* October 2005, pp. 785–812.

6. P. Aurier, S. Jean, and J. L. Zaichkowsky, "Consideration Set Size and Familiarity with Usage Context," *Advances in Consumer Research,* vol. 27, eds. S. J. Hoch and R. J. Meyer (Provo, UT: Association for Consumer Research, 2000), pp. 307–13; and K. K. Desai and W. D. Hoyer, "Descriptive Characteristics of Memory-Based Consideration Sets," *Journal of Consumer Research,* December 2000, pp. 309–23.

7. E. M. Felcher, P. Malaviya, and A. L. McGill, "The Role of Taxonomic and Goal-Derived Product Categorization in, within, and across Category Judgments," *Psychology & Marketing,* August 2001, pp. 865–87.

8. R. R. Brand and J. J. Cronin, "Consumer-Specific Determinants of the Size of Retail Choice Sets," *Journal of Services Marketing* 11, no. 1 (1997), pp. 19–38.

9. See S. C. Mooy and H. S. J. Robben, "How Consumers Learn from and about Products," *Advances in Consumer Research,* vol. 25, eds. J. W. Alba and J. W. Hutchinson (Provo, UT: Association for Consumer Research, 1998), pp. 318–23.

10. L. R. Klein and G. T. Ford, "Consumer Search for Information in the Digital Age," *Journal of Interactive Marketing,* Summer 2003, pp. 29–49; and B. T. Ratchford, M.-Soo Lee, and D. Talukdar, "The Impact of the Internet on Information Search for Automobiles," *Journal of Marketing Research,* May 2003, pp. 193–209.

11. H. Li, T. Daugherty, and F. Biocca, "The Role of Virtual Experience in Consumer Learning," *Journal of Consumer Psychology* 13, no. 4 (2003), pp. 395–407; A. E. Schlosser, "Experience Products in the Virtual World," *Journal of Consumer Research,* September 2003, pp. 184–98; and D. A. Griffith and Q. Chen, "The Influence of Virtual Direct Experience (VDE) on On-line Ad Message Effectiveness," *Journal of Advertising,* Spring 2004, pp. 55–68.

12. C. B. Jarvis, "An Exploratory Investigation of Consumers' Evaluations of External Information Sources in Prepurchase Search," *Advances in Consumer Research,* vol. 25, eds. Alba and Hutchinson, pp. 446–51; and M. Laroche, C. Kim, and T. Matsui, "Which Decision Heuristics Are Used in Consideration Set Formation?" *Journal of Consumer Marketing* 20, no. 3 (2003), pp. 192–209.

13. For a review and conflicting evidence, see A. A. Wright and J. G. Lynch, Jr., "Communications Effects of Advertising versus Direct Experience When Both Search and Experience Attributes Are Present," *Journal of Consumer Research,* March 1995, pp. 108–18.

14. See C. F. Mela, S. Gupta, and D. R. Lehmann, "The Long-Term Impact of Promotion and Advertising on Consumer Brand Choice," *Journal of Marketing Research,* May 1997, pp. 248–61; and M. J. Sirgy et al., "Does Television Viewership Play a Role in the Perception of Quality of Life?" *Journal of Advertising,* Spring 1998, pp. 125–42.

15. *World Internet Usage Statistics News and World Population Stats* (Bogota, Colombia: Miniwatts Marketing Group, March 2008).

16. See, e.g., *Internet Becomes More Mainstream,* Mediamark Research Inc., press release, July 16, 2002.

17. *Latinos Online,* Pew Internet & American Life Project, March 14, 2007, www.pewinternet.org.

18. *Older Americans and the Internet,* Pew Internet & American Life Project, March 25, 2004, www.pewinternet.org.

19. *A Nation Online* (Washington, DC: U.S. Department of Commerce, September 2004).

20. *Internet Activities*, Pew Internet & American Life Project, www.pewinternet.org, accessed June 9, 2008.

21. S. Hays, "Has Online Advertising Finally Grown Up?" *Advertising Age,* April 1, 2002, p. C1.

22. *Counting on the Internet*, Pew Internet & American Life Project, December 29, 2002, www.pewinternet.org; Klein and Ford, "Consumer Search for Information in the Digital Age"; Ratchford, Lee, and Talukdar, "The Impact of the Internet on Information Search for Automobiles"; *DoubleClick's Touch-points II*, DoubleClick research report, March 2004, www.doubleclick.com; *DoubleClick's Touch-points III*, DoubleClick research report, July 2005, www.doubleclick.com; and B. T. Ratchford, D. Talukdar, and M. Lee, "The Impact of the Internet on Consumers' Use of Information Sources for Automobiles," *Journal of Consumer Research,* June 2007, pp. 111–19.

23. *Search before the Purchase,* DoubleClick research report, February 2005, www.doubleclick.com.

24. Ratchford, Lee, and Talukdar, "The Impact of the Internet on Information Search for Automobiles."

25. J. L. Joines, C. W. Scherer, and D. A. Scheufele, "Exploring Motivations for Consumer Web Use and Their Implications for E-commerce," *Journal of Consumer Marketing* 20, no. 2 (2003), pp. 90–108.

26. L. Gentry and R. Calantone, "A Comparison of Three Models to Explain Shop-Bot Use on the Web," *Psychology & Marketing,* November 2002, pp. 945–56.

27. B. Bickart and R. M. Schindler, "Internet Forums as Influential Sources of Consumer Information," *Journal of Interactive Marketing,* Summer 2001, pp. 31–40; and P. Chatterjee, "Online Reviews," *Advances in Consumer Research,* vol. 28, eds. M. C. Gilly and J. Meyers-Levy (Provo, UT: Association for Consumer Research, 2001), pp. 129–33.

28. Klein and Ford, "Consumer Search for Information in the Digital Age."

29. A. Parmar, "Student e-union," *Marketing News,* April 1, 2004, pp. 14–15.

30. "Ethnic Groups Online," *eMarketer,* June 20, 2005.

31. N. Singh and H. Matsuo, "Measuring Cultural Adaptation on the Web," in *Advances in Consumer Research,* vol. 30, eds. P. A. Keller and D. W. Rook (Provo, UT: Association for Consumer Research, 2003), pp. 271–72.

32. "U.S. Online Ad Spending by Format," in *Advertising Age Digital Marketing & Media Fact Pack* (New York: Crain Communications, April 23, 2007).

33. J. Halliday, "Half Hit Web before Showrooms," *Advertising Age,* October 4, 2004, p. 76.

34. E-mail material based on *DoubleClick's 2004 Consumer E-mail Study*, DoubleClick, October 2004, www.doubleclick.com.

35. Information from DoubleClick's Web site, www.doubleclick.com.

36. J. S. Ilfeld and R. S. Winer, "Generating Web Traffic," *Journal of Advertising Research,* October 2002, pp. 49–61.

37. *Best Practices for Optimizing Web Advertising Effectiveness*, DoubleClick, May 2006, www.doubleclick.com.

38. Ibid.

39. C. McCarthy, "MySpace Gets 'Hyper' with Targeted Ads," *CNET News.com,* November 5, 2007, http://news.cnet.com/; and J. Kirk, "MySpace User Ad Targeting Will Be Optional," *The Industry Standard,* April 29, 2008, www.thestandard.com.

40. W. Dou, R. Linn, and S. Yang, "How Smart Are 'Smart Banners'?" *Journal of Advertising Research* 41, no. 4 (2001), pp. 31–43.

41. K. Oser, "Snapple Effort Finds Women as They Browse," *Advertising Age,* May 3, 2004, p. 22.

42. D. Sullivan, "Intro to Search Engine Optimization," *SearchEngineWatch.com,* October 14, 2002.

43. See, e.g., T. P. Novak, D. L. Hoffman, and Y.-F. Yung, "Measuring the Customer Experience in Online Environments," *Marketing Science,* Winter 2000, pp. 22–42; and J. R. Coyle and E. Thorson, "The Effects of Progressive Levels of Interactivity and Vividness in Web Marketing Sites," *Journal of Advertising,* Fall 2001, pp. 65–77.

44. R. A. Westbrook and C. Farnell, "Patterns of Information Source Usage among Durable Goods Buyers," *Journal of Marketing Research,* August 1979, pp. 303–12; and J. E. Urbany, P. R. Dickson, and W. L. Wilkie, "Buyer Uncertainty and Information Search," *Journal of Consumer Research,* September 1989, pp. 208–15.

45. Consumer Insight 15–1 is based on M. Kamvar and S. Baluja, "A Large Scale Study of Wireless Search Behavior," in *Proceedings of SIGCHI Conference on Human Factors in Computing Systems,* eds. R. Ginter et al. (Montreal: Conference on Human Factors in Computing Systems, 2006), pp. 701–709; "Search Marketing," in *Advertising Age Fact Pack 2007* (New York: Crain Communications, November 5, 2007); *Best Practices: A Blueprint for Building a Retail Mobile Marketing Program,* (Irvine, CA: SmartReply, 2007); "Case Studies," *MobileMarketing Magazine,* November 19, 2007, p. 22; and "Special Report: Interactive Marketing," *promomagazine.com,* accessed April 15, 2008.

46. Urbany, Dickson, and Wilkie, "Buyer Uncertainty and Information Search"; and *Warranties Rule Consumer Follow-Up* (Washington DC: Federal Trade Commission, 1984), p. 26.

47. Ratchford, Lee, and Talukdar, "The Impact of the Internet on Information Search for Automobiles."

48. G. Katona and E. Mueller, "A Study of Purchase Decisions," in *Consumer Behavior: The Dynamics of Consumer Reaction,* ed. L. Clark (New York: New York University Press, 1955), pp. 30–87; J. Newman and R. Staelin, "Prepurchase Information Seeking for New Cars and Major Household Appliances," *Journal of Marketing Research,* August 1972, pp. 249–57; J. Claxton, J. Fry, and B. Portis, "A Taxonomy of Prepurchase Information Gathering Patterns," *Journal of Consumer Research,* December 1974, pp. 35–42; G. C. Kiel and R. A. Layton, "Dimensions of Consumer Information Seeking Behavior," *Journal of Marketing Research,* May 1981, pp. 233–39; J. B. Freiden and R. E. Goldsmith, "Prepurchase Information-Seeking for Professional Services," *Journal of Services Marketing,* Winter 1989, pp. 45–55; Urbany, Dickson, and Wilkie, "Buyer Uncertainty and Information Search"; G. N. Souter and M. M. McNeil, *Journal of Professional Services Marketing* 11, no. 2 (1995), pp. 45–60; and Klein and Ford, "Consumer Search for Information in the Digital Age."

49. See W. K. Darley, "The Relationship of Antecedents of Search and Self-Esteem to Adolescent Search Effort," *Psychology & Marketing,* August 1999, pp. 409–27.

50. J. G. Lynch, Jr., and D. Ariely, "Wine Online," *Marketing Science,* Winter 2000, pp. 83–103; D. Ariely, "Controlling the Information Flow," *Journal of Consumer Research,* September 2000, pp. 233–48; and Ratchford, Lee, and Talukdar, "The Impact of the Internet on Information Search for Automobiles."

51. For a similar model of online search, see S. Kulviwat, C. Guo, and N. Engchanil, "Determinants of Online Search," *Internet Research* 14, no. 3 (2004), pp. 245–53.

52. D. R. Lichtenstein, N. M. Ridgway, and R. G. Netemeyer, "Price Perceptions and Consumer Shopping Behavior," *Journal of Marketing Research,* May 1993, pp. 234–45.

53. M. N. Bergen, S. Dutta, and S. M. Shugan, "Branded Variants," *Journal of Marketing Research,* February 1996, pp. 9–19.

54. J. Srivastava and N. Lurie, "A Consumer Perspective on Price-Matching Refund Policies," *Journal of Consumer Research,* September 2001, pp. 296–307.

55. D. Grewal and H. Marmorstein, "Market Price Variation, Perceived Price Variation, and Consumers' Price Search Decisions for Durable Goods," *Journal of Consumer Research,* December 1994, pp. 453–60.

56. See B. G. C. Dellaert, "Investigating Consumers' Tendency to Combine Multiple Shopping Purposes and Destinations," *Journal of Marketing Research,* May 1998, pp. 177–89.

57. See C. Moorman, "Market-Level Effects of Information," *Journal of Marketing Research,* February 1998, pp. 82–98; and A. D. Miyazaki, D. E. Sprott, and K. C. Manning, "Unit Prices on Retail Shelf Labels," *Journal of Retailing* 76, no. 1 (2000), pp. 93–112.

58. See C. M. Fisher and C. J. Anderson, "The Relationship between Consumer Attitudes and Frequency of Advertising in Newspapers for Hospitals," *Journal of Hospital Marketing* 7, no. 2 (1993), pp. 139–56.

59. S. Widrick and E. Fram, "Identifying Negative Products," *Journal of Consumer Marketing,* no. 2 (1983), pp. 59–66.

60. See D. D'Rozario and S. P. Douglas, "Effect of Assimilation on Prepurchase Information-Search Tendencies," *Journal of Consumer Psychology* 8, no. 2 (1999), pp. 187–209; and C. Merrill, "Where the Cars Are Caliente," *American Demographics,* January 2000, pp. 56–59.

61. J. Lee and J. Cho, "Consumers' Use of Information Intermediaries and the Impact on Their Information Search Behavior in the Financial Market," *The Journal of Consumer Affairs* 39, no.1 (2005), pp. 95–120.

62. J. W. Alba and J. W. Hutchinson, "Knowledge Calibration," *Journal of Consumer Research,* September 2000, pp. 123–49.

63. C. M. Heilman, D. Bowman, and G. P. Wright, "The Evolution of Brand Preferences and Choice Behaviors of Consumers New to a Market," *Journal of Marketing Research,* May 2000, pp. 139–55. See also D. Mazursky, "The Effects of Invalidating Information on Consumers' Subsequent Search Patterns," *Journal of Economic Psychology,* April 1998, pp. 261–77.

64. See J. A. Barrick and B. C. Spilker, "The Relations between Knowledge, Search Strategy, and Performance in Unaided and Aided Information Search," *Organizational Behavior and Human Decision Processes* 90 (2003), pp. 1–18.

65. See T. Williams, M. Slama, and J. Rogers, "Behavioral Characteristics of the Recreational Shopper," *Journal of Academy of Marketing Science,* Summer 1985, pp. 307–16; J. R. Lumpkin, J. M. Hawes, and W. R. Darden, "Shopping Patterns of the Rural Consumer," *Journal of Business Research,* February 1986, pp. 63–81; and W. W. Moe, "Buying, Searching, or Browsing," *Journal of Consumer Psychology* 13, no. 1/2 (2003), pp. 29–39.

66. See U. M. Dholakia, "Involvement-Response Models of Joint Effects," *Advances in Consumer Research,* vol. 25, eds. Alba and Hutchinson, pp. 499–506.

67. T. H. Dodd, B. E. Pinkleton, and A. W. Gustafson, *Psychology & Marketing,* May 1996, pp. 291–304. See also J. R. McColl-Kennedy and R. E. Fetter, Jr., "An Empirical Examination of the Involvement to External Search Relationship," *Journal of Services Marketing* 15, no. 2 (2001), pp. 82–98.

68. G. R. Dowling and R. Staelin, "A Model of Perceived Risk and Intended Risk-Handling Activity," *Journal of Consumer Research,* June 1994, pp. 119–34. See also J. B. Smith and J. M. Bristor, "Uncertainty Orientation," *Psychology & Marketing,* November 1994, pp. 587–607.

69. A. Chaudhuri, "Product Class Effects on Perceived Risk," *International Journal of Research in Marketing,* May 1998, pp. 157–68; and K. Mitra, M. C. Reiss, and L. M. Capella, "An Examination of Perceived Risk, Informational Search, and Behavioral Intentions," *Journal of Services Marketing* 13, no. 3 (1999), pp. 208–28.

70. See, e.g., M. W. H. Weenig and M. Maarleveld, "The Impact of Time Constraint on Information Search Strategies in Complex Choice Tasks," *Journal of Economic Psychology* 23 (2002), pp. 689–702. For an exception, see C. J. Hill, "The Nature of Problem Recognition and Search in the Extended Health Care Decision," *Journal of Services Marketing* 15, no. 6 (2001), pp. 454–79.

71. A. G. Abdul-Muhmin, "Contingent Decision Behavior," *Journal of Consumer Psychology* 8, no. 1 (1999), pp. 91–111.

72. "L&M Lights Up Again," *Marketing and Media Decisions,* February 1984, p. 69.

73. L. L. Garber, "The Package Appearance in Choice," in *Advances in Consumer Research,* vol. 22, eds. F. R. Kardes and M. Sujan (Provo, UT: Association for Consumer Research, 1995), pp. 653–60.

74. Oser, "Snapple Effort Finds Women as They Browse."

75. See, e.g., Erdem and Swait, "Brand Credibility, Brand Consideration, and Choice."

76. R. Gray, "Chrysler Hinges Price on Popularity," *Advertising Age,* October 5, 1981, p. 7.

# Alternative Evaluation and Selection

In Chapter 15 we discussed online shopping services that help consumers with information search. These services, sometimes called recommendation agents or bots, can also aid in the decision-making process. For example, some shopping services simply list available brands or look for the lowest price. If lowest price is all a consumer is worried about, then they can simply pick that offering. For example, a consumer might reason that all flights from New York to Denver are the same and they simply want the lowest price. Having found it, their alternative selection process is simple—pick the lowest-priced offering.[1]

Other decisions are more complex and there are shopping services and bots that help consumers with that complexity. For example, Price Grabber allows consumers to filter the available alternatives based on various evaluative criteria, thus helping consumers form their evoked set. That is, the consumer decides what their acceptable levels are on various attributes and Price Grabber only presents the brands that are left that meet those criteria. This remaining set is what we referred to in Chapter 15 as the consid-

eration set. The challenge here for the consumer is to evaluate the brands in the consideration set and to make a final choice.

Some shopping services or bots help consumers actually make decisions when there are numerous evaluative criteria and the decision is relatively complex. Yahoo Shopping is one example. It allows consumers to rate the importance of each evaluative criteria and then provides recommendations that are ranked on the basis of this input. The top-ranked alternative is the one that Yahoo Shopping deems the best fit for consumer preferences. This feature, called Smart Sort, mimics the trade-offs that consumers would naturally make given the importance they place on various evaluative criteria. Such "smart" recommendation agents are important because they help consumers make choices that are more closely matched to their preferences rather than simply telling consumers what's available. In addition, Yahoo Shopping provides an explanation, based on product attributes and consumer input, of why the brand is recommended. This explanation is important because it increases consumer trust in the recommendation.

**FIGURE 16–1**   Alternative Evaluation and Selection Process

As the opening examples suggest, consumers make decisions in a variety of ways and the decisions they make range from simple to complex. The process by which consumers evaluate and choose among alternatives is illustrated in Figure 16–1.

We will organize our discussion around four basic areas. First, we will provide an overview of the processes consumers use to select among alternatives. Then, we will describe the nature and characteristics of evaluative criteria (the benefits the product should provide). After examining evaluative criteria, we will focus on the ability of consumers to judge the performance of products on the evaluative criteria. Finally, we will examine the decision rules that consumers use in selecting one alternative from those considered.

It is important to remember that many purchases involve little or no evaluation of alternatives. Nominal decisions do not require the evaluation of any alternatives. The last purchase is repeated without considering other information. Limited decisions may involve comparing a few brands (small evoked set) on one or two dimensions (I'll buy Heinz or Del Monte ketchup, depending on which is cheaper at Safeway).

# HOW CONSUMERS MAKE CHOICES

Any attempt to describe a complex, nonlinear process such as consumer choice necessarily simplifies it and removes much of its richness. Thus, our discussion will make consumer choice seem more logical, structured, rational, and deliberate than it often is. Fortunately, we have all made numerous consumer choices, so we know that they are frequently circular, emotional, and incomplete, and may be based on expediency rather than optimality. We also know that the situation plays an important role in the processes we use to make consumer choices. For example, when we are tired or hurried, we are very likely to use different choice processes than we would if we had more energy or time.

A substantial amount of research and marketing strategy has assumed a rational consumer decision maker with well-defined, stable preferences. The consumer is also assumed to have sufficient skills to calculate which option will maximize his or her value, and will choose on this basis. This approach is referred to as *rational choice theory*. The task in rational choice theory is to *identify* or discover the one optimal choice for the decision confronting the decision maker. The decision maker simply collects information on the levels of the attributes of the alternatives, applies preexisting values to those levels, applies the appropriate choice rule, and the superior option is revealed.

In reality, all consumers have **bounded rationality**—*a limited capacity for processing information*. Moreover, consumers often have goals that are different from, or in addition

## Consumer Choice Metagoals

Consumer choice goals are usually described in terms such as "getting the least expensive calculator with the functions I need" or "selecting a dress that makes me feel great." These are the specific purchase goals or outcomes the consumer wants to obtain. A **metagoal** refers to *the general nature of the outcome being sought.*[2] The purchase goals just described are examples of a metagoal of *maximizing the accuracy of the decision.* This is the only goal assumed in many studies of consumer decision making. However, other metagoals exist.

Consumers often seek to *minimize the cognitive effort required for the decision.* This is often the goal in nominal and limited decision making. However, it can also play an important role in extended decision making as well. Consumers seeking to minimize effort tend to use simple choice rules, consider fewer alternatives, place more importance on the dominant attribute, and evaluate fewer attributes of each alternative.[3] Consumers may also delay or avoid the decision.[4]

Choices that involve conflicts between valued goals such as having an attractive, low-effort lawn versus avoiding the use of pesticides and herbicides can generate significant negative emotions.[5] Thus, another consumer metagoal is to *minimize the experience of negative emotion while making the decision.* One strategy consumers use for this purpose is to avoid or delay the decision and stay with the status quo.

A fourth metagoal is to *maximize the ease with which a decision can be justified.* Consumers are social beings and often feel compelled to justify a decision

to others or to themselves.[6] This is particularly true for luxury items and items that are different or more extravagant than those used by one's reference groups. Anticipating the need for such justification can affect how a consumer makes the initial decision.

Many decisions are characterized by multiple goals with differing levels of importance. Further, the relative importance of the goals may change as the consumer moves through the decision process. For example, while buying a lawn mower, as the consumer learns of incompatible features (the model that pollutes the least costs the most and does not perform as well), minimizing negative emotion may become more salient. Finally, regulatory focus can cause consumers to trade off goals. As we saw in Chapter 10, those with a promotion orientation prefer decision speed and ease over accuracy while those with a prevention orientation prefer decision accuracy over speed and ease. Regulatory focus is a motivational factor that is influenced by individual and situational characteristics.

### Critical Thinking Questions

1. Do you agree with the four metagoals described above? What others do you think are common?

2. What are the marketing implications of each of the metagoals described above (assume all four are widely used by consumers)?

3. What are the motivational aspects behind regulatory focus that cause the metagoal trade-offs on speed and ease versus accuracy?

to, selecting the optimal alternative (see Consumer Insight 16–1). Further, recent research indicates that preferences are not stable. That is, if an individual is comparing brands A and B, he or she might prefer brand A. However, if brand C is added to the evoked set, the consumer's preference might shift to brand B.[7] Therefore, for many decisions, consumers do not engage in a strictly rational choice; instead, they construct a decision process that is appropriate for the situation at hand.

In addition, many consumer decisions do not involve the comparison of brands on their features at all. Instead, they are based on emotional responses to the brand or overall impressions of the brand. In this section, we will examine three types of consumer choice processes: affective choice, attitude-based choice, and attribute-based choice. Keep in mind that these are not mutually exclusive and combinations may be used in a single decision.

# Affective Choice

Consider a consumer buying a camcorder. She inspects several models, noticing many differences among them. Some models have high definition while others have standard. Recording media options include tape, disc, and digital. Zoom ranges from 10x to 20x. LCD screen sizes range from 2 to 4 inches. Weight ranges from under 1 pound to over 2.5 pounds. Some models are Energy Star compliant and others are not. And there are price differences. She reviews her relative preference for these diverse features and chooses the model that gives her the best combination of the desired features.

Now consider her buying a dress for an upcoming big social event. Scanning a rack full of dresses in a store, she pulls out a few that seemed nice. One of them particularly caught her eye: she tries it on, and thinks she looks great in it. She tries another one which she thought made her look too conservative. A third one made her look too sexy. Somehow, the first one looked so right for her: a few more minutes of contemplation about what a great impression she would make donning that dress in the party, and she has made up her mind about that dress.[8]

The purchase of the camcorder is an example of an attribute-based choice, discussed in the following section. It is based on a conscious evaluation of the various features of the camcorders considered. The purchase of the dress is primarily an **affective choice.** Affective choices tend to be more holistic in nature. The brand is not decomposed into distinct components, each of which is evaluated separately from the whole. The evaluation of such products is generally focused on the way they will make the user feel as they are used. The evaluation itself is often based exclusively or primarily on the immediate emotional response to the product or service:

I'm getting married, and we were looking for a place to have the wedding and we had been to about five or six places . . . this (place) was not quite right . . . and this other place was not quite right . . . but then we went to a place called The Highlander in Glens Falls. I went in the lobby and I knew immediately that this was right. It was immaculately clean, the floor was not just marble but inlaid different types of patterns on the floor . . . its restaurant, the doors were lead and glass and you just knew that this was right. . . . You go in there and sure enough they had a wedding coordinator.[9]

Decisions based on affect use the "How do I feel about it" heuristic or decision rule.[10] Consumers imagine or picture using the product or service and evaluate the feeling that this use will produce.[11] For example, a consumer choosing between a weekend at a bed-and-breakfast on a beach and a weekend in a nice hotel in a city might imagine each episode to see how he or she feels. The decision would then be made largely or completely on these expected feelings.[12]

Underlying motives influence the use of affective choice. One framework is consummatory versus instrumental motives. Affective choice is most likely when the underlying motive is consummatory rather than instrumental. **Consummatory motives** *underlie behaviors that are intrinsically rewarding to the individual involved.* **Instrumental motives** *activate behaviors designed to achieve a second goal.* For example, one person might read a best-seller for the pleasure of reading the book (consummatory motive), whereas another might read the same book to be able to appear "with it" to his or her friends (instrumental motive).[13] Illustration 16–1 shows ads appealing to each of these motives.

Another motivation framework is regulatory focus. Affective choice is more likely when a consumer's regulatory focus is promotion-based rather than prevention-based (see Chapter 10). Relevant motives for promotion-focused consumers include hopes, aspirations, and growth. For prevention-focused consumers, motives include security and maintaining the status quo.

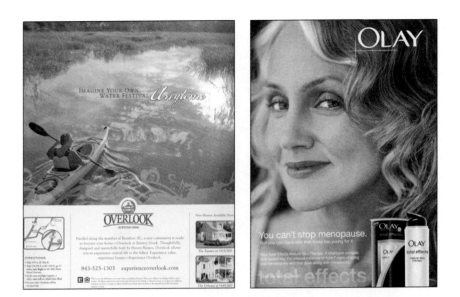

ILLUSTRATION 16–1

The ad on the left appeals to a consummatory motive by showing that the product or consumption is rewarding in and of itself. The ad on the right appeals to an instrumental motive by showing that the product is a means to an end.

Marketers continue to learn more about affect-based decisions.[14] It is clear that such decisions require different strategies than the more cognitive decisions generally considered in marketing. For those decisions that are likely to be affective in nature (largely triggered by consummatory motives), marketers should design products and services that will provide the appropriate emotional responses.[15] They also should help consumers visualize how they will feel during and after the consumption experience.[16] This is particularly important for new brands or products and services. Consumers who have experience with a product or brand have a basis for imagining the affective response it will produce. Those who do not may incorrectly predict the feelings the experience will produce. For example, individuals imagining a white-water rafting trip may conclude that it would produce feelings of terror rather than exhilaration. Such differences can be related to regulatory focus where terror is a negative emotion relating to avoidance tendencies and prevention, whereas exhilaration is a positive emotion relating to approach tendencies, fulfillment, and promotion. Illustration 16–2 shows an ad that helps consumers envision the positive experiences and accompanying feelings they would have if they owned the product.

## Attribute-Based versus Attitude-Based Choice Processes

Consider the following two processes a consumer might use to purchase a digital camera:

*Process 1:* After consulting the Internet to determine what features she is most interested in, the consumer then goes to her local electronics store and compares the various brands on the features most important to her—namely, camera size, zoom, automatic features, and storage size. She mentally ranks each model on these attributes and her general impression of each model's quality. On the basis of these evaluations, she chooses the Olympus Stylus.

*Process 2:* The consumer remembers that her friend's Olympus Stylus worked well and looked "good"; her parents had a Kodak Easyshare that also worked well but was rather large and bulky; and her old Fujifilm FinePix had not performed as well as she had expected. At her local electronics store she sees that the Olympus and Kodak models are about the same price and decides to buy the Olympus Stylus.

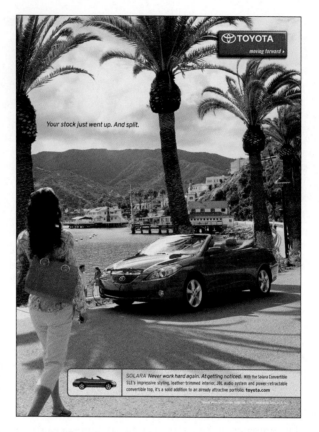

The first example above is attribute-based choice. **Attribute-based choice** *requires the knowledge of specific attributes at the time the choice is made, and it involves attribute-by-attribute comparisons across brands.* The second example above is attitude-based choice. **Attitude-based choice** *involves the use of general attitudes, summary impressions, intuitions, or heuristics; no attribute-by-attribute comparisons are made at the time of choice.*[17] There can also be combinations of these forms. A common combination would be for an evoked set (also known as a consideration set) to be formed using attitude-based processing, with the final choice being made on the basis of a brand-by-brand comparison.

Attribute-based choices require the comparison of each specific attribute across all the brands considered. This is a much more effortful and time-consuming process than the global comparisons made when attitude-based choice is involved. It also tends to produce a more nearly optimal decision.

Motivation, information availability, and situational factors interact to determine which choice process will be used. As one would suspect, the greater the motivation to make an optimal decision, the more likely an attribute-based choice will be made. In general, the importance of making an optimal decision increases with the value of the item being considered and consequences of a nonoptimal decision. Thus, attribute-based processing is more likely for a laptop computer or an athletic shoe for a marathoner than it is for an inexpensive calculator or an athletic shoe to wear around campus.

The easier it is to access complete attribute-by-brand information, the more likely attribute-based processing will be used. This can be used by marketers of brands that have important attribute-based advantages but that lack strong reputations or images in the target market. The approach would be to provide attribute-based comparisons in an easy-to-process format, such as a brand-by-attribute matrix. Such a matrix could be presented in ads, on packages, in point-of-purchase displays, in brochures, or on the brand's Web site.

A firm using such a strategy should use an appropriate comparison format and structure the information so that its brand will be the focal point of comparison.[18] This could be done by listing it first, perhaps in bold or colored type.

A variety of situations influence which choice approach is most likely. As we saw in Chapter 13, task definition influences the importance assigned to purchases, with gift purchases often being assigned more importance than similar purchases for oneself. Thus, gift purchases would be more likely to produce attribute-based decision processes. Time pressure is a major determinant of choice process used, with increasing time pressures producing more use of attitude-based decisions.

It is important to note that many decisions, even for important products, appear to be attitude-based. Recall from the previous chapter that most individuals collect very little product information from external sources immediately before a purchase. They are most likely making attitude-based decisions.

The ads in Illustration 16–3 illustrate the differences between attribute-based and attitude-based choice strategies. The ad on the left focuses on specific features of the brand and would be consistent with an attribute-based choice. The ad on the right focuses on the brand and an overall impression of the product and its users and would be consistent with an attitude-based choice.

Marketers for most products and services, even expensive, important ones, have a dual task. They must provide information and experiences that produce a strong attitude-based position (for those consumers making an attitude-based choice) *and* they must provide performance levels and supporting information that will result in preference among those consumers making attribute-based choices.

**ILLUSTRATION 16–3**

The ad on the left encourages attribute-based choice with primacy given to its key product features. Ads that assume or encourage attitude-based choice focus on brand, overall performance, and image rather than specific product features.

# EVALUATIVE CRITERIA

As the prior discussion described, consumers often make decisions based on affect or on overall attitude toward the brand or to minimize effort or negative emotion. Many of these types of decisions involve very little consideration of specific product features. However, most decisions involve an evaluation of the likely performance of the product or service on one or more dimensions. **Evaluative criteria** are *the various dimensions, features, or benefits a consumer looks for in response to a specific problem.* Before purchasing a computer, you might be concerned with cost, speed, memory, operating system, display, and warranty. These would be your evaluative criteria. Someone else could approach the same purchase with an entirely different set of evaluative criteria.

## Nature of Evaluative Criteria

*Evaluative criteria* are typically product features or attributes associated with either benefits desired by customers or the costs they must incur. Thus, many consumers who want to avoid cavities use toothpaste that contains fluoride. For these consumers, fluoride is an evaluative criterion associated with the benefit of cavity prevention. In this case, the evaluative criterion and the desired benefit are not identical, and fluoride is important as a feature only to the extent that it helps prevent cavities. In such cases, marketers should emphasize the benefit the feature will provide the consumer, not just the feature itself. The ad in Illustration 16–4 focuses primarily on the benefits of the product rather than its technical specifications.

**ILLUSTRATION 16–4**

Consumers are generally interested in product features only in relation to the benefits those features provide. This ad emphasizes core benefits rather than the technical characteristics that generate those benefits.

In other situations, the product feature and the benefit or cost are the same. For example, price is often an evaluative criterion that is identical to one aspect of cost (although it can also be a quality signal, as discussed in Chapter 8).

As we saw earlier, products and services purchased primarily for emotional reasons may involve anticipating the effect of purchase or use on feelings rather than on analysis of product attributes per se. Likewise, a product purchased for use in a social situation often involves anticipation of the reaction of others to the product instead of an analysis of its attributes. In these cases, the anticipated feelings or reactions would be the evaluative criteria.

Evaluative criteria can differ in type, number, and importance. The *type of evaluative criteria* a consumer uses in a decision varies from *tangible* cost and performance features to *intangible* factors such as style, taste, prestige, feelings generated, and brand image.[19]

Illustration 16–5 shows how two similar products stress very different types of evaluative criteria. The ad on the left stresses tangible attributes and technical performance. The ad on the right focuses more on intangible attributes and feelings.

Evaluative criteria may exist in terms of extremes (lower price or more miles per gallon is better), limits (it must not cost more than $100; it must get more than 25 miles per gallon), or ranges (any price between $85 and $99 is acceptable).[20] For new product categories, consumers must often determine which levels of a various criteria are desirable. For example, a consumer who buys a barbecue grill for the first time and has very limited experience with such grills may have to determine if he prefers gas to charcoal, domed or traditional shape, appropriate size, and so forth. After purchase and use, these preference levels are likely to become more firmly established and stable.[21]

For fairly simple products such as toothpaste, soap, or facial tissue, consumers use relatively few evaluative criteria. On the other hand, the purchase of an automobile, stereo system, or house may involve numerous criteria. Characteristics of the individual (such as product familiarity and age) and characteristics of the purchase situation (such as time pressure) also influence the number of evaluative criteria considered.[22] For example, recent research shows that time pressure reduces the amount of ingredient information that consumers examine in making choices about packaged goods.[23]

The *importance* that consumers assign to each evaluative criterion is of great interest to marketers. Three consumers could use the same six evaluative criteria shown in the following table when considering a notebook computer. However, if the importance rank they assigned each criterion varied as shown, they would likely purchase different brands.

| Criterion | Importance Rank for | | |
|---|---|---|---|
| | Consumer A | Consumer B | Consumer C |
| Price | 1 | 6 | 3 |
| Processor | 5 | 1 | 4 |
| Display quality | 3 | 3 | 1 |
| Memory | 6 | 2 | 5 |
| Weight | 4 | 4 | 2 |
| After-sale support | 2 | 5 | 6 |

Consumer A is concerned primarily with cost and support services. Consumer B wants computing speed and power (as represented by processor and memory). Consumer C is concerned primarily with ease of use (as represented by display and weight). If each of these three consumers represented a larger group of consumers, we would have three distinct market segments based on the importance assigned the same criteria.

Evaluative criteria, and the importance that individuals assign them, influence not only the brands selected but if and when a problem will be recognized. For example, consumers who attach more importance to automobile styling and product image relative to comfort and cost buy new cars more frequently than do those with the opposite importance rankings.[24]

Marketers must understand the criteria consumers use to evaluate their brands for two reasons. First, as we saw in the opening example, understanding these criteria is essential for developing or communicating appropriate brand features to the target market. In addition, marketers frequently want to influence the evaluative criteria used by consumers.[25]

## Measurement of Evaluative Criteria

Before a marketing manager or a public policy decision maker can develop a sound strategy to affect consumer decisions, he or she must determine

- Which evaluative criteria are used by the consumer.
- How the consumer perceives the various alternatives on each criterion.
- The relative importance of each criterion.

Consumers sometimes will not or cannot verbalize their evaluative criteria for a product. Therefore, it is often difficult to determine which criteria they are using in a particular brand-choice decision, particularly if emotions or feelings are involved. This is even more of a problem when trying to determine the relative importance they attach to each evaluative criterion.

**Determination of Which Evaluative Criteria Are Used**   To determine which criteria are used by consumers in a specific product decision, the marketing researcher can use either direct or indirect methods of measurement. *Direct* methods include asking consumers what criteria they use in a particular purchase or, in a focus group setting, noting what consumers say about products and their attributes. Of course, direct measurement techniques assume that consumers can and will provide data on the desired attributes.

However, direct questioning is not always successful. For example, Hanes Corporation suffered substantial losses ($30 million) on its L'erin cosmetics line when, *in response to consumer interviews,* it positioned it as a functional rather than a romantic or emotional product. Eventually, the brand was successfully repositioned as glamorous and exotic, although consumers did not *express* these as desired attributes.[26]

*Indirect* measurement techniques differ from direct in that they assume consumers will not or cannot state their evaluative criteria. Hence, frequent use is made of indirect methods such as **projective techniques** (see Appendix A, Table A-1), which allow the respondent to indicate the criteria someone else might use. The "someone else" will likely be a projection of the respondent, of course—thus, the marketer can indirectly determine the evaluative criteria that would be used.

**Perceptual mapping** is another useful indirect technique for determining evaluative criteria. First, consumers judge the similarity of alternative brands. This generally involves having the consumer look at possible pairs of brands and indicate which pair is most similar, which is second most similar, and so forth until all pairs are ranked. These similarity judgments are processed via a computer to derive a perceptual map of the brands. No evaluative criteria are specified by the consumer. The consumer simply ranks the similarity between all pairs of alternatives, and a perceptual configuration is derived in which the consumer's still unnamed evaluative criteria are the dimensions of the configuration.

For example, consider the perceptual map of beers shown in Figure 16–2. This configuration was derived from a consumer's evaluation of the relative similarity of these brands of beer. The horizontal axis is characterized by physical characteristics such as taste, calories, and fullness. The vertical axis is characterized by price, quality, and status. Naming each axis, and thus each evaluative criterion, is done using judgment. This procedure allows marketers to understand consumers' perceptions and the evaluative criteria they use to differentiate brands.

There may be attributes that consumers consider important but that they do not use in choosing among brands.[27] Such attributes will generally not be discovered in the techniques we have described. This situation would occur when consumers consider all brands either to be equivalent on the attribute or to be above their desired level. Thus, a consumer might consider all brands of bottled water to be safe to drink (not contaminated). Therefore, they do not use this as a criterion when comparing brands.

**Determination of Consumers' Judgments of Brand Performance on Specific Evaluative Criteria**   A variety of methods are available for measuring consumers' judgments of brand performance on specific attributes. These include *rank ordering scales, semantic differential scales,* and *Likert scales* (see Appendix A and Appendix Table A-3). The semantic differential scale is probably the most widely used technique.

None of these techniques are very effective at measuring emotional responses to products or brands. Projective techniques can provide some insights. SAM, the graphical approach designed to tap more directly into the pleasure-arousal-dominance dimensions of emotions (see Chapter 11), is also a useful option.

**Determination of the Relative Importance of Evaluative Criteria**   The importance assigned to evaluative criteria can be measured either by direct or by indirect methods.

FIGURE 16–2          Perceptual Mapping of Beer Brand Perceptions

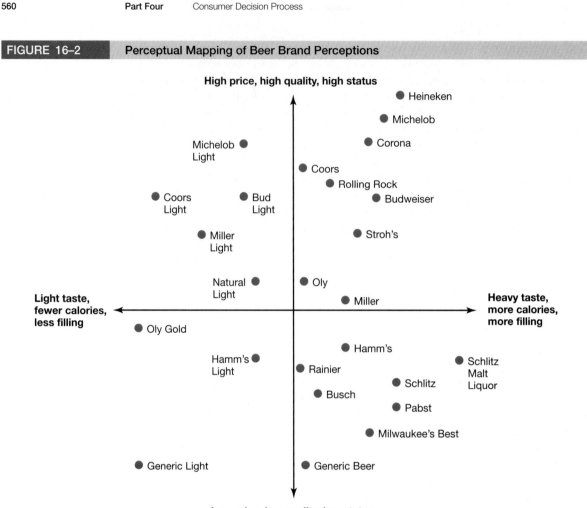

No matter which technique is used, the usage situation should be specified as attribute importance varies with the situation. The *constant sum scale* is the most common method of direct measurement (see Chapter 11).

The most popular indirect measurement approach is **conjoint analysis.** In conjoint analysis, the consumer is presented with a set of products or product descriptions in which the evaluative criteria vary. For example, the consumer may be presented with the description of 24 different notebook computers that vary on four criteria. Two might be

| | |
|---|---|
| Pentium M 2.0 GHz | Pentium M 1.6 GHz |
| Energy Star compliant (yes) | Energy Star compliant (no) |
| 5.1 pounds | 3.5 pounds |
| $2,000 | $1,500 |

The consumer ranks all 24 such descriptions in terms of his or her preference for those combinations of features. Using these preference ranks, sophisticated computer programs derive the relative importance consumers assign to each level of each attribute tested (see Appendix A and Appendix Figure A-1 for details).

Conjoint analysis was used by Sunbeam in reformulating its food processor line for various segments. Sunbeam tested 12 different attributes: price, motor power, number of blades, bowl shape, and so forth. Various segments emerged *based on the relative importance of these attributes.* In order of importance, the key attributes for two segments were as follows. These results helped Sunbeam develop models specifically for each of these segments and to better meet their needs on important evaluative criteria.

| **Cheap/Large Segment** | **Multispeed/Multiuse Segment** |
| --- | --- |
| $49.99 price | $99.99 price |
| 4-quart bowl | 2-quart bowl |
| Two speeds | Seven speeds |
| Seven blades | Functions as blender and mixer |
| Heavy-duty motor | Cylindrical bowl |
| Cylindrical bowl | Pouring spout |

# INDIVIDUAL JUDGMENT AND EVALUATIVE CRITERIA

If you were buying a notebook computer, you would probably make direct comparisons across brands on features such as price, weight, and display clarity. These comparative judgments might not be completely accurate. For example, the display that is the easiest to read in a five-minute trial might not be the easiest to read over a two-hour work session. For other attributes, such as quality, you might not be able to make direct comparisons. Instead, you might rely on brand name or price to indicate quality. In addition, consumer perceptions of the importance of product features are influenced by various external factors. The accuracy of direct judgments, the use of one attribute to indicate performance on another (surrogate indicator), and variations in attribute importance are critical issues for marketers.

## Accuracy of Individual Judgments

The average consumer is not adequately trained to judge the performance of competing brands on complex evaluative criteria such as quality or durability. For more straightforward criteria, however, most consumers can and do make such judgments. Prices generally can be judged and compared directly. However, even this can be complex. Is a six-pack of 12-ounce cans of Coca-Cola selling for $2.49 a better buy than two liters priced at $.99 each? Consumer groups have pushed for unit pricing (pricing by common measurements such as cost per ounce) to make such comparisons simpler. The federal truth-in-lending law was passed to facilitate direct price comparisons among alternative lenders.

*The ability of an individual to distinguish between similar stimuli* is called **sensory discrimination** (see Chapter 8). This could involve such variables as the sound of stereo systems, the taste of food products, or the clarity of display screens. The minimum amount that one brand can differ from another with the difference still being noticed is referred to as the *just noticeable difference (j.n.d.).* As we saw in Chapter 8, this ability is not well developed in most consumers. In general, research indicates that *individuals typically do not notice relatively small differences between brands or changes in brand attributes.* In addition, the complexity of many products and services as well as the fact that some aspects of performance can be judged only after extensive use makes accurate brand comparisons difficult.[28]

The inability of consumers to accurately evaluate many products can result in inappropriate purchases (buying a lower-quality product at a higher price than necessary).[29] This is a major concern of regulatory agencies and consumer groups as well as for marketers of high-value brands.

## Use of Surrogate Indicators

Consumers frequently use an observable attribute of a product to indicate the performance of the product on a less observable attribute.[30] For example, a consumer might infer that since a product has a relatively high price it must also be high quality. *An attribute used to stand for or indicate another attribute* is known as a **surrogate indicator.** As discussed in Chapter 8, consumers often use such factors as price, advertising intensity, warranties, brand, and country of origin as surrogate indicators of quality—what we termed quality signals. Illustration 16–6 shows a company that is attempting to take advantage of Germany's (its country of origin) reputation for engineering and manufacturing excellence.

In general, surrogate indicators operate more strongly when consumers lack the expertise to make informed judgments on their own, when consumer motivation or interest in the decision is low, and when other quality-related information is lacking. Unfortunately, the relationship between surrogate indicators and functional measures of quality is often modest at best.[31] Obviously, when consumers rely on surrogates that have little relationship to actual quality, they are likely to make suboptimal decisions.

**ILLUSTRATION 16–6**

Consumers often use a product's country of origin as an important indicator of product quality.

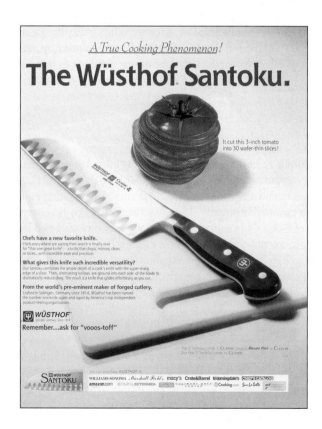

*A True Cooking Phenomenon!*

# The Wüsthof Santoku.

It cut this 3-inch tomato into 30 wafer-thin slices!

**Chefs have a new favorite knife.**
Chefs everywhere are saying their search is finally over for "that one great knife"—a knife that chops, minces, dices or slices...with incredible ease and precision.

**What gives this knife such incredible versatility?**
Our Santoku combines the ample depth of a cook's knife with the super-sharp edge of a slicer. Then, alternating hollows are ground into each side of the blade to dramatically reduce drag. The result is a knife that glides effortlessly as you cut.

**From the world's pre-eminent maker of forged cutlery.**
Crafted in Solingen, Germany since 1814, Wüsthof has been named the number one knife again and again by America's top independent product-testing organization.

**WÜSTHOF**

Remember...ask for "vooos-toff"

Surrogate indicators are based on consumers' beliefs that two features such as price level and quality level generally go together. Consumers also form beliefs that certain variables do not go together—such as *lightweight* and *strong; rich taste* and *low calories;* and *high fiber* and *high protein.*[32] Marketers attempting to promote the presence of two or more variables that many consumers believe to be mutually exclusive have a high risk of failure unless very convincing messages are used. Thus, it is important for marketers to fully understand consumers' beliefs about the feasible relationships of attributes related to their products.

## The Relative Importance and Influence of Evaluative Criteria

The importance of evaluative criteria varies among individuals and also within the same individual over time. That is, although consumers often have a general sense of how important various criteria are, this can be influenced by a number of factors. These include:

- *Usage situation.* The situation in which a product or service is used (Chapter 13) can have important influences on the criteria used to make a choice. For example, speed of service and convenient location may be very important in selecting a restaurant over a lunch break but relatively unimportant when selecting a restaurant for a special occasion.[33]
- *Competitive context.* Generally speaking, the lower the variance across competing brands on a given evaluative criterion, the less influence it is likely to have in the decision process.[34] For example, you might think that the weight of a notebook computer is important. However, if all the brands you are considering weigh between 3.5 and 5 pounds, this attribute may suddenly become less of a factor in your decision.

  When one evaluative criterion becomes less important, others generally become more important. We saw this in Chapter 11, where *decision irrelevant* advertising cues (peripheral cues) such as endorser fame became more important determinants of brand choice when competing brands were comparable in terms of important product features (central cues) such as price and quality.[35]
- *Advertising effects.* Advertising can affect the importance of evaluative criteria in a number of ways. For example, an ad that increases attention and elaborative processing of an attribute can increase its perceived importance and/or influence in the decision.[36] As we saw in Chapters 8 and 9, contrast, prominence, and imagery are just a few of the tactics that can be used to enhance attention and elaboration.

  A recent study suggests the power of imagery. Specifically, when consumers were encouraged to elaborate on prior usage experiences for a given product, attributes strongly related to the quality of the usage experience became much more important. As a consequence, they chose brands that were stronger on use-related attributes (e.g., suction power for a vacuum cleaner) over brands that were stronger on transaction-related attributes such as price.[37]

## Evaluative Criteria, Individual Judgments, and Marketing Strategy

Obviously, marketers must understand the evaluative criteria consumers use relative to their products and develop products that excel on those features. All aspects of the marketing communications mix must then communicate this excellence.

Marketers must also recognize and react to the ability of individuals to judge evaluative criteria, as well as to their tendency to use surrogate indicators. For example, most new consumer products are initially tested against competitors in **blind tests.** A blind test is one in which *the consumer is not aware of the product's brand name.* Such tests enable the marketer to evaluate the functional characteristics of the product and to determine if an advantage over a particular competitor has been obtained without the contaminating, or halo, effects of the brand name or the firm's reputation. *Can you see any drawbacks to only using blind tests in evaluating the market potential of products?*

Marketers also make direct use of surrogate indicators. Andecker was advertised as "the most expensive taste in beer." This was an obvious attempt to take advantage of the price–quality relationship that many consumers believe exists for beer. On occasion, prices are raised to increase sales because of the presumed price–quality relationship. For example, a new mustard packaged in a crockery jar did not achieve significant sales priced at $.49, but it did at $1.[38]

Marketers frequently use brand names as an indicator of quality. Elmer's glue emphasized the well-established reputation of its brand in promoting a new super glue: Ads for Elmer's Wonder Bond said, "Stick with a name you can trust." Firms with a limited reputation can sometimes form *brand alliances* with a reputable firm and gain from the quality associated with the known brand. Thus, a new brand of ice cream that used a branded ingredient such as M&Ms would gain from M&Ms quality image.[39] Country-of-origin themes such as "Made in America," "Italian Styling," or "German Engineering" are also common.

Marketers must also understand the various factors that can influence consumer perceptions of the importance of evaluative criteria. Understanding that attributes may be important but wield relatively little influence on consumer decisions because of similarity across competitors is a critical insight. It speaks to the need for marketing managers to examine critical points of differentiation on which the brand can be positioned. Advertising themes that emphasize specific usage occasions for which the brand is particularly appropriate can be effective, as can strategies such as imagery that draw consumer attention to an attribute on which the firm's brand is particularly strong.

# DECISION RULES FOR ATTRIBUTE-BASED CHOICES

As we describe some of the choice rules consumers use to select among alternatives, remember that these rules are representations of imprecise and often nonconscious or low-effort mental processes. The following example is a good representation of a consumer using a complex choice rule (compensatory with one attribute weighted heavily):

> I really liked the Ford [minivan] a lot, but it had the back tailgate that lifted up instead of the doors that opened. I suspect that if that had been available we might have gone with the Ford instead because it was real close between the Ford and the GM. The lift gate in the back was the main difference, and we went with the General Motors because we liked the doors opening the way they did. I loved the way the Ford was designed on the inside. I loved the way it drove. I loved the way it felt and everything, but you are there manipulating all these kids and groceries and things and you have got to lift this thing, and it was very awkward. It was hard to lift, and if you are holding something you have got to steer all the kids back, or whack them in the head. So that was a big thing. You know it was a lot cheaper than the GM. It was between $1,000 and $2,000 less than General Motors, and because money was a factor, we did go ahead and actually at one point talk money with a [Ford] dealer. But we couldn't get the price difference down to where I was willing to deal with that tailgate is what it comes down to.[40]

TABLE 16–1

Performance Levels on the Evaluative Criteria for Six Notebook Computers

| Evaluative Criteria | Consumer Perceptions* | | | | | |
|---|---|---|---|---|---|---|
|  | Acer | HP | Compaq | Dell | Lenovo | Toshiba |
| Price | 5 | 3 | 3 | 4 | 2 | 1 |
| Weight | 3 | 4 | 5 | 4 | 3 | 4 |
| Processor | 5 | 5 | 5 | 2 | 5 | 5 |
| Battery life | 1 | 3 | 1 | 3 | 1 | 5 |
| After-sale support | 3 | 3 | 4 | 3 | 5 | 3 |
| Display quality | 3 | 3 | 3 | 5 | 3 | 3 |

*1 = Very poor; 5 = Very good.

Despite the fact that the choice rules we describe are not precise representations of consumer decisions, they do enhance our understanding of how consumers make decisions and provide guidance for marketing strategy.

Suppose you have six notebook computers in your evoked set and that you have assessed them on six evaluative criteria: price, weight, processor, battery life, after-sale support, and display quality. Further, suppose that each brand excels on one attribute but falls short on one or more of the remaining attributes, as shown in Table 16–1.

Which brand would you select? The answer would depend on the decision rule you utilize. Consumers commonly use five decision rules: conjunctive, disjunctive, elimination-by-aspects, lexicographic, and compensatory. More than one rule may be used in any given decision. The most common instance of this is using a relatively simple rule to reduce the number of alternatives considered and then to apply a more complex rule to choose among the remaining options.[41] An example would be eliminating from consideration all those apartments that are too far from campus or that rent for more than $700 per month (conjunctive decision rule). The choice from among the remaining apartments might involve carefully trading off among features such as convenience of location, price, presence of a pool, and size of rooms (compensatory rule). Note that some online shopping services such as Price Grabber mimic this process. That is, they allow consumers to set their minimum acceptable levels on various evaluative criteria. Price Grabber then filters out all brands that don't meet the consumer's criteria. However, the consumer is still left to choose one brand from among this consideration set. The advantage is that this first "phase" has substantially reduced the size of the consideration set, thus making the final choice easier.

The first four rules we will describe are *noncompensatory* rules. This means that a high level of one attribute cannot offset a low level of another. In the apartment example, the consumer would not consider an apartment that was right next to campus if it cost more than $700 per month. An excellent location could not compensate for an inappropriate price. In contrast, the last rule we will describe is a *compensatory* rule in which consumers average across attribute levels. This allows a high level of one value to offset a low value of another.

Finally, note that the conjunctive and disjunctive decision rules may produce a set of acceptable alternatives, whereas the remaining rules generally produce a single "best" alternative.

## Conjunctive Decision Rule

The **conjunctive decision rule** establishes minimum required performance standards for each evaluative criterion and selects the first or all brands that meet or exceed these minimum standards. Thus, in making the decision on the computer, you would say, "I'll consider all (or I'll buy the first) brands that are acceptable on the attributes I think are important." For example, assume that the following represent your minimum standards:

| | |
|---|---|
| Price | 3 |
| Weight | 4 |
| Processor | 3 |
| Battery life | 1 |
| After-sale support | 2 |
| Display quality | 3 |

Any brand of computer falling below any of these minimum standards (cutoff points) would be eliminated from further consideration. Referring to Table 16–1, we can see that four computers are eliminated—Lenovo, Acer, Dell, and Toshiba. These are the computers that failed to meet all the minimum standards. Under these circumstances, the two remaining brands may be equally satisfying. Or you might use another decision rule to select a single brand from these two alternatives.

Because individuals have limited ability to process information, the conjunctive rule is frequently used to reduce the size of the information processing task to some manageable level. This is often done in the purchase of such products as homes, computers, and bicycles; in the rental of apartments; or in the selection of vacation options. A conjunctive rule is used to eliminate alternatives that are out of a consumer's price range, are outside the location preferred, or do not offer other desired features. After eliminating those alternatives not providing these features, the consumer may use another decision rule to make a brand choice among those remaining alternatives that satisfy these minimum standards.

The conjunctive decision rule is commonly used in many low-involvement purchases as well. In such a purchase, the consumer generally evaluates a set of brands one at a time and selects the first brand that meets all the minimum requirements.

If the conjunctive decision rule is used by a target market, it is critical to meet or surpass the consumers' minimum requirement on each criterion. For low-involvement purchases, consumers often purchase the first brand that does so. For such products, extensive distribution and dominant shelf space are important. It is also necessary to understand how consumers "break ties" if the first satisfactory option is not chosen. The ad in Illustration 16–7 tries to assure consumers that its brand has every feature the consumer might need.

## Disjunctive Decision Rule

The **disjunctive decision rule** *establishes a minimum level of performance for each important attribute* (often a fairly high level). All brands that meet or exceed the performance level for *any* key attribute are considered acceptable. Using this rule, you would say, "I'll consider all (or buy the first) brands that perform really well on any attribute I consider important." Assume that you are using a disjunctive decision rule and the attribute cutoff points shown below:

| | |
|---|---|
| Price | 5 |
| Weight | 5 |
| Processor | Not critical |
| Battery life | Not critical |
| After-sale support | Not critical |
| Display quality | 5 |

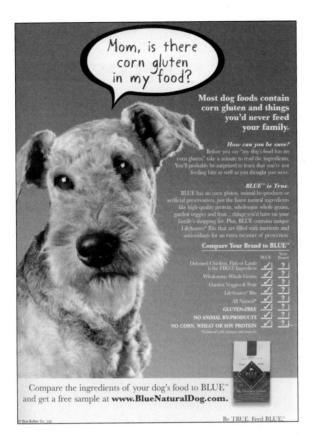

You would find Acer (price), Compaq (weight), and Dell (display quality) to warrant further consideration (see Table 16–1). As with the conjunctive decision rule, you might purchase the first brand you find acceptable, use another decision rule to choose among the three, or add additional criteria to your list.

When the disjunctive decision rule is used by a target market, it is critical to meet or surpass the consumers' requirements on at least one of the key criteria. This should be emphasized in advertising messages and on the product package. Because consumers often purchase the first brand that meets or exceeds one of the requirements, extensive distribution and dominant shelf space are important. Again, it is also necessary to understand how consumers break ties if the first satisfactory option is not chosen. Illustration 16–8 stresses one important attribute and would be appropriate for consumers who placed a high importance on this attribute and used a disjunctive decision rule.

## Elimination-by-Aspects Decision Rule

The **elimination-by-aspects decision rule** requires the consumer to rank the evaluative criteria in terms of their importance and to establish a cutoff point for each criterion. All brands are first considered on the most important criterion. Those that do not meet or exceed the cutoff point are dropped from consideration. If more than one brand remains in the set after this first elimination phase, the process is repeated on those brands for the second most important criterion. This continues until only one brand remains. Thus, the consumer's logic is, "I want to buy the brand that has a high level of an important attribute that other brands do not have."

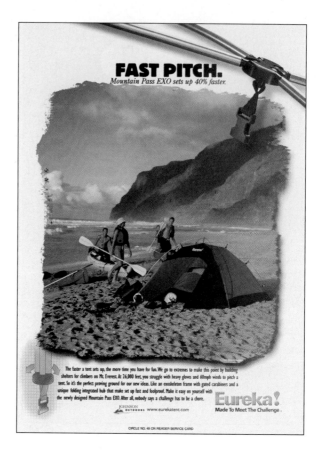

Consider the rank order and cutoff points shown below. What would you choose using the elimination-by-aspects rule?

|                    | Rank | Cutoff Point |
|--------------------|------|--------------|
| Price              | 1    | 3            |
| Weight             | 2    | 4            |
| Display quality    | 3    | 4            |
| Processor          | 4    | 3            |
| After-sale support | 5    | 3            |
| Battery life       | 6    | 3            |

Price would eliminate Lenovo and Toshiba (see Table 16–1). Of those remaining, Compaq, HP, and Dell meet or exceed the weight hurdle (Acer is eliminated). Notice that Toshiba also meets the minimum weight requirement but would not be considered because it had been eliminated in the initial consideration of price. Only Dell meets or exceeds the third requirement, display quality.

Using the elimination-by-aspects rule, you end up with a choice that has all the desired features of all the other alternatives, plus one more.

For a target market using the elimination-by-aspects rule, it is critical to meet or surpass the consumers' requirements on one more (in order) of the criteria used than the competition. This competitive superiority should be emphasized in advertising messages and on

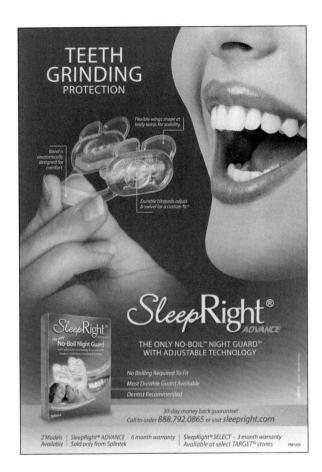

the product package. Firms can also attempt to alter the relative importance that consumers assign to the evaluative criteria. The ad in Illustration 16–9 is consistent with this rule. It indicates that the brand has desirable features other competitors do not have.

## Lexicographic Decision Rule

The **lexicographic decision rule** *requires the consumer to rank the criteria in order of importance.* The consumer then selects the brand that performs *best* on the most important attribute. If two or more brands tie on this attribute, they are evaluated on the second most important attribute. This continues through the attributes until one brand outperforms the others. The consumer's thinking is something like this: "I want to get the brand that does best on the attribute of most importance to me. If there is a tie, I'll break it by choosing the one that does best on my second most important criterion."

The lexicographic decision rule is similar to the elimination-by-aspects rule. The difference is that the lexicographic rule seeks maximum performance at each stage, whereas the elimination-by-aspects seeks satisfactory performance at each stage. Thus, using the lexicographic rule and the data from the elimination-by-aspects example above would result in the selection of Acer, because it has the best performance on the most important attribute. Had Acer been rated a 4 on price, it would be tied with Dell. Then, Dell would be chosen based on its superior weight rating.

When this rule is being used by a target market, the firm should try to be superior to the competition on *the* key attribute. This competitive superiority should be emphasized

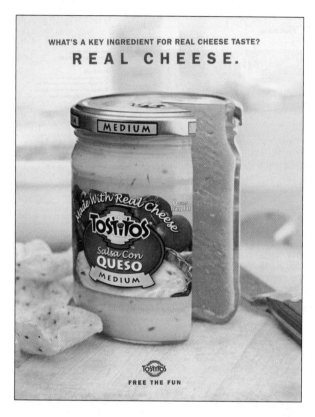

in advertising. It is essential that the product at least equal the performance of all other competitors on the most important criterion. Outstanding performance on lesser criteria will not matter if a competitor is superior on the most important attribute. If a competitive advantage is not possible on the most important feature, attention should be shifted to the second most important (assuming equal performance on the most important one). If it is not possible to meet or beat the competition on the key attribute, the firm must attempt to make another attribute more important.

The ad shown in Illustration 16–10 emphasizes one key feature, presumably the most important to their target market. To the extent that their customers use a lexicographic rule, this ad should be effective in driving choice of this brand.

## Compensatory Decision Rule

The four previous rules are *noncompensatory* decision rules, because very good performance on one evaluative criterion cannot compensate for poor performance on another evaluative criterion. On occasion, consumers may wish to average out some very good features with some less attractive features of a product in determining overall brand preference. That appears to be the case with the new minipackage craze being used by companies such as Frito-Lay, Nabisco, and Keebler. Some consumers have complained that the prices are high on a per-serving basis. Frito-Lay and others are counting on the fact that the convenience and calorie-control elements of their new 100-calorie packets will offset price in the minds of their target consumer. That is, they assume the target market will use a compensatory decision rule for this product. It appears this is the case, as explained by one customer who balked at the notion of buying in bulk and then measuring out 100-calorie servings into baggies:

> If you want to mess with those baggies, that's fine. But for those of us in the real world, we'll take the 100 cal packs. Sure, we might pay a few more pennies per ounce, but we also can't sneak any extra in while refilling.[42]

The **compensatory decision rule** states that *the brand that rates highest on the sum of the consumer's judgments of the relevant evaluative criteria will be chosen.* This can be illustrated as

$$R_b = \sum_{i=1}^{n} W_i B_{ib}$$

where $R_b$ = overall rating of brand $b$
$\quad W_i$ = importance or weight attached to evaluative criterion $i$
$\quad B_{ib}$ = evaluation of brand $b$ on evaluative criterion $i$
$\quad n$ = number of evaluative criteria considered relevant

This is the same as the multiattribute attitude model described in Chapter 11. If you used the relative importance scores shown below, which brand would you choose using the compensatory rule?

|  | Importance Score |
|---|---|
| Price | 30 |
| Weight | 25 |
| Processor | 10 |
| Battery life | 05 |
| After-sale support | 10 |
| Display quality | 20 |
| Total | 100 |

Using this rule, you would choose Dell, since it has the highest preference (see Table 16–1). The calculations for Dell are as follows:

$$R_{\text{Dell}} = 30(4) + 25(4) + 10(2) + 5(3) + 10(3) + 20(5)$$
$$= 120 + 100 + 20 + 15 + 30 + 100$$
$$= 385$$

Products and services targeting consumers likely to use a compensatory rule can offset low performance on some features with relatively high performance on others. However, it is important to have a performance level at or near the competition's on the more important features because they receive more weight in the decision than do other attributes. Recall the description of the minivan purchase from the beginning of this section. This customer preferred most of the features of the Ford but bought the GM because Ford was very weak on one key attribute. However, the consumer did express a willingness to change the decision had the price differential been greater. Thus, for compensatory decisions, the total mix of the relevant attributes must be considered to be superior to those of the competition.

The compensatory rule tends to be the most time consuming and mentally taxing. Also, consumers often find it difficult to consider more than a few attributes at a time in the trade-off process. However, the new shopping bots such as Yahoo Shopping's Smart Sort make it relatively easy for consumers to use a compensatory decision rule with numerous brands and attributes since that is the rule that underlies the Smart Sort feature. Smart Sort essentially weights each brand's performance on each criteria using the importance weights that the consumer has assigned and then sorts brands from best to worst based on their overall score.

## Summary of Decision Rules

As shown below, each decision rule yields a somewhat different choice. Therefore, marketers must understand which decision rules are being used by target consumers in order to position a product within this decision framework.

| Decision Rule | Brand Choice |
|---|---|
| Conjunctive | HP, Compaq |
| Disjunctive | Dell, Compaq, Acer |
| Elimination-by-aspects | Dell |
| Lexicographic | Acer |
| Compensatory | Dell |

Research clearly indicates that people do use these decision rules.[43] Low-involvement purchases generally involve relatively simple decision rules (conjunctive, disjunctive, elimination-by-aspects, or lexicographic), because consumers will attempt to minimize the mental cost of such decisions.[44] High-involvement decisions and purchases involving considerable perceived risk tend to increase evaluation efforts and often may involve not only more complex rules (compensatory) but stages of decision making, with different attributes being evaluated using different rules at each stage.[45] Of course, individual, product, and situational characteristics also influence the type of decision rule used.[46]

A marketing manager must first determine which rule or combination of rules the target consumers will most likely use in a particular purchase situation and then develop the appropriate marketing strategy.

## SUMMARY

During and after the time that consumers gather information about various alternative solutions to a recognized problem, they evaluate the alternatives and select the course of action that seems most likely to solve the problem. Consumer choices are sometimes based on extremely simple decision rules such as "buy the cheapest brand available." At other times, they are extremely complex, involving multiple stages and processes.

There are a number of ways consumers make choices. *Affective choice* is most likely when the underlying motive is consummatory rather than instrumental. *Con-*

*summatory motives* underlie behaviors that are intrinsically rewarding to the individual involved. *Instrumental motives* activate behaviors designed to achieve a secondary goal.

Affective choice tends to be holistic in nature. The brand is not decomposed into distinct components, each of which is evaluated separately from the whole. The evaluation of such products is generally focused on the way they will make the user *feel* as they are used. Decisions based on affect are said to use the "How do I feel about it" heuristic or decision rule. Consumers imagine or picture using the product or service and evaluate the feeling that this use will produce.

*Attribute-based choice* requires the knowledge of the specific attributes of the alternatives at the time the choice is made, and it involves attribute-by-attribute comparisons across brands. *Attitude-based choice* involves the use of general attitudes, summary impressions, intuitions, or heuristics; no attribute-by-attribute comparisons are made at the time of choice. There can also be combinations of these forms. A common combination would be for the evoked or consideration set to be formed using attitude-based processing, with the final choice being made on the basis of a brand-by-brand comparison on the price attribute.

*Rational choice theory* assumes a rational decision maker with well-defined preferences that do not depend on how the options are presented. Each option or alternative in a choice set is assumed to have a value to the consumer that depends only on the characteristics of that option. The consumer is also assumed to have sufficient skill to calculate which option will maximize his or her value and will choose on this basis.

Although useful, rational choice theory is incomplete. An emerging view is that many choices are constructed by the consumer as the decision is made. All consumers have *bounded rationality*—a limited capacity for processing information. In addition, consumers often have goals that are different from, or in addition to, selecting the optimal alternative. A *metagoal* refers to the general nature of the outcome being sought in a decision. Four metagoals characterize many consumer choices—maximizing the accuracy of the decision, minimizing the cognitive effort required for the decision, minimizing the experience of negative emotion while making the decision, and maximizing the ease with which a decision can be justified. These goals may shift in importance as the consumer moves through the decision process.

*Evaluative criteria* are the various features or benefits a consumer looks for in response to a specific problem. They are the performance levels or characteristics consumers use to compare different brands in view of their particular consumption problem. The number, type, and importance of evaluative criteria used differ from consumer to consumer and across product categories. And the importance of various evaluative criteria can be influenced by usage situation, competitive context, and advertising.

The measurement of (1) which evaluative criteria are used by the consumer, (2) how the consumer perceives the various alternatives on each criterion, and (3) the relative importance of each criterion is a critical first step in utilizing evaluative criteria to develop marketing strategy. The measurement task is not easy; however, a number of techniques, ranging from direct questioning to projective techniques and multidimensional scaling, are available.

Evaluative criteria such as price, size, and color can be judged easily and accurately by consumers. Other criteria, such as quality, durability, and health benefits, are much more difficult to judge. In such cases, consumers often use price, brand name, or some other variable as a *surrogate indicator* of quality.

When consumers judge alternative brands on several evaluative criteria, they must have some method to select one brand from the various choices. Decision rules serve this function. A decision rule specifies how a consumer compares two or more brands. Five commonly used decision rules are *disjunctive, conjunctive, lexicographic, elimination-by-aspects,* and *compensatory*. The decision rules work best with functional products and cognitive decisions. Marketing managers must be aware of the decision rule(s) used by the target market, because different decision rules require different marketing strategies.

## KEY TERMS

Affective choice  552
Attitude-based choice  554
Attribute-based choice  554
Blind tests  564
Bounded rationality  550
Compensatory decision rule  571
Conjoint analysis  560

Conjunctive decision rule  565
Consummatory motives  552
Disjunctive decision rule  566
Elimination-by-aspects decision rule  567
Evaluative criteria  556
Instrumental motives  552

Lexicographic decision rule  569
Metagoal  551
Perceptual mapping  559
Projective techniques  559
Sensory discrimination  561
Surrogate indicator  562

## INTERNET EXERCISES

1. Monitor several chat sites or interest groups for a week. Prepare a report on how a marketer could learn about the following used by consumers by doing this.
   a. Evaluative criteria
   b. Decision rules

2. Use Dell's recommendation feature to select a laptop computer (hint: go to www.dell.com, select "small and medium business," then click on "laptop."). What decision rule or combination of rules does this decision aid reflect? What type of consumer would be most likely to utilize this advisor function?

3. Visit Orbitz.com. What decision rule and evaluative criteria seem to dominate? Why do you think this is?

4. Visit three Web sites for brands in the same product category. Using the brand information provided and the manner in which it is provided, determine what decision rule each brand appears to assume its market uses. If there are differences, how would you explain them?

## DDB LIFE STYLE STUDY™ DATA ANALYSES

1. Based on the DDB Tables 1B through 7B, what characterizes an individual who would say, "In making big decisions, I go with my heart rather than my head"? How does this relate to affective decision making? What are the marketing implications of this?

## REVIEW QUESTIONS

1. What is *rational choice* theory?
2. What is meant by *bounded rationality*?
3. What is a *metagoal*?
4. What are four common metagoals for consumer decisions?
5. What is *affective choice,* and when is it most likely to occur?
6. What is the difference between *consummatory motives* and *instrumental motives*?
7. How does *attribute-based choice* differ from *attitude-based choice*? When is each most likely?
8. What are *evaluative criteria,* and on what characteristics can they vary?
9. How can you determine which evaluative criteria consumers use?
10. What methods are available for measuring consumers' judgments of brand performance on specific attributes?
11. How can the importance assigned to evaluative criteria be assessed?
12. What is *sensory discrimination,* and what role does it play in the evaluation of products? What is meant by a *just noticeable difference*?
13. What are *surrogate indicators*? How are they used in the consumer evaluation process?
14. What factors influence the *importance* of evaluative criteria?
15. What is the *conjunctive decision rule*?
16. What is the *disjunctive decision rule*?
17. What is the *elimination-by-aspects decision rule*?
18. What is the *lexicographic decision rule*?
19. What is the *compensatory decision rule*?
20. How can knowledge of consumers' evaluative criteria and criteria importance be used in developing marketing strategy?
21. How can knowledge of the decision rules consumers might use in a certain purchase assist a firm in developing marketing strategy?

22. Respond to the questions in Consumer Insight 16–1.

23. Would you use an attribute-based or an attitude-based decision approach to purchasing (or renting or giving to) the following? Which, if any, situational factors would change your approach?
    a. A present for your romantic partner
    b. A movie
    c. A sports car
    d. A BBQ grill
    e. A personal trainer
    f. Athletic shoes
    g. A new shampoo
    h. An apartment
    i. A camera phone
    j. Habitat for Humanity

24. Repeat Question 23, but speculate on how your instructor would answer. In what ways might his or her answer differ from yours? Why?

25. For which, if any, of the options in Question 23 would you make an affective decision? What role would situational factors play?

26. What metagoals might you have, and what would be their relative importance to you, in purchasing (or renting or giving to) the options in Question 23?

27. List the evaluative criteria and the importance of each that you would use in purchasing (or renting or giving to) the options in Question 23. Would situational factors change the criteria? The importance weights? Why?

28. Repeat Question 27, but speculate on how your instructor would answer. In what ways might his or her answer differ from yours? Why?

29. Describe a purchase decision for which you used affective choice, one for which you used attitude-based choice, and one for which you used attribute-based choice. Why did the type of decision process you used vary?

30. Identify five products for which surrogate indicators may be used as evaluative criteria in a brand choice decision. Why are the indictors used, and how might a firm enhance their use (i.e., strengthen their importance)?

31. The table below represents a particular consumer's evaluative criteria, criteria importance, acceptable level of performance, and judgments of performance with respect to several brands of mopeds. Discuss the brand choice this consumer would make when using the lexicographic, compensatory, and conjunctive decision rules.

| Evaluative Criteria | Criteria Importance | Minimum Acceptable Performance | Alternative Brands | | | | | |
|---|---|---|---|---|---|---|---|---|
| | | | Motron | Vespa | Cimatti | Garelli | Puch | Motobecane |
| Price | 30 | 4 | 2 | 4 | 2 | 4 | 2 | 4 |
| Horsepower | 15 | 3 | 4 | 2 | 5 | 5 | 4 | 5 |
| Weight | 5 | 2 | 3 | 3 | 3 | 3 | 3 | 3 |
| Gas economy | 35 | 3 | 4 | 4 | 3 | 2 | 4 | 5 |
| Color selection | 10 | 3 | 4 | 4 | 3 | 2 | 5 | 2 |
| Frame | 5 | 2 | 4 | 2 | 3 | 3 | 3 | 3 |

Note: 1 = Very poor; 2 = Poor; 3 = Fair; 4 = Good; and 5 = Very good.

32. Describe the decision rule(s) you used or would use in buying, renting, or giving to the options listed for Question 23. Would you use different rules in different situations? Which ones? Why? Would any of these involve an affective choice?

33. Describe your last two major and your last two minor purchases. What role did emotions or feelings play? How did they differ? What evaluative criteria and decision rules did you use for each? Why?

34. Discuss surrogate indicators that could be used to evaluate the perceived quality of the products or activities listed in Question 23.

## APPLICATION ACTIVITIES

35. Interview five students about a recent purchase decision. What metagoals characterize these different decisions? Do your results support Consumer Insight 16–1? How would you explain any differences?

36. Conduct an extensive interview with two students who recently made a major purchase. Have them describe the process they went through. Report your results. If each represented a market segment, what are the strategy implications?

37. Develop a list of evaluative criteria that students might use in evaluating alternative apartments they might rent. After listing these criteria, go to the local newspaper or student newspaper, select several apartments, and list them in a table similar to the one in Question 31. Then have five other students evaluate this information and have each indicate the apartment they would rent if given only those alternatives. Next, ask them to express the importance they attach to each evaluative criterion, using a 100-point constant sum scale. Finally, provide them with a series of statements that describe different decision rules and ask them to indicate the one that best describes the way they made their choice. Calculate the choice they should have made given their importance ratings and stated decision rules. Have them explain any inconsistent choices. Report your results.

38. Develop a short questionnaire to elicit the evaluative criteria consumers might use in selecting the following. Also, have each respondent indicate the relative importance he or she attaches to each of the evaluative criteria. Then, working with several other students, combine your information and develop a segmentation strategy based on consumer evaluative criteria and criteria importance. Finally, develop an advertisement for each market segment to indicate that their needs would be served by your brand.
    a. Cologne/perfume
    b. Running shoes
    c. Movie
    d. Nice restaurant
    e. Credit card
    f. Charity
    g. Home theatre system
    h. Health club

39. Set up a taste test experiment to determine if volunteer taste testers can perceive a just noticeable difference between three different brands of the following. To set up the experiment, store each test brand in a separate but identical container and label the containers L, M, and N. Provide volunteer taste testers with an adequate opportunity to evaluate each brand before asking them to state their identification of the actual brands represented as L, M, and N. Evaluate the results and discuss the marketing implications of these results.
    a. Colas
    b. Diet colas
    c. Lemon-lime drinks
    d. Carbonated waters
    e. Chips
    f. Orange juices

40 For a product considered high in social status, develop a questionnaire that measures the evaluative criteria of that product, using both a *direct* and an *indirect* method of measurement. Compare the results and discuss their similarities and differences and which evaluative criteria are most likely to be used in brand choice.

41 Find and copy or describe an ad that uses a surrogate indicator. Is it effective? Why? Why do you think the firm uses this approach?

42 Find and copy or describe an ad that attempts to change the importance consumers assign to product class evaluative criteria. Is it effective? Why? Why do you think the firm uses this approach?

43 Find and copy or describe two ads that are based on affective choice. Why do you think the firm uses this approach? Are the ads effective? Why?

44. Interview a salesperson for one of the following products. Ascertain the evaluative criteria, importance weights, decision rules, and surrogate indicators that he or she believes consumers use when purchasing this product. What marketing implications are suggested if their beliefs are accurate for large segments?
    a. Luxury cars
    b. Kitchen furniture
    c. Air purification systems
    d. Cosmetics
    e. Ski clothes
    f. Fine art

# REFERENCES

1. Chapter 16 opening examples are based on A. Ansari, S. Essegaier, and R. Kohli, "Internet Recommendation Systems," *Journal of Marketing Research,* August 2000, pp. 363–75; D. Lacobucci, P. Arabie, and A. Bodapati, "Recommendation Agents on the Internet," *Journal of Interactive Marketing,* Summer 2000, pp. 2–11; G. Haubl and K. B. Murray, "Preference Construction and Persistence in Digital Marketplaces," *Journal of Consumer Psychology* 13, no. 1/2 (2003), pp. 75–91; K. Diehl, L. J. Kornish, and J. G. Lynch, Jr., "Smart Agents," *Journal of Consumer Research,* June 2003, pp. 56–71; V. Swaminathan, "The Impact of Recommendation Agents on Consumer Evaluation and Choice," *Journal of Consumer Psychology* 13, no. 1/2 (2003), pp. 93–101; W. Wang and I. Benbasat, "Recommendations for Electronic Commerce," *Journal of Management Information Systems,* Spring 2007, pp. 217–46; G. N. Punj and R. Moore, "Smart Versus Knowledgeable Online Recommendation Agents," *Journal of Interactive Marketing,* Autumn 2007, pp. 46–60; *and* L. Aksoy et al. "Should Recommendation Agents Think Like People?" *Journal of Service Research*, May 2006, pp. 297–315.

2. J. R. Bettman, M. F. Luce, and J. W. Payne, "Constructive Consumer Choice Processes," *Journal of Consumer Research,* December 1998, pp. 187–217.

3. See C. A. Mandrik, "Consumer Heuristics," in *Advances in Consumer Research,* vol. 23, eds. K. P. Corfman and J. G. Lynch (Provo, UT: Association for Consumer Research, 1996), pp. 301–7; and J. Swait and W. Adamowicz, "The Influence of Task Complexity on Consumer Choice," *Journal of Consumer Research,* June 2001, pp. 135–48.

4. See R. Dhar and S. M. Nowlis, "The Effects of Time Pressure on Consumer Choice Deferral," *Journal of Consumer Research,* March 1999, pp. 369–84.

5. See E. C. Garbarino and J. A. Edell, "Cognitive Effort, Affect, and Choice," *Journal of Consumer Research,* September 1997, pp. 147–58; M. F. Luce, "Choosing to Avoid," *Journal of Consumer Research,* March 1998, pp. 409–33; M. F. Luce, J. W. Payne, and J. R. Bettman, "Emotional Trade-Off Difficulty and Choice," *Journal of Marketing Research,* May 1999, pp. 143–59; and A. Drolet and M. F. Luce, "The Rationalizing Effects of Cognitive Load on Emotion-Based Trade-off Avoidance," *Journal of Consumer Research,* June 2004, pp. 63–77.

6. See C. L. Brown and G. S. Carpenter, "Why Is the Trivial Important?" *Journal of Consumer Research,* March 2000, pp. 372–85; and J. J. Inman and M. Zeelenberg, "Regret in Repeat Purchase versus Switching Decisions," *Journal of Consumer Research,* June 2002, pp. 116–28.

7. J. R. Doyle et al., "The Robustness of the Asymmetrically Dominated Effect," *Psychology & Marketing,* May 1999, pp. 225–43; M. Bhargava, J. Kim, and R. K. Srivastava, "Explaining Context Effects on Choice Using a Model of Comparative Judgment," *Journal of Consumer Psychology* 9, no. 3 (2000), pp. 167–77; and R. Dhar, S. M. Nowlis, and S. J. Sherman, "Trying Hard or Hardly Trying," *Journal of Consumer Psychology* 9, no. 4 (2000), pp. 189–200. See also A. Drolet, "Inherent Rule Variability in Consumer Choice," *Journal of Consumer Research,* December 2002, pp. 293–305.

8. B. Mittal, "A Study of the Concept of Affective Choice Mode for Consumer Decisions," in *Advances in Consumer Research,* vol. 21, eds. C. T. Allen and D. R. John (Provo, UT: Association for Consumer Research, 1994), p. 256.

9. J. F. Durgee and G. C. O'Connor, "Why Some Products 'Just Feel Right,'" in *Advances in Consumer Research,* vol. 22, eds. F. R. Kardes and M. Sujan (Provo, UT: Association for Consumer Research, 1995), p. 652.

10. See M. T. Pham et al., "Affect Monitoring and the Primacy of Feelings in Judgment," *Journal of Consumer Research,* September 2001, pp. 167–87. See also P. R. Darke, A. Chattopadhyay, and L. Ashworth, "The Importance and Functional Significance of Affective Cues in Consumer Choice," *Journal of Consumer Research*, December 2006, pp. 322–28.

11. M. T. Pham, "Representativeness, Relevance, and the Use of Feelings in Decision Making," *Journal of Consumer Research,* September 1998, pp. 144–59.

12. For a more elaborate model of affective appraisal and its influence on subsequent judgment, see C. W. M. Yeung and R. S. Wyer, Jr., "Affect, Appraisal, and Consumer Judgment," *Journal of Consumer Research*, September 2004, pp. 412–24.

13. See also R. Dhar and K. Wertenbroch, "Consumer Choice between Hedonic and Utilitarian Goods," *Journal of Marketing Research,* February 2000, pp. 60–71.

14. See B. Shiv and A. Fedorikhin, "Heart and Mind in Conflict," *Journal of Consumer Research,* December 1999, pp. 278–91.

15. J. A. Ruth, "Promoting a Brand's Emotional Benefits," *Journal of Consumer Psychology* 11, no. 2 (2001), pp. 99–113; and J. C. Sweeney and G. N. Soutar, "Consumer Perceived Value," *Journal of Retailing* 77 (2001), pp. 203–20.

16. See P. Krishnamurthy and M. Sujan, "Retrospection versus Anticipation," *Journal of Consumer Research,* June 1999, pp. 55–69. See also B. Shiv and J. Huber, "The Impact of Anticipating Satisfaction on Consumer Choice," *Journal of Consumer Research,* September 2000, pp. 202–16; and C. P. S. Fong and R. S. Wyer Jr., "Cultural, Social, and Emotional Determinants of Decisions under Uncertainty," *Organizational Behavior and Human Decision Processes* 90 (2003), pp. 304–22.

17. This section is based on S. P. Mantell and F. R. Kardes, "The Role of Direction of Comparison, Attribute-Based Processing, and Attitude-Based Processing in Consumer Preference," *Journal of Consumer Research,* March 1999, pp. 335–52. For a discussion of the specific role of advertising-based attitudes, see W. E. Baker, "The Diagnosticity of Advertising Generated Brand Attitudes in Brand Choice Contexts," *Journal of Consumer Psychology* 11, no. 2 (2001), pp. 129–39.

18. See R. Dhar, S. M. Nowlis, and S. J. Sherman, "Comparison Effects on Preference Construction," *Journal of Consumer Research,* December 1999, pp. 293–306.

19. P. H. Bloch, "Seeking the Ideal Form," *Journal of Marketing,* July 1995, pp. 16–29; and Dhar and Wertenbroch, "Consumer Choice between Hedonic and Utilitarian Goods." See also D. Horsky, P. Nelson, and S. S. Posavac, "Stating Preference for the Ethereal but Choosing the Concrete," *Journal of Consumer Psychology* 14, no. 1/2 (2004), pp. 132–40.

20. G. Kalyanaram and J. D. C. Little, "An Empirical Analysis of Latitude of Price Acceptance in Consumer Package Goods," *Journal of Consumer Research,* December 1994, pp. 408–18.

21. See S. Hoeffler and D. Ariely, "Constructing Stable Preferences," *Journal of Consumer Psychology* 8, no. 2 (1999), pp. 113–39; and A. V. Muthukrishnan and F. R. Kardes, "Persistent Preferences for Product Attributes," *Journal of Consumer Research,* June 2001, pp. 89–102.

22. D. J. Mitchell, B. E. Kahn, and S. C. Knasko, "There's Something in the Air," *Journal of Consumer Research,* September 1995, pp. 229–38; D. R. Lichtenstein, R. G. Netemeyer, and S. Burton, "Assessing the Domain Specificity of Deal Proneness," *Journal of Consumer Research,* December 1995, pp. 314–26; D. R. Lichtenstein, S. Burton, and R. G. Netemeyer, "An Examination of Deal Proneness across Sales Promotion Types," *Journal of Retailing* 2 (1997), pp. 283–97; and V. Ramaswamy and S. S. Srinivasan, "Coupon Characteristics and Redemption Intentions," *Psychology & Marketing,* January 1998, pp. 50–80.

23. R. Pieters and L. Warlop, "Visual Attention during Brand Choice," *International Journal of Research in Marketing* 16 (1999), pp. 1–16.

24. B. L. Bagus, "The Consumer Durable Replacement Buyer," *Journal of Marketing,* January 1991, pp. 42–51.

25. A. Kirmani and P. Wright, "Procedural Learning, Consumer Decision Making, and Marketing Choice," *Marketing Letters* 4, no. 1 (1993), pp. 39–48; G. S. Carpenter, R. Glazer, and K. Nakamoto, "Meaningful Brands from Meaningless Differentiation," *Journal of Marketing Research,* August 1994, pp. 339–50; and S. M. Broniarczyk and A. D. Gershoff, "Meaningless Differentiation Revisited," in *Advances in Consumer Research,* vol. 24, eds. M. Bruck and D. J. MacInnis (Provo, UT: Association for Consumer Research, 1997), pp. 223–28.

26. B. Abrams, "Hanes Finds L'eggs Methods Don't Work with Cosmetics," *The Wall Street Journal,* February 3, 1983, p. 33.

27. See R. Dhar and S. J. Sherman, "The Effect of Common and Unique Features in Consumer Choice," *Journal of Consumer Research,* December 1996, pp. 193–203; and A. Chernev, "The Effect of Common Features on Brand Choice," *Journal of Consumer Research,* March 1997, pp. 304–11.

28. See S. H. Ang, G. J. Gorn, and C. B. Weinberg, "The Evaluation of Time-Dependent Attributes," *Psychology & Marketing,* January 1996, pp. 19–35.

29. P. M. Parker, "Sweet Lemons," *Journal of Marketing Research,* August 1995, pp. 291–307; S. Shapiro and M. T. Spence, "Factors Affecting Encoding, Retrieval, and Alignment of Sensory Attributes in a Memory-Based Brand Choice Task," *Journal of Consumer Research,* March 2002, pp. 603–17; and B.-K. Lee and W.-N. Lee, "The Effect of Information Overload on Consumer Choice Quality in an On-Line Environment," *Psychology & Marketing,* March 2004, pp. 159–83.

30. See A. Kirmani and A. R. Rao, "No Pain, No Gain," *Journal of Marketing,* April 2000, pp. 66–79.

31. See, e.g., V. P. Norris, "The Economic Effects of Advertising," *Current Issues and Research in Advertising,* 1984, pp. 39–134; S. Burton and D. R. Lichtenstein, "Assessing the Relationship between Perceived and Objective Price-Quality," in *Advances in Consumer Research,* vol. 27, eds. M. E. Goldberg, G. Gorn, and R. W. Pollay (Provo, UT: Association for Consumer Research,

1990), pp. 715–22; and D. J. Faulds, O. Grunewald, and D. Johnson, "A Cross-National Investigation of the Relationship between the Price and Quality of Consumer Products," *Journal of Global Marketing* 8, no. 1 (1994), pp. 7–25.

32. K. M. Elliott and D. W. Roach, "Are Consumers Evaluating Your Products the Way You Think and Hope They Are?" *Journal of Consumer Marketing,* Spring 1991, pp. 5–14; and J. Baumgartner, "On the Utility of Consumers' Theories in Judgments of Covariation," *Journal of Consumer Research,* March 1995, pp. 634–43.

33. See S. Ratneshwar et al., "Benefit Salience and Consumers' Selective Attention to Product Features," *International Journal of Research in Marketing* 14 (1997), pp. 245–59; R. Dhar and I. Simonson, "Making Complementary Choices in Consumption Episodes," *Journal of Marketing Research,* February 1999, pp. 29–44; and J. K. H. Lee and J. H. Steckel, "Consumer Strategies for Purchasing Assortments within a Single Product Class," *Journal of Retailing* 75, no. 3 (1999), pp. 387–403.

34. See, e.g., P. W. J. Verlegh, H. N. J. Schifferstein, and D. R. Wittink, "Range and Number-of-Levels Effects in Derived and Stated Measures of Attribute Importance," *Marketing Letters* 13, no. 1 (2002), pp. 41–52.

35. See, e.g., T. B. Heath, M. S. McCarthy, and D. L. Mothersbaugh, "Spokesperson Fame and Vividness Effects in the Context of Issue-Relevant Thinking," *Journal of Consumer Research,* March 1994, pp. 520–34.

36. M. P. Gardner, "Advertising Effects on Attributes Recalled and Criteria Used for Brand Evaluations," *Journal of Consumer Research,* December 1983, pp. 310–18; S. B. MacKenzie, "The Role of Attention in Mediating the Effect of Advertising on Attribute Importance," *Journal of Consumer Research,* September 1986, pp. 174–95; and G. D. Olsen, "Creating the Contrast," *Journal of Advertising,* Winter 1995, pp. 29–44.

37. C. Huffman, "Elaboration on Experience," *Psychology & Marketing,* August 1997, pp. 451–74.

38. K. B. Monroe, *Pricing* (New York: McGraw-Hill, 1979), p. 38.

39. A. R. Rao, L. Qu, and R. W. Ruekert, "Signaling Unobservable Product Quality through a Brand Ally," *Journal of Marketing Research,* May 1999, pp. 258–68; and C. Janiszewski and S. M. J. van Osselaer, "A Connectionist Model of Brand-Quality Associations," *Journal of Marketing Research,* August 2000, pp. 331–50.

40. C. J. Thompson, "Interpreting Consumers," *Journal Marketing Research,* November 1997, p. 443. Published by the American Marketing Association; reprinted with permission.

41. See G. Haubl and V. Trifts, "Consumer Decision Making in Online Shopping Environments," *Marketing Science,* Winter 2000, pp. 2–21.

42. S. Thompson, "Food Marketers Count on Snacks," *Advertising Age,* April 24, 2006, p. 4.

43. M. L. Ursic and J. G. Helgeson, "The Impact of Choice and Task Complexity on Consumer Decision Making," *Journal of Business Research,* August 1990, pp. 69–86; P. L. A. Dabholkar, "Incorporating Choice into an Attitudinal Framework," *Journal of Consumer Research,* June 1994, pp. 100–18; and T. Elrod, R. D. Johnson, and J. White, "A New Integrated Model of Noncompensatory and Compensatory Decision Strategies," *Organizational Behavior and Human Decision Processes* 95 (2004), pp. 1–19.

44. See E. Coupey, "Restructuring," *Journal of Consumer Research,* June 1994, pp. 83–99.

45. See D. L. Alden, D. M. Stayman, and W. D. Hoyer, "Evaluation Strategies of American and Thai Consumers," *Psychology & Marketing,* March 1994, pp. 145–61; and J. E. Russo and F. Lecleric, "An Eye-Fixation Analysis of Choice Processes for Consumer Nondurables," *Journal of Consumer Research,* September 1994, pp. 274–90.

46. See J. G. Helgeson and M. L. Ursic, "Information Load, Cost/ Benefit Assessment and Decision Strategy Variability," *Journal of the Academy of Marketing Science,* Winter 1993, pp. 13–20; W. J. McDonald, "The Roles of Demographics, Purchase Histories, and Shopper Decision-Making Styles in Predicting Consumer Catalog Loyalty," *Journal of Direct Marketing,* Summer 1993, pp. 55–65; M. S. Yadav, "How Buyers Evaluate Product Bundles," *Journal of Consumer Research,* September 1994, pp. 342–53; A. V. Muthukrishnan, "Decision Ambiguity and Incumbent Brand Advantage," *Journal of Consumer Research,* June 1995, pp. 98–109; and D. E. Hansen and J. G. Helgeson, "Consumer Response to Decision Conflict from Negatively Correlated Attributes," *Journal of Consumer Psychology* 10, no. 3 (2001), pp. 150–69.

# Outlet Selection and Purchase

■ Technology continues to transform the way consumers shop and make purchases. Internet shopping is one of the more obvious examples. But there are numerous other ways in which retailers are using technology to enhance the in-store experience, influence consumer choices, and ease the purchase process. Consider the following:

• Consumers, manufacturers, and retailers continue to be frustrated with the sizing system used in apparel. Consumers end up having to try on numerous brands and items to find what fits. There is also the issue of returns when items don't fit as intended. To combat this problem, Intellifit has developed a product called the Intellifit Virtual Fitting Room. It is a full-body scanner that collects full-body measurements in under 15 seconds. It then prints out a confidential ticket indicating which brands and sizes will fit the best and which retailers have them. Intellifit is also using the aggregated anonymous data to help retailers and manufacturers match their approach to sizing to "create and stock clothes that fit real people." Beyond working

with clients such as David's Bridal and Levi Strauss, Intellifit has its own line of custom-fit jeans, which it sells through its Intellifit Design Studio.[1]

• IBM has developed the Shopping Buddy, a computerized touchscreen PC that can be attached to shopping carts. Stop & Shop has tested this new technology in a number of its stores. The Shopping Buddy makes for a better in-store experience by allowing customers to do such things as order deli items remotely so they don't have to wait in line, scan and bag their items as they go to speed checkout, and browse recipes as they shop. While grocery retailing tends to be a highly competitive price-driven industry, technologies such as the Shopping Buddy are a reaction to research indicating that customers would pay more for groceries if the shopping experience were more positive.[2]

• Tired of boring mirrors in dressing rooms? Well, get ready for interactive mirrors that operate by outfitting a regular mirror with RFID (radio frequency identification), audio and video software, touch screen, and wireless messaging. Now with MagicMirror a "customer approaching the mirror with RFID-tagged garments activates customized ads and messages. A tailored suit might prompt James Bond-like images of martini glasses and go-go dancers. Or words and images can float on the glass to inquire about fit, suggest coordinating items, and take requests for other merchandise."[3]

Technology will continue to transform retailing as marketers work to improve the shopping experience and attract customers to their retail outlets. *What's next on the retail horizon?*

Selecting a retail outlet involves the same process as selecting a brand, as described in the previous chapters.[4] That is, the consumer recognizes a problem that requires an outlet to be selected, engages in internal and possibly external search, evaluates the relevant alternatives, and applies a decision rule to make a selection. We are not going to repeat our discussion of these steps. Instead, we will describe the evaluative criteria that consumers frequently use in choosing retail outlets, consumer characteristics that influence the criteria used, and in-store and online characteristics that affect the amounts and brands purchased.

# OUTLET CHOICE VERSUS PRODUCT CHOICE

Outlet selection is obviously important to managers of retail firms such as Amazon.com, Sears, and L.L. Bean. However, it is equally important to consumer goods marketers. There are three basic sequences a consumer can follow when making a purchase decision: (1) brand (or item) first, outlet second; (2) outlet first, brand second; or (3) brand and outlet simultaneously.

Our model and discussion in the previous two chapters suggest that brands are selected first and outlets second. This situation may arise frequently. For example, a consumer considering buying a notebook computer may first select a brand and then purchase it from the outlet with the lowest price (or easiest access, best image, service, or other relevant attributes). However, stores rather than brands can form the evoked set.[5] In our computer example, the consumer might be familiar with one store—Campus Computers—and decide to visit that store and select a computer from the brands available there. A third strategy is to compare the brands in one's evoked set at the stores in the evoked set. The decision would involve a simultaneous evaluation of both store and product attributes. Thus, a consumer might choose between a second-preferred computer at a store with friendly personnel and excellent service facilities versus a favorite computer at an impersonal outlet with no service facilities.

The appropriate marketing strategies for both retailers and manufacturers differ depending on the decision sequence generally used by the target market. How would a manufacturer's strategy differ depending on whether the brand or store was selected first? A brand-first decision sequence would suggest strategies such as brand image and feature advertising, brand availability advertising (e.g., manufacturer ad introduces the brand and indicates "available now at . . . "), and possibly a limited distribution strategy. An outlet-first choice would tend to produce a focus on point-of-purchase materials, distribution through key outlets, and programs to encourage good shelf space and support from store personnel. Table 17–1 highlights additional strategic implications.

Manufacturers often provide advertising dollars to retailers in exchange for featuring their products in the retailers' ads. At other times, the manufacturer lists one or more retailers as

TABLE 17–1

Marketing Strategy
Based on the
Consumer Decision
Sequence

| Decision Sequence | Level in the Channel | |
|---|---|---|
| | Retailer | Manufacturer |
| (1) *Outlet First, Brand Second* | Retailer image advertising<br>Margin management on shelf space, displays<br>Location analysis<br>Appropriate pricing | Distribution in key outlets<br>Point-of-purchase, shelf space, and position<br>Programs to strengthen existing outlets |
| (2) *Brand First, Outlet Second* | Many brands and/or key brands<br>Co-op ads featuring brands<br>Price special on brands<br>Retailer-sponsored search engine links | More exclusive distribution<br>Brand availability advertising<br>Brand image management |
| (3) *Simultaneous* | Margin training for sales personnel<br>Multiple brands or key brands<br>High service or low price structure | Programs targeted at retail sales personnel<br>Distribution in key outlets<br>Co-op advertising |

a source for its products. This both creates product demand and directs consumers to the appropriate retail outlet (see Illustration 17–1). Retailers often share in the cost of such ads. In other cases, firms use retailers' names in the ads as an inducement for the retailer to carry or display the brand.

## THE RETAIL SCENE

We use *retail outlet* to refer to any source of products or services for consumers. In earlier editions of this text, we used the term *store*. Increasingly, however, consumers see or hear descriptions of products in catalogs, direct-mail pieces, or various print media; on television or radio; or on the Internet or through their cell phones; they then acquire the products through mail, telephone, or computer orders. Generally referred to as **in-home shopping,** these sources represent an important and growing percentage of total retail sales. Consider this view of the future of retailing:

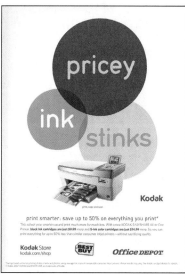

ILLUSTRATION 17–1

Marketers often use advertising to create brand demand and to direct consumers to appropriate outlets.

You're watching "Seinfeld" on TV, and you like the jacket he's wearing. You click on it with your remote control. The show pauses and a Windows-style dropdown menu appears at the top of the screen, asking if you want to buy it. You click "yes." The next menu offers you a choice of colors; you click on black. Another menu lists your credit cards asking which one you'll use for this purchase. Click on MasterCard or whatever. Which address should the jacket go to, your office or your home or your cabin? Click on one address and you're done—the menus disappear and "Seinfeld" picks up where it left off.

  Just as you'll already have taught the computer about your credit cards and addresses, you will have had your body measured by a 3-D version of supermarket scanners, so the system will know your exact size. And it will send the data electronically to a factory, where robots will custom tailor the jacket to your measurements. An overnight courier service will deliver it to your door the next morning.[6]

This quote is from Bill Gates, founder of Microsoft, in a statement nearly 15 years ago. It seemed far-fetched at the time, but today various aspects of this scenario are not only possible but actually exist. Computers can learn about your personal information, full-body scanners do exist that allow for custom-fitted apparel, and TiVo offers interactive tags for its advertisers, which allow viewers to click on the icon and go to more detailed brand information. As the line between computer and TV continues to blur and new interface technologies, wireless messaging, and RFID (radio frequency identification) become more commonplace, Gates's vision appears to be very much on target and right around the corner. Clearly, retailing is one of the most exciting areas of business in most developed economies.

We describe Internet (online) retailing and store (bricks-and-mortar) retailing in the next sections. We focus on Internet retailing because of its increasing prominence and rapid growth. However, other forms of nonstore retailing (catalogs, telemarketing, direct mail, television, and so forth) continue to be important and, in some cases, are being integrated with the Internet to produce powerful *multi-channel* approaches. These multi-channel approaches are also discussed.

## Internet Retailing

In Chapter 15 we saw the increasingly important role that the Internet plays as an information source prior to purchase. In addition, Internet retailing continues to evolve and grow as a strong retail channel, as shown below.[7]

|  | 2007 | 2012 |
|---|---|---|
| U.S. Internet users (millions) | 188 | 217 |
| Total nontravel U.S. retail expenditures online (billions) | $175 | $232 |
| Total Web-influenced in-store sales (billions) | $471 | $1,124 |

Several aspects of this table are worth noting. First, annual growth in the number of Internet users is relatively low, at about 2 to 3 percent. This is because most of the U.S. adult population is already online, as seen in Chapter 15. Second, growth in nontravel sales continues to be strong with a range of 10 to 20 percent, depending on the specific product. Third, estimates indicate that between 66 and 88 percent of Internet users have purchased a product online at some point. Thus, future growth in online sales will come more from increasing the amount of online spending from existing buyers than from increasing the number of Internet users. Finally, the Internet has a major influence on in-store sales, which further increases its importance as a retail channel. Such "cross-channel" effects are discussed later in the chapter.

Research suggests that products and services can be categorized into three groups based on their purchase characteristics relative to Internet shopping.

- *Replenishment goods:* moderate cost, high-frequency purchases. Items that are relatively expensive and easy to ship will be most successful. Examples include health care items such as vitamins, beauty aids, and gourmet foods.
- *Researched items:* high-information, big-ticket, planned purchases. Internet sales will be led by items with low style content and those for which "touch" is not important. Examples are leisure travel, computer hardware, and consumer electronics.

• *Convenience items:* low-risk discretionary items. Internet sales will be most successful for those where huge selection and deep discounts are important and easy shipping is available. Examples are books, CDs, flowers, and event tickets.[8]

As Figure 17–1 indicates, there is substantial growth across all categories. One of the more interesting categories is apparel, where lack of touch can be a major barrier for non-store retailers. Apparel is one of the largest and fastest-growing categories on the Internet. Part of the reason for this growth is that women make up a large proportion of online shoppers and they have considerable experience buying apparel from catalogs. This experience and comfort with other forms of in-home retailing appears to have transfered to the online context.[9] The growth of apparel also suggests that online marketers are increasingly finding ways to deal with the "touch" issue. For example, zoom features that allow for better viewing of items, free "swatches" from the clothing item being considered, and other such strategies to overcome the "touch" issue are being used increasingly by online apparel retailers.[10] In addition, across product categories including apparel, consumers are utilizing multiple channels in combination to satisfy their shopping needs. These various shopping channels often have complementary benefits that, when combined, can maximize a consumer's experience. For example, consumers may browse a catalog or retail store and then buy online.

Internet sales continue their strong growth and are expected to represent 11 percent of total retail sales by 2012. The penetration of Internet sales (as a percent of all sales in a category) in many categories is substantial and growing. By 2012 the most prominent categories will be computer hardware, software, and peripherals (55 percent); event tickets (43 percent); gift cards and certificates (35 percent); and music and videos (35 percent).[11]

Consumers shop online for various reasons, many of them similar to those for shopping from catalogs:[12]

| Reason | Online Shopping | Catalog Shopping |
| --- | --- | --- |
| Convenience | 67% | 62% |
| Price was right | 41 | 40 |
| Unique merchandise | 33 | 40 |
| Past experience with company | 28 | 39 |
| Wanted product delivered | 16 | 31 |
| No time to go to store | 13 | 17 |
| Recommendation from a friend | 7 | 7 |
| Impulse | 4 | 5 |

Source: *Catalog Age.* Reprinted with the permission of Primedia Business Magazines & Media Inc. Copyright 2001. All rights reserved.

Until recently, many industry experts predicted the demise of catalogs. However, catalogs and the Internet appear to work in a complementary fashion. For example, a recent study found that when consumers received a physical catalog, it nearly doubled their chances of buying at the retailer's Web site and increased their spending by 16 percent.[13]

**Characteristics of Online Shoppers**    Obviously, online shoppers must first be Internet users. As we saw in Chapter 15, Internet users tend to be younger and have higher income and education levels than the general population, although these differences are diminishing. Pew Internet and American Life estimates that currently 66 percent of all U.S. adult Internet users have made a purchase online at some time. The table below provides information about the demographic and technological characteristics of Internet buyers.

| FIGURE 17–1 | Online Sales by Categories (in $ billions) |
| --- | --- |

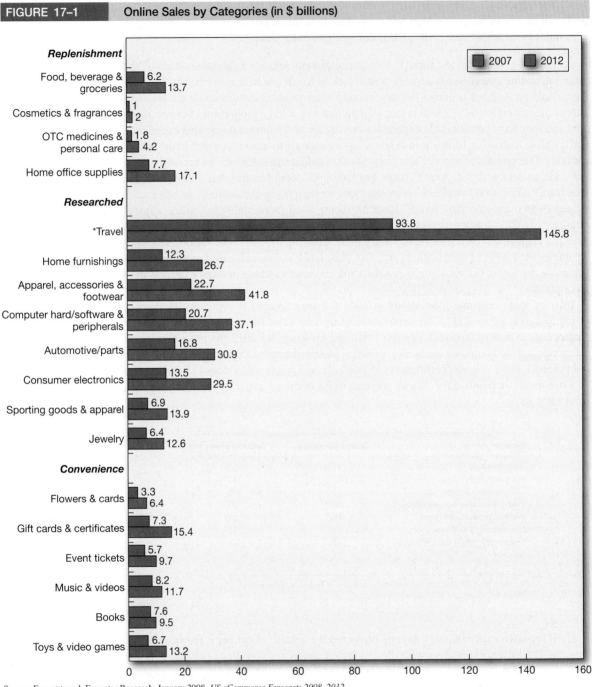

Source: Except travel, Forrester Research, January 2008, *US eCommerce Forecast: 2008–2012.*

*Travel is for 2007 and 2010 respectively and based on eMarketer, 2007.

| Characteristic | Ever Bought | Index* |
|---|---|---|
| **Gender** | | |
| Male | 66% | 100 |
| Female | 66 | 100 |
| **Age** | | |
| 18–29 | 68 | 103 |
| 30–49 | 71 | 107 |
| 50–64 | 62 | 93 |
| 65+ | 49 | 75 |
| **Race** | | |
| White | 69 | 104 |
| Black | 64 | 97 |
| Hispanic | 52 | 79 |
| **Education** | | |
| < High school | 52 | 78 |
| High school | 69 | 105 |
| Some college | 54 | 81 |
| College+ | 78 | 119 |
| **Income** | | |
| < $25,000 | 57 | 87 |
| $25,000–$40,000 | 61 | 92 |
| $40,000–$60,000 | 65 | 98 |
| $60,000–$100,000 | 73 | 110 |
| 100,000+ | 74 | 112 |
| **Geography** | | |
| Urban | 64 | 97 |
| Suburban | 67 | 102 |
| Rural | 65 | 98 |
| **Technology** | | |
| Broadband | 74 | 112 |

*Base is online buyers, where the average index is 100, which represents the 66 percent who are online buyers.

Source: Pew Internet & American Life Project, 2008.

As the table indicates, Internet buyers tend to be younger, non-Hispanic, higher-education, higher-income consumers with access to broadband technology.

Online experience also matters, with one study showing that those who have been online 10 or more years spend roughly 75 percent more than those who have been online 2 years or less.[14] Another study identified eight online shopper segments based on online attitudes, experiences, and behaviors.[15] Notice the variation in online spending across segments as a function of their attitudes and experiences.

- *Shopping Lovers* (11 percent of online households [HHs], 24 percent of online spending) enjoy buying online and do so frequently. They are competent computer users and will likely continue their shopping habits. They also spread the word to others about joys of online shopping whenever they have the opportunity. They represent an ideal target for retailers.
- *Adventurous Explorers* (9 percent of online HHs, 30 percent of online spending) are a small segment that presents a large opportunity. They require little special attention by Internet vendors because they believe online shopping is fun. They are likely the opinion leaders for all things online. Retailers should nurture and cultivate them to be online community builders and shopping advocates.
- *Suspicious Learners* (10 percent of online HHs, 15 percent of online spending) constitute another small segment with growth potential. Their reluctance to purchase online

more often hinges on their lack of computer training, but they are open to new ways of doing things. In contrast to more fearful segments, they don't have a problem giving a computer their credit card number. Further guidance and training would help coax them into online buying.

- *Business Users* (13 percent of online HHs, 19 percent of online spending) are among the most computer literate. They use the Internet primarily for business purposes. They take a serious interest in what it can do for their professional life. They don't view online shopping as novel and aren't usually champions of the practice.

- *Fearful Browsers* (11 percent of online HHs, 5 percent of online spending) are on the cusp of buying online. They are capable Internet and computer users, spending a good deal of time "window shopping." They could become a significant buying group if their fears about credit card security, shipping charges, and buying products sight unseen were overcome.

- *Shopping Avoiders* (16 percent of online HHs, 3 percent of online spending) have an appealing income level, but their values make them a poor target for online retailers. They don't like to wait for products to be shipped to them, and they like seeing merchandise in person before buying. They have online shopping issues that retailers will not easily be able to overcome.

- *Technology Muddlers* (20 percent of online HHs, 3 percent of online spending) face large computer literacy hurdles. They spend less time than any other segment online and show little excitement about increasing their online comfort level. They are not an attractive market for online retailers.

- *Fun Seekers* (12 percent of online HHs, 2 percent of online spending) are the least wealthy and least educated market segment. They see entertainment value in the Internet, but buying things online frightens them. Although security and privacy issues might be overcome, the spending power of the segment suggests that only a marginal long-term payback would be possible.

A recent study of Asian consumers yielded a similar set of segments, with online buyers tending to have more positive attitudes about, and experience with, online shopping and purchasing than traditional in-store buyers.[16]

**Barriers to Internet Shopping**    For some products, people, and situations, the Internet offers a better combination of selection, convenience, price, and other attributes than do catalogs, traditional stores, or other outlets. However, in many cases, consumers prefer traditional retail stores. Indeed, traditional offline stores are still the top-ranked purchasing channel for consumers (74 percent), followed by the Internet (52 percent), and catalogs (50 percent). An obvious barrier to Internet shopping is online access, although as we've seen in Chapter 15, this is diminishing rapidly. For those who are online, other barriers exist. A recent Forrester Research study found that for those who where online but had never made a purchase, the following reasons contributed.[17] Research suggests similar reasons for Asian consumers as well.[18]

| Reason | Percent |
| --- | --- |
| Credit card security concerns | 44% |
| Lack of "touch" | 40 |
| Don't have a credit/debit card | 21 |
| Want to research online and buy offline | 20 |
| Heard about bad online buying experiences of others | 18 |
| Delivery costs too high | 14 |
| Don't want to wait for delivery | 10 |

Source: Forrester Research, January 2008

Increasing online sales means converting Web site visitors to buyers, regardless of whether the visitor has ever made an online purchase or made an online purchase with your company. Consumer Insight 17–1 discusses some of the issues involved.

## Store-Based Retailing

The majority of retail sales take place in physical stores, and this will remain true for the foreseeable future. However, traditional store-based retailing is certainly vulnerable in ways that play into the hands of in-home retailers. Consider the results of a Roper survey asking consumers why they don't like shopping in stores:[19]

| Reason | Percent |
| --- | --- |
| Salespeople are poorly informed | 74% |
| Waiting in long lines | 73 |
| Hard time finding things | 64 |
| Parking and traffic | 64 |
| Dealing with crowds | 58 |
| Hard to get someone to wait on you | 54 |
| The time it takes to shop | 38 |
| Don't like shopping | 34 |

Source: From Roper Reports Telephone Survey, August 2003.

Obviously, for many people, in-store shopping is perceived as neither fun nor an efficient use of time. However, retailers are fighting back with an explosion of store-based retailing activities and technologies to improve the shopping experience.[20] Lifestyle centers are emerging to generate excitement and adapt to the changing shopping habits of consumers, as we saw in Consumer Insight 1–1. Brand stores are emerging as major sales volume outlets as well as promotional devices for brands, such as Levi's, Nike, Reebok, and OshKosh B'Gosh.

Other approaches are being tried, including kiosks, ministores, and stores within stores. Sunglass Hut operates small kiosks in malls, airports, and other high-traffic areas. Giant superstores such as Staples, Home Depot, and Costco are opening ministores in small towns, tiny shopping centers, and downtown areas.[21] And fast-food restaurants operate stores inside other outlets such as Wal-Mart, Home Depot, and gas stations.

Traditional department stores are fighting back by creating "destination areas" within their stores that enhance their overall image and drive ongoing store traffic. For example, Macy's has Elizabeth Arden Salons in their stores, which offer such services as manicures, pedicures, and facials. Saks Fifth Avenue has developed Club Libby Lu for girls where they can have birthday parties, get makeovers with friends, and so on. Club Libby Lu pushes the excitement and social aspects of shopping and terms its customers VIPs—Very Important Princesses!

Target has definitely gotten into the game and "reinvented the whole discount store concept." It has "been able to carve out the ultimate retail positioning with both a perception of having higher-quality and trendier products and brands and, at the same time, a perception of being a low-price leader."[22] And its use of designer collections has created a trendier image than that created by Wal-Mart and others.

Malls are becoming giant entertainment centers. For example, the Mall of America near Minneapolis is built around an amusement park. It also has a miniature golf course,

**Converting Web Site Visitors to Buyers**

With roughly 75 percent of U.S. adults online and roughly two-thirds having made an online purchase, increases in online sales will have to come by increasing the likelihood of buying and the amount spent by experienced online buyers. The following provides a set of guidelines for online retailers to help them convert Web site visitors to buyers.

- *Appropriate Landing Page.* Bad landing pages can be purchase killers. An example is clicking on an Esurance-sponsored link after searching for homeowner's insurance and having the landing page be about *auto* insurance. Companies are trying to target their landing pages specifically to the type of consumer who is clicking through. For example, Elite Island Resorts set up two landing pages to target different travel buyers.[23]

- *Deal with Privacy and Security Concerns.* Online privacy and security is the number one online buying deterrent and represents billions in lost sales. **Online privacy concerns** *relate to consumer fears regarding how personal information about them that is gathered online might be used.* Online privacy concerns include targeting children, being inundated with marketing messages, and identity theft.[24]

  Four approaches to reducing online privacy concerns seem possible. First is direct control through "opt in" features that let consumers choose directly how their information is used.[25] Second is the use of direct trust signals such as privacy statements and the incorporation and communication of security verification systems such as VeriSign.[26] These signals can increase trust, reduce privacy

concerns, and enhance purchases, but sometimes do not. A third approach is to use an indirect signal relating to a firm's investment in its Web site. An example would be a firm that uses "Shockwave technology to allow a user to experience an online demonstration and roll over the product image to gather additional information," versus one that conveys the same information but does so "through text and static graphics." Research shows that when consumers perceive that firms have invested more in their web site, that this increases trust and online purchase likelihood.[27] A final approach is to use brand as an indirect signal of trust. Research shows that consumers are more likely to provide transaction-specific information to a trusted retailer than to one they are unfamiliar with.[28]

The approach a firm should use depends on the type of Web visitor, with searchers (search-task directed) more responsive to the indirect Web site investment signal and browsers (pleasure directed) more responsive to the direct privacy statement signal.

- *Deal with Lack of Touch.* The lack of touch or ability to physically handle, test, or try products prior to purchase is the second-largest concern and affects product categories such as apparel and home decorating where it can be difficult to simulate experience attributes (e.g., fit for apparel, color and texture for home decorating).[29] Internet marketers are becoming much more sophisticated in terms of creating *virtual product experiences* using such techniques as 3-D simulations and rich media, made practical by the increased

nightclubs, theme-restaurants, and an aquarium (see Illustration 17–3).[30] Retailing is clearly an exciting, competitive area. Those retailers who best understand their consumers will be the ones to prosper in the future.

## The Internet as Part of a Multi-Channel Strategy

There is a tendency to think of Internet retailers as distinct from store-based retailers and other forms of in-home shopping such as catalogs. However, *pure play* Internet retailers penetration of broadband. For example, MVM (My Virtual Model) is available on various online apparel sites (see Illustration 17–2). MVM allows customers to create virtual models by entering their body dimensions and then "try on" the retailer's clothes to see how they "fit." Its use decreases returns and boosts purchase likelihood.[31]

- *Deal with Lack of Social Element.* In-store retailing allows for the social element, which is a major shopping motive and lacking in many online shopping sites. To deal with this, some online retailers

are creating sites that incorporate a social shopping experience. One example is Kaboodle, which combines online shopping with social networking to allow consumers to shop online with their friends.

## Critical Thinking Questions

1. What other strategies can online retailers use to increase the purchase likelihood of Web site visitors?

2. Do you think the social element even matters online? Explain.

3. Why is it important that MVM use reduces return rates?

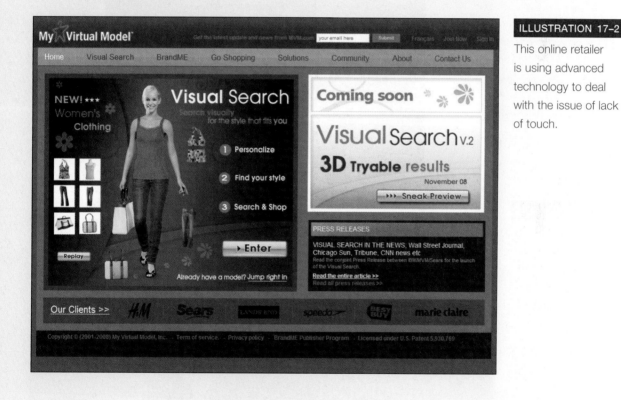

**ILLUSTRATION 17–2**

This online retailer is using advanced technology to deal with the issue of lack of touch.

such as eBay, Amazon.com, and Priceline are only part of the picture. Most large store-based retailers and catalog firms also have Internet sales sites. In fact, such multi-channel retail strategies are increasingly essential.[32] Thus, firms such as Eddie Bauer and The Gap actively market through physical retail stores, catalogs, and the Internet. In fact, over 70 percent of the top 100 online retailers in the United States are multi-channel retailers.[33]

A multi-channel approach can take many forms and can be successful for a number of reasons. For example, regional in-store retailers such as that shown in Illustration 17–4 can use the Internet to instantly become national and international in scope. On the flip side,

**ILLUSTRATION 17–3**

One way store-based retailers add value for their customers is by providing a fun shopping environment.

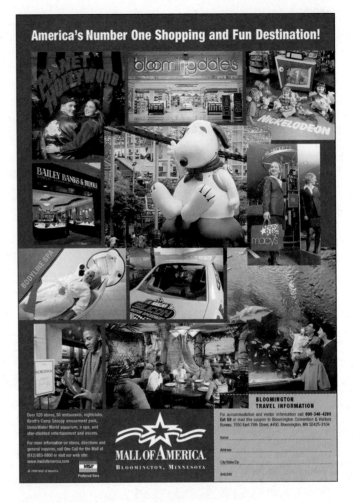

**ILLUSTRATION 17–4**

An Internet sales site instantly converts a local or regional firm into a national and even international one.

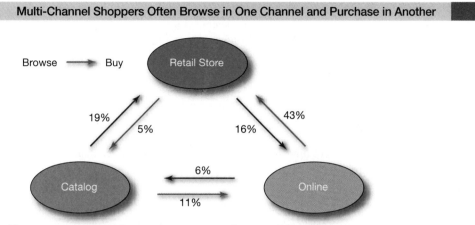

**Multi-Channel Shoppers Often Browse in One Channel and Purchase in Another** — FIGURE 17–2

The arrow start point indicates where consumer browse occurs; the arrow end point indicates where the consumer buy occurs. For example, 19 percent browsed/searched in the catalog and then purchased the product at the retail store.

Source: Multi-Channel Shopping Study (New York: DoubleClick, 2004), Copyright DoubleClick, Inc., 2005.

the Internet allows traditional retailers such as JCPenney and Saks Fifth Avenue to reach smaller communities where they could not otherwise operate economically.

Another option is the use of Internet shopping kiosks in traditional outlets. These kiosks allow consumers to purchase items not carried at that store or that are out of stock. In addition, consumers can use this service to purchase items for delivery to their homes or to be delivered as gifts. As a consequence, these kiosks represent a complementary rather than competing channel.

The increased use of a multi-channel approach relates to shifts in consumer shopping patterns.[34] Specifically, consumers are increasingly likely to be **multi-channel shoppers**—that is consumers who browse and/or purchase in more than one channel. Research by DoubleClick suggests the following:

- Multi-channel shoppers spend more than single-channel shoppers, with triple-channel shoppers (Internet, catalog, and retail store) spending the most.
- Multi-channel shoppers often browse/search in one channel and use that information to make a purchase in another channel. For example, a consumer might research jewelry at JCPenney's Web site but make the purchase at a JCPenney store.

Figure 17–2 shows the *channel-switching* behavior engaged in by multi-channel shoppers who browsed in one channel but purchased in another. Consistent with Chapter 15, many consumers browse/research online but then purchase offline in retail stores. However, the overall message here is that consumers are utilizing multiple channels in *complementary* ways since no retailing format is optimal on all dimensions. Thus, the Internet can be used to overcome a lack of informed salespeople or the inconvenience of researching products in-store, while in-store can provide "touch" and immediacy of purchasing.[35] Figure 17–2 also emphasizes the ongoing importance of catalogs as drivers of both online and retail store purchases.

# ATTRIBUTES AFFECTING RETAIL OUTLET SELECTION

The selection of a specific retail outlet involves a comparison of the alternative outlets on the consumer's evaluative criteria. This section considers a number of evaluative criteria commonly used by consumers to select retail outlets. While much of the research on outlet selection relates to choosing among retail stores (e.g., JCPenney versus Sears), when applicable we also draw linkages to choosing among online retailers (e.g., Buybooks.com versus Amazon.com) based on emerging evidence.

## Outlet Image

A given consumer's or target market's perception of all the attributes associated with a retail outlet is generally referred to as the **store image.** This is the same as the concept of *brand image* discussed in Chapter 9. One study found the following nine dimensions and 23 components of these nine dimensions of store image.[36] Notice that the store atmosphere component is primarily affective or feeling in nature.

| Store Image | |
|---|---|
| **Dimension** | **Components** |
| Merchandise | Quality, selection, style, and price |
| Service | Layaway plan, sales personnel, easy return, credit, and delivery |
| Clientele | Customers |
| Physical facilities | Cleanliness, store layout, shopping ease, and attractiveness |
| Convenience | Location and parking |
| Promotion | Advertising |
| Store atmosphere | Congeniality, fun, excitement, comfort |
| Institutional | Store reputation |
| Posttransaction | Satisfaction |

Source: J. D. Lindquist, "Meaning of Image," *Journal of Retailing,* Winter 1974, pp. 29–38.

This study focused on stores; the components and, probably, the dimensions will require adjusting for use with other types of retail outlets. For example, a recent study of *online retailer image* found the following seven dimensions and related components that influenced online outlet selection.[37] *Which dimensions and components of store image translate the most to an online context and which the least?*

| Online Retailer Image | |
|---|---|
| **Dimension** | **Components** |
| Usefulness | Good product offers and information, value, aligned with interests |
| Enjoyment | Fun, attractive, pleasant to browse |
| Ease of use | Easy to use and navigate, flexible site |
| Trustworthiness | Reputation, information safety and security |
| Style | Helpful, friendly, knowledgeable, calm |
| Familiarity | Advertising online and offline, general familiarity |
| Settlement | Fast and flexible delivery and transactions |

Source: Reprinted from H. van der Heijden and T. Verhage, "Online Store Image," *Information and Management* 41 (2004), pp. 609–17.

As these studies suggest, overall retailer image (both Internet and store-based) relates to both functional and affective dimensions. The importance of the affective component cannot be underestimated. A study that focused on the affective component of store image or personality found the following differences across stores (the higher the number, the more the component fits the outlet):[38]

| Store | Affective Component | | | |
| | Pleasant | Unpleasant | Active | Sleepy |
|---|---|---|---|---|
| Penney's | 18.5 | 12.8 | 13.7 | 14.3 |
| Kmart | 15.2 | 12.6 | 14.8 | 12.9 |
| Macy's | 25.2 | 7.2 | 19.0 | 6.7 |
| Sharper Image | 23.5 | 7.8 | 22.4 | 6.9 |
| Victoria's Secret | 25.5 | 9.5 | 16.0 | 12.7 |

Source: Reprinted from W. R. Darden and B. J. Badin, "Exploring the Concept of Affective Quality," *Journal of Business Research,* February 1994, p. 106.

Notice that JCPenney and Kmart are about as strong on the unpleasant component as on the pleasant component, and they are viewed as being neither active nor sleepy. This suggests that shopping motives will have to come from price, selection, or other functional features. In contrast, Macy's is a pleasant, active place to shop. Consumers will shop at stores such as Macy's because they are pleasant and active rather than, or in addition to, their functional characteristics. Victoria's Secret and Sharper Image are both pleasant places to shop, but the former is a less active experience than the latter. While Sharper Image does well on affective dimensions, it has recently run into problems. There is a lesson here in that both the affective and functional dimensions need to be balanced in ways that meet customer needs and expectations. As one commentator noted, the problem may have been in part that "people loved to look at (but not buy) fancy things with grossly inflated prices."[39]

Marketers make extensive use of image data in formulating retail strategies.[40] First, marketers control many of the elements that determine an outlet's image. Second, differing groups of consumers desire different things from various types of retail outlets. Thus, a focused, managed image that matches the target market's desires on both affective and functional elements is essential for most retailers. For example, fashion retailers build affective image by relying on designer collections to enhance their high-end, fashion-forward appeal, as shown in Illustration 17–5.

Other outlets focus on more functional attributes. For example, Amazon.com and Buy.com focus heavily on breadth of merchandise and price. And stores like 7-Eleven focus almost exclusively on convenience (easy access, extended hours, and quick service) for consumers in those situations where convenience is the key attribute.

## Retailer Brands

Closely related to store image are **store brands.** At the extreme, the store or outlet is the brand. The Gap, Victoria's Secret, and Body Shop International are examples. All the items carried in the store are the store's own brand. Traditionally, retailers carried only manufacturers' brands, and only a few, such as Sears and Wards, developed their own house or store brands. In the 1970s, many stores began to develop store brands as low-price alternatives to national brands, and many continue with this approach.[41]

Increasingly, however, retailers such as Wal-Mart and Target are developing and promoting high-quality brands with either the store's name or an independent name. Such brands not only provide attractive margins for these outlets; if they are developed appropriately, they also become an important attribute of the outlet. That is, they are another reason for the consumer to shop that store.[42] And importantly, no other outlet can carry this brand. The key to success of store brands seems clear—high quality at a reasonable price. The traditional pattern of providing reasonable quality at a low price is no longer necessarily optimal.[43] In fact, emphasizing quality over price may be particularly beneficial if the brand carries the store's name or will become associated with the store.

## Retail Advertising

Retailers use advertising to communicate their attributes, particularly sale prices, to con-sumers. It is clear that price advertising can attract people to stores. Revealing results were obtained in a major study involving newspaper ads in seven cities for a range of product categories (motor oil, sheets, digital watches, pants, suits, coffee makers, dresses, and mat-tresses). The impact of the retail advertisements varied widely by product category. For example, 88 percent of those who came to the store in response to the advertisement for motor oil purchased the advertised item, compared with only 16 percent of those respond-ing to the dress ad. Approximately 50 percent of the shoppers overall purchased the adver-tised item that attracted them to the store.

As Figure 17–3 illustrates, purchases of the advertised item understate the total impact of the ad. *Sales of additional items to customers who came to purchase an advertised item* are referred to as **spillover sales.** Spillover sales in this study equaled sales of the adver-tised items; that is, for every $1 spent on the sale item by people who came to the store in response to the advertising, another $1 was spent on some other item(s) in the store.[44]

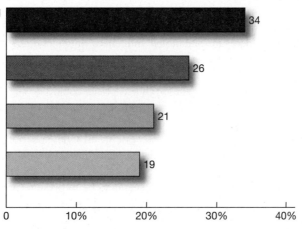

**Expenditures of Individuals Drawn to a Store by an Advertised Item**    FIGURE 17–3

Purchased the advertised item and one or more additional items — 34

Purchased only the advertised item — 26

Did not purchase the advertised item but purchased one or more other items — 21

Did not purchase anything — 19

Another study produced the results shown below:[45]

| | Reason for Visiting Store | |
| Action | Purchase Promoted Item | Other Reason |
| --- | --- | --- |
| Dollars spent on promoted items | $11.30 | $ 3.27 |
| Dollars spent on regular items | 18.48 | 21.90 |
| Total | $29.78 | $25.17 |
| Store profit | $ 5.64 | $ 5.77 |

Retailers evaluating the benefits of price or other promotions must consider the impact on overall store sales and profits, not just those of the advertised item. And while a large percentage of retail advertising stresses price, particularly sales price, studies continue to show that price is frequently not the prime reason consumers select a retail outlet.[46] Thus, many retailers could benefit by emphasizing service, selection, or the affective benefits of their outlets. Affective benefits may be particularly effective for hedonic rather than utilitarian products.[47]

Online retailers advertise in mass media both to attract consumers to their sites and to build an image. Price and value are clearly important attributes for online shoppers,[48] and many sites promote this feature. In addition, recent research suggests that customization of online promotions such as e-mail to better match the characteristics and needs of target customers can dramatically increase online store traffic.[49]

**Price Advertising Decisions**    Retailers face three decisions when they consider using price advertising:

1. How large a price discount should be used?
2. Should comparison or reference prices be used?
3. What verbal statements should accompany the price information?

Consumers tend to assume that any advertised price represents a price reduction or sale price. Showing a comparison price increases the perceived savings significantly. However, the strength of the perception varies with the manner in which the comparison or reference price is presented. A **reference price** is *a price with which other prices are compared.* In the claim, "Regularly $9.95, now only $6.95," $9.95 is the reference price. An **external reference price** is *a price presented by a marketer for the consumer to use to compare with the current price.* An **internal reference price** is *a price or price range*[50] *that a consumer retrieves from memory to compare with a price in the market.*[51]

Although there are situational influences and individual differences,[52] most consumers understand external reference prices and are influenced by them but do not completely believe them.[53] The reason for the lack of belief is the practice of some retailers of using inflated reference prices. These inflated prices could be "suggested list prices" in markets where virtually all sales are at a lower level. Or they may reflect prices that the store set for the merchandise originally that were too high and produced few sales. The price reduction being shown then merely corrects an earlier pricing error but does not provide meaningful benefit to the consumer. Since price and sale advertising have a strong impact on consumer purchases, the FTC and many states have special guidelines and regulations controlling their use.[54]

The best approach for retailers seems to be to present the sale price and (1) the dollar amount saved if it is large, (2) the percentage saved when it is large, and (3) both if both are large. Thus, $10 savings on a $200 item should show the dollar savings but not the percentage savings. A $10 saving on a $20 item could emphasize both the dollar and the percentage savings. A $1 saving on a $3 item should focus on the percentage savings.[55] The regular price could be shown in any of these conditions.[56] The regular price (the price on which the savings are calculated) should be the price at which the store normally sells a reasonable volume of the brand being discounted.

Such words or phrases as "now only," "compare at," or "special" appear to enhance the perceived value of a sale. However, this varies by situation, initial price level and discount size, consumer group, and retail outlet.[57] Is "50 percent off" or "buy one, get one free" likely to be perceived as a better value? It depends in large part on the nature of the item being promoted. For stock-up items such as detergent, they are viewed as equivalent. However, for perishable items such as bread, the "50 percent off" is seen as a better value.[58]

Retailers need to use caution in how they use price advertising. Such advertising signals not only the price of the advertised items but also the price level of the store.[59] And because price level, quality, service, and other important attributes are often linked in the consumer's mind, inappropriate price advertising can have a negative effect on the store's image.[60]

The ad in Illustration 17–6 places primary emphasis on the dollar savings but not the reference price or the sale price. To the extent that the target audience "knows" that the regular price for this item is high, they will use this internal reference price or range in making a judgment. And, since the dollar savings are relatively large, the research we have reviewed suggests that presenting the dollar savings is sound strategy.

## Outlet Location and Size

Location plays an important role in consumer store choice. If all other things are approximately equal, the consumer generally will select the closest store.[61] Likewise, the size of an outlet is an important factor. Unless the customer is particularly interested in fast service or convenience, he or she would tend to prefer larger outlets over smaller outlets, all other things being equal.[62] Interestingly, some of the major online players are "superstores" such as Amazon.com. Thus, retailer size appears to play a role online as well.

The **retail attraction model,** also called the **retail gravitation model,** is used to calculate the level of store attraction based on store size and distance from the consumer. In the retail gravitation model, store size is measured in square footage and assumed to be a measure of breadth of merchandise. The distance or travel time to a store is assumed to be a measure of the effort, both physical and psychological, to reach a given retail area.

**ILLUSTRATION 17–6**

This sale ad focuses primarily on the dollar savings. Should the percentage savings also be stressed?

The effect of distance or travel time varies by product.[63] For a convenience item or minor shopping good, distance is important, since shoppers are unwilling to travel very far for such items. However, major high-involvement purchases such as automobiles or specialty items such as wedding dresses generate greater willingness to travel.

Willingness to travel also varies with the size of the shopping list for that trip.[64] Thus, a consumer who would not be willing to travel very far to purchase three or four convenience items may willingly go much farther if 20 or 30 such items are to be purchased on the same trip.

Consumers often combine shopping trips and purposes.[65] Thus, a consumer may visit a health club, have lunch with a friend, pick up the laundry, shop for food for the next few days, and pick up a prescription on one trip. Thus, retail patronage is in part a function of an outlet's location in relation to other outlets and consumers' travel patterns. Combining outlets or adding departments in response to such shopping patterns can produce value for customers and increased revenue for the firm.[66] For example, supermarkets such as Safeway and Albertson's have added pharmacies to their outlets.

# CONSUMER CHARACTERISTICS AND OUTLET CHOICE

The preceding discussion by and large has focused on store attributes independently of the specific characteristics of the consumers in the target market. However, different consumers have vastly differing desires and reasons for shopping. This section of the chapter examines two consumer characteristics that are particularly relevant to store choice: perceived risk and shopper orientation.

## Perceived Risk

The purchase of products involves the risk that they may not perform as expected. As described in Chapter 15, such a failure may result in a high

- *Social cost* (e.g., a hairstyle that is not appreciated by one's peers).
- *Financial cost* (e.g., an expensive pair of shoes that become too uncomfortable to wear).
- *Time cost* (e.g., a television repair that requires the set to be taken to the shop, left, and then picked up later).
- *Effort cost* (e.g., a memory stick that is loaded with several hours of work before it fails).
- *Physical cost* (e.g., a new medicine that produces a harmful side effect).

The first of these is generally termed *social risk;* the next three are often considered to be *economic risk.* Product categories vary in the level and type of risk generally associated with them.[67] Table 17–2 shows that socks and gasoline are low in economic and social risk, while hairstyles and small gifts are low in economic risk but high in social risk. Other products, such as personal computers and auto repairs, are low in social risk but high in economic risk. Finally, automobiles and living room furniture are high in both economic and social risk.[68] Table 17–2 also indicates the role of the situation in perceived risk. Wine is shown as low in both social and economic risk when used for personal consumption but high in social risk when served while entertaining.

The perception of these risks differs among consumers, depending in part on their past experiences and lifestyles. For this reason, **perceived risk** is considered a consumer characteristic as well as a product characteristic.[69] For example, while many individuals would feel no social risk associated with the brand of car owned, others would.

Like product categories, retail outlets are perceived as having varying degrees of risk. Traditional outlets are perceived as low in risk, whereas more innovative outlets such as online are viewed as higher risk.[70]

The above findings lead to a number of insights into retailing strategy,[71] including the following:

- Nontraditional outlets need to minimize the perceived risk of shopping, particularly if they sell items with either high economic or social risk. Lands' End attempts to reduce

**TABLE 17–2**

The Economic and Social Risk of Various Types of Products

| Social Risk | Economic Risk | |
|---|---|---|
| | Low | High |
| *Low* | Wine (personal use) | Personal computer |
| | Socks | Auto repairs |
| | Kitchen supplies | Clothes washer |
| | Pens/pencils | Insurance |
| | Gasoline | Doctor/lawyer |
| *High* | Fashion accessories | Business suits |
| | Hairstyles | Living room furniture |
| | Gifts (inexpensive) | Automobile |
| | Wine (entertaining) | Snowboard |
| | Deodorant | Ski suit |

perceived risk by emphasizing toll-free ordering, 24-hour toll-free customer service telephones with trained assistants, and a 100 percent satisfaction guarantee. Word of mouth from satisfied customers reinforces these advertised policies.

- Nontraditional outlets need brand-name merchandise in those product categories with high perceived risk. Most Internet retailers feature such items.
- Traditional outlets and Web sites of well-known retailers have a major advantage with high-perceived-risk product lines. These lines should generally be their primary strategy focus. Low-risk items can be used to round out the overall assortment.
- Economic risks can be reduced through warranties, reasonable return policies, security verification systems, and so forth. As we've seen, such factors are critical to online shopping where financial security concerns are high. Social risk is harder to reduce. A skilled sales force, known brands, and satisfaction guarantees can help reduce this type of risk.

Illustration 17–7 shows how one retailer reduces perceived risk by providing a product-replacement guarantee.

## Shopping Orientation

Individuals go shopping for more complex reasons than simply acquiring a product or set of products. Diversion from routine activities, exercise, sensory stimulation, social interactions, learning about new trends, and even acquiring interpersonal power ("bossing" clerks) are nonpurchase reasons for shopping.[72] Of course, the relative importance of these motives varies both across individuals and within individuals over time as the situation changes.[73] See again Illustration 17–3, which shows how malls can provide an inviting environment for activities in addition to shopping.

**ILLUSTRATION 17–7**

Guaranteeing complete satisfaction no matter what can greatly reduce the perceived risk of a purchase, particularly one made via catalog or online.

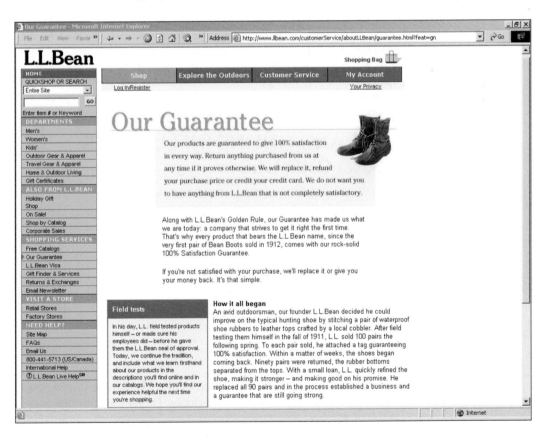

*A shopping style that puts particular emphasis on certain activities or shopping motivations* is called a **shopping orientation.** Shopping orientations are closely related to general lifestyle and are subject to similar influences. One study used projective techniques to ascertain the ways college students approach shopping.[74] It had consumers "[t]hink about an animal that best describes you as a shopper . . . [and] explain what it is about your behavior that makes this animal an appropriate metaphor." This projective approach uncovered six shopping orientations:

1.  *Chameleons* indicated that their shopping styles are situation-specific or constantly changing. Their shopping approach is based on product type, shopping impetus, and purchase task.
2.  *Collectors/Gatherers* are characterized by their propensity to stockpile items and to purchase large quantities to either save money or alleviate the need for shopping. They attempt to get the best price and take advantage of retailer guarantees.
3.  *Foragers* are particular and are motivated to purchase only the desired items. They are willing to search extensively and have little store loyalty. They like to shop alone.
4.  *Hibernants* are indifferent toward shopping. Their shopping patterns are opportunistic rather than need driven and they will often postpone even required purchases.
5.  *Predators* are purposive and speed oriented in their shopping. They plan before shopping and like to shop alone. They don't enjoy shopping and tend to shop outlets where they are assured of getting the items they need quickly.
6.  *Scavengers* enjoy shopping both to make purchases and as an activity. They like to go to sales and consider shopping to be entertainment. They make numerous unplanned purchases.

The opportunities for developing segment-specific marketing strategies are clearly evident.[75] For example, predators might respond to home delivery. Scavengers would respond well to entertainment-focused malls and outlets. However, as a single store attempts to target more of the segments, the risk of failure with all groups increases, as many of their desires are, if not mutually exclusive, difficult to meet within the same outlet. *Which of these groups would shop at Wal-Mart? Banana Republic? Sears? Which are the best targets for Internet outlets?*

# IN-STORE AND ONLINE INFLUENCES ON BRAND CHOICES

It is not uncommon to enter a retail outlet with the intention of purchasing a particular brand but to leave with a different brand or additional items. Influences operating within the retail outlet induce additional information processing and subsequently affect the final purchase decision. This portion of the chapter examines six variables that singularly and in combination influence brand decisions inside a retail outlet: *point-of-purchase materials, price reductions, outlet atmosphere, stockout situations, Web site design,* and *sales personnel.* Our focus is specifically on factors within *physical stores* or *online retailer Web sites* that influence purchase behavior. We begin by examining the extent and nature of unplanned purchases.

## The Nature of Unplanned Purchases

The fact that consumers often purchase brands different from or in addition to those planned has led to an interest in unplanned purchases. **Unplanned purchases** are defined as *purchases made in a retail outlet that are different from those the consumer planned to make prior to entering that retail outlet.* While the term *unplanned purchase* implies a lack of rationality or alternative evaluation, this is not necessarily true. For example, the decision to purchase Del Monte rather than Green Giant peas because Del Monte is on sale is certainly not illogical.

Viewing most in-store and online purchase decisions as the result of additional information processing within the retail outlet leads to more useful marketing strategies than does viewing such purchases as random or illogical.[76] This approach allows the marketer to utilize knowledge of the target market, its motives, and the perception process to increase sales of specific items. The Point-of-Purchase Advertising International (POPAI) uses the following definitions regarding in-store purchases:

- *Specifically planned.* A specific brand or item decided on before visiting the store and purchased as planned.
- *Generally planned.* A prestore decision to purchase a product category such as vegetables but not the specific item.
- *Substitute.* A change from a specifically or generally planned item to a functional substitute.
- *Unplanned.* An item bought that the shopper did not have in mind on entering the store.
- *In-store decisions.* The sum of generally planned, substitute, and unplanned purchases.

Unplanned purchases as defined above can be further subdivided into two categories—reminder purchases and impulse purchases. A *reminder purchase* would occur when a consumer notices Band-Aids in a store and remembers that she is almost out at home.[77] An **impulse purchase** would occur when a consumer sees a candy bar in the store and purchases it with little or no deliberation as the result of a sudden, powerful urge to have it.[78]

Figure 17–4 and Table 17–3 illustrate the extent of purchasing (in the United States and Canada) that is not specifically planned. It reveals that consumers make most item or brand decisions *after* entering the store. Interestingly, high levels of in-store decision making have also been found in the United Kingdom (76 percent), France (76 percent), Belgium (69 percent), Holland (80 percent), Australia (70 percent), and Brazil (88 percent).[79] *Can you explain differences in terms of cultural values?*

As a consequence, marketers not only must strive to position their brand in the target market's evoked set but also must attempt to influence the in-store and online decisions of their potential consumers. Retailers not only must attract consumers to their outlets but should structure the purchasing environment in a manner that provides maximum encouragement for unplanned purchases, particularly of high-margin items.[80] The appropriate way to do this would depend on the type of unplanned purchase associated with the product category.

We now turn our attention to some of the strategies that manufacturers and retailers can use to influence in-store and online decisions.

## Point-of-Purchase Materials

Point-of-purchase (P-O-P) materials are common in the retailing of many products, and the impact these materials have on brand sales can be substantial. Recent research by POPAI examined the sales increase or "lift" generated by the addition of various types of P-O-P materials in supermarkets.[81] They examined both store-shelf and product-display materials. Shelf-based materials are placed in the main shelf for the product category and include price signage, coupon dispensers, shelf talkers, and dangling signage. Product display

| FIGURE 17–4 | Supermarket Decisions: Two-Thirds Are Made In-Store |
|---|---|

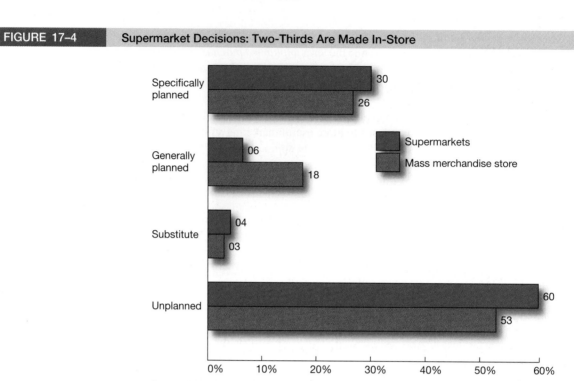

Source: *1995 POPAI Consumer Buying Habits Study* (Washington, DC: Point-of-Purchase Institute, 1995), p. 18, www.popai.com.

| TABLE 17–3 |
|---|
| In-Store Purchase Behavior |

| Product | Specifically Planned | Generally Planned | + | Substituted | + | Unplanned | = | In-Store Decisions |
|---|---|---|---|---|---|---|---|---|
| Total study average* | 30% | 61% | | 4% | | 60% | | 70% |
| Hair care* | 23 | 4 | | 5 | | 68 | | 77 |
| Magazines/newspapers* | 11 | 3 | | 1 | | 84 | | 89 |
| Oral hygiene products* | 30 | 5 | | 5 | | 61 | | 71 |
| Automotive oil* | 21 | — | | — | | 79 | | 79 |
| Tobacco products* | 32 | 6 | | — | | 61 | | 68 |
| Coffee* | 42 | 5 | | 6 | | 47 | | 58 |
| First-aid products* | 7 | 10 | | — | | 83 | | 93 |
| Cereal* | 33 | 9 | | 6 | | 52 | | 67 |
| Soft drinks* | 40 | 3 | | 5 | | 51 | | 60 |
| Mixers | 23 | 6 | | 4 | | 68 | | 77 |
| Fresh fruits, vegetables* | 67 | 7 | | 1 | | 25 | | 33 |
| Cold remedies[†] | 28 | 35 | | 19 | | 18 | | 72 |
| Toothpaste/toothbrushes[†] | 38 | 31 | | 16 | | 15 | | 62 |
| Antacids/laxatives[†] | 39 | 37 | | 12 | | 12 | | 61 |
| Facial cosmetics[†] | 40 | 34 | | 11 | | 15 | | 60 |

Source: *1995 POPAI Consumer Buying Habits Study* (Englewood, NJ: Point-of-Purchase Advertising Institute, 1995); [†]*1992 POPAI/Horner Canadian Drug Store Study* (Englewood, NJ: Point-of-Purchase Advertising Institute, 1992).

materials are those included with product displays located at the ends of aisles (end caps), on the store floor, and so on. Figure 17–5 provides a visual representation of the lift provided by four different shelf-based P-O-P materials.

This figure demonstrates that the effectiveness of P-O-P materials can vary substantially. Effectiveness can also vary across brands and products. Factors such as frequency

**FIGURE 17–5** The Sales Impact of Shelf-Based Point-of-Purchase Materials

Source: *2001 POPAI P-O-P Measure UP: Learnings from the Supermarket Class of Trade Study* (Washington, DC: POPAI, 2001), www.popai.com.

of promotion, brand familiarity, prevalence of certain types of P-O-P, and extent of P-O-P change can influence effectiveness. Many of these factors relate to the ability to capture consumer attention (Chapter 8). Consider the following comment from a POPAI report:

> When consumers visit the main shelf and the same types of P-O-P advertisements are presented from week to week and brand-to-brand, they appear to be less receptive to the message.[82]

Thus, the relative prevalence of price promotion signs and coupon dispensers may help to explain why they provide less lift than do other approaches. Despite variability across type, category, and brand, P-O-P materials are an important and increasingly measurable in-store influence.[83] P-O-P materials are important globally, as shown in Illustration 17–8.

**ILLUSTRATION 17–8**

Point-of-purchase displays are effective across cultures.

## Price Reductions and Promotional Deals

Price reductions and promotional deals (coupons, multiple-item discounts, and gifts) are generally accompanied by the use of some point-of-purchase materials. Therefore, the relative impact of each is sometimes not clear.[84] Nonetheless, there is ample evidence that in-store price reductions affect decision making and choice.[85] The general pattern, observed in the United States, the United Kingdom, Japan, and Germany, is a sharp increase in sales when the price is first reduced, followed by a return to near-normal sales over time or after the price reduction ends.[86]

Sales increases in response to price reductions come from four sources:[87]

1. Current brand users may buy ahead of their anticipated needs (stockpiling). Stockpiling often leads to increased consumption of the brand, since it is readily available.
2. Users of competing brands may switch to the reduced price brand. These new brand buyers may or may not become repeat buyers of the brand.
3. Nonproduct category buyers may buy the brand because it is now a superior value to the substitute product or to "doing without."
4. Consumers who do not normally shop at the store may come to the store to buy the brand.

High-quality brands tend to benefit more than brands from lower quality tiers when prices are reduced, and they suffer less when prices are raised.[88]

As discussed earlier under price advertising, consumers judge store quality and image in part on the basis of the number and nature of reduced-price items in the store.[89] Therefore, retailers need to carefully consider their sale price policies in view of both the sales of the discounted items and the impact these discounts will have on the store image. In addition, shoppers who purchase a large number of items at one time prefer stores with "everyday low prices"—all items in the store have relatively low prices but few are reduced beyond that level ("on sale")—to stores with somewhat higher standard prices but many sale items.[90] Is a shirt from an Internet retailer priced at $24.95 plus $5.00 shipping and handling a better or worse deal than the same shirt priced at $29.95 with shipping and handling free? Consumers tend to perceive the former to be a better deal than the latter. Research has shown that *partitioned prices* (the first scenario above) produced greater demand and a lower recalled total cost than the combined price (the second scenario).[91]

## Outlet Atmosphere

**Store atmosphere** is influenced by such attributes as lighting, layout, presentation of merchandise, fixtures, floor coverings, colors, sounds, odors, and the dress and behavior of sales and service personnel (see Chapter 13).

Atmosphere is referred to as **servicescape** when describing a service business such as a hospital, bank, or restaurant.[92] **Atmospherics** is the process managers use to manipulate the physical retail or service environment to create specific mood responses in shoppers. Internet retailers also have *online atmospheres* that are determined by graphics, colors, layout, content, entertainment features, interactivity, tone, and so forth.[93] *What type of atmosphere is portrayed in the site shown in Illustration 17–9?*

A store's atmosphere affects the shopper's mood/emotions and willingness to visit and linger. It also influences the consumer's judgments of the quality of the store and the store's image.[94] Similarly, recent research shows that online atmospherics influence shopping behavior. For example, one study found that designing a Web site to elicit affective responses such as pleasure and arousal leads to increased willingness to browse.[95] Another

ILLUSTRATION 17–9

Retail Web site designs should create an appropriate atmosphere or feelings as well as provide content and functionality.

study found that when a Web site offers restricted navigation, negative emotions (due to consumers' felt loss of control) occur, which lead to Web site avoidance.[96] Perhaps more important, positive mood/emotion induced while in the store or Web site increases satisfaction with the store or Web site, which can produce repeat visits and store loyalty.[97]

A major component of store atmosphere is the *number, characteristics, and behavior of other customers*.[98] Crowding must be considered since it can generate negative emotions and reduce browsing. And training staff how to appropriately deal with unruly customers is critical since the behaviors of other customers can influence the overall atmosphere.[99]

*Music* can have a major impact on the store environment (see Chapter 13). It can influence the time spent in the store or restaurant, the mood of the consumer, and the overall impression of the outlet.[100] However, it is important to match the music to the target audience. As shown below, baby boomers responded positively to classic rock music in a supermarket setting, but older adults did not:[101]

|  | Baby Boomers | | | Older Adults | | |
|---|---|---|---|---|---|---|
|  | Classic Rock | Big Band | Top 40 | Classic Rock | Big Band | Top 40 |
| Items purchased | 31 | 11 | 15 | 4 | 12 | 14 |
| Dollars spent | 34 | 21 | 21 | 16 | 17 | 24 |
| Shopping minutes | 27 | 16 | 29 | 21 | 30 | 28 |

Marketers are also beginning to investigate the impact of *odors* on shopping behaviors (see Chapter 13).[102] Early studies suggest that odors can have a positive effect on the shopping experience, particularly if they are consistent with other aspects of the atmosphere such as the music being played.[103] However, like music, odor preference varies across customers, so caution must be used to ensure that the aroma is not offensive to target customers.[104]

Figure 17–6 illustrates the way store atmosphere influences shopper behavior. Several things in this figure are noteworthy. First, the physical environment interacts with individual characteristics. Thus, an atmosphere that would produce a favorable response in

| FIGURE 17–6 | Store Atmosphere and Shopper Behavior |

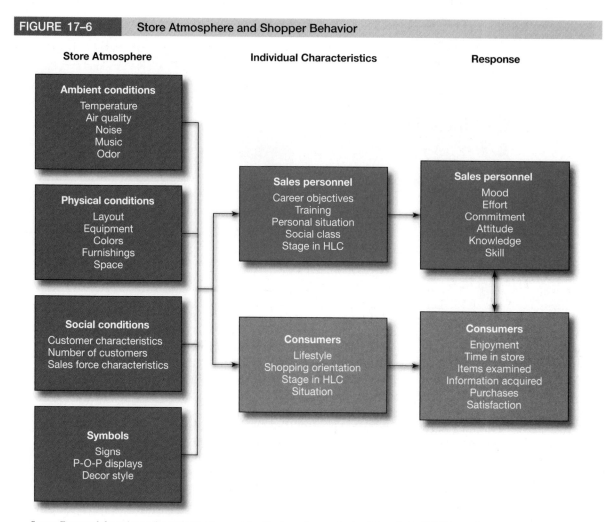

Source: Framework for understanding environment user relationships in service organizations," from the April 1992 issue of the *Journal of Marketing*. Used by permission.

teenagers might produce a negative response in older shoppers. Second, store atmosphere influences sales personnel and customers, whose interactions then influence each other. Finally, while this model focuses on store-based retailing, emerging research will continue to advance our understanding of online atmospherics.

## Stockouts

**Stockouts,** *the store being temporarily out of a particular brand,* obviously affect a consumer's purchase decision. The customer then must decide whether to buy the same brand but at another store, switch brands, delay the purchase and buy the desired brand later at the same store, or forgo the purchase altogether. In addition, the consumer's verbal behaviors and attitudes may change. Table 17–4 summarizes the impacts that a stockout situation may have.

Three types of perceived costs affect the likely response of a consumer to a stockout.[105] *Substitution costs* refer to the reduction in satisfaction the consumer believes a replacement size, brand, or product will provide. This is a function of the consumer's commitment or loyalty to the preferred brand and the perceived similarity of potential substitutes.[106]

| | |
|---|---|
| I. Purchase Behavior<br>  A. Purchase a substitute size, brand, or product at the original store. The substitute brand or product may or may not replace the regular brand or product in future purchases.<br>  B. Delay the purchase until the brand is available at the original store.<br>  C. Forgo the purchase entirely.<br>  D. Purchase the desired brand at a second store. All the items initially desired may be purchased at the second store or only the stockout items. The second store may or may not replace the original store on future shopping trips.<br><br>II. Verbal Behavior<br>  A. The consumer may make negative comments to peers about the original store.<br>  B. The consumer may make positive comments to peers about the substitute store.<br>  C. The consumer may make positive comments to peers about the substitute brand or product.<br><br>III. Attitude Shifts<br>  A. The consumer may develop a less favorable attitude toward the original store.<br>  B. The consumer may develop a more favorable attitude toward the substitute store.<br>  C. The consumer may develop a more favorable attitude toward the substitute brand/product. | **TABLE 17–4**<br><br>Impact of a<br>Stockout Situation |

*Transaction costs* refer to the mental, physical, time, and financial costs of purchasing a substitute product or brand. *Opportunity costs* are the reduction in satisfaction associated with forgoing or reducing consumption of the product. How these costs will be perceived and thus which of the outcomes, or combinations of outcomes, in Table 17–4 will occur depends on the particular consumer, product, and situation.[107]

## Web Site Functioning and Requirements

Recent research suggests that only 5 percent of those who visit an online outlet make a purchase.[108] One reason is that consumers often research online then buy in traditional stores. However, losses also occur during the online shopping process, when consumers who planned to make a purchase do not. One study finds that 57 percent of consumers abandon their online shopping carts without making a purchase, with the overall result being that for every $1 spent online, roughly $4 is left in abandoned shopping carts.[109] Various Web site factors can hamper online purchasing including security issues, return policies, and desired items being out of stock.[110] DoubleClick found the following reasons for shopping cart abandonment:[111]

| | |
|---|---|
| Additional charges (e.g., shipping) too high | 84% |
| Buying process (complicated, confusing, technical difficulties) | 44 |
| Changed mind | 32 |
| Desired item not available | 24 |
| Inaccurate initial product description | 5 |

Copyright © 2005, DoubleClick, Inc.

    Clearly, there are many areas in which the design and functioning of retail Web sites can be improved. Obviously, managing shipping charges is important and companies are responding. Amazon.com offers Amazon Prime, a member-based program where consumers pay a fixed annual fee for free second-day shipping and reduced-rate overnight. Some experts are even advocating that consumers be prompted when they attempt to abandon their carts and offered a better price or reduced or free shipping. *Can you think of any drawbacks to such an approach?* Complexity of the online buying process is also a problem. As a consequence, online retailers such as T.J. Maxx are adopting simplified shopping-cart technology that streamlines the online check-out process.[112] Some companies, such as Lands' End, are offering live chat, which connects consumers to a customer service representative at any point in the checkout process to answer questions and offer help. Security is an ongoing concern. Various Web site strategies are possible as we discussed earlier. In addition, credit card companies are getting into the game with *single-use numbers*. Consumers who were offered and adopted this controlled payment option increased their online purchases between 50 and 200 percent.[113]

## Sales Personnel

For most low-involvement purchases in the United States, self-service is predominant. As purchase involvement increases, the likelihood of interaction with a salesperson also increases. Thus, most studies of effectiveness in sales interactions have focused on high-involvement purchases such as insurance, automobiles, or industrial products. There is no simple explanation for effective sales interactions. Instead, the effectiveness of sales efforts is influenced by the interactions of

- The salesperson's knowledge, skill, and authority.
- The nature of the customer's buying task.
- The customer–salesperson relationship.

Thus, specific research is required for each target market and product category to determine the optimal personnel selling strategy.

Consider the following shopping experience:

> I also had lousy service in the store. The sales guy seemed to be trying to sell me the cheaper shoe to get me out the door. . . . The thing that irritated me was that I thought I was a fairly knowledgeable shopper and I thought that they should understand some of these things. . . . They weren't very knowledgeable. . . . I got the impression they didn't like their jobs.[114]

Is this consumer likely to return to this outlet? Will he recommend it to his friends? It is clear that knowledgeable, helpful salespeople enhance the shopping experience, while those who are not have the opposite effect.

In the online context, marketers are testing online sales clerks that interact with customers as they shop on their Web site. These online sales clerks are called *avatars* and can be defined as "virtual characters that can be used as company representatives." One study found that avatars increased store attitude, product attitude, and purchase likelihood. It also found that for high involvement products, expert avatars were more influential because of their increased credibility, while for lower involvement products, attractive-looking avatars were more effective as a result of their likeability.[115]

# PURCHASE

Once the consumer has selected the brand and retail outlet, he or she must complete the transaction. This involves what is normally called *purchasing* or *renting* the product. In traditional retail environments, this was straightforward and did not generally stop or delay purchases, with the possible exception of major and more complex purchases such as a home or car. However, as we saw earlier, many consumers starting to make an online purchase quit without making one for a variety of reasons. Increasing the percentage of potential purchasers who actually purchase is a major challenge for most online retailers.

Credit plays a major role in consumer purchases, and new technologies are being tested on an ongoing basis, as we saw earlier. And research indicates that the ability to pay by credit card rather than cash substantially increases consumers' willingness to pay and the amount they purchase.[116] Thus, it may be to the retailer's advantage to encourage credit card use even though it must pay a percentage of these sales to the credit card companies.

Businesses need to simplify the actual purchase as much as possible. This involves strategies as simple as managing the time spent in line at the checkout register to more complex operations, such as computerized credit checks to minimize credit authorization time. Many businesses appear to overlook the fact that the actual purchase act is generally the last contact the consumer will have with the store on that trip. Although first impressions are important, so are final ones. Store personnel need to be not only efficient at this activity but also helpful and personable. And online retailers need to minimize the complexity, hassle, and stress involved.

## SUMMARY

Consumers generally must select outlets as well as products. There are three general ways these decisions can be made: (1) *simultaneously;* (2) *item first, outlet second;* or (3) *outlet first, item second.* Both the manufacturer and the retailer must be aware of the decision sequence used by their target market, as it will have a major impact on their marketing strategy.

Internet retailing and other forms of in-home retailing including catalogs are increasingly important retail outlets. While store-based retailing continues to dominate in terms of overall sales, consumers increasingly use in-home options such as the Internet and catalogs in combination with retail stores in what is known as *multi-channel shopping.* Retailers often operate in various formats (catalog, retail store, and Internet) to leverage the benefits that consumers derive from each.

The decision process used by consumers to select a retail outlet is the same as the process described for selecting a brand. The only difference is in the nature of the evaluative criteria used. Retail outlet *image* is an important evaluative criterion. Store-based image and online retailer image are both important, although the dimensions consumers use to judge them vary. *Store brands* can both capitalize on a store's image and enhance, or detract from, it. *Outlet location and size* are important, with closer and larger outlets generally being preferred over more distant and smaller ones. Consumer characteristics such as *perceived risk* and *shopping orientation* are also important determinants of outlet choice.

While in a retail outlet, consumers often purchase a brand or product that differs from their plans before entering. Such purchases are referred to as *unplanned purchases.* Most of these decisions are the result of additional information processing induced by in-store or online stimuli. However, some are impulse purchases made with little or no deliberation in response to a sudden, powerful urge to buy or consume the product. Such variables as *point-of-purchase displays, price reductions, outlet atmosphere, Web site design, sales personnel,* and brand or product *stockouts* can have a major impact on sales patterns.

Once the outlet and brand have been selected, the consumer must acquire the rights to the item. This often involves credit.

## KEY TERMS

Atmospherics  606
External reference price  598
Impulse purchase  603
In-home shopping  583
Internal reference price  598
Multi-channel shoppers  593
Online privacy concerns  590

Perceived risk  600
Reference price  597
Retail attraction (gravitation)
    model  598
Servicescape  606
Shopping orientation  602
Spillover sales  596

Stockouts  608
Store atmosphere  606
Store brands  595
Store image  594
Unplanned purchases  602

## INTERNET EXERCISES

1. Visit three Internet retail outlets and evaluate them on the dimensions of Internet retailer image discussed in the text. Are there other dimensions or components you might add? Explain.
2. Visit two Internet retailers for the same product category. Evaluate the outlet atmosphere of each. What, if anything, in the atmosphere provides the following?
   *a.* Encouragement for impulse purchases
   *b.* Nonpurchase reasons for visiting

   *c.* Risk reduction
   *d.* Service
   *e.* Fun
3. Visit two online retailers and select an item of interest. Go through the checkout process up to the last step (don't buy it unless you want it!). What aspects of the process at each store might cause a user to stop before completing the purchase?

## DDB LIFE STYLE STUDY™ DATA ANALYSES

1. Based on the DDB Tables 1B through 7B, what most characterizes those who feel *making purchases over the Internet with a credit card is too risky*? What are the online marketing implications?
2. Using the DDB Tables 1B through 7B, describe the characteristics of those who have purchased event (concert/play/sports) tickets online. What is the role of the *tech-savvy* trait in terms of this behavior?
3. What most characterizes someone who frequently uses mail-order catalogs to make purchases (DDB Tables 1A through 7A)? Does there seem to be any relationship between characteristics of Internet buyers (Question 2) and catalog buyers? Explain.
4. What are the characteristics of heavy *store brand* buyers (Tables 1A through 7A)? What are the retail implications?

## REVIEW QUESTIONS

1. The consumer faces the problems of both what to buy and where to buy it. How do these two types of decisions differ?
2. How does the sequence in which the brand/outlet decision is made affect the brand strategy? The retailer strategy?
3. How is the retail environment changing?
4. Describe Internet retailing.
5. What is *multi-channel shopping* and what implications does it hold for retailer strategy?
6. What is meant by *online privacy concern*? Why is it a particularly important issue for online shoppers?
7. Describe the eight segments of online shoppers.
8. What is a *store image,* and what are its dimensions and components?
9. Describe *Internet retailer image* and compare/contrast it with *store image.*
10. What is a *store brand*? How do retailers use store brands?
11. What key decisions do retailers make with respect to retail price advertising?
12. What is meant by the term *spillover sales*? Why is it important?
13. How does the size of and distance to a retail outlet affect store selection and purchase behavior?
14. How is store choice affected by the *perceived risk* of a purchase?
15. What is meant by *social risk*? How does it differ from *economic risk*?
16. What is a *shopping orientation*?
17. Describe six motivation-based shopping orientations of college students.
18. What is meant by an *in-store purchase decision*? Why is it important?

19. What is meant by an *impulse purchase*? Why is it important?

20. Once in a particular retail outlet, what in-store and/or online characteristics can influence brand and product choice? Give an example of each.

21. Describe the impact of point-of-purchase displays on retail sales.

22. Describe the impact of price reductions and deals on retail sales.

23. What is meant by *store atmosphere*? *Online atmosphere*? How do they affect consumer behavior?

24. What is a *servicescape*?

25. Why do consumers planning to make a purchase at an online outlet often fail to do so?

26. What are frequent problems consumers encounter while shopping online?

27. What can happen in response to a *stockout*?

## DISCUSSION QUESTIONS

28. Name two product categories for which the brand is generally selected first and the outlet second, two for which the reverse is true, and two for which these decisions are generally made simultaneously. Justify your selections. How should marketing strategy differ across these products?

29. Does the image of a retail outlet affect the image of the brands it carries? Do the brands carried affect the image of the retail outlet?

30. What challenges face multi-channel retailers in managing their image across channels?

31. Respond to the questions in Consumer Insight 17–1.

32. How are social and economic risks associated with the following products likely to affect the outlet choice behavior of consumers? How would the perception of these risks differ by consumer? Situation?
    a. Men's suit
    b. Athletic shoes (for running)
    c. Wine (as a gift)
    d. Hairdresser
    e. Mountain bike
    f. Mouthwash
    g. Cell phone
    h. Movie for a date

33. Describe an appropriate strategy for an online store such as Target for each of the motivation-based shopping orientations described in the text (pages 601–602).

34. Describe an appropriate strategy for an online store such as J. Crew for each of the eight online shopper types described in the text (pages 587–588).

35. The motivation-based shopping orientations described in the text were developed using a small sample of students. Do you think these are accurate descriptions of the shopping orientations of students on your campus? How should they be modified?

36. How should retailer strategies to encourage unplanned purchases differ depending on the type of unplanned purchase generally associated with the product category?

37. What in-store characteristics could traditional retailers use to enhance the probability of purchase among individuals who visit a store? Describe each factor in terms of how it should be used, and describe its intended effect on the consumer for the following products:
    a. Cologne
    b. Ice cream
    c. Coffee after a meal
    d. Flowers from a supermarket
    e. Herbal supplements
    f. Motor oil

38. What site characteristics could online retailers use to enhance the probability of purchase among individuals who visit their sites? Describe each factor in terms of how it shou!d be used, and describe its intended effect on the consumer for the following products:
    a. Dorm furniture from Target.com
    b. Electronics from Amazon.com
    c. Laptop from HP.com
    d. Backpack from REI.com
    e. Apparel from JCPenney.com
    f. Cosmetics from Macys.com
    g. Tools from Sears.com

39. What type of store atmosphere is most appropriate for each of the following retailer types? Why?
    a. Bookstore serving college students
    b. Cosmetic section of Sears

c. Auto dealership service department
d. Consumer electronics
e. Mercedes automobiles
f. Inexpensive furniture
g. Thai food restaurant

40. Repeat Question 39 (except for *c* and *g*) for online retailers.

41. How would you respond to a stockout of your preferred brand of the following? What factors other than product category would influence your response?
    a. Suntan lotion
    b. Cereal
    c. Deodorant
    d. Dress shirt/blouse
    e. Perfume/aftershave lotion
    f. Soft drink

## APPLICATION ACTIVITIES

42. Describe the current state of Internet retailing.

43. Pick a residential area in your town and develop a gravitational model for (*a*) nearby supermarkets or (*b*) shopping malls. Conduct telephone surveys to test the accuracy of your model.

44. Develop a questionnaire to measure the image of the following. Have 10 other students complete these questionnaires. Discuss the marketing implications of your results.
    a. Target
    b. Kaboodle.com
    c. Subway
    d. Local coffee shop
    e. eBay
    f. Wal-Mart
    g. Saks Fifth Avenue

45. Have 10 students on your campus describe their shopping orientations in terms of animals as discussed in the section of the text on motivation-based shopping orientations. Combine your descriptions with those of two other students. Do any patterns emerge? Do they match those described in the text? How would you explain the differences?

46. For several of the products listed in Table 17–3, interview several students not enrolled in your class and ask them to classify their last purchase as specially planned, generally planned, substitute, or unplanned. Then combine your results with those of your classmates to obtain an estimate of student behavior. Compare student behavior with the behavior shown in Table 17–3 and discuss any similarities or differences.

47. Arrange with a local retailer (convenience store, drugstore, or whatever) to temporarily install a point-of-purchase display. Then set up a procedure to unobtrusively observe the frequency of evaluation and selection of the brand before and while the display is up. Describe your findings.

48. Visit two retail stores selling the same type of merchandise and prepare a report on their use of P-O-P materials. Explain any differences.

49. Interview the manager of a drug, department, or grocery store on their views of P-O-P materials and price advertising.

50. Develop an appropriate questionnaire and construct a new version of Table 17–2, using products relevant to college students. What are the marketing implications of this table?

51. Determine, through interviews, the general shopping orientations of students on your campus. What are the marketing implications of your findings?

52. Interview 10 students on your campus and determine their attitudes toward and use of the Internet and online shopping. Place each into one of the eight online shopper segments described in the text. Do they fit into these segments? Combine your results with those of four other students. What do you conclude?

## REFERENCES

1. S. Schubert, "The Size-atron," *Business 2.0,* June 2005, p. 2c; and information from Intellifit's Web site, at www.intellifit.com.

2. P. Bhatnagar, "Supermarkets Strike Back," *CNNMoney,* May 2, 2005, money.cnn.com.

3. "Mirror, Mirror, Talk to Me," *BusinessWeek,* July 9 and 16, 2007, p. 12.

4. See, e.g., M. Laaksonen, "Retail Patronage Dynamics," *Journal of Business Research,* September 1993, pp. 3–174.

5. R. R. Brand and J. J. Cronin, "Consumer-Specific Determinants of the Size of Retail Choice Sets," *Journal of Services Marketing* 1 (1997), pp. 19–38.

6. S. Sherman, "Will the Information Superhighway Be the Death of Retailing?" *Fortune,* April 18, 1994, p. 17.

7. Internet users from *US Online Population,* eMarketer, research report, January 2008. Internet sales from *US eCommerce Forecast: 2008 to 2012,* Forrester Research, Inc., January 18, 2008. Web-influenced store sales from *Multi-Channel Retailing,* eMarketer, research report, February 2008.

8. See, e.g., A. Bhatnagar, S. Misra, and H. R. Rao, "On Risk, Convenience, and Internet Shopping Behavior," *Communications of the Association for Computing Machinery* 43 (2000), pp. 98–105.

9. E. Yoh et al., "Consumer Adoption of the Internet," *Psychology & Marketing,* December 2003, pp. 1095–1118.

10. See, e.g., "New Belk.com Web Site Debuts with Innovative Design, Enhanced Shopping Experience and Outstanding Assortments of Top Fashion Brands," *PR Newswire,* October 13, 2008.

11. *US eCommerce Forecast: 2008 to 2012.*

12. S. Chiger, "Consumer Shopping Survey: Part III," *Catalog Age,* November 1, 2001, pp. 1–4. Used by permission of Multichannel Merchant Magazine (formerly Catalog Age). See also P. Miller, "Live from NEMOA," *Multichannel Merchant,* March 27, 2003, www.multichannelmerchant.com.

13. "USPS Study Shows Mailed Catalogs Boost Online Spending," *directmag.com,* September 28, 2004.

14. S. M. Kerner, "More Broadband Usage Means More Online Spending," *clickz.com,* October 8, 2004.

15. Adapted from W. R. Swinyard and S. M. Smith, "Why People (Don't) Shop Online," *Psychology & Marketing,* July 2003, pp. 567–97. For an alternative typology, see A. J. Rohm and V. Swaminathan, "A Typology of Online Shoppers Based on Shopping Motivations," *Journal of Business Research* 57 (2004), pp. 748–57.

16. See, e.g., A. K. Kau, Y. E. Tang, and S. Ghose, "Typology of Online Shoppers," *Journal of Consumer Marketing* 20, no. 2 (2003), pp. 139–56.

17. *US eCommerce Forecast: 2008 to 2012.*

18. Kau, Tang, and Ghose, "Typology of Online Shoppers."

19. From Roper Reports Telephone Survey, August 2003.

20. See A. Z. Cuneo, "What's in Store?" *Advertising Age,* February 25, 2002, p. 1; and R. V. Kozinets et al., "Themed Flagship Brand Stores in the New Millennium," *Journal of Retailing* 78 (2002), pp. 17–29.

21. S. A. Forest, "Look Who's Thinking Small," *BusinessWeek,* May 17, 1999, pp. 67–70.

22. A. Z. Cuneo, "On Target," *Advertising Age,* December 11, 2000, p. 1.

23. A. Klaassen, "Ion Interactive Develops System to Turn Online Visitors into Customers," *Advertising Age,* December 11, 2006, p. 32.

24. P. Paul, "Mixed Signals," *American Demographics,* July 2001, pp. 45–49.

25. For a description of the FTC's approach in this area and its fit with consumer concerns, see K. B. Sheehan and M. G. Hoy, "Dimensions of Privacy Concern among Online Consumers," *Journal of Public Policy & Marketing,* Spring 2000, pp. 62–73. See also J. Phelps, G. Nowak, and E. Ferrell, "Privacy Concerns and Consumer Willingness to Provide Personal Information," *Journal of Public Policy & Marketing,* Spring 2000, pp. 27–41; and K. B. Sheehan and T. W. Gleason, "Online Privacy," *Journal of Current Issues and Research in Advertising,* Spring 2001, pp. 31–41.

26. See, e.g., A. D. Miyazaki and A. Fernandez, "Consumer Perceptions of Privacy and Security Risks for Online Shopping," *Journal of Consumer Affairs* 35, no. 1 (2001), pp. 27–44; E. B. Andrade, V. Kaltcheva, and B. Weitz, "Self-Disclosure on the Web," in *Advances in Consumer Research,* vol. 29, eds. S. M. Broniarczyk and K. Nakamoto (Provo, UT: Association for Consumer Research, 2002), pp. 350–53; A. D. Miyazaki and S. Krishnamurthy, "Internet Seals of Approval," *Journal of Consumer Affairs* 36, no. 1 (2002), pp. 28–49; G. R. Milne and M. J. Culnan, "Strategies for Reducing Online Privacy Risks," *Journal of Interactive Marketing,* Summer 2004, pp. 15–29; and T. B. White, "Consumer Disclosure and Disclosure Avoidance," *Journal of Consumer Psychology* 14, no. 1/2 (2004), pp. 41–51.

27. A. E. Schlosser, T. B. White, and S. M. Lloyd, "Converting Web Site Visitors into Buyers," *Journal of Marketing,* April 2006, pp. 133–48.

28. *Personal Information that US Internet Users Are Willing to Share with Internet Retailers, by Trust Level, 2004* (New York: eMarketer, 2005).

29. See, e.g., K.-Pin Chiang and R. R. Dholakia, "Factors Driving Consumer Intention to Shop Online," *Journal of Consumer Psychology* 13, no. 1/2 (2003), pp. 177–83.

30. K. Labich, "What It Will Take to Keep People Hanging Out at the Mall?" *Fortune,* May 1995, pp. 102–6.

31. L. R. Klein, "Creating Virtual Product Experiences," *Journal of Interactive Marketing,* Winter 2003, pp. 41–55; and J. Nantel, "My Virtual Model," *Journal of Interactive Marketing,* Summer 2004, pp. 73–86.

32. R. Gulati and J. Garino, "Getting the Right Mix of Bricks & Clicks," *Harvard Business Review,* May 2000, pp. 107–14.

33. M. Brohan, "The Top 400 Guide," *InternetRetailer.com,* June 2005.

34. The remainder of this section is based on *Multi-Channel Shopping Study,* DoubleClick, research report, January 2004.

35. See also K. C. Gehrt and R.-N. Yan, "Situational, Consumer, and Retailer Factors Affecting Internet, Catalog, and Store Shopping," *International Journal of Retail and Distribution Management* 32, no. 1 (2004), pp. 5–18.

36. J. D. Lindquist, "Meaning of Image," *Journal of Retailing,* Winter 1974, pp. 29–38; see also M. R. Zimmer and L. L. Golden, "Impressions of Retail Stores," *Journal of Retailing,* Fall 1988, pp. 265–93.

37. H. van der Heijden and T. Verhagen, "Online Store Image," *Information and Management* 41 (2004), 609–17. See also J. R. Coyle and E. Thorson, "The Effects of Progressive Levels of Interactivity and Vividness in Web Marketing Sites," *Journal of Advertising,* Fall 2001, pp. 65–77; C. Page and E. Lepkowska-White, "Web Equity," *Journal of Consumer Marketing* 19, no. 3 (2002), pp. 231–48; E. J. Johnson, S. Bellman, and G. L. Lohse,

"Cognitive Lock-In and the Power Law of Practice," *Journal of Marketing*, April 2003, pp. 62–75; and P. Katerattanakul and K. Siau, "Creating a Virtual Store Image," *Communications in ACM*, December 2003, pp. 226–32.

38. W. R. Darden and B. J. Badin, "Exploring the Concept of Affective Quality," *Journal of Business Research*, February 1994, p. 106.

39. B. White, "Sharper Image Lives on as a Brand Name, Coming to a Retailer Near You," *bloggingstocks.com*, June 26, 2008.

40. See N. Sirohi, E. W. McLaughlin, and D. R. Witink, "A Model of Consumer Perceptions and Store Loyalty Intentions for a Supermarket Retailer," *Journal of Retailing* 2 (1998), pp. 223–45; and K. Macarthur, "What's in a Name?" *Advertising Age*, April 17, 2006, p. 43.

41. See S. Burton, D. R. Lichtenstein, R. G. Netemeyer, and J. A. Garretson, "A Scale for Measuring Attitude toward Private Label Products," *Journal of the Academy of Marketing Science*, Fall 1998, pp. 293–306.

42. See M. Corstjens and R. Lal, "Building Store Loyalty through Store Brands," *Journal of Marketing Research*, August 2000, pp. 281–91.

43. P. S. Richardson, A. K. Jain, and A. Dick, "Household Store Brand Proneness," *Journal of Retailing* 2 (1996), pp. 159–85; and S. C. Choi and A. T. Coughlan, "Private Label Positioning," *Journal of Retailing* 82, no. 2 (2006), pp. 79–93. For a conflicting view, see K. L. Ailawadi, S. A. Neslin, and K. Gegdenk, "Pursuing the Value-Conscious Consumer," *Journal of Marketing*, January 2001, pp. 71–89.

44. *The Double Dividend* (New York: Newspaper Advertising Bureau Inc., February 1977).

45. F. J. Mulhern and D. T. Padgett, "The Relationship between Retail Price Promotions and Regular Price Purchases," *Journal of Marketing*, October 1995, pp. 83–90. For similar results, see S. Burton, D. R. Lichtenstein, and R. G. Netemeyer, "Exposure to Sales Flyers and Increased Purchases in Retail Supermarkets," *Journal of Advertising Research*, September 1999, pp. 7–14.

46. See, e.g., V. Severin, J. J. Louviere, and A. Finn, "The Stability of Retail Shopping Choices over Time and across Countries," *Journal of Retailing* 77 (2001), pp. 185–202.

47. See, e.g., P. Chandon, B. Wansink, and G. Laurent, "A Benefit Congruency Framework of Sales Promotion Effectiveness," *Journal of Marketing*, October 2000, pp. 65–81.

48. See, e.g., van der Heijden and Verhagen, "Online Store Image."

49. A. Ansari and C. F. Mela, "E-Customization," *Journal of Marketing Research*, May 2003, pp. 131–45.

50. See C. Janiszewski and D. R. Lichtenstein, "A Range Theory of Price Perception," *Journal of Consumer Research*, March 1999, pp. 353–68.

51. See R. A. Briesch, L. Krishnamurthi, and T. Mazumdar, "A Comparative Analysis of Reference Price Models," *Journal of Consumer Research*, September 1997, pp. 202–14; R. W. Niedrich, S. Sharma, and D. H. Wedell, "Reference Price and Price Perceptions," *Journal of Consumer Research*, December 2001, pp. 339–54; and P. K. Kopalle, and J. Lindsey-Mullikin, "The Impact of External Reference Price on Consumer Price Expectations," *Journal of Retailing* 79 (2003), pp. 225–36. For a different approach, see K. B. Monroe and A. Y. Lee,

"Remembering versus Knowing," *Journal of the Academy of Marketing Science*, Spring 1999, pp. 207–25.

52. See V. Kumar, K. Karande, and W. J. Reinartz, "The Impact of Internal and External Reference Prices on Brand Choice," *Journal of Retailing* 3 (1998), pp. 401–26.

53. T. A. Suter and S. Burton, "Reliability and Consumer Perceptions of Implausible Reference Prices in Retail Prices," *Psychology & Marketing*, January 1996, pp. 37–54; M. S. Yadav and K. Seiders, "Is the Price Right?" *Journal of Retailing* (1998), pp. 311–29; and L. D. Compeau and D. Grewal, "Comparative Price Advertising," *Journal of Public Policy & Marketing*, Fall 1998, pp. 257–73. See also M. J. Barone, K. C. Manning, and P. W. Miniard, "Consumer Response to Retailers' Use of Partially Comparative Pricing," *Journal of Marketing*, July 2004, pp. 37–47.

54. See A. Biswas et al., "Consumer Evaluation of Reference Price Advertisements," *Journal of Public Policy & Marketing*, Spring 1999, pp. 52–65.

55. T. B. Heath, S. Chatterjee, and K. R. France, "Mental Accounting and Changes in Price," *Journal of Consumer Research*, June 1995, pp. 90–97.

56. See S.-F. S. Chen, K. B. Monroe, and Y.-C. Lou, "The Effects of Framing Price Promotion Messages on Consumers' Perceptions and Purchase Intentions," *Journal of Retailing* 3 (1998), pp. 353–72; and M. R. Stafford and T. F. Stafford, "The Effectiveness of Tensile Pricing Tactics in the Advertising of Services," *Journal of Advertising*, Summer 2000, pp. 45–60.

57. See A. Biswas and S. Burton, "Consumer Perceptions of Tensile Price Claims in Advertisements," *Journal of the Academy of Marketing Science*, Summer 1993, pp. 217–30; K. N. Rajendran and G.-J. Tellis, "Contextual and Temporal Components of Reference Price," *Journal of Marketing*, January 1994, pp. 22–39; and D. Grewal, H. Marmorstein, and A. Sharma, "Communicating Price Information through Semantic Cues," *Journal of Consumer Research*, September 1996, pp. 148–55.

58. I. Sinha and M. F. Smith, "Consumers' Perceptions of Promotional Framing of Price," *Psychology & Marketing*, March 2000, pp. 257–75.

59. See D. Simester, "Signaling Price Image Using Advertised Prices," *Marketing Science* 14, no. 2 (1995), pp. 166–88; and J. Srivastave and N. Lurie, "A Consumer Perspective on Price-Matching Refund Policies," *Journal of Consumer Research*, September 2001, pp. 296–307.

60. G. S. Bobinski, Jr., D. Cox, and A. Cox, "Retail 'Sale' Advertising, Perceived Retailer Credibility, and Price Rationale," *Journal of Retailing* 3 (1996), pp. 291–306.

61. See, e.g., Severin, Louviere, and Finn, "The Stability of Retail Shopping Choices over Time and across Countries."

62. See I. Simonson, "The Effect of Product Assortment on Buyer Preferences," and R. E. Stassen, J. D. Mittelstaedt, and R. A. Mittelstaedt, "Assortment Overlap," both in *Journal of Retailing* 75, no. 3 (1999), pp. 347–70 and 371–86, respectively.

63. C. S. Craig, A. Ghosh, and S. McLafferty, "Models of the Retail Location Process: A Review," *Journal of Retailing*, Spring 1984, pp. 5–33.

64. See D. R. Bell, T.-H. Ho, and C. S. Tang, "Determining Where to Shop," *Journal Marketing Research*, August 1998, pp. 352–69.

65. See B. G. C. Dellaert et al., "Investigating Consumers' Tendency to Combine Multiple Shopping Purposes and Destinations," *Journal Marketing Research,* May 1998, pp. 177–88.

66. See P. R. Messinger and C. Narasimhan, "A Model of Retail Formats Based on Consumers' Economizing on Shopping Time," *Marketing Science* 1 (1997), pp. 1–23.

67. A. Chaudhuri, "Product Class Effects on Perceived Risk," *International Journal of Research in Marketing,* May 1998, pp. 157–68; and R. Batra and I. Sinha, "Consumer-Level Factors Moderating the Success of Private Label Brands," *Journal of Retailing* 76, no. 2 (2000), pp. 175–91.

68. Based on V. Prasad, "Socioeconomic Product Risk and Patronage Preferences of Retail Shoppers," *Journal of Marketing,* July 1975, p. 44.

69. G. R. Dowling and R. Staelin, "A Model of Perceived Risk and Intended Risk-Handling Activity," *Journal of Consumer Research,* June 1994, pp. 119–34; L. W. Turley and R. P. LeBlanc, "An Exploratory Investigation of Consumer Decision Making in the Service Sector," *Journal of Services Marketing* 7, no. 4 (1993), pp. 11–18; and J. B. Smith and J. M. Bristor, "Uncertainty Orientation," *Psychology & Marketing,* November 1994, pp. 587–607.

70. R. B. Settle, P. L. Alreck, and D. E. McCorkle, "Consumer Perceptions of Mail/Phone Order Shopping Media" *Journal of Direct Marketing,* Summer 1994, pp. 30–45; C. R. Jasper and S. J. Ouellette, "Consumers' Perception of Risk and the Purchase of Apparel from Catalogs," *Journal of Direct Marketing,* Spring 1994, pp. 23–36; and D. Biswas and A. Biswas, "The Diagnostic Role of Signals in the Context of Perceived Risks in Online Shopping," *Journal of Interactive Marketing*, Summer 2004, pp. 30–45.

71. See also J. C. Sweeney, G. N. Soutar, and L. W. Johnson, "The Role of Perceived Risk in the Quality–Value Relationship," *Journal of Retailing* 75, no. 1 (1999), pp. 75–105.

72. See K. L. Wakefield and J. Baker, "Excitement at the Mall," *Journal of Retailing* 74, no. 4 (1998), pp. 515–39; H. McDonald, P. Darbyshire, and C. Jevons, "Shop Often, Buy Little," *Journal of Global Marketing* 13, no. 4 (2000), pp. 53–71; J. A. F. Nicholls et al., "Inter-American Perspectives from Mall Shoppers," *Journal of Global Marketing* 15, no. 1 (2001), pp. 87–103; B. Jin and J.-O. Kim, "Discount Store Retailing in Korea," *Journal of Global Marketing* 15, no. 2 (2001), pp. 81–107; and J. L. Joines, C. W. Scherer, and D. A. Scheufele, "Exploring Motivations for Consumer Web Use and Their Implications for E-commerce," *Journal of Consumer Marketing* 20, no. 2 (2003), pp. 90–108.

73. See M. A. Eastlick and R. A. Feinberg, "Gender Differences in Mail-Catalog Patronage Motives," *Journal of Direct Marketing,* Spring 1994, pp. 37–44; "The Call of the Mall," *EDK Forecast,* October 1994, pp. 1–3; "Black, Hip, and Primed to Shop," *American Demographics,* September 1996, pp. 52–58; and J. A. F. Nicholls et al., "The Seven Year Itch?" *Journal of Consumer Marketing* 19, no. 2 (2002), pp. 149–65.

74. D. N. Hassay and M. C. Smith, "Fauna, Foraging and Shopping Motives," in *Advances in Consumer Research,* vol. 23, eds. K. P. Corfman and J. G. Lynch (Provo, UT: Association for Consumer Research, 1996), pp. 510–15. Reprinted with permission of the Association for Consumer Research.

75. See N. Paden and R. Stell, "Using Consumer Shopping Orientations to Improve Retail Web Site Design," *Journal of Professional Services Marketing* 20, no. 2 (2000), pp. 73–85; and K. E. Reynolds and S. E. Beatty, "A Relationship Customer Typology," *Journal of Retailing* 75, no. 4 (1999), pp. 509–23.

76. See J. E. Russo and F. Lecleric, "An Eye Fixation Analysis of Choice Processes for Consumer Nondurables," *Journal of Consumer Research,* September 1994, pp. 274–90.

77. See L. G. Block and V. G. Morwitz, "Shopping Lists as an External Memory Aid for Grocery Shopping," *Journal of Consumer Psychology* 8, no. 4 (1999), pp. 343–75.

78. See D. W. Rook and R. J. Fisher, "Normative Influences on Impulsive Buying Behaviors," *Journal of Consumer Research,* December 1995, pp. 305–13; R. Puri, "Measuring and Modifying Consumer Impulsive Buying Behavior," *Journal of Consumer Psychology* 5, no. 2 (1996), pp. 87–113; U. M. Dholakia, "Temptation and Resistance," *Psychology & Marketing,* November 2000, pp. 955–82; and R. F. Baumeister, "Yielding to Temptation," *Journal of Consumer Research,* March 2002, pp. 670–76.

79. R. Liljenwall, "Global Trends in Point-of-Purchase Advertising," in *The Power of Point-of-Purchase Advertising,* ed. R. Liljenwall (Washington, DC: Point-of-Purchase Advertising International, 2004), p. 191.

80. See S. E. Beatty and M. E. Ferrell, "Impulse Buying," *Journal of Retailing* 2 (1998), pp. 169–91; and M. Koufaris, "Applying the Technology Acceptance Model and Flow Theory to Online Consumer Behavior," *Information Systems Research,* June 2002, pp. 205–23.

81. *P-O-P Measures Up* (Washington, DC: Point-of-Purchase Advertising Institute, 2001).

82. Ibid.

83. See *POPAI/Horner Drug Store Study* (Englewood, NJ: Point-of-Purchase Advertising Institute, 1992); A. J. Greco and L. E. Swayne, "Sales Response of Elderly Consumers to P-O-P Advertising," *Journal of Advertising Research,* September 1992, pp. 43–53; *POPAI/Kmart/Procter & Gamble Study of P-O-P Effectiveness* (Englewood, NJ: Point-of-Purchase Advertising Institute, 1993); *P-O-P Measures Up*; and T. Lee, "Experts Say Point-of-Purchase Advertising Can Influence Shoppers' Choices," *Knight Ridder Tribune Business News,* January 19, 2002. For an exception, see C. S. Areni, D. F. Duhan, and P. Kiekeer, "Point-of-Purchase Displays, Product Organization, and Brand Purchase Likelihoods," *Journal of the Academy of Marketing Science,* Fall 1999, pp. 428–41.

84. See E. T. Anderson and D. I. Simester, "The Role of Sale Signs," *Marketing Science* 2 (1998), pp. 139–55.

85. See, e.g., G. A. Taylor, "Coupon Response in Services," *Journal of Retailing* 77 (2001), pp. 139–51; C. M. Heilman, K. Nakamoto, and A. G. Rao, "Pleasant Surprises," *Journal of Marketing Research*, May 2002, pp. 242–52; and D. M. Hardesty and W. O. Bearden, "Consumer Evaluations of Different Promotion Types and Price Presentations," *Journal of Retailing* 79 (2003), pp. 17–25.

86. A. S. C. Ehrenberg, K. Hammond, and G. J. Goodhardt, "The After-Effects of Price-Related Consumer Promotions," *Journal of Advertising Research,* July 1994, pp. 11–21; and P. Papatla and L. Krishnamurthi, "*Journal of Marketing Research,* February 1996, pp. 20–36.

87. See C. F. Mela, K. Jedidi, and D. Bowman, "The Long-Term Impact of Promotions on Consumer Stockpiling Behavior," *Journal of Marketing Research,* May 1998, pp. 250–62; and J. E. Urbany, P. R. Dickson, and A. G. Sawyer, "Insights into Cross- and Within-Store Price Search," *Journal of Retailing* 76, no. 2 (2000), pp. 243–58. See also M. Zeelenberg and M. van Putten, "The Dark Side of Discounts," *Psychology & Marketing,* August 2005, pp. 611–22 for the negative effects of postpromotion when loyal customers miss a discount opportunity.

88. K. Sivakumar and S. P. Raj, "Quality Tier Competition," *Journal of Marketing,* July 1997, pp. 71–84; and S. M. Nowlis and I. Simonson, "Sales Promotions and the Choice Context as Competing Influences on Consumer Decision Making," *Journal of Consumer Psychology* 9, no. 1 (2000), pp. 1–16.

89. D. Grewal, R. Krishnan, J. Baker, and N. Borin, "The Effect of Store Name, Brand Name, and Price Discounts on Consumers' Evaluations and Purchase Intentions," *Journal of Retailing* 3 (1998), pp. 331–52.

90. D. R. Bell and J. M. Lattin, "Shopping Behavior and Consumer Preference for Store Price Format," *Marketing Science* 1 (1998), pp. 66–88. See also R. Lal and R. Rao, "Supermarket Competition," *Marketing Science* 1 (1997), pp. 60–80.

91. V. G. Morwitz, E. A. Greenleaf, and E. J. Johnson, "Divide and Prosper," *Journal of Consumer Research,* November 1998, pp. 453–63.

92. K. L. Wakefield and J. G. Blodgett, "The Effect of the Servicescape on Customers' Behavioral Intentions in Leisure Service Settings," *Journal of Services Marketing,* no. 6 (1996), pp. 45–61; and K. L. Wakefield and J. G. Blodgett, "Customer Response to Intangible and Tangible Service Factors," *Psychology & Marketing,* January 1999, pp. 51–68; and B. D. Keillor, G. T. M. Hult, and D. Kandemir, "A Study of the Service Encounter in Eight Countries," *Journal of International Marketing* 12, no. 1 (2004), pp. 9–35.

93. See C. Mathwick, N. Malhotra, and E. Rigdon, "Experiential Value," *Journal of Retailing* 77 (2001), pp. 39–56; P. D. Lynch, R. J. Kent, and S. S. Srinivasan, "The Global Internet Shopper," *Journal of Advertising Research,* May 2001, pp. 15–23; T. P. Novak, D. L. Hoffman, and A. Duhachek, "The Influence of Goal-Directed and Experiential Activities on Online Flow Experiences," *Journal of Consumer Psychology* 13, no. 1/2 (2003), pp. 3–16; and A. P. Vrechopoulos et al., "Virtual Store Layout," *Journal of Retailing* 80, no. 1 (2004), pp. 13–22.

97. E. Sherman, A. Mathur, and R. B. Smith, "Store Environment and Consumer Purchase Behavior," *Psychology & Marketing,* July 1997, pp. 361–78; and J. Baker et al., "The Influence of Multiple Store Environment Cues on Perceived Merchandise Value and Patronage Intentions," *Journal of Marketing,* April 2002, pp. 120–41.

95. S. A. Eroglu, K. A. Machleit, and L. M. Davis, "Emprical Testing of a Model of Online Store Atmospherics and Shopper Responses," *Psychology & Marketing,* February 2003, pp. 139–50. See also S. Menon and B. Kahn, "Cross-Category Effects of Induced Arousal and Pleasure on the Internet Shopping Experience," *Journal of Retailing* 78 (2002), pp. 31–40.

96. L. Dailey, "Navigational Web Atmospherics," *Journal of Business Research* 57 (2004), pp. 795–803.

97. B. Babin and W. R. Darden, "Good and Bad Shopping Vibes," *Journal of Business Research,* March 1996, pp. 210–60; K. Chang, "The Impact of Perceived Physical Environments on Customers' Satisfaction and Return Intentions," *Journal of Professional Services Marketing* 21, no. 2 (2000), pp. 75–85; D. Grewal et al., "The Effects of Wait Expectations and Store Atmosphere Evaluations on Patronage Intentions in Service-Intensive Retail Stores," *Journal of Retailing* 79 (2003), pp. 259–68; Menon and Kahn, "Cross-Category Effects of Induced Arousal and Pleasure on the Internet Shopping Experience"; and Eroglu, Machleit, and Davis, "Empirical Testing of a Model of Online Store Atmospherics and Shopper Responses."

98. See K. A. Machleit, S. A. Eroglu, and S. P. Mantel, "Perceived Retail Crowding and Shopping Satisfaction," *Journal of Consumer Psychology* 9, no. 1 (2000), pp. 29–42; K. Harris and S. Baron, "Consumer-to-Consumer Conversations in Service Settings," *Journal of Service Research,* February 2004, pp. 287–303; and J. J. Argo, D. W. Dahl, and R. V. Manchanda, "The Influence of Mere Social Presence in a Retail Context," *Journal of Consumer Research,* September 2005, pp. 207–12.

99. S. J. Grove and R. P. Fisk, "The Impact of Other Customers' Service Experiences," *Journal of Retailing* 1 (1997), pp. 63–85.

100. See, e.g., S. Oakes, "The Influence of Musicscape within Service Environments," *Journal of Services Marketing* 4, no. 7 (2000), pp. 539–56; J. C. Sweeney and F. Wyber, "The Role of Cognitions and Emotions in the Music-Approach-Avoidance Behavior Relationship," *Journal of Services Marketing* 16, no. 1 (2002), pp. 51–69; C. Caldwell and S. A. Hibbert, "The Influence of Music Tempo and Musical Preference on Restaurant Patrons' Behavior," *Psychology & Marketing,* November 2002, pp. 895–917; and S. Morin, L. Dube, and J. C. Chebat, "The Role of Pleasant Music in Servicescapes," *Journal of Retailing* 83, no. 1, (2007), pp. 115–30.

101. C. S. Gulas and C. D. Schewe, "Atmospheric Segmentation," in *Enhancing Knowledge Development in Marketing,* eds. R. Achrol and A. Mitchell (Chicago: American Marketing Association, 1994), pp. 325–30. Similar results are in J. D. Herrington and L. M. Capella, "Effects of Music in Service Environments," *Journal of Services Marketing* 2 (1996), pp. 26–41.

102. D. J. Mitchell, B. E. Kahn, and S. C. Knasko, "There's Something in the Air," *Journal of Consumer Research,* September 1995, pp. 229–38; A. R. Hirsch, "Effects of Ambient Odors on Slot-Machine Usage in a Las Vegas Casino," *Psychology & Marketing,* October 1995, pp. 585–94; M. Wilkie, "Scent of a Market," *American Demographics,* August 1995, pp. 40–49; P. Sloan, "Smelling Trouble," *Advertising Age,* September 11, 1995, p. 1; E. R. Spangenberg, A. E. Crowley, and P. W. Henderson, "Improving the Store Environment," *Journal of Marketing,* April 1996, pp. 67–80; and P. F. Bone and P. S. Ellen, "Scents in the Marketplace," *Journal of Retailing* 75, no. 2 (1999), pp. 243–62.

103. A. S. Mattila and J. Wirtz, "Congruency of Scent and Music as a Driver of In-Store Evaluations and Behavior," *Journal of Retailing* 77, no. 2 (2001), pp. 273–89.

104. See A. M. Fiore, X. Yah, and E. Yoh, "Effects of Product Display and Environmental Fragrancing on Approach Responses and Pleasurable Experiences," *Psychology & Marketing,* January 2000, pp. 27–54.

105. K. Campo, E. Gijsbrechts, and P. Nisol, "Towards Understanding Consumer Response to Stock-Outs," *Journal of Retailing* 76, no. 2 (2000), pp. 219–42.

106. G. J. Fitzsimons, "Consumer Response to Stockouts," *Journal of Consumer Research,* September 2000, pp. 249–67.

107. See, e.g., L. M. Sloot, P. C. Verhoef, P. H. Franses, "The Impact of Brand Equity and the Hedonic Level of Products on Consumer Stock-Out Reactions," *Journal of Retailing* 81, no. 1, (2005), pp. 15–34.

108. *E-Commerce Site Trend Report,* DoubleClick, research report, November 2004.

109. Ibid.

110. S. L. Wood, "Remote Purchase Environments," *Journal of Marketing Research*, May 2001, pp. 157–69; information reported by Pacific Online, Inc., www.pon.net/service/ecommerce/etailors, July 30, 2002; J. Goldeen, "Consumers More Likely to Stay Loyal to Stores with Easy Return Policy," *Knight Ridder Tribune Business News,* December 25, 2003, p. 1; and V. Vara, "Tabs on Tech," *The Wall Street Journal Online,* November 8, 2004.

111. *Holiday Multi-Channel Retail Study*, DoubleClick, research presentation, July 15, 2005. Similar results can be found in a recent study by PayPal and comScore, cited in J. Teixeira, "Why Are People Abandoning My Shopping Cart?" at *www.morevisibility.com*, June 2, 2008.

112. M. Prince, "Online Retailers Turn to New Shopping Carts to Drive Sales," *The Wall Street Journal Online,* November 10, 2004.

113. "Single-use Numbers Increase Confidence, Boost Online Spending, Study Says," *InternetRetailer.com,* February 3, 2005.

114. B. B. Stern, G. J. Thompson, and E. J. Arnould, "Narrative Analysis of a Marketing Relationship," *Psychology & Marketing* 3 (1998), pp. 195–214.

115. M. Holzwarth, C. Janiszewski, and M. M. Neumann, "The Influence of Avatars on Online Consumer Shopping Behavior," *Journal of Marketing*, October 2006, pp. 19–36.

116. D. Prelec and D. Simester, "Always Leave Home without It," *Marketing Letters*, February 2001, pp. 5–12; and D. Soman, "Effects of Payment Mechanism on Spending Behavior," *Journal of Consumer Research,* March 2001, pp. 460–74.

# Postpurchase Processes, Customer Satisfaction, and Customer Commitment

■ Customer relationship management (CRM) programs are increasingly common in American firms. The objective of such programs is to increase the satisfaction, commitment, and retention of key customers. *BusinessWeek* recently published its ranking of the Top 25 Service Organizations. The companies ranged from insurance and financial services to package carriers to cell phone service providers. A few of the companies and their *BusinessWeek* profiles are presented below.[1]

- USAA Insurance. Service representatives are highly rewarded, with recent bonuses of over 16 percent. They also instituted a call center tool that tracks frontline suggestions for customer-friendly innovations.
- Four Seasons Hotels. They rely on their customer service personnel heavily and understand that CRM is more than just a database management program. Each hotel employs a "guest historian" who is in charge of tracking guest preferences.

- Wegmans Food Markets. Knowing that good service requires lots of time, they reorganized their "back-of-store" operations and even moved some of it off site to free up service employee time and energy. These employees are now trained on how to help customers on the store floor.
- Porsche. Porsche drivers love their cars and according to the company "should not have to drive a car like everyone else's." So, when owners bring their Porsche in for service and repairs, they only loan them another Porsche.
- Amica Insurance. This company is dedicated to loyalty. They could assume their customers have made their purchase and will remain loyal. However, they don't take this for granted. One example is that when serious weather like a tornado strikes, they call customers who they haven't heard from!

As you can see, the best companies appear to blend technology and people in a way that is appropriate for their industry and their target customer. Firms that struggle often make the mistake of thinking that CRM is as simple as buying a computer program. These companies often fail to create great service organizations, and they damage long-term customer loyalty by failing to satisfy their customers' core needs.

CRM programs, whether complex and sophisticated database systems or a simple phone call, are designed to increase satisfaction and loyalty among target customers. In all the examples in the chapter opener, customers have made a purchase decision (they have purchased the insurance, are staying at the hotel, are shopping at the store, have bought the car). What is key is how these companies work to *keep* those customers coming back. In this chapter, we will examine the postpurchase processes that produce customer satisfaction and loyalty and the marketing strategies these processes suggest.

Figure 18–1 illustrates the relationships among the postpurchase processes. As the figure indicates, some purchases are followed by a phenomenon called *postpurchase dissonance*. This occurs when a consumer doubts the wisdom of a purchase he or she has made. Other purchases are followed by nonuse. The consumer keeps or returns the product without using it. Most purchases are followed by product use, even if postpurchase dissonance is present. Product use often requires the disposition of the product package or the product itself. During and after use, the purchase process and the product are evaluated by the consumer. Unsatisfactory evaluations may produce complaints by those consumers. Appropriate responses by the firm may reverse the initial dissatisfaction among those who complained. The result of all these processes is a final level of satisfaction, which in turn can result in a loyal, committed customer, one who is willing to repurchase, or in a customer who switches brands or discontinues using the product category.

| FIGURE 18–1 | Postpurchase Consumer Behavior |
|---|---|

# POSTPURCHASE DISSONANCE

I still like it [a dining room set] a whole lot better than what we used to have. But I think if we had taken longer we would have gotten more precisely what we wanted. I mean we got a great deal. You couldn't get that for that price, so I am happy with the money part of it, but some days I wish we had spent more and gotten something a bit different.[2]

This is a common consumer reaction after making a difficult, relatively permanent decision. Doubt or anxiety of this type is referred to as **postpurchase dissonance.**[3] Figure 18–1 indicates that some, but not all, consumer purchase decisions are followed by postpurchase dissonance. The probability of a consumer's experiencing postpurchase dissonance, as well as the magnitude of such dissonance, is a function of

- *The degree of commitment or irrevocability of the decision.* The easier it is to alter the decision, the less likely the consumer is to experience dissonance.
- *The importance of the decision to the consumer.* The more important the decision, the more likely dissonance will result.
- *The difficulty of choosing among the alternatives.* The more difficult it is to select from among the alternatives, the more likely the experience and magnitude of dissonance. Decision difficulty is a function of the number of alternatives considered, the number of relevant attributes associated with each alternative, and the extent to which each alternative offers attributes not available with the other alternatives.
- *The individual's tendency to experience anxiety.* Some individuals have a higher tendency to experience anxiety than do others. The higher the tendency to experience anxiety, the more likely the individual will experience postpurchase dissonance.

Dissonance occurs because making a relatively permanent commitment to a chosen alternative requires one to give up the attractive features of the unchosen alternatives. This is inconsistent with the desire for those features. Thus, nominal and most limited decision making will not produce postpurchase dissonance, because these decisions do not consider attractive features in an unchosen brand that do not also exist in the chosen brand. For example, a consumer who has an evoked set of three brands of detergent could consider them to be equivalent on all relevant attributes except price and, therefore, always purchases the least expensive brand. Such a purchase would not produce postpurchase dissonance.

Because most high-involvement purchase decisions involve one or more of the factors that lead to postpurchase dissonance, these decisions often are accompanied by dissonance. And since dissonance is unpleasant, consumers generally attempt to avoid or reduce it.

Decisions that involve giving up some or all of a desirable feature to obtain a slightly more desirable feature often generate negative emotions while the decision is being made. These negative emotions may be sufficient to cause the consumer to avoid or delay the decision (I'll just keep this car a while longer).[4] This suggests that firms marketing products such as automobiles, vacation homes, expensive vacation packages, and similar products train their salespeople to help minimize these negative emotions. Advertising that emphasizes the fun and positive emotions of the decision outcome and incentive programs that encourage consumers to continue with the purchase process could also be effective.

Consumers may also use decision rules designed to minimize the experience of postpurchase doubt. Such a rule or tactic would focus on minimizing the regret or doubt that a decision might produce rather than maximizing the value or benefits of the decisions.[5] The following choice exemplifies this rule:

> And I think that fear was one reason that we bought the General Motors van because we were afraid that if we bought the Ford . . . Well, there is a feeling that if something is too much less, then you start asking yourself why is it that much less. . . . We had read how Ford uses more automatization in their manufacturing and we knew that it cost them less to make a car than GM. So we knew that there was a real reason for why theirs is so much cheaper, but you keep asking yourself, "Am I going to kick myself for this? Am I going to wish that I spent more and gotten the other one?"[6]

After the purchase is made, the consumer may use one or more of the following approaches to reduce dissonance:

- Increase the desirability of the brand purchased.
- Decrease the desirability of rejected alternatives.
- Decrease the importance of the purchase decision.
- Reverse the purchase decision (return the product before use).

Although postpurchase dissonance may be reduced by internal reevaluations, searching for additional external information that serves to confirm the wisdom of a particular choice is also a common strategy. Naturally, information that supports the consumer's choice acts to bolster confidence in the correctness of the purchase decision.

Consumer search for, or heightened receptiveness to, information *after* the purchase greatly enhances the role that advertising and follow-up sales efforts can have. To build customer confidence in choosing their brand, many marketers of consumer durables such as major appliances and automobiles send recent purchasers direct-mail materials designed in large part to confirm the wisdom of the purchase. Local retailers can place follow-up calls to make sure the customer is not experiencing any problems with the car or appliance and to reduce any dissonance. Obviously e-mail is an option as well. For example, Johnston & Murphy (high-end footwear and accessories) sends follow-up e-mails thanking customers for their recent purchase, pointing them to its Web site, and soliciting feedback. Such communications can go a long way in reducing dissonance and increasing satisfaction.

Many advertisements help recent buyers confirm the wisdom of their purchase as well as attract new buyers. Imagine a consumer who just purchased a BMW 5 Series after a lengthy and difficult decision process involving it and several other options. At this point the buyer would be very receptive to positive information about the 5 Series and likely to watch an ad he or she might see on TV, read a print ad encountered in a magazine, or even scan blogs or relevant Web sites for positive reinforcement. The ad in Illustration 18–1 provides an additional example of the reinforcement potential of advertising in the postpurchase process.

A concept very similar to postpurchase dissonance is **consumption guilt.** Consumption guilt occurs when *negative emotions or guilt feelings are aroused by the use of a product or a service.* A person driving a large car may experience some negative feelings due to concern over resource utilization and pollution. The example below illustrates consumption guilt quite clearly:

> I have to count calories much more than I did before. I still buy a sundae once in a while but the joy of eating ice cream will probably forever be connected with guilt over eating something so unhealthy. When I think about it, I realize that most products make me feel good and bad at the same time.[7]

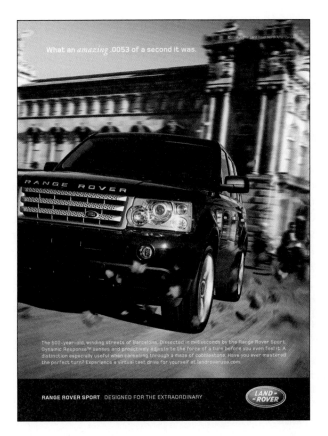

Marketers of products whose target markets might experience consumption guilt need to focus on validating the consumption of the product. They need to find ways to give the consumer permission or a rationale for indulging in that consumption act.[8]

# PRODUCT USE AND NONUSE

## Product Use

Most consumer purchases involve nominal or limited decision making and therefore arouse little or no postpurchase dissonance. Instead, the purchaser or some other member of the household uses the product without first worrying about the wisdom of the purchase. And as Figure 18–1 shows, even when postpurchase dissonance occurs, it is still generally followed by product use.

Marketers need to understand how consumers use their products for a variety of reasons. Understanding both the functional and symbolic ways in which a product is used can lead to more effective product designs. For example, Nike uses observation of basketball players at inner-city courts to gain insights into desired functional and style features. One insight gained through these observations is that the process of putting on and tying/buckling basketball shoes before a game is full of meaning and symbolism. In many ways, it is the equivalent of a knight putting on armor before a jousting match or combat. Nike has used this insight in several aspects of its shoe designs.

**Use innovativeness** refers to *a consumer using a product in a new way.*[9] Marketers who discover new uses for their products can greatly expand sales. Two products famous for this are Arm & Hammer's baking soda and WD-40. Arm & Hammer discovered that consumers were using its baking soda for a variety of noncooking uses, such as deodorizing refrigerators. It now advertises such uses and has developed product packaging, such as its Fridge Fresh Air Filters, specific to such uses. WD-40, a lubricant, is renowned for the wide array of applications that consumers suggest for it, including as an additive to fish bait and for removing gum from a carpet.

Many firms attempt to obtain relevant information on product usage via surveys using standard questionnaires. Such surveys can lead to new-product development, indicate new uses or markets for existing products, or indicate appropriate communications themes. Online surveys make this easier than ever before. Arm & Hammer has a page on its Web site where consumers can register for special offers, tips, and recipes. In return, they are asked several use-related questions, shown below. *What sorts of insights regarding use innovativeness do you think these questions are hoping to tap into? Which aspects get most directly at use innovativeness for Arm & Hammer?*

---

1. I most often find myself using ARM & HAMMER Baking Soda for:
    ___ Baking
    ___ Household Cleaning
    ___ Deodorizing my Refrigerator
    ___ Balancing my pool's pH
    ___ Boosting my laundry detergent performance
    ___ Oral care, skin care, hair care
    ___ Other [please specify: _____ ]

2. How often do you change the box of baking soda in your refrigerator or freezer?
    ___ Every 3 months
    ___ Twice a year
    ___ Once a year
    ___ Other
    ___ I currently don't keep baking soda in my refrigerator or freezer

---

Surveys can provide useful information, but observation, depth interviews, and case studies often produce deeper insights:

- During the summer, several Chicago organizations offer "architectural boat cruises" on the Chicago River. They compete on the architectural credentials of their guides, the sites shown, and the boats used. One company did a standard survey and virtually all the respondents checked "interest in architecture" as a "very important" or "extremely important" reason for taking the cruise. However, depth research with 50 passengers showed that architecture was a relatively minor reason for their being there. Most of the Chicago residents were there as a means to entertain out-of-town guests on a nice day. This finding resulted in very different positioning and advertising themes for the sponsoring firm.

- A few years back, a number of upscale frozen gourmet dinner entrées were introduced with great expectations—which none achieved. Researchers observed the frozen food cases that still sold the product and found that, while most consumers ignored it, a few bought substantial quantities. Interviews with these consumers revealed that they were not using them for home meals but rather were preparing them in the office microwave for lunch. They stated that good restaurants were too slow, inconvenient, and expensive for lunch and fast-food places lacked quality and nutrition. This led to opportunities to reposition a line for office-based lunch consumption.[10]

**Consumer Stories Help Bounce Cash In on Off-Label Uses**

Companies are often hesitant to encourage off-label uses, that is, uses for which the product was not originally intended.[11] This can stem from legal concerns surrounding the promotion of product uses that haven't been fully tested by the company. However, blogs and social network sites have increased the online chatter about alternative product uses. This was the case with Proctor & Gamble's Bounce dryer fabric sheets. At first P&G was hesitant, but eventually decided to capitalize on the buzz and draw on its consumers' unique usage stories to help foster additional product sales. As noted by one executive, P&G decided to take a risk and try to "capture the consumers' passion for the product and use it as a lever." The company used an integrated campaign that started with an online contest in which consumers posted their stories, with the best one to be featured in a print ad. The ad campaign, called "Bounce beyond the dryer," involves TV, radio, and print ads featuring actual consumer ideas for alternative uses for Bounce dryer sheets:

In one spot, a mother sticks the dryer sheet under her child's car seat to counter the smell of spilled milk and dirty diapers.

The campaign is ongoing, with the online component, located at www.bounceeverywhere.com, still providing consumers with the opportunity to post their own stories, view other people's stores, and rate the "cleverness" of the idea. So far, P&G has received over 26,000 stories, including putting Bounce sheets in camping tents, workout bags, and trash cans. P&G lawyers "scrubbed" the site of ideas that could be harmful to consumers or the environment.

Given the outpouring of stories by consumers, P&G may be wondering why it didn't consider this approach earlier. Indeed, executives predicted that if 25 percent of existing customers used one more sheet per month for nondryer use, this could lead to substantial growth. This growth appears to have been realized as Bounce sales increased $5 million in the two-quarter period following its launch.

### Critical Thinking Questions

1. How does the approach of P&G with Bounce differ from the survey approach utilized by Arm & Hammer? Can both be effective? Explain.

2. How has the Internet changed the nature of consumer input and corporate access to this input?

3. Why are companies so worried about promoting off-label uses for their products?

Consumer Insight 18–1 shows how a company used an integrated campaign, including an Internet contest, to collect and advertise so-called "off-label" uses for its product using consumer stories.

Marketers can frequently take advantage of the fact that the use of one product may require or suggest the use of other products (see Illustration 18–2). Consider the following product sets: houseplants and fertilizer, bikes and helmets, cameras and carrying cases, sport coats and ties, and dresses and shoes. In each case, the use of the first product is made easier, more enjoyable, or safer by the use of the related product. Retailers can promote such items jointly, display them together, or train their sales personnel to make relevant complementary sales.

Stringent product liability laws and aggressive civil suits also are forcing marketing managers to examine how consumers use their products. These laws have made firms responsible for harm caused by products *not only when the product is used as specified by the manufacturer but in any reasonably foreseeable use of the product.* Thus, the manufacturer

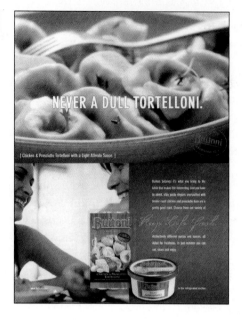

[ Chicken & Prosciutto Tortelloni with a Light Alfredo Sauce. ]

NEVER A DULL TORTELLONI.

must design products with both the primary purpose *and* other potential uses in mind. This requires substantial research into how consumers actually use products.

When marketers discover confusion about the proper way to use a product, it is often to their advantage to teach consumers how to use it and engage in marketing communications that increase the chances of proper use. After all, how many consumers blame themselves when a product failure occurs as a result of their own failure to follow usage instructions?[12] At other times, a firm can gain a competitive advantage by redesigning the product so that it is easier to use properly.

## Product Nonuse

As Figure 18–1 indicates, not all purchases are followed by product use. **Product nonuse** occurs when a consumer actively acquires a product that is not used or used only sparingly relative to its potential use.[13]

For many products and most services, the decisions to purchase and to consume are made simultaneously. A person who orders a meal in a restaurant is also deciding to eat the meal at that time. However, a decision to purchase food at a supermarket requires a second decision to prepare and consume the food. The second decision occurs at a different point in time and in a different environment from the first. Thus, nonuse can occur because the situation or the purchaser changes between the purchase and the potential usage occasion. For example, a point-of-purchase display featuring a new food item shown as part of an appealing entrée might cause a consumer to imagine an appropriate usage situation and to purchase the product. However, without the stimulus of the display, the consumer may not remember the intended use or may just never get around to it. Nonuse situations such as the following are common:[14]

Wok. "I wanted to try and cook stirfry, but I didn't take time out to use it."

Skirt. "My ingenious idea was that I'd lose a few pounds and fit into the size 4 rather than gain a few and fit into the size 6. Obviously, I never lost the weight, so the skirt was snug."

Gym membership. "Couldn't get in the groove to lift."

In such cases, the consumer has wasted money and the marketer is unlikely to get repeat sales or positive referrals. Many such purchases are difficult for the marketer to correct after the purchase. In other cases, consumers would have used the product if reminded or motivated at the proper time. In the last example above, good records would indicate that this member was not using the gym. A personal letter, e-mail, or telephone invitation to come in might be enough to get this person started.

Some products are known to be kept on hand by consumers; that is, they stock up on certain items. In this case, a major goal of advertising should be to encourage people to consume the product at the next appropriate occasion and perhaps even suggest situations that would be appropriate. Since consumers have the product available, the task is not to encourage purchase but to motivate near-term consumption, as in Illustration 18–3.

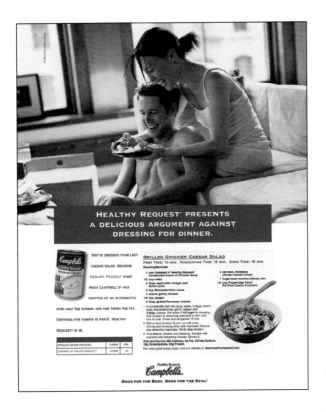

The division between the initial purchase decision and the decision to consume is particularly strong with catalog and online purchases. In effect, two decisions are involved in these purchases—the initial decision to order the product, and a second decision to keep or return the item when it is received. Not only is it likely that several days will have passed between the two decisions, but substantially different information is available at the "keep or return" decision point. In particular, consumers can physically touch, try on, or otherwise experience the item.

Obviously, online and catalog retailers want to maximize the percentage of items kept rather than returned. Intuitively, one might think that a strict return policy would accomplish this. However, such a policy might also reduce the number of initial orders. In fact, a liberal return policy appears to maximize initial orders and may also minimize returns. Such a policy reduces perceived risk and signals higher quality (surrogate indicator), which increases initial orders. Consumers also tend to perceive items ordered under liberal return policies as having higher quality after receiving them, which reduces returns.[15] In addition to return policies, online tools that can better represent products so that a maximal fit to consumer needs is attained can help. The My Virtual Model technology discussed in Chapter 17 has been shown to reduce the amount of returns by 40 percent, thus increasing consumer satisfaction and decreasing company costs.

# DISPOSITION

Disposition of the product or the product's container may occur before, during, or after product use. Or for products that are completely consumed, such as an ice cream cone, no disposition may be involved.

The United States produces several hundred million tons of household and commercial refuse a year, more than 1,500 pounds per person, not including industrial waste.[16] Many landfills are rapidly being filled. Collection and dumping costs for most urban and suburban areas continue to climb. Environmental concerns involving dioxins, lead, and mercury are growing. Clearly, disposition is a major concern for marketers.

Millions of pounds of product packages are disposed of every day. These containers are thrown away as garbage or litter, used in some capacity by the consumer, or recycled. Creating packages that utilize a minimal amount of resources is important for economic reasons as well as being a matter of social responsibility. Many firms are responding to this issue, as the examples below illustrate:

- Crate & Barrel stopped using white bleached board in its famous black and white boxes and switched instead to more renewable fiber that contains postconsumer recyclable material. They also did away with petroleum-based packing peanuts and foam in favor of eco-friendly recyclable alternatives.
- Casio has redesigned both its consumer and channel-based packaging so as to reduce the total amount of materials used.

For many product categories, a physical product continues to exist even though it may no longer meet a consumer's needs. A product may no longer function physically (instrumental function) in a manner desired by a consumer. Or it may no longer provide the symbolic meaning desired by the consumer. An automobile that no longer runs is an example of instrumental function, while one that runs but is out of style is an example of symbolic function. In either case, once a replacement purchase is made, or even before the purchase, a disposition decision must be made.

Exploding demand and short product life spans for high-tech gadgets such as cell phones, personal computers, and various other personal electronics devices is creating growing concerns over **e-waste.** Both instrumental and symbolic considerations can drive e-waste. Consumer and corporate solutions are necessary and evolving. For example:

- TechForward is a new company that is offering a guaranteed buy-back plan for electronics products.[17]
- Sony has developed a recycling plan whereby it will offset pound-for-pound that amount of materials recycled for new products produced. Sony is partnering with a recycling company and banking on the project's paying for itself as a result of the value of such ingredients as copper typically found in e-waste. Big issues are consumer awareness and convenience.[18]
- Companies such as HP, Office Depot, and PrintPal are engaged in ongoing efforts related to print cartridges. HP provides a self-addressed, postage-paid envelope in which you can return used ink cartridges to its recycling center. Office Depot offers discounts on new cartridges to those who bring in their used cartridges. And PrintPal offers a filler kit which allows consumers to reuse their cartridges.

Figure 18–2 illustrates the various alternatives for disposing of a product or package. Unfortunately, while "throw it away" is only one of many disposition alternatives, it is by far the most widely used by consumers. Environmental groups work hard to change these behaviors, as do some firms and other organizations (see Illustration 18–4). Other firms, however, continue to use unnecessary or hard-to-recycle packaging and product components. Some of these same firms also spend millions of dollars campaigning against stricter laws on recycling and product/package disposition.

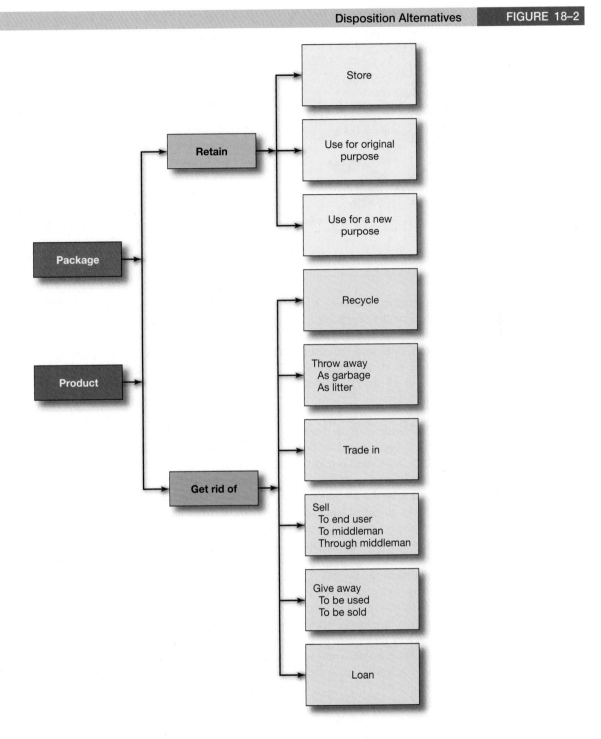

## ILLUSTRATION 18–4

Proper product disposition is important to many consumers and therefore to many firms and industries

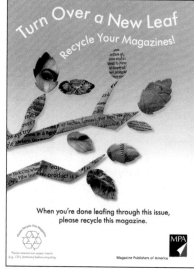

# Product Disposition and Marketing Strategy

Why should a marketing manager be concerned about the disposition of a used product? Perhaps the best reason is the cumulative effect that these decisions have on the quality of the environment and the lives of current and future generations. However, there are also short-term economic reasons for concern. Disposition decisions affect the purchase decisions of both the individual making the disposition and other individuals in the market for that product category.

There are five major ways in which disposition decisions can affect a firm's marketing strategy. First, for most durable goods, consumers are reluctant to purchase a new item until they have "gotten their money's worth" from the old one. These consumers mentally depreciate the value of a durable item over time. If the item is not fully mentally depreciated, they are reluctant to write it off by disposing of it to acquire a new one. Allowing old items to be traded in is one way to overcome this reluctance.[19]

Second, disposition sometimes must occur before acquisition of a replacement because of space or financial limitations. For example, because of a lack of storage space, a family living in an apartment may find it necessary to dispose of an existing bedroom set before acquiring a new one. Or someone may need to sell his current bicycle to raise supplemental funds to pay for a new bicycle. Thus, it is to the manufacturer's and retailer's advantage to assist the consumer in the disposition process.

Third, frequent decisions by consumers to sell, trade, or give away used products may result in a large used-product market that can reduce the market for new products. A **consumer-to-consumer sale** occurs when *one consumer sells a product directly to another with or without the assistance of a commercial intermediary.* Garage sales, swap meets, flea markets, classified ads, and postings on electronic bulletin boards are growing rapidly. And companies such as eBay and Yahoo! Auctions are flourishing as a result of consumer demand to buy and sell used items.

In addition to engaging in consumer-to-consumer sales, consumers may give or sell their used items to resellers. Thrift stores, featuring used clothing, appliances, and furniture, run by both commercial and nonprofit groups, are an important part of the economy.

A fourth reason for concern with product disposition is that the United States is not completely a throwaway society. Many Americans continue to be very concerned with waste and how their purchase decisions affect waste.[20] Such individuals might be willing to purchase, for example, a new vacuum cleaner if they were confident that the old one would be rebuilt and resold. However, they might be reluctant to throw their old vacuums away or to go to the effort of reselling the machines themselves. Thus, manufacturers and retailers could take steps to ensure that products are reused.

The fifth reason is that environmentally sound disposition decisions benefit society as a whole and thus the firms that are part of that society. Firms' owners and employees live and work in the same society and environment as many of their consumers. Their environment and lives are affected by the disposition decisions of consumers. Therefore, it is in their best interest to develop products, packages, and programs that encourage proper disposition decisions.

# PURCHASE EVALUATION AND CUSTOMER SATISFACTION

As we saw in Figure 18–1, a consumer's evaluation of a purchase can be influenced by the purchase process itself, postpurchase dissonance, product use, and product/package disposition. Further, the outlet or the product or both may be involved in the evaluation. Consumers may evaluate each aspect of the purchase, ranging from information availability to price to retail service to product performance. In addition, satisfaction with one component, such as the product itself, may be influenced by the level of satisfaction with other components, such as the salesperson.[21] For many products, this is a dynamic process, with the factors that drive satisfaction evolving over time.[22] However, keep in mind that nominal decisions and many limited decisions are actively evaluated only if some factor, such as an obvious product malfunction, directs attention to the purchase.[23]

## The Evaluation Process

A particular alternative such as a product, brand, or retail outlet is selected because it is thought to be a better overall choice than other alternatives considered in the purchase process. Whether that particular item is selected because of its presumed superior functional performance or because of some other reason, such as a generalized liking of the item or outlet, the consumer has a level of expected performance for it. The expected level of performance can range from quite low (this brand or outlet isn't very good, but it's the only one available and I'm in a hurry) to quite high.[24] As you might suspect, expectations and perceived performance are not independent. Up to a point, consumers tend to perceive performance to be in line with their expectations.[25]

While and after using the product, service, or outlet, the consumer will perceive some level of performance. This perceived performance level could be noticeably above the expected level, noticeably below the expected level, or at the expected level. As Table 18–1 indicates, satisfaction with the purchase is primarily a function of the initial performance expectations and perceived performance relative to those expectations.[26]

Table 18–1 shows that an outlet or brand whose performance confirms a low-performance expectation generally will result in neither satisfaction nor dissatisfaction but rather with what can be termed *nonsatisfaction*. That is, the consumer is not likely to feel disappointment or engage in complaint behavior. However, this purchase will not reduce the likelihood that the consumer will search for a better alternative the next time the problem arises.

A brand whose perceived performance falls below expectations generally produces dissatisfaction. If the discrepancy between performance and expectation is sufficiently large,

| | Expectation Level | |
|---|---|---|
| **Perceived Performance Relative to Expectation** | **Below Minimum Desired Performance** | **Above Minimum Desired Performance** |
| Better | Satisfaction* | Satisfaction/Commitment |
| Same | Nonsatisfaction | Satisfaction |
| Worse | Dissatisfaction | Dissatisfaction |

**TABLE 18–1**

Expectations, Performance, and Satisfaction

*Assuming the perceived performance surpasses the minimum desired level.

or if initial expectations were low, the consumer may restart the entire decision process. Most likely, he or she will place an item performing below expectations in the inept set (see Chapter 15) and no longer consider it. In addition, the consumer may complain or initiate negative word-of-mouth communications.

When perceptions of product performance match expectations that are at or above the minimum desired performance level, satisfaction generally results. Likewise, performance above the minimum desired level that exceeds a lower expectation tends to produce satisfaction. Satisfaction reduces the level of decision making the next time the problem is recognized; that is, a satisfactory purchase is rewarding and encourages one to repeat the same behavior in the future (nominal decision making). Satisfied customers are also likely to engage in positive word-of-mouth communications about the brand.

Product performance that exceeds expected performance will generally result in satisfaction and sometimes in commitment. Commitment, discussed in depth in the next section, means that the consumer is enthusiastic about a particular brand and is somewhat immune to actions by competitors.

Table 18–1 focuses on only the chosen alternative. However, the evaluation of the chosen alternative is somewhat dependent on the quality of the set of alternatives from which it was selected. A clearly superior choice may be held to lower standards than one that was nearly equal to one or more unchosen alternatives.[27] Other situational factors such as mood also affect how individuals evaluate products and services,[28] as do individual characteristics[29] and the general shopping environment.[30]

The need to develop realistic consumer expectations poses a difficult problem for the marketing manager. For a brand or outlet to be selected, the consumer must view it as superior on the relevant combination of attributes. Therefore, the marketing manager naturally wants to emphasize its positive aspects. If such an emphasis creates expectations in the consumer that the item cannot fulfill, a negative evaluation may occur. Negative evaluations can produce brand switching, unfavorable word-of-mouth communications, and complaint behavior. Thus, the marketing manager must balance enthusiasm for the product with a realistic view of the product's attributes.

**Determinants of Satisfaction and Dissatisfaction**   Because performance expectations and actual performance are major factors in the evaluation process, we need to understand the dimensions of product and service performance. A major study of the reasons customers switch service providers found competitor actions to be a relatively minor cause. Most customers did not switch from a satisfactory provider to a better provider. Instead, they switched because of perceived problems with their current service provider. The nature of these problems and the percentage listing each as a reason they changed providers follow (the percentages sum to more than 100 because many customers listed several reasons that caused them to switch):[31]

- *Core service failure* (44 percent). Mistakes (booking an aisle rather than the requested window seat), billing errors, and service catastrophes that harm the customer (the dry cleaners ruined my wedding dress).
- *Service encounter failures* (34 percent). Service employees were uncaring, impolite, unresponsive, or unknowledgeable.
- *Pricing* (30 percent). High prices, price increases, unfair pricing practices, and deceptive pricing.
- *Inconvenience* (21 percent). Inconvenient location, hours of operation, waiting time for service or appointments.

- *Responses to service failures* (17 percent). Reluctant responses, failure to respond, and negative responses (it's your fault).
- *Attraction by competitors* (10 percent). More personable, more reliable, higher quality, and better value.
- *Ethical problems* (7 percent). Dishonest behavior, intimidating behavior, unsafe or unhealthy practices, or conflicts of interest.
- *Involuntary switching* (6 percent). Service provider or customer moves, or a third-party payer such as an insurance company requires a change.

Other studies have found that waiting time has a major impact on evaluations of service. Consumers have particularly negative reactions to delays over which they believe the service provider has control and during which they have little to occupy their time.[32] *What are the marketing strategy implications of these results?*

Other research has found that negative performance on a feature such as waiting time or ease of use has a stronger effect on satisfaction than does positive performance on that same feature.[33] This suggests that both products and services focus on meeting expectations across all relevant features before maximizing performance on a few.

Not surprisingly, the nature and extent of personal contact with customers in service encounters are of critical importance in determining customer satisfaction. Although extended, personalized customer contact is expensive, it is very effective at increasing satisfaction and repeat purchase intentions.[34] However, increasingly services are delivered by self-service technologies such as ATMs and online stores. A recent study found the following dissatisfaction-causing incidents:[35]

| Incident Type | Example |
| --- | --- |
| Technology failure | The ATM broke down. Kept my card. I had to have the card reissued. |
| Service design flaw | I did not realize that some ATM machines limit how much you can get out. The machine did not tell me I went over my limit for the day. It just spit my card back out so I kept trying . . . |
| Process failure | After a month passed from placing my original order, I e-mailed the customer service center at Disney with my order confirmation number. They had lost my order. |
| Technology design flaw | I was trying to order books from a book club online. The system was confusing, and I ordered two copies of the same title without knowing it. |
| Customer failure | I was attempting to get money from an ATM and couldn't remember my number. I was leaving for Japan in an hour and it took my card. |

Many firms now guarantee their services. These guarantees can range from inclusive and general—"Satisfaction guaranteed"—to specific in terms of coverage and pay out—"Delivery in 30 minutes or it's free." Such service guarantees can increase expected performance levels and patronage—but can also increase costs.[36]

For many products, there are two dimensions to performance: instrumental, and expressive or symbolic. **Instrumental performance** relates *to the physical functioning of the product.* **Symbolic performance** relates to *aesthetic or image-enhancement performance.* For example, the durability of a sport coat is an aspect of instrumental performance, whereas styling represents symbolic performance. Complete satisfaction requires adequate performance on both dimensions. However, for at least some product categories such as clothing "Dissatisfaction is caused by a failure of instrumental performance, while complete satisfaction also requires the symbolic functions to perform at or above the expected levels."[37]

In addition to symbolic and instrumental performance, products also provide affective performance. **Affective performance** is *the emotional response that owning or using the product or outlet provides.*[38] It may arise from the instrumental or symbolic performance or from the product itself; for example, a suit that produces admiring glances or compliments may produce a positive affective response. Or the affective performance may be the primary product benefit, such as for an emotional movie or novel.

We continue to better understand the factors that lead to satisfaction with online retailers. One study found that convenience, site design, and financial security are the dominant factors. These are illustrated by the following statements from focus groups:[39]

It is easy to browse for books online. There is only a select group of authors that I read and I want to read everything they write. . . . I can give them the name of the author and a list will pop up (convenience, satisfaction).

It seems to take forever to navigate down far enough into the site to find what I'm looking for. And frankly, I've gotten really tired of the advertising (site design, dissatisfaction).

I don't like giving my credit card to someone online. They keep it on file. I don't like the thought of someone having my card number on file (financial security, dissatisfaction).

Another study found that Web site design (including adequate product information and selection), reliability of order fulfillment, privacy and financial security, and customer service can play a role. In addition, some factors were more important for some consumers than others. For example, the privacy/security issue was more important for frequent buyers and customer service was more important for buyers than browsers.[40] A study of German consumers finds similar drivers of satisfaction with online retailers.[41] Finally, research suggests that in multi-channel contexts involving the Internet, the issue of integration is critical in that content, processes, image and so on should be consistent to the extent possible and appropriate across different channels within a company or brand.[42]

# DISSATISFACTION RESPONSES

Figure 18–3 illustrates the major options available to a dissatisfied consumer.[43] The first decision is whether or not to take any external action. By taking no action, the consumer decides to live with the unsatisfactory situation. This decision is a function of the importance of the purchase to the consumer, the ease of taking action,[44] the consumer's existing level of overall satisfaction with the brand or outlet,[45] and the characteristics of the consumer involved.[46] It is important to note that even when no external action is taken, the consumer is likely to have a less favorable attitude toward the store or brand.

Consumers who take action in response to dissatisfaction generally pursue one or more of five alternatives. As Figure 18–3 indicates, the most favorable of these alternatives from a company's standpoint is for consumers to complain to them. This at least gives the company a chance to resolve the problem. Many times, however, consumers do not complain to the company, but instead take actions such as switching brands or engaging in negative word of mouth (WOM).

Consumers are satisfied with the vast majority of their purchases. Still, because of the large number of purchases they make each year, most individuals experience dissatisfaction

**Dissatisfaction Responses**    **FIGURE 18–3**

with some of their purchases. For example, one study asked 540 consumers if they could recall a case in which one or more of the grocery products they normally purchase were defective. They recalled 1,307 separate unsatisfactory purchases.

These purchases produced the following actions (the study did not measure negative word-of-mouth actions such as warning friends):

- 25 percent of these unsatisfactory purchases resulted in brand switching.
- 19 percent caused the shopper to stop buying the products.
- 13 percent led to an in-store inspection of future purchases.
- 3 percent produced complaints to the manufacturer.
- 5 percent produced complaints to the retailer.
- 35 percent resulted in the item's being returned.

In a similar study of durable goods, 54 percent of the dissatisfied customers said they would not purchase the brand again (brand switching), and 45 percent warned their friends (negative WOM) about the product.[47]

As we discussed in Chapter 7, WOM is a critical factor in consumer behavior. Consumers trust WOM more than many other sources and, therefore, tend to rely on it heavily when making decisions. Unfortunately for companies, when it comes to WOM, there appears to be an asymmetry—that is, dissatisfaction yields more WOM than does satisfaction. One estimate puts the ratio at 2 to 1, with consumers telling twice as many people about a negative product or service experience than a positive one.[48]

One of the reasons for the asymmetry in WOM is the motivational force behind the emotions surrounding dissatisfaction, which can range from disappointment to frustration to rage. The results clearly point to the fact that the stronger the negative emotion, the more consumers are motivated to hurt the company in some way. That is, rather than trying to explain their problem to the company in hopes of fixing the situation, angry customers want to "get even." Learning how to avoid situations which would provoke such negative emotions is critical, as is training customer service employees to identify and deal with these strong emotions when they occur.[49]

Obviously, marketers should strive to minimize dissatisfaction *and* to effectively resolve dissatisfaction when it occurs. However, marketers also need to strive to maximize the chances that consumers will complain to their firm rather than engage in negative WOM and brand switching. We discuss these issues next.

## Marketing Strategy and Dissatisfied Consumers

I feel mad. I put it in my Christmas letter to 62 people across the country. I mean, I told everybody don't buy one of these things because the transmission is bad.[50]

The above example is a marketer's nightmare. And the ease of communicating by e-mail and on Web sites and blogs makes such scenarios even more frightening:

I'm the founder of this Web site and like everyone else, I got scammed by First USA. Of course, at the time I thought it was just me. After battling First USA and getting nowhere, I decided to throw up a quick Web page. I was surprised when I got bombarded with e-mails from people saying the same thing happened to them. Since then, this site has grown tremendously.[51]

Firms need to satisfy consumer expectations by (1) creating reasonable expectations through promotional efforts and (2) maintaining consistent quality so the reasonable expectations are fulfilled. Since dissatisfied consumers tend to engage in negative WOM and since WOM is such a powerful decision influence, one dissatisfied consumer can cause a ripple or multiplier effect in terms of discouraging future sales. Movies are a great example of how powerful negative *buzz* about a new movie can quickly kill its box office take, even in the face of strong promotional support from the studio.

When a consumer is dissatisfied, the most favorable consequence is for the person to communicate this dissatisfaction to the firm but to no one else. This alerts the firm to problems, enables it to make amends where necessary, and minimizes negative word-of-mouth communications. Many firms have discovered that customers whose complaints are resolved to their satisfaction are sometimes even more satisfied than are those who did not experience a problem in the first place.[52] This appears to be more likely when the problem is minor or moderate rather than severe,[53] and when problems are isolated rather than ongoing.[54]

Unfortunately, many individuals do not communicate their dissatisfaction to the firm involved. Some people find it difficult to complain because of a lack of resources (e.g., income and education), while others have personality traits (e.g., introversion) that make the complaint process emotionally painful.[55] Consider the following:

I find it hard to say anything when I'm unhappy [with a purchase]. It takes talking to myself all the way to the store. I say, "how do I say that?" I practice it. If I can get my husband to do it, I will. I'm very uncomfortable, even afterwards. I don't want people to think that I'm such a crab or not be liked or not think, "That's not such a nice lady."[56]

As we saw in Chapter 2, cultural factors also play a role. However, demographics, personality, and culture do not completely explain consumers' generally negative attitude toward complaining. Companies often make it difficult to complain or are unresponsive to complaints. As a consequence, consumers "learn" that complaining to the company is not worth the effort. Thus, it is critical that companies not only create processes and an atmosphere that encourages consumers to direct their complaints to them, but also train and empower their employees to respond to and resolve consumer problems in a timely and effective manner.[57]

Toll-free call centers and hotlines are one approach used by many companies. These can be effective in handling complaints and also serve as an opportunity to learn how to improve. Procter & Gamble provides the following examples of benefits received from its hotline:

- Duncan Hines brownie mix: "We learned that people in high-altitude areas need special instructions for baking, and these soon were added to the packages. We also found that one of the recipes on a box label was confusing, so we changed it."
- Toothpaste: "We spotted a pattern of people complaining that they couldn't get the last bit of toothpaste out of the tube without it breaking, so the tubes were strengthened."
- P&G also receives calls with positive testimonials. These are forwarded to the appropriate advertising agency, where they are analyzed for insights into why people like the product. Several P&G campaigns have been based on these unsolicited consumer comments.[58]

Obviously consumers increasingly expect to be able to express complaints via e-mail. Research shows firms that receive and respond quickly to such complaints can greatly increase customer satisfaction.[59]

Although hotlines and other procedures increase the ease with which consumers can express a complaint, they are not sufficient. Most consumers who complain want a tangible result. Further, the results desired vary by customer type and the nature of the problem, requiring customized response capabilities.[60] Failure to deal effectively with this expectation can produce increased dissatisfaction. Therefore, firms need to resolve the cause of consumer complaints, not just give the consumers the opportunity to complain.[61]

In fact, for many firms, retaining customers by encouraging and responding effectively to complaints is more economical than attracting new customers through advertising or other promotional activities. It has been estimated that it costs only one-fifth as much to retain an old customer as to obtain a new one.[62] Training *front-line employees* who deal directly with customers to use appropriate communication styles and empowering them to resolve problems as they arise is one way firms can increase customer satisfaction and retention.[63]

Unfortunately, many corporations are not organized to effectively resolve and learn from consumer complaints. This area represents a major opportunity for many businesses.[64] Consider the following:[65]

When Sprint's new CEO Gary Forsee joined the company last March, he wanted to know why hundreds of millions of dollars were being spent on bringing in new wireless customers, while existing unsatisfied customers went out the back door. Mr. Forsee, a 30-year veteran of telephone companies including AT&T and BellSouth, wanted Sprint to put customer service in its place, right next to customer acquisition. So, Sprint changed—a lot. In fact, Sprint business units were completely reorganized around a new focus: the customer experience. No longer are customers acquired and then "thrown over the wall" to customer service. Marketing, customer service and sales are no longer three different silos, but reside in a combined unit working together.

Sprint's companywide approach has already yielded dividends, with customer turnover down since the reorganization. Illustration 18–5 shows another company that is aligning its processes to proactively deal with customer issues and the customer experience in an online context.

This online company is aligning its internal processes toward proactively responding to consumer issues and needs.

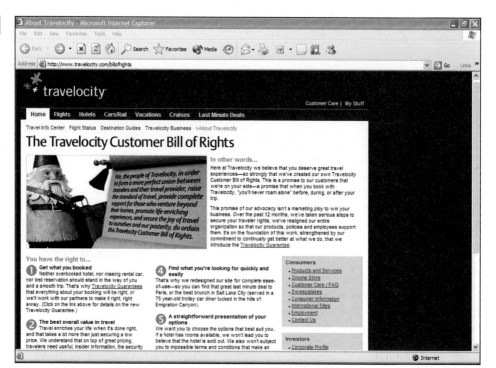

# CUSTOMER SATISFACTION, REPEAT PURCHASES, AND CUSTOMER COMMITMENT

Satisfaction is an important driver of customer loyalty and many organizations are investing in programs to enhance customer satisfaction, as shown by the following excerpt about New York–Presbyterian Hospital (NYP):

> NYP has looked very carefully at best practices for improving patient satisfaction across the country. To improve the patient experience, NYP implemented the Commitment to Care philosophy. Commitment to Care is a set of service expectations for all staff to follow in their work and interaction with patients, families and colleagues. The expectations are based on feedback that comes directly from patients and address their key priorities and needs. It was created to give employees clarity about what is expected of them and a clear set of standards by which to evaluate and recognize staff for issues related to service. Metrics [on key service dimensions] are an important tool for both the hospital and for our patients.[66]

Given increasingly sophisticated and value-conscious consumers and multiple brands that perform at satisfactory levels, producing satisfied customers is necessary but not sufficient for many marketers. Instead, the objective is to produce committed or brand-loyal customers.

Figure 18–4 illustrates the composition of the buyers of a particular brand at any point in time. Of the total buyers, some percentage will be satisfied with the purchase. As we have seen, marketers are spending considerable effort to make this percentage as high as possible. The reason is that, while many satisfied customers will switch brands,[67] satisfied customers are much more likely to become or remain repeat purchasers than are dissatisfied customers.[68] **Repeat purchasers** continue to buy the same brand though they do not have an emotional attachment to it.

**Creating Committed Customers Is Increasingly the Focus of Marketing Strategy**    FIGURE 18–4

As we saw earlier, some dissatisfied customers may also become or remain repeat purchasers. These individuals perceive the **switching costs**—*the costs of finding, evaluating, and adopting another solution*—to be too high.[69] However, they may engage in negative word of mouth and are vulnerable to competitors' actions.

Repeat purchasers are desirable, but *mere* repeat purchasers are vulnerable to competitor actions. That is, they are buying the brand out of habit or because it is readily available where they shop, or because it has the lowest price, or for similar superficial reasons. These customers have no commitment to the brand. They are not brand loyal. **Brand loyalty** is defined as

> a biased (i.e., nonrandom) behavioral response (i.e., purchase/recommend) expressed over time by a decision-making unit with respect to one or more alternative brands out of a set of such brands that is a function of psychological (decision-making, evaluative) processes.[70]

Service and store loyalty are generally defined in the same or a similar manner.[71] Thus, a consumer loyal to a brand (store or service), or a **committed customer,** has an emotional attachment to the brand or firm. The customer likes the brand in a manner somewhat similar to friendship. Consumers use expressions such as "I trust this brand," "I like this outlet," and "I believe in this firm" to describe their commitment, as in the following customer quote:

> I tried it myself one time and eventually adopted a taste for it. Now I drink it all the time. I have it every morning after I come in from my run. I drink it after I clean the house. I always have a glass of it in my hand. That's me. I am very loyal to Gatorade. I would say that I am very loyal to that. I know they have other brands of that now, I see coupons all the time, but I have never even picked up a bottle of them. Never even tried them. Because I like Gatorade a lot. I really do.[72]

In a higher involvement context, NYP Hospital, discussed earlier, goes well beyond having, measuring, and reporting on key metrics to high-touch efforts that deliver personalized and humane service to its patients and treat patients and family with compassion and respect. Such efforts go well beyond mere satisfaction toward building a committed, loyal customer base.

Brand loyalty can arise through identification, where a consumer believes the brand reflects and reinforces some aspect of his or her self-concept. This type of commitment is most common for symbolic products such as beer and automobiles. It is also likely in service situations that involve extended interpersonal encounters.[73] Research in services has also found that loyalty can arise from *consumer comfort*. Consumer comfort is "a psychological state wherein a customer's anxiety concerning a service has been eased, and he or she enjoys peace of mind and is calm and worry free concerning service encounters with [a specific] provider."[74] Service employees likely play a strong role in developing comfort given the high-contact nature of many services. Brand loyalty may also arise through performance so far above expected that it delights the customer.[75] Such superior performance can be related to the product, the firm itself, or, as mentioned earlier, the manner in which the firm responds to a complaint or a customer problem. Delight has been demonstrated for high-involvement services as well as for more mundane customer Web site visits.[76]

Given the above, it is obvious that it is more difficult to develop brand-loyal consumers for some product categories than for others. Indeed, for low-involvement product categories with few opportunities for truly distinct performance or customer service, most firms should focus on creating satisfied repeat purchasers rather than loyal or committed customers.[77]

Committed customers are unlikely to consider additional information when making a purchase. They are also resistant to competitors' marketing efforts—for example, coupons. Even when loyal customers do buy a different brand to take advantage of a promotional deal, they generally return to their original brand for their next purchase.[78] Committed customers are more receptive to line extensions and other new products offered by the same firm. They are also more likely to forgive an occasional product or service failure.[79]

Finally, committed customers are likely to be a source of positive word-of-mouth communications. This is extremely valuable to a firm. Positive word-of-mouth communications from a committed customer increase the probability of the recipient's both becoming a customer and sharing the positive comments with a third person[80]—"I haven't eaten at Aron's yet, but Kim raves about the food and service."

It is for these reasons that many marketers have attempted to create committed customers as well as satisfied customers. Committed customers are much more profitable to the firm than mere repeat purchasers, who in turn are more profitable than occasional buyers.[81]

## Repeat Purchasers, Committed Customers, and Profits

**Churn** is a term used to refer to *turnover in a firm's customer base*. If a firm has a base of 100 customers and 20 leave each year and 20 new ones become customers, it has a churn rate of 20 percent. Reducing churn is a major objective of many firms today. Why? It typically costs more to obtain a new customer than to retain an existing one, and new customers generally are not as profitable as longer-term customers. Consider the profits generated by one credit card firm's customers over time:[82]

| Year | Profits |
| --- | --- |
| Acquisition cost | ($51) |
| Year 1 | $30 |
| Year 2 | $42 |
| Year 3 | $44 |
| Year 4 | $49 |
| Year 5 | $55 |

Acquisition costs include such expenses as advertising, establishing the account, mailing the card, and so forth. First-year profits are low because many new customers are acquired as a result of a promotional deal of some type. In addition, their initial usage rate tends to

| Sources of Increased Customer Profitability over Time | FIGURE 18–5 |

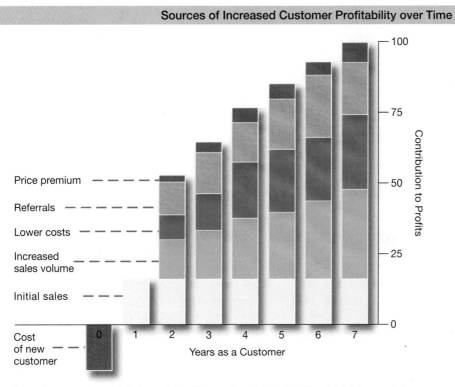

Source: "Sources of Increased Customer Profitability over Time." © 1999 TIME Inc. Reprinted by permission.

be low and they don't use all the features. This is a common pattern for both consumer and industrial products. Auto service profits per customer increased from $25 the first year to $88 in the fifth year, and an industrial laundry found they went from $144 to $258.

Figure 18–5 shows the sources of the growth of profit per customer over time. *Price premium* refers to the fact that repeat and particularly committed customers tend to buy the brand consistently rather than waiting for a sale or continually negotiating price. *Referrals* refers to profits generated by new customers acquired as a result of recommendations from existing customers. *Lower costs* occur because both the firm and the customer learn how to interact more efficiently over time. Finally, customers tend to use a wider array of a firm's products and services over time.[83]

Although committed customers are most valuable to a firm, reducing churn can have a major impact on profit even if the retained customers are primarily repeat purchasers. Reducing the number of customers who leave a firm in a year increases the average life of the firm's customer base.[84] As we saw earlier, the longer a customer is with a firm, the more profits the firm derives from that customer. Thus, a stable customer base tends to be highly profitable per customer. Reducing the number of customers who leave various types of firms each year by 5 percent has been found to increase the average profits per customer as follows:[85]

| Firm Type | Percent Increase in Average Profits per Customer |
|---|---|
| Auto service | 30% |
| Branch banks | 85 |
| Credit card | 75 |
| Credit insurance | 25 |
| Insurance brokerage | 50 |
| Industrial laundry | 45 |

**Not All Customers Are Created Equal**

Sophisticated data systems allow many firms to closely monitor the profitability as well as preferences of individual customers.[86] For example, every one of Continental Airlines' gate, reservation, and service agents can instantly access the history and economic value of every customer. This information includes very personal data such as past disagreements with gate agents. As a company vice president said, "We even know if they put their eyeshades on and go to sleep."

As you would expect, there are wide variations in profitability across customers. For example, at a typical commercial bank, the top 20 percent of customers generate six times more revenue than they cost. In contrast, the bottom 20 percent generate three to four times more costs than they do revenue.

In many industries, firms now utilize this individual profitability information to segment customers into service levels. Highly profitable customers receive excellent service, whereas those who generate low or negative profits receive little or no service.

One electric utility serves its top 350 business clients with six customer service representatives. The next 700 are served by six more, and the remaining 30,000 are served by two. The 300,000 residential customers must deal with an automated 800 number.

One financial institution rates its 2 million customers on a profitability scale from one to five. "Ones" get substantial personal attention; "fives" do not.

Another financial institution codes its credit card customers with colors that appear when their accounts appear on a service rep's screen. Green (profitable) customers are granted waivers and otherwise given white-glove treatment. Red (unprofitable) customers have no bargaining power. Yellow (marginal profit) customers are given a moderate level of accommodation.

**Critical Thinking Questions**

1. What ethical issues, if any, do you see from collecting and using individual data this way?

2. What risks, if any, do you see from this approach to providing service?

The motivation for marketers to retain customers is obvious. Phil Bressler, the co-owner of five Domino's Pizza outlets in Maryland, found that a regular customer was worth more than $5,000 over the 10-year life of the franchise agreement. He makes sure that every employee in every store is constantly aware of that number. Poor service or a bad attitude may cost the outlet several thousands of dollars, not just the $10 or $15 that might be lost on the single transaction![87]

However, as Consumer Insight 18–2 indicates, retaining some customers is more profitable than retaining others.

## Repeat Purchasers, Committed Customers, and Marketing Strategy

An important step in developing a marketing strategy for a particular segment is to specify the objectives being pursued. Several distinct possibilities exist:

1. Attract new users to the product category.
2. Capture competitors' current customers.
3. Encourage current customers to use more.
4. Encourage current customers to become repeat purchasers.
5. Encourage current customers to become committed customers.

**Customer Satisfaction Outcomes**    FIGURE 18–6

Each of the objectives listed above will require different strategies and marketing mixes. The first two objectives require the marketer to convince potential customers that the marketer's brand will provide superior value to not using the product or to using another brand. Advertisements promising superior benefits, coupons, free trials, and similar strategies are common approaches. While some firms are content to consider the sale the last step, smart firms now realize the critical importance of retaining customers after the initial sale. This is true even for infrequently purchased items—rather than repeat sales, the marketer wants positive, or at least neutral, word-of-mouth communications.

The last three objectives, listed earlier, focus on marketing to the firm's current customers. All require customer satisfaction as a necessary precondition. As Figure 18–6 indicates, this requires that the firm deliver the value expected by the customer. Techniques for creating satisfied customers were described earlier. Marketing efforts focused on a firm's current customers are generally termed *relationship marketing.*

**Relationship Marketing**    *An attempt to develop an ongoing, expanding exchange relationship with a firm's customers* is called **relationship marketing.**[88] In many ways, it seeks to mimic the relationships that existed between neighborhood stores and their customers many years ago. In those relationships, the store owner knew the customers not only as customers but also as friends and neighbors. The owner could anticipate their needs and provide help and advice when needed. Relationship marketing attempts to accomplish the same results, but because of the large scale of most operations, the firm must use databases, customized mass communications, and advanced employee training and motivation.[89]

Consider the following example:

Lees Supermarkets, a family-owned and -operated company, started a Shoppers Club that records the purchases of members. Frequent or heavy shoppers are offered special incentives and deals. These offers can be customized on the basis of past purchasing patterns. In addition, last Thanksgiving, 600 regular, high-volume members were rewarded with free turkeys. Such an unexpected reward can produce delight and loyalty among key customers.[90]

Relationship marketing has five key elements:[91]

1.    Developing a core service or product around which to build a customer relationship.
2.    Customizing the relationship to the individual customer.

3. Augmenting the core service or product with extra benefits.
4. Pricing in a manner to encourage loyalty.
5. Marketing to employees so that they will perform well for customers.

This list of elements makes it clear that relationship marketing is centered on understanding consumer needs at the individual consumer level.[92]

A substantial amount of effort is currently being focused on **customer loyalty programs.** In addition to frequent-flier programs offered by most major airlines, programs designed to generate repeat purchases include the following:

- Marriott has Marriott Rewards. Members earn points for staying at Marriott hotels and are classified into Silver, Gold, or Platinum, based on number of stays per year. This classification system and its large customer database help Marriott customize its amenities and promotions based on each customer's individual profile.
- Sports franchises use card-based reward programs where members earn points for attending events and can redeem those points for team memorabilia, food, and drinks. Teams can also use the member data to create personalized communications and offerings, including season-ticket packages to their most attractive members.[93]

However, it is important to distinguish between programs that simply generate repeat purchases and those that generate committed and loyal customers.[94] Committed customers have a reasonably strong emotional attachment to the product or firm. Generating committed customers requires that the firm consistently meet or exceed customer expectations. Further, customers must believe that the firm is treating them fairly and is, to some extent at least, concerned about their well-being. Thus, *generating committed customers requires a customer-focused attitude in the firm.* It also requires that this attitude be translated into actions that meet customers' needs.[95]

Loyalty programs can be effective in generating committed customers if they understand and fulfill key customer needs, as shown in Illustration 18–6.

**ILLUSTRATION 18–6**

Successful customer loyalty programs are based on understanding the needs of key customers and providing benefits of value to them.

Research continues to investigate online loyalty. While differences in type of site and purpose of visit (buying versus browsing) are likely to exist, evidence supports Figure 18–6 in suggesting that perceived value and satisfaction are important determinants of online loyalty just as they are for products, services, and traditional retail outlets.[96] In addition, research has identified factors unique to online settings that drive e-loyalty. For example, one study finds security and privacy to be critical.[97] Other research identifies customization and personalization, interactivity, convenience, and online community as factors that drive *e-loyalty,* WOM, and willingness to pay.[98] Interestingly, the importance of these factors seems to depend on the amount of Internet experience. For example, personalization is more important for those with greater online experience, while community is more important for those with less online experience.[99]

## SUMMARY

Following some purchases, consumers experience doubts or anxiety about the wisdom of the purchase. This is known as *postpurchase dissonance.* It is most likely to occur (1) among individuals with a tendency to experience anxiety, (2) after an irrevocable purchase, (3) when the purchase was important to the consumer, and (4) when it involved a difficult choice between two or more alternatives.

Whether or not the consumer experiences dissonance, most purchases are followed by product use. This use may be by the purchaser or by some other member of the purchasing unit. Monitoring product usage can indicate new uses for existing products, needed product modifications, appropriate advertising themes, and opportunities for new products. Product liability laws have made it increasingly important for marketing managers to be aware of all potential uses of their products.

Product nonuse is also a concern. Both marketers and consumers suffer when consumers buy products that they do not use or use less than they intended. Thus, marketers frequently attempt to influence the decision to use the product as well as the decision to purchase the product.

Disposition of the product or its package may occur before, during, or after product use. Understanding disposition behavior is important to marketing managers because of the ecological concerns of many consumers, the costs and scarcity of raw materials, and the activities of federal and state legislatures and regulatory agencies. *E-waste* is an emerging area of concern related to disposition.

Postpurchase dissonance, product usage, and disposition are potential influences on the purchase evaluation process. Consumers develop certain expectations about the ability of the product to fulfill instrumental and symbolic needs. To the extent that the product meets these needs, satisfaction is likely to result. When expectations are not met, dissatisfaction is the likely result.

Taking no action; switching brands, products, or stores; and engaging in negative WOM (e.g., warning friends) are all common reactions to a negative purchase evaluation. A marketing manager generally should encourage dissatisfied consumers to complain directly to the firm and to no one else. Unfortunately, only a fairly small, unique set of consumers tends to complain. Developing strategies and processes that minimize the costs and hassles of complaining are critical in encouraging dissatisfied consumers to complain to the firm.

After the evaluation process and, where applicable, the complaint process, consumers have some degree of repurchase motivation. There may be a strong motive to avoid the brand, a willingness to repurchase it some of the time, a willingness to repurchase it all of the time, or some level of brand loyalty or customer commitment, which is a willingness to repurchase coupled with a psychological commitment to the brand. As online retailing continues to grow, marketers are examining ways in which e-satisfaction and e-loyalty can be bolstered.

Marketing strategy does not always have the creation of brand loyalty as its objective. Rather, the manager must examine the makeup of the brand's current and potential consumers and select the specific objectives most likely to maximize the overall organizational goals.

Relationship marketing attempts to develop an ongoing, expanding exchange relationship with a firm's customers. It is used to increase brand usage, repeat sales, or customer commitment.

## KEY TERMS

Affective performance  636
Brand loyalty  641
Churn  642
Committed customer  641
Consumer-to-consumer sale  632
Consumption guilt  624

Customer loyalty programs  646
E-waste  630
Instrumental performance  635
Postpurchase dissonance  623
Product nonuse  628
Relationship marketing  645

Repeat purchasers  640
Switching costs  641
Symbolic performance  635
Use innovativeness  626

## INTERNET EXERCISES

1. Monitor several product- or activity-related chat sites, interest groups or blogs for a week. Prepare a report on how a marketer could learn about the following by doing this.
   a. Customer satisfaction levels and customer commitment
   b. Product use
   c. Customer evaluation processes

2. Pick a brand that offers an online newsletter and sign up for it. Evaluate its role in customer satisfaction and relationship marketing.

3. Find a company site that helps the company in terms of relationship marketing. Describe and evaluate this effort.

4. Find an independent complaint Web site (go to Yahoo and search for "complaints about _____") for the following firms. What insights does it provide? How should the targeted company respond?
   a. Wal-Mart
   b. Disney
   c. Saturn

5. Does the use of video excerpts of service failures by consumers on sights such as YouTube enhance their influence? Find an example and justify.

6. Find a product, company, or brand site that helps the consumer use a product properly or effectively. Describe and evaluate this effort.

## DDB LIFE STYLE STUDY™ DATA ANALYSES

1. What characterizes individuals who feel they have acquired too much debt (DDB Tables 1B through 7B)? What are the marketing implications of this? What are the regulatory implications of this?

2. Using DDB Tables 1B through 7B, what characterizes people who become committed enough to favorite brands to resist other brands when they are on sale? What are the marketing implications of this?

## REVIEW QUESTIONS

1. What are the major postpurchase processes engaged in by consumers?

2. How does the type of decision process affect the postpurchase processes?

3. What is *postpurchase dissonance*? What characteristics of a purchase situation are likely to contribute to postpurchase dissonance?

4. What actions do consumers take to avoid postpurchase dissonance before the purchase?

5. In what ways can a consumer reduce postpurchase dissonance?

6. What is *consumption guilt*?

7. What is *use innovativeness*?

8. What is an *off-label use,* and why is it important to companies?

9. Why are surveys not always the most effective way to get at innovative product uses?

10. What is meant by *product nonuse,* and why is it a concern of marketers?

11. What is meant by the disposition of products and product packaging, and why does it interest governmental regulatory agencies and marketers?

12. What is *e-waste,* and why is it a growing concern?

13. What factors influence consumer satisfaction? In what way do they influence consumer satisfaction?

14. What is the difference between *instrumental* and *symbolic performance,* and how does each contribute to consumer satisfaction?

15. What is *affective performance*?

16. What courses of action can a consumer take in response to dissatisfaction? Which are used most often?

17. What determines satisfaction for online retailers?

18. What would marketers like consumers to do when dissatisfied? How can marketers encourage this?

19. What is *churn*? How does it affect profits?

20. What are the sources of increased profits from longer-term customers?

21. What is the relationship between *customer satisfaction, repeat purchases,* and *committed customers*?

22. What is the difference between *repeat purchasers* and *committed customers*?

23. What are *switching costs*?

24. Why are marketers interested in having committed customers?

25. What are five objectives that a marketing strategy for a particular segment might have? How will marketing strategies differ across the five objectives that a firm might have for a particular segment?

26. What is *relationship marketing*? What strategies are involved?

27. What are *loyalty programs*? What do most of them actually do?

28. What factors influence e-loyalty?

## DISCUSSION QUESTIONS

29. How should retailers deal with consumers immediately after purchase to reduce postpurchase dissonance? What specific action would you recommend, and what effect would you intend it to have on the recent purchaser of (gift of) the following?
    *a.* PBS donation
    *b.* A condominium
    *c.* Dance lessons
    *d.* A hybrid automobile
    *e.* Microwave oven
    *f.* Tropical fish

30. What type of database should your university maintain on its students? In general, what ethical concerns surround the use of such databases by institutions and companies?

31. How should manufacturers deal with consumers immediately after purchase to reduce postpurchase dissonance? What specific action would you recommend, and what effect would you intend it to have on the recent purchaser of the following?
    *a.* Printer
    *b.* Expensive watch

    *c.* Cell phone
    *d.* Corrective eye surgery

32. Respond to the questions in Consumer Insight 18–1.

33. Discuss how you could determine how consumers actually use the following. How could this information be used to develop marketing strategy?
    *a.* Microwave
    *b.* Golf cart
    *c.* Online banking services
    *d.* Movies on demand
    *e.* Hair color
    *f.* Hotel reward points

34. How would you go about measuring consumer satisfaction among purchasers of the following? What questions would you ask, what additional information would you collect, and why? How could this information be used for evaluating and planning marketing programs?
    *a.* Cell phone service
    *b.* Target.com
    *c.* Car insurance
    *d.* Six Flags theme parks

e. Health care services

f. Laptop computers

35. What level of product dissatisfaction should a marketer be content with in attempting to serve a particular target market? What characteristics contribute to dissatisfaction, regardless of the marketer's efforts?

36. Describe the last time you were dissatisfied with a purchase. What action did you take? Why?

37. Are you a *mere* repeat purchaser of any brand, service, or outlet? Why are you not a committed customer? What, if anything, would make you a committed customer?

38. Respond to the questions in Consumer Insight 18–2.

39. How could an automobile dealership use the service segmentation strategy described in Consumer Insight 18–2?

40. Are you a committed customer to any brand, service, or outlet? Why?

41. Design a customer loyalty program for the following.

a. Dry cleaning service

b. Grocery store chain

c. Cosmetics line

d. Catering service

## APPLICATION ACTIVITIES

42. Develop a brief questionnaire to determine product nonuse among college students and the reasons for it. With four other classmates, interview 50 students. What do you conclude?

43. Develop a questionnaire designed to measure consumer satisfaction of a clothing purchase of $50 or more. Include in your questionnaire items that measure the product's instrumental, symbolic, and affective dimensions of performance, as well as what the consumer wanted on these dimensions. Then interview several consumers to obtain information on actual performance, expected performance, and satisfaction. Using this information, determine if consumers received what they expected (i.e., evaluation of performance) and relate any difference to consumer expressions of satisfaction. What are the marketing implications of your results?

44. Develop a survey to measure student dissatisfaction with service purchases. For purchases they were dissatisfied with, determine what action they took to resolve this dissatisfaction and what the end result of their efforts was. What are the marketing implications of your findings?

45. Develop a questionnaire to measure repeat purchase behavior and brand loyalty. Measure the repeat purchase behavior and brand loyalty of 10 students with respect to the following. Determine why the brand-loyal students are brand loyal.

a. Batteries

b. Spaghetti sauce

c. Coffee

d. Lightbulbs

e. Clothing stores

f. Online stores

46. With the cooperation of a durables retailer, assist the retailer in sending a postpurchase letter of thanks to every other customer immediately after purchase. Then, approximately two weeks after purchase, contact the same customers (both those who received the letter and those who did not) and measure their purchase satisfaction. Evaluate the results.

47. Interview a grocery store manager, a department store manager, and a restaurant manager. Determine the types of products their customers are most likely to complain about and the nature of those complaints.

48. Measure 10 students' disposition behaviors with respect to the following. Determine why they use the alternatives they do.

a. Car battery

b. Cell phones

c. Mattress

d. Televisions

e. Plastic items

49. Interview 20 students to determine which, if any, customer loyalty programs they belong to, what they like and dislike about them, and the impact they have on their attitudes and behaviors. What opportunities do your results suggest?

# REFERENCES

1. Chapter 18 opener is based on J. McGregor, "Customer Service Champs," *BusinessWeek*, March 5, 2007, pp. 52–64.

2. G. J. Thompson, "Interpreting Consumers," *Journal of Marketing Research,* November 1997, p. 444. Published by the American Marketing Association; reprinted with permission.

3. See J. C. Sweeney, D. Hausknecht, and G. N. Soutar, "Cognitive Dissonance after Purchase," *Psychology & Marketing,* May 2000, pp. 369–85.

4. M. F. Luce, "Choosing to Avoid," *Journal of Consumer Research,* March 1998, pp. 409–33.

5. See M. Tsiros and V. Mittal, "Regret," *Journal of Consumer Research,* March 2000, pp. 401–17; J. J. Hetts et al., "The Influence of Anticipated Counterfactual Regret on Behavior," *Psychology & Marketing,* April 2000, pp. 345–68; and A. D. J. Cooke, T. Meyvis, and A. Schwartz, "Avoiding Future Regret in Purchase-Timing Decisions," *Journal of Consumer Research,* March 2001, pp. 447–59.

6. See Thompson, "Interpreting Consumers."

7. S. J. Gould, "An Interpretative Study of Purposeful, Mood Self-Regulating Consumption," *Psychology & Marketing,* July 1997, pp. 395–426.

8. See, e.g., R. Kivetz and I. Simonson, "Self-Control for the Righteous," *Journal of Consumer Research,* September 2002, pp. 199–217.

9. See S. Ram and H.-S. Jung, "Innovativeness in Product Usage," and N. M. Ridgway and L. L. Price, "Exploration in Product Usage," both in *Psychology & Marketing,* January 1994, pp. 57–69 and 70–84, respectively; and K. Park and C. L. Dyer, "Consumer Use Innovative Behavior," in *Advances in Consumer Research,* vol. 22, eds. F. R. Kardes and M. Sujan (Provo, UT: Association for Consumer Research, 1995), pp. 566–72.

10. G. Berstell and D. Nitterhouse, "Looking 'Outside the Box,'" *Marketing Research,* Summer 1997, pp. 5–11. See also K. Parker, "How Do You Like Your Beef?" *American Demographics,* January 2000, pp. 35–37.

11. Consumer Insight 18–1 is based on A. A. Newman, "Apply Liberally," *Adweek*, July 14, 2008, pp. 20–21; and information garnered from www.bounceeverywhere.com.

12. V. A. Taylor and A. B. Bower, "Improving Product Instruction Compliance," *Psychology & Marketing,* March 2004, pp. 229–45; and D. Bowman, C. M. Heilman, and P. B. Seetharaman, "Determinants of Product-Use Compliance Behavior," *Journal of Marketing Research,* August 2004, pp. 324–38.

13. A. B. Bower and D. E. Sprott, "The Case of the Dusty Stair-Climber," in *Advances in Consumer Research,* vol. 22, eds. Kardes and Sujan, pp. 582–87. See also B. Wansink and R. Deshpande, *Marketing Letters* 5, no. 1 (1994), pp. 91–100.

14. Bower and Sprott, "The Case of the Dusty Stair-Climber," p. 585.

15. S. L. Wood, *Journal of Marketing Research,* May 2001, pp. 157–69.

16. For detailed statistics, visit the U.S. Environmental Protection Agency Web site at www.epa.gov.

17. "Cashing in on Old Gadgets," *CNN.com,* accessed January 17, 2008.

18. K. Hall, "Sony Likes the Yield from Its Junk," *BusinessWeek*, September 17, 2007, p. 40.

19. E. M. Okada, "Trade-ins, Mental Accounting, and Product Replacement Decisions," *Journal of Consumer Research,* March 2001, pp. 433–66.

20. A. Biswas, "The Recycling Cycle," *Journal of Public Policy & Marketing,* Spring 2000, pp. 93–105.

21. See B. G. Goff, J. S. Boles, D. N. Bellenger, and C. Stojack, "The Influence of Salesperson Selling Behaviors on Customer Satisfaction with Products," *Journal of Retailing* 2 (1997), pp. 171–83.

22. V. Mittal, P. Kumar, and M. Tsiros, "Attribute-Level Performance, Satisfaction, and Behavioral Intentions over Time," *Journal of Marketing,* April 1999, pp. 88–101; and R. J. Slotegraff and J. J. Inman, "Longitudinal Shifts in the Drivers of Satisfaction with Product Quality," *Journal of Marketing Research,* August 2004, pp. 269–80.

23. See, e.g., A. S. Mattila, "The Impact of Cognitive Inertia on Post-consumption Evaluation Processes," *Journal of the Academy of Marketing Science* 31, no. 3 (2003), pp. 287–99.

24. See, e.g., K. E. Clow, D. L. Kurtz, J. Ozment, and B. S. Ong, "The Antecedents of Consumer Expectations of Services," *Journal of Services Marketing* 4 (1997), pp. 230–48.

25. See J. Ozment and E. A. Morash, "The Augmented Service Offering for Perceived and Actual Service Quality," *Journal of the Academy of Marketing Science,* Fall 1994, pp. 352–63; and G. B. Voss, A. Parasuraman, and D. Grewal, "The Roles of Price, Performance, and Expectations in Determining Satisfaction in Service Exchanges," *Journal of Marketing,* October 1998, pp. 48–61.

26. See, e.g., C. P. Bebko, "Service Intangibility and Its Impact on Customer Expectations," *Journal of Services Marketing* 14, no. 1 (2000), pp. 9–26; B. Bickart and N. Schwartz, "Service Experiences and Satisfaction Judgments," *Journal of Consumer Psychology* 11, no. 1 (2001), pp. 29–41; D. M. Szymanski and D. H. Henard, "Customer Satisfaction," *Journal of the Academy of Marketing Science,* Winter 2001, pp. 16–35; J. C. Sweeney and G. N. Soutar, "Consumer Perceived Value," *Journal of Retailing* 77 (2001), pp. 203–20; P. K. Kopalle and D. R. Lehmann, "Strategic Management of Expectations," *Journal of Marketing Research,* August 2001, pp. 386–94; J. Wirtz and A. Mattila, "Exploring the Role of Alternative Perceived Performance Measures and Needs-Congruency in the Customer Satisfaction Process," *Journal of Consumer Psychology* 11, no. 3 (2001), pp. 181–92; E. Garbarino and M. S. Johnson, "Effects of Consumer Goals on Attribute Weighting, Overall Satisfaction, and Product Usage," *Psychology & Marketing,* September 2001, pp. 929–49; and M. Heitmann, D. R. Lehmann, and A. Herrmann, "Choice Goal Attainment and Decision Consumption Satisfaction," *Journal of Marketing Research*, May 2007, pp. 234–50.

27. See C. Droge, D. Halstead, and R. D. Mackoy, "The Role of Competitive Alternatives in the Postchoice Satisfaction Formation Process," *Journal of the Academy of Marketing Science,* Winter 1997, pp. 18–30.

28. A. Mattila, "An Examination of Consumers' Use of Heuristic Cues in Making Satisfaction Judgments," *Psychology & Marketing,* August 1998, pp. 477–500.

29. See, e.g., T. A. Mooradian and J. M. Oliver, "I Can't Get No Satisfaction," *Psychology & Marketing,* July 1997, pp. 379–92; and R. A. Preng and T. J. Page, Jr., "The Impact of Confidence in Expectations on Consumer Satisfaction," *Psychology & Marketing,* November 2001, pp. 1187–1204.

30. M. Griffin, B. J. Babin, and D. Modianos, "Shopping Values of Russian Consumers," *Journal of Retailing* 76, no. 31 (2000), pp. 33–52.

31. S. M. Keaveney, "Customer Switching Behavior in Service Industries," *Journal of Marketing,* April 1995, pp. 71–82. See also D. Grace and A. O'Cass, "Attributions of Service Switching," *Journal of Services Marketing* 14, no. 4 (2001), pp. 300–21; and V. Mittal, J. M. Katrichis, and P. Kumar, "Attribute Performance and Customer Satisfaction over Time," *Journal of Services Marketing* 15, no. 5 (2001), pp. 343–56.

32. See, e.g., S. Taylor, "The Effects of Filled Waiting Time and Service Provider Control over the Delay on Evaluations of Service," *Journal of the Academy of Marketing Science,* Winter 1995, pp. 38–48; and M. K. Hui, M. V. Thakor, and R. Gill, "The Effect of Delay Type and Service Stage on Consumers' Reactions to Waiting," *Journal of Consumer Research,* March 1998, pp. 469–79.

33. V. Mittal, W. T. Ross, Jr., and P. M. Baldsare, "The Asymmetric Impact of Negative and Positive Attribute-Level Performance on Overall Satisfaction and Repurchase Levels," *Journal of Marketing,* January 1998, pp. 33–47. See also G. J. Gaeth et al., "Consumers' Attitude Change across Sequences of Successful and Unsuccessful Product Usage," *Marketing Letters,* no. 1 (1997), pp. 41–53.

34. See B. Mittal and W. M. Lassar, "The Role of Personalization in Service Encounters," *Journal of Retailing* 1 (1996), pp. 95–109; R. A. Spreng and R. D. Mackoy, "An Empirical Examination of a Model of Perceived Service Quality and Satisfaction," *Journal of Retailing* 2 (1996), pp. 210–14; N. Sirohi, E. W. McClaughlin, and D. R. Wittink, "A Model of Consumer Perceptions and Store Loyalty Intentions for a Supermarket Retailer," *Journal of Retailing* 2 (1998), pp. 223–45; and W. O. Bearden, M. K. Malhotra, and K. H. Uscategui, "Customer Contact and the Evaluation of Service Experiences," *Psychology & Marketing,* December 1998, pp. 793–809.

35. M. L. Meuter et al., "Self-Service Technologies," *Journal of Marketing,* July 2000, pp. 50–64. See also M. J. Bitner and M. L. Meuter, "Technology Infusion in Service Encounters," and A. Parasuraman and D. Grewal, "The Impact of Technology on the Quality-Value-Loyalty Chain," both in *Journal of the Academy of Marketing Science,* Winter 2000, pp. 138–49 and 168–74, respectively.

36. See G. H. G. McDougall, T. Levesque, and P. VanderPlaat, "Designing the Service Guarantee," *Journal of Services Marketing* 4 (1998), pp. 278–93; and A. M. Ostrom and D. Iacobucci, "The Effect of Guarantees on Consumers' Evaluation of Services," *Journal of Services Marketing* 5 (1998), pp. 362–78.

37. I. E. Swan and L. J. Combs, "Product Performance and Consumer Satisfaction: A New Concept," *Journal of Marketing,* April 1976, pp. 25–33.

38. See H. Mano and R. L. Oliver, "Assessing the Dimensionality and Structure of the Consumption Experience," *Journal of Consumer Research,* December 1993, pp. 451–66; and L. W. Turley and D. L. Bolton, "Measuring the Affective Evaluations of Retail Service Environments," *Journal of Professional Services Marketing* 19, no. 1 (1999), pp. 31–44. See also S. M. Nowlis, N. Mandel, and D. B. McCabe, "The Effect of a Delay between Choice and Consumption on Consumption Enjoyment," *Journal of Consumer Research,* December 2004, pp. 502–10.

39. D. M. Szymanski and R. T. Hise, "e-Satisfaction," *Journal of Retailing* 76, no. 3 (2000), pp. 309–22. See also Q. Chen and W. D. Wells, ".Com Satisfaction and .Com Dissatisfaction," in *Advances in Consumer Research,* vol. 28, eds. M. C. Gilly and J. Meyers-Levy (Provo, UT: Association for Consumer Research, 2001), pp. 34–39.

40. M. Wolfinbarger and M. C. Gilly, "eTailQ," *Journal of Retailing* 79 (2003), pp. 183–98. See also A. Parasuraman, V. A. Zeithaml, and A. Malhotra, "E-S-QUAL," *Journal of Service Research,* February 2005, pp. 213–33.

41. H. Evanschitzky et al., "E-satisfaction," *Journal of Retailing* 80 (2004), pp. 239–47.

42. R. Sousa and C. A. Voss, "Service Quality in Multichannel Services Employing Virtual Channels," *Journal of Service Research,* May 2006, pp. 356–71.

43. See., e.g., J. Singh, "A Typology of Consumer Dissatisfaction Response Styles," *Journal of Retailing,* Spring 1990, pp. 57–97; J. Singh, "Voice, Exit, and Negative Word-of-Mouth Behaviors," *Journal of the Academy of Marketing Science,* Winter 1990, pp. 1–15; K. Gronhaug and O. Kvitastein, "Purchases and Complaints," *Psychology & Marketing,* Spring 1991, pp. 21–35; and S. W. Kelley and M. A. Davis, "Antecedents to Customer Expectations for Service Recovery," *Journal of the Academy of Marketing Science,* Winter 1994, pp. 52–61.

44. M. A. Jones, D. L. Mothersbaugh, and S. E. Beatty, "Switching Barriers and Repurchase Intentions in Services," *Journal of Retailing* 76, no. 2 (2000), pp. 259–74; J. Lee, J. Lee, and L. Feick, "The Impact of Switching Costs on the Customer Satisfaction-Loyalty Link," *Journal of Services Marketing* 15, no. 1 (2001), pp. 35–48; and I. Roos, B. Edvardsson, and A. Gustafsson, "Customer Switching Patterns in Competitive and Noncompetitive Service Industries," *Journal of Service Research,* February 2004, pp. 256–71.

45. M. A. Jones and J. Suh, "Transaction-Specific Satisfaction and Overall Satisfaction," *Journal of Services Marketing* 14, no. 2 (2000), pp. 147–59.

46. See, e.g., K. P. N. Morel, T. B. C. Poiesz, and H. A. M. Wilkie, "Motivation, Capacity and Opportunity to Complain," in *Advances in Consumer Research,* vol. 24, eds. M. Bruck and D. J. MacInnis (Provo, UT: Association for Consumer Research, 1997), pp. 464–69.

47. See also S. P. Brown and R. F. Beltramini, "Consumer Complaining and Word-of-Mouth Activities," in *Advances in Consumer Research,* vol. 16, ed. T. K. Srull (Provo, UT: Association for Consumer Research, 1989), pp. 9–11; and J. E. Swan and R. L. Oliver, "Postpurchase Communications by Consumers," *Journal of Retailing,* Winter 1989, pp. 516–33.

48. J. Goodman and S. Newman, "Understanding Customer Behavior and Complaints," *Quality Progress,* January 2003, pp. 51–55. For additional research and statistics, visit www.tarp.com.

49. See, e.g., A. K. Smith and R. N. Bolton, "The Effect of Consumers' Emotional Responses to Service Failures on Their Recovery Effort Evaluations and Satisfaction Judgments," *Journal of the Academy of Marketing Science,* Winter 2002, pp. 5–23; N. N. Bechwati and M. Morrin, "Outraged Consumers," *Journal of Consumer Psychology* 13, no. 4 (2003), pp. 440–53; and R. Bougie, R. Pieters, and M. Zeelenberg, "Angry Customers Don't Come Back, They Get Back," *Journal of the Academy of Marketing Science,* Fall 2003, pp. 377–93.

50. Thompson, "Interpreting Consumers."

51. L. J. Harrison-Walker, "E-Complaining," *Journal of Services Marketing* 15, no. 5 (2001), pp. 397–412.

52. See R. A. Spreng, G. D. Harrell, and R. D. Mackoy, "Service Recovery," *Journal of Services Marketing* 9, no. 1 (1995), pp. 15–23; and L. Dube and M. F. Maute, "Defensive Strategies for Managing Satisfaction and Loyalty in the Service Industry," *Psychology & Marketing,* December 1998, pp. 775–91. For an alternative view, see T. W. Andreassen, "From Disgust to Delight," *Journal of Service Research,* August 2001, pp. 39–49.

53. S. Weun, S. E. Beatty, and M. A. Jones, "The Impact of Service Failure Severity on Service Recovery Evaluations and Post-Recovery Relationships," *Journal of Services Marketing* 18, no. 2 (2004), pp. 133–46.

54. J. G. Maxham II and R. G. Netemeyer, "A Longitudinal Study of Complaining Customers' Evaluations of Multiple Service Failures and Recovery Efforts," *Journal of Marketing,* October 2002, pp. 57–71.

55. A literature review and model is in N. Stephens and K. P. Gwinner, "Why Don't Some People Complain?" *Journal of the Academy of Marketing Science,* Summer 1998, pp. 172–89. See also A. L. Dolinsky et al., "The Role of Psychographic Characteristics as Determinants of Complaint Behavior," *Journal of Hospital Marketing* 2 (1998), pp. 27–51; E. G. Harris and J. C. Mowen, "The Influence of Cardinal-, Central-, and Surface-Level Personality Traits on Consumers' Bargaining and Complaining Behavior," *Psychology & Marketing,* November 2001, pp. 1115–85; J. C. Chebat, M. Davidow, and I. Codjovi, "Silent Voices," *Journal of Service Research,* May 2005, pp. 328–342; and K. Bodey and D. Grace, "Contrasting 'Complainers' with 'Non-complainers' on Attitude Toward Complaining, Propensity to Complain, and Key Personality Characteristics," *Psychology & Marketing,* July 2007, pp. 579–594.

56. Ibid.

57. See, e.g., C. Kim et al., "The Effect of Attitude and Perception on Consumer Complaint Intentions," *Journal of Consumer Marketing* 20, no. 4 (2003), pp. 352–71.

58. J. A. Prestbo, "At Procter & Gamble, Success Is Largely Due to Heeding Consumer," *The Wall Street Journal,* April 29, 1980, p. 23.

59. J. Strauss and D. J. Hill, "Consumer Complaints by E-Mail," *Journal of Interactive Marketing,* Winter 2001, pp. 63–73. See also A. S. Mattila and J. Wirtz, "Consumer Complaining to Firms," *Journal of Services Marketing* 18, no. 2 (2004), pp. 147–55.

60. See A. K. Smith, R. N. Bolton, and J. Wagner, "A Model of Customer Satisfaction with Service Encounters Involving Failure and Recovery," *Journal of Marketing Research,* August 1999, pp. 356–72; A. Palmer, R. Beggs, and C. Keown-McMullan, "Equity and Repurchase Intention Following Service Failure," *Journal of Services Marketing* 14, no. 6 (2000), pp. 513–28; A. S. Mattila, "The Effectiveness of Service Recovery in a Multi-Industry Setting," *Journal of Services Marketing* 15, no. 7 (2001), pp. 583–96; J. G. Maxham III and R. G. Netemeyer, "Modeling Customer Perceptions of Complaint Handling over Time," *Journal of Retailing* 78 (2002), pp. 239–52; M. Davidow, "Organizational Responses to Customer Complaints," *Journal of Service Research,* February 2003, pp. 225–50; and C. Homburg and A. Furst, "How Organizational Complaint Handling Drives Customer Loyalty," *Journal of Marketing,* July 2005, pp. 95–114.

61. See C. Goodwin and I. Ross, "Consumer Evaluations of Response to Complaints," *Journal of Consumer Marketing,* Spring 1990, pp. 39–47; J. G. Blodgett, D. J. Hill, and S. S. Tax, "The Effects of Distributive, Procedural, and Interactional Justice on Postcomplaint Behavior," *Journal of Retailing* 2 (1997), pp. 185–210; and C. M. Voorhees, M. K. Brady, and D. M. Horowitz, "A Voice from the Silent Masses," *Journal of the Academy of Marketing Science* 34, no. 4, (2006), pp. 514–27.

62. P. Sellers, "What Customers Really Want," *Fortune,* June 4, 1990, pp. 58–62.

63. B. A. Sparks, G. L. Bradley, and V. J. Callan, "The Impact of Staff Empowerment and Communication Style on Customer Evaluations," *Psychology & Marketing,* August 1997, pp. 475–93.

64. See F. F. Reichheld, "Learning from Customer Defections," *Harvard Business Review,* March 1996, pp. 56–69. See also H. Estelami, "The Profit Impact of Consumer Complaint Solicitation across Market Conditions," *Journal of Professional Services Marketing* 20, no. 1 (1999), pp. 165–95; and N. A. Morgan, E. W. Anderson, and V. Mittal, "Understanding Firms' Customer Satisfaction Information Usage," *Journal of Marketing,* July 2005, pp. 131–51.

65. B. S. Bulik, "Brands Spotlight Customer Experience," *Advertising Age,* April 19, 2004, pp. 1, 14.

66. R. Liebowitz, "Putting Patients First," *Healthcare Executive,* July–August 2008, pp. 42–44.

67. T. O. Jones and W. E. Sasser, Jr., "Why Satisfied Customers Defect," *Harvard Business Review,* November 1995, pp. 88–95; P. P. Leszczyc and H. J. P. Timmermans, "Store-Switching Behavior," *Marketing Letters,* no. 2 (1997), pp. 193–204; B. Mittal and W. M. Lassar, "Why Do Customer Switch?" *Journal of Services Marketing,* no. 3 (1998), pp. 177–94; and C. Homburg and A. Giering, "Personal Characteristics as Moderators of the Relationship between Customer Satisfaction and Loyalty," *Psychology & Marketing,* January 2001, pp. 43–66.

68. See V. Mittal and W. Kamakura, "Satisfaction, Repurchase Intent, and Repurchase Behavior," *Journal of Marketing Research,* February 2001, pp. 131–42.

69. For a discussion of switching costs and repurchase intentions, see Jones, Mothersbaugh, and Beatty, "Switching Barriers and Repurchase Intentions in Services"; P. G. Patterson and T. Smith, "A Cross-Cultural Study of Switching Barriers and Propensity to Stay with Service Providers," *Journal of Retailing* 79 (2003),

pp. 107–20; T. A. Burnham, J. K. Frels, and V. Mahajan, "Consumer Switching Costs," *Journal of the Academy of Marketing Science,* Spring 2003, pp. 109–26; and M. A. Jones et al., "The Positive and Negative Effects of Switching Costs on Relational Outcomes," *Journal of Service Research*, May 2007, pp. 335–55.

70. J. Jacoby and D. B. Kyner, "Brand Loyalty versus Repeat Purchasing Behavior," *Journal of Marketing Research,* February 1973, pp. 1–9. See also S. Rundle-Thiele and M. M. Mackay, "Assessing the Performance of Brand Loyalty Measures," *Journal of Services Marketing* 15, no. 7 (2001), pp. 529–46; A. Chaudhuri and M. B. Holbrook, "The Chain of Effects from Brand Trust and Brand Affect to Brand Performance," *Journal of Marketing,* April 2001, pp. 81–93; C. F. Curasi and K. N. Kennedy, "From Prisoners to Apostles," *Journal of Services Marketing* 16, no. 4 (2002), pp. 322–41; and V. Liljander and I. Roos, "Customer-Relationship Levels," *Journal of Services Marketing* 16, no. 7 (2002), pp. 593–614.

71. See, e.g., R. G. Javalgi and C. R. Moberg, "Service Loyalty," *Journal of Services Marketing* 3 (1997), pp. 165–79.

72. S. Fournier, "Consumers and Their Brands," *Journal of Consumer Research,* March 1998, p. 355.

73. See E. Garbarino and M. S. Johnson, "The Different Roles of Satisfaction, Trust, and Commitment in Customer Relationships," *Journal of Marketing,* April 1999, pp. 70–87; J. Singh and D. Sirdeshmukh, "Agency and Trust Mechanisms in Consumer Satisfaction and Loyalty Judgments," *Journal of the Academy of Marketing Science,* Winter 2000, pp. 150–67; D. Sirdeshmukh, J. Singh, and B. Sabol, "Consumer Trust, Value, and Loyalty in Relational Exchanges," *Journal of Marketing,* January 2002, pp. 15–37; and C. B. Battacharya and S. Sen, "Consumer–Company Identification," *Journal of Marketing*, April 2003, pp. 76–88.

74. D. F. Spake et al., "Consumer Comfort in Service Relationships," *Journal of Service Research,* May 2003, pp. 316–32.

75. R. L. Olvier, R. T. Rust, and S. Varki, "Customer Delight," *Journal of Retailing* 3 (1997), pp. 311–36; and R. T. Rust and R. L. Oliver, "Should We Delight the Customer?" *Journal of the Academy of Marketing Science,* Winter 2000, pp. 86–94.

76. A. Finn, "Reassessing the Foundations of Customer Delight," *Journal of Service Research*, November 2005, pp. 103–16.

77. R. L. Oliver, "Whence Consumer Loyalty," *Journal of Marketing,* Special Issue 1999, pp. 33–44.

78. See J. Deighton, C. M. Henderson, and S. A. Neslin, "The Effects of Advertising on Brand Switching and Repeat Purchasing," *Journal of Marketing Research,* February 1994, pp. 28–43.

79. See D. Bejou and A. Palmer, "Service Failure and Loyalty," *Journal of Services Marketing* 1 (1998), pp. 7–22; and R. L. Hess Jr., S. Ganesan, and N. M. Klein, "Service Failure and Recovery," *Journal of the Academy of Marketing Science,* Spring 2003, pp. 127–45.

80. M. Johnson, G. M. Zinkham, and G. S. Ayala, "The Impact of Outcome, Competency, and Affect on Service Referral," *Journal of Services Marketing* 5 (1998), pp. 397–415.

81. E. W. Anderson, C. Fornell, R. T. Rust, "Customer Satisfaction, Productivity, and Profitability," *Marketing Science* 2 (1997), pp. 129–45.

82. F. F. Reichheld and W. E. Sasser, Jr., "Zero Defections," *Harvard Business Review,* September 1990, pp. 105–11; and R. Jacob, "Why Some Customers Are More Equal than Others," *Fortune,* September 19, 1994, pp. 215–24. See also V. A. Zeithaml, "Service Qualilty, Profitablity, and the Economic Worth of Customers," *Journal of the Academy of Marketing Science,* Winter 2000, pp. 67–85.

83. For additional research examining these various outcomes, see T. Hennig-Thurau, K. P. Gwinner, and D. D. Gremler, "Understanding Relationship Marketing Outcomes," *Journal of Service Research,* February 2002, pp. 230–47; P. C. Verhoef, P. H. Franses, and J. C. Hoekstra, "The Effect of Relational Constructs on Customer Referrals and Number of Services Purchased from a Multiservice Provider," *Journal of the Academy of Marketing Science* 30, no. 3 (2002), pp. 202–16; H. S. Bansal, P. G. Irving, and S. F. Taylor, "A Three-Component Model of Customer Commitment to Service Providers," *Journal of the Academy of Marketing Science* 32, no. 3 (2004), pp. 234–50; C. Homburg, N. Koschate, and W. D. Hoyer, "Do Satisfied Customers Really Pay More?" *Journal of Marketing,* April 2005, pp. 84–96; and K. Seiders, G. B. Voss, D. Grewal, and A. L. Godfrey, "Do Satisfied Customers Buy More?" *Journal of Marketing*, October 2005, pp. 26–43.

84. See S. Li, "Survival Analysis," *Marketing Research,* Fall 1995, pp. 17–23.

85. Reichheld and Sasser, "Zero Defections," p. 110.

86. Based on D. Brady, "Why Service Sucks," *BusinessWeek,* October 23, 2000, pp. 118–28. See also J. Ganesh, M. J. Arnold, and K. E. Reynolds, "Understanding the Customer Base of Service Providers," *Journal of Marketing,* July 2000, pp. 65–87.

87. See also S. Lingle, "How Much Is a Customer Worth?" *Bank Marketing,* August 1995, pp. 13–16.

88. See G. S. Day, "Managing Market Relationships," *Journal of the Academy of Marketing Science,* Winter 2000, pp. 24–30.

89. See the special issue on relationship marketing, *Journal of the Academy of Marketing Science,* Fall 1995; and G. E. Gengler and P. P. Leszczyc, "Using Customer Satisfaction Research for Relationship Marketing," *Journal of Direct Marketing,* Winter 1997, pp. 23–29.

90. L. Freeman, "Marketing the Market," *Marketing News,* March 2, 1998, p. 1. Other examples are in G. B. Voss and Z. G. Voss, "Implementing a Relationship Marketing Program," *Journal of Services Marketing* 11 (1997), pp. 278–98; B. G. Yovovich, "Scanners Reshape the Grocery Business," *Marketing News,* February 16, 1998, p. 1; and G. Brewer, "The Customer Stops Here," *Sales & Marketing Management,* March 1998, pp. 31–36.

91. L. L. Berry, "Relationship Marketing of Services," *Journal of the Academy of Marketing Science,* Fall 1995, pp. 236–45.

92. See N. Bendapudi and L. L. Berry, "Customers' Motivations for Maintaining Relationships with Service Providers," *Journal of Retailing* 1 (1997), pp. 15–37.

93. J. Raymond, "Home Field Advantage," *American Demographics,* April 2001, pp. 34–36.

94. See G. Levin, "Marketers Flock to Loyalty Offers," *Advertising Age,* May 24, 1993, p. 13; C. Miller, "Rewards for the Best Customers," *Marketing News,* July 5, 1993, p. 1; J. Fulkerson, "It's in the Cards," *American Demographics,* July 1996, pp. 38–43; and J. Passingham, "Grocery Retailing and the Loyalty Card,"

*Journal of the Market Research Society,* January 1998, pp. 55–63. See also L. O'Brien and C. Jones, "Do Rewards Really Create Loyalty?" *Harvard Business Review,* May 1995, pp. 75–82; R. N. Bolton, P. K. Kannan, and M. D. Bramlett, "Implications of Loyalty Programs Membership and Service Experiences for Customer Retention and Value," *Journal of the Academy of Marketing Science,* Winter 2000, pp. 95–108; and A. W. Magi, "Share of Wallet in Retailing," *Journal of Retailing* 79 (2003), pp. 97–106.

95. See F. Rice, "The New Rules of Superlative Services," and P. Sellers "Keeping the Buyers," both in *Fortune,* Autumn–Winter 1993, pp. 50–53 and 56–58, respectively; and G. A. Conrad, G. Brown, and H. A. Harmon, "Customer Satisfaction and Corporate Culture," *Psychology & Marketing,* October 1997, pp. 663–74.

96. J. Holland and S. M. Baker, "Customer Participation in Creating Site Brand Loyalty," *Journal of Interactive Marketing,* Autumn 2001, pp. 34–45; R. E. Anderson and S. S. Srinivasan, "E-Satisfaction and E-Loyalty," *Psychology & Marketing,* February 2003, pp. 123–38; L. C. Harris and M. M. H. Goode, "The Four Levels of Loyalty and the Pivotal Role of Trust," *Journal of Retailing* 80 (2004), pp. 139–58.

97. J. Gummerus et al., "Customer Loyalty to Content-based Web Sites," *Journal of Services Marketing* 18, no. 3 (2004), pp. 175–86.

98. S. S. Srinivasan, R. Anderson, and K. Ponnavolu, "Customer Loyalty in E-commerce," *Journal of Retailing* 78 (2002), pp. 41–50.

99. H. Thorbjornsen et al., "Building Brand Relationships Online," *Journal of Interactive Marketing,* Summer 2002, pp. 17–34.

# Part Four | Cases

Sears has struggled over the years. While some categories, such as Craftsman tools, have been a perennial hit, other categories, particularly apparel, have struggled. Sears has made numerous efforts, including the addition of Lands' End and the Covington collection, as well as the refurbishing of out-of-date stores. While Sears may not be the coolest brand around, the data in Table A for tween and teen girls suggest that in terms of store visits, Sears beats out retailers such as Gap, Macy's, and Wet Seal.

Sears is definitely not done trying to redefine itself. And particularly with the recent struggles by specialty retailers like Gap, there may be opportunities to gain ground. Their most recent effort targets tweens and teens in the "back-to-school" shopping arena. Their

tool? Social networking! Their message? "Don't Just Go Back. Arrive." According to one source:

> Thirteen sites have partnered with Sears to create custom animation, virtual worlds and social networking applications aimed at driving the target market to the Sears online "Arrive Lounge." [Arrive Lounge] features exclusive, interactive content from the entire Sears 2008 back to school offering.

Some of the features of Arrive Lounge include:

- A five-part video series that focuses on Vanessa Hudgens (star of *High School Musical*), on her quest to pick a style for the first day of school.

## TABLE A

Store Shopped in Last Three Months by Girls Age 12 to 17

| 12–14-Year-Old Girls | Percent Shopped | 15–17-Year-Old Girls | Percent Shopped |
|---|---|---|---|
| Wal-Mart | 69.1% | Wal-Mart | 66.4% |
| Target | 51.6 | Target | 48.9 |
| Old Navy | 42.5 | JCPenney | 45.1 |
| JCPenney | 40.8 | Old Navy | 43.1 |
| Kohl's | 35.5 | American Eagle | 36.4 |
| American Eagle | 29.1 | Kohl's | 31.9 |
| Family Dollar Store | 26.9 | Victoria's Secret | 27.7 |
| Payless ShoeSource | 25.8 | Abercrombie & Fitch | 27.6 |
| Dollar General | 25.7 | Hot Topic | 25.8 |
| Abercrombie & Fitch | 25.3 | Payless ShoeSource | 25.8 |
| Kmart | 25.3 | Family Dollar Store | 24.6 |
| Sears | 24.8 | Sears | 23.8 |
| Victoria's Secret | 24.3 | Kmart | 20.3 |
| Gap | 20.8 | Gap | 19.6 |
| Nike | 18.5 | Macy's | 18.5 |
| Sam's Club | 18.2 | Wet Seal | 18.4 |
| Hot Topic | 18.0 | Dollar General | 18.4 |
| Macy's | 17.7 | Dillard's | 17.3 |
| Costco | 17.6 | Nike | 17.2 |
| T.J. Maxx | 16.9 | Lady Foot Locker | 17.1 |
| Famous Footwear | 15.6 | Foot Locker | 16.9 |
| Big Lots | 15.1 | Express | 16.2 |
| Limited Too | 14.9 | Costco | 15.7 |

Source: Simmons Market Research Bureau, Teens National Consumer Survey, Fall 2006.

- MTV's "The American Mall," which includes product placement throughout for Sears products.
- Registration for VIP Access Cards, one part of a Sears loyalty program.

Partner sites that are designed to drive perceptions and awareness of Sears include:

- Zwinky. Virtual world Zwinky.com, highly popular with teens, created a Sears virtual store. The store, located in their Zwinchester Mall, offers exclusive apparel for users' personal avatars, will host a "Fashion Forward" event celebrating the best of back-to-school fashion, and so on.
- Addicting Games. This online gaming site created a fully Sears branded back-to-school hub with integrated content from Arrive Lounge throughout.
- MySpace. Sears has a custom back-to-school page featuring Arrive Lounge content and applications.

Says a Sears executive of these efforts:

> Expanding our marketing strategy into the online world of user communities and social networking is a critical means of developing engagement and brand loyalty within the youth demographic. By modifying our strategy to reach tweens in their own environment we are demonstrating to them how Sears can be a part of their life, from their entertainment to their school wardrobe.

### Discussion Questions

1. What image is Sears attempting to create with its "Don't Just Go Back. Arrive," its Arrive Lounge, and other partnerships with social network sites? Do you think it worked? Explain.

2. What do you think the existing store image prior to the campaign was for Sears for tween and teens in the apparel and fashion category?

3. Create a survey to capture what tweens and teens actually think of Sears in terms of its retailer image and personality in apparel and fashion targeted at them. With parental permission, gather data from six tween/teen girls and boys. For a point of comparison, also collect data on several other retailers listed in Table A. What do you conclude?

4. Visit a Sears store near you and visit their tween and teen apparel section. Does their in-store image match that which they were attempting to create via their promotional campaign and social network sites? Explain.

5. Explain which of the strategies relating to information search patterns, shown in Table 15–2, that Sears is enacting with its new campaign.

6. Discuss clothes shopping from a family decision-making standpoint, including parent–child dynamics. What dynamic is Sears attempting to influence by using social network sites?

7. Do you think teen and tween apparel decisions are attribute, attitude, or affect based? Explain and discuss how Sears' new online and social network efforts either are or are not effective in this context.

Source: N. Zmuda, "Sears Tries to Alter Image, Co-Opt Cool in Web Push," *Advertising Age*, July 14, 2008, p. 3; "Sears 'Arrives' on the Social Networking Scene with Multiple Partnerships Aimed at Increasing User Engagement among Teens and Tweens," *Forbes.com*, July 15, 2008; "Sears 'Arrives' on the Social Networking Scene with Multiple Partnerships Aimed at Increasing User Engagement among Teens and Tweens," *PR Newswire*, July 15, 2008; M. Warner, "Sears Uses Virtual Worlds for Back-to-School Marketing Strategy," *Virtual World News*, July 20, 2008; and information from the Sears Arrive Lounge Web site.

## CASE 4–2 ADIDAS 1—AHEAD OF ITS TIME?

In 2005, after three years of product development, Adidas announced the launch of Adidas 1, a $250 running shoe that used a computer sensor in the heel of the shoe to adjust the amount of cushion in real time 1,000 times per second. Adidas executives were ecstatic:

> Adidas executives believe the shoe could be their iPod, a technology so ready for prime-time that it can be adapted to the company's basketball and soccer shoes and eventually enter the profitable league of "gotta-have" sneakers among urban youth. Says a hopeful Erich Stamminger, CEO of Adidas North America: "This is the biggest thing to hit this industry in decades."

Early signs were positive, including an endorsement by *Runner's World*'s Warren Greene. However, there were concerns, including price, which was more than 50 percent higher than the most expensive sneaker currently on the market. In addition, the technology added weight to the shoe, which can be a big deal to serious runners.

Adidas was counting on this technology to gain an edge over its closest rivals, Nike and Reebok, who also claimed to be developing sensor technology. However, by 2006, there were already signs of trouble. Nike came out with its Air Max 360, which included air sole technology it had been working on for 20 years, with a price tag of $160. As one industry commentator noted:

> Pushing past the $100 is risky in the running business. From experienced marathoners to novices, runners have resisted the kind of marketing flash that has allowed shoe companies to seek higher price points in basketball shoes, where the target is impressionable teen boys wowed by sports stars like LeBron James. Instead, runners focus on comfort and fit, and often obsessively stick to one brand. What's more, consistent runners need to buy new shoes after several hundred miles, which they can rack up in months or so. That makes pricey running shoes an even harder sell.

Perhaps in response to these issues, Adidas announced plans for a 2007 launch of two less expensive versions of the Adidas 1 to "spur sales and draw a larger audience." The new models, the Adidas 1 Runner and the Adidas Runner DLX were designed to be lighter than the original model and retail for $150. As of 2008, however, the Adidas 1 appeared to have been discontinued, although remaining inventory could still be purchased from retailers such as Amazon and Overstock. After all the investment, corporate press, and industry buzz, no mention of the Adidas 1 or their sensor technology could be found on the Adidas Web site.

## Discussion Questions

1. What type of innovation was the Adidas 1?
2. Conduct an innovation analysis of Adidas 1 using Table 7–2 as the basis. What insights does the innovation analysis provide into the failure of Adidas 1?
3. How might shoe weight have been used in the decision process for *serious runners* that could account for the failure of Adidas 1?
4. When Adidas lowered its price for the 2007 season, what assumptions were they making about the decision-making process?

5. Is the serious runner a repeat purchaser or loyal committed customer? Explain and relate to how this may have contributed to the failure of Adidas 1.

For the remaining questions, assume you have been hired by Adidas to revive their Adidas 1 and its related sensor technology. This time they want to avoid the mistakes of the past and move beyond a novelty technology to a mass-marketed item.

6. Analyze the market for Adidas 1 and its sensor technology as you move from the innovators to the early adopters to the mass market. In doing so:
   a. Detail the types of consumers the market will or should consist of in terms of users (e.g., professional vs. amateur, sport, type of shoe, etc.) at each of the stages.
   b. Detail what you think the "optimal" product would look like for each of the groups (innovators versus early adopters versus mass market) in terms of price and other features, such as styling, comfort, and support.
   c. What types of decision making (affective, attitude-based, attribute-based) should Adidas attempt to encourage for each of the identified markets? Explain.
7. Develop an advertisement for each of the markets identified in Question 6. Identify such factors as core positioning, theme, copy points, visuals, and so on.
8. Develop a retail strategy for Adidas as its technology moves from innovators, to early adopters, and finally, to the mass market.
9. How might Adidas capitalize on reference group influence, WOM, and buzz to influence the diffusion process? Outline a strategy for creating a cascading influence from innovators, to early adopters, to the mass market.

Source: "The Machine of a New Sole," *BusinessWeek,* March 14, 2005, p. 99; S. Kang, "Gear: Feet of Gold," *The Wall Street Journal*, March 18, 2006, p. 4; and E. Newman, "Could New Styles Energize Adidas 1?" *Footwear News*, June 19, 2006, p. 2.

## CASE 4–3 SUPERMARKET SHOPPING IN EUROPE

The Point-of-Purchase Advertising Institute (POPAI) conducted a major study of supermarket shopping in four European countries. Almost 3,000 consumers age 16 or older were interviewed while shopping at a major supermarket. Respondents were first screened to ascertain that they were on a "major shopping trip"

before the interview. Part of the results are shown in Table A.

## Discussion Questions

1. What are the most significant shopping differences across these four countries?

| | UK | Holland | Belgium | France |
|---|---|---|---|---|
| **Age** | | | | |
| 55 and over (%) | 32 | 32 | 15 | 22 |
| 35–54 (%) | 49 | 48 | 50 | 43 |
| Under 35 (%) | 20 | 20 | 34 | 35 |
| Female (%) | 84 | 87 | 83 | 77 |
| Shop alone (%) | 57 | 79 | 65 | 62 |
| **How often do you use this store?** | | | | |
| Some of the time (%) | 18 | 32 | 47 | 27 |
| Most of the time (%) | 32 | 52 | 32 | 24 |
| All of the time (%) | 50 | 16 | 21 | 49 |
| Average time on a major trip (minutes) | 48 | 23 | 38 | 53 |
| Number of items bought on a major trip | 30 | 15 | 14 | 26 |
| Number of major trips per week | 1.1 | 1.2 | 1.1 | 1.0 |
| Total number of grocery trips per week | 2.1 | 3.4 | 3.4 | 3.7 |
| Use a written shopping list (%) | 61 | 70 | 74 | 76 |
| Store is over 5 km from home (%) | 32 | 9 | 24 | 46 |
| Amount spent ($) | 74 | 36 | 52 | 86 |
| **Shopping patterns** | | | | |
| Visited aisles where intended purchases were (%) | 29 | 45 | 51 | 45 |
| Visited most aisles (%) | 35 | 28 | 34 | 38 |
| Visited all aisles (%) | 36 | 27 | 15 | 17 |
| **In-store decision making** | | | | |
| Specifically planned (%) | 25 | 20 | 31 | 24 |
| Generally planned (%) | 8 | 24 | 9 | 12 |
| Substitute (%) | 4 | 4 | 4 | 6 |
| Unplanned (%) | 64 | 53 | 56 | 58 |

**TABLE A**

Cross-Country Variations in Major Shopping Trips to Supermarkets

Source: "Cross-Country Variations in Major Shopping Trips to Supermarkets," *The 1997/98 POPAI Europe Consumer Buying Habits Study* (POPAI Europe, 1998).

2. What causes the most significant shopping differences across these four countries?

3. What are the strategy implications of the most significant shopping differences across these four countries for an EU-wide supermarket chain?

4. What, if any, are the strategy implications of the most significant shopping differences across these four countries for a manufacturer of products sold in supermarkets throughout the European Union?

## CASE 4–4  A SHIFTING RETAIL SCENE—CAN BLOCKBUSTER SURVIVE?

There's no question about it—consumers prefer to watch movies at home. A recent survey finds that 73 percent prefer watching a movie at home to going to the theater. You might think that's good news for Blockbuster. Think again. While Blockbuster is still a major player in the movie rental business, it has been slow to recognize or adapt to competitive threats. These include:

- *Consumer purchases of new DVDs.* Consumers appear to want to own movies, and studios now offer relatively low-priced movies through discounters like Wal-Mart. While Blockbuster now buys used DVDs from consumers and resells them at a considerable markup, it admits that it can't match the low new-DVD prices offered by the discount chains.

- *Online rentals and streaming video.* Netflix, which was a relatively small upstart just a few years ago, now dominates online rentals, with roughly 8.2 million of the 11 million U.S. households who rent online doing so through Netflix. Blockbuster basically matched this program with its own version, but it has been unprofitable for them. Netflix then increased the stakes again by offering streaming video to computers or TV from its Web site. The program, called "Watch Instantly," draws from a separate catalog but includes both movies and TV episodes. Both online rentals and streaming video require at least some changes in consumer behavior, which represent a challenge to these new technologies, at least among some segments of the market. For example, online rentals require consumers to "plan ahead" for their entertainment needs rather than spontaneously stop in at the video store on the way home from work.

- *Video-on-demand (VOD) offered by cable companies.* While still somewhat new, this service could revolutionize the industry *and* make obsolete all existing models. VOD offers the convenience of in-home ordering, instant delivery, and automatic billing. Assuming studios back the system and rental options remain current and broad, this could spell the end for Blockbuster as we know it. One aspect of current VOD offered by cable companies is that it doesn't include computer viewing as an option.

As one analyst notes:

Blockbuster's problems are not just a tale of a business struggling with technological obsolescence, but a compelling illustration of how more general changes in consumer behavior can affect a business.

Blockbuster has taken steps, as we've seen. First, it eliminated the late charge (sort of), but it cost them $50 million in advertising and $250 million in revenues. In addition, since consumers who didn't return the movie in the designated time were billed for the cost of the movie minus rental fees, on the assumption they had decided to purchase it, lawsuits surrounding the misleading nature of the "no late fee" claim surfaced. Other steps have included matching the Netflix online model with one of its own. Perhaps the brightest spot for Blockbuster is video games, which account for 20 percent of its business.

## Discussion Questions

1. Detail the various options available for movie rentals. List what you feel are the most important evaluative criteria on which to judge these options. Do the evaluative criteria depend on consumer characteristics?

2. What are some of the "must have" attributes and features for online and VOD to spread to the mass market?

3. What marketing strategies can be developed to "teach" consumers to plan ahead for their entertainment needs?

4. Are there any benefits to the "brick and mortar" stores operated by Blockbuster that exist or could be developed that would be unique from VOD and get consumers into Blockbuster stores?

5. How might Blockbuster leverage its current strength in video games to make it a stronger part of its business model?

6. What, if any, switching barriers exist in a consumer's decision to switch from the traditional in-store Blockbuster model to other options, such as online and VOD? Are these barriers higher for some consumers than others?

7. Create an advertising campaign for Blockbuster to *increase* consumers' sense of regret, or so-called buyers' remorse, at having purchased a DVD (or many DVDs) they probably won't watch again and paid substantially more than the rental fee. Consider such appeals as:
   a. Emotional appeal
   b. Testimonials
   c. Utilitarian appeal

Source: "Poll: Most Prefer to Watch Movies at Home," *CNN.com*, accessed June 17, 2005; and D. McGinn, "Rewinding a Video Giant," *Newsweek*, June 27, 2005, pp. E9–E14; A. Harvey, "Is Downloading Movies Biting into Rental Stores' Profits?" *McClatchy-Tribune Business News*, July 16, 2008; and S. Murphy, "A Lesson in Change," *Chain Store Age*, July 2008, p. 58.

## CASE 4–5 HYUNDAI'S TURNAROUND

In 1998, Hyundai was at a crossroads in the U.S. market. After a decade of dwindling sales and nagging quality concerns, Hyundai needed to do something to turn their brand around. And they took some bold moves. Among them:

- A 10-year, 100,000-mile warranty
- Quality improvements
- Product line and pricing reconfiguration
- "Buy-in" from its dealers, a critical customer link

The changes were dramatic and so were the results. Sales jumped from a low of 90,200 vehicles in 1998 to 400,200 in 2003 and 467,000 in 2007! In 2004, Hyundai tied with Honda for second place in the J.D. Power Initial Quality Survey, and was only one point behind the leader, Toyota. In 2007, three of its models received the number one quality rating in their segment according to a survey by Strategic Vision. In the survey, respondents were asked about quality problems they had encountered as well as perceived quality, or "what they got for their money."

Obviously, Hyundai has come a long way. However, the company realizes there are still obstacles to overcome. Consider a story related by Chris Perry, Hyundai Motor America's National Advertising Manager:

During a product clinic, where we introduce one of our new models, we asked people to tell us what they thought of Hyundai. A woman in the focus group said, "Wow, I just love that vehicle, but I've worked too hard to drive a Hyundai."

Perry goes on to state:

Now, this [the focus group statement] happened a couple of years ago, and perceptions of Hyundai have improved quite a bit since then. But we still think of that comment to remind ourselves that we have a long way to go, in spite of our sales success. In fact, research from NOP World Automotive shows that a large percentage of new vehicle intenders who are aware of Hyundai say that they would not consider purchasing the brand. A lot of this lingering reluctance has to do with product cycles. Most experts say that in our industry it takes one to two product cycles for perceptions to catch up to reality.

Indeed, it appears that Hyundai continues to have mixed brand associations that may help explain the "I've worked too hard to drive a Hyundai" statement. On the plus side—great warranty, good value, affordable, independent minded, and a perception that Hyundai is probably better than its reputation. On the minus side—unfamiliar, cheap, low quality, economy car, and boring. And despite its quality improvements, Hyundai's Korean heritage may still be a problem area. A recent *American Demographics* study found that U.S. consumers "of all ages, incomes and education levels gave Korea the lowest marks for car quality."

In taking its next steps, Hyundai has worked with NOP to conduct a segmentation analysis. One intriguing finding is that within their critical target markets consumers "strive for an authentic lifestyle." In addition, however, they also recently launched their first ever luxury model in the Hyundai Genesis. The company had debated whether to brand and distribute this model as a Hyundai, which was their ultimate decision. The alternative was to utilize a "new brand strategy" (as was done by Toyota, for Lexus, for example) in which a new brand name is selected separate from Hyundai and a new distributor/dealer network is created just for that new brand.

Obviously, Hyundai is working hard and making headway in the U.S. automotive market. Where it goes in the future remains to be seen.

## Discussion Questions

1. What role do you feel Hyundai's 10-year, 100,000-mile warranty played in its turnaround? Can you relate this to postpurchase dissonance? Would this warranty be as important an evaluative criterion today as it was 10 years ago? Explain.

2. How much influence do you think Hyundai's value-pricing strategy plays in consumers' ongoing mixed perceptions about Hyundai's quality?

3. Based on Hyundai's efforts thus far, have they been taking more of a utilitarian approach or a value-expressive approach in their overall strategy and marketing efforts?

4. Assume that Hyundai successfully upgrades its quality image among all U.S. consumers so that they are universally recognized for high quality. Will this result in greater sales and loyalty? Are there other factors driving consumer decisions and satisfaction that Hyundai could focus on *beyond* quality that could drive even greater sales increases?

5. To which VALS segment(s) does the woman belong who indicated "I've worked too hard to drive a Hyundai"? If Hyundai sticks with its current positioning efforts, do you think this person will ever change her mind?

6. Research indicates that "authenticity" is critical to Hyundai's target consumers. To what VALS segments do you think these consumers belong?

7. Based on your answers to Questions 5 and 6, which VALS segment(s) would you strive to target? Justify your selection. Develop an advertising campaign for one of these chosen segments to include core positioning statement, theme, copy points, and visuals. Justify your ad in terms of the characteristics of your selected target segment.

8. Do you agree with Hyundai's branding strategy for the Genesis? Explain.

Source: D. Kiley, "Hyundai Improves Dramatically in Quality Survey," *USA Today,* April 28, 2004; B. Johnson, "American Consumers Largely Ignore 'Made in USA' Pitch," *AdAge.com,* June 6, 2005; C. Perry, "Driving Your Brand Forward . . . by Narrowing Your Focus," *NOP World Perspectives,* Spring 2005; and "Hyundai Tops New Quality List," at *blogs.cars.com/kickingtires,* accessed August 4, 2008.

## CASE 4–6 VESPANOMICS

Vespa was a popular motor scooter in the United States until it withdrew from the market as a result of its inability to meet federal emission standards. In 2000 it returned. Since its reintroduction, Vespa has run ads that position it as fun, sexy, and hip. Examples include:

- A 30-second TV spot: Set in a backyard on a summer afternoon; a young man appears to heap praise on a woman reading in a nearby lawn chair. "You take me places I've never been before," he says in an Italian accent as he praises "her" curves and sleek figure. "Your petite but powerful body will purr with excitement when we are together." When he continues with "I must mount you now," the camera pans out to reveal a new Vespa, which he climbs aboard.

- A campaign by Vespa of Greater New York: Ads showcased words ending in "issimo," such as "vroomisimo," and "sexissimo," and featured "barely clothed women sprawled over and around Vespas."
- Billboards in San Francisco: Three billboards were developed that featured a woman's hands, arms, or legs grasping a male driver.
- Guerrilla marketing: Teams of 12 models visited cafés and colleges in cities with Vespa boutiques. Their mission was described as "looking cool, sipping coffee, and tacitly pitching the Vespa."

While Vespa's general marketing and advertising strategy is certainly unique for a motor scooter, its distribution strategy is even more so. Vespa is distributed through a limited but growing number of Vespa boutiques, which were designed to exude the fun and style of Vespa along with a prestige or luxury feel. These outlets sell only Vespas, Vespa merchandise, and espresso and pastries. Vespa merchandise includes product accessories, helmets, and apparel. In announcing the launch of the boutiques, the Vespa Web site indicated that:

> Since 1946, Vespa has been synonymous with entertainment, pleasure, freedom; feelings directly influencing the design of the new Vespa boutiques—unique retail environments created to showcase all the products which comprise the Vespa Lifestyle.

In commenting on Vespa's promotional tactics and positioning, a spokesman states: "Vespa is a passion brand that has been discovered by style leaders. Vespa is the sexiest way to get from A to B, and its Italian heritage allows us to own that."

Fast-forward to 2008. Gas prices hover around $4 per gallon. Global warming is a serious concern. *Eco-friendly* is the new buzzword. Vespa sales increase dramatically, so much so that some showrooms are selling out of all their stock. Vespa launched its "Vespanomics Platform" on its Web site. On it, they define Vespanomics as "the ecological, economic, and personal satisfaction one achieves after buying a Vespa scooter. Vespanomics promotes embracing motor scooters as an alternative form of transportation to reduce oil consumption,

pollution, and traffic congestion." Excerpts from the platform are as follows:

> If America is serious about ending its "oil addiction," consumers must be encouraged to curb their rampant use of gasoline for transportation purposes—by far the largest and fastest growing use of oil in the U.S.
>
> Piaggio Group Americas, manufacturer of the Vespa scooter, is at the forefront of this issue. Along with other scooter and motorcycle manufacturers, Piaggio believes that motor scooters and other street-legal two-wheel vehicles offer an important and viable means of transportation in many situations, and could bring a lasting, positive impact on domestic energy stability and America's dependence on foreign oil.
>
> Independent research shows that Americans would consider utilizing motor scooters for up to 10% of the mileage currently traveled in a car, truck or SUV. If they did the savings would be (a) Oil consumption per day—savings of 14.4–18.4 million gallons, (b) Carbon dioxide emissions per day—a decrease of 324 million lbs.

In addition, they provide a comparative analysis of the fuel costs of a Vespa versus other options, such as the Hummer, the Toyota Camry, and the Toyota Prius. A surprising aspect of this analysis is just how competitive the Prius is with the Vespa, with a mileage differential of only 17 miles per gallon.

In describing one of its current models, Vespa attempts to convey the brand's core values as follows:

> Take a new spin on an original classic. From the same pedigree as the first Vespa prototype built by Piaggio in 1946, the LX is 60 years in the making. Witness the evolution of style, comfort, and performance with the core values of Vespa that never change: eco-friendly engineering, passion, individualism, and integrity.

## Discussion Questions

1. What brand image was Vespa trying to create in the early part of this decade through its advertising, guerilla tactics, and boutiques?

2. What brand image is emphasized with its Vespanomics Platform?

3. Are the elements of its earlier image and that created by its Vespanomics Platform compatible?

4. Before $4-per-gallon gasoline, was the need for a Vespa Scooter active or inactive? Explain and discuss implications for marketing strategy.

5. Describe what you currently see as at least three segments of the market for Vespa and other scooters. List

the different needs, demographics, and psychographics for owning a scooter for each of these segments.

6. Based on your analysis in Question 5, develop ads for each segment. Be sure to include key positioning statements, key copy points, visuals, and so forth for each, and defend your decisions.

7. Evaluate Vespa's Web site (www.vespausa.com).

8. In this age of $4-per-gallon gasoline and concern about global warming, discuss how Vespa can be both a utilitarian decision and a value-expressive decision.

9. How do gas prices or fuel costs factor into the decision-making process for consumers in terms of influencing the consideration set and decision-

making rule used in selecting a transportation option? Detail and explain.

10. Which of the six environmental activism segments discussed in Chapter 3 (p. 90) does Vespa appeal to most? Explain.

Source: J. Halliday, "Scooters and Pastry," *Advertising Age,* November 6, 2000, p. 4; K. Greenberg, "Reintroduced Vespa Takes a New Turn," *Brandweek,* May 28, 2001, p. 1; S. J. Heim, "Vespa's Sex Appeal Promoted in KBP Ads," *Adweek Western Edition,* April 22, 2002, p. 2; M. Anderson, "Vespa Gets Sexy in New Dealer Ads," *Adweek Eastern Edition,* May 13, 2002, p. 1; K. Roundtree, "Viewpoint Studios Intros Racy TV Work for Vespa," *Adweek New England Edition,* July 2002, p. 1; "Make Your Reality a Dream," *InternetAutoguide.com,* featured news article, August 3, 2005; B. Shlachter, "High Gas Prices Spur Local Scooter Sales," *McClatchy-Tribune Business News,* August 4, 2008; and information from the Vespa Web site, www.vespausa.com.

## CASE 4–7 CREATING A LOYALTY PROGRAM AT THINGS REMEMBERED

Things Remembered provides personalized gifts for special occasions. It has catalogs, physical stores, and an online store. It provides personalization through embroidery and engraving of initials, words, and designs specified by the customer. Although successful, the company noted the challenge of its position:

> The strength of a business such as Things Remembered can also become a challenge. Customers see the Things Remembered brand as being all about occasions. That is good, because the brand is about occasions. However, many customers begin to limit the occasions and think that it is just about anniversaries, graduations, Christmas and weddings.

Earlier in the decade, Things Remembered was struggling because its *repeat purchase rate* was lower than other retailers' rates. Its goal was to create a marketing program that would get customers to buy at Things Remembered (a) for a wider set of occasions, and (b) more frequently. The solution was a loyalty program called "Rewards Club." The key features of the Rewards Club were as follows:

- One-time $5 membership fee
- Earn $10 rebate for every $100 purchased
- Automatic tracking and distribution of reward certificates
- Certificates good for 90 days
- $50 limit in rebates earned in a given month
- One transaction every 18 months required to maintain membership

To help encourage internal buy-in to the program, Things Remembered gave store associates incentives to enroll customers as members. Initial results were positive, with enrollments at targeted levels. However, one concern is that they enrolled more low spenders (spend less than $50) than high spenders (spend more than $100).

### Discussion Questions

1. Define loyalty as you understand it from the text. Do you think the Rewards Club at Things Remembered helps create loyalty? Explain.

2. Beyond earning $$ for purchases, can you think of other aspects that could be added to their program that would enhance loyalty?

3. The marketing program was designed to achieve two goals, namely, increasing the number of occasions for which consumers purchased from Things Remembered, and increase the frequency with which they purchased from Things Remembered. Which goal is best achieved by the Rewards Club? Explain.

4. Design a marketing program from the ground up to achieve the goal of increasing the number of occasions for which consumers think of and purchase from Things Remembered. Note: It may or may not involve a rewards program.

5. What explains the fact that lower spenders are more likely to enroll? Is this a good or bad thing? Explain.

Source: T. Mulhern and D. Duffy, "Building Loyalty at Things Remembered," *Journal of Consumer Marketing* 21, no. 1 (2004), pp. 62–66; and www.thingsremembered.com.

# Organizations as Consumers

External
Influences

Firmographics
Culture
Government
Reference Groups
Marketing Activities

Experiences and Acquisitions

Organizational
Culture

Internal
Influences

Organizational Values
Perception
Learning
Memory
Motives
Emotions

Experiences and Acquisitions

The stereotype of organizational buying behavior is one of a cold, efficient, economically rational process. Computers rather than humans could easily, and perhaps preferably, fulfill this function. In reality, nothing could be further from the truth. In fact, organizational consumer behavior is as human as individual and household consumer behavior.

Organizations pay price premiums for well-known brands and for prestige brands. They avoid risk and fail to properly evaluate products and brands both before and after purchase. Individual members of organizations use the purchasing and consumption process as a political arena and attempt to increase their personal, departmental, or functional power through purchasing. Marketing communications are perceived and misperceived by organization members. Likewise, organizations learn correct and incorrect information about the world in which they operate.

Organizational purchase decisions take place in situations with varying degrees of time pressure, importance, and newness. They typically involve more people and criteria than do individual or household decisions. Thus, the study of organizational buying behavior is a rich and fun-filled activity.

On this and the facing page is a version of our model of consumer behavior modified for organizational buying. Chapter 19 explains these modifications.

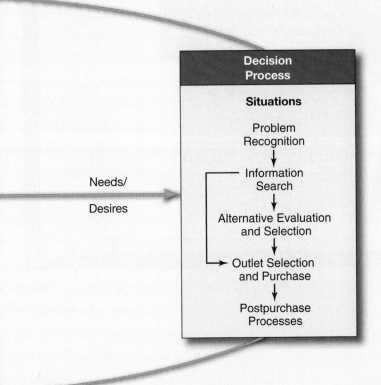

Needs/Desires

**Decision Process**

**Situations**

Problem Recognition
↓
Information Search
↓
Alternative Evaluation and Selection
↓
Outlet Selection and Purchase
↓
Postpurchase Processes

# Organizational Buyer Behavior

■ It may sound funny to say it this way, but businesses are customers too! They have needs and wants, are influenced by internal factors like values, and by external factors like reference groups. Relationships matter, as do efforts to build and foster brand image. Understanding what drives businesses, and the people who run them, is critical to marketing success. Consider the following:

*Segmentation.* While small and moderate-sized businesses often get lost in the shuffle, marketers increasingly realize that this segment has a lot of potential. However, tapping this potential requires adapting to the unique needs and wants of this customer base. For example, in the North American IT industry, slightly more than half of all spending comes from companies with fewer than 1,000 employees. IBM is aggressively courting these customers with a program called IBM Express, which offers flexible and reasonably priced products and services tailored to this market.[1]

*Technology.* Technology helps businesses in many ways. An interesting twist is in the area of online business networking (think Friendster for

business), particularly for salespeople. Consider the following:

Most business networking sites work in similar ways. You can create a profile with your name, title, and other basic information, then have the option of uploading your personal address book and inviting colleagues to join the network. After you sign up you can search the database by job title, geographic location, company name, and more. If the site indicates you know someone who knows a person at a company you want to pursue, you can request an introduction. If that person agrees to be an intermediary, you exchange information with his contact, and go from there.[2]

Sites such as LinkedIn, Ryze, and Spoke offer online networking services, and results are encouraging. However, having a strong set of intermediaries is critical and the less direct a linkage you have to the person you want to contact, the lower the chances of success.

*Branding.* Think brands don't matter in the world of organizational buying? Don't tell that to New Pig Corporation. New Pig makes products such as absorbent socks (pigs) for soaking up oil spills on factory floors. New Pig has built a strong brand reputation not only by providing innovative products and delivering on its quality and service promises, but also with unique marketing efforts built around its name. For example, it has giveaways such as pig hats, "Oink" T-shirts, and piggy banks. This all might sound a bit over the edge. However, New Pig's loyal customers seem to love it and have, themselves, become apostles for the brand. One customer went so far as wearing her pig hat to get married—now that's devotion![3]

Purchase decisions by businesses are often described as "rational" or "economic." However, as the chapter opener suggests, various factors beyond functional utility influence organizational decisions. This is not so surprising when you consider that businesses and other organizations are made up of individuals, and that these individuals, not "the organization," make the purchase decisions.

Understanding organizational purchasing requires many of the same concepts used to understand individual consumer or household needs (see Illustration 19–1). Although larger and often more complex than individual consumers and households, organizations too develop preferences, memories, and behaviors through perceptions, information processing, and experience. Likewise, organizations develop cultures that create relatively stable patterns of behaviors over time and across situations.

Like households, organizations make different types of buying decisions. In some instances, these buying decisions are routine replacement decisions for a frequently

**ILLUSTRATION 19–1**

Communicating with organizational buyers often involves many of the same principles used to reach household buyers— in this case fear appeal.

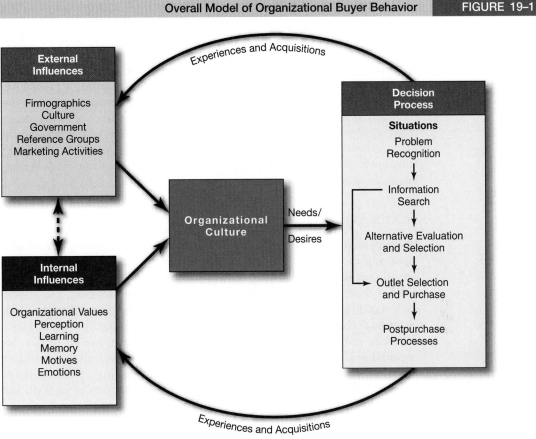

**Overall Model of Organizational Buyer Behavior**     FIGURE 19–1

purchased commodity product or service such as paper or pens. At the other end of the continuum, organizations face new, complex purchase decisions that require careful problem definition, extensive information search, a long and often technical evaluation process, perhaps a negotiated purchase, and a long period of use and postpurchase evaluation.

Because there are many similarities between analyzing consumer behavior and analyzing organizational buyer behavior, our basic conceptual model of buyer behavior still holds. However, organizations are not just a collection of individuals. Organizations do develop unique rules and cultures that influence the behavior of their members. Thus, it is important that we understand the unique characteristics of organizations that relate to their purchasing behavior.

Figure 19–1 shows our basic model of buyer behavior modified to be applicable to an organizational buying context. We will begin our discussion by examining the organization decision process. Then we will examine the internal and external factors that determine organizational culture, the organizational equivalent of household lifestyle.

# ORGANIZATIONAL PURCHASE PROCESS

Organizational buying decisions are often compared with family purchases. Although the comparison is useful, there are important distinctions. Organizations generally have relatively objective and clearly articulated criteria, such as profit maximization, that guide purchases. Families lack such explicit, overarching goals.

Most organizational purchases are made by individuals unknown to other organizational members, and most purchases have little effect on most other members of the organization. On the other hand, many family purchases are inherently emotional and strongly affect the relationships between the family members.[4] For example, the decision to buy a child a requested toy or new school clothes is more than an acquisition; it is a symbol of love and commitment to the child. Such processes are not likely to operate with such intensity for most organizational buying decisions, although emotions certainly can play a role.

Finally, businesses often engage in reciprocal purchases (they buy from their customers when possible), form strategic alliances with their suppliers, and are proactive in helping suppliers develop products that meet their unique needs. These are not common options for households. Thus, while organizational decision making has some things in common with family decision making, it is not the same.

## Decision-Making Unit

**Decision-making units (DMUs)** are the individuals (representing functional areas and management) within an organization who participate in making a given purchase decision. These often function as **buying centers** when they consist of individuals from various areas of the firm, such as accounting, engineering, manufacturing, and marketing, who meet specifically to make a purchase decision. They are often relatively permanent for recurring decisions and ad hoc for nonroutine ones. Large, highly structured organizations ordinarily involve more individuals in a purchase decision than do smaller, less formal organizations. Important decisions are likely to involve individuals from a wider variety of functional areas and organizational levels than are less important purchase decisions.

The following describes a Hewlett-Packard salesperson's view of the DMU and the buying process for very expensive imaging systems for large hospitals:

> Selling in the hospital market is a two-stage process and the buying cycle ranges from 3 to 12 months. In the first stage, I deal with medical professionals. They are most concerned with image quality, product reliability, and service. I must establish relationships and awareness of our products' functionality and reliability with a number of people, and the product demonstration is critical.
>
> The second stage is negotiations with administrators, who are more driven by price and cost issues. But much depends on the hospital's situation. For example, if a hospital is renowned for cancer treatment, they want the best available systems in that area and are more price sensitive with other equipment.[5]

In Table 19–1, we see that buyers in retail and wholesale firms assign different priorities to the performance of suppliers than do the operations people in those same firms. Organizations marketing to these firms must meet the needs of each group and communicate that to each group. Note that focusing only on the buyers, a common strategy, is not likely to be successful.

How the final purchase decision is made is determined in part by individual power, expertise, the degree of influence each functional area possesses in this type of decision, how the organization resolves group decision conflicts, and the nature of the decision.[6]

Members of the decision-making unit play various roles, such as information gatherer, key influencer, decision maker, purchaser, or user. A plant manager could play all five roles, while corporate engineers may simply be sources of information.

Decision-making units are likely to vary over the product life cycle (new products versus older ones). Consider the changes in the decision-making unit that took place in the purchase of microprocessors by an original equipment manufacturer over the stages of the

| Attribute* | Buyer Rating | Operations Rating |
|---|---|---|
| Ease of placing orders | **4.01** | 3.71 |
| Line-item availability | **4.55** | 4.31 |
| Package clearly identified | 4.46 | **4.82** |
| Meets appointments | 4.46 | **4.73** |
| Delivers when requested | **4.87** | 4.70 |
| Delivered sorted and segregated | 4.36 | **4.75** |
| Palletizing/unitizing capability | 3.72 | **4.37** |
| Master carton packaging quality | 3.81 | **4.48** |
| Shelf unit packaging quality | 3.97 | **4.29** |
| Complete/accurate documentation | 4.54 | **4.81** |
| Well-documented deal/style codes | 4.36 | **4.60** |
| Length of order cycle | **4.14** | 3.61 |
| Consistency of order cycle | **4.38** | 3.88 |

**TABLE 19–1**

Service Attribute Importance for Retail and Wholesale Buyers and Operations Personnel

*Measured on a scale of 1 to 5, with 5 being very important and 1 being not at all important. All are significantly different at the .05 level.

Source: Adapted from M. B. Cooper, C. Droge, and P. J. Daugherty, "How Buyers and Operations Personnel Evaluate Service," *Industrial Marketing Management* 20 (1991), p. 83, with permission from Elsevier.

microprocessor's product life cycle. Early stages in the life of the new microprocessor presented a difficult, important decision that required a large DMU. As the product grew in its utilization, a simpler decision evolved, as did a change in the structure of the DMU. Finally, as the microprocessor moved into a mature stage, it became a routine low-priority decision involving primarily the purchasing function. These changes are illustrated below:

| Stage of Product Life Cycle | Size of DMU | Key Functions Influencing the Purchase Decision |
|---|---|---|
| Introduction | Large | Engineering and R&D |
| Growth | Medium | Production and top management |
| Maturity | Small | Purchasing |

## Purchase Situation

The buying process is influenced by the importance of the purchase and the complexity and difficulty of the choice. Simple, low-risk, routine decisions are generally made by an individual or even an automated process without extensive effort. At the other extreme are decisions that are complex and have major organizational implications. A continuum of purchase situations lies between these two extremes. A useful categorization of organizational purchase situations is provided in Table 19–2 and described in the following paragraphs.[7]

Note that this is similar to the purchase involvement construct discussed in Chapter 14. For consumers, we divided the purchase involvement continuum into three categories—nominal, limited, and extended. These correspond closely to the straight rebuy, modified rebuy, and new task purchase situations shown in Table 19–2.

**Straight Rebuy**    This situation occurs when the purchase is of minor importance and is not complex. This is generally the case when reordering basic supplies and component parts. In such cases, the reordering process may be completely automated or done routinely by clerical personnel. Such purchases are often handled under a contract that is reviewed and perhaps rebid periodically. Price or reliability tend to be the dominant evaluative criteria. No consideration is given to strategic issues.

**TABLE 19–2**

Organizational
Purchase Situations
and Buying
Responses

|  | Straight Rebuy | Modified Rebuy | New Task |
|---|---|---|---|
| *Situational characteristics* | | | |
| Purchase importance | Low | Moderate | High |
| Choice complexity | Low | Moderate | High |
| *Purchasing characteristics* | | | |
| Size of DMU | Very small | Medium | Large, evolving |
| Level of DMU | Low | Mid-level | Top of organization |
| Time to decision | Very brief | Moderate | Long |
| Information search | None/very limited | Moderate | Extensive |
| Analysis techniques | None/price companions | Several | Extensive, complex |
| Strategic focus | None | Limited | Dominates |

**Modified Rebuy**    This strategy is used when the purchase is moderately important to the firm or the choice is more complex. This typically involves a product or service that the organization is accustomed to purchasing but the product or the firm's needs have changed. Or because the product is important to the firm (it is simple but the firm uses a lot of it or it is an important component of the firm's output), the firm may periodically reevaluate brands or suppliers. The DMU is likely to include several representatives, including some midlevel managers. More information is gathered and more evaluative criteria are analyzed. Strategic issues also begin to play a role.

**New Task**    This approach tends to occur when the buying decision is very important and the choice is quite complex. This would involve decisions on such things as an initial sales automation system or a new advertising agency. The buying organization will typically have had little experience with the decision and perhaps with the product or service. The DMU is likely to be large and evolve over time. Top management will be involved in the decision, and strategic issues will be of prime importance. The time involved is frequently quite long; for example, from problem recognition to implementation of a sales automation system typically takes 21 to 30 months.

Clearly, the marketing strategy and tactics for one particular type of purchase situation would be inappropriate for others. Thus, marketers must understand the purchase task confronting their organizational consumers and develop appropriate marketing strategies.

## Steps in the Organizational Decision Process

Because organizational decisions typically involve more individuals in more complex decision tasks than do individual or household decisions, marketing efforts to affect this process are much more complex.[8] Shown in Table 19–3 are the likely stages in the decision process and sources of influence at each stage in a large company's decision to acquire a new customer relationship management (CRM) system. Obviously, such decisions won't be made the same way for every organization. However, the key here is recognizing that this is a new task buy situation in which the DMU will involve many sources of influence, with varying criteria, varying levels of power, and varying media habits. The company trying to sell the CRM system must provide relevant information to each source of influence in order to be successful. This is no easy task in such a complex and large DMU.

**Problem Recognition**    In Table 19–3, the sales manager and director of operations play the key role in recognizing the need. Triggers for this problem recognition could be numerous including conflicts between field sales agents and sales assistants, ongoing customer service problems identified by field sales agents or customers themselves and passed on to the sales manager.

TABLE 19–3

Decision Process in
Purchasing a New
CRM System

| Stages of the Purchase Decision Process | Key Influences within Decision-Making Unit | Influences Outside the Decision-Making Unit |
|---|---|---|
| Problem recognition | Director of operations<br>Sales manager | Field sales agents<br>Administrative staff<br>Sales assistants<br>CRM sales representative |
| Information search | Data/CRM specialist<br>Director of operations<br>Purchasing manager | Operations personnel<br>CRM sales representative<br>Other corporate users<br>Office systems consultant |
| Alternative evaluation | Vice president of sales<br>Data/CRM specialist<br>Director of operations<br>Sales manager<br>Purchasing manager | Office systems consultant<br>CRM sales representative |
| Purchase decision | General management<br>Vice president of sales<br>Purchasing manager | |
| Product usage | Director of operations<br>Sales manager | Field sales agents<br>Administrative staff<br>Sales assistants<br>CRM sales representative |
| Evaluation | Director of operations<br>Sales manager<br>Vice president of sales<br>General management | Field sales agents<br>Administrative staff<br>Sales assistants |

Table 19–4 shows that in high-tech markets, the head of a department is most likely to recognize a problem or need to purchase. Perhaps more important is that purchasing managers are not a source of problem recognition. This points out the danger of salespeople calling on purchasing agents only. As shown in Table 19–4, problem recognition and determining specifications often occur without much involvement of purchasing personnel.

**Information Search**    Information search can be both formal and informal.[9] Site visits to evaluate a potential vendor, laboratory tests of a new product or prototype, and investigation of possible product specifications are part of formal information search. Informal

TABLE 19–4    Group Involvement in the Decision Process in High-Tech Organization

| | Percent Involved in Each Stage of Decision Process | | | | | |
|---|---|---|---|---|---|---|
| Stages of Decision Process | Board of Directors | Top Management | Head of Department | Lab Technician or Operator | Purchasing Manager or Buyer | Finance Manager or Accountant |
| Recognizing the need to purchase | 7% | 26% | 70% | 30% | 0% | 3% |
| Determining product specifications | 0 | 33 | 74 | 33 | 3 | 0 |
| Deciding which suppliers to consider | 3 | 33 | 56 | 14 | 19 | 0 |
| Obtaining quotations and proposals | 0 | 26 | 52 | 19 | 14 | 3 |
| Evaluating quotations and proposals | 7 | 63 | 63 | 3 | 11 | 7 |
| Final product or supplier selection | 21 | 48 | 48 | 7 | 11 | 0 |

Source: Reprinted from R. Abratt, "Industrial Buying in Hi-Tech Markets," *Industrial Marketing Management* 15 (1986), p. 295. Copyright 1986; reprinted with permission from Elsevier Science.

information search can occur during discussions with sales representatives, while attending trade shows, or when reading industry-specific journals. Industrial buyers search for information both to help make the best decision and to support their actions and recommendations within the organization.[10]

For complex technology products, organizational buyers often hire consultants both to provide information and to help evaluate alternatives. Consider the role played by consultants in the purchase of sales automation systems:

> The second step in the buying cycle was to evaluate the potential to automate existing processes. . . . Customers were usually not equipped to do this in-house. It was common for SA consultants to help them. Their deep understanding of the industry, and their skills and experience, made them the best option for this step.
>
> In the third step, the customer decided how the different functions to be automated were related, and determined how data was to be collected, stored, and analyzed. This again was usually done by SA consultants with the support of the customer's information systems department.
>
> The customer decided the type of SA software and hardware to be purchased. . . . Here again, the customer relied heavily on the consultant.[11]

Organizational buyers often search for product and price information on the Internet. The company in Illustration 19–2 even offers an online tool that businesses can

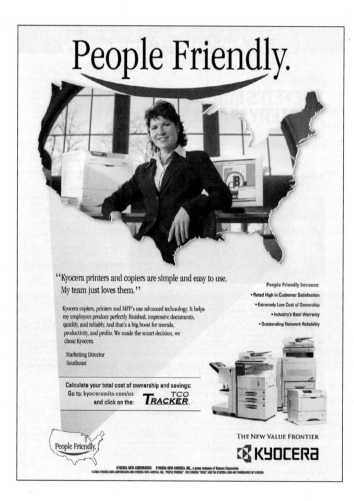

use to determine ownership costs and savings (note that the ad, as shown here, is not full size).

**Evaluation and Selection**    The evaluation of possible vendors and selection of a given vendor often follow a **two-stage decision process.**[12] The first stage is making the buyer's approved vendor list. A conjunctive decision process is very common. In this manner, the organization can screen out potential vendors that do not meet all its minimum criteria. In a government missile purchase, 41 potential manufacturers of a given missile electronics system were first identified. After site visits to inspect manufacturing capability and resources, the organization pared this list of 41 down to 11 that met the government's minimum criteria.

A second stage of organizational decision making could involve other decision rules, such as disjunctive, lexicographic, compensatory, or elimination-by-aspects. For the government purchase discussed above, a lexicographic decision process was next used, with the most important criterion being price. Using this decision rule, the organization selected two vendors.

The process of evaluation and selection is further complicated by the fact that different members of the decision-making unit have differing evaluative criteria.[13] Recall the difference in criteria for imaging systems between hospital administrators and medical professionals described earlier. Table 19–5 shows that purchasing, management, engineering, and operations use differing sets of performance criteria. For example, purchasing is more concerned with pricing policies, terms and conditions, and order status; engineers are more concerned with product knowledge, product operations, and applications knowledge. A salesperson calling on these accounts would need to understand and respond to the unique as well as the shared criteria of these purchase influencers.

It is generally assumed that business purchases are strictly economic, with the goal of maximizing the profits of the purchasing organization.[14] However, power, prestige,

| Evaluative Criteria Used in Purchase Decision | Functional Role in Organization | | | |
|---|---|---|---|---|
| | Purchasing | Management | Engineering | Operations |
| Vendor offers broad line | X | X | | |
| Many product options available | X | X | | |
| Ease of maintenance of equipment | | | X | X |
| Competence of service techniques | | X | X | X |
| Overall quality of service | | X | X | |
| Product warranty | X | X | X | X |
| Delivery (lead time) | | | | X |
| Time needed to install equipment | X | | | X |
| Construction costs | X | | X | X |
| Vendor has lowest price | X | X | X | |
| Financial stability of vendor | X | | X | X |
| Vendor willing to negotiate price | X | | | |
| Vendor reputation for quality | X | X | X | |
| Salesperson competence | | X | X | X |
| Compatibility with equipment | X | X | | |
| Available computer interface | X | | | |

**TABLE 19–5**

Evaluative Criteria and Organizational Role

Source: Adapted from D. H. McQuiston and R. G. Walters, "The Evaluative Criteria of Industrial Buyers: Implications for Sales Training," *Journal of Business and Industrial Marketing,* Summer–Fall 1989, p. 74.

security, and similar noneconomic criteria also play important roles in business purchase decisions.[15] Research finds that there are organizations that buy "green," similar to the "green consumers" described in Chapter 3. These organizations have policies or individual champions for socially responsible buying behavior by the organization.[16] Firms wishing to do business with these organizations must meet their requirements for products produced in an environmentally sound manner. The ad in Illustration 19–3 would appeal to these firms.

Brand image and equity also play a role in the evaluation process for organizations. Obviously, brand can be a surrogate indicator of quality (see Chapter 16). And research suggests that while brand may not always be the most important consideration, it can result in organizational buyers' paying a price premium.[17]

**Purchase and Decision Implementation**    Once the decision to buy from a particular organization has been made, the method of purchase must be determined. From the seller's point of view, this means how and when they will get paid. In many purchases, payment is not made until delivery. Others involve progress payments. For a firm working on the construction of a building or highway or developing a new military aircraft that will take several years, payment timing is critical.

On an international basis, purchase implementation and method of payment are even more critical. Some countries prohibit the removal of capital from their country without an offsetting purchase. This led Caterpillar Tractor Company to sell earthmoving equipment in South America in exchange for raw materials, such as copper, which it could sell or use in its manufacturing operations.

**Terms and conditions**—payments, warranties, delivery dates, and so forth—are both complex and critical in business-to-business markets. One U.S. manufacturer of steam turbines lost a large order to a foreign manufacturer because its warranty was written too much to the advantage of the seller.

Firms marketing to organizations increasingly use the Internet to sell their products directly to customers or through online wholesalers (see Illustration 19–4).[18] They also use it to generate leads for telephone or direct sales calls and to solicit orders either on the Internet or via an 800 number.

**Usage and Postpurchase Evaluation**    After-purchase evaluations of products are typically more formal for organizational purchases than are household evaluations of purchases. In mining applications, for example, a product's life is broken down into different components such that total life-cycle cost can be assessed. Many mines will operate different brands of equipment side by side to determine the life-cycle costs of each before repurchasing one in larger quantities.

A major component of postpurchase evaluation is the service the seller provides during and after the sale.[19] Table 19–6 indicates the importance that one group of customers and managers assigned to different aspects of after-sales service. Notice that the managers did not have a very good understanding of what was important to their customers. Clearly, this firm needs a better understanding of its customers' needs.

Similar to households, dissatisfied organizational buyers may switch suppliers or engage in negative word-of-mouth communications.[20] Firms marketing to organizations pursue strategies similar to those followed by consumer marketers in dealing with dissatisfied customers. They seek to minimize dissatisfaction and to encourage those who become dissatisfied to complain to them and to no one else.[21]

Otis Elevator uses customer problems and a sophisticated database not only to increase customer satisfaction but to improve the design and functioning of its elevators. Below is

**ILLUSTRATION 19–4**

The Internet is a major source of supply for many organizational buyers.

TABLE 19–6 Customer and Management Perceptions of the Importance of After-Sale Services

| After-Sales Service Item | Importance of Service Item | | | Ratings of Service | | |
|---|---|---|---|---|---|---|
| | Customers | Managers | Gap | Customers | Managers | Gap |
| Attitude and behavior of technician | 11.5 | 8.4 | 3.1 | 7.04 | 7.56 | −0.52 |
| Availability of technical service staff | 16.1 | 12.9 | 3.2 | 7.64 | 8.12 | −0.48 |
| Repair time when service needed | 15.4 | 17.4 | −2.0 | 6.36 | 7.71 | −1.35 |
| Dispatch of breakdown call | 15.5 | 9.8 | 5.7 | 6.92 | 7.57 | −0.65 |
| Availability of spare parts during call | 10.0 | 10.1 | −0.1 | 7.16 | 7.49 | −0.33 |
| Service contract options | 5.2 | 6.8 | −1.6 | 6.88 | 7.48 | −0.60 |
| Price–performance ratio for services rendered | 8.1 | 14.5 | −6.4 | 6.12 | 7.30 | −1.18 |
| Response time when service needed | 18.2 | 20.1 | −1.9 | 5.92 | 7.09 | −1.17 |

Source: Reprinted from H. Kasper and J. Lemmink. "After-Sales Service Quality: Views between Industrial Customers and Service Managers," *Industrial Marketing Management* 18 (1989), p. 203, with permission from Elsevier.

an excerpt regarding their OTISLINE service center:

> Imagine you are a building maintenance supervisor. It is 5 o'clock in the morning. You awaken and prepare to go to work. Unbeknownst to you, one of the elevators in your building has had a malfunction. If ignored, it could cause a bigger problem, delaying thousands of people on their way to their office suite. As you make your coffee, the monitoring system on the elevator detects the problem and makes a service call. Even before you get on the road to the office, a mechanic has arrived with the part and fixed the glitch. You enter, board the same elevator and know nothing about the problem until you pass the Otis mechanic on his way out the door.
>
> The preceding scenario could be a true story written by Otis Elevator, thanks to the OTISLINE system. Simply put, OTISLINE is a communications service center for customers. Operators work 24 hours a day, handling emergency calls, dispatching mechanics and entering and updating information on the elevators. Close to 1.35 million elevators are handled by Otis call centers at 325 locations around the globe.[22]

*Relationship marketing* is at least as important in industrial marketing as it is in consumer marketing.[23] The basic idea at the organizational level is for the seller to work closely with the buyer over time with the objective of enhancing the buyer's profits or operations while also making a profit. Consumer Insight 19–1 examines various dimensions of organizational relationships, the perceptual gaps between buyer and seller, and relationship evolution over time.

## The Internet's Role in the Organizational Decision Process

Just as the Internet has become a major force in consumer decisions, so too is it an important tool in organizations. In fact, business-to-business (B-to-B) e-commerce in the United States is estimated at over $6 trillion and represents a substantial proportion of all B-to-B sales.[24] As we have seen, the Internet can play a variety of roles in the decision process from lead generation, to information provision, to efficient and automated order fulfillment.[25] Yankelovich and Harris Interactive surveyed purchasers and purchase influencers within organizations about the Internet's role relative to other sources for "providing information," and "influencing/supporting decisions." The percentages are those who said a source was either somewhat or extremely valuable:[26]

## Organizational Relationship Dimensions

Both buyers and sellers have perceptions of the quality or health of a relationship.[27] Clearly delivered performance of the core product or service is critical. But additional dimensions matter as well. One study examined the following four dimensions of organizational relationships:

- *Legitimacy and Compatibility.* This dimension deals with actual delivered quality, perceived quality as represented by brand reputation, as well as trust and reliability.
- *Social Relations.* This dimension deals with friendship, closeness, and the extent of buyer–seller communication.
- *Economic and Shared Values.* This dimension deals with the extent to which buyer and seller are integrated through joint manufacturing, information technology, and values.
- *Learning Bonds.* This dimension deals with the extent to which buyer and seller cooperate in learning through joint research and development, staff exchanges, and training.

The researchers found that while buyers and sellers placed very similar importance on each of these dimensions, there were perceptual gaps between buyers and sellers regarding how the relationship was actually performing. The table shows these gaps.

Notice how sellers tend to think the relationship is stronger or healthier than do buyers but that these gaps tend to go away the longer the relationship lasts.

| Relationship Length | Buyer | Seller |
|---|---|---|
| *Short Term* | | |
| Legitimacy/compatibility | 4.9 | 5.7* |
| Social | 4.7 | 5.2* |
| Economic/shared values | 4.5 | 4.8 |
| Learning | 2.8 | 3.1 |
| *Medium Term* | | |
| Legitimacy/compatibility | 4.9 | 5.4* |
| Social | 4.8 | 4.9 |
| Economic/shared values | 4.5 | 4.7 |
| Learning | 3.3 | 2.9 |
| *Long Term* | | |
| Legitimacy/compatibility | 5.4 | 5.3 |
| Social | 5.2 | 5.4 |
| Economic/shared values | 5.1 | 5.0 |
| Learning | 3.8 | 3.4 |

Note: Higher numbers mean higher perceived performance, with asterisk denoting dimensions on which buyers' and sellers' differences are statistically significant.

Source: Adapted from B. R. Barnes et al., "Perceptual Gaps and Similarities in Buyer–Seller Dyadic Relationships," *Industrial Marketing Management* 36 (2007), p. 667.

### Critical Thinking Questions

1. Why is it important to go beyond core product and service importance in understanding organizational relationships?

2. Should all organizational relationships involve high levels of integration in terms of manufacturing, research and development, and so on? Explain.

3. What explains the fact that buyer–seller gaps seem to disappear as relationships move from short term to long term?

| | Information | Decision |
|---|---|---|
| B-to-B magazines | 56% | 51% |
| B-to-B trade shows | 51 | 49 |
| Salespeople | 48 | 47 |
| B-to-B Web sites | 47 | 44 |
| Professional organizations | 44 | 40 |
| Online database services | 34 | 29 |
| Newspapers | 34 | 23 |
| General business press | 17 | 11 |
| Television business networks | 15 | 11 |

Source: *Business-to-Business Media Study Final Report* (October 14, 2001), p. 14. © American Business Media.

As this information shows, the Internet rivals salespeople, trade shows, and trade magazines as a source of information and influence. In terms of Web site design, recent research suggests that site organization (ease of navigation), customization, privacy/security, information value, and personalization are important drivers of B-to-B Web site effectiveness.[28] These characteristics are similar to those found to be important in business-to-consumer (B-to-C) contexts (see Chapter 17).

Having examined organizational purchasing behavior in some detail, let us now apply the remainder of our revised model to further our understanding of organizations as consumers.

# ORGANIZATIONAL CULTURE

At the hub of our consumer model of buyer behavior is self-concept and lifestyle. Organizations also have a type of self-concept in the beliefs and attitudes the organization members have about the organization and how it operates. Likewise, organizations have a type of lifestyle in that they have distinct ways of operating. We characterize these two aspects of an organization as its **organizational culture** (see Figure 19–1). Organizational culture is much like lifestyle in that organizations vary dramatically in how they make decisions and how they approach problems involving risk, innovation, and change.[29] The term **corporate culture** is often used to refer to the organizational culture of a business firm.

Organizational culture reflects and shapes organizational needs and desires, which in turn influence how organizations make decisions. For example, the Environmental Protection Agency, the Red Cross, and IBM are three large organizations. Each has a different organizational culture that influences how it gathers information, processes information, and makes decisions.

# EXTERNAL FACTORS INFLUENCING ORGANIZATIONAL CULTURE

## Firmographics

We discussed earlier the important role of consumer demographics in understanding consumer behavior. Firmographics are equally important. **Firmographics** involve both *organization characteristics*—for example, size, activities, objectives, location, and industry category—*and characteristics of the composition of the organization*—for example, gender, age, education, and income distribution of employees.

Size    Large organizations are more likely to have a variety of specialists who attend to purchasing, finance, marketing, and general management; in smaller organizations, one or two individuals may have these same responsibilities. Larger organizations are generally more complex because more individuals participate in managing the organization's operations. That there are often multiple individuals involved in the purchase decision in a large organization means advertising and sales force efforts must be targeted at various functions in the firm. Each message might need to emphasize issues of concern only to that function. The same purchase decision in a smaller firm might involve only the owner or manager. Different media would be required to reach this person, and one message would need to address all the key purchase issues.

Activities and Objectives    The activities and objectives of organizations influence their style and behavior. For example, the Navy, in procuring an avionics system for a new

| General Organizational Objective | Nature of Organizational Activity | | |
|---|---|---|---|
| | Routine | Complex | Technical |
| Commercial | Office management | Human resource management | New-product development |
| Governmental | Highway maintenance | Tax collection | Space exploration |
| Nonprofit | Fund-raising | Increase number of national parks | Organ donor program |
| Cooperative | Compile industry statistics | Establish industry standards | Applied research |

**TABLE 19-7**

Organizational Activities Based on Organizational Objective and Nature of Activity

fighter plane, operates differently than Boeing does in purchasing a similar system for a commercial aircraft. The Navy is a government organization carrying out a public objective, whereas Boeing seeks a commercial objective at a profit.

Table 19–7 is a matrix that provides examples of the interface between broad organizational objectives and activities. Organizational objectives can be categorized as commercial, governmental, nonprofit, and cooperative. The general nature of organizational activity is described as routine, complex, or technical. For example, a government organization purchasing highway maintenance services would operate differently from a government organization procuring missiles. Likewise, a cooperative wholesale organization set up as a buying cooperative for several retailers would have a different organizational culture from a cooperative research institute set up by firms in the semiconductor industry. And a nonprofit organization involved in organ donations is likely to differ from one organized to gather industry statistics.

Commercial firms can be usefully divided into public firms (stock is widely traded) and private firms (one or a few individuals own a controlling share of the firm). In public firms, management is generally expected to operate the firm in a manner that will maximize the economic gains of the shareholders. These organizations face consistent pressures to make economically sound, if not optimal, decisions.

However, about half of all business purchases involve privately held firms whose CEO is often the controlling shareholder. In this situation, the firm can and frequently does pursue objectives other than profit maximization. One study found that the following motives drive the management of such firms:[30]

- Building a place for the entire family to work and be involved.
- Having complete, autocratic control over an environment.
- Build a lasting "empire."
- Becoming wealthy.
- Doing what the family expects.
- Avoiding corporations or working for others.
- Obtaining status.
- Improving the world or the environment.

Segmenting these firms according to the motives of the owners is a useful approach for developing sales messages. For example, Micron Electronics targeted the owners and managers of smaller, entrepreneurial firms. Its ads positioned it as understanding and caring about the needs and concerns of these individuals more than the larger firms do. One ad stated, "They wouldn't give you the time of day. They said you weren't a player. . . . They're holding on line three." The firm in Illustration 19–5 is also clearly targeting this group with an ad designed to appeal to concerns regarding long-term wealth management.

**Location**   As we saw in Chapter 5, there are a number of regional subcultures in the United States. These subcultures influence organizational cultures as well as individual lifestyles. For example, firms on the West Coast tend to be more informal in their operations than those on the East Coast. Dress is more casual, relationships are less formalized, and business is on more of a personal level in the West than elsewhere in the country. The Midwest and South also have unique business styles. Marketing communications and sales force training need to reflect these differences.

Location-based differences are magnified when doing business in foreign cultures. Firms that open branches outside their home countries frequently experience some difficulties managing the workforce and operating within the local community. Selling to organizations outside a firm's home culture poses as many challenges as selling to households in that culture (see Chapter 2). For example:

> To get a bank in China's Sichuan province last year to buy more than 100 ATMs, Diebold had to offer the bank 23 units for free. Diebold's distributor was coerced into buying a floor in a building the bank had invested in. And the distributor, as well as Thorpe McConville, Diebold's general manager and CEO, and Kevin Wu, a deputy GM, needed to get approval from 10 people in a variety of the bank's departments. "You've always got to meet with 8 to 12 people, all of whom have a different agenda," Wu says. "And you've got to be prepared for political chaos." The sales cycle took six months. McConville paid four visits to Sichuan, each time taking the prospects out for lunch, dinner, or karaoke.[31]

**Industry Category**   Two firms can be similar in terms of size (large), location (Illinois), activity (manufacturing), objective (profit), and ownership (public), and still have sharply differing cultures due in part to being in differing industries. If one of the two firms described above manufactured heavy equipment and the other, computers, we would expect differing cultures to exist.

**Organization Composition**    Organization cultures influence the behaviors and values of those who work in the organizations. However, the types of individuals who work in the organization also heavily influence organization cultures. An organization composed primarily of young, highly educated, technically oriented people (say, a software engineering firm) will have a different culture from an organization composed primarily of older, highly educated, nontechnical individuals (say, an insurance firm). While the culture of most organizations is influenced more by the characteristics of the founder and top managers, the overall composition of the organizational membership is also important.[32]

**Macrosegmentation**    Organizations with distinguishing firmographics can be grouped into market segments through a process called **macrosegmentation.** These segments, based on differences in needs due to firmographics, are called *macrosegments.*[33] Micron Electronics' decision to focus on smaller firms, described earlier, is an example. First Chicago Bank stated,

> We've tried too long to be everything to everyone. We're in the process of rolling out a strategy in all our branches where we segment customers and tailor our marketing campaigns to those segments.

Two of the macrosegments the bank is targeting are midsized and small businesses. Each segment will have a marketing team that focuses on that segment.[34]

## Culture/Government

Variations in values and behaviors across cultures affect organizations as well as individuals.[35] For example, in most American firms, shareholder or owner wealth is a dominant decision criterion. Corporate downsizing has resulted in hundreds of thousands of workers and managers losing their jobs in order to enhance profitability. These actions have been acceptable in American society. Similar corporate behavior would not be accepted in much of Europe or Japan. In these societies, worker welfare is often on a par with or above concern about corporate profit. Plant closure laws, layoff regulations, and worker benefits tend to be much higher than in America.

In America, Japan, and most of Europe, bribery and similar approaches for making sales are not acceptable, and these governments enforce a wide array of laws prohibiting such behaviors. In America, both the legal and social constraints against bribery are strong enough to make corporate gift giving from a supplier to a buyer difficult or impossible.[36] In other parts of the world, "bribes" are an expected part of many business transactions. This poses a difficult ethical dilemma for firms doing business in these regions. Ignoring any legal constraints imposed by the American government, *should an American firm provide an expensive "gift" to the purchasing agent in a foreign country where it is common knowledge that such gifts are essential to do business with the country's firms?*

In many parts of the world, businesses and governments are partners or at least work closely together. In the United States, an arm's-length or even adversarial relationship is more common. One example of this was Microsoft's battle with the U.S. government regarding anti-competitive practices. *How do you think this might have influenced Microsoft's culture over time?*

# Reference Groups

Reference groups influence organizational behavior and purchasing decisions. Perhaps the most powerful type of reference group in industrial markets is that of lead users. **Lead users** are *innovative organizations that derive a great deal of their success from leading change*. As a result, their adoption of a new product, service, technology, or manufacturing process is watched and often emulated by the majority.[37] This statement from a Hewlett-Packard salesperson illustrates their role:

> Another aspect of hospital buying behavior is the role of key accounts. A pyramid of influence operates in this market, with smaller and medium-sized hospitals often relying on larger research and teaching hospitals for technology cues. Therefore, maintaining a strong position in influential hospitals is critical.[38]

Other reference groups such as trade associations, financial analysts, and dealer organizations, also influence an organization's decision to buy or not buy a given product, or to buy or not buy from a given supplier. **Reference group infrastructure** refers to *the flow of purchase influence within an industry*. As an example, the success of a new technology product depends on how the firm influences the reference groups located along the continuum separating it from its market. The more the firm gains positive endorsement or use throughout this infrastructure, the greater its chances of customers' treating it as a preferred source of supply.

If we combine the concept of lead users with reference group infrastructure, as shown in Figure 19–2, we have a more comprehensive picture of organizational reference group systems. Because the lead users play such a critical role, their adoption of a product,

| FIGURE 19–2 | Combining Lead User and Infrastructure Reference Groups |
|---|---|

Source: Roger Best and Reinhard Angelihard, "Strategies for Leveraging a Technology Advantage," *Handbook of Business Strategy*, 1988.

technology, or vendor can influence the overall infrastructure in two powerful ways. First, a lead-user's decision to adopt a given supplier's innovative product adds credibility to the product and supplier. This in turn has a strong positive impact on the infrastructure that stands between the firm and its remaining target customers. Second, a lead-user decision to purchase will have a direct impact on firms inclined to follow market trends.

The strategy implication of this is clear. Marketers of new industrial products, particularly technology products, should focus initial efforts on securing sales to visible lead users.

# INTERNAL FACTORS INFLUENCING ORGANIZATIONAL CULTURE

## Organizational Values

Hewlett-Packard and Apple Computer both manufacture and market computers. However, each organization has a distinct organizational culture. Hewlett-Packard is corporate, formal, and takes itself seriously. Apple is less formal, creative, and promotes a more open organizational culture. Marketing managers must understand these differences in order to best serve the respective organizational needs.

As you examine the eight common business values shown below, think of how Hewlett-Packard might differ from Apple, Macy's from Target, Amazon.com from Buy.com, or FedEx from the U.S. Postal Service. Each is a large organization, but each has a unique set of values that underlies its organizational culture. To the degree that organizations differ on these values, a firm marketing to them will have to adapt its marketing approach.

1. Risk taking is admired and rewarded.
2. Competition is more important than cooperation.
3. Hard work comes first, leisure second.
4. Individual efforts take precedence over collective efforts.
5. Any problem can be solved.
6. Active decision making is essential.
7. Change is positive and is actively sought.
8. Performance is more important than rank or status.

The values as stated above are representative of an innovative organization that seeks change, views problems as opportunities, and rewards individual efforts.[39] It is hard to imagine the U.S. Postal Service or many other bureaucratic organizations encouraging such values. On the other hand, these values underlie many high-technology start-up organizations.

The ad in Illustration 19–6 would appeal to organizations and individuals with an orientation toward efficiency and active problem solving.

## Perception

To process information, a firm must go through the same sequential stages of exposure, attention, and interpretation as consumers. Of course, given the

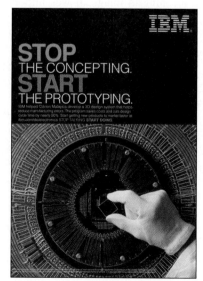

**ILLUSTRATION 19–6**

Ads should appeal to the values of the organizations they are targeting. This ad will appeal to businesses and individuals that value efficiency and active problem solving.

more complex nature of organizations, the processes involved are also more complex.[40]
A business customer develops certain images of seller organizations from their products,
people, and organizational activities. Like people, organizations have memories and base
their decisions on images or memories they have developed. Once an image is formed by
an organization, it is very difficult to change. Therefore, it is important for an organization to develop a sound communications strategy to build and reinforce a desired image or
brand position.[41]

Illustration 19–7 shows an ad from 3M's 1, 2, 3M campaign, which was very successful. The challenge was to unify 3M's 60,000 products and provide the organization with
a meaningful image. It was important to show that not only are 3M products exciting
technologically but they are useful and make a difference in peoples' lives. The campaign was highly successful in the United States, France, Latin America, and Australia.
Research showed that perception of 3M as an innovative company with innovative products went from 10 to 51 percent, overall favorable impression of 3M increased from 65 to
85 percent, and the likelihood of recommending 3M and its products moved from 71 to
91 percent.[42]

Ad size and repetition have a positive effect on awareness and action. One major study
found a 20 percent gain in awareness when two or more ads are placed in the same issue
of a specialized business magazine compared with only one.[43] The size of the advertisement also affects action in the form of inquiries generated by the advertisement. Research
examining business-to-business magazine advertisements shows that full-page ads are
much more effective at generating inquiries than smaller ads.

The potential power of industrial advertising can be seen in its impact on sales of an
industrial safety product. Sales in the first year of the ad campaign increased almost four-
fold, with advertising in one trade publication using an eight-page advertising schedule:
six black-and-white ads and two color ads. When three color spreads were added to the
schedule, sales continued to climb. When ad frequency was again increased, this time to

six black-and-white single-page ads and 11 color spreads, product sales rose to 6.7 times pre-campaign sales.[44]

While advertising plays an important role in communicating to organizations, direct sales calls are the most important element of the communications mix in most industrial markets. This is the case despite the high cost of such calls, which is thought to be in the range of $300 per call.

One reason for the significant role of salespeople is that businesses are not just economic entities. Business buyers prefer to do business with firms they know, like, and trust. Those relationships are most often formed between members of the firms involved, with sales personnel being the most common representative of the selling organization. As one successful salesperson stated:

> You have to have a great product but you also have to make the customer like you as a salesperson.[45]

## Learning

Like individuals, organizations learn through their experiences and perceptions.[46] Positive experiences with vendors are rewarding and tend to be repeated. Purchasing processes and procedures that prove effective tend to be institutionalized in rules and policies. Likewise, negative experiences with vendors produce learning and avoidance behavior, and purchasing procedures that don't work are generally discarded. Developing the capacity to learn efficiently is increasingly a key to organizational success.[47]

## Motives and Emotions

Organizational decisions tend to be less emotional than many consumer purchase decisions. However, because humans with psychological needs and emotions influence these decisions, this aspect of marketing to an organizational customer cannot be overlooked or underestimated.

Quite often there is considerable personal or career risk in organizational purchase decisions. The risk of making a bad purchase decision can elicit feelings of self-doubt or psychological discomfort. These are personal emotions that will influence purchase decisions. FedEx appeals to risk avoidance with ads that ask, in essence,

> How do you explain to your boss that the important papers didn't arrive but you saved the company $5 by using a less expensive overnight mail service?

## SUMMARY

Like households, organizations make many buying decisions. In some instances, these buying decisions are routine replacement decisions; at other times, they involve new, complex purchase decisions. Three purchase situations are common to organizational buying: *straight rebuy, modified rebuy,* and *new task.* Each of these purchase situations will elicit different organizational behaviors.

The organizational decision process involves problem recognition, information search, evaluation and selection, purchase implementation, and postpurchase evaluation. As with household decisions, the Internet is an important element across various phases of the organizational decision process, including the information search and decision phases. A conjunctive process is typical in establishing an evoked set, and other decision rules are used for selecting a specific vendor. While functional attributes such as price and quality certainly play a critical role, brand image can also be important, in some cases even increasing the prices that organizational buyers are willing to pay.

Purchase implementation is more complex and the terms and conditions more important than in household decisions. How payment is made is of major importance. Finally, use and postpurchase evaluation are often quite formal. Many organizations will conduct detailed in-use tests to determine the life-cycle costs of competing products or spend considerable time evaluating a new product before placing large orders. Satisfaction depends on a variety of criteria and on the opinions of many different people. To achieve customer satisfaction, each of these individuals has to be satisfied with the criteria important to him or her.

Organizations have a style or manner of operating that we characterize as organizational culture. *Firmographics* (organization characteristics such as size, activities, objectives, location, and industry category, and characteristics of the composition of the organization such as the gender, age, education, and income distribution of employees) have a major influence on organizational culture. The process of grouping buyer organizations into market segments on the basis of similar firmographics is called *macrosegmentation*.

Reference groups play a key role in business-to-business markets. *Reference group infrastructures* exist in most organizational markets. These reference groups often include third-party suppliers, distributors, industry experts, trade publications, financial analysts, and key customers. *Lead users* have been shown to be a key reference group that influences both the reference group infrastructure and other potential users.

Other external influences on organizational culture include the local culture in which the organization operates and the type of government it confronts. Internal factors affecting organizational culture include organizational values, perception, learning, memory, motives, and emotions.

Organizations hold values that influence the organization's style. Individuals in the organization also hold these values in varying degrees. Organizations also develop images, have motives, and learn. Seller organizations can affect how they are perceived through a variety of communication alternatives. Print advertising, direct mail, sales calls, and the Internet are common. Whereas organizations have rational motives, their decisions are influenced and made by people with emotions. A seller organization has to understand and satisfy both to be successful.

## KEY TERMS

Buying centers  670
Corporate culture  680
Decision-making units
     (DMUs)  670

Firmographics  680
Lead users  684
Macrosegmentation  683
Organizational culture  680

Reference group infrastructure  684
Terms and conditions  676
Two-stage decision process  675

## INTERNET EXERCISES

1. Evaluate the Otis Elevator Web site (www.otis.com).
2. Visit Sun Microsystem's Web site (www.sun.com). How does their site leverage the power of reference groups in an organizational setting?
3. Evaluate *Advertising Age*'s Web site (www.adage.com).
4. Pick an industrial market and compare the Web sites of three firms. Which is best? Why?

## REVIEW QUESTIONS

1. How can an organization have a culture? What factors contribute to different organizational cultures?
2. How would different organizational activities and objectives affect organizational culture?

3. What are *organizational values*? How do they differ from personal values?

4. What are *firmographics* and how do they influence organizational culture?

5. Define *macrosegmentation* and describe the variables used to create a macrosegmentation of an organizational market.

6. What types of reference groups exist in organizational markets?

7. What are *lead users* and how do they influence word-of-mouth communication and the sales of a new product?

8. What is a *decision-making unit*? How does it vary by purchase situation?

9. How can a seller organization influence perceptions of a buyer organization?

10. What are *organizational motives*?

11. What is a *two-stage decision process*?

12. Why is purchase implementation a critical part of the organizational decision process?

13. What are the three purchase situations commonly encountered by organizations? How do organizations typically respond to each situation?

14. In what ways does the Internet play a role in the organizational decision process?

## DISCUSSION QUESTIONS

15. Describe three organizations with distinctly different organizational cultures. Explain why they have different organizational cultures and the factors that have helped shape the style of each.

16. Respond to the questions in Consumer Insight 19-1.

17. Describe how Hewlett-Packard might vary in its organizational culture from the following. Justify your response.
    a. Dell Computer
    b. Compaq
    c. Apple

18. Discuss how the following pairs differ from each other in terms of organizational activities and objectives. Discuss how these differences influence organizational cultures.
    a. Wal-Mart, Target
    b. DHL, the US Post Office
    c. Buy.com, Banana Republic
    d. Mercedes Benz, Kraft Foods

19. What role does brand/brand image play in the organizational decision process?

20. Discuss how Compaq might use a macrosegmentation strategy to sell computers to businesses.

21. Discuss how a small biotechnology firm could influence the reference group infrastructure and the lead users to accelerate adoption of its products in the market.

22. "Industrial purchases, unlike consumer purchases, do not have an emotional component." Comment.

23. For each of the three purchase situations described in the chapter (Table 19–2), describe a typical purchase for the following:
    a. Wendy's
    b. A local radio station
    c. Target
    d. Your university
    e. Rite Aid drugstores

## APPLICATION ACTIVITIES

24. Interview an appropriate person at a large and at a small organization, and ask each to identify purchase situations that could be described as straight rebuy, modified rebuy, and new task. For each organization and purchase situation, determine the following:
    a. Size and functional representation of the decision-making unit
    b. The number of choice criteria considered
    c. Length of the decision process
    d. Number of vendors or suppliers considered

25. Review two issues of a magazine targeting organization buyers or purchase influencers. What percent of the ads contain emotional or other noneconomic appeals?

26. Interview a representative from a commercial, governmental, and nonprofit organization. For each,

determine its firmographics, activities, and objectives. Then relate these differences to differences in the organizational cultures of the organizations.

27. Interview a person responsible for purchasing for a business or government agency. Have that person describe and evaluate any attempts at relationship marketing by its suppliers. What do you conclude?

28. For a given organization, identify its reference groups. Create a hierarchical diagram, as shown in Figure 19–2, and discuss how this organization could influence groups that would in turn create favorable communication concerning this organization.

29. Interview a manager at a business or government agency who has recently been involved in an important purchase decision (e.g., a capital equipment acquisition). Have them describe the key influences at each phase of the decision process as shown in Table 19–3. Discuss how this information might be used in developing a marketing strategy for this industry.

## REFERENCES

1. J. Gilbert, "Small but Mighty," *Sales & Marketing Management,* January 2004, pp. 30–35.

2. D. Tynan, "Tech Advantage," *Sales & Marketing Management,* April 2004, pp. 46–51.

3. B. Lamons, "Even Small Companies Can Build Big Brands," *Marketing News,* October 27, 2003, pp. 7–8.

4. See J. Park, P. Tansuhaj, and E. R. Spangenberg, "An Emotion-Based Perspective of Family Purchase Decisions," *Advances in Consumer Research,* vol. 22, eds. F. R. Kardes and M. Sujan (Provo, UT: Association for Consumer Research, 1995), pp. 723–28.

5. F. V. Cespedes, "Hewlett-Packard Imaging Systems Division," Harvard Business School case 9-593-080, September 6, 1994, p. 4.

6. R. Ventakesh, A. K. Kohli, and G. Zaltman, "Influence Strategies in Buying Centers," *Journal of Marketing,* October 1995, pp. 71–82; and M. A. Farrell and B. Schroder, "Influence Strategies in Organizational Buying Decisions," *Industrial Marketing Management* 25 (1996), pp. 393–403.

7. See W. J. Johnson and J. E. Lewin, "Organizational Buying Behavior," *Journal of Business Research,* January 1996, pp. 1–15; and E. J. Wilson, R. C. McMurrian, and A. G. Woodside, "How Buyers Frame Problems," *Psychology & Marketing,* June 2001, pp. 617–55. See also L. C. Leonidou, "Industrial Buyers' Influence Strategies," *Journal of Business and Industrial Marketing* 21, no. 1 (2005), pp. 33–42.

8. S. J. Puri and C. M. Sashi, "Anatomy of a Complex Computer Purchase," *Industrial Marketing Management,* January 1994, pp. 17–27; and E. Day and J. C. Barksdale, Jr., "Organizational Purchasing of Professional Services," *Journal of Business and Industrial Marketing* 9, no. 3 (1994), pp. 44–51.

9. See A. M. Weiss and J. B. Heide, "The Nature of Organizational Search in High-Technology Markets," *Journal of Marketing Research,* May 1993, pp. 220–33.

10. P. M. Doney and G. M. Armstrong, "Effects of Accountability on Symbolic Information Search and Information Analysis by Organizational Buyers," *Journal of the Academy of Marketing Science,* Winter 1996, pp. 57–65; and P. L. Dawes, D. Y. Lee, and D. Midgley, "Organizational Learning in High-Technology Purchasing Situations," *Industrial Marketing Management* 36, 2007, pp. 285–99.

11. D. Narayandas, "SalesSoft, Inc.," Harvard Business School case 9-596-112, March 24, 1998.

12. J. B. Heide and W. M. Weiss, "Vendor Consideration and Switching Behavior for Buyers in High-Technology Markets," *Journal of Marketing,* July 1995, pp. 30–43.

13. J. E. Stoddard and E. F. Fern, "Buying Group Choice," *Psychology & Marketing,* January 2002, pp. 59–90.

14. See K. N. Thompson, B. J. Coe, and J. R. Lewis, "Gauging the Value of Suppliers' Products," *Journal of Business and Industrial Marketing* 9, no. 2 (1994), pp. 29–40.

15. See, e.g., A. Kumar and D. B. Grisaffe, "Effects of Extrinsic Attributes on Perceived Quality, Customer Value, and Behavioral Intentions in B2B Settings," *Journal of Business-to-Business Marketing* 11, no. 4 (2004), pp. 43–63.

16. M. E. Drumwright, "Socially Responsible Organizational Buying," *Journal of Marketing,* July 1994, pp. 1–19. See also D. Pujari, K. Peattie, and G. Wright, "Organizational Antecedents of Environmental Responsiveness in Industrial New Product Development," *Industrial Marketing Management* 33 (2004), pp. 381–91.

17. M. Bendixen et al., "Brand Equity in the Business-to-Business Market," *Industrial Marketing Management* 33 (2004), pp. 371–80. See also P. Michell, J. King, and J. Reast, "Brand Values Related to Industrial Products," *Industrial Marketing Management* 30 (2001), pp. 415–25.

18. See, e.g., G. S. Lynn et al., "Factors Impacting the Adoption and Effectiveness of the World Wide Web in Marketing," *Industrial Marketing Management* 31 (2002), pp. 35–49; and H. Min and W. P. Galle, "E-Purchasing," *Industrial Marketing Management* 32 (2003), pp. 227–33.

19. K. Smith, "Service Aspects of Industrial Products," *Industrial Marketing Management* 27 (1998), pp. 83–93.

20. S. Y. Lam et al., "Customer Value, Satisfaction, Loyalty, and Switching Costs," *Journal of the Academy of Marketing Science* 32, no. 3 (2004), pp. 293–311; R. E. Plank and S. J. Newell, "The Effect of Social Conflict on Relationship Loyalty in Business Markets," *Industrial Marketing Management* 36 (2007), pp. 59–67; and C. Jayawardhena, "Outcomes of Service Encounter Quality in a Business-to-Business Context," *Industrial Marketing Management* 36 (2007), pp. 575–88.

21. S. W. Hansen, J. E. Swan, and T. L. Powers, "Encouraging 'Friendly' Complaint Behavior in Industrial Markets," *Industrial Marketing Management* 25 (1996), pp. 271–81.

22. "UTC Products at a Glance: OTISLINE," United Technologies, press release, http://utc.com, accessed July 28, 2008.

23. See, e.g., A. Walter et al., "Functions of Industrial Supplier Relationships and Their Impact on Relationship Quality," *Industrial Marketing Management* 32 (2003), pp. 159–69; J. N. Sheth and R. H. Shah, "Till Death Do Us Part . . . But Not Always," *Industrial Marketing Management* 32 (2003), pp. 627–31; and T. L. Keiningham, T. Perkins-Munn, and H. Evans, "The Impact of Customer Satisfaction on Share-of-Wallet in a Business-to-Business Environment," *Journal of Service Research*, August 2003, pp. 37–50.

24. "B to B E-Commerce," *The Marketing Site,* www.themarketingsite.com, accessed July 29, 2008.

25. H. H. Bauer, M. Grether, and M. Leach, "Building Customer Relations over the Internet," *Industrial Marketing Management* 31 (2002), pp. 155–63; J. B. MacDonald and K. Smith, "The Effects of Technology-Mediated Communication on Industrial Buyer Behavior," *Industrial Marketing Management* 33 (2004), pp. 107–16; G. Easton and L. Araujo, "Evaluating the Impact of B2B E-commerce," *Industrial Marketing Management* 32 (2003), pp. 431–39; and L. M. Hunter et al., "A Classification of Business-to-Business Buying Decisions," *Industrial Marketing Management* 33 (2004), pp. 145–54.

26. *Business-to-Business Media Study Final Report,* prepared by Yankelovich Partners and Harris Interactive (Rochester, NY: Harris Interactive, October 4, 2001), p. 14.

27. Consumer Insight 19–1 is based on B. R. Barnes, P. Naude, and P. Mitchell, "Perceptual Gaps and Similarities in Buyer–Seller Dyadic Relationships," *Industrial Marketing Management* 36 (2007), pp. 662–75. See also C. Steinman, R. Deshpande, and J. U. Farley, "Beyond Market Orientation," *Journal of the Academy of Marketing Science* 28, no. 1 (2000), pp. 109–19; and P. H. Andersen and R. Kumar, "Emotions, Trust and Relationship Development in Business Relationships," *Industrial Marketing Management* 35 (2006), pp. 522–35.

28. G. Chakraborty, V. Lala, and D. Warren, "What Do Customers Consider Important in B2B Web sites?" *Journal of Advertising Research,* March 2003, pp. 50–61; and G. Chakraborty, P. Srivastava, and D. L. Warren, "Understanding Corporate B2B Web Sites' Effectiveness from North American and European Perspective," *Industrial Marketing Management* 34 (2005), pp. 420–29.

29. See S. Kitchell, "Corporate Culture, Environmental Adaptation, and Innovation Adoption," *Journal of the Academy of Marketing Science,* Summer 1995, pp. 195–205; and P. Berthon, L. F. Pitt, and M. T. Ewing, "Corollaries of the Collective," *Journal of the Academy of Marketing Science,* Spring 2001, pp. 135–50.

30. K. M. File and R. A. Prince, "A Psychographic Segmentation of Industrial Family Businesses," *Industrial Marketing Management,* May 1996, pp. 223–34.

31. G. Brewer, "An American in Shanghai," *Sales & Marketing Management,* November 1997, p. 42. See also N. D. Albers-Miller and B. Gelb, "Business Advertising Appeals as a Mirror of Cultural Dimensions," *Journal of Advertising,* Winter 1996, pp. 57–70.

32. See J. E. Stoddard and E. F. Fern, "Risk-Taking Propensity in Supplier Choice," *Psychology & Marketing,* October 1999, pp. 563–82.

33. See R. L. Griffith and L. G. Pol, "Segmenting Industrial Markets," *Industrial Marketing Management,* January 1994, pp. 39–46.

34. G. Brewer, "Selling an Intangible," *Sales & Marketing Management,* January 1998, pp. 52–58. See also S. P. Kalafatis and V. Cheston, "Normative Models and Practical Applications of Segmentation in Business Markets," *Industrial Marketing Management* 26 (1997), pp. 519–30.

35. See, e.g., C. Nakata and K. Sivakumar, "Instituting the Marketing Concept in a Multinational Setting," *Journal of the Academy of Marketing Science* 29, no. 3 (2001), pp. 255–75.

36. See F. Gibb, "To Give or Not to Give," *Sales & Marketing Management,* September 1994, pp. 136–39.

37. A. N. Link and J. Neufeld, "Innovation vs. Imitation: Investigating Alternative R&D Strategies," *Applied Economics* 18 (1986), pp. 1359–63.

38. Cespedes, "Hewlett-Packard Imaging Systems Division."

39. For a discussion of innovativeness, see G. T. M. Hult, R. F. Hurley, and G. A. Knight, "Innovativeness," *Industrial Marketing Management* 33 (2004), pp. 429–38.

40. D. I. Gilliland and W. J. Johnston, "Toward a Model of Business-to-Business Marketing Communications Effects," *Industrial Marketing Management* 26 (1997), pp. 15–29.

41. See S. M. Mudambi, P. Doyle, and V. Wong, "An Exploration of Branding in Industrial Markets," *Industrial Marketing Management* 26 (1997), pp. 433–46; J. Lapierre, "The Role of Corporate Image in the Evaluation of Business-to-Business Professional Services," *Journal of Professional Services Marketing* 1 (1998), pp. 21–41; and D. H. McQuiston, "Successful Branding of a Commodity Product," *Industrial Marketing Management* 33 (2004), pp. 345–54.

42. L. Hochwald, "It's the Sizzle That Sells," *Sales & Marketing Management,* April 1997, p. 51.

43. *CARR Report No. 120.3* (Boston: Cahners Publishing Co., undated).

44. "Study: Increase Business Ads to Increase Sales," *Marketing News,* March 14, 1988, p. 13.

45. G. Conlon, "A Day in the Life of Sales," *Sales & Marketing Management,* September 1997, pp. 42–63.

46. See J. M. Sinkula, "Market Information Processing and Organizational Learning," *Journal of Marketing,* January 1994, pp. 35–45; G. T. M. Hult and E. L. Nichols, Jr., "The Organizational Buyer Behavior Learning Organization," *Industrial Marketing Management,* May 1996, pp. 197–207; and S. J. Bell, G. J. Whitwell, and B. A. Lukas, "Schools of Thought in Organizational Learning," *Journal of the Academy of Marketing Science,* Winter 2002, pp. 70–86.

47. D. A. Garvin, "Building a Learning Organization," *Harvard Business Review,* July 1993, pp. 78–91; S. F. Slater and J. C. Narver, "Market Orientation and the Learning Organization," *Journal of Marketing,* July 1995, pp. 63–74; and G. T. M. Hult, "Cultural Competitiveness in Global Sourcing," *Industrial Marketing Management* 31 (2002), pp. 25–34.

# Part Five | Cases

The global steel market has been historically plagued with overcapacity and slow growth. This has created fierce competition and a perception among industrial buyers that steel is a commodity. The result has been that in many cases the deciding factor in a purchase decision is price, with resulting downward pressure on profitability.

One strategy that some steel manufacturers have used is to cut operating costs to help protect profit margins. Another strategy that some manufacturers have been attempting is a product differentiation approach accompanied by a strong brand name around which to build a distinctive image. But is branding useful in an industrial (B-to-B) context? The answer appears to be yes:

> [I]ndustrial firms hold very positive views about the benefits of brand names and feel that branding is valuable to marketing success and is a major corporate asset. In addition, industrial firms perceive a number of competitive differential benefits in the use of manufacturer brands, with quality, reliability, and performance rated as primary factors.

Clearly, industrial marketers see value in branding. However, do industrial buyers? The answer here depends on the extent to which the brand (*a*) creates benefits of value to buyers and (*b*) consistently delivers these core benefits. When these two factors are present, brand name becomes the symbol of these benefits and core values and provides for differentiation in the marketplace. In addition, consistent delivery over time results in increased trust, stronger relationships, and enhanced loyalty.

Rautaruukki Ojy (RO) is a steel manufacturer in Finland. It has a strong reputation in Europe but is relatively small. Rather than go the cost-cutting route, it decided to take the differentiation route. Its opportunity came when laser cutting technology became available. After hearing initial grumbling about steel quality problems associated with laser cutting, RO conducted intensive research to understand the nature of the problem/opportunity.

RO found that laser cutting involves preprogrammed computer settings. These settings involve considerable setup time, so users want to be able to save the cutting specs for use later on. However, being able to reuse the specs requires very high consistency in terms of the chemical composition and quality of the steel both within a batch of steel and across batches. The nature of the industry was also one where companies outsourced their laser cutting needs to specialty "job shops." Order quantity from these job shops was highly variable and not predictable. Given the technical nature of laser cutting, an educated customer service department was also critical.

As a result of this research, RO created RAEX LASER brand steel. The value components included:

- Consistent quality steel within and across batches to meet laser cutting specifications.
- Flexibility in order size acceptance through its distributors. The supply chain for RO is one of manufacturer (RO) to distributors, to end users (job shops who do laser cutting). Since the job shops had highly variable order size needs and they were unpredictable, RO had to provide flexibility in order size fulfillment. In managing supply, RO also created a cooperative atmosphere among its distributors whereby they would share inventories if needed to keep the supply chain running. Educational seminars and an annual retreat are part of this process.
- Customer service. Since education was critical, RO engaged in extensive training of its internal customer service personnel to provide them with the tools to deliver the highest customer service possible.

The results have been very positive. Sales have been on the increase since the introduction of the RAEX LASER brand and its value components. Customer loyalty has increased, and buyers are now willing to pay a *price premium* to get RAEX LASER steel and all that goes with it. And its efforts even caught the attention of the largest laser cutter manufacturer, which now recommends RAEX to new buyers of its machines!

### Discussion Questions

1. Create a diagram linking the value drivers for RAEX LASER steel to buyer satisfaction, trust, relationship quality, and loyalty. Explain how RAEX branding was much more than a promotion-driven process.

2. Should promotion and advertising come first or last in the brand building process? Does this depend on whether the promotion is targeted at the "external consumer" (in this case the job shops) or the "internal consumers" (in this case customer service employees)? Explain.

3. Discuss the importance of "internal marketing efforts" discussed in Question 2 to the success of RAEX's branding strategy.

4. Are buyers of RAEX LASER just "paying more for the name" or is it due to the economic benefits associated with the name? What, if any, economic benefits accrue to buyers of RAEX LASER steel?

5. Does the fact that job shops use brand name in their decision process mean that they are irrational decision makers?

6. Describe the various ways reference groups and word of mouth might operate in this setting.

7. Could RO use the RAEX name to expand beyond laser applications? Which of its value propositions do you think would transfer successfully?

Source: D. H. McQuiston, "Successful Branding of a Commodity Product," *Industrial Marketing Management* 33 (2004), pp. 345–54; and www.ruukki.com.

---

## CASE 5–2 PACCAR—MORE THAN SHINY TRUCKS

Paccar makes two of the most recognizable names in trucking—Kenworth and Peterbilt. These trucks represent the premium end of the over-the-road (OTR) truck market. They sell and lease their products to a large array of businesses with varying needs, wants, and resources. The truck industry is considered a commodity market for the most part, with price generally topping the list of buying criteria. In this market, Paccar and its trucks stand out. They have created a strong brand image for premium trucks, high quality, technology, and intense brand loyalty. Consider the following:

> Herbert J. Schmidt is a truck guy, but not just any truck. It's Kenworth or nothing. For the past 20 years, Contract Freighters Inc. has bought only Kenworth rigs, and the chief executive of the Joplin (Mo.) trucking company intends to stick with Kenworth . . . with plans to order at least 700 new trucks. Sure, these 10-wheel diesels cost 10% more than rivals' trucks. But when Schmidt factors in everything else—reliability, trade-in value, even the plush interiors that attract better drivers—he says they're worth it. "It's not the price," he says, "It's the quality."

Paccar's success can be attributed to a number of factors:

- *Quality.* In a commodity market, these trucks are premium quality, luxury products. Freight hauling companies love them because of their quality, reliability, and trade-in values. Drivers love them because of the plush and comfortable interiors among other things (consider that OTR drivers spend days on end in their trucks and often sleep in them). Both Kenworth and Peterbilt recently won J.D. Power and Associates awards.

- *Benchmarking.* Paccar is unusual in that it doesn't benchmark its products only against other truck brands. It specifically picks the leader in each area of concern and benchmarks against them. So, in IT it's Microsoft, in custom manufacturing it's Dell.

- *Technology.* Paccar actually considers itself a technology company as much as a trucking company. More accurately, it applies technological expertise to the trucking industry to remain a leader. Examples include its Electronic Fleet Management System, which is a computerized module that can be installed in the trucks and integrated into an owner's IT system to increase efficiency, help with regulatory compliance, and reduce paperwork.

- *Customization.* No "off-the-lot" purchases necessary here. With its custom manufacturing process, Paccar can offer buyers the opportunity to select from thousands of options and within six to eight weeks take delivery of their custom-built truck.

- *Industry reputation.* Paccar and its trucks are recognized throughout the industry as a leader in quality (J.D. Powers), technology (National Medal of Technology), and computing (Computer World Honors). These awards help further solidify an already strong reputation.
- *Lease options.* If you are buying 700 trucks like Herbert Schmidt, you have the technology, capital, and human resources to manage and operate your own fleet. However, smaller carriers have problems in these areas. A growing business for Paccar is its leasing operation, which provides services such as truck maintenance, which eliminates the need for the carrier to maintain a staff of trained technicians—a huge overhead expense.

Finally, in response to environmental issues and rising fuel prices, Paccar is taking the lead with Hybrid trucks. It is starting with medium-size trucks and is working on full-size models.

## Discussion Questions

1. Define loyalty as you understand it from the text. Does Paccar with its Kenworth and Peterbilt trucks create loyalty? Explain.

2. What type of buying process (straight rebuy, modified rebuy, new task) is the decision to buy Kenworth for Herbert Schmidt? Would the buying process be the same for all carriers? Explain.

3. Using all possible sources of information, including the case, the Internet, OTR truck dealers, develop what you think the decision-making unit looks like for a truck purchase. Does its size depend on the size of the company or other factors? Explain.

4. Using all possible sources of information, including the case, the Internet, OTR truck dealers, complete the following information in Table A. What implications does this have for Paccar and other truck companies in terms of their marketing efforts?

5. Explain the role of reference groups for Paccar and its trucks.

6. Describe the differences you would expect between a company that owned their own trucks versus those that lease. Relate these to the internal and external influences shown in Figure 19–1.

7. How does Paccar's hybrid offering fit into its current brand image?

Source: M. Arndt, "Built for the Long Haul," *BusinessWeek*, January 30, 2006, p. 66; and information from Paccar's Web site, www.paccar.com.

| Evaluative Criteria Used in Purchase Decision | Functional Role in Organization | | | |
|---|---|---|---|---|
| 1. | | | | |
| 2. | | | | |
| 3. | | | | |
| 4. | | | | |
| 5. | | | | |
| . | | | | |
| . | | | | |
| . | | | | |
| . | | | | |
| . | | | | |

**TABLE A**

Evaluative Criteria and Organizational Role

# Consumer Behavior and Marketing Regulation

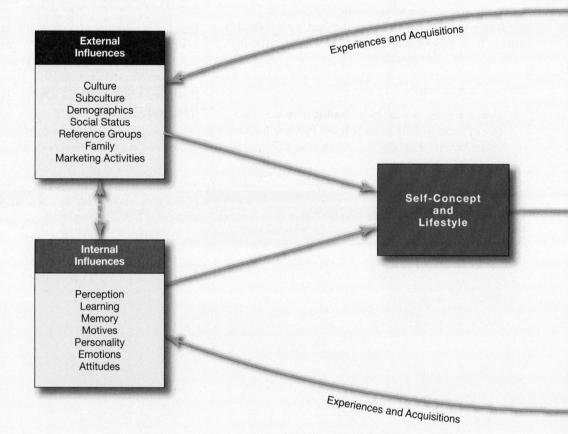

**External Influences**

Culture
Subculture
Demographics
Social Status
Reference Groups
Family
Marketing Activities

**Internal Influences**

Perception
Learning
Memory
Motives
Personality
Emotions
Attitudes

**Self-Concept and Lifestyle**

Experiences and Acquisitions

Experiences and Acquisitions

Throughout the text, we have emphasized that knowledge of consumer behavior is as important to those who would regulate consumer behavior as it is to those who engage in marketing activities. Government officials, consumer advocates, and citizens all need to understand consumer behavior to develop, enact, and enforce appropriate rules and regulations for marketing activities. Consumers in particular need to understand their own behaviors and how their purchase and consumption behaviors help determine the type of marketplace and society we have.

In this section, we will analyze the role of consumer behavior principles in regulating marketing practices.

We will pay particular attention to the regulation of marketing activities focused on children. We also discuss regulations covering advertising, product, and pricing practices aimed at adults.

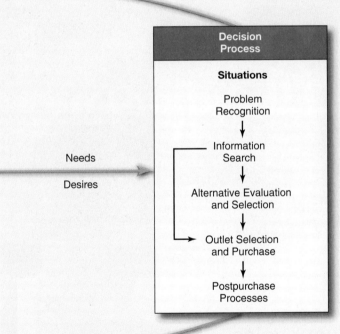

Needs

Desires

**Decision Process**

**Situations**

Problem Recognition

Information Search

Alternative Evaluation and Selection

Outlet Selection and Purchase

Postpurchase Processes

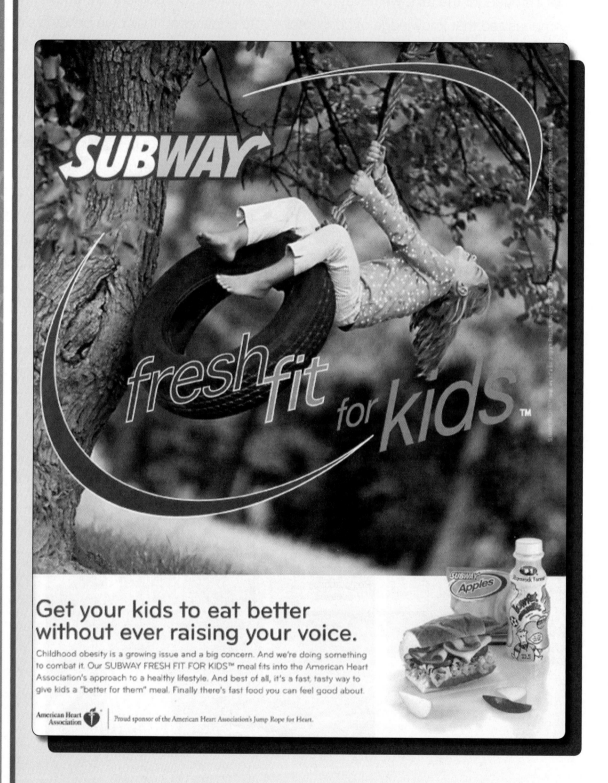

# Marketing Regulation and Consumer Behavior

A battle is raging over childhood obesity.[1] On the one hand, consumer groups, lawyers, and policy makers often claim that food marketing and advertising are major contributing factors, citing among other things that childhood obesity has increased in the face of a doubling of advertising targeted at children, food advertising is often in high-fat and high-sugar categories, and food advertising can influence children's food choices. On the other hand, food marketers and their proponents have often argued that a strong, solid link between food advertising and obesity has not been established and further suggest that inactivity and parents are to blame.

At a two-day workshop on marketing, self-regulation, and childhood obesity, the chairperson of the Federal Trade Commission (FTC) was quick to point out the complex and multifaceted nature of the problem, noting that suburban sprawl, the cutting of physical education programs in schools, video games competing with physical play time, increased portion sizes in restaurants, as well as an abundance of good-tasting, calorie-laden foods, marketed in ways that are highly appealing to children are all part of the problem.[2] The FTC chairperson went on to say, however, that the food industry must be accountable and play a positive, proactive, role:[3]

> [F]rom the FTC's perspective, based on years of experience with advertising, a government ban on children's food advertising is neither wise nor viable. It would be, however, equally unwise for industry to maintain the status quo. Not only is downplaying the concerns of consumers bad business, but if industry fails to demonstrate good faith commitment to this issue and to take positive steps, others may step in and act in its stead.

In response, the food industry has reacted with self-regulatory initiatives, including the following:[4]

- In concert with the Alliance for a Healthier Generation (AHG), "The nation's top beverage manufacturers—Coca-Cola, PepsiCo and Cadbury-Schwepps—agreed . . . to revise their product distribution in schools to include only water, tea, and low-calorie drinks."

- In another joint effort with AHG, five major food manufacturers worked to "establish nutrition guidelines that will lead to healthier food choices for millions of children in schools across the nation." Just a few examples of specific actions to be taken include Dannon, which will further decrease the sugar content of Danimals yogurt cups even though they currently meet AHG guidelines, and Mars, which will create a new line of snacks for kids that meet the AHG guidelines.

- Ten leading food and beverage companies that account for 66 percent of all children's TV ads worked in concert with the Better Business Bureau (BBB) to establish the Children's Food and Beverage Advertising Initiative (CFBAI). Among other "pledges" made by the companies involved, such as Campbell's, Coca-Cola, and Hershey, the initiative specifies that they "use at least half of their ads to children to promote more healthful dietary choices and/or to encourage healthful lifestyles."

Many, even those in the industry, admit that these efforts are just a start. And some critics have deemed the moves more public relations than substance. However, significantly, in discussing the CFBAI, the FTC chairperson indicated:

The pledges are a significant step forward in industry self-regulation. While changes in food marketing alone will not solve the nation's childhood obesity problem, these actions will help make a healthy choice the easy choice for parents and kids.

---

As the opening example indicates, marketing practices are sometimes controversial. Marketing is a highly visible, important activity. It affects the lives of individuals, the success of nonprofit groups, and the profits of businesses. As indicated throughout the text, there are many issues where the appropriate ethical action for marketers is not clear-cut. As a marketing manager, you will face many such situations in your career. However, society has declared that some marketing actions are clearly inappropriate. It has done so by enacting laws and regulations that prohibit or require specific marketing actions. In this chapter, we examine the regulation of marketing practices. Regulating marketing activities requires the same level of understanding of consumer behavior as does managing marketing programs. Our consideration of the regulation of marketing practices will separate regulations designed to protect children from those designed to protect adults.

# REGULATION AND MARKETING TO CHILDREN

The regulation of marketing activities aimed at children focuses primarily on product safety, advertising and promotions, and privacy protection. Product safety issues focus on appropriate product design and materials. We will concentrate on privacy protection and advertising and other promotional activities[5] targeting children as consumers. The regulation of these activities rests heavily on theories of children's consumer behavior, particularly their information-processing skills.

There are a variety of state, federal, and voluntary guidelines and rules governing marketing to children. Despite these rules, many feel that some marketers continue to take advantage of children and that the overall marketing system, particularly advertising, is socializing children to value things (products) rather than intangibles such as relationships and integrity.

One basis for the concern over marketing to children is based on *Piaget's stages of cognitive development* (Chapter 6), which indicate that children lack the ability to fully process and understand information, including marketing messages, until around 12 years of age.[6] This and related theories are the basis for most regulation of advertising aimed at children and, according to critics, for some marketing programs that deliberately exploit children.

## Concerns about the Ability of Children to Comprehend Commercial Messages

The American advertising industry's primary self-regulatory body, the National Advertising Division (NAD) of the Council of Better Business Bureaus, maintains a special unit to review advertising aimed at children—the **Children's Advertising Review Unit (CARU).** Four of the eight principles that underlie CARU's guidelines for advertising directed to children relate to their ability to comprehend commercial messages:[7]

1. Advertisers have special responsibilities when advertising to children or collecting data from children online. They should take into account the limited knowledge, experience, sophistication, and maturity of the audience to which the message is directed. They should recognize that younger children have a limited capacity to evaluate the credibility of information, may not understand the persuasive intent of advertising, and may not even understand that they are being subjected to advertising.
2. Advertising should be neither deceptive nor unfair, as these terms are applied under the Federal Trade Commission Act, to the children to whom it is directed.
3. Advertisers should have adequate substantiation for objective advertising claims, as those claims are reasonably interpreted by the children to whom they are directed.
4. Advertising should not stimulate children's unreasonable expectations about product quality or performance.

Some of the specific guidelines relating to information processing that guide CARU's policing of children's advertising are shown in Table 20–1.

| TABLE 20–1 |
| --- |

Information Processing–Related Guidelines of CARU

1. Whether an advertisement leaves a misleading impression should be determined by assessing how reasonable children in the intended audience would interpret the message, taking into account their level of experience, sophistication, and maturity; limits on their cognitive abilities; and their ability to evaluate the advertising claims.
2. Claims should not unduly exploit a child's imagination. While fantasy, using techniques such as animation and computer-generated imagery, is appropriate for both younger and older children, it should not create unattainable performance expectations nor exploit the younger child's difficulty in distinguishing between the real and the fanciful.
3. Advertisements should demonstrate the performance and use of the product in a way that can be duplicated by a child for whom the product is intended.
4. All disclosures and disclaimers material to children should be understandable to the children in the intended audience, taking into account their limited vocabularies and level of language skills.
5. Program personalities, live or animated, should not be used to advertise products, premiums or services in or adjacent to a television program primarily directed to children under 12 years of age in which the same personality or character appears.

Source: *Self-Regulatory Program for Children's Advertising,* Children's Advertising Review Unit, Council of Better Business Bureaus, 2006.

CARU and others are interested in the impact that the *content* of children's advertising has, as well as the ability of children to process advertising messages. However, our current focus is limited to children's abilities to *comprehend* advertising messages. There are two main components to this concern: (1) Do children understand the selling intent of commercials? and (2) Can children understand specific aspects of commercials, such as comparisons?

**Do Children Understand the Selling Intent of Commercials?**    Research suggests that younger children have at least some difficulty understanding the selling intent of commercials.[8] Currently, the advertising industry strives to separate children's commercials from the programs by prohibiting overlapping characters and by using *separators,* such as "We will return after these messages."

This problem is growing in intensity, as children's products are often the "stars" of animated children's films and television programs. Increasingly, product lines and television programs (and movies) are being designed jointly with the primary objective being sales of the toy line. Parents have expressed concerns ranging from the effects that toy-based programming has on their children's behaviors and emotional development to the fear that such programming may replace other more creative and child-oriented programs.[9]

This concern has led to a variety of proposals to restrict or eliminate such programs. These proposals have produced an ongoing debate about who controls the television set. One argument is that it is the parent's responsibility to monitor and regulate their children's viewing behaviors. If a sufficient number of parents find such programs inappropriate and refuse to let their children watch them, advertisers will quit sponsoring them and they will no longer be available. Another argument is that today's time-pressured parents do not have time to screen all the shows their children watch. Furthermore, tremendous peer pressure can develop for children to watch a particular show or own the products associated with it. Denying a child the right to watch such a show then causes arguments and resentments. Therefore, society should set appropriate standards within which broadcasters should operate. *Which, if either, of these views matches your own?*

**Can Children Understand the Words and Phrases in Commercials?**    The second aspect of comprehension involves specific words or types of commercials that children might misunderstand. For example, research indicates that disclaimers such as "Part of a nutritious breakfast," "Each sold separately," and "Batteries not included," are ineffective with preschool children.[10] Not only do young children have a difficult time understanding these phrases, the problem is compounded when such disclaimers are presented in a manner that does not meet the Federal Trade Commission's "Clear and Conspicuous" requirements for such disclaimers.[11] For example, consider the following toy ad disclaimer:

The disclaimer noted that "TV Teddy comes with one tape. Other tapes sold separately." However, it appeared near the bottom of the screen in lettering that measured only 3.5 percent of the screen height against a multicolor background. It was not repeated by an announcer and appeared for less than three seconds. A child would have to read at 200 words per minute to read the message!

In relation to words and phrases, CARU recommends wording and language that is age appropriate (such as simple words for young audiences) and prohibits price minimizations such as "only" and "just." It also suggests specific phrasing for certain situations, such as "you have to put it together," rather than "assembly required." Several cases involving CARU and the information-processing skills of children include the following:

- Nintendo agreed to discontinue advertising in which groups of four people such as a family or young girls at a slumber party are shown playing Mario Party 8 [on the Wii system] each with her or his own separate remote control. Even though a small video super indicated "Game and system sold separately," CARU was concerned that "children watching the advertisement could be confused by what is included in the initial purchase of the Wii game system."[12]

- Nabisco, Inc., agreed to change its advertising for KoolStuf Oreo Toaster Pastries after CARU brought a consumer complaint to its attention. The commercial showed Oreo cookies going into a toaster and popping up as KoolStuf toaster pastries. A four-year-old saw the commercial and tried to do the same thing by putting Oreos into a toaster. When they melted, he tried to remove them with a pair of metal tongs before being stopped by his mother.[13]
- Rose Art Industries agreed to alter its packaging after CARU concluded that the size of the product relative to the size of the child shown in the package picture could lead a child to believe the Super Lite toy is larger than it is.[14]

## Concerns about the Effects of the Content of Commercial Messages on Children

Even if children accurately comprehend television ads, there are concerns about the effects the content of these messages has on children. These concerns stem in part from the substantial amount of time American children spend viewing television. The large amount of time children devote to watching television, including commercials, gives rise to two major areas of concern:

- The impact of commercial messages on children's values.
- The impact of commercial messages on children's health and safety.

Four of the eight basic principles that underline CARU's guidelines for advertising directed at children focus on these concerns (the other four, as we saw, are concerned with children's information-processing capabilities). They are:[15]

1. Products and content inappropriate for children should not be advertised directly to them.
2. Advertisers should avoid social stereotyping and appeals to prejudice, and are encouraged to incorporate minority and other groups in advertisements and to present positive role models whenever possible.
3. Advertisers are encouraged to capitalize on the potential of advertising to serve an educational role and influence positive personal qualities and behaviors in children, e.g., being honest, and respectful of others, taking safety precautions, engaging in physical activity.
4. Although there are many influences that affect a child's personal and social development, it remains the prime responsibility of the parents to provide guidance for children. Advertisers should contribute to this parent–child relationship in a constructive manner.

Several of the specific guidelines derived from these principles are provided in Table 20–2.

**Health and Safety**  CARU challenged a television commercial for 4 Wheelers by Skechers, which ran during traditional children's viewing time. The ad featured teens skating and performing a stunt without the use of any safety gear such as helmets or pads. According to CARU, this violates the third guideline in Table 20–2. Skechers appealed the ruling, stating that there are no children shown in the commercial; protective gear while skating or roller-blading is not required by law; it warns purchasers to "always" wear protective gear in the safety pamphlet that comes with the product; and the skates are not being portrayed in an athletic or sporting manner.[16] *What do you think? Was CARU correct or was Skechers?*

TABLE 20–2

TABLE 20–2

Examples of
Specific Guidelines
of the Children's
Advertising Review
Unit

1. Advertising should not urge children to ask parents or others to buy products. It should not suggest that a parent or adult who purchases a product or service for a child is better, more intelligent or more generous than one who does not.
2. Advertisers should not convey to children that the possession of a product will result in greater acceptance by peers or lack of a product will result in less acceptance by peers.
3. Advertisements should not portray adults or children in unsafe situations, or in acts harmful to themselves or others. For example, when athletic activities (such as bicycle riding or skateboarding) are shown, proper precautions and safety equipment should be depicted.
4. Advertising of food products should encourage responsible use of the product with a view toward healthy development of the child. For example, advertising of food products should not discourage or disparage healthy lifestyle choices or the consumption of fruits or vegetables, or other foods recommended for increased consumption by current USDA Dietary Guidelines for Americans and My Pyramid, as applicable to children under 12.

Source: "Examples of Scientific Guidelines of Children's Advertising Review Unit," *Self-Regulatory Program for Children's Advertising,* CARU, 2006.

In many instances, children and teenagers are exposed to advertising directed at adults. For example, CARU found that Proactiv Solution cleansing system which is labeled as "keep out of reach of children," was being advertised in time slots and locations likely to involve children's programming and viewership. The company responded by removing the ad from those time slots and locations.[17]

Even ads clearly not targeting children can have potentially harmful consequences:

A television commercial for Calgonite automatic dishwasher detergent showed a woman inside an automatic dishwasher. The commercial was withdrawn voluntarily after CARU received a complaint that a three-year-old child had climbed into a dishwasher shortly after viewing the commercial.[18]

The problem caused by the Calgonite commercial illustrates the difficulty marketers face. This commercial was not aimed at children nor shown during a children's program. The fact that children watch prime-time television extensively places an additional responsibility on marketers.[19]

Ensuring that advertisements portray only safe uses of products is sometimes difficult, but it is not a controversial area. Advertising of health-related products, particularly snack foods and cereals, is much more controversial. The bulk of the controversy focuses on the heavy advertising emphasis placed on sugared and high-fat products. Advertising sugared products, such as presweetened breakfast cereals, does increase their consumption. However, this same advertising may also increase the consumption of related products, such as milk. What is not known, and probably cannot be determined, are the eating patterns that would exist in the absence of such advertising. That is, if children did not know about cereals such as Cap'n Crunch, would they eat a more nutritious breakfast, a less nutritious breakfast, or perhaps no breakfast at all? Recent self-regulatory efforts by food marketing companies highlighted in the chapter opener suggest a move in the right direction when it comes to food-related safety and children. However, issues still remain, as can be seen in the following example:

Advertising for "Cookie Crisp" came to the attention of CARU. It opens with the cereal's mascot, "Chip the Wolf," as he describes the cereal and plots to steal the box of Cookie Crisp from children who are sitting at a table, each eating a bowlful of cereal. Chip ultimately drops the box into the arms of the happy children, one of whom adds more cereal to his bowl. CARU was concerned that the ad depicted over-consumption and General Mills responded by removing the segment showing the child adding extra cereal to his bowl.[20]

**Values**    Advertising is frequently criticized as fostering overly materialistic, self-focused, and short-term values in children:

> We cannot afford to raise a generation of children that measures its own value by the insignia on their clothes—not by the compassion in their hearts or the knowledge in their minds.[21]

One reason is the magnitude of advertising focused on kids. One estimate is that marketers spend $15 billion per year advertising to children.[22] In addition, estimates of the number of TV ads that children are exposed to ranges from 18,000 to 40,000 per year.[23] Obviously, these numbers are conservative in terms of total ad exposure since they exclude other popular media such as the Internet. Many are concerned that this consistent pressure to buy and own things is producing negative values in children.

Numerous cosmetics companies and day spas are now targeting children at increasingly younger ages with both products and advertisements. Most position the products in terms of fun rather than sensuality. For example, Disney's products are packaged in boxes with pictures of Tinkerbell, Winnie the Pooh, and similar characters.[24] According to an industry expert, girls 8 to 12 are now wearing platform heels and "low-rise jeans, tight miniskirts and midriff-baring T-shirts."[25]

There is also an increase in concern about looking thin and in eating disorders in children as young as 6.[26] Many find this apparent shortening of childhood and the related body image problems inappropriate. They assign a large part of the blame to the marketing of products such as cosmetics and personalities such as Britney Spears.

**Summary of Advertising and Children**    Available evidence suggests that the vast majority of ads meet CARU guidelines.[27] CARU reviews thousands of ads every year and has over a 95 percent success rate in resolving issues related to children's advertising.[28] However, given the enormous amount of time children spend with all forms of media, most will see many ads that are in violation of these guidelines. Clearly, CARU does not cover all aspects of advertising. For example, it does not, nor could it, oppose generating desires for products that many families cannot afford. Nonetheless, CARU has greatly enhanced the level of responsibility in advertising aimed at children. Many consumer advocates would like it to expand the areas it covers and increase the stringency of its rules.

## Controversial Marketing Activities Aimed at Children

There are a number of marketing activities targeted at children in addition to television advertising that are controversial and for which various regulatory proposals are being considered. For example, violent entertainment products (movies, videos, and music) labeled for those 17 and older were, until recently, routinely marketed to kids. Highly publicized acts of violence by teenagers produced threats of regulation and improved self-regulation by the industries.[29] However, it remains a problem.

Another area of ongoing concern is kids' clubs, which typically provide a membership certificate, a magazine or Web site, the chance to win prizes, and discounts or coupons for products offered by the sponsor. Kids' clubs vary widely in what they offer the members and how ethically they are run. A major concern is that these clubs disguise commercial messages, for example, when ad messages come disguised as "advice from your club."[30]

Three additional issues are described in this section.

**Mobile Marketing and Children**    Sometimes referred to as the "third screen," cell phones are an increasingly integral part of our lives. And marketers see younger children as the next big growth market. Consider the following:

Appealing to kids is rich terrain for wireless companies, which have already locked up nearly 70 percent of the U.S. population through service contracts. In the past year, the industry's biggest growth has come from 14- to 24-year-olds buying from specialized brands like Virgin Mobile or Boost Mobile LLC. Now, 55 percent of teens have wireless phones, so companies see green in the even younger market, where 25 percent of kids 12 and under own phones, according to the Yankee Group.[31]

Various types of promotional efforts are being used, including the following:[32]

- *Ringtones*. Customized ringtones are quite the craze. Movies have gotten into the mix in a big way and allow downloads of ringtones such as Samantha's "nose wiggle" ring tone for the movie *Bewitched*. An example targeting an even younger audience is the Pokemon ringtone.
- *Mobile games*. General mobile games are a major market. Increasingly, mobile games are being customized to a brand or event. *Batman Begins* was promoted with a mobile game custom-designed around the movie. In the United Kingdom, Dennis the Menace mobile games, which feature characters from the comic strip, will be distributed.
- *Text-in contests*. Text message codes are being used by numerous companies for contests and other promotions. Text-in a specific code provided in an ad or on the package and you can enter to win various prizes. Recent examples include Starburst and Nesquik.

The ability of marketers to infiltrate yet another media domain with promotions and materials that are seen as further blurring the line between advertising and entertainment has many parents and consumer advocate groups worried. Several years back when Disney announced that it would, in a partnership with Sprint, offer cellular phone service targeted specifically at children in the 8- to 12-year range, concerns grew even stronger. Consider an excerpt from a letter to Congress by Commercial Alert, a nonprofit consumer advocate group:

If Disney Corporation and the others just wanted to give children a way to contact parents in emergencies, that would be one thing. The telecommunications companies—to parents at least— are playing up this angle. Telecommunications lobbyists in Washington will harp on it as well. But despite the industry's rhetoric, Disney and the telecommunications companies really want to use children as conduits to their parents' wallets. And marketers want another way to bypass parents and speak directly to the nation's children.

*Advertising Age* reported on July 11th that many corporations, including McDonald's, Coca-Cola, and Timex, are moving "from small [mobile phone advertising] tests to all-out campaign[s]." Children already are bombarded with too much advertising. They don't need more advertising through their mobile phones, whether it is telemarketing, text message marketing, adver-games, or any other type of commercial messages.[33]

Obviously, the battle lines are being drawn. *Which side of this debate do you come down on more—that of the marketers or the consumer advocates? Does your answer depend on the age of the children and the nature of the tactics utilized?*

**Commercialization of Schools**      There has been ongoing concern and controversy around the commercialization of elementary and high schools. Schools are often motivated by money as budgets continue to be tight. The issue of commercialization covers a broad sphere of activities. Consumers Union has the following classification system:[34]

- *In-school ads*. Ads in such places as school buses, scoreboards, bulletin boards, as well as coupons and free samples. For example, Sonic Drive-in launched Sonic Invasion, which included in-school ads and e-mail blasts designed to get students to go to a Web site and vote for their school. Although the call to action wasn't buying burgers, the exposure for Sonic clearly was a positive aspect of the campaign for the company. Other aspects might include schools' selling naming rights to companies and distributing ads in student newspapers. For example, advertisers can now get national runs in high school newspapers through Campus Media Group.

Kraft recently announced that it would stop school advertising aimed at younger children. However, Krispy Kreme has come under fire for offering free donuts to children who get A's on their report cards.

- *Ads in classroom.* Ads in classroom magazines and television programs. This also includes ads in magazines distributed in school libraries. Channel One has created substantial controversy in this area. It provides 12 minutes of news to participating schools, but contains two minutes of commercials. Research indicates that the commercials have an impact on students.[35]

  Recently, *Time* and *Newsweek* were applauded for agreeing to remove tobacco ads from school library editions of *Time, Sports Illustrated,* and *Newsweek.*

- *Corporate-sponsored educational materials and programs.* Also called sponsored educational materials, or SEMs. SEMs are teaching materials provided by corporations, usually for free. They come in various forms, including posters, activity sheets, and multimedia teaching aids.

  While many criteria can be used to evaluate these materials, one of the main criteria is the level of commercialism. Highly commercialized SEMs that are thinly veiled ads with little educational value draw the most scrutiny. However, there are trade-offs in that compliance with a completely noncommercial standard would greatly reduce the motivation of firms to provide valuable (sometimes) material to the schools.[36]

- *Corporate-sponsored contests and incentive programs.* When companies gain access through various contests and incentives, including prizes such as travel and free pizza.

Another area of great concern includes direct sales, usually by food products companies. The chapter opener provides examples of how the major food and beverage companies are working to develop and comply with voluntary guidelines designed to deal with this issue.

**Internet Marketing and Children**    Children are major users of the Internet. Not surprisingly, marketers use the Internet to communicate with kids. Two major concerns have emerged: invading children's privacy and exploitation of children through manipulative sales techniques. We will consider the online privacy issue in the next section.

Concern regarding manipulative Internet practices often revolves around the creation of sites that blur the line between entertainment and advertising. This goes back to concerns touched on earlier in terms of difficulties that children have in discerning selling intent and their ability to distinguish commercial from noncommercial content. An emerging concern is "adver-games." These customized games, which are placed on a company's Web site, prominently feature or integrate the company's brands and products as part of the game itself. Consider the following excerpt:

Kraft's Nabiscoworld.com features adver-games for at least 17 brands, plus classic games such as chess, mah-jongg and backgammon. Some games integrate brands into the play. In Ritz Bits Sumo Wrestling, for example, players control either the Creamy Marshmallow or the Chocolatey Fudge cracker in a belly-smacking showdown, which results in the "S'more"-flavored cracker.[37]

An early set of guidelines set forth by the Center for Media Education (CME) recommends the following principles for development of online commercial services:[38]

1.  Personal information should not be collected from children, nor should personal profiles of children be sold to third parties.
2.  Advertising and promotions targeted at children should be clearly labeled and separated from content.
3.  Children's content areas should not be directly linked to advertising sites.
4.  There should be no direct interaction between children and product spokespersons.
5.  There should be no online microtargeting of children (commercials or promotions developed for individual children), and no direct-response marketing.

Two examples of companies putting Principle 2 to work are Kraft and Burger King. Kraft has an "Ad Break" icon that is an explicit indication that the material is a commercial message designed to sell something. Burger King Kids section has various notices that indicate, "Hey Kids! This is Advertising!" *What effect, if any, do you think such notifications have on the effectiveness of this online advertising to children? Should so-called adver-games be subject to such notification?*

## Children's Online Privacy Issues

Online privacy relates to the collection and use of information from Web sites. Collecting information from children is a sensitive issue, as well it should be, given all we know about their information-processing deficits relative to those of adults. An example of an online children's privacy issue involved the KidsCom communications playground (targeting kids 4 to 8), which required children to provide their name, age, sex, and e-mail address in order to enter the site. It also requested their favorite TV show, music groups, and the name of the child who referred them to KidsCom. Once in the playground, they could earn "KidsCash," which could be redeemed for prizes by supplying additional personal information. KidsCom has since been modified (see its privacy statement at www.kidscom.com).

Concern over the invasion of children's privacy prompted Congress to pass the **Children's Online Privacy Protection Act (COPPA)** in October 1998. It authorizes the FTC to develop specific rules to implement the provisions of the act. In 1999, the FTC issued the *Children's Online Privacy Protection Rule*, also referred to as The Rule. Key provisions of The Rule under COPPA are detailed in Table 20–3.

The Rules became effective in April 2000 and appear to be working, although clearly, ongoing diligence on the part of the FTC and commercial entities is required.

CARU adopted similar but more detailed rules. Privacy issues now dominate CARU cases:

*   CARU was concerned that the Web site for the Jonas Brothers (a band popular with children) collected personally identifiable information from children without obtaining verifiable parental consent and that it used "tip-off" language that would alert younger children to enter a false age. The company worked to get its site into compliance.[39]
*   Pinkspage, the fan site for the artist Pink, did not contain a privacy statement. In addition, CARU was concerned that a visitor of any age could submit personal identifying information such as an e-mail or street address at the "Fan Club" registration.[40]
*   Scan-command.com features online games designed to be played by children ages 8 and up. It agreed to cease collecting parents' offline contact information from children under 13 without prior parental consent.[41]

The importance of consumer education also plays a prominent role in the FTC's approach. This can be seen in the fact that it has created a privacy Web site designed to educate kids and parents about online privacy issues (see Illustration 20–1).

The Rule applies to (a) operators of commercial web sites or online services directed to children under 13 that collect personal information from children, (b) operators of general audience sites that knowingly collect personal information from children under 13, and (c) operators of general audience sites that have a separate children's area and that collect personal information from children. Nonprofits are not covered.

**Privacy Policy.** Post privacy policy on the homepage of the web site and link to the privacy policy everywhere personal information is collected.

**Parental Notice.** Provide parents notice about the site's information collection practices and, with some exceptions, get verifiable parental consent *before* collecting personal information from children.

**Parental Consent.** Give parents the choice to consent to the collection and use of a child's personal information for internal use by the web site, and give them the chance to choose not to have that personal information disclosed to third parties.

**Parental Access.** Provide parents access to their child's information, and the opportunity to delete the information and opt out of the future collection or use of the information.

**Conditional Access.** Do NOT condition a child's participation in an activity on the disclosure of more personal information than is reasonably necessary for the activity.

**Confidentiality.** Maintain the confidentiality, security, and integrity of the personal information collected from children.

Source: *You, Your Privacy Policy and COPPA* (Washington, DC: Federal Trade Commission).

**TABLE 20–3**

Key Provisions of The Rule under COPPA

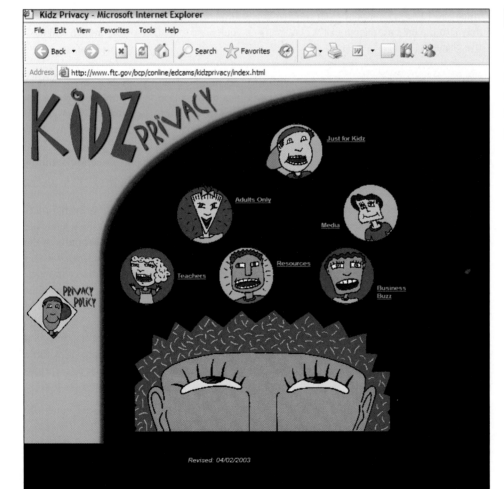

**ILLUSTRATION 20–1**

Education is an important aspect of the FTC's fight against online privacy invasion among children.

# REGULATION AND MARKETING TO ADULTS

Regulation of marketing activities aimed at adults focuses on marketing communications, product features, and pricing practices. There is increasing demand for regulation to protect the privacy of adults. Many magazines sell their subscription lists to various firms who use the information for direct marketing campaigns. Some charities sell or otherwise make available their donor lists. While the dissemination of credit card, subscription, and donation data is a concern, most attention is currently focused on the privacy of data collected on the Internet.[42]

Consider the following from the online privacy statement found on the American Express Web site:

> American Express does not sell or share customer information with entities outside of American Express who may want to market to you their own products and services. You don't need to take any action for this benefit. American Express uses your information to process applications, complete transactions, respond to your requests, deliver the products and services in which you enroll or for which you apply, and notify you of promotions, updates, or special offers that we think may interest you. We also use your information to provide you with a more effective customer experience while on our web site. In order to do this, we may process your information or combine it with other information that is publicly available. This enables us to customize your American Express experience and provide you with more relevant offers. American Express may also use the information that we collect from you online to market to you through alternative channels.

Parts of this statement would be comforting to most consumers. Other parts, such as that dealing with how American Express combines information from public sources with its own information to customize the experience or how it can use information collected online to market to consumers through other channels, make some consumers uncomfortable. Companies argue that data collection and mining in order to offer a more targeted offering is beneficial to consumers. Consumer advocates often argue that such procedures are invasive. *Which side do you most agree with and why? Does it depend on what types of information are collected?*

One of the reasons the concern about Internet privacy is so strong is that information is often collected without the consumer's explicitly providing it. A person visiting a Web site can have that fact recorded (his or her IP address at a minimum) as well as what parts of the site are visited, what information is requested, what links are accessed, and so forth without consent or even knowledge. Other information may be collected in a more direct manner. Information from various sites and sources can be pooled to develop individual profiles. Consumer Insight 20–1 provides the FTC's evolving and ongoing approach to regulating Internet privacy practices.

The Better Business Bureau has a Code of Online Business Practices that is "designed to guide ethical business-to-consumer conduct in electronic commerce." It provides three broad requirements, each with substantial details and examples, with respect to information practices:

- Post and adhere to a privacy policy that is open, transparent, and meets generally accepted fair information principles.
- Provide adequate security for the type of information collected, maintained, or transferred to third parties.
- Respect customers' preferences regarding unsolicited e-mail.

**Online Privacy and the Federal Trade Commission**

In May 2000, the Federal Trade Commission issued its third report on online privacy issues to Congress.[43] This report concluded that self-regulation was not providing adequate privacy regulation and recommended national legislation. It recommended that consumer-oriented commercial Web sites that collect personal identifying information from or about consumers comply with four standards:

1. *Notice.* Web sites would be required to provide consumers clear and conspicuous notice of their information practices, including what information they collect; how they collect it (e.g., directly or through nonobvious means such as cookies); how they use it; how they provide *choice, access,* and *security* to consumers; whether they disclose the information collected to other entities; and whether other entities are collecting information through the site.
2. *Choice.* Web sites would be required to offer consumers choices as to how their personal identifying information is used beyond the use for which the information was provided (e.g., to consummate a transaction). Such choice would encompass both internal secondary uses (such as marketing back to consumers) and external secondary uses (such as disclosing data to other entities).
3. *Access.* Web sites would be required to offer consumers reasonable access to the information a Web site has collected about them, including a reasonable opportunity to review information and to correct inaccuracies or delete information.
4. *Security.* Web sites would be required to take reasonable steps to protect the security of the information they collect from consumers.

However, in 2001 the new chairman of the FTC concluded that "it is too soon to conclude that we can fashion workable legislation." At the same time, he did conclude that privacy protection in general and online privacy protection in particular are important issues. He indicated that the FTC was going to increase the resources it devotes to privacy protection by 50 percent.

While legislative initiatives (e.g., OPPA, which was designed to incorporate the four key features above) continue to be debated, the FTC's position as of 2008 as described on its Web site is as follows:

A key part of the Commission's privacy program is making sure companies keep the promises they make to consumers about privacy and, in particular, the precautions they take to secure consumers' personal information. To respond to consumers' concerns about privacy, many Web sites post privacy policies that describe how consumers' personal information is collected, used, shared, and secured. Indeed, almost all the top 100 commercial sites now post privacy policies. Using its authority under Section 5 of the FTC Act, which prohibits unfair or deceptive practices, the Commission has brought a number of cases to enforce the promises in privacy statements, including promises about the security of consumers' personal information. The Commission has also used its unfairness authority to challenge information practices that cause substantial consumer injury.[44]

Thus, in dealing with online privacy, the FTC operates within already established legislative guidelines.

### Critical Thinking Questions

1. Should there be national legislation such as that proposed above? Why or why not?
2. In the absence of legislation, how should a firm collect and use data from those who visit its Web site?

## Marketing Communications

There are three major concerns focused on the information that marketers provide to consumers, generally in the form of advertisements—the accuracy of the information provided, the adequacy of the information provided, and the cumulative impact of marketing information on society's values. We will briefly look at advertising's impact on society's values before focusing on the accuracy and adequacy of consumer information.

Advertising and Values   We discussed the impact of advertising on values in the previous section on advertising to children. The concern is the same for advertising directed at adults—the long-term effect of a constant flow of messages emphasizing materialistic or narcissistic values may be negative for both individuals and society. For example, an ad for Musk by Alyssa Ashley appeared in a magazine read by teenage females. It consisted of a picture of a teenage girl on the back of a motorcycle driven by a scruffy-looking man with long hair, a beard, and a tattoo. The girl's dress is pulled up to the top of her thigh. The only other content was a picture of the product package and the headline—"Sometimes even good girls want to be bad." Many would argue that this ad promotes inappropriate values and behaviors.

Most ads for women's cosmetics and clothing emphasize beauty or sex appeal as major benefits. Each individual ad is probably harmless. However, critics charge that when people see such themes repeated thousands of times for hundreds of products, they learn to consider a person's looks to be more important than other attributes.[45] This can lead to injurious consumption patterns such as excessive tanning or inappropriate dieting despite knowledge of the associated health hazard.[46] These harmful effects may be most severe in younger women.[47] Further, those who cannot afford such products or who are not "good-looking" suffer. Others argue that individuals have been concerned with their looks and possessions in virtually all cultures and times. They argue that advertising does not cause a society's values; it merely reflects them.

Portrayals of beauty and casual attitudes toward sex are not the only ways advertisements are argued to influence values. The portrayal of women in the mass media in general and in advertising in particular often has been limited to stereotypical roles or as decoration.[48] This in turn can influence the concepts girls develop of themselves and their role choices. Of course, many firms now portray females in a more positive, realistic fashion, as shown in Illustration 20–2.

A Nike campaign generated a positive response from many women as well as advertising critics. A television ad in the campaign combined quick camera takes and slow-motion shots of teenage girls on a playground, with images of girls playing on swing sets and monkey bars. The sound portion is a variety of girls' voices describing the long-term benefits of female participation in sports:

> I will like myself more; I will have more self-confidence if you let me play sports. If you let me play, I will be 60 percent less likely to get breast cancer. I will suffer less depression if you let me play sports.
>
> I will be more likely to leave a man who beats me. If you let me play, I will be less likely to get pregnant before I want to; I will learn what it means to be strong.[49]

**ILLUSTRATION 20–2**

Many firms now portray females in a more positive, realistic fashion.

THE MORE MULTITASKING I DO, THE MORE MULTIGRAINS I'M GONNA NEED.

-RACHAEL RAY

DUNKIN' DONUTS

DUNKIN' DONUTS NEW FIBER-RICH, MULTIGRAIN BAGEL WITH REDUCED FAT BLUEBERRY CREAM CHEESE. IT'S THE DELICIOUS WAY TO A HEALTHIER DAY.

The manner in which ethnic groups, the elderly, and other social groups are portrayed in ads and the mass media can affect the way members of these groups view themselves as well as the way others see them.[50] Marketers need to ensure that their ads reflect the diversity of the American society in a manner that is realistic and positive for all the many groups involved. These portrayals should involve both the content of the ads and the shows sponsored by the ads.[51] For example, the relative absence of Hispanic roles and actors on network television has been an ongoing concern among Hispanics, although evidence suggests that this is changing.[52]

**Consumer Information Accuracy**    The salesperson tells you, "My brand is the best there is." Does he or she need scientific proof to make such a statement? At what point does permissible puffery become misleading and illegal? Does it vary by the situation? The consumer group involved?[53]

An ad shows a pair of attractive female legs. The headline reads, "Her legs are insured for $1,000,000. Her policy came with one minor stipulation. Schick Silk Effects." Schick Silk Effects is a women's razor. How do you interpret this ad? Many would assume that the insurance company insisted on her using only this brand as a condition of the policy. This suggests that the insurance company considers this razor to be very good at protecting women's legs while they shave. However, in exceedingly fine print at the very bottom of the ad is this disclaimer: "Policy condition included by insurer at the request of Warner-Lambert Co." Warner-Lambert is the firm that markets Silk Effects. In other words, the firm that owns the razor had the requirement that this razor be used in the insurance policy. This leads to a very different interpretation of the ad. *Should this ad be illegal? Is it unethical?*

Research shows that the more baking soda toothpaste contains, the more effective it is in cleaning away plaque and deep stains. How much baking soda should a brand of toothpaste contain before it can be called "baking soda" toothpaste? There is no rule. Arm & Hammer's contains 65 percent baking soda, but Crest Baking Soda Toothpaste has only 20 percent.[54] *Should there be rules for names such as this or is the required listing of the contents enough?*

Illustration 20–3 shows several major national brands and several competing brands with similar packages. *Are consumers misled by such packages? Or are these legitimate attempts to position competing products as being similar to the brand leaders?*[55]

Because of such problems, various businesses, consumer groups, and regulatory agencies are deeply concerned with the interpretation of marketing messages. However, determining the exact meaning of a marketing message is not a simple process. The National Advertising Division (NAD) of the Council of Better Business Bureaus recently asked Bayer to alter an *accurate* commercial for Aleve. The commercial accurately stated that Aleve provided longer-lasting relief with a smaller dosage than Tylenol ("Just 2 Aleve can stop the pain all day; it would take 8 Tylenol to do that"). The concern was that this would unintentionally convey a message of superior efficacy (it would stop more pain than Tylenol).[56]

Table 20–4 illustrates some of the areas where controversy over the interpretation of various marketing messages has existed.

Obtaining accurate assignments of meaning is made even more difficult by the variation in information-processing skills and motivations among different population groups.[57] For example, this warning was ruled inadequate in a product liability case involving a worker who was injured while inflating a truck tire:

Always inflate tire in safety cage or use a portable lock ring guard. Use a clip-on type air chuck with remote valve so that operator can stand clear during tire inflation.

Is imitation the sincerest form of flattery or a source of consumer confusion?

TABLE 20-4

Regulation and the Interpretation of Marketing Messages

- Gillette was forced to relabel 6.5 million M3 Power razor packages when a court ruled that the claim "gentle micropulses stimulate hair up and away from skin" was literally false. The court indicated that "The use of the term 'up and away' in conjunction with the term 'stimulates' is literally false as it connotes an angle change."[58]
- The 4th U.S. Circuit Court of Appeals ruled that meat from a turkey thigh can be called a "turkey ham" even if it contains no pork. A lower court had reached the opposite conclusion. The ruling appeared to rely heavily on a technical definition of the term *ham*.
- Maximum Strength Anacin's claim that it is "the maximum strength allowed" was ruled illegal because it "implies that an appropriate authority has authorized the sale of products like Maximum Strength Anacin." No such authorization exists.
- Keebler Company's claim of "Baked not fried" for Wheatables and Munch'ems snack crackers was challenged before the NAD. Although the crackers are baked, they are sprayed with vegetable oil after baking and have a fat content similar to that of fried products.
- Under the Federal Trademark Dilution Act (FTDA), Hasbro was able to stop the use of the Internet name candyland.com for a sexually explicit Web site because the site would injure the value of its registered trademark Candy Land (a line of children's games). Courts have generally held that only the owners of registered trademarks can use them as Web site addresses.

The court held that (1) "there is a duty to warn *foreseeable* users of all hidden dangers" and (2) "in view of the unskilled or semiskilled nature of the work and the existence of many in the workforce who do not read English, warnings *in the form of symbols* might have been appropriate since the employee's ability to take care of himself was limited."[59]

Thus, marketers must often go to considerable lengths to provide messages that the relevant audience will interpret correctly.

Fortunately, marketers are developing considerable knowledge on how to effectively present difficult messages about such issues as product risks, nutrition, and affirmative disclosures (see Chapter 8). In addition, consumer research is being used by both marketers and the courts to determine if an ad is misleading.[60]

Regulating the explicit verbal content of ads is difficult. Regulating the more subtle meanings implied by the visual content of ads is much more difficult.[61] For example, some are critical of beer advertisements that portray active young adults in groups having fun and consuming beer. These critics contend that the visual message of these ads is that alcohol consumption is the appropriate way for young adults to be popular and have fun.

Both government and business self-regulatory groups have begun regulating visual communications.

- The FTC challenged ads for Beck's beer that featured young adults drinking on a sailing ship. It charged that the ads promoted unsafe marine conduct.
- The NAD required Balance Bar to drop all claims referring to clinical studies and *visuals of physicians* in its advertising after ruling that its formula was not proved to be "clinically effective for the general population."

**Corrective advertising** is advertising run by a firm to cause consumers to unlearn inaccurate information they acquired as a result of the firm's earlier advertising. Three examples of corrective advertising messages follow:

- "Do you recall some of our past messages saying that Domino sugar gives you strength, energy, and stamina? Actually, Domino is not a special or unique source of strength, energy, and stamina. No sugar is, because what you need is a balanced diet and plenty of rest and exercise."
- "If you've wondered what some of our earlier advertising meant when we said Ocean Spray cranberry juice cocktail has more food energy than orange juice or tomato juice, let us make it clear: we didn't mean vitamins and minerals. Food energy means calories. Nothing more.

    "Food energy is important at breakfast since many of us may not get enough calories, or food energy, to get off to a good start. Ocean Spray cranberry juice cocktail helps because it contains more food energy than most other breakfast drinks.

    "And Ocean Spray cranberry juice cocktail gives you and your family vitamin C plus a great wake-up taste. It's . . . the other breakfast drink."
- Sugar Information, Inc.: "Do you recall the messages we brought you in the past about sugar? How something with sugar in it before meals could help you curb your appetite? We hope you didn't get the idea that our little diet tip was any magic formula for losing weight. Because there are no tricks or shortcuts; the whole diet subject is very complicated. Research hasn't established that consuming sugar before meals will contribute to weight reduction or even keep you from gaining weight."

Although the effectiveness of corrective advertising has been debated, the FTC considers it a useful tool in protecting the public. Likewise, firms injured by the false claims of competitors often request it as a remedy (Power Bar requested the FTC to require Balance Bar to run corrective ads concerning the clinical claims described earlier). Indeed, the threat of lawsuits by competitors can serve as a strong deterrent of comparative advertising. For example, Procter & Gamble is revisiting its aggressive advertising strategy across its various brands in light of all the substantial litigation it has created (e.g., lawsuits by Playtex, J&J-Merck, Kimberly-Clark, and Georgia Pacific).[62]

With regard to corrective advertising, a court ruling has challenged the conditions under which the FTC can require it. Significantly, the challenge centers on how strongly the false impression must be learned before corrective advertising is necessary to erase it.[63]

**Adequacy of Consumer Information**    It is important that consumers have not only accurate information but adequate information as well. To ensure information adequacy, a number of laws have been passed, such as the federal truth-in-lending legislation.

Nutritional labeling has been required for years and was significantly revised in 1990. Research findings on the impact of such labels are mixed, but the labels do provide valuable information to many consumers. A consistent stream of consumer behavior research since these rules were enacted has uncovered a number of potential improvements in the manner in which the information should be presented. Unfortunately, as with many such programs, those who are relatively disadvantaged in terms of education and income are least able to use this type of information.[64]

A new FDA labeling rule deals with trans fats. While the Nutritional Labeling and Education Act (NLEA) of 1990 led to the nutrition fact box on food packaging that includes a line for total fat, the new rule requires a new line for trans fats as well. The logic behind this change, which involves costs to companies in terms of research into trans fat content and label redesign, is explained here:

> The latest health threat is so-called trans fats, which are hydrogenated oils used to make margarine, deep fried foods, cookies, cakes and crackers. They give foods the texture consumers expect, and help foods stay fresh longer than alternative ingredients. Trans fats have an effect similar to saturated fats in the body and raise the level of LDL (bad) cholesterol, but they also lower HDL (good) cholesterol levels. Because of this, the U.S. Food and Drug Administration . . . issued a ruling requiring food manufacturers to modify their package labels to reflect the *total amount* of trans fats used in their products.[65]

Obviously, this ruling will provide opportunities for some food marketers and challenges for others. Given consumer health concerns, marketers of products such as Weetabix (Illustration 20–4) can use trans fats as a point of differentiation not just in the nutrition facts box but also in more prominent locations like the box front.

Marketers, consumer groups, and public officials would like consumers to have all the information they need to make sound choices. One approach is to provide all potentially relevant information. This approach is frequently recommended by regulatory agencies and is required for some product categories such as drugs.

Problems with this approach can arise, however. The assumption behind the full-disclosure approach is that each consumer will utilize those specific information items required for the particular decision. Unfortunately, consumers frequently do not react in this manner. This is true particularly for low-involvement purchases, but can also be true of higher-involvement purchases as well. Instead, consumers may experience *information overload* (see Chapter 8) and ignore all or most of the available data. For example:

> A federal act required banks belonging to the Federal Reserve to explain to their customers the detailed protections built into money transfer systems available in electronic banking. Thus, Northwestern National Bank of Minneapolis was forced to create and mail a pamphlet explaining Amended Regulation E to its 120,000 customers. At a cost of $69,000 the bank created and mailed the 4,500-word pamphlet.
>
> In 100 of the pamphlets, the bank placed a special paragraph that offered the reader $10 just for finding that paragraph. The pamphlets were mailed in May and June. As of August, not one person had claimed the money![66]

ILLUSTRATION 20–4
The new trans fat rule will require packaging adaptations by companies and will serve as a way for certain brands to differentiate themselves from the competition on an attribute of importance to consumers.

In the drug category, relatively simple print ads require attached disclosures, usually printed in small type, telling of dosage, precautions, and warnings in order to comply with federal full-disclosure regulations. Many marketers claim that such ads add to the costs of advertising and therefore reduce the available consumer information without an offset in consumer benefit.[67] Many consumer advocates agree that the current approach is not meeting the needs of consumers.

In the area of online privacy policies which appear to be increasing in length, there is considerable variation in format which can affect consumer information overload and comprehension.[68] The disclosure shown in Illustration 20–5 shows a retailer trying to help organize and chunk the information for consumers to avoid overload.

A new issue confronting marketers and regulators is disclosure in Internet advertising. Disclosure involves providing relevant qualifiers to advertising claims such as "limited to stock on hand," or "available at participating outlets only." The FTC requires disclosures to be "clear and conspicuous," and this standard has been translated into clear guidelines for print, television, and radio ads. The FTC provides the following general guidelines to online marketers. *Are these general guidelines enough?*

- Place the disclosure near the claim it is qualifying.
- Make the disclosure prominent.

Organizing informa-
tion in certain ways
can reduce informa-
tion overload.

- Avoid having other aspects distract from the disclosure.
- Repeat the disclosure if ad length warrants it.
- Make sure disclosures are adequate in volume, size, and duration.
- Make the language of the disclosure understandable to the intended audience.

## Product Issues

Consumer groups have two major concerns with products—*Are they safe?* and *Are they environmentally sound?* A variety of federal and state agencies are involved in ensuring that products are safe to use. The most important are the Food and Drug Administration and the Consumer Product Safety Commission. Product safety is generally not a controversial issue. However, it is impossible to remove all risk from products.

Should tricycles be banned? Accidents involving tricycles are a major cause of injury to young children. Manufacturers, consumer groups, and individuals differ on where the line should be drawn and who should draw it. Some feel that tricycles should indeed be banned. Others feel that parents should decide if their children should ride tricycles. However, both would agree that information on both the risks of tricycle riding and ways of reducing the risk should be made available to purchasers, though there is disagreement on who should make the information available and how it should be made available. Of course, tricycles represent only one of many products subject to such a debate.

We examined consumers' desires for environmentally sound products in some detail in Chapter 3. As indicated there, many consumers want products whose production, use, and disposition produce minimal environmental harm. Many marketers are striving to produce such products. Nonetheless, consumer groups continue to push for more stringent regulation in this area.

Potentially injurious products such as guns, tobacco products, and alcoholic beverages are subject to a wide variety of regulations at the federal, state, and even city level. So-called safer cigarettes such as R. J. Reynolds' Eclipse brand with its claim "may present less risk of cancer" are drawing significant attention.[69]

# Pricing Issues

Consumer groups want prices that are fair (generally defined as competitively determined) and accurately stated (contain no hidden charges). The FTC is the primary federal agency involved in regulating pricing activities.

Perhaps the most controversial pricing area today is the use of reference prices. An **external reference price** is *a price provided by the manufacturer or retailer in addition to the actual current price of the product*. Such terms as "compare at $X," "usually $X," "suggested retail price $Y—our price only $X" are common ways of presenting reference prices (see Chapter 17). The concern arises when the reference price is one at which no or few sales actually occur. Most states and the federal government have regulations concerning the use of reference prices, but they are difficult to enforce. Given the history of abuse of reference prices, it is not surprising that many consumers are skeptical of them.

## SUMMARY

Marketing to children is a major concern to regulators and consumer groups. A major reason for this concern is evidence based on Piaget's theory of cognitive development that children are not able to fully comprehend commercial messages. This has led to rules issued by both the Federal Trade Commission and the Children's Advertising Review Unit (CARU) of the National Advertising Division of the Council of Better Business Bureaus. These rules focus mainly on being sure that commercials are clearly separated from the program content and that the words and pictures in the commercials do not mislead children having limited cognitive skills.

In addition to concerns about children's comprehension of advertisements, there is concern about the effect of the content of commercials on children. The extensive advertising of high-fat and high-sugar products raises a concern about its effect on the health of children, although recent initiatives by the food and beverage industry may help. Since children watch a substantial amount of prime-time television, there is also a danger that ads aimed at adults will inspire children to take inappropriate actions. In addition, there is concern that the enormous amount of advertising that children view will lead to values that are overly materialistic.

There are a number of marketing activities aimed at children other than television advertising that cause concerns. Marketing to children through mobile devices is an emerging concern. Corporate programs that place strong sales messages in "educational" materials supplied to schools have also come under attack. Children's advocates are now particularly concerned about marketing to children on the Internet. The federal government has passed legislation to protect children's online privacy (Children's Online Privacy Protection Act). CARU also has guidelines on this topic.

Regulators and businesses alike are also concerned that adults receive accurate and adequate information about products. The cumulative impact of numerous ads focusing on narcissistic values and product ownership on society's values is a controversial issue.

The regulators and responsible marketers want consumers to have sufficient, adequate information to make sound purchase decisions. Attempts to regulate the amount of information provided sometimes overlook information overload and are not effective.

The focus of consumer concern and regulation of products is twofold: Are they safe? and Are they environmentally sound?

Concern with pricing is that prices be fair and accurately presented in a manner that allows comparison across brands.

## KEY TERMS

Children's Advertising Review Unit (CARU)  701

Children's Online Privacy Protection Act (COPPA)  708

Corrective advertising  715

External reference price  719

## INTERNET EXERCISES

1. Visit the Federal Trade Commission Web site (www.ftc.gov). Describe the issues the FTC is concerned with in terms of consumer protection and marketing.

2. Visit the CARU Web site (www.caru.org). Examine the past six months' news releases. Place each case in a category (such as privacy protection). What do you conclude?

3. Visit the TrustE Web site (www.truste.org). Evaluate its approach to privacy. Will such a seal increase consumer confidence in a site? Justify your response.

4. Visit one of the sites listed below. Evaluate the effectiveness of the site in terms of marketing to children and the degree to which it meets the requirements of The Rules under COPPA (Table 20–3).
   a. www.nick.com
   b. www.barbie.com
   c. www.nabiscoworld.com
   d. www.bk.com/kids.

5. Visit three companies' Web sites. Evaluate their privacy statements and policy.

6. Visit the Better Business Bureau Web site (www.bbb.org). Describe the issues the BBB is concerned with in terms of consumer protection and marketing to adults.

7. Visit an adult-oriented site such as Mike's Hard Lemonade (www.mikeshardlemonade.com). How hard would it be for a 10-year-old to access inappropriate content on this site?

## DDB LIFE STYLE STUDY™ DATA ANALYSES

1. Based on DDB Tables 1B through 7B, what characterizes individuals who feel *TV commercials place too much emphasis on sex*? What are the marketing and regulatory implications of this?

2. Using the DDB Tables (1B through 7B), determine what characterizes people who *avoid buying products advertised on shows with sex or violence*. What are the marketing and regulatory implications of this?

3. What characterizes individuals who feel that *advertising directed at children should be taken off TV* (DDB Tables 1B through 7B)? What are the marketing and regulatory implications of this?

4. Based on DDB Tables 1B through 7B, what characterizes those who feel that *there is not enough ethnic diversity in commercials today*? What are the marketing and regulatory implications of this?

## REVIEW QUESTIONS

1. What are the major concerns in marketing to children?

2. What are the main issues concerning children's ability to comprehend advertising messages?

3. What is *CARU*? What does it do? What are some of its rules?

4. What are the major concerns about the *content* of commercial messages targeting children?

5. What are the issues concerning the impact of advertising on children's health and safety?

6. What are the issues concerning the impact of advertising on children's values?

7. What are the concerns associated with mobile marketing to children?

8. What is meant by "commercialization of schools"? What are the various areas in which commercialization can occur, and what are the major concerns?

9. Why are consumer advocates worried about marketing to kids on the Internet?

10. Describe the key provisions of The Rules under *COPPA*.

11. How would you go about deciding if COPPA has been effective?

12. What are the major concerns with marketing communications targeting adults?

13. What are the issues concerning the impact of advertising on adults' *values*?

14. What are the concerns with *consumer information accuracy*?

15. What are the concerns with *consumer information adequacy*?

16. What is *information overload*?

17. What is *corrective advertising*?

18. What are the FTC's general guidelines for "clear and conspicuous" *disclosure* in an online setting?

19. What are the major regulatory issues with respect to products?

20. What are the major regulatory issues with respect to prices?

21. What is a *reference price*? What is the concern with reference prices?

## DISCUSSION QUESTIONS

22. A television advertisement for General Mills' Total cereal made the following claim: "It would take 16 ounces of the leading natural cereal to equal the vitamins in 1 ounce of fortified Total." The Center for Science in the Public Interest filed a petition against General Mills claiming that the advertisement is deceptive. It was the center's position that the claim overstated Total's nutritional benefits because the cereal is not 16 times higher in other factors important to nutrition.

    a. Is the claim misleading? Justify your answer.

    b. How should the FTC proceed in cases such as this?

    c. What are the implications of cases such as this for marketing management?

23. Turkey ham looks like ham and tastes like ham but it contains no pork; it is all turkey. A nationwide survey of consumers showed that most believed the meat product contained both turkey and ham. The USDA approved this label based on a dictionary definition for the term *ham:* the thigh cut of meat from the hind leg of any animal. Discuss how consumers processed information concerning this product and used this information in purchasing this product. (One court ruled the label to be misleading but was overruled by a higher court.)

    a. Is the label misleading?

    b. How should the FTC proceed in such cases?

24. How much and what type of (if any) advertising should be allowed on television programs aimed at children of the following ages?

    a. Under 6

    b. 6 to 9

    c. 10 to 12

25. Are the self-regulatory attempts by the food and beverage industry enough in regard to regulating food marketing to children? What if anything additional would you propose? Explain.

26. Does advertising influence children's values? What can the FTC or CARU do to ensure that positive values are promoted? Be precise in your responses.

27. What rules, if any, should govern mobile marketing to children?

28. What rules, if any, should govern marketing to kids on the Internet?

29. What rules, if any, should govern advertising and promotional messages presented in the classroom?

30. Does advertising influence or reflect a society's values?

31. Do you agree that beer advertisements portraying groups of active young adults having fun while consuming beer teach people that the way to be popular and have fun is to consume alcohol?

32. Respond to the questions in Consumer Insight 20–1.

33. Do you think corrective advertising works? Evaluate the three corrective messages described in the text.

34. "Since riding tricycles is a major cause of accidental injury to young children, the product should be banned." State and defend your position on this issue (the first part of the statement is true).

35. To what extent, if at all, do you use nutrition labels to guide your purchases? Why?

36. Do you believe reference prices generally reflect prices at which substantial amounts of the product are normally sold? Does this vary by store, season, or other circumstances?

## APPLICATION ACTIVITIES

37. Watch two hours of Saturday morning children's programming on a commercial channel (not public broadcasting). Note how many commercials are run. What products are involved? What are the major themes? Would hundreds of hours of viewing these commercials over the course of several years have any impact on children's values or behaviors?

38. With parental consent, interview a child 2 to 4 years of age, one between 5 and 7, and one between 8 and 10. Determine their understanding of the selling intent and techniques of television commercials.

39. Interview two grade-school teachers and get their responses to material provided by corporations and the level of educational versus commercial content.

40. Repeat Question 37 for prime-time television and adults.

41. Find and copy or describe an ad that you feel is misleading. Explain why.

42. Visit a large supermarket. Considering both cost and nutrition, identify the best and worst breakfast cereal focused on children. What do you conclude?

## REFERENCES

1. Chapter 20 opener is based on B. Young, "Does Food Advertising Influence Children's Food Choices?" *International Journal of Advertising* 22 (2003), pp. 441–59; *The Role of Media in Childhood Obesity* (Washington, DC: Kaiser Family Foundation, Research Report, February 2004); D. Kunkel et al., *Report of the APA Task Force on Advertising to Children* (Washington, DC: American Psychological Association, February 20, 2004); M. M. Cardona, "Marketers Bite Back as Fat Fight Flares Up," *Advertising Age,* March 1, 2004, pp. 3, 35; J. Pereira, "Coming Up Next . . ." *The Wall Street Journal,* March 15, 2004, pp. B1, B3; D. J. Wood, "Anti-Ad Crusaders Miss Point," *Advertising Age,* April 12, 2004, p. 30; J. Pereira, "Junk-Food Games," *The Wall Street Journal,* May 3, 2004, pp. B1, B4; S. Vranica, "Kraft Limits on Kids' Ads May Cheese Off Rivals," *The Wall Street Journal Online,* January 13, 2005, p. B3, www.wsj.com; I. Teinowitz, "Politicians Feast on Food Fight," *Advertising Age,* March 14, 2005, pp. 1, 37; R. Berman, "Sloth, Not Ads, Is Responsible for Fat Kids," *Advertising Age,* April 18, 2005, p. 30; I. Teinowitz, "Marketer Obesity Efforts Get Low Consumer Marks," *AdAge.com,* June 7, 2005; I. Teinowitz, "Food Industry Braces for Two-Day FTC Hearing," *AdAge.com,* July 13, 2005; and D. Majoras, *FTC/HHS Marketing, Self-Regulation, and Childhood Obesity Workshop,* Washington, DC, Federal Trade Commission, Opening Remarks, July 15, 2005, http://www.ftc.gov/speeches/majoras.

2. Majoras, *FTC/HHS Marketing, Self-Regulation, and Childhood Obesity Workshop.*

3. Ibid.

4. In order, these examples come from (*a*) "Marketers Regroup on Junk Food Marketing," *Marketing News,* December 15, 2006, pp. 18, 20; (*b*) "Nutrition Guidelines Fact Sheet," Alliance for a Healthier Generation, www.HealthierGeneration.org, accessed July 31, 2008; and (*c*) I. Teinowitz, "More Major Food Marketers Establish Kids-Advertising Limits," *Advertising* Age, July 18, 2007; and *The Children's Food & Beverage Advertising Initiative in Action* (Arlington, VA: Council of Better Business Bureaus, July 2008).

5. For an overview of this area, see S. Bandyopadhyay, G. Kindra, and L. Sharp, "Is Television Advertising Good for Children?" *International Journal of Advertising* 20, no. 1 (2001), pp. 89–116.

6. See D. R. John, "Consumer Socialization of Children," *Journal of Consumer Research,* December 1999, pp. 183–209.

7. *Self-Regulatory Program for Children's Advertising,* Children's Advertising Review Unit (CARU), Council of Better Business Bureaus, 2006.

8. See M. C. Martin, "Children's Understanding of the Intent of Advertising," *Journal of Public Policy & Marketing,* Fall 1997, pp. 205–16.

9. L. Carlson, R. N. Laczniak, and D. D. Muehling, "Understanding Parental Concern about Toy-Based Programming," *Journal of Current Issues and Research in Advertising,* Fall 1994, pp. 59–72.

10. M. A. Stutts and G. G. Hunnicutt, "Can Young Children Understand Disclaimers?" *Journal of Advertising* 1 (1987), pp. 41–46.

11. R. H. Kolbe and D. D. Muehling, "An Investigation of the Fine Print in Children's Television Advertising," *Journal of Current Issues and Research in Advertising,* Fall 1995, pp. 77–95; and D. D. Muehling and R. H. Kolbe, "A Comparison of Children's and Prime-Time Fine-Print Advertising Disclosure Practices," *Journal of Advertising,* Fall 1998, pp. 37–47.

12. "CARU Recommends Nintendo Modify Advertising for Wii Game System, Game," CARU, Council of Better Business Bureaus, January 30, 2008.

13. "Nabisco Puts Safety First in TV Ads," CARU, Council of Better Business Bureaus, October 4, 2000.

14. "Rose Art Industries, Inc., and Hasbro Participate in CARU Self-Regulatory Forum," CARU, Council of Better Business Bureaus, February 22, 2000.

15. *Self-Regulatory Program for Children's Advertising.*

16. "Skechers USA, Inc. Appeals CARU Decision," CARU, Council of Better Business Bureaus, April 10, 2002.

17. "CARU Recommends Guthy-Renker Discontinue Advertising Proactiv to Children," CARU, Council of Better Business Bureaus, June 9, 2008.

18. "B-M Drops Spots after Query by NAD," *Advertising Age,* April 20, 1981, p. 10.

19. See C. Preston, "The Unintended Effects of Advertising upon Children," *International Journal of Advertising* 18, no. 3 (1999), pp. 363–76.

20. "CARU Reviews Advertising for General Mills' 'Cookie Crisp,'" CARU, Council of Better Business Bureaus, August 23, 2007.

21. H. Clinton, "FTC Action," *Advertising Age,* October 9, 2000, p. 58. For an opposing view, see R. Bergler, "The Effects of Commercial Advertising on Children," *International Journal of Advertising* 18, no. 4 (1999), pp. 411–25.

22. "Advertising Strategies to Target Kids Raise Questions," *10News.com,* July 11, 2005.

23. See, e.g., *The Role of Media in Childhood Obesity* (Washington, DC: Kaiser Family Foundation); and P. M. Ippolito, *TV Advertising to Children 1977 v. 2004* (Washington, DC: Bureau of Economics, FTC, Research Presentation, July 14, 2005).

24. M. M. Cardona, "Young Girls Targeted by Makeup Companies," *Advertising Age,* November 27, 2000, p. 15.

25. M. Scott, "Girls Clamoring for Grown-up Shoe Styles," *Marketing News,* November 19, 2001, p. 25.

26. M. Irvine, "More Young Children Fret over Body Image," *Eugene Register Guard,* July 23, 2001, p. 1.

27. S. W. Colford, "Top Kid TV Offender: Premiums," *Advertising Age*, April 29, 1991, p. 52.

28. *Guidance for Food Advertising Self-Regulation,* New York, National Advertising Review Council, White Paper, May 28, 2004.

29. See K. Anders, "Marketing and Policy Considerations for Violent Video Games," *Journal of Public Policy & Marketing,* Fall 1999, pp. 270–73; I. Teinowitz, "FTC Report Refuels Debate on Violent Entertainment," *Advertising Age,* April 30, 2001, p. 4; I. Teinowitz, "Violence Revisited," *Advertising Age,* December 3, 2001, p. 3; and I. Teinowitz, "Entertainment Gets a Pass," *Advertising Age,* December 10, 2001, p. 16.

30. See *Selling America's Kids* (Yonkers, NY: Consumers Union Educational Services, 1990), p. 15.

31. Y. Noguchi, "Connecting with Kids, Wirelessly," *Washington Post,* July 7, 2005, p. A1.

32. See "Blue Sphere Games Announces Licence Agreement with DC Thomson," *phonegamereview.com,* May, 25, 2005; A. Z. Cuneo, "Marketers Get Serious about the 'Third Screen,'" *Advertising Age,* July 11, 2005, p. 6; and "Please Hold," *Dallas Morning News,* July 14, 2005.

33. *Children's Advocates Ask Congress to Investigate Marketing of Mobile Phones to Kids,* Portland, OR, Commercial Alert, press release, www.commercialalert.org, July 26, 2005.

34. Classification scheme and descriptions come from *Captive Kids* (Yonkers, NY: Consumers Union, 1995 Research Report, copyright 1998). Various examples, unless otherwise listed, from Teinowitz, "Marketer Obesity Efforts Get Low Consumer Marks"; M. M. Cardona, "High School Papers Group to Take Ads," *Advertising Age,* March 29, 2004, p. 13; "NAAG Bans Tobacco Ads in Library Magazines," *Promo Magazine,* June 21, 2005; *Krispy Kreme in Florida Schools,* Portland, OR: Commercial Alert, press release, www.commercialalert.org, August 30,

2004; and A. Enright, "Food, Drink Firms Take New Path to Reach Youths In, Out of Class," *Marketing News,* August 15, 2006, pp. 8–10.

35. See J. E. Brand and B. S. Greenberg, "Commercials in the Classroom," *Journal of Advertising Research,* January 1994, pp. 18–27.

36. See S. Thompson, "Pepsi Hits High Note with Students," *Advertising Age,* October 9, 2000, p. 30; and S. Jarvis, "Lesson Plans," *Marketing News,* June 18, 2001, p. 1.

37. Pereira, "Junk-Food Games," p. B1.

38. K. Montgomery and S. Pasnik, *Web of Deception* (Washington, DC: Center for Media Education, 1996).

39. "Echo Participates in CARU Process," CARU, Council of Better Business Bureaus, May 21, 2008.

40. "CARU Refers Fansite of Singer Pink to Federal Trade Commission," CARU, Council of Better Business Bureaus, April 10, 2002.

41. "Scan-Command.Com Works with CARU," CARU, Council of Better Business Bureaus, April 17, 2002.

42. See K. B. Sheehan and M. G. Hoy, "Flaming, Complaining, and Abstaining," *Journal of Advertising,* Fall 1999, pp. 37–51; K. B. Sheehan, "An Investigation of Gender Differences in On-Line Privacy Concerns," *Journal of Interactive Marketing,* Autumn 1999, pp. 24–38; and E. M. Caudill and P. E. Murphy, "Consumer Online Privacy," J. Phelps, G. Nowak, and E. Ferrell, "Privacy Concerns and Consumer Willingness to Provide Personal Information," and K. B. Sheehan and M. G. Hoy, "Dimensions of Privacy Concern among Online Consumers," all in *Journal of Public Policy & Marketing,* Spring 2000, pp. 7–19, 27–41, and 62–73, respectively. See also K. B. Sheehan and T. W. Gleason, "Online Privacy," *Journal of Current Issues and Research in Advertising,* Spring 2001, pp. 31–41; P. Paul, "Mixed Signals," and R. Gardyn, "Swap Meet," both in *American Demographics,* July 2001, pp. 47 and 51–55, respectively; and J. E. Phelps, G. D'souza, and G. J. Nowak, "Antecedents and Consequences of Consumer Privacy Concerns," *Journal of Interactive Marketing,* Autumn 2001, pp. 2–17.

43. Based on R. Pitofsky, "Privacy Online," testimony before the U.S. Senate, May 25, 2000; and T. J. Muris, "Protecting Consumers' Privacy: 2002 and Beyond," speech at the Privacy 2001 Conference, both available at www.ftc.gov.

44. From the FTC Web site, www.ftc.gov/privacy/privacyinitiatives/promises.html, accessed August 1, 2008.

45. See B. G. Englis, M. R. Solomon, and R. D. Ashmore, "Beauty *before* the Eyes of Beholders," *Journal of Advertising,* June 1994, pp. 49–64; C. R. Wiles, J. A. Wiles, and A. Tjernlund, "The Ideology of Advertising," *Journal of Advertising Research,* May, 1996, pp. 57–66; M. C. Martin and J. W. Gentry, "Stuck in the Model Trap," *Journal of Advertising,* Summer 1997, pp. 19–33; M. K. Hogg, M. Bruce, and K. Hough, "Female Images in Advertising," *International Journal of Advertising* 18, no. 4 (1999), pp. 445–73; and T. Reichert, "The Prevalence of Sexual Imagery in Ads Targeted to Young Adults," *Journal of Consumer Affairs,* Winter 2003, pp. 403–12.

46. S. Burton, R. G. Netemeyer, and D. R. Lichtenstein, "Gender Differences for Appearance-Related Attitudes and Behaviors," *Journal of Public Policy & Marketing,* Fall 1994, pp. 60–75.

47. R. Gustafson, M. Popovich, and S. Thompson, "Subtle Ad Images Threaten Girls More," *Marketing News,* June 4, 2001, p. 12.

48. For research in these areas, see R. W. Pollay and S. Lysonski, "In the Eye of the Beholder," *Journal of International Consumer Marketing* 6, no. 2 (1993), pp. 25–43; D. Walsh, "Safe Sex in Advertising," *American Demographics,* April 1994, pp. 24–30; and R. H. Kolbe and D. Muehling, "Gender Roles and Children's Television Advertising," *Journal of Current Issues and Research in Advertising,* Spring 1995, pp. 49–64.

49. C. Rubel, "Marketers Giving Better Treatment to Females," *Marketing News,* April 22, 1996, p. 10.

50. See L. Langmeyer, "Advertising Images of Mature Adults," *Journal of Current Issues and Research in Advertising,* Fall 1993, pp. 81–91; C. R. Taylor and J. Y. Lee, "Not in *Vogue,*" *Journal of Public Policy & Marketing,* Fall 1994, pp. 239–45; T. H. Stevenson and P. E. McIntyre, "A Comparison of the Portrayal and Frequency of Hispanics and Whites in English Language Television Advertising," and M. T. Elliott, "Differences in the Portrayal of Blacks," both in *Journal of Current Issues and Research in Advertising,* Spring 1995, pp. 65–86; J. M. Bristor, R. G. Lee, and M. R. Hunt, "Race and Ideology," *Journal of Public Policy & Marketing,* Spring 1995, pp. 48–59; E. J. Wilson and A. Biswas, "The Use of Black Models in Specialty Catalogs," *Journal of Direct Marketing,* Autumn 1995, pp. 47–56; and K. Karande and A. Grbavac, "Acculturation and the Use of Asian Models in Print Advertisements," *Enhancing Knowledge Development in Marketing* (Chicago: American Marketing Association, 1996), pp. 347–52.

51. See L. J. Shrum, "Television and Persuasion," *Psychology & Marketing,* March 1999, pp. 119–40.

52. See, e.g., *Fall Colors* (Oakland, CA: Children Now, 2003–04).

53. See A. Simonson and M. B. Holbrook, "Permissible Puffery versus Actionable Warranty in Advertising and Salestalk," *Journal of Public Policy & Marketing,* Fall 1993, pp. 216–33.

54. J. Pollack, "Arm & Hammer Brand Fights Toothpaste Rivals," *Advertising Age,* July 27, 1998, p. 2.

55. See J.-N. Kapferer, "Brand Confusion," *Psychology & Marketing,* September 1995, pp. 551–68; and D. J. Howard, R. A. Kerin, and C. Gengler, "The Effects of Brand Name Similarity on Brand Source Confusion," *Journal of Public Policy & Marketing,* Fall 2000, pp. 250–64.

56. "Bayer & McNeil Participate in NAD Self-Regulatory Process," CARU, Council of Better Business Bureaus, July 8, 2002.

57. C. A. Cole and G. J. Gaeth, "Cognitive and Age-Related Differences in the Ability to Use Nutritional Information in a Complex Environment," *Journal of Marketing Research,* May 1990, pp. 175–84; and W. Mueller, "Who Reads the Label?" *American Demographics,* January 1991, pp. 36–40.

58. Gillette example from J. Neff, "Court Rules against Gillette Razor Package Claim," *AdAge.com,* June 23, 2005.

59. B. Reid, "Adequacy of Symbolic Warnings," *Marketing News,* October 25, 1985, p. 3.

60. M. L. Retsky, "Survey Research Is Useful in False Advertising Cases," *Marketing News,* April 27, 1998, p. 8; M. L. Retsky, "Misleading Ads Could Be as Litigious as Outright Lies," *Marketing News,* August 3, 1998, p. 5; and I. L. Preston, "Dilution and Negation of Consumer Information by Antifactual Content," *Journal of Consumer Affairs,* Summer 2003, pp. 1–21.

61. See G. V. Johar, "Consumer Involvement and Deception from Implied Advertising Campaigns," *Journal of Marketing Research,* August 1995, pp. 267–79.

62. S. Ellison and B. Steinberg, "P&G Is Settling Disputes on Ads as Suits Pile Up," *The Wall Street Journal,* November 26, 2003, pp. B1, B3.

63. I. Teinowitz, "FTC Faces Test of Ad Power," *Advertising Age,* March 30, 1998, p. 26.

64. See, e.g., A. Mitra et al., "Can the Educationally Disadvantaged Interpret the FDA-Mandated Nutrition Facts Panel?" *Journal of Public Policy & Marketing,* Spring 1999, pp. 106–17; J. A. Garretson and S. Burton, "Effects of Nutrition Facts Panel Values, Nutrition Claims, and Health Claims," *Journal of Public Policy & Marketing,* Fall 2000, pp. 213–27; G. Baltas, "The Effects of Nutrition Information on Consumer Choice," *Journal of Advertising Research,* March 2001, pp. 57–63; and S. K. Balasubramanian and C. Cole, "Consumers' Search and Use of Nutrition Information," *Journal of Marketing,* July 2002, pp. 112–27.

65. D. L. Vence, "The Lowdown on Trans Fats," *Marketing News,* March 15, 2004, pp. 13–14.

66. "$10 Sure Thing," *Time,* August 4, 1980, p. 51. See also M. A. Eastlick, R. Feinberg, and C. Trappey, "Information Overload in Mail Catalog Shopping," *Journal of Direct Marketing,* Autumn 1993, pp. 14–19. For a different explanation, see Y. Ganzach and P. Ben-Or, "Information Overload, Decreasing Marginal Responsiveness, and the Estimation of Nonmonotonic Relationships in Direct Marketing," *Journal of Direct Marketing,* Spring 1996, pp. 7–12.

67. See M. Wilkie, "Rx Marketers 'Test' FDA Guides on Print DTC Ads," *Advertising Age,* April 6, 1998, p. 18.

68. G. R. Milne, M. J. Culnan, and H. Greene, "A Longitudinal Assessment of Online Privacy Notice Readability," *Journal of Public Policy and Marketing*, Fall 2006, pp. 238–49.

69. V. O'Connell, "As 'Safer Smokes' Multiply, States Probe Marketing Claims," *The Wall Street Journal,* May 18, 2004, pp. B1, B10.

# Part Six | Cases

Table A provides a grid that can be used to evaluate how well various Web sites targeted toward children under 13 years of age adhere to The Rules under COPPA (Children's Online Privacy Protection Act). Each row represents one of the key provisions of The Rules under COPPA (for more detail on each provision, see Table 20–3). Each column represents a different company Web site.

| COPPA Provision | Company A | Company B | Company C |
|---|---|---|---|
| Privacy Policy | | | |
| Parental Notice | | | |
| Parental Consent | | | |
| Parental Access | | | |
| Conditional Access | | | |
| Confidentiality | | | |

**TABLE A**

The Rules Under COPPA—Evaluation Grid

Each company Web site can be rated in terms of its adherence to each COPPA provision on the following scale: 1 = very poor; 2 = poor; 3 = adequate; 4 = good; 5 = very good. Alternatively, a check box procedure might be used in which a check mark is placed in each cell where the provision is met.

## Discussion Questions

1. Visit at least three Web sites designed to appeal to children under 13 (e.g., Nick.com, Disney.com and so on) and complete the COPPA Evaluation Grid.

2. Prepare a report including the COPPA Evaluation Grid and discuss how well these companies appear to be adhering to the The Rules under COPPA. Are there areas in which you see room for improvement? Explain.

3. Do you feel COPPA is adequate? Detail any areas where COPPA could be strengthened in order to better protect children's online privacy.

4. CARU (Children's Advertising Review Unit) has its own self-regulatory program, which is an FTC-approved Safe Harbor. Participants (companies) who adhere to CARU's Guidelines are deemed in compliance with COPPA. Visit CARU's Online Privacy Program area at www.caru.org/program/index.asp, and address the following:

   a. In what ways do CARU's guidelines (under CARU's compliance checklist tab) help companies interpret the broad mandates of COPPA?

   b. Do CARU's guidelines help you make finer-grade assessments of the companies you evaluated in Questions 1 and 2 above? Do your assessments remain the same, or do they change? Explain.

   c. Describe and evaluate any tools provided by CARU to help companies evaluate their Web sites with respect to children's online privacy.

## CASE 6–2 SAFER CIGARETTES?

For some years, there has been an ongoing debate over the marketing of so-called safer cigarettes—cigarettes with lower levels of cancer-causing substances that could be seen as healthier alternatives to regular cigarettes. One brand that was tested in recent years but is currently not on the market is Advance. Advance was produced by Brown & Williamson Tobacco (now owned by R.J. Reynolds). "Safer" cigarette brands have not done well in the U.S. market, although some in the industry think there is a niche in this area. As such, the test and various reactions to it, which are detailed next, are instructive regarding the issues surrounding this product.

In November 2001, Brown & Williamson Tobacco placed Advance cigarettes into Indianapolis stores for a sales test. Ads supporting the brand featured part of a man's or woman's face focusing on one clear eye. The headline was "New ADVANCE . . . A step in the right direction." The tagline was, "All of the taste . . . Less of the toxins." The text credited the toxin reduction to a "revolutionary new filter design," and a "patented new method for growing tobacco." The text again stated, "Less toxins and great taste." In addition to the required Surgeon General's warning, the ads contained a boxed statement: "There is no such thing as a safe cigarette, nor is there enough medical information to know if Advance with less toxins will lower health risks." This statement was also on the back of the package.

At the time, there are four views of the likely impact of this product and its message. Brown & Williamson felt it met a market need. It used the "less toxins" claim because

[i]t seems to be the clearest and most impactful statement we could make of the facts that are behind Advance and the product itself. We did not want to get into polysyllabic chemical names.

One analyst felt that the tagline would backfire and remind smokers of the harmful effects of smoking:

People are aware of the fact that when they purchase cigarettes, there are significant adverse health consequences, but it doesn't seem to be a winning proposition to remind them every time.

Mathew Myers, president of the Campaign for Tobacco-Free Kids, felt it was unethical and misleading:

It's always a good thing to remove a known carcinogen from cigarettes, but it is irresponsible to make statements in marketing that will lead consumers to believe that the product is safer. And that's exactly what happens when a manufacturer touts a product as having fewer toxins, no matter how many disclaimers they put on it.

A final view was expressed by an analyst who saw very little demand for a safer or less toxic cigarette:

Cigarette smokers are risk-takers. If they're truly concerned about health, they quit.

### Discussion Questions

1. Which of the four positions described above is (are) most likely accurate? Why?
2. Why would consumers believe that Advance was a safer, if not a safe, cigarette despite the disclaimer?
3. What are the ethical issues involved surrounding Brown & Williamson's launch of this product?
4. What regulations, if any, should be applied to promoting toxin reduction in cigarettes?
5. Less-educated individuals are much more likely to smoke and smoke heavily. Does this fact impose additional ethical or regulatory requirements on companies trying to market a so-called safer cigarette?

Source: C. B. DiPasquale, "B&W Smoke Boasts Fewer Toxins," *Advertising Age,* November 5, 2001, p. 3; "Blowing Smoke," *Advertising Age,* November 12, 2001, p. 26; B. Garfield, "Softly Lit or Blunt, 'Less Toxic' Cigarette Ads Hint at Health," *Advertising Age,* November 12, 2001; C. B. DiPasquale, "B&W Leads Lower-Toxin Pitch," *Advertising Age,* June 24, 2002, p. S22; "B&W Seeks to Advance 'Safer Smokes' Category," *Brandweek,* July 26–August 2, 2004, p. 10; and *Cigarette Smoking among Adults—United States, 2006* (Atlanta: Centers for Disease Control, 2006).

# Consumer Research Methods

In this appendix, we want to provide you with some general guidelines for conducting research on consumer behavior. While these guidelines will help you get started, a good marketing research text is indispensable if you need to conduct a consumer research project or evaluate a consumer research proposal.

## SECONDARY DATA

Secondary data is basically existing information or data. Any research project should begin with a thorough search for existing information relevant to the project at hand. Internal data, such as past studies, sales reports, and accounting records, should be consulted. External data, including reports, magazines, government organizations, trade associations, marketing research firms, advertising agencies, academic journals, trade journals, and books, should be thoroughly researched.

Computer searches are a fast, economical means of conducting such searches. University and large public libraries, as well as companies, often subscribe to various databases that can be invaluable sources of information, reports, and data. These include, but are not limited to, (a) ABI Inform—electronic access to trade and academic publications, (b) MarketResearch.com—an online source of detailed industry reports, (c) Simmons Market Research Bureau data, (d) Mediamark data, and (e) Standard Rate and Data Service (SRDS). Publicly available demographic information can be found at the U.S. Census (www.census.gov). And a great source for global information is *The World Fact Book* (www.cia.gov/cia/publications/factbook/).

## PRIMARY DATA COLLECTION: ISSUES AND METHODS

If the specific information required is not available from secondary sources, we must gather primary data. Primary data is information or data that we collect for the first time in order to answer a specific research question. Thus, we might use the U.S. Census data to better understand the demographics driving gardening (secondary data), but conduct a survey to collect information (primary data) regarding the specific brand name we will use for our new garden tool.

## Sampling

Collecting primary data generally involves talking to or observing consumers. However, it could involve asking knowledgeable others, such as sales personnel, about the consumers. In either case, time and cost constraints generally preclude us from contacting every single potential consumer. Therefore, most consumer research projects require a sample—a deliberately selected portion of the larger group. This requires a number of critical decisions, as described below. Mistakes made at this point are difficult to correct later in the study. The key decisions are briefly described below.

**Define the Population**    The first step is to define the consumers in which we are interested. Do we want to talk to current brand users, current product-category users, or potential product-category users? Do we want to talk with the purchasers, the users, or everyone involved in the purchase process? The population as we define it must reflect the behavior on which our marketing decision will be based.

**Specify the Sampling Frame**    A sampling frame is a list or grouping of individuals or households that reflects the population of interest. A phone book and shoppers at a given shopping mall can each serve as a sampling frame. Perfect sampling frames contain every member of the population one time. Phone books do not have households with unlisted numbers; many people do not visit shopping malls, while others visit them frequently. This is an area in which we generally must do the best we can without expecting a perfect frame. However, we must be very alert for biases that may be introduced by imperfections in our sampling frame.

**Select a Sampling Method**    The major decision at this point is between a random (probability) sample and a nonrandom sample. Nonrandom samples, particularly judgment samples, can provide good results. A judgment sample involves the deliberate selection of knowledgeable consumers or individuals. For example, a firm might decide to interview the social activity officers of fraternities and sororities to estimate campus attitudes toward a carbonated wine drink aimed at the campus market. Such a sample might provide useful insights. However, it might also be biased, since such individuals are likely to have a higher level of income and be more socially active than the average student.

The most common nonrandom sample, the convenience sample, involves selecting sample members in the manner most convenient for the researcher. It is subject to many types of bias and should generally be avoided.

Random or probability samples allow some form of a random process to select members from a sample frame. It may be every third person who passes a point-of-purchase display, house addresses selected by using a table of random numbers, or telephone numbers generated randomly by a computer. If random procedures are used, we can calculate the likelihood that our sample is not representative within specified limits.

**Determine Sample Size**    Finally, we must determine how large a sample to talk to. If we are using random sampling, there are formulas that can help us make this decision. In general, the more diverse our population is and the more certain we want to be that we have the correct answer, the more people we will need to interview.

# DATA COLLECTION METHODS

## Depth Interviews

Depth interviews can involve one respondent and one interviewer, or they may involve a small group (8 to 15 respondents) and an interviewer. The latter are called **focus group**

**interviews,** and the former are termed **individual depth interviews** or one-on-ones. Groups of four or five are often referred to as minigroup interviews. Depth interviews in general are commonly referred to as qualitative research. Individual depth interviews involve a one-to-one relationship between the interviewer and the respondent. The interviewer does not have a specific set of prespecified questions that must be asked according to the order imposed by a questionnaire. Instead, there is freedom to create questions, to probe those responses that appear relevant, and generally to try to develop the best set of data in any way practical. However, the interviewer must follow one rule: He or she must not consciously try to affect the content of the answers given by the respondent. The respondent must feel free to reply to the various questions, probes, and other, more subtle ways of encouraging responses in the manner deemed most appropriate.

Individual depth interviews are appropriate in six situations:

1. Detailed probing of an individual's behavior, attitudes, or needs is required.
2. The subject matter under discussion is likely to be of a highly confidential nature (e.g., personal investments).
3. The subject matter is of an emotionally charged or embarrassing nature.
4. Certain strong, socially acceptable norms exist (e.g., child care) and the need to conform in a group discussion may influence responses.
5. A highly detailed (step-by-step) understanding of complicated behavior or decision-making patterns (e.g., planning the family holiday) is required.
6. The interviews are with professional people or with people on the subject of their jobs (e.g., finance directors).

Focus group interviews can be applied to (1) basic need studies for product ideas creation, (2) new-product ideas or concept exploration, (3) product-positioning studies, (4) advertising and communications research, (5) background studies on consumers' frames of reference, (6) establishment of consumer vocabulary as a preliminary step in questionnaire development, and (7) determination of attitudes and behaviors.

The standard focus group interview involves 8 to 12 individuals. Normally, the group is designed to reflect the characteristics of a particular market segment. The respondents are selected according to the relevant sampling plan and meet at a central location that generally has facilities for recording the interviews. The discussion itself is led by a moderator. The competent moderator attempts to develop three clear stages in the one- to three-hour interview: (1) establish rapport with the group, structure the rules of group interaction, and set objectives; (2) attempt to provoke intense discussion in the relevant areas; and (3) attempt to summarize the group's responses to determine the extent of agreement. In general, either the moderator or a second person prepares a summary of each session after analyzing the session's transcript.

## Observation

Observation can be used when (1) the behaviors of interest are public; (2) they are repetitive, frequent, or predictable; and (3) they cover a relatively brief time span. An observational study requires five decisions:

1. *Natural versus contrived situation.* Do we wait for a behavior to occur in its natural environment, or do we create an artificial situation in which it will occur?
2. *Open versus disguised observation.* To what extent are the consumers aware that we are observing their behavior?
3. *Structured versus unstructured observation.* Will we limit our observations to predetermined behaviors, or will we note whatever occurs?
4. *Direct or indirect observations.* Will we observe the behaviors themselves or merely the outcomes of the behaviors?

5. *Human or mechanical observations.* Will the observations be made mechanically or by people?

## Physiological Measures

Physiological measures are direct observations of physical responses to a stimulus such as an advertisement. These responses may be controllable, such as eye movements, or uncontrollable, such as the galvanic skin response. Eye-tracking cameras allow researchers to determine how long a consumer looks at each element in a stimulus, such as a point-of-purchase display, ad, or package, and the sequence in which the elements are examined. Galvanic skin response can be measured (via a lie detector) to detect the intensity of emotional responses to ads or packages.

## Projective Techniques

Projective techniques are designed to measure feelings, attitudes, and motivations that consumers are unable or unwilling to reveal otherwise. They are based on the theory that the description of vague objects requires interpretation, and this interpretation can be based only on the individual's own attitudes, values, and motives.

Table A–1 provides descriptions and examples of the more common projective techniques.

## Surveys

Surveys are systematic ways of gathering information from a large number of people. They generally involve the use of a structured or semi-structured questionnaire. Surveys can be

**TABLE A–1**

Motivation Research Techniques

| **Association Techniques** | |
|---|---|
| Word association | Consumers respond to a list of words with the first word that comes to mind. |
| Successive word association | Consumers give the series of words that come to mind after hearing each word on the list. |
| Analysis and use | Responses are analyzed to see if negative associations exist. When the time to respond (response latency) is also measured, the emotionality of the word can be estimated. These techniques tap semantic memory more than motives and are used for brand name and advertising copy tests. |
| **Completion Techniques** | |
| Sentence completion | Consumers complete a sentence such as "People who buy a Cadillac _____ _____." |
| Story completion | Consumers complete a partial story. |
| Analysis and use | Responses are analyzed to determine what themes are expressed. Content analysis—examining responses for themes and key concepts—is used. |
| **Construction Techniques** | |
| Cartoon techniques | Consumers fill in the words or thoughts of one of the characters in a cartoon drawing. |
| Third-person techniques | Consumers tell why "an average woman," "most doctors," or "people in general" purchase or use a certain product. Shopping lists (describe a person who would go shopping with this list) and lost wallets (describe a person with these items in his wallet) are also third-person techniques. |
| Picture response | Consumers tell a story about a person shown buying or using a product in a picture or line drawing. |
| Analysis and use | Same as for completion techniques. |

administered by mail, telephone, in person, or online. Personal interviews generally take place in shopping malls and are referred to as mall intercept interviews. Each approach has advantages and disadvantages.

- **Personal interviews** allow the use of complex questionnaires, product demonstrations, and the collection of large amounts of data. They can be completed in a relatively short period of time. However, they are very expensive and are subject to interviewer bias.
- **Telephone surveys** can be completed rapidly, provide good sample control (who answers the questions), and are relatively inexpensive. Substantial amounts of data can be collected, but it must be relatively simple. Interviewer bias is possible.
- **Mail surveys** take the longest to complete and must generally be rather short. They can be used to collect modestly complex data, and they are very economical. Interviewer bias is not a problem.
- **Online surveys** are increasingly popular since they are highly cost effective (respondents enter the data), fast, and easy to conduct. A major concern with online survey research historically has been the demographic skew or bias due to income, education, ethnic, and gender gaps. As the online population continues to become more representative of the general population, such concerns are reduced.

A major concern in survey research is nonresponse bias. In most surveys, fewer than 50 percent of those selected to participate in the study actually do participate. In telephone and personal interviews, many people are not at home or refuse to cooperate. In mail surveys, many people refuse or forget to respond.

We can increase the response rate by callbacks in telephone and home personal surveys. The callbacks should be made at different times and on different days. Monetary inducements (enclosing $1) increase the response rate to mail surveys, as do prenotification (a card saying that a questionnaire is coming) and reminder postcards.

If less than a 100 percent response rate is obtained, we must be concerned that those who did not respond differ from those who did. A variety of techniques are available to help us estimate the likelihood and nature of nonresponse error.

## Experimentation

Experimentation involves changing one or more variables (product features, package color, advertising theme) and observing the effect the change has on another variable (consumer attitude, repeat purchase behavior, learning). The variable(s) that is changed is called an *independent variable*. The "change" is called a "manipulation," which simply means that we are systematically varying a factor at different levels. For example, if we presented different groups of consumers with a product priced at $1.00, $1.50, and $2.00, then we would have manipulated price at three levels.

The variable(s) that may be affected by the manipulation(s) is called a *dependent variable*. The objective in experimental design is to structure the situation so that any change in the dependent variable is very likely to have been caused by a change in the independent variable. The way this is done is through high levels of "control," which generally means that we manipulate variables of interest and hold all other factors constant. Thus, we could present three different product concepts that differed only in terms of price. Everything else, including design, package color, and so on, would be held constant (or remain the same) across the different price levels. The logic is that since only the manipulated variable changed, we have high confidence that it was the reason (cause) for any observed changes in the dependent variable.

There are numerous experimental designs depending on the number and level of independent variables the researcher wishes to investigate. There are different kinds of experiments that reflect the level of control that we can achieve. In a laboratory experiment, we carefully control for all outside influences and can conclude with confidence that our independent variables *caused* the changes in our dependent variable(s). Lab experiments thus yield high levels of *internal validity*.

In a field experiment, we conduct our study in the most relevant environment possible. This generally means giving up the pristine control of a lab setting. However, the reason for doing so is to see how consumers actually react in "real-world" settings. Field experiments are important because they help establish *external validity*—which is the extent to which our results are likely to hold true in real-world settings. This can mean that unusual outside influences may distort our results (that is, reduce internal validity). However, careful planning can often avoid these unusual influences.

### Conjoint Analysis: Examining Attribute Importance Using Experimentation

Conjoint analysis is an application of experimentation. In conjoint analysis, the consumer is presented with a set of products or product descriptions in which the potential evaluative criteria vary (are manipulated). For example, consider a notebook manufacturer who is interested in the importance of four different attributes: Processor (2 levels: Pentium M 1.6 Ghz versus Pentium M 2.0 Ghz), Energy Star compliant (2 levels: yes versus no), weight (2 levels: 3.5 lbs versus 5.1 lbs), and price (3 levels: $1,000, $1,500, and $2,000). This would result in 24 different notebook computer configurations ($2 \times 2 \times 2 \times 3 = 24$) that vary on four criteria. Two might be

| | |
|---|---|
| Pentium M 2.0 Ghz | Pentium M 1.6 Ghz |
| Energy Star compliant (yes) | Energy Star compliant (no) |
| 5.1 lbs | 3.5 lbs |
| $1,500 | $2,000 |

The consumer ranks all 24 such descriptions in terms of his or her preference for those combinations of features. Based on these preference ranks, sophisticated computer programs derive the relative importance consumers assign to each level of each attribute tested.

For example, in Figure A–1, imagine a consumer was asked to rank in terms of overall preference 24 different computer designs featuring different levels of four key evaluative criteria. The preferences were then analyzed in light of the variations in the attributes. The result is a preference curve for each evaluative criterion that reflects the importance of that attribute. On the basis of the data in Figure A–1, processor is a particularly important evaluative criterion for this consumer while weight (at least in the range examined) is of almost no importance.

Conjoint analysis is limited to the attributes listed by the researcher. Thus, a conjoint analysis of soft-drink attributes would not indicate anything about calorie content unless the researcher listed it as a feature. If an important attribute is omitted, incorrect market share predictions are likely to result. In addition, conjoint analysis is not well suited for measuring the importance of emotional or feeling-based product choices. For example, what types of attributes would you use to perform a conjoint analysis of perfumes?

## Questionnaire Design

All surveys and many experiments use questionnaires as data collection devices. A questionnaire is simply a formalized set of questions for eliciting information. It can measure (1) behavior—past, present, or intended; (2) demographic characteristics—age, gender,

**Using Conjoint Analysis to Determine the Importance of Evaluative Criteria for a Notebook Computer**

**FIGURE A–1**

**Design features**

Processor
• Pentium M 1.6 GHz
• Pentium M 2.0 GHz

Energy Star compliant
• Yes
• No

Weight
• 3.5 lbs
• 5.1 lbs

Price
• $1,000
• $1,500
• $2,000

**Design options**

These design attributes produce 24 alternative computer design configurations

**One design possibility**

Processor: Pentium M 2.0 GHz
Energy Star compliant: No
Weight: 5.1 lbs
Price level: $2,000

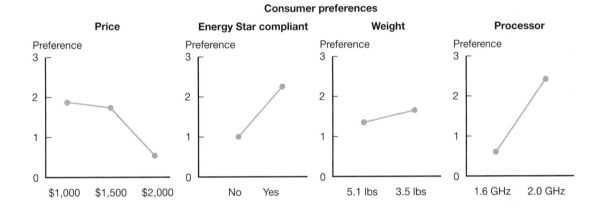

**Consumer preferences**

**Relative importance**

| Evaluative criteria | Importance |
|---|---|
| Processor | 45% |
| Weight | 5 |
| Energy Star compliant | 25 |
| Price | 25 |

■ Processor is the most important feature in this example, and Pentium M 2.0 GHz is the preferred option.

■ While price and Energy Star compliant are also important, price becomes important only between $1,500 and $2,000.

income, education, occupation; (3) level of knowledge; and (4) attitudes and opinions. The process of questionnaire design is outlined in Table A–2.

## Attitude Scales

Attitudes are frequently measured on specialized scales, as detailed below. The instructions indicate that the consumer is to mark the blank that best indicates how accurately one or the other term describes or fits the attitude object.

| TABLE A–2 |
| --- |

**Questionnaire Design Process**

1. *Preliminary decisions*
   Exactly what information is required?
   Exactly who are the target respondents?
   What method of communication will be used to reach these respondents?
2. *Decisions about question content*
   Is this question really needed?
   Is this question sufficient to generate the needed information?
   Can the respondent answer the question correctly?
   Will the respondent answer the question correctly?
   Are there any external events that might bias the response to the question?
3. *Decisions about the response format*
   Can this question best be asked as an open-ended, multiple-choice, or dichotomous question?
4. *Decisions concerning question phrasing*
   Do the words used have but one meaning to all the respondents?
   Are any of the words or phrases loaded or leading in any way?
   Are there any implied alternatives in the question?
   Are there any unstated assumptions related to the question?
   Will the respondents approach the question from the frame of reference desired by the researcher?
5. *Decisions concerning the question sequence*
   Are the questions organized in a logical manner that avoids introducing errors?
6. *Decisions on the layout of the questionnaire*
   Is the questionnaire designed in a manner to avoid confusion and minimize recording errors?
7. *Pretest and revise*
   Has the final questionnaire been subjected to a thorough pretest, using respondents similar to those who will be included in the final survey?

Various types of attitude scales exist, including the following:

**Noncomparative Rating Scale**    Noncomparative rating scales require the consumer to evaluate an object or an attribute of the object without directly comparing it to another object. An example would be:
   *"How do you like the taste of Diet Pepsi?"*

| Like it very much | Like it | Dislike it | Strongly dislike it |
| --- | --- | --- | --- |
| _____ | _____ | _____ | _____ |

**Comparative Rating Scale**    Comparative rating scales provide a direct comparison point (a named competitor, "your favorite brand," "the ideal brand"). An example would be:
   *"How do you like the taste of Tom's of Maine compared with Ultra Bright?"*

| Like it much more | Like it more | Like it about the same | Like it less | Like it much less |
| --- | --- | --- | --- | --- |
| _____ | _____ | _____ | _____ | _____ |

**Semantic Differential Scale**    The semantic differential scale requires the consumer to rate an item on a number of scales bounded at each end by one of two bipolar adjectives. For example:
   *"Rate the Honda Accord on the following attributes."*

Fast _____ _____ _____ _____ _____ _____ _____ Slow

Fancy _____ _____ _____ _____ _____ _____ _____ Plain

The end positions indicate "extremely," the next pair in from the ends indicate "very," the middlemost pair indicate "somewhat," and the middle position indicates "neither/nor."

**Likert Scale**   Likert scales ask consumers to indicate a degree of agreement or disagreement with each of a series of statements related to the attitude object, such as the following:

1. *Macy's is one of the most attractive stores in town.*

| Strongly agree | Agree | Neither agree nor disagree | Disagree | Strongly disagree |
|---|---|---|---|---|
| _____ | _____ | _____ | _____ | _____ |

2. *The service at Macy's is not satisfactory.*

| Strongly agree | Agree | Neither agree nor disagree | Disagree | Strongly disagree |
|---|---|---|---|---|
| _____ | _____ | _____ | _____ | _____ |

To analyze responses each response category is assigned a numerical value. For example, in the Likert scales above we could assign values such as 1 (Strongly agree) through 5 (Strongly disagree). Or a +2 through −2 system could be used with 0 representing the neutral point (Neither agree nor disagree).

## Measuring the Three Attitude Components

As we discussed in Chapter 11, attitude can be broken into its cognitive, affective, and behavioral components. Table A–3 provides a detailed set of items for each attitude component.

**Cognitive Component (Measuring Beliefs about Specific Attributes Using the Semantic Differential Scale)**

Diet Coke

| | | | | | | |
|---|---|---|---|---|---|---|
| Strong taste | ____ | ____ | ____ | ____ | ____ | Mild taste |
| Low priced | ____ | ____ | ____ | ____ | ____ | High priced |
| Caffeine free | ____ | ____ | ____ | ____ | ____ | High in caffeine |
| Distinctive in taste | ____ | ____ | ____ | ____ | ____ | Similar in taste to most |

**Affective Component (Measuring Feelings about Specific Attributes or the Overall Brand Using Likert Scales)**

| | Strongly agree | agree | Neither agree nor disagree | Disagree | Strongly disagree |
|---|---|---|---|---|---|
| I like the taste of Diet Coke. | ____ | ____ | ____ | ____ | ____ |
| Diet Coke is overpriced. | ____ | ____ | ____ | ____ | ____ |
| Caffeine is bad for your health. | ____ | ____ | ____ | ____ | ____ |
| I like Diet Coke. | ____ | ____ | ____ | ____ | ____ |

**Behavioral Component (Measuring Actions or Intended Actions)**

The last soft drink I consumed was a _____.
I usually drink _____ soft drinks.
What is the likelihood you will buy Diet Coke the next time you purchase a soft drink?

_____ Definitely will buy
_____ Probably will buy
_____ Might buy
_____ Probably will not buy
_____ Definitely will not buy

# EVALUATING ADVERTISING EFFECTS

A successful advertisement, or any other marketing message, must accomplish four tasks:

1. *Exposure.* It must physically reach the consumer.
2. *Attention.* The consumer must attend to it.
3. *Interpretation.* It must be properly interpreted.
4. *Memory.* It must be stored in memory in a manner that will allow retrieval under the proper circumstances.

Advertising evaluation covers all these tasks. However, most of the effort is focused on attention and, to a lesser extent, memory.

## Measures of Exposure

Exposure to print media is most frequently measured in terms of circulation. Data on circulation are provided by a variety of commercial firms. Frequently, however, these data are not broken down in a manner consistent with the firm's target market. Thus, a firm may be targeting the lower-middle social class, but circulation data may be broken down by income rather than social class.

Diary reports, in which respondents record their daily listening patterns, and telephone interviews are the two methods used to measure radio listening. Television viewing is measured primarily by **people meters** (mechanical observation), which are electronic devices that automatically determine if a television is turned on and, if so, to which channel. They allow each household member to log on when viewing by punching an identifying button. The demographics of each potential viewer are stored in the central computer so viewer profiles can be developed.

Web sites can automatically record (mechanical observation) the number of total and unique (from distinct computers) visits per time period. Banner ads and the sites on which they appear are often evaluated on the *clickthrough rate*—the percentage of site visitors or total number of people who click on the banner ad.

## Measures of Attention

The attention-attracting powers of commercials, packages, and Web sites can be partially measured in a direct manner using **eye tracking** (mechanical observation) or eye fixations. While a consumer looks at images of print ads, billboards, store shelves, packages, or Web sites, a camera underneath the screen sends an invisible beam of light off the consumer's pupil. The camera indicates exactly what the consumer is attending to. This technology allows marketers to determine (1) what parts of the message were attended to, (2) what sequence was used in viewing the message, and (3) how much time was spent on each part.

Indirect measures of attention, which also tap at least some aspects of memory, include theater tests, day-after recall, recognition tests, and Starch scores. *Theater tests* involve showing commercials along with television programs in a theater. Viewers complete questionnaires designed to measure which commercials, and what aspects of those commercials, attracted their attention. **Day-after recall (DAR)** is the most popular method of measuring the attention-getting power of television commercials. Individuals are interviewed the day after a commercial is aired on a program they watched. Recall of the commercial and recall of specific aspects of the commercial (assessed through questionnaires) are interpreted as a reflection of the amount of attention.

DAR measures of television commercials have been criticized as favoring rational, factual, hard-sell ads and high-involvement products while discriminating against feeling, emotional, soft-sell ads. However, for many product–target market combinations, the latter approach may be superior. In response, substantial work has been done to develop recognition measures for television commercials. In **recognition tests,** the commercial of interest, or key parts of it, along with other commercials are shown to target market members. Recognition of the commercial, or key parts of it, is the measure.

**Starch scores** are the most popular technique for evaluating the attention-attracting power of print ads. The respondents are shown advertisements from magazine issues they have recently read. For each advertisement, they indicate which parts (headlines, illustrations, copy blocks) they recall reading. Three main scores are computed:

1. *Noted.* The percentage of people who recall seeing the ad in that issue.
2. *Seen-associated.* The percentage of those who recall reading a part of the ad that clearly identifies the brand or advertiser.
3. *Read most.* The percentage of those who recall reading 50 percent or more of the copy.

Starch scores allow an indirect measure of attention to the overall ad and to key components of the ad.

## Measures of Interpretation

Marketers investigating *interpretation* can use any number of the research methods we've discussed, including focus groups, surveys, and projective techniques. A critical task for marketers is to move beyond cognitive interpretation and tap emotions and feelings as well. Techniques such as the AdSAM® discussed in Chapter 11 can be quite useful in this regard.

# Consumer Behavior Audit*

In this appendix, we provide a list of key questions to guide you in developing marketing strategy from a consumer behavior perspective. This audit is no more than a checklist to minimize the chance of overlooking a critical behavioral dimension. It does not guarantee a successful strategy. However, thorough and insightful answers to these questions should greatly enhance the likelihood of a successful marketing program.

Our audit is organized around the key decisions that marketing managers must make. The first key decision is the selection of the target market(s) to be served. This is followed by the determination of a viable product position for each target market. Finally, the marketing mix elements—product, place, price, and promotion—must be structured in a manner consistent with the desired product position. This process is illustrated in Figure B–1.

| FIGURE B–1 | Consumer Influences Drive Marketing Decisions |
| --- | --- |

*Consumer influences*

**External influences**
Culture, subcultures, values
Demographics, income, and social class
Reference groups and households
Marketing activities

**Internal influences**
Needs, motives, and emotions
Perceptions and memory
Personality and lifestyle
Attitudes

**Situational influences**
Physical, time, social, task, and antecedent

**Decision process influences**
Problem recognition
Information search
Alternative evaluation
Outlet selection
Purchase
Postpurchase processes

*Marketing decisions*

**Marketing segmentation**
Target segment(s)
Single or multiple target segments

**Product positioning**
Key product differentiation variables
Position relative to competition

**Market mix**
Product features
Price level
Promotional appeal
Place (distribution)
Services

*Revised by Richard Pomazal of Wheeling College.

# MARKET SEGMENTATION

Market segmentation is the process of dividing all possible users of a product into groups that have similar needs the products might satisfy. Market segmentation should be done prior to the final development of a new product. In addition, a complete market segmentation analysis should be performed periodically for existing products. The reason for continuing segmentation analyses is the dynamic nature of consumer needs.

A.  External influences
1.  Are there cultures or subcultures whose value system is particularly consistent (or inconsistent) with the consumption of our product?
2.  Is our product appropriate for male or female consumption? Will ongoing gender-role changes affect who consumes our product or how it is consumed?
3.  Do ethnic, social, regional, or religious subcultures have different consumption patterns relevant to our product?
4.  Do various demographic or social-strata groups (age, gender, urban/suburban/rural, occupation, income, education) differ in their consumption of our product?
5.  Is our product particularly appropriate for consumers with relatively high (or low) incomes compared with others in their occupational group?
6.  Can our product be particularly appropriate for specific roles, such as students or professional women?
7.  Would it be useful to focus on specific adopter categories?
8.  Do groups in different stages of the household life cycle have different consumption patterns for our product? Who in the household is involved in the purchase process?

B.  Internal influences
1.  Can our product satisfy different needs or motives in different people? What needs are involved? What characterizes individuals with differing motives?
2.  Is our product uniquely suited for particular personality types? Self-concepts?
3.  What emotions, if any, are affected by the purchase and/or consumption of this product?
4.  Is our product appropriate for one or more distinct lifestyles?
5.  Do different groups have different attitudes about an ideal version of our product?

C.  Situational influences
1.  Can our product be appropriate for specific types of situations instead of (or in addition to) specific types of people?

D.  Decision process influences
1.  Do different individuals use different evaluative criteria in selecting the product?
2.  Do potential customers differ in their loyalty to existing products or brands?

# PRODUCT POSITION

A product position is the way the consumer thinks of a given product or brand relative to competing products or brands. A manager must determine what a desirable product position would be for each market segment of interest. This determination is generally based on the answers to the same questions used to segment a market, with the addition of the consumer's perceptions of competing products or brands. Of course, the capabilities and motivations of existing and potential competitors must also be considered.

A.  Internal influences
   1.  What is the general semantic memory structure for this product category in each market segment?
   2.  What is the ideal version of this product in each market segment for the situations the firm wants to serve?
B.  Decision process influences
   1.  Which evaluative criteria are used in the purchase decision? Which decision rules and importance weights are used?

# PRICING

The manager must set a pricing policy that is consistent with the desired product position. Price must be broadly conceived as everything a consumer must surrender to obtain a product. This includes time and psychological costs as well as monetary costs.

A.  External influences
   1.  Does the segment hold any values relating to any aspect of pricing, such as the use of credit or conspicuous consumption?
   2.  Does the segment have sufficient income, after covering living expenses, to afford the product?
   3.  Is it necessary to lower price to obtain a sufficient relative advantage to ensure diffusion? Will temporary price reductions induce product trial?
   4.  Who in the household evaluates the price of the product?
B.  Internal influences
   1.  Will price be perceived as an indicator of status?
   2.  Is economy in purchasing this type of product relevant to the lifestyle(s) of the segment?
   3.  Is price an important aspect of the segment's attitude toward the brands in the product category?
   4.  What is the segment's perception of a fair or reasonable price for this product?
C.  Situational influences
   1.  Does the role of price vary with the type of situation?
D.  Decision process factors
   1.  Can a low price be used to trigger problem recognition?
   2.  Is price an important evaluative criterion? What decision rule is applied to the evaluative criteria used? Is price likely to serve as a surrogate indicator of quality?
   3.  Are consumers likely to respond to in-store price reductions?

# DISTRIBUTION STRATEGY

The manager must develop a distribution strategy that is consistent with the selected product position. This involves the selection of outlets if the item is a physical product, or the location of the outlets if the product is a service.

A.  External influences
   1.  What values do the segments have that relate to distribution?
   2.  Do the male and female members of the segments have differing requirements of the distribution system? Do working couples, single individuals, or single parents within the segment have unique needs relating to product distribution?

3. Can the distribution system capitalize on reference groups by serving as a means for individuals with common interests to get together?
4. Is the product complex such that a high-service channel is required to ensure its diffusion?

B. Internal influences
1. Will the selected outlets be perceived in a manner that enhances the desired product position?
2. What type of distribution system is consistent with the lifestyle(s) of each segment?
3. What attitudes does each segment hold with respect to the various distribution alternatives?

C. Situational influences
1. Do the desired features of the distribution system vary with the situation?

D. Decision process factors
1. What outlets are in the segment's evoked set? Will consumers in this segment seek information in this type of outlet?
2. Which evaluative criteria does this segment use to evaluate outlets? Which decision rule?
3. Is the outlet selected before, after, or simultaneously with the product or brand? To what extent are product decisions made in the retail outlet?

# PROMOTION STRATEGY

The manager must develop a promotion strategy, including advertising, nonfunctional package design features, publicity, promotions, and sales force activities that are consistent with the product position.

A. External factors
1. What values does the segment hold that can be used in our communications? Which should be avoided?
2. How can we communicate to our chosen segments in a manner consistent with the emerging gender-role perceptions of each segment?
3. What is the nonverbal communication system of each segment?
4. How, if at all, can we use reference groups in our advertisements?
5. Can our advertisements help make the product part of one or more role-related product clusters?
6. Can we reach and influence opinion leaders?
7. If our product is an innovation, are there diffusion inhibitors that can be overcome by promotion?
8. Who in the household should receive what types of information concerning our product?

B. Internal factors
1. Have we structured our promotional campaign such that each segment will be exposed to it, attend to it, and interpret it in the manner we desire?
2. Have we made use of the appropriate learning principles so that our meaning will be remembered?
3. Do our messages relate to the purchase motives held by the segment? Do they help reduce motivational conflict if necessary?
4. Are we considering the emotional implications of the ad and/or the use of our product?

5. Is the lifestyle portrayed in our advertisements consistent with the desired lifestyle of the selected segments?

6. If we need to change attitudes via our promotion mix, have we selected and properly used the most appropriate attitude-change techniques?

C. Situational influences

1. Does our campaign illustrate the full range of appropriate usage situations for the product?

D. Decision process influences

1. Will problem recognition occur naturally, or must it be activated by advertising? Should generic or selective problem recognition be generated?

2. Will the segment seek out or attend to information on the product prior to problem recognition, or must we reach them when they are not seeking our information? Can we use low-involvement learning processes effectively? What information sources are used?

3. After problem recognition, will the segment seek out information on the product or brand, or will we need to intervene in the purchase decision process? If they do seek information, what sources do they use?

4. What types of information are used to make a decision?

5. How much and what types of information are acquired at the point of purchase?

6. Is postpurchase dissonance likely? Can we reduce it through our promotional campaign?

7. Have we given sufficient information to ensure proper product use?

8. Are the expectations generated by our promotional campaign consistent with the product's performance?

9. Are our messages designed to encourage repeat purchases, brand-loyal purchases, or neither?

# PRODUCT

The marketing manager must be certain that the physical product, service, or idea has the characteristics required to achieve the desired product position in each market segment.

A. External influences

1. Is the product designed appropriately for all members of the segment under consideration, including males, females, and various age groups?

2. If the product is an innovation, does it have the required relative advantage and lack of complexity to diffuse rapidly?

3. Is the product designed to meet the varying needs of different household members?

B. Internal influences

1. Will the product be perceived in a manner consistent with the desired image?

2. Will the product satisfy the key purchase motives of the segment?

3. Is the product consistent with the segment's attitude toward an ideal product?

C. Situational influences

1. Is the product appropriate for the various potential usage situations?

D. Decision process influences

1. Does the product or brand perform better than the alternatives on the key set of evaluative criteria used by this segment?

2. Will the product perform effectively in the foreseeable uses to which this segment may subject it?

3. Will the product perform as well as or better than expected by this segment?

# CUSTOMER SATISFACTION AND COMMITMENT

Marketers must produce satisfied customers to be successful in the long run. It is often to a firm's advantage to go beyond satisfaction and create committed or loyal customers.

1. What factors lead to satisfaction with our product?
2. What factors could cause customer commitment to our brand or firm?

# PHOTO CREDITS

## CHAPTER 11:

P. 390, Neuter & Spay Stamp Designs © 2002 United States Postal Service. Used with pemission. All rights reserved. Written authorization from the Postal Service is required to use, reproduce, post, transmit, distribute, or publicly display these images. P. 396, Courtesy Verizon Wireless. P. 397, Courtesy ASICS America Corporation. P. 401, Courtesy of the Almond Board of California. P. 402, Courtesy Aldo Group, Inc. P. 408, Courtesy National Fluid Milk Processor Promotion Board; Agency: Lowe Worldwide, Inc. P. 410, Courtesy AFLAC, Inc. P. 411, Courtesy State Street Global Advisors. P. 412, Courtesy Peanut Board. P. 413, Courtesy Daewoo. P. 414, Courtesy The Humane Society of the United States. P. 415, Courtesy Keen, Inc. P. 415, Courtesy Tyrell, Inc.; Agency: Richards Partners/ Dallas.

## CHAPTER 12:

P. 426, Chase Jarvis/Getty Images. P. 429, © The Procter & Gamble Company. Used by permission. P. 434, © 2008 Wyeth Consumer Healthcare. P. 436, Courtesy Concussion Magazine. P. 438, Courtesy Toshiba American Information Systems, Digital Products Divisions. P. 441, © British Airways plc 2005. P. 442, Courtesy Garmin International Inc. P. 443, Courtesy New Mexico Tourism Board. P. 443, Courtesy Central Boiler. P. 448, Courtesy ALMAP/ BBDO, Sáo Paulo.

## CHAPTER 13:

P. 468, Courtesy Fiestas The Party Magazine, Inc. P. 473, Courtesy Coach USA, Inc.; Creative Director: Reed Krakoff; Photographer: Steven Sebring. P. 474, The McGraw-Hill Companies, Inc./Lars A. Niki, photographer. P. 474, © Tannen Maury/ The Image Works. P. 478, Courtesy Allen Edmonds. P. 480, Courtesy Shopzilla. P. 482, © 2005 Jelly Belly Candy Company.® Reg. TM's of Jelly Belly Candy Company. Used with permission from Jelly Belly Candy Company. P. 483, Copyright GlaxoSmithKline. Used with permission. P. 484, Courtesy of 1-800-FLOWERS.COM, Inc. P. 486, Courtesy McDonald's USA, LLC.

## CHAPTER 14:

P. 494, Courtesy The Quaker Oats Company. P. 500, © Veterinary Pet Insurance Company. P. 503, Courtesy Nestle Purina Pet Care. P. 503, Abreva® is a trademark of the GlaxoKline Group of Companies. P. 505, Courtesy The American Cancer Society. P. 507, Courtesy Church & Dwight, Co. P. 509, Courtesy National Fluid Milk Processor Promotion Board; Agency: Lowe Worldwide, Inc. P. 509, Courtesy Merial Limited. P. 510, *No credit.* P. 511, Courtesy American Honda Co.

## CHAPTER 15:

P. 516, © Copyright 2008, Eastman Kodak Company. P. 520, Courtesy The Hertz Corporation. P. 527, Courtesy Zappos.com. P. 529, Courtesy mySimon, Inc. P. 538, © The Coca-Cola Company. Used with permission. P. 539, Courtesy White Wave. P. 540, Courtesy Papa John's International, Inc. P. 541, © 2005 General Motors Archive.

## CHAPTER 16:

P. 548, Copyright © 2008 Yahoo! Inc. P. 553, Courtesy of PEC Development Group/Experience FBC, LLC. P. 553, © The Procter & Gamble Company. Used by permission. P. 554, Courtesy Toyota Motor Sales, U.S.A., Inc.; Agency: Saatchi & Saatchi/Los Angeles. P. 555, Courtesy Visa, USA. P. 555, Courtesy MGI Luxury Group S.A.—Ebel Division. P. 556 , Courtesy Samsung Telecommunications America, LLP. P. 557, Reprinted by permission of the Andrew Jergen Company. P. 557, © The Procter & Gamble Company. Used by permission. P. 562, Courtesy Wusthof-Trident of America, Inc. P. 567, Courtesy The Blue Buffalo Co. P. 568, Printed with permission of the Eureka!® Tent Brand, Johnson Outdoors, Inc. P. 569, Courtesy Splintek, Inc. P. 570, Courtesy FritoLay, Inc.

## CHAPTER 17:

P. 580, Courtesy Intellifit Corporation. P. 583, Copyright © 2008 Eastman Kodak Company. P. 591, Courtesy My Virtual Model, Inc. P. 592, Courtesy Mall of America. P. 592, Courtesy Eastern Mountain Sports. P. 596, © Lars Niki. P. 599, Courtesy La-Z-Boy, Inc. P. 601, Courtesy L.L.Bean, Inc. P. 605, Courtesy STI Group/Germany; Nestlé S.A. P. 607, Courtesy RedEnvelope, Inc.

## CHAPTER 18:

P. 620, Courtesy Four Seasons Hotels & Resorts. P. 625, Courtesy YR Irvine. P. 628, Materials courtesy of Nestle Prepared Foods Company. P. 629, Courtesy Campbell Soup Company. P. 632, Copyright © 2008, Magazine Publishers of America, Inc. Used with permission. P. 640, © 1996–2008. All rights reserved. Travelocity, The Roaming Gnome and the Stars Design are trademarks of Travelocity.com LP. P. 646, Courtesy Marriott International, Inc.

## CHAPTER 19:

P. 666, Courtesy New Pig Corporation. P. 668, © Tekelec. All rights strictly reserved. Reproduction by any third party in any manner is strictly prohibited. P. 674, Courtesy Kyocera Mita America, Inc. P. 676, Courtesy The Dow Chemical Company. P. 677, Courtesy Afflink. P. 682, Courtesy SunTrust Banks, Inc.; Photograph by Jim Bastardo. P. 685, Courtesy IBM Corporation. P. 686, Courtesy 3M.

## CHAPTER 20:

P. 698, Courtesy Subway Sadwiches & Salads. P. 709, © 2005 Federal Trade Commission. P. 712, Courtesy Dunkin Brands, Inc. P. 714, © Paul F. Kilmer. P. 717, Integrated Solutions, LLC. P. 718, Courtesy Amazon.com.

# NAME INDEX

Page numbers followed by n refer to notes.

# CASE INDEX

# SUBJECT INDEX

role of, 370
satisfaction of, 23–24
Need sets
customers with similar, 18
product-related, 16–17
Negative products, 535
New Age Nurturers, 438
New green mainstream, 90
New Pig Corporation, 667–668
New task approach, 672
New Zealand, 359–360
Nextel, 409–410
NextTag.com, 528
Nike, 17, 31, 177, 377, 517, 625, 712
Niketown, 13
Nokia, 65
Nominal decision making, 497, 498
Noncomparative rating scale, 734
Noncompensatory decision rules, 565, 570
Nonfamily households, 195
Nonfocused attention
explanation of, 291–292
hemispheric lateralization and, 292–293
subliminal stimuli and, 293
Nonverbal communications
advertisements and, 416
agreements and, 61
cultural variations in, 56–57
effects of, 63
etiquette and, 62–63
explanation of, 57
possessions and, 62
relationships and, 60–61
space and, 59
symbols and, 59, 60
time and, 57–59
Normative influence, 234
Norms, 43
Numbers, 60
Nutritional Labeling and Education Act
(NLEA), 9, 716
NYP Hospital, 641

O

Objectification need, 364
Observation
explanation of, 729–730
to obtain product use information, 626
Occupation, consumption and, 117, 119
Odors, 376, 607
Office Depot, 39, 40, 94, 630
Oil of Olay, 349
Oita Prefecture Fisherman's Cooperative,
317–318
Older people
products and services for, 124
targeting to, 126–127
in United States, 2, 124
Older single households, 205–206

One Laptop Per Child (OLPC), 6, 8
One-sided messages, 415
Ongoing searches, 519
Online business networking, 667
Online communities, 231–233
Online loyalty, 647
Online marketing, overview of, 5
Online privacy concerns, 590, 708–711
Online shoppers, 585, 587–588. *See also*
Internet retailing
Online social networks
communication and, 239
explanation of, 231–233
Online surveys, 731
Operant conditioning
explanation of, 328–329, 333
marketing applications for, 330
Opinion leaders
characteristics of, 242–244
explanation of, 240–241
marketing strategy and, 244–247
situations for, 241, 242
Orbitz, 99
Organic food, 83
Organizational culture
explanation of, 680
firmographics and, 679–683
learning and, 687
local culture and government and, 683
motives and emotions and, 687–688
organizational values and, 685
perception and, 685–687
reference groups and, 684–685
Organizational purchase process
decision-making units and, 670–671
evaluation and selection and, 675–676
implementation stage of, 676–677
information search and, 673–675
Internet role in, 678, 680
overview of, 669–670
problem recognition and, 672–673
purchase situation and, 671–672
steps in, 672–678
usage and postpurchase evaluation and,
677–678
Organizations
activities and objectives of, 680–682
as component of market analysis, 15
composition of, 683
industry category of, 682–683
internal and external factors affecting,
667–668
location of, 682
outcomes of, 23
relationship dimensions of, 679
Other-oriented values
competition/cooperation as, 50–51, 93
diversity/uniformity as, 51, 91–92
explanation of, 45, 91
extended/limited family as, 48–49, 92

individualism/collectivism as, 46–47, 91
masculine/feminine, 49–50, 93
youth/age as, 47–48, 92–93
Otis Elevator, 677–678
Outcomes
firm, 23
individual, 23–25
society, 25–26
Outdoor advertising, 280–281
Outlet atmosphere, 606–608
Outlet choice
consumer characteristics and, 598–602
perceived risk and, 600–601
product choice vs., 582–583
retail advertising and, 596–598
shopping orientation and, 601–602
Overwhelmed, 90

P

Pace, 378
Packaging, design of, 306–307
Papa John's, 5
Passive approach, 53, 87
Peak experience, 430
People meters, 736
PepsiCo, 132, 160, 174, 346, 409
Perceived risk
in diffusion process, 253
outlet choice and, 600–601
of product performance, 536
Perception
attention and, 283–293
consumer characteristics and, 535–536
explanation of, 278
exposure and, 279–283
interpretation and, 293–302
marketing strategy and, 302–307
nature of, 278–279
organizational culture and, 685–686
problem recognition and, 502
rhetorical figures and, 297
Perceptual defenses, 279
Perceptual mapping, 559, 560
Perceptual relativity, 293
Performance-oriented values
explanation of, 51–52
in United States, 90–91
Permission-based e-mail (PBE), 530
Permission-based marketing, 283
Personal interviews, 731
Personality
explanation of, 360, 373–374
family decision roles and, 211
marketing strategy and, 375–378
multitrait approach to, 374–375
single-trait approach to, 375
Personal sales, 237–238
Personal space, 59
Person-situation segmentation matrix, 486, 487